D1587500

Yale Language Series

CANTONESE DICTIONARY

Cantonese-English

English-Cantonese

by Parker Po-fei Huang

New Haven and London
Yale University Press

Library of Congress catalog card number: 72–110727
International standard book number: 0–300–01293–4
Printed in the United States of America by
The Murray Printing Co., Westford, Mass.

13 12 11 10 9 8 7 6 5

CONTENTS

PREFACE

One may define a lexicographer as one who loves words. My love of words has often tempted me to include in this dictionary more words than I should have, and it has been very difficult to resist every temptation. Nonetheless, the struggle has forced me to examine each word for inclusion, and I hope that such scrutiny has made the entries worthwhile. Further, I hope the extension of this scrutiny to the whole entry has produced clear definitions and useful illustrative sentences. I hope also that this work will serve as an adequate first response to the many requests for a Cantonese dictionary from those who have been using my Speak Cantonese series. No literary expressions are included, because the primary object has been to help the English-speaking student understand and communicate in the oral-aural mode of Cantonese.

In compiling this dictionary I owe much to many people. A few I want to mention in particular. Professor Roy Andrew Miller, the director of the Institute of Far Eastern Languages of Yale University, has supported me morally and financially in seeing this dictionary to completion, ever since he prevented me from throwing away the index cards a few years ago. Mrs. Judith G. Blatchford has patiently and painstakingly checked the correspondence of meaning between each English and Cantonese word and sentence. Mr. Peter Sargent has written the section on Cantonese pronunciation in the Introduction. My wife Mabel has furnished me as usual with systems of arranging cards and keeping files, a process in which I have always found myself lost. By freeing me from teaching summer school in the Institute in 1967, the Yale-in-China Association has contributed greatly to this project. In every language I assume there is an expression for "Thank you." To these people and institutions mentioned and to all who have given me advice and help, the appropriate Cantonese words are "Dò·jeh, dò·jeh!"

Parker Po-fei Huang

New Haven
June 1969

INTRODUCTION

This dictionary is composed of the following parts:

1. An introduction to the phonetic and structural systems of Cantonese
2. An English-Cantonese section of 20,000 entries, with phrases or sentences to illustrate accepted usages
3. A Cantonese-English section, in which each romanized Cantonese word is listed with appropriate characters, part of speech (according to the system designed at Yale), and the English equivalent with illustrative sentences when necessary
4. A character index
5. A list of geographical names and common Chinese surnames

The student may find the dictionary most useful by first familiarizing himself with the phonetic and structural system. The English-Cantonese section is designed to help even a beginner speak Cantonese. The illustrative sentences given under each use of an English word are simple and direct, and all are for use in an actual situational conversation. To find the Cantonese equivalent of an English phrase, the user should look under the key English word in the phrase. For instance, if he wishes to translate the English phrase "this way," he should turn to "way" and choose a Cantonese version of the phrase. The Cantonese-English section is intended to be used for both the comprehension and the production of Cantonese. It will be useful not only to those who are learning Cantonese but also to those relatively fluent in it who will find that it provides a source for increasing the size of vocabulary and for checking on words which have been forgotten or are little used. The dictionary may be used as an aid in reading, as the character index has listed the Chinese characters that are most frequent. Although Cantonese is not a written language, the bulk of its spoken vocabulary is similar to that of written Chinese. The student may use the index to look up the pronunciation of characters he has seen on a street sign, in a store name, or in any reading, and then he can look up the meaning in the Cantonese-English section. Names of important cities and names of famous people are compiled in a short list, along with the most common Chinese surnames. In this list Chinese characters are used side by side with romanization.

There are several existing romanization systems for Cantonese. The reasons for using the Yale system here are that it has been used in a series of widely adopted textbooks and supplementary materials and that it has been in use for almost twenty years. For those unfamiliar with it, however, a comparative table for conversion of Yale romanization to that of other major systems is included at the end of the dictionary.

PRONUNCIATION GUIDE

In describing the pronunciation of Cantonese, it is most convenient to take the single syllable as the point of departure, and to consider it as composed of three elements— initial, final, and tone.

The initial is the consonantal element which begins the syllable; it includes everything before the main vowel. In the syllables tìng, chè, gwóng, and ngáan, the initials are t, ch, gw, and ng respectively. A few syllables in Cantonese do not begin with a consonantal element; we describe these as having zero initial: àh.

The final consists of the main vowel of the syllable along with any consonants or semi-vowels that follow it. In the syllables fā, chēut, gwai, gwóng, the finals are a, eut, ai, and ong respectively.

The initial and final exhaust the consonant-and-vowel aspect of the syllable. But in Cantonese there is a third element that is an indispensable part of every syllable: in pronouncing the syllable the pitch of the voice must move in a prescribed pattern, called the tone. The tone of a syllable is just as vital to its pronunciation as its initial or its final: two syllables differing only in tone are just as different as two syllables differing in initial consonant or main vowel. The syllables sī, sî, sí are all different. The first has the high level tone (⌐), the second the high falling tone (⑁), and the third the high rising tone (⑂).* Other syllables may have the mid level (—⑂) or the low falling, low rising, or low level tones (↓, ⊿, ⊿).

Initials

Cantonese has nineteen initials. They can be grouped as follows:

Stops	{Aspirated	p,t,k,kw
	{Unaspirated	b,d,g,gw
Affricates	{Aspirated	ch
	{Unaspirated	j
Fricatives and Continuants		f,s,h
Nasals and Lateral		m,n,ng,l
Semivowels		y,w

Of the stops, p, t, k, and kw are pronounced very nearly as in English. The aspiration (i.e. the puff of breath accompanying the production of this type of stop) of these consonants is more forceful in Cantonese than in English.

Cantonese b, d, g, and gw differ from the English sounds spelled with these letters. The point of difference will become clear if we consider first the situation in English. In the production of a stop consonant, two factors (other than position of articulation) are crucial: aspiration and voicing. The English initial stops p, t, and k are aspirated but not voiced—that is, their production is accompanied by a fairly strong puff of breath, but not by vibration of the vocal cords. On the other hand, English b, d, and g are voiced but not aspirated—that is, their production is accompanied by vibration of the vocal cords but not by a puff of breath. The situation in English can be summarized graphically:

	Unvoiced	Voiced
Aspirated	p t k	
Unaspirated		b d g

In Cantonese, on the other hand, no initial stops are ever voiced. The two kinds of Cantonese stops are differentiated only by being (strongly) aspirated or not aspirated at all. Cantonese p, t, k, and kw are unvoiced and aspirated. Cantonese b, d, g, and gw are unvoiced and unaspirated:

	Unvoiced
Aspirated	p t k kw
Unaspirated	b d g gw

---

*The figures in parentheses are tone-letters, used to represent pitch-contours graphically. The horizontal or oblique line represents the change (or constancy) of pitch during the pronunciation of the syllable, and the vertical line provides a scale against which similar movements in different pitch registers can be distinguished.

It happens that in English the stops p, t, and k lose their aspiration (become like Cantonese b, d, and g) when they are not initial but instead follow initial s. By comparing the sounds of these stops in spill, still, skill, squill with those in pill, till, kill, quill, it is possible to get a feeling for the kind of contrast required in Cantonese.

The two affricate initials are distinguished in the same way: ch is aspirated and un-voiced, while j is unaspirated and unvoiced. But these sounds in Cantonese are articulated in a different position from that of English ch and j: Cantonese ch is articulated midway between the positions of English ch and ts.

Among the fricatives and continuants, the English speaker will have no difficulty with f and h. In pronouncing Cantonese s he will again have to make a slight adjustment in position of articulation: the position of s is intermediate between those of English s and sh.

The semivowels y and w have in Cantonese virtually the same articulation as in English; so do the nasals m, n, and ng and the lateral l. The sound of ng is always as in singer, never as in finger. In English, ng never occurs at the beginning of a word; to learn its use as an initial in Cantonese will be simply a matter of getting used to an unfamiliar arrangement of familiar sounds, not a matter of acquiring a new articulatory skill.

The initials are listed below with their pronunciations in modified IPA phonetic symbols ([y] used in place of IPA [j]).

Stops	Affricates	Fricatives & Continuants	Nasals & Lateral	Semivowels
p:[p'] b:[p]	ch:[tɕ']j:[tɕ]	f:[f]	m:[m]	y:[y]
t:[t'] d:[t]		s:[ɕ]	n:[n]	w:[w]
k:[k'] g:[k]		h:[h]	ng:[ŋ]	
kw:[k'w]gw:[kw]			l:[l]	

Finals

The basic part of the Cantonese final is the main vowel. Some finals consist only of the main vowel, while others consist of the main vowel followed by a terminal, which may be a consonant or a semivowel. The possible terminals are consonants p, t, k, m, n, and ng, and semivowels i, u (these could also be written y and w, since they are identifiable with the initial semivowels y and w). The semivowels and the consonants m, n, and ng re-quire no comment except that, as when initial, ng is always pronounced as in singer. The consonants p, t, and k in terminal position have an additional articulatory peculiarity: in this position, when the stop is formed the air pressure which would otherwise be built up behind it and explosively released is not allowed to build up at all, so that the release of the stop is noiseless (it is "swallowed"). The time between formation and release of the stop is longer than if it were explosively released.

There are seven vowels which occur in Cantonese finals: a, e, eu, i, o, u, and yu. Each vowel has a simple sound (see the phonetic transcriptions below), even though several of them are spelled with compound symbols.

In the section below, approximate pronunciations from English, German, and French are given for some of the finals. In most cases the approximation is very rough; it is intended only to serve as a mnemonic aid, not to supplant the hearing of the actual sounds from a native speaker of Cantonese.

Before discussing individually the vowels and the finals they form, we should clarify the operation of vowel length in Cantonese. In the pronunciation of the Cantonese finals the length of time taken in producing the main vowel is an essential feature. A vowel may be longer in one of its finals than in another, or two finals may differ only in the fact that the vowel of one is short while the vowel of the other is long. The mastery of vowel length in Cantonese is not just a matter of having a good accent; it is essential in making one's meaning intelligible.

In practice, differences in vowel length are generally accompanied by other pronunciation differences which serve to reinforce one's perception of the length difference. In Cantonese we find two such subordinate differences. The first concerns the relation of the vowel to its following terminal. When the vowel is long, its duration is considerably greater than that of the terminal; when the vowel is short, the impression of shortness is enhanced by corresponding prolongation of the terminal. Schematically, for instance, we might represent the difference between aai (long) and ai (short) as *aai/aii. Similarly, ou with short o sounds like *ouu, and eun with short eu sounds like *eunn.† The vowel-terminal relation should be carefully observed in learning the finals.

The second subsidiary difference involves vowel quality. A vowel when pronounced only briefly may be slightly altered in quality from its sound when pronounced long. Thus, the final aam, with long a, rhymes (approximately) with English calm, while the final am, with short a, rhymes with come (with the terminal m drawn out). The vowel o is long in on, which rhymes with English lawn; it is short in ou, which rhymes with low (with terminal u drawn out). The change of quality according to length affects every vowel except yu, which never occurs short.

The vowel a is written doubled (aa) when it is long, single when it is short (except that the final a with no terminal is always long). The long vowel aa has about the sound of English a in father in all its finals:

a	aam	aap
aai	aan	aat
aau	aang	aak

Short a when followed by i or u has nearly the same quality as long aa (a as in father). The short finals ai and au are distinguished from the long finals aai and aau only by the brevity of the a sound and the prolongation of the terminal.

In all its other finals the short a has altered quality; it sounds like English u in sun:

am	ap
an	at
ang	ak

None of the other vowels is written doubled when long.

The vowel e has when long approximately the sound of English ai in air: e, eng, ek. It occurs short in the final ei, which rhymes with English day (terminal i prolonged).

The vowel eu has no English equivalent. When long, it has about the sound of French eu in veuve or German ö in zwölf:

eu eung euk

Its short sound differs somewhat in quality, being slightly higher and further back:

eui eun eut

The vowel i when long has roughly the sound of ee in English see. This English sound, however, ends in a y element; phonetically it is [iy], while the Cantonese sound is the [i] only. A more accurate comparison is with French i in mari:

i	im	ip
iu	in	it

---

†Note that *aii, *ouu, and *eunn are not actual Cantonese finals; they are schematic representations intended to illustrate the relative length of vowel and terminal.

Table of Cantonese Finals

		-#	-i	-u	-m	-n	-ng	-p	-t	-k
(long)	aa	aa [a:]	aai [a:i]	aau [a:u]	aam [a:m]	aan [a:n]	aang [a:ŋ]	aap [a:p]	aat [a:t]	aak [a:k]
(short)	a		ai [ai]	au [au]	am [əm]	an [ən]	ang [əŋ]	ap [əp]	at [ət]	ak [ək]
(long)	e	e [ɛ:]					eng [ɛ:ŋ]			ek [ɛ:k]
(short)	e		ei [ei]							
(long)	eu	eu [œ:]					eung [œ:ŋ]			euk [œ:k]
(short)	eu		eui [ɵü]			eun [ɵn]			eut [ɵt]	
(long)	i	i [i:]		iu [i:u]	im [i:m]	in [i:n]		ip [i:p]	it [i:t]	
(short)	i						ing [eŋ]			ik [ek] (or [Ik])
(long)	o	o [ɔ:]	oi [ɔ:i]			on [ɔ:n]	ong [ɔ:ŋ]		ot [ɔ:t]	ok [ɔ:k]
(short)	o			ou [ou]						
(long)	u	u [u:]	ui [u:i]			un [u:n]			ut [u:t]	
(short)	u						ung [oŋ]			uk [ok]
(long)	yu	yu [ü:] or [yü:]*				yun [ü:n] or [yü:n]*			yut [ü:t] or [yü:t]*	

*After zero initial.

In iu, it should be remembered, the main vowel is i; the u is terminal and brief.

   The i is short in ing and ik; in these finals it has roughly the sound of English e in pet, more accurately the sound of French é in été.†

   When the vowel o is long, it has about the sound of English o in long:

o
oi on ot
ong ok

---

†The compiler of this dictionary pronounces the final ik to rhyme with sick.

It is short in the final <u>ou</u>, which rhymes approximately with English <u>tow</u> (terminal <u>u</u> prolonged).

The long form of <u>u</u> has roughly the sound of <u>oo</u> in English <u>food</u>. This English sound, however, ends in a <u>w</u> element; it is phonetically [uw], while the Cantonese sound is the [u] only:

u
<u>ui</u>   <u>un</u>   <u>ut</u>

The short form of <u>u</u> is somewhat lowered, tending toward the <u>o</u> of <u>yoke</u> (which is phonetically [ow], while the Cantonese sound is simply [o]):

<u>ung</u>   <u>uk</u>

The vowel <u>yu</u> is always long. It has the sound of French <u>u</u> in <u>su</u> or German <u>ü</u> in <u>kühn</u>:

<u>yu</u>   <u>yun</u>   <u>yut</u>

When this final stands after zero initial, it begins with a <u>y</u>-glide ([yü]).

A few syllables fall outside the above scheme of initials and finals. These consist of <u>m</u> or <u>ng</u> functioning (with tone) as the whole syllable. Syllabic <u>m</u> is common in English as an expression of approval (<u>mmm</u>); syllabic <u>ng</u> is the sound obtained by drawing out the final sound of <u>sing</u>.

The accompanying table shows the Cantonese finals along with their pronunciations transcribed in modified IPA symbols (<u>y</u> for IPA <u>j</u>, <u>ü</u> for IPA <u>y</u>).

Tones

Cantonese has seven tones. They can be grouped according to their pitch-contours (level, rising, or falling) and according to their pitch-registers (high, mid, low) as follows:

	Level	Rising	Falling
High	˥	˧˥	˥˩
Mid	˧		
Low	˨	˨˧	˨˩

The pitch-contours are represented in the romanization by the use of diacritics: the mark ` is used for both falling tones and the mark ´ for both rising tones. Of the level tones, only the <u>high</u> one is marked, by use of the sign ⁻; the mid and low level tones have no diacritic at all. It remains to distinguish the low tones from the rest, which is accomplished by inserting an <u>h</u> after the vowels (and before any terminals) of all low-register syllables.* Thus, such pairs as

bīn (˥)   si (˧)   tòng (˥˩)   múi (˧˥)
bìhn (˨)   sih (˨)   tòhng (˨˩)   múih (˨˧)

---

*The romanization used in this dictionary differs from that used in <u>Speak Cantonese</u>, by Parker Huang and Gerard P. Kok (New Haven: Yale University, Far Eastern Publications, 1960) by using the inserted <u>h</u> consistently for <u>all</u> low-tone syllables; in <u>Speak Cantonese</u> the <u>h</u> was omitted for low-tone syllables beginning with <u>m, n</u> or <u>ng</u>. When these syllables occurred in mid level or high rising or high falling tones, the initial was underscored. Thus, this book has

múi (˧˥)   múih (˨˧)   m̀h (˨˩)   ńgh (˨˧)   néuih (˨˧)   néui (˧˥)   ngóh (˨˧)

where <u>Speak Cantonese</u> has

<u>mú</u>i (˧˥)   múi (˨˧)   m̀ (˨˩)   ńg (˨˧)   néui (˨˧)   n<u>é</u>ui (˧˥)   ngo (˨˧)

differ only in regard to the pitch-register; the pitch-contours are the same for both members of each pair, as are initial and final. The lower member of each pair has one of the low tones.

By combining the use of the diacritics and the inserted h, we can represent all the Cantonese tones. Below are written out all the tonal representations for the initial-final combinations si and yun (the latter does not occur in high-level tone):

	Level	Rising	Falling			Level	Rising	Falling
High	sī	sí	sì		High	(yūn)	yún	yùn
Mid	si				Mid	yun		
Low	sih	síh	sìh		Low	yuhn	yúhn	yùhn

Note also the following spellings: m̀h (↓), ńgh (⌐).

In describing the pronunciation of the Cantonese tones, we cannot give their absolute pitches, since a speaker with a high voice will pronounce his tones at a higher pitch than a speaker with a low voice will. But no matter how high or low the speaker's voice is, his tones will be in the same relation to each other as any other speaker's tones. For instance, the level tones—high, mid, and low—will be in very nearly the relation sol mi re for all speakers. By specifying the beginning and ending points of the rising and falling tones as degrees of this scale we can describe the relationships of the whole seven-tone system in a way that is independent of the pitch of the speaker's voice.

Before we proceed to the description, however, a caution is in order. The pitch relationships of the tones in actual speech are by no means as rigidly defined and unvarying as they will appear in this presentation. For one thing, the mood of the speaker will often influence the pitch relationships of his tones; when excited, for instance, he may extend the pitch range of his voice so that the distance between higher and lower tones becomes greater and the rising and falling tones rise and fall farther than usual. Besides this, even in normal, unexcited speech the individual will show slight variations in the pitch-levels or end-points of his tones. But in spite of these difficulties, there is a great deal of pedagogical advantage to be gained by presenting the learner with a normalized representation of tone shapes and heights. Such a normalization, even if it is a bit more rigid than living speech, will nonetheless give him a good idea what to listen for, and will function as a detailed guide to the production of acceptable tones at an early stage of the learning process, thus serving as a convenient stepping-stone to the acquisition of natural-sounding speech. A presentation made in less specific terms (relying, for instance, solely upon tone-letters of the kind used above), might not err on the side of overspecification, but would run the risk of providing the learner with insufficiently firm ground for his first steps toward acquisition of the tones.

A range of pitch that contains all seven tones extends from do upward to sol and also from do downward to la. On this scale, the positions of the level tones can be diagrammed as follows:

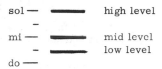

    sol — ———— high level
      -
    mi —   ———— mid level
      -    ———— low level
    do —

The rising tones can be represented as follows:

    sol —
      -          high rising
    mi —
      -          low rising
    do —

The low-rising tone may ordinarily rise as little as a half step or as much as a full step (re-mi).

The falling tones are diagrammed below. In the case of the low-falling tone there are two possible contours: while this tone may indeed have a falling contour, for many speakers (including the compiler of the present dictionary) it has in fact a level contour at a pitch lower than that of the low-level tone. An individual speaker will use one or the other of these contours, but not both; the difference appears to be dialectal.

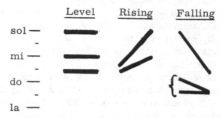

The whole system of Cantonese tones, then, looks like this:

	Level	Rising	Falling

sol —
  -
mi —
  -
do —
  -
la —

Tone Sandhi

When two syllables come together in speech, the tone of the first may be altered so that it combines more smoothly with the tone of the second; this phenomenon is called tone sandhi. In Cantonese, tone sandhi affects only the high-falling tone. When this tone precedes another high-falling tone or a high-level tone, it changes to a high-level tone. Thus:

$$\text{Y} + \text{Y} \rightarrow \text{⌐} \; \text{Y}$$
$$\text{Y} + \text{⌐} \rightarrow \text{⌐} \; \text{⌐}$$

For example, the syllables sàam and jèung occurring together in speech are pronounced sáam jèung; the syllables sàam and màn occurring together are pronounced sáam màn. In this dictionary, any word of two or more syllables in which the constituent syllables are affected by tone sandhi is given with the rules already applied; that is, in the form that actually occurs in speech. For example, the word listed in the dictionary as sìnsàang ("Mr.") is composed of the syllables sìn and sàang; the tone of the first syllable has been altered by tone sandhi. *

---

*In the speech of the compiler, a few words and phrases do not follow the sandhi rule: for instance sài·gwà. These forms are transcribed in the text in accordance with the compiler's usage.

A more detailed discussion of the pronunciation of Cantonese, which differs at some points from the present treatment, will be found in Yuen Ren Chao's Cantonese Primer (Cambridge: Harvard University Press, 1947).

Convenient materials for practice in the pronunciation of Cantonese, including an extensive section dealing with the tones both alone and in combination, are found in Cantonese Sounds and Tones by Parker Po-fei Huang (New Haven: Yale University, Far Eastern Publications, 1962).

GRAMMATICAL NOTATIONS

Abbreviations

A	adverb	Pat	patterns
At	attributive	Ph	phrase
AV	auxiliary verb	PN	pronoun
BF	boundform	PW	placeword
CV	coverb	Q	question word
EV	equative verb	PV	postverb
I	interjection	RV	resultative verb
IE	idiomatic expression	RVE	resultative ending
M	measure	SP	specifier
MA	movable adverb	SV	stative verb
N	noun	V	verb (functive verb)
NU	number	VO	verb-object compound
ON	onomatopoeia	TW	timeword
P	particle		

Description of Usage

1. Verbal Expressions

1.1 Stative verbs (SV) express a quality or condition, and never take an object. They may be preceded by the adverb hóu ("very"). A stative verb may function:

a) As a predicate:

Nī·gāan ngūk gòu.
This house is tall.

b) As a noun modifier (with or without the particle ge) like an English adjective:

Ngóh yiu yāt·gàan daaih (ge) ngūk.
I want a big house.

Certain stative verbs which function only as noun modifiers (with optional ge) and cannot be preceded by the adverb hóu ("very") are known as attributives (At).

sī·lahp (ge) hohk·haauh   private school
yàhn·jouh sī   artificial silk

1.2 Functive verbs (V) denote actions; they may take objects.

Gó·gàan pou·táu maaih syù.
That store sells books.

Kéuih·ge pàhng·yáuh yáuh hóu·dò syù.
His friend has many books.

Hohk·sāang lèih·jó la.
The students came.

1.3 Equative verbs (EV) stand between nouns or nominal expressions, connecting and equating them. The most common equative verb is haih ("be") in the sense that one thing is (the same thing as) another; others in everyday use are giu (·jouh) ("be called or named"), sing ("be surnamed"), and dáng·yù ("is [mathematically] equal to").

Kéuih haih ngóh·ge pàhng·yáuh.
He is my friend.

Gó·go sai·mān·jái giu Jùng·hàhng.
That child's name is Jung·hahng.

Kéuih sing māt·yéh a?
What is his surname?

Yìh gà yih dáng·yù sei.
Two plus two equals four.

1.4 **Coverbs (CV).** The term coverb refers not to a separate class of verbs but rather to a separate function of functive verbs. A coverb always has an object and is never separated from it; together with the object, the coverb acts as a modifier of the main verb.

Ngóh·deih yuhng faai·jí sihk·faahn.
We eat with chopsticks.

Ngóh chóh hei·chè heui.
I go by car.

Kéuih tùhng ngóh heui hohk·haauh.
He's going to school with me.

1.5 **Postverbs (PV).** hái ("at" or "in"), béi ("give"), dou ("arrive" or "to"), and occasionally other verbs may be suffixed to functive verbs to indicate certain relationships. The resulting compound requires an object, just as a coverb does. A verb used in this way is called a postverb.

Kéuih jyuh·hái Hèung·góng.
He lives in Hong Kong.

Ngóh sung·béi kéuih yāt·bún syù.
I gave him a book (as a gift).

Ngóh·deih duhk·dou nī·syu.
We have read up to here.

1.6 **Resultative verbs (RV).** Many verbs are compounded with a second verb which indicates the result of the action of the first verb. The second verb in such a compound is called resultative verb ending (RVE). A simple compound of this type indicates the actual result; the same compound with dāk ("be able to," "can") or m̀h ("not") inserted between the verbs indicates potential or negative results.

Ngóh wán·dóu ngóh·ge bīu la.
I have found my watch.

Néih tái·dāk·gin hei·chè léuih·bihn gó·go yàhn ma?
Can you see the person inside the car?

Ngóh tái·m̀h·gin gó·ga chē.
I can't see that car.

1.7 **Auxiliary verbs (AV).** An auxiliary verb immediately precedes the verb which it aids. When the context makes the meaning clear, the main verb is often omitted, as in English.

Kéuih wúih góng Yìng·màhn ma?
Does he know how to speak English?

Kéuih <u>wúih</u>.
Yes, he <u>does</u>.

Néih <u>jùng·yi</u> cheung·gō ma?
Do you <u>like</u> to sing?

Ngóh·<u>jùng yi</u>.
Yes, I <u>do</u>.

1.8 Adverbs modify verbs or other adverbs. The fixed adverb (A) immediately precedes the verb it modifies, with a few exceptions like <u>sìn</u> ("first"). Ex. Néih
hàahng sìn. ("You walk first.") The movable adverb (MA) must likewise precede
the verb but may be separated from it by the subject of the sentence. Most monosyllabic adverbs are fixed.

Kéuih·deih <u>dōu</u> sihk tòhng·chāan.
They eat Chinese food <u>also</u>.

<u>Waahk·jé</u> kéuih m̀h·lèih.
<u>Perhaps</u> he won't come.

Kéuih <u>waahk·jé</u> m̀h·lèih.
<u>Perhaps</u> he won't come.

1.9 Verb-object compound (VO). Certain Chinese verbs always occur with a noun object of closely connected meaning directly after them. These combinations, called
verb-object compounds, generally correspond to single verbs in English.

<u>VO</u>	<u>Lit. trans.</u>	<u>Normal trans.</u>
<u>sihk·faahn</u>	eat cooked rice	eat
<u>fan·gaau</u>	sleep sleep	sleep
<u>cheung·gō</u>	sing song	sing
<u>góng·wá</u>	speak speech	speak

2. Nominal Expressions

2.1 Nouns (N) are words which can be preceded by the combination specifier-number-
measure (SP-NU-M) or some portion of it. A noun may function as the subject or
object of a verb or as a modifier of another noun.

2.2 Measures (M) are bound forms (see 4 below) which can be preceded by a number
(NU), a specifier (SP), or some other indicator of quantity. Together with its NU
and/or SP, a measure functions as a noun. Many nouns may also be used as
measures. The measure of widest occurrence is <u>go</u>; when a noun commonly occurs
with a measure other than <u>go</u>, this form is listed in the entry with the noun. When
no measure is listed, the form <u>go</u> should be used.

yāt·<u>go</u>	one (of something)
yāt·<u>bún</u> syù	one book
yāt·<u>wùh</u> jáu	a <u>pot</u> of wine

2.3 Numbers (NU) are essentially counters. In simple counting or in lists, numbers
are free forms. Elsewhere they are bound forms and must be followed by a measure.

<u>léuhng</u>·go	<u>two</u> (of something)
<u>bun</u>·go sài·gwà	<u>half</u> of a watermelon

2.4 Specifiers (SP) are noun modifiers that make the noun refer to a specific thing or
things ("this" and "that" for example). They can stand before the combination
NU-M-N or any portion of it.

nī(·yāt)·go	this one
gó·sei·bún syù	those four books

2.5 Pronouns (PN). Pronouns in Chinese are a small group of words used to replace
nouns after their first occurrence in a context: ngóh ("I," "me"), néih ("you"),
kéuih ("he," "she," "him," "her"), ngóh·deih ("we," "us"), néih·deih ("you"
[plural]), kéuih·deih ("they," "them"). The particle ge may be added to pronouns
to make them possessive.

ngóh·ge	my, mine
ngóh·deih·ge	our, ours

2.6 Placewords (PW) are indicators or names of places. Like nouns, they may function as the subject or the object of the verb.

Jùng·gwok haih yāt·go daaih gwok.
China is a big country.

Ngóh jyuh·hái gó·syu.
I live there.

Léuih·bihn hóu·gwo ngoih·bihn.
The inside is better than the outside.

2.6.1 A noun can be used as a PW by adding a positional suffix or localizer— seuhng·
bihn ("on"), yahp·bihn ("in"), or the like:

tói·seuhng·bihn	on the table
fóng·yahp·bihn	in the room

2.7 Timewords (TW), which denote days, months, years, and other times, have the
same uses as placewords, except that they also function adverbially.

Gàm·yaht haih láih·baai·sàam.
Today is Wednesday.

Néih gàm·yaht heui m̀h·heui a?
Are you going today?

3. Particles

Particles (P)·have no denotative meanings, but only grammatical functions. There
are two general categories:

a) The interrogative particles, ma, a, àh, gwa, and mē, which mark various types
of questions:

Néih yám jáu ma?	Do you drink?
Néih yám m̀h·yám jáu a?	Do you want a drink?
Néih m̀h·yám jáu àh?	Don't you want a drink?
Néih m̀h·yám jáu gwa?	You probably don't drink, do you?
Néih m̀h·yám jáu mē?	You don't drink?

b) Aspect particles which follow verbs and add certain shades of meaning to the
verb action.

Kéuih (yìh·gā) hóu gòu <u>la</u>.   She is very tall now.
   (change of status)

Ngóh sihk·<u>jó</u> faahn <u>la</u>.   I have already eaten.
   (completed action)

Kéuih haih kàhm·yaht lèih <u>ge</u>.   He came yesterday.
   (emphasis on attendant
   circumstance rather than
   the action itself)

Kéuih fan·<u>gán</u> gaau.   He is sleeping.
   (continuing action)

Chéng néih daai·<u>màaih</u> dī   Please bring your children (and come)
   sai·mān·jái lèih.   along.
   (accompanying action)

Ngóh meih sihk·<u>gwo</u> tòhng·chāan.   I haven't ever eaten Chinese food.
   (previously experienced
   action)

4. Boundforms (BF) are elements which cannot be used as free, independent words. As a group they do not follow any set grammatical pattern. These should not be confused with some boundforms, such as attributives, resultative endings, postverbs, particles, etc., which follow definite patterns to warrant giving them separate notations.

fòng   as in <u>dùng·fòng</u> ("east")
                              [<u>dùng</u> ("east"), <u>fòng</u> ("direction")]

fu   as in <u>fu·jyú·jihk</u> ("vice-chairman")
                              [<u>fu</u> ("vice"), <u>jyú·jihk</u> ("chairman")]

A

a   (one) yāt; one, yāt·go; **a book** yāt·bún syù; **a pair of shoes** yāt·deui hàaih; **a table** yāt·jèung tói.
    (use as an article): **a short while** yāt·jahn·gāan; **a good while** hóu noih; **a few words** géi·geui wá

abacus   syun·pùhn

abalone   bàau·yùh

abandon   fong·hei: **abandon one's duty** fong·hei jaak·yahm

abbey   sàu·douh·yún

abbot   sàu·douh·yún yún·jéung

abbreviate   sūk·syé

abbreviation   gáam·bāt·jih

A.B.C.   yahp·mùhn: **the A.B.C. of English Grammar** yìng·màhn màhn·faat yahp·mùhn

abdicate   (to relinquish or renounce a throne) teui·waih

abdomen   tóuh, fūk·bouh

abduct   gwáai·daai

ability   nàhng·lihk, bún·sih

able   nàng·gau, hó·yíh, wúih: **able to do** nàhng·gau jouh; **able to arrive** hó·yíh dou·dāk; **able to help** hó·yíh bòng; **able to speak** wúih góng; **able to manage** wúih dá·léih.
    (competent) hóu·bún·sih ge, hóu·jouh·dāk ge. /He is very able. Kéuih hóu bún·sih ge.

able-bodied man   jong·dīng

abnormal   bāt·jing·sèung ge, bin·taai ge: **abnormal condition** bāt·jing·sèuhng ge chìhng·yìhng

aboard   hái . . . syu: **aboard a ship** hái syùhn·syu; **aboard a plane**. hái fèi·gèi·syu

abolish   fai·chyùh: **abolish a treaty** fai·chyùh tíuh·yeuk

abominable   hāk·yàhn·jàng

aboriginal   bún·déi ge, bún·deih ge

aborigines   tóu·yàhn, bún·deih·yàhn

abortion   síu·cháan; **criminal abortion** lohk·tòi, dá·tòi

abound   yáuh·hóu·dò ge, yáuh·hóu·fùng·fù ge

about   gwàan·yù; góng; gam·seuhng·há; jauh·lìeh . . . la. /I don't know anything about this matter. Gwāan·yù nī·gihn sih ngóh yāt·dī dōu m̀h·jî. /This book is about China. Nī·bún syù haih góng Jùng·gwok ge. /About three dollars. Sāam·mān gam·seuhng·há. /The train is about to leave. Fó·chè jauh·lèih hòi la.

above   seuhng·bihn. /The plane is flying above the cloud. Fèi·gèi hái wàhn·seuhng·bihn fèi. /What's mentioned above isn't correct. Seuhng·bihn só·góng·ge m̀h·ngāam.

1

abreast   yāt·paak: **walk abreast** yāt·paak gám hàahng

abridge   sūk·dyún

abroad   chēut·yèuhng, hái ngoih·gwok. /When is he going abroad? Kéuih géi·sí chēut·
yèuhng a? /Is he studying abroad? Kéuih hái ngoih·gwok duhk·syù àh?

abscess   chōng, nùhng·chōng

absent   móuh lèih, kyut·jihk. /He is absent. Kéuih móuh lèih. /There were quite a few
members absent in yesterday's meeting. Kàhm·yaht ge wúi yáuh hóu·dò wúi·yùhn kyut·
jihk.

absolute   jyuht·deui: **absolutely right** jyuht·deui móuh cho

absorb   sok, kāp·sàu: **absorb water** sok·séui; **absorb a new idea** kāp·sàu sān jī·sīk

abstain   gaai: **abstain from smoking** gaai·yīn; **abstain from alcoholic drinks** gaai·jáu;
abstain from meat (for religious reasons), sihk·jàai

abstract   (opposite to concrete) chàu·jeuhng (SV); (summary) daaih·yi (N)

absurd   (foolish) sòh, ngohng, ngauh; (unreasonable) móuh·léih·yàuh; hóu·siu: /This is
absurd! Jàn·haih móuh·léih·yàuh la! or Jàn·haih hóu·siu la!

abuse   (misuse) laahm·yuhng: **abuse one's power** laahm·yuhng kyùhn·lihk; (revile)
naauh·yàhn (VO); (corrupt custom) baih, baih·behng (N)

abyss   sàm·yùn.

academic degree   hohk·wái

academic world   hohk·syuht·gaai

academy   hohk·haauh, hohk·yún

accent   yām, háu·yām. /He speaks English without even a trace of local accent. Kéuih
góng Yìng·mahn yāt·dī bún·deih háu·yām dōu móuh.

accept   jip·sàuh: **accept other's kindness** jip·sàuh yàhn·deih ge hóu·yi; **accept a gift**
jihp·sauh láih·maht; **accept terms of a treaty** jip·sàuh tiuh·gín
        sàu. Has that school accepted you? Gó·gàan hohk·haauh sàu·jó néih meih a? /Do
you accept American dollars? Néih sàu m̀h·sàu Méih·gām a?
        yìng·sìhng. /Have you accepted his offer? Néih yìng·sìhng·jó kéuih meih a?

accessary   fuh·suhk·bán

accident   (unforseen events) yi·ngoih: **have an accident** sāt sih, faat·sàng yi·ngoih; or
the action may be expressed more specifically: /They had an automobile accident yesterday. Kéuih·deih kàhm·yaht johng·chè (collided with another car), or pung·chàn yàhn
(ran into someone).

acclimatize   jyun·séui·tóu: **acclimatized** jyun jo séui·tóu la.

accommodate   yùhng·naahp. /How many people can it accommodate? Hó·yih yùhng·naahp
géi·dò yàhn a?

accompany   pùih, tùhng·màaih. /Can you accompany me there? Néih hó·yíh pùih ngóh
heui ma? or Néih hó·yíh tùhng·màaih ngóh heui ma?

accomplish   jouh·sìhng, yùhn·sìhng. /When can you accomplish it? Néih géi·sí hó·yíh
jouh·sèhng kéuih a? /He needs some time before he can accomplish this. Kéuih sèui·
yiu dò·síu sìh·gaan sìn·jí hó·yíh yùhn·sìhng nī·gihn sih.

according   jiu, yî·jiu. /According to the weather report, it'll rain tonight. Jiu tìn·hei
bou·gou gám góng, gàm·máahn wúih lohk·yúh boh. /According to the law, he should be
punished. Yî·jiu faat·leuht kéuih yìng·gòi sauh chyúh·faht. /According to the local custom

no one will do business on New Year's Day. Yì·jiu bún·deih ge jaahp·gwaan, nîhn·chō· yāt móuh yàhn jouh sàang·yi ge. /According to what you say, he won't come today will he? Jiu néih gám wah kéuih gàm·yaht m̀h·lèih lo boh, haih m̀h·haih a?

accordion   sáu·fùng·kàhm

account   (financial) sou, sou·muhk. /Have you figured out the account? Néih gai·chēut tiuh sou meih a? /This company's accounts are in good order. Nī·gāan gūng·sī ge sou· muhk hóu chìng·chó. **on no account** /On no account should you allow him to do it. Néih jyuht·deui bāt·nàhng béi kéuih jouh nī·gihn sih. **charge to one's account** yahp·sou /Please charge to my account. M̀h·gòi néih, yahp ngóh ge sou là.

accountant   wuih·gai, wuih·gai·sī

accumulate   jīk·maai. /What did you accumulate that many lanterns for? Néih jīk·màaih gam dò dàng·lùhng jouh māt·yéh a?

accurate   jéun·kok

accuse   jí·jaahk, hung·gou. /He accuses him of being dishonest. Kéuih jí·jaahk kéuih góng·daaih·wah. /He was accused of stealing a car. Kéuih béi yàhn hung·gou kéuih tàu chè.

accused (the)   beih·gou (N)

accustomed   gwaan·jó. /I'm accustomed to it. Ngóh yìh·gìng gwaan·jó la.

ache   tung. Nominal expressions plus tung are used to express an ache in a particular part of the body: **have a headache** tàuh·tung; **have a toothache** ngàh·tung; **have a stomach ache** tóuh·tung, waih·tung; etc. /I have a headache. Ngóh tàuh·tung. /I have a toothache. Ngóh ngàh·tung. /Do you have a stomach ache? Néih tóuh·tung àh?

acid   (chemical) syūn. /Is there any acid in that solution? Gó·jek yùhng·yihk yahp·bihn yáuh móuh syūn a?

acknowledge   sìhng·yihng: **acknowledge a fault** sìhng·yihng jouh cho

acquainted with   sīk. /Are you acquainted with the manager? Néih sīk gó·go gìng·léih ma?

acquire   hohk·dóu. /It's easy to forget but difficult to acquire a foreign language. Hóu nàahn hohk·dóu yāt·júng ngoih·gwok·wá, daahn·haih hóu yùhng·yih jauh m̀h·gei·dāk ge la.

acquit   fong. /That man has already been acquitted. Gó·go yàhn yìh·gìng fong·jó la.

acre   yìng·máuh: one acre, yāt·yìng·máuh

across   (in combination with verbs) gwo: **walk across** hàahng·gwo. /As soon as you walk across the bridge, you'll see it. Néih yāt hàahng·gwo douh kìuh jauh tái·dóu la. **across** the street, road, river, etc. . . . hái . . . deui·mihn. /The restaurant is across the street from the hotel. Gó·gàan chāan·gún jauh hái gó·gàan jáu·dim deui·mihn.

act   (give a performance) /He acted very well. Kéuih bíu·yín dāk hóu hóu. (of a play) mohk: **the third act** daih·sàam·mohk **act like** hóu·chíh. /Don't act like a child. M̀h·hóu hóu·chih go sai·màn·jái gám. **act in one's place** doih·léih. /Who'll act in your place after you're gone. Néih jáu·jó jī·hauh bīn·go doih·léih néih a? **act when you see a chance** gin·gèi·yìh·jok. /You may act when you see a chance. Néih hó·yíh gin·gèi·yìh·jok. **act without noise or ostentation** bāt·duhng·sīng·sīk gám (A)

acting   doih·léih: **acting principal** doih·léih haauh·jéung.

action   (person's behavior) géui·duhng. /His actions have been strange lately. Ni·páai kéuih ge géui·duhng hóu kèih·gwaai.

be in action jeun·hàhng. /The plan is under way. Nī·go gai·waahk jing·joih jeun·hàhng·gán.

put into action saht·hàhng. /When are you going to put this plan into action? Néih géi·sí saht·hàhng nī·go gai·waahk a?

active   (of a child) wuht·put (SV); (in political or social life) wuht·duhng (SV), wuht·yeuhk (SV).

activities   wuht·duhng: **extracurricular activities** fo·ngoih·wuht·duhng

actor   (opera) hei·jí; (drama or movies) yín·yùhn; (male actor who takes female parts) fà·dáan

actress   (opera) hei·ji, lóuh·gùn; (drama or movies) néuih·yín·yùhn

actual   saht·joih ge: **the actual condition** saht·joih ge chìhng·yìhng

actually   kèih·saht, jàn·haih. /Actually, he's wrong. Keih·saht kéuih cho·jó. /He actually came! Kéuih jàn·haih lèih·jó!

acute   gán·yiu, gāau·gwàan (ref. C – E section). **acute pain** tung dāk hóu gāau·gwàan.

A.D.   géi·yùhn·hauh, gùng·yùhn, Jú·hauh. **300 A.D.** géi·yùhn hauh sāam·baak·nìhn.

Adam   A·dōng

adapt   sīk·ying. /You should adapt yourself to the circumstance. Néih yiu sīk·ying wàahn·gíng ji·dāk.

add   gà. /Add some water to it. Gà dī séui ji·dāk.

add together gà·màaih yāt·chái. /Add these two numbers together. Jèung nī·léuhng·go sou·muhk gà·màaih yāt·chái. /Please add up this list of figures. M̀h·gòi jèung nī·dī sou·muhk gà·màaih kéuih.

add up to gà·màaih yāt·guhng yáuh géi·dò. /How much do these figures add up to? /Nī·dī sou·muhk gà·màaih yāt·guhng yáuh géi·dò a?

add a little more gā dī tìm

add ten times as much gà·dò sahp·púih

adding machine   gai·syun·gèi

addicted to   yáuh . . . yáhn. /He is addicted to heroin. Kéuih yáuh baahk·mihn yáhn.

addition   gà·faat: addition, subtraction, multiplication, and division; gà·(faat),gáam·(faat) sìhng·(faat), chèuih·(faat)

(result of adding). /Is my addition correct? <u>is expressed as</u> Have I added (calculated) correctly? Ngóh gā dāk ngāam m̀h·ngāam a?

(thing added). haih hauh·lèih gà·lohk·heui ge <u>or</u> haih hauh·lèih gà·séuhng·heui ge. /This part is an addition to the original. Nī·bouh·fahn haih hauh·lèih gà·lohk·heui ge.

(person needed). /We need to hire additional clerks to handle the extra work. Ngóh deih sèui·yiu jāng·gà dī jīk·yùhn.

in addition chyùh·chí·jí·ngoih. /Do you need anything else in addition? Chyùh·chí·jí·ngoih néih juhng yiu dī māt·yéh ma?

in addition to chyùh·jó . . . jí·ngoih. /In addition to these two items, which one (of the rest) do you want? Chyùh·jó ni·léuhng·gihn ji·noih néih juhng yiu bīn gihn a?

address   (place of residence or business) deih·bouh, deih·jí; (place of residence) jyuh·jí; (mailing address) tùng·seun·chyúh. /My address is . . . Ngóh ge deih·jí haih . . . /Please write down your address for me. M̀h·gòi néih sé(·dài) go deih·jí béi·ngóh.

to give an address yín·góng, yín·syut. /The President is going to address the Congress tomorrow. Júng·túng tìng·yaht deui gwok·wúi yín·góng.

address to sé·béi. /To whom should I address this letter? Nī·fùng seun ngóh yìng·gòi sé·béi bīn·go a?

address as chìng·fù. /How should I address him? Ngóh yìng·dòng dím·yéung chìng·fù kéuih a?

addressee   sàu·seun·yàhn

adequate   sīk·dong (ge) (SV)

adhere   chí·jyuh

adhesive tape   gàau·bou

adjacent   jó·gán, fuh·gahn, lèuhn·gahn.   /His house is adjacent to the school. Kéuih gàan ngūk hái hohk·haauh jó·gán.

adjective   yìhng·yùhng·chìh.

adjoin   lìhn·màaih.   /This house adjoins that one. Nī·gāan ngūk haih tùhng gó·gāan ngūk lìhn·màaih ge.

adjust   gaau·ngāam, jíng·hóu

administer   gún·léih

administration   (of a government) hàhng·jing·dòng·guhk; (of a school) hohk·haauh·dòng· guhk; (of an enterprise) gìng·léih·bouh·mùhn, (administering punishment) chìhng·faht ge jāp·hàhng

admiral   hói·gwān seuhng·jeung

admire   (respect) pui·fuhk, yàm·pui.   /I admire him. Ngóh hóu pui·fuhk kéuih. /I admire Confucius. Ngói hóu yàm·pui Húng·fù·jí.
      (enjoy) yàn·séung.   /I'm admiring the scenery. Ngóh jing·joih yàn·séung nī·dī fùng· gíng.

admission   (price of entrance) piu·ga.   /How much is the admission? Piu·ga géi·dò chín a?

admission ticket   fēi, yahp·chèuhng·hyun (M: jèung)

admit   sìhng·yihng.   /He admits that he has made a mistake. Kéuih sìhng·yihng kéuih jouh·cho·jó.
      (admission given by a school or an institution) sàu, chéui·luhk.   /The school wouldn't admit him. Gó·gàan hohk·haauh m̀h·sàu kéuih. /Has the college admitted you? Gó·gàan daaih·hohk chéui·luhk·jó néih meih a?
      (allow, permit to enter) béi . . . yahp·lèih.   /Don't admit them! M̀h·hóu béi kéuih· deih yahp·lèih!

admonish   hyun·gaai

adopt   (to take and apply) chói·yuhng.   /I'm sorry, we can't adopt your plan. Deui·m̀h· jyuh, ngóh·deih bat·nàhng chói·yuhng néih ge gai·waahk.
      (a child, or parent) yihng.   /Would you like to adopt him as your son? Néih séung yihng kéuih jouh jái ma?

adore   (to worship or honor) chùhng·baai; (to feel or express reverent admiration for) ging·pui.

adorn   jōng·sīk.

adult   daaih·yàhn.

adulterer   gàan·fù.

adultery   tùng·gàan: . . . and . . . commit adultery . . . tùhng . . . tùng·gàan; commit adultery (as a crime) faahn tùng·gàan jeuih.

advance   (progress) jeun·bouh. (in battle) jeun·jín
      in advance yuh·sìn.   /Let me know in advance if you're coming. Yùh·gwó néih lèih m̀h·gòi néih yùh·sìn tùhng·jí ngóh.

to advance <u>money</u> (informal), sìn je . . . béi; (formal), yuh·jì. /Can you advance me thirty dollars? Néih hó·yíh yuh·sìn béi sà'ah mān ngóh ma? <u>or</u> Ngóh séung yuh·jì sà'ah mān, dāk m̀h·dāk a?

advanced class   gōu·kāp·bāan

advantage   leih. **have advantages** yáuh leih; **have disadvantages** yáuh bāt·leih. /If this is to your advantage, of course you should take it. Yùh·gwó nī·gihn deui néih yáuh·léih gáng·haih jouh lā. /This method has advantages and disadvantages. Nī·go baahn·faat yáuh leih yihk yáuh bāt·leih.

advantageous   jeuhk·sou

adventure   mouh·hím (ref. C – E section)

adverb   fu·chìh

adversary   deui·tàuh

adverse   **adverse wind** ngahk·fùng; **adverse fortune** sèui·wahn

adversity   waahn·naahn

advertise   (in newspaper, magazine) maaih·gou·baahk; (on walls) tip·gāai·jīu

advertising department   gwóng·gou·bouh

advertisement   gwóng·gou, gou·baahk

advice   yi·gin, jùng·gou. /It's good advice from you. Néih·ge yi·gin hóu hóu. /Your advice has worked well. Néih·ge jùng·gou faat·sàng haauh·lihk boh.

advise   wah . . . yìng·dòng, hyun. /What do you advise me to do? Néih wah ngóh yìng· dòng dím baahn a? /I advise you to take a rest. Ngóh hyun néih yáu sīk háh.
advise against m̀h·jyú·jèung. /I advise against going. Ngóh m̀h·jyú·jèung heui.

aerodrome   fèi·gèi·chèuhng

affable   hóu·sèung·yúh

affair   sih·gon, sih, sih·chihng

affect   (cause a change) yíng·héung; (move the feelings) gáam·duhng

affidavit   syùn·saih·syù

affection   gáam·chihng; **filial affections** tin·leuhn ji ngoi, chàn·chihng

affectionate   chàn·ngoi (ge), chihng·sàm (ge); **affectionate mother** chìh·móuh

affinity   (having an attraction for) yùhn·fahn; **have affinity with** yáuh yùhn·fahn

affirm   (say firmly) góng·m̀ihng; (say that something is true) góng·saht

affirmative   háng·dihng·ge

affix   nìhm, tip; dám; chìm. **affix a postage stamp** nìhm sih·dāam; **affix a seal** dám yan <u>or</u> dám tòuh·jèung; **affix a signature** chìm méng

affliction   fú·naahn

afford   gūng·dāk·héi, gùng·m̀h·héi; máaih·dāk·héi, máaih·m̀h·héi. /Can you afford to send him to school? Néih gūng·dāk·héi kéuih duhk·syù ma? /Can you afford to buy it? No, I can't. Néih máaih·dāk·héi ma? Ngóh m̀h·máaih·dāk·héi.

afraid   pa. /Don't be afraid. M̀h·sái pa.
be afraid of pa. /What are you afraid of? Néih pa māt·yéh a?
be afraid to pa. /I'm afraid to go out alone. Ngóh pa yāt·go yàn chēut·gāai.
be afraid that húng·pa. /I'm afraid I can't go. Ngóh húng·pa ngóh bāt·nàhng heui.

after　yih·hauh, jì·hauh, hauh (ref. C – E section)
　　(next in order) /What's the next street after this? Hah·yāt·tìuh gāai haih māt·yéh
　gāai a? /What is the next picture after this? Hah·yāt·kèih yíng māt·yéh wá a?
　　after all　gau·gíng, dou·dái. /After all, is he coming or not? Gau·gíng kéuih lèih
　m̀h·lèih a? /You're right, after all. Dou·dái haih néih ngāam.
　　after that, afterward　hāu·mēi. /What happened after that? Hāu·mēi dím a?
　　day after day　yaht yaht gám; **year after year**　nìhn nìhn gám (A)

after death　séi·hauh, sàn·hauh: **after his death** kéuih séi·hauh, or kéuih sàn·hauh

afternoon　hah·jau

afterwards　hāu·mēi. /What happened afterwards? Hāu·mēi dím a?

again　joi; yauh. /Don't go again. M̀h hóu joi heui la. /I forgot again. Ngóh yauh
　m̀h·gei·dāk·jó la.
　　again and again　joi·sàam, yāt·chi yauh yāt·chi gám. /I told him again and again . . .
　Ngóh joi·sàam góng kéuih jì . . .

against　be against a person, policy, proposal, idea, etc. fáan·deui, fáan. /Everyone
　is against him. Go·go dōu fáan·deui kéuih.
　　be against the law, faahn faat, wàih·faahn faat·leuht. /If you're doing that, it is
　against the law. Yùh·gwó néih gám jouh, faahn·faat ge boh.
　　against the current, current opinion, wind, ngahk: **against the current** ngahk·séui;
　against the wind ngahk·fùng; **against current opinion** ngahk daaih·gā ge yi·si
　　be against (of subordinate to higher authority), fáan·kong. /A group of soldiers are
　against their officers. Yāt·bouh·fahn (sih·)bìng fáan·kōng kéuih·deih ge gwān·gùn.
　　bring action against　hung·gou, gou. /He wants to bring action against that firm.
　Kéuih yiu hung·gou gó·gàan gūng·sī.
　　against one's will　mìhn·kéuhng. /I think he did it against his will. Ngóh tái kéuih
　mìhn·kéuhng gám jouh ge jē.
　　go against one's conscience wàih·bui. /I'd never go against my own conscience.
　Ngóh jyuht·deui m̀h·wàih·bui ngóh ge lèuhng·sàm.

agate　máh·nóuh

age　(year of age) seui, nình·géi; (formal) nìhn·lìhng. /How old are you? Néih géi·dò
　seui la? /How old is your father? Néih bàh·bā māt·yéh nìhn·géi a? /Please fill in your
　age here. Chéng néih jèung néih ge nìhn·lìhng sé·hái nī·syu.
　　(era) sìh·doih. /This is the space age. Yìh·gā haih taai·hùng sìh·doih.
　　the aged (people) baak·yē·gūng baak·yē·pó, lóuh·nìhn·yàhn, lóuh·yàhn
　　to age　lóuh. /He's aged a great deal lately. Kéuih gahn·lói lóuh·jó hóu·dò.

agency　doih·léih, doih·léih·chyúh

agenda　yih·chìhng, yih·sih·chìhng·jeuih

agent　doih·léih

aggression　chàm·leuhk

aggressive　(indifferent to others' rights) ba·douh. /He is very aggressive. Kéuih hóu
　ba·douh ge. (enterprising) háng·gon. /I need an aggressive agent. Ngóh séui·yiu yāt·
　go hóu háng·gon ge doih·léih.

aggressor　chàm·leuhk·jé; (a country) chàm·leuhk·gwok(·gà)

agitate　gīk·duhng, sin·duhng

ago　chìhn, yíh·chìhn. /Two years ago I was in America. Léuhng·nìhn chìhn ngóh hái
　Méih·gwok.

a while ago yāt·jahn·gāan la. /He left a while ago. Kéuih jáu·jó Yāt·jahn·gāan la.
long ago hóu noih, hóu noih yíh·chìhn. /He left long ago. Kéuih jáu·jó hóu noih la.
/It happened long ago. Yíh gìng haih hóu noih yíh·chìhn ge sih la.
not very long ago móuh géi nói jì·chìhn, bāt·gáu jì·chìhn. /He was here not very long
ago. Móuh géi nói jì·chìhn kéuih juhng hái nī·syu.

agony   tung·fú

agree   (be in accord) sèung·fùh; (have the same opinion) tùhng·yi; (be the same) yāt·yeuhng,
seung·tùhng. /The translation and the original don't agree. Fàan·yihk tùhng yùhn·màhn
m̀h·sèung·fùh. /If he doesn't agree, you had better not do it. Yùh·gwó kéuih m̀h·tùhng·yi
jauh m̀h·hóu jouh la. /The ideas of the two parties agree to some extent. Léuhng·dóng ge
yi·gin yáuh yāt·bouh fahn sèung·tùhng.
 agree to something jip sauh. /I can't agree to your terms. Ngóh bāt·nàhng jip·sauh
néih ge tìuh·gín.
 agree with an idea or proposition jaan·sìhng. /I don't agree with this measure.
Ngóh m̀h·jaan·sìhng nī·go baahn·faat.
 agree with certain kind of (food, climate) sauh·dak. /Does coffee agree with you?
Néih sauh m̀h·sauh·dāk ga·fē a? /I'm afraid that the climate there wouldn't agree with
me. Ngóh pa ngóh m̀h·sauh dāk gó·syu ge tìn·sìh.

agriculture   nùhng·yihp

aground   gok·chín

ahead   chìhn, chìhn·bihn /Go straight ahead. Yāt·jihk heung chìhn gám hàahng. /Do you
know whose car is ahead of us? Néih jì m̀h·jì chìhn·bihn gó·ga chē haih bīn·go ga?

aid   gau·jai. /We need some money to aid the refugees there. Ngóh·deih sèui·yiu dī chín
gau·jai gó·syu dī naahn·màhn.
 financial aid: (money for study) jéung·hohk·gām; (pension) yéuhng·lóuh·gām; (compensation) gau·jai·gām; (subsidy) jèun·tip.
 foreign aid ngoih·yùhn; **American aid** Méih·yùhn

aide-de-camp   fu·gùn

ailment   behng, behng·tung

aim   (goal) muhk·dīk. /My aim is to finish writing this book. Ngóh ge muhk·dīk haih
sé·yùhn nī·bún syù.
 (plan) dá·syun, séung. /What do you aim to do? Néih dá·syun jouh māt·yéh a?
 to aim a weapon mìuh·jéun, heung . . . mìuh·jéun. /Don't shoot until you aim.
Mìuh·jéun sìn·ji hóu hōi·chēung. /Aim at that target. Heung gó·go muhk·bīu mìuh·jéun.
 (purpose of an association, etc.) jùng·jí. /What is the aim of this organization? Nī·
go tyùhn·tái ge jùng·jí haih māt·yéh a?

air   (atmosphere) hùng·hei; (sky, weather) tìn·hei. /I'm going out for some fresh air.
Ngóh yiu chēut·heui kāp·háh sàn·sìn hùng·hei. /The air is clear today. Gàm·yaht ge
tìn·hei hóu chìn·sóng.
 (sky) (tìn·)hūng·jùng /Suddenly the air was filled with chattering birds. Fāt·yìhn·
gāan tīn·hūng·jùng yáuh hóu dò jéuk hái syu chèung.
 by air (for passengers) chóh fēi·gèi; (for freight or mail), gei fēi·gèi; (for mail)
gei hòhng·hùng·seun. /I want to go by air. Ngóh séung chóh fèi·gèi heui.
 be on the air gwóng·bo. /This program will be broadcast tonight. Nī·go jit·muhk
gàm·máahn gwóng·bo.
 open-air louh·tìn. /Tonight there will be an open-air concert. Gàm·máahn yáuh
yāt·go louh·tìn ge·yàm·ngohk·wúi.
 be airtight m̀h·lauh·hei
 to air (of a room, etc.) tùng·háh·fùng. /Please open the window to air the room.

Mh·gòi dá·hòi go chēung·mún tùng·háh·fùng; (of clothing) sáu. /Take these clothes out and air them. Nīk nī·dī sāam chēut·heui sáu·háh keuih.

aircraft carrier   hòhng·hùng·móuh·laahm (M: jek)

airfield   fēi·gèi·chèuhng

air force   hūng·gwān

air letter   hòhng·hùng·yàuh·gáan

airmail   fēi·gèi·seun, hòhng·hùng·seun.   **by airmail** gei fèi·gèi, yùhng fèi·gèi gei

airplane   fēi·gèi (M: ga)

airport   fēi·gèi·chèuhng

airline   hòhng·hūng·gūng·sī

air raid   hùng·jaahp

air raid alarm   fòhng·hùng·gíng·bou

air raid shelter   fòhng·hùng·duhng

alarm   gíng·bou.   **fire alarm** fó·gíng; **burglar alarm** fòhng·chahk gíng·jūng.
   alarm clock naauh·jūng
   to alarm gíng·duhng. /The noise alarmed the whole town. Sìng·yàm gìng·duhng·jó chyùhn·sèhng.
   be alarmed gèng, gèng·fòng. /Don't be alarmed. Mh·sái gèng·fòng.
   be alarming dāk·yàhn·gèng. /The situation was quite alarming. Dòng·sih ge chìhng· yìhng hóu dāk·yàhn·gèng.

album   géi·nìhm·chaak; **photograph album** seung·pín·bóu

alcohol   (medicinal) fó·jáu; (liquor) jáu·jīng

alert   sìng·séui, gèi·gíng

Algebra   doih·sou

alias   biht méng, yauh mìhng

alien   ngoih·gwok (At); ngoih·gwok·yàhn (N).

alight   lohk·hái, lohk·joih

alike   sèung·tùhng ge, yāt·yèuhng ge. /These materials are all alike. Nī·di chòih·líu dōu haih yāt·yeuhng ge.
   look alike hóu·chíh. /They look alike. Kéuih·deih léuhng·go hóu·chíh.

alive   sàang; sàang·máahng. /Is she still alive? Kéuih juhng sàang ma? /The fish is still very much alive. Gó·tìuh yú juhng hóu sàang·máahng.

all   go·go (or any measure in reduplication plus noun) dōu. /All are fine. Go·go dōu hóu hóu. /All of these watches are good. Go go bīu dōu hóu hóu.
   só·yáuh·ge. /All my students are Americans. Ngóh só·yáuh·ge hohk·sāang dōu haih Méih·gwok yàhn. /Give me all your money. Jèung néih só·yáuh·ge chín béi·saai ngóh.
   saai. /We've eaten all of them. Ngóh·deih sihk·saai lo.
   sèhng. **all day** sèhng·yaht, **all night** sèhng·máahn sèhng is also used for week, month, year, century, etc.
   all kinds of gok·sīk gok·yeuhng, gok·júng
   all the same móuh·fàn·biht, dōu haih yāt·yeuhng ge
   all the way yāt·louh·gám. /He ran all the way there. Kéuih yāt·louh·gám jáu·heui gó·syu.
   not at all yāt·dī·dōu·mh, yùhn·chyùhn·mh, chí·jùng·meih. /I don't know it at all. Ngóh

yāt·dī·dōu·m̀h·jî. /I don't know how to read it at all. /Ngóh yùhn·chyùhn·m̀h·sīk duhk.
/I haven't been there at all. Ngóh chí·jùng·meih heui·gwo.

alley   hóng·jái, láahng·hóng (M: tìuh)

alliance   lyùhn·màhng, tùhng·màhng

allied troops   lyùhn·gwān, màhng·gwān

alligator   ngohk·yùh (M: tìuh)

allot   fàn·paai

allow   (permit) béi (informal), jéun (formal). /She won't allow me to go. Kéuih m̀h·béi
(or m̀h·jéun) ngóh heui. /Each person is allowed fifty pounds of baggage without extra
charge. Múih·yàhn jéun míhn·fài daai ńgh·sahp·bohng hàhng·léih.
    allow so much for (pay, or loan on security). /How much will you allow me for this?
Nī·gihn yéh néih dá·syun béi géi·dò chín a?

allowance   jèun·tip: **housing allowance** fòhng·ngūk jèun·tip

alluring   yáhn·yau·lihk, yáhn·yau·sing

ally   (tùhng·)màhng·gwok

alma mater   móuh·haauh

almanac   tùng·syù, tùng·sing

almighty   mòuh·só·bāt·nàhng, chyùhn·nàhng, màahn·nàhng

almond   hahng·yàhn

almost   jāang·dī, chà·m̀h·dō, gèi·fùh. /I almost forgot. Ngóh jāang·dī m̀h·gei·dāk·jó.
(with reference to time) jauh·lèih. /It's almost three o'clock. Jauh·lèih sàam·dím
la. /I'm almost done. Ngóh jauh·lèih jouh·yùhn la. /We're almost there. Ngóh·deih
jauh·lèih dou la.

alone   (by oneself) jih·géi, jih·gēi. /Can you do it alone? Néih jih·géi jouh·dāk ma?
(to oneself) yāt·go·yàn. /I came alone. Ngóh yāt·go·yàn lèih ge. (orphaned) gù·duhk.
/He is all alone in the world, not even a single relative. Kéuih fèi·sèuhng gù·duhk, yāt
go chàn·yàhn dōu móuh. **Leave me alone!** Hàahng·hòi dī la!

along   (as a road or a coast) yùhn. **along a road** yùhn louh; **along the shore** yùhn ngohn;
along the coast yùhn hói (or ngohn).
    along with tùhng·màaih; **carry along with** daai·màaih

aloud   daaih·sèng. /Please read it aloud. Chéng néih daaih·sèng duhk.

alphabet   jih·móuh, jih·júng

already   yíh·gìng. /He has come already. Kéuih yíh·gìng lèih·jó la.

also   yihk·dōu, dōu, yihk (ref. C – E section)

altar   (for public use) jai·tàahn; (in a household) sàhn·tói

alter   gói, gàng·gói, gói·jing

alterable   gói·dāk. /Is it alterable? Gói·dāk ma?

alternate   (in turns) lèuhn·láu (A); **alternate days** gaak·yaht (A).

although   sèui·yìhn (often followed in the next part of the sentence by daahn·haih); or
sometimes expressed by daahn·haih without sèui·yìhn. /Although I'll be busy, I shall
go to his party. Sèui·yìhn ngóh m̀h·dāk·hàahn, daahn·haih ngóh yiu chàam·gà kéuih ge
yin·wuih. /Although they don't have much money, they live in quite a leisurely way.
Kéuih·deih móuh māt chín daahn·haih kéuih·deih gwo·dāk hóu yàu·yàuh.

alum   baahk·fàahn, mîhng·faahn

aluminium   léuih

altitude   gòu·douh

always   sîh·sîh, sîh·sîh·dou·haih. /Are you always so busy? Néih sîh·sîh·dōu·haih gam mh·dāk·hàahn àh? /It's always raining here in the springtime. Nī·syu chēun·tīn sîh·sîh lohk·yúh ge.
     (since some remote point of time) yāt·heung, heung·lòih, chùhng·lòih. /He has always been this way. Kéuih yāt·heung dōu haih gám ge la.

am   haih

a.m.   seuhng·jau

amah   gùng·yàhn, pòh·mā, má·jé

amalgamate   hahp·bihng

amateur   yihp·yùh: **amateur soccer team** yihp·yùh jūk·kàuh·déui

ambassador   daaih·si

amber   fú·paak

ambiguous   mh·chìng·chó, mh·chìng·mh·chó

ambition   (in good sense) ji·hei; (pejorative) yéh·sàm

ambitious   yáuh·ji·hei; yáuh·yéh·sàm

ambulance   gau·sèung·chè, sahp·jih·chè; **ambulance corps** gau·sèung·déui

ambush   maaih·fuhk (N); **to ambush** chit·hah màaih·fuhk lèih gūng·gīk

amend   (of a law or rule) sàu·jing, sàu·gói, gói·jing

amendment   sàu·jing·on

America   (the continent) Méih·jàu: **North America** Bāk·méih·jàu; **South America** Nàahm·méih·jàu; **United States of America** Méih·lèih·gīn·hahp·jung·gwok (full name) or Méih·gwok

American   Méih·gwok·yàhn (N); Meih gwok ge (At); **American currency** méih·gām, fà·kèih·ngān, fà·kèih·jí

amiable   wòh·hei, hóu·sèung·yúh

ammonia   a·mò·nàih·a

ammunition   gwàn·fó

among   (in the midst of) hái . . . léuih·bihn. /You'll find it among those books. Néih hái gó·dī syù léuih·bihn jauh wán·dóu ge la.
     (in the number or class of) kèih·jùng·jī·yāt. /He is one of them. Kéuih haih kèih·jùng·jī·yāt.
     (by the reciprocal action of) /They were quarreling among themselves. Kéuih·deih béi·chí ngaai·héi·gāau séuhng·lèih.

amount   (numerical sum) sou·muhk; (quantity) sou·leuhng. /This isn't the right amount. Nī·go sou·muhk mh·ngāam.

amplifier   fong·daaih·hei

amplify   fong·daaih

amputate   geu·heui

amulet   fùh; wuh·sàn·fùh

amuse   (of a child) tam: **amuse a child** tam sai·mān·jái. (of adult) lihng . . . hòi·háh·
sàm. /Tell him a joke to amuse him. Góng go siu·wá lìhng kéuih hòi·háh·sām la.
   amuse oneself sìu·hín. /How do you amuse yourself? Néih yáuh māt sìu·hín a?
   be amusing hóu siu. Do you find this movie amusing? Néih gok·dak nī·chēut hei hóu
siu ma?

amusement   yùh·lohk, yàuh·ngaih

amusement park   yàuh·lohk·chèuhng

anaemia   pàhn·hyut

anaesthetic   màih·mùhng·yeuhk, màh·jeui·yeuhk

anaesthetize   màih·mùhng, màh·jeui

analyze   fān·sīk, fàn·gáai; (in chemistry) fa·yihm

analysis   fān·sīk

anatomy   gáai·páu; gáai·páu·hohk

ancestor   jóu·sīn, jóu·jùng

ancestral hall   chìh·tóng

ancestral home   jóu·gà; jóu·ngūk

ancestral tablet   sàhn·jyú·páai

ancestral worship   baai jóu·sīn

anchor   màauh: **cast anchor** pàau màauh, lohk maauh; **weigh anchor** héi·màauh

ancient   gú·doih; gú (BF): **ancient people** gú·yàhn; **ancient time** gú·sìh; **ancient remains**
gú·jīk; **ancient city** gú·sèhng; **ancient and modern times** gú·gàm

and   (between nouns) tùhng, tùhng·màaih (Ref. C – E section)
   'and' between some nouns in English is often not expressed by a separate Chinese
word: **father and mother** fuh·móuh; **mother and child** móuh·jí; **man and wife** fù·fúh;
brothers and sisters hìng·daih jí·mui; **table and chairs** tòih·yí
   (between adjectives) yauh . . . yauh . . . (Ref. C – E section)
   (between verbs). /I called and called, but no one answered. Ngóh dá·jó yāt·chi yauh
yāt·chi dōu móuh yàhn jip. /I can wash and shave at the hotel. Ngóh hó·yíh hái jáu·dim
sái·mihn tùhng tai·sòu.
   (between clauses) in a sentence like He came and then I left. 'and' is not expressed
in Chinese. Instead, one says After he came I left. Kéuih lèih·jó jī·hauh ngóh jauh jáu·
jó la.
   and so só·yíh, yàn·chí /And so he quit. Só·yíh kéuih jauh jáu·jó la.
   and so forth jī·léui (ge yéh), dáng dáng. /I need towels, soap, and so forth. Ngóh
seui·yiu sáu·gān, fàan·gáan jī·léui ge yéh.
   and then gàn·jyuh (immediately after); jī·hauh, yìhn·hauh (secondly, after); plus jauh
if the event is in the past, ji if the event is in the future. /And then he said . . . Keuih
gàn·jyuh wah . . . /He locked the door and then he left. Kéuih sàan·màaih muhn jī·hauh
jauh jáu·jó la.
   both . . . **and** . . . yauh . . . yauh . . . /This vase is both beautiful and inexpensive.
Ni·go fā·jēun yauh leng yauh pèhng.
   come and lèih . . . Vháh. /Come and take a look. Lèih tái·háh.
   go and heui . . . Vháh. /Go and try it. Heui si·háh.

anecdote   yaht·sih

anew   joi·chi, chùhng·sàn

angel   tīn·si (one who carries messages from God); sàhn·sīn (being that never dies) angle   gok·douh

Anglo-American   Yìng·méih

angry   nàu. /What are you angry about? Néih nāu māt·yéh a?

animal   duhng·maht

ankle   geuk·ngau, geuk·ngáahn

anklet   (jewelry) geuk·ngák

annex   hahp·bihng

annihilate   sîu·miht, jíu·miht

anniversary   jàu·nîhn·géi·nihm

annotate   jyu·gáai

annotation   jyu·gáai

announce   syùn·bou (formally); gùng·bou (declare); gwong·bo; bou·gou (report). /They
    just announced that they're engaged. Kéuih·deih ngāam·ngāam syùn·bou dehng·fàn.
    /The government has announced the budget for next year. Jing·fú yíh·gîng gùng·bou·jó
    mîhng·nîhn ge yuh·syun la. /That news was announced on the radio. Gó·dyuhn sàn·
    mán háih mòuh·sin·dihn gwóng·bo ge.

announcement   tùng·gou; bou·gou (on a bulletin board)

announcer   (radio) gwóng·bo·yùhn, bou·gou·yùhn

annoying   fàahn·hei

annual   múih·nîhn, nîhn·nîhn, nîhn (BF): **annual meeting** nîhn·wúi

annuity   yéuhng·lóuh·gām

annul   chéui·sîu

anonymous   mòuh·mîhng ge, nihk·mîhng ge: **anonymous letter** nihk·mîhng·seun.

another   (different) daih·yih, lihng·ngoih, lihng·ngói. /I don't like this one, may I have
    another? Ngóh m̀h·jùng·yi nī·go, béi daih·yih·go ngóh dāk ma? /This is another matter.
    Nī·gihn haih lihng·ngói yāt·gihn sih. /Let's talk about it another day. Daih·yih·yaht
    sìn·ji góng la.
        (additional) joi, yauh, juhng. /Please give me another cup of coffee. M̀h·gòi joi béi
    bùi ga·fē ngóh. /He has drunk another cup of coffee. Kéuih yauh yám·jó yāt·bùi ga·fē.
    /He said, he wants another cup of coffee. Kéuih wah kéuih juhng yiu yāt·bùi ga·fē wóh.
        one after another yāt·go yāt·go gám. /Please walk in there one after another.
    Chéng néih·deih yāt·go yāt·go gám hàahng·yahp·heui gó·syu.
        one another béi·chí. People should love each other. Yàhn yìng·dòng béi·chí sèung·
    ngoi.
        one way or another júng·jì. /I'll fix it one way or another. Júng·jì ngóh gáau·dihm
    kéuih là.

answer   (respond to a question) wùih·daap, daap. /Why didn't you answer this question?
    Dím·gáai néih m̀h·wùih·daap nī·go mahn·tàih a?
        (when one's name is called) ying. /Why don't you answer him? Dím·gáai néih m̀h·
    ying kéuih a?
        (of a letter) wùih·seun, fūk·seun. /Why don't you answer his letter? Dím·gáai néih
    m̀h·wùih·seun béi kéuih a?
        answer a telegram fūk·dihn (·bou)
        answer the phone jip·dihn·wá
        (reply) wùih·daap /He gave a poor answer. Kéuih wùih·daap dāk m̀h·hóu.

(to a mathematical problem or to a question) daap·ngon. /The answers are in the back of the book. Daap·ngon hái bún syù hauh·bihn.

ant   ngáih (M: jek)

antagonists   deui·tàuh

antarctic   nàahm·gihk

Antarctic Ocean   Nàahm·bìng·yèuhng

antenna   (radio, television) tìn·sin; (feelers) chūk·gok

anthology   (of prose) màhn·syún; (of verse) sī·syún

anthem   (sung in churches) jaan·méih·sī; **national anthem** gwok·gō

anthropology   yàhn·leuih·hohk

anti-   fáan-: **anti-communist** fáan·guhng; **anti-imperialism** fáan·dai; **anti-war** fáan·jin; **anti-Soviet Russia** fáan·Sòu <u>or</u> fáan·Ngòh; **anti-British** fáan·Yìng; **anti-American** fáan·Méih; **anti-opium campaign** kéuih·duhk wahn·duhng <u>or</u> gam·yīn wahn·duhng

antiaircraft gun   gou·seh·paau

anticipate   yùh·liuh

antidote   gáai·duhk·jāi, gáai·duhk ge yeuhk

antimony   tài

antiquated   (out of date, old-fashioned) gú·lóuh ge

antique   (a relic or object of ancient art) gú·maht; (curios) gú·dúng (M: gihn)

antonym   fáan·yih·jih

anus   gòng·mùhn, sí·fāat (vulgar)

anxious   **be anxious about** gwa·jyuh /Your mother has been anxious about you. Néih màh·mā sìh·sìh gwa·jyuh néih.
be anxious (to) /I'm anxious to go there. Ngóh hóu séung heui go·syu.
be very anxious (to) gāp·yù /I'm very anxious to see him. Ngóh gāp·yù séung gin kéuih.

any   bīn·go . . . dōu, yahm·hòh, māt·yéh . . . dōu, /Anyone will help you. Bīn·go dōu wúih bòng néih ge la. /Any college teaches that subject. Yahm·hòh daaih·hohk dōu gaau nī·yāt fō. /Any string will do. Māt·yéh síhng·jai dōu dāk.
not . . . any yāt dī dōu m̀h . . . /I don't feel any pain. Ngóh yāt·dī dōu m̀h·tung.
anyone, anybody bīn·go dōu. /Anyone will do. Bīn·go dōu dāk. /I don't want to see anyone today. Gàm·yaht ngóh bīn·go dōu m̀h·gin.
anything māt·yéh dōu. /Anything will do. Māt·yéh dōu móuh·só·waih. /Is there anything for me? Yáuh móuh ngóh ge yéh a?
anywhere bīn·syu dōu /I'm not going anywhere. Ngóh bīn·syu dōu m̀h·heui.
any more /Do you have any more? Néih juhng yáuh ma? (also see 'more')
any time géi·sí·dōu /Any time will do. Géi·sí·dōu·dāk.

anyway   wàahng·dihm. /You won't believe it anyway. Néih wàahng·dihm dōu m̀h·seun ge la.

apart   (of distance) gaak. /Those houses are thirty feet apart. Gó·dī ngūk gaak sàam·sahp·chek yāt·gàan.
keep apart fān·hòi /Keep the children apart. Jēung dī sai·màn·jái fān·hòi.
take something apart jèung . . . chak·hòi. /Take the alarm clock apart. Jèung go naauh·jūng chak·hòi.
tell apart tái m̀h·chēut . . . /I can't tell them apart. Ngóh tái m̀h·chēut bīn·go wàahn bīn·go.

aperture   lūng, háu

apiece   múih·go. /One dollar apiece. Múih·go yāt·mān.

apologize   douh·hip, pùih·jeuih. /He should apologize to you. Kéuih yìng·gòi heung néih douh·hip.

apoplexy   jung·fùng

apostle   sí·tòuh

apparatus   (tools) hei·geuih; (instruments) hei·haaih; (scientific apparatus) yìh·hei

apparent   mìhng·baahk

apparition   gwái·wàhn, yīu·mò·gwái·gwaai

appeal   (earnestly for something) chíng·kàuh; (in law) seuhng·sou; (to one's interest) jùng·yi. /Does this appeal to you? Néih jùng·yi nī·go ma?

appear   (come into view) /A boat appeared on the horizon. Yāt·jek syùhn hái tīn·bīn chēut·yihn.
      (in court) chēut·tìhng. /The defendant didn't appear in court today. Beih·gou gàm·yaht móuh chēut·tìhng.
      appear to be hóu·chi /He appears to be very sick. Kéuih hóu·chi behng dak hóu gán·yiu gám.

appearance   yéung (face); (of a man) seung maauh; (of a woman) yùhng·maauh. /Her appearance is pleasing. Kéuih ge yéung sāang dak hóu lihng·yàhn·jùng·yi.

appendicitis   màahng·chéung·yìhm, wàahng·a·chéung faat·yìhm

appendix   fuh·luhk; màahng·chéung, wàahng·à·chéung (Med.)

appetite   waih·háu

applaud   (by clapping the hands) paak·sáu·jéung, paak·jéung, paak sáu; (by vocal sounds) hot·chói

apple   pìhng·gwó

applicant   sàn·chíng·yàhn

application   (document) sàn·chíng·syù; (for a school) yahp·hohk sàn·chíng·syù
      (of medicine). /This medicine is only for external application. Nī·jek yeuhk haih chàh ge m̀h·haih sihk ge.
      application blank bíu·gaak

apply   (place in contact) chàh. /Apply the ointment first. Sìn chàh yeuhk·gōu.
      (have bearing) ying·yuhng. /I want to apply this theory to prove it. Ngóh séung ying·yuhng nī·go léih·lyuhn lèih jing·mìhng kéuih.
      apply for sàn·chíng, jeun·hàhng. /You may apply for this position. Néih hó·yíh sàn·chíng nī·go jīk·waih. **apply for permission** ló·yàhn·chìhng
      (to use specifically) sīk·yuhng. /The rule doesn't apply in this case. Nī·tiuh kwāi·jāk m̀h·sīk·yuhng·yù nī·go chìhng·yìhng.
      apply oneself yuhng·sàm. /You should apply yourself to your studies. Néih yiu yuhng·sàm duhk·syù.

appoint   (general) paai; (to an office) yahm·mihng, wái·yahm. /He appointed me to represent him. Kéuih paai ngóh lèih doih·bíu kéuih.
      (a time or place) yeuk·dihng. **appoint a time** yeuk·dihng yāt·go sìh·gaan; **appoint a place** yeuk·dihng yāt·go deih·dím

appointment   (engagement) yeuk·wuih; (assignation) wái·yahm(·johng)
      have an appointment yeuk·jó. /Do you have an appointment to see him? Néih haih m̀h·haih yéuk·jó sìh·gaan lèih gin kéuih a? /Sorry, I've an appointment this morning.

Deui·m̀h·jyuh, Ngóh gàm·jìu yáuh go yeuk·wuih.

make an appointment dihng·go sìh·gaan . . . /I'd like to make an appointment to see him. Ngóh séung tùhng kéuih dihng go sìh·gaan gin·háh·mihn (or kìng·háh).

apportion   fàn·wàhn

appraise   (fix the value of) gú·ga

appreciate   (of art, scenery, etc.) yàn·séung. /I appreciate your paintings very much. Ngóh hóu yàn·séung ǹéih·ge wá.
(of a favor or kindness) gam·gīk. /I appreciate your help very much. Ngóh hóu gám·gīk néih ge bòng·mòhng.
(of characteristics such as talent, ability, etc.) séung·sīk. /He really appreciates your ability. Kéuih hóu séung·sīk néih ge bún·sih.
(recognize) líuh·gáai. /I can appreciate your difficulty, but there is nothing I can do. Ngóh hóu líuh·gáai néih ge kwan·nàahn, daahn·haih móuh·faat·jí bòng·mòhng.

apprehend   (arrest) làai; (understand) mìhng·baahk

apprehensive   (to anticipate with dread) gèng

apprentice   hohk·sî·jái

approach   (method) fòng·faat, faat·jí. /This is the wrong approach. Nī·go faat·jí m̀h·ngāam.
be approaching jauh·lèih V . . . la. /The train is approaching the station. Fó·chè jauh·lèih màaih jaahm la.
(of an enemy) bīk·gahn. /The enemy has already approached the station. Dihk·yàhn yíh·gīng bīk·gahn fó·chè·jaahm la.
approach a person about something wán. /Is it all right to approach him about this matter? Nī·gihn sih ngóh hó·yíh wán kéuih ma?

appropriate   sīk·hahp, sīk·dong, ngāam (SV)

approve   (by high authority) pài·jéun. /Has it been approved? Yíh·gīng pài·jéun meih a?
approve of jaan·sìhng. /His parents do not approve it. Kéuih ge fuh·móuh m̀h·jaan·sìhng.
be approved (by a group) tùng·gwo. /Has this plan been approved? Nī·go gai·waahk tùng·gwo meih a?

approximate   chā·m̀h·dō, gam·seuhng·háh, yeuk·mók

apricot   hahng

April   sei·yuht

apron   wài·kwán

aquarium   (bldg.) séui·juhk·gún; (pond) gàm·yùh·chìh; (glass bowl) gàm·yùh·gòng

Arabian   A·lā·baak·yàhn

arch   wùh

arched entrance   gúng·mùhn

archaeology   háau·gú·hohk

archbishop   daaih·jyú·gaau

archery   jin·seuht

archipelago   kwàhn·dóu

architect   waahk·jaak·sī, gin·jūk·sī

architecture   gin·jūk·hohk

archway   gúng·mùhn

artic   bāk·gihk·ge

Arctic Ocean   Bāk·bìng·yèuhng

ardent   yiht·sàm

are   haih. /Are you Mr. Gou? Néih haih m̀h·haih Gōu sīn·sàang a? **are in** or **at a place**
hái. /Where are you now? Néih yîh·gā hái bīn·syu a? **How are you?** Néih hóu ma?

area   yāt·daai; deih·fong; mihn·jīk (a particular extent of surface)

arena   ging·geih·chèuhng, gaau·chéung

argue   ngaai, ngaai·gāau, ngaau·géng, jàang·bihn. /What are they arguing about? Kéuih·
deih hái syu ngaai māt·yéh a? /He likes to argue with people. Kéuih hóu jùng·yi tùhng
yàhn ngaau·géng ge. /Don't argue please. Mh·hóu jàang(·bihn) la.

argument   (disputation) is expressed verbally as to argue.
(reasons offered in proof) léih·yàuh. /I don't follow your argument. Ngóh m̀h·haih
géi mìhng·baahk néih só góng ge léih·yàuh.

arise   (appear) faat·sàng, chēut·yihn; (get up) kéih·héi·sàn

aristocracy   gwai·juhk

arithmetic   syun·seuht

arm   (of the body) sáu·bei. /My arms hurt. Ngóh·ge sáu·béi tung.
   arm in arm sáu·làai·sáu, tō·làai·sáu. /They walk down the street arm in arm.
Kéuih·deih léuhng·go sáu·làai·sáu gám hàahng·gāai.
   arms (weapons) chēung, gà·sàang(vulgar)
   be armed (carry or have arms) daai chēung. /All personnel should be armed. Go
go dōu yiu daai chēung.
   to arm someone jèung . . . móuh·jōng héi·lòih. /Arm all the farmers. Jēung·dī
nùhng·yàhn móuh·jōng héi·lòih.

armistice   yàu·jin, tìhng·jin: **armistice day** yàuh·jin·géi·nìhm·yaht

armor   (for body) fùi·gaap; (for a vehicle or battleship) tit·gaap

armpit   gaap·lāp·dái

army   (as dist. from Navy) luhk·gwān
(as a force in the field) gwàn·déui
(armed forces or major subdivision thereof) gwān; the First army daih·yāt·gwān
send an army to . . . paai bìng heui . . . , paai gwàn·déui heui . . .
serve in the Army hái gwàn·déui fuhk·mouh

aroma   hèung, hèung meih

around   (approximately) jó·yáu, gam·seuhng·há. /I'll be there around two o'clock. Ngóh
léuhng·dím·jūng gam·seuhng·há jauh dou la.
(circumference) jàu·wàih, sei·wàih. /How big around is this city? Nī·go sèhng jàu·
waih yáuh géi dáai a? /There are hills all around that city. Gó·go sèhng sei·wàih dōu
yáuh sàan.
(walk, go, run, etc.) wàih·jyuh. /We strolled around the lake after supper. Ngóh·deih
sihk·yùhn máahn·faahn jî·hauh wàih·jyuh go wùh saan·bouh.
other expressions: /Turn around! (facing me) jyun·gwo·lèih nī·bihn! (facing away
from me) jyun·gwo·heui gó·bihn! /Is there any doctor around? Nī·syu jó·gán yáuh móuh
yī·sāng a? /I'll have to look around for it. Ngóh yiu wán·háh. /The store is just around
the corner. Gó·gàan pou·táu jauh hái jyun·wáan gó·syu jē. /See you around. Joi·gin.

arouse (awaken) giu·séng, jíng·séng; (to a sense of guilt) wuhn·séng, séng·ngh; **arouse one's anger** gīk·yàhn·nàau

arrange (put in order) báai, báai·hóu, chaap·hóu /Have you arranged (or set) the table? Néih báai·hóu tói meih a? /Wait until I've arranged the furniture. Dáng ngóh báai·hóu dī gā·sī sìn. /Have you arranged the flowers yet? Néih chaap·hóu dī fā meih a?
(make plans) séung·faat·jí, chi·faat. /I can arrange to have them sent to your home. Ngóh hó·yíh séung·faat·jí sung·heui néih ngūk·kéi.
(straighten out) jāp·hóu. /Please arrange the things on the desk. Mh·gòi néih jāp·hóu jèung tói.
(take care of) baahn·léih, liuh·léih. /Can you arrange this for me? Néih hó·yíh tùhng nógh baahn·léih nī·gihn sih ma?
(prepared) jéun·beih·hóu, jéun·beih·tóh·dong. /Everything has been arranged. Yeuhng·yeuhng dōu jéun·beih tóh·dong la.
arrange with tùhng . . . sèung·lèuhng. /You may arrange it with him. Néih hó·yíh tùhng kéuih sèung·lèuhng.

arrest làai. /The police arrested two men. Gíng·chaat làai·jó léuhng·go yàhn. /Who was arrested by the police? Bīn·go béi gíng·chaat làai·jó a?

arrive dou. /When will we arrive there? Ngóh·deih géi·sí hó·yíh dou (gó·syu) a?

arrogant gīu·ngouh, ngáahn·gok·gòu, gòu·dau

arrow jin (M: jī)

arrowhead jin·jéui

arsenal bìng·gùng·chóng

arsenic pēi·sèung

arson fong·fó

art méih·seuht (includes wuih·wá, painting; dīu·hāk, sculpture, etc.)
(more inclusive term) ngaih·seuht; (skill, craftmanship) sáu·ngaih; **industrial arts** gùng·ngaah; **liberal arts program** mành·fō; **liberal arts school** màhn·hohk·yún; **art gallery** méih·seuht·gún

artery (blood vessel) duhng·mahk

arthritis gwāt·jit·yìhm

article yéh: **articles of value** jihk·chìn·ge yéh; bán (used in compounds): **article of food** sihk·bán, **article of luxury** chè·chi·bán, **toilet articles** fa·jōng·bán
(in a document) tìuh, hohng: **article one**, daih·yāt·tìuh
(written composition) màhn·jèung. /Have you read his article on Chinese philosophy? Néih yáuh móuh tái kéuih góng Jùng·gwok Jit·hohk ge màhn·jèung a?

artificial yàhn·jouh·ge, yàhn·gùng ge: **artificial silk** yàhn·jouh sī

artillery (guns) daaih·paau; (troops) paau·bìng

artisan (man) sáu·jok·jái; (master) sī·fú

artist (general) ngaih·seuht·gā; (painter) wá·gā; (sculptor) dīu·hāk·gā; (a caligrapher) syù·faat·gā

as jiu·jyuh, hóu·chíh. /Do it as you're told by the teacher. Jiu·jyuh sīn·sàang gám góng heui jouh. or Sīn·sàang dím góng néih jauh dím jouh. /It is to be done as before. Hóu·chíh yíh·chìhn gám jouh.
as a matter of fact kèih·saht. /As a matter of fact, I don't know very much about this matter. Kèih·saht ngóh deui nī·gihn sih mh·haih hóu chìng·chó.
as follows yùh·hah. /The terms are as follow. Tìuh·gín yùh·hah.

as a rule jìu·kwèi·géui
as if, as though hóu chíh: **as if it's flying** hóu·chih fèi·gán gám
as regards deui·yù: **as regards his family** deui·yù kéuih ge gà·tìhng
as to, as for ji·yu: **as to this matter** ji·yù nī·gihng sìh
as soon as yāt . . . jauh . . . /Can we go as soon as we've eaten? Ngóh·deih yāt sihk· yùhn·faahn jauh heui, dāk ma?
as usual jiu·sèuhng, tùhng yíh·chìhn yāt·yeuhng gám V . . . /Schools open as usual. Hohk·haauh jiu·sèuhng séuhng·fo.
as you please chèuih néih bīn
be the same as tùhng . . . yāt·yeuhng. /This is the same as that. Nī·go tùhng gó·go yāt·yeuhng.
be V as dong . . . V. /It may be used as a knife. Nī·go hó·yíh dong dōu·jái sái. /It may be worn as a hat. Nī·go hó·yíh dong móu daai.
such as hóu·chíh . . . jī·léui: **such as books, magazines, newspapers, etc.** hóu·chíh syù, jaahp·ji, bou·jí, jī·léui.
take (or treat) A as B jèung A dong·jok <u>or</u> dong·waih B. /Treat him as his own child. Jèung kéuih dong·jok jih·gēi ge sai·mān·jái gám.

asbestos   sehk·mìhn

ascend   sìng: **ascend to Heaven** sīng·tīn

Ascension Day   Yèh·sōu sīng·tīn·jit

ash   fùi

ash tray   yīn·fùi·díp

ashamed   (embarrassed) m̀h·hóu·yi·si. /I'm ashamed to ask him for help. Ngóh m̀h·hóu· yi·si chéng kéuih bòng·mòhng.
    (have a sense of shame) /I'm ashamed to have done the job so poorly. Ngóh hóu chàahm·kwai nī·gihn sih ngóh m̀h·jouh·dāk tóh·dong.

ashore   (on shore) hái ngohn·seuhng; **to go ashore** séuhng·ngohn

Asia   A·jàu

Asian   A·jàu·yàhn; A·jàu·ge

aside   /Put it aside. Jài·màaih kéuih.

ask   (inquire of) mahn. /May I ask . . . Chéng·mahn . . . /Ask him if he can come tomor-row. Mahn kéuih tìng·yaht lèih m̀h·lèih·dāk. /May I ask is there a restaurant nearby? Chéng·mahn nī·syu jó·gán yáuh móuh chāan·gún a?
    ask <u>someone to do something</u> chéng. /Ask him to come tomorrow. Chéng kéuih tìng·yaht lèih. /Ask him to show it to us. Chéng kéuih béi ngóh·deih tái·háh.
    ask for yiu, yìu·kàuh. /How much is he asking for it? Kéuih yiu géi·dò chín a? /He is asking for a raise. Kéuih yìu·kàuh gà yàhn·gùng.
    ask about dá·tìng, mahn. /He is asking about the sailing date of the ship. Kéuih dá· tìng gó·jek syùhn ge syùhn·kèih.
    ask for <u>someone</u> wán. /Was there anyone asking for me? Yáuh móuh yàhn wán(·gwo) ngóh a?
    ask after mahn·hauh. /Please ask after him for me. Chéng néih tùhng ngóh mahn· hauh kéuih.
    ask leave of absence chéng·ga, gou·ga. /He wants to ask for two days' leave. Kéuih séung chéng léuhng·yaht ga. **ask sick leave** chéng behng·ga
    ask the way mahn louh. /Please go and ask the way. M̀h·gòi néih heui mahn·háh louh lā.
    ask a blind man the way mahn-douh-yù-màahng (IE)

askew   mé, m̀h·jeng

asleep (sleeping) fan·gán·gaau, fan·jeuhk(·gaau). /The baby is asleep. Bìh·bī fan·gán·gaau. <u>or</u> Bìh·bī fan·jeuhk·gaau la.
(numb) bei. /My arm asleep. Ngóh ge sáu bei.

asparagus louh·séun

aspect chìhng·yìhng, johng·fong: **aspect of affairs** chìhng·yìhng

asphalt laahp·chēng

aspirin ā·sī·pāt·līng, a·sì·pāt·lìhng

ass (animal) lèuih·jái

assail (lit.) dá. (fig.) gūng·gīk

assassin chi·haak

assassinate ngaam·saat, hàhng·chi

assault (lit.) dá. (fig.) gūng·gīk

assay (test) fa·yihm, fān·sīk

assemble (gather together) jeuih·jaahp. (fit together) gaap·màaih, dau·maaih

assembly (meeting) wúi

assembly hall wuih·tòhng, wuih·chèuhng

assent (agree to) tùhng·yi, yìng·sìhng: **assent to a petition** pài·jeun

assets chòih·cháan

assign (appoint) jí·dihng. (allot) fàn·paai

assimilate tùhng·fa

assist bòng

assistant joh·sáu, bòng·sáu

assistant manager fù·gìng·léih

associate (associate with) tùhng . . . lòih·wóhng. /Who does he associate with? Kéuih tùhng bīn·go lòih·wóhng a? (colleague) tùhng·sih

association wúi, gùng·wúi: **teachers' association** gaau·sī (gùng·)wúi

assure wah . . . yāt·dihng. /He assured us that he would be here. Kéuih wah kéuih yāt·dihng lèih.
assure that gáam dàam·bóu /I assure you that he will do a good job. Ngóh gáam dàam·bóu kéuih yāt·dihng jouh dāk hóu hóu.

asthma ché·hā

astonishing chēut·kèih

astray (go astray) dohng·sāt·louh

astrologer sìng·seung·gā, jaahk·yaht·ji ge sīn·sàang

astronomer tìng·màhn·gā

astronomy tìng·màhn·hohk

asylum yún: **asylum for the insane** dìn·kwòhng yún

at hái (ref. C – E section)

at <u>a time</u> (specifying time when) hái <u>is often omitted</u>. /Please be there at 10 A.M.

Chéng néih seuhng·jau sahp·dím·jūng dou gó·syu. /You may do it any time. Néih géi·sí jouh dōu dāk.

at any rate mòuh·leuhn·dím

at ease jih·yìhn, jih·joih; sāau·sīk (military command)

at first tàuh·táu, héi·táu, héi·sìn

at last sāu·mēi, jeui·hauh

at least ji·síu

at some length hóu noih. /He spoke at some length. Kéuih góng·jó hóu noih.

at most ji dò, jeui do. /He is most six feet tall. Kéuih ji dò luhk·chek jē.

at once jīk·hāk, lahp·hāk. /Please come at once. Chéng néih jīk·hāk lèih. /Ask him to come at once. Chéng kéuih jīk·hāk lèih.

at the same time tùhng·sìh. /I'll try to find it at the same time. Ngóh tùhng·sìh yihk heui wán·háh.

at times yáuh·sìh. /Do you have a headache at times? Néih yauh·sìh tàuh tung ma?

ate   sihk·jó

athlete   wahn·duhng·yùhn, wahn·duhng·gā

athletics   wahn·duhng

Atlantic Charter   Daaih·sai·yèuhng hin·jēung

Atlantic Ocean   Daaih·sài·yèuhng

atlas   deih·tòuh

atmosphere   (air in any locality) hùng·hei, hei; (air surrounding the earth) daaih·hei

atom   yùhn·jí; **atomic bomb** yùhn·jí·dáan; **atomic energy** yùhn·jí·nàhng

attach   (as a label) nìhm, tip; (adhere) chì; (join) lìhn; (belong to) suhk·yù; **attach to the end** lìhn·hái hauh·bihn, or fuh·gà·hái hauh·bihn.

attaché   (civilian) chèuih·yùhn; (military) móuh·gùn

attack   (lit.) dá; gūng·dá, jeun·gùng (military); (fig.) gūng·gīk

an attack of yáuh·gwo (or dāk·gwo) chi. /Has he ever had a heart attack? Kéuih yáuh móuh si·gwo sàm·johng·behng a? /Yes, he has had two of them. Yáuh, kéuih yáuh·gwo léuhng·chi.

attain   (achieve) dāk·dóu; **attain good marks** dāk·dóu hóu ge sìhng·jīk; (reach) daahk·dou; **attain one's object** daahk·dou muhk·dīk

attempt   (see 'try')

attend   (of a patient) dá·léih. /Which doctor attended you? Bīn·go yī·sāng dá·léih néih a?

attend a meeting heui (or lèih) hòi·wúi. I'm sorry, I have to attend a meeting. Deui·mh·jyuh, ngóh yiu heui hòi·wúi.

attend to baahn. /Excuse me, I have something to attend to. Deui·mh·jyuh ngóh yauh dī sih yiu baahn.

attendance register   chìm·dou·bóu

attention   **pay attention** làuh·sàm; léih·wuih, sòu (vulgar). /Please pay attention to what he says. Chéng làuh·sàm tèng kéuih góng ge syut·wah. /No one pays attention to him. Móuh yàhn léih·wuih kéuih. **Attention, everyone!** Chéng gok·wái jyu·yi!

attentively   hóu làuh·sàm gám

attitude   taai·douh

attorney   leuht·sī, johng·sī

attract   kāp·yáhn; (as a magnet) sip

attraction   kāp·yáhn·lihk

attractive   (pretty) leng

auction   haam·lāang, paak·maaih

audience   tèng·jung, gùn·jung

auditor   chàh·jeung·yùhn

August   baat·yuht

aunt   (paternal older brother's wife) baak·móuh; (paternal younger brother's wife) a·sám; (paternal sister married) gū·mā; (paternal sister unmarried) gū·jē; (maternal sister married) yìh·mā; (maternal sister unmarried) yī·jái; (maternal brother's wife) káuh·móuh, a·káhm; (paternal sisters in general) a·gù; (maternal sisters in general) a·yī

auspicious   daaih·gāt·daaih·leih; **auspicious day** hóu·yaht·jí

authentic   (genuine) jàn·jîng·ge

author   jok·jé, jok·gā, jyu·jok·gā

authority   (power) kyùhn, kyùhn·lihk, kyùhn·wài. (govt.) jing·fú, jing·fú·dòng·guhk

authorize   sauh·kyùhn

autobiography   jih·jyún

autograph book   géi·nihm·chaak

automatic   jih·duhng·ge

automobile   hei·chè (M: ga)

autumn   chāu·tīn

auxiliary   fuh·joh (ge)

avail   **avail** (oneself) **of an opportunity** chàn·gèi·wuih

available   /Is that book available? Hó·yíh wán·dāk·dóu gó·bún syù ma? /Is he available? Hó·yíh wán·dāk·dóu kéuih ma?

avarice   tāam·sàm

avenge   bou·sàuh

avenue   daaih·gāai, louh (M: tìuh)

average   pìhng·gwān·sou (N), pìhng·gwān·fān (N). /What's the average of these numbers? Nī·dī sou·muhk ge pìhng·gwān·sou haih géi·dò a? /What is the average grade of this examination? Nī·chi háau·si ge pìhng·gwān·fān haih géi·dò a?
      to average /Would you please average these figures for me? M̀h·gòi néih jēung nī·dī sou·muhk·jih ge pìhng·gwān·sou gai·béi ngóh dāk ma?
      average speed pìhng·gwān·chūk·douh; **average age** pìhng·gwān nìhn·lìhng

aviator   fèi·hàhng·gā

avoid   (of a thing) beih·míhn: **avoid dangers** beih·míhn ngàih·hím; **avoid accidents** beih·míhn faat·sàng yi·ngoih
      (of people) bèi·hòi. /Is there any way to avoid him? Yáuh māt faat·jí hó·yíh beih·hòi kéuih a?

awake   (naturally) fan·séng. /Is he awake? Kéuih fan·séng làh?
      (wake someone up) giu·séng, jíng·séng
      (give new life to) gok·ngh

award   séung (V); jéung (N)

away   **be away** (from one's usual place) /Have you been away this summer? Nǐ·go syú·
kèih néih yáuh heui bīn·syu ma? /He has been away for three months now. Kéuih yíh·
gīng heui·jó sàam·go·yuht la. /He is away (from home). Kéuih m̀h·hái kéi.
    be away (by such and such a distance) lèih . . . (yáuh) . . . /How far away is the
hospital? Nǐ·syu lèih yì·yún yáuh géi yúhn a? /It's only three miles away. Lèih gó·syu
sàam·léih(·louh) jē.
        other expressions: /Don't take it away. M̀h·hóu nīk·jáu. /They've already moved
away. Kéuih·deih yíh·gīng bún·jáu·jó la. /I'm too busy, I can't go away. Ngóh hóu m̀h·
dāk·hàahn, Ngóh m̀h·hàahng·dāk·hòi. /Go away! Hàahng hòi!

awful   (dreadful) dāk·yàhn·pa; (fearful) dāk·yàhn·gèng. /It's awful! Jàn·haih dāk·yàhn·pa
la!
    (not handsome) nàahn·tái. /You look awful in that hat. Néih daai déng gám ge móu
jàn·haih nàahn·tái la.

awhile   yāt·jahn·gāan, yāt·háh

awkward   (clumsy) leuhn·jeuhn

awl   yēui

awning   yàhm·pùng

ax   fú·tàuh

axle   juhk, chè·juhk

azure   tīn·chēng·sīk

B

baby   bìh·bī, bìh·bī·jái

bachelor   dāan·sān·jái, gwá·lóu (vulgar); **bachelor's degree** hohk·sih; **Bachelor of Arts**
màhn·hohk·sih; **Bachelor of Science** léih·hohk·sih; **Bachelor of Laws** faat·hohk·sih

back   (of the body) bui·jek. (reverse side) bui·mihn. (space behind anything) hauh·bihn
    back to back bui·deui·bui
        be back fàan·lèih; **bring back** daai·fàan·lèih; **move back** bùn·fàan·lèih; **go back** fàan·
heui; **give back** béi·fàan; **pay back** wàahn·fāan dī chín; **send back** teui·fàan; **back up** (a
vehicle) tan·hauh; **back down** yeuhng·bouh; **back** (support) jì·chìh, jaan·joh; **back into**
tan·yahp; **to be in back of** hái . . . bui·hauh; **back out** tan·táaih

backbone   jek·gwāt, yīu·gwāt

background   bui·gíng

bacon   yīn·yuhk, hàahm·yuhk

bacteria   mèih·sàng·maht, sai·kwán

bad   (unfavorable) m̀h·hóu: **bad weather** tìn·hei m̀h·hóu; **bad news** m̀h·hóu ge sīu·sīk;
    (defective) yáih; **bad material** chòih·líu hóu yáih; (below standard) dauh·nàih; **a bad re·
porter** dauh·nàih gei·jé; (naughty) yáih, kwàaih. /You're a bad boy. Néih jàn·haih yáih
la. (morally evil, wicked) kwàaih; **bad man** kwàaih·yàhn. (spoiled, decayed) waaih,
laahn; **bad egg** waaih·dáan; **bad apple** laahn·pìhng·gwó. (injurious, hurtful) deui . . .
m̀h·hóu; **bad for the health** deui sàn·tái m̀h·hóu. (distressed, sorry) gok·dāk nàahn·gwo·
(severe) leih·hoih, gàau·gwàan. /He has a bad cold. Kéuih séung·fùng dāk hóu leih·hoih.
(worthless) **bad debt** laahn·jeung
        other expressions: **bad luck** m̀h·leih·sih, sèui. **bad temper** pèih·hei·m̀h·hóu. **smell
bad** chau. /That's too bad! Māt gám a! Gòi·jyùn lo!

badge   fāi·jēung, kām·jēung

badminton   yúh·mòuh·kàuh

bag   doih. (made of cloth) bou·doih; (made of paper) jí·dói; **bag for books** syū·bāau;
   handbag sáu·dói; **sandbag** sā·bāau

baggage   hàhng·léih

bail   (a person out) bóu . . . chēut·lèih. (security) bóu·jing gām

bait   néih, yùh·néih

bake   guhk

bakery   mìhn·bāau·chóng

balance   (deposit) chyùhn·fún. /What's my bank balance? Ngóh juhng yáuh géi·dò chyùhn·
   fún a?
      (of an account) chēut·yahp·sèung·fùh; **not be balanced** chēut·yahp m̀h sèung·fùh.
   /Does this account balance? Nī·bāt jeung sèung·fùh ma? **the balance of an account** sou·
   méih
      (scales) lèih·dáng (small scale with two matched hanging pans); (steelyard) ching
      balance sheet jeung·muhk
      keep one's balance V wán: **standing in balance** kéih·wán; **walking in balance** hàahng·
   wán
      balance of power sai·lihk·gwàn·dáng

balcony   (on the outside of a building) kèh·láu·jái, jáu·máh·kèh·láu; (of a theater) bāau·
   sēung

bald-headed person   gwòng·tàuh·lóu

bale   bàau: **a bale of cotton** yāt·bàau mìhn·fà

ball   bō; kàuh (BF): **football** (soccer) jūk·kàuh; **basketball** làahm·kàuh; **tennis ball**
   móhng·kàuh; **volleyball** pàaih kàuh; **baseball** bong·kàuh
      play ball dá·bō
      (dance) tiu·móuh·wúi

ballad   màhn·gō, sāan·gō

balloon   hei·kàuh

ballot   (the printed or written slip) syún·géui·piu. (to cast a ballot) tàuh·piu syún·géui,
   piu·syún

balm   (herb) hèung·líu; (ointment) hèung·yàuh

balustrade   làahn·gōn

bamboo   jūk (M: jì): **bamboo blinds** jūk·lím; **bamboo poles** jūk·gòu; **bamboo shoots** jūk·
   séun; **bamboo splints** jūk·mit

ban   gam·jí

banana   jīu, hēung·jīu

band   (instrumental group) ngohk·déui; (group) bàan
      to band together hahp·màaih yāt·chái

bandage   sà·bou, bàng·dáai (N); bóng, jaat, chìhn (V)

bandit   chaak, chak

banish   kèui·juhk·chēut·gíng

bank   (for money) ngàhn·hòhng; **banker** ngàhn·hòhng·gā
      (open a bank account) hòi wuh·háu; **to bank money** chyùhn·chín; **bank note** ngàhn·jí;
   bank book chyùhn·jíp
      (shore) ngohn·bīn, hòh·bīn, hói·bīn

(heap or pile) dèui

bankrupt   pò·cháan, bou·kùhng

banner   kèih (M: jì)

banquet   yin·wuih

banyan   yùhng·syuh

baptism   sái·láih

Baptist Mission   Jam·seun·wúi, Jam·láih·wúi

baptize   (give baptism) sì·sái; (to be baptized) líhng·sái, sauh·sái

bar   (where drinks are served) jáu·bā; (of wood or metal) gwan; (across a door) mùhn·
wáang. **bar the way** jó·jyuh

barbarous   yéh·màahn

barber   fèi·faat·lóu; **barber shop** fèi·faat·póu

bare   dá·chek·laak. /The children swim bare. Dī sai·mān·jái dá·chek·laak hái syu yàuh·
séui.
       bare footed dá·chek·geuk

barge   (for goods) bok·téhng, dán·syùhn; (for pleasure) jí·dúng, fà·téhng

bark   syuh·pèih (N); (of a dog) faih (V)

barley   yi·máih

barometer   fùng·yúh·bíu

barracks   bìng·fòhng, bìng·yìhng

barrel   túng

barren land   fòng·deih

barrier   jeung·ngoih·maht

base   (foundation) gèi·chó; (not noble) hah·jihn. **base of operation** gàn·geui·deih

baseball   lùih·kàuh

basement   deih·lòuh

bashful   pa·cháu

basic   gèi·bún: **basic English** gèi·bún yìng·yúh

basin   pùhn: **basin for washing the face** mihn·pún

basis   gèi·chó

basket   lēi, láam

basketball   làahm·kàuh

bass   (in music) dāi·yām

bat   fèi·syú, bín·fūk, fūk·syú (M: jek)

bathe   (wash) sái; (wash the body, take a bath) sái·sàn; (take a shower) chùng·lèuhng

bathing suit   yàuh·séui·sāam, yàuh·wihng·yī

bathroom   sái·sàn·fóng, chùng·lèuhng·fóng

bathtub   sái·sàn·pùhn

battalion   yìhng

battery   (electrical) dihn·chǐh, dihn·sām

battle   jeung, jin·sih (M: chèuhng); **fight a battle** dá·jeung. /How long will this battle last? Nǐ·chèuhng jeung yiu dá géi noih a?
    air battle hùng·jin. **sea battle** hói·jin

battlefield   jin·chèuhng

battleship   jyú·lihk·laahm (M: jek)

bay   hói·wāan

bayonet   chi·dōu (M: bá)

B.C.   géi·yùhn·chǐhn, Yèh·sū gong·sàng chǐhn

be   (am, are, is, was, were, been, being). followed by a noun (denoting merely classifi- cation) haih; (indicating profession or function) jouh, dòng (only the latter if the function is that of a soldier). /We're Americans. Ngóh·deih haih Méih·gwok yàhn. /He is a policeman. Kéuih jouh gíng·chaat. /He has been in the service for two years. Kéuih yíh·gǐng dòng·jó léuhng·nìhn bìng la.
    followed by an adjective (denoting temporary or relative description) the Chinese stative verb (SV) is used without any separate word for be; (denoting general classifica- tion) haih . . . ge. /The sky is blue. (at the moment) Tīn·sǐk hóu làahm. (statement of a general truth) Tīn·sǐk haih làahm·sǐk ge. /I'm thirsty. Ngóh hóu géng·hot.
    followed by an expression of place hái; (if there is an idea of arriving) dou. /The books are on the table. Dī syù hái tói seuhng·bihn. /Is he home? No, he isn't. Kéuih hái kéi ma? Kéuih m̀h·hái kéi. /Be here at nine tomorrow. Tìng·jiu gáu·dím dou nǐ· douh.
    followed by an adjective (serving as a suggestion or command) yiu (optional) or m̀h· hóu. /Be sure to be there at eight o'clock. Baat·dím·jūng yiu dou gó·douh. /Be careful! (yiu) hóu·sēng boh. /Be yourself! [Yiu] jih·yìhn dī. /Be quiet! M̀h·hóu chòuh.
    be . . . ing V gán. /They're eating dinner right now. Kéuih·deih sihk·gán·faahn.
    be . . . ing (referring to an event in the future) yiu (or omitted). /I'm going to England tomorrow. Ngóh tìng·yaht yiu heui Yìng·gwok.
    with the past participle of a transitive verb to form the passive voice béi, beih. /If you do this, you probably will be scolded by people. Yùh·gwó néih gám jouh, néih wúih béi yàhn naauh ge bo. /He was beaten by a group of hoodlums. Kéuih béi laahn·jái dá·chàn.

beach   hói·pèih

bead   jyū·jái

beak   (of birds) jéui

beam   (timber) ngūk·lèuhng; (ray) gwòng·sin

bean   dáu, dauh. **bean curd** dauh·fuh; **bean sauce** dauh·jèung; **bean sprouts** ngàh·choi

bear   huhng·yán (animal); (give birth to) sàang; (fruit of a tree) git·gwo; (endure) dái·dāk; (on a pole) dàam; (between two people) tòih; (on the palm) tok; (support) jì·chìh. **bear responsibility** dàam (or dāam·dāk·héi) jaak·yahm. /Can he bear this responsibility? Kéuih dàam·m̀h dāam·dāk·héi nǐ·go jaak·yahm a? **bear witness** jouh·gin·jing, jouh·jing· yàhn

beard   sòu: **grow a beard** làuh·sòu

beast   máahng·sau, yéh·sau

beat   (hit, strike) dá: **beat a drum** dá·gú; **beat a gong** dá loh. (time in music) paak·jí (N); **beat time** dá·paak·jí. **beat an egg** faak gài·dáan; **beat a carpet** faak·háh jēung·jīn (in games) yèhng (win), syù (lose). /Who beat whom? Bīn·go yèhng·jó a? or Bīng· go syù·jo a?

(unusually rapid beating of the heart) tiu. /His heart was beating very fast. Kéuih
ge sàm tiu dāk hóu faai.

beautiful   hóu, leng (specifically of a person). /What a beautiful day! Tīn·hei jàn·haih
hóu la! /The scenery there is quite beautiful. Gó·syu ge fùng·gíng hóu hóu. /Your
dress is beautiful. Néih gihn sāam jàn·haih leng la. /Don't you think she is beautiful?
Néih wah kéuih leng ma?

beauty parlour   méih·yùhng·yún

because   yàn·waih, yàn·waih . . . só·yíh . . . /He didn't come because he got sick. Yàn·
waih kéuih behng·jó só·yíh kéuih móuh lèih. **because of this** yàn·chí. /I sent her home
because of this. Yàn·chí ngóh sung·jó kéuih fàan ngūk·kéi.

become   bin·sèhng, sèhng or sìhng, sìhng·wàih. /You may either become a hoodlum or
a good man. Néih hó·yíh bin·sèhng yāt·go laahn·jái yihk hó·yíh bin·sèhng yāt·go hóu
yàhn. /He said, he would like to become an immortal. Kéuih wah kéuih séung sìhng sīn
woh. /He has become a very devoted Christian now. Kéuih yíh·gìng sìhng·wàih yāt·go
hóu kìhn·sìhng ge Gēi·dūk·tòuh la.

bed   chòhng (M: jèung): **bed sheet** chòhng·dāan; **bedspread** chòhng·kám; **bedroom** fàn·
fóng; **bedbug** muhk·sāt; **make a bed** pòu·chòhng; **go to bed** (séuhng·chòhng) fan·gaau

bedding   chòhng·pòu

bee   maht·fūng; **beehive** maht·fūng·dau

beef   ngàuh·yuhk; **beefsteak** ngàuh·pá

beer   bē·jáu

beetle   ngaahng·hok·chùhng

beet   hùhng·choi·tàuh

before   (earlier) yíh·chìhn, jì·chìhn, sìn·ji. /I've met him before. Ngóh yíh·chìhn gin·gwo
kéuih. /I can't leave before I finish this. Ngóh meih jouh·yùhn nī·gihn sih jì·chìhn mh·
jáu·dāk. /We'll not go before eating. Ngóh·deih sihk·yùhn sìn·ji heui.
(in front of people) /Don't cry before people. Mh·hóu hái yàhn mihn·chìhn haam.
(in front of a thing) /Who's standing before the table. Kéuih hái jeung tói chìhn·bihn
gó·go haih bīn·go a?
(confronting) dòng·chìhn, muhk·chìhn. /The question before us is how to solve this
problem. Ngóh·deih dòng·chìhn ge mahn·tàih haih dím·yéung gáai·kyut nī·gihn sih.
before long mh·sái·géi·nói, jauh·lèih. /He'll be here before long. Mh·sái·géi·nói
kéuih jauh lèih·dou la.

beg   (for something) yiu. /I won't beg you for it. Ngóh jàn·haih mh·yiu a. **beg** (some·
one) **to** /They begged us to help them. Kéuih·deih kàuh ngóh·deih bòng·joh kéuih·deih.
beg (as a beggar) hāt. **I beg your pardon.** Deui·mh·jyuh.

beggar   hāk·yī

begin   héi·sáu, hòi·chí, hòi·sáu. /We must begin work right away. Ngóh·deih yiu jīk·hāk
héi·sáu jouh la. /When will the summer begin? Hah·tīn géi·sí hòi·chí a? /When did
you begin to have the headache? Néih géi·sí hòi·sáu tàuh·tung ga?
begin at (with, from) chùhng . . . héi. /Begin at lesson five. Chùhng daih·ngh·fo héi.
(of a movie) hòi·yín. /When will the movie begin? Dihn·yíng géi·sí hòi·yín a? (of
an opera) hòi·tòih; (of a play) hòi·chèuhng
from the beginning yāt·héi·sáu. /He knew it right from the beginning. Kéuih yāt·
héi·sáu jauh jì la.
from beginning to end yàuh tàuh ji méih. /Please take charge of this matter from
beginning to end. Nī·gihn sih chéng néih yàuh tàuh ji meih fuh·jaak.

beginner   chò·hohk·ge

beginning   (of the month) yuht·táu, yuht·tàuh. (month of the year) nìhn·táu, nìhn·tàuh.

behalf   (on behalf of) doih. /I have come to speak to you on behalf of our president (of a firm). Ngóh doih ngóh·deih ge júng·ging·léih lèih tùhng gok·wái góng géi·geui syut·wah.

behavior   hàhng·wàih, géui·duhng

behind   hái hauh·bihn. /Please stand behind him. Chéng néih kéih·hái kéuih hauh·bihn. /What is behind that door? [Hái] gó·douh mùhn hauh·bihn yáuh mát·yéh a?
     leave behind làuh·dài. /He would like to leave the furniture behind. Kéuih séung làuh·dài dī gā·sī.
     left behind lauh·jo. /Have you left anything behind? Néih yáuh móuh lauh·jó yéh a?

belch   dá·sī·īk

believe   sèung·seun. /I believe you won't lie to me. Ngóh sèung·seun néih m̀h·wúih góng·daaih·wah ge.
     (religiously) seun. /What religion do you believe in? Néih seun māt·yéh gaau a?

believer   seun·tòuh

bell   (large) jūng; (small) lāang·jūng. **door bell** dihn·jūng; **press a bell** gahm·jūng

belly   tóuh

belong   haih . . . ge; suhk·yù; haih. /This book belongs to me. Nī·bún syù haih ngóh·ge. /Which firm does that ship belong to? Gó·jek syùhn suhk·yù bīn·go gūng·sī ga? /He belongs to the Nationalist party. Kéuih haih Gwok·màhn·dóng dóng·yùhn.

below   hah·bihn. /It's downstairs, one floor below this one. Hai nī·chàhng hah·bihn gó·yāt·chàhng. /What is said below is quoted from the Bible. Hàh·bihn só·góng·ge haih Sing·gìng léuih·bihn ge syut·wah.
     (a certain scale) yíh·hah. /I'll buy it if it's below ten dollars. Yùh·gwó haih sahp·mān yíh·hah ngóh jauh máaih.

belt   (for trousers) fu·tàuh·dáai; (at the waist) yīu·dáai; (of leather) pèih dáai. **life belt** gau·sāng·yī, gau·sāng·hyūn

bench   chèuhng·dang

bend   wāt: **bend . . . into** wat·sèhng. /Bend this wire into a circle. Jēung nī·tìuh dihn·sin wāt·sèhng yāt·go yùhn·hyūn.
     bend down wū·dai (tìuh yīu). /You can't get in if you won't bend down. Néih m̀h wū·dài tìuh yīu néih m̀h·yahp·dāk·heui.

beneath   hái hah·bihn, hái·hah·dài

benefactor   (to help an individual) yàn·yàhn; (to help an institution) jaan·joh·yàhn

benefit   hóu·chyúh, leih·yīk. **to benefit** deui . . . yáuh hóu·chyúh. /This will benefit all of us. Nī·gihn sih deui go·go dōu yáuh hóu·chyúh.

beri-beri   geuk·hei·behng; geuk·júng

beseech   chíng·kàuh, hán·kàuh

beside   hái pòhng·bīn. /Please sit beside him. Chéng néih chóh·hái kéuih pòhng·bīn.

besides   (in addition to) chèuih·jó . . . jī·ngoih. /What do you have besides this? Chèuih·jó nī·dī jī·ngoih néih jung yáuh ma?
     (moreover) yìh·ché. /I haven't got that much money; besides I haven't time. Ngóh móuh gam dò chín, yìh·ché ngóh yihk móuh gam dò sìh·gaan.

best   jeui hóu ge, ji hóu ge

best man   buhn·lòhng, nàahm·bàn·seung

bestow   béi, séung·chi. **bestow blessings** chi·fūk

bet   syù·dóu. /I'll bet you that it will rain tomorrow. Ngóh tùhng néih syù·dóu lā nah,
tìn·yaht yāt·dihng lohk·yúh.

betel nut   bàn·lòhng

betray   chēut·maaih. **betray one's country** maaih·gwok

betroth   dihng·fàn, dehng·fàn

betrothed   yíh·gìng déhng·jó·fàn

better   hóu·gwo; béi (ref. C – E sect.) /This one is better than that one. Nī·go hóu·gwo
gó·go. **getting better** hóu dī. /He (a sick person) is getting better. Kéuih yíh·gā hóu di
la. **(had) better** jeui hóu. /You'd better do it now. Néih jeui hóu yìh·gā jouh·jó kéuih la.
/You'd better not go. Néih jeui hóu m̀h·heui la.

between   tùhng . . . jī·gàan. /Is there a highway between Hong Kong and Canton? Hèung·
góng tùhng Gwóng·jàu jī·gàan yáuh móuh gùng·louh a?
     (in the interval which separates) . . . ji . . . jī·gàan. /I'll come to see you between
six and seven o'clock. Ngóh luhk·dím ji chāt·dím jī·gàan lèih gin néih.

beware   síu·sàm; tàih fòhng; **beware of fire** tàih·fòhng·fó·jūk, **beware of imitation** tàih·
fòhng·gá·mouh. **beware of pickpockets** tàih·fòhng·síu·sáu

bewitch   màih·waahk

beyond   (on the far side of) hái . . . gó·bihn: **beyond the hill** hái go sàan gó·bihn. **go beyond** gwó·jó. /We can't go beyond that line. Ngóh·deih bāt·nàhng gwó·jó gó·tìuh gaai·sin.
     beyond control gún·m̀h·dihm. /These circumstances are beyond our control. Gám
ge chìhng·yìhng ngóh·deih gún·m̀h·dihm la.
     beyond doubt hòuh·mòuh·yìh·yih. /Beyond any doubt, this is done by him. Nī·gihn
sih hòuh·mòuh yìh·yih haih kéuih jouh ge.
     beyond hope móuh hèi·mohmg. /This is beyond hope. Nī·gihn sih móuh hèi·mohng
ge la.

bias   pìn·gin

bib   háu·séui·gīn

Bible   Sing·gìng (M: bouh). **bible class** chàh·gīng·bāan

bicycle   dāan·chē (M: ga)

bid   chēut. /Would you bid ten dollars? Néih háng m̀h·háng chēut sahp·man a?
     (to order) giu, fan·fu. /You must do as he bids you. Kéuih giu néih dím jouh néih
jauh dím jouh.
     enter a bid tàuh·bīu (VO). /Have you entered the bid? Néih tàuh·jó bīu meih a?
/Who got the bid? Bīn·go tàuh·dóu a?

big   daaih. /Is this big enough? Nī·go gau daaih ma? **big shot** daaih·nāp·lóu, daaih·yàhn·
mát. /What's the big idea? Néih jouh·māt yéh a? or Néih séung dím a?

bill   (for things bought, etc.) dāan. (of a bird) jéui. (paper money) jí: **five-dollar bill**
ngh·mān·jí. (proposed law) yih·ngon. **bill of exchange** wuih·dāan, wuih·piu. **to bill** hōi·
dāan. /Please bill me at this address. Mh·gòi néih hòi·tìuh dāan gei·heui nī·go deih·jí
béi ngóh.

billiards   tói·bō. **play billiards** dá·tói·bō

billion   sahp·maahn·maahn

bind   bóng. /Bind it up. Bóng·héi kéuih. (of a wound) jaak·hóu (go sèung·háu)
     (of papers, book, etc.) dèng·màaih, dèng·hóu. /Has the book been bound? Bún syù
dèng·hóu meih a?

bind together bóng·héi, jaat·màaih. /Bind these together. Jēung nī·dī bóng·hei kéuih. or Jēung nī·dī jaat·màaih kéuih.

binoculars   mohng·yúhn·geng

biography   jyuhn·gei, jyún

biology   sàng·maht·hohk

bird   jéuk, jeuk·jái (M: jek)

bird cage   jeuk·lùhng

bird feather   jeuk·mòuh

bird's nest   jeuk·dau; **bird's-nest** (delicacy) yin·wō

bird seed   jeuk·sūk

birth   chēut·sai ge. /What is the date of your birth? Néih géi·sí chēut·sai ga? **give birth to** sàang. /She has just given birth to a boy. Kéuih jing·wah sàang·jó go jái.

birth certificate   chēut·sai·jí, chēut·sāng·jí, bou·sāng·jí

birth control   sāng·yuhk·jit·jai, jit·yuhk

birthday   sàang·yaht. /When is your birthday? Néih géi·sí sàang·yaht a? **celebrate a birthday** jouh saang·yaht. Happy birthday! (to seniors) Gùng·héi, gùng· héi! (to children) chèuhng·mehng·baak·seui

birthmark   ji, mahk·sí

birthplace   jihk·gun, yùhn·jihk

birth rate   sāng·cháan·leuht

biscuit   (in the English sense, i.e. American 'cooky') béng·gōn

bishop   (Protestant) wuih·dūk; (Catholic) jyú·gaau

bit   (a drilling or boring tool) jyun. **a little bit** dī, yāt·dī, dī·gam·dēui. /I only want a little bit. Ngóh yiu dī jē.

bite   ngáauh. /He was bitten by a dog. Kéuih béi gáu ngáauh·chàn. **a bite** yāt·daahm

bitter   fú (taste)

black   hāk; hāk·sīk ge: **black dress** hāk·sīk ge sāam. **black at heart** hāk·sām. **black spot** hāk dím

blackboard   hāk·báan (M: faai)

blackmail   lahk·sok

black market   hāk·síh

blackout   dāng·fó gún·jai

blacksmith   dá·tit·lóu

bladder   (human) pòhng·gwòng; (animal) síu·tóuh

blade   (razor) dōu·pín; (of a knife) dōu·háu; **a blade of grass** yāt·tìuh chóu

blame   gwaai. /Don't blame him, he hasn't done anything wong. Mh·hóu gwaai kéuih, kéuih móuh jouh·cho. **blame one's fate** yun·mehng

blank   (empty) hùng. **blank space** (to be filled in) hùng·gáak

blanket   jīn (M: jēung)

blaspheme   sit·duhk: **blaspheme the gods** sit·duhk sàhn·mîhng

bleach   piu·baahk: **bleaching powder** piu·baahk·fán

bleed   làuh·hyut: **bleeding nose** bèih·gō làuh·hyut; **bleeding piles** jih·lauh

blend   chàm, kàu: **blend with** chàm·màaih, kàu·màaih

bless   jūk·fūk. /The minister blessed us. Muhk·sī jūk·fūk ngóh·deih. God bless you. Seuhng·dai bóu·yauh néih (in singular, néih·deih, in plural).

blind   màahng. /How long has he been blind? Kéuih màahng·jó géi noih la? **blind person** màahng·gūng (man); màahng·mūi (girl)

blinds   (Venetian) baahk·yihp·chēung; (bamboo) jūk·lím

blink   jáam·jáam·há. /The stars in the sky are blinking. Tìn·seuhng dī sīng jáam·jáam· há.

blister   séui·jì, séui·póuh

bliss   fūk, fūk·hei

block   (solid piece of) gauh: **a block of wood** yat gauh muhk; **to block up** (a hole) sāk· jyuh; (a way) jó·jyuh

blood   hyut

blood poisoning   hyut jung·duhk

blood pressure   hyut·ngaat

bloodstain   hyut·jīk

blood transfusion   syù·hyut

blood vessel   hyut·gwún

bloom   (flower) fā; (have flowers) hōi·fá

blotter   yan·séui·jí, kāp·mahk·jí

blow   chèui: **blow a trumpet** chèui la·bā; **blow a flute** chēui·sīu. (by pressing a button) gahm: **blow the horn** gahm hōn. (by pulling a chord) làai: **blow on a whistle** lāai bē·sán
blow out chēui·sīk; **blow out the lamp** chēui·sīk jáan dāng
blow out (of a tire) baau·tāai. /My car has a tire blown out. Ngóh ga chè baau·jó tāai.
blow the nose sing·beih, sing·beih·tai. /Blow your nose! Sing·háh go beih kéuih!
a blow dá·gīk. /He suffered a terrible blow. Kéuih sauh·jó yāt·go hóu daaih ge dá· gīk.

blue   làahm ge, làahm·sīk ge; **blue color** làahm·sīk

bluff   (deceive) pàau·lohng·tàuh, chè·daaih·paau

blunt   deuhn

blurred   mùhng, mòuh·wùh

blush   mihn·hùhng, pa·cháu

boa   móhng, móhng·sèh (M: tîuh)

board   báan (M: faai). (committee) wúi; **board of directors** dúng·sih·wúi
Board of Health waih·sāng·gúk
(eat meals as a boarder) bàau·sihk. /He boards with Mrs. Chang. Kéuih·hái Jèung· táai·syu bàau sihk.

(room and board) sihn·sūk. /Does this fee include room and board? Nī·bāt fai·yuhng bàau m̀h·bàau·màaih sihn·sūk a?

(get on a vehicle or boat) séuhng; **board a ship** séuhng syùhn
to board (eat or serve meals) bàau·faahn (VO), bàau·fó·sihk (VO)
on board hái . . . seuhng·bihn; **on board** (of a train), hái fó·chè seuhng·bihn

boast   kwà·háu, chèui·ngàuh, chè·daaih·paau

boaster   daaih·paau·yáu

boat   (vessel) syùhn; (small) téhng; (rowboat) sàam·báan (M: jek)

Boat-people   Daahn·gā, Daahn·gà·lóu (man); Daahn·gà·pó (woman); Daahn·gā·mūi (girl)

body   sàn·tái; (corpse) sī·sáu, sī·sàn

boil   bòu: **boil water** bòu séui, **boil tea** bòu chàh. (on the body) chōng

boiling   gwán: **boiling water** gwán·séui

boiler   bōu

bold   daaih·dáam

bolt   (used in fastening a door) mùhn·sāan, mùhn·wáang. **bolt the door** seut·hóu douh mùhn

bomb   ja·dáan. **to bomb** gwàng·ja

bomber   gwàng·ja·gèi (M: ga)

bonds   gùng·jaai

bone   gwāt (M: tĩuh or gauh)

book   syù (M: bún). **telephone book** dihn·wá bóu. **to book** dehng; **to book a seat** dehng wái; **to book a passage on a ship** dehng·syùhn·wái

bookcase   syù·gwaih

book cover   syù·pèih, fùng·mín

bookkeeper   bouh·gei·yùhn

bookkeeping   bouh·gei

bookshelf   syù·gá

bookshop   syù·póu (M: gàan)

bookstore   syù·gúk (M: gàan)

bookworm   syù·māi, syù·chùhng

boot   hèu (M: deui, a pair; jek, one)

booty   chak·jòng

borax   pàahng·sà

border   (of anything) bīn; (land) bīn·gaai

born   chēut·sai. /When were you born? Néih géi·sí chēut·sai ga? /Were you born in China? Néih hái Jùng·gwok chēut·sai gàh?

borrow   je

bosom friend   jī·géi·pàhng·yáuh

boss   sih·táu

botanical garden   jihk·maht·yùhn

botany   jihk·maht·hohk

both   léuhng . . . dōu . . . /Both are Mr. Lee's daughters. Léuhng·go dōu haih Léih sīn·
sàang ge néui.   **both ends** léuhng·tàuh; **both hands** léuhng jek·sáu; **both of us** léuhng·gā;
both parties léuhng·fòng·mihn, sēung·fòng; **both sides** léuhng·bihn

bother   gáau; gwán·gáau. /Don't bother him. M̀h·hóu gwán·gáau kéuih. /Sorry that I've
bothered you. Gwán·gáau·saai.

bottle   jēun. **to bottle** yahp·jēun

bottom   dái: **the bottom of the sea** hói·dái; **the bottom of the boat** syùhn·dái. Bottoms
up (in drinking)! Yám sing kéuih!

bough   syuh·jī

bounce   daahn: **bounce back** daahn·fàan·héi, daahn·fàan·fàan·lèih

bound   faahn·wàih (N). **bound to** bīt·dihng. /He's bound to lose (as in a game). Kéuih
bīt·dihng syù ge.

boundless   mòuh·haahn

boundary   bìn·gaai, gàau·gaai ge deih·fòng; boundary stone, gaai·jī

bouquet   yāt·jaat·fā

bow   (weapon) gùng; (for the violin) gùng; (of a ship) syùhn·tàuh; (neck wear) léhng·fā.
to bow gūk·gùng. **bow and arrow** gùng·jin

bowel   (intestine) chéung. **move the bowels** chēut·gùng, daaih·bihn

bowl   wún (M: jek): **a bowl of rice** yāt·wún faahn. **bowls and plates** wún·dihp

box   (small) háp; (large) sēung

boxing   kyùhn·seuht

boy   (male child) nàahm·jái, sai·lóu·gō; (domestic servant) sih·jái; (in hotels, shops,
etc.) fó·gei

boyfriend   nàahm·pàhng·yáuh

boycott   dái·jai

boy scout   tùhng·jí·gwān

bracelet   sáu·ngáak

bracket   kwut·wùh (sign)

brag   kwà·háu, chèui·ngàuh

brain   nóuh

bran   hòng, mahk·hòng

branch   (of a tree) syùh·jī. (division) fàn, jī: **branch school** fàn·haauh; **branch office**
fàn·gúk; **branch of a firm** fān·gūng·sī; **branch of a store** fàn·dim or jī·dim

brand   (trademark) māk·tàuh, jih·houh. **brand new** chyùhn·sàn ge

brandish   móu: **brandish a sword** móu·gim

brandy   baahk·lāan·déi (·jáu)

brass   wòhng tùhng; **brass wire** tùhng·sín

brass band   tùhng·ngohk·déui (M: deuih)

brave   yúhng·gáam. **to brave danger** mouh·hím

bravo   hóu yéh!

breach   (of a law) waih·faahn; **breach of contract** wàih·bui hahp yeuk; **breach of trust**
sāt·seun

bread   mihn·bāau (M: faai, slice; tiuh, loaf; go, roll)

breadth   fut·douh

break   jíng·laahn; (smash) dá·laahn; (by dropping) dit·laahn; (with fingers) mīt·laahn.
break a law wàih·faahn faat·leuht; **break a record** dá·po·géi·luhk; **break an appointment
or engagement** sāt·yeuk; **break a promise** sāt·seun; **break the law** faahn·faat; **break
into two pieces** jíng·tyúhn; **break off relations** dyuhn·jyuht-gwàan·haih.

breast   (chest) hùng·bouh, hùng·chìhn; (of a woman) nīn, náaih

breath   hei: **breathless** móuh hei; **breath stopped** tyúhn hei. /Take a deep breath.
Daaih·daahm gám sok yāt·daahm hei.

breathe   táu·hei, fū·kāp

breeze   fùng (M: jahm)

brew   yeuhng

brewery   yeuhng·jáu·chóng

bribe   (to bribe) sái·hāk·chín; (take a bribe) sauh·hāk·chín

brick   jyùn: **brick kiln** jyùn·yìuh; **bricklayer** nàih·séui·sì·fú, nàaih séui·lóu

bride   sàn·néung

bridegroom   sàn·lóng, sàn·lòhng·gō

bridge   kìuh (M: douh, tìuh)

bridle   máh·gèung

brief   dyún

briefcase   gùng·màhn·doih, gùng·sih·bāau

brigade   léuih (M): **two brigades of infantry** léuhng·léuih bouh·bìng

bright   (of light) gwòng; (of a person) chùng·mìhng

bring   nìng·lèih, nīk·lèih, daai·lèih; nìng . . . lèih, nīk . . . lèih, daai . . . lèih. /Bring
it here. Nìng·lèih nī·syu. /Bring a glass of water to me, please. Mh·gòi néih nìng bùi
séui lèih béi ngóh. /Bring your children with you. Daai néih·dī sai·mān·jái lèih.
bring back here nìng·fàan·lèih. /Remember to bring it back! Gei·jyuh nìng·fàan·
lèih!
bring down (here) nìng·lohk·lèih. **bring in (here)** nìng·yahp·lèih. **bring up** yéuhng·
daaih. /Their grandmother brought them up. Kéuih·deih ge jó·móuh yéuhng·daaih
kéuih·deih ge.

bristle   jyū·jùng

Britain   Yìng·gwok

British pound   Yìng·bohng

British subject   Yìng·gwok·jihk·màhn, Yìng·jihk·màhn

brittle   cheui

broad   fut

broadcast   gwóng·bo

broadcasting station   gwóng·bo·dihn·tòih

broken   laahn·jó

broken hearted   sēung sàm. /She is broken hearted. Kéuih hóu sēung·sàm.

broil   sìu

broker   gìng·géi

brokerage   gìng·sáu·fai, hàaih·gām

bronchial tubes   hei·gún

bronchitis   hei·gún·yìhm

bronze   gú·tùhng: **bronze color** gú·tùhng·sīk ge; **Bronze age** tùhng·hei sìh·doih, **bronze statue** tùhng·jeuhng

brook   kài·séui

broom   sou·bá (M: bá)

broth   tòng (M: wún, bowl)

brother   (general term) **older brother** gòh·gō, a·gō; **younger brother** sai·lóu; **brothers** hìng·daih. /They are two brothers. Kéuih·deih haih léuhng·hìng·daih. (polite term) **your older brother** lihng·hìng; **your younger brother** lihng·dái; **my older brother** gā·hìng; **my younger brother** séh·dái
   brother-in-law: **elder sister's husband** jé·fù; **younger sister's husband** muih·fù, **husband's elder brother** daaih·baak; **husband's younger brother** sìu·sūk; **wife's elder brother** daaih·káuh; **wife's younger brother** sìu·káuh; **wife's elder sister's husband** kām·hìng; **wife's younger sister's husband** kàm·dái
   brother's daughter jaht·néui; **brother's son** ját

brotherly   yáuh·ngoi

brow   ngaahk·tàuh

brown   jūng·sīk ge, jyū·gōn·sīk ge

brown sugar   wòhng·tòhng

bruise   kaat·sèung; yú·hāk (N)

brush   cháat (N). chaat (V): **brush teeth** chaat ngàh; **brush shoes** chaat hàaih; **brush clothes** chaat sāam; **brush up** wàn·jaahp. /I'm brushing up on my Cantonese. Ngóh jing·joih wàn·jaahp ngóh ge Gwóng·jàu·wá.

brutal   chàahn·yáhn, móuh·yàhn·douh

bubble   póuh, séui póuh (N). héi·póuh (VO)

bucket   túng: **water bucket** séui·túng

bud   (in general) ngàh; (of a flower) lām. **to bud** chēut·ngàh, chēut

Buddha   faht, pòuh·saat; faht·jóu

Buddhism   Faht·gaau

Buddhist   Faht·gaau·tòuh; **Buddhist scripture** faht·gìng; **Buddhist disciple** faht·gaau·tòuh; **Buddha's image** faht·jeuhng; **Buddhist nun** sī·gū; **Buddhist priest** wòh·séung

budget   yuh·syun, yuh·syun·bíu (N). yuh·syun (V)

buffalo   séui·ngàuh (M: jek)

bug   ngaahng·hok·chùhng

bugle   la·bā

build   (of a house or building) héi; (of a road) jūk; (of a ship) jouh

building   (house) ngūk (M: gaan), láu (M: joh); (thing that is built) gin·jūk·maht (M: joh)

bulb   (electrical) dāng·dáam, dihn·dāng·daam

bulky   (clumsy) lauh·bauh

bull   ngàuh·gūng (M: jek)

bullet   máh·jí, jí·dáan (M: nāp)

bulletin   (official report) gùng·bou

bully   hà, hèi·fuh (V)

bump   pung (V); làuh (N): **bump into** pung·gin, yuh·gin. /I bumped into him on the street this morning. Ngóh gàm·jiu·jóu hái gāai·syu pung·gin kéuih.

bunch   (of green vegetables) bá, jaat; (of flowers) jaat; (of keys) chàu, lang; (of people) bàan, jah. /There is a bunch of kids running around. Sèhng·bàan sai·mān·jái hái gó·syu jáu·lèih jáu·heui.

bund   hói·pèih, tàih·ngohn

bundle   bàau: **a bundle of clothes** yāt·bàau yì·fuhk

buoy   séui·póuh, fàuh·bīu. **Life buoy** gau·sāng·hyūn

burden   fuh·dàam

bureau   (office) gúk; (furniture) yì·gwaih

burglar   chahk, chák

burglary   tàu·yéh. /There was a burglary on this street last night. Kàhm·máahn nī·tìuh gāai·syu yáuh yàhn tàu·yéh.

burial   màaih·jong; **burial place** sàan·fàhn; **burial ground for free use** yih·jōng

burn   sìu (V); béi·fó sīu·chàn. /He has a burn on his hand. Kéuih jek sáu béi·fó sīu·chàn. **burned** nùng·jó. /Don't let the piece of bread burn. Mh·hóu béi faai mihn·bāau nùng·jó.

bursar   chēut·naahp

burst   (crack or split open) baau, lik. /If you put that many things into your pocket, it's going to burst. Néih jài gam dò yéh yahp·heui, néih ge dói jauh·lèih baau la. /The tire is so old, it'll burst easily. Tìuh tāai gam gauh hóu yùhng·yih baau ge la.

bury   màaih·jong, jong

bus   bā·sí (M: ga); **bus driver** sī·gēi; **bus conductor** sàuh·piu·yùhn; **bus inspector** chàh· piu·yùhn; **bus stop** bā·sí·jaahm

bush   syuh·jái

business   (trade) sàang·yi. /He is in business. Kéuih jouh·gán sàang·yi. /How's business? Sàang·yi géi hóu ma? /The business is slow. Sàang·yi hóu daahm. /The business is fairly good. Sàang·yi géi hóu.
    (matter) sih, sih·gon. /This is his business. Nī go haih kéuih ge sih. /It's none of your business. Mh·gwàan néih sih.
    business man sèung·yàhn, sàang·yi lóu (colloq.); **business transaction** gàau·yihk

bustling   yihk·naauh

busy (of a person) m̀h·dāk·hàahn. /He's very busy. Kéuih hóu m̀h·dāk·hàahn. (of a place) yihk·naauh. /That is a busy street. Gó·tìuh gāai hóu yihk·naauh. (of a telephone) yáuh yàhn góng·gán. /The line is busy. Yáuh yàhn góng·gán. (not busy) dāk·hàahn. /You may go in, he's not busy now. Kéuih yìh·gā dāk·hàahn la, néih hó·yíh yahp·heui la.

but daahn·haih. /I thought I could go, but I can't. Ngóh yíh·wàih ngóh heui·dāk, daahn· haih m̀h·dāk. (except) chèuih·jó. /The library is open everyday but Sunday. Tòuh·syù·gún chèuih·jó láih·baai·yaht jì·ngoih yaht yaht dōu hòi·mùhn.

butcher (of pigs) tōng·jyū·lóu; (of cows) tòng·ngàuh·lóu. (meat seller) maaih·yuhk·lóu

butter ngàuh·yàuh

butterfly wùh·díp (M: jek)

buttocks sí·fāt

button ngáu (M: nāp)

buy máaih. /I do not want to buy it. Ngóh m̀h·máaih. **buy things** máaih yéh. **a buy** hóu dái. /It's a good buy. Máaih dāk hóu dái.

buyer (customer) haak·jái, gu·haak; (in a firm) máaih sáu; (of property, etc.) máaih· jyú

by (location) hái . . . pòhng·bīn. /Please sit by him. Chéng néih chóh·hái kéuih pòhng· bīn; **by** (a means of transportation), chóh. /He'll come by bus. Kéuih chóh bā·sí lèih; **by** (a means of shipping) gei. /Send it by air. Gei fēi·gèi. **by** (a quantity, as in buying) dyun. /Do you sell this by the pound? [Nī·tíng yéh] haih m̀h·haih dyun bòhng maaih ga? **by** (someone or something who causes an event) béi, beih. /He was beaten by the hood- lums. Kéuih béi laahn·jái dá·chàn. /He was burned by fire. Kéuih béi fó sīu·chàn. **by** (on or before a time). /Please be here by two o'clock. Chéng néih léuhng·dím·jūng lèih·dou nī·syu; **by** (oneself) ji·géi, ji·géi yāt·go·yàhn. /He did it by himself. Kéuih jih· géi jouh ge. **by order of** fuhng . . . mihng·lihng. /I come by the order of my govern- ment to study the situation here. Ngóh fuhng ngóh·deih jing·fú ge mihng·lihng lèih diuh· chàh nī·syu ge chìhng·yìhng. **by way of** yàuh. /They will go back to the United States by way of Europe. Kéuih·deih yàuh Ngāu·jàu fàan Méih·gwok. **by the way** waih; **day by day** yāt·yaht . . . gwo yāt·yaht. /She is prettier day by day. Kéuih yāt·yaht leng·gwo yāt·yaht. **near by** jó·gán. /Is there a restaurant near by? Nī·syu jó·gán yáuh móuh chāan·gún a? **by mistake** m̀h·gok·yi . . . cho·jó. /I said it by mistake, please excuse me. Ngóh m̀h·gok·yi góng·cho·jó, chéng néih m̀h·hóu gwaai ngóh. **by** (a period of time) on . . . gai. /The house is rented by the month. Ngūk·jòu on yuht gai. **by all means** chìn·kèih. /By all means don't go there. Chìn·kèih m̀h·hóu heui gó·syu. **by turns** lèuhn·láu. /How about doing it by turns? Lèuhn·láu jouh, hóu ma?

cabaret tiu·móuh·tēng (M: gàan); **cabaret girl** tiu·móuh·néui

cabbage (brassica) yèh·choi; **Chinese cabbage** baahk·chòi (M: pò, a head)

cabin (in a ship) chōng·fóng

cabinet (furniture) gwaih. (council) noih·gok: **cabinet meeting** noih·gok·wuih·yi, gwok· mouh·wuih·yi

cable (rope) laahm (M: tìuh). (message) dihn·bou

cactus sìn·yàhn·jéung (M: pò)

cafe ga·fē·sāt, ga·fē·dim (M: gàan)

cage lùhng

cake (ordinary) béng; (sponge) daahn·gōu; **a cake of soap** yāt·gauh fàan·gáan calamity   jòi·naahn

calculate   gai, gai·syun

calculator   (machine) gai·syun·gèi (M: ga)

calculus   mèih·jīk·fān

calendar   (almanic) yaht·lihk; (monthly) yuht·fahn·pàaih; **solar calendar** sàn·lihk, yèuhng lihk; **lunar calendar** gauh·lihk, yàm·lihk

calf   ngàuh·jái (M: jek)

calibre   háu·gihng

calico   (plain white) baahk·bou; (printed) fà·bou

calisthenics   yàuh·yúhn·tái·chòu

call   (shout, cry out) giu. /Please call him to come see me. Mh·gòi giu kéuih lèih gin ngóh. /Whom is he calling? Kéuih giu bīn·go a? /Call him back. Giu kéuih fàan·leih.
     (visit) taam. /Shouldn't we call on him someday? Ngóh·deih yiu m̀h·yiu heui taam kéuih a?
     (address) giu, giu jouh; chǐng·fù (formal). /What should I call you? Ngóh dím giu néih a? /You may call me "elder brother." Néih giu ngóh jouh a-gō la. /How should I address your father? /Ngóh dím chǐng·fù néih bàh·bā a?
     (name) giu . . . jouh . . . /He named his motor boat the "Tiny Whale." Keuih giu kéuih jek syùhn·jái jouh Kìhng·yùh·jái. /What do you call this in Cantonese? Gwóng jàu·wá nī·go giu·jouh māt·yéh a? /It's called a sampan. Giu·jouh sàam·báan.
     call for help yiu yàhn heui gau (in danger), yiu yàhn heui bòng (in doing something). /Is he calling for help? Kéuih haih m̀h·haih yiu yàhn heui gau kéuih a?
     call off chéui·sìu·jó. /The meeting has been called off. Gàm·yaht ge wúi yíh·gìng chéui·sìu·jó la.
     call . . . up dá·dihn·wá béi . . . (by phone). /Please call me up this afternoon. Chéng néih gàm·yaht hah·ńgh dá·dihn·wá béi ngóh.
     a call (on the telephone) dihn·wá. /Were there any calls for me? Ngóh yáuh móuh dihn·wá a? /Please put the call through right away. Chéng néih jīk·hak tùhng ngóh bok·tùng kéuih.

calm   daahm·dihng (for a person), pìhng·jihng (for the sea, etc.)

Cambridge University   Gim·kìuh·daaih·hohk

camel   lohk·tòh (M: jek)

camellia   chàh·fā

camera   séung·gèi, yíng·séung·gèi

camouflage   yím·sīk

camp   (for soldiers) yìhng·fòhng, yìhng·pùhn; **make a camp** jaat·yìhng; **camp out** louh·yìhng

camphor   jèung·nóuh; **camphor wood** jèung·muhk; **balls of camphor** chau·yún

can   (know how to) wúih. /Can your boss speak English? Néih ge sìh·táu wúih góng Yìng·màhn ma? /Can you type? Neih wúih dá·jih ma?
     (be able to) hó·yíh, -dāk; (not able to) m̀h . . . dāk . . . /Can you give me a hand? Néih hó·yíh bòng·háh ngóh ma? /Can he come? Kéuih lèih·dāk ma? /No, he can't. Kéuih m̀h·lèih dāk. /Can you see? Néih tái·dāk·gin ma? /No, I can't. Ngóh m̀h·tái·dāk·gin. or Ngóh tái·m̀h·gin (ref. Resultative Verb in the Introduction)
     (container) gun; **canned food** gun·táu. /Give me a can of soup. Béi gun tòng ngóh.
     can opener gun·táu·dōu

canal   wahn·hòh (M: tìuh)

cancer   duhk·láu, yùng: **have cancer** sàang duhk·láu, sāang yùng; **cancer of the breast** yúh·yūng

cancel   chéui·sîu

candidate   hauh·syún·yàhn

candle   laahp·jūk (M: jì): **candlestick** laahp·jūk·tói

candy   tóng (M: gauh): **candy store** tòhng·gwó·póu

cannon   daaih·paau, paau (M: hám): **cannonball** paau·má

cannot   m̀h·wúih, m̀h . . . dāk, . . . m̀h . . . (also refer to Resultative Verb in the Introduction) /She cannot swim. Kéuih m̀h·wúih yàuh·séui. /He cannot walk. Kéuih m̀h·hàahng·dāk. /I cannot find it. Ngóh wán·m̀h·dóu. /You cannot go. Néih m̀h·heui·dāk. /She cannot hear. Kéuih tèng·m̀h·gin.
      cannot bear it m̀h yáhn dāk jyuh; **cannot blame him** m̀h gwaai dāk kéuih; **cannot lift it** m̀h·nīk·dāk·héi; **cannot get it** ló·m̀h·dóu; **cannot help but do it** m̀h·jouh m̀h·dāk; **cannot part with** m̀h·sé·dāk; **cannot recognize** yihng·m̀h·chēut; **cannot recollect** séung·m̀h·chēut; **cannot say certainly** m̀h·wah·dāk·saht; **cannot see** tái·m̀h·gin, m̀h·tái·dāk·gin; **cannot sell** maaih·m̀h·heui; **cannot trust him** m̀h·seun·dāk·kéuih·gwo

canoe   duhk·muhk·jàu (M: jek)

canon   gìng·dín, gìng

canteen   (metal container) séui·wú

Canton   Gwóng·jàu **Cantonese** Gwóng·jàu·yàhn, sáang·sèhng·yàhn (one who lives in Canton), Gwóng·fú·yàhn (one who lives in the area where Cantonese is spoken), Gwóng·dùng·yàhn (one who lives in the province of Kwangtung). **Cantonese** (language) Gwóng·jàu·wá, (in general) sáahng·wá, sáang·sèhng·wá (term used by people of Kwangtung Province), Gwóng·dùng·wá (term used by people from other provinces)

canvas   fàahn·bou; **canvas cot** fàahn·bou·chòhng (M: jèung)

cap   (for the head) móu·jái; (for a bottle) jēun·goi

capable   bún·sih. /Your son is very capable. Néih·ge jái hóu bún·sih.

capacity   yùhng·leuhng. /The bottle has a capacity of one quart. Nī·go jēun ge yùhng·leuhng haih yāt·go·gwāt·dá. or Nī·go jēun hó·yíh jòng yāt·go gwāt·dá. /The church has a seating capacity of 400. is expressed as: Nī·gàan gaau·tòhng hó·yíh chóh sei·baahk·yahn.

capital   (money) bún·chìhn, jì·bún. /He doesn't have enough capital to run this business. Kéuih m̀h·gau bún·chìhn jouh nī·hohng sàang·yi.
      (city) sáang·sèhng, sáang·wuih; sáu·dòu. /Canton is the capital of Kwangtung Province. Gwóng·jàu haih Gwóng·dùng ge sáang·sèhng. /Washington, D.C. is the capital of the United States. Wàh·sihng·deuhn haih Méih·gwok ge sáu·dòu.
      capital letter daaih·sé ge jih·júng; **capital offense** séi·jeuih; **capital punishment** séi·yìhng

capitalism   jì·bún·jyú·yih

capitalist   jì·bún·gā

captain   (of a ship) syùhn·jéung; (of a team) deuih·jéung; (Navy rank) seuhng·gaau; (of a warship) laahm·jéung; (Army rank) seuhng·wai; (of a company in the army) lìhn·jéung

captive   fù·lóuh

capture   (people) jūk·dóu; (place) jim·líhng

car   (automobile) chè, hei·chè (M: ga)

carat   kā

carbolic acid   Gā·bō·līk chau·séui; **carbolic soap** Gā·bō·līk·gáan, yeuhk·gáan (M: gauh)

carbon   taan; **carbon paper** fūk·sé·jí (M: jèung, sheet)

card   kāt·pín (M: jēung); (calling card) mìhng·pín, kāt·pín; (invitation card) chéng·típ; (playing card) páai, jí·páai; (postal) mìhng·seun·pín

cardboard   ngaahng·jí·pèih (M: faai)

cardinal   hùhng·yî·jyú·gaau

care   (love) ngoi, sek. /Don't you care for your children? Néih m̀h·ngoi néih·dī sai·mān·jái àh?

    (look after) dá·léih, jiu·liuh. /Is anyone caring for your children? Yáuh yàhn dá·léih néih dī sai·mān·jái ma? /I need someone to take care of my children. Ngóh sèui·yiu yāt·go yàhn tùhng ngóh dá·léih sai·mān·jái. /I want to hire a person to take care of my children. Ngóh séung chéng yāt·go yàhn dá·léih ngóh dī sai·mān·jái.

    (be interested in) gwāan·sàm. /We care greatly about the health of your children. Ngóh·deih hóu gwāan·sàm néih·dī sai·mān·jái ge sàn·tái.

    (attention) síu·sàm. /Please do this with great care. Chéng néih dahk·biht síu·sàm jouh nī·gihn sih.

    care of (of mail) gei . . . jyún·gàau·béi . . . /Please address the letter in care of our church. Chéng gei·heui ngóh·deih gaau·tòhng jyún·gàau·béi ngóh.

    care for hei·fùn; **care** (worry) sàuh; **take care of people** jiu·liuh; **take care of guest** jīu·fù; jîu·doih. /Take care of yourself! Dō·dò bóu·juhng!

careful   síu·sàm. **be careful!** síu·sàm boh! hóu·sēng boh! gu·jyuh boh! /Be careful with fire and lights! Síu·sàm fó·jūk boh! **carefully** hóu síu·sàm gám

careless   m̀h·síu·sàm

career   sih·yihp

cargo   fo (M: dī): **cargo boat** fo·syùhn (M: jek)

carp   (fish) léih·yú (M: tìuh)

carpet   deih·jīn (M: jèung)

carriage   máh·chè (M: ga)

carpenter   dau·muhk·sî·fú, dau·muhk·lóu

carpentry   muhk·gūng

carrot   hùng·lòh·baak, gàm·séun

carry   (in the hand) nìng, nīk; (at two ends of a pole) dàam; (between two people with a pole) tòih; (in the arms, as carry a child) póuh; (in the pocket) doih·jyuh; (on the back) mè; **carry a child** mè·jái; **carry a pack** mè·jyuh go bàau·fuhk; (on the head) díng·jyuh; (on the palm) tok·jyuh; (on the shoulder) dàam·jyuh; (up with both hands) púng·jyuh

    Carry on! Jip·jyuh jouh. Mh·hóu tìhng! **carry out** (a contract) léuih·hàhng, (a plan) jāp·hàhng; **carry passengers** joi·haak; **carry cargos** joi·fo

    /How many passengers can that plane carry? Gó·ga fēi·gèi hó·yíh joi géi·dò haak a? /How many tons can that truck carry? Gó·ga fo·chè hó·yíh joi géi·dò dēun a?

cart   chē

carton   jí·háp

cartoon   maahn·wá (M: fūk); **cartoonist** maahn·wá·gā

carve   hāk, dīu·hāk

case   (small box) háp, hahp·jái; (large box) sēung; (of soft material) tou; (cabinet)
gwaih; **bookcase** (with a door), syù·gwaih, (without a door) syù·gá
(legal) ngon, ngon·gín: **in case** yùh·gwó. /In case you can't find the place, come
back right away. Yùh·gwó néih wán·m̀h·dóu gó·daat deih·fòng, jīk·hāk fàan·lèih; **in that
case** yùh·gwó haih gám. /In that case don't buy it. Yùh·gwó haih gám, m̀h·hóu maaih
la. **in any case** mòuh·leuhn·yùh·hòh. /In any case I don't want to go. Mòuh·leuhng·yùh·
hòh ngóh m̀h·séung heui.

cash   yihn·chín, yihn·fún

cashier   sàu·ngán·yàhn, chēut·naahp

cask   túng

cast   (throw) pàau, diuh; **cast the anchor** pàau·màauh; **cast away** diuh·hòi
(form in a mold) jyu; **cast a bell** jyu·jūng; **cast a vote** tàuh·piu
(actors) yín·yùhn

caste   gāai·kāp; **caste system** gāai·kāp·jai·douh

castor oil   se·yàuh

casually   mòuh·yi·jùng

casualty   séi·sèung ge yàhn. /There were many casualties. is expressed as Séi·sèung
ge yàhn hóu dò.

cat   māau (M: jek)

catalogue   muhk·luhk

catch   (seize and hold) jūk; **to catch a thief** jūk·chahk, jūk·chák; **caught a thief** jūk·dóu
yāt·go chák; **catch fish** (with a net) dá·yú, (with a rod) diu·yú; **catch a ball** jip·bō; **catch
a cold** sēung·fùng, láahng·chàn; **catch a disease** sàang·behng; **catch up** jēui·dāk·séuhng

cathedral   láih·baai·tòhng (M: gàan)

Catholic   Tìn·jyú·gaau; **Catholic priest** sàhn·fuh

catty   gàn

cauliflower   yèh·choi·fà

cause   (reason) yùhn·yàn, yùhn·gu; **cause of death** séi·yàn; **the immediate cause** gahn·
yàn; **the underlying** cause yúhn·yàn
to cause yáhn·héi. /This caused us a lot of trouble. Nī·gihn sih yáhn·héi bāt·jì géi·
dò màh·fàahn. /What caused the accident? Nī·gihn sìh dím·yéung faat·sàng ga? /Sorry
to cause you so much trouble. Lòuh·fàahn·saai néih.

cavalry   kèih·bing, kèh·bing, máh·déui

cave   sāan·lūng

cease   tìhng, tìhng·jí; **cease hostilities** tìhng·jin; **cease fire** tìhng·fó, tìhng·jin

cedar   chaam·muhk

ceiling   tìng·fà·báan

celebrate   **celebrate a festival** jouh jit; **celebrate one's birthday** jouh sàang·yaht; **celebrate the birthday of a country** hing·jūk gwok·hing; **celebrate the 30th day after a con-
finement for childbirth** jouh múhn·yuht

celery   hèung·kán, kàhn·choi (M: jaat, bunch)

cell   (of living matter) sai·bāau; (in a prison) gāam·fòhng

cellar   deih·lòuh

cement   hùhng·mòuh·nàih

cemetery   fàhn·chèuhng

censor   (examine) sám·chàh, gím·chàh; (an official) gím·chàh·gùn

censure   jāk·beih, jaak·beih

census   yàhn·háu·diuh·chàh

cent   (coin) sīn, sīn·sí; **per cent** baahk·fahn·jì . . .; **one hundred per cent** baak·fahn·jì·baahk, **sixty per cent** baak·fahn·jì·luhk·sahp, **five percent** baak·fahn·jì·ńgh

center   jūng·sām, jūng·gāan, jūng·sām·dím

centipede   baak·jūk (M: tìuh)

central   jūng·gàan (ge), jūng·yèung (ge); **central government** jūng yèung·jing·fú

centralize   jaahp·jùng

century   sai·géi: **the twentieth century** yih·sahp·sai·géi

ceramics   tòuh·hei; (pottery) gòng·ngáh

cereal   (plants that produce grain) gūk, gūk·liuh

ceremony   dín·láih; -láih: **ceremony of baptism** sái·láih; **ceremony of burial** jong·láih; **ceremony of ship launching** hah·séui·láih, **ceremony of marriage** fàn·láih

certain   (positive, sure) yāt·dihng (A); dihng·saht (V). /The weather report said that rain was certain. Tìn·hei·bou·gou wah yāt·dihng lohk·yúh. /He is not certain he can go until he asks his father. Kéuih meih dihng·saht heui m̀h·heui, kéuih yiu mahn·gwo kéuih bàh·bā sìn·ji jì.
    (special but not named) máuh: **certain kind of** máuh·júng; **certain month and a certain day** máuh·yuht máuh·yaht; **certain person** máuh yàhn; **certain place** máuh daat deih·fòng, máuh chyúh; **certain reason** máuh·júng léih·yàuh.

certainly   (with be) yāt·dihng; (with verb to be) jàn·haih. /I will certainly be there by eight o'clock. Ngóh baat·dím·jūng yat·dihng heui·dou gó·syu. /Your wife certainly is a good cook. Néih·ge taai·táai jàn·haih hóu·sáu·sai la.

certificate   jing·mìhng·syù, jāp·jiu (M: jèung)

certify   jing·mìhng

chaff   (of grain) hòn

chain   lín (M: tìuh) **watch chain** bīu·lín; **iron chain** tit·lín

chair   yí (M: jèung): **sofa** sō·fá yí; **rattan chair** tàhng·yí; **bamboo chair** jūk·yí

chairman   jyú·jihk

chalk   (for writing) fán·bāt (M: jì)

chamber   (room) fóng; **Chamber of Commerce** sèung·wúi

champagne   hēung·bān (·jáu) (M: jèun, bottle)

champion   gun·gwān

chance   gèi·wuih; **take a chance** si·háh, johng·háh sáu·sàhn; **take chances** mouh·hím

chancellor   (of a university) daaih·hohk·haauh·jéung

chandler's shop   (grocery) jaahp·fo·póu (M: gàan)

change   (alter, correct) gói. /You must change your bad habits. Néih yāt·dihng yiu gói néih dī m̀h·hóu ge jaahp·gwaan. /Bad habits are hard to change, but if you do it serious-

ly they will be changed. Waaih·jaahp·gwaan haih hóu nàahn gói ge, daahn·haih néih yihng·
jàn heui gói, néih yāt·dihng gói·dāk ge.

  bin. /The weather surely changed fast. Tìn·hei bin dāk jàn·haih faai la.

  change into bih·sehng. /Do you want to change yourself into a fairy? Néih séung m̀h
séung bin·sèhng yāt·go sìn·néui a?

  (exchange) wuhn. /May I change seats with you? Ngóh hó·yíh tùhng néih wuhn go
wái ma? /Do you change American money? Néih wuhn Méih·gām ma?

  change appearance jyun·yéung; **change clothes** wuhn sāam; **change a date** gói yaht·jí;
change hands jyun·sáu; **small change** seui·ngán

chant nihm: **chant a liturgy** nihm·gìng; **chant poetry** yàhm·sī

chapel fūk·yām·tòhng, láih·baai·tòhng (M: gàan)

chapter jèung

character sing·gaak. (written symbol) jih. /Can you teach me to read the characters?
Néih hó m̀h·hó·yíh gaau ngóh yihng jih a?

characteristic dahk·sing

charcoal taan (M: gauh, piece)

charge (of money) gai. /Is there an extra charge for this? Haih m̀h·haih lihng·ngoih
gai chín a? /How much do you charge me? Néih gai ngóh géi·do chín a?

  be in charge fuh·jaak. /Who is in charge here? Nī·syu bīn·go fuh·jaak a? _or_ Bīn·go
haih fuh·jaak·yàhn a? /You take charge of this section. Néih fuh·jaak nī·bouh·fahn.

  be in charge of (a place) fuh·jaak. /Who is in charge of this place? Bin go fuh jaak
gun·léih nī·daat deih·fòng a?

  charge to an account yahp·sou, séuhng·sou. /Charge it to my account. Yahp ngóh
ge sou là.

  charge for board and lodging sihn·sūk·faai

charitable chìh·sihn·ge

charity (kindness) hóu·sih; (philanthropy) chìh·sihn·sih·yihp

charm (word) jau; (symbol) fùh (M: douh)

charming hó·ngoi

chart (list or diagram) tòuh·bíu; (sea map) hòhng·hói·tòuh (M: fūk)

charter (hire) bàau, jòu

chase jèui

chat kìng·gái

chatter box hou·góng ge. /He's a chatterbox. Kéuih hóu hou·góng ge.

chauffeur chē·fū

cheap pèhng, sèung·yìh. **cheaper** pèhng dī. /Which one is cheaper? Bīn·go pèhng dī a?

cheat ngāk, hèi·pin; **be cheated** séuhng·dong. /I've been cheated again. Ngóh yauh
séuhng·jó·dong la.

check (examine) chēk. /Please check it. Chéng néih chēk·háh, ngāam m̀h·ngāam.
  (the number) dim; (compare) chàh, deui; **check an account** deui·háh tìuh sou
  a check chēk, chēk·jí, jì·piu (M: jēung)
  (receipt) sàu·geui; páai (made of metal or cardboard)
  other expressions: Check! ngāam la! (correct); Check! Jēung·gwàn! (in chess);
  checkup (physical examination) gím·chàh·sàn·tái

cheek mihn·jyū·dān

cheerful   fùn·héi, faai·wuht, gòu·hing

cheese   chī·sí, jī·sí

chef   chyùh·sī, sì·fú

chemicals   fa·hohk·bán

chemist   fa·hohk·gā, fa·hohk·sī

chemistry   fa·hohk

cheque   chēk, chēk·jí, jì·piu (M: jēung)

cherry   yìng·tòuh

chess   kéi (M: pùhn, a game): **chess board** kèih·pún; **chess book** kèih·póu; **chessman** keih·jí; **play chess** jūk·kéi

chest   (breast) hùng·háuh; (box) gwaih, sēung, lùhng

chestnut   fùng·léut

chew   jiuh; **chew it well** jiuh·laahn·kéuih

chewing gum   hèung·háuh·gàau

chicken   (fowl) gāi; (young fowl) gāi·jái (M: jek); **chicken broth** gāi·tòng; **chicken coop** gāi·lùhng; **chickenhearted** sai·dáam

chicken pox   séui·dáu; **have chicken pox** chēut·séui·dáu

chief   (important) gán·yiu, jyú·yiu. /What is the chief thing in your life? Néih yāt·sàng jeui gán·yiu (or jyú·yiu) ge sih haih māt·yéh?
    (a leader) táu, tàuh·yàhn. /Who's the chief among you? Néih·deih bīn·go haih táu a? /Who is your chief? Néih·deih ge táu haih bīn·go a?
    chief executive yùhn·sáu; **chief justice** daaih·faat·gùn; **chief mate** daaih·fó; **chief of a tribe** yàuh·jéung; **chief of general staff** chàam·màuh·júng·jéung; **chief of police** gíng·chaat·guhk·jéung

child   sai·mān·jái, sai·lóu·gō; (female) néuih·jái; **child education** yîh·tùhng·gaau·yuhk

childish   sai·mān·jái(·pèih)·hei

children   sai·mān·jái; (one's sons and daughters) jái·néui

chili   (pepper) laaht·jîu

chill   (med.) **have a chill** dá·láahng·jan

chilly   mèih·méi·dung

chimney   yìn·tùng; (of an oil lamp) dāng·túng, dāng·jaau

chin   hah·pàh

China   Jūng·gwok; **China proper** Jùng·gwok bún·bouh

China Inland Mission   Noih·deih·wúi

Chinese   (people) Jùng·gwok·yàhn; tòhng·yàhn (term used by overseas Chinese). **Chinese characters** Jùng·gwok·jih; **Chinese emigrants** wàh·kìuh; **Chinese spoken language** Jùng·gwok·wá; tòhng·wá; **Chinese style of dress** tòhng·jōng; **Chinese written language** Jùng·mmàhn, wàh·màhn, hon·màhn

chisel   jók (N); johk (V)

chivalry   yih·haahp·ge

chloroform   (Chem.) màh·yeuhk

chocolate   jyū·gū·lēut; (candy) jyū·gū·lēut tóng

choir   (of a church) gō·sī·bāan, sing·sī·bāan

choke   (have a blocking or checking of the breathing) juhk·chàn. /He choked while he was drinking water. Kéuih yám·séui juhk·chàn. (clog; fill up) sāk·múhn. /The river was choked with small boats. Tìuh hòh sāk·múhn téhng·jái.

cholera   fok·lyuhn, fok·lyuhn·jing

choose   gáan, syún·jaak

chop   (with an axe) pek; (cut into small pieces) deuk, chit. (a seal) yan; to chop, dám·yan

chopper   (for chopping meat) choi·dòu (M: bá)

chopping board   jàm·báan (M: faai)

chopsticks   faai·jí (M: fu, sèung, a pair)

chop suey   jaahp·seui (term used by overseas Chinese); cháau sahp·gám

chorus   (a choir) hahp·cheung·tyùhn; **sing in chorus** hahp·cheung

Christ   Gēi·dūk

Christian   Gēi·dūk·tòuh

Christianity   Gēi·dūk·gaau

Christmas   Yèh·sōu·daan, Yèh·sōu·sing·daan; **Christmas card** sing·daan·kāat; **Christmas Eve** sing·daan·chìhn·jihk; **Christmas tree** sing·daan·syuh (M: pò)

chronic   maahn·sing·ge

chrysanthemum   gūk·fà (M: déu, a flower; po, a plant; pùhn, a pot)

church   (building) láih·baai tòhng, gaau·tòhng; (congregation) gaau·wúi; (church member) gaau·yáuh

cicado   sím, chàu·sìhm (M: jek)

cigar   léuih·sung·yīn (M: háu)

cigarette   yīn·jái (M: háu)

cinema   yíng·hei·yún, dihn·yíng·yún, yíng·wá·yún

cinnabar   jyū·sà

cinnamon   yuhk·gwai

circle   (a ring) yùhn·hyūn. /Draw a circle. Waahk·yāt·go yùhn·hyūn. (government, business, educational, etc.) gaai: **government circle** jing·gaai; **business circle** sèung·gaai; **educational circle** hohk·gaai; **to circle, go around in a circle** wàih·jyuh . . . tàhm·tàhm·jyun

circular   (advertisement) chyùhn·dāan; (announcement) tūng·jî·syù; (in a form of a circle) yùhn·ge

circulation   (of a newspaper, periodical) chēut . . . fahn. /That newspaper has a circulation of fifty thousand copies. Gó·gàan bou·jí yāt·yaht chēut nǵh·maahn fahn. **blood circulation** hyut·chèuhn·wàahn

circumcision   got·láih

circumference   yùhn·jàu

circumstance   (condition) chìhng·yìhng, gwōng·gíng; (surroundings) wàahn·gíng; (state of affairs) chìhng·sai, guhk·sai circus   (show) máh·hei; (company) máh·hei·bāah

cistern   séui·chòuh

citizen   gùng·màhn

citizenship   gwok·jihk

city   (theoretically, a wall-city) sèhng; (municipality) síh; (in contrast with rural area) sèhng·síh; **city life** sèhng·síh sàng·wuht

civil   gùng·màhn(ge) **civil airport** màhn·yùhng fēi·gèi·chèuhng; **civil case** màhn·sih·ngon; **Civil Defense Corps** màhn·fòhng·déui; **civil engineer** gùng·chîhng·sī; **civil engineering** tóu·muhk·gùng·chîhng; **civil service examination** màhn·gun háauh·si; **civil law** màhn·faat; **civil officer** màhn·gùn; **civil war** noih·jin

civilians   pîhng·màhn

civilization   màhn·mîhng

civilized world   màhn·mîhng·sai·gaai

clam   hín (M: jek)

clamorous   bà·bai

clan   juhk; **clan's association** . . . sih·gùng·só (or gùng·wúi); The Wong's Association, Wòhng·sîh·gùng·só

clap   (applaud) paak·jéung, paak·sáu

clash   (as in opinion) chùng·daht

class   (grade) dáng; **first class** tàuh·dáng; **second class** yih·dáng
(sort, kind) tíng, leuih. /Don't associate with that class of people. Mh·hóu tùhng gó·tíng yàhn lòih·wóhng.
(a studying group) bāan; tòhng. /How many students do you have in your class? Néih gó bāan yáuh géi·dò hohk·sāang a? /Sorry, I must go to my class. Deui·m̀h·jyuh ngóh yiu heui séuhng·tòhng la. /I'll see you after the class. Ngóh lohk·jó tòhng gin néih. /Come to see me after class. (as a teacher talks to his student) Lohk·jó tòhng lèih gin ngóh.
    classmate tùhng·bāan, tùhng·bāan syù·yáu; **classroom** fo·sāt, fo·tòhng

classics   gìng·dín

classified   fàn·leuih·ge: **classified advertisement** fàn·leuih gwóng·gou

classify   jèung . . . fàn·leuih. /We should classify these books. Ngóh·deih yiu jèung nī·dī syù fàn·leuih

clause   (in grammar) dyún·geui; (of a treaty) tîuh

claw   (of animal) jáau (M: jek)

clay   nàih (M: dī)

clean   gòn·jehng (SV); sái·gòn·jehng (RV) (by washing); maat·gòn·jehng (RV) (by wiping); chaat·gòn·jehng (RV) (by rubbing)

clear   (general term) chîng·chó. /His voice was very clear over the radio. Kéuih ge sīng·yàm bo·sung dāk hóu chîng·chó. (of water) chîng; (of the head) chîng síng; (understandable). /Is it clear? Néih mîhng·baahk meih a?
    be cleared of one's debt waahn·chîng; **clear up**. /The skies are clearing now. Jauh·lèih hóu·tîn la.

cleft   la

clergyman   (Protestant) muhk·sī; (R. Catholic) sàhn·fuh

clerk   syù·gei, jīk·yùhn

clever   (in learning) chùng·mìhng; (smart and quick) lìhng·leih; lēk(·máh)

client   (at a shop) haak·jái; (of a lawyer) sih·jyú

cliff   sàan·ngàaih

climate   hei·hauh; séui·tóu. /Someone said the climate over there is good, but it doesn't
    agree with me. Yáuh yàhn wah gó·syu ge hei·háuh hóu hóu, daahn·haih ngóh m̀h·hahp
    gó·syu·ge séui·tóu.

climax   (as in a novel, drama, etc.) gòu·chìuh

climb   pàh: **climb a mountain** pàh·sàan; **climb up** pàh·séuhng·heui

clinic   chán·lìuh·só

clip   gíp (N); (cut) jín (V)

clippers   gaau·jín (M: bá)

clock   jūng; **clock tower** daaih·jūng·làuh

clod   **a clod of earth** yāt·gauh nàih

clog   (shoes with wooden soles) kehk, muhk·kehk (M: deui); **clogged** sāk·jyuh·ge

close   (in general) sàan·muhn; sàu·síh (for business firm only). /When does the museum
    close? Bok·maht·yún géi·dím·jūng sàan·mùhn a? /What time do you close? Néih·deih
    géi·dím jūng sàu·síh a?
        to close: close the book hahp·màaih bún syù; **close a box** kám·màaih ge háp; **close
    the eyes** hahp·màaih sèung ngáahn; **close the door** yím·màaih (or sàan·màaih) douh
    mùhn; **close the suitcase** sàan·màaih go pèih·gíp; **close the trunk** kám·màaih go lúhng
        (for a holiday) fong·ga. /When will your school be closed for the summer vacation?
    Néih·deih gàan hohk·haauh géi·sí fong·syú·ga a?

close   (near) lèih . . . káhn (ge). /I would like to find a place close to the school. Ngóh
    séung wán gàan ngūk lèih hohk·haauh hóu káhn ge.
        (approaching) /It's close to New Year's. Jauh·leih gwo·nìhn la.

clot   (coagulate) git·màaih·yāt·gauh·gauh

cloth   bou

clothes   sāam, yì·fuhk; **clothes horse** sāam·gá, yì·gá

cloud   wàhn

cloudy   yām·tìn. /Another cloudy day! Gàm·yaht yauh haih yām·tìn!

clown   cháu·gok, síu·cháu

club   (group of people) kèui·lohk·bouh, wúi; **club member** wuih·yáuh, wúi·yùhn; (a stick)
    gwan; **to club** bōk

clue   tàuh·séuih, sin·sok (as in a criminal case, etc.)

clumsy   leuhn·jeuhn

coach   máh·chè; (an instructor or trainer) gaau·lihn

coal   mùih: **coal yard** mùih·chóng; **coal mine** mùih·kwong

coalition   lyùhn·hahp

coarse   chòu

coast   hói·bīn, hói·pèih; **coast line** hói·ngohn·sin

coat   (garment) daaih·lāu (M: gihn); (covering) douh, jahm

cobbler   bóu·hàaih·lóu

cobra   faahn·cháan·tàuh, ngáahn·géng·sèh (M: tìuh)

cobweb   kàhm·lòuh·sī·mōng

cock   gāi·gūng, sāang·gāi; **cock fighting** dau·gāi; **cock's crow** gāi·tàih; **cocktail** party gài·méih·jáu·wúi

cockroach   gàh·jáat (M: jek)

cockscomb   gāi·gūn; **cockscomb flower** gāi·gūn·fā

coconut   yèh·jí; **coconut milk** yèh(·ji) jāp, yèh·jí·séui; **coconut pulp** yèh·yuhk; **coconut shell** yèh·hok

cocoon   gáan; (of a silkworm) chàahm·gáan

codfish   máhn·yùh; **cod-liver oil** yùh·gòn·yàuh, máhn·yùh·yàuh

code   ngam·máh; **code book** dihn·máh·bóu, maht·máh·bóu; **code signals** ngam·máh

coeducation   nàahm·néuih·tùhng·hohk

coerce   kéuhng·bīt

coffee   ga·fē; **coffee cup** gà·fēi·būi; **coffeepot** gà·fē·wùh; **coffee stall** ga·fē·dong

coffin   gùn·chòih, sauh·muhk, sauh·báan (M: fu)

coiffure   gái

coil   (wind up) gyún·màaih

coin   (small change) sáan·ngán

coincide   fùh·hahp

cold   (not warm) láahng, dung; (sickness) sēung·fùng. /You have such a bad cold, you'd better go home and take a rest. Néih sēung·fùng dak gam gán·yiu, bāt·yùh fàan ngūk·kéi táu·háh la. (not friendly) láahng·daahm

colic   tóuh·tung

collapse   (fall down) daat·dài; (figurative usage) kĭng·fūk

collar   (of a coat) léhng (M: tìuh)

colleague   tùhng·sih

collect   (receive) sàu. /Please collect the examination papers and hand them to me. Chéng néih tùhng ngóh sàu dĭ háu·si·gyún lèih béi ngóh. /How much money has he collected so far? Kéuih yíh·gĭng sàu·jó géi·dò chín la. /Who is in charge of collecting the money? Bīn·go fuh·jaak sàu chín a?
     (as a hobby) sàu·chòhng. /I'm interested in collecting stamps. Ngóh jùng·yi sàu·chòhng sih·dāam.
     (gather together in a group) jeuih·màaih. /A large crowd collected to hear his preaching. Yāt·daaih·kwàn yàhn jeuih·màaih kéuih·syu tèng kéuih góng douh.

college   (university in general) daaih·hohk (M: gàan); syù·yún (term used in Hong Kong). **college student** daaih·hohk·sāang

colloquial   **colloquial expressions** tùng·juhk ge jih·ngáahn

colonel   seuhng·gaau

colony   jihk·màhn·deih

color   sīk·séui, ngàahn·sīk, sīk; **color T.V.** chói·sīk dihn·sih; **color film** chói·sīk·pín

color-blind   sīk·màahng

colors   (flag) kèih (M: mihn, fūk; jì, on a pole). **colors of a nation** gwok·kèih; **colors of a school** haauh·kèih

colt   máh·jai (M: jek)

column   (pillar) chyúh (M: tìuh); (of characters) hòhng; (in newspaper) làahn; (of soldiers) jūng·déui

comb   sò: **comb the hair,** sò·tàuh

combine   hahp·màaih

come   lèih, làih. /When will he come? Kéuih géi·sí làih a? /Is he coming? Kéuih lèih m̀h·lèih a? /I'm coming. Ngóh jauh lèih la. /Have you come before? Néih yíh·chìhn yáuh móuh lèih·gwo a? /When did he come? Kéuih géi·sí lèih ga?
       come <u>plus an infinitive</u>. /He said he'd come to see you. Kéuih wah kéuih lèih taam néih.
       come across tái·gin, yuh·gin. /Let me know if you come across his name. Yùh·gwó néih tái·gin kéuih ge méng, m̀h·gòi néih góng ngóh jì.
       come back fàan·lèih; **come by boat** chóh syùhn lèih; **come by foot** hàahng·louh lèih; **come down** lohk·leih; **come downstairs** lohk·láu; **come here** lèih nī·syu; **come in** yàhp·leih; **come late** lèih·chìh·jó; **come nearer to me** hàahng·màaih·lèih ngóh·syu; **come out** chēut·lèih; **come quickly** faai·dī lèih; **come up** séuhng·leih

comedian   síu·cháu

comedy   héi·kehk (M: chēut)

comet   sou·bá·sīng

comfort   (cheer up) ngòn·wai. /Go and comfort him and make him forget his fears. Heui ngòn·wai kéuih, giu kéuih m̀h·hóu pa.
       (freedom from trouble or worry) ngòn·lohk. /They live in great comfort now. <u>is expressed as</u>: Kéuih·deih yìh·gā hóu ngòn·lohk la.

comfortable   (physically) syù·fuhk. /This chair is very comfortable. Nī·jèung yí hóu syu·fuhk; (contented) ngòn·lohk

comic book   gūng·jái·syù (M: bún)

comical   fùi·hàaih, waaht·kài

comma   dauh·dím

command   (an order) mihng·lihng. (take charge of) jí·fài. /He commands forty thousand troops. Kéuih jí·fài sei·maahn bìng. **commandant** sī·lihng·gùn; **commander** sī·lihng·gùn, -jéung: **company commander** lìhn·jéung; **battalion commander** yìhng·jéung; **regiment commander** tyùhn·jéung; **brigade commander** léuih·jéung; **division commander** sī·jéung; **army commander** gwàn·jéung; **commander in chief** júng·sī·lihng, daaih·yùhn·seui

commandment   gaai·mihng; **the Ten Commandments** sahp·gaai

commemorate   géi·nihm; **commemoration day** géi·nihm·yaht, géi·nihm·yát

commemorative monument   géi·nihm·bēi; **commemorative stamp** géi·nihm·yàuh·piu

commence   héi·sáu, hòi·sáu

comment   (notes) jyu·gáai; (criticize) pài·pìhng; **commentary** jyu·gáai

commerce   sèung·yihp. /There is much commerce between Hong Kong and the United States. Hèung·góng tùhng Méih·gwok ge sèung·yihp hóu wohng·sihng.

commercial   sèung·yihp·ge. **commercial city** sèung·yihp sìhng·síh; **commercial competition** sèung·yihp ging·jàng; **commercial law** sèung·faat; **commercial war** sèung jin; **commercial world** sèung·gaai

commission   wái·yahm (V); (brokerage) yúng, hàaih gām. **commission of inquiry** diuh chàh·wái·yùhn·wúi

commissioner   -sī: **commissioner of police** gíng·mouh·sī; **commissioner of customs** seui·mouh·sī

commit   faahn; **commit a crime** fàahn·jeuih; **commit suicide** jih·saat; **commit suicide by hanging** diu·géng; **commit suicide by drowning** tàuh·séui jih·saat

committee   wái·yùhn·wúi; **committee member** wái·yùhn; **committee chairman** jyú·jihk; **scholarship committee** jéung·hohk·gām wái·yùhn·wúi

commodity   fo·maht, sèung·bán; **daily commodity** yaht·yuhng·bán

common   pìhng·sèuhng, póu·tùng; **common people** lóuh·baak·sing, pìhng·màhn; **common saying** juhk·yúh; juhk·wá; **common sense** sèuhng·sīk

commonwealth   lyùhn·bòng: **The Commonwealth of Australia** Ngou·jàu·lyùn·bòng

communicate   tūng sīu·sīk, lyuhn·lok. /Is there any way to communicate with him? Yáuh móuh faat·jí hó·yíh tùhng kéuih tūng sīu·sīk a?

communication   gāau·tùng. /There is no communication whatsoever from here to there. Nī·syu tùhng gó·syu yùhn·chyùhn dyuhn·jyuht gāau·tùng.

communion   (Lord's Supper) sing·chāan; **to take the Holy Communion** sáu sing·chāan

communique   gùng·bou

communism   guhng·cháan·jyú·yih

communist   guhng·cháan·dóng; **communist party** guhng·cháan·dóng

community   séh·wúi, tyùhn·tái; **community service** séh·wúi·fuhk·mouh

companion   (in general) pún, (literary) tùhng·buhn, (friend) pàhng·yáuh

company   (in business) gūng·sī; (group) kwàhn, deuih; (military) lìhn; (companions) pàhng·yáuh. /We're having company for dinner tonight. Ngóh·deih gàm·máahn chéng pàhng·yáuh sihk·faahn. (companionship) jouh·pún. /I enjoy her company. Ngóh hóu jùng·yi kéuih tùhng ngóh jouh·pún.

comparatively   béi·gaau·seuhng, béi·gaau. /This one is comparatively practical. Nī·go béi·gaau saht·jai dī. /This one is comparatively cheap. Nī·go béi·gaau pèhng dī.

compare   béi·gaau. /You may compare these two and see which one is better. Néih hó·yíh béi·gaau nī·léuhng·go, tái bīn·go hóu dī.

compass   (for mariners) lòh·pùhn, lòh·gàang, jí·nàahm·jām; (for making circles) yùhn·kwài

compassion   chìh·bèi, lìhn·máhn

compatriot   tùhng·bàau

compel   kéuhng·bīt

compensate   (for loss or injury) bóu·sèuhng, pùih·sèuhng; (for trouble) chàuh·lòuh

compensation   bou·chàuh

compete   ging·jàng

competent   nàhng·sing·yahm·ge, hahp·gaak·ge

competition   ging·jàng; **competition in business** sèung·yihp ging·jàng

competitor   dihk·sáu

compile   pìn, pìn·chāp

complain   ngàhm·chàhm, san·yùn, màaih·yun. /What is he complaining about? Kéuih
    hái syu ngàhm·chàhm māt·yéh a? /He always complains, but he never tells you exactly
    what he is complaining about. Kéuih sìh·sìh dōu hái syu san·yùn, daahn·haih kéuih
    wìhng m̀h·góng néih jī kéuih waih māt sih san·yùn.

complete   (finish) jouh·hóu, jouh·sèhng, yùhn·sèhng. /When can you complete this? Néih
    géi·sí hó·yíh jouh·sèhng nī·gihn sih a?
        (without damage or loss) chàih. /Is this set of books complete? Nī·tou syù chàih
    m̀h·chàih a?
        (entire) sèhng, chyùhn. /Would it be cheaper if I buy the complete set? Yùh·gwó
    ngóh sèhng tou máaih, haih m̀h·haih pèhng dī a?

complex   fūk·jaahp

complexion   (of the face) mihn·sīk; (of the skin) pèih·fù·ge ngàahn·sīk

complicated   fūk·jaahp

complimentary ticket   jahng·hyun, yàu·doih·hyun (M: jèung)

compose   (write) jok, sé, (print) jāp·jih. **compose a poem** jok·sī; **compose a song**
    jok·kūk; **compose an essay** jok·mán, jok·mahn·jèung

composer   jok·kūk·gā

composition   (essay) mán, leuhn·màhn; (a subject in the curriculum) jok·mán; (construc-
    tion) jóu·jīk

compositor   jap·jih·gùng·yàhn

compradore   máaih·báan

comprehend   mìhng·baahk

comprise   bàau·hahm

compromise   béi·chí sèung·yeuhng·háh, béi·chí sèung·jauh·háh. /Let's compromise!
    Daaih·gā sèung·yeuhng·háh lā!

compulsory   kéuhng·bīt; **compulsory education** kéuhng·bīt·gaau·yuhk

comrade   tùhng·ji

concave   nāp·ge; **concave and convex** nāp·daht

conceal   yím·chòhng, beng·màaih

conceited   jih·gòu·jih·daaih

concentrate   jaahp·jùng; **concentration camp** jaahp·jùng·yìhng

concept   koi·nihm; **general concept** yāt·bùn·ge koi·nihm

concern   (worry) dāam·sàm, gwāan·sàm, gwa·sàm. /His illness caused his parents con-
    siderable concern. Kéuih ge behng lìhng kéuih ge fuh·móuh hóu dàam·sàm. /She is very
    much concerned about her daughter's health. Kéuih deui kéuih ge néui ge sàn·tái fèi·
    sèuhng gwa·sàm.
        (involvement or interest) tùhng . . . yáuh (or móuh) gwàan·haih. /Which people were

concerned in this matter? /Bīn·dī yàhn tùhng nī·gihn sih yáuh gwàan·haih a? /Does this concern you? Nī·gihn sih tùhng néih yáuh móuh gwàan·haih a? /This doesn't concern me. Nī·gihn sih tùhng ngóh móuh gwàan·haih.
(business) gūng·sī, pou·táu, sèung·dim

concerning   (regarding) gwāan·yù (M: gàan)

concert   yàm·ngohk·wúi: to give a concert hōi yàm·ngohk wúi, géui·hàhng yàm·ngohk·wúi

concise   (succinct) gáan·mìhng

conclude   git·chūk; conclude a treaty sèung·dihng yāt·go tiuh·yeuk; conclude a work yùhn·gung

conclusion   git·léun

concrete   (not abstract) geuih·tái·ge, saht·joih·ge; (for building) sehk·sí

concubine   chip·sih, yih·nāai

condense   kìhng·màaih; condensed milk lihn·náaih

condition   (state) chìhng·yìhng; (terms) tiuh·gín; living conditions sāng·wuht·chìhng·yìhng

condole   heui diu·sòng

conduct   (behaviour) bán·hahng, hàhng·wàih; (lead) yáhn·douh, daai; (direct) jí·douh
(business), jí·fài (music).   conduct electricity chyùhn·dihn; conduct heat chyùhn yiht

conductor   the conductor of an orchestra ngohk·déui jí·fài

confection   (sweets) tòhng·gwó; confectionery tòhng·gwó·dim

confer   (give) béi; confer baptism sī·sái; confer medical aid gratuitously jàhng·yi; confer a degree bàan·faat hohk·wái

conference   wuih·yi; hold a conference géui·hàhng wuih·yi

confess   sìhng·yìhng; confess a fault or mistake yihng·cho; confess sin yìhng jeuih

confidence   seun·yahm. /I have perfect confidence in them. Ngóh yùhn·chyùhn seun·yahn keuih·deih.

confident   kok·seun. /I'm confident that everybody will do his duty. Ngóh kok·seun go·go dōu yāt·dihng jeun kéuih ge jīk·jaak.

confidential   /This is confidential. is expressed as: Nī·gihn sih chéng néih chìn·kèih sáu bei·maht. or Nī·gihn sih chìn·kèih bāt·nàhng góng·béi daih·yih·go yàhn jí.

confirm   jing·saht. /This report has not been confirmed. Nī·go sīu·sīk juhng meih jing·saht.

confiscate   chūng·gùng, muht·sàu

conflict   chūng·daht

Confucian temple   Húng·miuh

confucianism   Yùh·ga·ge·gaau·yih

Confucianist   (an adherent) Húng·gaau·tòuh; Yùh·ga·ge (At)

Confucius   Húng·jí, Húng·fù·jí

confuse   jing·lyuhn, gáau·lyuhn. confused lahp·lyuhn. /I'm confused. Ngóh·ge sàm hóu lahp·lyuhn. confusion lyuhn. /It was in a great state of confusion. Bāt·jì géi lyuhn.

congeal   kìhng, kìhng·màaih

congee   jūk (M: wún, bowl)

congestion   (of blood) chùng·hyut; **congestion of the brain** nóuh chùng·hyut; **congestion of the lungs** fai chùng·hyut

congratulate   gùng·héi, gùng·hoh; **congratulate on a birthday** hoh sàang·yaht, baai·sauh; **congratulate on the new year** baai·nìhn; **congratulatory presents** hoh·láih

congress   (meeting) daaih·wúi, wuih yih; (legislature) gwok·wúi

connect   (as a chain) lìhn màaih; jip·màaih; (as beads) chyun·màaih; (by a knot) bok·màaih

conquer   (a country) jìng·fuhk; (one's bad habits, etc.) hāk·fuhk

conscience   lèuhng·sàm

conscientious   yihng·jàn. /He's a very conscientious worker. Kéuih jouh·sih hóu yìhng·jàn ge.

conscription   jīng·bìng; **escape conscription** tòuh·beih bìng·yihk; **exempted from conscription** míhn·chyùh bìng·yiht

consecutive   luhk·juhk ge

consent   (agree) yìng·sìhng. /Has he consented? Kéuih yìng·sìhng·jó meih a? (approval) jéun·héui, ngahp·táu. /His consent is absolutely necessary. Yāt·dihng yíu kéuih jéun·héui sìn·ji dāk.

consequence   (result) git·gwó

consequently   yàn·chí, yùh·sih

conservative   bóu·sáu ge, sáu·gauh ge; **Conservative party** bóu·sáu·dóng

consider   (think about) háau·leuih. /We are considering whether we should give him this money or not. Ngóh·deih háau·leuih·gán yìng mh·yìng·gòi béi nī·bāt chín kéuih. /Please consider it. Chéng néih háau·leuih·háh.
    (pay attention to) gu·gahp. /He never considers the feelings of others. Kéuih wihng·yúhn mh·wúih gu·gahp yàhn·deih dím ge gáam·gok ge.

considerable   sēung·dòng . . . ge . . . /We have had considerable rain this summer. Gàm·nìhn hah·gwai lohk·yúh lohk dāk sēung·dòng dò.

consist   yáuh. /What does this dish consist of? Nī·meih sung léuih·bihn yáuh dī māt·yéh a? /It consists of fish, meat and vegetables. Léuih·bihn yáuh yúh, yáuh yuhk, yihk yáuh choi.

console   ngòn·wai

consonant   (sound) jí·yām; (letter) jí·yām·jih·móuh

constantly   sìh·sìh. /Do they constantly quarrel? Kéuih·deih haih mh·haih sìh·sìh ngaai·gāau a? /It's constantly so. Sìh·sìh (or Wòhng·wòhng) haih gám ge la.

constellation   sīng·sūk, sīng·joh

constipation   daaih bihn mh·tùng, bihn·bei

constitution   (of the body) tái·gaak; (of a state) hin·faat

construct   **construct a bridge** jūk yāt·douh kìuh; **construct a house** héi yāt·gàan ngūk; **construct a sentence** jouh yāt·geui géui; **construct a wall** jūk yāt·buhng chèuhng

constructive   yáuh gin·chit·sìhng ge

consul   líhng·sí; **consul general** júng·líhng·sí; **consulate,** líhng·sih·gún

consult   sèung·lèuhng, jàm·jeuk. /I think I shall consult him on this. Nī·gihn ngóh yiu tùhng kéuih sèung·lèuhng·háh. **consult a dictionary** chàh·jih·dín; **consult a lawyer** tùhng leuht·sī sèung·lèuhng; **consult with friends** tùhng pàhng·yáuh s<u>èung lèuhng</u> (<u>or</u> jàm·jeuk)

contact   /We tried to contact you, but we couldn't locate you. Ngóh·deih sîh·gwo wán néih daahn·haih wán·m̀h·dóu néih. **contact lenses** yán·yîhng·ngáahn·géng

contagious   chyùhn·yíhm·sing ge, wúih chyùhn·yíhm ge; **contagious disease** chyùhn yíhm· behng

contain   yáuh. /What does this bottle contain? Nī·go jēun léuih·bihn yáuh dī māt·yéh a? /It contains some cough syrup. Léuih·bihn yáuh dī kāt·yeuhk.
    (hold) jòng. /How many catties will it contain? Hó·yíh jòng·dāk géi·dò gàn a?

contemn   (despise) tái·síu

contemporary   tùhng·sîh ge, tùhng·yāt·go·sîh·doih ge

contempt   tái·hèng, tái·dài, tái·síu

contend   (fight) jàang; **contend for merit** jāang·gùng

content   **be contented with one's lot** ngòn·fahn; **be contented with what one possesses** jī·jūk; **contentment is a continual feast** jī·jūk·sèuhng·lohk

contents   noih·yùhng; **table of contents** muhk·lúk, muhk·luhk

contest   (competition) béi·choi: **music contest** yàm·ngohk béi·choi; **calligraphy contest** jaahp·jih béi·choi; **drawing contest** wuih·wá béi·choi

context   seuhng·hah·màhn

continent   daaih·luhk: **the continent of Asia** Nga·jàu·daaih·luhk; **the continent of America** Méih·jàu·daaih·luhk

continually   jip·juhk·bāt·dyuhn ge

continue   jip·jyuh (<u>or</u> gai·juhk) . . . lohk·heui. /We shall continue our work without stopping until we are finished. Ngóh·deih yiu jip·jyuh jouh·lohk·heui m̀h·hóu tîhng, yāt·jihk ji·dou jouh·yùhn wàih·jí. /You continue (to tell this story). Néih jip·jyuh góng là.

continuously   lihn·juhk·bāt·dyuhn gám (A). /It has been raining continuously the last few days. Nī·syu nī·géi·yaht lihn·juhk·bāt·dyuhn gám lohk·jó géi·yaht yúh.

contraband   (smuggled goods) sî·fo, jáu·sî·fo; (prohibited goods) wàih·gam·bán

contraception   beih·yahn·faat

contract   (agreement) hahp·tùhng: **make a contract** dá·yāt·go hahp·tùhng

contractor   sîhng·baahn·yàhn; (builder) sîhng·jip gùng·chîhng ge yàhn, sîhng·gihn·sèung

contradict   **contradict oneself** jih·sèung·màauh·téuhn

contradictory   béi·chi·màauh·téuhn ge

contrary   yúh . . . sèung·fáan (ge). /Driving on the right side of the street is contrary to law in Hong Kong. Hái Hèung·góng hái gāai·syu kaau yauh·bihn hàahng·chè haih yúh faat·leuht sèung·fáan ge. **on the contrary** sîk·ngāam·sèung·fáan

contribute   (money, supplies) gyùn·joh, gyùn. /Would you like to contribute some? Chéng néih gyùn·joh dò síu lā. /Would you like to contribute more? Chéng néih gyùn· joh dō dī la. (article for publication) tàuh·góu (VO)

contribution   (money) gyùn·fún. /We should have a committee to handle this contribution. Ngóh·deih yîng·fahn yáuh yāt·go wái·yùhn·wúi bóu·gún nī·bāt gyùn·fún.
    (for a common cause) gung·hin. /His discovery was a great contribution to mankind. Kéuih ge faat·mîhng deui yàhn·leuih hàih yāt·go hóu daaih ge gung·hin.

control   gún·léih, gún. /Is she good at controlling children? Kéuih wúih m̀h·wúih
gún·léih sai·māan·jái a? /Can you control your men? Néih gún m̀h·gún·dāk·dihm
néih dī yàhn a?

    controlled price gún·ga; **control one's temper** ngaat·jai jih·géi ge pèih·hei; **out of**
control gún·m̀h·dihm, gáau·m̀h dihm (unmanageable); gèi·gín waaih·jó (unworkable);
controls gèi·gín, gèi·hei. /Are the controls in order? Gèi·gín dōu móuh sih lā ma?
/Take over the controls for a while. Néih lèih sái (referring to a plane or train, etc.)
yāt·jahn·gāan.

controversy   dáu·fàn

convene   jiuh·jaahp; **convene a meeting** jiuh·jaahp hòi·wúi

convenient   fòng·bihn

convenience   seuhn·bín. /Can you buy me a book at your convenience? Néih seuhn·bín
tùhng ngóh máaih bún syù dāk ma?

convent   (Buddhist) sī·gū·ngām, jàai·tóng; (Catholic) gù·nèuhng·tòhng

convention   daaih·wúi (M: chi; gaai, a session)

conventional   jaahp·gwaan·seuhng ge, sèuhng·yuhng ge; **conventional expressions** sèuhng·
yuhng go oyut wah; **conventional greeting** haak tou wá

conversation   expressed verbally as converse, kìng(·gái). /We had a cordial conversation. Ngóh·deih kìng dāk hóu tàuh·gèi. /We had a long conversation. Ngóh·deih kìng·jó
hóu noih.

converse   kìng, kìng·gái (ref. conversation)

convert   bin·sèhng, bin·wàih. /Heat converts water into steam. /Yiht jèung séui bin·wàih
hei. /Water is converted into ice at 32 degrees Fahrenheit. Wàh·sih·bíu sà·ah·yih·douh
ge sih·hauh, séui bin·sèhng bīng.

    (from one religion to another religion) seun·fuhng, gói·seun. /He was converted to
Christianity. Kéuih seun·fuhng Gēi·dūk·gaau la.

    gáam·fa. /Have we ever thought seriously how to convert people's hearts? Ngóh·
deih yáuh móuh yihng·jàn séung·gwo dím·yéung heui gáam·fa yàhn·sām nē?

convey   (as news, information) chyùhn·daaht

convict   faahn·yàhn, jeuih·fáan, faahn·gwo·ngon·ge·yàhn (N)

convince   lihng . . . seun·fuhk. /Can you convince me what you've said is true? Néih
nàhng m̀h·nàhng·gau lihng ngóh seun·fuhk néih só·góng·ge haih jàn ga?

convoy   wuh·sung (V); wuh·sung·déui, wuh·hòhng·déui (for vessels)

convulse   (of the muscles) chāu·gàn

cook   jyú·faahn (in general); jyú·sung (preparing dishes); jyú·faahn (cook rice). /I don't
know how to cook rice, nor any dishes, but I can eat. Ngóh m̀h·wúih jyú·faahn, yihk m̀h·
wúih jyú·sung, daahn·haih ngóh wúih sihk. /Do you know how to cook? Néih wúih jyú·
faahn ma?

    cook in particular ways (boil) jyú; (bake) guhk; (roast, or broil) sìu; (deep fry) jaau,
ja; (pan-fry) jìn, cháau; (steam) jìng; (barbecue) kaau

    cook a little longer jyú noih dī; **cook thoroughly until it's tender** jyú·nàhm dī; **cook-**
ing time sufficient gau·fó, **cooking time not sufficient** m̀h·gau·fo

    cookbook sihk·póu; **a cook** chyùh·fóng (male), jyú·fáan (female). /We want to hire
a cook. Ngóh·deih yiu chéng yāt·go jyú·fáan. /She is a very good cook. Kéuih hóu wúih
jyú·sung. /You certainly are a very good cook! Néih jàn·haih wúih jyú·sung la!

cooky   béng·jái, béng·gōn

cool   lèuhng, lèuhng·sóng (cool and airy). /It was cool last night, wasn't it? Kàhm-máahn jàn·haih lèuhng la, haih m̀h·haih a? /Your house is really cool. Néih gàan ngūk jàn·haih lèuhng·sóng la.

coolie   gū·lēi

cooperate   hahp·jok

cooperative   hahp·jok·séh

copper   tùhng **copper nail** tùhng·dēng; **copper wire** tùhng·sín

copy   (by writing) chàau; (by typing) dá; (by tracing) mìuh. /Can you copy down these words for me? Néih hó·yíh tùhng ngóh chàau·dài nī géi·go jih ma?
    make a copy /Make ten copies of this letter. Jēung nī·fùng seun chàau· (by writing, or dá by typing) sahp·fahn.
    a copy of a book yāt·bún; **a copy of a newspaper or periodical** yāt·fahn

copyright   báan·kyùhn

coral   sàan·wùh: **coral island** sàan·wùh·dóu

cord   (string) síng (M: tìuh)

core   (of a fruit) sām

cork   (stopper) sāk; (stop with a cork) sāk·jyuh; **cork of a bottle** jēun·sāk

corn   **Indian corn** sūk·máih; (on the foot) gài·ngáahn

corner   gok, gok·lōk·táu. **corner of the eyes** ngáahn·gok; **corner of the room** chèuhng·gok·lōk·táu; **corner of the street** gāai·gok; **corner of the table** tói·gok

coronation   gà·mìhn: **coronation ceremony** gà·mìhn láih

coroner   yihm·sī·gùn

corporation   gūng·sī, yáuh·haahn·gūng·sī (M: gàan)

corpse   séi·sì, sì·sáu

correct   (right) ngāam; (to make right) gói, gói·jing
    correct one's errors gói·gwo; **correct compositions** gói·mán; **correct examination papers** gói·gyún

correspond   (writing to one another) tùng·seun. /Have you corresponded with him? Néih yáuh móuh tùhng kéuih tùng·seun a? (to be in agreement) sèung·fùh. /Does the figure in your checkbook correspond to the bank statement? Néih ngàhn·hònhng chyùhn·jíp ge sou·muhk tùhng ngahn·hòhng tūng·jì ge sou·muhk sèung·fuh ma?

correspondence school   hàahm·sauh hohk·haauh (M: gàan)

correspondent   (to a newspaper, etc.) tùng·seun·yùhn

corrupt   fuh·baaih ge; **corrupt officials** tāam·gùn·wù·leih; **corrupt practices** tāam·wù

cosmetics   fa·jōng·bán, yīn·jì·séui·fán

cost   yiu. /What does this article cost? Nī·gihn yéh yiu géi·dò chín a? /How much does it cost to have this watch repaired? Jíng·fàan nī·go bìu yiu géi·dò chín a?
    (expense) fai·yuhng. /The cost is too great. Fai·yuhng taai daaih. /The cost of living is getting higher and higher. Sàng·wuht ge fai·yuhng yuht·lèih·yuht gòu.
    (sacrifice) hèi·sàng. /It's not worthwhile obtaining a diploma at the cost of your son's health. Hèi·sàng néih ge jái ge sàn·jí heui bok yāt·jèung màhn·pàhng taai m̀h·jihk·dāk.

costume   fuhk·jōng

cot   (made of canvas) fàahn·bou·chòhng (M: jèung)

cottage   ngūk·jái (M: gàan)

cotton   mìhn·fà; **sterilized cotton** yeuhk·mìhn, yeuhk·mìhn·fà

cough   kāt. /How long has he been coughing? Néih kāt·jó géi·nói la? /He has been coughing for more than two months. Kéuih kāt·jó léuhng·go·géi·yuht la. **cough syrup** kāt·yeuhk; **cough drops** kāt·tóng

counselor   gu·mahn

count   sóu. /Please count it. Chéng néih sóu·háh. /Please count this for me. M̀h·gòi néih tùhng ngóh sóu·háh.
        (include) gai. /This room cost me fifteen dollars not counting the tips. Gó·gàan·fóng sái·jó ngóh sahp·ngh·mān m̀h·gai siu·fai.
        (rely on) kaau. /We are counting on you. Ngóh·deih chyùhn·kaau néih ge la.

countenance   mihn·maauh

counter   (of a shop) gwaih·mín, gwaih·tói

counterfeit   gá ge, gá·mouh ge; **counterfeit a label** gá·mouh jih·houh

counteroffensive   fáan·gùng

country   (nation) gwok. /Do you think that Hawaii will become a country someday? Néih gú Hah·wài·yih jèung·lòih wúih m̀h·wúih bin·sèhng yāt·gwok a?
        (rural area) hèung·há. /Do you like to live in the country? Néih jùng·yi hái hèung·háh jyuh ma?

couple   (two) léuhng. /Give me a couple of them. Béi léuhng·go ngóh. **a couple of days** léuhng·yaht; **a couple of hours** léuhng·go jūng·dím; **a couple of years** léuhng·nìhn; **a married couple** léuhng·gùng·pó, leuhng·fù·fúh

coupon   jahng·hyun (M: jèung)

courage   dáam·leuhng, yúhng·hei

course   (of instruction) fō (M); gùng·fo (M: mùhn). /How many courses have you taken? Néih duhk géi·dō fō a? /Which course is most interesting to you? Néih deui bīn·yāt·fō (or bīn·yāt·mùhn gùng·fo) jeui yáuh hin·cheui a?
        (direction of a boat or airplane) hòhng·sin; (of a meal) meih

court   (law) faat·yún, faat·tìhng, kōt; (for games) kàuh·chèuhng; (royal residence) wòhng·gùng; (courtyard) tìn·jéng; **to court** jèui·kàuh

courteous   yáuh·láih

courtesy   láih·maauh

cousin   (paternal uncle's elder son) sò·tòhng·a·gō; (younger son) sò·tòhng sai·lóu; (elder daughter) sò·tòhng ā·jē; (younger daughter) sò·tòhng a·múi; (paternal or maternal aunt's elder son) bíu·gō, (younger son) bíu·dái, (elder daughter) bíu·jé, (younger daughter) bíu·múi
    cousins (sons of paternal uncle) sò·tòhng hìng·daih, (daughters of paternal uncle) sò·tòhng jí·múi; (sons of paternal or maternal aunt) bíu·hìng·daih, (daughters of paternal or maternal aunt) bíu·jí·múi

cover   (an object or a person) kám. /Put the lid on the teapot. Kám hóu go chàh·wú. /Cover him with the quilt. Tùhng kéuih kám·hóu jèung péih.
        (with a fitted case) tou. /Cover up the sofa. Tou·hóu jèung sō·fá.
        (with the hand) ngám·jyuh. /Use your hand to cover your right eye. Yuhng sáu ngám·jyuh néih ge yauh ngáahn.

(spread on) pòu. /Use this tablecloth to cover that table. Yuhng nī·jèung tói·bou pòu·hai gó·jèung tói·mín·syu.

(protect) /Is your car covered by insurance? Néih ga chè yáuh móuh yin·sō a?

covet   tàam

covetous   tàam·sàm

cow   ngàuh, ngàuh·ná (M: jek)

crab   háaih (M: jek)

crack   lit (V), lit·hòi (V); la (N) (M: tîuh)

cracker   hàahm·béng·gōn

cradle   yìuh·làahm

craft   sáu·gùng

crafty   gwéi·máh, dò·gái

cramp   (convulsion) chàu·gàn

crane   (bird) hók; (machine) héi·chúhng·gèi (M: fu)

crater   fó·sàan·háu

crawl   pàh, làan

crazy   faat·dìn, sàhn·gìng

cream   (of milk) geih·līm

create   chong·jouh, jouh. **create trouble** gáau·sih·gáau·fèi

Creator, the   jouh·maht·jyú

creature   (living things) sàang·maht

credit   (reputation for paying bills) seun·yuhng. /Your credit is good. Néih ge seun·yuhng hóu·hóu.

creditor   jaai·jyú

cremate   fó·jong; **crematory** fó·jong·chèuhng

crescent moon   ngòh·mèih·yuht

crevice   la (M: tîuh)

crew   (of a ship) séui·sáu, syùhn·yùhn

cricket   jīk·jēut, sīk·sēut (M: jek)

crime   jeuih; **commit a crime** faahn·jeuih

criminal   (person) jeuih·fáan. **criminal case** yìhng·sih·ngon; **criminal law** yìhng·faat; **criminal offense** faahn·faat, faahn·jeuih

crimson   (deep red) daaih·hùhng ge, sàm·hùhng ge

cripple   /He is crippled. Kéuih bài·jó jek geuk. **a cripple** bài·geuk·lóu

crisis   ngàih·gèi

crisp   cheui

critic   pài·pìhng·gā

critical   ngàih·gāp

criticize   pài·pìhng

crocodile   ngohk·yùh (M: tîuh)

crooked   (bent) lyūn·gūng ge

crop   (harvest) sàu·sîhng. /The litchi crop this year is very good. Gam·nín laih·jī ge sàu·sîhng hóu hóu.

cross   (religious symbol) sahp·jih·gá. to cross gwo; cross a bridge gwo kîuh; cross a harbor gwo hói; cross a river gwo hòh; cross a sea gwo hói; cross a street gwo gāai cross out waahk·jó kéuih. /Cross out the items you don't want. Jèung néih m̀h·yiu go·dī waahk·jó kéuih. make a cross waahk go sahp·jih or dá go gāau·chā

crow   wū·ngà (M: jek); giu (V)

crowd   yāt·kwàhn yàhn. crowded bīk

crown   wòhng·gùn; crown land wòhng·gà·deih; crown of the head tàuh·hok·déng; crown prince taai·jí

crucify   jèung . . . dèng sahp·jih·gá

cruel   chàahn·yáhn

cruiser   chèuhn·yèuhng·laahm (M: jek)

crumbs   (of bread) mihn·bāau·séui; (of cake) béng·séui

crusader   sahp·jih·gwān

crumple   jau·màaih

crush   (pressure from above) jaahk; (pressure from the sides) gihp; (pressure from a moving and rolling object) ngaat; (collide) johng. These verbs are used to form a re-sultative compound with other verbs such as: laahn (be broken); seui (be shattered); bín (be flat); lit (be cracked); sáan (be in scattered parts), etc. crushed and broken jaahk·laahn·jó; crushed and shattered jaahk·seui·jó; crushed and flat jaahk·bín·jó; crushed to death jaahk·séi·jó

crust   crust of bread mihn·bāau·pèih; crust of the earth deih·hok

cry   (shout) ngaai. /Cry louder! Daaih·sèng ngaai! (weep) haam. /Please stop crying. M̀h·hóu haam la. /Is it someone crying for help? Haih m̀h·haih yáuh yàhn ngaai 'gau mehng a'?

cub   bear cub hùhng·yán·jái; lion cub sì·jí·jái; tiger cub lóuh·fú·jái

cubic foot   lahp·fōng·chek

cuckoo   douh·gyūn (M: jek)

cucumber   wòhng·gwā

cue   (hint) ngam·sih

cuff   jauh·háu

cultivate   cultivate rice jung·wòh; cultivate the soil jung·tîhn; cultivate flowers jung·fā

culture   màhn·fa

cunning   gwái·máh

cup   būi (M: jek); a cup of tea yāt·bùi·chàh; teacup chàh·būi

Cupid   ngoi·sàhn

curable   yî·dāk·hóu ge

cure (heal) yî; (as meat, etc.) yìm. **cure a disease** yì·behng; **cure of the habit of taking drugs** gaai kāp·duhk; **cured ham** fó·téui, yìm·yuhk

curfew gaai·yìhm

curio gú·dúng, gú·wún (M: gihn); **curio shop** gú·wún·dim, gú·dúng·dim

curiosity hou·kèih·sàm

curious hou·kèih

curl **curl one's hair** gyún·tàuh·faat

current (present) /Is this the current issue? Nī·kèih haih·m̀h·haih jeui·gahn ge yāt·kèih a? (of electricity) dihn·làuh; (of water) séui·làuh; **current events** sìh·sih; **current price** sìh·ga; **current account** wuht·kèih·chyùhn·fún

curriculum fo·chìhng

curse (swear at) naauh. /Whom is she cursing? Kéuih naauh·gán bīn·go a?

curry ga·lēi: **curry powder** ga·lēi·fán

curtain (of doors, windows) lím (M: fūk); (of a theater) mohk

curve kūk·sin; **curves of a beauty** kūk·sin·méih

curved lyùn·ge, lyūn·kūk ge

cushion jín: **cushion for a chair** yí·jín

custom (habit) fùng·juhk; (rule) kwài·géui

customary jiu·láih·ge, jiu·kwài·géui

customer haak·jái, gu·haak

customs seui; **customs house** seui·gwāan, hói·gwāan; **customs broker** bou·gwāan·hóng; **customs cruiser** chāp·sî·téhng (M: jek)

cut (with a knife) got; (by slicing) chit; (with scissors) jín; (with an ax) pek; (with a sword) jáam
 (reduce) gáam. /These prices will be cut next month. Nī·dī ga·chìhn hah·go·yuht jauh wúih gáam ge la.
 cut hair jín·faat, fèi·faat. /Where do you go for your haircut usually? Néih pìhng·sìh heui bīn·syu jín·faat ga?
 /Be careful, don't cut your hand. Hóu·sēng, m̀h·hóu got·chàn sáu.

cute dāk·yi, cheui·ji

cymbal chàh·chá

D

daddy bàh·bā

daffodil séui·sīn·fā

dagger dyún·gim (M: bá)

daily yaht·yaht, múih·yaht. **daily expenditure** múih·yaht ge sái·yuhng; **daily necessities** yaht·yuhng·bán; **daily newspaper** yaht·bou; **daily use** yaht·yuhng ge

damage syún·waaih, jíng·waaih, waaih. /He damaged my car. Kéuih syún·waaih·jó ngóh ga chè. /How was the damage done? Dím·yéuhng jíng·waaih ga? /How much damage? Waaih sèhng dím a? **pay damage** pùih·fàan·béi, pùih·sèuhng syún·sāt, pùih·chín. /He should pay your damages. Kéuih yiu pùih·fàan·béi néih. /He sued for damages. Kéuih yìu·kàuh (demand) pùih·sèuhng syún·sāt.

damp   chìuh·sāp

dance   tiu·móuh (VO). /Do you dance? Néih tiu·móuh ma? /No. I don't know how to dance. Ngóh m̀h·tiu·móuh, Ngóh m̀h·sīk tiu·móuh. /Do you know how to dance the fox trot? Néih sīk tiu wùh·bouh·móuh ma? /I know a little, I've danced the fox trot a couple of times. Ngóh sīk·sīk·dei, Ngóh tiu·gwo léuhng·chi.
    dancing tiu·móuh; **dancing girl** móuh·néui; **tea dance** chàh·móuh; **a dance or ball** tiu·móuh·wúi

dandruff   tàuh·pèih

dangerous   ngàih·hím

dare   gáam (AV). /Do you dare to go? Néih gáam heui ma?

daring   m̀h·pa·séi·ge, daaih·dáam·ge

dark   (without light) hāk; (lack of light) ngam. /It will get dark soon, let's hurry up. Jauh·lèih hāk la, faai dī la. /This room is too dark. Nī·gàan fóng taai ngam.
    (of a color) sàm. /This color is not dark enough. Nī·go ngàahn·sīk m̀h·gau sàm.
/I want a darker shade of this color. Ngóh yiu go sàm·sīk dī ge.
    dark blue sàm·làahm·sīk; **dark brown** jyū·gōn·sīk; **dark red** sàm·hùhng·sīk

date   (the exact time) yaht·kèih. /Have you set the date yet? Néih dihng·jó yaht·kèih meih a? (fruit) sài·jóu. **out of date** gwo·sih. /This style is out of date. Nī·jek fún yíh·gìng gwo·sìh la.

daughter   néui; **daughter's son** ngoih·syūn; **daughter-in-law** sàn·póuh

dawn   tīn·gwòng

day   yaht. **day and night** yaht·yeh; **in a day or two** yāt·léuhng·yaht; **every other day** gaak·yāt·yaht; **day before yesterday** chìhn·yaht; **day after tomorrow** hauh·yaht; **in a few days** géi·yaht·noih; **some other day** daih·yih·yaht; **the next day** daih·yih·yaht. /How many days did you spend there? Néih hái gó·syu jyuh·jó géi·dò yaht a? /We spent three days there. Ngóh·deih hái gó·syu jyuh·jó sàam·yaht. /What day of the week is today? Gàm·yaht láih·baai·géi a? /What day of the month is today? Gàm·yaht géi·dò houh a? /You will be paid every other day. Néih ge yàhn·gùng gaak·yāt·yaht béi·yāt·chi.
    day by day yaht·yaht; **daytime** yaht·táu; **let's call it a day** sāu·gùng lo

dead   séi ge, séi-; **be dead** séi·jó, gwo·jó·sàn (passed away). /The dog that was hit by the car is not dead; it is still alive. Béi chè pùhng·chàan gó·jek gáu juhng meih séi, juhng sàang. /Get rid of the dead goldfish. Diuh·jó go·géi·tìuh séi gàm·yú kéuih. /His father is dead. Kéuih fuh·chàn yíh·gìng gwo·jó·sàn la. **dead-end street** gwaht·tàuh·hóng

deadly   ló·mehng·ge; ji mehng ge; **a deadly disease** ló·mehng·ge jing·hauh; **a deadly weapon** ji·mehng·ge leih·hei

deaf   lùhng, yíh·lùhng. /Is he deaf? Kéuih haih m̀h·haih yíh·lùhng ga?

deal   (business) sàang·yi, gàau·yihk. /Did you close that deal? Gó·dàan sàang·yi sèhng· jó meih a? /The deal was off. Móuh gàau·yihk.
    (amount) /He smokes a good deal. Kéuih sihk·yīn sihk dāk hóu gán·yiu. /He lost a great deal of weight. Kéuih sau·jó hóu·dò.
    deal with ying·fuh, deui·fuh, gún (juniors). /He dealt with those people superbly. Kéuih ying·fuh gó·dī yàhn ying·fuh dāk fèi·seuhng hóu. /That man is very hard to deal with. Gó·go yàhn hóu nàahn ying·fuh. /That boy is really very hard to deal with. Gó· go sai·màn·jái jàn·haih nàahn gún la.
    to deal (cards) paai·páai. **It's a deal!** Haih gám là!

dealer   (in business) doih·léih; (in playing cards) jōng, jōng·gà

dean   (of the faculty) gaau·mouh·jéung, gaau·mouh·jyú·yahm

dear   (term of endearment) <u>No special term is used in Cantonese.</u> /He said there has never been anyone dear to him. Kéuih wah chùhng·lòih dōu móuh yàhn sek·gwo kéuih. **Oh dear!** Báih la! **dear** gwai (expensive)

death   séi, séi·mòhng, gwo·sàn. /He met such a tragic death. Kéuih sék dāk jàn·haih cháam lo. /I am sorry to hear of the death of our friend. Ngóh tèng·màhn néih ge pàhng·yáuh gwo·jó·sàn, Ngóh hóu nàahn·gwo.

   death certificate séi·mòhng·jing·mìhng·syù; **death penalty** séi·yìhng; **death rate** séi·mòhng·léut

debate   bihn·leuhn, bihn·bok; **debating society** bihn·leuhn·wúi

debt   jaai, jaai·hohng; **in debt** him·jaai, him·chín. /He is in debt. Kéuih him·yàhn chín. **debtor** jaai·jyú

decadent   (of morals) doh·lohk; (of health) sèui·lóuh

decay   laahn, fuh·laahn. /The apples are beginning to decay. Dī pìhng·gwó hòi·sáu laahn la.

   tooth decay chùhng·jyu·ngàh

deceased   **the deceased** séi·jé

deceive   ngāk

December   sahp·yih·yuht

decide   kyut·dihng

decision   kyut·dihng. /We haven't decided yet. Ngóh·deih juhng meih kyut·dihng. /We'll follow your decision. Néih kyut·dihng dím jouh, ngóh·deih jauh dím jouh.

deck   syùhn·mín

declaration   syùn·yìhn. **Declaration of Independence** duhk·lahp·syùn·yìhn; **declaration of war** syùn·jin

declare   (announce) syùn·bou. /The two countries have declared an armistice. Léuhng·gwok yíh·gìng syùn·bou tìhng·jín la.
   (at customs) bou·gwāan, bou. /Have you declared these goods yet? Nī·dī fo néih bou·jó gwāan meih a?

   declare martial law syùn·bou·gaai·yìhm; **declare one's opinion** faat·bíu yi·gin; **declare a meeting adjourned** syùn·bou saan·wúi; **declare war** syùn·jin

decline   (refuse) tèui·chìh. /Is there any way to decline (the invitation)? Yáuh móuh faat·jí tèui·chìh a?

decorate   jōng·sīk, jōng·sàu (decorate and remodel)

decorum   láih·maauh, láih·jit

decrease   gáam·síu

decree   (by a government) faat·lihng (N); gùng·bou (V); (by a court) pun·kyut (N)

dedicate   fuhng·hin

deduct   kau; **deduct from one's wages** hái yàhn·gùng·syu kau

deed   (act) hàhng·wàih; (exploit) sih·yihp; (a legal statement) kai, kai·yeuk (M: jèung)

deep   sàm; **deep blue** sàm·làahm·sik; **deep breathing** sām·fū·kāp; **deep red** daaih·hùhng·sīk

deeply   sahp·fàn, fèi·sèuhng: **deeply affected** sahp·fàn gám·gīk; **deeply grieved** sahp·fàn bèi·sèung; **deeply distressed** fèi·sèuhng bei·tung deer   lúk (M: jek)

defame   dái·wái

defeat   (win a victory over: war, battle, or game) yèhng, dá·yèhng; dá·sing (in a battle);
(being beaten) syù, dá·syù; dá·baaih (in a battle)

defect   mòuh·behng

defend   (against physical attack) fòhng·sáu, fòhng·waih (a city, a position, etc.); bóu·waih
(a country)
(against verbal attack) jàang·jyuh, waih·jyuh, bòng·jyuh

defendant   beih·gou

defense   **national defense** gwok·fòhng, gwok·fòhng gùng·jok; **self defense** jih·waih

deficit   kwāi·hùng

defile   (to befoul) jíng·wū·jòu

definite   kok·saht, jéun·kok, -saht. /When can you give me a definite answer? Néih géi·
si hó·yih béi ngóh yāt·go kok·saht ge daap·fūk a? /The sentence doesn't have a definite
meaning. Nī·geui wáh ge yi·si mh·jéun·kok. /Are you definitely going? Néih dihng·saht
heui lā ma? /I can't say definitely. Ngóh mh·wah·dak·saht.

definition   (explanation) gáai·sīk, dihng·yih

defy   (disregard) mh·léih

degenerate   teui·fa

degrade   (to reduce in rank) gong·kāp; (deprive of office) gaak·jīk

degree   (unit of measurement) douh. /It's so hot today, it must be over a hundred degrees. Gàm·yaht gam·yiht, yāt·dihng gwo yāt·baak douh la.
(academic) hohk·wái (ref. bachelor, master, Ph.D.)
degree of latitude wáih·douh; **degree of longitude** gìng·douh

deity   sàhn

dejected   bai·ngai, sāt·yi

delay   jó·chìh·jó, dàam·gok jó. /The mail has been delayed for two days. Dī seun jó·
chìh·jó léuhng·yaht.

delegate   (representative) doih·bíu; (appoint) wái·yahm; (authorize) sauh·kyùhn

delegation   doih·bíu·tyùhn

deliberate   háau·leuih

delicacy   (food) hóu hóu·sihk·ge yéh

delicate   (as a situation) mèih·miuh; (as the structure of body) dàan·bohk

delicious   hóu·sihk, hóu·meih·douh

delight   jeui fùn·héi jouh ge sih, jeui jùng·yi jouh ge sih. /Listening to music is her
greatest delight. Tèng yàm·ngohk haih kéuih jeui fùn·héi jouh ge sih.
be delighted /I'll be delighted to have you come. Néih lèih·dāk, ngóh jàn·haih fùn·héi
la. /I am delighted that you've come. Néih lèih dak, ngóh jàn·haih fùn·héi la.
delight in hóu jùng·yi. /He delights in studying. Kéuih hóu jùng·yi duhk·syu.

deliver   (send, bring) sung, sung·heui, sung·lèih, sung·dou. /Do you deliver? Néih·deih
sung·mh·sung ga? /Please deliver these to the school, those to my home. Nī·dī sung·
heui hohk·haauh, gó·dī sung·heui ngóh·ngūk·kēi. /When will they be delivered? Géi·
si hó·yih sung·dou a?

deliver a baby jip·sāng. /The doctor went to deliver a baby. Yī·sāng heui·jó jip·sāng. **deliver a speech** yín·góng

delta   (of river) sàam·gok·jàu

demand   yîu·kàuh (V), (N)

democracy   màhn·jyú jing·jih, màhn·jyú

democratic   **democratic country** màhn·jyú gwok·gà; **Democratic party** màhn·jyú·dóng

demolish   chaak; **demolish a house** chaak·ngūk

demon   gwái

demonstrate   /Can you demonstrate it for us? Néih jouh·béi ngóh·deih tái·háh, dāk·ma?

demonstration   (public protest) sih·wài·yàuh·hàhng

den   (animal's living place) dau

denomination   (of a religion) gaau·wúi

dense   maht

dent   jíng·nāp·jó (V)

dentist   ngàh·fō yī·sāng

dentistry   ngàh·fō

deny   (claim a statement is not true) fáu·yihng

department   (general) bouh·fahn, bouh, chyu. /What department does he work in? Kéuih hái bīn bouh·fahn jouh a? /He works in the accounting department. Kéuih hái wuih·gai·chyu jouh.
   (of the government) -yún, -bouh, -tēng, -chyu, etc. **State Department** (U.S.) gwok·mouh·yún; (Republic of China) ngoih·gàau·bouh (i.e. Ministry of Foreign Affairs); **Defense Department** gwok·fòhng·bouh; **Department of Finance** (provincial) chòih·jing·tēng; **Department of Public Health** waih·sāng·chyu
   (of a university) -haih. **Department of History** lihk·sí·haih
   department store baak·fo·gūng·sī

depend   yí·laaih. /Don't depend on him to help you. M̀h·hóu yí·laaih kéuih bòng néih. /That depends. Gám yiu·tái dím ge chîhng·yîhng sìn.

deposit   (put away to keep safe) chyùn, chyùhn fún (VO). /I want to deposit six hundred dollars. Ngóh séung chyùhn luhk·baak mān. (I am going to make a deposit of six hundred dollars.)
   (a payment indicating trust) dehng, ngon·gwái, jaahk·gwái, ngon·gām

depreciation   jit·gauh

depress   lihng . . . hóu m̀h ngòn·lohk. /The letter he received depressed him. Kéuih jip·dóu fùng seun lihng kéuih hóu·m̀h ngòn·lohk.

depth   sàm·douh

deputy   doih·léih

derail   chēut·gwái

descend   lohk; **descend from the mountain** lohk sāan

describe   (by telling about) góng·háh. /Can you describe what kind of work you had been doing in that factory? Néih hó·yíh góng·hah gauh·sîh hái gó·gàan gùng·chóng jouh dī māt·yéh gūng ma?

(by writing) yìhng·yùhng (dāk·chēut). /I can't describe it, can you? Ngóh móuh·faat·
jí yìhng·yùhng·dāk·chēut, Néih hó·yíh yìhng·yùhng·háh ma?

desert   (run away from) pàau·hei. /You can't desert your family. Néih bāt·nàhng pàau·
hei néih ge gà·tìhng. (sandy place) sà·mohk

deserter   tòuh·bìng

deserve   (something good) /You deserve it. Hóu gùng·douh, nī·go haih néih yìng·fahn
dāk ge. (something bad) /It's my mistake, I deserve it. Haih ngóh·ge cho, yìng·fahn
yùh·chí. /I don't deserve it. (overly good treatment) Ngóh saht·haih (or dīk·kok)
m̀h·gáam·dòng.

design   (drawing) tòuh·yéuhg; (pattern) tòuh·ngon; **designer** chit·gai·sī; **to design** chit·
gai

desire   séung yiu. /What do you desire most of all? Néih jeui séung yiu ge haih māt·
yéh? **a desire** (for something particular), hóu séung. /He has a great desire to meet
you. Kéuih hóu séung gin néih. **a desire** (for luxury, etc.), yuhk·mohng

desk   syù·tói, sé·jih·tói (M: jèung)

desolate   fòng·lèuhng

despair   sāt·mohng, jyuht·mohng

desperate   **a desperate situation** jyuht·mohng ge gíng·deih; **a desperate** (critical) **illness**
mòuh·hó·gau·yeuhk ge behng·jing; **a desperate man** mòhng·mihng·jī·tòuh. /He is desperate. Kéuih yíh·gìng bīt·dou mòuh·louh·hó·jáu la.

despise   tái·síu, tái·hèng

destination   muhk·dīk·deih

destine   **be destined for** jyu·dihng·ge

destiny   (fate) mehng·séui; **destiny with luck** hóu·mehng·séui, hóu·mehng; **destiny with**
bad luck m̀h·hóu mehng·séui, fú·mehng

destroy   often expressed by resultative verbs: /That building was destroyed by fire.
Gó·joh láu sìu lam·jó. /The bridge was destroyed by floods. Douh kìuh béi séui chùng·
lam·jó. /The flood destroyed all the village. Daaih séui jèung sèhng tìuh chyūn chùng·
lam·saai.
        (military) wái·miht, sìu·miht. **destroy evidence** wái·miht jing·geui, or sìu·miht jing·
geui

destroyer   kèui·juhk·laahm (M: jek)

destruction   expressed verbally as destroy. See destroy

detail   **in detail** chèuhng sai (ge). /Please tell me in detail. Chéng néih chèuhng·sai (ge)
góng béi ngóh tèng. **details** chèuhng·sai ge chìhng·yìhng, sai·jit

detain   (seize) kau·làuh; (detain from departure) làuh·jyuh

detect   (find out) tái·chēut, faat·gok

detective   jìng·taam: **detective story** jìng·taam síu·syut

determination   (resolution) kyut·sàm

determine   kyut·dihng. /Who is going to determine this? Nī·gihn sih bīn·go kyut·dihng
a?
        determined to kyut·dihng yiu, kyut·sàm yiu. /I am determined to see this through.
Ngóh kyut·dihng yiu jouh·yùhn nī·gihn sih. /She is determined to raise a fund for building a hospital. Kéuih kyut·sàm yiu chàuh·chín héi yāt·gāan yī·yún.

be determined gám yiu tái. /This will be determined by the situation. Gám yiu tái dòng·sìh ge chìhng·yìhng dím.

determined yáuh·kyut·dyuhn ge, gìn·kyut ge (SV)

detestable hó·wu·ge

Deuteronomy Sàn·mihng·gei

develop (grow) jéung·sìhng. /To help a boy to develop into a man, we need food; but, there is something more important, education. Bòng·joh yāt·go sai·màn·jái jéung· sìhng·wàih yāt·go daaih·yàhn, sèui·yiu hóu·dò máih·faahn, daahn·haih, yáuh dī yéh juhng· gà gán·yiu ge, jauh·haih gaau·yuhk.

(of undertakings) jeun·jín. /How is his project developing? Kéuih gihn sih jeun·jín· sèhng dím a?

(of film) saai. /Can you develop this film for me right away? Néih hó·yíh tùhng ngóh jīk·hāk saai nī dī fēi·lám ma?

devil (Satan) mò·gwái; **meet a devil** johng·gwái

devise séung·chēut (go faat·jí)

devote (apply) jyūn·sàm, yuhng·sàm (A). /He devotes himself to study. Kéuih hóu jyùn· sàm duhk·syu.

dew louh·séui, louh

diabetes tòhng·niuh·behng

diagnose chán·dyuhn, tái·jing

diagonal che, chèh; **diagonal line** chèh·sin

diagram (drawing, plan) tòuh, tòuh·yéung; (chart) bíu

dial (sun dial) yaht·kwāi; (of a watch) bīu·mín. **to dial** dá·dihn·wá. /Dial the police station. Dá·dihn·wa béi 'chàai·gwún' (Hong Kong expression, 'máh·dá·lìuh' Malayan expression).

dialect tóu·wá; (local dialect) bún·deih·wá

dialogue mahn·daap

diameter jihk·ging

diamond jyun·sehk, fó·jyun, sék (M: nāp); **diamond ring** jyun·sehk·gaai·jí

diaper si·pín (M: faai)

diarrhea tóuh·ngò, tóuh·se, ngò·leih. /How long has he had diarrhea? Kéuih tóuh·ngò· jó géi·dò yaht la. /He has had it for two days. Kéuih ngò·jó léuhng·yaht la.

diarrhea and vomiting yauh ngò yauh ngáu

diary yaht·gei; (book) yaht·gei·bóu

dice sīk·jái; **to roll the dice** jaahk sīk·jái; **to play dice** jaahk sīk·jái

dictation (a school exercise) mahk·syù

dictator duhk·chòih·jé

dictionary (of single characters) jih·dín; (of words and compounds) chìh·dín.
English-Chinese dictionary Yìng·Hon chìh·dín; **Chinese-English dictionary** Hon· Yìng chìh·dín; **to consult a dictionary** chàh·jih·dín

die séi. /He is not going to die. Kéuih m̀h·wúih séi gé. /How did he die? Kéuih dím· yéung séi ga? /He died of an illness. Kéuih behng·séi ge. /He died by drowning. Kéuih jahm·séi ge.

(euphemistic) gwo·sàn. /When did your father pass away? Néih fuh·chàn géi·sí gwo·sàn ga?

be dying to bā·bāt·dāk, hahn·bāt·dak. /He is dying to try. Kéuih bā·bāt·dāk si·háh.

diet   (on a special diet) gaai·háu. /I am on a special diet. Ngóh gaai·gán·háu. (can't eat anything fattening) m̀h·sihk·dāk fèih·neih

differ   tùhng . . . m̀h·tùhng; jàang; m̀h·(sèung·)tùhng. /My car differs from his in color. Ngóh ga chè tùhng kéuih ga chè m̀h·tùhng sīk·séui. This color differs a little from that one. Nī·go sīk·séui tùhng gó·go sīk séui jàang sè·síu. /Our views differ on only two points. Ngóh·deih ge tái·fáat jí·yáuh léuhng·dím m̀h·(seung·)tùhng.

different   . . . m̀h·tùhng, m̀h·sèung·tùhng. /These two are different. Nī·léuhng go m̀h·tùhng. (another) lihng·ngoih. /This is a different matter. Nī·gihn haih lihng·ngoih yāt·gihn sih. /This color is a little different from that one. Nī·go ngàahn·sīk tùhng gó·go ngàahn·sīk yáuh dī m̀h·tùhng.

difficult   (not easy) nàahn, ngok. **difficult to believe** hóu nàahn seun; **difficult to comprehend** hóu nàahn mìhng·baahk; **difficult to do** hóu nàahn jou, hóu ngok jouh; **difficult to learn** hóu nàahn hohk; **difficult to manage** hóu nàahn·baahn; **difficult to obtain** hóu nàahn dāk; **difficult to say** hou nàahn góng

difficulty   (hardship) kwan·nàahn; (distress) gàan·nàahn

dig   gwaht. **dig a hole** gwaht yāt·go lūng; **dig a well** gwaht yāt·go jéng; **dig out,** gwaht·chēut

digest   (as food) sīu·fa; (understand) mìhng·baahk

digit   (figures) sou·jih

dignity   jyùn·yìhm

dilemma   jeun·teui·léuhng·nàahn

diligent   kàhn·lihk; **diligent and frugal** kàhn·gihm

dilute   kàu·hèi

dim   ngam; (obscure) mùhng·chàh·chàh

dime   hòuh·jí

dimension   mihn·jīk; **in three dimensions** lahp·tái

diminish   (make small) sūk·síu; jíng·sai; (lessen) gáam·síu. /The swelling is diminishing. Sīu·júng la.

dimple   jáu·nāp

din   chòuh (V)

dine   sihk·máahn·faahn

dining hall   chāan·tēng; **dining room** faahn·tēng, sihk·faahn·tēng; **dining table** chāan·tói, sihk·faahn·tói (M: jèung)

dinner   máahn faahn; **dinner party**. /We are going to a dinner party tonight. Ngóh·deih gàm·máahn yáuh yàhn chéng sihk máahn·faahn.

dip   tíhm: **to dip something in the soy sauce** tíhm baahk·yáu

diphtheria   baahk·hàuh, ngòh·hàuh

diploma   màhn·pàhng (M: jèung)

diplomacy   ngoih·gàau; (fig.) sáu·dyuhn, sáu·wún

diplomat   ngoih·gàau·gùn, ngoih·gàau yàhn·yùhn; **diplomatic circles** ngoih·gàau·gaai

direct   (oversee) jí·fài; (guide) jí·douh; (lead) yáhn·douh. (straight) jihk

direction   (way) fòng·heung; (use) yuhng·faat

directly   jihk·jip. /Why don't you speak to him directly? Dím·gáai néih m̀h jihk·jip tùhng kéuih góng nē?

director   jyú·yahm, yún·jéung (of a hospital, institute, etc.), gún·jéung (of a library, museum, etc.), dúng·sí (of a company or firm). **board of directors** dúng·sih·wúi

directory   (of names) yàhn·mìhng·lúk; **telephone directory** dihn·wá·bóu

dirt   nàih

dirty   wū·jòu, laaht·taat, láh·já

disabled   chàahn·fai

disadvantageous   bāt·leih. /It's disadvantageous to you. Nī·gihn sih deui néih bāt·leih.

disagree   /I disagree with you. Ngóh tùhng néih ge tái·fáat m̀h·tùhng. (make sick) /Cold milk disagrees with her. Kéuih m̀h·sauh·dāk dung ngàuh·náaih.

disappear   m̀h·gin·jó

disappointed   sāt·mohng

disapprove   m̀h·jéun, fáan·deui

disarm   gíu·haaih; **disarmament conference** chòih·gwàn·wuih·yi

disaster   jòi·naahn, jòi·woh

disband   gáai·saan

discern   (distinguish) bihn·biht; **discern truth and falsehood** bihn·biht jàn·gá; (make out) tái·m̀h·chēut. /I can't discern his true intention. Ngóh tái·m̀h·chēut kéuih dou·dái haih māt·yeh yi·si.

disciple   mùhn·tòuh

discipline   (control of behavior) géi·leuh; (training) fan·lihn; (force to obey) yeuk·chūk; (punish) jāk·faht

disclose   (as a secret) sit·lauh: **disclose a secret** sit·lauh bei·maht

discomfort   (of body) m̀h·syù·fuhk; (of mind) m̀h·ngòn·lohk

discontented   m̀h·jī·jūk; (not satisfied) m̀h·múhn·yi

discontinue   tìhng·jí, tìhng

discount   jit·tàuh, jit·kau. /Is there any discount? Yáuh móuh jit·tàuh a? /There is a twenty per cent discount. Baat·jit. (baat·jit means the remaining eighty per cent) Thirty per cent discount. Chāt·jit.

discourage   lihng . . . fūi·sàm. /The news has discouraged him a great deal. Nī·go sīu·sīk lihng kéuih hóu fūi·sàm. discouraged, fūi·sàm. /He's very discouraged. Kéuih hóu fūi·sam.

discover   faat·yihn. /Someone said America wasn't discovered by Columbus. Yáuh yàhn wah Méih·jàu m̀h haih Gò·lèuhn·bou faat·yihn ge. (from investigation) chàh·chēut

discrimination   kèih·sih: **racial discrimination** júng·juhk kèih·sih

discuss   tóu·leuhn, (consult about) sèung·lèuhng, (talk about) kìng·taahm·háh

discussion   expressed verbally as discuss. See discuss

disease   behng, behng·jing (M: tíng); **contagious disease** chyùhn·yíhm·behng

disembark   séuhng·ngohn

disgrace   dìu . . . ge gá. /If you keep on acting like this, you will disgrace your family.
Yùh·gwó néih gai·juhk gám jouh, néih jauh dìu néih ngūk·kéi ge gá ge la.

disgraceful   dìu·gá (ge). /How disgraceful! Jàn·haih dìu·gá la! /Don't do such a disgraceful thing! Chìn·kèih m̀h·hóu jouh dī gam dìu·gá ge sih!

disguise   gá·baahn

disgust   **disgusted** lihng yàhn tóu·yim; **disgusting** hāk yàhn jàng

dish   (plate) díp; (food) sung

disheartened   fūi·sàm

dishonest   m̀h·lóuh·saht

disinfect   sìu·duhk; **disinfectant** sìu·duhk yeuhk·séui

dislike   yìhm, m̀h·jùng·yi

dislocate   gwāt·gaau sùng·jo

dismiss   (discharge, as an employee) chìh; (expel from school) hòi·chèuih; (as workman,
for the day) fong·gùng. **dismiss the class** lohk·tòhng; **dismiss the meeting** saan·wúi

disobedient   m̀h·tèng·wah

disobey   m̀h·tèng; **disobey the order** m̀h·tèng·mihng·lihng; **disobey one's parents** m̀h·
haau·seuhn

disorder   móuh·diht·jeuih

dispensary   yeuhk·fòhng (M: gàan)

disperse   saan·hòi

display   (exhibit) chàhn·liht; (manifest) bíu·yihn

disposition   sing·chìhng; (temper) pèih·hei

disproportionate   m̀h·sèung·ching, m̀h·dahng·chan

dispute   jàang leuhn, jàang (V); **dispute on family property** jàang gà cháan

disqualify   (for a position) chéui·sìu jì·gaak. /He was disqualified from the competition
because he broke the rule. Yàn·waih kéuih po·waaih·jó wúi·chèuhng ge jèung·chìhng,
só·yíh beih chéui·sìu·jó jì·gaak.

disregard   m̀h·gu, m̀h·yiu; m̀h·léih; **disregard one's life** m̀h·yiu·mehng gám (A); **disregard one's reputation** m̀h·gu mìhng·yuh

disreputable   hah·làuh (ge)

disrespect   m̀h·jyùn·ging

dissatisfied   m̀h·múhn·yi

dissimilar   m̀h·sèung·tùhng

dissolve   yùhng, yùhng·gáai; **dissolve a partnership** chaak·gú; **dissolve phlegm** fa·tàahm

distance   kéuih·lèih

distant   yúhn: **distant and near** yúhn·gahn; **distant relative** yúh·chàn; **distant view** yúhn·
gíng

distil   **to distil wine** jìng jáu; **distilled water** jìng·làuh·séui distinct   chìng·chó

distinction   dahk·sing, dahk·dím

distinguish   fàn·biht, bihn·biht; **distinguish right from wrong** bihn·biht sìh·fèi; **distinguish the true from the false** bihn·biht jàn·gá; **distinguished** yáuh·méng·ge

distort   kūk·gáai. /You distort my idea. Néih kūk·gáai ngóh·ge yi·si.

distress   tung·fú

distressing   chài·lèuhng, bai·ngai

distribute   fàn, fàn·pui, paai

district   (of a city or a country) kēui

distrust   m̀h·seun

disturb   gáau. /Don't disturb them. M̀h·hóu gáau kéuih·deih. (disarrange) gáau·lyuhn. /Don't disturb my papers. M̀h·hóu gáau·lyuhn ngóh dī jí. (alarm, excite) gìng·duhng. /Don't disturb the others (as one is leaving a party). M̀h·hóu gìng·duhng kèih·tà gok· wái. **be disturbed** (emotionally) hóu nàahn·gwo, sàm·léuih·bihn hóu fàahn. /I am disturbed to hear that news. Ngóh tèng·jó gó·go sīu·sīk jì·hauh hóu nàahn·gwo.
    disturb the peace yíuh·lyuhn·jih·ngòn

ditch   kèuih (M: tìuh)

ditto   tùhng seuhng

dive   (of a bather) tiu·séui; (swim under water) meih·séui

divide   fàn. /Please divide the ice cream and give it to the children. Chéng néih jēung dī syut·gōu fàn·béi dī sai·mān·jái. /Divide the money among you. Nī·dī chín néih·deih daaih·gā fàn. /Let me divide it for you. Dáng ngóh tùhng néih·deih fàn.
    divided by chèuih. /Four divided by two equals two. Yih chèuih sei (four) dáng·yù yih. **divide equally** deui·fàn, pìhng fàn

dividend   (on stock) hùhng·leih, gú·sīk

division   (arith.) chèuih·sou, chèuih·faat; (segment) bouh·fahn; (army) sī; **divisional commander** sī·jéung

divorce   lèih·fàn

dizzy   tàuh·wàhn

do   (perform) jouh, (fix) jíng. /Is this the right way to do it? Haih m̀h·haih gám jouh a? or Gám jouh ngāam m̀h·ngāam a? /Let me see you do it? Néih jouh·béi ngóh tái·háh. /I am busy, you do it. Ngóh m̀h·dāk·hàahn néih jouh là. /You can't do it that way. Néih gám jouh m̀h·ngāam. /Does he know how to do it? Kéuih wúih m̀h·wúih jíng a? /No, he doesn't. Kéuih m̀h wúih (jíng).
    did, done is expressed by using a resultative verb. /How did he do it? Kéuih dím jíng ga? /Is it done yet? Jíng·héi (or jíng·hóu; or jouh·héi, jouh·hóu) meih a? /Yes, it's done. Jíng·héi la. No, not yet. Meih jíng·héi.
    as an auxiliary verb in questions. /Does he go? Kéuih heui m̀h·heui a? /What do you want? Néih yiu māt·yéh a? /Why did he say that? Dím·gáai kéuih gám góng a? /Don't do that! M̀h·hóu gám jouh!
    as an emphatic word, jàn·haih. /I do wish we could finish today. Ngóh jàn·haih hèi· mohng gàm·yaht jouh·yùhn kéuih. /We do need your help. Ngóh·deih jàn·haih sèui·yiu néih bòng·mòhng.
    do . . . good deui . . . hóu. /This drug will do you good, but don't take too much. Nī·jek yeuhk deui néih hóu, daahn·haih m̀h·hóu sihk dāk taai dò. **do good** jouh·hóu·sih. /He has done a lot of good. Kéuih jouh·jó hóu dò hóu sih.

　　do one's best jeuhn·lihk (followed by jouh or other verbs). /I'll do my best. Ngóh jeuhn·lihk jouh lā. /Do your best. Néih jeuhn·lihk jouh là.
　　will do dāk m̀h·dāk. /Do you think this will do? Nī·go dāk m̀h·dāk a? /That'll do. Dāk. /That won't do. Mh·dāk.
　　do harm deui . . . yáuh māt·yéh hoih·chyúh. /It won't do him any harm. Mh·wúih deui kéuih yáuh māt yéh hoih·chyúh.
　　do away with chéui·sìu. /Do you think we should do away with these regulations or not? Néih wah ngóh·deih yìng m̀h·yìng·fahn chéui·sīu nī·dī kwài·géui nē?
　　do without. /Can you do without it? Néih m̀h·yuhng kéuih dāk m̀h·dāk a? /We can't do without you. Ngóh·deih mouh·jó néih m̀h·dāk.
　　easy does it hóu·sēng (be careful); maahn·máan, maahn dī (be slower), hēng di sáu (more lightly), dihng dī (don't get excited)
　　do as you like chèuih bín néih, chèuih dāk néih; **do business** jouh·sàang·yi; **do it by turns** lèuhn·láu jouh; **do it when convenient** seuhn·bín jouh; **do one's duty thoroughly** jeuhn bún·fáhn, jeuhn·jīk; **do you believe or not** néih seun m̀h·seun. **Well done.** Jouh dāk hóu hóu.

dock　　(for ships) syùhn·ngou; **dockyard** syùhn·chóng, jouh·syùhn·chóng

doctor　　(medical) yī·sāng, yī·sī; (academic) bok·sih. **Doctor of Divinity** sàhn·hohk bok· sih; **Doctor of Law** faat·hohk bok·sih; **Doctor of Literature** màhn·hohk bok·sih; **Doctor of Medical Science** yī·hohk bok·sih; **Doctor of Philosophy** jit·hohk bok·sih; **Doctor of Science** Léih·hohk bok·sih

doctorate　　bok·sih·hohk·wái

doctrine　　(of a political party) jyú·yih; (of a school of thought, or a philosophy of a church) douh·léih

document　　màhn·gín (M: gihn)

dog　　gáu (M: jek)

dogmatic　　móuh·dyuhn

doll　　gūng·jái

dollar　　mān, ngàhn·chín (M: go): **one dollar** yāt·mān, yāt·go ngàhn·chín

domestic　　gà·tìhng ge; ga-: **domestic affairs** gà·sih; **domestic animals** gā·chūk; **domestic expenses** gà·yuhng

dominion　　(territory) líhng·tóu; (of the British Empire) jih·jih·líhng: **Dominion of Canada** Gà·nàh·daaih jih·jih·líhng

dominoes　　gwāt·páai (M: fu, set; piece, jek)

donate　　gyùn; **donate to** gyùn·béi

donation　　gyùn·fún (M: bāt)

donkey　　lèuih·jái (M: jek)

don't　　m̀h·hóu, m̀h·sái, máih. **don't be afraid** m̀h·sái pa; **don't be in such a rush** m̀h·sái gam gāp; **don't do it** m̀h·hóu jouh; **don't do so** m̀h·hóu gám jouh; **don't drink so much** m̀h·hóu yám gam dò; **don't move** m̀h hóu yūk, máih yūk; **don't speak so loud** máih góng gam daaih sèng; **don't stand on ceremony.** m̀h·sái kèui, m̀h·sái haak·hei; **don't touch** m̀h·hóu dau; máih dau

door　　mùhn (M: douh). **doorbell** dihn·jūng; **doorplate** mùhn·pàaih; **doorway** mùhn·háu

dormitory　　sūk·se (M: gàan)

dose　　(medicine taken at one time) chi, fuhk; jài (for Chinese herbs) dot   dím; **dotted line** hèui·sin

double   (twice as much) gā·dò yāt·púih, sèung púih. /His income was doubled last year. Kéuih gauh·nìn ge sàu·yahp gā·dò·jó yāt·púih. /He asks a double price. Kéuih yiu sèung· púih gam dò chín. **double bed** sèung·yàhn·chòhng; **double room** sèung·yàhn·fóng

doubt   sî·yìh. /I doubt if this story is true. Ngóh sî·yìh nī·gihn sih m̀h·haih jàn ge. /Doubtless so. Dīk·kok haih gám.

dove   baahk·gáap (M: jek)

down   lohk. /Come down (toward the speaker)! Lohk·lèih! /Go down (away from the speaker) there. Lohk·heui gó·syu! /Put that thing down. Jài·dài gó·gihn yéh. But /Put that thing down there. Jài gó·gihn yéh hái gó·syu. no translation for the word down. /The sun is going down, let's go home. Yaht·táu jauh lohk la, fāan ngūk·kéi lo. /Please sit down. Chéng·chóh.
      write down sé·dài. /Please write down your address on this paper. Chéng néih hái nī·jèung jí·syu sé·dài néih·ge deih·jí.
      calm down dihng dī. /Down with Imperialism! Dá·dóu dai·gwok jyú·yih!

downstairs   làuh·hah

dowry   ga·jòng

doze   hāp·ngáahn·fan

dozen   dā: **one dozen** yāt·dā; **two dozens** léuhng·dā

draft   héi·góu (V); (of a document) chóu·góu; (of a law) chóu·ngon; (bill) wuih·piu, wuih· dāan (M: jèung)

draftsman   waahk·jīk·sī

drag   (pull) làai, tò

dragon   lùhng (M: tìuh); **dragon boat** lùhng·syùhn; **dragon boat festival** ngh·yuht·jit, dyùn· ngh·jit; **dragon boat race** dau·lùhng·jàu, choi·lùhng·jàu, choi·lùhng·syùhn

dragonfly   chìn·tìhng, tòhng·mēi (M: jek)

drain   (a means of draining) kèuih (M: tìuh); **covered drain** ngam·kèuih; **open drain** mìhng·kèuih

drama   hei, hei·kehk; **drama school** hei·kehk hohk·haauh

drastic   gīk·liht; **drastic measure** gīk·liht sáu·dyuhn

draw   **draw a dog** waahk jek gáu; **draw away** làai·jó heui; **draw a knife** màng·bá gim· jái chēut·lèih; **draw lots** jāp·cháu, chāu·chīm; **draw money** jì chín; **draw out a nail** baht·héi háu dēng; **draw pictures** waahk wá; **draw up a draft** héi góu; **draw up a list** hòi yāt·jèung dāan; **draw a bucket of water from the well** dá yāt·túng séui
      a draw (tie) bāt·fàn·sing·fuh; **a drawback** kyut·dím

dreadful   hó·pa(·ge)

dream   muhng; **have dreams** faat·muhng; **dream about** muhng·gin

dredge   (in deep water) làauh; (in shallow water) mò

drench   sāp·saai

dress   (woman's garment in general) sāam (M: gihn). /She went to buy a dress. Kéuih heui·jó máaih sāam.
      to dress (put on clothes) jeuk (must be followed by a word for clothes). /He is too small, he can't dress himself yet. Kéuih juhng sái, juhng meih wúih jeuk sāam.
      dress the wound fù·yeuhk. /When was this wound dressed? Nī·go sèung·háu géi·sí fù·gwo·yeuhk a?

dried gòn·jó ge; **dried fish** yùh·gōn; **dried lichee** laih·jī·gōn; **dried persimmons** chî·béng

drift (on or in water) pìu·làuh; **drift about** pìu·làuh

drill (train or practice) lyan; **drill soldiers** lihn·bìng; **drill typing** lìhn dá·jih; (tool) jyun; **drill a hole** jyun yāt·go lūng

drink yám. /Drink plenty of water. Yám dō·di séui. /Does he drink? Kéuih yám jáu ma? /Quit drinking, or you'll never get well. Mh·hóu yám jáu la, yeuhk·mh·haih néih jauh mh·hóu·dāk·fàan ge la.
    drink to (toast). /Let's drink to your health. Jūk néih sān·tái pìhng·ngòn.
    a drink. /May I have a drink of water? is expressed as Ngóh séung yám dī séui. (I want a little water to drink.) or Mh·gòi béi bùi séui ngóh. (Please give me a glass of water.)

drip dihk·lohk·làih (V)

drive (operate a mechanical vehicle) sái. /Do you know how to drive a car? Néih wúih sái chè ma? /Drive slowly. Sái maahn dī. /Don't drive so fast. Mh·hóu sái dāk gam faai. /Don't drive too fast. Mh·hóu sai dāk taai faai.
    (take a person somewhere in a car). /Can you drive me to the President Hotel? Néih hó·yíh sái ngóh heui Júng·túng jáu·dim ma? /Would you like to go for a drive? Néih séung heui yàuh chè·hó ma?
    drive a nail dám yāt·háu dēng; **drive a screw** séuhng yāt·háu lòh·sī(·dēng); **drive the screw harder** séuhng gán dī; **go for a drive** yàuh chè·hó; **drive a pile**; dá jòng

driver (of a car) sī·gēi

drizzle lohk·yúh·mēi. /It has been drizzling all day. Sehng·yaht dōu haih gám lohk·yúh·mēi.

drop (to fall or let fall) dit·jó. /Don't drop the glass. Mh·hóu dit·jó go būi.
    (of liquid) dihk. /Take three drops each time. Múih·chi sihk sāam·dihk.
    /Drop in to see me tomorrow morning. Tìng·jiu·jóu lèih gin ngóh. Drop it! (drop the argument) Syun sou la! mh·jéun góng la!

drought tìn hóhn. /There was a drought this year, therefore the crop is bad. Gàm·nìhn tìn hóhn só·yíh sàu·sìhng mh·hóu.

drown **drown in water** jahm·séi; **drown one's self in the sea** tàuh hói, tiu hói

drowsy ngáahn·fan

drug yeuhk; **drugstore** yeuhk·fòhng (M: gàan)

drum gú; **beat a drum** dá·gú

drunk yám·jeui. /Don't get drunk. Mh·hóu yám·jeui boh. **drunkard** jeui·jáu lóu, jeui·māau

dry (not wet) gòn; (of wine) mh·tìhm ge; **to dry in the air** lohng·gòn; **to dry in the sun** saai·gòn

duck ngáap (M: jek): **duckling** ngaap·jái

due (to be paid or done) /When will the rent be due? Ngūk·jòu géi·sí dou·kèih a?
    (arrive) yìng·fahn dou. /When is the plane due? Ga fēi·gèi yìhng·fahn géi·sí dou a?
    dues wuih·fai. /Have you paid the dues? Néih béi·jó wúih·fai meih a?
    overdue gwo·kèih

duel kyut·dau

dugout (in battlefield) jin·hòuh; (against air raid) fòhng·hùng·hòuh

duke gùng·jeuk

dull   (monotonous) dàan·diuh; (uninteresting) móuh·cheui·meih; (boring) lihng yàhn hāp·ngáahn·fàn; (not sharp) deuhn

dumb   ngá; **dumb person** ngá·lóu (man), ngá·jái (boy); (stupid) chún

dummy   (a figure) gá·yàhn; **dummy gun** gá·chēung (M: jì)

dump   (empty out) dóu; **dump rubbish** dóu·laahp·saap; (commerce) kìng·sìu

dung   (manure) sí

duplicate   (of document) chyùhn·dái (N); (of check) chyùhn·gān (N)

durable   (lasting) kàm·sái

during   . . . gó·jahn·sí. /Where were you during the war? Dá·gán·jeung gó·jahn·sí néih hái bīn·syu a? /They were very good friends during their school days. Kéuih·deih hái hohk·haauh duhk·syù gó·jahn·sí haih hóu hóu ge pàhng·yauh.
      during the day yaht·táu gó·jahn·sí; **during the night** máahn·táu gó·jahn·sí; **during a year** yāt·nìhn jì·noih. /He went to the United States three times during last year. Kéuih gauh·nín yāt·nihn jì·noih heui·jó sàam·chi Méih·gwok. /He wrote four articles during the six days. Kéuih luhk·yaht jì·gāan sé·jó sei·pín màhn·jèung.

dusk   ngāai·māan sìh·hauh

dust   yìn·chàhn, fùi·chàhn

duster   (feather) gài·mòuh·sóu (M: bá)

duty   bún·fahn, jīk·jaak, jaak·yahm

dwarf   ngái·jái

dye   yíhm (V), yíhm·liuh, ngàahn·liuh (N)

dying   seuhng·háh séi

dynamite   ja·yeuhk

dynasty   chìuh: **Ming dynasty** Mìhng·chìuh

dysentery   hùhng·leih; **have dysentery** ngò hùhng·leih

E

each   yāt, múih. /Each has his own share. Yāt·yàhn yāt·fahn. /Issue three of these to each person. Múih·yàhn faat sàam·go. /Please give me one of each kind. M̀h·gòi néih múih·yeuhng béi yāt·go ngóh.
      (apiece) yāt. /These chairs are fifty dollars apiece. Nī·dī yi ńgh·sahp·go ngàhn·chín yāt·jèung.
      each of us múih (yāt·go) yàhn. /This is the responsibility of each of us. Nī·go haih ngóh·deih múih yāt·go·yahn ge jaak·yahm.
      each other béi·chí, wuh·sèung. /We should help each other. Ngóh·deih yìng·dòng béi·chí bòng·mòhng. /If we would like to have world peace, first we should enable countries to understand each other. Yùh·gwó yiu sai·gaai wòh·pìhng, ngóh·deih sáu·sìn yiu jouh·dou gwok yú gwok jì·gāan nàhng·gau wùh·sèung líuh·gáai.
      each one has his own preference gok yáuh só hou. /Each one has his own preference, you can't force it. Gok yáuh só hou, bāt·nàhng míhn·kéuhng.

eager   (to do something) hóu séung (AV). /I am very eager to learn Chinese; is it true that Chinese is very difficult to learn? Ngóh hóu séung hohk Jùng·màhn (Chinese language as a whole), Jùng·màhn haih m̀h·hahh jàn·haih hóu nàahn hohk a?

eagle   ngàh·yīng (M: jek): **eaglet** ngàh·yīng·jái

ear   yíh·jái (M: jek). /Does your ear hurt? Néih yíh·jái tung ma? /Which ear hurts?
   Bīn·jek yíh·jái tung a? **earache** yíh·tung; **eardrum** yih·mók; **an ear of corn** yāt·go sūk·
   máih; **ear pick** (a swab for cleaning the ears) yih wáat; **earring** yíh·wáan; **ear of wheat**
   mahk·seui; **ear wax** yíh·sí

early   jóu. /You are early today. Néih gàm·yaht lèih dāk jàn·haih jóu la. /Am I too
   early? Ngóh haih m̀h·haih lèih dāk taai jóu a? /It's still early. Juhng hóu jóu jē.
   /Please call me early tomorrow. Tìng·yaht jóu dī giu ngóh. /How early? Géi jóu a?
   /The earlier the better. Yuht jóu yuht hóu. /Please let us have an early reply from
   you. Chéng néih jóu dī daap·fūk ngóh·deih.

earn   (receive as pay or profit) wán; (receive as profit in business) jaahn. /How much
   do you earn per day? Néih yāt·yaht wán géi(·dò) chín a? /How much does your stall
   earn a month, is it enough for you to support your family? Néih ge dong·háu múih·yuht
   wán géi chín a? Gau m̀h·gau néih yéuhng ngūk·kéi a?

earnest   saht·joih, yihng·jàn. /He is an earnest worker. Kéuih jouh·sih hóu saht·joih.

earnestly   hán·chit

earning   yahp·sīk, sàu·yahp

earth   (the planet) deih·kàuh; (the world) sai·gaai; (ground) deih; (soil) nàih; **heaven and
   earth** tīn·deih

earthenware   (utensils) gòng·ngáh

earthquake   deih·jan

earthworm   wòhng·hyún (M: tìuh)

easily   hóu·yùhng·yih, hóu.yih

east   (direction) dùng. /We'll walk east. Ngóh·deih heung dùng hàahng. (indicating a
   part or an area) dùng·bouh, dùng·bihn, dùng·bín. /I lived in the east for ten years.
   Ngóh hái dùng·bouh jyuh·jó sahp·nìhn. /The airfield is just east of the highway. Fēi·
   gèi·chèuhng jauh hái gùng·louh dùng·bín.
       Far East Yúhn·dùng; **Near East** Gahn·dùng; **northeast** dūng·bāk; **southeast** dùng·
   nàahm
       East Asia Dùng·nga; **eastbound** heung·dùng·hàahng(·ge); **eastern China** Jùng·gwok
   dùng·bouh, wah·dùng

Easter   Fuhk·wuhk·jit

easy   yùhng·yih. /Is it easy to do? Yùhng·yih jouh ma? /Very easy. Hóu yùhng·yih.
   (comfortable) ngòn·lohk. /He leads an easy life. Kéuih gwo dāk hóu ngòn·lohk.
       Take it easy! m̀h·hóu gam pàhn·làhn (Don't hurry!); maahn·máan lèih! (slowly,
   lightly); **Easy does it!** (ref. do.); **easy going** mòuh·yàu mòuh·leuih

eat   sihk. /I want something to eat. Ngóh yiu sihk dī yéh. /Is there anything to eat?
   Yáuh móuh yéh sihk a? /Have you ever eaten this before? Néih yáuh móuh sihk·gwo
   nī·dī yéh a? /You mean to eat it raw? Jauh gám sāang sihk àh?
       (to have a meal) sihk·faahn. /Have you eaten? Néih sihk·jó faahn meih a? /How
   about going out to eat with me? Tùhng ngóh chēut·heui sihk·faahn hóu ma? /Let's take
   turns eating, you go first. Ngóh·deih leuhn·láu sihk·faahn, néih heui sīn lā.

eaves   yìhm·háu

eavesdrop   tāu·tèng (V)

ebb   (of the tide) séui teui. /The tide will begin to ebb at six o'clock. Luhk·dím·jūng
   jauh séui teui la.

ebony   syūn·jī, wù·muhk

Ecclesiastes   Chyùhn·douh·syù

echo   wùih·sìng

eclipse   **eclipse of the moon**   yuht·sihk; **eclipse of the sun**   yaht·sihk

economic   **economic problem**   gìng·jai mahn·tàih

economical   gìng·jai

economics   gìng·jai·hohk

economist   gìng·jai·hohk·gā

economy   gìng·jai; **the economy of Taiwan**   Tòih·wāan ge gìng·jai(·chìhng·yìhng)

edge   (border) bīn; **edge of a knife**   dōu·háu; **edge of a table**   tói·bīn

edible   sihk·dāk.   /Is it edible? Sihk m̀h·sihk dāk ga?

edibles   sihk·maht, sihk·bán

edict   tùng·gou

edit   pīn·chāp; **editor**   pīn·chāp

edition   (printed at one time) báan; **second edition**   daih·yih·báan; **deluxe edition**   jīng·
   jōng·bún; **pocket edition**   jauh·jān·bún

editorial   séh·léun (M: pìn, article)

educate   gaau·yuhk; **an educated person**   sauh·gwo gaau·yuhk ge yàhn

education   gaau·yuhk: **children's education**   yìh·tùhng gaau·yuhk; **adult education**   sìhng·
   yàhn gaau·yuhk; **women's education**   fúh·néuih gaau·yuhk
      educational institutions   gaau·yuhk gei·gwàan; **educational supplies**   gaau·yuhk yuhng·
   bán; **educational system**   gaau·yuhk jai·douh; **educationalist**   gaau·yuhk·gā

educational   yáuh gaau·yuhk·sing(·ge)

eel   síhn (M: tìuh)

effect   (result) gùng·haauh, haauh·gwó.   /What is the effect of this medicine? Nī·jek yeuhk
   yáuh māt yéh gùng·haauh a? /Has his speech had the desired effect? Kéuih ge yín·góng
   yáuh móuh sàu·dou yuh·kèih ge haauh·gwó a?
      (influence) yíng·héung; **good effect**   hóu ge yíng·héung; **bad effect**   waaih ge yíng·héung.
   /Living in these places has many bad effects on the children. /Hái dī gám ge deih·fòng
   jyuh deui dī sai·mān·jái yáuh hóu waaih ge yíng·héung.
      no effect   taking effect.   /This medicine had no effect at all. Nī·dī yeuhk yāt·dī gùng·
   haauh dōu móuh. /This medicine is beginning to take effect. Nī·dī yeuhk jihm·jím gìn·
   gùng la. /Government programs to help the poor have had no effect on their lives as
   yet. Jing·fú tùng·gwo ge fàat·lìhng deui·yù pìhng·màhn ge sang·wuht juhng meih yáuh
   māt bòng·joh.
      in effect   saht·hàhng.   /The recently passed law is not yet in effect. Jeui·gahn tùng·
   gwo ge faat·lihng juhng meih saht·hàhng.
      effects   yéh; **personal effects**   go·yàhn só·yuhng·ge yéh

efficacious   ying·yihm

efficient   yáuh·haauh·leuht

effective   yáuh·gùng·haauh

effort   nóuh·lihk.   /The success of our school is due to the effort of you ladies and
   gentlemen. Ngóh·deih hohk·haauh ge sìhng·gùng yùhn·chyùhn haih yàuh yùh néih·deih
   gok·wái ge nóuh·lihk.

egg   dáan (M: jek): **boiled eggs** saahp·dáan; **duck's eggs** ngaap·dáan; **hen's eggs** gài·dáan; **eggshell** dáan·hok; **a bad egg** waaih·dáan (literal and figurative)

eight   baat; **eighteen** sahp·baat; **eighty** baat·sahp; **eighth** daih·baat; **the eighth month of the year** baat·yuht

either   (negative of also) yihk. /If you won't go, I won't go either. Yùh·gwó néih m̀h·heui, ngóh yihk m̀h·heui.

      (both). /There are no windows on either side of the building. Gó·gàan ngūk léuhng·bihn dōu móuh chēung.

      (one of). /Does either of these roads lead to the bus stop? Nī·léuhng tìuh louh bīn·tìuh tùng(·heui) bā·sí·jaahm a?

      either . . . or . . . /Either you go or he goes. M̀h·haih néih heui jauh·haih kéuih heui. or waahk·haih néih heui waahk·haih kéuih heui. /Either take it or leave it, as you please. Waahk·haih yiu waahk·haih m̀h·yiu, chèuih néih bín. /Either today or tomorrow will do. Waahk·haih gàm·yaht waahk·haih tìng·yaht dōu dāk.

elastic   yáuh·daahn·sing·ge

elbow   sáu·jàang

elder   (older) daaih. /Who is the elder of the two children? Nī·léuhng·go sai·mān·jai bīn·go daaih a?

    elder brother daaih·lóu; **elder sister** daaih·jí; **elder sister's husband** jé·fù

eldest   ji·daaih·ge. **eldest brother** daaih·gō; **eldest sister** daaih·jē; **eldest son** daaih·jái, jéung·jí; **eldest daughter** daaih·néui, jéung·néui

elect   syún, syún·géui. /Have you elected a chairman? Néih·deih syún·jó jyú·jihk meih a?

    be elected dòng·syún. /Who was elected? Bīn·go dòng·syún a?

electric   dihn; **electric power** or **electric current** dihn·lihk. /Are there electric lights in the mine? Kwòng yahp·bihn yáuh móuh dihn·dāng a?

    electric appliances dihn·hei, dihn·hei yuhng·geui; **electric bell** dihn·jūng; **electric circuit** dihn·lauh; **electric clock** dihn·jūng; **electric fan** dihn·sin, dihn fùng·sin; **electric heater** dihn·nyúhn·lòuh; **electric iron** dihn·tong·dáu; **electric lamp** dihn·dāng; **electric light** dihn·dāng; **electric light bulb** dihn·dāng·dáam; **electric stove** dihn·lòuh; **electric wires** dihn·sin; **electric meter** dihn·bīu

electrician   dihn·dāng·lóu

electricity   dihn. /There is no electricity. Móuh dihn.

electrometer   dihn·bīu

elegant   (of persons) sì·màhn, màhn·ngáh; (of things) leng, jìng·ji

element   (chemical) yùhn·sou (M: júng)

elementary   **elementary education** chò·dáng gaau·yuhk; **elementary English** chò·kāp Yìng·yúh; **elementary school** chō·kāp síu·hohk

elephant   daaih·bahn·jeuhng, jeuhng (M: jek)

elevator   (electric lift) dihn·tài, sìng·gong·gèi

eleven   sahp·yāt; **eleventh** daih·sahp·yāt

elf   yīu·jīng

eligible   (for office, etc.) hahp·gaak

eloquence   háu·chòih

else   daih·go, daih·yéung. /Everyone else has gone. Daih·go jáu·saai la. /What else can we do? Juhng yáuh māt daih·yéung ma?

(otherwise) yùh·gwó m̀h·haih. **elsewhere** daih·yih·syu

embankment   ba (M: tìuh)

embargo   gam·wahn

embark   lohk·syùhn, séuhng·syùhn (Use 'séuhng' when climbing up to a ship; use 'lohk' when climbing down from a pier to a ship.)

embarrass   lihng . . . nàahn·wàih·chìhng. /Don't embarrass him. Mh·hóu lihng kéuih nàahn·wàih·chìhng. **embarrassed** /He's very embarrassed. Kéuih hóu m̀h·hóu·yi·si. **embarrassing.** /It's very embarrassing. Hóu m̀h·hóu·yi·si·ge. or Hóu nàahn·wàih chìhng ge.

embassy   daaih·sí·gún (M: gàan)

embrace   (in the arms) póuh; (include) bàau·hàhm

embroider   sau (V); sau·fā (VO); **embroidery** chi·sau

emerald   féi·cheui, luhk·bóu·sehk (M: gauh, large; nāp, small)

emerge   yihn·chēut·lèih, chēut·yihn

emergency   gán·gāp ge chìhng·yìhng, gán·gāp ge sih, chìhng·yìhng gán·gāp
     emergency door taai·pìhng·mùhn; **emergency law** gān·gāp faat·lihng

emigrant   kìuh·màhn

emigrate   kìuh·gèui; **emigration** yìh·màhn

emigration   yih·mahn; **emigration office** yih·mahn·guk

eminent   chēut·méng·ge

emit   **emit fire** chēut fó; **emit light** faat gwòng; **emit smoke** chēut yìn, pan yìn; **emit sparks** chēut fó·sīng

emotion   gáam·chìhng, chìhng·gáam

emperor   wòhng·dai; **emperor's father** taai·seuhng·wòhng; **emperor's mother** wòhng taai·hauh

emphasize   jyu·juhng; **emphasize children's education** jyu·juhng yìh·tùhng gaau·yuhk

empire   dai·gwok. /Have you studied the history of the British Empire? Néih yáuh móuh duhk·gwo Daaih·yìng·dai·gwok ge lihk·sí a?

employ   (to use; of persons or tools) yuhng; (hire) chéng. /How many workers are employed here? Néih·deih nī·syu yuhng·gán gei·dò yàhn a? /We plan to employ five doctors and twenty nurses. Ngóh·deih dá·syun chéng ngh·go yī·sāng, yih·sahp·go hòn·wuh.
     be employed jouh·sih. /Are you employed here? Néih haih m̀h·haih hái nī·syu jouh·sih a?
     employment gùng, jīk·yihp; **employment agency** jīk·yihp gaai·siuh·só, jin·yàhn·gún; **employer** sih·táu, dūng·gā, lóuh·báan

emporium   (shop) baak·fo·sèung·dim, sèung·dim

empower   sauh·kyùhn

empress   wòhng·hauh; **empress dowager** wòhng·taai·hauh

empty   hùng: **empty bottle** hūng jēun; **empty box** hùng háp; **empty barrel** hùng túng; **empty-handed** hùng sáu; **empty house** hūng ngūk; **empty stomach** hùng tóuh

encamp   jaap·yìhng (VO)

encircle   wàih·jyuh; (by the army) bàau·wàih

enclose waih·jyuh, wàih·héi. /Can we use something to enclose the building before it is finished? Gaan láu héi·hóu jī·chìhn, ngóh·deih hó m̀h·hó·yíh béi dī yéh wàih·jyuh kéuih a? **enclosing wall** wàih·chèuhng

encounter (meet) johng·dóu. /I encountered your good friend Mr. Lee on the street yesterday. Ngóh kàhm·yaht hái gāai·syu johng·dóu néih ge hóu pàhng·yáuh Léih sīn·sàang.

encourage gú·laih; **encourage by reward** jéung·laih; **encourage each other** wuh·sèung míhn·laih

encroach chàm·faahn; chàm·jim. **encroach upon other's liberty** chàm·faahn yàhn·deih ge jih·yàuh; **encroach upon other's land** chàm·jim yàhn·deih ge tóu·deih

encyclopedia baak·fō·chyùhn·syù (M: bún, a volume; tòu, a set)

end (the tip) tàuh. /You hold this end and I'll take the other. Néih jà·jyuh nī·tàuh, ngóh jà gó·tàuh.
(of a street) gaai·tàuh (where usually used as the entry), gāai·méih (the other end of the street)
(edge or side) bihn. /Seal up both ends. Léuhng·bihn dōu yiu fùng·hóu kéuih. /Is the other end of the building also finished? Gàan láu gó·bihn yihk dōu jouh hóu làh?
/The story is ended. Gu·sih góng·yùhn la. **at the end of the story** gú·jái git·méih gó·jahn·sí, sāu·mēi. /I didn't read the story from beginning to end. Ngóh móuh yàuh tàuh ji méih tái·yùhn gó·go gú·jái.
(conclusion) git·chūk. /How does the story end? Go gú·jái dím·yéung git·chūk ga? /How did the war come to an end? Jin·sih haih dím·yéung git·chūk ga?
(ending) méih, dái. /I'll pay you at the end of the month. Ngóh yuht·méih (or yuht· dái) béi chín néih. /Do you think we can finish this by the end of the year? Nī·gihn sih néih wah ngóh·deih gàm·nín nìhn·méih jouh·dāk·yùhn ma?
no end. /There is no end of these kind of things. Nī·dī gám ge sih móuh líuh ge.
(objective). /To what end (for what) are you working so hard? Néih wàih māt sih jouh dāk gam sàn·fú nē?
(result) git·gwo, git·guhk. /The end will certainly be great. Git·gwó yāt·dihng hóu hóu.
odds and ends sāp·sīng ge yéh, sāp·sāp·sīng·sīng ge yéh. /There are some odds and ends that have to be tidied up. Juhng yáuh dī sāp·sāp·sīng·sīng ge yéh meih jāp· hóu.
to end. /I think this thing will end next month. Ngóh tái nī·gihn sih hah·go·yuht hó· yíh jouh·yùhn la.

endless mòuh·jeuhn·ge, mòuh·jí·gíng·ge

endorse chìm·méng. /Please endorse this check. Chéng néih hái nī·jēung chēk·syu chìm go méng.

endow gyùn·joh; **endowment fund** gēi·gām

endure ngàaih, dái, yáhn·noih. **endure hardship** ngaaih·dāk fú; **endure hunger** dái·tóuh· ngoh; **able to endure** ngáaih·dāk·jyuh; **cannot endure** m̀h·ngàaih·dāk·jyuh

enemy (personal) sàuh·yàhn; (in war, a single individual or the group) dihk·yàhn; (country) dihk·gwok; (nationals) dihk·kìuh; (properties) dihk·cháan; (airplane) dihk·gèi; (army) dihk·gwān; (warship) dihk·laahm

energetic háng·jouh, kàhn·lihk

energy (mental power) jìng·sàhn; (physical power) hei·lihk

enforce (carry out) jāp·hàhng; **enforce a law** jāp·hàhng faat·lihng

engage (employ) chéng. /We have already engaged two teachers to teach Chinese. Ngóh·deih yíh·gìng chéng·jó léuhng·wáih sīn·sàang gaau Jùng·màhn la.

(be doing) jing·joih . . . gán. /I was engaged in composing a poem when you called me on the phone. Néih dá·dihn·wá béi ngóh gó·jahn·sí, ngóh jing·joih jok·gán yāt·sáu sī. (betroth) dihng·fàn. /I didn't know that your daughter has become engaged. Congratulations! Ngóh m̀h·jī néih ge néui dihng·jó fàn, gùng·héi gùng·héi.

engagement   (an appointment). /Do you have an engagement with Dr. Wohng this morning? Néih yáuh móuh yeuk·jó Wòhng yī·sāng gàm·jiu·jóu néih lèih gin kéuih a? (betrothal) dihng·fàn. /What should I give them for their engagement? Kéuih·deih dihng·fan ngóh sung dī māt·yéh béi kéuih·deih hóu a?

engine   (motor) mō·dá, gèi·hei, faat·duhng·gèi. /Is it engine trouble? Haih m̀h·haih mō·dá waaih·jó a? (locomotive) chè·tàuh, fó·chè·tàuh

engineer   gùng·chìhng·sī; **civil engineer** tóu·muhk·gùng·chìhng·sī; **electrical engineer** dihn·gèi·gùng·chìhng·sī; **mechanical engineer** gèi·haaih·gùng·chìhng·sī (in military service; individual or group) gūng·bìng; (of a train) sī·gēi

England   Yìng·gwok; **the Queen of England** Yìng·néuih·wòhng

English   (of England) Yìng·gwok(·ge), Yìng·màhn-, yìng-. /Is your car an English car? Néih ga chè haih m̀h·haih Yìng·gwok chè a? **English book** Yìng·màhn syu; **English-Cantonese dictionary** Yìng·Yuht·jih·dín; **English-Chinese dictionary** Yìng·Hòn·jih·dín; **English language** Yìng·màhn; **Englishman** Yìng·gwok·yàhn; **English mile** Yìng·léih; **English pound** Yìng bohng; **English school** Yìng·màhn hohk·haauh; **English version** Yìng·mahn fàan·yihk

engrave   tìu, hāk, tìu·hāk. **engrave figures** tìu·fā; **engrave Chinese characters** hāk·jih

enjoy   There is no Chinese equivalent for the word 'enjoy.' It has to be expressed in the following ways: /Did you enjoy yourself? Néih wáan dāk géi hóu lā ma? /He knows how to enjoy himself. Kéuih hóu wúih héung·fūk. /Did you enjoy the movie? (Néih gok·dāk) chēut dihn·yíng hóu·tái ma? /Yes, I enjoyed it. Hóu hóu·tai. /I didn't enjoy it at all. Yāt·dī dōu m̀h·hóu·tái.

enlarge   (a photo) fong·daaih; (make large) jíng daaih

enlighten   kái·faat

enlist   (enroll) dàng·gei; **enlist soldier** jīu·bìng, mouh·bìng

enmity   (hatred and hostility) yùn·sàuh

enormous   fèi·sèuhng·daaih ge

enough   (sufficient) gau; (eating to one's fill) báau. /Do you have enough money? Néih gau m̀h·gau chín a?/Is that enough? Gáu meih a? /Yes, it is. Gau la. /No, it is not. M̀h·gau. /That's enough sugar, I don't want any more. Gau tòhng la, ngóh m̀h·yiu la.

enrage   gīk·nàu

enroll   bou·méng; **enrollment fee** bou·méng·faai

entangle   (involve in difficulty) lìhng·leuih. /Don't entangle him in this. M̀h·hón lìhn·leuih kéuih.

enter   (come into a place) yahp·lèih; (go into a place) yahp·heui. /Can we enter now? Ngóh·deih hó·yíh yahp·heui meih a? /Please come in and have a seat. Chéng yahp·lèih chóh.

    enter by walking or **walk in** hàahng·yahp (lèih or heui); **enter by driving** or **drive in** sái·yahp (lèih or heui)

    (to join an organization) yahp, gà·yahp. /When are you going to enter a university? Néih géi·sí yahp daaih·hohk a? /He entered the Democratic Party two years ago. Kéuih léuhng·nìhn chìhn (ga·)yahp·jó Màhn·jyú·dóng.

(to register) bou·méng. /He entered his name as a candidate. Kéuih bou·jó méng
jouh hauh·syún·yàhn.
>   **enter a port** yahp·háu; **enter a society** yahp·wúi

enterprise   (industrial, etc.) kei·yihp; **International Enterprise Co.** Gwok·jai kei·yihp
gūng·sī; (undertaking) sih·yihp

entertain   (show hospitality to) jîu·doih, fún·doih

entertainment   yùh·hing, yùh·lohk jit·muhk, hóu·wáan ge deih·fòng, sîu·hín ge deih·fong.
/Is there any entertainment after the party? Sihk·yuhn faahn yáuh māt·yéh yùh·hing ma?
/Is there any entertainment in town? Nī·syu yáuh māt hóu·wáan ge deih·fòng ma?

enthusiasm   yiht·sàm

enthusiastic   yiht·sàm

entice   yáhn·yáuh, yáuh·waahk

entire   (whole) sèhng (M) . . .; **entire building** sèhng·joh láu; **entire duck** sèhng·jek
ngāap; **entire house** sèhng·gāan ngūk; **entire room** sèhng·gàan fóng; **entire school**
sèhng·gàan hohk·haauh

entirely   yùhn·chyùhn. /It's entirely wrong. Yùhn·chyùhn m̀h·ngāam.

entitle   /You are entitled to this reward. Nī·go haih néih yīng dāk ge chàuh·bou.

entrance   /Where is the entrance? is expressed as: Hái bīn·syu yahp a? (Where does
one enter?) **entrance exam** yahp·hohk háau·si; **entrance fee of a society** yahp·wúi fai;
entrance to a lane hohng·háu; **entrance to a road** louh·háu; **entrance to a street** gāai·
háu; **entrance to the station** chè·jaahm mùhn·háu

entrust   wái·tok, seun·tok

entry   yahp. /Entry into the enemy's territory was dangerous but he made it. Yahp
dihk·yàhn ge tóu·deih fèi·sèuhng ge ngàih·hím, daahn·haih kéuih yahp·jó·heui.
>   **make an entry** (bookkeeping) yahp sou. /Have you made that entry yet? Gó·tîuh sou
néih yahp·jó meih a?

envelop   bàau·jyuh

envelope   (for letter) seun·fūng

envious   dou·geih, ngáahn·hùhng

envoy   dahk·si

envy   sihn·mouh; douh·geih

epidemic   làuh·hàhng·jing, sîh·jing, wàn·yihk

epilepsy   faat·yèuhng·diu

epitaph   mouh·ji

Epsom salt   se·yìhm

equal   dáng·yù, séung·dáng. /Two times two equals four. Yih sîhng yih dáng·yù sei.
/Are these two angles equal? Nī·léuhng·go gok·douh haih m̀h·haih sèung·dáng a?

equality   pìhng·dáng

equation   (in math.) fòng·chìhng·sīk

equator   chek·douh

equipment   chit·beih

era   sîh·doih

erase   (rub out) chaat·jó; **erased** chaat·lāt. /Please erase it. Chéng néih chaat·jó kéuih.
/Has it been erased? Chaat·lāt·jó meih a?

eraser   (for pencil marks) gàau·chāat (M: gauh); (for blackboard) fán·bāt·cháat

erect   (build) héi; (as a shed or stage) daap; (establish) chit·lahp

err   gáau·cho, jouh·cho

errand   **run errands** jouh dī sāp·seui ge sih

erroneous   cho·ge, cho·ngh ge

error   cho, cho·ngh, gwo·cho; **repent of one's error** fui·ngh

escape   (tòuh·)jáu. /When did you escape from the mainland? Néih géi·sìh hái daaih·luhk
jáu·chēut·lèih ga?
     (avoid) beih·hòi, dó·beih. /Is there any way to escape the crowd? Yáuh māt faat·jí
hó·yíh beih·hòi dī yàhn a?
     /We had a narrow escape. Ngóh deih jāang dī jauh jáu·m̀h·lāt (or johng·báan) la.

escort   sung, wuh·sung; (as prisoner) ngaat·heui

especially   dahk·biht

Esperanto   sai·gaai·yúh

essay   mán (M: pìn)

essence   jìng·wàh, yiu·sou

essential   bīt·yiu·ge, jyú·yiu·ge; **essential elements** yiu·sou; **essential points** yiu·dím

establish   (a business, school, or hospital privately) chong·baahn; (a government office,
hospital, church) chit·lahp, sìhng·lahp

estate   (property in general) cháan·yihp; (hereditary estate) wàih·cháan

estimate   gú·gai, gú. /Can you estimate the cost? Néih hó·yíh gú·gai·háh géi·dò chín
ma? (of price) gú·ga·dāan (N)

etc.   dáng·dáng

eternal   wìhng·yúhn; **eternal death** wìhng sí; **eternal life** wìhng sàng

ether   (chem.) yíh·taai

ethics   lèuhn·léih·hohk

etiquette   láih·jit

eunuch   taai·gaam

evacuate   sò·saan; **evacuate a house** būn·hūng·gāan·ngūk kéuih; **evacuate a place** chit·
teui

evade   dó·beih; **evade responsibility** dó·beih jaak·yahm

evangelist   chyùhn·douh·yàhn; **evangelical group** bou·douh·tyùhn

evangelization   bou·douh·gùng·jok

evangelize   chyùhn·douh, bou·douh

evaporate   jìng·faat

Eve   Hah·wā

eve   **Christmas Eve** Sing·daan·chìhn·jihk; **New Year's Eve** nìhn·sà·ah·máahn

even   (regular) wàhn·chèuhn. /His heartbeat is quite even. Kéuih ge ꜱàm tiu dāk hóu
wàhn·chèuhn.

(numbers) sèung. /Two, four, six, etc. are even numbers. Yih, sei, luhk, dáng·dáng dōu haih sèung·sou.

(exact) ngāam·ngāam. /We have an even dozen. Ngóh·deih ngāam·ngāam yáuh yāt·dā.

(for emphasis) lìhn . . . dōu . . . /Even you have to be innoculated. Lihn néih dōu yiu dá·jām. /He is my best friend, even he didn't come. Kéuih haih ngóh jeui hóu ge pàhng·yóuh, lihn kéuih dóu móuh leih. /Yes, even you have to go. Móuh·cho la, lìhn néih dōu yiu heui.

even so jīk·sí haih gám. /Even so, I don't believe it. Jīk·sí haih gám ngóh dōu m̀h·seun.

even if jīk·sí. /Even if you didn't tell us, we would do so. Jīk·sí néih m̀h·wah ngóh·deih tèng, ngóh·deih dōu haih gam jouh ge la.

even though sèui·yìhn. /Even though you are poor, we'll take care of you (to cure you). Don't worry. Sèui·yìhn néih móuh chín, ngóh·deih yāt·yeuhng gám yī néih, néih fong·sām lā.

even worse juhng baih·gwo gauh·sí, juhng baih dī

evening   ngāai·māan sìh·hauh; -máahn. /The view of the sea at evening is beautiful. Ngāai māan sìh·hauh ge hói·gíng jàn·haih leng la.   **this evening** gàm·máahn; **last evening** kàhm·máahn; **tomorrow evening** tìng·máahn; **evening meal** máahn·faahn, máahn·chāan; **evening paper** máahn·bou (Mı fahn)

event   (happening) sih; **current event** sih·sih; **a happy event** héi·sih; **important event** daaih·sih; **in any event** mòuh·leuhn yùh·hòh. /I'll be there waiting for you in any event. Mòuh·leuhn yùh·hoh ngóh yāt·dihng hái gó·syu dáng néih.

eventually   jēut·jí. /Eventually he did learn to speak Cantonese. Kéuih jēut·jí hohk·sīk góng Gwóng·jàu·wá.

ever   (at any time) gwo. /Have you ever been innoculated? Néih yáuh móuh dá·gwo jām a? /Have you ever been to Taiwan? Néih yáuh móuh heui·gwo Tòih·wāan a?

ever since jih·chùhng. /Ever since Dr. Lee came, I haven't had to work seven days a week. Jih chùhng Léih yī·sāng lèih·jó ngóh jauh m̀h·sái yāt·go láih·baai jouh chāt·yaht la.

every   múih M , M M /Every person gets three dollars. Muih·yàhn sāam·mān. /I see him every day. Ngóh yaht·yaht dōu gin·dóu kéuih. /It rains every day. yaht·yaht dōu lohk·yúh. /Every night there is a nurse on duty. Múih·máahn (or máahn máahn) dōu yáuh wuh·si jihk·bāan.

every now and then noih·bāt·nói, gáu·m̀h·gáu

every other day gaak yāt·yaht. /From now on, you come every other day. Chùhng·chí jí·hauh, néih gaak yāt·yaht lèih yāt·chi.

evidence   jing·geui, pàhng·geui

evident   hín·mìhng

evil   jeuih·ngok; **evil-hearted** hāk·sàm; **evil man** ngok·yàhn; **evil spirits** ngok·gwái; **evil thoughts** ngok·nihm; **evil world** jeuih·ngok ge sai·gaai

evolution   jeun·fa; **theory of evolution** jeun·fa·léun

exact   jéun·kok. /Are these figures exact? Nī·dī sou·muhk jéun·kok ma? /Is that information exact? Gó·go sīu·sīk jéun·kok ma?

exactly   ngāam·ngāam, jing·haih. /It's exactly four thirty. Ngāam·ngāam sei·dím·bun. /This is exactly what I want. Nī·go jing·haih ngóh só·yiu·ge. /This is exactly what I am thinking about. Ngóh jing·joih séung gám. /That's exactly it. Ngāam·saai la! or Yāt dī dōu móuh cho!

exaggerate   kwà-daaih-kèih-chìh, góng dāk yáuh gam gāau·gwàan dāk gam gāau·gwàan. /He is exaggerating. Kéuih góng dāk yáuh gam gāau·gwaan dāk gam gāau·gwāan jē.

examination   (test) háau·si; (inspection) chàh·mahn; **examination of goods** yihm fo.
/Who made the examination of these goods? Nī·dī fo bīn·go yihm ga?

examine   (test) háau, háau·si, si·yihm; (inspect) chàh, yihm; (scrutinize) yĭhn·gau
   examine a patient gím·chàh behng·yàhn, gím·yihm behng·yahn; **examine oneself**
   sing·chaat jih·géi, gím·tóu jih·géi

example   (pattern) yéung; (model) bíu·jéun; (precedent) laih. **for example** pei·yùh

excavate   gwaht

exceed   chĭu·gwo, gwo

excel   chĭu·gwo, sing·gwo

exceedingly   fèi·sèuhng

excellence   yāu·dím

excellent   hóu dou·gihk, gihk·jī hóu ge. /That was an excellent dinner last night. Kàhm·
   máahn chàan faahn hóu dou·gihk. /He is an excellent cook. Kéuih haih yāt·go gihk·jī
   hóu ge chyùh·sī.

except   (not including) chèuih·jó; (unless) chèuih·fèi

exception   laih·ngoih

exceptional   ngaahk·ngoih·ge, dahk·biht·ge

excessive   gwc·douh·ge

exchange   gàau·wuhn; (transpose) diuh·wuhn; **exchange** (money) wuhn·chín; **exchange of
   goods** gàau·wuhn maht·jí; **exchange of prisoners of war** gàau·wuhn fù·lóuh; **exchange
   rate of remittance** wuih·séui, wuih·ga

excite   (a body of people) gú·duhng, gīk·duhng; (a body of people to sedition) sin·duhng;
   (stir, stimulate) gīk·duhng

exclamation   gáam·taan·chìh

exclude   (not include) m̀h·gai, m̀h·lĭhn. /Exclude this one. Mh·gai nī·go.

exclusive   duhk·yáuh·ge; **exclusive of this** m̀h·gai joih noih; **exclusive right** jyūn leih·
   kyùhn

excrete   fàn·bei

excursion   léuih·hàhng

excuse   (pardon) yùhn·leuhng (V); (reason, explanation) léih·yàuh (N). /Please excuse
   him. Chéng néih yùhn·leuhng kéuih. /Excuse me. Deui·m̀h·jyuh. or Chéng néih
   yùhn·leuhng ngóh. /Excuse my leaving you. (said to other guests at a party) Sāt pùih.

execute   (carry out) saht·hàhng, jāp·hàhng; **to execute by shooting** chēung·kyut, chēung·
   baih, dá·bá (colloq.)

executives   (of the government) hàhng·jing yàhn·yùhn; (of a business firm) gìng·léih
   yàhn·yùhn; **executive secretary** gon·sí

exempt   míhn; **exempt from military service** mihn·yihk; **exempt from taxes** míhn·seui

exercise   (of the body) wahn·duhng; (practice) lihn·jaahp; (rights, etc.) hàhng·sái; (gym·
   nastic) tái·chòu; (in a lesson) lihn·jaahp; **exercise book** lihn·jaahp·bóu

exert   **exert one's self** chēut·lihk; **exert one's self for the country** wàih gwok·gà jeuhn·
   lihk; **exert one's self to the utmost** jeuhn·lihk

exhale   táu·hei

exhibit 85 explorer

exhibit   (as paintings, etc.) jín·láahm; (display, as goods) báai; (as objects in a court) maht·jing

exhibition   jín·láahm·wúi

exhort   hyun·gáai, hyun·míhn

exile   (forced) beih fong·juhk·ge yàhn; (voluntary) tòuh jyuh tā bòng ge yàhn

exist   chyùhn·joih. /He said ghosts do not exist in this world, but in another world. Do you believe that? Kéuih wah gwái m̀h·chyùhn·joih hái nī·go sai·gaai·seuhng, daahn·haih chyùhn·joih·hái lihng·yāt·go sai·gaai·seuhng, néih seun ma? /I said ghosts do not exist. Ngóh wah gàn·bún móuh gwái. or Gwái gàn·bún bāt chyùhn·joih.
    struggle for existence sàng·chyùhn·ging·jàng

exit   chēut·háu

Exodus   Chēut·ngòi·gahp·gei

expand   (develop) kwong·chùng; (to swell) pàahng·jeung

expect   (wait for) dáng. /Are you expecting someone? Néih haih m̀h·haih dáng·gán yàhn a?
    (count on someone for something) jí·yíh. /Don't expect that he will help you. Mh·sái jí·yíh kéuih wúih bòng néih.
    (hope for) hèi·mohng. /Don't expect too much. Mh·hóu hèi·mohng taai góu.
    not expected móuh séung·dou. /It's easier than I expected. Ngóh móuh·séung·dou gam yùhng·yih. /I never expected to see him again. Móuh·séung·dou juhng wúih gin·dóu kéuih.

expedient   leih·bihn

expedite   gà·gán·jeun·hàhng

expedition   (for recreation) léuih·hàhng·tyùhn; (for scientific research) taam·hím·déui; (for military purposes) yúhn·jīng·gwān

expel   (as from school) hòi·chèuih; (send away) gón·jáu, gón·chēut; **expel devils** gón·gwái

expense   fai·yuhng, hòi·sìu. /What will the expenses be? Yiu géi chín fai·yuhng a? **daily expenses** yaht·yuhng·fai; **expense account** baahn·gùng·fai; **household expenses** gà·yuhng; **miscellaneous expenses** jaahp·fai; **traveling expenses** (paid by an organization) chēut·chàai·fai

expensive   gwai

experience   gìng·yihm

experienced   yáuh·gìng·yihm, lóuh·lihn, suhk·hòhng

experiment   si·yihm

expert   (specialist) jyūn·gā; (in the trade) yáuh·gìng·yihm, nàh·sáu, suhk·hòhng. /He is an expert in that kind of work. Kéuih jouh gó tìng sih jeui yáuh·gìng·yihm ge la. /We need an expert carpenter. Ngóh·deih sèui·yiu yāt·go nàh·sáu ge dau·muhk sī·fú.

expire   /When will it expire? Géi·sí dou kèih (or múhn kèih) a?

explain   gáai, gáai·sīk, gáai·míhng. /Can you explain this for us? Néih hó·yíh gáai·bei ngóh·deih tèng ma? /Can you try to explain it to us in English? Néih hó·yíh si·háh yuhng yìng·màhn gáai·béi ngóh·deih tèng ma?

explanatory notes   jyu·gáai

explode   baau·ja

explorer   taam·hím·gā

explosive ja·yeuhk (N)

export chēut·háu; **export commodity** chēut·háu·fo; **export tax** chēut·háu·seui

expose **expose a film** sai fēi·lám; **expose to the public** béi yàhn tái, béi yàhn jì; **expose a secret** kit·chyùn bei·maht; **expose one's body** chèuih·sai·sāam·fu; **expose to disease** expressed as: tùhng . . . jyuh·màaih yāt·chai. /He was exposed to T.B., but luckily he didn't get it. Kéuih tùhng dī yáuh fai·behng ge yàhn jyuh·màaih yāt·chái, hóu·chói kéuih móuh chyùhn·yíhm·dóu.

express bíu·daaht, góng. /I have difficulty expressing myself in Cantonese. Ngóh yuhng Gwóng·jàu·wá hóu nàahn bíu·daaht ngóh ge yi·si. /Express yourself freely, don't be afraid. Néih hó·yíh chèuih·bín góng, m̀h·sái gèng. **express train** faai·chè

expression (facial) sàhn·chìhng, sàhn·hei. /He said nothing, but his expression was sad. Kéuih māt dōu móuh góng, daahn·haih kéuih ge sàhn·chìhng sahp·fàn yàu·sàuh.

extend (make longer) yìhn·chèuhng. /I have to extend my visa. Ngóh yāt·dihng yiu yìhn·chèuhng ngóh gèui·làuh ge kèih·haahn. /Do they plan to extend this road to the coast? Kéuih·deih haih m̀h·haih dá·syun jèung nī·tiuh louh yìhn·chèuhng dou hói·bīn a?

exterior ngoih·bouh ge

exterminate sîu·miht

external ngoih·mihn ge; **external piles** ngoih·jih

extinction miht·mòhng

extinguish (as a light) sīk; (as a fire) jíng·sīk; (destroy) wái·miht

extort lahk·sok

extra (additional) lihng·ngói ge, lihng·ngoih ge, ngaahk·ngoih ge. (of newspaper) houh·ngoih; **extra work** ngaahk·ngoih ge gūng·fù; **extra pay** ngaahk·ngoih ge yàhn·gùng

extradite yáhn·douh

extraordinary fèi·sèuhng ge, gaak·ngoih ge

extravagant chè·wàh

extract (pull) màng. /I think this tooth has to be extracted. Ngóh tái nī·jek ngàh yiu màng. (outline) jaahk·yiu

extreme fèi·sèuhng. /He is in extreme danger. Kéuih fèi·sèuhng ngàih·hím.

extremely fèi·sèuhng, . . . dou·gihk; . . . gāau·gwàan. /Today is extremely hot. Gàm·yaht fèi·sèuhng yiht. or Gàm·yaht yiht·dou·gihk. or Gàm·yaht yiht dāk gāau·gwàan.

eye ngáahn (M: jek, one; sèung, pair). /Close your eyes. Hahp·màaih sèung ngáahn. /Open your eyes. Maak·hòi sèung ngáahn. /Open your eyes wide. Maak·daaih sèung ngáahn. /It's right before your eyes. Jauh hái néih mihn·chìhn jē. /He is nearsighted in his left eye and astigmatic in the right. Kéuih jó·ngáahn gahn·sí, yauh ngàahn sáan·gwōng.
eyeball ngáahn·jyū; **eyebrows** ngáahn·mèih; **eyelashes** ngáahn·yāp·móu; **eyelids** ngáahn·goi; **eyesight** ngaahn·lihk, sih·lihk; **eye socket** ngáahn·kwōng; **eyesore** ngáahn·jūng·dēng (lit. the nail in the eye); **eye specialist** ngáahn·fō·yī·sāng; **eyewitness** chàn·ngáahn tái·gin; jing·yàhn (N)
keep an eye on hòn·jyuh, hàu·jyuh. /Be sure to keep an eye on the children. Chìn·maahn yiu hòn·jyuh dī sai·màn·jái a. /Keep an eye on (to tail or spy on) him. Hàu·jyuh kéuih.
see eye to eye. /I don't see eye to eye with him on this question. Nī·go mahn·tàih ngóh tùhng kéuih ge tái·faat m̀h·sèung·tùhng.

F

fable   yuh·yìhn

fabric   (cloth) bou·pāt

face   (human) mihn, mihn·maauh; (surface of anything) mín: **face of watch** bīu·mín; (look toward) heung(·jyuh), deui·jyuh. /This window faces south. Nī·go chēung·mún heung nàahm.
    (basin for washing the face) mihn·pún; **face each other** mihn·deui·mihn; **face to face** dòng mín

facilities   bihn·leih, fòng·bihn; **facilities for research** yìhn·gau·seuhng ge bihn·leih

fact   sih·saht

factor   yàn·sou, yùhn·yàn

factory   gùng·chóng (M: gàan)

faculty   (ability) chòih·gon; (teaching staff) gaau·jīk·yùhn

fade   (wither) jeh. /The color fades. Lāt·sīk. /The noise fades. Sìng·yàm yuht·lèih·yuht sai.

Fahrenheit   hòhn·syú·bíu, wàh·sih·bíu

fail   sāt·baaih; **fail to keep promise** sāt·yeuk; **fail to pass an examination** m̀h·gahp·gak, m̀h·hahp·gak

failure   sāt·baaih

faint   (not bright) ngam; (weak) yeuhk; (not loud) mèih·yeuhk

fair   (in price) gùng·douh; (in dealing or game, etc.) gùng·pìhng; (for grading) jùng·tíng; (in color) baahk·jehng; (of weather) hóu·tìn. /Is the weather going to be fair tomorrow? Tìng·yaht hóu·tìn ma?

fairly   sēung·dòng

fairy   sīn·gū; **fairyland** sìn·gíng; **fairy tales** tùhng·wá

faith   (a religion or belief) seun·yéuhng, seun·sàm. /What is his religious faith? Kéuih seun(·yéuhng) māt·yéh jùng·gaau a? /You should have faith in God. Néih yìng·dòng deui seuhng·dai yáuh seun·sàm.

faithful   jùng·saht

fall   (drop) dit, dit·lohk·lèih, dit·lohk·heui; **fall on the ground** dit·lohk·déi; **fall and hurt oneself** dit·chàn; **fall down** dit·dóu, dit·dài; **fall from virtue** doh·lohk; **fall in price** dit·ga; **fall of a city** haahm·lohk

false   (not true) gá·ge; (dishonest) hèui·ngaih; **false teeth** gá·ngàh; **false accusation** yùn·wóng (V). /You made a false accusation against him. Néih yùn·wóng·jó kéuih.

fame   mìhng·sìng, mìhng·yuh

familiar   (of relations) chàn·maht; (acquainted with) sèung·suhk; (knowing about) jīng·tùng. /He is familiar with several dialects. Kéuih jīng·tùng géi·júng tóu·wá.

family   gà·tìng (parents and children); (one's wife and children) gà·gyun, jyuh·gā; **family condition** gà·gíng; **family expenditure** gà·yuhng; **family letter** gà·seun; **family property** gà·cháan

famine   gēi·fòng

famous   chēut·méng (ge); yáuh·méng (ge); màhn·méng (ge); **famous doctor** mìhng·yì

fan   sin (M: bá); put (V)

fancy   (delusive imagination) waahn·séung, mohng·séung

far   yúhn. /Is the bridge far away? Douh kíuh lèih nī·syu yúhn ma? /How far is it from
here to there? Nī·syu lèih gó·syu yáuh géi yúhn a?
        as far as. /As far as I'm concerned, I'm satisfied. Yíh ngóh yíh leuhn, ngóh hóu
múhn·jūk la. /We drove as far as to the border. Ngóh·deih yāt·jihk sái·dou bīn·gaai
gam yúhn.
        /So far so good. Dou muhk·chìhn wàih·jí dōu géi tóh·dong.

Far East   Yúhn·dūng

fare   (the price of transportation by vehicle) chè·geuk; (by boat) séui·geuk, syùhn·geuk

farewell   **farewell dinner** jin·hàhng. /Shall we give him a farewell dinner? Ngóh·deih
sèui m̀h sèui·yiu tùhng kéuih jin·hàhng a? **farewell party** fùng·sung·wúi. Farewell!
Yāt·louh·pìhng·ngòn!

farm   gàang·tìhn, gàang·jùng (V); (cultivated land) tìhn; (with barns and houses) nùhng·
chèuhng; (place for raising cattle)·muhk·chèuhng

farmer   gàang·tìhn·lóu, nùhng·fù (bookish); (as a social class) nùhng·yahn, nùhng·màhn

farther   gang yúhn, juhng yúhn dī; **farthest** ji·yúhn·ge

fascinating   yáhn·yàhn·yahp·sing

fashion   (style) fún; (shape) yéung; **new fashion** sàn·fún; **old fashion** gauh·fún

fashionable   sìh·hīng, mō·dāng

fast   (quick) faai; (tight) gán; (firm) saht. **to fast** sáu·jàai, gam·sihk; **fast color** m̀h·lāt·
sīk; **hold fast** jà·saht

fasten   (tie, bind) bóng·jyuh. **fasten it in any way so as to be immovable** jíng·saht;
fasten it tighter bóng·gán dī; **fasten it well** bóng·hóu kéuih; **fasten it tightly** bóng·gán
kéuih; **fasten it with a nail** dèng·saht kéuih; **fasten it with string** bóng·hóu kéuih

fastidious   yīm·jīm

fat   fèih. /Don't get too fat. M̀h·hóu taai fèih. /I'm already too fat, am I not? Ngóh
yíh·gìng taai fèih la, haih m̀h·haih a? /Go and buy a fat chicken. Heui máaih yāt·jek
fèih gāi.
        faat·fūk (polite saying for people). /You are getting a bit fat. Néih faat·jó·fūk bo.
(part of the flesh) fèih·yuhk. /This piece of pork has too much fat on it. Nī·gauh
jyù·yuhk fèih·yuhk taai dò.
        fat boy fèih·jái; **fat girl** fèih néui; **fat man** fèih lóu; **fat woman** fèih pòh

fatal   ji·mehng ge

fate   (destiny) mehng, wahn·sou, mehng·wahn

father   (formal term) fuh·chàn; (more intimate term) bàh·bā, louh·dauh; **my late father**
sìn·fuh; **father and mother** fuh·móuh; (polite term) **your father** lihng·jyūn; **my father**
gà·fuh; **wife's father** (term used by husband) ngoih·fú; **husband's father** (term used by
wife), gā·gūng, lóuh·yèh; **father's elder brother** a·baak; **father's elder brother's wife**
baak·móuh; **father's elder sister** gū·mā; **father's sister's husband** gù·jéung; **father's
younger brother** a·sūk; **father's younger brother's wife** a·sám; **father's younger sister**
gū·jē; priest, sàhn·fuh; **fatherless** móuh·lóuh·dauh; **fatherless child** gù·yìh

fatigue   guih, sàn·fú

fatten   yéuhng feih

fault   cho, cho·ngh; (moral failing) gwo·sāt; **faultfinding** chèui·mòuh·kàuh·chì

fatherland   jóu·gwok

favor   (kindness, privilege) in statement, yàhn·chìhng, mín; in questions, the idea is expressed in words such as lòuh·fàahn (trouble), kàuh (beg). /It's a big favor that he lets
us use this hall as a meeting place. Kéuih béi ngóh·deih yùhng nī·go tēng hòi·wúi haih
yāt·go hóu daaih ge yàhn·chìhng. /May I ask you to do me a favor? Ngóh séung kàuh
néih yāt·gihn sih. /I want to ask you a favor. Ngóh yàuh dī sih séung kàuh néih. **favor
of elders** yàn·waih; **favor of divine mercy** yàn·dín
    in one's favor deui . . . yáuh·leih. /That's in our favor. Gám, deui ngóh·deih yáuh·
leih.
    be in favor of jaan·sìhng. /I'm in favor of immediate action. Ngóh jaan·sìhng jīk·
hak jouh.

favorable   **favorable opportunity** hóu gèi·wuih; **favorable current** seuhn·séui; **favorable
wind** seuhn·fùng; **everything favorable** sih·sih·yùh·yi

favorite   ji·jùng·yi·ge; ji·jùng·yi; (for close relationship such as parents to children)
ji·tung, ji·sek. /Which is your favorite color? Néih ji·jùng·yi bīn·go ngàahn·sīk a? or
Bīn·go haih néih ji·jùng·yi ge ngàahn·sīk a? /Who is your favorite movie star? Bīn·
go haih néih ji·jùng·yi ge mìhng·sīng a? /He is his father's favorite. Kéuih bàh·bā ji·
tung kéuih ge la. /You are your father's favorite, aren't you? Néih bàh·bā ji·tung néih
ge la, haih m̀h·haih?

fear   (emotion) is expressed verbally as **to fear** pa. /There are all kinds of fears in
his mind, it's no good for his future. Kéuih sàm·léuih·bihn yeuhng·yeuhng dōu pa, nī·go
deui kéuih gé chìhn·tòuh fèi·sèuhng m̀h·hóu.
    to fear pa, gèng. /Never fear! He'll take good care of you! M̀h sái pa! Kéuih wúih
hóu·hóu·déi jiu·ying néih gé!
    for fear of pa. /He didn't eat his breakfast for fear of missing the train. Kéuih pa
daap·m̀h·dóu fó·chè só·yíh móuh sihk·dou jóu·chāan.

fearful   hó·pa (ge)

feast   (banquet) yin·wuih; **give a feast** báai·jáu, chéng·yám

feather   jeuk·mòuh; **feather duster** gài·mòuh·sóu (M: jī); **feather fan** ngòh·mòuh·sin (M:
bá)

February   yih·yuht

federal government   lyùhn·bòng·jing·fú; **federal state** lyùhn·bòng

Federation of Malaysia   Máh·lòih·a lyùhn·bòng

fee   fai; **doctor's fee** chán·gām, yī·yeuhk fai (as in a clinic or hospital); **lawyer's fee**
johng·sī fai, leuht·sī·fai; **registration fee** jyu·chaak·fai; **tuition fee** hohk·fai

feeble   yúhn·yeuhk; **feeble body** sàn·jí yeuhk; **feeble-minded** yi·ji·bohk·yeuhk

feed   wai; **feed a baby** wai bìh·bī·(jái); **feed a bird** wai (or hei)·jéuk; **feed a pig** waih
(or hei)·jyū; **feed cattle** wai (or hei)·ngàuh

feel   (be aware of, have feeling about) gin·gok, gok·dāk, gin(·dāk); (think) gok·dāk. /Do
you feel a pain here? Néih nī·syu gin·gok tung ma? /Where do you feel a pain? Néih
bīn·syu gok·dāk tung a? /Do you feel hungry? Néih gin tóuh·ngoh ma? /How do you
feel? (to a patient) Néih gin·dāk dím a? /Do you feel better? Néih gin dāk (or gok·
dāk) hóu dī ma? **feel pain** gin(·dāk)·tung; **feel cold** gin(·dāk)·dung; **feel hot** gin(·dāk)·
yiht. /I feel you need a little exercise. Ngóh gok·dāk néih yìng·gòi yáuh dī wahn·duhng.
(touch) mó. /Feel it. Isn't it smooth? Mò·háh, géi yúhn·suhk?
    feel like séung, jùng·yi. /Do you feel like taking a walk? Néih séung saan·háh·bouh
ma?
    feel the pulse bá·mahk

feeling (emotion) chìhng·gáam; (to be in good or bad mood) sàm·chìhng: in good mood, sàm·chìhng hóu; in bad mood, sàm·chìhng m̀h·hóu. /I don't want to hurt his feelings. is expressed as Ngóh m̀h·séung lihng kéuih nàahn·hàm.

feign ja·dai; **feign death** ja·séi; **feign ignorance** ja·m̀h·jì; **feign illness** ja·behng; **feign madness** ja·dìn; **feign stupidity** ja·sòh; **feign sleep** ja·fan

fellow yàhn. **fellow countryman** tùhng·bàau; **fellow lodger in the same house** tùhng·ngūk jyuh ge; **fellow member** wuih·yáuh; **fellow student** tùhng·hohk; **fellow villager** tùhng·hēung; **fellow worker** tùhng·sih; **a fellow of a society** wúi·yùhn; **a fellow of a graduate school** gùng·fai·yìhn·gau·sāng

felt jīn (N) (M: faai): **felt hat** jīn·móu (M: déng)

female néuih-. **female laborer** néuih·gūng; **female sex** néuih·sing, néuih·gaai; **female teacher** néuih·sìn·sàang

feminine néuih·sing ge, néuih·yán ge

fence lèih·bā (M: douh); (metal mesh) móhng

ferment ngau; faat·hàau. /We can ferment this to make wine. Ngóh·deih hó·yíh yuhng nī·dī yéh lèih ngau jáu. /This thing is fermented. Nī·dī yéh yìh·gìng faat·hàau la.   **in ferment** gīk·duhng. /The students are in ferment. Dī hohk·sāang hóu gīk·duhng.

ferocious hùng·lòhng ge

ferry lèuhn·douh; **ferryboat** douh·syùhn

fertile fèih·yūk; **fertile land** fèih·tìhn

fertilizer fèih·tìhn·líu

festival jit, daaih·yaht·jí; **celebrate a festival** jouh·jit; **Dragon boat festival** Dyùn·ngh·jit, Ńgh·yuht·jit; **Mid-autumn festival** Jūng·chàu·jit

fetch (go and get) ló

feudal fùng·gin; **feudal lord** jyù·hàuh; **feudal system** fùng·gin jai·douh; **feudal times** fùng·gin sìh·doih

fever yiht (N), faat·yiht, faat·sìu (VO). /Does he still have a fever? Kéuih juhng·yáuh yiht ma? or Kéuih juhng faat·sìu ma? /He has had a fever for two days. Kéuih yìh·gìng faat·jo léuhng·yaht sìu la.   **scarlet fever** sìng·hùhng yiht; **yellow fever** wòhng·yiht·jing

few (not many) géi·M. /Please say a few words to our students. Chéng néih deui ngóh·deih ge hohk·sāang góng géi·geui syut·wah. /I know only a few words. Ngóh sīk géi·go jih jē. /I'd like to borrow a few of your chairs. Ngóh séung tùhng néih je géi·jeùng yí. (with emphasis) hóu·síu, móuh·géi·dò. /Few American know how to speak Cantonese. Hóu·síu Méih·gwok yàhn sīk góng Gwóng·jàu·wá. /Few students want to be doctors nowadays. Gahn·lói móuh·géi·dò hohk·sāang séung jouh yī·sāng.   **quite a few** bāt·síu. /There are quite a few students who would like to be doctors. Yáuh bāt·síu hohk·saang séung jouh yī·sāng.   **a few days** sàam·géi·yaht; **quite a few days** hóu géi·yaht

fiance meih·fān·fù; **fiancée** meih·fàn·chài

fickle (changeable) fáan·fūk ge; (uncertain) móuh·dihng·sing ge

fiction (story) gú·jái, gu·sih; (novel) síu·syut; (romance) chyùhn·kèih

field (tract of land) deih (M: faai); (cultivated) tìhn (M: faai); (for playing) chèuhng; **athletic field** wahn·duhng·chèuhng; **football field** jūk·kàuh·chèuhng

fierce (violent) kek·liht, máahng·liht

fifteen   sahp·ńgh; **fifteen cents** hòuh·bun·jí; **fifteen minutes** yāt·go·gwāt; **fifteenth** daih· sahp·ńgh

fifth   daih·ńgh; **fifth column(ist)** daih·ńgh·jùng·deuih; **one fifth** ńg·fahn·jí·yāt

fifty   ńgh·sahp

fig   mòuh·fà·gwó

fight   (between individuals, physically) dá gāau, dá. /Let's not start a fight. Mh·hóu dá· gāau. /How did the fight start? Dim·yéung dá·héi·séuhng·lèih ga?
     (verbally) /Are he and his wife fighting all the time? Kéuih haih mh·haih sìh·sìh tùhng kéuih lóuh·pòh ngaai·gāau ga?
     (in war) dá·jeung. /The Arabs and the Israelis have been fighting since the end of the Second World War. Jih·chùhng sai·gaai daih·yih·chi·daaih·jin jí·hauh, A·làai·baak yàhn tùhng Yíh·sīk·liht yàhn jauh dá·jeung yāt·jihk dá·dou yìh·gā.
     fight against cháan·chèuih. /We must fight against malaria, typhoid fever and cholera. Ngóh·deih yāt·dihng yiu cháan·chèuih faat·láahng·jing, sèung·hòhn, tùhng fok· lyuhn.

fighter   (plane) jin·dau·gēi (M: ga)

fighting line   jin·sin

figure   (number) sou·muhk·jih; (of body) sàn·chòi; (form) yìhng·jeuhng; (in art, human form) yàhn·mát; (price) ga·chìhn

file   (tool) cho; (for documents) dóng·ngon; **put it on file** gwài·dóng (term used in government organizations, not popular in business firms); **to file** cho; **rank and file** hòhng· ńgh; (row) hòhng

Filipino   Fēi·leuht·bān yàhn

filial   **filial piety** haau·seuhn; **filial reverence** haau·ging; **filial-minded son** haau·jí; **filial behavior to one's parents** haau·ging fuh·móuh

fill   (with liquids) jàm; (with dry things) jòng; (as a cavity; an office) bóu. **fill a tooth** bóu·ngàh; **fill a vacancy** bóu·kyut; **fill in (a hole)** tìhn, (a form) tìhn (sé); **fill in the name** tìhn·méng. /Have you filled in your name? Néih tìhn·jó méng meih a? /Fill in your name here. /Tìhn néih ge méng hái nī·syu. **fill up** jàm·múhn. /Fill it up. Jàm·múhn kéuih. but /Fill it (the gasoline tank) up. is Yahp (or gun)·múhn kéuih.

film   (photo) fēi·lám (M: gyún, roll); (movie) yíng·pín; (thin skin) mók; **film on the eye** ngáahn·mók

filter   sà·láu (N); gak, leuih (V)

filthy   wù·jòu, láh·já, laaht·taat

fin   yùh·chi

final   (last) sàu·mēi (ge), jeui·hauh (ge); (definite) dihng·saht·jó, kyut·dihng·jó. /This is final, you don't have to say any more. Yíh·gìng dihng·saht·jó la. Néih mòuh·waih dò góng la. **final examination** daaih·háau; **final outcome** git·gwó; **finals (in competition)** kyut·choi

finally   sàu·mēi, git·gwó

finance   chòih·jing (N)

financial   gìng·jai; **financial problem** gìng·jai mahn·tàih; **financial condition** gìng·jai johng·fong; **financial difficulties** gìng·jai·seuhng ge kwan·nàahn

find   (search) wán, wán·dóu. /Could you find him and bring him back? Néih nàhng·mh· nàhng·gau wán kéuih fàan·lèih a? /Have you found him? Néih wán·dóu kéuih meih a?

/Where did you find him? Néih hái bīn·syu wán·dóu kéuih ga? /His father has found him. Kéuih bàh·bā yíh·gīng wán·dóu kéuih la.
  (discover) tái·dóu, faat·yihn. /I found my car was not in the garage. Ngóh tái·dóu ngóh ga chē m̀h·hái chē·fòhng·syu. /I found her staring at me. Ngóh tái·dou kéuih mohng·jyuh ngóh.
  (through research) yìhn·gau·dóu. /They found a new way to cure diabetes. Kéuih· deih yìhn·gau·dóu yāt·júng sàn fòng·faat yi·jih tòhng·neuih.
  (accidentally) jāp·dóu, yuh·dóu. /I found a five-dollar bill on the street. Ngóh hái gāai·syu jāp·dóu yāt·jèung ńgh·mān·jí. /We found a tail wind with us while we were traveling north. Ngóh·deih heung bāk hàhng gó·jahn·sí yuh·dóu seuhn·fùng.
  find out mahn·dóu (by asking), chàh·dóu (by investigating). /Have you found out who he is? Néih yáuh·móuh mahn·dóu (or chàh·dóu) kéuih haih bīn·go a?

fine   (minute) yau·sai; (elaborate, of workmanship) jìng·háau
  (nice or well) hóu. /I'm fine, thank you. Ngóh hóu hóu, yáuh·sàm. /It's a fine day, today. Gàm·yaht tìn·hei jàn·haih hóu la. /That's fine. Hóu hóu.
  fine arts méih·seuht; **fine gold** sahp·jūk gàm; **a fine** faht·fún; **to fine** faht

finger   sáu·jí (M: jek) thumb, móuh·jí; **index finger** sihk·jí, yih·jí; **middle finger** jùng·jí; **fourth finger** mòuh·mìhng·jí; **little finger** mēi·jí; **fingernail** sáu·jí·gaap; **fingerprint** sáu·jí·mòuh, jí·mòuh, sáu·jí·yan

finish   -yùhn (RVE). **finish eating** sihk·yùhn; **finish reading** tái·yùhn; **finish speaking** góng·yùhn; **finish working** jouh·yùhn. /Have they finished eating? Kéuih·deih sihk·yùhn faahn meih a? /I'll come as soon as I finish reading this letter. Ngóh tái·yúhn fùng seun jauh lèih. /After he finished speaking he left. Kéuih góng·yùhn jí·hauh jauh jáu·jó la. /When will it (work, or job) be finished? Géi·sí hó·yíh jouh·yùhn a? /Let's finish this job tonight. Gàm·máahn jouh·yùhn nī·gihn sih kéuih, hóu ma.

fire   (conflagration) fó·jūk. /Fire! Fire! Fó·jūk a! Fó·jūk a! /That building burned down. Gó·gāan ngūk fó·jūk sìu·jó.
  catch fire sìu·jeuhk. /This material doesn't catch fire easily. Nī·jek chòih·líu m̀h·yùhng·yih sìu·dāk·jeuhk ge.
  fire a cannon hòi paau; **fire a gun** hòi chēung; **fire alarm** fó·gíng; **firearms** chēung· haaih; **fire a blank cartridge** fong hūng·chēung; **fire brigade** gau·fó·déui, sìu·fòhng·déui; **firecracker** paau·jéung; **to set off firecracker** sìu·paau·jéung; **fire insurance** fó·hím; **fireman** gau·fó·yùhn; **fireplace** bīt·lòuh; **fireproof** m̀h·pa·sìu ge, fòhng·fó ge; **fire station** séui·chè·gún (Hong Kong), fó·jūk·gún (Malaya), sìu·fòhng·gūk (Mainland); **fire tongs** fó·kìhm (M:bá); **firewood** chàaih; **fireworks** yìn·fó
  (discharge from employment) chìh. /If he really did something wrong, you may fire him. Yùh·gwó kéuih jàn·haih jouh·cho·jó, néih hó·yíh chìh kéuih.

firm   (solid) saht, git·saht; (steady) wán·jahn. /Is it firm enough? Gáu·m̀h·gau saht a? /This chair is not firm, be careful of it. /Nī·jèung yí m̀h·wán·jahn, yiu sìu·sàm. (trading co.) jih·houh, gūng·sī, hóng. **your firm** (polite), gwai·gūng·sī, gwai·hóng

firmly   -wán; **hold it firmly** jà·wán; **place it firmly** jài·wán

first   (in time) sìn; (in place) daih·yāt. /You first. Néih sìn. /Who is first? Bīn·go sìn a? /Who is the first one? Bīn·go daih·yāt a?
  at first héi·sáu. /He didn't like his car at first; now he just loves it. Héi·sáu kéuih m̀h·haih géi jùng·yi kéuih ga chè, yìh·gā kéuih hóu jùng·yi la.
  the first (of a month) yāt·houh (**solar calendar**) chò·yāt (**lunar calendar**); **first aid** gau·sèung; **first class** tàuh·dáng; **first floor** yih·láu; **first of all** daih·yāt; **first prize** tàuh·jéung, táu·chói; **win the first prize** jung·jó tàuh·jéung

fish   yú (M: tìuh); **freshwater fish** taahm·séui·yú; **saltwater fish** hàahm·séui·yú; **fish bait** yùh·néih; **fish bone** yùh·gwāt; **fisherman** dá·yùh·lóu; **fishery** yùh·yihp; **fishhook** yùh·ngàu; **fishing line** diu·yùh·síng; **fishnet** yùh·móhng; **fishing rod** diu yùh·gòn; **fish pond** yùh·tòhng; **fish scales** yùh·lèuhn; **fish spawn** yùh·chēun fist   kyùhn·tàuh

fit   ngāam. /It fits you perfectly. Nĭ·go jàn·haih ngāam néih la. /Does it fit (as of a
suit or dress) all right? Ngāam·sān ma? /You may act as you see fit. Néih gok·dāk
dím·yéung ngāam jauh dím jouh là.
    fit in (to a schedule). /The doctor is very busy today, but he will try to fit you in
somewhere. Yĭ·sāng gàm·yaht hóu m̀h·dāk·hàahn, daahn·haih kéuih yāt·dihng wán chēut
go sih·gaan lèih tái néih ge.
    convulsive fit faat yèuhng·diu; convulsion in children, gèng·fùng

five   ńgh; **five senses** ńgh·gùn

fix   jíng, jíng·fàan, jíng·fàan·hóu. /Can you fix this watch? Néih hó·yíh jíng·fàan hóu
nĭ·go bĭu ma? /Do you know how to fix it? Néih wúih m̀h·wúih jíng a? /Can it be fixed?
Jíng m̀h·jíng·dāk·fàan a? /It's all fixed. Jíng·fàan·hóu la.
    (set in order) jāp. /I need someone to fix up my room. Ngóh séung wán go yàhn
lèih tùhng ngóh jāp fóng.
    (prepare, as food) jíng. /Can you fix something for us to eat? Néih hó·yíh jíng dĭ
yéh béi ngóh·deih sihk ma?
    (establish) dihng. /Let's fix a date. Ngóh·deih dihng go yaht·jí (or yaht·kèih), hóu
ma?
    fixed date yaht·kèih; **fixed deposit** dihng·kèih chyùhn·fún; **fixed price** dihng·ga

flag   kèih (M: jì): **flag at half mast** hah bun·kèih; **flagship** kèih·laahm; **flag signals**
kèih·yúh; **flagstaff** kèih·gōn (M: jì)

flake   pin; **snowflake** syut·fā

flame   fó·mìuh

flannel faht·lāan·yúng

flare   **flare up** faat·pèih·hei, faat·fó

flash   (of light) sím; **flashlight** dihn·túng (M: jì); **flash of lightning** sím·dihn

flat   (even) pìhng; (of an object) bín; (story) yāt chàhng (láu); **two flats** léuhng chàhng·
láu

flatten jíng·pìhng; jíng·bín

flatter tok·daaih·geuk. /He's an expert at flattering people. Kéuih hóu wúih tok·daaih·
geuk ge.

flavor meih·douh (N); tìuh meih, gaau meih (V); **lost its flavor** jáu·jó dĭ meih·douh

flaw   mòuh·behng; **flawless** yāt·dĭ mòuh·behng dōu móuh

flea   **cat flea** māau·sāt (M: jek); **dog flea** gáu·sāt (M: jek)

flee   **flee from danger (or disaster)** jáu·naahn, beih·naahn

fleet   **fleet of warships** laahm·déui; **the Seventh fleet** daih·chāt·laahm·déui

flesh   yuhk; (opp. to spirit) yuhk·tái

flexible (able to bend without breaking), yìn·ngahn

flight (in the schedule of an airline), bāan·kèih; (flying) fèi·hàhng; (of stairs, or steps),
kāp

fling   fihng, diuh, deng

flint   fó·sehk (M: gauh)

float   pòuh, fàuh. /What is floating on the water? Pòuh·hái séui·mín gó·go haih māt·yéh
a? **floating bridge** fàuh·kìuh (M: douh)

flock   kwàhn: **a flock of sheep** yāt·kwàhn yèuhng·mē

flog   (beat) dá; (with whip) bīn

flood   daaih·séui, séui·jòi. **flooded** séui·jam.   /The village has been flooded for five days. Tìuh chyūn yíh·gìng séui·jàm·jó ńgh·yaht la.

floor   (wooden only) deih·báan; (of a room or house) deih·háh.
    (story of a building) láu.   /Which floor do you live on? Néih jyuh géi láu a?   /I live on the fourth floor. Ngóh jyuh ńgh·láu.

flour   mìhn·fán; **rice flour** máih·fán

flourish   (prosper) hìng·wohng

flow   (as water does) làuh; **flow in** làuh·yahp; **flow into the sea** làuh·yahp hói; **flow out** làuh·chēut `

flower   fā (M: déu): **flower basket** fā·láam; **flowerpot** fà·pùhn; **flower vase** fā·jēun

fluently   làuh·leih.   /She speaks English fluently. Kéuih góng Yìng·màhn góng dāk hóu làuh·leih.

fluid   (water) séui; (chem. term) yiht·tái, làuh·jāt

flush   (face) mihn·hùhng

flute   sīu (M: jì): **play the flute** chēui sīu

fly   (as birds) fèi; (as a kite) fong; **fly a kite** fong jí·yíu; **fly the national flag** gwa gwok· kèih; (insect) wū·yīng (M: jek)

foam   póuh (N); héi·póuh (V)

focus   jìu·dím (N)

fodder   jih·liuh

foe   sàuh·yàhn

fog   mouh.   /The fog usually disperses around ten o'clock. Dī mouh sahp·dím·jūng jó· yáu jauh saan la.

foggy   /It was very foggy this morning; now it has cleared up. Gàm·jìu·jóu hóu daaih mouh, yìh·gā saan·jó la.

fold   (bend) jip, jip·hóu.   /Fold the clothes and put them away. Jip·hóu dī sāam jài·màaih kéuih.   /Do you know how to fold a suit? Let me teach you. Néih wúih m̀h·wúih jip sāi· jōng a? Dáng ngóh gaau néih.

folklore   màhn·gàan chyùhn·syut; màhn·gàan·gu·sih; **folk song** màhn·gō; **folk tale** màhn· gàan gu·sih

follow   gàn·jyuh.   /Follow him. Gàn·jyuh kéuih hàahng.   /Don't look now, I think there is someone following us. M̀h·hóu nihng·jyun·tàuh tái, ngóh gú yáuh yàhn gàn·jyuh ngóh· deih.
    (understand) mìhng·baahk.   /Do you follow me? Néih mìhng·baahk ngóh ge yi·si ma?
    (obey) fuhk·chùhng.   /Follow your leader. Fuhk·chùhng néih ge líhng·jauh.
    (go along a road, a river, etc.) seuhn·jyuh.   /Follow this road, it will lead you to the bridge. Seuhn·jyuh nī·tiuh louh jauh wúih hàahng·dou tìuh kìuh·syu la.
    (after one already mentioned) **the following class** hah·yāt·tòhng; **the following day** daih·yih·yaht; **the following visit** hah·yāt·chi
    following or **as follows** yíh·hah, hah·bihn, hah·liht, yùh·hah.   /My reasons are as follows. Yíh·hah haih ngóh ge géi·go léih·yàuh.   /Translate the following sentences in· to Chinese. Jèung hah·bihn nī·géi·geui wá yihk·sìhng Jùng·màhn.   /Please pay attention

to the following points. Chéng gok·wái jyu·yi hah·liht gók·dím. /The new regulations announced by the school are as follows. Hohk·haauh syùn·bouh ge sàn·gwāi·jāk yùh·hah.

fond   hóu hou, hóu jùng·yi. /He is fond of joking. Kéuih hóu hou góng·síu ge. /She is very fond of music, isn't she? Kéuih hóu jùng·yi yàm·ngohk haih m̀h·haih a?

food   (edibles) sihk maht, sihk ge yéh; (a meal or cooking) fó·sihk (served in a mess); -chāan (as in Western food, sāi·chāan; Chinese food, tòhng·chāan); choi (served in restaurants), sung (served at home). /How is the food in school? Hohk·haauh ge fó·sihk hóu m̀h·hóu a? /Do you like to eat Western food or Chinese food? Néih jùng·yi sihk sāi·chāan yīk·waahk tòhng·chāan (or Jūng·chāan) a? /Which restaurant serves the best food here? Nī·syu bīn·gàan jáu·gún ge choi jeui hóu a?

fool   sòh·jái

foolish   sòh, bahn, chéun

foot   (of the leg) geuk; (the measure) chek. **football** (soccer) jūk·kàuh; **football match** jūk·kàuh béi·choi; **foot of a hill or mountain** sàan·geuk; **footprint** geuk·yan; **footsore** geuk tung

for   (instead of, in place of) tai. /Do you need someone to teach for you? Néih sèui m̀h sèui·yiu yàhn tai néih séuhng·tòhng a?
  (on behalf of) waih, hòng. /She bought this house for her mother. Nī·gaan ngūk kéuih waih kéuih lóuh·móu máaih ge. /Will you do something for me? Néih bòng ngóh jouh dī yéh, dāk ma?
  (adapted to) béi, waih. /Is that movie for children? Gó·chēut dihn·yíng haih mh·haih béi sai·mān·jái tái ga?
  (with reference to) deui. /Milk is good for you, drink some. Ngàuh·náaih deui néih hóu, yám dī lā.
  (in favor of) jaan·sìhng. /He is always neither for nor against it. Kéuih géi·sí dōu haih yihk m̀h·jaan·sìhng yihk m̀h·fáan·deui.
  (throughout; of time or space). /He has been waiting for you for an hour. Kéuih hái syu dáng·jó néih sèhng dím·júng la. /Go straight ahead for five miles and you'll be there. Heung chìhn yāt·jihk hàahng ńgh·yìng·léih jauh dou la.
  (because) waih(·yan). /I can't go for these three reasons: first . . . Ngóh m̀h·heui·dāk waih(·yàn) sàam·go yùhn·yàn: daih·yāt . . . /She did it for her mother's sake. Kéuih waih kéuih lóuh·móu sìn·ji gám jouh ge.
  for a short time jaahm·sìh; **for example** pei·yùh, laih·yùh; **for my part** yíh ngóh lèih góng; **for sale** chēut maaih; **for the time being** jaahm·sìh, muhk·chìhn; **for the sake of** waih·jó; **for what reason** waih·māt·yéh, dím·gáai

forbearance   noih·sing

forbid   gam·jí

force   lihk (N); míhn·kéuhng, kéuhng·bīk (V); (troops) gwàn·déui

forceps   kím

forearm   sáu·bei

forecast   yuh·chāk, yuh·bou

forefather   jóu·jùng, jóu·sīn

forefinger   sihk·jí

forehead   ngaahk·tàuh

foreign   (of foreign origin) ngoih·gwok ge; **foreign affairs** ngoih·gàau; **foreign exchange** ngoih·wuih; **foreign country** ngoih·gwok; **foreign firm** yèuhng·hóng; **foreign goods** yèuhng·fo; **foreign language** ngoih·gwok·wá, fàan·wá (colloq.); **foreign loan** ngoih·jaai;

foreign minister ngoih·gàau bouh·jéung; **Ministry of Foreign Affairs** ngoih·gàau·bouh; **foreign relations** ngoih·gàau

foreigner   sài·yàhn, ngoih·gwok·yàhn, fàan·gwái(·lóu) (lit. foreign devil)

foreman   gùng·táu

forenoon   seuhng·jau, seuhng·ńgh

forerunner   sīn·fūng

foresaid   seuhng·bihn só·góng·ge syut·wah

forest   syuh·làhm

foretell   yuh·yìhn

forever   wìhng·yúhn

forewarn   yuh·sìn gíng·gou

foreword   jéui

forge   gá·mouh; **forge a name** mouh·méng

forget   m̀h·gei·dāk, mòhng·gei

forgetful   móuh·gei·sing

forgive   fùn·syu, yùhn·leuhng; (religious) se·míhn; **forgive sins** se·jeuih

fork   chā

form   (shape, appearance) yéung, yeuhng·jí. /Follow this form to make it. Jiu nī·go yéung (or yeuhng·jí) jouh.
   (style, written) gaak·sīk. /Copy it down according to that form. Jiu·jyuh gó·go gaak·sīk chāau yāt·fahn.
   (a blank) bíu(·gaak). /Did you fill out all the forms? Néih tìhn·hóu·saai gó·dī bíu meih a?
   (make, organize) -sèhng, jóu·jīk. /Please form a circle. Chéng néih·deih waih·sèhng yāt·go yùhn·hyūn. /They want to form a new party. Kéuih·deih séung jóu·jīk yāt·go sàn jing·dóng.
   (in art or literature) yìhng·sīk. /It's written in the form of a poem. Haih yuhng sī ge yìhng·sīk sé ge. **order form** dihng·fo·dāan

formal   (in due form) jing·sīk·ge; (ceremonial) yī·jūk·láih·faat·ge

formality   (ceremony) yìh·sīk

former   yìh·chìhn (ge), chìhn·sìh (ge). /He is a former student of mine. Kéuih haih ngoh yìh·chìhn ge yāt·go hohk·sāang. **in former times** wóhng·sí, gauh·sìh
   (first) sìn·tàuh gó·go. /Of these two suggestions, which one do you prefer, the former one or the latter one? Nī·léuhng·go tàih·yi néih syún·jaak bīn·yāt·go nē, sìn·tàuh gó·go nē, yihk·waahk hāu·mēi gó·go nē?

formidable   hó·pa (ge)

formula   (med.) yeuhk·fōng; (prescribed form) fòng·chìhng·sīk; (in math.) gūng·sīk

forsake   pàau·hei; **forsake evil ways and return to the right** hei-chèh-gwài-jing

fort   paau·tói, paau·tòih

forth   **and so forth** dáng·dáng (ge) plus yéh of articles, sih of affairs, deih·fong of place, etc. /They went shopping for jade, pearls, and so forth. Kéuih·deih heui·jó máaih yúk a, jān·jyù a, dáng·dáng ge yéh.

back and forth . . . lèih . . . heui. /He kept walking back and forth. Kéuih hàahng. lèih hàahng·heui. /She rocked the baby back and forth. Kéuih jèung go bìh·bī·jái yìuh· lèih yìuh·heui.

fortieth daih·sei·sahp

fortnight léuhng·go láih·baai, leuhng·go sìng·kèih; **fortnightly** (publication) bun·yuht·hón, sèung·jàu·hón

fortress paau·tói

fortunate gau·wahn, hóu·mehng

fortunately hóu·chói, hóu·joih

fortune mehng wahn, mehng; **fortune teller** syun·mehng sīn·sàang; **fortune telling** syun·mehng

forty sei·sahp

forward lèih chìhn·bihn; heui chìhn·bihn. /Come forward. Hàahng·lèih chìhn·bihn. /Walk forward and take a look. Hàahng·heui chìhn·bihn tái·háh.
   look forward to paan·mohng. /I'll look forward to your letters. Ngóh paan·mohng jip·dóu néih ge seun. /I am looking forward to meeting him. Ngóh paan·mohng tùhng kéuih sèung·gin.
   to forward jyún. /Would you please forward this letter to Mr. Lee? Chéng néih jyún nī·fùng seun béi Léih sīn·sàang. /Please forward my mail to this new address. Chéng néih jèung ngóh ge seun jyún·heui nī·go sàn deih·jí.

fossil fa·sehk

foster **foster daughter** yéuhng·néui; **foster father** yéuhng·fuh; **foster mother** yéuhng· móuh; **foster son** yéuhng·jái, ló·jai

foul (smell) chau; (filthy) wū·jòu

found (establish) chong·lahp; (as metals) jyu

foundation deih·gèi; (fig.) gèi·chó; (for a statement) gàn·geui

founder (of an institution) chong·baahn·yàhn; (of a state) hòi·gwok·yùhn·fàn; (of a religion) gaau·jyú

foundling home yuhk·yīng·tóng (M: gàan)

fountain (spring) chyùhn; (artificial) pan·séui·chìh

fountain pen mahk·séui·bāt (M: jì)

four sei; **fourfold** sei·púih; **four limbs** sei·jì; **four seasons** sei·gwai; **four sides** sei· mihn, sei·bihn

fourteen sahp·sei; **fourteenth** daih·sahp·sei

fourth daih·sei; **fourth finger** mòuh·mìhng·jí

fox wùh·léi (M: jek); **fox-trot** wù·bouh·móuh

fraction (part) bouh·fahn; (arith.) fahn·sou

fragile (easily broken) yih laahn ge; (weak) yúhn·yeuhk ge

fragment síu bou·fahn, pin·dyuhn

fragrant hèung

frame **frame of a picture** geng·kwōng; **frame for spectacles** ngáahn·géng·kwóng

franc faat·lòhng

frank   táan·baahk (ge), sēut·jihk (ge)   /I want to be frank with you, you have to stop gambling.   Ngóh louh·saht tùhng néih góng, néih bāt·nàhng joi dóu chín la.

fraud   (deceit, breach of confidence) pin·guhk

freckle   mahk·sí (N)

free   (having leisure) dāk·hàahn.   /When will he be free? Kéuih géi·sí dāk·hàahn a? /Are you free now? Néih yìh·gā dāk·hàahn meih a? /No, I'm busy. Ngóh yìh·gā m̀h·dāk· hàahn. /Yes, I am. Ngóh yìh·gā dāk·hàahn la.
    (without cost) sung (ge), m̀h·sái·chín. /This is a free sample. Nī·go haih báan, haih sung·béi néih ge. /This is free of charge. Nī·go m̀h·sái chín.
    free from   /He is free from trachoma. Kéuih móuh sà·ngáahn.
    free to; feel free to   /He's free to eat anything he wants. Kéuih jùhg·yi sihk māt yéh dōu dāk. /He's free to leave at any time. Kéuih jùng·yi géi·sìh jáu dōu dāk. /Please feel free to tell me what you honestly think. Chéng néih jihk·baahk góng béi ngóh jí néih ge yi·gin.
    free education yih·mouh gaau·yuhk; **free port** jih·yàuh·góng; **free translation** yihk· yi

freedom   jih·yàuh; **freedom of speech** yìhn·leuhn jih·yàuh; **freedom of thought** sí·séung jih·yàuh; **freedom of work** gùng·jok jih·yàuh; **freedom of religion** seun·gaau jih·yauh; **freedom of the press** chēut·báan jih·yàuh

freeze   (congeal) git·bìng, git·maaih, kîhng·maaih. /Water will freeze when it gets cold enough. Séui duhng dāk gán·yiu jauh git·bìng ge la. **freezing point** git·bìng·dím

freight   (goods) fo (M: dī; pài, shipment); (charge for transport) séui·geuk, joi·geuk

French   (in general) Faat·gwok (ge) (At); (people) Faat·gwok·yàhn; (language) Faat·gwok· wá

frequent   (often) sìh·sìh, jàu·sìh; (often go to) sìh·sìh heui

fresh   sān·sìn; **fresh water** táahm séui

friction   mòh·chaat

Friday   láih·baai·ńgh

fried   (deep fried) ja, jaau; (sautéd) cháau; **fried rice** cháau·faahn

friend   pàhng·yáuh

friendless   móuh·pàhng·yáuh, gū·dàan

friendly   hóu·sèung·yúh, hóu·pàhng·chîhng (loyal to a friend). /He is very friendly. Kéuih hóu hóu·sèung·yúh ge.

friendship   gàau·chîhng, yáuh·yìh

frighten   haak; gèng. /Don't frighten him. M̀h·hóu haak kéuih. /Don't be frightened. M̀h·sái gèng.

frightful   hó·pa (ge), dāk·yàhn·gèng (ge); **frightful noise** chouh dāk hóu gāau·gwàan. /There was a frightful noise. Dòng·sìh chòuh dāk hóu gāau·gwàan.

frigid   (unfeeling) láahng·daahm

fringe   (as on a drapery, etc.) seui

frivolous   hèng·fàuh

fro   **to and fro** lòih heui, lòih wóhng

frog   tìhn·gāi (M: jek) (edible); gaap·ná (M:jek) (inedible) from   hái, yàuh. /Where did you come from just now? Néih (jing·wah) hái bīn·syu lèih a? /Where do you come from? Néih hái bīn·syu lèih ga? or expressed as Of what place are you from? Néih haih bīn·syu yàhn a? /Choose any one from those three. Yàuh (or hái) nī·sàam·go léuih·bihn gáan yāt·go. /Look out from here. Yàuh (or hái) nī·syu mohng·chēut·heui. /Why don't you go from here? Dím·gáai néih m̀h yàuh (or hái) nī·syu heui nē? /I got it from the corner store. Ngóh hái gāai·gok gó·gàan pou·táu máaih ge.

    (of distance) yàuh; lèih. /How far is it from here to there? Yàuh nī·syu heui gó·syu yáuh géi yúhn a? or Nī·syu lèih gó·syu yáuh géi yúhn a? /Do you live far from school? Néih jyuh dāk lèih hohk·haauh hóu yúhn àh?

    (of gifts, mail, etc.) /That's from school. Hohk·haauh sung·lèih (sent) ge. or Hohk·haauh gei·lèih (mailed) ge. /This is from me. Nī·go haih ngóh sung·béi néih ge. /I got a letter from my elder brother. is expressed as Ngóh sàu·dou (received) ngóh a·gō yāt·fùng seun. /I got it from him. is expressed as Haih kéuih béi (give) ngóh ge. or Hái kéuih·syu dāk·lèih ge.

    (as a result of) yàn·waih . . . só·yíh . . . /He suffers from high blood pressure. Yàn·waih kéuih hyut·ngaat gòu só·yíh m̀h·jih·yìhn. /He got the cold from exposure in the rain. Yàn·waih kéuih dahp·chàn só·yíh láahng·chàn.

    (in defining limits of number) yàuh . . . ji . . . /This classroom is for the use of children from eight to twelve years old. Nī·gàan fo·sāt haih béi yàuh baat·seui ji sahp·yih·seui ge sai·mān·jái yuhng ge.

    from beginning to end yàuh tàuh ji méih; **from door to door** juhk gāan fóng gám; **from every point of view** chùhng gok fòng·mihn lèih tái; **from house to house** juhk gàan ngūk gám; **from this time on** chùhng·gàm·yíh·hauh

front   chìhn·bihn. /I want a room in the front. Ngóh yiu gàan hái chìhn·bihn ge fóng. /A big crowd is standing in front of the post office. Hóu·dò yàhn kéih·hái yàuh·jing·gūk chìhn·bihn.

    in front of (people) hái . . . mihn·chìhn. /Don't say that in front of him. Hái kéuih mihn·chìhn m̀h·hóu góng nī·gihn sih. /It's right in front of you. Jauh hái néih mihn·chìhn jē.

    front door chìhn·mún (M: douh); **front tooth** mùhn·ngàh (M: jek); **the front** (mil.) chìhn·sin

frontier   bìn·gaai, bìn·gíng

frost   (hoar) sòng; **frost falls** lohk·sòng

frown   jau·héi mèih·tàun

frozen   **frozen foods** láahng·chòhng ge (or syut·chòhng ge) sihk·maht

frugal   hàan(·gihm). /He is very frugal. Kéuih hóu hàan (or sīk hàan) ge.

fruit   sàang·gwó; **fruit juice** gwó·jāp; **fruit stall** sàang·gwó·dong

fry   (sauté) cháau; (with little oil) jìn; (with a lot of oil) jaau, ja; **fry eggs** cháau·dáan (scrambled), jìn·daan (sunny side up); **fried rice** cháau·faahn; **frying pan** wohk

fuel   (firewood) chàaih; (any substance) yìhn·liuh

fulfill   **fulfill one's promise** wah·gwo gám jauh gám, sáu seun, sáu yeuk. /He always fulfills his promise. Kéuih wah·gwo gám jauh gám ge la. **fulfill one's wish** muhn·jūk . . . yuhn·mohng; **fulfill one's duty** jeuhn . . . jīk·jaak

full   (containing many) dou·syu·dōu·haih. /Hong Kong is full of people. Hèung·góng dou·syu·dōu·haih yàhn.

    (filled). /We still have a full bottle of wine. Ngóh·deih juhng yáuh sèhng jèun jáu. /I'm full, I can't eat any more. Ngóh sihk·báau la, Ngóh m̀h·sihk·dāk·lohk la.

    (as in a hotel) /No vacancy. Jyuh·múhn la. or Móuh·fóng la. Full house. Múhn·joh. or Móuh·wái la.

full moon yuht·yùhn; **full name** sing·mìhng; **full powers** chyùhn·kyùhn; **full session** chyùhn·tái daaih·wúi; **full text** chyùhn màhn

fully **fully paid** béi·saai la; **fully satisfied** sahp·fàn múhn·yi

fun /Fishing is a lot of fun. Diu·yú hóu hóu·wáan. /We had a lot of fun. Ngóh·deih wáan dāk hóu tung·faai (or hóu gwo·yáhn).

function (of an organ) yuhng·chyúh, gùng·yuhng, jok·yuhng

fund (capital) gēi·gām; **raise funds** chàuh·fún

fundamental (basal) gàn·bún·seuhng ge (must be followed by a noun); (essential) jyú·yiu· ge

funeral **funeral affairs** sòng·sih; **funeral rites** sòng·láih; **funeral service** hòi·diu (traditional Chinese service), jèui·douh·wúi; **attend a funeral procession to the grave** sung· ban

fungus (from trees, edible) muhk·yíh

funnel (for pouring liquids) lauh·dáu; (smokestack) yīn·tùng

funny hóu·siu, dāk·yi

fur (pelt) péi

furious hóu nàu; (violent) máahng·lihk

furl gyún·màaih

furlough yàuh·ga

furnish (supply) gūng·kāp; (equip) chit·beih. /Is the house furnished? Gāan ngūk lìhn m̀h·lihn gā·sî a?

furniture gā·sî (M: gihn, a piece; tou, a set)

furthermore juhng yáuh, yìh·ché

fuse fīu·sî, bóu·hím·sī (M: tìuh); yùhng (V)

fuss /Don't make a big fuss about it. M̀h·hóu daaih·gèng·síu·gwaai.

fussy dò·sih. /Don't be so fussy. M̀h·hóu gam·dò sih.

future (time to come) jèung·lòih; (prospect) chìhn·tòuh; **future events** jèung·lòih ge sih; **future generations** hauh·doih

G

gain (obtain) dāk (·dóu). /What does he gain by doing that? Kéuih gám yéung jouh wúih dāk·dóu dī māt·yéh nē?

(make profit) wán·dóu. /How much did he gain last year? Gauh·nín kéuih wán·dóu géi·dò chín a?

Galatians Gà·làai·taai·syù

gale daaih·fùng

gall dáam

gallant (brave) yúhng·gáam

gallery **art gallery** méih·seuht·gún, méih·seuht·jín·láahm·sāt

gallon gā·léun

gamble dóu·chín, dóu·bok

gambling   dóu·chìn, dóu·bok; **gambling house** dóu·gún, dóu·chèuhng

game   (contest) is usually expressed in Chinese by a verb-object form of the specific game such as: play cards, dá·páai; play chess, juk kéih; play tennis, dá·móhng·kàuh, etc. The term 'yauh·hei' is used, but rather limitedly. /That's a good game for the children. Nī·go deui sai·màn·jái haih yāt·júng hóu hóu ge yàuh·hei.

   a game chi, chèuhng (ball game), pùhn (chess only). /We have time for one more game. Ngóh·deih hó·yíh joi wáan yāt·chi.

   win or lose a game, yèhng (win), syù (lose)
   Olympic games sai·gaai·wahn·duhng·wúi

gang   dóng

gangplank   tiu·báan

gap   (opening) la

garage   chē·fòhng

garbage   laahp·saahp

garden   fà·yún; **gardener** fā·wòhng

gargle   nóng·háu (V)

garlic   syun·tàuh, syun·jí

garment   (clothes) yì·fuhk, sāam·fu

garoupa   (fish) sehk·bàan·yú (M: tìuh)

garrison   jyu·gwān

gas   gē·sí, mùih·hei; **gas cooker** gē·sí·lòuh; **gas lamp** mùih·hei·dāng; **gas mask** fòhng·duhk·mihn·geuik

gasoline   dihn·yàuh; **gasoline station** dihn·yàuh·jaahm

gasp   chyún, chyúhn·hei

gate   daaih·mùhn; **gate of a walled city** sèhng·mùhn

gather   **gather flowers** jaahk·fā; **gather fruits** jaahk·gwó; **gather together** jeuih·jaahp

gauge   lèuhng, dohk (V); yìh·hei (N)

gauze   sà; (med.) sà·bou

gay   (merry) faai·wuht; (showy) leng, wài

gaze   tái·saht

gazette   hin·bou

gem   bóu·sehk

gendarme   hin·bìng

gender   (gram.) sing

genealogy   **genealogy of a clan** juhk·póu; **genealogy of a family** gà·póu

general   (not local or particular) póu·tùng (ge), pìhng·sèuhng (ge), yāt·bùn (ge). /This is not a book for specialists; it's for the general reader. Nī·bún syù mh·haih waih jyūn·gā yuhng ge, jí·haih waih póu·tùng yàhn yuhng ge. /What he has been doing is not understood by the people in general. Yāt·bùn yàhn mh·mìhng·baahk kéuih dou·dái jouh·gán māt·yéh.

   (of everyone) daaih·gā ge. /The general opinion is that he is right. Daaih·gā ge yi·gin dōu yihng·wàih kéuih ngāam.

in general daaih·tái·seuhng lèih tái, daaih·tái·seuhng lèih góng. /In general, the outlook is bright. Daaih·tái·seuhng lèih·tái, chìhn·tòuh lohk·gùn.

general outline daaih·gōng. /Can you write a general outline for me? Néih hó·yíh sé go daaih·gōng béi ngóh ma?

a general jeung·gwàn (collective term), jēung·gwàn (individual); **major general** siu·jeung; **lieutenant general** jùng·jeung; **general** (full) seuhng·jeung
   (of the civil service and civilian organizations) may be expressed by júng or -jéung.
consul general júng·líhng·sí; **general agent** júng·doih·léih; **general manager** júng·gìng·léih; **secretary general** bei·syū·jéung, júng·gon·sí

general aspects yāt·bùn ge chìhng·yìhng; **general assembly** daaih·wúi; **general attack** júng·gūng·gīk; **general average** júng·pìhng·gwàn; **general condition** yāt·bùn ge chìhng·yìhng; **general idea** daaih·yi; **general meeting** daaih·wúi; **general staff** chàam·màuh; **general store** jaahp·fo·póu; **general strike** júng·bah·gùng

generally   yāt·bùn·lèih·góng

generate   **generate electricity** faat·dihn

generation   (step in genealogy) doih, sai·doih

generator   faat·dihn·gèi

generous   (noble) daaih·leuhng; (not mean or stingy) kóng·koi; **generous minded** daaih·fòng

Genesis   Chòng·sai·géi

Genghis Khan   Sìhng·gāt·sî·hon

genial   wàn·wòh

genie   sàhn·sīn

genital organ   sàng·jihk·hei

genius   tìn·chòih

gentle   (mild) wàn·wòh, wàn·yàuh; (well mannered) sî·màhn

gentleman   (as distinguished from lady) sīn·sàang; (well-bred) sî·màhn·yàhn. Gentle-men! Gok·wái sīn·sàang!

gently   (lightly) hehng·hēng·déi; (slowly) maahn·māan·déi

genuine   (not false) jàn·ge

geography   deih·léih

geology   deih·jāt·hohk

geomancy   fùng·séui

geometry   géi·hòh

germ   (of a disease) behng·kwán; (microbe) meih·sàng·maht; (bacillus) sai·kwán

German   Dāk·gwok (ge); (people) Dāk·gwok·yàhn; (language) Dāk·gwok·wá (spoken), Dāk·màhn (written)

Germany   Dāk·gwok

germinate   faat·ngàh

gesticulate   jouh·sáu·sai

gesture   (with the hand) sáu·sai

get   (obtain or acquire) ló. /Can you get a pencil for me? Néih hó·yíh ló jî yùhn·bāt lèih béi ngóh ma?

(fetch a person). /Go and get him. Heui giu (or chéng, more polite) kéuih lèih nī·
syu.

(find, as a job; reach, as a person by phone). /Did he get a job? Kéuih wán·dóu sih
(or gūng for manual work) meih a?

get a disease, yihm·dóu. /How did he get this disease? Kéuih dím·yéung yihm·dóu
nī·go behng ga?

get plus an adjective or expression of action. /She got sick. Kéuih behng·jó. /Who
got hurt? Bīn·go sèung·jo a? /Why are you getting thinner? Dím·gáai néih yuht leih
yuht sau a? /Do you get tired very easily? Néih haih m̀h·haih hóu yùhng·yih guih a?
/My feet got wet. Ngóh sèung geuk sāp·jó. /He got a cold, it's nothing.serious. Kéuih
sèung·fūng jē, móuh sih ge.

get something wet, dirty, etc. /Don't get yourself wet! M̀h·hóu jing·sāp go sàn!
/Don't get your dress dirty! M̀h·hóu jíng·laaht·taat gihn sāam.

get to a place, heui·dou. /How can we get to the railroad station? Ngóh·deih dím·
yéung hó·yíh heui·dou fó·chè·jaahm a? /I have to get there by five o'clock. Ngóh ńgh·
dím·jūng yāt·dihng yiu heui·dou gó·syu.

get together sèung·jeuih, jeuih·wuih. /How about getting together at my house tonight? Gàm·maahn hái ngóh ngūk·kéi sèung·jeuih hóu ma?

get up héi·sàn. /What time do you get up in the morning? Néih jìu·tàuh·jóu géi
dím·jūng héi·sàn a?

get in yahp·lèih. /How did he get in? Kéuih dím·yéung yahp·lèih ga?

get out. /Get the dog out of here. Gón jek gáu chēut·heui. /I saw three men get
out of the car. Ngóh tái·gin sàam·go yàhn hái ga chè lohk·lèih.

get off. /I want to get off at the next stop. Ngóh hái daih·yih·go jaahm lohk·chè.

get away. /Can you get away for a few minutes? Néih hó·yíh hàahng·hòi yāt·jahn·
gāan ma? /No, I'm very busy. Ngóh m̀h·hàahng·dāk·hòi, Ngóh hóu m̀h·dāk·hàahn.

get the idea. /Do you get the idea? Néih mìhng·baahk meih a? No, I don't. Ngóh
m̀h·mìhng·baahk.

get something off jíng·lāt. /Can you get it off? Néih hó·yíh jíng·lāt kéuih ma?

get a sun-stroke jung·syú; **get angry** nàu·héi·séuhng·lèih; **get engaged** dihng·fàn;
get down or out from the car lohk·chè; **get drunk** yám·jeui; **get fat** faat·fūk; **get hold
of** wán·dóu; **get married** git·fàn; **get ready** jéun·beih·hóu; **get rich** faat·chòih; **get
rusty** sàang·sau; **get sick** behng, sàang·behng; **get smallpox** chēut·dáu, chēut tīn·fà;
get sores sàang·chōng; **get well again** hóu·fàan

ghost   gwái

giant   (tall fellow) gòu lóu; (person of great stature) geuih·yàhn

giddy   tàuh·wàhn

gift   (a present) láih·maht (M: gihn); (talent) tìn·chòih; **a gifted musician** yàm·ngohk
tìn·chòih

giggle   siu

gild   douh·gām: **gilded** douh·gām ge

ginger   gēung, gèung: **preserved ginger** tòhng·gēung

ginseng   yàhn·sàm

giraffe   chèuhng·géng·lúk (M: jek)

girdle   (worn round the waist) yìu·daai, yìu·dáai

girl   néuih·jái; síu·jé, gù·nèuhng (all mean especially young lady); néui. /Who is that
girl? Gó·go néuih·jái haih bīn·go a? /That girl is Miss Chan. Gó·go néuih·jái haih
Chàn síu·jé. /Is it a boy or a girl? Haih jái behng néui a? It's a girl. Haih néui.

girls' school néuih (·jí) hohk·haauh; **girl student** néuih hohk·sāang

give   (generally) béi; (as a present) sung. /Who gave you this? Nī·go haih bīn·go béi néih ga? /It was given me by my mother. Haih ngóh màh·mā béi ngóh ge. /Give me a cup of tea. Béi bùi chàh ngóh. /Give him something to eat. Béi dī yéh kéuih sihk. /What did you give her for her birthday? Néih sung·jó dī māt·yéh béi kéuih jouh sàang·yaht a? /Can you give him a job? Néih hó·yíh béi gihn sih kéuih jouh ma?
     The meaning of 'give' is not used at all in some translations, such as: /Give him an injection. Tùhng kéuih dá háu jām. /We are planning to give him a birthday party. Ngóh·deih dá·syun tùhng kéuih jouh sàang·yaht. /We are planning to give him a fare-well party. Ngóh·deih dá·syun tùhng kéuih jihn·hàhng.
     give back béi·fàan, wàahn·fàan·béi. /Have you given it back to him? Néih béi·fàan kéuih meih a? /Don't forget to give it back to me. Gei·jyuh béi·fàan ngóh.
     give birth to sàang. /She gave birth to a baby boy. Kéuih sàang·jó go jái.
     give in yihng·syù. /He never gives in. Kéuih wíhng m̀h·yihng·syù ge.
     give up m̀h·jai la, sāu·fò la, syun·sou la. /I give up. Ngóh m̀h·jai la.
     give a hand bòng. /Give him a hand. Bòng·háh kéuih.
     give a light. /Will you give me a light? Je go fó, dāk ma? or Yáuh fó·chái ma? (Do you have a match?)
     give a hint béi go ngam·houh; **give a signal** béi go seun·houh; **give a thought** séung·háh; **give alms** sí·sé; **give free medical treatment to the poor** sí·yì; **give him my best regards** tùhng ngóh mahn·hauh kéuih; **give it to someone personally** dòng·mihn gàau béi kéuih; **give up smoking** gaai·yīn

glad   fùng·héi. /I'm glad to see you. Hóu fùng·héi gin·dóu néih.

gland   sin: **thyroid gland** gaap·johng·sin

glare   sím: **glaring light** sím·gwòng

glass   (substance) bō·lēi; (drinking vessel) bō·lēi·būi; **glasses** (spectacles) ngáahn·géng (M: fu); **a glass of** yāt·bùi. /Please give me a glass of water. Chéng néih béi (yāt) bùi séui ngóh.

glide   **glide down** sin·lohk·lèih, waaht·lohk·lèih; **glider** waaht·chèuhng·gēi

glitter   sím·sím·há: **glittering** sim·sim·há ge

globe   (planet) deih·kàuh; (teaching aid) deih·kàuh·yíh

gloomy   (of a person) sàuh·muhn

glorify   jaan meih: **glorify God** jaan·méih Seuhng·daih

glorious   wìhng·yiuh

glory   gwòng·wìhng, wìhng·yiuh

glossy   gwōng·waaht

glove   sáu·māt, sáu·tou (M: fu, pair; jek, single)

glucose   pòuh·tòuh·tóng

glue   gàau (N); chi·jyuh (V); **glue it back** chi·fàan kéuih

glutton   daaih·sihk·wòhng, faahn·túng

gluttonous   waih·sihk (ge)

glycerine   gàm·yàuh

go   (purpose of going) heui. /Where are you going? Néih heui bīn·syu a? /I'm going to see a friend, I'll be back at eleven o'clock. Ngóh heui taam yāt·go pàhng·yáuh, sahp·yāt dím·jūng jauh fàan·lèih. /Let's go for a walk. Ngóh·deih chēut·heui hàahng háh, hóu ma? /Is he going? Kéuih heui m̀h·heui a? /No, he won't go. Kéuih m̀h·heui. /Go and ask him where he wants to go. Heui màhn·háh kéuih séung heui bīn·syu. /He says he wants to go swimming. Kéuih wah kéuih séung heui yàuh·séui. /Go and see whether there are lotus flowers for sale. Heui tái·háh yáuh móuh lìhn·fà maaih. /How about going out to dinner with us? Tùhng·màaih ngóh·deih yāt·chái heui sihk·faahn, hóu ma? /She went from America to England. Kéuih hái Méih·gwok heui·jó Yìng·gwok. /When did he go to America? Kéuih géi·sí heui Méih·gwok ga? /He went two years ago. Kéuih léuhng·nìhn chìhn heui ge.

(indicating direction) -heui. /Go upstairs and see whether she is there? Séuhng· heui làuh·seuhng tái·háh kéuih hái mh·hái·syu. /He went downstairs just a minute ago. Kéuih ngāam·ngāam lohk·jó·heui làuh·hah. /Go out and see it. Chēut·heui tái·háh. /Can we go in and see it? Ngóh·deih hó·yíh yahp·heui tái·háh ma?

(leave) jáu, ché. /It's time to go. Ngóh·deih hóu jáu la boh. /Let's go. Jáu la. /Has he gone? Kéuih ché·jó meih a? No, he hasn't. Juhng meih ché.

(walk or drive) hàahng. /Who goes first? Bīn·go hàahng sìn a? (the same sentence is used for 'whose car goes first?') /You go first. Néih hàahng sìn. /Go straight ahead and you'll be there. Néih yāt·jihk hàahng jauh dou la.

(be done away with, finished, spent, sold) /All the headaches (fig.) are gone. Gáau· dihm·saai la. /The brandy is all gone. Dī Baahk·làan déi yám·saai la. /All my money will be gone by the end of this month. Ngóh dī chín nī·go yuht·dái jauh sái·saai la. /The pain is gone. Mh·tung la. or Yíh·gìng jí (stopped) tung la.

going to do something yiu. /We are going to build a church here. Ngóh·deih yiu hái nī·syu héi yāt·gàan gaau·tòhng. /We are also going to build a hospital and a school here. Ngóh·deih yihk yiu hái nī·syu héi yāt·gàan yī·yún, yāt·gàan hohk·haauh.

go ahead (polite). Chíngchíng. (You first.) meaning you may do it is expressed by the specific verb required. /Go ahead (and eat). Sihk lā. Go ahead (and talk). Góng lā. /I'll go ahead then. Gám, Ngóh jauh gám jouh la. (I'll go ahead to do as we agreed.)

go by means of chóh. /How do we go there? By boat or by train? Ngóh·deih dím· yéung heui a? Chóh syùhn heui, yīk·waahk chóh fó·chè heui a? /We'll go by plane. Ngóh·deih chóh fēi·gèi heui.

go around fàn. /Do we have enough to go around? Ngóh·deih nī·dī yéh gau mh·gau fàn a?

go into business jouh·sàang·yi. /Are you planning to go into business? Néih haih mh·haih dá·syun jouh·sàang·yi a?

go on (continue) gai·juhk·lohk·heui. /I can't go on like this. Ngóh gám gai·juhk·lohk· heui mh·dāk. /What's going on here? Māt·yéh sih a? or Jouh māt·yéh a?

go over, go through (to check). /Let's go over this carefully once. Ngóh·deih joi chēk yāt·chi.

go to (attend). /What school do you go to? is expressed as Néih hái bīn·gàan hohk· haauh duhk·syù a? (lit. You at which school study.)

go to bed. /It's time to go to bed. Hóu fan·gaau la.

go up (in price) héi·ga. /The price went up again? Yàuh héi·gà làh?

let go (release). /Don't let go of the rope! Mh·hóu fong·hòi tìuh síng a!

go abroad heui ngoih gwok; **go again** joi heui; **go alone** jih·géi yāt·go yàn heui; **go along well** hóu seuhn·leih; **go and get it** heui ló; **go and return at once** jīk·hak heui jīk·hāk fàan; **go ashore** séuhng ngohn; **go astray** dohng sāt louh; **go at once** jīk·hāk heui; **go back** fàan·heui; **go back on one's word** móuh·háu·chí (lit. no mouth and teeth); **go-between** jūng gāan yàhn; gìng·géi (broker), mùih·yán (matchmaker); **go by** haang· gwo, ging·gwo (pass); **go down** lohk·heui; **go downstairs** lohk·láu; **go fast** hàahng faai·dì; **go first** hàahng sìn; **go for a walk** chēut·heui hàahng·háh; **go home** fāan ngūk· kéi; **go in** yahp·heui; **going to rain** jauh·lèih lohk·yúh; **going mad**: /I'll go mad if things don't improve soon. Yùh·gwo juhng haih gám, ngóh jauh yiu sàhn·gìng ge la. **go near** hàahng·màaih; **go on board a boat** séuhng syùhn; **go on duty** séuhng·bāan; **go out** chēut· heui; **going out and coming in** chēut·yahp; **going out into the street** chēut·gāai (for a walk, shopping, etc.); **going away for a trip** chēut mùhn; **going out** (to meet a guest), yìhng·jip; **go over** tái, duhk (read); **go over** wàn·jaahp (review); **go slowly** maahn·māan hàahng; **go straight on** yāt·jihk heui; **go this way** yàuh nī·douh heui; **go through** gìng·

gwo, tùng gwo·heui; **go to** heui; **go to a foreign country** heui ngoih·gwok; **go to heaven** séuhng tìn·tòhng; **go to hell** lohk deih·yuhk; **go to meet** heui jip; **go to the restroom** heui chi·só; **go to school** fàan·hohk, séung·hohk; **go to sleep** heui fan·gaau; **go up** séuhng·heui; **go up by foot** hàahng·séuhng·heui; **go upstairs** séuhng·láu; **go to the w.c.** heui chi·só; **go with** tùhng·màaih heui; **go with me** tùhng·màaih ngóh heui; **go wrong** gáau·cho·jo. /Don't let it go wrong. Mh·hóu gáau·cho·jo.

goal   (of ambition) muhk·bīu; (of a race) jùng·dím; (of the soccer game) kàuh·mùhn

goat   sàan·yèuhng, yèuhng·mē (M: jek); **goat's milk** yèuhng·náaih

god   (deity) sàhn, sahn·sīn; **goddess** néuih sàhn; **godfather** gaau·fuh, kài·yèh; **godmother** gaau·mouh, kài·mā

God   (common Protestant term) Seuhng·dai; (Roman Catholic term) Tìn·jyú

godown   fo·chōng

gold   gām, wòhng·gàm: **gold bar** gam tíu; **gold bracelet** gām·ngāak; **gold chain** gām lín; **gold coin** gām·chín; **gold mine** gām kwòng; **gold ring** gām·gaai·jí

golden   gām ge, gàm·wòhng·sīk ge: **golden age** wòhng gām sìh doih; **golden color** gām·sīk ge, gàm·wòhng·sīk ge; **golden image** gām·jeuhng; **golden opportunity** daaih hóu gèi·wuih; **golden wedding** gām·fàn

goldfish   gàm·yú (M: tìuh)

goldsmith   (store) gām·póu

golf   gòu·yíh·fū·kàuh

gong   lòh (M: mihn)

good   (of outstanding quality) hóu. /He's a very good child. Kéuih nī·go sai·màn·jái hóu hóu. /Is this a good watch? Nī·go haih mh·haih hóu bīu a? /You are a good teacher. Néih haih yāt·go hóu sīn·sàang.
    (referring to persons as good in a certain profession, field, or way of life) /He's a good cook. Kéuih hóu wúih jyú·sung. /She's a good amah (for taking care of children). Kéuih hóu wúih chau sai·màn·jái. /He's a good teacher. Kéuih hóu wúih gaau·syù.
    (referring to persons in their treatment of others). /She's very good with children. Kéuih doih sai·màn·jái hóu hóu. /He has always been good to his students. Kéuih doih kéuih dī hohk·sàang géi·sìh dōu haih gam hóu ge. /It's good of you to think of us. Dò·jeh néih sìh·sìh gwa·jyuh ngóh·deih.
    (referring to a specific object) /This medicine is good for you. Nī·jek yeuhk deui néih hóu hóu ge. /This is a good meal. Nī·chàan faahn jàn·haih hóu la.
    be good at. /Are you good at this sort of thing? Néih haih mh·haih jàn·haih wúih jouh nī·dī yéh a?
    for one's (own) good wàih . . . jih·géi ge hóu·chyúh. /This is for your own good. Nī·gō haih waih néih jih·géi ge hóu·chyúh.
    in greetings. /Good morning. Jóu·sàhn. /Good night. Jóu·táu. /Good-bye. Joi·gin.
    good appetite hóu waih·háu. /Have you had a good appetite today? Néih gàm·yaht waih·háu hóu ma?
    good boy gwàai·jái; **good deal** (a lot) hóu dò; **good doctor** hóu yī·sāng; **good figure** hóu sàn·chòih; **good for nothing** mouh·yuhng; **good for the price** jeuhk·sou, dái; **Good Friday** Yèh·sōu sauh·naahn·yaht; **good-hearted** hóu·sàm; **good looking** leng; **good luck** hóu wahn·chìhng; **good many** hóu dò; **good-natured** hóu pèih·hei; **good news** hóu sìu·sīk; **good opportunity** hóu gèi·wuih; **good time:** /Have a good time. Hóu·hóu·déi wáan·háh. /Did you have a good time? Wáan dāk géi hóu ma? **good to drink** hóu yám; **good to eat** hóu sihk; **good to look at** hóu tái; **good weather** hóu tìn

goods   fo, fo·maht

goose   ngó (M: jek); **goose feather** ngòh·mòuh

gorgeous   wàh·laih, tòhng·wòhng

gorilla   sīng·sīng (M: jek)

gospel   fūk·yām; (book) fūk·yām·syù; **preach the gospel** chyùhn fūk·yām

gossip   (ill-natured talk) sih·fèi; **to gossip** góng sih·fèi

gourd   gwā: **bottle gourd** wùh·lòuh·gwā; **winter gourd** dūng·gwà

govern   gún, gún·léih

government   (the governing body) jing·fú; (the act of governing) jing·jih; **government gazette** hin·bou (term used in Hong Kong); **government land** gùng·deih, wòhng·gā·deih (in Hong Kong); **government office** jing·fú·baahn·sih·chyúh; **government official** jing·fú·baahn·sih yàhn, gùng·mouh·yùhn (in the Republic of China); gùn (in colonies)

governor   (of a colony) júng·dūk; (of a province) sáang·jyú·jihk (as in Taiwan); **governor's residence** júng·dūk·fú (as in a colony)

gown   chèuhng·sāam; **nightgown** seuih·yī

grace   (refinement) sî·màhn, màhn·ngáh; (of God) yàn·dín; (prayer) kèih·tóu

graceful   daaih·fòng

gradation   dáng·kāp

grade   (class of things of one quality) dáng: **best grade** sèuhng·dáng; **medium grade** jùng·dáng; **low grade** hah·dáng
    (class in school) nìhn·kāp, nìhn·bāan. /What grade do you teach? Néih gaau géi nìhn·kāp a? /What grade is he in? Kéuih duhk géi nìhn·bāan a?
    grade in, grade into fàn, fàn sehng. /Grade these oranges into three sizes. Jēung dī cháang fàn·sèhng sāam·dāng.

gradually   maahn·māan gám

graduate   (as from a school) bāt·yihp: **graduate from a grammar school** síu·hohk bāt·yihp; **graduate from a high school** jùng·hohk bāt·yihp; **graduate from a college** (university) daaih·hohk bāt·yihp; **graduating class** bāt·yihp·bāan; **graduation ceremony** bāt·yihp(·dín)·láih

graft   bok·jī; **graft a tree** bok·syuh, bok·jī

grain   (cereal) ngh·gūk; **a grain of** yāt·nāp; **a grain of rice** yāt·nāp·máih, **a grain of sand** yāt·nāp·sà

grammar   màhn·faat

grammatical   màhn·faat·seuhng ge: **grammatical error** màhn·faat·seuhng ge chò·ngh

gramophone   làuh·sīng·gèi; **gramophone record** cheung·díp, cheung·pín

granary   máih·chōng

grand   **grandchild** syūn; **granddaughter** néuih·syūn (son's daughter), ngoih·syūn·néui (daughter's daughter); **grandfather** a·yèh (paternal), a·gùng (maternal); **grandmother** a·màh (paternal), a·pòh (maternal); **grandnephew** jaht·syūn; **grandniece** jaht·syūn·néui; **grandson** syūn (son's son); ngoih·syūn (daughter's son); **grand scale** daaih·kwài·mòuh

granite   màh·sehk

grant   (permit) jéun (V); **grant** (a petition) pài·jéun (V)

granulated   **granulated sugar** sà·tòhng

grape   pòuh·tàih·jí; **grape juice** pòuh·tàih·jāp; **grape wine** pòuh·tòuh·jáu

grasp   (with the hand) jà; (understand, learn) líuh·gáai, mìhng·baahk; **grasp firmly** jà·gán; **grasp the meaning** líuh·gáai, mìhng·baahk; **grasp the power of** jà·kyùhn

grass   chóu: **grass mat** chóu jehk (M: jèung)

grasshopper   máang (M: jek)

grateful   gáam·jeh, gáam·gīk. /I'm grateful to you for your help. Ngóh hóu gáam·gīk néih bòng joh·ngóh. or Ngóh fèi·sèunng gáam·gīk.

gratitude   gáam·jeh. /I don't know how to express my gratitude. Ngóh m̀h·jî dím·yéung gáam·jeh néih sìn·ji haih.

grave   (serious, of an affair) yìhm·juhng; (severe) yìhm·sūk; (tomb) fàhn·mouh; **grave-stone** mòuh·bèi; **graveyard** fàhn·chèuhng

gravel   sehk·jái

gravy   jāp

gray   fūi·sīk ge; **gray color** fūi·sīk

graze   (of cattle) sihk·chóu. /The cattle are grazing there. Dī ngàuh hái gó·syu sihk·gán chóu.

grease   yàuh (N); séuhng·yáu (V)

greasy   fèih·neih (ge), yàuh·meih (ge); **greasy spot** yáuh·jīk

great   daaih, wáih·daaih ge. /He's a great statesman. Kéuih haih yāt·go daaih (or wáih·dáaih ge) jing·jih·gā. /There's a great difference between these two men. Nī·léuhng·go yàhn yáuh hóu daaih ge fàn·biht.
      /Were you in great pain yesterday? Néih kàhm·yaht haih m̀h·haih tung dāk hóu gán·yiu a? /Isn't that great! Néih wah géi hóu a? /That's great news. Jàn·haih hóu la. /That's great! Hóu dou·gihk.
      great deal, great many hóu dò, daaih bá; **great reduction** daaih gáam ga (sale); **Great Wall** maahn·léih·chèuhng·sìhng; **the Great War** sai·gaai·daaih·jin

greediness   tāam·sàm

greedy   tāam·sàm, tàam; (for money) tàam chín; (for fame) tàam méng; (for food) waih sihk; (for drink) tàam yám

green   luhk ge, chèng ge; (unripe) sàang; **green color** luhk·sīk, chēng·sik; **green horn** sàang·sáu; **greens** chèng·choi

Greenwich time   sai·gaai·bìu·jéun·sìh·gaan

greet   mahn·hauh

grenade   sáu·làuh·dáan

grief   yàu·sàuh

grievance   yūn, yūn·wāt

grieve   yàu, yàu·sàuh

grill   sìu (V)

grind   (as coffee bean) mòh; **grind a knife** mòh·dōu; **grind Chinese ink** mòh·mahk; **grind it sharp** mòh leih kéuih; **grindstone** mòh·dōu·sehk

groan   ngàhng·ngáng·sèng. /Why is he groaning? Kéuih jouh·māt·yéh ngàhng·ngáng·sèng a?

grocery   jaahp·fo·póu (M: gàan)

grope   (feel) mó; **grope in the dark** màahng mó mó

gross   **gross amount** júng·gai; **gross weight** júng·leuhng

grotesque   (absurd) fòng·tòhng; (fantastic) gú·gwaai

ground   (earth) deih; (on the surface of the earth) deih·há; (authority, as for a statement) gàn·geui; (reason) léih·yàuh; (of painting, flag, etc.) dái; (foundation) gèi·chó; (of a ship) gok·chín; **ground floor** deih·há, làuh·hah

group   kwàhn, bàan: **a group of children** yāt·kwàhn (or bàan) sai·mān·jái

grove   syuh·làhm

grow   (become larger physically) daaih, jéung. /He is growing fast. Kéuih daaih dāk jàn·haih faai la! /He's growing taller and taller. Kéuih yuht jéung yuht gòu.
     (raise crops) jung. /What are you growing this year? Néih gàm·nín jung māt·yéh a? /He likes to grow roses. Kéuih jùng·yi jùng mùih·gwai·fā.
     grow a beard làuh sòu; **grow rusty** sàang sau; **grow sour** bin syùn; **grow to man-hood** sìhng yàhn; **grow up** jéung daaih. /Where did you grow up? Néih hái bīn·syu jéung daaih ga? **grow worse and worse.** /The situation grows worse and worse. Chìhng·yìhng yuht bin yuht wàaih.

grudge   **bear a grudge** wàaih·hahn

grumble   ngàhm·ngàhm·chàhm·chàhm

guarantee   dàam·bóu, bóu·jing. /I guarantee that there will be no trouble. Ngóh dàam·bou móuh sih. **guarantee to change** (as goods) bàau wuhn; **guarantee to cure** bāau yî

guarantor   dàam·bóu·yàhn

guard   (a person or place) hòn (jyuh); (a place only) bá·sáu; (protect) bóu·wuh; **guard against** tàih·fòhng. /Be always on guard against the devil. Yiu sìh·sìh tàih·fòhng mò·gwái.
     a guard (a person who guards) waih·déui, dá·sáu (bodyguard); waih·bìng (military); hòn·gàang·ge (watchman); **guard of honor** yìh·jeuhng·déui; **advance guard** chìhn·fūng; **rear guard** hauh·waih

guardian   gàam·wuh·yàhn, bóu·wuh·yàhn

guerrilla   yàuh·gīk·déui; **guerrilla warfare** yàuh·gīk·jin; **to fight guerrilla warfare** dá yàuh·gīk·jin

guess   gú, chàai; **guess a riddle** dá·go·gú, chàai·mái; **guess right** gú·jung; **guess wrong** gú·mh·jung; **guess fingers** (in a finger game) chàai·múi; **make a guess** gú·háh
     /Guess who it is. Gú·háh haih bīn·go. /Let me guess. Dáng ngóh gú·hah. /Let's see if you can guess. Tái néih gú mh·gú·dāk·dóu. /You guessed it! Néih gú·dóu (or gú·jung) la! /You guessed wrong. Néih gú·cho·jó.

guest   yàhn·haak. /How many guests did you invite? Néih chéng·jó géi·dò yàhn·haak a? **guest of honor** jyú·haak; **honored guest** gwai·bàn

guide   daai. /Please guide us to the bridge. Mh·gòi néih daai ngóh·deih heui douh kìuh·syu. **a guide** daai·louh·ge, héung·douh; **guidebook** léuih·hàhng·jí·nàahm; **guidebook to Hong Kong** Hèung·góng·jí·nàahm; **guidebook to Singapore** Sìng·ga·bō·jí·nàahm; **guide-post** louh·pàaih

guild   tùhng·yihp gùng·wúi

guilt   jeuih

guilty   yáuh jeuih. /He's guilty. Kéuih yáuh jeuih.

gulf   (bay) (hói·) wān

gulp   (swallow) tàn; **a gulp** yāt·daahm; **gulp down** tàn·lohk·heui

gum   (of the mouth) ngàh·yuhk; (glue) gàau·séui; **chewing gum** hèung·háu·gàau; **to gum with glue** nìhm, chì, tip

gun   (small arms) chēung (M: jī, hám); **machine gun** gēi·gwāan·chēung (M: hám); cannon, paau, daaih·paau (M: hám)

gunboat   paau·laahm (M: jek)

gunpowder   fó·yeuhk

H

habit   jaahp·gwaan: **good habit** hóu·(ge) jaahp·gwaan; **bad habit** m̀h·hóu (ge) jaahp·gwaan, waaih·jaahp·gwaan

Hades   yàm·gàan: **lord of Hades** yìhm·lòh·wòhng

hail   bohk (N); lohk·bohk (V); (salute) fūn·fù

hair   (on a human head) tàuh·faat. /I would like to have my hair cut shorter. Ngóh séung jín·dyún dī ngóh·ge tàuh·faat. /I want my hair washed. Ngóh yiu sái·tàuh (head). (on the rest of the body) hohn·mòuh, mòuh; (on animals) mòuh
    hairdresser léih·faat·sī; beauty parlor, méih·yùhng·yún; **hairnet** faat·móhng; **hairpin** faat·gíp

Hakka   (people) Haak·gà·yàhn; **Hakka dialect** haak·(gà) wá

half   **a half** yāt·bún, bun·go; **half of** bun-M; **NU and a half** Nu-M-bun. /I want this half Ngóh yiu nī·yāt·bun. /You can eat half of a watermelon? I don't believe it. Néih hó·yíh sihk bun·go sài·gwà? Ngóh m̀h·seun. /I lived there for two and a half years. Ngóh·hái gó·syu jyuh·jó léuhng·nìhn·bun.
    half a bottle bun·jèun; **half a century** bun·go sai·géi; **half a cup** bun·bùi; **half a dozen** bun·dā; **half a month** bun·go·yuht; **half a year** bun·nìhn; **half an hour** bun dím·jūng; **half and half** yāt·bun yāt·bun; **half asleep** bun·séng·bun·fan; **half boiled** bun·sàang·suhk ge; **half day** bun·yaht; **half dollar** bun·go ngàhn·chín, bun·mān; **half each** yāt·yàhn·yāt·bun; **half-mast** hah·bun·kèih; **half past one (o'clock)** yāt·dím·bun; **half past six** luhk·dím·bun; **half price** bun·ga; **half way** bun·lóu, bun·louh

hall   **dining hall** faahn·tòhng; **reception hall** haak·tēng; **lecture hall** góng·tòhng; **assembly hall** láih·tohng, wuih·chèuhng

halt   tìhng (·jí)

ham   fó·téui

hammer   chéui (N); dám (V)

hammock   diu·chòhng (M: jèung)

hamper   jó·ngoih

hand   (part of the body) sáu (M: jek). /Where can I wash my hands? Bĭn·syu hó·yíh sái·sáu a? /What's that in your hand? Néih sáu leuih·bihn jà·jyuh ge haih māt·yéh a?
    to hand daih·béi. /Will you please hand me the sugar. Mh·gòi néih daih dī tòhng béi ngóh. /Be sure to hand him the letter. Gei·jyuh gàau fùng seun béi kéuih.
    hand in gàau (·béi), chìhng·béi (to government or superior). /Have you handed in your report to Mr. Lee? Néih gàau·jó go bou·gou béi Léih sīn·sàang meih a? /Yes, I have. Ngóh gàau·jó la.
    by hand yuhng sáu. /Are these all done by hand? Nī·dī tūng·tūng haih yuhng sáu jouh gàh?
    hands off. /Hands off! Mh·jéun dau.

in hand, out of hand. /The situation is well in hand. Yeuhng·yeuhng dōu hóu seuhn·leih. /At that moment the situation in the theater was out of hand. Gó·jahn·sí sèhng·go hei·yún lyuhn·saai·luhng.

firsthand, secondhand jihk·jip; gaan·jip. /Is this firsthand information? Nī·go sīu·sīk haih m̀h·haih jīhk·jīp dāk·lèih ga? /No, it's secondhand information. M̀h·haih, haih gaan·jīp dāk·lèih ge. **firsthand material** jihk·jip chàam·háau jí·líu; **secondhand material** gaan·jip·chàam·háau·jí·líu. **secondhand goods** yih·sáu·fo; **secondhand store** haam·lāang·póu, gauh·fo·póu

(style of writing) bāt·jīk. /Is this signature in his hand? Nī·go chìm·jí, haih m̀h·haih kéuih ge bāt·jīk a?

on hand. /I've only a small amount on hand. Ngóh sáu·seuhng jí yáuh dò·sīu jē. /He's never on hand when I want him. Ngóh yiu yuhng kéuih ge sìh·hauh, kéuih wìhng m̀h·hái syu ge.

on the other hand chùhng lihng yāt·fòng·mihn lèih tái (look) or góng (speak). /As you say, he's a good man, but on the other hand he hasn't had much experience. Néih góng dāk móuh cho, daahn·haih chùhng lihng yāt·fòng·mihn lèih tái, kéuih móuh māt (yéh) gìng·yihm.

hand down (to posterity) chyùhn·lohk·béi ji·syùn; **hand over to** gàau·béi; **hand over to a successor** gàau·doih; **hand in hand** sáu·lāai·sáu; **hands off** (let go) fong·sáu; **hands up** géui sáu

handbag   sáu·dói

handbill   (pasted up) gāai·jīu, gou·baahk; (given out by hand) chyùhn·dāan

handbook   sáu·chaak (M: bún)

handcuffs   sáu·lìuh (M: fu)

handful   yāt·jah, yāt·jāp

hand grenade   sáu·làuh·dáan

handicap   fòhng·ngoih (V) & (N)

handicraft   sáu·gùng, sáu·gùng·ngaih

handiwork   sáu·gùng·jouh ge

handkerchief   sáu·gān·jái (M: tìuh)

handle   (shaft) beng; (of a cup, etc.) yíh; (take in the hand) nìng; **handle of a cup** būi·yíh; **handle of a hoe** chòh·táu·beng; **handle of a knife** dōu·beng

(manage, deal with). /Can you handle the situation? Néih gáau m̀h·gáau·dāk·dihm a? /Can you handle those students? Néih gáau m̀h·gáau·dāk·dihm gó·bàan hohk·saang a?

handrail   fùh·sáu

handsome   piu·leuhng

handwriting   sáu·bāt, bāt·jīk

handy   (conveniently near) fòng·bihn; (dexterous) dái·sáu ge

hang   (suspend) gwa, dèng. /Hang the picture here. Gwa·fūk wá hái nī·syu. /Why did they hang a lantern in front of the house? Kéuih·deih jouh·māt·yéh hái mùhn·háu gwà go dàng·lùhng a? /Hang it on the wall with a nail. Yuhng háu dēng dèng·hái buhng chèuhng·syu.

(naturally) dam. /The litchi fruits are like little lanterns hanging on the trees. Dī·laih·jī dam·hái syuh·seuhng hóu·chíh dàng·lùhng·jái gám.

hang on. /Hang on, don't let it go! Jà·gán kéuih m̀h·hóu fong·sáu!

hang up gwa·héi; sàu·sin (telephone). /Hang up your coat. Gwa·héi gihn daaih·lāu kéuih. /The other party has already hung up. Gó·tàuh yíh·gìng sàu·jó·sin la.

hanging (execution) gáau·yìhng; **hang one's self** díu·géng; **hang out a signboard** gwa·jìu·pàaih; **hang up to dry in the air** lohng. /Hang this dress up and dry it in the air. Lohng·héi nī·gihn sāam kéuih.

hanker   (long for) hahn; **hanker after wealth** hahn faat·chòih

happen   /What happened to you? Do you feel sick? Néih jouh·māt·yéh a? Néih m̀h·jìng·sàhn a? /What happened to this typewriter? Nī·go dá·jih·gèi jouh·māt·yéh a?
    (occur) /Were you there when the accident happened? Nī·gihn sih faat·sàng ge sìh·hauh néih joh·chèuhng ma? /How did it happen? Haih dím·yéung faat·sàng ga? /It happened this way. Haih gám·yéung faat·sàng ge. /How could such a thing happen? Dím wúih yáuh dī gám ge sih faat·sàng ge nē?
    happen to, happen that yùh·ngāam. /It happened that that day was my day off. Yùh·ngāam ngóh gó·yaht yīu·sīk. /It happened that that day was a holiday. Yùh·ngāam gó·yaht fong·ga. /I happened to be there when the accident happened. Gó·gihn sih faat·sàng ge sih·hauh ngóh ngāam·ngāam hái syu.

happiness   fūk·hei, fūk·fahn

happy   faai·lohk, fùng·héi, faai·wuht. /He's always happy. Kéuih géi·sìh dōu haih hóu faai·lohk ge. /This is the happiest day of my life. Gàm·yaht haih ngóh yāt·sàng jeui faat·lohk ge yaht·jí.
    Happy New Year! Gùng·héi·faat·chòih!; **happy occasion** héi·sih; **Many happy returns!** Maahn·sih·yùh·yi!

harass   sòu·yíuh (V)

harbor   (port) góng·háu, hói·hau; (conceal) sàu·chòhng; **harbor ill-feeling** wàaih·hahn·joih·sàm

hard   (not soft) ngaahng; (not easy) nàahn. /Is it hard? Nàahn m̀h·nàahn a? /It isn't hard at all. Yāt·dī dōu m̀h·nàahn. /It looks easy, but it's really quite hard. Tái·héi séuhng·lèih yùhng·yih, jouh·héi séuhng·lèih jauh nàahn la.
    (strenuous; diligent). /You have to work hard. Néih yāt·dihng yiu chēut·lihk jouh ji dāk. /He has to study hard, if he wants to be promoted. Yùh·gwó kéuih séung sīng·bāan yāt·dihng yiu kàhn·lihk duhk·syu ji dāk.
    hard of hearing yíh·lùhng. /You have to speak louder, because he's hard of hearing. Néih yiu daaih·sèng dī góng, kéuih yáuh dī yíh lùhng.
    hard to bear nàahn·dái, nàahn·sauh; **hard to believe** nàahn seun; **hard to deal with** hóu nàahn ying·fuh; **hard to do** nàahn jouh; **hard to explain** naahn gáai·sīk; **hard to find** naahn wán; **hard to get** naahn dāk; **hard to get over** ngàahn·gwo; **hard to say** nàahn góng; **hard to tell** nàahn góng, ngok góng; **hard to tolerate** nàahn yáhn

hardly   (scarcely) gán·gán: **hardly enough** gán·gán gau

hardship   gàan·nàahn, sàn·fú

hare   yéh·tou (M: jek)

harm   sèung·hoih (V)

harmful   yáuh·hoih. /This kind of thinking is harmful to the society. Nī·dī gam ge sī·séung deui séh·wúi yáuh·hoih.

harmonica   háu·kàhm

harmonious   (musically) wòh·hàaih; (cordial) wòh·muhk

harmonize   wòh·sìng

harmony   (musical) wòh·hàaih; (color) tîuh·wòh; (between persons) wòh·muhk; **in harmony** tîuh·wòh; (in action) yāt·ji

harsh   (rough) chòu, chòu·lóuh; (to touch) hàaih; (stern) yìhm·laih; **harsh words**   hāk· bohk syut·wah

harvest   sàu·sìhng; sàu·got (V); **harvest time**   sàu·got sìh·hauh; **good harvest**   fūng·sàu

haste   **in haste**   gāp·gāp·mòhng·mòhng gám (A); **make haste**   góng·gán. /I must make haste with my task.   Ngóh yiu gón·gán jouh ngóh ge gùng·jok.

hasten   gón·jyuh. /I must hasten back before night comes.   Ngóh yiu gón·jyuh tīn·hāk jì·chìhn fàan·lèih. /I must hasten to Macao.   Ngóh yiu gón·jyuh heui O·mún.

hasty   (of temper) gāp; (speedy) pàhn·làhn; (done without due deliberation) gáu·gáan

hat   móu (M: déng); **wear a hat**   daai·móu

hatch   bouh; **hatch chicks**   bouh gāi·jái

hatchet   fú·tàuh·jái

hate   (dislike) jàng; (with intense aversion) sàuh·hahn

hateful   hāk·yàhn·jàng, hó·wu

hatred   sàuh·hahn

haughty   gìu·ngouh, sà·chàhn

haul   **haul in**   làaih·màaih, làai·yahp; **haul up**   ché·héi, ché·gòu

haunted   yáuh·gwái; **a haunted house**   gwái·ngūk

have   (possess) yáuh. /Do you have any? Néih yáuh móuh a? /Do you have any more? Néih juhng yáuh ma? /What do you have in your hand? Néih sáu léuih·bihn yáuh māt· yéh a? /What do you have on your mind? Néih sàm leuih·bihn yáuh māt·yéh sih a?
    (describing physical condition or characteristics). /Do you have a headache? Néih tàuh tung ma? /I have a headache. Ngóh tàuh tung. /I have a slight headache. Ngóh yáuh dī tàuh tung. /I have a terrible headache. Ngóh tàuh tung dāk hóu gāau·gwàan. /He has large hands. Kéuih sèung sáu hóu daaih.
    Sometimes indirectly translated by other verbal expressions: /May I have one? Béi yāt·go ngóh, dāk ma? /Let me have a look. Béi ngóh tái·háh.
    (before a verb, indicating past time or completed action. ref. -jó, -gwo, in C-E section) /Have you read today's newspaper? Néih tái·jó gàm·yaht ge bou·jí meih a? /I haven't yet. Meih·tái. /I've read it. Tái·jo la. /Have you ever been to Taiwan? Néih yáuh móuh heui·gwo Tòih·wāan a? /Has he taken the medicine? Kéuih sihk·jó yeuhk mcih a? /Has he gone home? Kéuih fàan·jó ngūk·kéi meih a? /Yes, he has. Kéuih yih·gīng fàan·jó ngūk·kéi la. /He hasn't come for two weeks. Kéuih léuhng·go láih·baai móuh lèih la. /Have you finished your work? Néih jouh·yùhn meih a? /Have you found it yet? Néih wán·dóu meih a?
    (give birth to). /Is she going to have a baby? Kéuih haih m̀h·haih yáuh·jó sai·mān jái a?
    (experience). /I had a hard time buying it. Ngóh yuhng·jó hóu dò sìh·gaan sìn·ji máaih·dóu.
    (eat) sihk. /Have you had dinner yet? Néih sihk·jó faahn meih a? /Please have some more. Sihk dī tīm lā. /Let's have dinner at six, how about it? Luhk·dím·jūng sihk·faahn, hóu ma?
    have a word with. /May I have a word with you. Ngóh yáuh geui wá séung tùhng néih góng·háh.
    have in mind. /Do you have anyone in mind (for this job)? Néih sàm·muhk·jùng yáuh móuh bīn·go yàhn a?
    have to   sih·bīt yiu. /He has to sell his car before leaving here. Kéuih sih·bīt yiu màaih·jó ga chè sìn·ji lèih·hòi nī·syu. /Excuse me, I have to go now. Deui·m̀h jyuh, ngóh sih·bīt·yiu jáu la.

have a baby yáuh·jó sai·mān·jái, yáuh·jó sai·lóu·gō; **have a cold** sēung·fùng; **have a fever** faat·yiht, faat·sìu; **have a headache** tàuh tung; **have a holiday** fong ga; **have everything** māt yéh dōu yáuh; **have nothing to do with:** /It has nothing to do with him. Mh·gwàan kéuih sih. **have nothing to say** móuh dāk góng; **have pain** tung; **have acute pain** tung dāk hóu gāau gwàan; **have surplus** yáuh dò, yáuh yùh; **have the heart** to yáuh sàm yiu; **have the measles** chēut·má

hawk   ngàh·yīng (M: jek)

hawker   síu·fáan

hawthorn   sāan·jà

hay   gòn·chóu

hazardous   ngàih·hím (ge)

hazy   hàh·mouh (N). /Today is very hazy. Gàm·yaht hàh·mouh hóu daaih.

he   kéuih

head   (part of the body) tàuh, tàuh hok; **nod one's head** ngahp·táu; **shake one's head** nihng táu; **turn one's head** nihng jyún go tàuh
      (leader) gà·jéung (of a family), sìh·táu (employer), guhk jéung (of a bureau), fō·jéung (of a section of department), haih·jyú·yahm (of a department of college)
      (of workmen or an informal group) táu, tàuh·yàhn, (of bandits) chahk·táu
      head office júng·hóng, júng·dim; **head ornaments** sáu·sīk; **head wind** ngaahk·fùng

headache   tàuh tung. /I have a headache. Ngóh tàuh tung.

headlight   chē·tàuh·dāng (M: jáan)

headline   daaih·bìu·tàih

headquarters   (of political party, etc.) júng·bouh; (mil.) júng·sī·lihng·bouh

headstrong   ngaahng·géng

heal   yì; **healed** yì·hóu·jó, hóu·fàan la

health   gihn·hòng; **health department** wàih·sāng·gúk

healthy   (in good health) gihn·hòng, hòng·gihn

heap   dèui: **heap of refuse** yāt·dèui laahp·saap; **heap of firewood** yāt·dèui·chàaih; **heap it together** deui·màaih kéuih; **heap it up** deui·héi kéuih

hear   (simple perception) tèng·gin; (more clear perception) tèng·chìng·chó. /Did you hear anything? Néih tèng·gin māt·yéh héung ma? /Can you hear it? Néih tèng·dāk·gin ma? /Do you hear it? Néih tèng·gin ma? /No, I don't. Ngóh tèng·mh·gin. /Yes, I do. Ngóh tèng·gin la.
      hear that tèng·màhn·wah. /I hear that there will be no school tomorrow, is that true? Ngóh tèng·màhn·wah tìng·yaht fong·ga, haih mh·haih a?
      hear of tèng·gin·gwo. /Have you ever heard of such a thing? Néih tèng·gin·gwo gám ge sih ma? /I never heard of such a thing. Ngóh chùhng·lòih meih tèng·gin·gwo gám ge sih.

heart   (physical) sàm, sàm·johng. /He has a weak heart. Kéuih ge sàm sēung·dòng yeuhk. /He has heart disease. Kéuih yáuh sàm·johng·behng.
      (emotional) sàm. /She has a soft heart. Kéuih hóu chìh·sàm ge. /Don't lose heart. Mh·hóu fūi·sàm. /If you are going to do that you'll break your mother's heart. Yùh·gwó néih gám jouh, néih lóuh·móuh yāt·dihng fèi·sèuhng sēung·sàm.
      (central part) jūng·sàm. /The theater is in the heart of the city. Gó·gàan hei·yún hái sèhng·jūng·sàm.
      by heart nihm·suhk. /Learn this poem by heart. Nihm·suhk nī·sáu sī kéuih.

heat   yiht (seldom used as a noun except in scientific statements). /In July and August
the heat is quite intense. Chāt·yuht baat·yuht yiht dāk sēung·dòng leih·hoih.
(of a heating system) nyúhn·hei, fó·lòuh. /Is there any heat in this house? Nī·gāan
ngūk yáuh móuh nyúhn·hei ga?
to heat bòu·yiht, jíng·yiht. /Heat some water and give the baby a bath. Bòu·yiht dī
séui tùhng bìh·bī·jái sái·sàn. /Heat up the fish. Jíng·yiht dī yú kéuih.

heaven   (sky) tìn; (paradise of Christian belief) tìn·tòhng, tìn·gwok; (paradise of Buddhist belief) sāi·tìn, sāi·tìn·gihk·lohk·sai·gaai; **the heavens** tìn, tìn·hùng

heavenly   **heavenly body** tìn·tái; **Heavenly Father** Tìn·fuh

heavy   (of weight) chúhng. /Is it too heavy for you? Haih m̀h·haih taai chúhng a?
/How heavy is it? Yáuh géi chúhng a? /How heavy are you? Néih yáuh géi chúhng a?
heavy rain. /There was a heavy rain this morning. Gàm·jìu·jóu lohk·yúh lohk dāk
hóu daaih.
heavy burden fuh·dàam hóu chúhng; **heavy fine** faht dāk hóu chúhng; **heavily taxed**
chàu seui chāu dāk hóu chúhng

Hebrew   Hèi·baak·lòih: **Hebrew language** Hèi·baak·lòih·wá

hedge   (fence) lèih·bā

heel   geuk·jāang; **heel of a shoe** hàaih·jàang; **high-heeled shoe** gōu·jàang·hàaih

height   gòu·douh

heir   hauh·yàhn, hauh·doih; (leg.) sìhng·gai·yàhn

helicopter   jihk·sīng (·fēi)·gèi (M: ga)

hell   deih·yuhk

helm   tòh; **helmsman** tòh·gūng; **hold the helm** bá·táaih, bá·tòh

helmet   tàuh·fùi; **helmet and mail** fùi·gaap

help   (give assistance to) bòng, bòng·joh, bòng·sáu. /Can you help me to do this? Néih
hó·yíh bòng ngóh jouh nī·gin sih ma? /We should help each other. Ngóh·deih yiu wuh·
sèung bòng·joh. /Come and help! Faai·dī lèih bòng sáu!
(save) gau. /Help! Gau mehng a! /If the lifeguard hadn't come to help him, the boy
would have drowned. Yùh·gwó gau·sàng·yùhn m̀h·lèih gau kéuih, gó·go sai·mān·jái jauh
jahm·séi la.
(prevent) /Sorry, it can't be helped. Deui·m̀h·jyuh, móuh·faat·ji la. /She couldn't
help crying. Kéuih yáhn·m̀h·jyuh haam·héi·séuhng·lèih.
(serve) /Help yourself. Jih·gēi lèih la. or Jih bín la.
(persons who help) bòng·sáu (in general), gùng·yàhn (servant)
(assistance) bòng·joh, bòng·mòhng, gau·jai; or expressed verbally as in the first
paragraph above. /We need your help. Ngóh·deih sèui·yiu néih·deih ge bòng·joh.
/Thank you for your help. Dò·jeh néih bòng·mòhng. /The stricken area needs our immediate help. Jōi·kēui sèui·yiu ngóh·deih lahp·hāk gau·jai.

hem   (of a garment) kwán·tíu (N); kwán (V); kwán·bīn (VO)

hemisphere   bun·kàuh: **Eastern hemisphere** Dùng·bun·kàuh; **Western hemisphere** Sài·
bun kàuh

hemp   màh: **hemp cloth** màh·bou; **hemp rope** màh·síng (M: tìuh)

hen   (chicken) gài·ná (M: jek)

henceforth   chùhng·gàm·yíh·hauh

henpecked   pa·lóuh·pòh(·ge)

her   kéuih; (possessive) kéuih ge; **hers** kéuih·ge; **herself** kéuih jih·gēi

herb   chóu·yeuhk

herd   kwàhn: **a herd of cattle** yāt·kwàhn ngàuh; **to herd cattle** hòn·ngàuh; **herdboy** hòn· ngàuh·jái

here   (this place) nī·syu, nī·douh. /Come here. Lèih nī·syu (or nī·douh). /Here it is. Hái nī·syu. /Are we going to sit here? Ngóh·deih haih m̀h·haih chóh·hái nī·syu a? /Look here, see what I got! Tái·hah, tái·hah nī·go haih māt·yéh!

heretofore   dou·gà·jahn·wàih·jí

hereditary   (of property) jóu·chyùhn ge; (of rank) sai·jaahp ge; (of disease) wàih·chyùhn ge; **hereditary disease** wàih·chyùhn·behng

heredity   wàih·chyùhn, wàih·chyùhn·sing

heritage   wàih·cháan

hermit   yáhn·sih

hernia   síu·chèuhng·hei

hero   yìng·hùhng; (in romance, drama, etc.) nàahm·jyú·gok

heroin   hói·lohk·yīng

heroine   néuih·yìng·hùhng; (in romance, drama, etc.) néuih·jyú·gok

heroism   yìng·hùhng·jyú·yih; yìng·hùhng·hei·koi

heron   baahk·louh·chìh

hesitate   chàuh·chèuih, chàuh·chèui·bāt·kyut. /Don't hesitate. Mh·hóu·chàuh·chèuih la. /You shouldn't hesitate. Néih m̀h yìng·goi chàuh·chèuih·bāt·kyut.

hexagon   luhk·gok·yìhng

hiccup   dá·sí·īk

hide   (conceal) nì (·màaih) (a person); beng (·màaih) (a thing). /Where is he hiding? Kéuih nì·màaih hái bīn·syu a? /Where did you hide my pen? Néih beng·màaih ngóh jī bāt hái bīn·syu a? /It's hidden under the pillow. Beng·hái jám·tàuh·dái.
(keep from sight by an obstruction) jè·jyuh, dóng(·jyuh). /She hides her face behind a fan. Kéuih yuhng bá sin jè·jyuh go mihn. /The building hides the view of the harbor. Joh láuh dóng·saai hói·wāan ge fùng·gíng.

high   (by measurement) gòu. /Is that high enough? Gau gòu meih a? /How high do you want it? Néih yiu géi gòu a? /I want it ten feet high. Ngóh yiu sahp·chek gòu. /Can you hang it higher? Gwa gōu dī dāk m̀h·dāk a? /How high is today's temperature? Gàm·yaht ge wàn·douh yáuh géi gòu a? /Don't climb that high! M̀h·hou pàh gam gòu!
(of price) gòu, gwai. /The price is too high. Ga·chìhn taai gòu.
(of hopes) gòu. /Don't let your hopes fly too high. M̀h·hóu hèi·mohng dāk taai gòu.
be in high spirits gòu·hing. /Why is he in such high spirits today? Kéuih gàm·yaht dím·gáai gam gòu·hing a?
have a high opinion of pui·fuhk. /I have a high opinion of him. Ngóh hóu pui·fuhk kéuih.
(of speed) is expressed as fast faai. /How high a speed will this car reach? Nī·ga chè hó·yíh hàahng dāk géi faai a?
high blood pressure gòu hyut·ngaat. /He has high blood pressure. Kéuih hyut·ngaat gòu. **high class** gòu·dáng (ge), gōu·kāp (ge); **high court** gòu·dáng faat·yún; **high-heeled shoes** gōu·jàang·hàaih; **high jump** tiu·gōu; **high land** gòu·deih, sàan·deih; **high-minded** gòu·seuhng (ge); **high position** deih·waih hóu gòu; **high school** jùng·hohk; **the high sea** gùng·hói; **high tide** séui daaih; **highway** daaih·louh, gùng·louh; **highway robbery** dá geuk·gwāt, laahn·louh dá·gip

hill   sàan: **hill road** sàan·louh; **hillside** sāan·bīn; **hilltop** sàan·déng

hilly   dō·sàan (ge)

him   kéuih: **himself** kéuih jih gei

hind legs   hauh·geuk

hinder   jó·ngoih, fòhng·ngoih

Hindu   (people) Yàn·douh·yàhn; **Hinduism** Yan·douh·gaau; **Hindi** Yàn·douh·wá

hinge   gaau (N); **put on a hinge** ngòn go gaau

hint   ngam·sih

hip   daaih·béi

hippopotamus   hòh·máh (M: jek)

hire   (person) chéng; (things) giu, jòu; **hire a boat** giu jek téhng; **hire a car** giu ga che

his   kéuih ge

historian   lihk·sí·gā

history   (general) lihk·sí; (personal experience) léih·lihk, gìng·lihk; **history of China** Jùng·gwok·sí; **history of the United States** Méih·gwok·sí

hit   (general) dá; (by colliding) pung, pung·chàn; (by throwing) deng, deng·chàn. /Who hit him? Bĭn·go dá kéuih a? /I saw that car hit the boy. Ngóh tái·gin gó·ga chè pung· chàn gó·go sai·mān·jái. / That boy hit him with a stone. Gó·go sai·mān·jái béi sehk deng·chan kéuih.
    hit the bull's-eye dá·jung. /He made four hits. Kéuih dá·jung·jó sei·chi.

hive   maht·fūng·dau

hoard   dán (V)

hobby   dahk·biht·ge ngoi·hou

hoe   chòh·táu

hog   jyū (M: jek)

hoist   **hoist a flag** sîng·kèih; **hoist up** sìng·héi, ché·héi

hold   (general term) jà. /Will you hold this package a minute for me? M̀h·gòi néih tùhng ngóh jà·jyuh nī·bàau yéh yāt·jahn·gāan.
    (in both hands, with arms partially stretched out) púng (·jyuh); (in one hand, with arm stretched out) tok (·jyuh); (in the hand with arm stretched overhead) géui (·héi); (in the arms, in an embrace) láam (·jyuh); (in one arm or both arms, embrace and lift up, as of a baby) póuh (·jyuh). /May I hold him for a while? Ngóh póuh·hah kéuih dāk m̀h·dāk a? (support with the hand or arm) fùh (·jyuh). /Hold him or he'll fall. Fùh· jyuh·háh kéuih yeuhk·m̀h·haih kéuih jauh wúih dit ge la.
    (contain) jòng. /Can your suitcase hold all these things? Néih go pèih·gīp jòng·m̀h· jōng·dāk·saai gam dò yéh a? /Will this box hold all these books? Nī·go hāp jong m̀h· jōng·dāk·saai nī·dī syù a?
    (of persons in an auditorium, hotel, etc.) chóh. /Will your car hold six people? Néih ga chè chóh m̀h·chóh·dāk luhk·go yàhn a? /That plane can hold more than a hun- dred people. Gó ga fēi·gèi hó·yíh chóh baahk géi yàhn.
    hold a meeting hòi·wúi. /When will be the best time to hold the meeting? Géi·sí hòi·wúi jeui hóu a?
    hold one's breath m̀h·hóu táu·hei. /Hold your breath until I say OK. Mh·hóu táu· hei, dáng ngóh wah 'Dāk la' sìn·ji hóu táu·hei.

hold it. Mh·hou yūk (don't move). Maih jáu ji (don't leave).

hold water (fig., of reasoning) chūng·jūk; (of a plan) tóh·dong. /Your argument won't hold water. Néih só·góng·ge léih·yàuh mh·chūng·jūk. /Your plan won't hold water. Néih ge baahn·faat mh·tóh·dong.

hold on jà·jyuh, mh·hóu fong·sáu. /Hold on to me when we cross the street. Gwo·gaai·ge sìh·hauh jà·jyuh ngóh ge sáu.

hold up (rob) chéung. /They were held up last night. Kéuih·deih kàm·máahn béi yàhn chéung·jó.

hole   lūng. /Why is there a hole in the wall? Dím·gáai chèuhng·syu yáuh go lūng a?

holiday   fong·ga. /Is today a holiday? Gàm·yaht haih mh·haih fong·ga a? /Will there be a holiday for the Chinese New Year? Gwo·gauh·lihk·nìhn (the new year day of the old calendar) fòng mh·fong ga a? /For how many days? Fòng géi·do yaht a? /Today is a bank holiday. Gàm·yaht ngàhn·hòhng fong·ga.

     (day off) yāu·sīk, táu·gùng

holiness   sàhn·sing

hollow   (empty) hùng; (concave) nāp

Hollywood   Hòh·léih·wuht

holy   sàhn·sing: **Holy Bible,** Sing·gìng; **holy city,** sing·sìhng; **Holy Communion** Sing·chāan; **holy disciple** sing·tòuh; **Holy Father** Sing·fuh; **Holy Ghost** Sing·Lìhng; **Holy Land** Sing deih; **holy orders** sing·jīk; **Holy Scripture** Sing gìng; **Holy Son** Sing·jí; **Holy Spirit** Sing·lihng, Sing·sàhn; **holy war** sing·jin; **holy water** sing·séui

homage   **pay homage to** baai·mohng, jìm·yéuhng

home   (abode of one's family) ngūk·kéi, jyuh·gā. /Where is your home? Néih ngūk·kéi hái bīn·syu a? /My home is at No. 15 Kennedy Road. Ngóh ngūk·kéi hái Gìn·neih·deih douh sahp·ńgh·houh. /How many persons are in your home? Néih ngūk·kéi yáuh géi·dò yàhn a? /I have to go home. Ngóh yiu fàan ngūk·kéi la. /Can you see her home? Néih hó·yíh sung kéuih fāan ngūk·kéi ma? /Make yourself at home. Mh·hóu haak·hei. (native) /Where is your home town? (common) Néih haih bīn·syu yàhn a? (polite) Néih gwai·chyúh a? or Sìhng hèung a?

     home address jyuh·jí; **foundling home** yuhk·yīng·yún; **old people's home** yéuhng·lóuh·yún; **homeless** mòuh·gà·hó·gwài

homeland   tòhng·sàan (term used by the overseas Chinese in America), jóu·gà (term used by the overseas Chinese in Southeast Asia), jóu·gwok (formal term)

homemade   gā·gēi ge; (as opp. to foreign) tóu·jai ge, tóu·cháan ge

homesick   /Is he homesick? Kéuih haih mh·haih séung fàan ngūk·kéi (or tòhng·sàan, jóu·gà; ref. 'homeland') a?

homework   gùng·fo

honest   (upright or frank) lóuh·saht. /Is he honest? Kéuih go yàhn lóuh·saht ma? **be honest** or **speak honestly** lóuh·saht·góng. /I tell you honestly, if your grades are not improved next term, there is no hope for you to get the scholarship. Ngóh lóuh·saht·góng néih jì, yùh·gwó néih hah·go hohk·kèih ge fān·sou mh·gōu dī, néih móuh hèi·mohng dāk·dóu jéung·hohk·gāam.

honey   maht·tòhng, fùng·maht: **honeycomb,** maht·fung·dau

honeymoon   maht·yuht

honeysuckle   gàm·ngàhn·fà

honor   (personal glory, privilege) wìhng·hahng. /I consider it a great honor to be elected president of this association. Sìhng gok·wái syún ngóh jouh bún·wúi ge wuih·

jéung, ngóh gok·dāk sahp·fàn ge wìhng·hahng. /It is a great honor to speak to you today. Gàm·yaht yáuh gèi·wuih tùhng gok·wái góng géi·geui syuht·wah, hìng·daih (polite form for 'I' in formal speech) gok·dāk fèi·sèuhng wìhng·hahng.

(revere, respect) **honor father and mother** haau·ging fuh·móuh; **honor a teacher** jyùn·ging sīn·sàang

honors (at school, etc.) jéung. /How many honors has he got for this term? Kéuih gàm·nín dāk·jó géi·dō·go jéung a?

honorary   mìhng·yuh: **honorary degree** mìhng·yuh hohk·wái; **honorary member** mìhng·yuh wúi·yùhn; **honorary president** mìhng·yuh wuih·jéung

hoodlum   laahn·jái; **young hoodlum** fēi·jái

hoof   tàih (M: jek)

hook   ngāu: **fishhook** diu·yùh·ngāu

hoop   (of a tub, etc.) kū; (to fasten with a hoop or a band) kù·jyuh

hoot owl   māau·tàuh·yīng (M: jek)

hop   tiu

hope   (expect, desire) hèi·mohng. /I hope you can come. Ngóh hèi·mohng néih nàhng· gau lèih. /I hope the weather is good tomorrow. Ngóh hèi·mohng tìng·yaht hóu·tìn. (desire, expectation) hèi·mohng. /There is still hope. Juhng yáuh hèi·mohng.
 give up hope is expressed as fūi·sàm (be disheartened). /Don't give up hope. M̀h·hóu fūi·sàm.

hopeful   yáuh hèi·mohng

hopeless   móuh hèi·mohng

horizon   tīn·bìn

horn   (of an animal) gok (M: jek): **ox's horn** ngàuh·gok; (wind instrument) hōn, la·bā, hèuh·dēu; **sound a horn** héung hōn, gahm hōn

hornet   wòhng·fūng (M: jek)

horrible   hó·pa

horse   máh (M: pāt): **horse race** páau·máh, choi·máh

horsepower   máh·lihk (M: pāt)

hose   (tube) séui·hàuh (M: tìuh); (stockings) maht (M: jek, one; seung, pair)

hospitable   hóu·haak·chìhng (ge), hóu jiu·fù, hou·haak (ge)

hospital   yī·yún (M: gàan)

host   jyú·yán: **hostess** néuih·jyú·yán

hostel   jiu·doih·só, sūk·se (M: gàan)

hostile   dihk·deui: **hostile action** dihk·deui hàhng·duhng; **hostile attitude** dihk·deui taai· douh; **hostile country** dihk·gwok

hot   (of temperature) yiht. /What a hot day it is. Jàn·haih yiht la. /It's so hot outside, don't go out. Ngoih·bihn gam yiht, m̀h·hóu chēut·heui la. /Is there any hot water? Yáuh móuh yiht·séui a?
 (pungent) laaht. /Is this hot? Nī·dī laaht m̀h·laaht ga?
 (violent, of temper) bouh·chou. /I didn't know he had such a hot temper. Ngóh m̀h· jì kéuih gam bouh·chou ge.

hot spring   wàn·chyùhn

hotel   (modern, western) jáu·dim (M: gàan); (conventional Chinese) léuih·gún, haak·
jáan (M: gàan)

hound   lihp·gáu (M: jek)

hour   dím·jūng; jūng·tàuh (M: go), jūng·dím (M: go). /I'll be back in about half an hour.
Ngóh bun·dím·jūng dóu jauh fàan·leih. /We've been waiting for more than two hours.
Ngóh·deih yíh·gìng dáng·jó léuhng·dím·géi·jūng la. /Can you fix it within an hour?
Néih yāt·go jūng·tàuh·noih jíng·dāk·héi ma?
   every hour on the hour daahp·jeng múih·dím·jūng. /The bus leaves every hour on
the hour. Bā·si daahp·jeng múih·dím·jūng hòi yāt·chi.
   office hours gùng·jok sìh·gaan, baahn·gùng sìh·gaan. /Come to see me during my
office hours. Baahn·gùng ge sìh·gaan lèih gin ngóh.

house   (dwelling place) ngūk (M: gàan). /Is there any house to let in this neighborhood?
Nī·syu jó·gán yáuh móuh ngūk chēut·jòu a? /There are two houses for rent, go and take
a look. Gó·syu yáuh léuhng·gāan ngūk chēut·jòu, néih heui tái·há. /Five generations of
the Chans have lived in this house. Chàhn·gà yíh·gìng hái nī·gāan ngūk jyuh·jó ngh·doih
la.
   House of Commons Hah·yi·yún; **House of Lords** Seuhng·yi·yún; **House of Representatives** Jung·yi·yún; **Senate** Chàam·yih·yun
   house rent ngūk·jòu; **housing allowance** fòhng·ngūk·jèun·tip

how   (in what way) dím(·yéung). /Can you teach me how to use chopsticks? Néih gaau
ngóh dím sái faai·jí, dāk ma? /How do you feel? Néih gok·dāk dím a? /How do you
sell this, by the pound or by the piece? Nī·dī yéh dím maaih·faat a? Dyun bòhng yīk·
waahk leuhn go a?
   (the way) gám. /Is this how to do it? Haih m̀h·haih gám jouh a? /No. M̀h haih gám
jouh.
   (to what extent) géi. /How high is the door? Gó·douh mùhn géi gòu a? /How far is
it from here? Lèih nī·syu géi yúhn a? /How long is this table? Nī·jèung tói géi chèuhng a? /How long have you waited? Néih dáng·jó géi nói la? /How heavy is this fish?
Nī·tìuh yú yáuh géi chúhng a?
   (in exclamations) géi gam, jàn·haih. /How beautiful that house is! Gó·gàan ngūk
géi gam leng a! or Gó·gàan ngūk jàn·haih leng la.
   (amount) **how much, how many** géi·dò. /How much does it cost? Géi·dò chín a?
/How many do you want? Néih yiu géi·dò go a? /How many people are coming? Yáuh
géi·dò·go yàhn lèih a?
   how is it that dím·gáai. /How is it that he didn't come? Kéuih dím·gáai móuh lèih
a?
   know how wúih. /Do you know how to swim? Néih wúih m̀h·wáih yàuh·séui a?
   other expressions: /How do you do? Néih géi hóu a? /How are you getting along?
Gahn·lói géi hóu ma? /How come? Dím·gáai a?
   show someone how gaau. /Please show me how to use chopsticks. Chéng néih gaau
ngóh dím·yéung sái faai·jí.

however   m̀h·léih, mòuh·leuhn, daahn·haih. /However difficult it may be, I must try to
do it. M̀h·léih kéuih géi nàahn, ngóh yāt·dihng yiu si·háh. /However rich he may be,
he is never contented. Mòuh·leuhn kéuih géi yáuh·chín kéuih dōu m̀h·múhn·jūk. /How-
ever expensive it is, he still wants to buy it. Mòuh·leuhn géi gwai, kéuih juhng·haih yiu
máaih. /He wants to buy it, however he doesn't have any money. Kéuih séung máaih
daahn·haih kéuih móuh chín.

howl   (yell) ngaai

hubbub   chòuh, chòuh·hyùn·bà·bai. /What is this hubbub about? Gó·dī yàhn hái syu
chòuh māt·yéh a? or Gó·dī yàhn jouh·māt·yéh hái syu chòuh·hyùn·bà·bai a?

hue   sīk, sīk·séui

hug   láam(·jyuh) (V), póuh(·jyuh) (V)

huge   daaih

hula-hula dance   chóu·kwàhn·móuh

hull   (husk) hok; (of a vessel) syùhn·hok, syùhn·sàn; **to hull** jùng; **to hull the rice** jùng máih; **hulled rice** baahk·máih

human   yàhn ge. /Is this a human skull or a monkey's? Nī·go haih yàhn ge tàuh·gwāt yihk·waahk haih máh·lāu ge tàuh·gwāt a? **human being** yàhn; **human nature** yàhn·sing; **human race** yàhn·leuih

humane   yàhn·chìh

humanitarianism   yàhn·douh·jyú·yih

humanity   (people) yàhn·leuih; (the nature of man) yàhn·sing; (kindness) yàhn·douh, hóu· sàm

humble   hìm·hèui, hìm·bèi

humbug   (deceive) ngāk, tam

humid   chìuh·sāp

humidity   sāp·hei

humiliate   móuh·yuhk

humorous   fùi·hàaih, hóu·siu, yàu·mahk

humpback   tòh·bui

Hun   Hùng·nòuh

hunchback   tòh·bui

hundred   baak: **one hundred and one** yāt·baak·lihng·yāt; **one hundred and ten** yāt·baahk· yāt·sahp; **a hundred times** yāt·baak·púih

hunger   ngoh, gèi·ngoh. /Many people died of hunger during the Second World War. Daih·yih·chi sai·gaai·daaih·jin ngoh·séi hóu dò yàhn.

hungry   tóuh·ngoh. /Are you hungry? Néih tóuh·ngoh ma? /Yes, I am. Ngóh hóu tóuh· ngoh.

hunt   (chase, game) dá: **hunt birds** dá jéuk; (try to find) wán; **hunting** dá·lihp; **hunter** lihp· yàhn; **hunting dog** lihp·gáu

hurricane   daaih·fùng

hurried   chùng·mòhng

hurry   (move faster) faai·dī. /Hurry up! Faai·dī! (make haste in doing something) gón. /Please hurry to have this done before five o'clock. Mh·gòi néih ngh·dím·jūng yíh·chìhn gón·héi kéuih. (cause to move quickly) chèui. /Hurry him a little bit. Chèui·háh kéuih lā. **a hurry**. /What's the hurry? Jouh·māt gam pàhn·làhn a?

hurt   (pain) tung. /Where does it hurt? Bīn·douh tung a? /My arm hurts. Ngóh sáu·bei tung. /Does it still hurt? Juhng tung ma? /Does it hurt badly? Hóu tung àh? /Yes. Hóu tung. (injure or wound) sèung, sauh·sèung. /He hurt his foot. Kéuih sèung·jó jek geuk. or Kéuih jek geuk sauh·jó sèung. (distress) lihng . . . sèung·sàm. /Please excuse me, I didn't mean to hurt your feelings. Chéng néih yùhn·leuhng ngóh, ngóh m̀h·haih yáuh·yi lìhng néih sèung·sàm ge. /Don't hurt her feelings. M̀h·hóu lìhng kéuih sèung·sàm.

(have a bad effect on) yíng·héung. /Weather like this hurts the business greatly. Gám yéung ge tìn·sìh yíng·héung sàang·yi hóu daaih.

husband   sīn·sàang, lóuh·gùng (colloq.), nàahm·yán (vulgar); **husband and wife** léuhng· gùng·pó, léuhng·fù·fúh; **husband's father** gà·gūng; **husband's mother** gà·pó; **husband's elder brother** daaih·baak; **husband's elder sister** daaih·gù; **husband's younger brother** sìu·sūk, sūk·jái; **husband's younger sister** sìu·gù, gū·jái

husk   (as of rice) hòn; (as of beans) hok

husky voice   sàh·sàh·sèng

hut   (small house) ngūk·jái; (thatched house) màauh·lìuh

hydrogen   hèng·hei: **hydrogen bomb** hèng·hei·dáan

hygiene   waih·sāng

hymen   (anat.) chyúh·néuih·mōk

hymn   jaan·méih·sī (M: sáu)

hymnal   jaan·méih·sī

hyperemia   chùng·hyut: **hyperemia of the brain** nóuh·chùng·hyut

hypnotism   chèui·mìhn·seuht

hypnotize   chèui·mìhn

hypocrite   gá·mouh·wàih·sihn ge yàhn, ngaih·gwàn·jí

hypocritical   gá·mouh·wàih·sihn ge

hypodermic   pèih·hah: **hypodermic injection** pèih·hah jyu·seh

hypothesis   gá·chit

hypothetical   gá·chit ge, gá·dihng ge

I

I   ngóh. /She phoned me this morning but I wasn't home. Kéuih gàm·jiu dá·dihn·wá béi ngóh daahn·haih ngóh m̀h·hái kéi.

ice   syut, bìng: **iceberg** bìng·sàan; **icebox** syut·gwaih, bìng·sēung; **ice cream** syut·gōu; **iced** syut·chòhng ge; **ice manufactory** syut·chóng; **ice water** syut·séui

idea   (plan) baahn·faat, faat·ji. /This is a good idea. Nī·go baahn·faat géi hóu.
    (opinion) yi·gin. /Do you have any ideas on the subject? Deui·yù nī·gihn sih néih yáuh māt yi·gin ma?
    (viewpoint) gin·gáai. /The idea of a philosopher is different from a scientist. Jit· hohk·gā ge gin·gáai tùhng fò·hohk·gā ge gin·gáai m̀h·tùhng.
    other expressions: /What's the big idea? Dím·gáai a? or Jouh·māt·yéh a? /I haven't any idea where he is. Ngóh yùhn·chyùhn m̀h·jì kéuih hái bīn·syu. /That's the idea! Ngāam la. /The idea is to get this done today. Jeui gán·yiu ge haih gàm·yaht (jèung nī·gihn yéh) jouh·héi kéuih.

ideal   (aim) léih·séung. /One should have a high ideal in life. Yāt·go yàhn yāt·sàng yìng·gòi yáuh yāt·go gòu·seuhng ge léih·séung.
    (model) /Who is his ideal? Kéuih séung jouh dím·yéung ge yāt·go yàhn a? /Is Con- fucius his ideal? Kéuih haih m̀h·haih séung jouh hóu·chíh Húng·jí gám·yéung ge yāt·go yàhn a?
    be ideal (existing as a mere mental image) léih·séung ge; (model) mòuh·faahn (ge); (best) jeui hóu ge; (nothing better) mòuh·yíh·seuhng·jì ge. /Ideal beauty is hard to attain.

Léih·séung ge méih haih hóu nàahn daaht·dou ge. /He's an ideal teacher. Kéuih haih yāt·go mòuh·faahn (ge) sīn·sàang. /He's the ideal man for the job. Kéuih jouh nī·gihn sih jeui hóu bāt·gwo la. /A summer resort like that would be ideal. Yáuh gám ge beih·syú ge deih·fòng jauh jàn·haih mòuh·yíh·seuhng·jī la.

identify   yihng·cheut, jing·mìhng. /Can you identify in which country it was made? Néih yihng·dāk·chēut haih bīn·gwok jouh ge ma? /Can you identify yourself? Néih hó·yíh jing·mìhng néih haih bīn·go ma?

identity card   sàn·fahn·jing

ideograph   jeuhng·yìhng·màhn·jih; **Chinese ideographs** Jung·gwok·jih, Hon·jih

idiom   sìhng·yúh (M: geui)

idiot   ngòih·lóu, sòh·gwā, sáhn·jái

idle   (lazy) láahn·sáan, láahn·doh

idler   yàuh·sáu·hou·hàahn ge yàhn, mòuh·yihp·yàuh·màhn

idol   (image of a god) ngáuh·jeuhng; **idol worshiping** chùhng·baai ngáuh·jeuhng

idolatry   chùhng·baai·ngáuh·jeuhng

if   yùh·gwó, yeuhk·gwó, yeuhk·haih. /If you do not study, you'll never learn. Yùh·gwó néih m̀h·duhk·syù, néih wìhng·yúhn m̀h·sīk. /If it rains we won't go. Yeuhk·gwó lohk·yuh ngóh·deih jauh mh·heui la. /I wouldn't have known it at all if you hadn't told me. Yeuhk·haih néih m̀h·góng, ngóh yāt·dī dōu m̀h·jī. /If anyone asks for me, say I'll be right back. Yùh·gwó yáuh yàhn wán ngóh, néih wah ngóh jauh fàan·lèih. /What if it rains? Yùh·gwó lohk·yúh jauh dím a?
    (whether) /See if there is any mail for me. Tái·háh yáuh móuh ngóh·ge seun. /Ask her if she would like to go home. Mahn·háh kéuih haih m̀h·haih séung fàan·ngūk·kéi.
    as if hóu·chíh. /He talks as if he is your old friend. Kéuih góng·héi·séuhng·lèih hóu·chíh néih·ge lóuh pàhng·yáuh gám. /He walks as if he were crippled. Kéuih hàahng·héi·séuhng·lèih hóu·chíh bài·bài·déi gám.
    if only. /If you had only come earlier, nothing would have happened. Yùh·gwó néih jóu dī lèih jauh móuh sih la.

ignorance   mòuh·jī

ignorant   (without knowledge) móuh·jī·sīk (ge); (not aware) m̀h·jī

ignore   m̀h·léih

ill   (sick) behng. /She is ill. Kéuih yáuh behng. (not feeling well) m̀h·jing·sàhn, m̀h·syu·fuhk. /The teacher is ill today. Sīn·sàang gàm·yaht m̀h·jing·sàhn. (bad, evil) ngok. /If you do ill, you must expect to be punished. Ngok yáuh ngok bou. (a Chinese proverb)
    ill-fated fú·mehng; **ill-natured** m̀h·hóu·pèih·hei; **ill-treat** neuhk·doih; **ill will** yun·hahn

illegal   m̀h·hahp·faat ge, fèi·faat ge, faahn·faat ge

illegible   lóuh·chóu, nàahn·duhk ge

illegitimate   mh·hahp·faat ge; **illegitimate child** sī·sàang·jí

illicit   wàih·faat ge

illiterate   m̀h·sīk·jih (ge). /He is illiterate. Keuih m̀h·sik·jih. /It's very difficult for an illiterate to find a job. M̀h·sīk·jih ge yàhn hóu nàahn wán·dóu sih jouh.

illness   behng, behng·jing

illogical   m̀h·tùng (ge), m̀h·hahp·lòh·chāp (ge), bāt·tùng (ge) illuminate   jiu

illusion   waahn·jeuhng, cho·gok

illustrate   syut·mìhng, gáai·sīk: **illustrate with pictures** yùhng tòuh lèih gáai·sīk

illustration   (picture) chaap·tòuh (M: fūk); (act of) gáai·sīk; (example) pei·yuh

image   (idol) ngáuh·jeuhng; (mental picture) séung·jeuhng; (effigy) jeuhng; (reflection) yíng; **image of Buddha** faht·jeuhng

imaginary   séung·jeuhng ge, gá·séung ge: **imaginary enemy** gá·séung·dihk

imagine   (conceive) séung·jeuhng

imagination   séung·jeuhng; (creative power) séung·jeuhng·lihk

imitate   hohk. /Can you imitate bird calls? Néih wúih hohk jéuk giu ma? (act like) mòh·fóng. /The children always try to imitate their parents. Sai·mān·jái sìh·sìh dōu séung mòh·fóng kéuih·deih ge fuh·móuh.

imitation   mòh·fóng ge, fóng·haauh ge; **imitation leather** gá·péi

immaterial   (unimportant) m̀h·gán·yiu (ge)

immediate   (instant) jīk·hāk, lahp·hāk

immense   gihk·jì·daaih ge

immerse   (put in liquid) jam; **baptism by immersion** jam·láih

immigrant   yìh·màhn

immigrate   yìh·màhn

immigration   yìh·màhn; **immigration office** yìh·màhn·gūk

immoderate   gwo·leuhng (ge), m̀h·jì·jit·jai (ge)

immoral   m̀h·douh·dāk ge, móuh·douh·dāk ge: **immoral conduct** móuh·douh·dāk ge hàhng·wàih

immortal   (undying) chèuhng·sàng·bāt·lóuh (ge); (being) sàhn·sīn; **immortal life** wíhng·sàng

immovable   (fixed) m̀h·yūk·dāk (ge); **immovable property** bāt·duhng·cháan

imp   (mischievous child) fáan·dáu·jìng, baak·yim·jìng; (mischief-making fairy) yìu·gwaai

impart   (give) chyùhn, chyùhn·sauh: **impart knowledge** chyùhn·sauh jì·sīk; (communicate) chyùhn·daaht: **impart some news** chyùhn·daaht sīu·sīk

impartial   gùng·pìhng (ge), daaih·gùng·mòuh·sì (ge)

impatient   móuh·noih·sing, sām·gāp, sing·gāp

impeach   (in court) hung·gou; (an official) tàahn·hāk

imperial   dai·wòhng ge

imperialism   dai·gwok jyú·yih

imperil   ngàih·hoih

implement   (equipment) ga·sàang, hei·geuih; (carry out) saht·hàhng, léih·hàhng: **implement a treaty** léih·hàhng tìuh·yeuk

implicate   (involve) tòh·leuih, hìn·lìhn

implore   (beg) ngài·kàuh

imply   (hint) ngam·sih

impolite   sāt·láih; (rude) móuh·kwài·géui

import   syù·yahp, yahp·háu (V); yahp·háu·fo (N); **import duty** yahp·háu·seui; **importer** yahp·háu·sēung

important   gán·yiu (ge), juhng·yiu (ge); **important points** yiu·dím

impose   **impose a fine** faht·chín; **impose a tax** chàu·seui

impossible   bāt·hó·nàhng (ge), m̀h·hó·nàhng (ge)

impostor   gwòng·gwan, pin·jí

impotence   yèuhng·wái

impracticable   jouh·m̀h·dou ge

impress   (have an effect on someone's mind) lihng . . . gok·dāk, lihng . . . yáuh yāt·go hóu ge yan·jeuhng. /He impressed me as a good worker. Kéuih lihng (or sí) ngóh gok· dāk kéuih hóu jouh·dāk·sih. /He tried very hard to impress his teacher. Kéuih jeuhn· lihk lihng sīn·sàang deui kéuih yáuh yāt·go hóu ge yan·jeuhng.

impression   (effect on someone's mind) yan·jeuhng

imprison   gàam·gam, wan, chóh·gāam. /He was imprisoned for three months. Kéuih chóh·jó sàam·go yuht gāam. or Kéuih béi yàhn wan·jó sàam·go yuht.

improper   m̀h·jing·dong ge

improve   (make better) gói·lèuhng: **improve the breeds of animals** gói·lèuhng duhng· maht ge bán·júng; **improve on the method of study** gói·lèuhng duhk·syù ge fòng·faat;
    (making progress) jeun·bouh. /Your English has improved a great deal. Néih ge Yìng·màhn hóu yáuh·jeun·bouh.
    (ameliorate) gói·sihn. /We should improve the living conditions of the poor right away. Ngóh·deih yìng·gòi jīk·hāk gói·sihn kùhng·yàhn ge sàng·wuht.

improvement   jeun·bouh, gói·lèuhng, gói·sihn

impulse   chung·duhng

in   (general) hái. /Is Dr. Chan in? Chàhn yī·sāng hái·syu ma? /No, Dr. Chan isn't in. Chàhn yī·sāng m̀h·hái syu.
    (location) (hái) . . . yahp·bihn. /Is there furniture in that house? Gó·gāan ngūk yahp·bihn yáuh·móuh gà·sī a?
    (location in time) . . . ge sih·hauh. /It gets very hot here in the daytime. Nī·syu yaht·táu ge sìh·hauh hóu yiht.
    (within a period of time) . . . ji·noih, most of the time just the term for the period of time. /Can you finish this in a week? Néih yāt·go láih·baai jouh·dāk·héi ma?
    (after a period of time). /I'll be back in a week. Ngóh yāt·go láih·baai jauh fàan· lèih.
    (using as a medium) yuhng. /Say it in English. Yuhng Yìng·màhn góng. /Write it in ink. Yuhng mahk·séui·bāt sé.
    (at, concerning). /Is he good in arithmetic? Kéuih ge syun·seuht hóu m̀h·hóu a?
    in case yùh·gwó, maahn·yāt; **in debt** jàang·yàhn·chín, him·jaai; **in detail** chèuhng· sai; **in fact** kèih·saht; **in a word** júng·jí, júng·yìh·yìhn·jì; **in other words** wuhn·geui· wá·góng; **in person** chàn·sàn; **in place of** tai, tai·doih; **in reality** saht·jai·seung; **in ro-tation** lèuhn·láu; **ins and outs** chèuhng·sai ge chíhng·yìhng; **in short** júng·jí; **in the end** dou·dái, git·gwó; **in the first place** daih·yāt; **in the presence of** dòng·mín; **in the second place** daih·yih; **in time** jéun·sìh; **in what way** dím·yéung

inaccurate   m̀h·jéun·kok

inactive   m̀h·wuht·put

inaudible   tèng·m̀h·dóu, tèng·m̀h·gin

inaugurate   (as an exibition) hòi·mohk; (as a building) lohk·sihng; (as a society) hòi sìhng·lahp daaih·wúi; (induct into an office) jauh·jīk, jauh·yahm; (as a new era) hòi· chí

inaugural   **inaugural ceremony for an official** jauh·jīk·dín·láih; **inaugural ceremony for exhibition, etc.** hòi·mohk·dín·láih

inauspicious   m̀h·leih·sih

inborn   sàang·sèhng

incalculable   gai·m̀h·dihm, gai·m̀h·chēut gam dò

incendiary   **incendiary bomb** sìu·yìh·dáan, yìhn·sìu·dáan

incense   (sticks) hēung (M: jī); **incense burner** hèung·lòuh; **burn incense sticks** sìu· hēung, dím·hēung

incessant   m̀h·tìhng ge, bāt·hit·ge

inch   chyun

incident   (accident) ngáuh·yìhn·ge sih, yi·ngoih·ge sih; (event) sih

incidental   ngáuh·yìhn ge

incidentally   ngáuh·yìhn

incise   (cut) got

incision   hán (M: tìuh)

incite   (stir up) sin·duhng

incline   (lean) che, jāk, pìn; (tend to) sìh·sìh (often), juhk·jím (gradually). /He's inclined to be late. Kéuih sìh·sìh dōu chìh·dou ge. /I'm inclined to believe him. Ngóh juhk·jím sèung·seun kéuih.
  an incline che·lóu, chèh·bō
  (to do) séung: **inclined to vomit** séung ngáu

include   bàau·kut, bàau·màaih, gai·màaih. /It includes the following points. Bàau·kut hah·bihn géi·dím. /Are tips included? Haih m̀h·haih bàau·màaih tīp·sí (or síu·fai) la?

income   yahp·sīk, sàu·yahp; **income tax** yahp·sīk·seui, só·dāk·seui

inconceivable   (that cannot be imagined) séung·m̀h·dou (ge)

inconsiderate   (careless) m̀h·síu·sàm; (not showing regard for other people) m̀h·wúih tái·leuhng yàhn·deih (ge)

inconsistent   yāt·sìh·yāt·yeuhng

inconstant   fáan·fūk, fáan·fūk·mòuh·sèuhng

inconvenient   m̀h·fòng·bihn

incorrect   m̀h·ngāam

incorruptible   m̀h·wúih·laahn (ge)

increase   (become more) dò; (become greater) daaih. /The sale of American cars is increasing. Nī·páai Méih·gwok hei·chè maaih dò hóu dò. /His power is increasing all the time. Kéuih ge sai·lihk yuht lèih yuht daaih.
  (make greater) jāng·gà. /The population has increased by fifty percent. Yàhn·háu jāng·gà·jó baak·fahn·jì ńgh·sahp.

(of rent, taxes, etc.) gà. **increase of rent** gā jòu; **increase of tax** gà seui
(of price) héi (ga). /The price of rice increased again. Máih·gà yauh héi·jó la.
an increase is expressed verbally as: gà. /Do you expect an increase in salary?
Kéuih·déih wúih m̀h·wúih gà néih sàn·séui a?

incredible   hóu·nàahn·sèung·seun (ge)

incurable   m̀h·yī·dāk·hóu. /His illness is incurable. Kéuih ge behng m̀h·yī·dāk·hóu ge
la.

indebted   (obliged) gáam·gīk. /He is deeply indebted to his teacher. Kéuih fèi·sèuhng
gáam·gīk kéuih·ge sīn·sàang.

indecisive   yàuh·yùh·bāt·kyut

indeed   (in reality) kok·haih. /He's very sick indeed. Kéuih kok·haih behng dāk hóu
gán·yiu.

indefinite   móuh·dihng·jeuhk

indemnity   pùih·sèuhng·fai; **indemnity for damage or loss** pùih·sèuhng·syún·sāt; **indemnity for defamation** pùih·sèuhng·mìhng·yuh

indent   iíng·ngàp·jó; indented nāp·jó, nāp·jó yahp heui

independent   (of people) jih·lahp. /He is independent now. Kéuih yìh·gā yíh·gìng jih·
lahp la.
(of country) duhk·lahp. /There are many small countries in Africa that have become independent recently. Fèi·jàu jeui·gahn yáuh hóu·dò gwok·gà duhk·lahp.
(separate) /She has an independent income. is expressed as: Kéuih yáuh kéuih
jih·géi ge sàu·yahp.
independent country duhk·lahp·gwok; **declare independence** syùn·bou·duhk·lahp

indescribable   góng·m̀h·chēut, nàahn·yíh·yìhng·yùhng. /Her beauty is indescribable.
Kéuih góng·m̀h·chēut·gam leng.

index   sok·yáhn

indicate   bíu·sih, bíu·mìhng, jyu·mìhng

indict   hung·gou

indifferent   (unconcerned) m̀h·gwāan·sàm; (not mattering much) mòuh·só·waih; (cold)
láahng·daahm

indigestible   nàahn·sîu·fa (ge)

indigo   làahm, làahm·dihn

indirect   gaan·jip

indispensable   bīt·sèui·ge

indisposed   m̀h·jih·yìhn, m̀h·syù·fuhk

individual   go·yàhn (ge), jih·géi (ge); **individual capital** go·yàhn jī·bún, jih·géi sàang·yi

individualism   go·yàhn jyú·yih

individuality   go·sing

indivisible   m̀h·fàn·dāk·hòi (ge)

indolent   (lazy) láahn, yàuh·sáu·hou·hàahn

induce   (lead) yáhn, yáhn·douh; (persuade) hyun; (bring upon) jiu; (cause) sái

indulge   (as a child) jung, jung·yùhng; **indulge in corrupt practice** jok·baih, móuh·baih industrial   gùng·yihp·ge, gùng·yihp·sing·ge **industrial area** gùng·yihp·kēui

industrious   kàhn·lihk

industry   gung·yihp: **heavy industry** juhng·gung·yihp

inefficient   m̀h·jùng·yuhng (ge)

inevitable   bāt·hó·beih·míhn (ge), m̀h·míhn·dāk (ge)

inexcusable   bāt·hó·yùhn·leuhng (ge)

inexpensive   pèhng, sèung·yîh

inexperienced   móuh·gìng·yihm, m̀h·suhk·hòhng, sàang·sáu

inexpressible   m̀h·góng·dāk·chēut (ge)

infancy   sōu·hāh·jái·ge sîh·hauh

infant   sōu·hā·jái, bîh·bī·jái

infantile paralysis   síu·yîh·màh·bei·jing, yìng·yîh·màh·bei·jing

infantry   bouh·bìng: **infantry man** bouh·bìng

infect   chyùhn·yîhm

infection   faat·yîhm

infectious   wúih·chyùhn·yîhm ge: **infectious disease** chyùhn·yíhm·behng

infer   tēui·chāk: **the rest may be inferred** yùh·hó·leuih·tèui (lit.)

inferior   (in quality) yáih; (in position) dài, dāi·kāp; (subordinates) sáu·hah; (subordinate, as an official) bouh·hah

infinite   mòuh·haahn ge

inflammable   yáhn·fó ge

inflammation   (med.) faat·yîhm

inflate   chèui·jeung: **inflate a balloon** chèui·jeung·go hei·kàuh

inflation   (monetary) tùng·fo·pàhng·jeung

influence   (effect) yíng·héung. /The experience of the last two years had tremendous influence on him. Gwo·heui nī·léuhng·nîhn ge gìng·yihm deui kéuih yáuh hóu daaih ge yíng·héung. /I believe your advice may have some influence on him. Ngóh sèung·seun néih ge jùng·gou hó·nàhng deui kéuih yáuh yíng·héung.
    (power) sai·lihk. /Who has the greatest influence here? Nī·syu bīn·go jeui yáuh sai·lihk a?
    to influence seui·fuhk. /I hope I can influence him not to gamble any more. Ngóh hèi·mohng ngóh nàhng·gau seui·fuhk kéuih m̀h·joi dóu·bok.
    sphere of influence sai·lihk·faahn·wàih

influential   yáuh·sai·lihk: **an influential man** daaih·nāp·lóu

influenza   gám·mouh, sèung·fùng

inform   (notify) tūng·jì; (tell) góng(·béi) ... jì. /Who will inform him that tomorrow we'll have a meeting? Bīn·go tūng·jì kéuih tìng·yaht ngóh·deih hòi·wúih a? /I was not informed in time. Kéuih·deih góng ngóh jì yíh·gìng taai chîh la.
    well informed. /He is really well informed! Kéuih jàn·haih ɛīu·sīk lîhng·tùng la!

informal   fèi·jing·sīk ge

information   (news) sīu·sīk; (intelligence) chîhng·bou

infringe   chàm·faahn; **infringe a copyright** chàm·faahn báan·kyùhn; **infringe on territory**
   ba·jin tóu·deih

ingenious   (clever) chùng·mîhng

ingot   **ingot of gold** gām·tíu

ingratitude   mòhng·yàn·fuh·yih

ingredient   sîhng·fahn; (of food) jeuk·liuh

inhabitant   gèui·màhn

inhale   sok·hei, kāp·hei; **inhale and exhale** fū·kāp

inherit   (as an heir) sîhng·gai; (by birth) chyùhn·sauh; (to come into possession of)
   sîhng·sauh

inheritance   (property) wàih·cháan; **inheritance tax** wàih·cháan·seui

inhuman   (unfeeling) móuh·yàhn·chîhng ge; (cruel) chàahn·yáhn ge

initial   (placed at the beginning) héi·táu ge, tàuh·yāt·go ge; **initial expenses** hòi·baahn·
   faai; **initial letter** tàuh·yāt·go jih·móuh; **initial stage** chò·kèih

initiate   (begin) faat·hói, tàih·chèung, jeuhk·sáu

inject   dá·jām (VO)

injection   dá·jām

injure   sèung·hoih: **injured** sauh·sèung

injustice   m̀h·gùng·pîhng, m̀h·gùng·douh

ink   (western) mahk·seui; (Chinese) mahk

inlaid   sèung: **inlaid with gold** sēung·gām; **inlaid with silver** sèung·ngán

inland   noih·deih

inmate   tùhng·jyuh ge

inn   haak·jáan (M: gàan)

innate   tìn·yîhn ge

inner   yahp·bihn ge; **inner tube of a tire** noih·tāai

innocent   (as a child) tìn·jàn; (free from guilt) móuh·jeuih

innumerable   mòuh·sou·gam·dò, gai·m̀h·dihm gam dò

inoculate   (against a disease) dá yuh·fòhng·jām: **inoculate against smallpox** jung·dáu

inoculation   dá·yuh·fòhng·jām: **inoculation against cholera** dá fok·lyuhn·jām; **inoculation
   against typhoid** dá sèung·hòhn·jām

inorganic chemistry   mòuh·gèi fa·hohk

inquire   (ask) mahn; mahn·gahp (make a search for information) dá·ting. /I want to inquire about schools in this neighborhood. Ngóh séung màhn·háh nī·syu jó·gán dī hohk·
   haauh ge chîhng·yîhng. /He inquired about you, and I said you were fine. Kéuih mahn·
   gahp néih ngóh wah néih géi hóu.
      inquire into (investigate) diuh·chàh. /We ought to form a committee to inquire into
   this matter. Ngóh·deih yiu jóu·jīk yāt·go wái·yùhn·wúi lèih diuh·chàh nī·gihn sih.

inquiry office   sèun·mahn·chyúh

inquisitive   (curious) hou·kèih; (improperly curious) hou·gún·hàahn·sih (ge) insane   faat·dìn

insanity   sàhn·gìng·behng, faat·dìn

insect   chùhng: **insect powder** saat·chùhng·yeuhk·fán

insecure   m̀h·wán·jahn

insensible (unconscious) wàhn·jó, bāt·sìng·yàhn·sih; (numb) màh·bei

inseparable fàn·m̀h·hòi (ge)

insert   chaap **insert in** chaap·yahp; **insert an advertisement** maaih·gou·baahk

inside   yahp·bihn, léuih·bihn, léuih·tàuh. /May I see the inside of the house? Ngóh hó·
            yíh tái·háh gāan ngūk yahp·bihn ma? /What's inside? Léuih·bihn yáuh māt·yéh a?

insipid   táahm, móuh·meih

insist   haih, haih·wah. /He insists that you're wrong. Kéuih haih·wah néih·m̀h·ngāam.
            /I insist that I know nothing about it. Ngóh haih m̀h·jì. but /He insists that he knows
            nothing about it. Kéuih haih·wah kéuih·m̀h·jì.
              insist on haih·yiu, yāt·yù·yiu. /Why does he insist on going? Dím·gáai kéuih haih·
            yiu heui nē? /He insists on paying. Kéuih yāt·yù·yiu béi chín. but /I insist (on paying).
            Ngóh·béi, ngóh·béi.

insomnia   sāt·mìhn

inspect   (as goods) gím·chàh; (documents) sám·chàh; (school, factory) sih·chaat; (troops)
            gím·yuht (as troops on review)

inspector   kài·chá, gim·chàh·gùn; (overseer) gāam·dūk; **inspector general** júng·gāam;
            inspector general of police gíng·chaat·júng·gāam; **inspector of schools** sih·hohk·gùn
            (most of the above terms are used only in Hong Kong)

inspiration lìhng·gáam; **divine inspiration** sing·lìhng ge kái·sih

install   (as a lighting system or home appliance) ngòn, jòng: **install a light** ngòn dihn·
            dāng; **install a telephone** ngòn dihn·wá; (induct) jauh·jīk (to place in an official position
            with formality or ceremony)

installation ngōn·jòng, jòng·ji: **installation fee** ngōn·jòng·fai, jong·ji·fai; (induction) jauh·
            jīk dín·láih (ref. install)

installment (as a device) fàn·kèih·fuh·fún; (as a payment) múih·kèih·ge fuh·fún

instance   **for instance** pèi·yùh

instant   (immediate) jīk·hāk (A), lahp·hāk (A), máh·seuhng (A), gón·gán (A). /Come this
            instant. Jīk·hāk·lèih. /The play had instant success. is expressed as: Gó·chēut hei
            jīk·hāk jouh chēut·jó méng la.
              instant coffee jīk·chùng·jīk·yám ge ga·fē; **instant tea** jīk·chùng·jīk·yám ge chàh

instead   (in the place of) (díng·)tai, tai (of someone or something); or use other indirect
            expressions. /Use the truck instead. Yùhng ga fo·chè lèih díng·tai là. /His brother
            did it instead of him. Kéuih ge sai·lóu tai kéuih jouh·jó. /Don't take that chair, take
            this instead. Mh·hóu chóh gó·jèung yí, chóh nī·jèung là.
              (in its stead). /I don't want that; give me this instead. is expressed as: Ngóh m̀h·
            yiu gó·go, ngóh yiu nī·go. /Would you like this instead? is expressed as: Néih jùng·yi
            nī·go má?

instinct   tìn·sing, bún·nàhng

institute   (set up) chit·lahp (V); (society) wúi, séh; (school) hohk·yún (M: gàan)

institution (society) séh·tyùhn; (organization) gèi·gwàan: **philanthropic organization**
            chìh·sihn·gèi·gwàan; (school) hohk·haauh; (college) hohk·yún

instruct   (teach) gaau, gaau·sauh; (order) fan·fu; (command) mihng·lihng

instruction   **instruction materials** gaau·chòih; **instructions** fan·lihng, mihng·lihng

instructor   sīn·sàang, gaau·sī

instrument   (tools) ga·sàang; (scientific devices) yìh·hei; **musical instrument** ngohk·hei

insufficient   m̀h·gau

insult   móuh·yuhk

insurance   yin·sō, bóu·hím; **life insurance** yàhn·sauh yin·sō; **insurance policy** yin·sō·jí; **insurance premium** bóu·fai

insure   máaih yin·sō, máaih bóu·hím: **insure against fire** bóu·fó·hím (VO)

intellect   (the power of knowing and reasoning) ji·lihk

intellectuals   jī·sīk·fahn·jí

intelligence   (the power of meeting any situation) chùng·mìhng, ji·waih; (the power or act of understanding) ji·lihk; (information) chìhng·bou; (news) sīu·sīk; **intelligence test** ji·lihk·chāk·yihm

intelligent   chùng·mìhng

intelligible   mìhng·baahk, chìhng·chó

intend   séung, dá·syun. /What do you intend to be in the future? Néih dá·syun jèung·lòih jouh māt·yéh a?

intention   (purpose) yi·si, muhk·dīk

intentionally   jyūn·dāng, dahk·dāng, gu·yi

intercalary   **intercalary month** yeuhn yuht; **intercalary (leap) year** yeuhn·nìhn

intercept   jiht·jyuh; (mil.) jiht·gīk

interchange   gàau·wuhn: **exchange opinions** gàau·wuhn yi·gin

intercourse   (social) gàau·jai, séh·gàau, lòih·wóhng; (between countries) ngoih·gàau; (sexual) sing·gàau, hàhng·fòhng

interest   (share) fán. /Do you have an interest in the business? Nī·go sàang·yi néih yáuh·fán ma?

    take an interest in (like) héi·fun; (be enthusiastic about) deui . . . faat·sàng hing·cheui /The children took great interest in hearing about the experiences of their parents during the war. Dī sai·mān·jái hóu héi·fùn tèng kéuih·deih fuh·móuh hái dá·jeung gó·jahn·sí ge gìng·yihm. /He has taken great interest in solving this problem. Kéuih deui yùh·hòh gáai·kyut nī·go mahn·tàih fāat·sàng hóu daaih ge hing·cheui.

    be interested in deui . . . yáuh hing·cheui. /I'm very much interested in this problem. Ngóh deui nī·go mahn·tàih hóu yáuh hing·cheui. /Would you be interested in going to a movie? is expressed as: Néih séung heui tái dihn·yíng ma?

    (advantage) leih·yīk. /He's only thinking of his own interests. Kéuih jí haih gu·jyuh kéuih jih·géi ge leih·yīk.

    (money return) leih·sīk. /How much interest does it pay? Béi géi chín leih·sīk a? /They pay 3% interest. Béi sāam·fān sīk.

    to interest someone. /The agent tried to interest me in buying that house. Gó·go gìng·géi séung ngóh máaih gó·gāan ngūk. /That book didn't interest me at all. is expressed as: Gó·bún syù yāt·dī yi·si dōu móuh.

interesting   hóu yáuh·cheui

interfere   (meddle) gòn·sip; **interfere verbally** chaap·jéui

interior (inside) léuih·tàuh, noih·bouh; (inland) noih·deih; (of a country) gwok·noih

interjection gáam·taan·chìh

interlude chaap·kūk

intermediate jūng·kāp ge

intern (med.) gin·jaahp·yī·sāng, jyuh·yún·yī·sāng

internal noih·bouh, léuih·tàuh; **internal parts of the body** sàn·tái·noih·bouh; **internal medicine** noih·fuhk·yeuhk, haih sihk ge yeuhk; **internal revenue** seui·sàu; **internal problem of a country** noih·jing; **internal strife** noih·lyuhn

international gwok·jai: **International Court of Justice** Gwok·jai faat·tìhng; **international exchange** gwok·jai wuih·deui; **international law** gwok·jai gung·faat; **International Red Cross** Maahn·gwok hung·sahp·jih·wui; **international status** gwo·jai deih·waih; **international trade** gwok·jai mauh·yihk; **international usage** gwo·jai gwaan·laih

interpret (explain) gáai·sik; (to act as an interpreter) chyùhn·wá, chyùhn·yihk, fàan·yihk. /We need a person to interpret for us. Ngóh·deih sèui·yiu go yàhn tùhng ngóh·deih chyùhn·wá. **interpret a dream** chèuhng·muhng (VO). /He said that he knows how to interpret dreams, is that true? Kéuih wah kéuih wúih chèuhng·muhng, haih m̀h·haih jàn ga?

interpretation (translation) fàan·yihk; (exposition) gáai·sik

interpreter chyùhn·wá (colloq.), fàan·yihk

interrogate sám·mahn

interrogation mark mahn·houh

interrupt jiht·tyúhn; **interrupt a conversation** chaap·jéui. /Excuse my interrupting you. is expressed as: Deui·m̀h·jyuh, ngóh jó néih yāt·jahn·gāam.

interruption tyúhn·jyuht, m̀h·tùng, bāt·tùng, sòu·yíuh, jó·ngoih, jó·jaahm; **interruption of communications** tyúhn·jyuht gàau·tùng; **interruption of telephone communications** dihn·wá m̀h·tùng; **interruptions in the execution of a piece of work** jeun·hàhng yāt·gihn sih ge sìh·hauh só·yuh·dóu·ge sòu·yíuh. /It's ill-mannered to make frequent interruptions while people are in conversation. Yàhn·deih góng·gán wá sìh·sìh chaap·jéui haih hóu sāt·láih ge.

inter-school haauh·jai: **inter-school examination** wuih·háau; **inter-school tournament** haauh·jai béi·choi

intersection (of roads) gāau·chā·louh·háu

interval yāu·sīk sìh·gaan

intervene (interfere) gòn·sip, gòn·yuh

intervention gòn·sip, gòn·yuh: **intervention by arms** móuh·lihk gòn·yuh

interview fóng·mahn (N) (by the press); **to interview** fóng·mahn (by the press); jip·gin (by a statesman, official, employer, celebrity, etc.)

intestinal chèuhng·johng ge; **intestinal discharge** daaih·bihn; **intestinal worms** wùih·chùhng

intestine chéung, chèuhng (M: tìuh); **large intestine** daaih·chéung; **small intestine** síu·chéung; **inflammation of the intestine** chéung·yìhm

intimate (very familiar) (sèung·)suhk, chàn·maht; **intimate friend** hóu pàhng·yáuh, hóu jì·géi·ge pàhng·yáuh

intimidate hāp

into   yahp preceded by a verb of motion, as go or walk into hàahng·yahp (heui or lèih)
ran into jáu·yahp (heui or lèih), etc. /May we got into that building and take a look?
Ngóh deih yahp·heui gó·gāan ngūk tái·háh, dāk m̀h·dāk a?
    for the other uses of 'into' in phrases, see the other word

intolerable   m̀h·dái·dāk, m̀h·yáhn·dāk; **intolerable heat** yiht·dou·séi

intoxicated   (drunk) yám·jeui

intoxicating   (by drinking) wúih·yám·jeui·yàhn ge

introduce   (to cause to be acquainted) gaai·siuh; (present someone to a superior) gin,
    gaai·siuh . . . gin. /Allow me to introduce you two. /Ngóh lèih tùhng néih·deih léuhng·
    wái gaai·siuh·háh. /I'd like to introduce you to my father. Ngóh séung tùhng néih heui
    gin·háh ngóh bàh·bā. /Can you introduce me to the headmaster? Néih hó·yíh gaai·siuh
    ngóh gin·háh néih·deih ge haauh·jéung ma?

introducer   gaai·siuh·yàhn

introduction   (preface) jéui (M: pìn); (formal preliminary treatise or guide) yahp·mùhn:
    An Introduction to Chinese Literature Jùng·gwok màhn·hohk yahp·mùhn; **letter of intro-**
    duction gaai·siuh seun (M: fùng)

intrude   (disturb) gwán·gáau; (in a conversation) chaap·jéui

introspection   fáan·sing

inundate   (to flood) séui·jam

invade   (with armed forces) dá (attack, hit), chàm·leuhk; (infringe, violate) chàm·faahn

invalid   (not valid) mòuh·haauh ge, jok·faai ge; (a sick person) chàahn·faai ge yàhn

invaluable   mòuh·ga·jì·bóu (N)

invariable   m̀h·bin·ge

invent   faat·mìhng

inventor   faat·mìhng·gā

inventory   chyùhn·fo; **check inventory** dím·fo, pùhn·fo

inverse   sèung·fáan ge; **inverse proportion** fáan·béi·làih

invert   fáan·jyun, dou·jyun, dìn·dóu

invest   tàuh·jì, lohk bún·chìhn (jouh·sàang·yi, in business; hòi·kwong, in mining)

investigate   (a case, or facts) diuh·chàh; (a subject of study) yìhn·gau; (a case judicial-
    ly) sám·mahn

investigator   diuh·chàh·yùhn

investment   tàuh·jì; (capital invested) jì·bún

invigorating   bóu

invincible   mòuh·dihk (ge)

invisible   tái·m̀h·gin ge, mòuh·yìhng ge

invitation   (written) chéng·típ (M: fahn); (oral) is expressed indirectly. /Should we send
    him an invitation? Ngóh·deih yìng m̀h·yìng·gòi gei go chéng·típ béi kéuih nē? /Thanks
    for the invitation. Néih jàn·haih haak·hei la. Ngóh yāt·dihng dou.

invite   chéng. /Aren't you going to invite him? Néih m̀h·chéng kéuih àh? /How many
    people have you invited? Néih chéng·jó géi·dò yàhn a? /I invite you to have lunch with

me, are you free? Ngóh chéng néih sihk ngaan·jau, néih dāk·hàahn ma? /Invite him to come in. Chéng kéuih yahp·lèih lā.

invoice   faat·piu, dāan: **to invoice** hōi·dáan, hòi·faat·piu

invoke   kàuh: **invoke God's blessing** kàuh Seuhng·daih bóu·yauh

involve   (implicate) lìhn·leuih, tòh·leuih. /I don't want to get involved. Mh·hóu lìhn·leuih ngóh a!

iodine   dīn·jáu

I.O.U.   him·geui, je·geui (M: jèung)

iron   (metal) tit. /Is this made of iron? Nī·go haih m̀h·haih yùhng tit jouh ga? /Has the iron gate been locked? Gó·douh tit·mùhn só·jó meih a?
  (instrument for ironing) tong·dáu; **electric iron** dihn·tong·dáu
  to iron tong. /Have you ironed my dress yet? Ngóh gihn sāam néih tong·jó meih a?
  to iron out is expressed by gáai·kyut (solve). /There are still a few problems to be ironed out. Juhng yáuh géi·go mahn·tàih yiu gáai·kyut ge.
  ironing tong·sāam. /Do you know how to iron? Néih wúih m̀h·wúih tong·sāam a?

irrigate   gun·koi

irritate   (provoke) gīk, (nettle) lìuh

is   haih; hái; yáuh. /Who is he? Kéuih haih bīn·go a? /He is busy. Kéuih m̀h·dāk·hàahn. /Is he home? Kéuih hái kéi ma? /Is there a restaurant there? Gó·syu yáuh·móuh chāan·gún a? /Yes, there is one. Yáuh.

Islam   (religion) Wùih·gaau; (follower of) wùih·gaau·tòuh

island   dóu

islet   síu·dóu

ism   jyú·yih

isolate   (place apart) gaak·hòi; **isolated island** gù·dóu

issue   (as order, licence, etc.) faat·chēut; (make public) faat·bíu; (put into circulation) faat·hàhng; (of books, etc.) chēut·báan
  an issue (publication) kèih (number, of a periodical); báan (edition or printing, of a newspaper, book, etc.)
  (problem, dispute) mahn·tàih. /The issue is whether or not we should have a student union. Mahn·tàih haih ngóh·deih sih·fáu yìng·gòi yáuh yāt·go hohk·sāang·wúi.
  at issue. /If this is not the point at issue, then what is it? is expressed as: Yùh·gwó néih·deih m̀h·haih jàang nī·yeuhng, gám néih·deih yauh jāang māt·yéh nē?
  take issue with (oppose) fáan·deui. /Why does he always take issue with what you say? Dím·gáai kéuih sèhng·yaht tùhng néih fáan·deui ga?

it   (as a demonstrative) is expressed by nī·go or gó·go; or is not expressed at all. /What is it? Gó·go haih māt·yéh a? or Haih māt·yéh a? or Māt·yéh a? /Who is it? Bīn·go a? /I can't do it. Ngóh m̀h·jouh·dāk. /It's very kind of you to say so. Hóu·wah. /It's here. Hái nī·syu. /It belongs to me. Haih ngóh·ge.
  (with the impersonal verb). /Is it raining? Lohk·gán yúh àh? /It's a beautiful day. Tīn·sìh jàn·haih hóu la. /It's five o'clock now. Ńgh·dím·jūng la.
  (as a substitute for a noun) is not expressed when the noun is elsewhere in the sentence; when the noun is not in the sentence, it is usually not expressed. /This house is nice, but it costs too much. Nī·gāan ngūk hóu hóu daahn·haih taai gwai. /I don't like this room, it has no window. Ngóh m̀h·jùng·yi nī·gāan fóng, móuh chēung·mún ge. /How long is this movie? Nī chēut dihn·yíng yíng géi nói a? It lasts two hours. Yíng léuhng·dím·jūng. or Yíng léuhng·go jūng·dím. /Do you like this book? Néih jùng yi nī·bún syù ma? /I like it. Ngóh jùng·yi.

it is plus an adjective. /It's hard to get a ticket. Hóu nàahn máaih·fēi. /It's impossible to get there by noon. Ngaan·jau ge sìh·hauh m̀h·dou·dāk. /Is it necessary for me to go? Ngóh yāt·saht yiu heui àh?

italic type che·tái·jih

itch hàhn

itchy hàhn. /Is it itchy? Hàhn m̀h·hàhn a?

item (general) go; (in document) tîuh, hohng

its kéuih·ge

itself kéuih jih·géi

ivory jeuhng·ngàh; **ivory chopsticks** jeuhng·ngàh faai·jí (M: sèung, fu, pair)

ivy chèuhng·chèun·tàhng

J

jacket ngoih·tou (M: gihn)

jade yúk (M: gauh, piece); **jade ornaments** yuhk hoi

jail gāam·fòhng, gāam·yuhk; **jailer** hōn·gāam·ge, gāam·dán

jam gwó·jeung; kāk·jyuh (V). /The drawer is jammed. Nī·go gwaih·túng yáuh yéh kāk·jyuh.

January (solar calendar) yāt·yuht

jar (glass with a stopper) bō·lēi·ngāang; (small-mouthed, medium-sized earthenware) chìhng, ngung;(large barrel-like earthenware) gòng: **water container** séui·gòng

jargon (secret vocabulary of a special group) buih·yúh; (technical vocabulary) seuht·yúh

jasmine muht·léi; **jasmine flower** muht·léi·fā; **Jasmine tea** Hèung·pin

jaundice wòhng·dáam·behng

jaw ngàh·gaau

jealous (in general) douh·geih, haap·chou; (of husband, wife, or lover) haap·chou

jeer dai, nán·fa

Jehovah Yèh·wòh·wàh

jelly je·lēi, jè·léi

jeep gāt·póu·chè, jīp·jái (M: ga)

jellyfish hói·jit

Jenghiz Khan Sìhng·gāt·sì·hon

Jerusalem Yèh·louh·saat·láahng

jest góng·síu (V); siu·wá (N)

Jesus Yèh·sōu; **Jesus Christ** Yèh·sōu·gēi·dūk

Jew Yàuh·taai·yàhn

jewel (collectively) jyù·bóu; **jeweler** jyù·bóu·sèung; (precious stone) bóu·sehk, sék: /This watch has seventeen jewels. Nī·go bīu haih sahp·chāt·nāp sék ge. **jeweled** sèung bóu·sehk ge jewelry   jyù·bóu

job   (permanent employment or work that requires mental effort) sih. /Are you looking
for a job? Néih séung wán sih jouh àh? /He has been looking for a job. Kéuih jing·joih
wán·gán sih. /Why don't you go find a job? Dim·gáai néih m̀h·heui wán sih jouh nē?
/How many men does this job require? Nī·gihn sih yiu yuhng géi·dò·go yàhn a?
       (permanent employment requiring manual labor) gūng (M: fahn). /Can you help him
to find a job? Néih hó·yíh bòng kéuih wán fahn gūng ma? /You can't find such a job anywhere else. Néih hái bīn·syu dōu wán·m̀h·dóu yāt·fahn gám ge gūng ge la. /Do you like
your job? Néih jùng·yi néih fahn gūng ma?
       (piece of work) gūng (M: gihn). /How many hands will this job require? Nī·gihn
gūng yiu géi·dò go yàhn jouh a?
       do a good job hóu·hóu·déi jouh; **did a good job** jouh dāk hóu hóu
       have the job of dá·léih. /You'll have the job of buying food; mine is to collect money,
and his is arranging transportation. Néih dá·léih máaih sihk·maht; ngóh dá·léih sàu·
chín; kéuih dá·léih wán chè.

Job   Yeuk·baak

John   Yeuk·hohn; (gospel) Yeuk·hohn·fūk·yām

join   (connect something) bok. /Join these pipes together. Jèung nī·léuhng·tìuh gún
bok·màaih kéuih.
       (connect, come together, combine, merge) hahp. /Shall we join in partnership?
Ngóh·deih hahp·gú hóu m̀h·hóu a? /Where do the two roads join? Nī·léuhng·tìuh louh
hái bīn·syu hahp·màaih a?
       join a group gà·yahp, chàam·gà. /Do you want to join us? Néih séung gà·yahp ma?
/Do you want to join our club? Néih séung gà·yahp ngóh·deih ge wúi ma? /Has he
joined any political party before? Kéuih yáuh móuh gà·yahp·gwo māt·yéh jing·dóng ma?
       join the army dōng·bìng, yahp·nǵh; **join the church** yahp·gaau

joint   (of bones) gwāt·jit, gwàan·jit

joke   góng·síu (V). /He likes joking. Kéuih hóu jùng·yi góng·síu ge. /I'm just joking.
Ngóh góng·síu jē.
       siu·wá (N). /Tell us some jokes. Góng géi·go siu·wá béi ngóh·deih tèng la.
       play a joke hòi·wàahn·siu. /I was only playing a joke on you. Ngóh tùhng néih hòi·
wàahn·siu jē.
       joking matter góng·síu ge. /This is no joking matter. Nī·gihn sih m̀h·haih góng·síu
ge boh.

jolly   (gay) faai·wuht, faai·lohk; (delightful) gòu·hing

jolt   jan·duhng

joss stick   hēung (M: jì; bá, bundle)

journalism   sàn·màhn·hohk

journalist   sàn·màhn·gei·jé

journey   (trip, expedition) léuih·hàhng; (distance traveled) louh·chìhng

joy   fùn·héi, gòu·hing, faai·lohk. /On hearing the news, she was filled with joy. Tèng
dóu nī·go sīu·sīk, kéuih múhn·sàm fùn·héi.

joyful   faai·lohk (ge), fùn·héi (ge)

Judaism   Yàuh·taai·gaau

judge   (in a law court) faat·gùn; tèui·sí;(in a contest) pìhng·pun·yùhn, chòih·pun·yùhn
       to judge pun·dyuhn (make a final judgment about); dúng·dāk (understand); kyut·dihng
(decide about). /He is a good judge of men. Kéuih wúih pun·dyuhn yàhn ge sing·gaak.

/Only God can judge who is right and who is wrong. Jí·yáuh Seuhng·dai hó·yíh pun·dyuhn bīn·go sih bīn·go fèi. /He's a good judge of art. Kéuih hóu dúng·dāk ngaih·seuht. /You'll have to judge it for yourself. Néih jih·gēi kyut·dihng la.

judgment tái dāk hóu jéun (good judgment) tái dāk m̀h·jéun (bad judgment); pun·dyun·lihk. /When driving, one needs good judgment. Sái·chè yiu tái dāk hóu jéun jí dāk. or Sái chè sèui·yiu hóu hóu ge pun·dyun·lihk.
  in my judgment yì ngoh·ge tái·fáat. /In my judgment, he is doing the wrong thing. Yì ngóh ge tái·fáat, nī·gihn sih kéuih jouh dāk m̀h·ngāam.
  the judgment in court pun·kyut, pun·kyut·syù

judicial (distinguished in general from legislative, executive, administrative, ministerial) sī·faat (At)

judo yàuh·seuht, yàuh·douh

jug jēun, ngāang

juggler luhng·bá·hei·ge

juice jāp; **orange juice** cháang·jāp; **grape juice** pòuh·tàih·jí jāp; **lemon juice** nìhng·mūng·jāp

jujitsu yàuh·seuht

jujube jóu

July chāt·yuht

jump tiu; **jump about** tiu·lèih tiu·heui; **jump aside** tiu·hòi; **jump down** tiu·lohk·heui (away from the speaker), tiu·lohk·lèih (toward the speaker); **jump out** tiu·chēut·heui (away from the speaker), tiu·chēut·lèih (toward the speaker); **jump over** tiu·gwo·heui; **jump up** tiu·héi; **jump up and down** tiu·séuhng tiu·lohk; **broad jump** tiu·yúhn; **high jump** tiu·gōu; **jump rope** tiu·síng
  (sudden rise). /There's been quite a jump in the temperature. Tìn·hei fāt·yìhn yiht·héi·séuhng·lèih. or Wān·douh fāt·yìhn gòu·jó.

junction gàau·gaai·ge deih·fòng; (crossroad) sahp·jih·louh·háu

juncture (emergency, crises) sìh·gèi; **at this juncture** gám ge sìh·gèi, douh jó nī·go deih·bouh

June luhk·yuht

jungle daaih·sàan·làhm, sàm·làhm

junior (of age) hauh·sāang, sai. /I'm his junior by many years. Ngóh hauh·sāang·gwo (or sai·gwo) kéuih hóu·dò nìhn. (subordinate) hah·kāp; **junior officer** (in armed forces) hah·kāp gwān·gùn; **junior class** chō·kāp; **junior high school** chō·kāp jùng·hohk

junk (Chinese ship) fàahn·syùhn; (rubbish) laahn·tùhng·laahn·tit

Jupiter (planet) muhk·sīng

jurisdiction (the legal power to determine) chòih·pun·kyùhn

jurist faat·leuht·gā

jury (law) pùih·sám·yùhn

just (fair) gùng·douh (ge), gùng·pìhng (ge); (impartial) gùng·jing (ge); (well-founded) jing·dong·(ge)
  (a moment ago) jing·wah. /I've just had my dinner. Ngóh jing·wah sihk·yùhn faahn. /They've just arrived. Kéuih·deih jing·wah lèih·dou. /He was here just a while ago. Kéuih jing·wah hái syu. /He just left a while ago. Kéuih ngāam·ngāam jáu·jó.

(at that moment) jíng·joih. /He was just leaving when I asked him. Ngóh mahn kéuih ge sìh·hauh, kéuih jíng·joih yiu jáu.

(only, nothing more than) jí·haih, jauh(·haih). /He just said he was very thirsty. Kéuih ji·haih wah kéuih hóu géng·hot. /He said he just had two dollars. Kéuih wah kéuih jauh yáuh léuhng·go ngàan·chín jē.

(simply) jàn·haih, gáan·jihk. /I just don't understand why he did it. Ngóh jàn·haih (or gáan·jihk) m̀h·mìhng·baahk dím·gáai kéuih yiu gám jouh.

just as, just like jàn·haih chíh, chíh·jūk. /It's just like spring. Jàn·haih chíh chēun·tīn la. /It was just like a dream. Jàn·haih chíh faat·jó chèuhng muhng gám. /He walks just like his father. Kéuih hàahng héi·séuhng·lèih chíh·jūk kéuih lóuh·dauh.

justice   (judge) faat·gùn; (fairness) <u>is expressed by verb phrases</u>: /Don't expect justice from him. <u>is expressed as</u>: Don't expect him to be just. M̀h·sái ji·yi kéuih wúih gùng·pìhng. /We must admit the justice of his demands. <u>is expressed as</u>: We must admit that his demands are just. Ngóh·deih bāt·nàhng·bāt sìhng·yihng kéuih ge yiu·kàuh haih jíng·dong ge.

jut out   daht·chēut

juvenile   siu·nìhn (At), yìh·tùhng (At); **juvenile court** siu·nìhn faat·tìhng; **juvenile education** yìh·tùhng gaau·yuhk

K

kaleidoscope   maahn·fà·tùhng

kangaroo   doih·syú (M: jek)

keel   (of a ship) lùhng·gwāt

keen   (acute of mind) jìng·mìhng, jèng; (sharp) leih

keep   (retain in good condition; save) làuh·fàan. /This milk won't keep until tomorrow, let's drink it. Nī·dī ngàuh·náaih m̀h·làuh·dāk·fàan tìng·yaht la, yám·jó kéuih là. /Do you think this fish will keep until tomorrow? Néih wah nī·tìuh yú hó·yíh làuh·fàan tìng·yaht ma? /Let's keep this and eat it later. Làuh·fàan kéuih yāt·jàn sìn·ji sihk. /Do you want to keep this picture (photograph)? Néih séung làuh·fàan nī·fūk séung ma? <u>but</u> /May I keep this picture? Béi nī·fūk séung ngóh dāk ma? (Can you give me this picture?)

(put away; keep in stock) sàu·màaih; chyùhn. /Where do you keep your stamps? Néih sàu·màaih dī sih·dāam hái bīn·syu a? /What do you keep in stock? Néih chyùhn·jó dī māt·yéh fo a?

(raise, tend) yéuhng. /Why don't you keep a dog? Dím·gáai néih m̀h·yéuhng jek gáu nē?

(continue doing something or being a certain way) bāt·hit, sèhng·yaht. /He keeps asking when his mother will come. Kéuih bāt·hit gám mahn kéuih màh·mā géi·sìh lèih. /He keeps bothering his mother. Kéuih sèhng·yaht gám lò·sò kéuih lóuh·móu. /Keep trying. Joi si·háh. /Keep quiet. M̀h·hóu chòuh.

keep <u>something</u> **on**. /Keep your eyes on that man. Néih hàu·jyuh gó·go yàhn. /Keep your shoes on. M̀h·sái chèuih hàaih.

keep <u>something or someone</u> **from**. /You'd better put a bandage on to keep the dirt from getting into the cut. Néih ge sèung·háu jeui hóu béi yéh jaat·jyuh mìhn·ji béi dī laaht·taat yéh jáu·jó yahp·heui. /You'd better close the window to keep the mosquitoes from coming in. Néih ji hóu sàan·màaih dī chēung·mún mìhn·ji dī mān fēi·yahp·lèih.

keep a person làuh. /Keep him here a while longer, the coffee is about ready. Làuh kéuih chóh dō yāt·jahn·gāan, dī ga·fē jauh dāk la.

keep accounts. /Can you keep accounts? Néih wúih dá·léih sou·muhk ma? <u>or</u> Néih wúih bouh·gei ma? (Do you know bookkeeping?)

keep a diary gei yaht·gei. /Do you keep a diary? Néih gei yaht·gei ma?

keep a promise or **keep one's word.** /He always keeps his promise. Kéuih yìng·
sìhng·jó néih yāt·dihng jouh·dou ge. /You'd better keep your promise this time. Néih
nī·yāt·chi yìng·sìhng·jó yāt·dihng yiu jouh·dou sìn·ji hóu.
    keep a secret. /Can he keep a secret? Kéuih hó·yíh sáu bei·maht ma?
    keep at. /Keep at it. Mh·hóu tìhng·sáu.
    keep good time (of a timepiece) jéun. /Does this watch keep good time? Nī·go bīu
jéun ma?
    keep house (manage a house) dá·léih ngūk·kéi. /I want to hire a person to keep house
for me. Ngóh yiu chéng yāt·go yàhn tùhng ngóh dá·léih ngūk·kéi.
    keep one's temper mh·faat pèih·hei. /He has promised me to keep his temper while
someone wakes him up in the morning. Kéuih yìng·sìhng ngóh jiu·tàuh·jóu yàhn·deih giu
kéuih héi·sàn gó·jahn·sí, kéuih mh·faat·pèih·hei la.
    keep away. /Keep away from here. Hàahng hòi, hàahng hòi.
    keep off. /Keep off the grass. Mh·hóu hàahng chóu·déi.
    keep the change. /You may keep the change. Mh·sái juhk·chín la.
    keep watch hòn. /Who will keep watch over this patient tonight? Gàm·máahn bīn·
go hòn nī·go behng·yàhn a?
    keep to. /Do I keep to the right or the left? Ngóh kaau yauh·bihn hàahng yīk·waahk
kaau jó·bihn hàahng a?
    keep up. /Keep it up. Mh·hóu tìhng. /Keep up the good work. Jouh dāk gam hóu,
gai·juhk jouh·lohk·heui lā.
    keep up with. /Do you have any trouble keeping up with your classmates? Néih
gàn·dāk·séuhng néih dī tùhng·bāan ma?
    keep in mind gei·jyuh; **keep it covered** kám·jyuh kéuih; **keep it under water** béi séui
jam·jyuh kéuih; **keep the rules** sáu kwài·géui

kerosene   fó·séui: **kerosene lamp** fó·séui·dāng

ketchup   ké·jāp (M: jèun, bottle)

kettle   chàh·bōu

key   (lock opener) só·sìh (M: tìuh). /Do you have a key for that door? Néih yáuh móuh
gó·douh mùhn ge só·sìh a?
    key of piano kàhm·jí; **key in music** díu, diuh: **key of C** C díu, C diuh

keyhole   só·sìh·lūng

khaki   (cloth) wòhng·ché

kick   tek: **kick the ball** tek bō, **kick shuttlecock** tek yín

kid   (child) sai·màn·jái, sai·lóu·gō

kidnap   (to carry away a child by unlawful force or fraud) gwáai·daai; (to seize and detain the victim for ransom) bīu·sām, bóng·piu. **kidnapper** gwáai·jí·lóu

kidney   sahn, sáhn, sahn·johng

kill   (put to death) jíng·séi, dá·séi; (murder) saat·séi; or expressed with séi alone. /How
did he kill the rat? Kéuih dím·yéung jíng·séi jek lóuh·syú ga? /How was he killed?
Kéuih dím yéung séi ga? /He was murdered. Kéuih béi yàhn saat·séi ge.
    kill by being . . . : by being stabbed béi yàhn gāt·séi; **by being hit by a car** béi chè
pung·séi; **being run over by a car** béi chè lūk·séi; **being killed by a falling rock** béi
sehk jaahk·séi; **by drowning** jahm·séi
    (fig.) is expressed with resultative compounds with séi as the second element, as
(by laughter) siu·séi; (by overwork) guih·séi; (by pain) tung·séi; (by boredom) fàahn·séi;
(by noise) chòuh·séi. /You are killing me! (by laughter) Néih jàn·haih siu·séi ngóh
la. /This is killing me! (by overwork) Jàn·haih guih·séi ngóh lo. or (by pain)
Tung·sei ngoh lo! or (boredom) Jàn·haih fàahn·séi ngóh lo.
    kill (animals) tòng: **kill a chicken** tòng gāi; **kill a pig** tòng jyū; **kill time** sìu·mòh
sìh·gaan; **killer** (murderer) hùng·sáu

kiln   yìuh: **brick kiln** jyùn yìuh

kilogram   gūng·gàn

kilometer   gùng·léih

kin   (relatives) chān·chīk

kind   hóu (good); hóu sèung·yúh (affable). /He's a very kind man. Kéuih go yàhn hóu
hóu ge. /The people here are very kind. Nī·syu ge yàhn go·go dōu hóu hóu·sèung·yúh
ge.

   (sort) tíng; (species) júng; (types distinguished by shape, form, or mannerisms)
yéung. /Do you like this kind of music? Néih jùng·yi nī·tíng yàm·ngohk ma? /This kind
of person is hard to deal with. Nī·tíng gám ge yàhn hóu nàahn sèung·yúh ge. /Do you
have any more of this kind of paper? Néih juhng yáuh móuh nī·tíng jí a? /What kind
(species) of dog is he? Nī·jek gáu haih māt·yéh júng ga? /We don't need this kind of
person. Ngóh deih m̀h·sèui·yiu gám yéung ge yàhn. /Do you like to wear this kind of
shoe? Néih jùng m̀h·jùng·yi jeuk gám yéung ge hàaih a?
   be kind enough to. /Would you be kind enough to help him? Chéng néih bòng·háh
kéuih?
   give kindest regards to mahn·hauh. /Give my kindest regards to your family.
Mahn·hauh fú·seuhng gok·wái.

kindergarten   yau·jih·yún

king   gwok·wòhng; (tycoon) daaih·wòhng: **oil king** mùih·yàuh·daaih·wòhng

kiss   sek·háh, jyut·háh. (used especially of kissing children; public or indiscriminate
kissing among adults, even as a merely friendly gesture or between relatives, is not
generally approved by Chinese custom). /She is so cute, let me kiss her. Kéuih gam
dāk·yi, dáng ngóh sek·háh kéuih dāk.

kitchen   chyùh·fóng; **kitchen knife** choi·dōu (M: bá)

kite   jí·yíu (M: jek); **fly a kite** fong jí·yíu

kitten   māau·jái (M: jek)

knee   sāt·tàuh·gō; **on one's knee** gwaih. /Why is he on his knee? Kéuih gwaih·hái syu
jouh māt·yéh a?

kneel   gwaih; **kneel down** gwaih·dài

knife   dōu (M: bá); **pocket knife** dōu·jái (M: bá); **knife and fork** dōu chā

knight   móuh·sih; (honorary title) jeuk·sih

knit   jīk; **knitting needle** jīk·jām, gwāt·jām

knock   (bump) pung. /Be careful not to knock anything down. Hóu·sēng m̀h·hóu pung·dit
dī yéh.
   (rap or tap) hàau; **knock on a door** paak·mùhn, hàau·mùhn, dá·mùhn
   knock down (reduce; of a price) gáam·ga; (of a person) dá·dài. /The detective knocked
down the thief. Go jìng·taam dá·dài go chahk.

knot   (in strings, etc.) lit. /Could you untie this knot for me? Néih tùhng ngóh gáai·hòi
nī·go lit, dāk ma?
   (nautical miles) hói·léih; **to knot** dá go lit

know   (have knowledge about) jî·dou. /Do you know what his last name is? /Néih jî·dou
kéuih sing māt·yéh ma? /Who knows? Bīn·go jî a? /No one. Móuh yàhn jî. /Does he
know? Kéuih jî m̀h·jî a? /He knows nothing about it. Kéuih yāt·dī dōu m̀h·jî.
   (be skilled in; know how to) sīk (V), sīk (AV); wúih (V), wúih (AV); sīk wúih (AV).
/Do you know English? Néih sīk Yìng·màhn ma? /Do you know how to speak English?

Néih sīk góng Yìng·màhn ma? /Does he know English? Kéuih wúih Yìng·màhn ma?
/He knows how to speak but not to write. Kéuih wúih góng m̀h·wúih sé. /Do you
know how to drive? Néih sīk (or wúih, or sīk wúih) sái chè ma?
   (be acquainted with) sīk. /Do you know Mr. Hòh? Néih sīk Hòh sīn·sàang ma?
   (by recognition) sīk, yihng·dāk. /Do you know (how to read) Chinese characters?
Néih sīk Jùng·gwok jih ma? /Do you know this character? Néih sīk nī·go jih ma? /Do
you know (still recognize) this character? Néih yihng·dāk nī·go jih ma?

knowledge   (understanding) jī·sīk; (experience) gin·sīk; (learning) hohk·mahn
   no knowledge of. /I have no knowledge of how it happened. Gó·gihn sih dím·yéung
   faat·sàng ge ngóh yāt·dī dōu m̀h·jī.

knuckle   sáu·jí·lit

Koran   Hó·làahn·gīng

kowtow   kau·tàuh (VO). /He kowtowed three times. Kéuih kau·jó sàam·go tàuh.

Kuomintang   Gwok·màhn·dóng

L

label   jīu·pàaih·jí, māk·tàuh·jí

laboratory   saht·yihm·sāt (M: gàan)

laborious   sàn·fú

labor   (work) gùng·jok; (a person) gùng·yàhn, dá·gùng·jái; **labor and material** gùng·líu;
   Labor Department Lòuh·gùng·bouh; **labor union** gùng·wúi

Labor Party   Gùng·dóng

lace   fā·bīn; **shoelace** hàaih·dáai

lack   kyut·síu, kyut·faat, kyut·fat

lacquer   chāt: **lacquerware** chāt·hei

lad   hauh·sāang·jái

ladder   tài (M: bá)

ladle   hok, séui·hok; **ladle out** fāt, yíu

lady   (woman) taai·táai, nàaih·náai, sī·naai (married); fù·yán (married, a polite term);
   young lady síu·jé. (as a prefix indicating the female sex) néuih: **lady friend** néuih·
   pàhng·yáuh, **lady doctor** néuih·yī·sāng; **lady guest** nćuih·haak; **ladies' room** néuih
   chi·só; **Ladies and gentlemen!** Gok·wái (nàahm néuih) lòih·bàn! **old lady** baak·yē·pó

lake   wùh

lama   lā·mā

Lamaism   Lā·mā·gaau

lamb   yèuhng·mē·jái; gòu·yèuhng (as it is used in the Bible)

lame   bài, bài·geuk

lament   ngòi·douh

lamp   dāng (M: jáan); **lamp shade** dāng·jaau. /Turn on the lamp (electric lamp)! Hoi·
   jeuhk jáan dāng kéuih. /Turn off the lamp! Sik·jó jaan dāng kéuih!

land   deih, tóu·deih; (in contrast to sea) luhk·deih; (disembark from ship) séuhng·ngohn;
   (as an airplane) gong·lohk

landlord   (of a house) ngūk·jyú; (of a piece of land) deih·jyú; (of a shop) pou·jyú; (of property) yihp·jyú; **landlady** ngūk·jyú·pòh

land mine   deih·lèuih

landscape   (scenery) fùng·gíng; (picture) sàan·séui·wá

lane   hóng (M: tîuh)

language   (spoken language) wá; màhn (BF) (written language) màhn (BF), màhn·jih; yúh·yîhn (technical word). /Do you speak English? Néih sīk góng Yìng·màhn ma? /Can you read English? Néih sīk Yìng·màhn ma? /Which country's written language is this? Nī·dī haih bīn·gwok ge màhn·jih a? /I like to study languages. Ngóh jùng·yi yîhn·gau yúh·yîhn.

    Hakka haak·ga·wá; **Swatownese** Saan·tàuh·wá, chìu·jàu·wa; **Fukienese** Fūk·gin·wá; **French** Faat·gwok·wá (spoken), Faat·màhn (spoken and written); **German** Dāk·gwok·wá (spoken), Dāk·màhn (spoken and written)

languid   móuh·jìng·sàhn, móuh·lihk

lantern   dàng·lùhng

Lao Tzu   Lóuh·jí

lap   sāt·tàuh (N); líhm (V)

lard   jyù·yàuh

large   daaih; **large part of** daaih·bouh·fahn·ge; **large quantity of** daaih·leuhng ge, hóu dò ge; **larger than** daaih·gwo; **a little larger than** daaih dī; **the largest** jeui·daaih·ge, ji daaih ge; **the larger the better** yuht·daaih·yuht·hóu

lark   baak·lîhng·níuh

larva   yau·chùhng

larynx   hàuh·lùhng, sèng·daai

last   (final) jeui·hauh (ge), jeui·sāu·mēi. /This is the last one. Nī·go haih jeui·hauh·ge yāt·go la. /He came last. Kéuih haih jeui sāu·mēi lèih ge. /This is your last chance. Nī·go haih néih jeui·hauh ge gèi·wuih.

    (most recent) seuhng: **last time** seuhng·chi; **last week** seuhng·go láih·baai; **last Monday,** seuhng·láih·baai·yāt; **last month** seuhng·go·yuht; **last night** kàhm·máahn, chàhm·maahn, johk·máahn; **last year** gauh·nín; **the night before last** chîhn·máahn; **the last few days** chîhn·géi·yaht; **the last few months** chîhn·géi·go·yuht, nī·géi·go yuht; **the last few years** chîhn·géi·nîhn, nī·géi·nîhn

    at last gīt·gwó. /At last we found the place. Git·gwó ngóh·deih wán·dóu·gó·daat deih·fòng la.

    to last yuhng. /How long will this battery last? Nī·go dihn·sām hó·yíh yuhng géi·nói a? **lasting** kàm·sái. /It'll last for a long time. Nī·gihn yéh hóu kàm·sái ge.

latch   gaau: **door latch** mùhn·gaau

late   (tardy) chîh. /Don't be late! M̀h·hóu lèih·chîh·jó! or M̀h·hóu chîh·dou. /I'm sorry, I've arrived late. M̀h·hóu·yi·si, Ngóh lèih·chîh·jo.

    (far advanced in time) ngaan. /I slept late this morning. Ngóh gàm·jîu·jóu héi·sàn héi dāk hóu ngaan. /It's quite late now, you'd better get up. Hóu ngaan la boh, néih hóu héi·sàn lo boh.

    (deceased) yîh·gìng gu·heui ge, sàn·gahn (recently) gu·heui ge, sin (BF): sìn·fuh (late father), sìn·móuh (late mother)

    late at night or **at a late hour** bun·yé; **lately** jeui·gahn; **latest** jeui·hauh ge (final), jeui·gahn·ge (most recent); **at the latest** jî chîh. /You have to be here by one o'clock at the latest. Néih ji·chîh yāt·dím·jung yiu dou nī·syu.

sooner or later chìh·jóu. /God will save you sooner or later. Seuhng·dai chìh·jóu wúih·gáai·gau néih ge.

lathe   chē·chòhng (M: fu)

lather   (from soap) fàan·gáan·póuh

Latin   Lāai·dǐng; (as a language) Lāai·dǐng·màhn, lā·dǐng·màhn

latitude   (geog.) wéih·douh

latrine   chi·só

latter   hauh·bihn gó·go, hauh·jé (lit.). /I like the latter, not the former. Ngóh jùng·yi hauh·bihn gó·go, m̀h haih chìhn·bihn gó·go.

lattice   gaak·jái: **lattice window** gaak·jái·chēung

laugh   siu. /What are you laughing about? Néih siu māt·yéh a? **laugh at** siu. /Don't laugh at him, he'll get mad. M̀h·hóu siu kéuih, kéuih wuih nàu ga. **laughable** hóu·síu. /What is so laughable (funny)? Yáuh māt gam hóu·siu a?

laughter   /They burst into laughter. Kéuih·deih fát·yìhn siu·héi séuhng·lèih.

launch   (N) fó·syùhn·jái; (V) lohk·séui (a boat); fong·seh, faat·seh (a rocket, etc.) **launching ceremony** hah·séui·láih

laundry   (establishment) sái·yì·dim, yì·sèuhng·gún (term used in Chinese community in North America); **clothes washed** sai·jó ge sāam. **clothes to be washed** yiu sái ge sāam

lavatory   chi·só

law   faat·leuht, faat (BF): **civil law** mahn·faat; **criminal law** yìhng·faat; **commercial law** sèung·faat; **military law** gwàn·faat; **international law** gwok·jai·faat, gwok·jai·gung· faat. **abide by the law** sáu·faat. **break the law** wàih·faat, faahn·faat

lawn   chóu·déi (M: pin, faai)

lawyer   johng·sī, leuht·sī: **lawyer's office** leuht·sī·làuh, johng·sī·làuh

lax   (not strict or firm) sùng

laxative   se·yeuhk

lay   (put) jài, fòng. /Lay the books here. Jeung dī syù jài·hái nī·syu. /Lay the baby on the bed. Jèung bìh·bī fong·hái chòhng·syu.
       (spread out) póu·hòi. /Please lay the carpet on the floor for me to examine. M̀h· gòi póu·hōi jèung deih·jīn béi ngóh tái·háh.
       lay bricks chai·jyùn; **lay a foundation** lahp or dá yāt·go gèi·chó; **lay an egg** sàang dáan. **lay aside** jài·dài, jài·màaih. /If you can't do it now, lay it aside and do it later. Yùh·gwó néih yìh·gā m̀h·jouh·dāk, jài·dài kéuih yāt·jahn·gāan sìn·ji jouh lā.

layer   chàhng, chùhng

layman   ngoih·hóng, mùhn·ngoih·hon; (not a clergyman) seun·tòuh

lazy   láahn, láahn·doh

lead   yùhn (N). (guide) daai. /Please lead me to the U.S. Consulate. M̀h·gòi néih daai ngóh heui Méih·gwok lìhng·sih·gún. (conduct) lìhng·douh. /He led the people to re- construct the country. Kéuih lìhng·douh yàhn·mahn jèung gwok·ga gin·chit·héi·lèih. **leading lady** néuih jyú·gok; **leading man** nàahm·jyú·gok

leader   táu, tàuh·yàhn (vulgar), líhng·jauh (formal). **leadership** líhng·douh ge nàhng· lihk

leaf yihp, syuh·yihp (M: faai, pin)

leaflet chyùhn·dāan (M: jèung)

league wúi, hip·wúi, lyuhn·hahp·wúi

leak lauh. (of electricity) lauh·dihn. **leak out** jáu·lauh: **let a secret leak out** jáu·lauh· sīu·sīk. /There is a leak in the room. Gaan·fóng lauh·yúh.

lean (thin) sau. **lean against** ngàai·màaih; **lean on** ngàai·jyuh, ngaai·màaih

leap tiu: **leap over** tiu·gwo. /He leaps over a puddle. Kéuih tiu·gwo yāt·táhm séui. **a leap** is expressed verbally as: /He made a four-foot leap. Keuih tiu·jó sei·chek gam gòu. **a leap year** yeuhn·nìhn

learn hohk. /How long have you been learning English? Néih hohk Yìng·màhn hohk·jó géi nói la? /Do you want to learn to type? Néih séung hohk dá·jih ma? **learn that** or **learn about** tèng·màhn, tèng·gin·wah, tèng·màhn·góng. /I learned that there is no ship to Macao tomorrow, is that true? Ngóh tèng·màhn tìng·yaht móuh syùhn heui Ngou·mún haih m̀h·haih a?

learned yáuh hohk·mahn ge

learning hohk·mahn: **having learning** yáuh·hohk·mahn

lease jòu (V); jòu·yeuk (N). **lease to** jòu·béi

least ji síu, jeui síu. /It'll take three days at least. Ji síu yiu sàam·yaht ji dāk.

leather pèih: **leather belt** pèih·dáai; **leather shoes** pèih·haaih (M: deui, pair); **leather boots** pèih·hèu (M: deui, pair)

leave jáu. /When do you leave? Néih géi·sí jáu a? (depart from a place) /When did he leave this place? Kéuih géi·sí lèih·hòi nī·syu ga? (do something when leaving) làuh· dài. /Has he left any word? Kéuih yáuh móuh làuh·dài māt·yéh syut·wah a? (intentionally) làuh·dài. /I want to leave these things here. Ngóh séung làuh·dài nī·dī yéh hái syu. (unintentionally) lauh·dài. /What did you leave behind? Néih lauh·dài·jó māt· yéh a? (depart of a train, ship, etc.) hòi, hōi·sàn. /When will the train leave? Fó· chè géi·sí hòi a? (remaining) /Are there any tickets left? Juhng yáuh móuh fēi a? (vacation) ga. **ask leave** chíng ga, gou ga. /He may ask for two days leave. Kéuih hó·yíh chíng leuhng·yaht ga. **leave it alone** yáu dāk kéuih lā. **leave it to you** yáu dāk néih. /I'll leave it to you. Yáu dāk néih jùng·yi dím jauh dím.

lecture yín·góng (M: pìn); **lecture hall** góng·tòhng; **lecture notes** góng·yih

lecturer (instructor) góng·sī

leech kèh·nā, séui·jaht

leek gáu·choi

left jó: **left-hand** jó·sáu; **left-hand side** jó·sáu·bihn. **leftover (food)** gaak·yéh ge, sihk· jihng ge. **left wing** jó·paai. /How much is there left? Juhng jihng géi dò a?

leg (lower part) geuk; (thigh) béi, daaih·béi

legacy wàih·cháan; **legacy tax** wàih·cháan·seui

legal (lawful) hahp·faat ge; (fixed by law) faat·dihng ge; **legal adviser** faat·leuht gu·mahn; **legal number** faat·dihng yàhn·sou; **legal price** gùn·ga; **legal wife** git·faat·chài, git· faat·lóuh·pòh

legation gùng·sí·gún (M: gàan)

legend chyùhn·syut

legible   duhk·dāk·chēut, yìhng·dāk·chēut

legislate   lahp·faat

legislative assembly   lahp·faat·yún. **The Legislative Yuan** (in the Republic of China) Lahp·faat·yún. **legislative body** lahp·faat·gēi·gwàan

legislator   yih·yùhn

leisure   dāk·hàahn. /He has plenty of leisure. Kéuih hóu dāk·hàahn.

lemon   nìhng·mūng, lìhng·mūng: **lemonade** nìhng·mūng·séui

lend   je . . . béi, je·béi. /Can you lend me ten dollars. Néih je sahp·mān béi ngóh dāk m̀h·dāk a? /Don't lend it to him. M̀h·hóu je·béi kéuih.

length   chèuhng·dyún. /Is this the right length? is expressed as Gam chèuhng ngāam m̀h·ngāam a? (lit. So long right not right?)

lengthen   (by pulling out) làai·chèuhng; (by adding something) bok·chèuhng; (extend) yìhn·chèuhng

lenient   fùn·yùhng. /The teacher is very lenient with the students. Gó·wái sīn·sàang hóu fùn·yùhng kéuih dī hohk·sāang ge.

lens   (of a camera) gēng·táuh

leopard   paau, gàm·chìhn·paau (M: jek)

leper   faat·fūng·lóu, màh·fūng·lóu

leper asylum   màh·fūng·behng·yún (M: gàan)

leprosy   màh·fūng; **show signs of leprosy** faat·fūng

less   (in quantity) síu dī. /Eat less. Sihk síu dī. /Give me less sugar. Bei síu dī tòhng ngóh. /Add less salt this time. Nī·tong jài síu dī yìhm.
(in size) sai dī. (minus) gáam. /Five less three is two. Ńgh gáam sàam haih yih.
less than síu·gwo, sai·gwo. /I have less money than he has. Ngóh ge chín síu·gwo kéuih. **less than** (not in comparison of parallel things) m̀h·gau. /Less than ten dollars. M̀h·gau sahp·mān. /Less than a week. M̀h·gau yāt·go láih·baai.

lessee   jōu·ngūk·yàhn, lahp·jòu·yeuk·yàhn

lesson   (learning unit) fo: **lesson nine** daih·gáu·fo. (instructive experience) gaau·fan. /The experience taught us a great lesson. Nī·yat·chi gìng·yihm béi ngóh·deih yāt·go hóu daaih ge gaau·fan. (homework) gùng·fo. /Have you finished your lessons yet? Néih jouh·yùhn néih dī gùng·fo meih a?

lest   mìhn·ji, yeuhk·m̀h·haih jauh . . . /You'd better do it now, lest you be lectured by him. Néih jeui hóu jik·hāk jouh·jó kéuih mìhn·ji béi kéuih naauh néih. or Néih jeui hóu jīk·hāk jouh·jó kéuih yeuhk·m̀h·haih jauh béi kéuih naauh ge la.

let   (may be rented) chēut·jòu. /House to let. Yáuh ngūk chēut·jòu.
(allow) béi, yáu. /Please let us in. M̀h·gòi béi ngóh·deih yahp·heui. /Let him go and play. Yáu kéuih heui wáan la. /Let me try. Béi ngóh si·háh. /Please let me see the menu. M̀h·gòi béi go chāan·dāan (or chòih·dāan) ngóh tái·háh.
let me see (to look at) dáng ngóh tái·háh; (to think over) dáng ngóh séung·háh.
let . . . know góng·béi . . . jì. /Please let me know. M̀h·gòi góng·béi ngóh jì.
let me explain to you dáng ngóh góng·béi néih jì. **let me do it** dáng ngóh lèih là.
let go one's hold fong·sáu. **let** (release) **him go** fong kéuih jáu la. **let off firecrackers** síu paau·jéung

letter   (message) seun (M: fùng). /Are there any letters for me? Ngóh yáuh móuh seun a? /I want to write a letter to her. Ngóh yiu sé fùng séun béi kéuih.

(of an alphabet) jih (also means a Chinese character). /These letters are not very clear. Nī·dī jih m̀h·chìng·chó. (a letter of the alphabet) jih·júng

letter box seun·sēung. **letter of introduction** gaai·siuh·seun. **letter paper** seun·jí

lettuce   sàang·choi (M: pò head, jaat bunch)

level   pìhng (SV); jíng·pìhng (V); **level ground** pìhng·deih

lever   beng, gung·gón (N); **pry with a lever** giuh·héi

levy   chàu: **levy a tax** chàu·seui

lexicon   chìh·dín, jih·dín

li   léih (about one third of a mile)

liar   daaih·paau·yáu

libel   dái·wái (V)

liberate   gáai·fong: **liberation army** gáai·fong·gwān

liberty   jih·yàuh: **liberty and equality** jih·yàuh pìhng·dáng. **be at liberty** chèuih·bín, chèuih·yi. /Are you at liberty to talk? Néih yìh·gā hó·yíh chèuih·bín góng·wá ma?

librarian   tòuh·syù gún·yùhn

library   tòuh·syù·gún (M: gàan)

license   pàaih·jiu, lāai·sán; **license plate** pàaih; **trading license** yìhng·yihp jāp·jiu

lick   lím

lid   goi (N); **to put on a lid** kám·jyuh, kám·goi

lie   fan·dài, fan·hái, buhk·hái. /You'd better lie down for a while. Néih fan·dài yāt·jahn·gāan lā. /Help him to lie down on the sofa and don't let him move. Fùh kéuih fan·hái jèung sō·fá syu, m̀h·hóu yūk. **lie down, face down** buhk·hái syu (deceive) góng daaih·wah. /Don't tell lies. M̀h·jéun góng daaih·wah.

life   mehng, sāang·mehng, sàng·mihng, sing·mihn (M: tìuh). /He saved my life. Kéuih gau·fàan ngóh tìuh mehng. (way of living) sàng·wuht. /He leads a very happy life. is expressed as: Kéuih sàng·wuht dāk hóu faai·lohk. (the extent in time one lives) yāt·sàng, yāt·sai·yàhn. /He never drank in his whole life. Kéuih yāt·sàng dōu m̀h·yám·jáu. (biography) jyuhn·gei. /I like to read the life of a great man. Ngóh hóu jùng·yi tái wáih·yàhn ge jyuhn·gei.

life imprisonment mòuh·kèih·tòuh·yìhng; **life-insurance** yàhn·sauh·yin·sō, or yàhn·sauh·bóu·hím; **life-preserver** (the ring-shaped type) gau·sàng·hyūn, (the jacket or May West type) gau·sàng·yī; **lifeboat** gau·sàng·téhng; **lifeguard** gau·sàng·yùhn; **life-span** sauh·mehng; **lives** (persons) yàhn mehng, yàhn

lift   (raise) nìng·héi; (with two hands) chàu·héi; (above the shoulder) géui·héi. (of raising a cover, curtain, rug, etc.) kín·hòi. /Lift up the cover and see what's inside. Kín·hòi kéuih tái·háh léuih·bihn yáuh māt·yéh. **lift (elevator)** dihn·tài

light   gwòng, gwòng·sin. /The light is bad here. Nī·syu m̀h gau·gwòng. or Nī·syu ge gwòng·sin taai yáih. /That bulb doesn't give enough light. Gó·go dāng·dáam m̀h·gau gwòng.

(source of artificial illumination) dāng; **electric light** dihn·dāng, **light bulb** dāng·dáam; **flashlight** dihn·túng; **lighthouse** dāng·taap; **headlight** chè·tàuh·dāng; **fluorescent light** gwòng·gún

to light dím, tau. **light a candle** dím yèuhng·jūk; **light a lamp** dím dāng. **light the stove** tau fó·lòuh. **light up** dím·jeuhk

(of weight) hèng. (of color) chín.
sunlight yaht·gwōng. **light year** gwòng·nìhn

lighter   (for cigarette) dá·fó·gèi

lightly   hehng·hēng

lightning   sím·dihn; **killed by lightning** béi lèuih pek·séi

like   fùn·héi, jùng·yi. /Do you like to sing? Néih fùn·héi cheung·gō ma? /What would
you like to eat? Néih jùng·yi sihk māt·yéh a? /Whom do you like? Néih fùn·héi bīn·go
a? /I like the tall one. Ngóh fùn·héi go gòu ge. /Which one do you like? Néih jùng·yi
bīn·go a? /I like the small one. Ngóh jùng·yi go sai ge. /Do you like fish? is expressed
as: Do you like to eat fish? Néih jùng·yi sihk·yú ma? /Do you like movies? is expressed as: Do you like to see a movie? Néih jùng·yi tái dihn·yíng ma?
    (indicating opinion) gok·dāk. /How do you like my dress? Néih gok·dak ngoh gihn
sāam leng ma? /How do you like the food at that restaurant? Néih gok·dāk gó·gàan
jáu· gún ge sung dím a?
    would like séung, yuhn·yi. /I'd like to visit your factory. Ngoh séung chāam·gùn·
háh néih·deih ge gùng·chóng. /Would you like to go there with me? Néih yuhn·yi tùhng·
màaih ngóh yāt·chái heui ma?
    (similar to) hóu·chíh, chíh. /She looks like her mother. Kéuih hóu·chíh kéuih màh·
mā. /Is it like this? Chíh m̀h·chíh nī·go gám a?

likely   (may be) wúih. /Is it likely to rain tonight? Gàm·máahn wúih lohk·yúh ma?
most likely daaih·kói. /He most likely won't come. Kéuih daaih·kói m̀h·lèih ge la.

likewise   jiu yéung gám. /Please do likewise. Chéng jiu yéung gám jouh.

lilac   dīng·hēung (bush), dīng·hēung·fā (flower)

lily   baak·hahp·fā; **water lily,** lìhn·fà, hòh·fā; **white lily** (tuberose) yuhk·jāam·fā

limb   (of the body) jì·tái; **the four limbs** sei·jì. **a limb of a tree** syuh·jì

lime   sehk·fùi; (fruit) chèng·nìhng·mūng

limit   haahn·jai (V); haahn·douh, haahn·jai (N). **limited** yáuh·haahn(ge). /Our capital is
limited. Ngóh·deih ge bún·chìhn yáuh·haahn. **limited company** yáuh·haahn gūng·sī.
limit to haahn: **limit to three days** haahn sàam·yaht

limp   **limping about** gaht·gaht·háh

line   (mark) sin (M: tìuh): **draw a straight line** waahk tìuh jihk·sin; **telephone line** dihn·
wá·sin; **line of defense** fòhng·sin; **battle line** jin·sin
    (of type or writing) hohn. (series of objects, as cars or trees) laaht, pàaih. **line up**
pàaih·déui, pàaih·chèuhng·lùhng. /What are these people lined up for? Dī·yàhn hái syu
pàaih·déui jouh·māt·yéh a?
    other expressions: /The lines are busy. Deui·m̀h·jyuh yáuh yáhn góng·gán. /What
is your line? Néih jouh bīn·hòhng a?

linen   màh·bou

liner   yàuh·syún

linguist   yúh·yìhn·hohk·gā

lining   (of a coat) léih, sāam·léih: **serve as a lining for** jouh léih

link   lìhn·màaih (V)

linoleum   chāt·bou

linotype   pàaih·jih·gèi (M: fu)

lion   sī, sî·jí (M: jek). **lion dance** móu·sī; **to dance a lion dance** móu·sī; **stone lions** sehk·sî·jí

lip   háu·sèuhn; **lipstick** háu·sèuhn·gōu

liquid   yiht·tái

liquidate   chǐng·syùhn

liquor   jáu: **liquor store** jáu·pou; **a man's capacity for liquor** jáu·leuhng. /He can drink like a fish. Kéuih ge jáu·leuhng hóu hóu.

list   dāan (M: jèung). /This is the list of the things I want to buy. Nī·jēung dāan seuhng·bihn haih ngó yiu máaih ge yéh. **list of books** syū·dāan; **list of errata** jing·ngh·bíu; **list of persons** mîhng·dāan; **black list** hāk·mîhng·dāan; **price list** ga·muhk·bíu **make a list** hōi·dāan. /Make a list of the things you need and give it to me. Néih jèung néih sèui·yiu gó·dī yéh hōi jēung dāan béi ngóh.

listen   tèng. /Please listen to what I say. Chéng néih tèng ngóh góng.

listless   móuh·sām·gèi, móuh·jîng·sàhn

litchi   laih·jī: **litchi nuts** làih·jī·gōn

literal   jiu jih·mín gáai: **in the literal sense of the word it is** . . . , jiu jih·mín gáai nī·go jih ge yi·si haih . . . ;**literal translation** jihk·yihk

literary   màhn·hohk (ge): **literary talent** màhn·hohk ge tîn·chòih; **literary club** màhn·hohk·wúi; **literary works** màhn·hohk jok·bán; **literary world** màhn·hohk·gaai

literati   màhn·yàhn, duhk·syù·yàhn

literature   màhn·hohk. /I like to study Chinese literature. Ngóh jùng·yi duhk Jùng·gwok màhn·hohk.

lithograph   sehk·yan

little   sai, jái (used as a suffix). /I want a little piece. Ngóh yiu yāt·gauh sai·gauh ge. /Whose little dog is that? Gó·jek gáu·jái haih bīn·go ga? **Little cat** māau·jái; **little box** háp·jái; **little chair** yí·jái
    a little dī; **a very little** dī gam·dēu. /Please give me a little. Mh·gòi béi dī ngóh. /Do you feel a little better? Néih gok·dāk hóu dī ma? /You know how to speak Cantonese, don't you? Néih wúih góng Gwóng·jàu·wá àh? /No, just a little. Dī·gam·dēu jē.
    a little while yāt·jahn·gāan. /I'll come in a little while. Ngóh yāt·jahn gāan jauh lèih.
    (of ability) sè·síu, síu·síu. /How much rice can you eat? Néih hó·yíh sihk géi·dò faahn a?
    a little better hóu dī; **a little longer** noih dī; **a little louder** daaih sēng dī; **little by little** yát dī yāt dī gám, juhk dī juhk dī gám. /You have to pour it in little by little. Néih yiu yāt dī yāt dī gám dóu·lohk·heui.

live   (dwell) jyuh. /Where does he live? Kéuih jyuh·hái bīn·syu a? /Does anyone live in this house? Nī·gāan ngūk yáuh móuh yàhn jyuh a?
    (be or remain alive) is expressed with a negative plus séi. /The doctor said he would live. Yī·sāng wah kéuih mh wúih séi ge.
    (spend one's life) sàng·wuht. /He lives well. Kéuih sàng·wuht dāk hóu hóu.
    (of biological life) sàang·máahng ge: **a live fish** sàang·máahng ge yú

lively   wuht·put. /She is always very lively. Kéuih sîh·sîh dōu hóu wuht·put.

liver   gòn (man); yéun, gòn (animal)

living   **living things** sàng·maht; **art of living** sàng·wuht ge ngaih·seuht; **earn one's living** wán·sihk, màuh·sàng

lizard   yìhm·sé (M: tìuh)

load   jòng: **load a cargo** jòng fo, lohk fo; **load a gun** yahp máh·jí, yahp jí·dáan
a load joi. /How much of a load can that boat carry? Gó·jek syùhn hó·yíh joi géi
chúhng a?

loafer   mòuh·yihp·yàuh·màhn

loan   je·chín. /You could ask for a loan from the bank. Néih hó·yíh heung ngàhn·hòhng
je chín.

lobe   **lobe of the ear** yíh·jái; **lobe of the liver** gòn·yihp; **lobe of the lungs** faai·yihp

lobster   lùhng·hā (M: jek)

local   bún·deih ge; **local products** bún·deih ge chēut·cháan; **local custom** bun·deih ge
fùng·juhk; **local dialect** bún·deih·wá; **local news** bún·deih sàn·mán
local authority deih·fòng dòng·guhk; **local court** deih·fòng faat·yún
local anaesthesia guhk·bouh màh·jeui; **local congestion** guhk·bouh chùng·hyut

location   (place) deih·dím; (position) waih·ji

lock   só (M: bá). só, só·màaih. /Have you locked the door? Néih yáuh móuh só mùhn
a? or Neih yáuh móuh só·màaih douh mùhn a? /The door is locked. Douh mùhn só·
jyuh.
    locksmith só·sìh·lóu; **lock up** só·màaih, wan·jyuh

locomotive   fó·chè·tàuh (M: ga)

locust   wòhng·chúhng, máang (M: jek)

log   muhk, muhk·tàuh (M: gauh)

logic   lòh·chāp; (as a science) lòh·chāp·hohk, leuhn·léih·hohk

loin   yìu, yìu·gwāt

lonely   jihk·mohk. /Aren't you lonely? Néih gok·dāk jihk·mohk ma?

long   (in space) chèuhng. /I need a long rope. Ngóh yiu yāt·tìuh chèuhng sing. /How
long is the table from here to there? Nī·jèung tói yàuh nī·syu dou gó·syu yáuh géi
chèuhng a?
    (in time) nói, noih. /How long should we wait? Yiu dáng géi nói a? /I haven't seen
you for a long time. Hóu noih móuh gin. /Sorry to make you wait for me for such a
long time. Deui·m̀h·jyuh giu (or yiu) néih dáng·jó gam noih.
    as long as jí yiu. /We'll finish it within an hour as long as it doesn't rain. Jí yiu
m̀h·lohk·yuh, m̀h·sái yāt·go jūng·dím ngóh·deih jauh hó·yíh jouh·yùhn la.
    in the long run fong·chèuhng lèih tái. /In the long run, certainly it will be richly
rewarded. Fong·chèuhng lèih tái jēung·lòih bīt·dihng yáuh hóu bou ge.

longevity   chèuhng·mehng, chèuhng·sauh

longitude   gìng·sin; **degrees of longitude** gìng·douh; **east longitude** dūng·gìng; **west longitude** sāi·gìng

look   tái. /Look this way. Tái nī·bihn. /What is he looking at? Kéuih tái·gán māt·yéh
a?
    (appear, seem) tái·gin hóu·chih. /He looks sick, is he really sick? Kéuih tái·gin
hóu·chíh yáuh behng gám, Kéuih haih m̀h·haih behng a?
    look like chíh. /You look very much like your father. Néih jàn·haih chíh néih lóuh·
dauh la.
    look after hòn (to guard), chau (to take care of) hòn or tái (to guard a place). /Is
there any one looking after your children? Yáuh móuh yàhn bóng néih chau·gán néih ge
sai·màn·jái a?

look for wán. /Whom are you looking for? Néih wán bīn·go a? /What are you looking for? Néih wán māt·yéh a? /I'm looking for my keys. Ngóh wán·gán ngóh ge só·sìh. /Is he looking for a job? Kéuih haih m̀h·haih wán gán gūng a?

look around sei·wàih tái·háh; **look down** tái m̀h·héi; **look into** diuh·chàh; **look here** waih. /Look here! You can't do that! Waih, gám m̀h·ngāam ge boh! /Look out! Waih, gu sàang boh! **look toward** mohng·heui

loop (in a rope) hyūn

loose (not tight) sùng. (not firm) yūk. /This tooth of yours is already loose. Néih nī· jek ngàh yíh·gìng yūk la.
  to loosen sūng·hòi, gáai·hòi

loot (plunder) chéung

loquacious dò·háu, dò·jéui

loquat pèih·pàh, pèih·pàh·gwó, làuh·gwāt

lord jyú: **Lord of Heaven** Tìn·jyú, Seuhng·dai; **Lord's Day** Jyú·yaht; **Lord's Prayer** Jyú·tóu·màhn

lorry fo·chè (M: ga)

lose (lost) (of objects) sāt·jó, m̀h·gin·jó. /Don't lose it! M̀h·hóu sāt·jó keuih! (in a game or gambling) syù·jó. /Who lost the game? Bīn·go syù·jó a? /I lost ten dollars. Ngóh syù·jó sahp·mān.
  lose one's way, be lost dohng·sāt·jó. /Don't get lost! M̀h·hóu dong·sāt·jó! **lose an opportunity** sāt·jó·gèi·wuih. **lose face** dìu·gá, sāt·mín, lāt·sòu (vulgar). **lose hope** fūi· sàm. /Don't lose hope! M̀h·hóu fūi·sàm! **lose sleep** sāt·mìhn. **don't lose sight** hòn· jyuh. /Don't lose sight of the dog. Hòn·jyuh jek gáu. **lose time** sàai·sìh·gaan. /Don't lose any more time. M̀h·hóu joi sàai·sìh·gaan la. **lose weight** sau·jó. /You've been losing weight, haven't you? Néih gahn·lói sau·jó boh, haih m̀h·haih a? **lose one's head** fōng·jèung. /Don't lose your head! M̀h·hóu fōng·jèung! **lose one's temper** faat·ngok. /He has lost his temper again. Kéuih yauh faat·ngok la. **lose in business** siht·bún. **lose one's heart** móuh·saai sām·gèi.

loss syún·sāt

lot (of land) deih. (much) hóu dò, daaih bá. /I've a lot of Chinese friends. Ngóh yáuh hóu dò Jùng·gwok pàhng·yáuh. /He has lots of money. Kéuih yáuh daaih bá chín.
  draw lots jāp·cháu, chāu·chìm. **lot** (as fate) mehng, mehng·wahn

lottery ticket chói·piu, máh·bīu (M: jèung)

lotus lín; **lotus flower** hòh·fà, lìhn·fà; **lotus leaf** hòh·yihp, lìhn·yihp; **lotus root** lìhn· ngáuh; **lotus seed** lìhn·jí

loud daaih·sèng. /Please speak louder. Chéng néih góng daaih·sēng dī.

loudspeaker fong·yām·gèi

lounge wuih·haak·sāt, haak·tēng

louse sāt·ná

lovable hó·ngoi·ge

love (between persons, general) ngoi, jùng·yi. /Don't you love her any more? Néih m̀h ngoi kéuih làh?
  (between elders and children involving close relationship) sek, tung. /You said that she doesn't love her grandchildren, I just don't believe it. Néih wah kéuih m̀h·tung kéuih dī syūn àh, Ngóh jàn·haih m̀h·seun.
  (between children and parents) haau·seuhn. /He loves his parents very much. Kéuih hóu haau·seuhn kéuih ge fuh·móuh.

(between brothers and sisters) deui . . . hóu hóu. /He loves his elder sister. Kéuih deui kéuih daaih·jí (or gā·jē) hóu hóu.

(of things) jùng·yi. /I love small cars. Ngóh jùng·yi sai che. /I love to drive. Ngóh jùng·yi sái·che. /I love Chinese food. is expressed as: Ngóh jùng·yi sihk (to eat) Jung· gwok·sung (or tòhng·chāan, in the community of the overseas Chinese).

(strong like of an action) hóu jùng·yi. /He loves to sing. Kéuih hóu jùng·yi cheung· gō. /He loves to race. Kéuih hóu jùng·yi dau faai.

love each other béi chí sèung ngoi. /We should love each other. Ngóh·deih yìng· fahn béi chí sèung ngoi; **love** letter chìhng·seun; **love one's country** ngoi gwok; **love song** chìhng·gō; **love story** ngoi·chìhng síu·syut (fiction).

lover   ngoi·yàhn, chìhng·yàhn, kai·gà·lóu (of the male sex, vulgar form), kai·gà·pòh (of the female sex, vulgar form). **lover of books** syū·māi; **lover of music** yàm·ngohk· màih

low   dài. /The plane is flying too low. Ga fēi·gèi fēi dāk taai dài.
(of rank, position, grade, etc.) dài. (in pitch) dài. /He has a very low voice. Kéuih ge sīng·yàm hóu dài. (of temperature) /The temperature of this room is too low. Nī· gàan fóng ge wàn·douh taai dài. (of price) dài, pèhng. /Can you lower the price? Gáam· dāi dī ga·chìhn, dāk m̀h·dāk a? /It's not low enough. Mh·gau pèhng. (of tide) séui teui. /When will it be low tide? Géi·dím jūng séui teui a?

lower   jèung . . . dāi dī. /Please lower the window. Jèung go chēung·mún sāan dāi dī. **lower the voice.** /Please lower your voice. Chéng néih sai sēng dī. /Is this the lowest price? Nī·go haih ji dài ge ga·chìhn làh?

loyal   jùng·sàm

lubricate   séuhng·yáu; **lubricating oil** waaht·gèi·yáu

luck   wahn·hei; **good luck** wahn·hei hóu; **in luck** hàahng wahn; **hard luck, bad luck** wahn· hei m̀h·hóu; **have bad luck** jaih·wahn, dóu·mùih. /He has had hard luck this year. Gàm· nín kéuih jàn·haih jaih·wahn la.

lucky   hàahng wahn, hóu chói. /You lucky chap! Néih jàn·haih hàahng wahn la! /How could he always be so lucky? Kéuih dím·gáai sìh·sìh dōu gam hóu·chói ga?

luggage   hàhng·léih (M: gihn)

Luke   **The Gospel of Luke** lòuh·gā fūk·yām

lukewarm   nyúhn·nyún·déi·ge

lullaby   chèui·mìhn·kūk, gó·jái (colloq.)

lumbago   yīu·gwāt·tung

lumber   muhk·líu

lump   gauh (M)

lunar calendar   yàm·lihk, gauh·lihk

lunatic   dìn: **become a lunatic** faat·dìn. /Suddenly he became a lunatic. Kéuih faat·yihn faat·hèi·dìn·séuhng·lèih. **lunatic asylum** dìn·kwòng behng·yún

lunch   ngaan·jau. /Where would you like to have lunch? Néih jùng·yi heui bīn·syu sihk ngaan·jau a?

lung   faai

lure   yáhn·yau

luxuriant   maauh·sihng

luxuries   chè·chi·bán

luxurious   chè·wàh, chè·chi

lye   gáan·séui

M

macaroni   tūng·sàm·fán

machine   gèi·hei

machine gun   gēi·gwāan·chēung (M: tíng)

machinery   gèi·gín, gèi·hei. /My watch has stopped; something must be wrong with the machinery. Ngóh ge bīu mh·hàahng yāt·dihng haih yáuh dī gèi·gín waaih·jó.

mad   (angry) faat·nàu, faat·ngok. /There is no reason to get mad. Mòuh·waih faat nàu ā. **be mad at** nàu. /Do you know who he is mad at? Néih jî·dou kéuih nàu bīn·go ma? (crazy, rabid) dìn. /Are you mad? Néih faat·dìn àh? **mad dog** dìn gáu. /Beware, mad dog. Tàih·fòhng dìn·gáu.

madam   taai·táai, sī·nāai, táai (BF). /Mrs. Wong. Wòhng·taai·taai, Wòhng·sī·nāai, Wòhng·táai

made   (done) jouh·héi. /Has my suit been made? Ngóh tyut sāam jouh·héi meih a? (manufactured) haih . . . jouh ge. /Is it made in Hong Kong? Haih mh·haih hái Hèung·góng jouh ga? **made of** haih béi . . . jouh ge. /What is it made of? Haih béi māt·yéh jouh ga? /It's made of silver. Haih béi ngán jouh ge. **made to order** dehng·jouh. /Is it made to order? Haih mh·haih dehng·jouh ga?

magazine   (pamphlet) jaahp·ji (M: bún); (powder) fó·yeuhk·fu

magic   mò·lihk; **the magic of love** ngoi·chìhng ge mò·lihk. mò·seuht, faat·seuht; **magician** mò·seuht·gā; **a performance by a magician** luhng bá·hei, luhng faat·seuht

magic lantern   waahn·dāng; **magic lantern slide** waahn·dāng·pín

magistrate   (of a district) yuhn·jéung

magnanimous   daaih·leuhng

magnate   daaih·wòhng; **oil magnate** mùih·yàuh daaih·wòhng

magnesia   (med.) seh·yìhm

magnet   chîh·sehk, sip·sehk

magnificent   wài·wòhng

magnifier   fong·daaih·geng (M: mihn); **magnifying glass** fong·daaih·geng

magpie   héi·jéuk (M: jek)

mahjong   màh·jéuk (M: fu, a set); **play mahjong** dá·màh·jéuk

maid   (servant) gùng·yàhn, pòh·mā, má·jé; sái·pó, àh·sám (terms used in Singapore and nearby Chinese communities). (maiden) chyúh·néuih; **maid of honor** néuih·bàn·seung; **old maid** lóuh·gù·pòh, lóuh·chyúh·néuih; **maiden voyage** chyúh·néuih·hòhng

mail   (letter) seun. /Has the mail come yet? Seun lèih·jó meih a? **mailbox** seun·sēung sēung. **mailman** seun·chàai, yàuh·chàai; **to mail** gei. /Please mail this letter. Mh·gòi gei·jó nī·fùng seun kéuih.

main   daaih, jing; **main door** daaih mùhn, jing mùhn; **main road** daaih louh, jing louh; **main force** jyú·lihk; **main office** júng guk; **main point** yiu·dím; **main switch** júng jai

mainland   daaih·luhk

maintain   **maintain order** wàih·chǐh·diht·jeuih; **maintain the peace** wàih·chǐh·wòh·pìhng; **maintain the status quo** wàih·chǐh·yihn·johng; **maintain temperature** bóu·chǐh·wàn·douh; **maintain that** gìn·chǐh. /I maintain that that is the way to do it. Ngóh gìn·chǐh nī·go haih jéui hóu ge fòng·faat.

maize   sūk·máih

major   (mil.) siu·gaau; **major-general** siu·jeung; (the principle subject of study) jyú·sàu (V)

majority   daaih·dò·sou, gwo·bun·sou, daaih·bouh·fahn. /The majority of children in this area go to our school. Nī·yāt·kēui ge sai·mān·jái daaih·dò·sou hái ngóh·deih hohk·haauh duhk·syu.

make   (construct) jouh, jing; (manufacture) jai·jou. /Can you make a lantern? Néih wúih jouh dàng·lùhng ma? /He wants you to make him a toy. Kéuih séung néih tùhng kéuih jíng go gūng·jái. /What does that factory make? Gó·gàan gùng·chóng jai·jouh māt·yéh ga?
　　(cause) lihng. /It makes me very embarrassed. Lihng ngóh hóu m̀h·hóu·yi·si. /You make me very happy. Néih lihng ngóh hóu fùn·héi.
　　make a copy dá (type) dò yāt·fahn, chàau (copy) dò yāt·fahn; **make a hole** johk go lūng; **make a mistake** (in hearing what is said) tèng·cho; **make a mistake** (in speaking) góng·cho; **make a motion** tàih·yíh; **make peace** góng wòh; **make a pretext of** jihk·háu; **make an entry in an account** séuhng sou; **make certain** góng dihng; **make clothes** jouh sāam; **make inquiries** dá·ting·háh; **make friends** gàau pàhng·yáuh; **make money** wán chín; **make one laugh** yáhn yàhn siu; **make out a bill** hòi dāan; **make out a list** hòi dāan; **make a sentence** jouh geui; **make tea** chùng chàh; **make the bed** pòu chòhng; **make up** (as an actor) fa·jōng; **make up one's mind** kyut·yi, dá·dihng jyú·yi, lahp·dihng jyú·yi; **make use of** yuhng; **make believe** ja·dai; **makeup** (cosmetics) fa·jōng·bán

malaria   faat·láahng, faat·láahng·jing

Malay language   Máh·lòih·wá

Malay peninsula   Máh·lòih·bun·dóu

Malaya   Máh·lòih·a

Malaysia, Federation of   Máh·lòih·a·lyùhn·bòng

male   (human) nàahm (BF): **male teacher** nàahm·sīn·sàang; (animals) gūng (BF), hùhng (BF): **male dog** gáu·gūng

malicious   hāk·sàm: **malicious person** hāk·sàm·gwéi

malignant   yàm·duhk; **malignant tumor** duhk·làuh, duhk·láu

malt   mahk·ngàh

maltreat   yeuhk·doih

mamma   màh·mā

mammal   póu·yúh·duhng·maht

man   (human being) yàhn; (a male, not specifying age) nàahm·yán; (adult) daaih yàhn. /I would like to hire a man to help me. Ngóh séung chéng go yàhn lèih bòng·hah ngóh. /Who is that man? Gó·go nàahm·yán haih bīn·go a?
　　man and wife fù·fúh. /Are they husband and wife? Kéuih·deih léuhng·go haih m̀h·haih fù·fúh a?

manacles   sáu·lǐuh (M: fu)

manage   gáau·dāk·dihm. /Can you manage it? Néih gáau·m̀h·gáau·dāk·dihm a? /Yes, I can. Gáau·dāk·dihm.

(control, have charge of) /Who manages this place? Bīn·go gún·léih nī·go deih·fòng a? /This place is well managed. Nī·daat deih·fòng gún·léih dāk hóu hóu.

manager (of a bank, shop, etc.) gìng·léih: **general manager** júng·gìng·léih

Mandarin (language) gwok·yúh

maneuver yín·jaahp; **anti-air-raid maneuver** fòhng·hùng yín·jaahp; **hold a maneuver** géui·hàhng yín·jaahp

manger máh·chòuh

mango mòng·gwó

manifest bíu·mìhng

manifesto syùn·yìhn

Manila Máh·nàih·lā; **Manila cigar** léuih·sung·yīn

mankind yàhn·leuih

manner yéung. /Do it in this manner. Gám·yéung jouh.

manners (social behaviour) kwèi·géui. /Your children have excellent manners. Néih dī sai·mān·jái jàn·haih hóu kwèi·géui la. **ill-mannered** móuh kwèi·géui; **well-mannered** hóu·kwèi·géui

mansion daaih·hah, daaih·ngūk (M: gàan)

mantis tòhng·lòhng (M: jek)

manual (handbook) jí·nàahm (BF): **car repair manual** hei·chè sàu·léih jí·nàahm. **manual labor** chòu·gūng. /Can you do some manual work? Néih hó·yíh jouh chòu·gūng ma?

manufactory gùng·chóng, jai·jouh·chóng (M: gàan)

manufacture jai·jouh

manure fáhn, sí

manuscript yùhn·góu

many hóu dò, dò. /There are still many people starving nowadays in this world. Yìh·gà sai·gaai·seuhng juhng·haih yáuh hóu dò yàhn móuh faahn sihk. /It's too many. Taai dò la! **how many** géi dò. /How many do you want? Néih yiu géi dò a? **many thanks** dò·jeh, dò·jeh·saai; **many times** hóu dò chi; **very many** hóu dò; **a great many** mòuh·haahn gam dò

map deih·tòuh (M: fūk). /I want to buy a map of Hong Kong. Ngóh séung máaih yāt·fūk Hèung·góng deih·tòuh.

marble wàhn·sehk; (play thing) bō·jí (M: nāp); **play marbles** dá bō·jí

March sàam·yuht

march (military) hàhng·gwàn: **while marching** hàhng·gwàn ge sìh·hauh; (piece of music) jeun·hàhng·kūk (M: jì); **marching song** gwàn·gō

mare máh·ná

margarine yàhn·jouh ngàuh·yàuh

Maria Máh·leih·a

marine **marine products** hói·cháan; **marine police** séui·seuhng gíng·chaat; **Marine Corps** Hói·gwàn·luhk·jin·déui; **a marine** hói·gwàn·luhk·jin·déui·déui·yùhn

mark (symbol) gei·yihng, gei·houh. /Is there any mark on it? Yáuh móuh gei·yihng a?

to make a mark jouh go gei·yihng, tĭk·héi. /I've marked the items I want. Ngóh yíh·gìng tĭk·héi ngóh yiu ge gó·di yéh la.
(grade) fān·sou. **to mark** (the grade) béi fān·sou
(a price on goods) bĭu ga·chìhn. /Have you marked those goods today? Gó·dĭ yéh (or fo) néih yíh·gìng bĭu·jó ga·chìhn meih a?
mark down (the price) bĭu dài ga·chìhn; **mark up** (the price) bĭu gòu ga·chìhn

market (place) síh·chèuhng; (demand for goods) sĭu·louh; (price) hòhng·chìhng. **market report** hòhng·chìhng bou·gou; **market value** síh·ga

marriage (wedding) fàn·láih. /The marriage will take place on June 1. Luhk·yuht yāt·houh géui·hàhng fàn·láih. (married life) fān·yàn. /Their marriage has been very successful. Kéuih·deih ge fān·yàn hóu méih·múhn.
marriageable age git·fàn nìhn·lìhng; **marriage ceremony** fàn·láih; **marriage certificate** git·fàn·jing·syù, fān·syù; **marriage engagement** dihng·fàn; **marriage law** fān·yàn·faat

married **married couple** léuhng·fù·fuh, léuhng·gùng·pó; **married man** yáuh·fúh·jì fù; **married woman** yáuh·fù·jì·fúh. /Is he married? Kéuih git·jó fàn meih a? or Kéuih ji·jó gà meih a? /Is she married? Kéuih git·jó fàn meih a? Kéuih ga·jó meih a?

marrow (anat.) gwāt·séuih

marry (of a woman) tùhng . . . git·fàn, ga·béi . . . /Do you know whom she will marry? Néih jì mh·jì kéuih yiu tùhng bīn·go git·fàn a? or Néih jì mh·jì kéuih yiu ga·béi bīn·go a?
(of a man) tùhng . . . git·fàn, ló . . . jouh lóuh·pòh. /He says he will marry a rich girl. Kéuih wah kéuih yiu tùhng yáuh·chín néui git·fàn. or Kéuih wah kéuih yiu ló yáuh·chín néui jouh lóuh·pòh.
get married (of a couple or an individual) git·fàn; (of a man) ló·lóuh·pòh; (of a woman) ga·lóuh·gùng. /Do you know when they are going to get married? Néih ji·dou kéuih·deih géi·sí git·fàn ma?

Mars fó·sīng

marshal (a high army officer) yùhn·seui

martial law (regulation for army) gwàn·faat; **proclaim martial law** gaai·yìhm. /The martial law (the curfew) is in effect from 6 p.m. till midnight tonight. Gàm·máahn yàuh luhk·dìm ji sahp·yih·dìm gaai·yìhm.

Martin Luther Louh·dāk máh·dīng

martyr (for a country) liht·sih; (for a religion) sèun·gaau ge yàhn; (for a cause other than country or religion) sèun·naahn·ge yàhn

Mary Máh·leih·a

masculine gender nàahm·sing

mask mihn·geuih: **a gas mask** fòhng·duhk·mihn·geuih; **to wear a mask** daai mihn·geuih

mason (bricklayer) nàih·séui sì·fú; (stonemason) dá·sehk sì·fú

mass (a lump) yāt·gauh; (people) kwàhn·jung; (a Roman Catholic service) nèih·saat; **high mass** daaih·nèih·saat; **mass production** daaih·leuhng sàng·cháan; **mass wedding** jaahp·tyùhn·git·fàn

massacre tòuh·saat

massage ngon·mò

mast ngàih·gōn (M: jì)

master (of a household) jyú·yán; (in a business) sih·táu, lóuh·báan; (of an apprentice) sì·fú

Master of Arts sehk·sih, màhn·fō·sehk sih; **Master of Science** léih·fō·sehk·sih
to master a subject of study jīng·tùng. /When will I have mastered Cantonese?
Ngóh géi·sìh sìn·ji hó·yíh jīng·tùng Gwóng·jàu·wá a?

match   (to make fire with) fó·cháai (M: jì, a stick; hahp, box). /Have you got a match?
Néih yáuh fó·cháai ma?
    (a contest) béi·choi; **a football match** jūk·kàuh béi·choi
    (an equal) paak·dāk·jyuh. /I'm no match for you. Ngóh m̀h·paak·dāk·jyuh néih.
    (a well-suited pair) pui·dāk·ngāam. /You and she are a good match. Néih·deih
léuhng·go jàn·haih pui·dāk·ngāam la.
    (find or make something the same as) pui, chan (especially in color). /I'd like to
buy a chair to match this table. Ngóh séung máaih jèung yí pui nī·jèung tói. /Do you
think this color matches the color of my dress? Néih gok·dak nī·go ngàahn·sīk chan
ngóh gihn sāam ge sīk·séui ma?

matchmaker   mùih·yán, mùih·yàhn·pó

mate   **schoolmate** syū·yáu, tùhng·hohk; **classmate** tùhng·bāan tùhng·hohk

material   (for building, sewing, etc.) chòih·líu; (for writing an article or book) jì·líu.
construction material gihn·jūk chòih·líu; **raw material** yùhn·líu. **materialistic civilization** maht·jāt màhn·mìhng; **materialism** wàih·maht·léun

maternity hospital   cháan·fō yì·yún (M: gàan), làuh·cháan·só

mathematics   sou·hohk

matinee   yaht·chèuhng

matriculation   daaih·hohk yahp·hohk háau·si

matron   (of a hospital) wuh·sih·jéung; (of a dormitory) séh·gāam

matter   (affair) sih, sih·gon. /This is a very important matter. Nī·gihn sih hóu gán·yiu.
/It's a matter of life and death. Nī·gihn sih sāang·sí gāau·gwàan. /We have only a few
matters to discuss. Ngóh·deih jí yáuh géi·gihn sih tóu·leuhn jē.
    (trouble). /What is the matter with him? Kéuih jouh·māt·yéh a?
    (substance) maht·jāt; (pus) nùhng. **as a matter of fact** kèih·saht; **no matter** (followed
by what, whether, how, etc.) mòuh·leuhn (ref. C-E section)

Matthew   **The Gospel of Matthew** Máh·taai fūk·yām

matting   jehk (M: jèung)

mattock   chòh·táu (M: bá)

mattress   jin·yúk (M: jèung)

mature   sìhng·yàhn, sìhng·nìhn. /He is mature now. Kéuih yíh·gìng sìhng yàhn la.

mausoleum   lìhng·mouh

maxim   gaak·yìhn (M: geui)

maximum   gihk·haahn, jeui gou ge sou·muhk. /It has already reached the maximum.
Yíh·gìng dou·jó gihk·haahn la.

may   (possibly will) wáahk·jé. /That may be true. Waahk·jé haih jàn ge. /I may go
with you tomorrow night. Tìng·máahn ngóh waahk·jé hó·yíh tùhng néih heui. /It may
be already too late. Waahk·jé yih·gìng taai chìh la.
    (be allowed or permitted) hó·yíh. May I have an apple? Ngóh hó·yíh sihk yāt·go
pìhng·gwó ma?
    may I ask chíng mahn. /May I ask, is there a restaurant nearby? Chíng mahn nī·
syu jó·gán yáuh móuh faahn·gún a?

May   nǵh·yuht; **May Day** (in Soviet Russia) làuh·duhng·jit

mayor   síh·jéung

me   ngóh

meal   chāan, chàan·faahn. /We eat three meals a day. Ngóh·deih yāt·yaht sihk sāam·
chàan. /This is a good meal. Nī·chàan·faahn jàn·haih hóu·sihk la.

mean   (base) hah·jihn

mean   (intend, signify) yi·si. /I don't know what you mean. Ngóh m̀h·jì néih haih māt·
yéh yi·si. /Does it mean that? Haih m̀h·haih gám ge yi·si a? /What does this word
mean? Nī·go jih haih māt·yéh yi·si a? /That was not what he meant. Kéuih m̀h·haih
gám ge yi·si.
      I mean that ngóh ge yi·si haih . . .; **by all means** chìn·kèih; **by no means** máih yíh·
wàih. /That's by no means the end of the matter. Máih yíh·wàih gám jauh syun·sou la.
by means of yuhng . . . faat·jí

meaning   yi·si

meaningful   yáuh·yi·yih·ge

meanwhile   tùhng·sìh, dòng·sìh

measles   má (M: chèuhng). **to have the measles** chēut·má. /Has he had measles before? Kéuih yáuh móuh chēut·gwo má a?

measure   dohk, lèuhng (V). /Measure it from here to there, and see how long it is.
Yàuh nī·syu dok·dou gó·syu tái·hah yáuh géi chèuhng.
      measure across dá wàahng lèuhng

measurement   chek·chyun; **take one's measurements** (for making a suit, etc.) dohk·sān

meat   yuhk; **meatball** yuhk·yún

mechanic   gèi·hei·jái, gèi·hei·lóu

mechanics   gèi·haaih·gùng·chìhng

mechanize   gèi·haaih·fa: **mechanized unit** gèi·haaih·fa bouh·déui

medal   jéung·jēung

mediate   tìuh·tìhng

mediator   wòh·sih·lóuh, jūng·gāan·yàhn

medical   yì·hohk·seuhng·ge. /This is a medical problem. Nī·go haih yī·hohk seuhng ge
mahn·tàih. **medical books** yī syù; **medical certificate** yī·sāng·jí; **medical college** yī·
fō daaih·hohk; **medical fee** yī·yeuhk·fai; **medical officer** yī gùn; **medical science**
yì·hohk

medicated spirits   yeuhk·jáu

medicinal powders   yeuhk·fán

medicine   (drug) yeuhk; (fluid) yeuhk·séui; (ointment) yeuhk·gōu; (pill) yeuhk·yún; (plaster) gòu·yeuhk; (tablet) yeuhk·béng; (herb) yeuhk·chòih; **take medicine** sihk·yeuhk

medium   jùng·dáng·ge; **medium size** jùng houh; mùih·gaai·maht (N)

meek   wàn·wòh

meet   (come upon) yuh·dóu, yuh·gin. /I did not expect to meet you here. Ngóh séung
m̀h·dou hái nī·syu yuh·gin néih. (welcome; greet) jip. /We are going to the station to
meet our friend. Ngóh·deih heui fó·chè·jaahm jip ngóh·deih·ge pàhng·yáuh. (join) sèung

yuh. /The two rivers meet here. Nī·léuhng tìuh hòh hái nī·syu sèung·yuh. (make the acquaintance of) gin·háh. /I would like to meet your friend Mr. Lee. Ngóh séung gin· háh néih ge pàhng·yáuh Léih sīn·sàang.

meeting   wúi, wuih·yi, jeuih·wuih. /When will the meeting be? Géi·sìh hòi·wúi a? /Is this a formal meeting? Nī·go haih m̀h·haih jing·sīk ge wuih·yi a? /There is a meeting at the church tonight. Gàm·máahn hái gaau·tòhng yáuh yāt·go jeuih·wuih.

mellow   (ripe and tender) nàhm

melodious   hóu·tèng

melon   gwà: **melon seed** gwà·jí; **a slice of melon** yāt·káai gwà

melt   yùhng

member   (limb) jī·tái; **church member** gaau·yáuh; **party member** dóng·yùhn; **member of a society** wuih·yáuh; **member of a team** deuih·yùhn; **member of a committee** wái· yùhn; **Member of Parliament** yíh·yùhn; **member of the House of Representatives** jung· yíh·yùhn; **member of the Senate** chàam·yíh·yùhn

membrane   mók (M: chàhng)

memorandum   beih·mòhng·lúk; (informal letter) bihn·jīn (M: jèung)

memorial   **memorial arch** pàaih·làuh; **memorial day** géi·nihm·yaht; **memorial hall** géi· nihm·tòhng; **memorial service** jèui·douh·wúi, gùng·jai; **memorial stone** géi·nihm·bèi

memorize   nihm·suhk, gei·jyuh. /Memorize this passage. Nihm·suhk nī·dyuhn syù kéuih. /Please memorize his address. Chéng néih gei·jyuh kéuih ge deih·jí.

memory   gei·sing. /I have a very bad memory. Ngóh ge gei·sing hóu yáih.

menace   wài·hip

Mencius   Maahng·jí

mend   bóu: **mend clothes** bóu·sāam; **mend shoes** bóu·hàaih. **mend one's ways** gói·gwo

meningitis   nóuh·mók·yìhm

menses   yuht·gìng

menstrual period   gìng·kèih

mental   **mental debility** sàhn·gìng·sèui·yeuhk; **mental disease** sàhn·gìng·behng; **mental power** ji·lihk

menthol   bohk·hòh

mention   góng, tàih(·héi). /Did he mention that he wanted to quit studying? Kéuih yáuh móuh góng·héi kéuih m̀h séung duhk·syu a? /Don't mention this in his presence. Hái kéuih mihn·chìhn m̀h·hóu tàih(·héi) nī·gihn sih.
     Don't mention it. Siu yi·si jē (in reply to thanks for a gift). M̀h·sái·haak·hei (in reply to thanks for a favor).

menu   choi·dāan, choi·páai

merchandise   fo, fo·maht, sèung·bán (technical term); **foreign merchandise** yèuhng·fo

merchant   jouh·sàang·yi ge, sàang·yi·lóu, sèung·yàhn (formal expression); **a very suc-cessful merchant** daaih·sèung·gā

merciful   chìh·bèi, hóu·sàm

mercury   séui·ngàhn; (the planet) **Mercury** séui·sīng

mercy   (pity) chìh·bèi. /God has mercy upon us and sends His only begotten Son to save

us from our sin. is translated: Seuhng·dài lìhn·máhn sai·yàhn hín·paai Kéuih ge duhk·
sāng·jí gong·sàng sai·seuhng lèih suhk ngóh·mùhn ge jeuih.
    (a kindness) yàn·waih. /On Thanksgiving Day, we thank God for his mercies. Gáam·
yàn·yaht (or Jeh·sàhn·jit) ngóh·deih gáam·jeh Seuhng·dai chi·béi ngóh·deih ge yàn·waih.

merely   jí·haih. /It's merely a suggestion. Ji·haih yāt·go gin·yi jē.

merge   hahp·bihng. /When will the two companies merge? Gó·léuhng·gāan gūng·sī géi·
sí hahp·bihng a?

meridian   jí·ngh·sin

merit   gùng·lòuh

mermaid   méih·yàhn·yùh, yàhn·tàuh·yú (M: tìuh)

mess   (untidy condition) wū·chì·máh·cháh, lyuhn·chì·bā·jāu. (upset) gáau·lyuhn·saai.
/Don't mess up the classroom. Mh·hóu gáau·lyuhn·saai go fo·tòhng. **mess hall** faahn·
tòhng

message   làuh·dài syut·wah. /Is there any message for me? Yáuh móuh yàhn làuh·dài
syut·wah béi ngóh a? /I want to leave a message for him. Ngóh séung làuh·dài géi·geui
syut·wah béi kéuih.

messenger   seun·chàai

Messiah   Gau·sai·jyú

messieurs   gok·wái sīn·sàang

metal   ngh·gām, gàm·suhk

metaphor   béi·yuh

meteor   làuh·sīng

meteorological observatory   hei·jeuhng·tòih

meter   **electric meter** dihn·bīu; **gas meter** mùih·hei·bīu; **water meter** séui·bīu;
(measure) gùng·chek, máih·daht·chek

method   faat·jí, fòng·faat; **method of treatment** yì·faat; **method of teaching** gaau·sauh·
faat

mice   lóuh·syú·jái (M: jek)

microphone   māai

microscope   hín·mèih·geng

Mid-autumn festival   Jūng·chàu·jit

middle   (of a space) jūng·gāan, dōng·jùng; **middle-aged** jùng·nìhn; **Middle Ages** jùng·
sai·géi; **middle finger** jùng·jí; **middleman** jùng·yán; **middle of the month** yuht·jūng;
middle school (high school) jùng·hohk; **middle class** jùng·dáng gāai·kāp

midnight   bun·yé, bun·yeh·sāam·gàang

midway   bun·lóu

midwife   jip·sāng·pó

midwifery   cháan·fō

might   (power) kyùhn·lihk; (strength) lihk·leuhng

mighty   hóu yáuh kyùhn·lihk ge

mild   (of manner) sì·màhn; (of character) wàn·wòh; (of disease) hèng; (of medicine) wòh·
pìhng. **mild and gentle** wàn·yàuh

mildew   mòu: **to have mildew** faat·mòu; **have mildewed** faat·jó mòu; **spoiled by mildew** mùih·jó

mile   yìng·léih: **nautical mile** hói·léih; **square mile** fòng·léih

military   gwàn·sih: **military academy** gwān gùn hohk·haauh; **military activity** gwàn·sih hàhng·duhng; **military affairs** gwàn·sih; **military attaché** luhk·gwān móuh·gùn; **military authorities** gwàn·sih dòng·guhk; **military band** gwàn·ngohk·déui; **military base** gwàn·sih gàn·geui·deih; **military circle** gwàn·gaai; **military conference** gwàn·sih wuih·yi; **military correspondent** chèuih·gwàn gei·jé; **military discipline** gwàn·géi; **military drill** gwān·chòu; **military hospital** luhk·gwān yī·yún; **military law** gwàn·faat; **military man** (man in service) gwān·yàhn; **military officer** gwān·gùn; **military operation** gwàn·sih hàhng·duhng; **military order** gwàn·lihng; **military police** hin·bìng; **military review** yuht·bìng; **military rites** gwàn·láih; **military secrets** gwàn·sih bei·maht; **military service** bìng·yihk: **to be in military service** fuhk·bìng·yihk; **military strategy** jin·leuhk; **military strength** bìng·lihk; **military supplies** gwān·sèui·bán; **military surgeon** gwān·yī; **military tactics** jin·seuht; **military training** gwàn·sih fan·lihn; **military weapon** bìng·hei, gwàn·hei

militia   màhn·bìng, màhn·tyùhn

milk   (general) náaih; (of a cow) ngàuh·náaih. /Is the milk fresh? Dī ngàuh·náaih sān·sìn ma?

Milky Way   ngàhn·hòh

mill   (for grinding rice) máih·jín, máih·gáau; **paper mill** jouh·jí·chóng; **sawmill** geui·muhk·chóng; **water mill** séui·chè

millet   sîu·máih, sūk

millimeter   gùng·léih

million   baak·maahn; **ten million** chìn·maahn; **hundred million** maahn·maahn, yāt·yīk; **millionaire** baak·maahn·fu·yūng

mince   deuk

mind   (that thinks) nóuh·gàn; (that feels, knows) sàm, sàm·gèi. /He has a good mind, he can learn a lot. Kéuih ge nóuh·gàn hóu hóu, kéuih hó·yíh hohk hóu dò. /Where is your mind? Néih ge sàm heui·jó bīn·syu a? /Keep your mind on your work. Béi sàm gèi jouh·gùng.

   (obey) tèng . . . wah. /Do you mind your parents? Néih tèng m̀h·tèng néih bàh·bā màh·mā wah a?

   (take care of) gu·jyuh·háh. /Please mind my children for a while, I'll be right back. Mh·gòi néih tùhng ngóh gu·jyuh·háh dī sai·mān·jái, Ngóh jīk·hāk jauh fàan·lèih.

   (pay attention to) gu·jyuh. /Mind the traffic when you cross the street. Néih gwo gāai gó·jahn·sí gu·jyuh chè boh.

   on one's mind. /What is on his mind? Kéuih yáuh dī māt·yéh sàm·sih a? or Kéuih séung gán māt·yéh a?

   (care about or dislike; of active dislike) /Do you mind if I bring my children along? Néih m̀h gai·daai ngóh daai·màaih dī sai·mān·jái lèih lā máh?

   never mind m̀h·gán·yiu, móuh·gán·yiu, hóu hàahn jē

   mind your own business m̀h hóu léih yàhn·deih gam·dò sih. or m̀h·hóu léih yàhn gà ge sih.

mine   (belonging to me) ngóh·ge. (pit) kwong; **to mine** hòi·kwong. (military) deih·lèuih (land); séui·lèuih (water); **lay a mine** fong deih·lèuih, or fong séui·lèuih

mineral   **mineral substance** kwong·maht; **mineral products** kwong·cháan; **mineral water** kwong·chyùhn·séui mingle   kàu·màaih

minimum   ji síu, ji dài; jeui síu, jeui dài: **the minimum price** jeui dài ge ga·chìhn

mining   /He is in the mining business. Kéuih gìng·yìhng kwong·mouh.

minister   (in a government) bouh·jéung; daaih·sàhn (in a monarchy); (as a diplomat) gūng·si; (pastor) muhk·sī
    to minister fuhk·sih. /We may have a nurse to minister to her needs. Ngóh·deih hó·yíh chéng go hòn·wuh lèih fuhk·sih kéuih.
    Prime Minister sáu·seung (in monarchy), noih·gok·júng·léih

ministry   (in government) bouh

minor   mèih·sai ge, síu ge, m̀h·gwàan juhng·yiu ge

minority   síu·sou; **in the minority** jìm síu·sou

mint   jouh·baih·chóng (M: gàan); **to mint** jyu. (herb) bohk·hòh

minus   gáam; **minus sign** gáam·houh

minute   (of time) fān (jūng). (very small) sái·sai ge; (detailed) chèuhng·sai ge; **minutes of a meeting** géi·luhk

miracle   kèih·jīk, sàhn·jīk

miraculous   sàhn·kèih mohk chāk ge

mirror   geng (M: mihn)

misapply   yuhng·cho

misapprehend   tèng·cho

miscalculate   nám·cho

miscarriage   (abortion) síu·cháan

miscellaneous   jaahp·hohng; **miscellaneous goods** jaahp·fo

mischievous   baak·yim

miser   gù·hòhn·gwéi

miserable   chài·lèuhng, hó·lìhn. /He is so miserable, we should help him as much as we can. Kéuih gam chài·lèuhng, ngóh·deih yīng·gòi jeuhn·lihk bòng·joh kéuih. /That little puppy looked so miserable, it must have been lost. Gó jek gáu·jái gam chài·lèuhng, yāt·dihng haih jáu·sāt·jó la.
    (bad or unpleasant) yáih. /The weather was so miserable yesterday, we stayed home the whole day. Kàhm·yaht tìng·sìh gam yáih, ngóh·deih sèhng·yaht hái kéi.

misfortune   jaih wahn

misinform   bou·cho síu·sīk. /I'm misinformed. Yáuh yàhn bou·cho síu·sīk béi ngóh.

misinterpret   chyùhn·cho

misplace   jài·cho; **misplaced** m̀h·gin·jó

misprint   yan·cho

misrepresent   chyùhn·cho syut·wah

miss   (unmarried woman) gù·nèuhng, síu·jé (formal); néuih·sih (very formal)

miss   (fail to catch a train, etc.) daap·m̀h·dóu. /Hurry up, otherwise you'll miss the train. Faai dī lā, yeuhk·m̀h·haih néih jauh daap·m̀h·dóu nī·douh fó·chè ge la. (fail to meet someone at the station, etc.) jip·m̀h·dóu; (fail to see) tái·m̀h·dóu. /It's just

around the corner; you can't miss it. Yāt jyun·wāan jauh haih la, néih m̀h·wuih tái·m̀h·
dóu ge. (fail to catch a ball) jip·m̀h·dóu go bō. (lose) sāt·jó, m̀h·gin·jó; /Is there anything missing? Yáuh móuh m̀h·gin·jó yéh a?
(be lonesome without) séung·nihm. /Do you miss him? Néih séung·nihm kéuih ma?
miss an opportunity cho·gwo gèi·wuih

missing   sāt·jùng, jūng·jīk bāt·mìhng

mission   (a sending forth) sí·mihng; (a religious body) gaau·wúi

missionary   chyùhn·douh·yàhn (N), chyùhn·gaau·sih (N). **missionary school** gaau·wúi
hohk·haauh; **missionary board** chàai·wúi (term used in Hong Kong)

misspell   chyun·cho

mist   hàh·mouh, mouh

mistake   cho. /Sorry, my mistake. Deui·m̀h·jyuh háih ngóh·ge cho.
to make a mistake jouh cho. /Anyone can make a mistake. Yàhn yàhn dōu wúih
jouh cho ge.
to mistake yihng·cho. /I mistook him for a friend of mine. Ngóh yihng·cho kéuih
haih ngóh yāt·go pàhng·yáuh.
by mistake m̀h·gok·yi. /Sorry, I did it by mistake. Deui·m̀h·jyuh, ngóh m̀h·gok·yi
jouh·cho·jó.

Mister   sīn·sàang

mistress   (of a household) jyú·fúh

misunderstood   ngh·wuih, tèng·cho

misuse   (use wrongly) yuhng·cho; (misapply, misappropriate) laahm·yuhng

mix   (stir) gáau. /You'll have to mix it with a spoon. Néih yiu yuhng chìh·gāng gáau·
háh kéuih.
(blended) kàu·màaih yāt·chái. /You should have the sand and cement mixed. Néih
yiu jèung dī sà tùhng hùhng·mòuh·nàaih kàu·màaih yāt·chái.
mix up (in identity) gáau·cho·saai (or fàn·m̀h·chēut). /I always mixed up which is
which. Ngóh sìh·sìh gáau·cho·saai bīn·go dá bīn·go.
mix up (disarrange) gáau·lyuhn. /Don't mix them up. M̀h·hóu gáan·lyuhn kéuih.

moan   ngàhng·ngáng·sèng. /I heard him moaning. Ngóh tèng·gin kéuih hái syu ngàhng·
ngáng·sèng.

mobilize   duhng·yùhn

mock   (ridicule) gèi·siu

mode   yéung, fún

model   (form for imitation or copying) yéung. /Give me a model to follow. Béi go
yéung ngóh jiu·jyuh jouh.
(imitation of a structure) mòuh·yìhng. /This is the model of that bridge. Nī·go haih
gó·douh kìuh ge mòuh·yìhng.
(person who poses) mō·dahk·yìh. **a model village** mòh·faahn·chyūn. **set a model for**
jouh mòh·faahn. /You should set yourself as the model for them. Néih jih·géi yīng·
dòng jouh go mòh·faahn béi kéuih·deih tái.

moderate   hāp hāp hóu ge, jùng·wòh ge

modern   mō·dāng; yihn·doih ge: **modern history** yihn·doih·sí; **modern sanitation** sān·
sīk ge waih·sāng chit·beih

modernize   yihn·doih fa. /We should modernize this factory. Ngóh·deih yīng·gòi jèung
nī·gàan gūng·chóng yihn·doih·fa.

modest   (of attitude) hīm·hèui; (of dress) pok·sou

modify   gói, gàng·gói

Mohammedan   (a follower) wùih·gaau·tòuh; **Mohammedan mosque** wùih·gaau·tòhng; **Mohammedanism** wùih·gaau

moist   sāp

moisten   jíng·sāp

moisture   sāp·hei, sāp·douh

molar tooth   daaih·ngàh (M: jek)

mold   móu (N)

mole   (on the skin) ji (M: nāp)

moment   yāt·jahn·gāan. /Please wait a moment. Chéng néih dáng yāt·jahn·gāan. /I'll
     be back in a moment. Ngóh yāt·jahn·gāan jauh fàan·lèih.
     at the moment yìh·gā. /You can't see him at this moment. Néih yìh·gā m̀h·gin·dāk
     kéuih. /I can't answer your question at the moment. Ngóh yìh·gā m̀h·daap·fūk·dāk néih
     ge mahn·tàih.

monarchy   gwàn·jyú gwok·gà

monastery   sàu·douh·yún; **Buddhist monastery** jih·mùhn; **Taoist monastery** douh·gun

Monday   láih·baai·yāt, sìng·kèih·yāt

monetary system   baih·jai; **monetary unit** fo·baih·dāan·wái

money   chín. /Do you accept American money? is expressed as: 'I pay U.S. money,
     O.K.?' Ngóh béi Méih·gām dāk ma? /What is the exchange rate for a U.S. dollar? Yāt·
     go ngàhn·chín Méih·gām wuhn géi·dò chín a? /How much do I owe you? Ngóh jàang néih
     géi dò chín a?
     money-changer's shop chìhn·tói, chìhn·jōng; **money-making** wán·chín; **money order**
     wuih·piu

Mongolia   Mùhng·gú: **Mongolian** mùhng·gú·yàhn

monk   (Buddhist) wòh·séung

monkey   máh·láu (M: jek)

monopolize   (the sale of certain merchandise) jyùn·leih; (the market) duhk·jim

monosyllable   dāan·yām·jih

monotonous   dàan·diuh

monsoon   gwai·hauh·fùng

monster   gwaai·maht (M: jek)

month   yuht: **monthly magazine** yuht·hón; **monthly ticket** yuht·piu; **once a month** (month-
     ly) múih·yuht yāt·chi; **last month** seuhng·go yuht; **next month** hah·go yuht; **this month**
     nī·go yuht

monument   géi·nihm·bèi

mood   (state of mind) sàm·chìhng. /Has he been in a good mood lately? Kéuih jeui gahn·
     ge sàm·chìhng dím a?

moon   yút, yuht·gwōng. /Look, how beautiful the moon is! Tái·háh go yút géi leng!
     Moon cake yuht·béng; **eclipse of the moon** yuht·sihk; **moonlight** yuht·gwōng

moral   (ethical) douh·dāk. /A person's morals are his life. Yàhn ge douh·dāk jauh·haih
     kéuih ge sàng·mihng.

(lesson) gaau·fan, yuh·yi. **a moral man** yáuh dāk·hàhng ge yàhn; **moral support** jìng·sàhn·seuhng ge yùhn·joh

morale   sih·hei

morality   douh·dāk: **commercial morality** sèung·yihp douh·dāk

more   juhng, joi. /Do you want some more? Néih juhng yiu ma? /I don't want any more. Ngóh m̀h·yiu la. /Please give me some more. Chéng néih joi béi dī ngóh. /I want two more. Ngóh juhng (or joi) yiu léuhng go. /There are two more guests coming. Juhng yáuh léuhng·go yàhn·haak lèih. /I'm going to stay here two weeks more. Ngóh juhng hái syu jyuh léuhng·go láih·baai tìm. /Is there any more? Juhng yáuh móuh a? /There are a few more left. Juhng yáuh géi·go. /Try once more. Joi·si yāt·chi. /I won't do it anymore (won't dare to). Ngóh joi m̀h·gáam la.
        dō dī. /Have some more (food)? Sihk dō dī la. /Give him more. Béi dō dī kéuih.
        more than . . . : **more than ten** sahp·géi·go; **more than a thousand** chìn·géi·go
        more or less gam·seuhng·há, jó·yáu, yeuk·mó
        more and more (ref. yuht lèih yuht . . . in C-E section); **the more** . . . **the** (ref. yuht dò yuht . . . in C-E section); **the more** . . . **the more** . . . (ref. . . . yuht . . . yuht . . . .)

moreover   yîh·ché, bihng·ché

morning   jìu·tàuh·jóu, jìu·jóu

morphia   mō·fē, máh·fē

mortal   ji·mehng·ge; **mortal wound** juhng·sèung

mortality   séi·mòhng·léut

mortar   (for building) hùhng·mòuh·fùi, fūi·sà; (for pounding) jùng·hám

mortgage   dái·ngaat

mortuary   tîhng·si·fòhng

Moses   Mō·sāi

Moslem   wùih·gaau·tòuh

mosque   wùih·gaau·tòhng

mosquito   mān (M: jek); **mosquito net** mān·jeung (M: chòhng)

moss   chèng·tòih

most   ji, jeui. /Which restaurant is the most famous? Bīn·gàan jáu·gún haih ji chēut·méng ga?
        Most likely it is so. Daaih koi haih gam. **most probably** daaih koi; **most proper to do** ji jeuhk haih, ji ngāam haih . . . ; **most urgent** ji gán·gāp ge; **most valuable** ji bóu·gwai ge

moth   fèi·ngòh (M: jek); dāng·ngòh (M: jek)

mother   (formal term) móuh·chàn; (more intimate term) lóuh·móu; a·mã, màh·mã. **your mother** (term used for special politeness) lihng·tóng; **my mother** (term used for special politeness) gà·móuh; **my mother** (if she is deceased) sìn·móuh; **stepmother** gai·móuh, hauh·móuh; **mother-in-law** (wife's mother) ngoih·móuh, ngoih·móu; (husband's mother) gà·pó, nàaih·náai
        one's mother country bún·gwok; (the country of one's ancestors) jóu·gwok. **Mother's Day** móuh·chàn·jit

motherly   chìh·ngoi

mother-of-pearl   wàhn·móuh·hok

motion   (suggestion to be voted on) tàih·yih; **make a motion** tàih·yih; **second a motion** fuh·yih; **a motion is passed** tùng·gwo

motive   duhng·gèi; nihm·tàuh, séung·tàuh

motor   mō·dá, faat·duhng·gèi. **motor boat** dihn·syùhn, dihn·syùhn·jái; **motorcycle** dihn·dāan·chē

motto   gaak·yìhn (M: geui)

mound   dèui: **mound of earth** nàih·dēui; **this mound of earth** nī·dèui nàih; **mound of sand** sā·dēui

mount   (get up on a horse) sèuhng máh; (to mount a picture) bíu; (mountain) sàan

mountain   sàan: **mountain cave** sāan·lūng; **mountaineering** pàh·sàan; **mountain path** sàan·louh; **mountain range** sàan·léhng; **mountain top** sàan·déng

mountainous   dō·sàan ge

mourn   ngòi·douh

mouse   lóuh·syú (M: jek); **mouse trap** lóuh·syú·gíp

moustache   sòu

mouth   háu, jéui; **mouth of a bottle** jēun·háu; **mouth of a well** jéng·háu; **mouth of a wound** sèung·háu

movable   wúih·yūk ge, yūk·dāk ge, wuht·duhng ge

move   (change position) yūk. /Don't move. M̀h·hóu yūk. (change the position of) bùn. /Please move the table over there. Chéng néih bùn jèung tói heui gó·syu. (change residence) bùn. /Where has he moved to? Kéuih bún·jó heui bīn·syu a? /I'll move in tomorrow. Ngóh tìng·yaht bùn·lèih. (propose) tàih·yih; (affect emotionally) gáam·duhng; (as troops) diuh·duhng; (in games) hàahng (V), bouh (M): **make a move** hàahng·yāt·bouh

movement   (for a special purpose) wahn·duhng: **anti-war movement** fáan·jin wahn·duhng

movie   dihn·yíng (M: chēut), yíng·wá, yíng·hei; **movie star** dihn·yíng mìhng·sīng; **movie theater** dihn·yíng·yún (M: gàan)

mow   got; **mowing the grass** cháan·chóu; **lawn mower** cháan·chóu·gèi; jín·chóu·gèi

Mrs.   táai, taai·táai; (for the wife of a teacher, minister) sī·nāai; (for the wife of a prominent man, particularly an official) fù·yàhn

much   géi·do. /How much do you want? Néih yiu géi·dò a? /I don't want much. Ngóh m̀h yiu géi·dō jē. /He doesn't have much money. Kéuih móuh géi·dò chín jē.
         hóu·dò. /You're much taller. Néih gòu hóu·dò. /This one is much more expensive. Nī·go gwai hóu·dò.
         sìh·sìh. /Don't go out too much. Mh·hóu sìh·sìh chēut·gāai. /Have you played Mahjong much? Néih sìh·sìh dá màh·jéuk ma?
         taai do. /Don't drink too much. Mh·hóu yám dāk taai dò.

mucus   (of the eye) ngáahn·sí; (of the nose) beih·tai; **mucus running from one's nose** làuh·beih·tai

mud   nàih·baahn

muff   sáu·mát (M: deui)

mulberry   (fruit) sòng·jí; (leaves) sōng·yihp; (tree) sōng·syuh

mule   lòh (M: jek)

multiplication   sìhng·faat; **multiplication table** sìhng·faat·bíu multiply   sîhng. /Two multiplied by two equals four. Yih sîhng yih dáng·yù sei.

multitude   **a multitude of men** yāt·kwàhn·yàhn

mumble   ngàhm·chàhm, ngàhm·ngàhm chàhm·chàhm

mummy   gēung·sî

mumps   ja·sòi: **have the mumps** sàang·jà·sòi

municipal area   sîh·kēui

murder   saat·séi (V); **murder case** yàhn·mehng·ngon; **murderer** hùng·sáu

murmur   ngàhm·chàhm

muscle   gèi·yuhk

museum   bok·maht·yún (M: gàan)

mushroom   (edible) sīn·gù, dūng·gù, chóu·gù

music   yàm·ngohk; (written notes) ngohk·póu (M: bún)

musical   **musical instrument** ngohk·hei

musician   (men who play Chinese music in funeral procession, etc.) dī·dá·lóu; (an artist) yàm·ngohk·gā

mussel   hín (M: jek)

must   yāt·dihng yiu, sih·bīt yiu. **must not** yāt·dihng m̀h·hóu, chìn·kèih m̀h·hóu

mustard   gaai·laaht; **mustard plant** gaai·choi; **mustard powder** gaai·muht

mutiny   bun·bin

mutton   yèuhng·yuhk

mutual   wuh·sèung; **mutual agreement** sēung·fòng·tùhng·yi; **mutual aid** wuh·sèung bòng·joh

muzzle   háu·jaau, háu·lāp

my   ngóh·ge

mysterious   sàhn·bei, sàhn·bei ge

mythology   sàhn·wá

N

nail   (of metal) dēng (M: háu); (of fingers) sáu·gaap; (of toes) geuk·gaap; (fasten by hammering) dèng; **nail securely** dèng·saht . . . kéuih, dèng·gáng . . . kéuih. **nail to** dèng·hái; **nail to the cross** dèng·hái sahp·jih·gá seuhng·bihn; **nail up** dèng·màaih . . . kéuih

naked   chèuih daaih·chek·laak, mōk·chīng·gwòng, ló·tái

name   méng. /What is your name? Néih giu(·jouh) māt méng a? (primarily to inferiors). **full name** sing·mîhng. /What is your (full) name? Gwai sing·mîhng a? (polite). /My name is Gwòng·wàh. Ngóh giu(·jouh) Gwòng·wàh.

     pen name bāt·méng; **nickname** fà méng; **trade name** pàaih, māk·tàuh

     to name (give a name to). /Who gave him this name? Bīn·go tùhng kéuih héi ge méng a? /All my children were named by their grandfather. Ngóh dī sai·màn·jái ge méng dōu haih kéuih·deih a·yèh héi ge.

     (of something other than a person) méng. /What is the name of the book? Gó·bún syù giu·jouh māt·yéh méng a? /What is the name of this place? Nī·daat deih·fòng giu·jouh māt·yéh méng a?

nap   **take a nap** hāp·yāt·jahn·gāan ngáahn·fan

napkin   chāan·gān (M: faai <u>or</u> tîuh)

narcissus   séui·sīn·fā

narcotic   (drug) màh·jeui·yeuhk, màh·jeui·bán

. narrate   góng

narrow   jaak; **narrow-minded** síu·hei

nasal cavity   bèih·gō·lūng

nation   (country) gwok, gwok·gà; (people) màhn·juhk

national   gwok·gà ge; **national affairs** gwok·gà ge sih; **national anthem** gwok·gō; **national assembly** gwok·màhn wuih·yih; **national bank** gwok·gà ngàhn·hòhng; **national credentials** gwok·syù; **national day** gwok·hing(·yaht); **national defense** gwok·fòhng; **national flag** gwok·kèih

nationality   gwok·jihk

native   bún·deih·ge, bún·déi·ge; **native dialect** bún·deih·wá; **native goods** bún·deih fo; **native products** tóu·cháan. **a native** bún·deih·yàhn, tóu·yàhn

natural   (not made by man) tīn·yín ge, tīn·sàang ge. /These 'rock hills' are natural. Nī·dī sehk·sāan haih tīn·yín ge.
     (innate) tīn·sàang ge. /She has a natural talent for singing. Kéuih tīn·sàang ge wúih cheung·gō.
     (unaffected) jih·yìhn. /He is a very natural person. Kéuih nī·go yahn hóu jih·yìhn.
     (normal) gáng haih. /It was a natural thing to do. Gáng haih gám jouh la.

naturally   (of course) dòng·yín

nature   (inborn nature) tīn·sing. /It's not in his nature to like swimming. Kéuih tīn·sing m̀h·jùng·yi yàuh·séui.
     (characteristic, of something other than a person) dahk·sing, sing·jāt. /Do you know the nature of this metal? Néih jì·dou nī·tíng gàm·suhk ge dahk·sing ma?

naughty   ngàn·pèih, baak·yim

nauseate   séung ngáu, jok muhn

nautical mile   hói·léih

naval   hói·gwān ge; **naval attaché** hói·gwān móuh·gùn; **naval base** gwàn·góng; **naval blockade** hói·seuhng fùng·só; **naval engagement** hói·jin; **naval flag** hói·gwān·kèih; **naval officer** hói·gwān gwān·gùn; **naval warfare** hói·jin

navel   tóuh·chìh; umbilical cord chìh·dáai (M: tîuh)

navigate   (a ship or airplane) sái

navigation   hòhng·hói·seuht

navigator   hòhng·hói·gā; líhng·hòhng·yùhn (air crew)

navy   hói·gwān

near   káhn·jyuh, lèih . . . káhn. /What is the school near? Gó·gàan hohk·haauh káhn· jyuh bīn·syu a? /Our church is very near your place, please come to see us. Ngóh· deih gaau·tòhng lèih néih nī·syu hóu káhn, lèih taam ngóh·deih lā.
     nearby jó·gán, fuh·gahn. /Is there a hotel near here? Nī·syu jó·gán yáuh móuh léuih·gún a?
     to near jauh·lèih dou . . . la. /We're nearing Macao. Jauh·lèih dou Ngou·mún la.
     nearsighted gahn·sí. /Are you nearsighted? Néih haih m̀h·haih gahn·sí a?

(closely related) gahn·bohng. /Your figure is very near the predicted total. Néih nī·go sou·muhk tùhng ngóh·deih só·gú·gai·ge sou·muhk hóu gahn·bohng la.

neat   kéih·léih, jíng·chàih

necessary   bīt·sèui ge. /There are some necessary arrangements you must settle before leaving. Yáuh dī bīt·sèui ge sáu·juhk, jáu jî·chîhn néih yāt·dihng yiu baahn·tóh ge.
    it is necessary to   sih·bīt. /It will be necessary to have a passport to travel abroad.
Néih sih·bīt yiu yáuh yāt·go wuh·jiu sîn·ji hó·yíh heui ngoih·gwok léuih·hàhng. /It's necessary for you to ask Mr. Lahm's permission before leaving the school. Néih sih·bīt
yiu mahn·jéun Làhm·sīn·sàang sîn·jí hó·yíh lèih·hòi hohk·haauh.

necessaries   bīt·sèui·bán; **daily necessaries** yaht·yuhng·bán

neck   géng (M: tîuh); **necklace** géng·lín; **necktie** tāai, léhng·dáai

need   (require something or someone) sèui·yiu. /We need a few men to come to help us.
Ngóh·deih sèui·yiu géi·go yàhn lèih bòng ngóh·deih. /If I need you, I'll let you know.
Yùh·gwó ngóh sèui·yiu néih, Ngóh yāt·dihng tùng·jî néih.
    need not m̀h·sái. /Do you need us to help you? Néih sái·m̀h·sái ngóh·deih bòng néih
a? /No. M̀h·sái. /Yes. Ngóh yiu néih·deih bòng ngóh.
    a need sèui·yiu or expressed verbally kyut·faht: /They have a need of food and
medicine. Kéuih·deih kyut·faht sihk·maht tùhng yeuhk·bán.
    needless to say m̀h·sái·góng. /Needless to say, he'll be the winner. M̀h·sái·góng
gáng·haih kéuih yèhng ge la.

needle   jām, jàm. (M: háu); **eye of a needle** jàm·ngáahn; **needlework** jàm·jí

negative   (photo) séung·dái (M: jèung); (opp. to positive, constructive) sîu·gihk. **negative
electricity** yàm·dihn; **negative sign** fuh·houh

neglect   m̀h·léih. /Is he neglecting the children? Kéuih haih·m̀h·haih m̀h·léih dī sai·mān·
jái a?
    should not neglect yiu hóu·hóu·déi dá·léih. /You should not neglect your health.
Néih yiu hóu·hóu·déi·dá·léih néih jih·géi ge sàn·jí.
    (apathy) mh·hóu·hóu·déi. /He's been neglecting his work lately. Kéuih nī·páai m̀h·
hóu·hóu·déi jouh·sih. /He's been neglecting his school work. Kéuih nī·páai m̀h hóu·
hóu·déi duhk·syù.

negotiate   gàau·sip, tàahm·pun

negro   hāk·yàhn

neighbor   gaak·lèih·lèuhn·séh, gāai·fōng; **neighboring** gaak·lèih; **neighboring village**
gaak·lèih·chyūn; **next-door neighbor** gāak·lèih·ngūk·jyú; **neighboring country** lèuhn·
gwok

neither   **neither . . . nor** (yauh) m̀h . . . (yauh) m̀h . . . , m̀h·haih . . . yauh (or yihk)
m̀h·haih . . . , . . . yauh m̀h . . . yauh m̀h . . . . /The climate over there is very interesting, it's neither cold nor hot. Gó·syu ge tìn·sîh hóu dāk·yi ge, yauh m̀h·láahng yauh
m̀h·yiht. /If it's neither you nor him, then who is it? Yauh m̀h·haih kéuih yauh m̀h·haih
neih, haih bīn·go a? /He said he could neither eat nor sleep. Kéuih wah kéuih yauh mh
sihk·dak yauh m̀h fan·dak. **neither of the two** léuhng·go dōu m̀h·haih

neon sign   gwòng·gún, ngàih·hùhng·dāng (M: jî)

nephew   (brother's son) ját; (sister's son) ngoih·sāang; (son of wife's brother) noih·ját

Neptune   (planet) Hói·wòhng·sīng

nerve   sàhn·gîng

nervous   gēng·sāt·sāt gám. /He has been very nervous recently. Kéuih nī·páai sìh·sìh
dōu haih gēng·sāt·sāt gám.

nervous breakdown sàhn·gìng sèui·yeuhk; **nervous disorder** sàhn·gìng·cho·lyuhn

nest   dau; **bird's nest** jeuk·dau

net   móhng; **net amount** saht·sou; **net price** saht·ga; **net profit** jihng·leih, seuhn·leih;
net weight jihng·chúhng
    to fish with a net jūk·yú, dá·yú; **to throw a net** saat·móhng

neuralgia   sàhn·gìng·tung

neutral   jùng·lahp: **neutral country** jùng·lahp gwok·gà; **neutral zone** jùng·lahp deih·daai;
remain neutral bóu·chìh jùng·lahp

never   (in past time) chùhng·lòih·meih, chùhng·lòih·móuh. /I've never been there before.
Ngóh chùhng·lòih meih heui·gwo.
    (habitually, present and future) m̀h, joi·m̀h, wíhng yúhn dōu m̀h. /I'll never go there
again. Ngóh joi m̀h·heui gó·syu la. /He's afraid that his eyes will never recover.
Kéuih pa kéuih sèung ngáahn wíhng·yúhn m̀h·hóu·dāk·fàan. /The color of this material
will never fade. Nī·jek bou wíhng·yúhn dōu m̀h·lāt·sīk ge.

nevertheless   sèui·yìhn haih gám . . . júng haih . . . /His hands were sore, nevertheless
he held onto the rope. Kéuih ge sáu yíh·gìng hóu tung la, sèui·yìhn haih gám, kéuih juhng
haih jà·jyuh tìuh síng.

new   (not old) sàn, sàn ge. /When was this new house built? Nī·gāan sàn ngūk géi·sìh héi
ga?
    (different) sàn <u>or expressed verbally as</u> wuhn·jó. /They have a new amah. Kéuih·
deih chéng jó go sàn pòh·mā. <u>or</u> Kéuih·deih wuhn·jó go pòh·mā.
    newborn infant sōu·hā·jái; **newcomer** sàn·haak (used in Southeast Asia), sàn·hèung·
léih (in America); **new-fashioned** sàn·fún ge, sān·sīk ge; **new hand** sàang·sáu; **New**
Testament Sàn·yeuk chyùhn·syù; **new year** sàn·nín, sàn·nìhn; **Happy New Year!** Baai
nihn! Baai nihn; Gùng·héi! Gùng·héi!; **New Year's Eve** nìhn·sà·ah·máahn

newly   **newly arrived** sàn dou ge; **newly bought** sàn máaih ge; **newly married couple**
sàn·gahn·git·fàn·ge, sàn·fàn·fù·fùh

news   (in a newspaper) sàn·mán, sīu·sīk. /What's the latest news? Yáuh māt·yéh sàn·
mán a?
    (personal) yàm·seun, sīu·sīk. /Is there any news from your son? Néih ge jái yáuh
māt yàm·seun ma?
    news agency tùng·seun·séh; **newsreel** sàn·màhn·pín

newspaper   bou·jí, sàn·màhn·jí; **morning paper** jóu·bou, yaht·bou; **evening paper** máahn·
bou; **newspaperman** sàn·màhn·gei·jé; **newspaper office** bou·gún

next   (after one thing or time) daih·yih. /We left there the next day. Ngóh·deih daih·yih·
yaht jauh lèih·hòi gó·syu la. /Who is next? Lèuhn·dou bīn·go a?
    (in a series of several things or times) **the next time** hah·yāt chi, **the next week**
hah·yāt·go láih·baai; **the next month** hah·yāt·go yuht; **the next year** (like school year,
etc.) hah·yāt·nìhn; **next year** (in general) chēut·nín, mìhn·nìhn
    (after that) . . . yìhn·hauh . . . /Do that one next. Jouh·yùhn nī·go yìhn·hauh jouh
gó·go.
    (in location) pòhng·bīn. /The next house is ours. Pòhng·bīn gó·gāan ngūk haih ngóh·
deih ge. /Please sit next to him. Chéng néih chóh·hái kéuih pòhng·bīn.
    next door gaak·lèih. /Who lives next door? Bīn·go jyuh·hái gaak·lèih a?

nice   hóu. /It's a nice day. Gàm·yaht tìng·hei jàn·haih hóu la. /He's a nice man. Kéuih
go yàhn hóu hóu.
    /Did you have a nice time? <u>is expressed verbally as</u>: Néih·deih wáan dāk hóu ma?

niche   (for religious images) sàhn·ngām

niece   (brother's daughter) jaht·néui; (sister's daughter) ngoih·sāang·néui

night   yeh·máahn, máahn·hāk, máahn·tàuh·hāk, yeh·máahn·hāk. /Don't go out at night.
Yeh·máahn m̀h·hóu chēut·gāai.
   máahn. /I spent two nights there. Ngóh hái gó·syu jyuh·jó léuhng·máahn. /I was
awake all night. Ngóh sehng máahn móuh fan.
   last night kàhm·máahn, chàhm·máahn, johk·máahn; **tomorrow night** tìng·máahn;
   night before last chìhn·máahn; **night after tomorrow night** hauh·máahn; **night after
   night** máahn·máahn; **every night** múih·máahn; **night duty** jihk·yé; **night school** yeh·
   hók

nightingale   yeh·ngāng (M: jek)

nightmare   **have a nightmare** faat ngok·muhng

nine   gáu: **nineteen** sahp·gáu; **ninety** gáu·sahp; **ninety nine** gáu·àh·gáu

nip   (pinch) nìm·jyuh; (with an instrument) gihp·jyuh, kìhm·jyuh, **nip up** nìm·héi, gihp
héi, kìhm·héi

nippers   kím·jái

nipple   nīn·tàuh, náaih·tàuh

nitric acid   kéuhng·séui

nitrogen   daahm·hei

no   (in answering a question) m̀h; meih. /No, I'm not going. Ngóh m̀h·heui. /Are you a
German? Néih haih·m̀h·haih Dāk·gwok·yàhn a? No. M̀h·haih. /Have you eaten yet?
Néih sihk·jó faahn meih a? No. Meih. /May I go now? Ngóh heui·dāk meih a? No.
Meih·dāk.
   no . . .-ing m̀h·jéun. /No smoking. M̀h·jéun sihk·yīn.
   no longer m̀h . . . la. /He's no longer here. Kéuih m̀h·hái nī·syu la.
   have no, there is (or are) no móuh. /They have no winter clothes, no heater, and
not even enough food. Kéuih·deih móuh láahng·tīn·sāam, móuh fó·lòuh, yihk m̀h·gau
yéh sihk.
   nobody móuh·yàhn; **no entry** m̀h·jéun yahp; **no matter** (followed by what, whether,
if, how, etc. ref. mòuh·leuhn in C-E section); **no means** móuh faat·jí; **no more** móuh
la; **no need** m̀h·sái; **no parking** m̀h·jéun tìhng·chè; **there is no rain** móuh·yúh; **no use**
móuh yuhng; **no wonder** m̀h·gwaai·dāk. /No wonder he doesn't want to go. M̀h·gwaai·
dāk kéuih m̀h·séung heui.

Nobel prizes   Nòh·bui·yíh·jéung·gām

noble-minded   gòu·seuhng

noise   sèng

noisy   chòuh

none   móuh, yāt·dī·dōu·móuh. /I've none. Ngóh yāt·dī dōu móuh.

nonsense   **talk nonsense** faat·ngahm·wah. /What he says is all nonsense. Kéuih hái·syu
faat·ngahm·wah. /I don't listen to his nonsense. Ngóh m̀h·tèng kéuih faat·ngahm·wah.

noon   ngaan·jau; **take a noon nap** fan·ngaan·gaau

nor   see neither

normal   (natural) jing·sèuhng; (usual) pìhng·sèuhng. /Is his weight normal? is usually
expressed verbally as: Kéuih haih·m̀h·haih gwo·chúhng (overweight) a? or Kéuih haih·
m̀h·haih m̀h·gau chúhng (underweight) a?
   normal school sî·faahn hohk·haauh

north   bāk (BF). **North America** Bāk·méih·jàu; **North Borneo** Bāk·bò·lòh·jàu; **northeast** dūng·bāk; **north pole** Bāk·gihk; **northward** heung bāk; **northwest** sāi·bāk; **north winds** bāk·fùng

Northern Malaya Bāk·máh; **northern regions** bāk·fòng; **northern side** bāk·bihn; **northerner** bāk·fòng·yàhn, bāk·lóu (vulgar), ngoih·gōng·lóu (vulgar)

nose   beih·gō; **running nose** làuh beih·séui, lauh beih·tai; **stuffed nose** beih·sāk

nostril   beih·gō·lūng

not   m̀h. /He says he's not going. Kéuih wah kéuih m̀h·heui. /It's not correct. M̀h·ngāam. /I think it's not expensive. Ngóh wah m̀h·gwai. /It's not enough. M̀h·gau. /He is not at home. Kéuih m̀h·hái kéi. /He's not here. Kéuih m̀h·hái nī·syu. /It's not included. M̀h·gai joih noih. /It's not worth it. M̀h·dái.

  not very m̀h·haih géi. /It's not very convenient. M̀h·haih géi fòng·bihn. /It's not very far. M̀h·haih géi yúhn. /It's not very good. M̀h·haih géi hóu. /It's not very many. M̀h·haih géi dò.

  do not m̀h·hóu. /Do not move! M̀h·hou yūk! /Not so fast! M̀h·hou gam faai! /Do not touch! M̀h·hóu mò! or M̀h·hóu dau!

  not much móuh māt. /It's not of much use. Móuh māt yuhng. /There is not much business. Móuh māt sàang·yi.

  not yet meih. /He's not twenty years old yet. Kéuih meih gau yih·sahp·seui. /It's not ready yet. Meih·dāk. /He's not qualified yet. Kéuih meih gau jì·gaak.

  not a bit yāt dī dōu m̀h. /It's not a bit the same. Yāt dī dōu m̀h·tùhng. /There's not a sound to be heard. Yāt dī sèng dōu móuh. **not certain** m̀h·yāt·dihng. **not for sale** fèi·màaih·bán. **not only . . . but also . . .** M̀h·jí . . . juhng . . . /He's not only lazy, but also steals. Kéuih m̀h·jí láahn juhng tàu·yéh tìm.

  not to be used for, not to be taken m̀h·haih ngoi·lèih · · · ge. /This medicine is not to be taken internally, it's only to be used externally. Nī·jek yeuhk m̀h·haih ngoi·lèih sihk ge, haih ngoi·lèih chàh ge.

note   (short letter) géi·go jih. /Drop me a note when you get there. Néih heui·dou jì·hauh sé géi·go jih béi ngóh.

  notes bāt·gei; **take notes** gei bāt·gei; **make a note of** gei·dài

  (comment) jyu·gáai; (paper money) ngàhn·jí; (observe) jyu·yi; (musical sound) yām; (written musical symbol) yām·fùh; **notebook** bóu·jái

nothing   móuh yéh; **nothing to do** móuh yéh jouh; **nothing to wear** móuh sāam jeuk

notice   (notification) tūng·jì, tūng·jì·syù. /Have you received the notice? Néih yáuh móuh jip·dóu tūng·jì a?

  (posted announcement) tùng·gou. **to notice** jyu·yi, làuh·sàm·dou

notify   tūng·jì

noun   mìhng·chìh

nourish   jì·bóu: **nourishing food** jì·bóu ge sihk·bán, bóu·bán

novel   síu·syut, chèuhng·pìn síu·syut; **novelist** síu·syut·gā

November   sahp·yāt·yuht

now   yìh·gā, gà·jahn, gà·háh, yihn·joih. /You may leave now. Néih yìh·gā hó·yíh jáu (or ché) la.

  now and then sìh·bāt·sìh, noih·bāt·nói. /He comes here now and then. Kéuih sìh·bāt·sìh lèih·háh.

nowadays   yìh·gā. /Everything is dear nowadays. Yìh·gā yeuhng·yeuhng yéh dōu gwai.

nowhere   móuh·deih·fong. /He has nowhere to go. Kéuih mouh·deih·fong hóu heui.

nucleus   haht·jì: **nuclear weapon** haht·jí móuh·hei

nude   ló·tái: **picture of a nude** ló·tái·wá; **statue of a nude** ló·tái·jeuhng

nuisance   /Don't be a nuisance! M̀h·hóu gam lihng yàhn tóu·yim. /What a nuisance!
Jàn·haih tóu·yim la!

numb   bei, màh·bei

number   (how many) sou·muhk, sou. /The number is incorrect. Nī·go sou·muhk m̀h·
ngāam. (No.) daih . . . (houh). /Who is number three? Bīn·go haih daih·sàam·houh a?
to number. /Have these been numbered? Nī·dī yáuh·saai nām·bá meih a? /Please
number the pages. M̀h·gòi néih juhk yihp béi go nām·bá.
numberless mòuh sou gam dò; **house number** mùhn·pàaih (door plate); **wrong number**
/You have the wrong number. Néih nī·go nām·bá m̀h·ngāam. or (in answering a wrong
telephone call) Daap·cho·sin.

numeral   sou·muhk·jih

numerous   hóu·dò, mòuh·haahn gam dò

nun   (Buddhist) sī·gū; (Roman Catholic) gù·nèuhng

nurse   hòn·wuh, wuh·sih; **head nurse** wuh·sih·jéung

nut   **chestnut** fùng·léut; **peanut** fā·sāng; **Spanish peanut** sai·fā·sāng; **walnut** hahp·tòuh.
(counterpart of a bolt) lòh·sī·móu

nutrition   yìhng·yéuhng: **want of nutrition** yìhng·yéuhng bāt·jūk or kyut·faht yìhng·yéuhng

nutritious   yáuh yìhng·yéuhng ge

O

oar   lóuh (M: tìuh)

oatmeal   mahk·pin

oath   saih·yuhn. **make an oath** saih·yuhn faat·saih; **take an oath** syùn·saih; **ceremony
of taking an oath** syùn·saih·láih

obedient   (children to adult) tèng·wah; (inferior to superior) seuhn·chùhng; (a child to
his parents) haau·seuhn

obey   fuhk·chùhng; **obey order** fuhk·chùhng mihng·lihng; **obey the teacher** tèng·sīn·sàang
wah; **obey my instruction** tèng ngóh·ge fàn·fu

obituary notice   fuh·màhn (M: fahn)

object   (thing) yéh. /What's that object in the road? Louh·seuhng gó·go haih māt·yéh a?
(purpose) muhk·dīk. /The object of this book is to tell you what English words mean
in Cantonese and show you how to use them. Nī·bun syù ge muhk·dīk haih góng·béi néih
jī Ying·màhn·jih ge Gwóng·jau·jih tùhng·màaih dím yuhng nī·dī Gwóng·jàu·jih. /We must
accomplish our objective. Ngóh·deih yāt·dìhng yiu daaht·dou muhk·dīk.
(oppose) fáan·deui. /Do you object to his proposal? Néih fáan·m̀h·fáan·deui kéuih
ge tàih·yih a?

objection   fáan·deui. /Is there any objection? is expressed verbally as: Yáuh móuh
yàhn fáan·deui a?

obligation   bún·fahn

oblige   /I'm very much obliged for the help you've given to us. Ngóh·deih fèi·sèuhng
gáam·gīk néih deui ngóh·deih ge bòng·mòhng. /He was obliged to tidy up the classroom
everyday. Kéuih muih·yaht yat·dihng yiu jap·hóu go fo·tòhng.

oblong   chèuhng·fōng ge

obscene   hàahm·sāhp ge, yàhm·dohng·ge

obscure   mùhng·chàh·chàh

observatory   tìn·màhn·tòih

observe   gùn·chaat, tái; **observe the law** jyùn·sáu faat·leuht

obsolete   gwo·sìh ge, gwo·hei ge

obstinate   ngàahn·gu

obstruct   jó·ngoih, jó·jyuh

obstruction   jeung·ngoih

obtain   dāk·dóu

obvious   mìhng·baahk

obviously   hín·yìhn

occasion   chèuhng·hahp, sih, sìh·hauh. **big occasion** daaih·sih; **happy occasion** héi·sih
(as a wedding, birthday, family reunion, etc.)

occasional   ngáuh·yìhn ge; **occasionally** ngáuh·yìhn

occupation   (business or work) jīk·yihp

occupy   (take up time or space) jim·jó, yuhng·jó. /Taking care of the house occupies
most of my wife's time. Dá·léih gà·mouh jim·jó ngóh taai·táai daaih·bouh·fahn ge sìh·
gaan.
(live or be in). /That room is already occupied. Gó·gaan fóng yìh·gìng yáuh yàhn
jyuh la.
(take over by military action) jim·lìhng. Napoleon's army occupied Italy. Nàh·po·
lèuhn ge gwàn·déui jim·lìhng·jó Yi·daaih·leih.
(busy). M̀h·dāk·hàahn. /The doctor is occupied at present. Yī·sāng yìh·gā m̀h·dāk·
hàahn.

occur   (take place or happen) faat·sàng. /When did that occur? Gó·gihn sih géi·sìh
faat·sàng ga?
(come to one's mind) séung·dou, séung·héi. /It didn't occur to me that I could explain
the situation to him. Ngóh dòng·sìh móuh·séung·dou ngóh hó·yíh jèung go chìhng·yìhng
gáai·mìhng béi kéuih tèng.
(be found) chēut·yihn. /The word 'God' occurs often in the Bible. Seuhng·dai nī·go
jih hái Sing·gìng sìh·sìh chēut·yihn.

occurence   sih, sih·gon; **common occurence** pìhng·sèuhng ge sih

ocean   yèuhng, daaih·hói: **Pacific Ocean** Taai·pìhng·yèuhng; **Atlantic Ocean** Daaih·sài·
yèuhng; **Indian Ocean** Yan·douh·yèuhng. **Oceania** Daaih·yèuhng·jàu

o'clock   dím·jūng: **three o'clock** sàam·dím·jūng

octagonal   baat·gok ge, baat·láng ge

October   Sahp·yuht

octopus   baat·jáau·yú (M: tìuh)

oculist   ngáahn·fō yī·sāng

odd   (number) dàan·sou; (extra, not matching) dāan·dǐng·ge; (strange or queer) gú·gwaai.
odd job sáan·gūng

odor   meih: **bad odor** chau·meih; **good odor** hèung·meih

of   There is no Cantonese equivalent. Some English expressions containing 'of' may be

<u>translated as follows</u>: (belonging to) ge, di (followed by a plural noun). /I met a friend of yours last night. Ngóh kàhm·máahn yuh·gin néih yāt·go pàhng·yáuh. /The children of the neighborhood are playing outside. Gāai·fōng dī sai·màn·jái go go dōu hái ngoih·bihn wáan·gán.

(expressing time before the hour) jàang . . . -dím. /It's a quarter of eight. Jàang yāt·go gwāt baat·dím.

(made from) ge. /I think a coat of silk is what she would like. Ngóh gú kéuih séung yiu yāt·gihn sī·faat ge sāam.

(in a place name) **the city of Canton** <u>is expressed as</u> Gwóng·jàu·sìh; **the province of Kwangtung** <u>is expressed as</u> Gwóng·dùng·sáang

(from) hái . . . ge . . . /Canton is west of Hong Kong. Gwóng·jàu hái Hèung·góng ge sài·bìn.

(between a measure and a noun) **a pound of beef** yāt·bohng ngàuh·yuhk; **a bottle of wine** yāt·jèun jáu; **a glass of water** yāt·bùi séui.

hear of tèng·màhn·gwo. /I've never heard of that place. Ngóh móuh tèng·màhn·gwo gó·daat deih·fong.

know of jì·dou. /I know that you don't know him personally, but do you know of him? Ngóh jì·dou néih m̀h·sīk kéuih, daahn·haih néih jì·dou kéuih haih bīn·go ma?

of course dòng·yín; **it's of no effect** móuh haauh·lihk; **it's of no importance** m̀h·gán·yiu, móuh·gán·yiu; **it's of no use** móuh·yuhng ge

off   (from one's body) chèuih·jó. /Take off the coat! Chèuih·jó gihn sāam kéuih!

(not on as it should be). /There's a button off your dress. Néih gihn sāam yáuh go náu lāat·jó.

(disconnect) sàan·jo. /Turn the water off! Sàan·jó go séui·hauh kéuih!

(in the future) juhng·jàang . . . jauh·haih . . . /Her birthday is two days off. Juhng jàang léuhng·yaht jauh·haih kéuih ge sàang·yaht la.

off and on yáuh sìh . . . yáuh sih . . . /The light works off and on, can you fix it? Jáan dāng yáuh·sìh jeuhk yáuh·sìh m̀h·jeuhk, néih wúih jíng ma?

offend   dāk·jeuih

offer   (a price) chēut. /I'm willing to offer one hundred dollars for it. Ngóh yuhn·yi chēut yāt·baak mān.

offer one's congratulations gùng·héi. /May I offer my congratulations? Gùng·héi, gùng·héi.

offering for sacrifice jai·bán

office   sé·jih·làuh, baahn·sih·chyúh; (govt.) baahn·gūng·tēng; **office boy** hauh·sāang; **office hours** baahn·gùng·sìh·gaan; **office supplies** màhn·geuih

officer   (of govt.) -gùn, gùng·mouh·yùhn; (of company, society, etc.) jīk·yùhn; **officer in charge** jyú·yahm; **officer of the day** jihk·yaht·gùn; **commanding officer** jí·fài·gùn, sī·lihng·gùn

official   (formal) jing·sīk ge. /Is that an official order? (Gó·go) haih·m̀h·haih jing·sīk mihng·lihng a?

(public, not personal) gūng·gā ge. /This is for official use. Nī·go haih gūng·gā yuhng ge.

official circle gùn·chèuhng, jing gaai; **official gazette** hin·bou; **official interpreter** fàan·yihk·gùn; **official letter** gùng·màhn; **official receipt** jing·sīk sàu·geui; **official report** gūn·fòng bou·gou; **official title** gùn·hàahm

often   sìh·sìh, jàu·sìh, sìh·sèuhng (A)

oil   yàuh. **lubricating oil** gèi·yáu, waaht·gèi·yáu; **castor oil** se·yàuh; **peanut oil** fā·sāng yàuh; **oil-mill** yàuh·chóng; **oil painting** yàuh·wá; **oilcloth** yàuh·bou

oily   yàuh·neih

ointment   yeuhk·gōu

old   (not young) lóuh. /My grandmother is very old, she's almost eighty. Ngóh·ge jóu·
móuh yíh·gìng hóu lóuh la, Kéuih jauh·lèih baat·sahp (seui) la.
        (not new) gauh. /I want to sell my old car, is there any buyer? Ngóh séung maaih·
jó ngóh ga gauh·chè, yáuh móuh yàhn máaih a?
        (one's age). /How old are you? (If said to a young person) is expressed as Néih
géi dáai la? or Néih géi dò seui la? (if said to an old person) Néih géi daaih nîhn·géi
la? /I'm thirty years old. Ngóh sàam·sahp seui.
        (ancient) gú·lóuh, yáuh hóu noih ge lihk·sí. /This is a very old city. Nī·go sèhng
hóu gú·lóuh ge la. or Nī·go sèhng yáuh hóu noih ge lihk·sí ge la.
        (former) gauh·sîh ge, lóuh. /Mr. Lee was my old colleague. Léih sīn·sàang haih
ngóh gauh·sîh ge tùhng·sih. /He's my old student. Kéuih haih ngóh gauh·sîh ge hohk·
saang.
        old-fashioned gú·lóuh ge; **old friend** lóuh pàhng·yáuh; **old goods** gauh fo; **old hand**
lóuh sáu; **old man** baak·yē·gūng; **old people's home** lóuh·yàhn·yún; **Old Testament**
Gauh·yeuk·chyùhn·syù; **old woman** baak·yē·pó

olive   baahk·láam, láam: **salted olive** hàahm·láam

Olympic games   Sai·gaai·wahn·duhng·wúi

omnipotent   maahn·nàhng ge, mòuh·só·bāt·nàhng ge

omnipresent   mòuh·só·bāt·joih ge

omniscient   mòuh·só·bāt·jî ge

on   (resting on top of) hái . . . seuhng·bihn. /The book is on the table. Bún syù hái tói·
seuhng·bihn.
        (used with other words to tell where, when, how, and the like). /Put it on the table.
Fong·hái tói·seuhng·bihn. /He's coming on Sunday. Kéuih láih·baai·yaht lèih. /You
must be on time. is expressed as: Néih yiu yì·sìh (or jéun·sìh) lèih·dou (for coming)
boh. /How can you go to sleep with your glasses on? Néih dím nàhng·gau daai·jyuh
ngáahn·géng fan·gaau ga? /Climb on! Pàh·séuhng·lèih! Jump on! Tiu·séuhng·lèih!
/Put your hat on. Daai·hóu déng móu kéuih!
        /Turn on the light! Hòi·jeuhk jáan dāng kéuih! /Is the motor on? Go mō·dá haih·
m̀h·haih hòi·gán a? /No, I forgot to turn on the motor. Móuh, Ngóh m̀h·gei·dāk·jó hòi·
jeuhk go mō·dá. /Please turn on the light. M̀h·gòi néih hòi·jeuhk jáan dāng.
        on behalf of doih·tai; **on duty** dōng gàang; **on either end** léuhng·tàuh; **on friendly
terms** sèung hóu; **on hand** hái sáu·seuhng; **on leave** táu·ga; yāu·sīk; **on probation** si·
yuhng; **on purpose** dahk·dāng (A), jyūn dāng (A); **on the average** làai ché lèih gai; **on
the right-hand side** hái yauh·sáu·bihn; **on the contrary** jing sèung·fáan; **on the ground**
hái deih·há·syu; **on the grounds of** yàn·waih; **on the other hand** lihng yāt·fòng mihn lèih
góng; **on the shore** hái ngohn·seuhng; **on the spot** dòng·tòhng (A); **on the street** hái gāai·
seuhng; **on the way** hái louh·seuhng lèih·gán; **on the whole** daaih·kói

once   yāt·chi: **once more** joi si yāt·chi; **at once** jīk·hāk; **not even once** yāt·chi dōu meih
si·gwo

one   yāt: **one plus a measure** yāt M̲. **one-act play** duhk·mohk·kehk; **one after the other**
yāt·go yāt·go gám, luhk·juhk gám. /One at a time, please. Yāt·go yāt·go lèih. **one by
one** yāt·go yāt·go gám; **one half** yāt·bun; **one-man exhibition** go·yàhn jín·láahm·wúi;
one or two yāt·léuhng·go; **oneself** jih·géi; **one tenth** sahp·fahn jī·yāt; **one third** sàam·
fahn jī·yāt; **by one's own hand** chàn·sáu (A)

onion   yèuhng·chūng; **green onion** chūng

only   (one, single) wàih yāt ge. /It's our only chance. Nī·go haih ngóh·deih wàih·yāt ge
gèi·wuih. /This is your only hope. Nī·go haih néih wàih yāt ge hèi·mohng.
        (no more than) ji haih. /I only want a little. Ngoh ji haih yiu di gam deu je. /I only
went there once. Ngóh jí·haih heui·gwo yāt·chi jē.

(only existing one) duhk (BF). /He's the Only Begotten Son of God. Kéuih haih Seuhng·dai ge duhk·sàng·jí. /She's an only child in the family. Kéuih haih go duhk néui.

(only if) chèuih·fèi. /Only if you repent of your sins will you be saved. Chèuih·fèi néih fui·gói néih yíh·chîhn ge gwo·cho, néih m̀h·wúih dāk·gau.

onward   heung·chîhn (A)

open   dá·hòi: **open a door** dá·hòi douh mùhn; **open a window** dá hòi douh chēung·mún; **open a book** dá·hòi bún syù; **open the lid** dá hòi go goi; **open the drawer** dá·hòi go gwaih· túng. /As soon as you open the drawer you'll find it. Néih yāt dá·hòi go gwaih·túng jauh wán·dóu ge la. **open (start) a meeting** hòi wúi; **open a lottery** hòi chói; **open fire** hòi· fó; **open letter** gūng·hòi·seun; **open up waste land** hōi fòng. /Open your eyes wide and look here! Maak·daaih sèung ngáahn tái·jyuh nī·syu! /Open your mouth wide! Maak daaih go háu!
    /Are you open on Sunday? Néih·deih láih·baai·yaht hòi·m̀h·hòi·mùhn a? /What time do you open every day? Néih·deih múih·yaht géi·dím·jūng hòi·mùhn a?

opening   hòi·mohk. /When is the (grand) opening of his store? Kéuih gàan pou·táu géi· sìh hòi·mohk a? **opening ceremony** hòi·mohk·láih; **opening speech** hòi·wúi·chîh

opera   (Chinese) daaih·hei; (European) gò·kehk; **opera glasses** chìn·léih·gèng

operate   gún, sái. /Can you operate this machine? Néih wúih gún nī·ga gèi·hei ma? /Can you operate a sewing machine? is expressed as: Néih wúih chē·yī ma?
    (surgery) hōi·dōu, got·jó (take out). /We have to operate on her and take out the tumor; she'll completely recover within two weeks. Ngóh·deih yiu tùhng kéuih hōi·dōu, got·jó go làuh, léuhng·go láih·baai jî·noih kéuih jauh yùhn·chùhn hóu fàan ge la.

operation   hōi·dōu, sì·sáu·seuht. /The operation will be done next Monday. Hah·láih· baai yāt hōi·dōu. **operating room** sáu·seuht·sāt

ophthalmologist   ngáahn·fō yī·sāng

opinion   yi·gin. /What is your opinion? Néih ge yi·gin dím a?

opium   ngà·pin, ngà·pin·yīn, yīn·sí: **smoke opium** sihk ngà·pin·yīn, sihk yīn·sí

opportunity   gèi·wuih. /This is a good opportunity for you. Nī·go haih néih yāt·go hóu hóu ge gèi·wuih.

oppose   (be against) fáan·deui; (resist) fáan·kong; **oppose violently** máahng·liht fáan·kong

opposite   (facing) deui·mihn. /The drugstore is just opposite the church. Yeuhk·fòhng jauh hái gaau·tòhng deui·mihn jē. /Please sit opposite Mr. Chahn. Chéng néih chóh·hái Chàhn·sīn·sàang deui·mihn.
    (different, reverse) sèung·fáan. /Your idea is just the opposite of his. Néih·ge yi· si tùhng kéuih ge ngāam·ngāam sèung·fáan.

opposition party   fáan·deui·dóng

oppress   ngaat·jai: **oppress the people** ngaat·jai dī lóuh·baak·sing

optician   pui·ngáahn·géng·ge yàhn

optimistic   lohk·gùn, lohk·gùn ge

optional   /It's optional. Chèuih néih syún·jaak (select); chèuih néih yiu·m̀h·yiu (take it or leave it).

or   (between choices) dihng, yīk·waahk. /Do you want this one or that one? Néih yiu nī· go dihng gó·go a?
    (between one number and other). /Give me two or three, that'll be enough. Béi léuhng·sàam·go ngóh jauh gau la.

either . . . **or** . . . waahk·haih . . . waahk·haih . . . /You may go either to England or to the United States. Néih waahk·haih heui Yìng·gwok waahk·haih heui Méih gwok dōu dāk.

oral   háu·tàuh·seuhng ge: **oral report** háu·tàuh·seuhng ge bou·gou (opposite to syù·mìn· seuhng ge bou·gou, written report); **oral examination** háu·si

orange   cháang; Sunkist gām·sāan·cháang; **local orange** bún·deih cháang; **orange juice** cháang·jāp

oration   yín·syut

orator   yín·syut·gā

orbit   gwái·douh (N)

orchard   gwó·yùhn

orchestra   yàm·ngohk·déui

orchid   làahn·fà (M: deu, one flower; ji, stem; puhn, pot); **orchid with aerial roots** diu· làahn

ordain   fùng . . . wàih, lahp . . . wàih. /When will he be ordained? Kéuih géi·sí fùng· wàih muhk sī a? /When was he ordained? Kéuih géi·sí fùng·wàih muhk·sī ga?

order   (discipline, orderliness, lawful conduct) diht·jeuih, jih·ngòn. /You'll be responsible for keeping order in this class. Néih fuh·jaak wàih·chìh nī·bāan ge diht·jeuih. /The government has already sent troops to maintain order in that area. Jing·fú yíh· gìng paai bìng heui wàih·chìh gó·daat deih·fong ge jih·ngòn la.
    (a request for goods) ō·dá, dehng; giu. /Have you ordered those goods yet? Néih ō·dá·jó gó·dī fo meih a? /I want to order something. Ngóh séung ō·dá dī yéh. /Have you received my order? Néih jīp·dóu ngóh ge ō·dá meih a? /You can order these things by mail. Néih hó·yíh sé seun dehng nī·dī fo. /May I order you a glass of wine? Ngóh tùhng néih giu bùi jáu, hóu ma? (order a meal) /Have you ordered yet? Néih giu·jó choi meih a? /Please order me a glass of orange juice. Mh·gòi néih tùhng ngóh giu yāt·bùi cháang·jāp.
    (command) mihng·lihng (V & N). (list of things wanted) dihng·dāan, dihng fo·dāan
    be in order (or **out of order** of machines). /Is the machinery in order? Nī·go gèi· hei sái·dāk ma? /The elevator is out of order. Dihn·tài waaih·jó.
    be in order jíng chàih; **be out of order** lyuhn. /Her daughter's room is in good order. Keuih ge néui gāan fóng hóu jíng·chàih. /Her son's room is not. Kéuih go jái gāan fóng hóu lyuhn.
    made to order dehng jouh ge. /The suit was made to order. Nī·tyut sāam haih dehng jouh ge.
    in order to jauh haih waih yiu . . . /We raised more money in order to build the hospital. Ngóh·deih gyùn dō dī chín jauh haih waih yiu héi nī·gāan yì·yún. /I came all the way in order to see you. Ngóh lèih nī·syu jauh haih waih yiu lèih taam néih.

ordinance   faat·lihng

ordinary   pìhng·sèuhng ge, póu·tùng ge; **ordinary events** pìhng·sèuhng ge sih; **ordinary meal** bihn·faahn

ore   kwong·sehk, kwong·maht; **iron ore** tit·kwong; **silver ore** ngàhn·kwong; **tin ore** sek· kwong

organ   (musical instrument) fùng·kàhm. (a part of the body) hei·gùn; **five sense organs** nǵh·gùn; **internal organs** noih·johng; **sex organs** sàng·jihk hei·gùn; **administrative organ** hàhng·jing gēi·gwàan

organic chemistry   yáuh·gèi fa·hohk

organization   tyùhn·tái, jóu·jīk

organize   jóu·jīk: **organize a political party** jóu·jīk jing·dóng; **organize a club** jóu·jīk yāt·go wúi

oriental   dūng·fòng (ge): **oriental art** dūng·fòng ngaih·seuht; **oriental culture** dūng·fòng màhn·fa

origin   (beginning) héi·yùhn; (cause) chí·yàn, yùhn·yàn: **the origin of a quarrel** ngaai·gāau ge héi·yàn

original   (first) jeui chò ge, yùhn·lòih ge. /The original site of the hospital was over there. Yî·yún jeui chò ge yùhn·jí haih hái gó·syu. /That was our original plan, now we have already changed it. Gó·go haih ngóh·deih yùhn·loih ge gai·waahk yîh·gā ngóh·deih yîh·gìng gói·jó la.
　　　original copy yùhn·bún; **original draft** yùhn·góu; **original sin** yùhn·jeuih; **original text** yùhn·màhn
　　　(new, novel) sàn·yîhng (ge), yúh·jung·bāt·tùhng (ge)
　　　the original jàn ge. /Where is the original of this painting? Jēung jàn ge (wá) hái bīn·syu a?

originally   bún·lòih. /This book was mine originally, but I gave it to him. Nî·bún syù bún·lòih haih ngóh·ge, daahn·haih ngoh béi·jó kéuih la.

oriole   wòhng·ngāng (M: jek)

ornament   jōng·sīk (V); jōng·sīk·bán (N)

orphan   gù·yìh: **orphanage** gù·yìh·yún (M: gàan)

ostrich   tòh·níuh (M: jek)

other   (more, additional) daih·yih·dī. /Have you any other tables? Néih yáuh móuh daih·yih·dī tói a? /Do you have any other things to do? Néih yáuh móuh daih·yih·dī sih yiu jouh a?
　　　(remaining) kèih·tà ge, kèih·yùh ge. /Are there any other reasons? Juhng yáuh móuh kèih·tà ge yùhn·yàn a? /Where are the other students? Kèih·yùh dī hohk·sāang hái bīn·syu a?
　　　the other daih·yih·go, gó·go. /Give me the other one. Béi daih·yih·go ngóh. /She doesn't want this one, but the other one. Kéuih m̀h·yiu nī·go, yiu gó·go.
　　　every other gaak . . . /Come every other day. Gaak yāt·yaht lèih yāt·chi. /The buses leave every other hour. Bā·sí gaak yāt·go jūng·dím hōi yāt·chi.
　　　other kind daih (yih) yéung ge; **other people** daih (yih) dī yàhn

otherwise   yeuhk·m̀h·haih. /I won't buy it otherwise. Yeuhk·m̀h·haih ngóh m̀h·máaih.

otter   séui·chaat (M: jek)

ought   yīng·gòi, yìng·fahn, yīng·dòng; **ought not** m̀h·yīng·gòi

ounce   ōn·sí

our   ngóh·deih·ge

ourselves   ngóh·deih jih·géi

out   (outside) ngoih·bihn. /We'll eat out tonight. Ngóh·deih gàm·máahn hái ngoih·bihn sihk·faahn. /Let the dog out. Fong jek gáu chēut·heui ngoih·bihn.
　　　(as a postverb with the proper verb) -chēut·lèih, -chēut·heui. /Move the chairs out (toward the speaker). Būn dī yí chēut·lèih (ngoih·bihn). /Move the chairs out (away from the speaker). Būn dī yí chēut·heui (ngoih bihn).
　　　(have none) . . . móuh·saai. /We're out of gasoline. Ngóh·deih móuh·saai dihn·yàuh la. or Ngóh·deih yuhng·saai dihn·yàuh la. /We're out of bread, we should buy some today. Ngóh·deih sihk·saai mihn·bāau la, gàm·yaht yiu máaih mihn·bāau la.

/It's out of my control. Ngóh gún m̀h·dim la. /Speak out! Góng la! /Are you out of your mind? Néih sàhn·gìng àh?

outing   gàau·ngoih léuih·hàhng. /Tomorrow we're going to have an outing, are you going? is expressed as: Tìng·yaht ngóh·deih heui gàau·ngoih léuih·hàhng, néih heui m̀h·heui a?

output   cháan·leuhng. /The output of cans in this factory is five thousand a day. Nī·gàan gùng·chóng gun·táu ge cháan·leuhng haih ńgh·chìn gun yāt·yaht.

outlet   chēut·háu; (commerce) sìu·louh

outline   (a general sketch of a plan, etc.) daaih·yi; (a short summary) daaih·gōng; (contour) lèuhn·kwok

outlook   (prospect for the future) chìhn·tòuh

out-of-date   gwo·saai·sìh, m̀h·hahp·sìh

outpatient   m̀h·jyuh·yún ge behng·yàhn

outside   ngoih·bihn

outsider   ngoih·yàhn, guhk·ngoih·yàhn

outskirt   gàau·ngoih

outspoken   jihk·baahk ge

outstanding   (conspicuous) bīu·chēng ge; **outstanding debt** meih wàahn·chìng ge jaai·hohng

oval   tòh·yùhn·yìhng ge; **oval face** gwà·jí háu·mihn

ovary   léun·chàauh

oven   guhk·lòuh

over   (more than) dò·gwo, chìu·gwo, . . . yí·seuhng, géi. /It's already over five pounds. Yíh·gìng dò·gwo ńgh·bohng la. /Anyone who is over sixty may not stand in line. Chìu·gwo luhk·sahp·seui ge (or luhk·sahp·seui yíh·seuhng ge) hó·yíh m̀h·sái pàaih·déui. /There are over three hundred children studying in our school. Yáuh sàam·baahk géi hohk·sāang hái ngóh·deih hohk·haauh duhk·syu.

(across) gwo alone or as postverb with a main verb. /How can we get over the river? Ngóh·deih dím·yéung gwo nī·tìuh hòh a? /Over there you'll see a bridge. You may walk across the bridge, but you can't drive the car across. Hái gó·syu néih hó·yíh tái·dóu yāt·douh kìuh, néih·deih hó·yíh hàahng·gwo douh kìuh daahn·haih ga chè m̀h·gwo·dāk. /Bring the chair over here. Būn jèung yí gwo·lèih nī·syu.

(above) hái . . . seuhng·bihn. /His room is directly over mine. Kéuih gàan fóng hái jeng ngóh gàan fóng seuhng·bihn.

go over yìhn·gau. /We have to go over it more carefully. Ngóh·deih yiu jí·sai yìhn·gau·háh.

over and over yāt·chi yauh yāt·chi. /He looked at it over and over and still couldn't find out what the trouble was. Kéuih tái·yùhn yāt·chi yauh yāt·chi juhng·haih wán·m̀h·chēut bīn·syu waaih·jó.

do it over. Joi jouh yāt·chi. /It (the trouble) is all over now! Yíh·gìng móuh sih la! or Yíh·gìng gáau·dihm·saai la!

over an hour dím·géi·jūng; **knock over** pung·dit·jó; **the typhoon is over** dá·yuhn fùng la!

overboard   dit·lohk·séui. /Someone is overboard! Yáuh yàhn dit·lohk·séui a!

overcharge   (ask a high price) hòi·daaih·ga

overcoat   daaih·lāu (M: gihn)

overcome   hāk·fuhk

overdo   jouh dāk taai gwo·fahn

overdose   gwo·leuhng. /Don't take an overdose! Mh·hóu sihk gwo·leuhng boh!

overdraw   tau·jî. /He was overdrawn three hundred dollars. Kéuih tau·jî·jó sàam·baahk·
màn.

overdue   gwo·kèih. /It's overdue. Yíh·gìng gwo·jó kèih la. /The freighter is overdue.
Jek fo·syùhn yíh·gìng gwo·jó kèih la juhng meih dou.

overeat   sihk dāk taai báau. /Don't overeat! M̀h hóu sihk dāk taai báau!

overflowing   múhn·gwo·tàuh

overhaul   daaih·sàu·jíng

overhear   tèng·dóu; (on purpose) tāu·tèng

overlap   sèung·chùhng

overload   joi dāk taai chúhng

overlook   sō·fāt, fāt·leuhk

overproduction   sàng·cháan·gwo·jihng

overseas   hói·ngoih

overseas Chinese   wàh·kìuh

overshadow   jè·jyuh

oversleep   fan·gwo·lùhng

overthrow   tēui·fàan

overweight   chúhng·gwo·tàuh

overwork   gùng·jok·gwo·douh

owe   him, jàang

owing to   yàn·waih

owl   māau·tàuh·yīng (M: jek)

own   yáuh. /He owns a whole block. Kéuih yáuh sèhng·tìuh gāai gam dō ngūk. /He owns
this house. is expressed as: This house is his. Nī·gāan ngūk haih kéuih ge. /Who
owns this property? Nī·go cháan·yihp haih bīn·go ga?
    one's own   jih·géi ge. /Are these your own things? Nī·di yéh haih néih jih·géi ge
ma?

owner   owner of a car chè·jyú; owner of a factory chóng·jyú; owner of a house ngūk·
jyú; owner of a ship syùhn·jyú; owner of a store pou·jyú; owner of land deih·jyú;
owner of lost property sāt·jyú; ownership yihp·kyùhn

ox   ngàuh·gūng (M: jek)

Oxford University   Ngàuh·jèun daaih·hohk

oxygen   yéuhng·hei

oyster   hòuh, sàang·hòuh (M: jek one, dī few); dried oysters hòuh·sí; oyster shell hòuh·
hok

P

pace   bouh: walk in a longer pace hàahng daaih bouh dī; keep pace with gān dāk séuhng,
paak dāk jyuh

pacify   (a country, uprising, etc.) pìhng·dìhng; (one's anger) hyun; (soothe) ngòn·wai

pack   jāp (sahp), jòng, dá. /She is packing (for a trip). Kéuih jāp·gán hàhng·léih. /The books are all packed (in a box). Dī syù yíh·gìng jòng·hóu la. /Has he packed up the bedding yet? Kéuih dá·hóu péih·bāau meih a?
    a pack of cigarettes yāt·bāau yīn; **a pack of cards** yāt·fu páai; **a charge for packing** bāau·jòng·faai

package   bàau (M): **a package** yāt·bàau yéh; bàau·gwó (N): **a package** yāt·go bàau·gwó. /Is this package yours? Nī·bàau yéh haih·m̀h·haih néih ga? /The mailman gave me this package and asked me to sign for it. I looked at it carefully and found out it wasn't mine. Yàuh·chàai béi go bàau·gwó ngóh yiu ngóh chìm·jí, ngóh tái·chìng·chó yùhn·lòih m̀h·haih ngóh ge.

pact   (agreement) tìuh·yeuk

pad   jin (V); **shoulder pad** jin·bok; **pad of paper** paak·jí·bóu

paddle   pàh (V); **paddle a boat** pàh·téhng; **paddle a dragon-boat** pàh·lùhng·syùhn

paddy   **paddy field** tìhn, wòh·tìhn

padlock   só (M: bá)

page   (one side of a leaf of a book) yihp; (one leaf of a book) pìn

pagoda   taap (M: joh)

paid   béi·jó. /It's paid. Yíh·gìng béi·jó la. /Has it been paid? Béi·jó méih a?

pail   túng

pain   tung. /Where is the pain? Bīn·syu tung a? /Do you feel any pain? Néih gok·dāk tung ma? /This shouldn't cause you any pain at all. M̀h·tung ge. or Yāt dī dōu m̀h·tung ge. /The tooth was so painful that I couldn't sleep. Ngàh tung·dou ngóh m̀h·fan·dāk.
    pain in the stomach tóuh tung; **pain in the back** bui·jek tung; **pain in the stomach** waih tung

painstaking   hóu sāai sām·gèi ge. /This is a very painstaking job. Nī·gihn sih hóu sāai sām·gèi ge. **painstakingly** hóu yuhng sām·gèi gám, hóu fú·sàm gám. /He has been working on it painstakingly. Kéuih hóu yuhng sām·gèi gám jouh·gán.

paint   yáu, yàuh·chāt. /What color of paint should we use for this building? Nī·joh láu yìng·gòi yuhng bīn·jek sīk·séui ge yáu (or yàuh·chāt) a?
    to paint yàuh. /How much will it cost to paint this building? Yàuh nī·joh láu yiu géi dò chín a? /This house needs a coat of paint (needs painting). Nī·gàan ngūk yiu yàuh yáu la. /How about painting it white? Yàuh baahk sīk, hóu ma?
    to paint pictures waahk, waahk wá (VO). /I like to paint. Ngóh jùng·yi waahk·wá. /What do you like to paint? Néih jùng·yi waahk māt·yéh a? /I like to paint horses. Ngóh jùng·yi waahk·máh. /How many paintings have you done this month? Nī·go yuht néih waahk·jó géi·dō fūk wá la.
    painting wá (M: fūk); **oil painting** yàuh·wá; **watercolor painting** séui·chói·wá; **painter** wá·gā (artist), yàuh·chāt lóu (artisan); **to paint a Chinese landscape painting** waahk sàan·séui·wá

pair   (for shoes, socks, earrings, chopsticks, etc.) deui: **a pair of shoes** yāt·deui hàaih; (for eyes, hands, feet, chopsticks) sèung: **her (a pair of) eyes** kéuih sèung·ngáahn; **a pair of hands** yāt·sèung sáu; (for glasses) fu: **this pair of glasses**, nī·fu ngáahn·géng; (for trousers) tìuh: **a pair of trousers** yāt·tìuh fu; (for scissors) bá: **a pair of scissors** yāt·bá gaau·jín

pajama   sèuih·yī (M: tyut)

palace   gùng·dihn

pale   chèng

palings   làahn·gōn (M: douh)

palm   (tree) jùng·syuh; (of hand) sáu·jéung; **carry on the palm** béi sáu tok·jyuh

palpitation   (of heart) sàm·tiu. /You said you had a palpitation, when was that? Néih
wah néih ge sàm tiu dāk hóu gán·yiu, haih géi·sí ge sih a?

pamper   jung

pamphlet   sîu·chaak·jí

pan   (for cooking) wohk; (all) faahn: **Pan-American** faahn·méih

pant   sok·hei

panther   paau (M: jek)

pantomime   ngá·kehk (M: chēut)

pants   fu (M: tîuh); **a pair of pants** yāt·tîuh fu

papa   bàh·bā, a·bā

papaya   muhk·gwā

paper   jí (M: jèung); (newspaper) bou·jí (M: fahn); **toilet paper** chóu·jí; **wallpaper** fà·jí
(M: gyún roll)
          (document) màhn·gín. /Some important papers are missing. Yáuh dī juhng·yiu màhn·
gín m̀h·gin·jó
          (essay) leuhn·màhn, màhn·jèung. /What is his paper about? Kéuih pìn leuhn·màhn
góng māt·yéh ga?
          papers (identification) jing·gín, jing·mìhng màhn·gín. /May I see your papers?
Ngóh hó·yíh tái·háh néih ge jing·mìhng màhn·gín ma? or Béi néih ge jing (mìhng màhn)
gín ngóh tái háh.
          paper money ngàhn·jí; **examination paper** si·gyún

parable   (allegory) pei·yuh, yuh·yîhn

parachute   gong·lohk·saan

parade   (an organized procession or march) yàuh·hàhng; (review of troops) yuht·bìng

paradise   (of the Christians) tìn·tòhng; (of the Buddhists) sài·fòng·gihk·lohk·sai·gaai

paragraph   dyuhn, jit

parallel   pìhng·hàhng: **parallel line** pìhng·hàhng·sin

paralyzed   (to become paralyzed) fùng·táan·jó; **paralyzed on one side of body** bun·sàn
bāt·seuih

paralysis   fùng·táan, màh·bei: **infantile paralysis** sîu (or yìng) yîh·màh·bei·jing

paralytic stroke   jung·fùng (VO). /He had a paralytic stroke. Kéuih jung·fùng.

parasite   (worm) gei·sàng·chùhng; (plant) gei·sàng·chóu (grass or vine)

paratroop   gong·lohk·saan bouh·déui; **paratrooper** saan·bìng

parcel   (package) bàau (M), bàau·yéh (M+N): **a parcel of books** yāt·bāau syù; **a parcel**
yāt·bàau yéh. /You have a parcel. Néih yáuh bàau yéh.

pardon   (excuse) yùhn·leuhng (V); (of a criminal) se·míhn; **to pardon sin** se·jeuih; **I beg
your pardon** M̀h·gòi. **Pardon me** M̀h·gòi.

pare	pài: **pare the potatoes** pài syùh·jái

parent	(father) lóuh·dauh (colloq.), fuh·chàn; (mother) lóuh·móu (colloq.) móuh·chàn; **parents** fuh·móuh

parenthesis	kut·wùh

parish	gaau·kēui

park	(a public place) gùng·yún; **to park** tìhng. /Where can we park (the car)? Ga chè tìhng·hái bīn·syu a? or Bīn·syu hó·yíh tìhng chè a? **parking lot** tìhng·chè·chèuhng

parliament	gwok·wúi

parlor	haak·tēng; **beauty parlor** méih·yùhng·yún

parrot	ngāng·gō (M: jek)

parson	(minister) muhk·sī

part	(portion) bouh·fahn. /You do that part, I'll do this part. Néih jouh gó·bouh fahn, ngóh jouh nī·bouh fahn. /Which part needs repairing? Bīn·bouh·fahn yiu sàu·jíng a?
	(length, or one of several continuous parts) gyuht, dyuhn. /This road is part cement and part asphalt. Nī·tìuh louh yāt·gyuht haih sehk·sí (or séui·nàih) ge, yāt·gyuht haih laahp·chēng ge.
	(piece of a machine) lìhng·gín. /Do you sell parts for this brand of car? Néih·deih maaih·m̀h·maaih nī·tíng hei·chè ge lìhng·gín a?
	(unit measurement) fahn. /Mix two parts of coca cola with one part of brandy. Jèung léuhng·fahn hó·háu·hó·lohk yāt·fahn baahk·lāan·déi kàu·màaih kéuih.
	(role in a play) geuk·sīk. /She plays that part very well. Kéuih yín (or baahn) gó·go geuk·sīk yín (or baahn) dāk hóu hóu.
	take part in chāam·gà. /Why don't you take part in the tournament? Dím·gáai néih m̀h·chāam·gà béi·choi a?
	part-time job sáan·gūng

partake	chāam·gà

partial	yāt·bouh·fahn ge; **partial view** pìn·gin

participant	chāam·gà ge yàhn

participate	chāam·gà

particular	dahk·biht

particularly	yàuh·kèih·sih, dahk·biht·haih

partition	(dividing) gaan·gaak

partly	yāt·bouh·fahn, yáuh·dī

partner	paak·sáu fó·gei, pāat·nā; **partnership** hahp·gú sàang·yi

partridge	je·gū (M: jek)

party	(social gathering) Chinese has no single term that covers the range of meaning of the English term party, but the following expressions are useful: chéng yám, chéng haak (have a formal dinner party); dá páai (have a card party); sihk chàan bihn·fàahn (have an informal party); baai sauh (birthday party for a venerable person); jouh múhn·yuht (celebration of the first month of a newborn baby); jip fùng (welcome dinner party); jihn·hàhng (farewell dinner party). /Are you going to Mr. Lahm's dinner party? Làhm sīn·sàang hah·láih·baai chéng·yám néih heui·m̀h·heui a? but Néih géi·sí chéng·yám a? may mean When are you going to (get married and) give a dinner party? /They are having a card party. Kéuih·deih dá·gán páai. /How about coming to my place for an informal party? Lèih ngóh·syu sihk chàan bihn·faahn hóu ma? /We're having a welcome party for Mr. Lee; can you come? Ngóh tìng·yaht tùhng Léih·sīn·sàang jip·fùng, néih lèih ma?

(political group) jing·dóng, dóng in combination: **Communist Party** Guhng·cháan· dóng; **Conservative Party** Bóu·sáu·dóng; **Democratic Party** Màhn·jyú·dóng; **Kupmingtong** Gwok·màhn·dóng; **Labour Party** Gùng·dóng; **Republican Party** Guhng·wòh·dóng

(in negotiation, a lawsuit, drawing up a contract, etc.) fòng. /Both parties agreed. Sèung·fòng tùhng·yi.

party member dóng·yùhn; **party newspaper** dóng·bou; **tea party** chàh·wúi

pass		(go by) gìng·gwo. /Are we going to pass the bank? Ngóh·deih gìng·gwo gó·gàan ngàhn·hòhng ma? /Please tell me when we pass that building. Gìng·gwo gó·joh láu gó· ﹨jahn·sí m̀h·gòi néih góng ngóh jì.

(of an examination) gahp·gaak (in school); gìng·gwo (undergo). /Did you pass? Néih gahp·gaak ma? /He must pass a test before he can go. Kéuih heui jì·chìhn yāt·dihng yiu gìng·gwo yāt·go háau·si.

(approve) tùng·gwo. /Do you think my proposal will be passed? Néih gok·dāk ngóh ge tàih·yi wúih tùng·gwo ma?

pass away gwo·sàn. /How long ago did his mother pass away? Kéuih lóuh·móu géi· sìh gwo·sàn ga?

pass out (faint) wàhn·jó. /He passed out. Kéuih wàhn·jó. /Come over here quickly, someone has just passed out. Faai dī lèih, jing·wah yáuh yàhn wàhn·jó.

pass sentence pun·jeuih. /The court will pass sentence on him today. Faat·yún gàm·yaht pun kéuih jeuih.

pass through gìng·gwo. /Do we have to pass through the town? Ngóh·deih yāt·dihng yiu gìng·gwo sèhng yahp·bihn àh?

pass up cho·gwo. /You shouldn't pass up an opportunity like that. Néih m̀h·hóu cho·gwo gam hóu ge gèi·wuih.

(permit) chēut·yahp·jing, yahp·mùhn·jing

passage		(act of passing) tùng·hàhng; (a way to go through) louh; (in a house) láahng· hóng; (a hole) lūng; (a bill) tùng·gwo; (fare) louh·fai (in general), syùhn·fai (by ship); (paragraph) jit, dyuhn; **passage money** séui·geuk (for people), joi·geuk (for goods)

passenger		daap·haak

passion		(capacity for emotion) chìhng, chìhng·gáam; (desire) yuhk·mohng; (fondness for) ngoi

passionate		hóu yùhng·yih gīk·duhng ge

passive		(negative) sìu·gihk; (acted upon) beih duhng ge: **passive resistance** sìu·gihk dái·kong

passport		wuh·jiu

past		(gone by, in space or time) gwo·jó, gwo·heui. /The worst part of the trip is past. Jeui yáih gó·dyuhn louh yíh·gìng gwo·jó la. /It's past four. Gwó·jó sei·dím la. or Sei·dím·géi la. /Don't worry about a thing that is past. Gwo·heui ge sih m̀h·hóu séung la.

(used as a PV) gwo, gwo·jó, gwo·heui. /Walk past that building and turn right. Hàahng·gwo gó·joh láu jyun yauh. /It's past noon; let's eat. Gwo·jó sahp·yih·dím la, sihk ngaan·jau la. /He didn't stop but drove right past. Kéuih móuh·tìhng·dou yāt·jihk gám sái·jó gwo·heui.

in the past yíh·chìhn, chùhng·chìhn. /In the past it's been very difficult to get tickets. Yíh chìhn hóu nàahn máaih dóu fēi ga.

the past week seuhng·go láih·baai; **the past month** seuhng·go yuht; **the past year** gauh·nín; **the past few years** chìhn·géi·nìhn

the past, one's past yíh·chìhn ge sih, chùhng·chìhn ge sih, yíh·wóhng ge sih. /When- ever she thinks of the past she starts to weep. Kéuih yāt séung·héi yíh·chìhn ge sih jauh haam·héi·séung·lèih. /Don't be depressed by the past. Mh·hóu waih yíh·wóhng ge sih sēung·sàm.

paste   jèung·wùh (N), nìhm, chì, tip, bíu (with a backing as Chinese paintings or scrolls). **paste up on** tip·hái: **paste up on the wall** tip·hái chèuhng seuhng·bihn

pasteurize   sìu·duhk. /How do you pasteurize these? Dím·yéung jèung nī·dī yéh sìu·duhk a? **pasteurized** sìu·duhk ge, sìu·gwo·duhk ge

pastime   (diversion, recreation) sìu·hin

pastor   muhk·sī

pastry   dím·sām, sài·dím

pasture   (grazing land) chóu·déi

pat   paak: **pat a person on the shoulder** paak bok·tàuh

patch   bóu: **to patch a hole in clothing** bóu·nà

patent   jyùn·maaih·kyùhn; **patented article** jyùhn·maaih·bán; **patent leather** chāt·péi; **patent medicines** sìhng·yeuhk; **patent right** jyùn·maaih·kyùhn

path   louh·jái

pathologist   behng·léih·hohk·gā

pathology   behng·léih; behng·léih·hohk

patience   noih·sing, yáhn·noih; **have no patience with** mh·yáhn·dāk

patient   yáhn·noih (V). behng·yàhn (N). yáuh·noih·sing (SV)

patrimony   jóu·yihp

patriot   ngoi·gwok·ge yàhn, ngoi·gwok jé

patriotism   ngoi·gwok·sàm

patrol   chèuhn·lòh (V); **patrol boat** chèuhn·lòh·téhng

patron   (customer) haak·jái; (of a society) jaan·joh·yàhn

patronize   (a shop) bòng·chan; (to sponsor) jaan·joh

pattern   (design) fún. /This rug has a very nice pattern. Nī·jèung deih·jīn hóu hóu·fún. (model) yéung. /Where did you get the pattern for your new dress? Néih gihn sāam ge fā·yéung hái bīn·syu lèih ga?

Paul   Bóu·lòh

pauper   kùhng·yàhn

pause   tìhng yāt·háh, tìhng·deuhn (V)

pave   pòu: **pave with pebbles** pòu sehk·jái; **paved with pebbles** pòu·múhn sehk·jái; **paved with moss** sàang·múhn chèng·tòih

pavement   sehk·sí·louh, sehk·jái louh

pavilion   (for spectators) tòih; (for resting by the roadside or in a garden) tíng, lèuhng·tíng

paw   jáau, jéung: **bear's paws** hùhng·jéung

pawn   dong: **pawnshop** dong·póu; **pawn ticket** dong·piu

pay   (make payment for something) béi·chín. /When will he pay you? Kéuih géi·sí béi chín néih a? /How much did he pay you? Kéuih béi néih géi dò chín a? /I paid him ten dollars. Ngóh béi·jó sahp·go ngàhn·chín kéuih. /I haven't paid for it yet. Ngóh juhng meih béi chín. /How much do you want to pay for it? Néih béi géi chín a?

(spend for buying) máaih ga, máaih ge, máaih jó, máaih. /How much did you pay for your watch? Néih go bīu géi chín máaih ga? /How much were you paid for your watch? Néih go bīu máaih·jó géi chín a? /You'll have to pay for your own ticket. Néih yiu jih gēi máaih piu.

(give a salary or wage) chēut·lèuhng, chēut·yàhn·gùng. /We pay our employees every Friday. Ngóh·deih múih·go láih·baai·ńgh chēut·lèuhng.

(of payments as rent, water, electricity, etc.) gàau. /When will you have to pay the rent? Néih géi·sí yiu gāau·jòu a? /How much do we pay for the water a month? Ngóh·deih múih·yuht gàau géi chín séui·fai a?

(debts, loans) wàahn·fàan(·béi). /We'll lend you fifty dollars, you pay us back next month. Ngóh·deih je·béi néih ńgh·sahp·mān, néih hah·go yuht wàahn fàan béi ngóh·deih.

(of damages) pùih. /Is he going to pay for it? Kéuih pùih ma? /Isn't he going to pay for it? Kéuih m̀h pùih àh?

(of taxes, duty, etc.) naahp. /How much income tax do you have to pay? Néih yiu naahp géi dò chín yahp·sīk·seui a?

(be worthwhile) jeuhk·sou, jihk·dāk. /Does it pay to sell it now? Yìh·gā maaih·jó kéuih jeuhk·m̀h·jeuhk·sou a? /He always asks himself: Does it pay to study so hard? Kéuih sìh·sìh mahn kéuih jih·gēi: jihk·m̀h·jihk·dāk hohk dāk gam sàn·fú nē?

be paid chēut·lèuhng, líhng·sàn·séui, jì·yàhn·gùng. /When are we going to be paid? Ngóh·deih géi·sí chēut·lèuhng a?

pay a visit taam·háh. /Should we pay him a visit? Ngóh·deih yìng·fahn heui taam·háh kéuih ma?

(salary) sàn·séui; (wages) yàhn·gùng. /Is the pay good on your job? Néih yìh·gā jouh·gán nī·fahn sih sàn·séui (or yàhn·gùng) dò ma?

pay a New Year's visit baai·nìhn; **pay attention to** jyu·yi; **pay in advance** béi seuhng·kèih; **payment on delivery of goods, C.O.D.** fo·dou·gàau·ngán; **pay no attention to** m̀h·léih, m̀h·chói; **pay deposit** lohk·dehng

payee   sàu·fún yàhn

payer   fuh·fún·yàhn

pea   chèng·dáu, hòh·lāan·dáu ngàhn, pī·dáu; **pea pod** hòh·lāan·dáu, syut·dau (used in the Chinese community in America)

peanut   fā·sāng (M: nāp) **peanut oil** fā·sāng·yàuh

peace   (national) wòh·pìhng, taai·pìhng. **the peace of the world** sai·gaai·wòh pìhng; **peace treaty** wòh (pìhng·tìuh)·yeuk; **peace conference** wòh·pìhng wuih·yih
when speaking of peace as the ending of a war, verbal expressions as m̀h·dá jeung la, dá·yùhn·jeung are used. /When will there be peace? Géi·sí sìn·ji m̀h·dá jeung a? /I hope peace will come soon. Ngóh hèi·mohng faai dī dá·yùhn·jeung la.

(domestic) wòh·muhk pìhng·ngòn. /God bless your family, may you be always at peace. Seuhng·dai bóu·yauh néih·deih gà·tìhng wòh·muhk, yàhn·háu pìhng·ngòn.

peace (and quiet) m̀h·hóu chòuh. /Can't we have a little peace (and quiet) around here? is expressed as: Néih·deih m̀h·hóu chòuh dāk ma?

peacemaker   wòh·sih·lóu

peach   tóu; **peach blossoms** tòuh·fà

peacock   húng·jéuk (M: jek)

peak   (of a mountain) sàan·déng

pear   (American variety) bē·léi; (Kwangtung and Kwangsi) sà·léi; (Tientsin) syut·lèih

pearl   jān·jyù, jyū (M: nāp); **cultured pearl** yéuhng·jyū peasant   (farmer) gàang·tìhn·lóu (colloq.), nùhng·fù

pebble   sehk·jái; ngòh·chēun·sehk (oval and smooth)

peck   (measurement) dáu; (strike with the beak) dèung

peculiar   (special) dahk·biht, dahk·syùh; (strange) gú·gwaai, kèih·gwaai

peculiarity   dahk·sing, dahk·sīk

pedal   daahp (V); geuk·daahp·báan

peddler   síu·fáan

peel   pèih (N); **to peel** mīt; mīt pèih (as a banana); mōk, mōk pèih (as an orange); (with
a knife) pài, pài pèih

peep   (look slyly) tàu·tái, jòng

peer   sèung gahn·chi ge yàhn (one's equals); gwai·juhk (aristocracy)

peerless   móuh·dāk béi·ping ge, géui·sai·mòuh·sèung ge

peevish   bouh·chou

peg   (of wood) muhk·dĕng; (of bamboo) jŭk·dĕng

Peking   Bāk·gìng

pen   (Chinese) mòuh·bāt; (foreign) mahk·séui·bāt; (enclosure) lāan

penknife   dōu·jái (M: bá)

penmanship   syù·faat

penname   bāt·méng

penal law   yìhng·faat

penalty   (punishment) yìhng·faht; (fine) faht·fún

pence   bihn·sih

pencil   yùhn·bāt (M: jì); **pencil sharpener** yùhn·bāt·páau

pending   meih·chàhng kyut·dihng ge

pendulum   jūng·báai

penetrate   (pierce) chaap·yahp, sàm·yahp

penguin   kei·ngòh (M: jek)

peninsular   bun·dóu

penniless   kùhng·dou·gwaht, kùhng·gwòng kùhng·gwaht

penny   bihn·sih (in England); sín·sí, sín (U.S. or Canadian)

pension   yéuhng·lóuh·gām, chèuhng·lèuhng

Pentecost   nǵh·chèuhn·jit

peony   máuh·dāan; cheuk·yeuhk

people   (persons) yàhn. /How many people were there at last night's meeting? Kàhm·
máahn hòi·wúi yáuh géi·dò yàhn a?
　　(others) yàhn·deih. /People will laugh at you. Yàhn·deih wúih siu néih ga.
　　(electorate) yàhn·mahn, màhn·jung. /A government must have the support of the
people. Jing·fú yāt·dihng yiu yáuh yàhn·màhn ge yúng·wuh.
　　(race) júng·juhk. /The natives in the mountains are a distinct people. Sàan·seuhng
ge tóu·yàhn haih lihng yāt·go júng·juhk ge.

pepper   wùh·jîu; ground pepper   wùh·jîu·fán

peppermint   bohk·hòh: **peppermint oil** bohk·hòh yàuh, **peppermint candy** bohk·hòh·tóng

per   /Three dollars per hour. Sàam·go ngàhn·chín yāt·dím·jūng. /Two hundred dollars per month. Léuhng·baak·mān yāt·go·yuht.

per cent   baak·fahn·jì followed by the number required. /What per cent? Baak·fahn·jì géi a? Ninety-six per cent. Baak·fahn·jì gáu·sahp·luhk (lit. 96 of 100 parts).

perceive   (see) tái·gin; (see clearly into) tái·chēut; (understand) mìhng·baahk; jì; (comprehend) líuh·gáai

percentage   (proportion) sìhng, sìhng·sou

perch   lòuh·yùh (M: tìuh)

perfect   there is no single word to express the idea of perfect, but the following expressions are used to convey the idea: hóu (good) or some other stative verbs plus dou·gihk (to the last detail); jàn·haih (really) plus hóu or another stative verb or a verb. There are also a few indirect expressions. /It's perfect! Hóu·dou·gihk! /She gave a perfect performance. Kéuih bíu·yín dāk jàn·haih hóu la. /He speaks perfect Cantonese. Kéuih góng dāk sahp·jūk·sahp ge Gwóng·jàu·wá. /He is a perfect stranger to me. is expressed as: Ngóh yāt dī dōu m̀h·sīk kéuih.

perforate   dá·lūng

perform   (on a stage) bíu·yín, yín. /She performed very well. Kéuih bíu·yín dāk hóu hóu. /Who performs next? Lèuhn·dou bīn·go bíu·yín la?
    (carry out a contract, obligation, etc.) léih·hàhng
    perform an operation hōi·dōu, duhng·sáu·seuht; **perform a duty** jāp·hàhng jīk·mouh

performance   expressed verbally. /It's a wonderful performance! Yín dāk jàn·haih hóu la!

perfume   (liquid) hèung·séui, fà·louh·séui

perhaps   waahk·jé, waahk·jé . . . dōu m̀h·díng. /Perhaps he forgot. Waahk·jé kéuih m̀h·gei·dāk·jó. /Perhaps it'll rain today. Waahk·jé gàm·yaht wúih lohk·yúh dōu m̀h·díng.

peril   (danger) ngàih·hím

period   (stretch of time) sìh·kèih. /He worked here for a short period. Kéuih hái syu jouh·gwo yāt·go dyún sìh·kèih. /The history of this school may be devided into three periods. Nī·go hohk·haauh ge lihk·sí hó·yíh fàn·wàih sàam·go sìh·kèih.
    (class hour) tòhng. I have no class the third period. Ngó daih·sàam·tòhng móuh tòhng. /How many periods do you have per day? Néih yāt·yaht yáuh géi·dò tòhng a?

periodical   dihng·kèih hón·maht, kèih·hón (N)

perish   (be destroyed) miht·mòhng; (die) sí·mòhng

perishable   (liable to spoil) wúih mùih·laahn ge

perjure   (swear falsely) saih·gá·yuhn

permanent   hóu noih m̀h·bin ge, wìhng·gáu ge

permit   jéun. /I won't permit you to go. Ngóh m̀h·jéun néih heui. /No one is permitted to enter this building without special permission. Yùh·gwó móuh daht·bihk héui·hó m̀h·jéun yahp nī·joh láu.
    (written permission) yàhn·chìhng, yàhn·chìhng jí, héui·hó·jing; jāp·jiu. /You have to get a permit to visit this factory. Néih yiu ló go yàhn·chìhng(·jí) sìn·ji chàam·gùn dāk nī·gàan gùng·chóng. /Do we have to get a permit to fish? Ngóh·deih diu·yú sái·m̀h·sái ló jāp·jiu ga?

perpendicular   (vertical) sèuih·jihk ge

perpetual   (eternal) wìhng·gáu (ge)

persecute   chàahn·hoih

perseverance   ngaih·lihk

persimmon   gāi·sàm·chí; **dried persimmon** chí·béng

persist   gìn·chìh·lohk·heui

person   yàhn. /What sort of a person is he? Kéuih haih dím·yéung yāt·go yàhn a? /She
seems like a different person. Kéuih hóu·chíh lihng·ngói yāt·go yàhn gám. **in person**
bún·yàhn (oneself); chàn·jih (personally); dòng·mín (face to face). /Tell him to bring it
here in person. Giu kéuih bún·yàhn nīk·lèih. /Please deliver this to him in person (by
yourself). Chéng néih chàn·jih daai·heui béi keuih. /Please deliver this to him (to himself) in person. Chéng néih dòng·mín gàau·béi kéuih.

personal   go·yàhn ge, sì·yàhn ge, jih·géi ge. /This is my personal opinion. Nī·go haih
ngóh go·yàhn ge yi·gin. /Don't mix personal affairs with business. Mh·hóu jèung sì·
yàhn ge sìh tùhng gùng·sih kàu·màaih yāt·chái. /Are these your personal belongings?
Nī·dī haih·mh·haih néih jih·géi ge yéh a?

   personal affairs sì·sih. /I was very busy the last few days because I had some
personal affairs to take care of. Chìhn·géi·yaht ngóh hóu mh·dāk·hàahn yàn·waih ngóh
yáuh dī sì·sih yiu dá·léih.

perspire   (sweat) chēut·hohn (VO); **perspire freely** bíu·hohn

perspiration   (sweat) hohn

persuade   hyun

pertaining   **pertaining to** suhk·yù

perturb   (disturb) gáau·lyuhn

perverse   (stubbornly contrary) hóu ngaahng·géng ge

pessimism   sìu·gihk jyú·yih, bèi·gùn·jyú·yih

pessimist   sìu·gihk·paai

pessimistic   bèi·gùn (ge)

pestilence   (disease) wàn·yihk, sìh·yihk; **pestilence among fowls** gāi·wàn; **pestilence
among pigs** jyū·wàn

pestle   (for pounding and grinding) jùng·hám

petal   fā·fáan

petition   chíng·yuhn (V); chíng·yuhn·syù

petrol   dihn·yàuh, hei·yàuh

petroleum   mùih·yàuh

petticoat   dái·kwùhn

petty cash   lìhng·yuhng·fai

pewter   sek: **pewter articles** sek·hei

pharmacy   (dispensary) yeuhk·fòhng; (study of) jai·yeuhk

pheasant   sāan·gāi (M: jek)

phenomenon   yihn·jeuhng, jih·yìhn ge yihn·jeuhng

philanthropic   chǐh·sihn (ge); **philanthropic works** chǐh·sihn sih·yihp

philanthropist   chǐh·sihn·gā

philosopher   jit·hohk·gā

philosophical   yáuh·jit·hohk·yi·meih (ge)

philosophy   jit·hohk

phlegm   tàahm

phoenix   fuhng·wòhng (M: jek)

Phonetic alphabet   jyuh·yām·jih·móuh; **phonetic symbols** jyuh·yām·fuh·houh (both terms are also commonly used for the Chinese National Phonetic Alphabet)

phonograph   làuh·sìng·gèi·hei

phosphorus   lèuhn, lèuhn·sou

photograph   séung (M: fūk), seung·pín (M: jèung). /Whose photograph is this? Nī·fūk haih bīn·go ge séung a? <u>or</u> Nī·fūk séung haih bīn·go ga? (This photograph belongs to whom?) /Remember to bring two photographs with you. Gei·jyuh daai léuhng·fūk séung lèih. /Please enlarge this photograph for me. M̀h·gòi néih tùhng ngóh fong·daaih nī· jèung séung.

    to photograph <u>or</u> **have a photograph taken** yíng·séung (VO). /How many photographs have you taken? Néih yíng·jó géi·dò fūk séung la? /I haven't taken a photograph for months. Ngóh hóu géi·go yuht móuh yíng·séung la. /I haven't had a photograph taken for months. Ngóh hóu géi·go yuht móuh yíng·séung la.

    photographer sip·yíng·sī, yíng·séung·láu (colloq.); **photographer's studio** yíng·séung· póu; **photograph negative** dái·pín

photography   (art) yíng·séung, sip·yíng·seuht (technical term). /This is excellent photography. Nī·fūk séung yíng dāk jàn·haih hóu la.

phrase   dyún·geui; sèuhng yuhng ge dyún·geui

physical   (bodily) sàn·tái·seuhng ge, sàng·léih·seuhng ge; (material) maht·jāt seuhng ge; **physical constitution** tái·gaak; **physical examination** tái·gaak gín·chàh; **physical exercise** tái·chòu, wahn·duhng; **physical training** tái·yuhk

physician   yī·sāng; noih·fō yī·sāng (as opposed to surgeon); ngoih·fō yī·sāng (surgeon)

physics   maht·léih (hohk)

physiognomist   tái·seung·lóu, tái·seung·sīn·sàang

physiognomy   seung·faat, seung·seuht; tái·seung (VO). /He said he knows physiognomy, is it true? Kéuih wah kéuih wúih tái·seung, haih·m̀h·haih a?

physiology   sàng·léih·hohk

physique   tái·gaak

pianist   gong·kàhm·sī (musician, instructor); gong·kàhm·gā (artist)

piano   gong·kàhm: **play piano** tàahn·gong·kahm. /Do you (know how to) play the piano? Néih wúih tàahn gong kàhm ma? /He really knows how to play the piano. Kéuih tàahn (gong) kàhm tàahn dāk hóu hóu.

pick   (choose) gáan. /Please pick two men to help me. M̀h·gòi néih gáan léuhng·go yàhn lèih bòng ngóh.

    (pluck) jaahk (fruit, vegetables, flowers). /Are the lichis ripe enough to pick? Dī laih·jī jaahk·dāk meih a?

    pick on (annoy) hà, hèi·fuh. /Stop picking on him! M̀h·jéun joi hà kéuih!

pick up (an object) jāp·héi (on ground, floor, bed, etc.); nìng·héi, nìm·héi. /Please pick up the papers. M̀h·gòi néih jāp·héi gó·dī jí kéuih. /He picked up the phone immediately and called the police (headquarters). Kéuih jīk·hāk nìng·héi go dihn·wá dá·béi chàai·gún.

pick out gáan·chēut; **pick a lucky day** gáan·go hóu yaht·jí; **pick teeth** tīu·ngàh, lìu·ngàh

pickpocket   pàh·sáu, chaap·sáu; dá·hòh·bāau. /Beware of the pickpockets! Gu·jyuh béi yàhn dá·hòh·bāau boh!

picket   (of a labor union) dáu·chaat·yùhn (N); **picketline** dáu·chaat·déui

pickle   yip (V); **pickled eggs** (thousand-year-eggs) pèih·dáan; **pickles** hàahm·syùn·choi; **pickled peach** hàahm·syùn·táu

picnic   yéh·chāan

pictorial   wá·bou (N), (M: bún)

picture   (painting) wá, tòuh·wá; (M: fūk) (drawing) tòuh·wá (M: fūk); (photograph) séung (M: fūk).

picture frame seung·gá; **picture framing** jòng seung·gá; **paint** (or draw) **a picture** waahk·wá; **take a picture** yíng·séung

picul   daam

piece   the following measures are used: faai, gauh (chuhk); jèung (sheet; also used of flat things not expressed in English as piece); gihn (of work, or an article of something made); dyuhn (section or piece of music); tìuh (a length); gyuht (a section of length); nāp (of candy, etc.). /How much does this piece of material cost? Nī·faai bou·líu géi chin a? /This piece of meat is too fat, I want a lean piece. Nī·gauh yuhk taai fèih, Ngóh yiu gauh sau ge. /Please give me a piece of paper. M̀h·gòi néih béi jèung jí ngóh. /That's a fine piece of work. (of a job or situation) Nī·gihn sih jouh dāk hóu hóu. (of an article, a composition) Nī·pin màhn·jèung sé dāk hóu hóu. /Can you play this piece of music for us? Néih hó·m̀h·hó·yíh wáan nī·dyuhn yàm·ngohk béi ngóh·deih tèng·háh a? /Can it be fixed with this piece of copper wire? Hó·yíh yuhng nī·tìuh tùhng·sín jíng·fàan kéuih ma? /Give me the short piece. Béi gyuht dyún ge ngóh. /How many pieces of candy has he eaten? Kéuih sihk·jó géi·dō·nāp tóng la? /Do you own this piece of land? Nī·daat deih haih·m̀h·haih néih ga?

(small broken pieces) seui. /Please sweep away these pieces of broken glass. Faai dī sou·jó nī·dī bō·lēi·séui kéuih. (crumbs) séui: bread crumbs mihn·bāau·séui

a piece of chalk yāt·jī fán·bāt; **a piece of stone** yāt·gauh sehk; **a piece of sugar cane** yāt·sóng je or yāt·lūk je

break to pieces resultative compounds with seui as second element. **break into pieces** jíng·seui; **chop into pieces** deuk·seui; **cut into pieces** (with scissors) jín·seui

timepiece (clock) jūng; (watch) bīu

to piece together dau·fàan·màaih, bok·fàan·màaih

pier   máh·tàuh

pierce   gāt; **pierce through** gāt·chyùn

piety   (towards God) kìhm·sìhng; (towards parents) haau·seuhn, haau·ging

pig   jyū (M: jek)

pigeon   baahk·gáap (M: jek)

pigment   ngàahn·liuh

pigmy   ngái·yàhn

pile   lahm (heap); dihp, daahp (stack up neatly). /Just pile it up in the corner. Lahm·hái chèuhng·geuk·syu jauh dāk la. /Pile the books on top of each other. Jèung dī syù yāt·bún yāt·bún gám dihp·hóu kéuih.

a pile dèui; daahp (a neat pile). /Carry this pile of clothes into the bedroom. Jùeng nī·daahp sāam nīk·yahp·heui fan·fóng. **a pile of paper** yāt·daahp jí
pile it up lahm·héi kéuih; **pile it evenly** daahp·hóu kéuih, lahm·hóu kéuih
(post) jōng; **drive piles** dá·jōng

piles (disease) jih·chōng

pilfer tàu; tàu·yéh (VO)

pilgrim (to a sacred place as Jerusalem, mecca, etc.) chìuh·sing ge yàhn, chàam·sing ge yàhn; (to a temple) hēung·haak

pill (med.) yún, yeuhk·yún (M: nāp)

pillage dá·gip, chéung·gip

pillar chyúh (M: tìuh)

pillow jám·tàuh: **pillowcase** jám·tàuh·dói

pilot (of airplane) fèi·hàhng·yùhn, gēi·sī; (of port) daai·séui, léhng·góng·yàhn

pimple ngam·chōng, jáu·máih (M: nāp)

pin (fastener) jām (M: jì), biht·jām (M: go); **hairpin** díng·gáap; **safety pin** kau·jām
to pin biht. /Would you please help me to pin this flower on my dress. Mh·gòi néih tùhng ngóh biht·hóu déu fā kéuih.

pincers kím

pinch (to squeeze) mīt

pine (tree) chùhng·syuh (M: pò); **pinecone** chùhng·jí; **pinewood** chaam·muhk

pineapple bò·lòh

ping pong pīng·pāang·bō, bīng·bām·bō

pink fán·hùhng·sīk ge, fán·húng ge

pioneer hòi·louh·sīn·fūng

pious sìhng·sàm

pipe (tube) gún, túng; (flute) sīu; (for smoking) yīn·dáu; **water pipe** séui·gún; **iron pipe** tit·gún

pirate hói·chahk (N); **to pirate** (a literary work, etc.) fàan·yan, tàu·yan

pistil fā·yéuih

pistol sáu·chēung

piston wuht·sāk

pit hāang

pitch (throw) deng, diuh, dám, pehk, fihng

pitch-dark hāk·mā·mà

pitcher séui·wùh, séui·wú

pitiable chài·lèuhng, chài·cháam

pity lìhn·máhn, hó·lìhn. /What a pity! Jàn·haih hó·sīk la!

pivot juhk·sām

place (location) deih·fòng; syu, douh, daat, daai (ref. each of these words in the C-E section). /Is there any place to put the car? Gó·syu yáuh móuh deih·fòng tìhng chè a?

/How about going to his place? Heui kéuih syu hóu ma? /His place is very noisy, would it be alright to go to your place? Kéuih syu chòuh dāk·jaih, heui néih syu dāk ma? /Where is the place you've just finished reading in this book? Nī·bún syù néih jing·wah tái·dou bīn·douh a? /I've lost my place, let me try to find it. Ngóh m̀h·gei· dāk tái·dou bīn·douh la, dáng ngóh si·háh wán·háh. /How far is this place from the railroad station? Nī·syu lèih fó·chè jaahm géi yúhn a? /Whose place (open area) is this? Nī·daat deih·fòng haih bīn·go ga? /Have you ever been to that place (region)? Néih yáuh móuh heui·gwo gó·yāt·daai deih·fòng a?

(vacancy) ngáak. /There are two places in the third grade. Sàam·nìhn·kāp yáuh léuhng·go ngáak.

(find employment for) waih·ji. /Could you place these three people? Néih hó·m̀h· hó·yíh waih·ji nī·sàam·go yàhn a?

out of place (not in the proper location) jāi (<u>or</u> báai) dāk m̀h·ngāam. /This table is out of place. Nī·jèung tói jāi·dāk m̀h·ngāam. (inappropriate) m̀h·chíh·yéung. /His action is certainly out of place. Kéuih gám jouh jàn·haih m̀h·chíh·yéung la.

take the place of (a person) tai (substitute for). /Can you find someone to take his place? Néih hó·yíh wán yàhn tai kéuih ma?

take place (happen) faat·sàng. /This must have taken place while he was away. Nī· gihn sih yāt·dihng haih kéuih m̀h·hái syu ge sìh·hauh faat·sàng ge.

to place (put) fong·hái, jài·hái. /Where do you want me to place this (potted) plant? Nī·pùhn fā fong (<u>or</u> jài, <u>or</u> báai)·hái bīn·syu a?

to place (an order) dehng·fo. /Have you placed that order (for goods)? Néih dehng· jó fo meih a?

take place (of a ceremony) géui·hàhng. /When will the marriage take place? Géi·sí géui·hàhng fàn·láih a?

plague (pestilence) wàn·yihk

plain (clear, understandable) chìng·chó, mìhng·baahk. /He made it perfectly plain that he didn't want to leave. Kéuih góng dāk hóu chìng·chó kéuih m̀h·sćung ché.

(clear, obvious) hín·yìhn. /It's perfectly plain that that is the case. Hín·yìhn haih gám.

(of design) lóuh·saht, pok·sou. /She always wears a plain dress. Kéuih sìh·sìh dõu jeuk dāk hóu pok·sou.

(of color) sèuhn. /She wore a plain white dress. Kéuih jeuk yāt·gihn sèuhn·baahk·ge sāam.

a plain (level land) pìhng·yùhn

plainclothesman (detective) bihn·yī jìng·taam

plaintiff yùhn·gou

plait baan (V); **to plait a pigtail** baan tìuh bīn·jái

plan (intend) dá·syun. /Where do you plan to spend your New Year's holiday? Nihn·ga néih dá·syun heui bīn·syu wáan a? /What is your plan? Néih dá·syun dím a?

(arrange). /I've already planned everything. Ngóh yeuhng·yeuhng yíh·gìng gai·waahk· hóu la.

a plan (method) gai·waahk, faat·ji. (diagram) tòuh, tòuh·jīk, jīk. /What is your plan? Néih yáuh māt gai·waahk (<u>or</u> faat·jí) a?

plane (level) pìhng; (geometry) pìhng·mihn; (carpenter's) páau; **to make smooth with a plane** pàauh·pìhng

plane geometry pìhng·mihn géi·hòh; **plane trigonometry** pìhng·mihn sàam·gok

planet hàhng·sīng

plank (board) báan (M: faai)

plant (vegetation) syuh (tree) (M: pò); chóu (grass or a grasslike leafy plant) (M: dī);

fā (a flower) (M: dī); choi (vegetable) (M: pò). /What kind of plants are these? Nī·dī haih māt·yéh syuh (or fā) a?

(factory) gùng·chóng; -chóng: **power plant** dihn·lihk·chóng. /Have you ever been to that plant? Néih yáuh móuh heui·gwo gó·gàan gùng·chóng a?

to plant jung. /What did you plant this spring? Néih gàm·nín chēun·tīn jung·jó dī māt·yéh a?

plaster   (med.) gòu·yeuhk (M: tip); (lime) fūi·sà; **plaster of Paris** sehk·gōu; **sticking plaster** gàau·bou

plastic   sok·gàau (ge), sou·gàau (ge)

plate   (dish) díp. /Pass your plate and I will give you some more food. Daih néih go díp lèih ngóh joi béi dī choi néih.

(sheet of metal) báan (M: faai): **iron plate** tit·báan; **steel plate** gong·báan
(license) pàaih. /Have you got the plate for your car yet? Néih ga chè ló·dóu pàaih meih a?

to plate douh; **electroplating** dihn·douh; **plated with gold** douh·gām; **plated with silver** douh·ngán. /This watch is gold-plated. Nī·go bīu haih douh·gām ge.

plateau   gòu·yùhn

platform   (in a railroad station) yuht·tòih; (in a classroom, auditorium, etc.) góng·tòih; (on a roof) tìn·páang; (political) jing·gōng

platinum   baahk·gām

platoon   pàaih: **platoon commander** pàaih·jéung

play   (amuse oneself) fáan, wáan. /What game are you playing? Néih·deih fáan·gán māt·yéh a? /Go out and play. Chēut·heui fáan lā. /Stop playing. M̀h·hóu fáan la. /Don't play with fire! M̀h·hóu wáan·fó nàh!

(of games) dá (tennis and other games in which a ball is hit; also cards); tek (games in which a ball is kicked); jūk (chess and checkers); when other games are mentioned, wáan may be used. /Do you play tennis? Néih dá·móhng·kàuh ma? /I don't like to play basketball, I like to play football. Ngóh m̀h·jùng·yi dá làahm·kàuh, ngóh jùng·yi tek jūk·kàuh. /Do you know how to play Chinese chess? Can you teach me? Néih wúih jūk jeuhng·kéi ma? Néih hó·yíh gaau ngóh ma? **play ball** dá·bō; **play dice** jaahk sīk·jái; **play football** dá jūk·kàuh or tek jūk·kàuh; **play golf** dá gò·yíh·fū·kàuh; **play shuttlecock** tek·yín; **play billiards** dá tói·bō; **play cards** dá·páai; **play dominoes** dá·páai; **play mahjong** dá màh·jéuk; **play poker** dá pūk·ká

(of musical instruments) làai (play with a bow); tàahn (play with the fingers); chèui (of wind instruments); dá (of percussion instruments). /Do you play the violin? Néih wúih lāai wāai·ō·līn (or síu·tàih·kàhm) ma? /He plays the piano very well. Kéuih tàahn·kàhm tàahn dāk hóu hóu. /Is it very difficult to learn to play the Chinese flute? Hohk chēui síu nàahn·m̀h·nàahn a? /Let me play the drum and you play the cymbals. Ngóh dá·gú néih dá·chàah·chá là. **play organ** tàahn fùng·kàhm; **play piano** tàahn gong·kàhm

(of music) jau·ngohk. /Listen; the orchestra is playing now. Néih tēng·háh, ngohk·déui yíh·gìng jau·gán ngohk la.

(compete) béi·choi. /When are we going to play their team? Ngóh·deih géi·sí tùhng kéuih·deih béi·choi a?

(act) yín, bíu·yín; **play the part of** yín, baahn, baahn·yín. /The actress plays her role very well. Gó·go néuih yín·yùhn yín dāk hóu hóu. /I want to play the part of the old man. Ngóh séung baahn·yín gó·go baak·yè·gūng.

play a joke hòi·wàahn·siu. /He is just playing a joke on us, you don't need to take it so seriously. Kéuih tùhng ngóh·deih hòi·wàahn·siu jē, néih m̀h·hóu gam yihng·jàn.

play fair with doih . . . gùng·pìhng. /He didn't play fair with you, did he? I'll punish him. Kéuih doih·néih m̀h·gùng·pìhng haih máh, dáng ngóh faht kéuih.

a play (drama) hei, wá·kehk, baahk·wá·kehk (M: chēut); (opera) daaih·hei (Chinese); gò·kehk (Western) (M: chēut)

plaything fáan·ge yéh; gūng·jái (doll)

play tricks (on people) nán·fa. /Are you playing tricks on me? Néih nán·fa ngóh àh?

playground   wahn·duhng·chèuhng

plead   (beg earnestly) chíng·kàuh, ngài·kàuh, hán·kàuh

pleasant   (enjoyable and interesting) gòu·hing. /We had a very pleasant talk. Ngóh·deih tàahm dāk hóu gòu·hing.
(enjoyable) hīng·sùng. ./It is a very pleasant job. Gùng·jok hóu hīng·sùng.
(friendly) hóu·sèung·yúh. /Your friend is a very pleasant person. Néih ge pàhng· yáuh hóu hóu·sèung·yúh.
(of a person's manner) haak·hei. /He asked me in a very pleasant way. Kéuih hóu haak·hei gám mahn ngóh.
in many cases hóu is used. /It was a pleasant day today (weather). Gàm·yaht tìn· hei hóu hou. /We had a pleasant time. Ngóh·deih wáan dāk hóu hóu.

please   (in requests) m̀h·gòi, lòuh·fàahn, chéng. /Please shut the door. M̀h·gòi (néih) sàan·màaih douh mùhn.
(be agreeable to) lihng . . . héi·fùn, lihng . . . gòu·hing; or, instead of saying that something pleases someone, Chinese often says that a person likes something, using fùn·héi or héi·fùn. /Does this please you, or do you want something else? Néih fùn·héi nī·go, yīk·waahk yiu daih·yih·go a? /What you said pleased him very much. Néih góng ge syut·wah lihng kéuih hóu fùn·héi.
(wish). /Do as you please. Chèuih·bín, m̀h·sái haak·hei. or Chèuih néih·bín.
please pardon me chéng néih yùhn·leuhng ngóh; please have some tea chéng yám chàh; please say it again chéng néih joi góng·gwo; please sit down chéng chóh; as you please chèuih·bín; if you please chéng

pleasure   faai·lohk

pledge   (solemn assurance) saih·yuhn. /You pledged that you would stop gambling, why did you gamble again? Néih saih·gwo·yuhn wah m̀h·dóu·chín la, dím·gáai néih yauh dóu la?

plentiful   hóu·dò, daaih·bá. /Oranges are plentiful this year. Gàm·nín yáuh hóu·dò cháang

plenty   (many or much) hóu·do, daaih·ba. /There's plenty more in the kitchen. Chyùh· fóng juhng yáuh hóu·dò (or daaih·bá). /He has plenty of money. Kéuih yáuh daaih·bá chín. /There's plenty of room here. Nī·syu juhng yáuh daaih·bá deih·fòng

plot   (conspiracy) yàm·màuh; plot against màuh·hoih

plough   gàang (V); làih (N)

pluck   (flowers and fruits) jaahk; (weeds and feathers) màng; pluck out māng·chēut

plug   (electric) chaap·sōu (N); plug in chaap·chaap·sōu

plum   léi; múi; plum blossom léi·fà or mùih·fà; plum tree léi·syuh or múi (M: pò)

plump   fèih, fèih·tàhn·tàhn

plunder   (rob) chéung·gip, dá·gip

plunge   plunge into pok·yahp·heui

plural   dò·sou ge

plus   (opp. of minus) gà

Pluto   (myth) yìhm·lòh·wòhng; (planet) mìhng·wòhng·sīng

pneumonia　　fai·yìhm

pocket　　dói, sāam·dói; doih·lohk·dói (VO); **pocket edition** jauh·jān·báan; **pocket knife** dōu·jái; **pocket money** lìhng·yuhng·chín

pockmark　　dauh·pèih

pod　　(bean) dauh·gaap

poem　　sī (M: sáu); **write a poem** jok·sī

poet　　sī·yàhn

poetical　　yáuh·sī·yi ge; **poetical form** sī·tái

poetry　　sī

point　　(sharp end) jīm; (having a sharp point) jìm.　/The point of this pencil is not sharp enough.　Nī·jì yùhn·bāt (jīm) juhng meih gau jìm.

　　(place) deih·fòng: **halfway point** jùng·gāan ge deih·fòng, or jùng·dím; (dot) dím: **decimal point** síu·sou·dím; (unit of scoring) fān; (degree) douh, dím: **boiling point** fāt·dím; (time) sìh·hauh; (stage, condition) deih·bouh; (characteristic, part) deih·fòng, -chyúh: **good points** hóu·chyúh; **bad points** waaih·chyúh; **essential points** yiu·dím

　　(purpose) waih.　/What was the point of his doing that? Kéuih waih māt·yéh gám yéung jouh a?

　　point of view yi·gin; **from** . . . **point of view** (on . . . basis) chùhng . . . nī·(or gó) fòng·mihn tái, chùhng . . . nī·fòng·mihn séung, or (on . . . opinion) yì·jìu . . . yi·gin, yì·jiu . . . yi·si.　/Your point of view is nearly the same as mine.　Néih ge yi·gin tùhng ngóh·ge chà·m̀h·dō.　/From his point of view the plan is, of course, impossible. Chùhng kéuih gó·fòng·mihn tái, nī·go gai·waahk gáng·haih hàahng·m̀h·tùng ge.　/From our point of view, it is the right thing to do.　Yì jiu ngóh·deih ge yi·si, nī·gihn sih yìng·dòng gám yéung baahn.

　　be on the point of jing joih yiu.　/I was on the point of leaving when he came back.　Ngóh jing joih yiu jáu ge sìh·hauh, kéuih fàan·fàan·lèih.

　　beside the point lèih·tàih·maahn·jeuhng, ngàuh·tàuh m̀h·deui máh·jéui

　　to the point yāt·jàm·gin·heut.　/His comments are always right to the point. Kéuih pìhng·leuhn yāt·gihn sih géi·sìh dōu haih yāt·jàm·gin·heut ge.

　　to point (indicate direction) jí; **point out** jí·chēut (lèih).　/Where is the place he pointed to? Kéuih jí·jyuh gó·syu haih bīn·syu a?　/Point out the place where you told me about.　Néih góng·béi ngóh tèng gó·daat deih·fòng hái bīn·syu a, néih jí·béi ngóh tái·há.　/Can you point out where the mistakes are?　Néih hó·yíh jí·chēut (lèih) bīn·syu cho·jó ma?

poise　　(weight on a steelyard) ching·tòh

poison　　duhk, duhk·yeuhk; **give poison to** lohk·duhk·yeuhk; **poison a person** (to death), duhk·séi·yàhn; **poison gas** duhk·hei; **poisoning** jung·duhk

poisonous　　yáuh·duhk (ge); **poisonous drug** duhk·yeuhk; **poisonous snake** duhk·sèh

poke　　(to thrust or prod) dūk

poker　　pūk·ká; **play a game of poker** dá·pūk·ká

pole　　(for flying a flag) kèih·gōn; (push along) chàang; **North Pole** Bāk·gihk; **South Pole** Nàahm·gihk; **pole a boat** chàang·syùhn; **bamboo pole** jūk·gòu; **carrying pole** daam·gòn; **telephone pole** dihn·dāng·chàam (M: tiuh)

police　　gíng·chaat, chàai·yàhn (Hong Kong expression), mā·dá (Malayan expression) **police dog** gíng·hyún; **police station** gíng·chaat·gúk, chàai·gún (Hong Kong expression), máh·dá·lìuh (Malayan expression); **police whistle** ngàhn·gāi

policy　　(of a government) jing·chaak: **foreign policy** ngoih·gàau jing·chaak; **policy of ag-**

gression chàm·leuhk jing·chaak; (settle course to be followed) kwài·géui. /It is the policy of our company never to cash checks. Ngóh·deih gūng·sī ge kwài·géui m̀h·sàu jì·piu. (aiming to a goal) jùng·jí, fōng·jām; **insurance policy** yin·sō·jí, bóu·dāan

polish   sáang (metals); chaat (shoes, etc.); **polish bright by rubbing** sáang·ling; **polish up one's knowledge** wàn·jaahp

polite   yáuh·láih, sì·màhn; **polite greeting** haak·tou; **politeness** láih·maauh. /Why are you not polite to her? Néih dím·gáai deui kéuih gam móu·láih a? /I don't think it would be polite for us to leave so soon. Ngóh·deih gam faai jauh jáu la m̀h·haih géi hóu yi·si boh.

political   jing jih (ge); in combination jing; **political activities** jing·jih wuht·duhng; **political conception** jing·jih sì·séung; **political criminal** jing·jih·fáan; **political party** jing·dóng; **political policy** jing·chaak; **political power** jing·kyùhn; **political situation** jing·guhk

politician   (good sense) jing·jih·gā; (bad sense) jing·haak

politics   jing·jih: **play politics** gáau·jing·jih

poll   (election) syún·géui; **polling district** syún·kēui; **poll tax** yàhn·tàuh·seui

pollen   fà·fán

polo   máh·kàuh; **water polo** séui·kàuh

pomegranate   sehk·láu

pomelo   lūk·yáu, sà·tìhn·yáu, sòng·màh·yáu

pompous   (in manner) ga·sai

pond   chìh, tòhng, chìh·tòhng

ponder   nám

pontoon bridge   fàuh·kìuh (M: douh)

pony   máh·jái (M: pāt)

pool   chìh: **swimming pool** yàuh séui chìh

poor   (poverty stricken) kùhng, móuh chín. /Is he really that poor? Kéuih haih·m̀h·haih jàn·haih gam kùhng a?
    (in quality) yáih, m̀h·hou, and other specific terms. /The workmanship is rather poor. Sáu·gùng sēung·dòng yáih. /That's a pretty poor job. Jouh dāk hóu yáih. or Jouh dāk m̀h·hóu. /His health is poor. Kéuih ge sàn·tái m̀h·hóu. /The soil is poor for planting flowers. Dī nàih m̀h·gau feih m̀h·jung dāk fā.
    the poor kùhng·yàhn. /We ought to take up a collection for the poor. Ngóh·deih yìng·gòi chàuh dī chín gau·jai dī kùhng·yàhn.
    (worthy of pity) hó·lìhn. /Don't you think we should help this poor fellow? Kéuih gam hó·lìhn, néih wah ngóh·deih m̀h·bòng kéuih dāk ma?

popcorn   sūk·máih·fā, baau·gūk

Pope   gaau·wòhng

poppy   ngāng·sūk, ngāng·sūk·fā

popular   is expressed by indirect expressions such as much liked, etc.; or làuh·hàhng, sìh·hīng. /This book is quite popular. Nī·bún syù hóu·dò yàhn jùng·yi tái. /Mr. Lee is the most popular teacher. Léih sīn·sàang haih jeui sauh hohk·sāang fùn·yìhng ge sīn·sàang. /He is very popular. Kéuih dou·chyu dōu sauh yàhn fùn·yìhng. /That song was very popular last year. Gó·jek gō gauh·nín hóu làuh·hàhng.

(of style of writing or speaking) tùng·juhk. /That book is written in a popular style. /Gó·bún syù sé dāk hóu tùng·juhk.

(of the people) yàhn·màhn. /No government can stand long without popular support. Yùh·gwó yāt·go jing·fú móuh yàhn·màhn ge yúng·wuh yāt·dihng m̀h·wúih chèuhng·gáu ge.

popular lecture tùng·juhk yín·góng; **popular song** làuh·hàhng·kūk, làuh·hàhng gō·kūk

population   yàhn·háu

populous   yàhn·háu hóu·dò

porcelain   chìh·hei (ge); **porcelain wares** chìh·hei

porcupine   jin·jyū (M: jek)

pores   mòuh·gún

pork   jyù·yuhk; **pork chop** jyù·pá; **pork ribs** pàaih·gwāt

porridge   (rice congee) jūk; **porridge with fish** yùh·sāang·jūk; **porridge with pork** jyù·yuhk·jūk

port   (harbour) hói·háu, góng·háu; (town) fauh, fauh·tàuh; **port clearance** chēut·háu·jí; **Port Office** góng·mouh·gūk; **port wine** būt·jáu

portable   sáu·tàih (ge); **portable typewriter** sáu·tàih dá·jih·gēi

porter   (luggage carrier) gū·lēi, dàam·daam·lóu

portfolio   gùng·màhn·dói, gùng·sih·dói; minister without portfolio (British), bāt·gún·bouh daaih·sàhn

portion   (part) bouh·fahn; (share) fahn

portrait   séung, chiu·jeuhng

Portugal   Pòuh·tòuh·ngàh

Portuguese   Pòuh·tòuh·ngàh·yàhn, Sài·yèuhng·yàhn

pose   (a bodily attitude) jì·sai

position   (location) -syu, -douh. /From this position you can see the whole city. Hái nī·syu néih hó·yíh tái·gin chyùhn·sèhng.

(posture) waih·ji, jì·sai. /If you are not comfortable, you may change your position. Yùh·gwó néih m̀h syù·fuhk néih hó·yíh jyun·háh néih ge waih·ji.

(situation) chìhng·yìhng (circumstances); deih·waih (high social position). /He's in a similar position; he doesn't know what to do either. Kéuih yihk·haih gám ge chìhng·yìhng, kéuih yihk m̀h·jì dím syun. /A man in his position has to be careful of what he says. Joih kéuih gám ge deih·waih, góng·wáh yāt·dihng yiu hóu síu·sàm. /This places me in a very difficult position. is expressed as: Gám·yéung (or nī·gihn·sih) lihng ngóh hóu wàih·nàahn.

(job). /He has a good position in a factory. Kéuih hái yāt·gàan gùng·chóng·syu jouh dāk géi hóu.

(attitude) yi·gin (opinion). /What is his position in this new policy? Kéuih deui·yù nī·go sàn jing·chaak yáuh māt yi·gin a?

positive   is mostly expressed indirectly. /I'm positive. Haih gám ge la, móuh cho ge la. (opp. to negative) jîk·gihk; (elec.) yèuhng -: **positive electricity** yèuhng·dihn

possess   (own, of property) yáuh; **possessed by a devil** gwéi·séuhng·sàn

possession   (things owned) só·yáuh·ge·yéh; (property, things owned) chòih·cháan

possessor   **possessor of property** yihp·jyú

possible   jouh·dāk·dou, hó·nàhng. /I'll come early if it's possible. Yùh·gwó jouh·dāk·dou ngó yāt·dihng jóu dī lèih. /Is it possible? Jouh m̀h·jouh·dāk·dou a?

(of something that may happen) waahk·je wúih, hó·nàhng. /It's possible to have a typhoon in the next couple days. Nī·léuhng·yaht waahk·jé wúih dá·fùng boh. /It's possible that the letter will come today. Gó·fùng seun gàm·yaht hó·nàhng sàu·dou la.

post   (job) jīk·waih, sih. /He has just been appointed to a new post in the government. Kéuih ngāam·ngāam hái jing·fú·syu wán·dóu go jīk·waih.

(of a fence) chyúh; **postbox** seun·sēung, seun·túng; **post card** mìhng·seun·pín; **postdated check** kèih·piu; **postgraduate** yìhn·gau·sāng; **postman** paai·seun·lóu, yàuh·chàai; **postmaster** yàuh·jing·guhk·jéung; **post mortem examination** yihm·sī; **post meridian** (p. m.) hah·jau; **post office** yàuh·jing·gūk; **postwar** jin·hauh

(put up) tip·hái, nìhm·hái (put on by sticking); dèng·hái (nail on); gwa·hái. /Post this on the bulletin board. Jèung nī·go tip·hái (or nìhm hái, dèng·hái, gwa·hái) bou·gou·pàaih·syu.

postage   yàuh·fai

postal   **postal matter** yàuh·gín; **postal money order** yàuh·jing·wuih·piu

poster   (printed bill) gou·baahk, gāai·jīu, gwóng·gou·wá (generally noncommercial); **post a poster** tip gou·baahk (or gāai·jīu, gwóng·gou·wá)

posterity   hauh·doih

postpone   jín·kèih

postscript   (to a letter) joi·jé; (to a periodical) fuh·kái; (to a book) fuh·lúk

posture   jī·sai

pot   wùh (M); bōu (M). /Please make a pot of tea for us. Mh·goi néih chùng wùh chàh béi ngóh·deih. /Don't move that pot of soup (off the fire). Mh·hóu yìh·hòi gó·bòu tòng. **flower pot** fà·pùhn; **teapot** chàh·wú; **water pot** séui·gòng

potato   syùh·jái, hòh·lāan·syú; **sweet potato** fàan·syú

pottery   gòng·ngáh

pouch   doih: **tobacco pouch** yīn·doih

poultry   gāi·ngaap (M: dī); **poultry shop** gāi·ngaap·póu

pound   (weight) bohng (M). /Give me a pound of sugar. Béi bohng tòhng ngóh.
(unit of money) yìng·bohng (British). /What is the exchange rate between the Hong Kong dollar and the pound? Yāt·go yìng·bohng wuhn géi·chín góng·ngán a?
(to hit) dám. **pound on the door** dám mùhn; **pound on the table** dám tói; **pound into small pieces** dám seui; (to pound with a pestle) jùng: **pound rice** jùng máih

pour   (heavily) dóu; **pour out water** dóu séui; **pour out the water** dóu dī séui chēut·lèih; **pour the water out** dóu·jó dī séui kéuih; **pour the water into the basin** dóu dī séui yahp go mihn·pún·syu
(gently) jàm. /Please pour me a cup of tea. Mh·gòi néih jàm·bùi chàh (béi) ngóh. /Please pour it full. Mh·gòi jàm·múhn kéuih.

pout   (to thrust out the lips) dyūt·héi tìuh jéui

poverty   /Most of the people in Hong Kong live in poverty. is expressed as: Hèung·góng daaih·dò·sou yàhn dōu sàng·wuht dāk hóu gàan·nàahn.

powder   (fine particles) fán: **medicinal powder** yeuhk·fán, yeuhk·sáan; (grind) ngàahn seui; (sprinkle with) sám. **powder the face** chàh fán; **gunpowder** fó·yeuhk

power   (energy) lihk·leuhng. /I believe the people always have the power to overthrow their government. Ngóh sèung·seun yàhn·màhn chí·jùng yáuh lihk·leuhng tèui·fàan kéuih·deih ge jing·fú.

(mechanical energy) lihk·leuhng; **electric power** dihn·lihk, dihn; **hydraulic power** séui·dihn, séui·lihk; **horsepower** máh·lihk. /This machine has more power than that one. Nī·go gèi·hei béi gó·go gèi·hei lihk·leuhng (or máh·lihk) daaih. /This is run by electric power. Ni·go haih yuhng dihn ge. /Hydraulic power is the cheapest source of electricity. Séui·lihk faat·dihn jeui pèhng. /Does your factory use a lot of electric power? Néih·deih gùng·chóng haih·m̀h·haih yuhng hóu·dò dihn a? /Suddenly the power was cut off. Fāat·yìhn·gāan tìhng·jó dihn. /How much power does this machine have? Nī·go gèi·hei yáuh géi·dō·pāt máh·lihk a?

(authority) kyùhn, kyùhn·lihk; (influence) sai·lihk; **come into power** <u>may be expressed as</u> séuhng·tòih; **out of power** (office),lohk·tòih; **be in power** <u>as</u> be in office dāk sai ge sìh·hauh; **be out of power** sāt·sai ge sìh·hauh. /Who has most of the power in their party? Kéuih·deih go dóng bīn·go jeui yáuh·kyùhn a? /We never know exactly how far his power goes. Ngóh·deih móuh·faat·jí jì·dou kéuih ge sai·lihk yáuh géi daaih. /Do you think, gentlemen, it is proper to limit the power of the president (of the school)? Néih· deih gok·wái gok·dāk haahn·jai haauh·jéung ge kyùhn·lihk ngāam ma? /When he came into power he forgot all his promises. Kéuih yāt séuhng·tòih jauh m̀h·gei·dāk·saai kéuih swó·yìng·sìhng·ge sih la. /That party won't be in power much longer. Gó·go dóng jauh· lèih sāt·sai la. /Who has the real power? Bīn·go jà·kyùhn a? or Bīn·go jeui yáuh saht· kyùhn a?

(ability) lihk, lihk·leuhng. /I'll certainly do everything in my power. Ngóh yāt·dihng jeuhn ngóh ge lihk heui jouh.

(great nation) -kèuhng, kèuhng·gwok. /Is France one of the five powers? Faat·gwok haih·m̀h·haih ńgh·kèuhng jī·yāt a? **the powers** liht·kèuhng

powerhouse, power station, power plant faat·dihn·chóng; **power of attraction** kāp· yáhn·lihk; **power of resistance** dái·kong·lihk; **power of the imagination** séung·jeuhng· lihk; **political power** jing·kyùhn

powerful (possessing authority) yáuh·kyùhn·lihk (ge); (efficacious) lèhng·kèhng; yáuh· gùng·haauh; (influential) yáuh·sai·lihk; (possessing strength) yáuh·lihk (ge) (of a country) kèuhng·sihng

practicable (that can be used) sái·dāk; (that can be done) jouh·dāk

practical saht·jai, sái·dāk, saht·yuhng. /Your suggestion is good, but it isn't practical. Néih ge yi·gin géi hóu, ji·haih m̀h·haih géi saht·jai. /Is his idea practical? Kéuih ge yi· gin sái·dāk ma? /If you want to be successful, you must be very practical. Yùh·gwó néih yiu sìhng·gùng, néih yāt·dihng yiu fèi·sèuhng saht·jai ji dāk. /This thing is not practical. Nī·gihn yéh m̀h·saht·yuhng.

practically (in reality) saht·joih haih. /It's practically impossible. Saht·joih haih m̀h· dāk. (almost) chà·m̀h·dō, gèi·fùh. /I was practically out of breath. Ngóh chà·m̀h·dō móuh·saai hei.

practice (perform repeatedly) lihn·jaahp, lihn. /If you want to speak well, you must practice constantly. Yùh·gwó néih séung góng dāk hóu, néih yāt·dihng yiu sìh·sìh lihn· jaahp. /He's practicing the piano. Kéuih yìh·gā lihn·gán kàhm.

practice law <u>is expressed as</u> be a lawyer. /How much longer do you have to study before you can practice law? Néih juhng yiu duhk géi·dò·nìhn syù sìn·ji jouh·dāk leuht· sī a?

practice medicine <u>is expressed as</u> be a physician. /How long has he been practicing (medicine) now? Kéuih jouh·jó géi·dò nìhn yī·sāng la? /Where does he practice? Kéuih hái bīn·syu hàhng·yì a?

be in practice, put into practice (use) yuhng; (make real) saht·hàhng; (apply) sí·hàhng; (try out) si·háh. /Your suggestion was put into practice immediately. Néih séung ge gó·go baahn·faat jīk·hāk jauh yuhng·jó la. /This suggestion was put into practice im- mediately. Nī·go baahn·faat yiu jīk·hāk saht·hàhng ji dāk. /When will this law be put into practice? Nī·go faat·leuht géi·sí sí·hàhng a? /Let's put your plan into practice and see whether it works. Ngóh·deih si·háh néih ge faat·jí tái·háh sái·m̀h·sái·dāk.

be out of practice hóu noih m̀h . . . /I know how to play tennis, but I'm a little out of practice. Ngóh wúih dá móhng·kàuh daahn·haih hóu noih m̀h·dá la.

make a practice of, make a practice to (always) gwaan·jó, heung·lòih. /We make it a practice to get up at six o'clock in the morning. Ngóh·deih gwaan·jó múih·yaht jìu·tàuh·jóu luhk·dím·jūng héi·sàn. /He makes it a practice to get to work on time. Kéuih heung·lòih dōu haih jéun·sìh fàan·gùng ge.

practice makes it natural jaahp·gwaan sìhng jih·yìhn

praise   (speak with approval of) chìng·jaan; (speak highly of) chìng·jaan (to one's superior), kwà·jéung (to one's inferior); (glorify) jaan·méih: **praise God** jaan·méih Seuhng·dai

prawn   hā (M: jek)

pray   (beg) kàuh. /They have prayed for rain the last few days. Kéuih·deih nī·géi·yaht yaht·yaht kàuh yúh.
(make a devout request) kèih·tóu, tóu·gou. /Have you ever tried to pray? Néih yáuh móuh si·gwo kèih·tóu a? /Let's pray to God to bless the world with peace. Ngóh·deih yāt·chàih tóu·gou Seuhng·dai bóu·yauh sai·gaai wòh·pìhng.

prayer   (words) kèih·tóu·màhn; **prayer book** kèih·tóu·màhn; **Lord's Prayer** Jyú·tóu màhn

preach   (proclaim a religious doctrine) chyùhn·douh, chyùhn·gaau; (deliver a sermon in church) góng·douh; **preach the gospel** chyùhn·fūk·yām

preacher   chyùhn·douh·yàhn

prearrange   yuh·sìn ngòn·pàaih

precaution   **take precaution against** yuh·fòhng. /We should take precautions against an epidemic. Ngóh·deih yiu yuh·fòhng làuh·hàhng·jing faat·sàng.

precautionary   **precautionary measures** yuh·fòhng ge fòng·faat, yuh·fòhng ge bouh·jauh

precede   (in time) joih·sìn; (go in front of) hàahng·sìn

precedent   chìhn·laih, sìn·laih, laih

preceding   **preceding chapter** chìhn·yāt·jèung; **preceding paragraph** chìhn·yāt·dyuhn

precious   bóu·gwai, gwai·juhng; **precious blood** bóu·hyut; **precious stone** bóu·sehk; **precious sword** bóu·dōu; **precious things** bóu·bui, jàn·bóu, bóu·maht; **precious words** gàm·yuhk·lèuhng·yìhn

precipice   sàan·ngàahm

precipitous   hím·jeun

precise   (exact) kok·saht

predecessor   chìhn·yàhn; (in office) chìhn·yahm

predestined   (destine) jíng·dihng ge, jyu·dihng ge

predetermine   yuh·dihng (ge)

predict   (prophesy) yuh·yìhn

prediction   (prophesy) yuh·yìhn

predominant   (superior in strength, numbers, etc.) jim·yàu·sai ge

preface   (of a book) jéui

prefer   (followed by a noun) béi·gaau héi·fun, gok·dāk . . . hóu di. /I prefer this brand of cigarettes. Ngóh béi·gaau héi·fùn nī·jek yīn. /Whom (or which) do you prefer? Néih gok·dāk bīn·go hóu dī a? <u>or</u> Néih béi·gaau héi·fùn bīn·go a?

(followed by a verb) chìhng·yún, nìhng·yún, bei·gaau héi·fùn. /I prefer to wait until tomorrow. Ngóh chìhng·yún dáng·dou tìn·yaht la. /I prefer not to go. Ngóh nìhng·yún m̀h·heui. /I prefer to eat fish. Ngóh béi·gaau héi·fùn sihk·yú.

prefer x to y béi·gaau héi·fun x m̀h·héi·fùn y. /I prefer a movie to an opera. Ngóh béi·gaau héi·fùn tái dihn·yíng, m̀h·héi·fùn tái hei. /He prefers pork to beef. Kéuih béi·gaau héi·fùn sihk jyù·yuhk m̀h·héi·fùn sihk ngàuh·yuhk.

prefer to x rather than y nìhng·hó x, dōu m̀h·y. /He is very stubborn, preferring to be sick rather than taking medicine. Kéuih hóu ngaahng·géng ge, nìhng·hó behng dōu m̀h·háng sihk·yeuhk ge.

pregnant   yáuh·jó sàn·géi, yáuh·jó sai·màn·jái, daaih (jó) tóuh (colloq.), yáuh·yahn; **a pregnant woman** yahn·fúh, daaih·tóuh·pó (colloq.)

prehistoric   yáuh·sí·yih·chìhn

prejudice   pìn·gin. /Don't hold any prejudice toward anyone. Deui yàhn m̀h·hóu yauh pìn·gin. **racial prejudice** júng·juhk·pìn·gin

preliminary   chò·bouh ge; **preliminary expense** hòi·baahn·fai; **preliminary measure** chò·bouh·gai·waahk

prelude   chìhn·jau·kūk, chìhn·jau

premature   jóu·suhk; **premature birth** sìu·cháan; **premature death** dyún·mehng

premier   (prime minister) sáu·seung (monarchical government); júng·léih

premise   (in logic) chìhn·tàih

premium   (of insurance) bóu·hím·fai, yin·sō·ngán

preparation   yuh·beih, jéun·beih

preparatory   **preparatory class** yuh·beih·bāan

prepare   (get ready) yuh·beih; (make careful preparation) jéun·beih; (make, as a report) jouh. /They've prepared to leave immediately. Kéuih·deih yíh·gìng yuh·beih hóu jǐk·hāak jáu la. /The two countries are preparing for war. Léuhng·gwok jing·joih jéun·beih jin·jàng. /He can't come because he has to prepare for tomorrow's examination. Kéuih m̀h·lèih·dāk yàn·waih kéuih yiu jéun·beih tìng·yaht háau·si. /Don't bother him, he is preparing a report. Mh·hóu gáau·kéuih, kéuih jing·joih jouh·gán yāt·go bou·gou. /We are well prepared. Ngóh·deih yíh·gìng yuh·beih (or jéun·beih) hóu la.

(cook) jyú, jíng. /Do you know how to prepare western food? Néih wúih jyú sāi·chāan ma? /That's not the way to prepare this kind of fish. Nǐ·tíng yú m̀h·haih gám jyú (or jíng) ge.

prepare someone for something hòi·douh. /You had better prepare him for the news. Néih jeui·hóu hòi·douh·háh kéuih, yìhn·jí·hauh góng·mìhng kéuih jì.

prepay   gàau·seuhng·kèih, béi·seuhng·kèih

preposition   chìhn·ji·chìh

Presbyterian Church   Jéung·láuh·wúi

prescribe   gwài·dihng

prescription   yeuhk·fōng (M: jèung); **make up a prescription** pui·yeuhk, jāp·yeuhk (Chinese); **write a prescription** hòi yeuhk·fōng

presence   (being present). /His presence is not going to make any difference. Kéuih dou m̀h·dou dōu móuh gán·yiu. /Her presence makes her parents very happy. Kéuih fuh·móuh tái·gin kéuih hóu fùn·héi.

in the presence of hái yàhn mihn·chìhn, dòng·jyuh yàhn mihn·chìhn. /Don't scold a child in the presence of other people. M̀h·hóu hái yàhn mihn·chìhn naauh sai·màn·jái.

/This must be signed in the presence of three witnesses. Nī·go yāt·dihng yiu dòng jyuh sàam·go jing·yàhn mihn·chìhn chìm·jí ji dāk.

present   (gift) láih, láih·maht. /This is the present I bought for him. Nī·gihn haih ngóh máaih·béi kéuih ge láih·maht. but /This watch is a present from my mother. is expressed as: Nī·go bīu haih ngóh màh·mā sung·béi ngóh ge.

(this time) yihn·joih (right now); muhk·chìhn, jaahm·sìh (temporarily); yìh·gā (this short period of time); yùh·gàm (the present as opposed to the past). /The present policy of the company is to hire younger men. Gūng·sī yihn·joih ge jing·chak haih chéng dī hauh· sāang·dī ge yàhn. /If there's no past, there's no present; if there's no present, there'll be no future. Yùh·gwó móuh gwo·heui jauh móuh yihn·joih, yùh·gwó móuh yihn·joih jauh móuh jèung·lòih. /What we need most at the present is medical supplies. Ngóh·deih muhk·chìhn jeui sèui·yiu ge haih yeuhk·báan. /That will be enough at the present. Jaahm·sìh gau la. /He is too busy to see you at present. Kéuih yìh·gā hóu m̀h·dāk· hàahn m̀h·gin·dāk néih. /The present situation in China is entirely different from its past. Yùh·gàm Jùng·gwok ge chìhng·yìhng tùhng yíh·chìhn daaih·bāt·sèung·tùhng lo.

to present sung . . . béi. /They presented him with a gold watch. Kéuih·deih sung· jó go gām·bīu béi kéuih.

(introduce). /Allow me to present Mr. Lee. is expressed as: I'll introduce you, this is Mr. Lee. Ngóh tùhng néih·deih gaai·siuh·háh, nī·wái haih Léih·sīn·sàang.

be present (not absent) expressed by the verbs dou (arrive) or join·chèuhng. /There are five hundred people present. Dou·jó ngh·baak yàhn. or Yáuh ngh·baak yàhn joih·chèuhng.

present (submit) a petition daih go bán; present a report (to a superior) chíhng·bou (béi); present at meeting dou·wúi, chēut·jihk; present circumstances muhk·chìhn ge wàahn·gíng; present condition yìh·gā ge chìhng·yìhng; present credentials chìhng·daih gwok·syù; present political situation (muhk·chìhn ge) sìh·guhk

preserve   (as health) bóu·juhng. /To preserve one's health is to love one's parents. Bóu·juhng sàn·tái jīk·sih haau·ging fuh·móuh.

(as eyesight) bóu·wuh. /If you would like to preserve your eyesight, you should not read in the dark. Yùh·gwó néih yiu bóu·wuh néih sèung ngáahn, chìn·kèih m̀h·hóu hái m̀h·gau·gwòng ge deih·fòng syu tái·syù.

preserves maht·jihn, maht·jihn tòhng·gwó; preserved dates maht·jóu; preserved fruits tòhng·gwó; preserved ginger tòhng·gēung; duck eggs preserved in lime (thousand year egg) pèih·dáan

preside   (act as chairman) jouh·jyú·jihk. /Who is going to preside at today's meeting? Gàm·yaht (nī·go·wúi) bīn·go jouh·jyú·jihk a?

president   (of a republic) júng·túng, daaih·júng·túng; (of a republic governed by a committee of which the president is chairman) jyú·jihk; (of a yún in the Chinese government) yún·jéung; (of a school) haauh·jéung; (of a business concern) júng·gìng·léih, gìng·léih; (of a bank) hòhng·jéung, júng·gìng·léih; (of a society or association) wuih·jéung; vice-president fu- plus any of the above terms.

presidium   jyú·jihk·tyùhn

press   (with finger or hand) gahm; (with foot) yáai (jyuh), daahp (jyuh); (apply weight to) jaahk·jyuh; (press down as with a roller) ngaat; (exert physical pressure) bīk. /Please press this end for me. M̀h·gòi néih tùhng ngóh gahm·jyuh nī·tàuh. /You may use your foot to press it. Néih hóh·yíh yùhng geuk yáai. /Press it with this dictionary until the glue dries. Yuhng nī·bún jih·dín jaahk·jyuh kéuih dáng·dou kéuih gòn wàih jí. /The only way to make it level is to press it with a roller. Wàih·yāt ge faat·jí jauh·haih yùhng go lūk ngaat·pìhng kéuih. /The crowd is pressing heavily against the door. Dī yàhn chēut· lihk gám bīk douh muhn. /Is this where it hurts? May I press it lightly? Haih·m̀h·haih nī·syu tung a? Ngóh hehng·hēng gahm·háh dāk·m̀h·dāk a?

(to iron) tong, tong·hóu. /Have this suit pressed for me. Tùhng ngóh tong·hóu nī·tyut sāam kéuih.

(force) bīk. /Don't press people too hard. M̀h·hóu bīk yàhn taai sahm. /If you press him a little further he'll talk. Yùh·gwó néih bīk·háh kéuih tìm, kéuih jauh wúih góng ge la.

(push or urge; an investigation) jèui·gau, jèui·mahn. /I wouldn't press this matter any further if I were you. Yùh·gwó ngóh haih néih, ngóh jauh m̀h·jèui·gau nī·gihn sih la.

(machine for printing) yan·jih·gèi; (printing house) yan·chaat·gún

(newspapers, collectively) bou·gaai, sàn·màhn·gaai. /These seats are reserved for the press. Nī·dī wái haih làuh·béi bou·gaai ge.

(journalists) (sàn·màhn) gei·jé. /Will the press be admitted to the conference? Nī·go wúi béi·m̀h·béi gei·jé yahp·heui a?

go to press fuh·yan. /This edition is ready to go to press. Nī·yāt báan hó·yíh fuh·yan la.

prestige   (due to reputation) mìhng·yuh; (due to public confidence and respect) mìhng·mohng

presume   (assume to be true) yíh·wàih; (suppose) gú

pretend   ja, ja·dai. /He pretends that he knows nothing about it. Gó·gihn sih kéuih ja·dai m̀h·jì.

pretend to be ill ja·behng; **pretend to be mad** (neurotic) ja·dìn, ja·dìn·baahn sòh; **pretend to sleep** ja·fan

pretext   (excuse) jihk·háu, ja·gā·yī. /The students are making a pretext of the inadequacy of the library and refusing to write any more papers. Hohk·sāang jihk·háu tòuh·syù·gún chit·beih m̀h·hóu, m̀h·háng joi sé leuhn·màhn. /He made a pretext of having a headache and left. Kéuih ja·gā·yī wah tàuh·tung jauh jáu·jó la.

pretentious   chùng·yéh, chùng·daaih·tói, chùng·hàhng·saai

pretty   (pleasing to the eye) hóu·yéung, leng. /She is a very pretty girl. Kéuih sāang·dāk hóu hóu·yéung.

(pleasing to the ear) hóu·tèng. /That's a pretty tune. Nī·jī kūk géi hóu·tèng.

(rather) hóu. /I've been pretty busy since I saw you last. Jih·chùhng ngóh seuhng·chi gin·gwo néih jì·hauh, ngóh yāt·jihk dōu hóu m̀h·dāk·hàahn.

prevent   (hinder) jó·jí. /Can you prevent him from drinking? Néih yáuh móuh faat·jí jó·jí kéuih yám·jáu a?

(keep something from occurring) yuh·fòhng. /We have to prevent cholera every summer. Ngóh·deih múih·nìhn dōu yiu yuh·fòhng fok·lyuhn.

previous   yíh·chìhn ge, seuhng·yāt·chi ge; **previous holder of an office** chìhn·yahm(ge); **previous time** seuhng·chi(ge), seuhng·yāt·chi (ge)

prewar   jin·chìhn (ge)

price   ga·chìhn. /The price you ask is too high. Néih yiu ge ga·chìhn taai góu.

prices maht·ga. /Prices are much higher than last year. Gàm·nín ge maht·ga gòu gwo gauh·nín hóu dò.

retail price lìhng·gù ge ga·chìhn; **wholesale price** faat·hòhng (ge) ga·chìhn; **fixed price** dihng·ga; **price has fallen** dit·ga; **price is dear** ga·chìhn hóu gwai; **price is going up** héi·ga; **price is too high** ga·chìhn taai gwai; **price list** ga·muhk·bíu

prick   (thorn) chi, lahk; (pierce) gāt: **prick so that it pains** gāt dāk yàhn hóu tung

prickly heat   yiht·fái: **to have prickly heat** chēut·yiht·fái; **itching of prickly heat** yiht·fái hàhn

prickle   (thistle) lahk, lak; (thorn) chi

pride   (self-respect) jih·jyūn·sàm. /Don't hurt his pride. M̀h·hóu sèung kéuih ge jih·jyūn·sàm.

(haughtiness) gìu·ngouh. /His pride hinders his advance. Kéuih·ge gìu·ngouh fòhng·
ngòih kéuih faat·jín
(gratification) dāk·yi. /We take a great pride in building this hospital. Ngóh·deih
héi·hóu nī·gàan yî·yún, ngóh·deih gok·dāk hóu dāk·yi.

priest   (Roman Catholic) sàhn·fuh; (Protestant) muhk·sī; (Buddhist) wòh·séung; (Taoist)
douh·sí; **become a priest** chēut·gà; **quit the priesthood** wàahn·juhk

primary   chò·bouh ge; **primary election** chò·syún; **primary school** sìu·hohk

prime   **prime minister** jói·seung (ancient term), sáu·seung (modern term), júng·léih (of
a republic); **of prime importance** ji gán·yiu ge

primitive   yùhn·chí (ge); **primitive people** yùhn·chí·yàhn

prince   (ruler) wòhng; (son of a king) wòhng·jí; Crown Prince taai·jí

princess   gùng·jyú

principal   (most important) jyú·yiu (ge), jeui juhng·yiu ge. /Sugar cane is the principal
crop in that area. Je haih gó·daat deih·fòng ge jyú·yiu chēut·cháan. /Is this his principal argument against our plan? Haih·m̀h·haih nī·go haih kéuih fáan·deui ngóh·deih ge
gai·waahk ge jyú·yiu léih·yàuh a?
(head of a school) haauh·jéung; (participant in a legal case) dòng·sih·yàhn; (sum of
money) bún·chìhn; **principal and interest** lìhn·bún·daai·leih

principle   (of conduct) dāk·hahng; douh·léih. /He is a man of principle. Kéuih haih yāt·
go yáuh dāk·hahng ge yàhn. /Treating people as you would like to have them treat you
is a good principle. Doih yàhn yùh géi haih yāt go hóu ge douh·léih
(as of physics) yùhn·léih. /These are the principles of modern physics. Nī·dī haih
yihn·doih maht·léih·hohk ge yùhn·léih.
(an originating or actuating agency or force) douh·leih. /The Book of Changes is a
book that explains the interacting principles of Yin and Yang. Yihk·gìng haih góng yàm
yèuhng sèung·sàng sèung·sìhng ge douh·léih ge syù.

print   (by printing press) yan. /How much will it cost to print three thousand sheets
of this? Nī·go yan sāam·chìn·jèung yiu géi·dò chín a?
(write like type) yuhng jing·káai sé. /Please print your name instead of writing it.
Chéng néih yuhng jing·káai sé néih ge méng.
(photographic positive) saai, saai·séung. /How many prints do you want? Néih yiu
saai géi·dò jèung a? /I'm going to have a few prints made. Ngóh yiu heui saai géi·
jèung séung.
be out of print jyuht·báan. /That book is hard to get because it's out of print. Gó·
bún syù hóu nàahn máaih, yàn·waih yíh·gìng jyuht·jó·báan la.
be printed yan·chēut·lèih. /I want this notice printed. Ngóh yiu jèung nī·go tūng·jì
yan·chēut·lèih.
print (type) jih (characters). /The print in this book is too small. Nī·bún syù ge
jih taai sai.
printed cotton cloth fà·bou; **printed matter** yan·chaat·bán; **printing cost** yan·chaat·
fai; **printing shop** yan·chaat·só, yan·jih·gún; **printing press** yan·chaat gèi; **fingerprint**
sáu·jí mòuh·yan

priority   yàu·sìn·kyùhn

prison   gāam·fòhng, gāam·yuhk; **be in a prison** (as a prisoner) chóh·gāam

prisoner   gāam·fáan; **prisoner of war** fù·lóuh

private   (not public; personal) jih·géi ge, go·yàhn ge. /This is his private matter. Nī·
dī haih kéuih jih·géi (or go·yàhn) ge sih.
(individual owned) sī·ga (ge). /This is his private car. Nī·ga haih kéuih ge sī·gā·chē.

(secret) sî·hah, bei·maht. /I'd like to discuss this matter with you in private. Ngóh séung tùhng néih sî·hah (or bei·maht) taam·háh nī·gihn sih.

(established by individual enterprise, as of school) sî·lahp (ge). /Is that school a private school or a public school? Gó·gàan hohk·haauh haih gùng·lahp ga sî·lahp ga?

private affair sî·sih; **private** (soldier),bìng·jái; **private life** sî·sàng·wuht, go·yàhn ge sàng·wuht

privately   (in an individual capacity) sî·jih, sî·hah; (not publicly) ngam·jùng

privilege   kyùhn·leih; **privilege and duty** kyùhn·leih tùhng yih·mouh; **special privilege** dahk·kyùhn

privy   **Privy Council** Syù·maht·yún; **privy seal** yuh·sái

prize   (monetary) jéung·gām; (non-monetary) jéung·bán

probably   waahk·jé, daaih·kói. /This is probably true. Waahk·jé haih dõu m̀h·díng boh. /He probably won't come. Kéuih daaih·kói m̀h·lèih la. /Probably not. Meih·bīt.

probation   /He is on six months' probation. Kéuih si·yuhng luhk·go·yuht.

problem   mahn·tàih. /How do you solve this problem? Nī·go mahn·tàih néih dím·yéung gáai·kyut a?

international problem gwok·jai mahn·tàih; **social problem** séh wúi mahn·tàih; **the problem of unemployment** sāt·yihp mahn·tàih

procedure   sáu·juhk

proceed   (continue) gai·juhk <u>must be followed by a verb describing the action continued.</u> /After the interruption they proceeded with their work. Jó·jó·háh jî·hauh kéuih·deih yauh gai·juhk jou·lohk·heui la. /Didn't he tell you to proceed? Kéuih móuh giu néih· deih gai·juhk jou lohk·heui mē?

(start out). /Now we can proceed to lesson one. Ngóh·deih yìh·gā hòi·chí gaau daaih·yāt·fo.

proceeds   sàu·yahp. /He sold his business and took the proceeds back to England. Kéuih maaih·jó pùhn sàang·yi, jèung dī sàu·yahp yùhn·chyùhn daai·fàan Yìng·gwok.

process   (method) fòng·faat; (procedure) sáu·juhk

procession   yàuh·hàhng

proclaim   (declare) syùn·bou; (as a law, etc.) gùng·bou; **proclaim martial law** syùn·bou gaai·yìhm; **proclaim war** syùn·jin

proclamation   gou·sih: **issue a proclamation** chēut·gou·sih; (manifesto) syùn·yìhn

procure   wán

prodigal   fa·gà, lohng·fai (SV); baaih·gà·jái (N)

produce   (manufacture) chēut. /How many thermos (vacuum) bottles does that factory produce per month? Gó·gàan gùng·chóng múih·go·yuht chēut géi·dò go nyúhn·séui·wú a?

(grow) chēut. /That place produces raw silk. Gó·syu chēut sāang·sī. /This soil ought to have produced better litchis than these. Nī·syu gám ge nàih·tóu yìng·fahn chēut dī hóu·gwo gám ge laih·jī.

(result in) faat·sàng or dāk·dou . . . git·gwó (result). /This kind of thing always pro-duces a tragic ending. Nī·dī gám ge sih júng·haih faat·sàng m̀h·hóu ge git·gwó ge.

(present; as facts, evidence) nàh·chēut. /You have to produce facts to prove your argument. Néih yāt·dihng yiu nàh·chēut jing·geui lèih jing·mìhng néih só·góng ge syut·wah.

(farm products) chēut·cháan, nùhng·cháan·bán. /Where do they sell their produce?

Kéuih·deih ge chēut·cháan maaih·heui bīn·syu a? /The amount of the produce of this area is lower than last year. Nī·yāt·kēui nùnng·cháan·bán ge cháan·leuhng dài·gwó gauh·nín.

producer (of a movie) jai·pín·yàhn; (distinguished from consumer sìu·fai·jé) sàang·cháan·jé

product (industrial) chēut·bán, jai·jouh·bán; (by nature) maht·cháan; **agricultural product** nùhng·cháan·bán; **local product** tóu·cháan

profession jīk·yihp, hòhng

professional **professional soccer player** jīk·yihp jūk·kàuh·yùhn; **professional man** jyūn·gā; **professional politician** jing·haak; **professional school** jyùn·mùhn·hohk·haauh

professor gaau·sauh

profit (financial) leih·chìhn, leih. /Is there very much profit in it? Leih·chìhn sàm ma? /The profits from the business will be divided equally. Só·dāk·ge leih·chìhn daaih·gā pìhng·fàn.
   make a profit jaahn·chín (VO). /Do you think this business will make a profit? Nī·dàan sàang·yi wúih jaahn·chín ma? /How much profit did you make on that sale? Néih gó·dàan sàang·yi jaahn·jó géi·dò chín a?
   profit by (of personal benefit). /I hope he profits by this experience. Ngóh hèi·mohng kéuih gìng·gwo nī·yāt·chèunng jì·hauh wúih dāk·dóu hóu hóu ge gaau·fan.

profound sàm

program (theater playbill) jit·muhk (of a concert, etc.); (entertainments) jit·muhk, diht·jeuih; (plan) gai·waahk. /Is there any good program on TV tonight? Gàm·máahn dihn·sih yáuh māt hóu jit·muhk ma?

progress (advance) jeun·bouh. /The students are progressing rapidly. Dī hohk·sāang jeun·bouh dāk hóu faai.
   (advancement) jeun·bouh. /Are they making any progress? Kéuih·deih yáuh móuh jeun·bouh a? /That country has made a lot of progress lately. Gó·go gwok·gà jeui gahn yáuh hóu daaih ge jeun·bouh.
   (continuation of some action) expressed by any verb of action, usually jouh. /Are you making any progress with your book? Néih bún syù jouh·sèhng dím la?
   had made progress yáuh jeun·bouh; **has made no progress** móuh jeun·bouh

prohibit gam·jí, gam. /Don't you think we should prohibit the students from smoking? Néih gok·dāk ngóh·deih yìng·gòi gam·jí dī hohk·sāang sihk·yīn ma?
   'smoking prohibited' gam·jí sihk·yīn

project (plan) gai·waahk; there is no equivalent for the word 'project' when it means 'undertaking' or 'task.' /How is your dictionary project? is expressed as Néih ge jin·dín (dictionary) jouh·sèhng dim·yéung la?

projector fong·yíng·gèi (M: ga)

prolong (as a time limit) yìhn·chèuhng, jín·kèih; (in length) jíng·chèuhng, màng·chèuhng, làai·chèuhng; (lengthen the pronunciation of) làai·chèuhng

prominent (distinguished) giht·chēut ge: **a prominent novelist** giht·chēut ge síu·syut·gā

promise yìng·sìhng. /I promised him that I would be here tomorrow. Ngóh yìng·sìhng·jó kéuih, tìng·yaht lèih. /Don't promise him anything. Māt dōu m̀h·hóu yìng·sìhng kéuih. /He has already promised to be my tutor. Kéuih yíh·gìng yìng·sìhng·jó jouh ngóh ge sīn·sàang la.
   break a promise sāt·seun, sāt·yeuk. /You can't break your promise. Néih m̀h·nàhng·gau sāt·seun ge boh.

keep a promise /We have to keep our promise. Ngóh·deih yìng·sìhng·jó gám yāt· dihng yiu gám.

promising   (of persons and undertakings) hóu yáuh·hèi·mohng ge, hóu yáuh·chìhn·tòuh ge

promote   (in rank) sīng, sīng·kāp (VO), sīng·gùn (VO). /Has he been promoted? Kéuih sīng·jó meih a? /He has been promoted three times in the last five years. Gwo·heui nī·ngh·nìhn kéuih yìh·gìng sīng·jó sàam·<u>chi</u> (<u>or</u> kāp) la.
    (as arts, etc.) tàih·chèung. /He devoted himself to promoting the arts throughout his whole lifetime. Kéuih yāt·sàng tàih·chèung ngaih·seuht.
    (as industry) gú·laih, jéung·laih. /The government decided to promote farming and handicraft. Jing·fú kyut·dihng gú·laih nùhng·yihp tùhng sáu·gùng·yihp.
    promote world peace, jàng·jeun sai·gaai wòh·pìhng; **to promote the development of resources of backward countries** tàih·chèung faat·jín lohk·hauh gwok·gà ge jī·yùhn

prompt   (quick) seun·chūk; (without delay) máh·seuhng

promulgate   (laws) syùn·bouh; (creed) chyùhn, syùn·chyùhn

pronoun   doih·mìhng·chìh

pronounce   (declare) syùn·bou; (utter sounds) duhk, faat·yām. /How do you pronounce that word? Gó·go jih néih dím·yéung duhk a?

pronunciation   (way of pronouncing) faat·yām. /Your pronunciation is incorrect; you should practice more. Néih ge faat·yām m̀h·jing·kok, yiu sìh·sìh lihn·jaahp ji dāk.

proof   (evidence) pàhng·geui, jing·geui. /What proof do you have that he has stolen your watch? Néih yáuh māt pàhng·geui wah kéuih tàu·jó néih ge bīu a?
    (in printing) góu. /Are you through reading the proof? Néih deui·gwo saai dī góu meih a?
    proofread gaau·deui. /I've just finished proofreading my book. Ngóh ngāam·ngāam gaau·deui yùhn ngóh nī·bún syù.
    bulletproof m̀h·pa·jí·dáan ge; **fireproof** m̀h·pa·fó·sìu ge; **waterproof** m̀h·pa séui· jam ge; **waterproof watch** yàuh·séui·bīu

prop   (support) díng·jyuh

propaganda   syùn·chyùhn

propagate   (pass on) chyùhn: **propagate doctrine** chyùhn douh

propeller   lòh·syùhn·jéung

proper   jiu·kwài·géui, ngāam·kwài·géui, ngāam. /The proper thing to do is to visit him. Jiu·kwài·géui yìng·gòi heui taam·háh kéuih. /It's not proper. Gám m̀h·ngāam kwài·géui. /This is the proper thing to do. Gám jouh ngāam la.
    proper time hahp·sìh; **China proper** Jung·gwok bún·bouh; **Japan proper** Yaht·bún bún·bouh

properly   **properly done** jouh dāk hóu tóh·dong; **properly said** góng dāk hóu ngāam; **do it properly** hóu·hóu·déi jouh; **not properly said** góng dāk m̀h·ngāam

property   (possessions) yéh (things); gà·dong (family possessions). /You should be more careful in using other people's property. Néih yùhng yàhn·deih ge yéh yiu dahk· biht sìu·sàm. /This is only a part of his property. Nī·dī jí·haih kéuih yāt bouh·fahn ge gà·dong.
    (real estate) cháan·yihp (general); deih, deih·cháan (land only); ngūk, ngūk·yihp, fòhng·cháan. /He owns a lot of property in the New Territories. Kéuih hái Sàn·gaai yáuh hóu·dò cháan·yihp.
    (attribute) sing·jāt. /This salt has the property of absorbing moisture from the air. Nī·tíng yìhm yáuh kāp·sàu séui·fahn ge sing·jāt.

prophecy   yuh·yìhn

prophet   sīn·jì

propitious   (auspicious) hóu·yi·tàuh, leih·sih

proportion   (part) bouh·fahn. /A great proportion of the fund is donated by the churches. Daaih·bouh·fahn ge gēi·gām haih gaau·wúi gyùn ge.
     (the relation between parts) wàhn·chèuhn, dahng·chan. /A well-written Chinese character has its strokes all written in proper proportion. Yāt·go sé dāk hóu ge Jùng·gwok jih haih só·yáuh·ge bāt·wahk dōu sé dāk sahp·fàn wàhn·chèuhn, gám sìn·jì syun haih. /The windows are too small, they are not in good proportion with the rest of the building. Dī chēung·mún taai sai, tùhng gāan ngūk m̀h·dahng·chan.

proposal   tàih·yi, tàih·yih, jyú·jèung; (motion) tàih·ngon; (of marriage) kàuh·fàn. A verbal expression is preferably used for each of these expressions, see **propose**

propose   (suggest) /I propose to have a picnic this Sunday. Ngóh tàih·yi nī·go láih·baai·yaht heui yéh·chāan.
     (intend) séung, dá·syun. /They propose to spread the gospel to the natives of that area. Kéuih·deih séung heung gó·syu ge tóu·yàhn chyùhn·bou fūk·yām.
     (ask to marry) kàuh·fan (VO). /He said he has already proposed to her but she told him that she had to ask her mother first before she accepted. Kéuih wah kéuih yíh·gìng hèung kéuih kàuh·fàn, daahn·haih kéuih wah yiu mahn·gwo kéuih màh·mā sìn·ji nàhng·gau daap·ying kéuih.

proprietor   sih·táu, lóuh·báan

propriety   láih, láih jit, kwài-géui

prose   sáan·màhn, sáan·mán

prosecute   (sue) gou. /He was prosecuted for driving through the red light. Kéuih sái·gwo hùhng dāng béi gíng·chaat (police) gou·jó. **prosecuting attorney** gím·chaat·gùn

prospect   (hope; something looked forward to) hèi·mohng, chìhn·tòuh. /The prospect of getting a better job pleased him. Kéuih hó·yih wán·dóu yāt·go hóu dī ge sih ge hèi·mohng lihng kéuih gok·dāk hóu fùn·héi. /There are no prospects in this kind of job. Jouh nī·tíng gám ge sih móuh chìhn·tòuh ge.
     (view) fùng·gíng. /The prospect from our front window is very beautiful. Ngóh·deih chìhn·mihn chēung·mún deui·jyuh ge fùng·gíng hóu leng.

prospectus   (of a business enterprise) jèung·chìhng; (of a plan, device) yi·gin·syù

prosper   (do well, be successful) hìng·wohng, wohng. /His new store is prospering. Kéuih gàan sàn pou·táu sàang·yi hóu (hìng·)wohng.

prosperous   hìng·wohng, faat·daaht, hóu·sai·gaai, fàahn·wìhng. /Their business is very prosperous. Kéuih·deih ge sàang·yi hóu hìng·wohng. /He has been very prosperous these last few years. Kéuih nī·géi·nìhn hóu faat·daaht (or hóu·sai·gaai). /Hong Kong was very prosperous a few years ago. Hèung·góng jóu géi·nìhn hóu fàahn·wìhng.

prostitute   lóuh·géui (colloq.), geih·néuih

prostrate   (to lay flat on the ground with the face downward) pà·hái deih·háh·syu

protect   (keep safe) bóu·wuh. /This law is designed to protect the poorer farmers. Nī·tìuh faat·leuht haih bóu·wuh dī kùhng·fú ge nùhng·màhn ge. /The doctor told me to wear these glasses to protect my eyes. Yī·sāng giu ngóh daai nī·fu ngáahn·géng bóu·wuh ngóh sèung ngáahn.
     (defend) fòhng·waih, fòhng·sáu. /To protect one village is easy, but to protect all the villages is impossible. The only thing to do is for each village to learn how to protect itself. Fòhng·waih yāt·tìuh chyūn yùhng·yih; fòhng·waih gam dò tìuh chyūn gàn·

bún bāt·hó·nàhng. Wàih·yāt ge baahn·faat jauh·haih múih·tìuh·chyūn yiu hòi·chí hohk· jaahp dím·yéung jih·waih.

(of the gods) bóu·yauh. /Let's pray and ask God to protect us. Ngóh·deih daaih·gā yāt·chái kèih·tóu, chéng Seuhng·dai bóu·yauh ngóh·deih.

protect from bóu·wuh . . . míhn·ji . . .; míhn·ji. /We should protect this village from flood. Ngóh·deih yiu bóu·wuh nī·tìuh chyūn míhn·ji béi daaih·séui chùng·jó kéuih. /Put this oil on, it protects your hands from chapping. Chà nī·dī yàuh hái sáu·syu míhn·ji baau·chaak.

protest   kong·yih (V)/(N)

Protestant   Gēi·dūk·tòuh

protrude   (stick out) daht·chēut

proud   (haughty) gìu·ngouh, sà·chàhn; (conceited) jih·gòu·jih·daaih
     (exulting in) in no case is the meaning of 'proud' used to express one's own accom-plishments, even of members of one's own family; it can only be expressed by various indirect expressions. /I feel very proud of myself for completing this task alone. is expressed as: Ngóh fèi·sèuhng hìu·hahng, go·yàhn yùhn·sìhng·jó nī·gihn sih. (It's just luck that I finished this job alone.) /I'm very proud of my younger brother's winning the scholarship. Ngóh sai·láu dāk·dóu nī·go jéung·hohk·gām, ngóh fèi·sèuhng gòu·hing. /I'm proud of you (for yourself). Néih jàn·haih hóu la. /I'm proud of you (for what you did). Néih jouh dāk jàn·haih hóu la. /I'm proud of you (for your ability). Néih jàn· haih lēk la.

prove   jing·mìhng. /Can he prove that he didn't do it? Kéuih hó·yíh jing·mìhng kéuih móuh jouh nī·gihn sih ma? /Can you prove your statement? Néih yáuh móuh faat·jí jing·mìhng néih só·góng·ge syut·wah haih ngāam ga?
     (try out) /The letter proved to be a forgery. is expressed as: Yùhn·lòih gó fùng seun haih gá ge. /The movie proved to be very bad. is expressed as: Yùhn·lòih gó· chēut dihn·yíng fèi·seuhng yáih.

proverb   gaak·yìhn, jàm·yìhn, juhk·yúh, juhk·wá: **there is a proverb which says** yáuh geui juhk·wá wah or juhk·wá yáuh wah

provide   (supply) chēut. /If they provide my traveling expenses I'll go. Yùh·gwó kéuih· deih chēut léuih·fai ngóh jauh heui.
     (stipulate) kwài·dihng. /The rule provides that the boarding student cannot leave the school without permission. Hohk·haauh kwài·dihng yùh·gwó meih dāk jéun·héui, gei· sūk·sāng bāt·dāk lèih·haauh.
     provide for gu·gahp. /Does your plan provide for that possibility? Néih ge baahn· faat yáuh móuh gu·gahp gó·chàhng a?
     provide with béi (give). /They were provided with only enough food to last two days. Béi kéuih·deih ge lèuhng·sihk jí·haih gau kéuih·deih sihk léuhng·yaht ge jē.
     provided (that) yùh·gwó, yeuhk·haih. /I'll go, provided (that) you'll go with me. Yùh·gwó néih tùhng ngóh yāt·chái heui ngóh jauh heui.

providence   tìn·yi; **have trust in providence** ting·tìn·yàuh·mihng

providential   seuhng·tìn jyu·dihng ge

province   (an administrative division) sáang (N/M); (proper duties or functions; sphere) faahn·wàih

provincial   **provincial capital** sáang·sèhng; **provincial government** sáang·jing·fú; **chair-man of provincial government** sáang (·jing)·fú jyú·jihk

provision   (food) lèuhng·sihk, fó·sihk, sihk·bán

provisional   làhm·sìh (ge); **provisional arrangement** làhm·sìh ge baahn·faat; **provisional government** làhm·sìh jing·fú

provoke   (to incite or stimulate a person, animal, etc.) lìuh. /Don't provoke that dog.
Mh·hóu lìuh gó·jek gáu. (enrage) gīk. /Why did you provoke him again? Dím·gáai néih
yauh gīk kéuih nē?

prow   syùhn·tàuh

prudent   (wisely careful) gán·sahn, sám·sahn. /He's a very prudent man. Kéuih go
yàhn hóu gán·sahn ge.

prune   sài·múi (N); (cut off parts of plants) jín . . . ge syuh·jī

Psalms   (Book of) Sī·pīn

pseudonym·   (penname) bat·méng

psychologist   sàm·léih·hohk·gā

psychology   sàm·léih·hohk

public   (all people) daaih·gā (everybody); chyùhn·gwok ge yàhn (all the people of the nation); and similar expressions with other place terms instead of gwok. /The public
likes him. Daaih·gā dōu héi·fùn kéuih. /The public considers he is the greatest president in their history. Chyùhn·gwok ge yàhn dōu yihng·wàih kéuih haih kéuih·deih lihk·
sí·seuhng jeui wáih·daaih ge júng·túng.
     (audience) is expressed as the people who hear a speaker tèng . . . ge yàhn, the
people who read a writer's writings tái . . . ge jok·bán ge yàhn. /His speech reached
a very small public. Kéuih ge yín·góng tèng ge yàhn hóu síu. /His novel reaches a
great public. Tái kéuih ge síu·syut ge yàhn hóu dò.
     in public   hái yàhn mihn·chìhn. /That's not the way to behave in public. Hái yàhn
mihn·chìhn mh·hóu gám yéung.
     open to the public   yahm yàhn followed by various verbs. /Is this section open to
the public? Nī·bouh·fahn haih·mh·haih yahm·yàhn chàam·gùn (visit, sightseeing) ga?
/Is this garden open to the public? Nī·go fà·yún haih·mh·haih yahm·yàhn yàuh·láahm
ga? /This library is only for members of the society; it is not open to the public. is
expressed as: Nī·go tòuh·syù·gún haih béi wúi·yùhn yuhng ge, daih·di·yàhn mh·béi yahp·
heui.
     public office   jing·gaai, jing·fú·gèi·gwàan, jing·fú·yahp·bihn. /He has held a public
office for the past twenty years. Kéuih hái jing·gaai (or either of the other two expressions) jouh·jó yih·sahp·nìhn sih la.
     public health   gùng·guhng waih·sāng; public opinion   gùng·yi; public organ   gùng·guhng
gèi·gwàan; public school   gùng·lahp hohk·haauh; public telephone   gùng·yuhng (or gùng·
guhng) dihn·wá; public welfare   gūng·yīk; public officer   (one who works in the civil
service) gùng·mouh·yùhn

publication   (periodicals, journals) hón·maht; (that which is published) chēut·báan·maht;
(of one's work) faat·bíu·gwo ge jok·bán. /Has he published anything? Kéuih yáuh móuh
faat·bíu·gwo ge jok·bán a? or Kéuih yáuh móuh faat·bíu·gwo māt·yéh màhn·jèung a?

publish   (a book, periodicals) chēut·báan. /Has your book been published yet? Néih·bún
syù chēut·báan meih a?
     (as in a newspaper) faat·bíu. /Why didn't the newspaper publish the speech he de-
livered yesterday? Dím·gáai bou·jí móuh faat·bíu kéuih kàhm·yaht ge yín·góng a?
     (announce) syùn·bou; (promulgate) gùng·bou
     publisher   chēut·báan·gā, faat·hòhng·yàhn, faat·hòhng·jé; publishing world   chēut·báan·
gaai

pull   (draw) màng, làai. /Give the rope a hard pull! Chēut·lihk màng tìuh síng! /Pull
it hard and make it tight. Màng·gán kéuih. /His car is stuck in the mud; we're looking
for a truck to pull it out. Kéuih ga chè jyut·hái nàih·leuih·bihn, Ngóh·deih yìh·gā wán·
gán ga fo·chè làai kéuih chēut·lèih.

(extract) màng, baht. /This tooth has to be pulled. Nī·jek ngàh yiu màng la.
(tear, rip) chaak. /They're going to pull it down and build a new one. Kéuih·deih
yiu chaak·jó kéuih héi·gwo go sàn·ge.
pull in dou. /When will the train pull in? Fó·chè géi·sìh dou a? /We pulled in last
night. Ngóh·deih kàhm·máahn dou ge.
pull out hòi. /Has the train already pulled out? Fó·chè hòi·jó làh?
pull through hóu·fàan, hóu·dāk·fàan. /She was very sick and we were afraid she
might not pull through. Kéuih behng dāk hóu gàau·gwàan, ngóh·deih yíh·wàih kéuih m̀h·
hóu dāk fàan ge la. /Do you think he will pull through? Kéuih hóu·dāk·fàan ma? /He
will. Kéuih hóu·dāk·fàan ge. /Thank God, he pulled through. Dò·jeh Seuhng·dai, kéuih
ngàaih·gwo·jó nī·chèuhng jòi·naahn, kéuih jauh·lèih hóu·fàan ge la.
pull apart màng·hòi, làai·hòi; **pull close together** màng·màaih, làai·màaih; **pull off**
màng·lāt; **pull out** màng·chēut; **pull the cork out** màng go jēut chēut·lèih; **pull tight**
màng·gán, màng·saht; **pull to pieces** ché·seui·saai; **pull up** màng·séuhng·leih, làai·
séuhng·lèih

pulp   (of a melon) nóng: **the pulp of a watermelon** sài·gwà·nóng

pulpit   góng·tòih

pulsate   (as the heart) tiu

pulse   (the regular throbbing of the arteries) mahk·bok; mahk(·bok). /Have you taken
his pulse? Néih yáuh móuh sóu kéuih ge mahk·bok a? /His pulse is beating very fast.
Kéuih ge mahk tiu dāk hóu faai.

pump   pām (N); pām (V). /Can you get a pump to pump some air in the tire? Néih hó·
yíh wán go pām lèih pām dī hei yahp·heui go tāai·syu ma? /Does this water pump work?
Nī go séui·pām sái·dāk ma?

pumpkin   fāan·gwà

punch   (beat) jùng, dá; (perforate) johk. /Punch a hole here. Hái nī·syu johk go lūng.

punctual   (not late; prompt) jéun·sìh (ge), sáu·sìh·hāk (ge). /He's always punctual.
Kéuih hóu jéun·sìh ge.

punctuate   bìu·dím

punctuation mark   bìu·dím fùh·houh

puncture   lūng (N)

punctured   chyūn·jó go lūng; chyūn·lūng ge; lauh·fùng (ge)

pungent   gùng·beih·ge

punish   faht, chyu·faht, chìhng·faht. /How do you think we should punish him? Néih gok·
dāk ngóh·deih yìng·gòi dím·yéung faht kéuih a? /Don't you think you should be punished?
Néih wah néih yìng m̀h·yìng·gòi faht a?

punishment   chìhng·faht; yìhng·faht (legal and physical); or expressed verbally. /This
punishment is too severe. Faht dāk taai chúhng la. /Who will handle the punishment?
Bīn·go fuh·jaak chìhng·faht a?

pupil   (of a teacher) hohk·sāang; (of the eye) tùhng·húng, tùhng·yán

puppet   muhk·tàuh·gūng·jái: **puppet show** muhk·tàuh·gūng·jái·hei; faai·léuih: **puppet government** faai·léuih·jing·fú

puppy   gáu·jái (M: jek)

purchase   (buy) máaih

purchaser   máaih·jyú

pure   (unmixed) sèuhn·seuih (ge). /He speaks pure Pekingese. Kéuih góng dāk yāt·háu
ge sèuhn·seuih gīng·hōng.
         (unpolluted) gòn·jehng. /Is the water pure enough to drink? Dī séui gòn·jehng ma,
yám·dāk ma? or expressed as: Is the water drinkable? Dī séui yám·dāk ma?
         (sheer) gaan·jihk, yùhn·chyùhn. /His statement is pure nonsense. Kéuih góng dī
syut·wah gáan·jihk móuh·léih·yàuh.
         (in accent) sèuhn·jeng; (in heart) sèuhn·git; **pure gold** jūk·gām, sèuhn·gām. /Is this
made of pure gold? Nī·go haih·m̀h·haih jūk·gām ga?

purgative medicine   se·yeuhk: **take purgative medicine** sihk se·yeuhk

purgatory   (Catholic) lihn·yuhk; (Buddhist) jihng·tóu

purge   (to cause evacuation of the bowels of a person) se; **vomiting and purging** yauh ò
yauh aú
         to purge a political party chìng·dóng; **to purge the members of a political party**
jíng·sūk

Puritan   chìng·gaau·tòuh

purple   jí·sīk·ge, chìng·lìn·sīk ge; **reddish purple,** jí·húng·sīk ge

purpose   (intention) yi·si; muhk·dìk; or expressed indirectly with waih (·jò). /What's
his purpose in doing this? Kéuih gám jouh haih māt·yéh yi·si a? /If this is what his
purpose is, I would say it's quite dishonorable. Yùh·gwó kéuih ge muhk·dīk haih gám,
gám jauh m̀h·haih géi hóu la (or gám jauh hóu dìu·gá la.). /What is the purpose of his
visit here? Kéuih waih·māt·sih lèih nī·syu a? /For the purpose of raising money.
Waih lèih nī·syu chàuh·fún.
         on purpose gu·yi, jyūn·dāng, dahk·dāng. /He did it on purpose. Kéuih gu·yi gám
jouh ge. /He asked on purpose to see what I would say. Kéuih gu·yi gám mahn ngóh
tái ngóh dím góng.
         serve a purpose yáuh yuhng (have use); yáuh hóu·chyúh. /It serves no purpose to
do it that way. Gám jouh móuh·yuhng ge. /What purpose does it serve to do it that
way? Gám jouh yáuh māt hóu·chyúh a?
         serve the purpose dāk (be satisfactory); míhn·kéuhng, deui·fuh (be a necessary sub-
stitute); jaahm·sìh hó·yíh deui·fuh (be a temporary substitute). /Would this serve the
purpose? Nī·go dāk ma? /Yes. Nī·go dāk la. /I guess this will serve the purpose until
we buy a new one. Ngóh tái meih máaih·dóu sàn·ge yíh·chìhn, nī·go hó·yíh míhn·kéuhng
(or deui·fuh) la. /I think this typewriter will serve the purpose for the next couple of
days. Ngóh nám nī·go dá·jih gēi jaahm·sìh nī·léuhng·yaht hó·yíh deui·fuh la.

purse   (moneybag; billfold) ngàhn·bāau; (prize money) jéung·gām; **purse one's lips** dyūt
(or míu)·héi tìuh·jéui

pursue   (chase) jèui; (to seek to accomplish) jèui·kàuh; saht·yihn. /Pursuing happiness
is the goal of some people's lives. Jèui·kàuh faai·lohk haih yāt·bouh·fahn yàhn ge yàhn·
sàng muhk·dīk. /How should one pursue one's goal in life? Yāt·go yàhn yìng·gòi dím·
yéung saht·yihn kéuih ge léih·séung?

push   (shove) ngúng, tèui. /Push the table over by the window. Ngúng jèung tói màaih·
heui go chēung·mún·syu. /Push it up not down. Ngúng·séuhng m̀h·haih ngúng·lohk.
/Push the books aside so you'll have some room to write. Ngúng·hòi dī syù, néih jauh
yáuh deih·fòng sé la. /Can you help me push the car? Néih bòng ngóh ngúng·háh ga
chè, dāk ma? /I pushed the door; it was locked. Ngón ngúng·háh douh mùhn, douh
mùhn só·jó.
         push someone **around** hà. /He likes to push everybody around, doesn't he? Kéuih
hóu jùng·yi hà yàhn ge, haih·m̀h·haih?
         other expressions in English: /Don't push your luck. M̀h·hóu tàam·sàm la. Hóu
sàu·fò la. /It's a pushover. Hóu yih jē.

put   (place, set) jài, fong, báai. /Put it here. Jài·hái nĭ·syu. /Where do you want me
to put it? Jài·hái bĭn·syu a? /Put it back into the drawer. Jài·fàan·hái gwaih·túng syu.
/(Just putting it) On the ground will do. Fong·hái go deih·há·syu jauh dāk la. /Where
shall I put these two vases? Nĭ·léuhng·go fā·jēun báai·hái bĭn·syu a? /Put that knife
down. Jài·dài bá dōu kéuih. /Put the tools away when you're through with them. Néih
yuhng·yùhn dĭ ga·sàang jì·hauh jài·fàan·màaih kéuih.

put on clothes jeuk (of articles of clothing which a part of the body passes through);
daai (of hats, gloves, ornaments). /Wait until I put on my coat and hat. Dáng ngóh jeuk·
fàan gihn daaih·lāu tùhng daai·fàan déng móu sìn.

put down (write) sé·dài. /Please put down your name and address. Chéng néih sé·
dài néih·ge méng tùhng deih·jí.

put in (of time) yuhng, jouh. /How many hours did you put in on that? Néih yuhng·
jó géi·dò·go jūng·dím a? /How many hours did you put in at the office last week? Néih
seuhng·go láih·baai hái sé·jih·làuh jouh·jó géi·dò·go jūng·dím a?

put (things) **in order** jíng·dihm. /I have to put my things in order before I leave.
Ngóh yiu jíng·dihm dĭ yéh sìn·ji jáu dāk.

put off (delay) yìhn·chìh. /You can't put it off; you must do it today. Néih joi bāt
nàhng yìhn·chìh ge la, gàm·yaht yāt·dihng yiu jouh ge la.

put off a person tò·yìhn, fù·yín. /Can't you put him off for a couple of days? Néih
hó·yíh tò·yìhn kéuih léuhng·yaht ma? /Can't you put him off until we have time to think
it over? Néih hó·fáu fù·yín·jyuh kéuih dáng ngóh·deih háau·leuih·háh a?

put out a light sīk; **put out** a fire jíng·sīk. /Put out the lights before you leave.
Néih jáu jì·chìhn sīk·jó dĭ dāng kéuih. /Put the fire out. Jíng·sīk go fó kéuih.

put through a telephone call dá·tùng. /Did you put through the telephone call? Néih
yáuh móuh dá·tùng go dihn·wá a?

put the children **to bed** chau dĭ sai·mān·jái fan·gaau. /I have to put the children to
bed. Ngóh yiu chau dĭ sai·mān·jái fan·gaau.

put to good use (of money). /You can be sure this money will be put to good use.
Néih fong·sàm, nĭ·bāt chín yāt·dihng hóu·hóu·déi yuhng.

put up (build) héi. /This building was put up in six months. Nĭ·gāan ngūk héi·jó
luhk·go·yuht.

put up (accommodate) jyuh·dāk·lohk. /Can you put up four more tonight? Néih gó·
syu hó·yíh jyuh·dāk·lohk sei·go yàhn tìm ma?

put up with yáhn·dāk. /Can you put up with him? Néih hó·yíh yáhn·dāk kéuih ma?
/I can, but I can't put up with his snoring. Yáhn·dāk, daahn·haih ngóh m̀h·yáhn·dāk
kéuih fan·gaau·sìh dá·beih·hòhn.

puzzle   (riddle) màih; (a perplexed condition) nàahn·tàih. /This matter puzzles me. is
  expressed as: Nĭ·gihn sih luhng dāk ngóh mohk·mìhng·kèih·miuh.

pygmy   ngái·yàhn

pyramid   (in Egypt) gàm·jih·taap

Q

quack   (a pretender to medical skill) wòhng·luhk·yī·sāng

quail   (game bird) ām·chēun (M: jek)

quaint   (peculiar) gú·gwaai

Quaker Oats   mahk·pin

qualification   jì·gaak /What's the qualification for this job? Yiu yáuh māt·yéh jì·gaak
sìn·ji jouh·dāk nĭ·gihn sih a?

qualified   gau·jì·gaak, hahp·gaak. /Is he qualified to be a music teacher? Kéuih gau·jì
gaak gaau yàm·ngohk ma? /Is he a qualified teacher? is expressed as: Kéuih gaau dāk
(syù) ma? (Is he able to teach?)

qualified teacher gîm·dihng·gaau·sī; **qualifying test** gîm·dihng·háau·si

quality   (property) sing·jāt. /Bamboo has two qualities: lightness, strength and elastici-
ty. Jūk yáuh léuhng júng sing jāt: hèng tùhng ngahn.
        (characteristics) deih·fòng; **good quality, best quality** hóu·chyúh; **bad quality** waaih·
chyúh. /He has many qualities people like. Kéuih yáuh hóu·dò deih·fòng lîhng yàhn jùng·
yi ge. /His best qualities are honesty and diligence. Kéuih ge hóu·chyuh haih yauh lóuh·
saht yauh kàhn·lihk.
        (grade) jāt·déi; **of good quality** hóu (jāt·déi) ge; **of superior quality** seuhng·dáng
(jāt·déi) ge, ji·hóu ge; **of medium quality** jùng·dáng (·jāt·déi) ge, jùng·tíng ge; **of poor
quality** hah·dáng (·jāt·déi) ge, yáih ge. /I want (good) quality, not (large) quantity.
Ngóh yiu hóu (·jāt·déi) ge, dò·siu móuh·gán·yiu. /Which kind has better quality? Bīn·
tíng jāt·déi hóu·dī a? /This is of the superior quality, that is of medium quality. Nī·
tíng haih seuhng·dáng ge, gó·tíng haih jùng·dáng ge.

quantity   leuhng; but more commonly expressed by words such as dò (many or much)
síu (few), sai (small), daaih (large) etc. /It's quality that's important, not quantity.
Joih jāt bāt joih leuhng. /He hoarded a large quantity of good liquor. Kéuih sàu·màaih
hóu·dò hóu jáu. /They said there are (large) quantities of Tungsten underground in
this region. Kéuih·deih wah nī·yāt·kèui deih·hah yáuh hóu·dò wù·kwong. /He said he
can only give us a small quantity. Kéuih wah kéuih jí nàhng béi síu·síu (or hóu·síu)
ngóh·deih jē.

quarantine   gîm·yihk: **quarantine station** gîm·yihk·só

quarrel   ngaai, ngaai·gāau (VO), chòuh. /What are they quarreling about? Kéuih·deih
hái syu ngaai māt·yéh a? /They quarreled again today. Kéuih·deih gàm·yaht yauh
ngaai·jó yāt·chèuhng gàau la. /What are the children quarreling about? Dī sai·màn·
jái hái syu chòuh māt·yéh a?
        a quarrel is expressed verbally as above. /They haven't seen each other since that
quarrel. Kéuih·deih léuhng·go ngaai·jó gāau jî·hauh meih gin·gwo·mihn. /It's said their
quarrel is about money. Yáuh·yàhn·wah kéuih·deih yàn·waih chín ngaai·héi·séuhng·lèih.

quarrelsome   jùng·yi ngaau·géng, jùng·yi díng·géng, jùng·yi (tùhng yàhn) ngaai·gāau

quarter   (one fourth) yāt·go·gwāt, sei·fahn·jī·yāt; **three quarters** sei·fahn·jī·sàam, sàam·
go·gwāt. /Give me a quarter of a pound of butter. Béi yāt·go·gwāt ngàuh·yàuh ngóh.
        (fifteen minutes) yāt·go·gwāt. /The train leaves at a quarter after three. Fó·chè
sàam·dím yāt·go·gwāt hòi. /I've been waiting for him for a quarter of an hour and he
still hasn't come. Ngóh hái syu dáng·jó kéuih sèhng·go·gwāt la, kéuih juhng meih·lèih.
/It's a quarter to six. Jàang go·gwāt luhk·dím. or Ngh·dím sàam·go·gwāt.
        industrial quarter gùng·yihp·kēui; **servants' quarters** gùng·yàhn·fóng

quay   (wharf) máh·tàuh

queen   (wife of king) wòhng·hauh; (reigning) néuih·wòhng; **queen mother** wòhng·taai hauh;
queen of England Yìng·néuih·wòhng

queer   kèih·gwaai; (odd) gú·gwaai

quench   (put out) jíng·sīk, see put out; **quench the thirst** jí·hot, gáai·hot

query   (ask) mahn

question   (inquiry or point of uncertainty) mahn·tàih; or often expressed as mahn (to
ask). /You didn't answer my question? Néih móuh·daap·fūk ngóh·ge mahn·tàih. /What
was your question? Néih jing·wah mahn māt·yéh a? /What is his question? Kéuih
mahn māt·yéh a? /I want to ask you. Ngóh séung mahn·háh néih. (polite) Ngóh yáuh
dī·sih séung chíng·mahn·háh néih.
        (matter of doubt) mahn·tàih. /Is there any question about his ability? Kéuih ge
nàhng·lihk yáuh móuh mahn·tàih a? /No. Móuh·mahn·tàih.

out of the question m̀h·sái·jí·yi. /It's out of the question to ask him to leave. M̀h·sái·jí·yi séung·giu kéuih jáu la!

without question gáng. /He'll be here without question. Kéuih gáng lèih ge.

to question someone (by authority) sám·mahn. /He has been questioned twice. Kéuih yih·gìng beih sám·mahn·gwo léuhng·chi la.

question something (doubt) sî·yíh (suspect that) or gok·dāk (feel that) followed by a negative verb. /Ngóh sî·yíh kéuih só·góng·ge·syut·wah m̀h·haih jàn ge.

queue (a braid of hair) bīn; (stand in a queue) pàaih·déui. /Everyone has to stand in a queue. Go go dōu yiu pàaih·déui.

quick (general term) faai, faai·cheui; (quick and efficient) faai·sáu, màh·leih. /Be quick about it! Faai·dī! or Faai·cheui·dī! /She's very quick in ironing. Kéuih tong·sāam hóu faai·sáu ge.

be quick is expressed as yāt·háh, yāt tái, yāt hohk, etc. /Don't be so quick to take offense. M̀h·hóu yāt·háh jauh nàu. /He was quick to catch on. Kéuih yāt·tái (by taking a look) jauh sīk la. or Kéuih yāt tèng (by listening) jauh mìhng·baahk la. or Kéuih yāt hohk (by learning) jauh sīk la.

the quicker the better yuht faai yuht hóu

quicksilver   séui·ngàhn

quickly   faai·dī, gón·faai; (immediately) máh·seuhng. /Shut the door, quickly! Faai·di sàan·màaih douh mùhn! /If we work quickly we can finish in two weeks. Yùh·gwó ngóh·deih gón·faai jouh, léuhng·go láih·baai hó·yíh jouh·héi la. /I'll be there as quickly as I can. Ngóh máh·seuhng jauh dou.

quick-tempered   bouh·chou

quiet (without noise or confusion) jihng, ngòn·jihng; (only of a place) chìhng·jihng; (of the sea) pìhng·jihng; (of a country) pìhng·jihng, taai·pìhng. /The place where I live is very quiet. Ngóh jyuh gó·daat deih·fòng hou jihng. /I would like to move to a quiet place. Ngóh séung bùn·heui yāt·daat jihng·dī ge deih·fòng. /That residential area is very quiet. Gó·go jyuh·jaahk·kēui hóu ngòn·jihng ge. /It's rather difficult to find a quiet place in Hong Kong now. Yìh·gā séung hái Hèung·góng wán daat chìhng·jihng ge deih·fòng hóu nàahn la. /The sea is very quiet today. Gàm·yaht ge hói·mihn hóu pìhng·jihng. /That area has been very quiet (peaceful) recently. Gó·yāt·kēui jeui·gahn hóu pìhng·jihng (or taai·pìhng).

quietly   jihng·jihng·déi. /He walked into that room very quietly. Kéuih jihng·jihng·déi hàahng·yahp gó·gàan fóng·syu.

quilt (cotton) mìhn·péih (M: jèung); **quilted garments** mìhn·naahp (M: gihn); **quilted gown** mìhn·póu (M: gihn)

quinine   gin·lìhn, gàm·gài·naahp

quit (stop doing something) /Quit it! (making trouble) M̀h·hóu gáau la nàh! (talking) M̀h·hóu chēut·sèng la nàh! or as a command M̀h·jéun chēut·sèng la nàh!

(stop work according to schedule) fong·gùng. /What time do you quit? Néih géi·dím·jūng fong·gùng a? /I quit at five. Ngóh ńgh·dím·jūng fong·gùng.

(leave something for a time) jài·dài. /Why don't you quit what you're doing and come out for a cup of coffee? Jài·dài dī yéh chēut·lèih yám bùi ga·fē lā!

(leave a job permanently) chìh·gùng, m̀h·jouh (labor work); chìh·jīk (office work). /When did you quit your job? Néih géi·sí chìh·gùng ga? /He said he'll quit his job the end of the month. Kéuih wah kéuih jouh·dou nī·go yuht·dái kéuih jauh m̀h·jou lo wóh. /Has he quit? Kéuih m̀h·jouh làh? or Kéuih chìh·jó·jīk làh?

quite   géi (fairly); hóu (very); sèung·dòng (fairly to very); sahp·fàn (very, hundred percent). /The eggs are quite fresh. Dī gài·dáan géi sàn·sīn. /The fish is quite fresh.

Tìuh yú hóu sàn·sìn. /The food (of the restaurant) is quite good. Dī choi sèung·dòng
hóu. /That chicken is quite well done. Gó·jek gāi jíng·dāk sahp·fàn hóu.
   not quite (is still lacking) juhng meih·dāk. /That's not quite what I wanted. Nī·go
juhng meih·dāk. /It's not quite finished. Juhng meih·dāk.
   quite good to eat géi hóu·sihk; **quite reasonable** géi yáuh·douh·léih; **quite right** géi
ngāam; **quite satisfied** hóu múhn·yi; **it's quite unexpected** gú·m̀h·dou; **the price is quite
reasonable** ga·chìhn géi sèung·yìh;

quiver   (tremble) jan; **quiver with fear** gèng·dou·jan

quiz   chāk·yihm; **quizzes on general knowledge** sèuhng·sīk chāk·yihm

quorum   faat·dihng·yàhn·sou

quota   ngáak, kōu·dá; **the quota of immigrants** yìh·màhn·ngáak

quotation   (from a classic, etc.) (jih gìng·dín (classics) <u>or</u> màhn·jèung (article)·jùng)
yáhn·yuhng ge jèung·geui; **quotation mark** yáhn·houh; (current price) síh·ga

quote   yùhn·yáhn, yáhn·yuhng: **quote a precedent** yùhn·yáhn chìhn·laih <u>or</u> yáhn·yuhng
chìhn·laih; **quote from the classics** yáhn·gìng·geui·dín
   quote . . . to prove yáhn (yuhng) . . . làih jing·mìhng. /Allow me to quote the Bible
to prove what I've said. It is in verse thirty-one of the Book of Luke. Jéun ngóh yáhn·
yuhng Sing·gìng yāt·geui syut·wah làih jing·mìhng ngóh só·góng·ge. Nī·geui syut·wah
haih hái Louh·gā fūk·yām daih·sàam·sahp·yāt·jit.

R

rabbit   tou·jái, tou (M: jek)

rabies   dìn·gáu·jing

race   (a contest of speed; competition) béi·choi, <u>in compounds</u> dau·; **race between persons** dau·jáu <u>or</u> dau·faai. **horse race** choi·máh, páau·máh; **dog race** choi·gáu. /The
races will be held next week. Hah·go láih·baai béi·choi. /How many races are there
per year? Yāt·nìhn yáuh géi·dò·chi béi·choi a? /When will there be a horse race?
Géi·sí choi·máh a? /He made a lot of money on horse races. Kéuih choi·máh yèhng·
jó hóu·dò chín.
   (people of same ancestry) júng·juhk, ·júng·yàhn: **white race** baahk·júng·yàhn; **yellow race** wòhng·júng·yàhn; **black race** hāk·júng·yàhn; **red race** hùhng·júng·yàhn.
/There are five major races in China. Jùng·gwok yáuh ńgh·go daaih·júng·juhk.
   (species) **the human race** yàhn·leuih; leuih <u>means</u> class <u>or</u> group <u>and is found in
compounds such as</u> sau·leuih (animal class), niuh·leuih (bird class), yú·leuih (fish
class). /Is there anyone who can predict the future of the human race? Yáuh móuh
yàhn nàhng·gau yuh·chāk yàhn·leuih ge jèung·lòih haih dím·yéung ge nē?
   to race dau, béi·choi. /I'll race you. Ngóh tùhng néih dau·háh leh. /I'll race you
to that schoolhouse. Ngóh tùhng néih dau·háh, tái·háh bīn·go heui·dou gó·gàan hohk·
haauh sìn.
   race course páau·máh·déi, páau·máh·chèuhng, máh·chèuhng; **race discrimination**
júng·juhk kèih·sih; **racial revolution** júng·juhk·gaak·mihng

rack   (frame, shelf) gá

racket   (a bat) kàuh·páak; (dishonest schemes or practices) hēi·ngāk·gwáai·pin ge
hàhng·wàih

radar   lèuih·daaht

radiate   fong·seh

radiator   (as in an automobile) séui·sèung

radical   (fundamental) gàn·bún·seuhng ge: **radical difference** gàn·bún·seuhng ge chà·
biht. (thoroughgoing) gàn·bún: **radical treatment** (of disease) gàn·bún jih·lìuh
(extremist) gīk·lihk fahn·jí
(one of 214 ideographic elements used in combination with phonetics to form thou-
sands of different Chinese characters) jih·bouh: the radical for yàhn, yàhn·jih·bouh; (at
the side of a character) jih·bīn: /It's the character 'hòh' with the radical for water at
the side of it. Haih séui·jih·bīn gó·go hòh. (at the top of a Chinese character) jih·tàuh.
/It's the character with the grass radical not the bamboo radical on the top of it. Haih
chóu·jih·tàuh gó·go (jih) m̀h·haih jūk·jih·tàuh gó·go (jih).

radio   mòuh·sin·dihn: (receiving set) sāu·yām·gēi. /Do you have a radio (radio set)?
Néih yáuh sāu·yām·gēi ma?
to radio (transmit a message by radio) yuhng mòuh·sin·dihn faat·chēut·heui (radio
out); Yuhng mòuh·sin·dihn faat·(or dá·) lèih
radio broadcast mòuh·sin·dihn·gwóng·bo; bo·yām; **radio broadcasting station** dihn·
tòih, gwóng·bo dihn·tòih, mòuh·sin·dihn·toih; **radio wave** dihn·bō, mòuh·sin dihn·bō

radish   lòh·baahk·jái, hùhng·lòh·baahk·jái

radium   lèuih·dihn

radius   bun·ging

raft   (of logs) muhk·pàaih

rag   (torn or worn cloth) laahn·bou (M: faai)

raid   (of police) sáu·chàh; (of troops or warships, etc.) daht·gīk; **air raid** hùng·jaahp;
air raid alarm fòhng·hùng gíng·bou

rail   (railing) làahn·gōn (M: tìuh or jì)

railroad   tit·louh; (company) tit·louh·gúk; (train) fó·chè; **railroad track** tit·gwéi; **railroad station** fó chè·jahm; **railroad ticket** chè·piu (M: jèung)

rain   yúh; **light rain** yúh·mēi; **rainstorm** lohk daaih yúh, yauh dá·fùng yauh lohk·yúh.
/We always have light rains rather than rainstorms here in spring. Chēun·tīn ge sìh·
hauh ngóh·deih nī·syu sìh·sìh dōu haih lohk yúh·mēi hóu síu lohk daaih yúh ge.
to rain lohk·yúh. /Is it raining? Lohk (·gán)·yúh àh? /Is it raining hard? Lohk
hóu daaih yúh àh? or Lohk dāk hóu daaih àh? /Will it rain today? Gàm·yaht wúih·m̀h·
wúih lohk·yúh a? /It's beginning to rain. Lohk·yúh la.
rainbow chói·hùhng, séui·hùhng; **raincoat** yúh·yī, yúh·lāu; **rainy season** yúh·gwai

raise   (grow) jung. /They raise sweet potatoes. Kéuih·deih jung fàan·syú.
(of farm animals) yéuhng. /He raises chickens; his younger brother raises ducks.
Kéuih yéuhng gāi, kéuih sai·lóu yéuhng ngáap.
(elevate) hòi. /We'd better get in, they've raised the curtain. Ngóh·deih hóu yahp·
heui la, yíh·gīng hòi·mohk la.
raise an army yéuhng·bīng. /A small country shouldn't raise such a large army.
Yāt·go síu·gwok m̀h·yìng·gòi yéunng gam dò bīng.
raise a family. /He raised a big family. is expressed as: Kéuih ngūk·kéi yáuh hóu
daaih dau yàhn.
raised (grown up) jéung·daaih ge. /Didn't you grow up in Shanghai? Néih haih m̀h·
haih hái Seuhng·hói jéung·daaih ga?
raise money gyùn(·chín), chàun(·fún), gaap(·chín). /How much money do they plan
to raise? Kéuih·deih dá·syun gyùn gei·do chín a? /We raise money each year to support the hospital. Ngóh·deih múih·nìhn chàuh yāt·chi fún lèih wàih·chìh nī·gàan yī·yún.
/How much money do they plan to raise? Kéuih·deih dá·syun gyùn (gyùn may mean
solicit or donate, it depends on the context) géi·dò chín a? /We're discussing how much
money we should raise to buy a gift for our Alma Mater. Ngóh·deih tóu·leuhn·gán yiu
gaap géi·dò chín lèih máaih yāt·gihn yéh béi ngóh·deih ge móuh·haauh.

raise a flag sìng·kèih (hoist), gwa·kèih (hang). /Why did they raise the flag today? Gàm·yaht jouh·māt·yéh sìng·kèih a?

raise a price héi·ga. /The price has been raised again? Yauh héi(·jó) ga làh? /The price of rice has been raised twice this month. Nī·go yuht dī máih·ga yìh·gìng héi·jó léuhng·chi la.

raise one's hand géui·sáu. /If anyone has a question please raise your hand. Bīn·go yáuh mahn·tàih hó·yíh géui·sáu.

raise one's head dàam·gòu go tàuh. /If you raise your head then you'll see the star. Néih dàam·gòu go tàuh jauh mohng·gin gó·nāp sīng la.

raise a question tàih·chēut·mahn·tàih. /He raised a very interesting question. Kéuih tàih·chēut yāt·go hóu yáuh·cheui ge mahn·tàih.

raise wages gà·yàhn·gùng; **raise salary** gà·sàn·séui. /Should we raise their wages? Ngóh·deih yìng·gòi gà kéuih·deih ge yàhn·gùng ma? /We raise your salary every year. Ngóh·deih múih·nìhn gà néih yāt·chi sàn·séui.

a raise (in pay) is expressed as raise wages or salary (see above). /He asked for a raise. Kéuih séung gà yàhn·gùng (wages). or Kéuih séung gà sàn·séui (salary). /Everybody will get a raise next month. Hah·go·yuht go·go·dōu gà yàhn·gùng.

raise one's spirits tàih·héi jìng·sàhn. /We should think of a way to raise his spirits. Ngóh·deih yìng·gòi séung go baahn·faat tàih·héi kéuih ge jìng·sàhn.

raisin   pòuh·tàih·jí (M: nāp)

rake   pá (N); pàh (V); **rake the lawn** pàh·háh go chóu·déi

ram   (a male sheep) yèuhng·gūng

range   (variety) is expressed indirectly. /He has a wide range of interests. is expressed as: Kéuih héi·fùn ge yéh hóu·dò. (The things he likes are many.)
      (distance) kéuih·lèih; (of firearms) seh·chìhng; **short range** dyún·kéuih·lèih ge, dyún·chìhng ge; **long range** chèuhng·kéuih·lèih ge, chèuhng·chìhng gc; (grazing land) chóu·déi; (stove) fó·lòuh, jou; **mountain range** sàan·mahk; **rifle range** lihn·bá·chèuhng
      to range (be within the limits of). /Prices range from one hundred to two hundred dollars. is expressed as: Ga·chìhn yàuh yāt·baak·mān jì yih·baak·mān jī·gāan.

rank   (position, title) gāai·kāp. /What rank does he have in the army? Kéuih hái gwàn·déui haih māt·yéh gāai·kāp a?
      (class, grade) dáng, làuh. /This is a first rank theater. Nī·gàan haih tàuh·dáng hei·yún. /That university is of the first rank. Gó·gàan daaih·hohk haih daih·yāt·làuh ge daaih·hohk.
      to rank (grade) is expressed as haih (be) or syun (count as). /He ranks second in achievements in the class. Chyùhn·bāan ge sìhng·jīk kéuih haih daih·yih·mìhng.

ransack   chéung·gip

ransom   suhk(·fàan) (V); suhk·fún (N)

rape   (ravish) kèuhng·gàan

rapid   faai

rapids   tāan

rapidly   faai. /He spoke so rapidly I missed what he said. Kéuih góng·dāk gam faai ngóh tèng·mh·dóu kéuih góng māt·yéh.

rare   (seldom met with) hèi·hón; (wonderful) hèi·kèih; **rarely seen** hóu síu gin

rash   (impetuous) lóuh·móhng; (acting hastily without due consideration) pàhn·làhn, lòhng·mòhng. /Don't be rash! Mh·sái pàhn·làhn!

rat   lóuh·syú (M: jek); mouse (rat) trap lóuh·syú·gíp, lóuh·syú·lùhng (cage); **rat poison** lóuh·syú·yeuhk

rate   (charge or fee) ga·chìhn. /This isn't the regular rate, is it? Nī·go m̀h·haih pìhng·
sìh ge ga·chìhn boh, haih·m̀h·haih a?
(class, grade) làuh, dáng. /This restaurant is definitely first rate. Nī·gàan jyuht·
deui haih <u>daih·yāt·làuh</u> (or tàuh·dáng) ge jáu·gún.
at any rate mòuh·leuhn·dím. /We think this is the best plan; at any rate we will
try it. Ngóh·deih gok·dāk nī·go haih jeui hóu ge baahn·faat; mòuh·leuhn·dím ngóh·deih
dōu yiu si·háh.
at the rate of. /You can pay for it at the rate of twenty dollars a month. <u>is expressed</u>
<u>as</u>: Néih hó·yíh múih·go yuht béi yih·sahp·mān. /This car can go at the rate of sixty
miles per hour. <u>is expressed as</u>: Nī·ga chè múih·dím·jūng hó·yíh hàahng luhk·sahp·
léih.
at this <u>or</u> **that rate** yùh·gwó haih gám. /The work is too much for one man; at this
rate we will need other helpers. Nī·gihn sih yāt·go yàhn m̀h·jouh·dāk, yùh·gwó haih gám,
ngóh·deih yāt·dihng yiu chéng dò géi·go bòng·sáu.
postage rate yàuh·jì, yàuh·fai. /The postage is six cents one ounce. Yàuh·jì haih
luhk·fān yāt ōn·sí.
special rate jit·tàuh. /Is there a special rate? Yáuh móuh jit·tàuh a?
(proportion) béi·laih; (degree) chìhng·douh; (degree of speed) chūk·douh; (charge)
ga·chìhn; (of exchange) hòhng·chìhng

rather   (a little) dōu géi, sèung·dòng, chíh·fùh. /It's rather cold this morning. Gàm·
jìu·jóu dōu géi láahng boh. /That movie was rather long. Gó·chēut hei sèung·dòng
chèuhng. /It seems rather early to decide what to do. Yìh·gā kyut·dihng dím jouh
chíh·fùh taai jóu dī.
. . . **rather than** . . . kèih·saht haih . . . m̀h·syun·dāk haih . . . /It's a song rather
than a poem. Kèih·saht haih yāt·sáu gō m̀h·syun·dāk haih yāt·sáu·sī.
would rather chìhng·yún, dōu haih, <u>all expressing a rather mild preference</u>; nìhng·
yún <u>expressing a strong preference</u>. /I would rather go with you. Ngóh chìhng·yún
tùhng néih·deih heui. /I don't feel well and I'd rather stay home. Ngóh m̀h·haih géi
jìng·sàhn, ngóh dōu haih làuh·hái ngūk·kéi bá la. /He said he would rather starve to
death than take this job. Kéuih wah kéuih chìhng·yún ngoh·séi dōu m̀h·jouh nī·gihn sih.

ratify   (sanction) pài·jéun

ratio   béi·laih, béi·leuht

rations   (food) fó·sihk, lèuhng·sihk

rational   hahp·léih (ge)

rattan   tàhng: **rattan chair** tàhng·yí; **rattan mat** tàhng·jehk; **rattan shield** tàhng·pàaih;
rattanware tàhng·hei

rattlesnake   héung·méih·sèh (M: tìuh)

raven   (crow) wū·ngà (M: jek)

ravine   sāan·gūk

raw   (uncooked) sàang (ge). /Don't eat any raw vegetables. M̀h·hóu sihk sàang ge choi.
raw silk sāang·sì; **raw cotton** mìhn·fà; **raw material** yùhn·líu

ray   (of light) gwòng·sin

razor   sòu·páau, tai·dōu; **razor blade** dōu·pín (M: faai)

reach   (reach something without much effort, as in one's pocket) ngàhm. /He reached
into his pocket to see if his wallet was still there. Kéuih ngàhm·háh kéuih ge ngàhn·
bāau tái·hah juhng hái·m̀h·hái syu.
(reach for something, when it involves stretching and effort) màan. /Can you reach
it with your hand? Néih ge sáu màan·m̀h·màan·dāk·dou gó·douh a?

(extend to) -dou. /The garden reaches to the river. Go fà·yún yāt·jihk heui·dou tîuh hòh·syu. /This curtain is too long; it almost reaches the floor. Nī·tîuh chēung·lìm taai chèuhng la, yāt·jihk dim·dou deih·báan·syu.

(arrive at) dou. /Your letter didn't reach me until today. Néih fùng seun gàm·yaht sìn·ji dou.

(find, get at) wán(·dāk)·dóu. /There was no way of reaching him. Móuh·faat·jí wán·dāk·dóu kéuih.

out of reach or **beyond one's reach.** /Put the candy out of his reach. is expressed as: Jèung dī tóng jài hóu, m̀h·hóu béi kéuih màan·dóu. (Put the candy so he can't reach it.) /Such food is beyond the reach of poor people. Nī·dī sihk·maht kùhng·yàhn m̀h·sihk·dāk·dóu ge.

react   (act in response to) fáan·ying; **react against oppression** fáan·kong

reaction   fáan·ying

reactionary   (a person) fáan·duhng·fahn·jí

read   (silently) tái; (aloud or study) duhk. /What books have you read recently? Néih jeui·gahn tái dī māt·yéh syù a? /Please read it to me. Chéng néih duhk·béi ngóh tèng. /This book is very easy to read. Nī·bún syù hóu yùhng·yih duhk.

reader   (of a newspaper, etc.) duhk·jé; (lecturer) góng·sī; (textbook) duhk·bún

readily   (quickly, without delay) làh·lá·sèng, máh·seuhng

reading   **reading matter** duhk·maht; **reading room** syù·fóng, yuht·láahm·sāt (for public)

ready   (prepared) hóu, dāk, yuh·beih·hóu la, jéun·beih hóu la. /Is dinner ready? Jyú·hóu·faahn meih a? /The coffee is ready. Ga·fē jyú·hóu la. or Ga·fē dāk la. /Every-thing is ready. Yeuhng·yeuhng dōu yuh·beih·hóu (or jéun·beih·hóu) la.

be ready to or **for** hó·yíh, -dāk. /Is the manuscript ready to be printed? Dī góu hó·yíh yan·dāk meih a? /Is it ready to eat? Sihk·dāk meih a?

get ready dāk, yuh·beih. /Can you get ready to go in five minutes? Néih ńgh·fān·jūng heui·dāk meih a? /I'll give you five minutes to get ready. Ngóh béi ńgh·fān·jūng néih yuh·beih.

ready cash yihn·chín, yihn·fún, yihn·ngán; **ready made** yihn·síng ge

real   jàn (ge), jàn·jing (ge). /Is this a real pearl or a cultured one? Nī·nāp haih jàn (·ge) jyú yīk·waahk haih yéuhng·jyū a? /This is the real Tiger-bone wine. Nī·dī haih jàn·jing ge fú·gwāt·jáu. /What was the real reason that he left home? is expressed as: Kéuih dou·dái waih·māt·yéh lèih·hòi ngūk·kéi a? /Do you know the real facts? Néih jì·dou nī·gihn sih ge jàn·seung ma? /It's a real pleasure to meet you. Gàm·yaht (nàhng·gau) gin·dóu néih, ngóh jàn·haih fùn·héi la.

real estate saht·yihp; **real thing** jing yéh, jing fo; **real Sunkist** jing gāam·sāan·cháang

reality   (state of being real) yihn·saht

realize   (come to understand) mìhng·baahk; (know) jî. /Do you realize what he did? Néih mìhng·baahk kéuih jouh·jó dī māt·yéh sih ma? /I didn't realize that you were in-terested in it. Ngóh m̀h·jî néih deui nī·gihn sih (business or nī·gihn yéh things) yáuh hing·cheui.

(achieve) saht·yihn. /If you want to realize what you are dreaming about, the only way is to work hard to gain it. Yùh·gwó néih séung saht·yihn néih ge léih·séung, jí·yáuh kàhn·lihk heui jouh.

really   jàn·haih, kèih·saht, jàn. /Are you really tired? Néih jàn·haih hóu guih àh? /He is really younger than he looks. Kéuih kèih·saht móuh kéuih ge yéung gam lóuh. /Really? Jàn gé?

ream   nīm, līm (M): **a ream of paper** yāt·nīm jí

reap   (cut) got: **reap rice** got·wòh

rear   hauh·bihn, hauh-. /There's a garden at the rear of the house. Ngūk·hauh·bihn yáuh go fà·yún. /The rear wheels got stuck in the mud. Hauh·lūk jyut·jó·hái nàih yahp·bihn. (raise or bring up) /Who reared him? Bīn·go yéuhng·daaih kéuih ga?
rear admiral hói·gwān·siu·jeung; **rear guard** hauh·waih

rearrange   chùhng·sàn báai·gwo (as furniture); chùhng·sàn pàaih·liht·gwo (as index cards, etc.)

reason   (cause) yùhn·yàn. /Do you know the reason he left here? Néih jī·dou kéuih jáu ge yùhn·yàn ma? /Yes, I know; there were three reasons that made him leave here. Ngóh jī, kéuih lèih·hòi nī·syu yáuh sàam·go yùhn·yàn.
(ground) léih·yàuh. /There's no reason for him not to attend this meeting. Kéuih móuh·léih·yàuh m̀h·lèih hòi·wúi.
listen to reason. /He won't listen to reason. Néih góng māt douh·léih kéuih dōu m̀h·tèng.
to reason (think logically). /Let's try to reason it out. Daaih·gā jí·sai séung·háh.
(persuade) hyun·hoi. /Try to reason with her. Hyun·hòi·háh kéuih lā.

reasonable   (fair and just) gùng·douh. /I think I'm reasonable in the amount of homework I assign you. Ngóh gok·dāk Ngóh paai·béi néih·deih ge gùng·fo hóu gùng·douh.
(logical, sensible) hahp·léih. /The way he proposes to solve this problem is quite reasonable. Kéuih tàih·chēut gáai·kyut nī·gihn sih ge baahn·faat sèung·dòng hahp·léih.
(moderate) gùng·douh. /This is a reasonable price. Nī·go ga·chìhn géi gùng·douh.

rebel   fáan·pun. /There's a small group of troops which is rebelling against the government. Yáuh yāt·siu·bouh·fahn ge gwàn·déui fáan·pun jing·fú.
(as a person) pun·tòuh. /The rebels tried to overthrow the government. Dī pun·tòuh dá·syun tèui·fàan kéuih·deih ge jing·fú.

rebellion   pun·lyuhn

rebound   daahn·fàan·jyun·tàuh

rebuild   chùhng·sàn héi·gwo, joi héi·gwo

rebuke   jāk·beih

recall   (remember) séung·dāk·héi (RV). /I couldn't recall which day I lost my watch. Ngóh m̀h·séung·dāk·héi bīn·yaht sāt·jó ngóh·ge bīu.
(call back). /He was recalled by his company last year. Kéuih·deih ge gùng·sī gauh·nín diuh·jó kéuih fàan·heui.

recapture   (as a fallen city) hāk·fuhk

receipt   (a written statement) sàu·tìuh, sàu·geui. /Can you write me a receipt? Néih hó·yíh sé·fàan jèung sàu·tìuh béi ngóh ma?
(money received) sàu·yahp. /The receipts from the show will be used to buy library books. Jouh hei ge sàu·yahp yùhng·lèih máaih tòuh·syù·gún yuhng ge syù.
(act of receiving) sàu·dóu, jip·dóu. /Upon receipt of the telegram, he immediately took the plane back to the United States. Kéuih yāt sàu·dóu gó·go dihn·bou jauh lahp·hāk chóh fēi·gèi fèi·fàan Méih·gwok la.

receive   (get or have given; accept something offered) sàu·dóu, jip·dóu. /We received a letter every week from him. Ngóh·deih múih·go·láih·baai dōu sàu·dóu kéuih ge seun. /Everyone will have a bonus at the end of the year. Mùih·yàhn nìhn·dái dōu yáuh fà·hùhng.
(experience; especially suffering) sauh. /If every child has an opportunity to receive a good musical education, he or she will grow up to be a happy adult. Yùh·gwó múih·go sai·mān·jái dōu yáuh gèi·wuih sauh(·dóu) lèuhng·hóu ge yàm·ngohk gaau·yuhk, daaih·jó yāt·dihng haih yāt·go hóu faai·lohk ge yàhn.

(greet or welcome) jip. /Should we receive him at the gate of the school? Ngóh·
deih sái·m̀h·sái chēut·heui hohk·haauh mùhn·háu jip kéuih a?

be received. /How was your suggestion received? is expressed as: Daaih·gā gok·
dāk néih ge yi·gin dím a? (How did everyone consider your idea?)

receive baptism (being baptized) líhng·sái, sauh·sái; **receive command from a superior officer** (being ordered by) fuhng·mihng; **receive a prize** léhng·jéung; **received
in full** sāu·chìng

receiver   **receiver** (of a letter) sàu·sèun·yàhn; **receiver** (of a telephone) tèng·túng, yíh·
túng

recent   jeui·gahn, sàn·gahn. /Is this a recent invention? Nī·go haih·m̀h·haih sàn·gahn
faat·mìhng ga? /Do you have the recent issue of <u>Life</u> magazine? Néih yáuh móuh jeui·
gahn nī·kèih ge sàng·wuht wá·bou a?

recently   gahn·lói, sàn·gahn. /How has he been recently? Kéuih gahn·lói géi·hóu ma?
/He bought another house recently. Kéuih sàn·gahn yauh máaih·jó gāan ngūk.

(very recently) jeui·gahn, nī·páai. /What have you been reading recently? Néih
jeui·gahn tái dī māt·yéh syù a? /Have you seen him recently? Néih jeui·gahn (<u>or</u> nī·
páai) yáuh móuh gin·dóu keuih a?

(a few days ago) nī·géi·yaht. /Did he come recently? Nī·géi·yaht kéuih yáuh móuh
lèih a?

receptacle   (spittoon) tàahm·túng, tàahm·yú

reception   (welcome meeting) fùn·yìhng·wúi; (ceremony with refreshments) chàh·wúi;
(act of receiving visitors) jìu·doih; (after a ceremony or some formal gathering as
news conference, etc.) jìu·doih·wúi; **afternoon tea reception** chàh·wúi

reception room ying·jip·sāt, jìu·doih·sāt

recess   yāu·sīk

recipient   **recipient of goods** sàu·fo·yàhn

recipe   (for preparing food) sihk·póu, jai·faat, but the sentence /Can you give me the
recipe? is generally expressed as: Néih hó·yíh góng ngóh jî dím·yéuhg jíng ge ma?
(Can you tell me how to make it?)

recite   (from memory) nihm, buih. /Can you recite this poem now? Nī·sáu sī, néih sīk
nìhm méih a?

recite incantation nihm·jau; **recite lessons** nihm·syù, buih·syù; **recite litanies**
nihm·gìng

reckless   (without care) m̀h·síu·sàm (ge); (rash) lóuh·móhng

reclaim   (land) hòi·hán; (demand the return) ló·fàan: **reclaim one's money** ló·fàan chín

recline   (lie down) fan·hái. /He's reclining on a couch, reading a book. Kéuih fan·hái
jèung seuih·yí·syu tái·gán syù.

recognize   (by looking) yihng·dāk, yihng·dāk·chēut; (by listening) tèng·dāk·chēut. /Do
you recognize these words? Néih yihng·dāk nī·dī jih ma? /Do you recognize me?
Néih yihng·dāk ngóh ma? /Do you recognize Mr. Lahm's son? Néih yihng·dāk·chēut
bīn·go haih Làhm·sìn·sàang ge jái ma? /Can you recognize whose voice it is? Néih
tèng·dāk·chēut haih bīn·go ge sèng ma?

recognize a government sìhng·yihng. /Do they recognize the new government?
Kéuih·deih sìhng·yihng nī·go sàn·jing·fú ma?

recollect   (call to mind again) séung·héi. /I can't recollect where I met him. Ngóh
séung·m̀h·héi (<u>or</u> m̀h·séung·dāk·héi) hái bīn·syu gin·gwo kéuih la.

recommend   (for employment) géui·jin, gaai·siuh. /Can you recommend him for this
job?   Néih hó·yíh géui·jin kéuih jouh nī·gihn sih ma? /I need a man to help me. Can

you recommend one? Ngóh sèui·yiu yāt·go yàhn bòng·sáu, néih hó·yíh gaai·siuh go yàhn béi ngóh ma? /Who recommended you? Bīn·go gaai·siuh néih lèih ga?

recommendation   gaai·siuh·seun. /Do you have a letter of recommendation? Néih yáuh móuh gaai·siuh·seun a?

recompense   (to reward for service) chàuh·bou, bou·chàuh; (to make resitution for loss) pùih, pùih·sèuhng; (to repay a favor) bou·daap, daap·jeh

reconcile   (other parties who disagree) tìuh·tìhng. /The British government works to reconcile the two hostile nations. Yìng·gwok jing·joih jeun·hàhng tìuh·tìhng nī·léuhng·go gwok·gà ge jàang·jāap. (become friendly again) wòh·gáai. /They argued for two days and finally reconciled (their differences). Kéuih·deih jàan·jāap·jó léuhng·yaht jì·hauh jēut·jì wòh·gáai·jó la.

recondition   sàu·jíng (V)

reconnaissance   jìng·chaat: **reconnaissance plane** jìng·chaat·gèi

reconsider   chùhng·sàn·háau·leuih, joi háau·leuih·háh

reconstruct   chùhng·sàn jíng·gwo, gói·jouh; (a building, etc.) héi·gwo

record   (written statement) géi·luhk; **keep records** géi·luhk. /These are the records of the works accomplished by our association. Nī·dī haih ngóh·deih nī·go wúi ge gùng·jok géi·luhk. /Have you (plural) kept records of what you have done? Néih·deih yáuh géi·luhk néih·deih jouh·jó ge gùng·jok ma?

    (financial) sou·muhk. **keep financial records of** sé·dài go sou·muhk. /Do you have a record to show us? Néih yáuh móuh sou·muhk béi ngóh·deih tái a? /Please keep a record of our expenses. Chéng néih sé·dài ngóh·deih ge fai·yuhng. or Chéng néih jèung ngóh·deih ge fai·yuhng sé·dài go sou·muhk.

    (recorded maximum) géi·luhk. /This new airplane broke all records for speed. Nī·ga sàn·sīk ge fēi·gèi dá·po fèi·hàhng chūk·douh ge géi·luhk. /The rainfall has set a new record this year. Gàm·nín ge yúh·leuhng chong·jouh·jó go sàn·géi·luhk. /We had a record crop this year. is expressed as: Ngóh·deih gàm·nín ge sàu·sìhng béi bīn·nìhn dōu hóu.

    (phonograph disk) cheung·díp, làuh·sìng gèi·hei·díp. /Do you have dance records? Néih yáuh móuh tiu·móuh ge cheung·díp a?

    (known past). /Has he a criminal record? is expressed as: Kéuih yíh·chìhn yáuh móuh faahn·gwo jeuih a? /He had a fine record in college. is expressed as: Kéuih daaih·hohk ge sìhng·jīk hóu hóu.

    the worst (or best, etc.) . . . **on record**. /This is the worst flood on record here. is expressed as: Nī·chi séui·jòi jàn·haih cháam la, chùhng·lòih meih si·gwo gam gán·yiu ge. (This flood is disastrous! We have never had anything like this before.)

    to record (in writing) gei·luhk. /Please record the proceedings of the meeting. Chéng néih gei·luhk·háh hòi·wúi ge chìhng·yìhng.

    (on disks) gun, gun·yām. /This disk was recorded when I was in college. Nī·go cheung·díp haih ngóh hái daaih·hohk sìh gun ge.

    (on tape) luhk·yām. /Do you want me to record this song on tape? Néih séung ngóh jèung nī·sáu gō luhk·yām ma?

recover   (get back) wán·fàan. /Is there a chance to recover our dog? Ngóh·deih jek gáu wán·m̀h·wán·dāk·fàan a?

    (from sickness) hóu·fàan. /Has he recovered? Kéuih hóu·fàan meih a?

    (as a captured city) sàu·fuhk. /The government troops recovered two cities. Jing·fú ge gwàn·déui sàu·fuhk·jó léuhng·go sìhng·síh.

recreation   (pastime) sìu·hín; (amusement) yùh·lohk; (sport) wahn·duhng; **recreation ground** (land set aside for games) wahn·duhng·chèuhng

recruit   jìng·mouh: **recruit soldiers** jìng·mouh sàn·bìng, jiu·bìng

rectify   (put right) gói·jing; (put straight) jíng·jing; (adjust) jíng·hóu

rectum   gòng·mùhn

red   hùhng·sīk (ge), hùhng-. /She likes to wear red clothes. Kéuih hóu jùng·yi jeuk
hùhng·sīk (ge) sāam ge. /Do you like this red dress? Néih jùng·yi nī·gihn hùhng·sāam
ma?
     red color hùhng·sīk; **Red Cross** (Society) hùhng·sahp·jih·wúi; **red corpuscle** hùhng·
hyut·kàuh; **Red Sea** Hùhng·hói

redeem   suhk, suhk·fàan. /He needs money to redeem his winter clothes. Kéuih sèui·
yiu dī chín suhk·fàan kéuih ge láahng·tīn·sāam. /Jesus redeems us from sin. Yèh·sōu
wàih sai·yàhn suhk·jeuih.

reduce   gáam, gáam·síu; **reduce the price** gáam·ga, gáam·dài ga·chìhn; **reduce the rent**
gáam·jòu; **reduce the penalty** gáam·hèng go jeuih; **reduce the fine** gáam·hèng faht·fún;
reduce the swelling sīu·júng

reed   séui·chóu

reel   (bobbin of thread) sin·lūk; (a spool on which a film is wound) gyún

reef   chìuh·sehk

refer   (to a person for information or decision) mahn. /You may refer this to our headmaster. Néih hó·yíh mahn ngóh·deih ge haauh·jéung.
    (go for information) chàh, chàam·háau. /Why don't you refer to the dictionary? Dím·
gáai néih m̀h·chàh·háh jih·dín nē? /You may refer to these two books. Néih hó·yíh chàam·
háau nī·léuhng·bún syù.
    (recommend) gaai·siuh. /Who referred you to that doctor? Bīn·go gaai·siuh néih
gin gó·go yī·sāng ga?
    (relate; point) góng. /To whom does he refer? Kéuih góng bīn·go a?

referee   (umpire) chòih·pun·yùhn

reference book   chàam·háau·syù

refine   (as metals) lihn

refined   (in manners) sì·màhn; **refined sugar** baahk·tòhng

refinery   **oil refinery** lihn·yàuh·chóng; **sugar refinery** lihn·tòhng·chóng

reflect   (light) fáan·seh. /The light is reflected from that mirror. Nī·go gwòng·sin haih
hái gó·go geng fáan·seh chēut·lèih ge.
    (cause blame) (fáan·) yíng·chēut. /His bad behavior reflects the way he was brought
up. Kéuih ge bán·hahng yíng·chēut kéuih móuh dī gà·gaau.
    (think over carefully) jí·sai séung·háh. /You should reflect on what has just happened.
Néih yìng·gòi jí·sai séung·háh jing·wah faat·sàng nī·go mahn·tàih.

reflection   (reflected image) yíng. /The dog looked into the water, saw his reflection,
and thought it was another dog so he barked. Jek gáu tái·gin séui·seuhng·bihn ge yíng,
yíh·wàih haih daih·yih·jek gáu, faih·héi·séuhng·lèih.
    (of light) fáan·gwòng. /It's just the reflection of the mirror. Haih go geng ge fáan·
gwòng jē.
    (serious consideration) gáam·séung. /What's your reflection about the war? Néih
deui·yù muhk·chìhn ge jin·sih yáuh māt gáam·séung a?

reform   (a process) gói·lèuhng; (a political condition) gói·gaak; (morally) gói·gwo is not
used transitively. /It's never too late to reform oneself. Yāt·go yàhn jí yiu háng gói·
gwo, géi·sí dōu m̀h·chìh.

reformatory   gáam·fa·yún

refrain   (keep oneself from doing something) gaai. /I think you should refrain from
   drinking. Ngóh gok·dāk néih yìng·dòng gaai·jáu. But when 'refrain' is used negatively,
   most of the time yán·m̀h·jyuh (·yiu) is used. /I cannot refrain from laughing when he
   tries to act like a child. Ngóh tái·gin kéuih baahn·sèhng yāt·go sai·mān·jái gám, ngóh
   jàn·haih yán·m̀h·jyuh siu. /He just can't refrain from drinking when there is wine.
   Kéuih yāt tái·gin yáuh jáu jauh yán·m̀h·jyuh yiu·yám ge la.

refreshments   chàh·dím

refrigerator   syut·gwaih

refuge   to take refuge beih·naahn. /There are many Chinese taking refuge in Hong Kong.
   Yìh·gā yáuh hóu·dò Jùng·gwo·yàhn hái Hèung·góng beih·naahn.
      (place) beih·naahn·só

refugee   naahn·màhn, jáu·naahn·ge yàhn; refugee camp nàahn·màhn sàu·yùhng·só

refund   /If it's not satisfactory, your money will be refunded. Yùh·gwó m̀h·múhn·yi, hó·
   yíh teui·fàan chín.

refuse   (of a proposal) kéuih·jyuht. /I feel the school should refuse this kind of request.
   Ngóh gok·dāk hohk·haauh yìng·gòi kéuih·jyuht nī·tíng gám ge yìu·kàuh.
      (of an invitation) tèui·chìh. /If I refuse to go, would it be impolite? Yùh·gwó ngóh
   tèui·chìh m̀h·heui, wúih·m̀h·wúih sāt·láih a?
      in other context it is expressed indirectly. /I offered him a drink, but he refused
   it. is expressed as: Ngóh chéng kéuih yám bùi jáu, daahn·haih kéuih m̀h·yám. /The
   manager refused to accept this resignation. is expressed as: Gìng·léih m̀h·jéun kéuih
   chìh·jīk.

regain   /He regained his position. Kéuih dāk·fàan kéuih·ge jīk·waih. /He is regaining
   his strength. Kéuih yáuh·fàan lihk la.

regard   (considered as) /I regard him as my younger brother. Ngóh dong kéuih haih
   ngóh·ge sai·lóu gám. /She is regarded as the best teacher in the school. Hohk·haauh
   go·go dōu yihng·wàih kéuih haih jeui hóu ge sīn·sàang.
      (respect or obey) /Children should have regard for their parents. Sai·mān·jái yìng
   gòi jyùn·juhng kéuih·deih fuh·móuh.
      (think well of) jyùn·juhng. /The students regard him very highly. Dī hohk·sàang hóu
   jyùn·juhng kéuih.
      be well regarded. /He's well regarded here. is expressed as: Kéiih hái nī·syu ge
   mìhng·mohng hóu hóu.
      with regard to, in regard to gwāan·yù, deui·yù. /We'll have to have a little discus-
   sion in regard to that last point. Gwāan·yù jeui hauh gó·yāt·dím, ngóh·deih juhng yiu
   tóu·leuhn·háh. /What is your opinion in regard to this matter? Néih deui·yù nī·gihn
   sih yáuh māt yi·gin a?
      send or give one's regards mahn·hauh. /Send my regards to your father. Tùhng
   ngóh mahn·hauh néih bàh·bā.

regent   sip·jing; the Prince regent sip·jing·wòhng

regime   (form of government) jing·kyùhn

regiment   (unit of troop) tyùhn; regimental commander tyùhn·jéung

region   (section or part of a country) deih·fòng; this region nī·yāt·daai deih·fòng; arctic
   regions bāk·gihk deih·fòng; tropical regions yiht·daai deih·fòng
      (part of the body) abdominal region fūk·bouh; the region of the breast hùng·bouh

register   (in official register) jyu·chaak (VO), dàng·gei; (at a hotel) dàng·gei (at a clinic,
   hospital) gwa·houh. /Have you registered? Néih gwa·jó·houh meih a? (as a trademark)
   jyu·chaak (VO), registered trademark jyuh·chaak sēung·bīu; (as in school) jyu·chaak (VO).
   /There are four hundred students already registered. Yíh·gìng yáuh sei·baak go hohk·

sāang jyu·jó chaak la. (of names) mìhng·chaak; (official) dàng·gei·bóu; **registered letter** gwa·houh·seun; **registered letter with return receipt** sèung·gwa·houh·seun

registrar (of school) jyu·chaak·jyú·yahm

regret (say that one is sorry for). /I regret that I cannot come to your party tonight. Ngóh hóu póuh·hip gàm·máahn bāt·nàhng lèih.
(feel sorry) hó·sīk. /I regret that I lost my dog. Ngóh m̀h·gin·jó jek gáu jàn·haih hó·sīk la.
(repent) hauh·fúi. /I regret that I haven't bought that car. Ngóh hauh·fúi móuh máaih·jó gó·ga chè.

regular (normal, customary) jing·sèuhng ge. /This is the regular procedure. Nī·go haih jing·sèuhng ge sáu·juhk. or expressed by using yìng·gòi (ought). /What is the regular way of writing this kind of letter? Nī·tìng seun yìng·gòi dím sé a?
(orderly) kwài·géui. /He lives a very regular life. Kéuih sàng·wuht dāk hóu kwài·géui.
regular customer suhk·haak·jái. /Treat him well, he is a regular customer. Hóu·hóu·déi jiu·fù kéuih, kéuih haih ngóh·deih ge suhk·haak·jái lèih ga.

regulate (adjust a mechanism) gaau·jéun; (put in good order) jíng·léih

regulation (rule) jèung·chìhng; (order or law) faat·lihng

rehearse (as a play, etc.) pàaih·yín, yáai·kehk, si·yín

reign túng·jih (V); túng·jih ge sìh·doih

rein gèung, máh·gèung (N)

reinforce **reinforce the troops** paai bìng jàng·yùhn, jàng·bìng (VO). /The commander-in-chief has just decided to reinforce the garrison in that area. Júng·si·lihng jing·wah kyuht·dihng paai bìng jàng·yùhn gó·kēui ge sáu·gwān.

reinforcements (additional troops) gau·bìng

reject (a proposal) kéuih·jyuht; (goods, etc.) jèung . . . dá·fàan·jyun·tàuh; (a petition) bok·wùih

rejoice fùn·héi

relapse (of sickness) fuhk faat. /You should be careful to prevent its relapse. Néih yiu síu·sàm fòhng·jí kéuih (or gauh·behng) fuhk·faat.

relate (of problems) sēung·gwàan ge. /These two problems are related. Nī·léuhng go mahn·tàih haih sēung·gwàan ge. (of people) /Are you related (as brothers)? Néih·deih haih·m̀h·haih hìng·daih a? /Are you related (by marriage)? Néih·deih haih·m̀h·haih chān·chīk a?

relation gwāan·haih, gáam·chìhng. /This chapter has no relation to the rest of the book. Nī·yāt·jèung tùhng nī·bún·syù kèih·yùh gok·bouh·fàhn hòuh·mòuh gwàan·haih. /Their relations with the press are excellent. Kéuih·deih tùhng bou·gaai ge gáam·chìhng hóu hóu.
in relation to. /You must judge his work in relation to the circumstances. is expressed as: Néih pài·pìhng kéuih ge gùng·jok ge sìh·hauh yìng·dòng tùhng·sìh séung·dou kéuih ge wàahn·gíng. (In judging his work, at the same time you must think of the circumstances.)
break off relations dyuhn·jyuht . . . gwàan·haih; (of countries) jyuht·gàau, dyuhn·jyuht ngoih·gaau gwàan·haih. /The two countries, therefore, have broken off relations. Yàn·chí léuhng·gwok jyuht·gàau la.

relative **relatives** (kin; members of the same family) ngūk·kéi·yàhn; (not in the same household) tùhng·jùng·ge, tùhng·juhk·ge; (by marriage) chān·chīk. **relatives and friends** chān·chīk·pàhng·yáuh, chàn·yáuh. /They invited all their friends and relatives to the wedding. Kéuih·deih git·fàn ge sìh·hauh chéng·saai gam dò chān·chīk·pàhng·yáuh.

relax   (release from tension) /Relax. M̀h·hóu gam gán·jèung. /Relax your muscles.
Fong·sùng kéuih. /He's always so relaxed. Kéuih géi·sìh dōu·haih gam jì·yàuh ge.

relay   (a message) chyùhn·daaht. /How are you going to relay this message to him?
Nī·go sīu·sīk néih dím·yéung chyùhn·daaht béi kéuih a?
     relay race jip·lihk·choi, jip·lihk·choi·páau

release   (set at liberty) fong, sīk·fong, fong·jó; **release one's hold** fong·sáu, fong·hòi·
sáu

reliable   kaau·dāk·jyuh. /He's very reliable. Kéuih hóu kaau·dāk·jyuh ge.

relics   gú·maht

relief   gau·jai. /The people of that area need relief badly. Gó·yāt·kēui ge yàhn sèui·
yiu jīk·hāk gau·jai.
     (bringing comfort). /He said this medicine brings great relief to him. Kéuih wah
nī·tíng yeuhk lìhng kéuih hóu hóu·dò.

relieve   (give aid to refugees, etc.) gau·jai; (from pain). /Take this pill, it will relieve
your pain. Nī·nāp yeuhk, néih sihk·jó jauh m̀h·wúih gam tung ge la.
     relieve guard or work wuhn·bāan

religion   gaau, jùng·gaau. /What is your religion? Néih seun māt·yéh gaau a? /Is
science a religion? Fò·hohk haih·m̀h·haih jùng·gaau a?
     the Buddhist religion Faht·gaau; **the Catholic religion** Tìn·jyú·gaau; **the Protestant
religion** Gēi·dūk·gaau; **the Mohammedan religion** Wùih·gaau

religious   (devout) sàhn·sàm. /He is a very religious man. Kéuih go yàhn hóu sàhn·sàm
ge.
     religious education jùng·gaau gaau·yuhk; **religious question** jùng·gaau mahn·tàih

relinquish   (give up) fong·hei; **relinquish rights or privileges** fong·hei kyùhn·leih, hei·
kyùhn

rely   (on a person for financial support or decision making) yí·kaau, yí·laaih. /She re-
lies on her elder brother to support her. Kéuih yí·kaau kéuih a·gō wàih·chìh kéuih ge
sàng·wuht.
     (put faith in someone to do something) seun·yahm. /Can we relay upon him to do
this? Ngóh·deih hó·(yíh) m̀h·hó·yíh seun·yahm kéuih jouh nī·gihn sih a?

remain   (stay) làuh. /Why is he remaining in Japan? Dím·gáai kéuih làuh·hái Yaht·bún
a?
     (be left over) jihng·fàan. /There are only two pencils remaining in the box. Háp·
léuih·bihn jí·haih jihng·fàan léuhng·jì yùhn·bāt jē.

remainder   (the part that is left) jihng·fàan gó·dī, jihng·fàan ge. /Cut the cake and give
me a piece, you may have the remainder. Chit gauh béng béi ngóh jihng·fàan gó·dī néih
sihk lā.
     (a number found by subtracting) jihng·fàan. /If you subtract four from six, the re-
mainder is two. Luhk gáam sei jihng·fàan yih.

remains   (that which is left or not used) yuhng·jihng ge (for thing), sihk·jihng ge (for
food). /We are eating the remains of the picnic we had at noontime. Ngóh·deih yìh·gā
sihk·gán gàm·yaht ngaan·jau yéh·chāan sihk·jihng ge yéh.
     (a body after death) sí·tái. /The man's remains have already been buried. Gó·go
yàhn ge sí·tái yíh·gìng màaih·jong·jó la.

remark   (say) góng. /He remarked to his friend that he felt a little sick. Kéuih gong
kéuih ge pàhng·yáuh jì, kéuih yáuh di m̀h·jih·yihn.

remarkable   fèi·sèuhng chēut·sīk(ge), fèi·sèuhng chēut·jung(ge). /He is a very remarkable man. Kéuih haih yāt·go fèi·sèuhng chēut·sīk ge yàhn. /This article is remarkable.
Nī·pìn màhn·jèung fèi·sèuhng chēut·sīk.

remedy   bóu·gau ge fòng·faat. /Is there a remedy for it? Yáuh móuh bóu·gau ge fòng·
faat a? (correct or make right) gói·jeng. /We will remedy the mistake at once. Ngóh·
deih máh·seuhng jauh gói·fàan·jeng kéuih.

remember   gei·dāk, gei·jyuh; (recall) séung·héi (RV). /It was last week, as I remember. Ngóh gei·dāk haih seuhng·go láih·baai. /Do you remember when he said that?
Néih gei·dāk kéuih géi·sìh gám góng·gwo ma? /Remember to turn out the lights. Gei·
jyuh sīk·saai dī dāng kéuih. /I can't remember when he was here. Ngóh séung·m̀h·héi
kéuih géi·sí lèih·gwo la.
      remember <u>someone</u> **to** doih . . . mahn·hauh . . . /Please remember me to your
mother. Doih ngóh mahn·hauh néih mà·mā.

remind   séung·héi. /She reminds me of my teacher. Kéuih lihng ngóh séung·héi ngóh·
ge sīn·sàang lèih.
      remind <u>someone to do something</u> tàih(·séng)·háh. /Please remind me, otherwise I
may forget it. M̀h·gòi néih tàih(·séng)·háh ngóh, yeuhk·m̀h·haih ngóh jauh wúih m̀h·gei·
dāk ge la.

remit   (send money) gei chín (VO), wuih. /I would like to send (remit) some money to
my family. Ngóh séung gei dī chín fàan ngūk·kéi. /How much do you want to send (remit)? Néih séung <u>gei</u> (<u>or</u> wuih) géi·dò a?

remnant   jihng·fàan ge, jihng·lohk ge; **the remnant of the bandits** chak·dóng ge chàahn·
yùh

remonstrate   (advise) hyun, hyun·gaan

remorse   hauh·fui, fui·hahn

remote   (far·off) lìuh·yúhn, yìuh·yúhn. /China was once a remote country to the Westerner, but it isn't anymore. Sài·fòng·yàhn yíh·chìhn yihng·wàih Jùng·gwok haih yāt·go
hóu lìuh·yúhn ge gwok·gà, yìh·gā m̀h·haih la.
      (long past, long ago) **remote times**, seuhng·gú sìh·doih. /In remote times people
lived in caves. Seuhng·gú sìh·doih ge yàhn yuht·gèui·yéh·chyúh.

remove   (of stains, ink spots, etc.) jíng·lāt (RV). /Can these ink spots be removed? Nī·
dī mahk·séui jíng·m̀h·jíng·dāk·lāt a?
      (of traces, clues, etc.). /They removed every trace of their presence before they
left. Kéuih·deih wái·miht·saai yāt·chai ge hàhn·jīk sìn·ji lèih·hòi.
      remove (one's hat or other garments). chèuih. /Please remove your hat. Chéng
néih chèuih·jó déng móu kéuih.
      remove <u>a growth, an appendix, etc.</u> got·jó. /We think this growth should be re-
moved. Ngóh·deih gok·dāk nī·go láu yìng·gòi got·jó kéuih.
      remove <u>an official</u> (by high authority) gaak·jīk, míhn·jīk; (by vote) (nī·chi) móuh syún·
dóu. /He was removed from office. Kéuih (nī·chi) móuh syún·dóu. <u>or</u> Kéuih beih gaak·
jó jīk. <u>or</u> Kéuih beih míhn·jó jīk.
      remove <u>someone from the room</u> **by force** dek . . . chēut·heui, gón . . . chēut·heui.
/He became boisterous and they had to remove him by force. Kéuih chòuh dāk taai gán·
yiu, béi yàhn·deih dek·jó chēut·heui.
      remove <u>objects from someplace</u> bùn; (of installations, as a telephone) chaak.
/We'll have to remove all these chairs first. Ngóh·deih yāt·dihng yiu bùn·hòi·saai nī·
dī yí sìn. /I want my telephone removed. Ngóh séung chaak·jó go dihn·wá kéuih.
      remove <u>a population</u> jèung . . . bùn·heui daih·syu. /We'll have to remove the people
who live in the valley before we can build the dam. Ngóh·deih yāt·dihng sìn yiu jèung
nī·syu ge yàhn bùn·heui daih·syu, sìn·ji héi·dāk nī·douh séui·jaahp.

remove pain jí·tung; **remove prohibitions** hòi·gam; **remove a restriction** hòi·gam; **remove a tooth** tyut·ngàh

remunerate   bou·chàuh, chàuh·làuh

remuneration   bou·chàuh, chàuh·bou, chàuh·làuh·fai; **remuneration for contributors of articles** góu·fai; **remuneration for loss** pùih·sèuhng·fai

renaissance   (revival of art, literature, and learning) màhn·ngaih·fuhk·hîng

renew   /I shall renew my driving license. Ngóh yiu wuhn·ngóh·ge sái·chè láai·sán la. /Do you renew your driving license here in Hong Kong every year or every three years? Hái Hèung·góng nî·syu múih·nîhn wuhn yāt·chi yīk·waahk múih·sàam·nîhn wuhn yāt·chi sái·chè lāai·sán a?

renovate   sàu·jíng·gwo. /The old house will have to be renovated before it is used as a school. Nî·gàan gauh ngūk yāt·dihng yiu sàu·jíng·gwo sìn·ji jouh dāk hohk·haauh.

rent   (of the person who acquires or of the thing transferred) jòu; (of the person who receives payment) jòu·béi, chēut·jòu. /I want to rent a motor boat. Ngóh yiu jòu jek dihn·syùhn·jái. /He rents boats to tourists. Kéuih yáuh syùhn jòu·béi yàuh·haak. /He has boats for rent. Kéuih yáuh syùhn chēut·jòu. /Is there a house for rent nearby? Nî·syu jó·gán yáuh móuh ngūk chēut·jòu a?
  (payment) jòu; **house rent** ngūk·jòu. /How much rent do you pay for the house? Néih múih·yuht béi géi·ngán ngūk·jòu a?
  rent payable in advance seuhng·kèih·jòu; **rent collector** sàu·jòu·yàhn

reorganize   gói·jóu

repair   sàu·jíng, jíng·fàan, sàu·léih, bóu·fàan, jāp·lauh (repair a leak in a house). /I need someone to repair my refrigerator. Ngóh yiu chéng go yàhn sàu·jíng syut·gwaih. /Can you repair my radio? Néih hó·yíh tùhng ngóh jíng·fàan go sàu·yàm·gèi ma? /The car only needs minor repairs. is expressed as: Nî·ga chè sáu·wàih sàu·léih·háh jauh dāk la. /A complete repair job will take ten days. is expressed as: Yùhn·chyùhn sàu·léih·hóu yiu sahp·yaht ji dāk. /Can you repair my shoes in a hurry? Néih hó·yíh jīk·hāk tùhng ngóh bóu·fàan deui hàaih ma? /Can you find a man to repair the leak of this house? Néih hó·yíh tùhng ngóh wán go yàhn lèih jāp·lauh ma?

repay   (money) wàahn, wàahn·fàan: **repay debt** wàahn·jaai; **repay money** wàahn·chín; (requite) bou·daap; (indemnify) pùih, pùih·fàan

repeat   expressed as 'again' joi (referring to a future action) or yauh (referring to a past action), with the specific verb for the thing done a second time; sometimes expressed adverbially as repeatedly joi sàam gám, joi chi gám, fàan fàan fūk fūk gám. /I am told the play will be repeated next week, is it true? Yáuh yàhn wah nî·chēut hei hah·go láih·baai joi jouh yāt·chi, haih·mh·haih a? /He repeated what he had just said. Kéuih jèung kéuih jing·wah só·góng·ge syut·wah yauh góng·jó yāt·chi. /He repeats the same instruction over and over again. Kéuih joi·sàam·gám gaau dī yàhn dím jouh.
  (pass on by word of mouth) góng béi daih·yih·go jî. /Don't repeat what I've told you. Ngóh góng béi néih tèng ge syut·wah mh·hóu góng·béi daih·yih·go·yàhn jî.
  repeat something **after** someone gàn·jyuh . . . góng. /Repeat this after me. Gàn·jyuh ngóh góng.

repent   hauh·fui, chaam·fui; **repent a fault** fui·gwo; **repent and reform** fui·gói

repetition   /This is a repetition. is expressed verbally: Nî·go chùhng·fūk·jó.

replace   (take the place of) doih·tai; (put back) jài·fàan yùhn·lòih ge waih·ji

reply   (verbal) daap, wùih·daap, daap·fūk. /It is wiser to make no reply to his angry words. Kéuih faat ngok naauh yàhn ge sîh·hauh, néih jeui hóu mh·daap kéuih. /You should reply to the question your teacher asked. Néih yîng·dòng wùih·daap (or daap·

fūk) néih sīn·sàang mahn ge mahn·tàih. /What is his reply? Kéuih dím daap·fūk ga?
/How did you reply to this? Néih dím·yéung daap·fūk ga?
   (written) wùih·seun (VO). /Sorry, I didn't reply to your letter. Deui·m̀h·jyuh, ngóh
móuh wùih néih ge seun. /Do you know why he didn't reply to our letter? Néih jì·dou
kéuih dím·gáai m̀h·wùih ngóh·dcih gc scun ma?

report   bou·gou (N); bou·gou (V). /It's reported that the fighting is still going on there.
   Jing·wah sàu·dóu go bou·gou wah gó·syu juhng dá·gán. /It is reported that he is wasting
   money. Yáuh yàhn wah béi ngóh tèng (or ngóh jip·dóu yāt·go bou·gou) kéuih lohng·fai·jó
   hóu·dò chín. /I'll report on this matter in our next meeting. Ngóh hah·chi hòi·wúi bou·
   gou nī·gihn sih·gon. /Why don't you report this to the police? Dím·gáai néih m̀h·bou
   (·gou) chàai·gún (see 'police' or 'chàai·gún') nē?
      (of a reporter or correspondent) is often expressed as write an account sé·sàn·mán.
   /He reports financial news. Kéuih sé gìng·jai sàn·mán. /He reported the fire for his
   paper. Kéuih jèung fó·jūk ge chìhng·yìhng sé·jó dyuhn sàn·mán béi kéuih·deih ge bou·
   gún.
      hear a report (rumor) that tèng·màhn·wah, tèng·gin·wah. /I heard a report that he
   is resigning, is it true? Ngóh tèng·màhn·wah kéuih yiu chìh·jīk boh, haih·m̀h·haih jàn
   ga?
      report card gà·tìhng bou·gou·bíu, sìhng·jīk·dāan

reporter   (of news) gei·jé, sàn·màhn gei·jé, fóng·yùhn

represent   (act for; politically) doih·bíu; (in court) chēut·tìhng. /He has represented us
   in convention for years. Kéuih doih·bíu ngóh·deih chēut·jihk daaih·wúi hóu·dò nìhn la.
   /Who will represent the defendant? Bīn·go doih·bíu beih·gou chēut·tìhng a?
      (symbolize) doih·bíu. /What does this symbol represent? Nī·go fùh·houh doih·bíu
   māt·yéh a? or it is expressed as: Nī·go fùh·houh haih māt·yéh yi·si a? (This symbol
   is of what meaning?)
      (report, make out). /He was represented to me as a first·rate teacher. is expressed
   as: Yàhn·deih góng ngóh jì kéuih haih yāt·go fèi·sèuhng hóu ge sīn·sàang.
      (exemplify). /He doesn't represent the typical miser. is expressed as: Kéuih m̀h·
   syun·dāk·haih jàn·jeng ge gù·hòhn·gwái.

representative   doih·bíu

repress   (one's feelings) ngaat·jai; repress a laugh yáhn·jyuh·siu; repress anger yáhn·
   hei

reprimand   (reprove) naauh, wah

reprint   (a second printing) joi·báan ge. /This is a reprint. Nī·go haih joi·báan ge.

reproach   (scold) naauh

reproduce   (a printed article) jyún·joi. /This article is reproduced from an American
   magazine. Nī·pìn màhn·jèung haih yàuh yāt·bún Méih·gwok jaahp·ji jyún·joi ge.
      (biological) fàahn·jihk. /Rabbits reproduce rapidly. Tòuh·jái fàahn·jihk dāk hóu
   faai.
      yuhng . . . V chēut·leih. /Can you reproduce this painting for me on silk? Néih hó·
   m̀h·hó·yíh yuhng sî·faat jeung ni·fūk wá sàu·chēut·lèih a?

reproductive   reproductive organs sàang·jihk·hei, sàang·jihk hei·gùn

reprove   (scold) naauh, wah

reptile   pàh·chùhng, pàh·chùhng·leuih ge duhng·maht

republic   (a nation) guhng·wòh·gwok. /China is a republic. Jùng·gwok hah yāt·go guhng·
   wòh·gwok. The Republic of China Jùng·wàh·màhn·gwok; The People's Republic of China
   Jùng·wàh·yàhn·màhn·guhng·wòh·gwok; the Republicans Guhng·woh·dóng·yàhn; the Republican party Guhng·wòh·dóng

repulse   (an enemy) gīk·teui

reputation   mîhng·sîng, mîhng·yuh: **bad reputation** m̀h·hóu·mîhng·sîng

request   chéng; (demand) yìu·kàuh; (pleading) chíng·kàuh; (beg) kàuh. /We would like to request further financial assistance. Ngóh·deih séung joi chíng dò·síu jèun·tip. /He requested us to take care of his child. Kéuih chíng(·kàuh) ngóh·deih jiu·liuh kéuih ge sai·mān·jái. /The student requested to postpone the examination till next week. Hohk·sāang chéng·kàuh hah·go láih·baai sìn·ji háau·si.
    a request chíng·kàuh; (written) sàn·chíng·syù; or expressed verbally as above. /Please file a written request. Chéng néih sé yāt·fahn sàn·chíng·syù lèih. /I am writing you at the request of a friend. Yáuh go pàhng·yáuh tok ngóh sé nī·fùng seun béi néih.

require   (demand something) sái (question), m̀h sái (negative), yiu (positive). /Does it require a deposit? Sái·m̀h·sái béi dehng a? /No. Mh·sái. /It does. Yiu béi dehng.
    (need) yiu, sèui·yiu. /How much do you require? Néih yiu (or sèui·yiu) géi·dò a?
    require someone to do something yiu, kwai·dihng. /They required us to take an examination first. Kéuih·deih yiu ngóh·deih sìn háau·si sìn. /The students are required (by the school) to wear uniforms. Hohk·haauh kwài·dihng hohk·sāang yiu jeuk jai·fuhk.

requisites   (things) bīt·sèui·bán; (courses) bīt·sāu·fō; (circumstances) tìuh·gín

requite   (to repay a benefit) bou·daap, bou: **to requite evil with good** yíh·sihn·bou·ngok, yíh·dāk·bou·yun; (to repay an injury) bou·sàuh, bou·fuhk

resale   jyún·maaih

rescind   chit·sìu, chéui·sìu

rescue   gau; (from poverty, famine, disasters, etc.) gau·jai

research   yîhn·gau. /He is doing research on racial discrimination. Kéuih yîhn·gau·gán yàhn·júng·kèih·sih ge mahn·tàih.

resemblance   sèung·chíh (see resemble)

resemble   hóu sèung·chíh, hóu·chíh. /They two resemble each other. Kéuih·deih léuhng·go hóu sèung·chíh. /You resemble very much your elder sister. Néih hóu·chíh néih gā·jē.

reserve   (set aside or hold) làuh·fàan. /How about reserving this day for an outing with the students? Làuh·fàan nī·yaht tùhng dī hohk·sāang heui léuih·hàhng hóu ma?
    (book) dihng. /Would you please call the theater to reserve four seats for us? Chéng néih dá·dihn·wá gó·gàan hei·yún tùhng ngóh·deih dihng sei·go wái.

reservoir   séui·tòhng, chūk·séui·chìh

reside   (dwell) jyuh

residence   (abode) jyuh·jáak, jyuh·gā

resident   gèui·màhn; **foreign residents** kìuh·màhn, ngoih·kìuh; **residential area** jyuh·jaahk·kēui; **residential dwelling** jyuh·gā·ngūk

resign   (as office) chîh·jīk. /He has already resigned. Kéuih yíh·gìng chìh·jó jīk la.

resist   (an attack, disease) dái·kong

resistance   (to an attack) dái·kong; (to disease) dái·kong·lihk

resolute   (resolved) gìn·kyut

resolution   (resoluteness, firmness) kyut·sàm; **make a resolution** hah kyut·sàm. /I've made a New Year's resolution to quit drinking. Ngóh sàn·nín hah·jó go kyut·sàm yíh·hauh m̀h·yám·jáu la.

(adopted by a meeting) yi·kyut·ngon, kyut·yih. /This is the resolution of the last meeting. Nī·go haih seuhng·yāt·chi wuih·yi ge yi·kyut·ngon.

resolve   (a problem) gáai·kyut; (decide) kyut·dihng; **resolve a chemical compound** fàn gáai; **resolve by vote** bíu·kyut

resourceful   /He is very resourceful. Kéuih hóu yáuh baahn·faat (or hóu·yáuh·bá·pau) ge.

resources   (of a country) fu·yùhn, jì·yùhn, chòih·yùhn; (financial means) chòih·lihk

respect   (as persons) jyùn·ging; (as another's right) jyùn·juhng

respiration   táu·hei, fū·kāp; **artificial respiration** yàhn·gùng·fū·kāp

respond   (answer) wùih·daap; (to treatment) fáan·ying

responsibility   jaak·yahm; **bear responsibility of** fuh·jaak; **sense of responsibility** jaak·yahm·sàm

responsible   jaak·yahm hóu chúhng ge, juhng·yiu ge. /It is a very responsible position. Gó·go jìk·waih jaak·yahm hóu chúhng ge. or Gó·go haih yāt·go hóu juhng·yiu ge jìk·waih.
(trustworthy) hó·kaau ge. /I consider him a thoroughly responsible person. Ngóh yihng·wàih kéuih haih yāt·go fèi·sèuhng hó·kàau ge yàhn.
be responsible for (give rise to). /His good conduct was responsible for the award. is expressed as: Yàn·waih kéuih bán·hahng hóu só·yíh kéuih dāk·jéung.
be responsible for (accountable for). /You are responsible for the books you take out of the library. Néih hái tòuh·syù·gún je chēut·lèih ge syù jauh yàuh néih fuh·jaak ge la.
be responsible to. /I'm only responsible to the general manager. Ngóh jí·haih deui júng·gìng·léih fuh·jaak ge jē.

rest   táu, yāu·sīk. /Rest awhile. Táu yāt·jahn·gāan. or Yāu·sīk yāt·jahn·gāan. /I hope you rest well. Ngóh hèi·mohng néih hóu·hóu·déi táu·háh. /Try to rest your eyes. Mì·màaih sèung ngáahn táu·háh.
rest one's head on jám·hái. /You may rest your head on this pillow. Néih hó·yíh jèung go tàuh jám·hái nī·go jám·tàuh·syu.
rest against (lean against) ngàai·hái (for people); baahng·hái (for things). /Why don't you rest against the wall? Dím·gáai néih m̀h·ngàai·hái buhng chèuhng·syu nē? /Let's rest the ladder against this wall. Jèung buhng tài·wáang baahng·hái nī·buhng chèuhng·syu.
rest in. /Our hope rests in you. Ngóh·deih ge hèi·mohng yùhn·chyùhn jí·yi néih la.
rest assured that fong·sàm. /You may rest assured that we'll take care of it. Fong·sām lā, ngóh·deih yāt·dihng baahn·tóh kéuih ge.
rest (freedom from activity) is expressed verbally as in the first definition. /A little rest will do you a lot of good. Néih táu·háh jauh hóu·hóu·dò ge la.
the rest (remainder) juhng·yáuh·dī, kèih·yùh ge, jihng·fàan·gó·dī, kèih·tà ge. /Where is the rest of the gang? Juhng·yáuh·dī·yàhn hái bīn·syu a? /I'll do the rest of the job. Jihng·fàan·gó·dī (or kèih·tà·ge yéh) ngóh lèih jou là. /I only understood a little and guessed the rest. Ngóh jí·haih jí·dou dī jē, kèih·tà ge dōu haih gú ge.

restaurant   (selling western food) chāan·gún, sāi·chāan·gún; (rather high class) jáu·làuh, jáu·gā; (tea·house) chàh·gēui, chàh·sāt

restore   fùi·fuhk, fùi·fuhk·fàan: **restore to the former condition** fùi·fuhk·yùhn·johng; **restore friendship** fùi·fuhk gáam·chìhng; **restore diplomatic relations** fùi·fuhk ngoih ·gàau gwàan·haih; fùi·fuhk bòng·gàau
(health) hóu·fàan. /When his health is restored, he will leave the hospital. Kéuih yāt hóu·fàan jauh chēut·yún la.
restored to office fuhk·jīk; **restored to the throne** fuhk·waih

restrain   (control) yeuk·chūk, gún·chūk, yáhn·jyuh: restrain oneself yeuk·chūk jih·gēi;
   restrain a child gún·chūk sai·mān·jái; **could not restrain one's laughter** yáhn·m̀h·jyuh
   siu

restrict   (limit) haahn·jai; (as one's vision) jè·jyuh

restriction   haahn·jai, haahn·douh

result   (consequence) git·gwó, git·guhk; (of an experiment, analysis, etc.) sìhng·jīk; (of
   medicine) gùng·haauh

resume   (recommence) fùi·fuhk: **the work resumes** fùi·fuhk·gùng·jok; (continue) gai·juhk:
   the train resumes fó·chè gai·juhk hòi·hàhng

resurrection   fuhk·wuht: **the Resurrection of Jesus** Yèh·sōu·fuhk·wuht

retail   lìhng·gù, sáan·maaih: **retail business** lìhng·gù sàang·yi, sáan·maaih sàang·yi;
   retail price sáan·maaih ge ga·chìhn, lìhng·gù ge ga·chìhn

retailer   lìhng·sauh·sēung, lìhng·gū·sēung

retain   (keep back) làuh·fàan; (continue to hold) bóu·làuh; **retain in office** làuh·yahm;
   (to ask a friend to stay for a meal) làuh go pàhng·yáuh sihk·faahn

retaliate   bou·fuhk, wàahn·sáu (to fight back with hands)

retard   (delay) jó·chìh; (impede) fòhng·ngoih: **retard progress** fòhng·ngoih jeun·bouh
   mentally retarded child baahk·chì·jái

retina   ngáahn·kàuh·móhng·mók

retinue   chèuih·yùhn, sih·chùhng

retire   (from service) gou·teui; (on account of age) gou·lóuh; (go to bed) heui fan·gaau

retreat   teui; (of an army) teui·bìng; **retreat to a position and make a stand** teui·sáu . . .
   (PW)

return   fàan·lèih, fàan·heui. /When will he return? Kéuih géi·sí fàan·lèih a? /I have
   to return to my house for the key. Ngóh yiu fàan·heui ngūk·kéi ló só·sìh.
      return something wàahn·fàan. /Will you return it (to me) when you're through?
   Chéng néih yuhng·yùhn wàahn·fàan·béi ngóh. /Have you returned the book to the library?
   Néih wàahn·fàan bún syù béi tòuh·syù·gún meih a?
      return (time of getting back) fàan·lèih ge sìh·hauh; (act of getting back) expressed
   verbally as in paragraph one. /I'll take this matter up on my return. Ngóh fàan·lèih
   jauh baahn nī·gihn sih. /His return was eagerly awaited by everyone. Go·go dōu mohng
   kéuih fàan·lèih.
      returns (results) git·gwó, sàu·yahp. /Did the election returns come in yet? Syún·
   géui ge git·gwó yáuh sīu·sīk meih a? /The returns from the exhibition were $500.00.
   Jín·láahm·wúi ge sàu·yahp haih n̄gh·baak·mān.
      return a courtesy wàahn·láih; **return a favor** bou·daap; **return a salute** wàahn·láih;
   return a visit wùih·baai; **return evil for good** yàn·jèung·sàuh·bou; **return good for evil**
   yíh·dāk·bou·yun; **return to one's country** wùih·gwok, fàan·jóu·gà; **return in victory** dāk·
   sing·gwài·lòih, hói·syùhn; **return to China** fàan·Jùng·gwok, fàan·tòhng·sàan

Reuters   Louh·tau·séh (news agency)

reveal   (let out a secret) sit·lauh. /The news was revealed by a cabinet minister. Nī·
   go sīu·sīk haih yāt·go bouh·jéung sit·lauh chēut·lèih ge.
      (indicate, display, or show) yín·chēut. Her voice revealed her nervousness. Kéuih
   ge sèng yín·chēut kéuih ge sàm hóu lyuhn.
      (by a deity) kái·sih: **Book of Revelations** Kái·sih·lúk

revenge   bou·sàuh

revenue   (of an individual) sàu·yahp, jeun·hohng, yahp·sīk; (of the state) seui·sàu, (customs) gwàan·seui; **revenue office** seui·mouh·gúk; **revenue stamp** yan·fā

revere   jyùn·ging

reverence   **show reverence to** (a person), jyùn·ging . . . ; **show reverence** (to God) ging·
waih . . . ; **show reverence** (to parents) haau·ging

Reverend   (Protestant) muhk·sī

reverse   /Write on the reverse side of the paper. is expressed as: Fáan·jyun jèung·jí
leih sé. /Move your car in reverse. Jèung ga chè tan·hauh. /Let's reverse it (to
turn it upside down). Fáan·jyun kéuih. or Dou·jyun kéuih.

review   wàn·jaahp: **review a lesson** wàn·jaahp gùng·fo; pìhng·leuhn: **review a book**
pìhng·leuhn yāt·bún syù; gím·tóu: **review a matter** gím·tóu yāt·gihn sih; **review troops**
gím·yuht, yuht·bìng

revise   (manuscript) gaau·jing; **revised edition** gaau·jing·báan, gaau·jing·bún

revival   (of learning, art, religion, etc.) fuhk·hìng: **the revival of the classical music**
gú·dín yàm·ngohk ge fuhk·hìng

revive   (recover life) fāan·sàang (V.I.), (from a faint) séng·fāan (V.I.)

revolt   jouh·fáan (V.I.); bouh·duhng (N); **to raise a righteous revolt** héi·yih

revolution   (political) gaak·mihng; (of a planet) gùng·jyún

revolutionary   **revolutionary party** gaak·mihng·dóng; **revolutionaries** gaak·mihng·dóng·
yàhn

revolve   (rotate) jyun

revolver   jó·léun, sáu·chēung (M: jì)

reward   bàan·jahng (by an institution or government); dá·séung (V) (by a master to a
servant, etc.). /We should reward him with a trophy. Ngóh·deih yìng·gòi bàan·jahng
yāt·go jéung·jēung béi kéuih. /Should we reward them for their service? Ngóh·deih
sái·m̀h·sái dá·séung kéuih·deih a?
    get a reward dāk·jéung. /You deserve a reward for your hard work. Néih gam
kàhn·lihk yìng·fahn dāk·jéung.
    give a reward (for the recovery of something lost or for the capture of fugitives)
chēut·fà·hùhng. /I offer five dollars reward for finding my pen. Ngóh chēut ńgh·go
ngàhn·chín fà·hùhng wán·fàan ngóh jī bāt.
    reward the troops (after a campaign) wai·lòuh gwàn·déui

rewrite   (joi) sé·gwo (V)

rhetoric   sàu·chìh·hohk

rheumatic   **rheumatic pains** fūng·sāp·tung

rheumatism   fūng·sāp, fūng·sāp·jing

rhinoceros   sài·ngàuh (M: jek)

rhyme   wán (N); ngaat·wán (VO)

rib   (anat.) lak·gwāt; (of meat) pàaih·gwāt (pork ribs)

ribbon   sī·dáai; (of typewriter) mahk·séui·dáai

rice   (growing in the field) wòh; (rice grain) gūk; (hulled) máih; (cooked) faahn; (well-
hulled rice) baahk·máih

rich   yáuh·chín, fut·cheuk. /His father is very rich. Kéuih lóuh·dauh hóu yáuh·chín.

/Most of the rich families are living in this area. Yáuh·chín ge yàhn·gà dò·sou jyuh·hái nī·kēui·syu.

(abounding) fùng·fu; (productive) hóu·dò, fèih, cháan·leuhng jeui dò. /Spinach is rich in iron. Bò·choi léuih·bihn tit·jāt hóu dò. /This country is rich in natural resources. Nī·go gwok·gà ge tìn·yìhn maht·cháan hóu fùng·fu. /This is a very rich bean land. Nī·faai deih jung dáu hóu fèih. /This is one of the richest oyster fields in South China. Nī·daat haih Jùng·gwok nàahm·bouh yāt·go cháan hòuh jeui dò ge deih·fòng.

the rich yáuh·chín·láu, fut·láu

rickshaw chē·jái (M: ga)

riddle gú, mái. /I have a riddle for you. Ngóh yáuh go gú béi néih gú·háh. /Whoever can answer this riddle, I'll treat him to a meal. Bīn·go gú·dóu nī·go gú (or Bīn·go chàai·dóu nī·go mái), ngóh chéng kéuih sihk·faahn.

ride (as a horse, etc.) kèh; (in a carriage, etc.) chóh; (as a bicycle) kèh, yáai. /Do you know how to ride a horse? Néih wúih kèh·máh ma? /Do you want to have a ride in this new car? Néih séung chóh·háh nī·ga sān·chē ma? /Shall we ride to the end of the line? Ngóh·deih haih·m̀h·haih yāt·jihk chóh·dou méih·jaahm a? /Do you like to ride a bike? Néih jùng·yi kèh dāan·chē ma?
(of the vehicle) hàahng. /This car rides smoothly. Nī·ga chè hàahng dāk hóu dihng.
a ride. /It's a short bus ride. Chóh yāt·jahn·gāan bā·sí jauh dou la. /They just went out for a ride. Kéuih·deih ngāam·ngāam chēut·jó heui yàuh chè·hó.

ridge bui·jek; **ridge of a mountain** sàan·jek; **ridge of a roof** ngūk·jek

ridicule dai (V)

ridiculous hóu·siu. /It's ridiculous. Jàn·haih hóu·siu la!

rifle bouh·chēung, lòih·fūk·chēung (M: jì)

right (correct, proper) ngāam. /That's right! Ngāam la. /Is this the right way? Gám ngāam·m̀h·ngāam a? /You're (i.e. What you have said is) absolutely right. Néih góng dāk hóu ngāam. /Is this the right answer? Nī·go wùih·daap ngāam·m̀h·ngāam a? /Is this the right time (on this clock)? Nī·go jūng ngāam ma?
(of a size) ngāam. /This one is the right size. Nī·go chek·chyun ngāam la.
(of good weather) hóu. /We'll leave tomorrow if the weather is right. Yùh·gwó tìng·yaht tìn·sìh hóu ngóh·deih jauh héi·chìhng la.
(opposite of left) yauh; **right hand** yauh·sáu; **right hand side** yauh·sáu·bihn. /Take the road on the right. Hàahng yauh·bihn (or yauh·sáu·bihn) gó·tìuh louh. /It seems my right foot is a little larger than my left one. Ngóh jek yauh·geuk hóu·chíh daaih·gwo ngóh jek jó·geuk dī.
(of one's mind). /It seems he isn't in his right mind this morning. Gàm·jiu·jóu kéuih ge nóuh·gàn hóu·chíh m̀h·haih géi chìng·chó.
(of something that has two sides) jing·mihn. /This tablecloth has a right side and a wrong side, don't put it on wrong. Nī·jèung tói·bou yáuh jing·mihn yáuh fáan·mihn m̀h·hóu pòu·cho·jó.
(true) haih. /Mr. Li says that you have a new car, is that right? Léih sīn·sàang wah néih yáuh ga sān chē boh, haih·m̀h·haih a?
(satisfactory) hóu hóu, móuh māt·sih. /His health is all right, since he gave up drinking. Jih·chùhng kéuih gaai·jáu jì·hauh, kéuih sàn·tái hóu·hóu (or móuh·māt·sih).
(precisely) jauh. /The book is right there on the shelf. Bún syu jauh·hái go syù·gá·syu jē.
(immediately) jauh, yāt·jihk (straight ahead). /I'll be right there. Ngóh jauh lèih. /Go right in. Yāt·jihk hàahng·yahp·heui lā. /Go right ahead. (when answering a request for permission to do something) Dāk.
(completely) yāt·jihk. /They fought right to the end. Kéuih·deih yāt·jihk dá·dou·dái.
a right (privilege; legal) kyùhn, kyùhn·leih; **right of ownership** só·yáuh·kyùhn; **right**

of priority yāu·sìn·kyùhn; **civil rights** màhn·kyùhn; **right to vote** syún·géui·kyùhn, tàuh·
piu·kyùhn; **sovereign right** jyú·kyùhn. (social) kyùhn. /I have a right to go if I wish.
Yùh·gwó ngóh yiu heui, ngóh yáuh kyùhn heui. /You have no right to behave like this.
Néih móuh kyùhn gám jouh.
    right away gón·gán, jík·hāk, máh·seuhng, all followed by jauh. /Let's go right
away or we'll be late. Ngóh·deih gón·gán heui, yeuhk·m̀h·haih jauh chìh la.
    right now jing·joih. /He's busy right now. Kéuih jing·joih m̀h·dāk·hàahn.
    all right hóu (fàan), seuhn·leih gáai·kyut, hóu. /The doctor said you'd be all right
in a few days. Yī·sāng wah chìh·sàam·léuhng·yaht néih jauh hóu·fàan ge la. /Don't
worry, everything will turn out all right. M̀h·sái dāam·sàm, yeuhng·yeuhng sih dōu
wúih seuhn·leih gáai kyut ge la.

righteous   (upright) jùng·jihk; (equitable) gùng·jing

righteousness   jing·yih

rigid   (stiff) gáng; (strict) yìhm

rigorous   (stern) yìhm, yìhm·gaak; (harsh) yìhm·laih

rim   bīn (N)

ring   (sound) héung. /Has the bell (for class) rung yet? Séuhng·tòhng·jūng héung·jó
meih a? /The phone is ringing. Dihn·wá héung.
    ring something (cause to sound) gahm (by pressing a button); dá (by striking). /Some-
one is ringing the doorbell. Yáuh yàhn gahm jūng. /Have you rung the bell? Néih dá·
jó jūng meih a?
    (on a finger) gaai·jí (M: jek); **jade ring** yuhk·gaai·jí; **gold ring** gām·gaai·jí; **engage-
ment ring** dihng·fàn gaai·jí; **wedding ring** git·fàn gaai·jí; **earring** yìh·wáan (M: deui,
fu 'pair')
    (any circular band) hyūn; **key ring** só·sìh·hyūn
    (circular arrangement) hyūn. /They stand in a ring. Kéuih·deih kéih·sèhng yāt·go
hyūn.
    (gang) dóng, móhng; **the ring of blackmarketeers** wòhng·ngàuh·dóng; **a spy ring**
gaan·dihp·móhng
    give someone **a ring** dá go dihn·wá béi . . . /Give me a ring tomorrow. Tìng·yaht
dá·go dihn·wá béi ngóh.

ringworm   sín; **have ringworm** sàang·sín

rinse   nóng. /Rinse it (clothing) until it's clean. Nóng gòn·jehng dī sāam kéuih. /Use
warm water to rinse your mouth. Yuhng nyúhn·séui nóng·háu.

riot   bouh·duhng

rioter   bouh·tòuh, bouh·duhng·fahn·jí

rip   (by tearing) chaak·hòi: **rip open a letter** chaak·hòi fùng seun

ripe   suhk; (lit. & fig.) sìhng·suhk

ripple   (of water) bò·màhn; (form into ripples) héi bò·màhn

rise   (of a person) héi·sàn (get up in the morning); kéih·héi·sàn (get up from sitting).
/The students all rose as we went in. Ngóh·deih yahp·heui gó·jahn·sí, dī hohk·sāang go·
go dōu kéih·héi sàn.
    (of the sun) chēut. /Has the sun risen yet? Yaht·táu chēut meih a?
    (of prices) héi, héi·ga. /Prices are still rising. Dī maht·ga juhng·haih héi·gán.
/Prices are rising sharply. Dī maht·ga héi dāk hóu gán·yiu. /The price has risen
again! Yauh héi·ga la!
    (of water) séui jeung, séui daaih. /The river will rise in about an hour. Juhng yáuh
yāt·dím·jūng gam·seuhng·háh jauh séui jeung (or séui daaih) la.

(move upward) sìng·séuhng·heui; fèi·séuhng·heui (flying, as a bird or plane). /The balloon rose slowly. Go hei·kàuh maahn·máan gám sìng·séuhng·heui. /The airplane rose and circled the field. Ga fēi·gèi fèi·séuhng·heui jî·hauh hái seuhng·bihn dāu·hyūn. **rise to fame** sìhng·mìhng. /He rose to fame overnight. Kéuih yāt·yeh sìhng·mìhng. (of temperature) gòu. /There was a sudden rise in his temperature this morning. Gàm·jîu·jóu kéuih ge yiht·douh fāt·yìhn gòu·héi·séuhng·lèih.

risk   (danger) ngàih·hím; **run a risk** mouh·hím; **risk one's life** mouh·hím, pìng·mehng

rite   láih: **funeral rites** jong·láih

rival   (compete with) gihng·jàng; dihk·sáu, deui·sáu (N); **rival in love** chìhng·dihk

river   hòh, gòng (M: tîuh). **Yellow River** Wòhng·hòh; **Yangtze River** Chèuhng·gòng, Yèuhng·jí·gòng; **Pearl River** Jyū·gòng; **river bank** hòh·bīn, gōng·bīn; **river bed** hòh·dái; **river valley** làuh·wihk: **the Yangtze valley** Cheuhng·gong làuh·wihk; **river water** hòh·séui

rivulet   hòh·jái, chūng (M: tîuh)

road   louh; (thoroughfare) máh·louh; (highway) gùng·louh; (main road) daaih·louh; (side road) síu·louh

roam   **roaming from place to place** dou·chyúh·làuh·lohng, làuh·lèih·lóng·dohng

roar   daaih·sèng gám giu; (with laughter) daaih·sèng gám siu; (of animals) giu; **the roar of cannon** paau·sèng lùhng·lùhng; **the roar of thunder** lèuih·sèng lùhng·lùhng

roast   sîu: **roast beef** sîu·ngàuh·yuhk; **roasted pig** sîu·jyù; **roasted duck** sîu·ngáap; **roast chicken** sîu·gāi; **roast goose** sîu·ngó

rob   chéung, dá·gip. /I've been robbed. Ngóh béi yàhn chéung·yéh. or (fig.) Ngóh béi yàhn wán·jó bahn. /The bank was robbed. Gó·gàan ngàhn·hòhng béi yàhn dá·gip.

robber   chahk; **robber's den** chahk·dau

robe   pòuh (M: gihn)

robust   (strong and sturdy) fèih·jong; (healthy) jong·gihn

roc   daaih·pàahng·níuh (M: jek)

rock   sehk (M: gauh); lūk: **rocking** lūk·lèih·lūk·heui; **rocking chair** lūk·yí

rocket   fó·jin (M: jî)

rod   **fishing rod** diu·yùh·gōn; **iron rod** tit·jī (M: jî)

roe   (fish eggs) yùh·chēun

rogue   (rascal) gwòng·gwan

roll   (turn over and over and move ahead) lūk. /Roll the barrel over here. Lūk go túng gwo·lèih nī·syu. /The ball rolled down the hill. Go bō lūk·jó lohk sàan·geuk. /Don't let the baby roll out of bed. Mh·hóu béi bìh·bī lūk·lohk chòhng.
   (shape a flat thing into a spiral) gyún·héi; (sleeves or pant legs only) ngaap·héi. /Roll up the rug. Gyún·héi go deih·jin kéuih. /Roll up that map. Gyún·héi gó·fūk deih·tòuh kéuih. /Roll up your sleeves. Ngaap·héi go sàam·jauh kéuih.
   (press something down by rolling something over it) lūk (if with a large roller, making it flat); ngàahn (make thin by rolling something over it). /We need a roller to roll it. Ngóh·deih yiu yáuh go lūk lèih lūk·háh kéuih. /Can you roll it thinner? Néih hó·yíh ngàahn bohk·dī ma?
   (of a ship) ngòuh. /The ship rolled violently. Jek syùhn ngòuh dāk hóu gán·yiu.
   roll something **into a ball** (with palms or fingers) chò·sèhng yāt·go bō gám
   a roll (list of names) mìhng·dāan; **call the roll** dím·méng. /I'm going to call the roll now. Ngóh yìh·gā dím·méng la.

a roll of gyún. /I want two rolls of toilet paper. Ngóh yiu léuhng·gyún chi·só·jí.

Roman   **Roman empire** Lòh·máh dai·gwok; **Roman letters** Loh·mah·jih; **Roman numerals** Lòh·máh sou·jih

Romanization   Lòh·máh·pīng·yām

romance   (fiction) síu·syut, chyùhn·kèih; **the Romance of the Three Kingdoms** (famous Chinese novel) Sàam·gwok (yín·yih); (love affair) lòh·maahn·sí, lohng·maahn·sí

roof   (of a house) ngūk·déng, ngáh·mín; (of a building) làuh·déng; **to roof** pòu·ngáh·mín; **roof of the mouth** seuhng·ngohk; **roof garden** tìn·tói fà·yún

room   fóng (M: gāan). /How many rooms does this house have? Nī·gāan ngūk yáuh géi·dò·gàan fóng a? **room to let** yáuh·fóng·chēut·jòu
    (space or place) deih·fòng; wái (seat). /There is no room to put these things. Móuh deih·fòng jài nī·dī yéh la. /Is there any room for her to sit down? Gó·syu yáuh móuh wái béi kéuih chóh a? /I see little room for improvement. is expressed as: Ngóh tái móuh māt hóu gói ge la.

root   (of plant, tooth, etc.) gàn (M: tìuh): **the root of a disease** behng·gàn; **the root of a tooth** ngàh·gàn; **the root of a tree** syuh·gàn; **the root of the trouble** woh·gàn
    root out cháan·chyùh. /I think it is impossible to root out their bad habits in a short time. Ngóh gú joih dyún·sìh·gàan·noih móuh·faat·jí cháan·chyùh kéuih·deih ge m̀h·hóu ge jaahp·gwaan.

rope   síng (M: tìuh)

rose   (flower) mùih·gwai, mùih·gwai·fā; (color) fán·hùhng·sīk ge; **wild rose** yéh·mùih gwai

rot   (as wood) laahn; (as meat) mùih

rotary   **rotary action** jyun; **Rotary Club** fùh·lèuhn·séh

rotate   (of a wheel) jyun

rotation   **in rotation** lèuhn·láu; **to do something in rotation** lèuhn·láu jouh; **rotation of a planet** jih·jyún

rotten   (decay) laahn; (very bad) yáih

rouble   lòuh·bou

rouge   yīn·jì

rough   (not smooth-surfaced) hàaih. /The piece of leather is too rough. Nī·faai péi taai hàaih.
    (of water). /The water is pretty rough today. Gàm·yaht lohng hóu daaih.
    (of road). /How well can this truck take rough ground. Nī·ga fo·chè hàahng dī nāp·daht·bāt·pìhng ge louh dāk·m̀h·dāk a?
    (sketchy) daaih·ji (ge). /This will give you a rough idea. Nī·go hó·yíh lihng néih jì·dou·háh daaih·jì ge chìhng·yìhng.
    (not gentle) chòu·lóuh. /His rough manner frightened the children. Kéuih gam chòu·lóuh hak·pa·saai dī sai·mān·jái.
    (severe, difficult). /They had a rough time of it. Kéuih·deih gìng·gwo bāt·jì géi·dò màh·fàahn.
    a rough draft chóh·góu. /This is the rough draft of my speech. Nī·go haih ngóh yín·góng ge chóh·góu.

round   yùhn: **round table** yùhn tói; **round bottle** yùhn jēun; **round trip ticket** lòih·wùih fēi
    to round a point of obstruction wahn·gwo. /We have to round the hill to get there. Ngóh·deih yāt·dihng yiu wahn·gwo gó·go sàan·jái sìn·ji dou·dāk gó·syu.

round a corner jyun·wāan. /As soon as you round the corner you'll see the store. Néih yāt jyun·wāan jauh tái·gin gó·gàan pou·táu ge la.

to go round. /Is there enough candy to go round? is expressed as: Dī tóng gau paai ma?

round and round tàhm·tàhm·jyun. /The children were dancing round and round. Dī sai·màn·jái tàhm·tàhm·jyun gám hái syu tiu·móuh.

round the edge of sei·wàih. /There's a border round the edge of it. Sei·wàih wàih· jyuh yāt·tîuh bīn.

all year round sèhng·nîhn. /I now live here all year round. Ngóh yîh·gā sèhng·nîhn jyuh·hái nī·syu.

rouse   (disturb, wake up) gáau·séng. /You may rouse the sleeping baby if you make so much noise. Yùh·gwó néih juhng haih gam daaih sèng, néih wúih gáau·séng go bìh·bī·jái ge boh.

(stir up or make angry) gīk·nàu. /It would be a very bad thing if you rouse this dog to anger. Yùh·gwó néih gīk·nàu nī·jek gáu jauh hóu leuhn·jeuhn la.

route   louh; **air route** hòhng·hùng louh·sin; **sea route** séui·louh

routed   (defeated) dá·syù·jó (as in games); dá·baaih·jó (as in battle); **completely routed** yāt·baaih·tòuh·deih

routine   laih·hàhng·gùng·sih. /It's merely a routine. Nī·dī bāt·gwo haih laih·hàhng gùng·sih jē.

row   laaht, hòhng. /Do you see the row of trees, his house is behind that. Néih tái·dóu gó·laaht syuh ma, kéuih gāan ngūk jauh hái gó·laaht syuh hauh·bihn. /This row of houses is all his. Nī·yāt·laaht ngūk dōu haih kéuih ge. /They are standing in a row waiting. Kéuih·deih pàaih·sèhng yāt·hòhng kéih·hái syu dáng.

to row jaauh, pàh. /You'll have to row too. Néih dōu yiu jaauh boh. /Who will row this boat with me? Bīn·go tùhng ngóh pàh nī·jek téhng a?

royal   dai·wòhng ge, wòhng·gà ge; **Royal Air Force** wòhng·gā hūng·gwān; **royal family** wòhng·sāt; **royal palace** wòhng·gùng

royalty   (to an author) báan·seui

rub   (out, off) chaat, maat. /Can you rub it off? Chaat·m̀h·chaat·dāk lāt a? (on) jēut. /Rub her back with alcohol. Yuhng fó·jáu tùhng kéuih jēut·háh go bui·jek. /Don't rub your eye. M̀h·hóu jēut néih ge ngáahn. /Rub this dress hard or it won't get clean. Chēut·lihk jēut·háh nī·gihn sāam yeuhk·m̀h·haih jauh m̀h·sái dāk gòn·jehng.

rub it in (fig.). /I know I'm wrong, so don't rub it in. Ngóh jī·dou cho la, m̀h·hóu joi góng la.

rubber   syuh·gàau, syuh·yuhng (term used in Malaya); (eraser) gàau·cháat (M: gauh)

rubbish   (refuse) laahp·saap. /It's rubbish. Faat·ngahm·wah.

ruble   (Russian money) lòuh·bou

ruby   hùhng·bóu·sehk (M: nāp)

rudder   táaih

rude   (impolite) móuh·láih; (lacking delicacy) chòu·lóuh

rudimentary   chò·bouh·ge

rueful   bai·ngai

rug   deih·jīn (M: jèung). /I want to buy a nine-by-twelve rug. Ngóh yiu máaih yāt·jèung gáu·chek fut sahp·yih·chek chèuhng ge deih·jīn.

rugged   (not smooth) chòu; (as mountain road) kēi·kèui

ruin   (destroy) wái·waaih·saai, po·waaih (fig.). /This typhoon has ruined the coming harvest. Nī·chèuhng fùng wái·waaih·saai gàm·nín ge sàu·sìhng. /I was told someone wants
to ruin our plan. Ngóh tèng·màhn·wah yáuh yàhn séung po·waaih ngóh·deih ge gai·waahk.
    (spoil) jíng·waaih, jòu·taat·saai. /Don't ruin it. Mh·hóu jíng·waaih kéuih. /If you
keep on drinking, it will certainly ruin your health. Yùh·gwó néih gai·juhk yám·jáu,
yāt·dihng wúih jíng·waaih néih·ge sàn·jí. /These materials are ruined. Nī·dī chòih·
líu yíh·gīng jòu·taat·saai la.
    (ancient remains) gú·jīk. /There are many ruins worth seeing in Rome. Lòh·máh
yáuh hóu·dò gú·jīk jihk·dāk tái ge.

rule   (regulation) kwài·géui, kwāi·jāk. /This is the rule of the school, everyone should
abide by it. Nī·go haih hohk·haauh ge kwài·géui, go·go dōu yiu jyùn·sáu ge. /Smoking
is against the rule here. is expressed as: Nī·syu·mh·jéun sihk·yīn. (Smoking is not
allowed here.)
    (act of ruling) is expressed verbally as: túng·jih (see to rule)
    as a rule chùhng·lòih. /As a rule I don't drink. Ngóh chùhng·lòih mh·yám·jáu.
    be the rule (be customary) chùhng·lòih. /That sort of thing is the rule around here.
Nī·syu chùhng·lòih jauh·haih gám ge la.
    to rule túng·jih. /The Manchus ruled China for 268 years. Múhn·jàu·yàhn túng·jih·
jó Jùng·gwok yih·baak·luhk·sahp·baat·nìhn. /He is ruled by his emotions. is expressed
as: Kéuih júng·haih gáam·chìhng·yuhng·sih.
    rule something out. /This doesn't entirely rule out all possibilities. is expressed
as: Gám mh·haih wah yùhn·chyùhn móuh daih·yih·dī baahn·faat.
    according to rule jiu kwài·géui; detailed rules sai·jāk; fundamental rule yùhn·jāk;
supplementary rule fuh·jāk

ruler   (for ruling lines) chek, gaan·chék (M: bá); (sovereign) yùhn·sáu; (king) wòhng;
(emperor) wòhng·dai

rumor   yìuh·yìhn

run   (go fast on foot) jáu. /See who can run faster. Tái bīn·go jáu dāk faai dī. /I can
walk faster than you can run, don't you believe it? Ngóh hàahng dāk juhng faai·gwo
néih jáu, néih mh·seun àh? /Don't run so quickly. Mh·hóu jáu gam faai.
    (be in operation) hàahng. /Don't get close to it while the engine is running. Gèi·hei
hàahng·gán mh·hóu hàahng·màaih·heui.
    (be in process). /The movie had been running for half an hour when we went in.
Ngóh·deih yahp·heui gó·jahn·sí, gó·chēut dihn·yíng yíh·gīng jouh·jó bun·dím·jūng lo.
    (flow, as water, etc.) làuh. /She forgot to turn off the water and it has run all over
the place. Kéuih mh·gei·dāk sàan séui·hàuh, dī séui làuh·dou bīn·syu dōu haih.
    (go; of something quoted or sung). /How does the first line run? (for reading)
Daih·yāt·hòhng dím·yéung duhk a? or Daih·yāt·hòhng haih māt·yéh a? (for singing)
Daih·yāt·hòhng dím·yéung cheung a? /The tune runs like this. Sáu gō gám·yéung
cheung.
    run an apparatus or machine sái. /Can you run a washing machine? Néih wúih mh·
wúih sái sái·yī gèi a?
    run a business jouh. /We are looking for a person who knows how to run a business.
Ngóh·deih séung wán go wúih jouh·sàang·yi ge yàhn.
    run a risk mouh·hím (VO). /It isn't worth it to run such a risk. Mh·jihk·dāk mouh
gam daaih ge (ngàih·)hím.
    run across an area jáu·gwo. /Don't run across the street. Mh·hóu jáu·gwo gāai.
    run across someone or something (see by accident) pung·gin, ngáuh·yìhn tái·gin. /I
ran across him yesterday on the street. Ngóh kàhm·yaht hái gāai·syu pung·gin kéuih.
/I ran across an article about him the other day. Jóu·géi·yaht ngóh tái·dóu yāt·pìn
gwàan·yù kéuih ge màhn·jèung.
    run aground gok·chín. /The radio said a ship ran aground fifteen miles from here.
Mòuh·sin·dihn wah yáuh jek syùhn lèih nī·syu sahp·ńgh·māai·syu gok·jó·chín.
    run along. /Run along now! Hàahng·hōi lā!

run around (go out for good times) sèhng·yaht gei·jyuh wáan. /He's running around too much, he'll never be able to pass the exams. Kēuih sèhng·yaht gei·jyuh wáan, kéuih móuh·faat·jí háau dāk gahp·gaak ge la.

run away (leave quickly) jáu·jó·heui. /Don't let it run away! M̀h·hóu béi kéuih jáu·jó·heui. /My dog ran away when he saw him. Ngóh jek gáu tái·gin kéuih jauh jáu·jó·heui la.

run away from a place (intending to stay away). /Did he run away from home? Kéuih haih·m̀h·haih hái ngūk·kéi jáu·chēut·lèih ga?

run away from (fig.) jáu·hòi. /You can't run away whenever you face anything which is difficult to handle. Néih móuh·faat·jí yāt·sai·yàhn yuh·dóu kwan·nàahn jauh jáu·hòi ge.

run away with someone jáu·lóu. /He and his accomplice both ran away. Kéuih túhng kéuih ge paak·sáu·fó·gei léuhng·go dōu jáu·jó·lóu.

run away with (one's imagination). /Don't let your imagination run away. M̀h·hóu wùh·sî·lyuhn·séung.

run by or **past** someone or something jáu·gwo. /He ran right by us without seeing us. Kéuih hái ngóh·deih sān·bīn jáu·gwo daahn·haih móuh·tái·gin ngóh·deih.

run by or **past** something (extend) hái . . . pòhng·bīn. /The road runs right by my house. Tîuh louh jauh hái ngóh gāan ngūk pòhng·bīn gwo.

run down a route (to a lower position; on foot) jáu·lohk·heui; (by flowing) làuh·lohk·heui; (on foot, but not to a lower position) hái . . . syu jáu. /He ran down the road as fast as he could go. Kéuih hái tîuh louh·syu jáu dāk yáuh gam faai dāk gam faai.

run someone **down** (struck down) pung·chàn. /He was run down by a truck. Kéuih béi ga fo·chè pung·chàn.

run someone **down** (speak ill of) pài·pìhng, naauh. /Don't run him down that way; he has done his best. M̀h·hóu gám pài·pìhng kéuih; kéuih yíh·gìng jeuhn·sàm·jeuhn·lihk gám jouh la.

be run down (of a house). /This house is run down. Nī·gāan ngūk yiu yihng·jàn sàu·jíng ji dāk la. (of a person) lohk·saai·yihng. /He looks terribly run down. Kéuih sèhng·go yàhn lohk·saai·yîhng.

run dry gòn. /The well never ran dry. Nī·go jéng chùhng·lòih móuh gòn·gwo.

run for a destination jáu·heui. /It's started to rain, let's run for that tree. Lohk·yúh la, jáu·heui gó·pò syuh beih·háh lā. but /Run for it! Faai·dí jáu lā!

run for an office gihng·syún. /Who ran for president that year? Gó·nîhn bīn·go gihng·syún júng·túng a?

run from A to B (of a vehicle on a route) hái A sái·dou B; (of a route) hai A tùhng·dou B. /This bus runs from the railroad station to the airport. Nī·ga bā·sī yàuh fó·chè·jaahm sái·dou fēi·gèi·chèuhng. /This railroad runs from the sea to the capital. Nī·tîuh tit·louh hái hói·bīn yāt·jihk tùhng·dou sáu·dòu.

run (all) **over** something (cover). /There was ivy running all over the wall. Chèuhng·seuhng·bihn sàang·múhn·saai chèuhng·chèun·tàhng.

run over a person or an animal (with a vehicle) lūk·chàn; (if it results in death) lūk·séi. /Someone was run over. Yáuh yàhn béi chè lūk·séi.

run over something (review) wàn·jaahp. /I think you should run over your speech again before you deliver it. Ngóh gú néih yín·góng jî·chîhn jeui hóu jèung néih·ge yín·chîh joi wàn·jaahp yāt·chi.

run someone **in**. /I'll have to run him in. Ngóh móuh·faat·jí m̀h·daai kéuih fàan·heui chàai·gún (or gíng·chaat·gúk, or máh·dá·lîuh — in Malaya).

run into an interior jáu·yahp. /He ran into the house. Kéuih jáu·yahp gāan ngūk·syu.

run into an obstruction (of a vehicle) johng·màaih. /The car ran into a tree. Ga chè johng·màaih pò syuh·syu.

run low yuht leih yuht síu la. /Our cash is running low. Ngóh·deih ge yihn·chín yuht lèih yuht síu la.

run off jáu. /Don't run off now! I have some other things to say. M̀h·hóu jáu·jih, Ngóh juhng yáuh dī yéh tùhng néih góng.

run out yuhng·saai la, yuhng·yùhn la. /Our supply of paper has run out. Ngóh·deih ge jí yíh·gìng yuhng·saai la. /We have run out of money. Ngóh·deih yíh·gìng yuhng· saai ngóh·deih ge chín la.

run out of an interior hái. /He ran out of the house. Kéuih hái gāan ngūk jáu·chēut· lèih.

run someone **out of** town, a country, etc. gón kéuih chēut·gíng. /He was run out of town by the government. Kéuih béi jing·fú gón·jó chēut·gíng.

run over (overflow) múhn·saai·chēut·lèih. /The water's running over. Dī séui múhn· saai·chēut·lèih la. /The tub is running over. Pùhn yahp·bihn ge séui múhn·saai·chēut· lèih la.

run over to a place jáu·heui. /Run over to the store and see if you can get some candles. Jáu·heui gó·gàan pou·táu syu tái·háh máaih·m̀h·máaih·dóu yèuhng·jūk.

run short jauh·lèih yuhng·yùhn la. /Our gasoline is running short. Ngóh·deih ge dihn·yàuh jauh·lèih yuhng·yùhn la. /We're running short of cash. Ngóh·deih ge yihn· chín jauh·lèih yuhng·yùhn la.

run through a passage (on foot) jáu·gwo·heui. /He ran through an alley as fast as he could. Kéuih pìng·mehng gam faai hái tìuh hóng·syu jáu·gwo·heui.

run something long **through** a narrow passage chyùn·gwo. /Run the rope through this loop. Jèung tìuh síng chyùn·gwo nī·go lūng·syu.

run to a place (on foot) jáu·heui or lèih . . . (syu); **to** a person jáu·heui or lèih . . . syu. /He ran to the school without stopping. Kéuih yāt·louh m̀h·tìhng gám jáu·heui hohk·haauh. /She saw her mother walk in, then ran to her. Kéuih tái·gin kéuih màh· mā hàahng·yahp·lèih jauh jáu·màaih·heui kéuih màh·mā·syu.

run to a place tùng (·dou). /All roads run to Rome. Tìuh·tìuh lóuh dōu tùng(·dou) Lòh·máh.

run up a route (to a higher position) jáu·séuhng. /They said they could run up the hill, but I didn't believe it. Kéuih·deih wah kéuih·deih hó·yíh jáu·séuhng gó·go sàan, daahn·haih ngóh m̀h·seun.

a run (trip) chi. /How many runs can the truck make per week. Ga fo·chē múih·go láih·baai hó·yíh jáu géi·dò·chi a?

in the long run dá chèuhng·lèih gai. /I think, in the long run, it's to your advantage. Ngóh yihng·wàih dá chèuhng·lèih gai, dōu·haih néih jeuhk·sou ge.

on the run. /He's coming on the run. Kéuih yāt·louh gám jáu·jyuh·lèih ge.

runway (for airplane) páau·douh

rupture (burst) lit·háu; **a rupture of diplomatic relations** dyuhn·jyuht bōng·gàau

rural hēung·chyùn, hèung·há; **rural area** hēung·chyūn·kēui, hèung·há; **rural life** hēung· chyūn·sàng·wuht; **rural scenery** hēung·chyūn·fùng·gíng

rush (do something in a hurry). /He rushed to the bank to withdraw some money. Kéuih gón·heui ngàhn·hòhng ló chín. /Rush him to the hospital. Gón faai sung kéuih yahp yī·yún.

a rush (hurry, tumult) is expressed in terms of bīk (be pressed or crowded) or jeui bà·bai, jeui m̀h·dāk·hàahn (be very busy). /At five o'clock there's always a rush in this area. Nī·yāt·daai ńgh·dím·jūng ge sìh·hauh géi·sí dōu haih gam bīk ge la. /This is the rush season for our business. Nī·go haih ngóh·deih nī·hòhng jeui bà·bai ge sìh· hauh.

(the plant) lòuh·wáih

rust sau (N); sàang·sau (V). /The knife has rusted. Bá dōu sàang·jó sau.

rustic (rural) hèung·há ge, hēung·chyùn ge; (simple and plain) pok·sou; (artless) lóuh· saht

rustling sàh·sàh·sèng

Sabbath   ngōn·sīk·yaht

sabotage   po·waaih (V); po·waaih·hàhng·duhng (N)

saber   (sword) jí·fāi·dōu, gwān·dōu (M: bá)

sack   (bag) doih

sacrament   **Holy Sacrament** sing·chāan; **to receive or take the sacrament** sáu·sing·
chāan

sacred   sàhn·sing·ge, sing —: **sacred book** sing·gìng; **sacred music** sing·ngohk; **sacred
place** sing·deih; **sacred service** láih·baai

sacrifice   (to a god) jai·láih (N); jai (V); (to one's ancestors) jai·bán, jai·láih (N); jai·jóu·
sīn; (to give up) hēi·sàng: **sacrifice money** hēi·sàng·gàm·chìhn; **sacrifice one's life** hēi·
sàng·sing·mihng; **sacrifice oneself** hēi·sàng jih·géi

sad   bai·ngai, m̀h·ngòn·lohk, hóu·ngàahn·gwo. /Why is he so sad? Dím·gáai kéuih gam
bai·ngai a? /This is very sad. Nī·gihn sih lihng yàhn hóu nàahn·gwo.

saddle   (horse) máh·ngòn; (bicycle) joh·wái

sadism   yeuhk·doih·kwòhng

safe   (reliable) wán·jahn, tóh·dong. /Is the bridge safe? Tìuh·kìuh wán·jahn ma? /Is
this method safe? Nī·go baahn·faat tóh·dong ma?
(free from danger). /He is safe now. Kéuih yìh·gā móuh·sih·la.
(not harmed). /The driver is safe, only the car is damaged. Sái chè ge yàhn móuh·
sih, jihng·haih ga chè waaih·jó jē.
a safe gaap·maahn, bóu·hím·sēung. /Should we put these things into the safe? Ngóh·
deih sái·m̀h·sái jèung nī·dī yéh jài·hái gaap·maahn·syu a?
safe and sound pìhng·ngòn mòuh·sih (not harmed or injured); móuh·behng móuh·tung
(in good health)

safeguard   bóu·jeung: **to safeguard the interests of the farmers** bóu·jeung nùhng·màhn
ge leih·yīk

safety   ngòn·chyùhn. /This is for your safety. Gám néih jauh ngòn·chyùhn la. or Gám
néih jauh m̀h·sái·pa la. (Then you'll have nothing to be afraid of.)
safety belt ngòn·chyùhn·daai; **Safety first.** Ngòn·chyùhn daih·yāt. **safety pin** biht·jām

sage   sing·yàhn

sail   léih. /Does this boat have a sail? Nī·jek syùhn yáuh móuh léih ga?
Go for a sail. /Let's go for a sail. Heui yàuh·hó lo.
to sail (of a ship) sái, hōi·sàn. /This boat sails too slowly, could it sail faster? Nī·
jek syùhn sái dāk taai maahn, hó·yíh sái dāk faai dī ma? /When do we sail? Jek syùhn
géi·sí hōi·sàn a?
(handle a sailboat) sái. /Can you sail a boat? Néih wúih sái fàahn·syùhn ma?

sailor   séui·sáu; (seaman) hàahng·syùhn·láu, hói·yùhn

saint   sing·yìhn, yìhn·yàhn; (Christian) sing·tòuh

sake   **for the sake of** waih·jó, waih yàn·waih. /You can't do this just for the sake of
money. Néih bāt·nàhng waih·jó chín jauh jouh dī gám ge sih. /We're doing this for the
sake of our security. Yìh·gā gám·yéung jouh yùhn·chyùhn haih waih daaih·gā ge ngòn·
chyùhn. /Don't you know that? Your parents saved the money merely for the sake of
seeing you through college? Néih m̀h·jî àh? Néih fuh·móuh chyùhn fàan dī chín yùhn·
chyùhn haih waih·jó gùng néih duhk·yùhn go daaih·hohk.
for someone's sake waih (because of); tái . . . fahn·seuhng (out of respect for).
/He did it for your sake. Kéuih yùhn·chyùhn haih waih néih sìn·ji gám·jouh ja. /For
my sake, don't say any more. Tái ngóh fahn·seuhng m̀h·hóu joi góng la.

Sakyamuni   Sīk·gà·mòuh·nàih

salable   maaih·dāk, hóu·maaih

salary   sàn·séui; (for manual or physical labor) yàhn·gùng

sale   (selling). /The government made a lot of money through the sale of the public
lands. Jing·fú jèung dī gùng·deih maaih·jó wán·jó hóu·dò chín.
(selling at a low price) gáam·ga. /Everything is on sale. Yeuhng·yeuhng yéh dōu
gáam·ga. /Is this on sale? Nī·yeuhng gáam·ga ma?
(amount sold) sàang·yi. /Our sales doubled this year. Gàm·nín ge sàang·yi dò·jó
yāt·púih.
(demand) sìu·louh. /There is no market for automobiles these days. Nī·páai hei·
chè móuh·māt sìu·louh.

saliva   háu·séui

salt   yìhm; **to salt** jài·yìhm, fong·yìhm. /Did you salt the soup? Tòng yahp·bihn jài·jó
yìhm meih·a? (treat with salt) yip. /This chunk of meat ought to be salted down. Nī·
gauh yuhk yiu yip·héi ji·dāk.
salted and sun-dried vegetables hàahm·choi; **salted black beans** dauh·sih; **salted
egg** hàahm·dáan; **salted fish** hàahm·yú

salute   (greet) ngahp·táu jìu·fù (by nodding one's head); (to honor) hàhng·láih ji·ging; (as
a mark of military respect) ging·láih. /Aren't you supposed to salute your senior officers? Néih gin·dóu néih ge jéung·gún dím·gáai m̀h (·tùhng kéuih) ging·láih a?

salvage   (for crew) gau·fàan (V); (for ship or cargo) làauh·fàan (V)

salve   (on wounds and sore) gòu·yeuhk

same   (be identical) yāt·yeuhng, tùhng . . . sèung·tùhng. /These two are the same. /Nī·
léuhng·go yāt·yeuhng. /Is this chair the same as the others? Nī·jèung yí tùhng kèih·tà
ge sèung·tùhng ma? /He's not the same as he was three years ago. Kéuih tùhng sàam·
nìhn chìhn m̀h·sèung·tùhng la. /This one is the same as that one. Nī·go tùhng gó·go
yāt·yeuhng.
the same thing (as that used before) yùhn·lòih ge. /You may take the same road going back. Néih hó·yíh hàahng·fàan yùhn·lòih gó·tìuh louh fàan·heui.
(one and the same) tùhng(·màaih) yāt M, tùhng·màaih . . . yāt M. /We graduated from
the same school. Ngóh·deih tùhng (màaih) yāt·gàan hohk·haauh bāt·yihp ge. /Did you
come in the same car? Néih·deih haih·m̀h·haih tùhng·màaih chóh yāt·ga chè lèih ga.
/You two may come on the same day. Néih·deih léuhng·go hó·yíh tùhng·màaih yāt·yaht
lèih.
(finish doing things in the same day) jīk·yaht. /Can I leave and be back on the same
day? Ngóh hó·m̀h·hó·yíh jīk·yaht fàan·lèih a?
at the same time tùhng·sih. /Did they come in at the same time? Kéuih·deih haih
·m̀h·haih tùhng·sìh yahp·lèih ga?
the same as someone else has done is expressed with yihk, yihk·dou. /I sang, and
he did the same. Ngóh cheung·gō, kéuih yihk cheung·gō. /I got up, and he did the same.
Ngóh héi·sàn, kéuih yihk·dōu héi·sàn la.
all the same (all one kind) tūng·tūng yāt·yeuhng ge. /They are all the same. Tūng·
tūng yāt·yeuhng ge. (make no difference). /That's all the same to me. Ngóh gok·dāk
móuh māt fàn·biht.
in the same boat is expressed as 'have the same sickness and therefore mutual sympathy.' tùhng·behng·sèung·lìhn. /They're in the same boat. Kéuih·deih jing só·waih
tùhng·behng·sèung·lìhn la.
just the same, all the same (regardless of argument or opposition) mòuh·leuhn·yùh
hòh. /We're going just the same. Mòuh·leuhn·yùh·hòh ngóh·deih dōu heui ge la.
same kind tùhng·yéung ge; **same size** yāt·yeuhng daaih; **same surname** tùhng·sing;
same trade or business tùhng·hòhng

sampan   téhng·jái, sàam·báan (M: jek)

sample   báan; yéung (pattern)

sanction   (approval) pài·jéun

sand   sà; **sandbag** sā·bāau; **sandpaper** sà·jí

sandal   tō·háai (M: deui 'pair'); lèuhng·hàaih (M: deui 'pair'); **sandalwood** tàahn·hēung·muhk

sandwich   sàam·màhn·jih

sanitarium   lìuh·yéuhng·yún (M: gàan)

sanitary   waih·sāng

Sanskrit   Fàahn·màhn

Santa Claus   Sing·daan·lóuh·yàhn

sap   (liquid) jāp

sardine   sā·dīn·yú: **a can of sardines** yāt·gun sā·dīn·yú

sarsaparilla   (the drink) sà·sí·séui

satchel   (of school children) syū·bāau; (in general) sáu·tàih·bāau

satin   dyún

satirize   dai, fúng·chi

satisfaction   múhn·jūk, múhn·yi

satisfied   (contented) múhn·yi

satisfactory   lihng·yàhn múhn·yi. /The result is not satisfactory. Git·gwó m̀h·lihng·yàhn·múhn·yi

satisfy   (end a need by filling it). /This will satisfy your thirst. Yám daahm nī·dī néih jauh m̀h·géng·hot la.
     (please) múhn·yi. /I'm satisfied with my old car. Ngóh deui·yù ngóh ge gauh chè hóu múhn·yi. /Are you satisfied? Néih múhn·yi ma?

saturate   (soak thoroughly) jam·tau; (make very wet) sāp·tau

Saturday   láih·baai·luhk, sìng·kèih·luhk

Saturn   (planet) Tóu·sīng (M: nāp)

sauce   **soy sauce** sih·yàuh, baahk·yáu, sih·yáu; **applesauce** pìhng·gwó·jeung; **tomato sauce** fàan·ké·jeung; (thick salty sauce made from bean & flour) jeung·liuh

saucer   (of teacup) chàh·būi·díp

sausage   yuhk·chéung; **Chinese dried sausage** laahp·chéung (M: tìuh; mà, a pair)

savage   (wild) yéh·màahn; (cruel) chàahn·yáhn; (uncivilized people) sāang·fāan, yéh·màahn·yàhn

save   (not spend) hàahn(·fàan). /By doing it this way, we will save some money. Gám jouh wúih hàahn·fàan dī chín. /Do you think this'll save some money? Gám wúih·m̀h·wúih hāahn dī chín a?
     (spare) m̀h·sái. /Then, you can save yourself the trouble of going. Gám néih jauh m̀h·sái·heui la.
     (keep, hold on to) làuh·fàan. /Could you save this for me? Néih hó·yíh làuh·fàan nī·go béi ngóh ma? /Save this for supper. Làuh·fàan nī·dī gàm·máahn ji sihk.

(reserve) làuh·fàan. /Is this seat being saved for anybody? Nī·go wái haih·m̀h·haih làuh·fàan béi daih·yih·go (yàhn) ga?

(rescue) gau. /He saved her life. Kéuih gau·fàan kéuih tìuh mehng. /The term used by the Buddhists for saving the people of this world is 'chìu·douh'; the term the Christians used is 'chìhng·gau.' Faat·gaau góng chìu·douh sai·yàhn, Gēi·dūk·gaau góng chìhng·gau sai·yàhn.

(collect) chóuh. /How much money can you save a month? Néih yāt·go·yuht hó·yíh chóuh géi·dò chín a? /Do you save stamps? Néih chóuh sih·dāam ma?

saving jīk·chūk. /How much savings do you have? Néih yáuh géi ngán jīk·chúk a?

savings bank chyúh·chūk·ngàhn·hòhng (M: gàan)

Saviour   Gau·jyú

saw   geui (M: bá); **to saw** geu. /Can you saw this in half? Néih hó·yíh jèung nī·go geu·sèhng (or geu·hòi) léuhng·gyuht ma?

sawdust muhk·hòn; **saw off** geu·tyúhn. /Please saw it off. M̀h·gòi néih geu·tyúhn kéuih.

say   góng, wah. /What did he say? Kéuih góng māt·yéh a? /The principal has just said there'll be no class today. Haauh·jéung ngāam·ngāam wah gàm·yaht móuh tòhng séuhng. /Please say it again. M̀h·gòi néih joi góng·gwo.

shall we say. /Shall we say twenty dollars? Yih·sahp·mān eh?

to say good-bye chìh·hàhng. /Have you said good-bye to him yet? Néih heui·jó kéuih syu chìh·hàhng meih a?

to say a prayer kèih·tóu. /Let's say our prayers together. Daaih·gā yāt·chái kèih·tóu.

saying gaak·yìhn. /Can you teach me some Chinese sayings? Néih hó·yíh gaau ngóh géi·geui Jùng·gwok gaak·yìhn ma?

scab   yìm; **form a scab** git·yìm

scaffold   pàahng; **to set up a scaffold** daap·pàahng

scald   (burn with hot water) luhk·chàn. /He scalded his hand with boiling water. Kéuih jek sáu béi gwáan·séui luhk·chàn.

scale   (layer of covering) lèuhn. /I prefer to have fish without scales. Ngóh séung yiu dī móuh·lèuhn ge yú.

(weighing machine, a balance) tìn·pìhng; (a Chinese scale) ching (M: bá); (for weighing gold, medicine powder, etc.) lèih·dáng; (a scale that weighs in pounds) bohng. /Put that on the scale. Ching·háh (or bohng·háh) gó·go géi chúhng?

(series of tones) yām·gāai. /She has to practice scales everyday. Kéuih múih·yaht dōu yiu lihn·jaahp yām·gāai.

(graded system) dáng·kāp, dáng. /What is the scale of wages in your factory? Néih·deih gùng·chóng ge gūng·jī (or yàhn·gùng) fàn géi·dò dáng·kāp a?

(series of marks at regular intervals for measurement; on a barometer, thermometer, protractor) douh·sou; (on a measuring cup, chemical flask, chart) gaak; (on a Chinese weighing instrument) ching·sīng

(proportion) béi·laih, béi·laih·chek. /This ship model is made exactly to scale. Nī·go mòuh·yìhng haih jiu·jyuh jek syùhn ge béi·laih jouh ge. /This map has a scale of one inch to one hundred miles. Nī·go deih·tòuh ge béi·laih·chek haih yāt·yìng·chyun dáng·yù yāt·baahk·yìng·léih.

a large scale daaih·kwài·mouh ge. /They have planned the improvements on a large scale. Kéuih deih gai·waahk daaih·kwài·mòuh gói·lèuhng.

to scale (remove scales) gwaat·lèuhn. /Please scale the fish. M̀h·gòi néih gwaat·jó dī yùh·lèuhn kéuih.

scale down gáam. /All their prizes have been scaled down. Kéuih·deih jèung ga·chìhn tūng·tūng gáam·dài·jó.

scalp   tàuh·pèih (N)

scandal   sih·fèi. /The discovery of bribery in the government caused a great deal of
   scandal. Jing·fú yahp·bihn yáuh yàhn móu·baih béi yàhn faat·yihn·jó, yéh·héi bāt·jì géi
   daaih ge sih·fèi.

scar   (mark) nà

scarce   (contrary of plentiful) hóu síu; (rare) hèi·hón; **scarcely any difference** hóu síu
   fàn·biht

scare   haak, haak·chàn; gèng. /Don't scare me! M̀h·hóu haak ngóh! /The thunder scared
   the baby. Lèuih·sèng haak·chàn go bìh·bī. /Don't be scared! M̀h·hóu gèng!
   scare one to death haak·séi·yàhn

scarf   géng·gān

scarlet   daaih·hùhng·sīk ge, sìng·hùhng·sīk ge

scatter   (toss or sprinkle in all directions) saat. /You may scatter a handful of rice to
   feed the chicks. Néih hó·yíh saat yāt·bá máih wai dī gāi·jái.
   (break up and go in different directions) saan·hòi. /The crowd scattered when it
   started to rain. Tái·gin lohk·héi·yúh·séuhng·lèih, gó·kwàhn yàhn jauh saan·hòi la.
   (cause to disband) gón·saan (by force); haak·saan, haak·jáu (by scaring). /Don't
   scatter the herd of cattle. M̀h·hóu haak·saan (or haak·jáu) gó kwàhn ngàuh a! /The ex-
   plosion (of a bomb) scattered the people. Gó·go ja·dáan haak·jáu·saai dī yàhn.

scene   (view) gíng·ji, fùng·gíng. /That's a beautiful scene. Jàn·haih hóu gíng·ji (or
   fùng·gíng) la. or Gó·go gíng·ji (or fùng·gíng) jàn·haih leng la.
   (environment) wàahn·gíng. /A change of scene will do you good. Wuhn·háh wàahn·
   gíng yāt·dihng wúih deui néih hóu.
   (part of a play) chèuhng. /This is the third scene of the second act. Nī·go haih daih·
   yih·mohk daih·sàam·chèuhng.
   (place at which anything occurs) chēut·sih deih·dím. /The police are investigating
   at the scene. Gíng·chaat jing joih chēut·sih deih·dím diuh·chàh·gán.
   make a scene hái yàhn mihn·chìhn dìu·gá. /Don't make a scene. M̀h·hóu hái yàhn
   mihn·chìhn dìu·gá.
   behind the scenes (in the theater) hauh·tòih; (out of the public view) mohk·hauh. /The
   plan for his running for election has already worked out behind the scenes. Kéuih
   chēut·lèih gihng·syún ge gai·waahk yíh·gìng hái mohk·hauh jouh·hóu·saai la.

scent   (smell) meih. (fragrance, pleasant smell) hèung, hèung·meih.
   (notice by smelling) màhn·dóu. /Later, we found out the dog had scented a squirrel.
   Sāu·mēi ngóh·deih faat·yihn jek gáu màhn·dóu yāt·jek chùhng·syú.

schedule   (list) bíu; (timetable) sìh·gaan·bíu

scheme   gai·waahk (N); gai·waahk (V)

scholar   (learned man) hohk·jé

scholarship   (financial aid) jéung·hohk·gām

school   (places of learning) hohk·haauh, syu·gun. (membership of a school, the whole
   school) chyùhn·haauh; (group of water animals) kwàhn (M); a school of fish yāt·kwàhn·
   yú; (as of philosophy) paai, hohk·paai. /He belongs to a new school of thought. Kéuih
   ge sì·séung haih suhk·yù sàn·paai ge. (academic division) -yún, hohk·yún: **the School
   of Law** Faat·hohk·yún; **the School of Liberal Arts** Màhn·hohk·yún; **the School of Natural Sciences** Léih·hohk·yún
   get out of school (at the end of school day) fong·hohk; (graduate) bāt·yihp. /What
   time does school get out? Géi·dím·jūng fong·hohk a? /What time does your child get
   out of school? Néih ge sai·màn·jái géi·dím·jūng fong·hohk a? /When did you get out of
   high school? Néih géi·sí jùng·hohk bāt·yihp ga?

go to school duhk·syù; (attending school) fàan·hohk. /Does your child go to school? Néih·ge sai·màn·jái yáuh móuh duhk·syù a? /Has he started school yet? Kéuih duhk·syù meih a? /What time do you go to school in the morning? Néih jiu·tàuh·jóu géi·dím·jūng fàan·hohk a?

school age yahp·hohk·nìhn·lìhng; **school badge** haauh·jēung; **schoolboy** nàahm·hohk·sāang; **schoolbook** gaau·fō·syù, fo·bún; **school building** haauh·se (M: gaan); **school bus** haauh·chè; **schoolgirl** néuih·hohk·sāang; **school hours** séuhng·fo·sìh·gàan; **schoolmate** syù·yáu, tùhng·hohk; **school physician** haauh·yī; **school supplies** hohk·haauh·yùhng·bán; **school term** hohk·kèih; **school uniform** haauh·fuhk; **school year** hohk·nìhn

science   fò·hohk. /Does he study natural science or social science? Kéuih duhk jih·yìhn· fò·hohk, yīk·waahk séh·wúi·fò·hohk a?

scientific   fò·hohk (ge); **scientific method** fò·hohk·fòng·faat; **scientific instruments** fò· hohk·yìh·hei

scientist   fò·hohk·gā

scissors   gaau·jín (M: bá); **to cut with scissors** jín·hòi

scoff   (mock) siu, gèi·siu

scold   naauh

scoop   hok (N & M). /She used the new scoop to scoop up a scoop of chocolate ice cream for her girl. Kéuih yùhng go sàn·hok fāt·jó yāt·hok ge jyū·gū·lēut syut·gōu béi kéuih ge néui.
    to scoop yíu (to ladle); waat (to dig); fāt (dig, on a small scale). /Have you scooped out all the water yet? Néih fāt·saai (or yíu saai) dī séui chēut·lèih meih a? /This machine is for scooping up the sand and gravel. Nī·go gèi·hei haih gwaht·nàih·sà ge.

scope   (sphere) faahn·wàih; **beyond the scope of** chēut·jó nī·go faahn·wàih jī·ngoih; **within the scope of** joih nī·go faahn·wàih jī·noih

scorch   (make dry and withered) -nùng. /The sun has scorched the grass. Go yaht·táu saai·nùng dī chóu. (burn slightly). /The iron was so hot I scorched a shirt while ironing it. Go tong·dáu taai yiht, ngóh tong·nùng·jó gihn sēut·sāam.

score   (points in a game) fān. /What was the score? Géi·dō fān la?
    (twenty) yih·sahp; **scores** (a considerable number) hóu·géi·sahp
    (musical) póu, ngohk·póu, gō·póu. /Can you read a score? Néih wúih tái póu ma?
    to score (make points) yèhng. /He scored four points in ten minutes. Kéuih sahp· fān·jūng·noih yèhng·jó sei·fān.
    (keep a record) gei·fān. /How does one score this? Dím·yéung gei·fān ga?
    (arrange musically). /This selection is scored for piano. Nī·go ngohk·póu haih waih gong·kàhm yuhng ge.

scoundrel   mòuh·láai, gwòng·gwan

scout   (a member of the Boy Scouts) nàahm·tùhng·jí·gwān; (a member of the Girl Scouts) néuih·tùhng·jí·gwān; (a spy) gaan·dihp
    to scout dá·taam chìhng·yìhng

scramble   (climb) pàh. /The students, one group after another, scrambled up the hill. Dī hohk·sāang yāt·kwàhn yāt·kwàhn gám pàh·jó séuhng·sàan.

scrap   **scrap iron** laahn·tit; **scraps** (left-over food) láahng·faahn; **scraps of cloth** bou· séui; **scraps of paper** jí·séui, jih·jí

scrape   (remove, using something sharp or rough) gwaat; **scrape off** gwaat·lāt. /You should scrape off the old paint before you paint it. Néih yiu gwaat·lāt dī yàuh·chāt sìn· ji yàuh yáu.

scratch   (an itching spot) ngàau, wá. /He wishes someone would scratch his back.
Kéuih séung yàhn tùhng kéuih ngàau·háh (or wá háh) kéuih· ge bui·jek.
   (with claws) wá. /He was scratched by the kitten. Kéuih béi māau·jái wá·chàn.
   (mark with something sharp) kaat. /Try not to scratch the floor when you move the
piano. Néih bùn go gong·kàhm gó·jahn·sí m̀h·hóu kaat·chàn ngóh ge deih·báan.
   scratch out waahk·jo·keuih, waahk·lāt·keuih. /You may scratch out the last line.
Néih hó·yíh jèung sáu·mēi gó·hòhng waahk·lāt kéuih.
   a scratch hán (M: tìuh). /How did you get that scratch on your face? Néih mihn·
syu gó·tìuh hán dím·yéung lèih ga? /After the crash he got out from his car without a
scratch. is expressed as: .Kéuih johng·chè jī·hauh hái ga chè·syu hàahng·chēut·lèih yāt
dī sih dōu móuh.
   from scratch (from the beginning) chùhng·tàuh jouh·gwo. /The whole job had to be
done over again from scratch. Nī·gihn sih yāt·dihng yiu chùhng·tàuh jouh·gwo.

scream   giu, ngaai. /She screamed in terror. Kéuih haak·dou daaih·sèng gám giu.
   a scream is expressed verbally as: /I thought I heard a scream. Ngóh tèng·dóu hóu·
chíh yáuh yàhn ngaai·gám léuhng·sèng, m̀h·jī haih·m̀h·haih nē?

screen   (standing) wàih·píng, pìhng·fūng; (hanging) lím; (of a cinema) ngàhn·mohk; (hide
with a screen) jè·jyuh. /We should screen that window with some pieces of cardboard.
Ngóh·deih yiu yuhng dī jí·pèih jè·jyuh gó·go chēung·mún.
   screen window sā·chēung; **smoke screen** yìn·mohk

screw   lòh·sī, lòh·sī·dēng (M: nāp); **screwdriver** lòh·sī·pāi
   (turn, twist) náu. /Please screw tight the cap of the jar. /M̀h·gòi náu·gán go jēun·
goi kéuih.
   to screw in a screw náu·saht go lòh·sī; **to screw out a screw** náu·sùng go lòh·sī
   fasten with a screw séuhng nāp lòh·sī

scribble   (write carelessly) sé dāk gam lóuh·chóu. /You're not permitted to scribble.
M̀h·jéun sé dāk gam lóuh·chóu. /Who can read your scribbling? is expressed as:
Néih sé dāk gam lóuh·chóu, bīn·go sīk tái a?

script   **cursive script** (Chinese) chóu·syù

Scriptures   Sing·gìng (M: bún)

scrofula   lék; **to have scrofula** sàang lék

scroll   (roll of paper) gyún (M); (of cloth scroll) juhk; **a pair of scrolls** (Chinese) yāt·fu
déui, yāt·deui dēui, yāt·fu deui·lyún; **a scroll** (of Chinese paintings) sáu·gyún

scrub   (clean by rubbing hard) chaat, maat. /Scrub this table with soapy water. Yùhng
fàan·gáan·séui chaat·gòn·jehng nī·jèung tói.

scrutinize   (behavior, etc.) jí·sai sám·chàh; (appearance) jí·sai jyu·yi

scull   lóuh

sculpture   dīu·hāk (V); dīu·hāk, dīu·hāk·maht (M)

scythe   lìhm·dōu (M: bá)

sea   hói. /How far are we from the sea? Ngóh·deih nī·syu lèih hói géi yúhn a? **heavy
sea, rough sea** is expressed as: fùng·lohng hóu daaih. /Yesterday when we went fishing, the sea was very rough. Kàhm·yaht ngóh·deih heui diu·yú, fùng·lohng hóu daaih.
   sea level hói·mihn; **above sea level** hoi·baht. /This land is 200 feet above sea level.
Nī·faai deih gòu·chēut hói·mín (or hói·mihn) yih·baak·chek. or Nī·faai deih hói·baht
yih·baak·chek.
   put to sea hòi. /When does the ship put to sea? Nī·jek syùhn géi·sí hòi a?
   sea captain syùhn·jéung; **seacoast** hói·ngohn; **sea-cucumber** hói·sàm; **seafarer**
hói·yùhn; **sea-fight** hói·jin; **seahorse** hói·máh; **seaman** (naval) séui·bìng, séui·sáu,

(commercial) hói·yùhn, syùhn·yùhn; **seaplane** séui·seuhng·fèi·gèi; **seaport** hói·háu; **seashore** hói·pèih, hói·bīn; **seasick** wàhn·lohng. /Do you get seasick? Néih wàhn·m̀h·wàhn·lohng ga? **seaside** hói·pèih

sea gull   hói·ngāu (M: jek)

seal   (a stamping device) yan, tòuh·jēung; (to mark with a stamp) kāp·yan, kāp·tòuh·jēung; (close tightly) fùng·màaih, fùng·hóu, fùng·saht. /Don't forget to seal up the letter. Gei·jyuh fùng·màaih fùng seun kéuih. /What do we use to seal the jars? Ngóh·deih yuhng māt·yéh lèih fùng·hóu dī jēun a?
    a seal (the animal) hói·gáu (M: jek); **sealing wax** fó·chāt; **to seal it with sealing wax** dá·fó·chāt. /Should we seal this letter with sealing wax? Nī·fùng seun sái·m̀h·sái dá·fó·chāt a? **a personal seal** sī·jēung, yan; **the imperial seal** yuhk·sái

seam   (in garment) gaap·háu; **to seam** lyùhn; **to seam it up** lyùhn·màaih·kéuih

search   wán. /I've searched everywhere. Ngóh bīn·syu dōu wán·wàhn·saai la.
    (look for something concealed) sáu, sáu·chàh; (examine) gím·chàh. /They said everyone will be searched. Kéuih·deih wah go·go dōu yiu sáu·sàn. /They're searching for smuggled goods. Kéuih·deih hái syu sáu·chàh sī·fo.

searchlight   taam·hói·dāng, taam·seh·dāng

season   gwai: **a season** yāt·gwai; **four seasons** sei·gwai; **spring season** chèun·gwai; **summer season** hah·gwai; **fall season** chàu·gwai; **winter season** dùng·gwai
    (period of the year) sìh·hauh, gwai·jit; **rainy season** yúh·gwai; **holiday season** ga·kèih. /This is the best season for outings. Nī·go sìh·hauh gàau·ngoih léuih·hàhng jeui hóu la. /When is the rainy season in this area? Nī·yāt·daai géi·sí haih yúh·gwai a? /Are you going anywhere during the holiday season? Ga·kèih ge sìh·hauh néih séung heui bīn·syu wáan ma?
    in season (be ripe) suhk; (come to market) séuhng·sih. /Are litchis in season yet? Laih·jī suhk meih a? or Laih·jī séuhng·sìh meih a?
    to season (flavor; add salt) jai yìhm; (add salt, sauce, or spices) gaau meih·douh. /Have you seasoned it yet? Gaau·jó meih·douh meih a?
    be seasoned (experienced) yáuh·gìng·yihm ge. /They all are seasoned sailors. Kéuih·deih go·go dōu haih hóu yáuh·gìng·yihm ge séui·sáu.

seat   wái. /There are two seats over there. Gó·syu yáuh léuhng·go wái.
    be seated chóh, chóh·dài. /Please be seated. Chéng·chóh. /May I be seated? Ngóh hó·yíh chóh·dài ma?
    take a seat chóh·dái. /Tell him to take a seat. Giu kéuih chóh·dài.
    seat of government (national) sáu·dòu, gwok·dòu, gìng·sèhng; (provincial) sáang·sèhng, sáang·wuih; (district) yuhn·sèhng
    seat someone giu . . . chóh. /Seat them in order. Giu kéuih·deih yī·jiu chi·jeuih chóh.
    to seat (have seats for). /This auditorium seats five hundred people. Nī·go láih·tòhng hó·yíh chóh ńgh·baak·yàhn.
    to book a seat dehng·wái. /Shouldn't we book our seats? Ngóh·deih sái·m̀h·sái dehng·wái sìn a?

seaweed   hói·daai

second   (following the first) daih·yih, yih. /Who is the second man from the left? Jó·sáu·bihn daih·yih·go haih bīn·go a? /My room is on the second floor. Ngóh gàan fóng hái yih·láu.
    (another) is expressed as: joi . . . (yāt) chi. /Give him a second chance. Joi béi chi gèi·wuih kéuih tīm lā.
    a second (of time) míuh (M). /There are sixty seconds in one minute. Yāt·fān·jūng yáuh luhk·sahp·míuh.

(a moment) yāt·jahn·gaan, yāt·sī·gāan. /Please wait a second. Chéng néih dáng yāt·jahn·gāan.

to second (parliamentary procedure) fuh·yi; (approve) jaan·sìhng. /I second the motion. Ngóh fuh·yi. or Ngóh jaan·sìhng nī·go tàih·yi.

second-hand gauh ge; **secondhand goods** yih·tói·fo, gauh·fo. /Where can I buy some secondhand furniture? Bīn·syu yáuh gauh (ge) gà·sī maaih a? /These are secondhand goods, how could you ask for that much? Nī·dī haih yih·tói·fo, néih dím yiu dāk gam gòu ga·chìhn a?

second lieutenant siu·wai; **the second of February** yih·yuht·yih houh; **the second show** daih·yih·chèuhng; **the second time** daih·yih·chi; **second rate goods** yih·dáng·fo

secondary   **secondary education** jùng·dáng gaau·yuhk; **secondary school** jùng·hohk

secret   (not generally known) bei·maht (ge). /Do you believe there's a secret agreement between these two countries? Néih sèung·seun nī·léuhng gwok jī·gāan yáuh móuh bei·maht hip·dihng nē?

(hidden, not obvious to the eye) ngam. /There's a secret lock on the closet. Go gwaih·syu yáuh douh ngam·só.

a secret bei·maht. /Can he keep a secret? Kéuih hó·yíh sáu bei·maht ma?

in secret bei·maht, ngam·jùng, jihng·jíng. /They met in secret to discuss their plan. Kéuih·deih bei·maht hòi·wúi tóu·leuhn kéuih·deih ge gai·waahk.

secret agent gaan·dihp, chìhng·bou yàhn·yùhn; **the secret of success** sìhng·gùng ge bei·kyut; **secret plot** yàm·màuh; **secret service** dahk·mouh; **secret society** wuih·dóng; **secret code** maht·dihn·máh

secretly   bei·maht (ge), ngam·jùng (ge), tāu·tāu·déi

secretariat   bei·syū·chyúh

secretary   (clerk) syù·gei; (confidential) bei·syū; (official of ministerial rank) bouh·jéung (in a republic), daaih·sàhn (in a monarchy); **Secretary of State** gwok·mouh·hīng

secrets   (emit as a secretion) fàn·bei

secretion   fàn·bei·maht

sect   (in religion) gaau·mùhn

section   (pieces) gyuht. /Cut this sugar cane into five sections. Jèung nī·tìuh je chit·sèhng ńgh·gyuht.

(of a citrus fruit) kái. /Can you guess how many sections in this orange? Néih gú·dāk·dóu nī·go cháang yáuh géi·dò kái ma?

(of a class) jóu. /What section of the class is he in? Kéuih hái bāan léuih·bihn bīn·yāt·jóu a?

(of a department) fō, chyúh, tēng, jóu, gú. /This is the third section of the department. Nī·go haih daih·sāam·fō.

(of a written composition) jit. /The part I'm referring to is in chapter one, section three. Ngóh só·góng·ge gó·bouh·fahn haih hái daih·yāt·jèung daih·sàam·jit.

(region) daai, kēui. /I was brought up in this section. Ngóh hái nī·yāt·daai jéung·daaih ge.

secure   (safe) wán·jahn. /Is this bridge secure? Nī·tìuh kìuh wán·jahn ma? /Do you feel your job is secure? Néih gok·dāk néih fahn gūng wán·jahn ma?

be secure from m̀h·sái·sàuh. /At least these kids are secure from starvation. Jeui dài hàahn·douh nī·bàan sai·mān·jái m̀h·sái sàuh móuh faahn sihk.

(to get or obtain) luhng·dóu. /We hope we can secure some money to buy books for the library. Ngóh·deih hèi·mohng luhng·dóu dī chín waih tòuh·syù·gún máaih·syú.

security   (safety) ngòn·chyùhn; (something pledged) dái·ngaat (bán): **security for a loan** dái·ngaat·bán; **Security Council of the U.N.** On·chyùhn·léih·sih·wúi.

sedan-chair   gíu (M: lehng); **sedan-chair bearers** tòih·gíu·lóu, giuh·fū

sediment   jà

seduce   yáhn·yau

see   (look at) tái (also ref. tái·gin, tái·dóu in C - E section). /He wants to see your identification. Kéuih yiu tái néih ge sàn·fahn·jing. /We've just seen a good movie. Ngóh·deih ngāam·ngāam tái·jó yāt·chēut hóu hóu ge dihn·yíng.

    (find out) tái·háh. /See what can be done to change it. Tái·háh yáuh māt faat·jí gói·háh kéuih.

    (make certain) tái·jéun. /See that the door is locked before you go to bed. Fan·gaau jī·chìhn tái·jéun douh mùhn sàan·hóu meih?

    (call on) gin. /You'd better take him to see a doctor right away. Néih jeui hóu jīk·hāk tùhng kéuih heui gin yī·sāng la.

    (understand) mìhng, mìhng·baahk. /I see what you mean. Ngóh mìhng(·baahk) néih ge yi·si la. /Do you see what I mean? Néih mìhng·baahk ngóh·ge yi·si ma?

    (realize, grasp) tái·chēut. /Do you see the point he made in this paragraph? Néih tái·chēut kéuih nī·yāt·dyuhn ge yi·si ma?

    (escort someone who is leaving) sung. /Can you see him home? Néih hó·yíh sung keuih tàan nguk·kéi ma?

    see light or objects **through** a window, etc. gaak·jyuh . . . tái·dāk·gin; **can't see through** tai·m̀h·dou gó·bihn. /Can you see anything through this glass? Gaak·jyuh nī·faai bō·lēi hó·yíh tái·dāk·gin gó·bihn ma? /This window is so dirty we can't see through it. Nī·go chēung·mún gam laaht·taat, ngóh·deih tái·m̀h·dóu gó·bihn.

    see something **through** (go through with) jouh·yùhn, yùhn·sìhng. Ngóh dá·syun jèung nī·gihn sih jouh·yùhn kéuih.

    see to (take care of). /Let me see to it. Dáng ngóh léih là.

    /I see! Oh, gám yéung! /Let me see. Dáng ngóh tái·háh. /See you again. Joi·gin.

    see a doctor gin yī·sāng; **see if it fits** si·háh ngāam·m̀h·ngāahm; **see in a dream** muhng·gin

seed   (of a plant) júng·jí (M: nāp); (stone) wát (M: nāp); **flower seeds** fà·ngàhn; **melon seeds** gwà·jí (M: nāp)

seek   (look for) wán. /They sought high and low but couldn't find him. Kéuih·deih dou syu wán kéuih dōu wán·m̀h·dóu kéuih.

    (ask for) kàuh. /We came here to seek your help. Ngóh·deih lèih nī·syu kàuh néih bòng·mòhng.

    seek a livelihood wán·sihk, wán·faahn·sihk; **seek employment** wán·gūng·jouh; **seek the opinions of** jìng·kàuh yi·gin. /I come here to seek your opinion. Ngóh lèih nī·syu jìng·kàuh néih·deih ge yi·gin.

seem   hóu·chíh . . . gám. /The door seems to be locked. Douh mùhn hóu·chíh só·jó gám.

    seem to someone gok·dāk. /It seems like a good idea to me. Ngóh gok·dāk gám géi hóu. /How does that seem to you? Néih gok·dāk gó·go yùh·hòh a? /It doesn't seem to me that he'll come. Ngóh gok·dāk kéuih m̀h·wúih lèih.

seize   jàu·jyuh, jāp·jyuh. /He seized my hand. Kéuih jàu·jyuh ngóh·ge sáu.

    seize an opportunity lá·jyuh go gèi·wuih. /You ought to seize this opportunity. Néih yìng·fahn lá·jyuh nī·go gèi·wuih.

    (take possession of; with or without force) jim, jim·geui; (with force, someone's personal property) ba·jim; (by government) (chàh·)fùng. /His property was seized by some rowdies. Kéuih gé cháan·yihp béi dī mòuh·láai jim·jó. /You have no legal right to seize his property. Néih móuh kyùhn ba·jim kéuih ge cháan·yihp. /His property was seized by the government. Kéuih ge cháan·yihp béi jing·fú (chàh·) fùng·jó.

seldom   hóu síu. /He is seldom at home. Kéuih hóu síu hái·kéi ge. /I seldom go to the movies. Ngóh hóu síu tái dihn·yíng ge.

select   gáan. /You may select the one you want. Yahm néih gáan. (You are free to select.) /Let her select the one she likes. Yáu kéuih jih·gēi gáan lā.
   (chosen as best) gáan·sáu (ge). /These are select Delicious apples. Nī·dī haih gáan·
sáu ge deih·lēi·gwó.

self   jih-: **self-confident** jih·seun; **self-satisfied** jih·múhn; **self-sufficient** jih·kāp jih·
jūk; be **self-centered** is expressed as géi·sìh dōu sìn séung·dou jih·géi sìn; be **self-sup-
porting** is expressed as jih·géi gūng·kāp jih·géi; be **self-conscious** is expressed as
(duhng·jok dāk) mh·jih·yìhn; be **self-possessed** is expressed as daahm·dihng
   self-control jih·jai ge nàhng·lihk; **self-defense** jih·waih. /I hit him in self-defense.
Ngóh waih·jó jih·waih sìn·ji wàahn·sáu ge. **self-respect** jih·jyūn·sàm. /Haven't you
any self-respect? Néih mh·tūng yāt·dī jih·jyūn·sàm dōu móuh?
   myself, ourselves, yourself, yourselves, himself, herself, themselves are expressed
by the proper pronoun plus jih géi, jih·gēi. /She did it herself. Haih kéuih jih·gēi jouh
ge. /She herself says so. Kéuih jih·gēi gám wah ge. /She cut herself. Kéuih got·chàn
jih·gēi. /She came by herself. Kéuih jih·gēi lèih ge. But /She isn't herself today.
is expressed as Keuih pìhng·sìh mh·haih gám ge. (She isn't usually this way.)
   self-contradictory jih·sèung·màauh·téuhn; **self-critical** jih·ngóh·pài·pìhng; **self-es-
teem** jih·juhng; **self-made man** baahk·sáu hìng·gà ge (yàhn); **self-sacrifice** jih·ngóh
hèi·sàng; **self-teaching** (book) móuh·sì·jih·tùng·ge syu.

selfish   jih·sì; **selfishness** jih·sì·sàm

sell   maaih. /What does he sell? Kéuih maaih māt·yéh a? /Sugar sells for twenty
cents a pound. Sà·tòhng màaih léuhng·hòuh·jí yāt·bohng.
   sell out (get rid of by selling) maaih·saai. /They're all sold out. Yíh·gìng maaih
·saai la.
   sell out (betray) chēut·maaih. /He never imagined that he would have been sold out
by his students. Kéuih chùhng·lòih móuh·séung·dou kéuih wúih béi kéuih ge hohk·sāang
chēut·maaih·jó kéuih.

semi-   **semi-circle** bun·yùhn·yìhng; **semi-civilized** bun·hòi·fa ge; **semi-transparent** bun·
tau·mìhng ge; **semi-literary** bun·màhn·yìhn ge

seminary   (theological) sàhn·douh·hohk·yún

send   sung; gei (mail); faat (send out); **send** a message dá. /Have you sent the manuscript off to the printers? Néih sung·jó dī góu heui yan·jih·gún meih a? /Have you
sent the letters yet? Néih gei·jó dī seun meih a? /Have the invitations been sent out
yet? Dī típ faat·jó meih a? /I've already sent him a telegram. Ngóh yíh·gìng dá·jó go
dihn·bou béi kéuih la.
   (cause to go) giu, béi. /Send him in. Giu kéuih yahp·lèih lā. /Why don't you send
him? Dím·gáai néih mh giu kéuih heui nē?
   send (someone) **for** sái or paai . . . lèih lo. /I'll send for it later. Ngóh yāt·ján sái
go yàhn lèih ló.
   send back sung·fàan·heui; **send for a person to come** giu go yàhn lèih; **send kind
regards** mahn·hauh. /Please send my best regards to your parents. Tùhng ngóh
mahn·hauh néih fuh·móuh. **send money** (remit) wuih·chín; **send a present** sung·láih

senior   (in age) chìhn·bui; (in a family or clan) jéung·bui; **senior staff** gōu·kāp jīk·yùhn;
senior class gōu·kāp·bāan

sense   (faculty of sensation) gáam·gok, jì·gok; **sense of hearing** ting·gok; **sense of sight**
sih·gok; **sense of smell** chau·gok; **sense of taste** meih·gok; **sense of touch** chūk·gok
   (meaning) yi·si, douh·leih. /I couldn't get the sense of the sentence. Ngóh·mh·
mìhng·baahk gó·geui wá ge yi·si. /Does it make sense to you? Néih mìhng·baahk haih
māt·yéh yi·si ma? /There is no sense in doing that. Móuh māt douh·léih yiu gám jouh.
   (feel or be aware of) gok·dāk. /I sensed that he is not telling the truth. Ngóh gok·
dāk kéuih só·góng·ge syut·wah mh·haih jàn ge.

common sense sèuhng·sīk. /That's common sense that every person should have.
Nī·dī haih yàhn·yàhn dōu yìng·dòng yáuh ge sèuhng·sīk.

in a sense (from one point of view) joih yāt·fòng·mihn lèih góng. /In a sense, that
is true. Joih yāt·fòng·mihn lèih góng, gám haih jàn ge.

come to one's senses (come out of a faint) séng·fàan. /Has he come to his senses
yet? Kéuih séng·fàan meih a? (be sensible at last). /Finally he came to his senses.
Jēut·jī kéuih mìhng·baahk la.

have a sense of gáam·gok·dāk. /He told me that he had a sense of danger while he
was there. Kéuih góng ngóh jī kéuih hái gó·syu gó·jahn·sí kéuih gáam·gok·dāk ngàih·
hím. /I have a strong sense of responsibility. Ngóh gok·dāk ngóh ge jaak·yahm hóu
chúhng.

sensible   mìhng·baahk·sih·léih ge. /He is a very sensible man. Kéuih go yàhn hóu
mìhng·baahk·sih·léih ge.

sensitive   sàhn·gìng·gwo·máhn

sensuality   sīk·yuhk

sentence   wá <u>with measure</u> geui. /What is the meaning of this sentence? Nī·geui wá
haih māt·yéh yi·si a?
     (pass official judgement on) pun. /The judge sentenced him to a year in prison.
Faat·gùn pun·jó kéuih chóh yāt·nìhn gāam.
     (decision of the court) pun·kyut. /Do you know the sentence of that case? Néih jī·
dou gó·go ngon dím·yéung pun·kyut ge ma?
     serve a sentence gàam·gam. /He has almost served his sentence. Kéuih gàam·
gam ge yaht·jī jauh lèih múhn la.

sentry   saau·bìng

separate   (divide) fàn, fān·hòi, lèih·hòi. /Separate this class into five sections. Jèung
nī·bāan fàn·sèhng ńgh·jóu. /We don't want to be separated. Ngóh·deih m̀h·séung fàn·
hòi. /Separate the yolks from the whites. Jèung dī dáan·wóng tùhng dáan·báak fàn·hòi.
/The child doesn't want to be separated from his mother. Go sai·màn·jái m̀h·háng
lèih·hòi kéuih lóuh·móu.
     (divide by putting something in between) gaak·hòi. /Can we put in a piece of board
to separate these two sections? Ngóh·deih hó·m̀h·hó·yíh yuhng faai báan lèih gaak·hòi
nī·léuhng·bouh·fahn a?
     (pull apart) lāai·hòi. /Hurry up, go and separate them (from fighting). Faai dī lāai·
hòi kéuih·deih lā.
     (as in marriage) fān·gèui. /When did she separate from her husband? Kéuih géi·
sí tùhng kéuih sīn·sàang fān·gèui ga.
     be separate. /These goods were delivered by separate trucks. Nī·dī fo haih yàuh
géi·ga fo·chè wahn·lèih ge. /I'd like to make a separate settlement. Ngóh yiu lihng·
ngói lahp yāt·go hahp·tùhng. (I'd like to make a separate contract.)

September   gáu·yuht

sergeant   sā·gín, seuhng·sih

serial   **serial number** houh·sou, houh·máh

series   (succession, etc., of things) chi·jeuih; (of books) chùhng·syù (M: tou)

serious   (in the way one works) yihng·jàn. /He's very serious about his work. Kéuih
jouh·sih hou yihng·jàn ge.
     (in one's moral attitude) yìhm·sūk. /He's a very serious man. Kéuih go yàhn hóu
yìhm sūk ge.
     (not joking). /Are you serious? Haih·m̀h·haih jàn ga? (Is it true?). /I wasn't
serious at all. I góng·síu jē.

(important) gán·yiu, juhng·yiu; (extremely important) yìhm·juhng. /This is a serious matter. Nī·gihn sih hóu yìhm·juhng.

(grave) yìhm·juhng; (of sickness) gán·yiu. /The international situation is getting more serious. Gwok·jai ge chìhng·yìhng yuht lèih yuht yìhm·juhng. /The doctor said his illness was quite serious. Yī·sāng wah kéuih bèhng dāk sèung·dòng gán·yiu.

(stern). /He always looks so serious and never smiles. Kéuih géi·sí dōu haih gám báan·jyuh go mín wìhng·yúhn m̀h·siu ge.

seriously   (earnestly) jàn·haih, kok·haih. /He is thinking seriously of becoming a doctor. Kéuih jàn·haih séung yiu jouh yī·sāng.

(not jesting) jàn·ge. /Seriously, did you tell him? Néih haih·m̀h·haih jàn ge góng·jó béi kéuih tèng la.

take someone or something **seriously.** /Don't take it so seriously. M̀h·sái gam yihng·jàn gé. /Don't take him so seriously. is expressed as M̀h·hóu seun kéuih. (Don't believe him.) /They're not taking this matter seriously. Kéuih·deui nī·gihn sih hóu·chíh fáan·fáan·háh gám. /I hope you will study this lesson seriously. Ngóh hèi·mòhng néih yihng·jàn duhk·sīk nī·fo syù.

sermon   (a religious talk) is always expressed verbally. /Who is going to give the sermon this week? Nī·go láih·baai bīn·go góng·douh a? /How do you like his sermon today? Néih gok·dāk kéuih gàm·yaht góng dāk dím a? /What's his sermon about? Kéuih góng dī māt·yéh a? /It's about discrimination. Kéuih góng júng·juhk·mahn·tàih.

serpent   sèh (M: tìuh)

serum   hyut·chīng

servant   gùng·yàhn; **female servant** pòh·mā, má·jé, sái·pó; **male servant** nàahm·gùng·yàhn

serve   (work, help, or do good for). /First you should learn how to serve the customers. Daih·yāt néih yiu hohk·sīk dím·yéung jiu·fù dī haak·jái. /If the mayor doesn't serve the people of the city, why don't we get a new one? Yùh·gwó go síh·jéung m̀h·waih síh·màhn fuhk·mouh dím·gáai ngóh·deih m̀h·wuhn·go yāt·go a? /It's everyone's duty to serve his country. Waih gwok·gà fuhk·mouh haih múih·yāt·go yàhn ge yih·mouh.

(wait on) fuhk·sih, dá·léih, kéih (used in Chinatowns in U.S. & Canada). /Who serves these three tables? Bīn·go fuhk·sih nī·sàam·jèung tói a? /Dinner is served. Chéng màaih·wái là.

(in armed forces) dōng·bìng. /He served in the army for three years. Kéuih hái luhk·gwān dòng·jó sàam·nìhn bìng.

(of a ball) faat·kàuh, 'serve' (used in Hong Kong). /It's your turn to serve. Lèuhn·dou neih faat·kàuh (or 'serve') la.

(of a prison term) chóh·gāam. /He is serving a prison term. Kéuih yìh·gā chóh·gán·gāam.

serve no purpose. /That serves no purpose at all. Gám jouh yāt·dī yuhng dōu móuh.

serve the purpose. /This will serve the purpose. Nī·go dāk la. /What purpose does it serve? Gám yáuh māt yuhng a?

serve a notice, a summons sung. /The landlord told me that he has already served a notice on the family to move. Ngūk·jyú wah ngóh jī kéuih yíh·gìng sung·jó jèung tùng·jì béi gó·gà yàhn giu kéuih·deih bùn·ché la.

service   (armed forces) gwàn·déui. /He enlisted in the service. Kéuih yahp·jó gwàn·déui.

(meeting for worship) láih·baai (Protestant); **hold a service** jouh·láih·baai; (nèih·saat (Catholic); say a Mass jouh·nèih·saat); **memorial service** jèui·douh·wúi (to hold a memorial service hòi jeui·douh·wúi); **military service** bìng·yihk, **to serve military service** fuhk·bìng·yihk

(employment). /Does she have a civil service job? Kéuih haih·m̀h·haih hái jing·fú jouh sih a? (Does she work for the government?)

(supplying of some need). /Do they have bus service there? <u>is expressed as</u>: Kéuih·
deih gó·syu yáuh móuh gùng·guhng·hei·chè a?

(performance of labor). /He gave us good service for more than ten years. (of an
employee) <u>is expressed as</u>: Kéuih hái syu jouh sih jouh·jó sahp·nìhn la, jouh dāk hóu
hóu.

be at one's service. /I'm at your service. Yùh·gwó yáuh māt·yéh sih, chéng néih
chèuih·sìh giu ngóh, m̀h·sái·haak·hei.

be of service yáuh·yuhng. /Will this book be of service? Nī·bún syù deui néih yáuh·
yuhng ma?

do a service (help) bòng·mòhng. /Could you do me a small service? Chéng néih
bòng·mòhng·háh dāk ma?

use the service of. /Can you use the service of a typist? <u>is expressed as</u>: Néih·
deih nī·syu chéng dá·jih·yùhn ma? (Will you hire a typist?)

to service dá·jíng (take care of); sàu·léih (repair). /They serviced my car pretty
well. Kéuih·deih dá·jíng ngóh ga chè dá·jíng dāk géi hóu. /I'm leaving my car here to
be serviced. Ngóh làuh·dài ga chè sàu·léih·háh.

sesame   jì·màh: **sesame oil** jì·màh·yàuh; **sesame seeds** jì·màh

session   (meeting) wuih·yi; **closing of the session** bai·wúi; **opening of the session** hòi·
wúi; **during the session** hòi·wúi·kèih·gaan; **extraordinary session** làhm·sìh·wuih yi;
full session chyùhn·tái·daaih·wúi

set   (put or place) jài. /Set it over there. Jài·hái gó·syu.

(established or fixed) dihng, kwài·dihng. /Have they set the time for the ball game
yet? Kéuih·deih dihng·jó géi·sí dá·bō meih a? /It is a set rule to get to school at 8
o'clock. Hohk·haauh kwài·dìhng baat·dím·jūng yiu dou hohk·haauh.

(put in proper condition or position): (a bone) jip. /The doctor said he would set
his broken bone. Yī·sāng wah yiu tùhng kéuih jip·fàan tìuh gwāt. (a table) báai. /Have
you set the table? Néih baai·jo·toi meih a? (alarm clock) gaau. /Does he know how to
set the alarm? Kéuih wúih·m̀h·wúih gaau naauh·jūng a? (a jewel) sèung. /I want to
have this diamond set in a gold ring. Ngóh séung jèung nī·nāp jyun·sehk sèung·hái go
gām·gaai·jí·syu.

(go down) lohk. /What time does the sun set today? Gàm·yaht géi·dím·jūng lohk·
yaht·táu a?

(get solid) kìhng. /Has the jelly set yet? Dī je·lēi kìhng·jó meih a?

(a group of articles used together) **a set of tools** yāt·tou ga·sàang; **a set of dishes**
yāt·fu wún·dihp; **a set of furniture** yāt·tou gā·sì; **a set of books** yāt·tou syù; **a set of
chessmen** yāt·fu kéi

set an example jouh go bóng·yeuhng. /He has set a good example for us. Kéuih
waih ngóh·deih jouh·jó yāt·go hóu hóu ge bóng·yeuhng.

set aside jài·màaih yāt·bihn. /This fund has been set aside for an emergency. Nī·
bāt chín haih jài·màaih yāt·bihn yuh·beih bāt·sìh·jì·sèui ge.

set at liberty, set free yáuh kéuih jáu, fong. /He will be set at liberty. Wúih fong
kéuih ge.

set off (start to go) héi·chìhng, chēut·faat; (increase the effect of) yíng·héi (cause to
explode) fong; (light) dím·jeuhk, sìu. /They're setting off tomorrow on their world tour.
Kéuih·deih tìng·yaht héi·chìhng wàahn·yàuh sai·gaai. /When are we setting off (on our
hike)? Ngóh·deih géi·sí chēut·faat a? /This ruby sets off her green dress nicely. Nī·
nāp hùhng·bóu·sehk yíng·héi kéuih gihn luhk·sāam gang·gà leng la. /Tell them not to
set off the firecrackers until the ceremony is over. Giu kéuih·deih dáng hàahng·yùhn·
láih sìn·ji hóu dím·jeuhk chyun paau·jéung. /Now you may set off the firecrackers.
Yìh·gā néih hó·yíh dím·jeuhk chyun paau·jéung la.

set sail hòi·sàn. /When will the ship set sail? Jek syùhn géi·sí hòi·sàn a?

set <u>someone</u> **on** (or against) <u>someone else</u> tíu·buht. /They wouldn't have fought if
he hadn't set them on one another. Yùh·gwó m̀h·haih kéuih tíu·buht, kéuih·deih m̀h·wúih
dá·héi·sèuhng·lèih ge.

set on fire sìu·jeuhk; **be set on fire** sìu·jeuhk·jó. /His cigarette set the sofa on fire. Kéuih háu yīn·jái sìu·jeuhk go sō·fā. /His house was set on fire last night. Kàhm·máahn kéuih gāan ngūk sìu·jeuhk·jó.

set straight góng chìng·chó. /Please set me straight on this. Chéng néih jèung nī·gihn sih tùhng ngóh góng chìng·chó.

set to music (compose). /Can you set this poem to music? Néih·hó·yíh waih nī·sáu sī sé go gō·póu ma?

set up (establish) gin·lahp, hòi. /I think first we should set up a system. Daih·yāt ngóh gok·dāk yiu gin·lahp·héi yāt·go jai·douh sìn. /Maybe we can help you to set up a shop. Waahk·jé ngóh·deih hó·yíh bòng néih hòi gàan pou·táu.

be set gu·jāp. /He has very set opinions. Kéuih go yàhn hóu gu·jāp ge.

radio set sāu·yām·gēi. /How much does this radio (set) cost? Nī·go sāu·yām·gēi géi·dò chín a?

(scenery) bou·gíng. /Who designed the sets for this play? Nī·chēut hei ge bou·gíng haih bīn·go chit·gai ga?

(ready, prepared) yuh·beih·hóu, tóh·dong. /Are you all set to go? Néih·deih yuh·beih·hóu héi·chìhng meih a? /Are you all set? Tóh·dong·saai lā máh?

settle   (make a permanent home, or go to live) dihng·gèui, jyuh. /I want to settle in the country when I am sixty. Ngóh·luhk·sahp·seui ge·sìh·hauh, ngóh jauh dihng·gèui·hái hèung·háh la. **settle down** òn·ji·hóu. /Has he settled down yet? Kéuih òn·ji·hóu meih a? or Kéuih jyuh·dihng meih a?

(decide) gáai·kyut. /Can you settle this question for me? Néih hó·yíh tùhng ngóh gáai·kyut nī·go mahn·tàih ma?

(arrange comfortably) hóu·jih·joih gám chóh (sit), . . . ngàai (recline, lean back). /He settled himself in the chair. Kéuih hóu·jih·joih gám chóh·hái jèung yi·syu.

(got to the bottom) chàhm·dái. /Wait until the tea leaves settle. Dáng dī chàh·yihp chàhm·jó·dái sìn.

(conclude by agreement) dihng·hóu. /Have you settled the terms of the contract yet? Néih·deih dihng·hóu·saai hahp·tùhng yahp·bihn ge tìuh·gín meih a?

(pay) wàahn·chìng. /I came to settle a bill. Ngóh lèih wàahn·chìng yāt·tìuh sou.

settle a bargain góng·sèhng·ga; **settled amicably** wòh·pìhng gáai·kyut; **settle by force** móuh·lihk gáai·kyut; **settle beforehand** yuh·sìn gáau·tóh; **settle** (a bill) **in full** wàahn·chìng

settlement   (solution) gáai·kyut; (a foreign settlement at a treaty port) jòu·gaai; **International Settlement** gùng·guhng·jòu·gaai; **Straits Settlements** Hói·haahp·jihk·màhn·deih

seven   chāt; **seventh** daih·chāt; **the seventh time** daih·chāt·chi

seventeen   sahp·chāt

seventy   chāt·sahp

sever   (separate) fān·hòi; **to sever with a knife** yuhng dōu chit·hòi (a small knife) . . . jáam·hòi (with a chopper)

several   géi plus a measure; for emphasis hóu géi plus a measure; **several days** géi·yaht; **several weeks** géi·go láih·baai; **several months** géi·go·yuht; **several years** géi·nìhn. /I want to stay here for several days. Ngóh yiu hái nī·syu jyuh géi·yaht. /There are several ways of doing this. Jouh nī·gihn sih yáuh hóu géi·go fòng·faat.

severe   leih·hoih, gāau·gwàan. /He has a very severe illness. Kéuih behng dāk hóu leih·hoih. /I have a severe pain in my tooth. Ngóh yáuh jek ngàh tung dāk hóu gāau·gwàan.

(for an accident) yìhm·juhng. /There was a severe accident this morning. Gàm·jìu·jóu faat·sàng yāt·gihn hóu yìhm·juhng ge yi·ngoih.

(hard to endure) gāau·gwàan, gán·yiu. /Is the winter severe here? Nī·syu ge láahng·tìn haih·m̀h·haih láahng dāk hóu gāau·gwàan ga?

(strict) yìhm. /Should we or shouldn't we be so severe with the students? Ngóh·
deih yìng·fahn m̀h·yìng·fahn gún dī hohk·sāang gún dāk gam yìhm a?

(difficult to be sustained) yihm·gaak ge. /This motor will have to undergo a severe
test before it is put into service. Nī·go mō·dá yāt·dihng yiu gìng·gwo yìhm·gaak ge si·
yihm sìn·ji yuhng dāk.

sew   lyùhn; (by machine) chē. /Do you sew? Néih wúih lyùhn sāam a? /Please sew
this button on for me. M̀h·gòi néih tùhng ngóh lyùhn·fàan nī·nāp náu. **sewing machine**
chē·yī·gēi, yī·chē (M: ga)

sewer   hàang·kèuih

shabby   **have on shabby clothes** yī·sāam·làahm·léuih. /They all had on shabby clothes.
Kéuih·deih go·go dōu yī·sāam·làahm·léuih.

sex   sing·biht (used only on written documents or when citing them). /The company
asks you to write down your name, age, and sex. Gūng·sī yiu néih sé·dài néih ge sing·
mìhng, nìhn·lìhng, tùhng sing·biht.

(for human) nàahm- (male), néuih- (female). /There are three hundred male students and two hundred female students in our school. Ngóh·deih hohk·haauh yáuh sàam·
baak nàahm·hohk·sāang, léuhng·baak néuih·hohk·sāang.

(for animals) gūng (ge), ná (ge). /What sex are these puppies? Nī·géi·jek gáu·jái
yáuh géi·dò·jek haih gūng yáuh géi dò jek haih ná a?

sex appeal sing·gáam; **sex education** sing·gaau·yuhk; **sexual desire** sing·yuhk;
sexual organ sing·hei·gùn, sàang·jihk·hei

shade   **shade of a tree** syuh·yàm. /Let's stand in the shade of the tree. Hái syuh·yàm
·hah kéih·háh là. /There's some shade, let's stand there. is expressed as: Gó·syu
yām·yām·déi hái gó·syu kéih·háh là.

(of color) ngàahn·sīk, sīk·séui. /I don't like this shade. Ngóh m̀h·jùng·yi nī·go
ngàahn·sīk.

(a blind) chēung·lím. /Pull down the shades. Lāai·dài dī chēung·lím.

to shade (screen) jè·jyuh; **to shade it with a fan** béi bá sin jè·jyuh; **to shade it with
the hand** béi jek sáu jè·jyuh

lamp shade dāng·jaau; **a parasol** taai·yèuhng·jē (M: bá)

shadow   yíng. /What are you afraid of? It's nothing but your own shadow. Sái·māt gèng
a, néih jih·gēi ge yíng jī ma.

to shadow (watch secretly)[am·jūng] gàam·sih;(follow secretly) diu·méih. /He said
he is shadowed. Kéuih wah yáuh yàhn gàam·sih kéuih. /I was shadowed again today.
Gàm·yaht yauh yáuh yàhn diu·ngóh·meih la.

shaft   (handle) beng

shake   ngòuh, nihng. /Shake the bottle well before using the medicine. /Nī·jèun yeuhk
sihk jī·chîhn yiu ngòuh·wàhn kéuih. /Don't shake the tree. M̀h·hóu ngòuh pò syuh. /He
shook his head and said no. Kéuih nihng·háh go táu wah m̀h·dāk·

(hold the end and shake up and down) yéung. /Can you help me to shake this rug?
Néih bòng·háh ngóh yéung·háh jèung deih·jīn dāk ma?

(quiver) jan. /He was shaking with cold. Kéuih láahng·dou jan·saai. /He can't stop
his hand from shaking. Kéuih ge sáu yāt·méi hái syu jan.

(move) yūk, ngòuh. /Our whole house shook during the earthquake. Deih·jan gó
jàhn·sî, ngóh·deih sèhng·gāan ngūk dōu yūk·yūk·háh.

shake hands làai·sáu, ngāk·sáu. /He said during the campaign his hand was sore
from shaking so many hands. Kéuih wah kéuih gihng·syún gó·jahn·sî, làai·sáu làai·dou
sáu dōu tung·saai.

shake off (fall off) lāt, ngòuh·lāt, fihng·lāt. /The mud will shake off your shoes
easily when it dries. Néih hàaih·seuhng·bihn gó·dī nàih gòn·jó jî·hauh jih·yìhn jauh lāt
ge la.

shake up (startle; give a shock to someone) haak dāk . . . hóu gāau·gwàan. /I was really shaken up by the accident. Gó·chi yi·ngoih haak dāk ngóh hóu gāau·gwàan.

shall   (expect or intend to) yiu. /I shall learn this lesson before school tomorrow. Ngóh tìng·yaht fàan·hohk jì·chìhn yiu duhk·sīk nī·fo syù.
    (be required) (yāt·dihng) yiu. /He shall return the book to the library tomorrow. Kéuih tìng·yaht yāt·dihng yiu jèung bún syù wàahn·fàan tòuh·syù·gún.
    (in asking someone). /Shall I wait? Ngóh sái·m̀h·sái dáng a? /Let's have dinner now, shall we? Ngóh·deih yìh·gā sihk·fàahn la, hóu ma? /Shall I close the window? Ngóh sàan·màaih douh chēung·mún, hóu ma?

shallow   chín. /The water is too shallow to swim in. Dī séui taai chín, m̀h·yàuh dāk· séui.

sham   (pretend to be) ja·dai, ja-: **sham dead** ja·séi; **sham sickness** ja·behng; **sham sleep** ja·fan

shame   (disgrace) cháu. /Doesn't he feel shame? Kéuih m̀h·gok·dāk cháu àh?

shameful   dìu·gá. /How shameful it is! Jàn·haih dìu·gá la!

shameless   m̀h·jì·cháu, mihn·pèih·háuh (thick skin). /He is shameless. Kéuih go yàhn hóu m̀h·jì cháu ge. or Kéuih mihn·pèih hóu háuh ge.

shampoo   (wash the hair) sái·tàuh; (liquid to wash the hair with) sái·tàuh·séui

shape   (form) yìhng·johng, -yìhng. /Isn't the shape of the mountain odd! Nī·go sàan ge yìhng·johng jàn·haih gwaai la! /I don't care whether it is in a round shape or square shape. Yùhn·yìhng, fōng·yìhng ge, ngóh dōu móuh·só·wáih.
    (condition) chìhng·yìhng. /His business is in bad shape. Kéuih pùhn sàang·yi ge chìhng yìhng m̀h·haih géi hóu. /I'm in bad shape. is expressed as: Ngóh nī·páai m̀h· haih géi jìng·sàhn. (Lately I haven't felt too good.)
    get something into shape jíng·léih. /I have to get my notes into shape before I can show them to you. Ngóh yiu jèung ngóh ge bāt·gei jíng·léih·hóu sìn·jì béi dāk néih tái.
    shape up (take a certain form). /How are things shaping up? Gihn sih luhng·sèhng dím la.
    be in shape. /Put your room in shape. Jāp·sahp·hóu gàan fóng kéuih. /Tell him to come this afternoon, the house is in such poor shape. Gāan ngūk gam làu·yàu giu kéuih gàm·yaht hah·jau sìn·ji lèih lā.

share   (part) fahn. /You'll have to do your share. Néih yiu jouh néih gó·fahn. /Let me pay my share of the bill. Dáng ngóh jih·gēi béi ngóh nī·fahn lā.
    (part ownership of a company) gú·fán, gú. /How many shares do you hold in that company? Gó·gāan gūng·sī néih yáuh géi·dò gú·fán a? /I have sixty shares. Ngóh yáuh luhk·sahp·gú.
    (use in common) hahp·màaih plus a suitable verb. /They share the kitchen. Kéuih deih hahp·màaih yùhng yāt·go chyùh·fóng.
    (have in common) dōu yáuh, dōu plus a suitable verb. /They share the habit of getting up late in the morning. Kéuih·deih léuhng·go dōu yáuh ngaan·héi·sàn ge jaahp· gwaan. /They shared the secret. is expressed as: Kéuih·deih léuhng·go dōu jì·dou nī· go bei·maht.
    to share (divide and use) fàn. /I know I can't finish this watermelon, let's share it. Ngóh jì·dou ngóh m̀h·sihk·dāk·saai nī·go sài·gwà, daaih·gā fàn·jó kéuih la.
    share certificate gú·piu; **shareholder** gú·dūng

shark   sà·yùh (M: tìuh); **shark's fins** yùh·chi

sharp   (not blunt) leih. /Give me a sharp knife. Béi bá leih ge dōu ngóh.

sharpen   (a pencil) pài: **sharpen a pencil** pài yùhn·bāt; (a razor) mòh: **sharpen a knife** mòh dōu; (to a point) seuk, seuk jìn; **pencil sharpener** yùhn·bāt·páau; **knife sharpener** mòh·dōu·sehk

shave   (with a razor) tai; (with a plane) pàauh. /Have you shaved? Néih tai·jó sòu meih
a? /I need a shave. <u>is expressed as</u>:   Ngóh yiu tai·sòu.

she   kéuih; **she cat** māau·ná; **she dog** gáu·ná

shear   (cut off) jín

shears   (large scissors) daaih·gaau·jín

sheath   dōu·hok

shed   (a building) pàahng·chóng, pàahng; **shed tears** làuh·ngáahn·leuih; (give off). /The
sun sheds light on the earth. Yaht·gwōng jiu·jyuh go deih·kàuh.

sheep   yèuhng·mē (M: jek), mìhn·yéung (M: jek)

sheet   (for bed) péih·dāan (M: jèung); (of paper) jèung: **a sheet of paper** yāt·jèung jí;
sheet copper tùhng·báan; **sheet of iron** tit·báan

shelve   gá; **book shelves** syù·gá

shell   (as on nuts, eggs, clams, oysters, etc.) hok; (projectile) paau·dáan (fire shells at)
hòi·paau gùng·dá. /The warship shelled the enemy's position. Jin·laahm hòi·paau gùng·
dá dihk·yàhn ge jahn·deih.
    to shell (remove shells) mīt: **shell the peas** mīt hòh·láan·dáu; mōk: **shell the wal-
nuts** mōk hahp·tòuh

shelter (protection). /We have to find a shelter for this homeless family. Ngóh·deih yāt·
dihng yiu wán daat deih·fòng béi nī·ga yàhn jaahm·sìh jyuh·jyuh sìn. /Can we find a
shelter from rain nearby? Yáuh móuh faat·jí hái jó·gán wán·dóu daat deih·fòng beih·
yúh a?
    air raid shelter fòhng·hùng·duhng; **fall-out shelter** yùhn·jí·chàhn fòhng·hùng·duhng
    to shelter jiu·liuh, jiu·gu, jiu·fù. /Who'll shelter the refugees? Bīng·go jiu·liuh dī
naahn·màhn a?

shepherd   muhk·yèuhng·yàhn, hòn·yèuhng ge yàhn; **to shepherd** jiu·gu

shield   deuhn·pàaih, pàaih: **rattan shield** tàhng·pàaih; **to shield** dóng·jyuh: **to shield with
one's hand** yuhng sáu dóng·jyuh

shift   (move) yìh; **day shift** yaht·bāan; **night shift** yeh·bāan; **change shift** wuhn·bāan

shilling   sìn·lìhng

shine   (give light) jiu; (dazzle) chàahng. /The moonlight is shining on the lake. Yuht·
gwōng jiu·jyuh go wùh. /The car's headlight is shining in my eyes. Jáan chē·dāng
chàahng·jyuh ngóh sèung ngáahn.
    (polish) sáang (like silver), chaat (like shoes). /This set of silver needs to be shined.
Nī·tou dōu·chā yiu sáang·háh la. /I want my shoes shined. Ngóh yiu chaat pèih·hàaih.
    (cause to give light) jiu. /Shine the light over here. Jiu·háh nī·syu.
    a shine (shoes). /Please give me a shine. Tùhng ngóh chaat·háh deui pèih·hàaih.
    have a shine (be shiny) líng. /Look at the shine of the car! Néih tái·háh ga chē géi
líng!

Shintoism   Sàhn·douh·gaau

ship   syùhn (M: jek); (send by freight) wahn; (dispatch, as troops) paai; (mail) gei.
/Have your goods been shipped yet? Néih·dī fo wahn·jó chēut·heui meih a? /The government shipped two thousand troops to the city to maintain order. Jing·fú yíh·gìng paai·
jó léuhng·chìn bīng heui gó·go sèhng wàih·chìh diht·jeuih la. /Where will the merchandise be shipped to? Nī·dī fo gei·heui bīn·syu ga?
    ship building jouh·syùhn; **ship launching** hah·séui·láih

shirk   **to shirk work** tàu·láahn; **to shirk danger** dó·beih; **to shirk responsibility** tèui·wái shirt   sēut·sāam (M: gihn)

shiver   jan, dá·láahng·jan

shock   (by electricity). /He was injured by electric shock. Kéuih béi dihn dihn·chàn.
  (something very upsetting) dá·gīk. /This is a very great shock to him. Nī·gihn sih
  deui kéuih jìng·sàhn·seuhng haih yāt·go hóu daaih ge dá·gīk.

shoe   hàaih (M: jek; pair, deui); **black shoes** hāk hàaih; **cloth shoes** bou·hàaih; **shoehorn**
  hàaih·chāu; **shoelace** hàaih·dáai; **shoe polish** hàaih·yáu (M: hahp); **sneakers** gàau·
  hàaih; **shoemaker** bóu·hàaih·lóu; **take off shoes** chèuih hàaih; **wear shoes** jeuk hàaih;
  white shoes baahk haaih

shoot   (as an arrow) seh: **shoot an arrow** seh·jin; (shoot with a gun) hōi chēung dá:
  shoot birds dá jéuk; **shoot down** dá·lohk; **shoot a cannon** hòi paau; **executed by shoot-**
  ing chēung·baih, chēung·kyut; (new growth) ngàh; **set forth shoots** chēut·ngàh; **shooting**
  star làuh·sīng; **bamboo shoots** séun
       shoot pictures yíng·séung. /We're planning to shoot a few pictures this morning.
  Ngóh·deih dá·syun gàm·jīu·jóu yíng géi·fūk séung.

shop   pou·táu (M: gàan); -póu (M: gaan): **bookshop** syù·póu; **barber shop** fèi·faat·póu;
  pawn shop dong·póu
       to shop máaih·yéh; **shop around** tái·háh; **shopping** máaih·yéh. /Where is the best
  place to shop? Hái bīn·syu máaih yéh jeui hóu a? /She went shopping. Kéuih heui·jó
  máaih yéh.
       shut up shop séuhng·pou, sàan·mùhn, sàu·dong, sàu·síh.

shore   ngohn. /How far are we from the shore? Ngóh·deih lèih ngohn yáuh géi yúhn a?
       go on shore séuhng·ngohn. /Don't go on shore yet? Ṁh·hóu séuhng·ngohn jih.

short   (in length) dyún. /This coat is too short. Nī·gihn sāam taai dyún. /I want my
  hair cut short. Ngóh séung (jèung ngóh ge tàuh·faat) jín·dyún dī.
       (in time) yāt·jahn·gāan. /He can only talk with you for a short time. Kéuih jí·nàhng
  tùhng néih góng yāt·jahn·gāan jē.
       (in height) ngái. /You say that he is short, I don't. Néih wah kéuih ngái àh, ngóh
  wah kéuih ṁh·ngái.
       be short (of) jàang. /We are short three chairs. Juhng jàang sāam·jèung yí.
       ran short ṁh·gau, **running short** jauh·lèih ṁh·gau. /We ran short of paper. Ngóh
  deih ṁh·gau jí la. /Our paper supplies are running short. Ngóh·deih jauh·lèih ṁh·gau
  jí la.
       cut short sūk·dyún. /He cut short his vacation because of his mother's illness.
  Kéuih yàn·waih kéuih lóuh·móuh behng só·yíh sūk·dyún kéuih ge ga·kèih.
       in short, make a long story short (as a whole) júng·jí, júng·yíh·yìhn·jí. /In short, I
  don't have the money. Júng·jí, ngóh móuh chín.
       short memory gei·sing ṁh·hóu. /I have a short memory. Ngóh gei·sing·ṁh·hóu.
       short temper cháu pèih·hei, bouh·chou. /He is known for his short temper. Kéuih
  hóu cháu pèih·hei ge, go·go dōu jí ge la.
       shorts dyún·fu (M: tîuh); **undershorts** dái·fu (M: tîuh); **short story** dyún·pìn síu
  syut; **short wave** dyún·bō

shortage   kyut·faht, kyut síu. /We have a shortage of fresh vegetables. Ngóh·deih kyut·
  faht sàn·sìn gwà·choi.

shortcoming   kyut·dím, dyún·chyúh

shortcut   jit·ging (N)

shorten   jíng·dyún; jín·dyún (by cutting)

shorthand chūk·gei. /Does she know shorthand? Kéuih wúih chūk·gei ma?

short-lived   dyún mehng

shortly   yāt·jahn·gāan. /I'll be with you shortly. Ngóh yāt·jahn·gāan jauh lèih.

shortsighted   gahn·sí. /Your child is shortsighted. Néih ge sai·mān·jái yáuh dī gahn·sí.

shot   (discharge of a gun) chēung héung. /Did you hear a shot? Néih yáuh móuh tèng·
gin chēung héung a?
(injection) dá·jām. /Have you had your cholera shots? Néih dá·jó fok·lyuhn·jām
meih a? /We'll give him a shot every four hours. Ngóh·deih múih sei·go jūng·tàuh
tùhng kéuih dá yāt·jām.
(photograph) séung. /Did you take any shots of the beautiful scenery? Néih yáuh
móuh yíng·dóu géi·fūk hóu ge fùng·gíng·séung a?

should   yīng·gòi, yīng·dòng. /I think we should leave now. Ngóh gú ngóh·deih yīng·gòi
jáu la. /They should be here by this time. Nī·go sìh·hauh kéuih·deih yīng·gòi lèih·dou
ge la.
(in a conditional clause). /If it should rain, do you still want to go? Yùh·gwó lohk·
yúh néih juhng heui ma?

shoulder   (part of the human body) bok·tàuh; **to shoulder the responsibility** fuh·jaak.
/We'll shoulder all the responsibility. Ngóh·deih yùhn·chyùhn fuh·jaak.
to shoulder (carry on one's shoulders or upper back; as a pack or person) tok;
(carry a pole, weighted at each end, on one shoulder) dàam. /He was shouldering a
bag of rice. Kéuih tok·jyuh yāt·bàau máih. /Do you think you can shoulder two buckets
of water with a pole and walk in good balance? Néih gú néih hó·m̀h·hó·yíh dàam·jyuh
léuhng·túng séui juhng hàahng dāk hóu dihng nē?

shout   daaih·sèng ngaai. /What are they shouting for? Kéuih·deih hái syu daaih·sèng
ngaai māt·yéh a?

shovel   cháan; **to shovel up** cháan·héi

show   (point out) jí·béi . . . tái. /Can you show me where he lives? Néih hó·yíh jí·béi
ngóh tái kéuih jyuh·hái bīn·syu ma? /Can you show me the place on the map? Néih hó·
yíh hái deih·tòuh·syu jí·béi ngóh tái gó·daat deih·fòng hái bīn·syu ma?
(go with and point out) daai . . . tái·háh. /Could you show us the house? M̀h·gòi néih
daai ngóh·deih tái·háh gāan ngūk, dāk ma? /Could you show us the way? M̀h·gòi néih
daai ngóh·deih heui, dāk ma?
(let someone see) nīk (jouh, etc.) béi . . . tái (háh). /Please show me some jade
rings. M̀h·gòi néih nīk dī yuhk·gaai·jí béi ngóh tái·háh. /Show me how to do it. Jouh·
béi ngóh tái·háh.
(instruct) góng béi . . . tèng or jì. /Show him how to do it. is expressed as: Góng
béi kéuih tèng dím jouh. (Tell him how to do it.) /Could you show me the way? Néih
hó·yíh góng·béi ngóh tèng dím heui ma?
(display). /His work shows signs of improvement. Kéuih ge gùng·jok tái·héi seuhng·
lèih géi yáuh jeun·bouh.
(indicate) wah. /The chart shows that you were absent (from school) twice this
week, is this true? Go bíu wah néih nī·go láih·baai kwong·fo léuhng·chi, haih·m̀h·haih
a? /What temperature is shown on the thermometer? Hòhn·syú·bíu wah géi·dò·douh
a?
(explain, prove) gáai·sīk, béi . . . tái·gwo. /They were not able to show why they
couldn't go. Kéuih·deih móuh·faat jí gáai·sīk kéuih·deih dím·gáai m̀h·heui. /I won't believe it unless it's shown to me. Yùh·gwó m̀h·béi ngóh tái·gwo, ngóh m̀h·sèung·seun.
(present, in a theater) yíng (movie); jouh (play, opera). /What are they showing at
the Queen's theater? Wòhng·hauh hei·yún gam·yaht yíng māt·yéh a? /I am told tonight
they are showing a play not an opera. Ngóh tèng·màhn·wah kéuih·deih gàm·máahn jouh
wá·kehk m̀h·haih jouh daaih·hei.
(present, in a store) báai. /Are those things shown in the show window for sale?
Báai·hái sīk·gwaih gó·dī yéh maaih·m̀h·maaih ga?

show off yín·yéh, yín. /He's showing off again. Kéuih yauh hái·syu yín·yéh la. /She is showing off her jewels again. Kéuih yauh hái·syu yín kéuih ge sáu·sīk la.

show up (appear, of a person). /We waited and waited for two hours, but he never showed up. Ngóh·deih dáng·jó léuhng·go jūng·dím, kéuih chí·jùng móuh·lèih·dou.

a show (play) wá·kehk (M: chēut); (movie) yíng·wá, dihn·yíng (M: chēut); (opera) daaih·hei (M: chēut). /Did you go to the show last night? Néih·deih kàhm·máahn yauh mouh tái wá·kehk (or yíng·wá, or daaih·hei) a?

showcase   sīk·gwaih

shower   (short rain) yāt·jahn·yúh. /Don't leave until this shower is over. Lohk·yùhn nī·jahn·yúh sìn·ji jáu la.

take a shower chùng·lèuhng. /You can take a shower here after the game. Dá·yùhn bō jī·hauh néih hó·yíh hái nī·syu chùng·lèuhng.

shrewd   jìng·mìhng ge. /He is very shrewd. Kéuih hóu jìng·mìhng ge.

shrimp   hā (M: jek)

shrine   sàhn·ngām (M: joh)

shrink   sūk·màaih; (as cloth) sūk·séui. /Will this kind of cloth shrink? Nī·tíng bou sūk· m̀h·sūk·séui ga?

shrub   syuh·jái

shuffle   **shuffle cards** sái·páai

shrug   sūk·háh go bok·tàuh

shut   sàan màaih. /Please shut the door when you leave. Néih jáu ge sìh·hauh chéng· néih sàan·màaih douh mùhn.

shut down. /This factory has already been shut down for two months. Nī·gàan gùng· chóng yíh·gìng tìhng·gùng léuhng·go·yuht la.

shut off sàan. /Shut off the water! Sàan séui·hàuh a! /Shut off the motor! Sàan·jó go mō·dá kéuih!

shut up (keep indoors) wan (héi). /He shut himself up to study for exams. Kéuih wan jih·gēi hái gàan·fóng·syu yuh·beih háau·si.

shut up (don't talk) Máih·chòuh! M̀h·hóu góng la! (more emphatic) M̀h·jéun góng la! (imprison or close in) wan. /Shut the dog in the garage. Wan jek gáu hái chē·fòhng· syu.

shut up shop at the end of the day séuhng·pou

shutter   baak·yihp·chēung

shuttle   sō

shuttlecock   yín; **play at shuttlecock** tek·yín (a Chinese sport)

shy   (coy) pa·cháu; (modest) haak·hei. /She is very shy. Kéuih hóu pa·cháu ge.

sick   (ill) behng. /Is he sick? Kéuih haih·m̀h·haih behng·jó a? or Kéuih haih·m̀h·haih behng a? /She is very sick. Kéuih behng dāk hóu gán·yiu.

(indisposed, out of sorts) m̀h·jih·yìhn, m̀h·jìng·sàhn, m̀h·syù·fuhk. /I'm feeling a little sick. Ngóh gok·dāk yáuh dī m̀h·jih·yìhn.

(sick with). /He's sick in bed with pneumonia. is expressed as: Kéuih dāk·jó fai· yìhm fan·hái chòhng·syu. (He got pneumonia and is lying in bed.)

(sick at the stomach) jok·muhn. /She often gets sick sailing. Kéuih sìh·sìh chóh· chàn syùhn jauh jok·muhn·ge la.

be sick of something V(O) . . . V dou·fàahn·saai. /We're sick of eating fish every-day. Ngóh·deih yaht·yaht sihk yú sihk·dou·fàahn·saai. /I'm sick of his shouting. Kéuih sìh·sìh gám daaih·sèng chòuh chòuh·dou ngóh fàahn·saai.

make one sick lihng . . . hóu fàahn·hei. /That sort of thing makes me sick. Gó dī gám ge sih lihng·dou ngóh hóu fàahn·hei.

the sick (sick people) behng·yàhn. /This hospital takes very good care of the sick. Nī·gāan yī·yún deui behng·yàhn jiu·fù dāk hóu·hóu ge.

sickness behng. /What kind of sickness does he have? Kéuih yáuh māt·yéh behng a? /His sickness was caused by eating the wrong food. Kéuih ge behng haih yàn·waih sihk·cho·jó yéh.

sick leave behng·ga. /He's on sick leave. Kéuih chéng behng·ga. /He wants to ask for sick leave. Kéuih séung chéng behng·ga.

sickle   lihm·dōu (M: bá)

side   (one of the surfaces of an object) bihn: **front side** chìhn·bihn; **back side** hauh·bihn; **left side** jó·bihn; **right side** yauh·bihn; **top side** seuhng·bihn; **bottom side** hah·bihn, dái·hah; (if the object has only two sides, like a mirror) **front side** jing·mihn; **back side** fáan·mihn. /Shall we start to paint this side first? Ngóh·deih sīn yàuh nī·bihn sīn, hóu·m̀h·hóu a? /Can you tell which is the right side of this material? Nī·gihn líu bīn·bihn haih jing·mihn, néih tái·dāk·chēut ma?

(surface, not top or bottom) pòhng·bīn, jāk·mihn. /There is a big garden at the side of the house. Gāan ngūk pòhng·bīn yáuh go hóu daaih ge fà·yún. /The picture is taken from the side. Fūk séung haih hái jāk·mihn yíng ge.

(line bounding a figure) bihn. /How long is each side of this land? Nī·faai deih múih·bihn géi chèuhng a?

(part) bihn, bín. /He lives on the east side of the city, I live on the south side. Kéuih jyuh·hái sèhng ge dùng·bihn (or bín), ngóh jyuh·hái sèhng ge nàahm·bihn (or bín).

(bank) deui·ngohn (the other side of a river), deui·mihn·hói (the other side of the harbor). /Can you take us across to the other side of the river? Néih joi ngóh·deih gwo·heui deui·ngohn, dāk ma?

(riverbank) hòh·bīn. /There are many litchi trees along the side of the river. Hòh·bīn·syu yáuh hóu dò laih·jī·syuh.

(partisan group) bihn. /Which side are you on? Néih haih bīn·bihn ga?

(aspect) fòng·mihn. /We should study this matter from every side. Ngóh·deih yiu chùhng gok·fòng·mihn yìhn·gau nī·go mahn·tàih.

(not front or center) pohng·bīn ge; **side door** wàahng·mún. /They went in through the side door. Kéuih deih chùhng pòhng·bīn ge mùhn·háu (or wàahng·mún) yahp·jó·heui.

take sides bòng . . . bihn. /I just don't know whose side I should take. Ngóh ján·haih m̀h·jī bòng bīn·yāt·bihn hóu.

sideline fuh·daai. /He carries cigarettes as a sideline. Kéuih fuh·daai maaih dī yīn·jái.

to side bòng·jyuh. /She always sides with us in any argument. Yáuh māt jàang·leuhn ge sih·hauh kéuih géi·sí dōu bòng·jyuh ngóh·deih ge.

sidewalk   hàahng·yàhn·louh (M: tìuh)

siege   (the besetting of a fortified place) bàau·wàih

siesta   fan·ngaan·gaau. /He's having a siesta. Kéuih fan·gán ngaan·gaau.

sieve   sāi, sāi·gēi

sift   (with a sieve) sài: **sift rice** sài·máih

sigh   taan·hei. /What made her sigh? Kéuih waih·māt·sih taan·hei a?

sight   (vision). /I have poor sight. is expressed as: /Ngóh sèung ngáahn m̀h·hàih géi hóu.

a sight. /It was a terrible sight. is expressed as: Jàn·haih nàahn·tái la.

in sight. /The end (of work) is in sight. is expressed as: Jauh·lèih jouh·yùhn la.

lose sight of (not be able to see) tái·m̀h·dóu. /I lost sight of him in the crowd. Kéuih hàahng·yahp gó·kwàhn yàhn·syu ngóh jauh tái·m̀h·dóu kéuih la.

out of sight. /The ship slowly sailed out of sight. Jek syùhn sái·háh sái·háh juhk· jím jauh tái·m̀h·gin la.

go sightseeing yàuh; (make a tour) yàuh·láahm, yàuh·lihk. /We spent the whole day sightseeing yesterday. Ngóh·deih kàhm·yaht sehng·yaht yàuh deih·fòng. /We plan to do some sightseeing when we go through Rome. Ngóh·deih gìng·gwo Lòh·máh gó·jahn· sí dá·syun heui yàuh·láahm·háh.

sign   (of wood or metal, or the bulletin board on which signs are posted) pàaih; (hung outside a store) jíu·pàaih

(gesture) yaahp·sáu (with the hand only). /The waiter gave us a sign to follow him. Go fó·gei yaahp·sáu giu ngóh·deih gàn·jyuh kéuih.

(indication) yi·tàuh (omen); **good omen** hóu·yi·tàuh; **bad omen** m̀h·hóu·yi·tàuh. /That's a good sign. Hóu·yi·tàuh boh.

(trace) yíng·jīk. /There's no sign of it. Yāt·dī yíng·jīk dōu móuh. But /Have you seen any sign of my friend? is expressed as: Néih yáuh móuh tái·gin ngóh·ge pàhng· yáuh a? (Have you seen my friend?)

(symbol) fùh·houh: **plus sign** jing·houh; **minus sign** gáam·houh

to sign one's name chìm·jí (formal); chìm·méng (informal). /I forgot to sign the letter. Gó·fùng seun ngóh m̀h·gei·dāk chìm·méng. /Has the President signed the bill yet? Gó·go yi·ngon júng·túng chìm·jó·jí meih a?

sign off. /Radio stations here sign off early in the evening. Nī·syu ge dihn·tòih máahn·tàuh·hāk hóu jóu jauh tìhng·jí gwóng·bo ge la.

sign someone **up** chéng . . . VO. /We've signed him up to teach English next year. Ngóh·deih chéng·jó kéuih chēut·nín hái syu gaau Yìng·màhn.

signal   seun·houh; **to make a signal** dá go seun·houh; **to make a signal with a flag** dá kèih·yúh. /We've already sent out an S.O.S. signal. Ngóh·deih faat·chēut kòuh·gau ge seun·houh la.

signature   chìm méng, chìm jí. /Is this your signature? Nī·go haih·m̀h·haih néih chim ge méng a?

significance   (meaning) yi·si; (importance) gán·yiu; (special meaning) yi·yih

significant   (full of import) gán·yiu; (containing special meaning) yáuh·yi·yih

signify   (mean) bíu·sih. /A red traffic light signifies danger. Hùhng·sīk·ge gāau·tūng· dāng bíu·sih ngàih·hím. /This sign signifies a note at the end of the chapter. Nī·go fùh·houh bíu·sih hái nī·yāt·jèung hauh·bihn yáuh go jyu·gáai.

(express) bíu·sih. /If you are pleased with the music, please signify it by clapping your hands. Yùh·gwó néih·deih gok·dāk yàm·ngohk hóu hóu, chéng néih·deih paak·sáu (bíu·sih).

silence   (quiet). /I like the silence of the country. is expressed as: Ngóh jùng·yi hèung· háh ge deih·fòng, jihng hóu dò. (I like the country, it's more quiet.) /The silence in the room was embarrassing. is expressed as: /Hái gàan fóng yahp·bihn daaih·gā dōu m̀h·góng·wá hóu gaam·gaai. /Silence! is expressed as: Chéng gok·wái ngòn·jihng dī. (A little quiet, please!); or as M̀h·hóu góng·wá la. (Don't talk!) or as M̀h·hóu chòuh! (Don't make any noise!); or as M̀h·hóu chēut·sèng! (Don't let out a sound!)

(make quiet). /Mother silenced the baby's crying by feeding her. is expressed as Màh·mā béi yéh go bìh·bī sihk, go bìh·bī jauh m̀h·haam la.

silent   jihng. /It's only eight o'clock and the street is already silent. Baat·dím·jūng·jē, tìuh gāai yíh·gìng hóu jihng la. /Before the teacher came out, the classroom was silent. Sīn·sàang hàahng·chēut·lèih jì·chìhn go fo·sāt hóu jihng.

(not speak) m̀h·chēut·sèng. /Why are you so silent? Dím·gáai néih m̀h·chēut·sèng a?

be silent about móuh·tàih·gahp. /They were silent about their plan. Kéuih·deih móuh·tàih·gahp kéuih·deih ge gai·waahk.

silently   jihng·jíng·gám

silk   sì, sì·faat; (silk material) sì·chàuh, chàuh·dyuhn; (satin) dyún; (thin silk material)
    chóu·jái. /Is this made of silk? Nī·go haih·m̀h·haih sī·jīk ga? /I'd like to buy some
    silk dresses. Ngóh séung máaih géi·gihn sì·faat ge sāam.
        silk stockings sì·maht; **silk store** chàuh·dyuhn·pou; **silk thread** sì·sin

silkworm   chàahm·chúng (M: tìuh)

silver   ngán (ge). **sterling** or **pure silver** sèuhn·ngán. /Does that place produce silver
    too? Gó·douh yihk·dōu chēut ngán àh? /I prefer to have a silver one. Ngóh jùng·yi yiu
    go ngán ge. /Is this made of sterling silver? Nī·go haih·m̀h·haih sèuhn ngán jouh ga?
        (utensils of silver) ngàhn·hei (M: gihn; set, tou). /Where did you buy this beautiful
    set of silver? Néih nī·tou ngàhn·hei hái bīn·syu máaih ga?
        plated with silver douh·ngán (ge). /She said she didn't want a silver plated one.
    Kéuih wah kéuih m̀h·yiu douh·ngán ge.

similar   tùhng . . . yāt·yeuhng. /She didn't buy the dress because it's so similar to the
    one she had. Kéuih móuh máaih gó·gihn sāam yàn·waih gó·gihn sāam chā·bāt·dō tùhng
    kéuih yíh·chìhn gó·gihn yāt·yeuhng.

simile   béi·yuh

simple   (plain) gáan·dàan. /He says a monk may live a simple life, but he himself is
    not a monk. Kéuih wah wòh·séung hó·yíh sàng·wuht dāk hóu gáan·dàan, daahn·haih kéuih
    m̀h·haih wòh·séung.
        (easy, easy to understand) gáan·dàan, yùhng·yih. /That's a simple matter. Gó·gihn
    sih hóu yùhng·yih jē. /That's simple. Hóu gáan·dāan jē. or Hóu yùhng·yih jē.
        (not fancy) pok·sou ge. /She likes simple dresses. Kéuih jùng·yi jeuk hóu pok·sou
    ge sāam.
        (sincere; not deceitful) sèuhn·háuh. /He is a very simple person. Kéuih haih yāt go
    hóu sèuhn·háuh ge yàhn.
        (weak-minded; stupid) tàuh·nóuh gáan·dàan. /He is too simple to bear this responsi-
    bility. Kéuih tàuh·nóuh taai gáan·dàan, m̀h·fuh·dāk nī·go jaak·yahm.

simpleton   sòh·jái (kid), sòh·lóu (man)

simply   (merely) jí·haih, bāt·gwo, mòuh·fèi. /This is simply a question of time. Nī·go
    jí·haih sìh·gaan mahn·tàih jē.
        (just). /It's easy to find our house, you simply turn left at the next corner. Ngóh·
    deih gāan ngūk hóu yùhng·yih wán ge, néih yāt hàahng·jyun go gāai·gok jauh wán·dóu ge
    la.

sin   jeuih·ngok; **sinful** yáuh·jeuih; **sinner** jeuih·yàhn; **original sin** yùhn·jeuih

since   (of something still going on) jih·chùhng (or chùhng) . . . yíh·lòih, . . . yíh·lòih . . .
    /The population has been growing fast since this place has become a port. Jih·chùhng
    nī·daat deih·fòng bing·sèhng sèung·fauh yíh·lòih, yàhn·háu jàng·gā dāk hóu faai. /There
    has been no typhoon since last summer. Gauh·nín hah·tīn yíh·lòih meih si·gwo dá·fùng.
        (at some time between that time and now) jih·chùhng (or chùhng) jì·hauh. /He didn't
    come to see us since we moved here. Jih·chùhng ngóh·deih bùn·lèih nī·syu jì·hauh,
    kéuih móuh·lèih taam·gwo ngóh·deih. /He hasn't been here since Monday. Kéuih jih·
    chùhng láih·baai·yāt jì·hauh jauh móuh lèih·gwo. /She gained a few pounds since you
    saw her last time. Jih·chùhng néih gin·gwo kéuih jì·hauh, kéuih chúhng·fàan géi·bohng
    la. /Since when have you worn glasses? is expressed as: Néih géi·sí héi·sáu daai
    ngáahn·géng ga? /Since when have you felt that it hurts? Yàuh géi·sí héi néih gok·dāk
    tung ga?
        (because) gei·yìhn. /Since they can't come to help us, we have to do it ourselves.
    Gei·yìhn kéuih·deih bāt·nàhng lèih bòng ngóh·deih, ngóh·deih jí·yáuh jih·gēi jouh.

sincere   (honest) lóuh·saht. /He is a very sincere person and will never fool you.

Kéuih hóu lóuh·saht ge, wíhng·m̀h ngāk néih ge.
(be real, come from a sincere heart) jān·sàm ge. /I believe he is sincere in what
he says. Ngóh sèung·seun kéuih góng ge haih jān·sàm ge syut·wah.

sinew   gàn (M: tîuh)

sing   (of people) cheung, cheung·gō; (of birds) cheung. /Which song are you going to
sing for us? Néih cheung bīn·jek gō béi ngóh·deih tèng a? /You said you like to sing
so sing for us please. Néih wah néih jùng·yi cheung·gō, cheung lèih béi ngóh·dieh tèng
háh lā. /The birds have been singing all morning. Dī jéuk cheung·jó sèhng·jîu la.

singe   sîu nùng·jó

single   (made for one only) **single room** dàan·yàhn·fóng (M: gàan); **single bed** duhk·séui·
chòhng (M: jèung). /I want a single room. Ngóh yiu yāt·gàan dàan·yàhn·fóng.
(unmarried) dāan·sān ge. /Is he single or married? Kéuih haih dāan·sān·ge, yīk·
waahk git·jó·fàn ga?

singular   **singular number** dàan·sou

sink   chàhm. /They sank the old ship (by shelling). Kéuih·deih dá·chàhm jek gauh
syùhn. /The old ship sank to the bottom of the sea. Gó jek gauh syùhn chàhm·lohk hói·
dái.

sinologist   hon·hohk·gā

sinology   hon·hohk

sip   jyut

sir   sīn·sàang. /Sir, could you tell me where the headmaster's office is? Sīn·sàang
néih hó·yíh góng ngóh jì haauh·jéung ge baahn·gūng·sāt hái bīn·syu ma?
<u>Chinese usually address a superior by his title, such as</u> jyú·jihk (chairman), júng·
sì·lihng (commander in chief), síh·jéung (mayor), haauh·jéung (headmaster), etc. /Yes,
sir. Haih, jyú·jihk (<u>or</u> Júng·sì·lihng, etc.). <u>but</u> /No, sir. <u>has no simple translation</u>
<u>but requires a statement which is negative or which clarifies the reasons for a negative</u>
<u>answer, as</u> /Is this yours? Nī·go haih·m̀h·haih néih ga? /No, sir. M̀h·haih ngóh ge.

siren   (alarm) gíng·bou; (the instrument) gíng·bou·gèi

sister   **sisters** jí·múi; **elder sister** daaih·jí, gā·jē; **younger sister** múi. /They are two
sisters. Kéuih·deih haih léuhng·jí·múi.
' **older sister's husband** jé·fù; **younger sister's husband** múi·fù, muih·fù
(Catholic nun) sàu·néuih, gù nèuhng

sit   chóh. /Where are we going to sit? Ngóh·deih chóh·hái bīn·syu a? /Would you please
sit over there? Chóh·hái gó·syu, hóu ma? /Sit down, please. Chéng·chóh.
sit a little closer chóh·màaih·dī; **sit a little further** chóh·hōi·dī; **sit down for a mo-**
ment, chóh·yāt·jahn·gāan; **sit properly** chóh·jeng; **sit steady** chóh·wán

site   deih·dím

situation   (condition) chìhng·yìhng. /The situation there is quite uneasy. Gó·syu ge
chìhng·yìhng sèung·dòng m̀h·ngòn·dihng.

six   luhk; **sixteen** sahp luhk; **sixty** luhk·sahp; **sixty-six** luhk·sahp·luhk; **six-fold** luhk·
púih, **one-sixth** luhk·fahn·jī·yāt; **the sixth** daih·luhk

size   (as of shirts, shoes, hats, etc.) houh, houh·sou. /What size shoes do you wear?
Néih jeuk géi·(dò·)houh ge hàaih a? /Let's try this size to see whether it fits or not.
Si·háh nī·go houh·sou ge, tái·háh ngāam·m̀h·ngāam? /What size is this? Nī·go haih géi·
houh ga? <u>or</u> Nī·go haih māt·yéh houh·sou ga?
(relative bigness) daaih·sai, chek·chyun; (length) chèuhng·dyún. /Try this for size.
Si·háh nī go daaih·sai ngāam·m̀h·ngāam.

what is the size of . . . (. . . is how big) . . . yáuh géi dáai, (. . . long) . . . yáuh géi chèuhng, (. . . high) . . . yáuh géi gòu, (. . . wide) yáuh géi fut, (. . . thick) . . . yáuh géi háuh. /What size is the room? Gàan fóng yáuh géi dáai a?

size up. /He sized up the situation at a glance. Kéuih yāt ngáahn jauh tái·chìng·chó dòng·sìh ge chìhng·yìhng la.

skate   syut·kehk, làuh·bìng·hàaih (M: deui); **to skate** yáai·syut·kehk, làuh·bìng; **skating rink** làuh·bìng·chèuhng

skeleton   hàaih·gwāt, gwāt·tàuh, kù·lòuh (M: fu)

ski   waaht·syut

skillful   hóu·bún·sih ge, hóu·hóu·sáu·sai ge. /He is very skillful in doing this. Kéuih jouh nī·yeuhng yéh hóu·bún·sih ge.

skill   (ability) geih·seuht, gūng·fù; **skilled worker** suhk·lihn ge gùng·yàhn

skim   pit. /Don't forget to skim the fat. M̀h·hóu m̀h·gei·dāk pit·jó dī yàuh keuih.

skin   (of a person) pèih·fù; (of fruits or vegetables) pèih: **banana skin** hēung·jīu·pèih; **potato skin** syùh·jái·pèih; (of animal) pèih: **alligator skin** ngohk·yùh·pèih
     thick-skinned háuh·mihn·pèih, mihn·pèih·háuh. /He is very thick-skinned. Kéuih hóu háuh mihn·pèih ge. or Kéuih mihn·pèih hóu háuh ge.
     thin-skinned mihn·peih·bohk. /Don't tease her, she is very thin-skinned. M̀h·hóu siu kéuih, kéuih mihn·pèih hóu bohk ge.
     to skin mōk·pèih. /Skin it. Mōk jó chàhng pèih kéuih.

skip   tiu; **skipping rope** tiu·síng; **skip rope** tiu·síng (VO)

skirt   kwàhn (M: tìuh)

skull   tàuh·hok, tàuh·goi·gwāt

sky   tìn. /What is the thing flying in the sky? Hái tìn·syu fèi·gán gó·go haih māt·yéh a? (weather) tìn·sìh. /How does the sky look today? Gàm·yaht tìn·sìh dím a? /It is cloudy. Gàm·yaht yām·tìn.

slacken   (cause to be loose) fong·sùng

slander   dái·wái

slanting   che; **rather slanting** chèh·ché·déi

slap   gwaak (V)

slate   sehk·báan (M: faai)

slaughter   (animal) tòng: **slaughter pig** tōng jyū; (human beings) saat; (massacre) tòuh· saat

slave   nòuh·daih

slay   saat·séi, jíng·séi, dá·séi

sleep   fan, fan·gaau. /Did you sleep well? Néih fan dāk hóu ma? /He is sleeping. Kéuih fan·gán gaau. /How long has she been sleeping? Kéuih fan·jó géi nói la? (have place for people to sleep) fan. /This room can sleep four persons. Nī·gàan fóng hó·yíh fan sei·go yàhn.
     get to sleep, go to sleep fan·jeuhk. /I couldn't get to sleep for hours. Ngóh fan·jó géi·dím·jūng dōu m̀h·fan·dāk·jeuhk. /I was so tired, I fell asleep as soon as I closed my eyes. Ngóh bāt·jì géi guih, yāt mì·màaih·ngáahn jauh fan·jeuhk·jó la.
     sleep (act of sleeping) is expressed verbally as in the first paragraph. I must get some sleep. Ngóh yāt·dihng yiu fan·háh ji dāk. /Did you have a good sleep? Néih fan dāk hóu ma?

sleepy   ngáahn·fan. /Why are you so sleepy? Dím·gáai néih gam ngáahn·fan a?

sleeve   sāam·jauh, jauh; **sleeveless** móuh·jauh ge

slender   yau

slice   (thin, flat piece) pin: **a slice of ham** yāt·pin fó·téui; **a slice of bread** yāt·faai
mihn·bāau

slide   (used for projector) wàahn·dāng·pín (M: fūk); **to slide** sin; **slide down** sin·lohk
(·heui)

slight   dī·gam·dēu, dī. /I have a slight cold. Ngóh yáuh dī·gam·dēu sēung·fùng. /She
says she has a slight headache. Kéuih wah kéuih yáuh dī tàuh·tung.
(slender, fragile, short and thin) sai·nāp. /She has a rather slight figure. Kéuih
hóu sai·nāp ge.

slightly   leuhk·léuk, mèih·méi. /The surface is slightly scratched. Go mín·syu leuhk·
léuk chaat·sèung dò·síu.

slip   (slide) sin. /She slipped and fell. Kéuih sin·dài.
(move stealthily) jihng·jíng gám gyùn. /He slipped into the cocktail party. Kéuih
jihng·jíng gám gyùn·yahp go gài·méih·jáu·wúi·syu. /This party is dull, let's slip away.
Nī·go wúi gam móuh yáhn, ngóh·deih sùng yàhn bá la.
(escape) cho·gwo. /Don't let the chance slip, if you can help it. Yùh·gwó néih jouh·
dāk·dou, m̀h·hóu cho·gwo nī·go gèi·wuih.
(say thoughtlessly) m̀h·gok·yi; **slip of the tongue** m̀h·gok·yi góng·jó chēut·lèih. /He
let the name slip before he thought. Kéuih m̀h·gok·yi jèung go méng góng·jó chēut·lèih.
slip one's mind. /The matter slipped my mind completely. is expressed as: Nī·
gihn sih ngóh yùhn·chyùhn m̀h·gei·dāk·jó. (I forgot the whole thing.)
(a casual mistake) cho; **make a slip.** /Did I make a slip? Ngóh yáuh móuh jouh·cho
a?
pillow slips jám·tàuh·tóu; **a slip of paper** jí·tíu

slipper   tō·háai (M: deui)

slippery   waaht

slit   (narrow opening) la (M: tìuh); (to cut a long line in) got, gaai. /The doctor slit his
coat so that he could dress his wound. Yī·sāng got·hòi kéuih gihn sāam hóu tùhng kéuih
jaat·hóu go sèung·háu.

slogan   (for rallying or battle cry) háu·houh; (printed sheet) bíu·yúh (M: jèung)

slope   (of a hill) chèh·pō; **to slope down** che·lohk·heui. /The hill slopes downward to
the river. Go·sàan yāt·louh gám che·lohk tìuh hòh·syu.
sloping road che·lóu

slow   maahn. /This clock is five minutes slow. Nī·go jūng maahn ńgh·fān·jūng.
(of thinking or general movements) chìh·deuhn. /He's very slow moving. Kéuih
duhng·jok hóu chìh·deuhn ge.
a slow fire maahn·fó. /Cook it over a slow fire. Yùhng maahn·fó jyú.
Slow down! Maahn dī! M̀h hóu gam faai!

slowly   maahn. /Walk slowly. Maahn·máan·hàahng. or Hàahng·maahn dī. /Drink
slowly. Maahn·māan yám. /Could you speak slowly? Chéng néih maahn·māan góng.
/The cars are moving very slowly because of the traffic. Yàn·waih louh·seuhng chè
taai dò, só·yíh dī chè hàahng dāk hóu maahn.

slums   pàhn·màhn·kēui

slump   (in business) hòhng·chìhng hóu daahm. /There was a slump in trade last month.
Seuhng·go·yuht hòhng·chìhng hóu daahm.

sly   (underhanded) gwéi·syú (ge), gàan·waaht (ge)

small   sai. /This room is too small. Nī·gàan fóng taai sai.
(small pieces) seui. /Chop it up small. Chit·seui kéuih.
a small matter siu·sih; m̀h·gán·yiu. /It's a small matter. Síu·sih jē. /Where we
stay is a small matter. Ngóh·deih hái bīn·syu jyuh m̀h·gán·yiu. /That's no small matter. Nī·gihn sih géi gán·yiu ge boh.
(diminutive, used before most nouns) -jái; **small box** háp·jái; **small room** fóng·jái;
small table tói·jái
small change sáan·chín, sáan·ngán; **small finger** mēi·jí, sáu·jí·mēi; **small letters**
sai·jih·júng, sai·sé ge jih·mouh; **small talk** ying·chàuh syut·wah

smallpox   dáu, tīn·fā; **to have the smallpox** chēut·dáu, chēut·tīn·fā. /Vaccination can
prevent smallpox. Jung·dáu hó·yíh fòhng·jí tīn·fā.

smart   (quick and clever) lēk(·máh), lìhng·leih; (stylish and good taste) leng, yauh leng
yauh daaih·fong; (sting or pain sharply) tung

smash   (to pieces) dá·laahn; (crush) jaahk·laahn. /Someone smashed the show window
last night. Kàhm·máahn yáuh yàhn jèung go sīk·gwaih dá·laahn·jó.

smear   chàh; **smear the face black** chàh hāk go mihn

smell   màhn. /Do you smell something? Néih màhn·dóu māt·yéh ma? /I smell something burning. Ngóh màhn·dóu yáuh dī yéh sīu nùng·jó.
smell bad ngok·màhn, nàahn·màhn; **smell good** hóu·màhn. /It smells bad. Hóu
ngok·màhn. /It smells good. Hóu·hóu·màhn.
a smell chèuih (M: buhng). /I don't like the smell. Ngóh m̀h·jùng·yi gó·buhng chèuih.
sense of smell chau·gok. /A dog has a very keen sense of smell. Gáu yáuh hóu
lìhng·máhn ge chau·gok.
good smell hèung·meih; **bad smell** chau·meih; **fishy smell** sèng·meih
(give off odor). /Roses smell sweet. is expressed as: Mùih·gwai·fā hóu hèung.
/The room smells of tobacco smoke. Sèhng·gàan fóng dōu haih yīn·chèuih.

smelt   yùhng

smile   siu, mèih·méi·siu. /She smiled and said, 'Will you have another helping?' Kéuih
siu·jyuh gám wah, 'Néih juhng yiu ma?'
a smile (cheerful appearance) siu·yùhng; (smiling appearance) is expressed verbally. /She always has a smile on her face. Kéuih géi·sí dōu haih hóu hóu siu·yùhng ge.
/You have a pretty smile. Néih siu dāk hóu hóu·yéung.

smoke   (fumes) yīn. /Why is there so much smoke? Dím·gáai gam dò yīn a? /Where
does the smoke come from? Dī yīn hái bīn·syu lèih ga?
(of cigarettes, cigars, etc.) sihk·yīn. /Do you smoke? Néih sihk·yīn ma? /No, I
don't. Ngóh m̀h·sihk·yīn.
give off smoke chēut·yīn. /The stove smokes too much. Go lòuh chēut·yīn chēut
dāk taai gán·yiu.
(cure) béi yīn fàn, bouh·yīn. /We may smoke these fish. Ngóh·deih hó·yíh béi yīn
fàn·jó nī·dī yú kéuih. /I like smoked fish. Ngóh hóu jùng·yi sihk bouh·yīn yú.
smoke it out béi yīn wāt kéuih chēut·lèih

smooth   (level and not rough) pìhng. /The road is very smooth. Tìuh louh hóu pìhng.
/The sea was very smooth. Go hói·mihn hóu pìhng.
(smooth and also slippery) waaht·lauh. /The cloth has a smooth surface. Nī·jek bou
ge bou·sān hóu waaht·lauh.

smoothly   yùhn·waaht. /He always handles things very smoothly. Kéuih sìh·sìh jouh sih
dōu hóu yùhn·waaht ge.

smother   (die from lack of air) guhk·séi. /Do not cover the baby's head too closely or she may smother. M̀h·hóu kám bìh·bī ge tàuh kám dāk taai hahm, wúih guhk·séi kéuih ge.

(extinguish by cutting air from) kám. /You may smother the fire by covering it with dirt. Néih hó·yíh yuhng nàih kám·sīk go fó.

smuggle   tàu·wahn, jáu·sī. /Those weapons were smuggled in recently. Gó·dī gwàn·fó haih jeui·gahn tàu·wahn·yahp·lèih ge. /Isn't there any way to stop smuggling? Yáuh móuh faat·jí fòhng·jí jáu·sī a? /The underworld has been smuggling in a large amount of narcotics. Nī·syu ge hāk·ngam·séh·wúi luhk·juhk·bāt·dyuhn gám tàu·wahn·jó daaih·leuhng ge duhk·bán yahp·háu.

snail   ló; **fresh water snail** tìhn·ló; **salt water snail** hàahm·séui·ló

snake   sèh (M: tìuh); **poisonous snake** duhk·sèh

snap   (as twig) ngáau·tyúhn; (as string) màng·tyúhn; (with the teeth) ngáauh

snare   (for catching rabbits, birds, etc.) lùhng; (net) móhng; (pit) haahm·jehng

snatch   (grab or catch hold of) chéung; jà·saht. /I saw him snatch the old lady's purse. Ngóh tái·jyuh kéuih chéung gó·go baahk·yē·pó ge ngàhn·bāau. /Hurry up, snatch at the rope! Faai dī jà·saht tìuh síng!

sneer   (to utter with a sneer) siu, gèi·siu

sneeze   dá·hāk·chì (VO)

sniff   béi go beih sok·háh

snore   beih·hòhn (N); ché·beih·hòhn (VO)

snow   syut. /Have you ever seen what snow looks like? Néih yáuh móuh tái·gin·gwo syut haih dím·yéung ga?
        to snow lohk·syut (VO). /Sometimes it snows hard. Yáuh·sìh lohk syut lohk dāk hóu daaih ge. /It snowed a lot last winter. Gauh·nín lohk·jó hóu dò syut.

snowflake   syut·fā

snowman   syut·yàhn

snuff   (pulverized tobacco) beih·yīn

so   (in this way) gám, gám·yeung. /If so, I'll have to go. Yùh·gwó haih gám, ngóh yāt·dihng yiu jáu la. /They say so. Kéuih·deih haih gám wah ge. /He's all right now and I hope he'll remain so. Kéuih yìh·gā móuh·sih la, Ngóh hèi·mohng kéuih yāt·louh dōu haih gám. /I told you so. Ngóh wah·gwo néih tèng haih gám ge la. /That's not so. M̀h·haih gám. /Is that so? Haih mē? (I don't believe you.) or Jàn·gé? (Is that true? I didn't know that.)
        (also) yihk·dōu. /If I can do it, so can you. Yùh·gwó ngóh jouh dāk, néih yihk dōu jouh dāk ge la. /You want to go and so does he. Néih yiu heui, kéuih yihk·dōu yiu heui.
        (very; very much) jàn·haih. /Your child is so clever. Néih ge sai·màn·jái jàn·haih chùng·mìhng la. /I'm so glad. Ngóh jàn·haih fùn·héi la.
        (therefore) só·yíh, yàn·chí. /They left early and so I missed them. Kéuih·deih jáu dāk jóu dī, só·yíh ngóh móuh gin·dóu kéuih·deih. /I wasn't feeling well so I didn't go. Ngóh gok·dāk m̀h·haih géi jih·yìhn yàn·chí móuh·heui·dou.
        or so jó·yáu. /The plane was an hour or so late. Fēi·gèi chìh·jó dím·jūng jó·yáu.
        so far (up to now) yāt·jihk dou yìh·gā. /So far so good. Yāt·jihk dou yìh·gā dōu géi hóu.
        so far as I know (according what I know) jiu·ngóh·só·jì. /So far as I know, he is still working in that company. Jiu·ngóh·só·jì, kéuih juhng·haih hái gó·gàan gūng·sī jouh·gán.
        so long (goodbye) is expressed as: Joi·gin (See you again.); Yāt·jahn·gāan·gin. (See you later.)
        so much gam·dò. /He has so much money he doesn't know what to do with it. Kéuih

yáuh gam dò chín gáau·dou kéuih m̀h·jī dím syun. /Don't eat so much. M̀h·hóu sihk gam dò.

so⸴so. /How are you feeling? Géi hóu lā máh? /So·so. Haih gam seuhng háh là. or Móuh māt dím lā.

so that (in order that). /You have to tell him how old your son is and what he looks like so that he can find him and send him back to you. Néih yāt·dihng yiu góng·béi kéuih jī, néih ge sai·mān·jái géi·dò seui, dím go yéung ge, gám kéuih sīn·ji hó·yíh tùhng néih wán·fàan kéuih, sung kéuih fàan·lèih néih·syu ga.

so that (with the result that) só·yíh. /It rained so hard, [so that] the streets were flooded. Lohk·yúh lohk dāk gam daaih, só·yíh hóu dò tíuh gāai dōu jam·saai.

so . . . (that). /He ran so fast he was all out of breath. Kéuih jáu dāk gam faai, jáu dou kéuih hei dōu móuh saai. /I'm so tired I can hardly keep my eyes open. Ngóh jàn·haih guih lo, guih dou ngóh ngáahn dou maak·m̀h·hòi.

so and so (a certain person) máuh máuh yàhn; **so as to avoid trouble** míhn·ji faat·sāng hauh·waahn; **So beautiful!** Jàn·haih leng la! **so called** só·waih; **so early** gam jóu; **so easy** gam yih; **so far** gam yúhn; **so heavy** gam chúhng; **so late** (in the day) gam ngaan; (in the evening) gam yeh; (not on time) gam chìh; **so little** gam síu; **so long** (time) gam noih; **so loud** gam daaih·sèng, gam héung; **so quick** gam faai. Let it be so. Jauh gám lā.

soak   jam; **soak in water** jam·séui; **soak through** jam·tau

soap   fàan·gáan (M: gauh)

soar   (as prices) gòu·jeung; (as a bird) gòu·fèi·séuhng·tīn

sob   (cry) haam

sober   (quiet; earnest) sàm·séui·chìng. /He is a very sober fellow. Kéuih go yàhn hóu sàm·séui·chìng ge.
(not drunk) chìng·síng. /He says he's still sober, do you believe him? Kéuih wah kéuih juhng haih hóu chìng·síng, néih seun kéuih ma?

soccer   (football) jūk·kàuh; **play soccer** dá·fūt·bō, wáan·fūt·bō, dá·jūk·kàuh

social   (fond of the company of others) jùng·yi gàau·jai. /She is a very social person. Kéuih hóu jùng·yi gàau·jai ge.
(having to do with people) séh·wúi: **social studies** séh·wúi·fò·hohk. /Geography and history are social studies. Deih·léih lihk·sí dōu haih séh·wúi·fò·hohk.
social gathering ying·chàuh, lyùhn·yìh·wúi; **social intercourse** séh·gàau, gàau·jai; **social life** séh·gàau sàng·wuht; **social problem** séh·wúi mahn·tàih; **social reconstruction** séh·wúi·gói·jouh; **social service** séh·wúi·fuhk·mouh; **social standing** sàn·fán; deih·waih; **social system** séh·wúi·jai·douh; **social welfare** séh·wúi·fūk·leih

socialism   séh·wúi·jyú·yih; **socialist** séh·wúi·dóng, séh·wuih·dóng

society   (social community) seh·wúi. /Can you tell me what we need most for our society? Néih hó·yíh góng béi ngóh jī, ngóh·deih nī·go séh·wúi jeui sèui·yiu ge haih māt·yéh ma?
(organization) wúi, tyùhn·tái, jóu·jīk. /Would you like to join our society? Néih séung gà·yahp ngóh·deih nī·go wúi ma?
(companionship). /I enjoy his society very much. is expressed as Ngóh hóu jùng·yi tùhng kéuih yāt·chái.
(fashionable group of people) seuhng·làuh séh·wúi. /She is very prominent in local society. Kéuih hái dòng·deih ge seuhng·làuh·séh·wúi hóu chēut·fùng·tàuh ga.

sociology   séh·wúi·hohk

sock   maht (M: jek; a pair, yāt·deui)

socket   sā·gét; (anatomy) ngáahn·kwōng

soda   sō·dá; **soda water** sō·dá·séui; **soda mint** sō·dá·yún

sofa   sō·fá (M: jèung)

soft   (not hard) yúhn. /Do you think the chair cushion is too soft? Néih gok·dāk nī·go yí·
jín haih·m̀h·haih taai yúhn·dāk·jaih a?
    (not bright) yàuh·wòh. /Don't you think a soft light would be better? Néih gok·dāk
yàuh·wòh dī ge dāng·gwòng wúih·m̀h·wúih hóu dī nē?
    (not loud) sai·sēng dī. /Please turn the radio down softer. Chéng néih jèung go sāu·
yām·gēi náu sai·sēng dī.
    (voice) wàn·yàuh, sai·sèng. /The hostess says to him in a soft voice, 'Please don't
smoke.' Go hùng·jùng·sīu·jé hóu wàn·yàuh gám deui kéuih wah, 'Chéng néih m̀h·hóu
sihk·yīn.'
    (tender-hearted) sàm·chèuhng . . . yúhn. /You are too soft to be an executive. Néih
go yàhn sàm·chèuhng gam yúhn, m̀h·jouh·dāk hàhng·jing ge sih ge.

soil   (land) deih. /What will grow in this soil? Nī·faai deih hó·yíh jung māt·yéh a.
/This is a good rich soil. Nī·faai deih hóu fèih.
    (make dirty) jíng·wū·jòu, jíng·laaht·taat. /Don't let it get soiled. M̀h·hóu jíng·wù·
jòu kéuih.

solar   **solar calendar** yèuhng·lihk, sàn·lihk; **solar eclipse** yaht·sihk

soldier   (private) bīng; (a man serving in the armed forces) gwàn·yàhn. /I'm a soldier.
It's my duty to protect my country. Ngóh haih yāt·go gwàn·yàhn, bóu·waih ngóh·ge gwok·
gà haih ngóh·ge jaak·yahm.

sole   (bottom of a shoe) hàaih·dái. /The soles of my shoes were worn out, I had to put
on a pair of new soles. Ngóh ge haaih·dái chyùn·jó, ngóh wuhn·jó deui sàn ge.
    (bottom of the foot) geuk·báan·(dái). /I walked so far that the soles of my feet were
sore. Ngóh hàahng·jó gam yúhn, hàahng dou ngóh geuk·báan (dái) dōu tung·saai.
    (single). /He is the sole agent of that firm. Kéuih duhk·gā gīng·léih gó·gāan gūng·
sī.

solemn   (look) yìhm·sūk; (ceremony) jòng·yìhm, yìhm·sūk

solicit   (seek support) jìng·kàuh

solicitor   (lawyer) johng·sī

solid   (firm, strong) wán·jahn, git·saht, saht·jehng. /Don't sit on that chair, it's not
solid. M̀h·hóu chóh gó·jèung yí, gó·jèung yí m̀h·wán·jahn. /The construction of the
building seems solid enough. /Nī·joh láu héi dāk géi gau saht·jehng. /His body is very
solid. Kéuih (ge sàn·tái) sāang dāk hóu git·saht.
    (the same throughout; pure) sèuhn: **solid gold** sèuhn·gām; **solid blue** sèuhn·làahm·
sīk ge
    (dependable) hó·kaau; (creditable) yáuh·seun·yuhng. /He seems to be a solid sort
of person. Kéuih go yàhn tái·lèih géi hó·kaau. /This is a solid firm. Nī·gàan pou·táu
hóu yáuh·seun·yuhng ge.
    solid food. /The doctor told him not to eat solid food for a few days. is expressed
<u>as</u> Yī·sāng giu kéuih nī·géi·yaht sihk làuh·jāt (liquid food) ge yéh.

solitary   (of people) gū·dàan; (of place) pīn·pīk

solitude   (loneliness) jihk·mohk

solo   (vocal) duhk·cheung; (instrument) duhk·jau

soluble   wúih·yùhng ge; (of a problem) hó·yíh·gáai·kyut ge

solution   (settlement of a problem) gáai·kyut ge baahn·faat; (liquid) yuhng·yiht; **medicinal**
solution yeuhk·séui

solve   (settle) gáai·kyut

some   (a little) dī. /Give me some water. Béi dī séui ngóh. /I want some fish. Ngóh
yiu dī yú.
    (a few) géi plus a measure. /Could I have some cups? Béi géi·go būi ngóh dāk ma?
/Take some samples and show them to your friends. Nīk géi·go báan heui béi néih dī
pàhng·yáuh tái·háh.
    (a fair quantity of) hóu géi. /He has been working here for some time. Kéuih hái
syu jouh·jó hóu géi·nìhn (years) la.
    (certain unspecified ones) yáuh·dī, yáuh. /Some of these chairs are broken. Nī·dī
yí yáuh dī haih laahn ge. /Some fellows didn't like this movie, but I liked it. Yáuh
yàhn m̀h·jùng·yi nī·chēut dihn·yíng, daahn·haih ngóh gok·dāk nī·chéut dihn·yíng géi hóu.

somebody   (unspecified person) yáuh·yàhn. /Somebody phoned you while you were out.
Néih chēut·jó heui gó·jahn·sí yáuh yàhn dá dihn·wá béi néih.
    (a person of some importance) daaih·yàhn·mát. /If you want to be somebody, you
must study hard. Yùh·gwó néih séung jèung·lòih jouh yāt·go daaih·yàhn·mát, néih yāt·
dihng yiu kàhn·lihk duhk·syù.

somehow   /I'll fix it for you somehow. Ngóh júng·jì tùhng néih jíng·fàan·hóu kéuih là.
/Somehow, I never did meet him. M̀h·jì dím·gáai ngóh yāt·jihk móuh gin·gwo kéuih.

someone   **someone else's** daih·yih·go·yàhn ge; yàhn·deih ge. /Last night I wore someone else's raincoat home. Kàhm·máahn ngóh jeuk·cho·jó daih·yih·go·yàhn ge yúh·lāu
fàan ngūk·kéi. /Would you like to ride in someone else's car? Néih jùhg·yi chóh yàhn·
deih ge chè ma?

somersault   dá·gàn·dáu; **turn a somersault** dá·gàn·dáu

something   (an unspecified thing) dī·yéh, māt·yéh. /Wouldn't you like a little something
to eat? Néih jùng·yi sihk dī·yéh ma? /If you want something, ring the bell. Yùh·gwó
néih sèui·yiu dī māt·yéh, néih gahm·jūng lā.
    (a little) dò·síu. /I know something about that area. Gó·daat deih·fòng ge chìhng·
yìhng ngóh jì·douh dò·síu.
    (some significance) /There's something in what he says. is expressed as Kéuih
góng ge sèung·dòng yáuh·douh·léih. (What he says is rather reasonable.)
    something else daih yéung yéh; lihng·ngói yāt·gihn sih. /He doesn't want to drink
coffee, he wants something else. Kéuih m̀h séung yám ga·fē, kéuih séung yám daih·
yéung yéh. /We are talking about something else. Ngóh·deih góng·gán lihng·ngói yāt·
gihn sih.

sometime   (in the future) jèung·lòih. /I want to go to Europe sometime. Ngóh dá·syun
jèung·lòih heui ngàu·jàu hàahng·háh.
    (in the near future). /I want to talk with you sometime today. Ngóh séung gàm·yaht
tùhng néih kìng·háh. /Can you come over sometime tomorrow? Néih tìng·yaht lèih·
dāk·m̀h·dāk a?
    (in the past) m̀h·jì·géi·sí. /A burglar broke into his house sometime last night.
Kàhm·máahn m̀h·jì·géi·sí yáuh go chahk yahp·jó kéuih gāan ngūk.

sometimes   yáuh·sìh. /After you take this medicine, sometimes you may throw up, but
it's nothing to be alarmed about. Sihk·jó nī·dī yeuhk jì·hauh, néih yáuh·sìh wúih ngáu ge,
daahn·haih m̀h·sái gèng, móuh·sih ge. /Do you ever see her sometimes? Néih yáuh sìh
wúih gin·dóu kéuih ma?

somewhat   yáuh·dī, sè·síu. /This differs somewhat from the usual type. Nī·tíng tùhng
pìhng·sìh gó·tíng yáuh dī m̀h·sèung·tùhng. /That is somewhat more expensive. Gó·go
gang gwai sè·síu.

somewhere   bīn·syu; yāt·daat·deih·fóng. /I'm sure I've seen her somewhere before.
Ngóh yíh·chìhn yāt·dihng hái bīn·syu gin·gwo kéuih. /Those refugees come from some-

where in the north. Gó·dī naahn·màhn haih chùhng bāk·fòng yāt·daat·deih·fòng lèih ge.
/I want to go somewhere in Japan for my summer vacation. Ngóh nī·go syú·ga séung
heui Yaht·bún yāt·daat·deih·fòng jyuh·háh.
>   (a certain place) -syu. /The letter must be somewhere in this drawer. Gó·fùng seun
>   yāt·dihng haih hái nī·go gwaih·túng syu.

son   jái; sai·mān·jái (child): my son ngóh·ge sai·mān·jái; (polite way of referring to
someone else's son) lihng·lóng, néih·ge gùng·jí. /This is my son. Nī·go haih ngóh ge
sai·mān·jái. /How old is your son now? Lihng·lóng géi·dò seui la? or Néih ge jái géi·
dò seui la.

>   **son-in-law** néuih·sái; **Son of Heaven** tìn·jí; **Son of Man** yàhn·jí; **sons and grandsons**
>   jí·syùn

song   (in general) gō (M: sáu); (melody) gō·kūk; (folksong) gō·jái (M: jek); (folksong sung
by mountain people) sāan·gō

soon   (in a short while) yāt·háh; móuh·géi·nói; bāt·gáu. /I'll be back soon. Ngóh yāt·háh
jauh fàan·lèih. /He came soon after you left. Néih jáu·jó móuh·géi·nói kéuih jauh lèih·
jó la. /The war was soon over. Jin·sih bāt·gáu jauh git·chōk la.
>   (quickly) faai. /The sooner the better. Yuht faai yuht hóu. /Why do you have to leave
>   so soon? Dím·gáai néih gam faai jauh jáu la?
>   **as soon as** (of time) yāt . . . jauh . . .; géi·sí yāt . . . jauh . . . . /Let me know as
>   soon as you get there. Néih yāt heui·dou gó·syu jauh jīk·hāk tùng·jī ngóh. /I'll tell you
>   as soon as I know myself. Ngóh yāt jī jauh jīk·hāk tùng·jī néih. /As soon as you feel
>   any pain, take a dose of this. Néih géi·sí yāt gok·dāk tung jauh jīk·hāk sihk yāt·chi yeuhk.
>   **sooner or later** chìh·jóu. /Sooner or later you have to make up your mind on this.
>   Néih chìh·jóu dōu yiu kyut·dihng nī·gihn sih ge la. /I'll have to see him sooner or later.
>   Ngóh chìh·jóu yiu gin kéuih.

soprano   néuih·gōu·yām

sore   (painful) tung. /Is your throat sore? Néih hàuh·lùhng tung ma? /Can you tell me
where it is sore? Néih hó·yíh góng ngóh tèng bīn·syu tung ma?
>   (a painful spot where the skin is broken or bruised) sèung·háu. /The sore is pretty
>   well healed up now. Go sèung·háu jauh·lèih hóu·fàan·saai la.

sorrow   expressed as **be sorrowful** nàahn·gwo, sèung·sàm; (unhappiness; trouble)
fàahn·nóuh. /He has caused his family a great deal of sorrow. Kéuih lìhng kéuih ngūk·
kéi·yàhn hóu nàahn·gwo. /She's sick with sorrow. Kéuih fèi·sèuhng sèung·sàm. /He is
a king, how could he have so many sorrows? Kéuih haih wòhng·dai, dím·gáai kéuih yáuh
gam dò fàahn·nóuh nē?

sorrowful   (full of sadness) bai·ngai. /Why is she so sorrowful lately? Dím·gáai kéuih
nī·páai gam bai·ngai a?

sorry   (apologetic) deui·m̀h·jyuh; (be embarrassed) m̀h·hóu·yi·si. /Did I bump you? I'm
sorry. Deui·m̀h·jyuh pung·chàn néih. /I'm sorry to be late. Deui·m̀h·jyuh, ngóh lèih·
chìh·jó. or Ngóh lèih·chìh·jó, jàn·haih m̀h·hóu yi·si la.
>   (repentant) hauh·fui. /I'm sorry I did it. Ngóh hauh·fui ngóh jouh·jó gó·gihn sih.
>   /Don't you feel sorry that you did it? Néih jouh·jó (gó·gihn·sih) jí·hauh, néih gok·dāk
>   hauh·fui ma?
>   **be** (or feel) **sorry for** someone hó·lìhn. /How can you be sorry for him, he is so
>   wealthy. Néih dím·gáai hó·lìhn kéuih a, kéuih gam yáuh·chín.

sort   (kind or type) tíng. /What sort of book do you like to read? Néih jùng·yi tái dī
bīn·tíng ge syù a? /What sort of a man is he? Kéuih haih bīn·tíng yàhn a? or Kéuih
haih yāt·go dím·yéung ge yàhn a? /You shouldn't mix with this sort of person. Néih
m̀h·yìng·gòi tùhng nī·tíng yàhn lòih·wóhng.
>   **sort of** dōu géi. /That movie was sort of funny. Gó·chēut dihn·yíng dōu géi lau·siu.
>   /I'd sort of like to go. Ngóh dōu géi séung heui.

to sort fàn·hóu, fān·hòi. /Please help me to sort these things. Chéng néih bòng ngóh fàn hóu nī·dī yéh kéuih.

soul   lìhng·wàhn, wàhn·pak

sound   (noise) sīng·yàm; héung. /I heard a funny sound. Ngóh tèng·gin yāt·go hóu kèih· gwaai ge sīng·yàm. /What was that sound? is expressed as /Māt·yéh héung a?
(reliable) kàau·dāk·jyuh; (steady) wán·jahn. /Do you think that business is sound? Néih wah gó·pùhn sàang·yi kaau·dāk·jyuh (or wán·jahn) ma?
(reasonable) yáuh·douh·léih. /I think he gave you very sound advice. Ngóh gok·dāk kéuih hyun néih hyun dāk hóu yáuh·douh·léih.
(valid; having a basis) yáuh·gàn·geui·ge; (legal) hahp·faat·ge; (real) jàn·jing·ge
to sound tèng·héi·lèih·hóu·chíh. /It sounds impossible. Tèng·héi·lèih·hóu·chíh m̀h· dāk·gám. /It sounds good. Tèng·héi·lèih hóu·chíh géi·hóu gám. but /How does that sound to you? is expressed as Néih gok·dāk dím a? (What do you think about it?)
sound sleep. /I had a sound sleep last night. Ngóh kàhm·máahn fan dāk hóu hóu.

soup   tòng: **a bowl of soup** yāt·wún tòng

sour   syùn; **sour pickles** hàahm·syùn·choi; **sweet and sour spareribs** tòhng·chou pàaih· gwāt, tìhm·syùn·pàaih·gwāt

source   (point of origin) lòih·yùhn. /Where is the source of this river? Nī·tìuh hòh ge lòih·yùhn haih bīn·syu a? /What is your source of information? is expressed as Néih ge sīu·sīk haih hái bīn·syu dāk·lèih ga? /He said the news came from a reliable source. Kéuih wah nī·go sīu·sīk haih chùhng hó·kàau fòng·mihn dāk·lèih ge.
(cause) yùhn·yàn. /Have you found the source of the trouble? Néih wán·dóu nī·gihn sih ge yùhn·yàn meih a?
(literary material) chòih·líu. /This book is based on several published sources. Nī·bún syù haih gàn·geui hóu géi·júng yíh·gīng chēut·báan·jó ge chòih·líu sé ge.

south   nàahm. /South wind is a dear, north wind is a fear. Nàahm·fùng hó·ngoi, bāk·fùng hó·pa. /There's a Cantonese saying, 'A house facing south is hardly obtainable even if you have money.' Gwóng·dùng·wá yáuh geui juhk·yúh wah, 'Yáuh chīhn nàahn máaih heung nàahm ngūk.'
(including a part or area) nàahm·bín, nàahm·fòng, nàahm·bouh. /Turn your face to the east. Your left hand is to the north, and your right hand is to the south. Yùh·gwó néih mihn heung dùng, néih ge jó·sáu·bihn haih bāk·bín, yauh·sáu·bihn haih nàahm·bín. /Some birds fly south in the summer. Yáuh dī jéuk hah·tīn fèi·heui nàahm·fòng. /My family lived in the South (of the United States). Ngóh ge ngūk·kéi jyuh·hái Meih·gwok nàahm·bouh.
(indicating an area beyond a border) naahm·bihn. /It's south of the tall building. Hái gó·gàan gòu·láu ge nàahm·bihn.
southeast dùng·nàahm; **southwest** sài·nàahm; **Southeast Asia** Dùng·nàahm·a; **South America** Nàahm·méih·jàu; **the South Seas** Nàahm·yèuhng, Nàahm·yéung; **South Pole** Nàahm·gihk

southern   naahm·fong·ge, naahm·bihn ge, naahm·bouh ge; **southern part** naahm·bouh. /They come from the southern part of Kwangtung province. Kéuih·deih haih hái Gwóng· dùng·sáang nàahm·bouh lèih ge. or Kéuih·deih haih Gwóng·dùng·sáang nàahm·bouh ge yàhn.

souvenir   géi·nihm·bán

sovereign   (supreme ruler) yùhn·sáu; (independent, of a country) yáuh·jyú·kyùhn ge

sovereignty   jyú·kyùhn

sow   bo·júng, saat·júng (V); **sow grass seeds** saat chóu·júng, saat chóu·máih

soy   **soy sauce** sih·yàuh, baahk·yáu; **soybean** baahk·dáu

space   (part marked off in some way) deih (land); hùng·wái, wái (emptiness). /Is this
space big enough to build an auditorium? Nī·faai deih gau·m̀h·gau héi go láih·tòhng a?
/How much space do you want between the two desks? Nī·léuhng·jèung tói jūng·gāan,
néih yiu làuh·fàan géi dò hùng·wái (or wái) a?
      (room) deih·fòng, wái. /Is there any space for my suitcase? Gó·syu yáuh móuh deih
fòng jài ngóh·ge pèih·gīp a? /We have to save some space for storage. Ngóh·deih yiu
làuh·fàan dī wái dán fo.
      (extension) hūng·gāan, tìn·hùng·jùng, taai·hùng (outer space). /Time and space de-
termine the existance of things. Sìh·gàan tùhng hūng·gàan kyut·dihng yāt·chai maht·jāt
ge chyùhn·joih. /Have you ever counted how many stars there are in space? Néih yáuh
móuh sóu·gwo tìn·hùng·jùng yáuh géi·dō·nāp sīng a?

spaceship   taai·hùng·syùhn (M: jek)

spacious   (roomy) fut·lohk

spade   cháan

spare   (extra) dò·yùh, sih·bē; **spare parts** (dò·yùh ge) lìhng·gín; **spare time** dāk·hàahn.
/Do you have a spare tire in your car? Néih ga chè yáuh móuh dò·yùh ge tāai a? or
Néih ga chè yáuh móuh sih·bē tāai a? /Do you carry spare parts for this radio? Néih
deih yáuh móuh nī·ting sāu·yām·gēi ge lìhng·gín a? /I'll do it in my spare time. Ngóh
yāt dāk·hàahn jauh jouh la.
      (give) béi. /Can you spare a cigarette? Néih béi háu yīn ngóh dāk ma? /Can you
spare a minute? is expressed as Ngóh gwán·gáau néih yāt·jahn·gāan dāk ma?
      (refrain from using) /Call him up on the phone, so you can spare yourself a trip.
Dá go dihn·wá béi kéuih, néih maih m̀h·sái jáu yāt·chi lō.
      (keep from destroying) fong·sàang. /The hunter spared the deer. Go lihp·yàhn fòng·
sàang jek lūk tìuh mehng.

spark   fó·sīng, fó·sí

sparkle   sím·sím·ling

sparrow   màh·jéuk, màh·jeuk·jái (M: jek)

sparse   hèi·síu

spasm   chàu·gàn. /I'm having a spasm in my foot. Ngóh jek geuk chàu·gàn.

spawn   (of fish) yùh·chēun

speak   góng, góng syut·wah. /Do you speak English? Néih góng Yìng·màhn ma? /Please
speak a little louder. Chéng néih daaih·sēng dī góng. /Whom should I speak to? Ngóh
tùhng bīn·go góng a? /Did you speak to me? Néih tùhng ngóh góng syut·wah àh?
      (make a speech) yín·góng, góng·wáh. /Who is speaking tonight? Gàm·máahn bīn·go
yín·góng a? /The headmaster is speaking to the students. Haauh·jéung jing·joih tùhng
dī hohk·sāang góng·gán wá.
      speak about góng·háh. /You have to speak to him about this. Nī·gihn sih néih yāt·
dihng yiu tùhng kéuih góng·háh.
      speak of góng·gahp. /He never spoke of this. Kéuih chùhng·lòih móuh góng·gahp
nī·gihn sih.
      speaking of góng·dou. /Speaking of the problem of poverty, ... Góng·dou pàhn
·kùhng mahn·tàih, ...
      speak for (represent) tai, waih, doih·bíu. /Why do you speak for him? Dím·gáai
néih yiu tai kéuih góng nē? /They need someone to speak for them. Kéuih·deih sèui·
yiu yàhn waih kéuih·deih góng syut·wah. /Can you speak for them? Néih hó·yíh doih·
bíu kéuih·deih ma?
      speak one's mind góng . . . ge yi·gin. /If you allow me to speak my mind, ...
Yùh·gwó néih jéun ngóh góng ngóh·ge yi·gin, ...

speak up Speak up! I can't hear you. Daaih·sēng dī góng, ngóh tèng·m̀h·gin néih góng māt·yéh.

generally speaking daaih·ji gám góng. /Generally speaking, the people here are living fairly well. Daaih·ji gám góng, nī·syu dī yàhn go·go dōu sàng·wuht dāk géi hóu.

special dahk·biht ge, dahk·syùh ge; dahk·dāng. /This is a special soap. It is good for your skin. Nī·tìng fàan·gáan haih yāt·tìng dahk·biht ge fàan·gáan, deui néih ge pèih·fū hóu hóu ge. /This is a special occasion. Nī·go haih yāt·go dahk·syùh ge chìhng·yìhng. /Don't make a special trip for it. Néih m̀h·sái dahk·dāng waih nī·gihn sih heui yāt·chi.

special correspondent dahk·yeuk gei·jé; **special meeting** làhm·sìh wuih·yi, dahk·biht wuih·yi; **special price** dahk·ga; **special right** dahk·kyùhn; **special train** jyūn·chè

specialist jyūn·gā

specialize (follow a special branch of work) jyūn jouh; (of study) jyūn·mùhn yìhn·gau. /This factory is specialized in making batteries. Nī·gàan gùng·chóng jyūn jouh dihn·sām. /He specializes in tuberculosis. Kéuih jyūn·mùhn yìhn·gau fai·behng.

specially dahk·biht. /I was specially hungry after swimming. Ngóh yàuh·yùhn séui jì·hauh dahk·biht tóuh·ngoh. /This dress is specially made for you. Nī·gihn sāam haih dahk·biht wàih néih jouh ge.

specialty (skill) dahk·syùh ge geih·nàhng; (art, like cooking; craftmanship) nàh·sáu, hóu·sáu·sai. /Does he have any specialty? Kéuih yáuh móuh dahk·syùh·ge geih·nàhng a? /Frying chicken is his specialty. is expressed as Kéuih jíng ja·jí·gāi jeui nàh·sáu.

species júng·leuih. /Are the rabbit and rat the same species? Tou tùhng lóuh·syú haih·m̀h·haih tùhng yāt·go júng·leuih ga?

specify (state clearly, fully) jí·mìhng. /Please specify what you need, so we can order for you. Chéng néih jí·mìhng yiu bīn·yeuhng, ngóh·deih hó·yíh tùhng néih ō·dá.

spectacles (eyeglasses) ngáahn·géng (M: fu); **pair of spectacles** yāt·fu ngáahn·géng; **wear spectacles** daai·ngáahn·géng

spectator (of a game, a play, etc.) gùn·jung; (bystander) pòhng·gùn·jé

speculate jouh tàuh·gèi·sàang·yi; cháau: **speculate in gold** cháau·gām

speech expressed verbally as: góng syut·wah, góng·wá. /Can you tell where he comes from by his speech? Néih tèng kéuih góng·syut·wah, néih tēng·dāk·chēut kéuih haih bīn·syu yàhn ma?
(address) yín·góng. /That was a very good speech. Gó·go yín·góng góng dāk hóu hóu. **make a speech** yín·góng. /We would like you to make a speech to our students next Monday. Ngóh·deih séung chéng néih hah·láih·baai·yāt lèih ngóh·deih hohk·haauh yín·góng.

speed chūk·douh (N); Speed it up! Faai·dī, faai·dī! /Speed limit 30 miles per hour. Chūk·douh múih·síu·sìh bāt·nàhng chìu·gwo sàam·sahp·léih.

speedometer chūk·douh·bíu

spell chyun·jih; pīng·yām. /Do you know how to spell this word? Néih wúih·m̀h·wúih chyun nī·go jih a? or Nī·go jih dím·yéung pīng·yām a?
(magic charm) fùh·jau; fùh; jau. /We don't believe in spells and charms. Ngóh·deih m̀h·seun fùh·jau dī gám ge yéh ge.
a spell /He had a coughing spell just a while ago. Kéuih jing·wah kāt·jó yāt·jahn. /Do you have fainting spells? is expressed as: Néih haih·m̀h·haih sìh·sìh wúih wàhn·dài (or wàhn·dóu) ga?

spend (use up, pay out) sái, yuhng. /I spent almost all my money. Ngóh dī chín chā·m̀h·dō sái·saai la. /I don't think we should spend all the money on building laboratories.

Ngóh gok·dāk ngóh·deih bāt·nàhng yuhng·saai dī chín léih héi saht·yihm·sāt. /Do not spend your money just because you have it. Néih bāt·nàhng yàn·waih néih yáuh chín jauh yiu sái·jó kéuih.

(of time) yuhng; (stay) gwo, jyuh; (for vacation) wáan. /We have spent several hours looking for a suitable gift, and we still haven't found one. Ngóh·deih yuhng·jó géi·go jūng·tàuh sìh·gaan séung wán yāt·gihn hahp·sīk ge láih·maht, yìh·gā juhng meih wán·dóu. /We want to spend the night here. Ngóh·deih séung hái nī·syu gwo yāt·máahn yeh (or jyuh yāt·máahn). /We plan to spend a few days there (for vacation). Ngóh·deih dá·syun hái gó·syu wáan géi·yaht.

sphere   (globe) deih·kàuh; (as of influence) faahn·wàih: **sphere of influence** sai·lihk·faahn·wàih

spice   hèung·líu; fā·jīu·baat·gok jī·léui

spider   kàhm·lóu (M: jek)

spill   /Watch him, don't let him spill the milk again. Tái·jyuh kéuih, m̀h·hóu béi kéuih joi dóu·sé dī ngàuh·náaih.

spin   (as thread) fóng, gáau: **spin yarn** fóng·sā, gáau·sā; **a silkworm spins silk** chàahm·chúng tou sī

spinach   bò·choi

spine   jek·gwāt (M: tìuh)

spiral   lòh·syùhn·yìhng ge; **spiral form** lòh·sī·màhn; **spiral staircase** lòh·sī·làuh·tài

spirit   (disposition) jīng·sàhn. /They are full of patriotic spirit. Kéuih·deih chùng·múhn ngoi·gwok ge jīng·sàhn. /Well, it's the spirit of the times. Nī·go haih yìh·gā nī·go sìh·doih ge jīng·sàhn.

(feeling, emotion) chìhng·séuih: **a spirit of revolt** fáan·paan ge chìhng·séuih

(liveliness) jīng·sàhn (of people or horses). /That kid has a lot of spirit. Gó·go sai·mān·jái jàn·haih jīng·sàhn la. /You have a horse with a lot of spirit there. Néih gó·pāt máh jàn·haih jīng·sàhn la.

(attitude) taai·douh. /That's the right spirit! Gám (ge taai·douh) jauh ngāam·saai la.

(supernatural beings) gwéi (ghost); sàhn (god); jīng (of animals of plants)

spirits sàm·chìhng. /He is in good spirits today. Kéuih gàm·yaht sàm·chìhng hóu hóu. or Kéuih gàm·yaht hóu gòu·hing.

spirits of wine jáu·jīng, fó·jáu; **spirit of lemon** nìhng·mūng·jīng

spiritual   jīng·sàhn·seuhng ge; **spiritual beings** gwéi·sàhn

spit   (release from the mouth) tou, léu, ngáu. /No spitting. M̀h·jéun tou tàahm. /If it tastes bad, spit it out. Yùh·gwó m̀h·sihk·dāk, léu kéuih chēut·lèih. /Has he ever spit blood? Kéuih yáuh móuh ngáu·gwo hyut a?

splendid   (very good) jeui hóu, jàn·haih hóu, miuh dou·gihk. /This is splendid weather for swimming. Gám ge tìn·hei jeui hóu yàuh·séui la. /I think what you have done is splendid. Ngóh gok·dak néih jouh dāk jàn·haih hóu la. /Splendid! Miuh dou·gihk!

splint   (surg.) gaap·báan (M: faai)

split   (rend) fàn·lit, fàn·lit·hòi; **split into** fàn·lit·sèhng. /The party now is split into four factions. Gó·go dóng yìh·gā yíh·gìng fàn·lit·sèhng sei·paai la.

spoil   (go bad) laahn, waaih. /These oranges are beginning to spoil. Dī cháang jauh·lèih laahn la. /Food spoils quickly in this kind of weather. Gám ge tìn·sìh dī sihk·maht jeui yùhng·yih waaih ge la.

(overindulge) jung·gwaan·saai, gwaan·waaih·saai. /He has been spoiled by his grand-mother. Kéuih béi kéuih a·màh jung·gwaan·saai. /Don't spoil him. M̀h·hóu jung·gwaan·saai kéuih. /He's a spoiled child. Kéuih gwaan·waaih·saai.

(ruin) cháh·wóh. /The bad weather spoiled our plan for hiking. Ngóh·deih dá·syun heui yúhn·jūk·léuih·hàhng·ge, béi dī gám ge tìn·sìh cháh·wóh·jó.

spoils hóu·chyúh. /I guess he got his share of the spoils. Ngóh gú kéuih yihk dāk· dóu yāt·fahn hóu·chyúh.

sponge   séui·póuh, hói·mìhn

spongy   sùng

spooky   gú·lìhng·jìng·gwaai

spool   lūk: **a spool of thread** yāt·lūk sin; gyún: **a roll of film** yāt·gyún fēi·lám

spoon   chìh·gāng (M: jek); **spoon up** fāt·héi; **soup spoon** tōng·gāng; **teaspoon** chìh·gāng· jái, chàh·gāng

spoonful   **a spoonful** yāt·chìh·gāng

sport   (exercise, physical games) wahn·duhng; **sports page** tái·yuhk·làahn; **sports coat** wahn·duhng·yī. /Do you like sports? Néih jùng·yi wahn·duhng ma? /What kind of sport do you like? Néih héi·fùn bīn·tíng wahn·duhng a?

(of a person) /He's a good sport. Kéuih go yàhn hóu daaih·leuhng ge. /He's a poor sport. Kéuih go yàhn hou sìu·hei ge.

spot   (small mark) dím; (dirty mark) láh·já. /She is wearing a white dress with red spots. Kéuih jeuk yāt·gihn baahk·dái yáuh hùhng·dím ge sāam. /Can you get these spots out of my coat? Néih hó·yíh jíng·lāt ngóh gihn sāam seuhng·bihn nī·dī láh·já ma?

(place) deih·fōng; (point) daat. /Show me the exact spot you mean. Jèung néih só· góng gó·daat deih·fōng jí·béi ngóh tái·háh. /Is this the spot? Haih·m̀h·haih nī·yāt·daat a?

on the spot (right there). /He said he was on the spot when it happened. Kéuih wah gó·gihn sih faat·sàng ge sìh·hauh kéuih ngāam·ngāam hái syu.

on the spot (immediately) jīk·hāk, dòng·tòhng. /They killed the snake right on the spot. Kéuih·deih jīk·hāk (or dòng·tòhng) jauh dá·séi tìuh sèh la.

be put on the spot /This really put me on the spot. Nī·gihn sih jàn·haih lìhng ngóh nàahn·jou la.

to spot /I spotted you in the crowd as soon as I saw your hat. is expressed as Hái gó·bàan yàhn jì·jùng ngóh yāt tái·dóu néih déng móu jauh jīk·hāk yihng·chēut haih néih la.

spout   **the spout of a teapot** chàh·wùh·jéui

sprain   wāt·chàn, náu·chàn. /He said he sprained his ankle. Kéuih wah kéuih wāt·chàn jek geuk.

spray   pan: **spray water** pan·séui

spread   (lay out, as a blanket, etc.) tàan·hòi, pòu·hòi, pòu·hóu. /Spread out the rug and let me look at it. Tàan·hòi jèung deih·jīn béi ngóh tái·háh. /Can you help me to spread out the tablecloth? Néih hó·yíh bòng ngóh pòu·hòi jèung tói·bou ma?

(open) maak·hòi. /Spread your fingers apart. Maak·hòi néih ge sáu·jí kéuih.

(extend) só·jim·ge deih·fōng. /The factory spreads over ten acres. Gùng·chóng só· jim ge deih·fōng yáuh sahp·máuh gam daaih.

(distribute; throw with the motion of sowing seed, a powdered fertilizer, etc.) sám; (smear butter, etc.) chàh. /Spread the fertilizer evenly. Jèung dī fèih·tìhn·líu sám· wàhn kéuih. /Do you want me to spread some butter on the bread? Néih yiu·m̀h·yiu ngóh tùhng néih chàh dī ngàuh·yàuh hái faai mihn·bāau·syu a?

(expand) chyùhn (of news, etc.); maahn·yìhn (of fire); chyùhn·yíhm (of disease); chyùhn· bo (of ideas or religion). /The news spread rapidly. Go sīu·sīk chyùhn dāk hóu faai. /The fire spread rapidly. Dī fó maahn·yìhn dāk hóu faai. /This kind of disease spreads very fast. Nī·tíng behng chyùhn·yíhm dāk hóu faai ge. /We should stop the disease from spreading. Ngóh·deih yiu fòhng·jí nī·tíng behng chyùhn·yíhm hòi·heui. /These ideas have already been spread all over the world. Nī·dī sî·séung yìh·gìng chyùhn·bo·dou sai·gaai gok·chyúh la.

spread under /Spread the towel under the baby. Pòu·hòi tìuh mòuh·gān jin·jyuh go bìh·bī·jái.

spread out to cool tàan·dung; **spread out to dry** lohng·hòi

spring   (season) chēun·tīn, chèun·gwai; **springtime** chēun·tīn ge sìh·hauh; **spring holidays** chèun·ga. /We have plenty of rain this spring. Gàm·nín chēun·tīn jàn·haih yúh·séui·jūk la.
(water source) chyùhn, sàan·chyùhn; **spring water** chyùhn·séui. /This mountain has three springs. Nī·go sàan yáuh sàam·go chyùhn.
(elastic metal device) daahn·gūng. /This bed has good springs. Nī·jèung chòhng ge daahn·gūng hóu hóu. /Thé springs seem to be broken. Hóu·chíh tìuh daahn·gūng waaih· jó.
(jump) tiu. /He sprang to his feet. Kéuih yāt tiu jauh tiu·héi·sàn la.

sprinkle   sá (fluid); sám (powder)

sprout   ngàh; **bamboo sprouts** jūk·séun; **bean sprouts** ngàh·choi; **wheat sprouts** mahk· ngàh; chēut·ngàh, faat·ngàh (V)

spurt   pan: **spurt water** pan séui

spy   gaan·dihp (N); dá·táam. /He was sent to spy on the enemy. Kéuih beih paai·heui dá· taam dihk·yàhn ge sīu·sīk.

squabble   ngaai·gàau, díng·géng

squad   sîu·deuih, deuih

squadron   jùng·deuih

square   (square-shaped) sei·fōng·(ge). /I want a square box. Ngóh yiu go sei·fōng ge háp.
(honest, fair) lóuh·saht; gùng·douh. /He's a fair and square man. Kéuih haih go lóuh·saht yàhn. /They gave him a square deal. Kéuih·deih deui kéuih hóu gùng·douh.
(square unit of measurement) dīng·fōng; square inch, fòng·chyun; square foot, fòng· chek; **square mile** fòng·léih. /I want a piece of cloth two feet square. Ngóh yiu yāt· fūk léuhng·chek dīng·fōng ge bou.

squash   jaahk: **squash flat** jaahk·bín·jó

squat   màu, màu·dài. /He squatted down there to weed the paddy field. Kéuih màu·hái go tìhn·syu màng·chóu.

squeeze   jà. /If she is thirsty, you may squeeze some orange juice for her to drink. Yùh·gwó kéuih géng·hot, néih hó·yíh jà dī cháang·jāp béi kéuih yám.
(extort) lahk·ja: **squeeze the people** lahk·ja dī yàhn·màhn
(press) ja: **squeeze the oil of** (beans, seeds, etc.) ja·yàuh

squirrel   chùhng·syú (M: jek)

stab   gāt. /Can you identify the man who stabbed you? Néih yihng·dāk·chēut [yuhng dóu· jái] gāt néih gó·go yàhn ma? /He was nearly stabbed to death. Kéuih jāang·dī béi yàhn gāt·séi.

stable   (steady) wán·jahn; (for horse) máh·fòhng

stadium   wahn·duhng·chèuhng

staff   (used to walk with) gwáai·jéung; (of an office) jīk·yùhn. /How many staff members do you have in your factory? Néih·deih gàan gùng·chóng yáuh géi·dò jīk·yùhn a? **staff officer** chàam·màuh

stag   luhk·gūng (M: jek)

stage   (theatrical) hei·tòih; (platform) góng·tòih; (to put on a play) séuhng·yín

stagger   (walk unsteadily) bài·bài·háh gám hàhng

stain   (make a soiled spot) jíng·wū·jòu. /Be careful, the juice may stain your dress.
Hóu·sěng a nàh, dī gwó·jāp wúih jíng·wù·jòu néih gihn sāam ga.
   blood stain hyut·jīk; **ink stain** mahk·séui·yan; **oil stain** yàuh·yan

stair   (a step) kāp; (leading to a door, outside a building) sehk·kāp; (leading from one
floor to another) làuh·tài. /Take the stairs to your right. Hàahng yauh·sáu·bihn gó·go
làuh·tài. **staircase** làuh·tài, làuh·tài·háu

stale   (not fresh) m̀h·sān·sìn; gaak·yeh: **stale bread** gaak·yeh mihn·bāau; **stale food**
gaak·yeh·sung; (vapid) móuh meih, jáu·jó meih·douh

stalk   (stem, of vegetables) kwáng

stall   (for selling goods) dong, dong·háu; dong (M). (stop when you don't want it to). /Our
motor stalled and we couldn't get it started. Ngóh·deih ge mō·dá waaih·jó, m̀h·dá·dāk·
héi·fó.

stallion   máh·gūng (M: pāt)

stamin   fā·yéuih

stammer   (stutter) lau·háu, háu·jaht·jaht. /He stammers whenever he gets excited.
Kéuih yāt gāp·héi·séuhng·lèih jauh lau·háu (or háu·jaht·jaht) ge la.

stamp   (postage stamp) yàuh·piu, sih·dāam (colloq.). /Have you put the stamp on?
Néih nìhm·jó sih·dāam meih a?
   (imprint or impress with a mark) dám·yan, dá·yan. /Please stamp the school name
on all these books. M̀h·gòi néih dám hohk·haauh ge yan hái nī·dī syù·seuhng·bihn.
   (step on with foot) yáai; dahm. /He stamped out the cigarette butt. Kéuih yáai·sīk·
jó go yīn·táu. /Tell the children not to stamp on the floor. Giu dī sai·mān·jái m̀h·hóu
dahm go deih·báan.
   rubber stamp jeuhng·pèih tòuh·jēung; **tax stamp** yan·fā; **stamp pad** yan·sīk; **stamp**
with a seal dám·yan, dám·tòuh·jēung.

stand   (on one's feet) kéih. /Stand over there. Kéih·hái gó·syu. /Stand where you are
and don't move. Kéih·hái syu m̀h·hóu yūk.
   (rise to one's feet) kéih·héi·sàn. /The students stood when they saw the teacher
come in. Dī hohk·sāang tái·gin sīn·sàang hàahng·yahp·lèih go·go dōu kéih·héi·sàn.
   (be upright; set upright) baahng·hái; duhng·héi. /The ladder is standing in the corner. Bá tài baahng·hái chèuhng·gok·lōk·táu·syu. /Stand the box on end. Duhng·héi go
háp kéuih.
   (endure) sauh·dāk (of people only); kām (dāk) (of people or thing). /They couldn't
stand the noise of the airplanes therefore they moved away. Kéuih·deih m̀h·sauh·dāk dī
fēi·gèi·sèng só·yíh kéuih·deih bùn·jáu·jó. /This cloth won't stand much washing. Nī·
tíng bou m̀h·kàm·sái.
   stand aside kéih·hòi; **stand by** kéih·hái pòhng·bīn; **stand by** (help) bòng·joh; **stand by**
(wait) dáng; **stand for** (uphold) jaan·sìhng; **stand for** (represent) doih·bíu; **stand firmly**
kéih·wán (physically); **stand in the way** jó·jyuh

standpoint   lahp·chèuhng

standstill   tìhng·deuhn

standard   (model) bìu·jéun; **standard time** bìu·jéun·sìh·gaan. /It isn't up to the standard.
M̀h·hahp bìu·jéun.
   (banner) kèih; **standard bearer** kèih·sáu, dàam·kèih·ge

stanza   jit

star　　(heavenly body) sīng (M: nāp). /Do you know the name of that star? Néih jĭ gó·
nāp sīng giu māt·yéh méng ma?
　　(in entertainment or sports) mìhng·sīng; **film star** dihn·yíng·mìhng·sīng
　　(play the leading role) jouh jyú·gok. /Who stars in that picture? Gó·chēut dihn·yíng
bīn·go jouh jyú·gok a?

starch　　(for cooking) lìhng·fán; (for clothes) jèung·fán; to starch the clothes jèung·sāan.
/This dress has to be starched. Nī·gihn sāam yiu jèung ge.

stare　　**stare at** ngáahn·gwòng·gwòng gám tái·jyuh. /Why do you stare at me? Néih
ngáahn·gwòng·gwòng gám tái·jyuh ngóh jouh·māt·yéh a?

start　　(begin) héi·sáu, hòi·chí; hòi—. /When are we going to start? Ngóh·deih géi sí
héi·sáu a? /The game has already started. Yíh·gìng hòi·chí béi·choi la. /When will
school start? Géi·sí hòi·hohk a? /When will the work start? Géi·sí hōi·gùng a? **start
of a boat** hòi·syùhn, hòi·sàn; **start of a train** hòi·chè, hòi·sàn; **start to do business** (in
a day) hòi·pou
　　(set out) héi·chìhng, duhng·sàn (depart for a journey); chēut·faat (as troops, etc.).
/When do we start? Ngóh·deih géi·sí héi·chìhng a? /It's starting to rain. Lohk·yuh la.
/Has the show started yet? Hòi·jó chèuhng meih a? /Start the engine! Hòi·jeuhk go
ēn·jín kéuih! /Start the fire. Tau·jeuhk go fó kéuih.

starve　　ngoh; **starve to death** ngoh·séi. /I'm starving, is there anything to eat? Ngóh
hóu tóuh·ngoh, yáuh móuh yéh sihk a?

state　　(nation) gwok·gà; **state department** gwok·mouh·yún. /The railroads are run by
the state. Tit·louh haih yàuh gwok·gà baahn ge. /All the states of Asia sent delegates
to the convention. Nga·jàu só·yáuh ge gwok·gà dōu paai yàhn heui chàam·gà gó·chi wuih·
yi.
　　(situation) chìhng·yìhng. /They are in a bad state. Kéuih·deih ge chìhng yìhng sèung·
dòng m̀h·hóu. /Anything is better than the present state of things. Dím dōu hóu·gwo
muhk·chìhn ge chìhng·yìhng.
　　(unit of a nation) jàu (one of the states of the United States); sáang (province, used
of the Chinese provinces)
　　to state góng (in speech); sé (in writing); **state clearly** góng (or sé) mìhng. /State
clearly what you.need. Góng (or sé)·mìhng néih yiu māt·yéh.
　　financial state of a family gà·gíng; **state of mind** sàm·gíng, sàm·chìhng

statement　　(notice sent to an individual) tūng·jì; (public bulletin) tùng·gou; (report) bou·
gou, bou·gou·syù; (bill) dāan. /The bank will send you a statement every four months.
Ngàhn·hòhng múih sei·go·yuht gei yāt·chi tūng·jì béi néih. /Has the store sent a statement of my account? Gó·gàan pou·táu yáuh móuh gei dāan lèih béi ngóh a?
　　(utterance) wá, syut·wah. /Have you any statement to make? Néih yáuh māt wá góng
ma?

statesman　　jing·jih·gā

station　　(stop) jaahm; **bus station** bā·sí·jaahm; **train station** fó·chè·jaahm. /I want to
get off at the next station. Ngóh yiu daih·yih·go jaahm lohk·chè. /Where is the train
station? Fó·chè·jaahm hái bīn·syu a?
　　(broadcasting unit) dihn·tòih. /What stations can you get on your radio? Néih ge
sāu·yām·gēi hó·yíh sàu·dóu bīn·géi·go dihn·tòih a?
　　(place for research) -chèuhng (field); -só (office or building); kēui (zone). /There
is an agricultural experiment station near here. Nī·syu fuh·gahn yáuh yāt·go nùhng·yihp
si·yihm·chèuhng.
　　fire station sìu·fòhng·gūk, séui·chè·gún (only used in Hong Kong); **police station** gíng·
chaat·gūk, chàai·gún (used in Hong Kong), máh·dá·lìuh (used in Singapore)
　　to station (assign) paai·jyuh, paai . . . sáu, jyuh·fòhng, jyuh·jaat. /His company
stationed him in Japan. Kéuih ge gūng·sī paai kéuih jyuh·hái Yaht·bún. /The police

stationed a man at the door. Gíng·chaat·gūk paai·jó yāt·go yàhn sáu·jyuh go mùhn·háu.
/Where is your battalion stationed? Néih·deih gó·yìhng yàhn hái bīn·syu jyuh·fòhng a?
<u>or</u> Néih·deih gó·yìhng yàhn jyuh·jaat·hái bīn·syu a?

stationary   màhn·geuih; (writing papers) seun·jí (M: jèung)

statistics   (figures) túng·gai sou·jih, túng·gai; (the science) túng·gai·hohk

statue   (bronze) tùhng·jeuhng; (stone) sehk·jeuhng

stature   (height) sàn·chòih

stay   (live) jyuh. /Where are you staying? Néih jyuh·hái bīn·syu a? /I'm staying with
friends. Ngóh jyuh·hái pàhng·yáuh·syu. /How long are you going to stay there? Néih
dá·syun jyuh·hái gó·syu géi nói a? /I intend to stay for a week. Ngóh dá·syun jyuh yāt·
go láih·baai.
    /Stay away from that place. M̀h·hóu hàahng·màaih gó·syu. /Stay where you are.
M̀h·hóu yūk.

steady   (firm, not shaky) wán·jahn. /Is the ladder steady enough? Bá tài gau wán·jahn
meih a?
    (regular) /Has he a steady job now? Kéuih yáuh fahn chèuhng·gūng meih a?

steak   (beefsteak) ngàuh·pá

steal   tàu. /My car was stolen. Ngóh ga chè béi yàhn tàu·jó. /Someone stole my watch.
Yáuh yàhn tàu·jó ngóh ge bīu.

steam   (vapor) hei; jìng·hei, séui·jìng·hei (hot vapor); **steam heat** nyúhn·hei; **steamship**
dihn·syùhn
    (cook by steaming) jìng. /Steam it half an hour. Jìng kéuih bun·dím·jūng.

steel   gong, gong·tit. /This is all steel. Nī·go sèhng·go haih gong ge. /He worked in a
steel mill before. Kéuih yìh·chìhn hái yāt·gàan gong·tit·chóng jouh·gwo sih.

steep   che. /The road is very steep when it is going down hill. Gó·tìuh louh lohk sàan
ge sih·hauh hóu che ge.

steer   **steering wheel** táaih. /Do you know how to steer? Néih wúih jà·táaih ma?

stem   (of flower) kwáng; (of a fruit) dìng

stench   chau·meih; chau (SV)

stencil   **paper for making a stencil master** yàuh·yan·jí

stenographer   chūk·gei·yùhn

stenography   chūk·gei. /Do you know stenography? Néih wúih chūk·gei ma?

step   (movement of the foot) bouh. /He took one step forward. Kéuih heung chìhn laam·
jó yāt bouh.
    (sound of walking) geuk·bouh·sèng. /He said he heard steps but I didn't. Kéuih wah
kéuih tèng·gin geuk·bouh·sèng, daahn·haih ngóh tèng·m̀h·dóu.
    (unit of action) bouh, bouh·jauh. /This is only the first step (in the process). Nī·go
jí·haih daih·yāt·bouh. /He mentioned three steps but I only remember the first one.
Kéuih góng·jó sàam·go bouh·jauh, daahn·haih ngóh jí gei·dāk yāt·go jē.
    (on a stairway) kāp; **steps** sehk·kāp (steps leading to the door of a building); làuh·
tài (a flight of stairs leading from one floor to another)
    step by step yāt·bouh yāt·bouh gám. /You should do it step by step. Néih yiu yāt·
bouh yāt·bouh gám jouh.
    take steps séung·baahn·faat. /We have to take steps to correct this mistake. Ngóh·
deih yiu séung baahn·faat gói·jing nī·go cho·ngh.
    watch one's step /Watch your step! <u>is expressed as</u> Hóu·sēng a! (Be careful!)

to step /Step aside. Hàahng·hõi dī. /Step back a little. Heung hauh·bihn tan·háh. (put the foot down on) yáai. /Don't step on the flowers. M̀h·hóu yáai·dī fā.

step up (increase) /Their factory had been trying to step up production. Kéuih· deih gàan gùng·chóng jing·joih séung·baahn·faat jàng·gà sàng·cháan.

stepfather hauh·fuh; **stepmother** hauh·móuh, gai·móuh

stern   yihm; (naut.) syùhn·méih

stethoscope   tèng·túng

stew   màn

steward   gún·sih

stick   (fasten with glue) nìhm. /Stick a ten cent stamp on the envelope. Nìhm yāt·go sahp·fān ge sih·dāam hái go seun·fūng·syu. /I'll stick these pictures in my album. Ngóh yiu jèung nī·dī seung·pín nìhm·hái ngóh·ge seung·bóu·syu.

(adhere) chì. /The glue sticks to my fingers. Dī gàau·séui chì·jyuh ngóh ge sáu·jí.

(thrust into) chaap. /She stuck a flower in her hair. Kéuih chaap·jó yāt·déu·fā hái tàuh·faat·syu.

(hook through something) biht. /She stuck a jade pin on her collar. Kéuih biht·jó go yuhk·kau·jām hái tìuh léhng·syu.

(slip, tuck in) sāk. /The little boy stuck all the candies into his pocket. Gó·go sai· mān·jái jèung dī tóng sāk·saai·yahp·heui go dói·syu.

(prick) gāt. /If you don't move away, I will stick you with a pin. Yùh·gwó néih juhng m̀h·hàahng·hòi, ngóh jauh ló jī jām gāt néih ge làh.

stick it out yáhn, yáhn·noih. /Try to stick it out a little longer. Yáhn (or yáhn·noih) yāt·jahn·gāan tim lā.

stick something out daht·chēut, gaht·chēut. /Your shirttail is sticking out. Néih gihn sēut·sāam daht·jó chēut·lèih. /Watch out for that pipe sticking up over there. Gu· jyuh gó·syu gó·tìuh gaht·chēut·lèih ge séui·gún.

get stuck /Our car got stuck. is expressed as Ngóh·deih ga chè waaih·jó.

a stick (walking stick) sih·dīk (M: jī), gwáai·jéung (M: tìuh)

sticky   chī·chì·nahk·nahk; (hot and humid) sāp·sāp·nahp·nahp. /Why is the table so sticky? Dím·gáai jeung toi gam chī·chì·nahk·nahk ga? /The summer here is always very sticky. Nī·syu ge hah·tīn géi·sìh dōu haih gam sāp·sāp·nahp·nahp ge.

stiff   (hard to bend) ngaahng. /This brush isn't stiff enough. Nī·go cháat m̀h·gau ngaahng. /Make it stiff when you starch my collars. Ngóh ge sāam·léhng yiu jèung ngaahng·dī.

(formal) /Don't be so stiff! M̀h·sái gam kèui·láih!

(difficult) /Is it a stiff examination? Háau·si háau dāk nàahn ma?

have a stiff neck /I have a stiff neck. Ngóh fan·làaih·jó géng.

still   (quiet) ngòn·jihng. /The whole school was still. Sèhng·gàan hohk·haauh dōu hóu ngòn·jihng.

(motionless) dihng, m̀h(·hóu) yūk. /Stand still. Kéih·dihng, m̀h·hóu·yūk. /Can you stay still? Néih m̀h·yūk dāk·m̀h·dāk a? /Keep your feet still. Néih sèung geuk m̀h·hóu yūk.

(calm and quiet; of water) móuh·fùng·móuh·lohng, pìhng·jihng. /The sea is still to-day. Gàm·yaht go hói móuh·fùng·móuh·lohng, hóu pìhng·jihng.

(as yet, now as before) juhng, juhng·haih, yìhng·yìhn. /We still need five teachers. Ngóh·deih juhng sèui·yiu ńg·go sīn·sàang. /He's still the same. Keuih juhng haih gám.

even so . . . still jīk·sí haih gám . . . yìhng·yìhn; **although . . . still** sèui·yìhn . . . daahn·haih . . . yìhng·yìhn. /Even so I still think you did the right thing. Jīk sí haih gám, ngóh yìhng·yìhn yihng·wàih néih jouh dāk hóu ngāam. /Although I don't like him, still I have to admit he's clever. Sèui·yìhn ngoh m̀h·héi·fùn keuih, daahn·haih ngóh yìhng·yìhn gok·dāk kéuih go yàhn hóu chùhng·mìhng. /This is still better. Nī·go juhng hóu. /It's still early. Juhng jóu jē.

still life painting jihng·maht sé·sāng

stimulant   (Med.) hǐng·fáhn·jài

stimulate   (as emotion) gīk·duhng

sting   (as done by an insect) dèng (V). /He was stung by a wasp. Kéuih béi wòhng·fūng dèng·chàn.

stingy   (not generous) gù·hòhn; **stingy fellow** gù·hòhn·júng, gù·hòhn·láu. /Don't be so stingy! Mh·hóu gam gù·hòhn là.

stink   chau (SV); chau·meih, chau·hei (N)

stir   (move or mix) gáau. /Stir it when it is cooking. Jyú·gán ge sìh·hauh yiu gáau·háh kéuih.
     stir up (arouse, excite). /He tried to stir up the students to oppose the president. Kéuih séung gú·duhng dī hohk·sāang fáan·deui haauh·jéung. /He stirs up trouble where- ever he goes. Kéuih dou·chyúh dōu gáau·fùng·gáau·yúh ge. or Kéuih dou·chyúh dōu gáau·sih·gáau·fèi ge.

stitch   (by hand) lyùhn(·màaih); (by machine) chè(·màaih); (a single passage of thread) jām, jām·bouh /Please stitch the hem for me. Mh·gòi néih tùhng ngóh lyùhn·màaih go bīn kéuih. /The doctor took five stitches in his wound. Yī·sāng hái kéuih ge sèung·háu· syu lyùhn·jó ngh·jām.

stock   chyùhn. /We should stock more goods before Christmas. Sīng·daan·jit chìhn ngóh·deih yiu chyùhn dō·dī fo.
     (a supply of things to sell) chyùhn·fo. /We have only a small stock of this brand radio. Nī·tìng ge sāu·yām·gēi ngóh·deih ge chyùhn·fo hóu síu.
     (share or holdings) gú·fán, gú·piu; **stock market** gú·piu sìh·chèuhng; (livestock) sàang·háu

stocking   maht (M: jek; pair, deui or sèung)

stomach   (for digesting food) waih; (the belly; abdomen) tóuh; **stomach ache** waih tung or tóuh tung; **empty stomach** hùng tóuh. /Don't drink on an empty stomach. Mh·hóu hùng tóuh yám jáu.
     to stomach sauh·dāk. /I can't stomach such rich food. Ngóh mh·sauh·dāk fèih·neih ge yéh. /No one can stomach such an insult. Móuh yàhn sauh·dāk dī gám ge móuh·yuhk ge.

stone   sehk; (pebble) sehk·jái. /This bridge is built entirely of stone. Nī·tìuh kìuh yùhn· chyùhn haih yuhng sehk héi ge.
     stone of a peach tòuh·wát; **stone of a litchi** laih·jī·wát; **gravestone** sehk·bèi

stool   dang, dang·jái

stoop   (bend down) lyùn·màaih go yīu; (let the shoulders and head lean forward) wù·dài go tàuh

stop   (halt) tìhng. /Stop the car! Tìhng chè! /My watch just stopped. Ngóh go bīu ngāam·ngāam tìhng·jó. /Stop the car at the next crossing. Hái daih·yih·go gāai·háu tìhng·chè.
     (stop someone from doing something) jó·jí . . . /Can you stop him from playing the record? Néih hó·yíh jó·jí kéuih cheung làuh·sìng·gèi ma? /No one can stop me from doing this. Móuh yàhn nàhng jó·jí ngóh jouh nī·gihn sih.
     (cease pain, bleeding, etc.) jí. /This medicine ought to stop the pain. Nī·jek yeuhk hó·yíh jí·tung ge la. /Can you stop the bleeding? Yáuh māt·faat·jí hó·yíh jí·hyut a?
     (cease) tìhng; (when asking someone to stop something) mh·hóu (don't). /Has it stopped raining? Tìhng·jó yúh meih a? /Stop doing that! Mh·hóu gám jouh.

(act of stopping) <u>is expressed verbally as in the first paragraph.</u> /We made several stops before we got here. Ngóh·deih lèih·dou jì·chìhn hái louh·seuhng tìhng·jó géi·chi.

(stay) /We stopped at a small village overnight. Ngóh·deih hái tìuh chyūn·jái jyuh·jó yāt·máahn.

a stop (stopping place) jaahm. /I want to get off at the next stop. Ngóh yiu hái daih·yih·go·jaahm lohk·chè.

(close or stuff up) sāk·jyuh. /Can you stop the leak? Néih yáuh móuh faat·jí sāk·jyuh kéuih m̀h béi kéuih lauh a?

/Stop him, don't let him get away! Jiht·jyuh (<u>or</u> jūk·jyuh 'seize') kéuih, m̀h·hóu béi kéuih jáu·lāt·jó!

stopper   jāt: **stopper of a bottle** jēun·jāt

storage   (place for goods) jaahn·fòhng; (charge for) jaahn·jòu

store   (shop) pou·táu (M: gàan); sih·dō (M: gàan) (term used in Hong Kong for grocery selling western canned food). /Where is this store? Nī·gàan pou·táu hái bīn·syu a?
to store jài·màaih, sàu·màaih, chyùhn·héi. /Where can we find a place to store these canned goods. Nī·dī gun·táu jài·màaih·hái bīn·syu a? /Can you find me a place to store these goods? Néih hó·yíh tùhng ngóh wán daat deih·fòng chyùhn·héi nī·dī fo ma?

storehouse   jaahn·fòhng, fo·chōng

storekeeper   (one in charge of stores) sih·táu

storey   (floor) láu; chàhng. /He lives on the third storey (British: second floor). Kéuih jyuh·hái sàam·láu. /It's a four-storey building. Gó·joh láu haih sei·chàhng ge.

stork   baahk·hók

storm   daaih·fùng·daaih·yúh. /Last night we had a storm, and now we have such a beautiful day. Kàhm·máahn daaih·fùng·daaih·yúh, gàm·yaht gam hóu tìn·sìh.

story   (a report of things that happened) gìng·gwo (ge) chìhng·yìhng. /Do you know the story of his life? Néih jì·dou kéuih yāt·sàng gìng·gwo ge chìhng·yìhng ma? /Can you tell me the whole story about it? Néih·hó·yíh jèung sèhng·gihn sih ge gìng·gwo chìhng·yìhng góng·béi ngóh tèng ma?
(short tale) gú·jái. /Can you tell the children a story? Néih hó·yíh góng go gú·jái béi dī sai·màn·jái tèng ma?
(account) só·góng·ge wá. /Their stories don't agree. Kéuih·deih só·góng·ge wá m̀h·sèung·tùhng. /It'll be another story tomorrow. Tìng·yaht jauh m̀h·tùhng·yéung ge la.

stove   (for cooking) fó·lòuh

stowaway   jáu·gwāan·ge (yàhn), tàu·douh·ge (yàhn)

straight   jihk, yāt·jihk. /Hold your arm straight. Sàn·jihk jek sáu. /Stand up straight. Kéih·jihk. /Go straight ahead. Yāt·jihk hàahng.
(directly) yāt·jihk. /Go straight home after school! Fong·jó hohk yāt·jihk fàan ngūk·kéi.
(honest) jihk·baahk. /He's always been straight with me. Kéuih deui ngóh géi·sìh dōu haih hóu jihk·baahk ge.
get something straight gáau·chìng·chó. /Be sure to get your facts straight before you put them into your report. Néih yiu gáau·chìng·chó dī sih·saht sìn·ji hóu sé·lohk go bou·gou·syu.
a straight face báan·jyuh go mín. /He always has a straight face. Kéuih géi·sí dōu haih gám báan·jyuh go mín ge.

strain   (sprain) náu·chàn. /He lifted a heavy rock and strained his back. Kéuih chàu·héi gauh daaih sehk náu·chàn go yīu·gwāt.
(stretch, pull too tight) jeuih gán. /The clothesline was strained by the wet clothes hanging on it. Tìuh lohng·sàam·síng béi dī sāp·sāam jeuih dāk bāt jì géi gán.

(sieve) gaak. /How (by using what) should I strain the coffee? Yuhng māt·yéh lèih gaak dī ga·fē a?
(work too hard) gwo·lòuh. /Don't strain yourself. M̀h·hóu jouh dāk gwo·lòuh a!

strainer   jaau·lēi

strait   hói·haahp

strand   (as ship) gok·chín. /The ship was stranded. Jek syùhn gok·jó chín. (as people) làuh·lohk. /Because communication was cut off he was stranded on the island. Yàn· waih gàau·tùng dyuhn·jyuht, kéuih làuh·lohk·hái gó·go dóu·syu.

strange   (unfamiliar) sàang·bóu; **stranger** sàang·bóu·yàhn. /When I came back to Hong Kong this time it seemed that I had come to a strange place. Ngóh nī·chi làih·dou Hèung· góng hóu·chíh làih·dou yāt·go sàang·bóu deih·fòng gám.
    (peculiar) gú·gwaai, kèih·gwaai; daht·biht, lèih·kèih (special, unusual). /He's a strange character. Kéuih go yàhn hóu gú·gwaai ge. /Strange to say, I didn't notice it. Góng·héi·séuhng·lèih yauh kèih·gwaai la, ngóh móuh jyu·yi·dou gihn gám ge sih. /There is something strange about this house. Nī·gāan ngūk yáuh dī daht·biht.

strangle   (with the hands) nín·séi; (with a cord, etc.) lahk·séi

strap   daai (N); baan. /Why don't you strap your basket onto your bicycle? Dím·gáai néih m̀h·yuhng tìuh dáai jèung go syù·láam baan·hái néih ga dāan·chē·syu nē?

stratagem   gai·màuh; (military) jin·leuhk

strategic   yáuh·jin·leuhk·sing ge, hím·yiu ge: **strategic position** hím·yiu ge deih·fòng

strategy   jin·leuhk

straw   wòh·gón, wòh·gón·chóu; **straw hat** chóu·móu (M: déng); (for drinking) yám·gún (M: jì)

stray   (wander) hàahng·cho·jó louh. /We strayed away from the path. Ngóh·deih hàahng· cho·jó louh. (lost) Ngóh·deih dohng·sāt·jó louh. /Can you ask this stray child where he lives? Néih hó·yíh mahn·háh nī·go dohng·sāt·jó·louh ge sai·mān·jái kéuih jyuh·hái bīn· syu ma?

streak   **a streak in a stone** sehk·màhn

stream   (small river) kài·séui, kài·gaan (M: tìuh)

streamline   làuh·sin·yìhng (ge)

street   gāai (M: tìuh) /Be careful when you cross the street! Hóu·sēng gwo·gāai! /What street do I get off at? Ngóh hái bīn·tìuh gāai lohk·chè a? /I ran into him on the street the other day. Ngóh gó·yaht hái gāai·syu yuh·dóu kéuih.

strength   lihk. /I can't lift it up, I don't have that much strength. Ngóh m̀h·gau·lihk, m̀h·géui·dāk·héi kéuih.
    (power) lihk·leuhng. /The strength of the Republican party is increasing. Guhng·wòh· dóng ge lihk·leuhng yuht lèih yuht daaih.

strengthen   gà·kèuhng (or jàng kèuhng) . . . lihk·leuhng. /They plan to strengthen their party. Kéuih·deih gai·waahk gà·kèuhng kéuih·deih ge dóng ge lihk·leuhng.

stretch   (extend a part of the body) sàn·chèuhng. /Try to stretch for it! Sàn·chèuhng jek sáu tái·háh ló·m̀h·ló·dāk·dóu!
    (extend or reach) yàuh . . . yāt·jihk heui·dou. /This lot stretches from the street to the shore. Nī·faai deih yàuh tìuh gāai yāt jihk heui·dòu hói·pèih.
    (become larger) sùng·jó. /Will this sweater stretch when I wash it? Nī·gihn lāang· sāam sái·séui jì·hauh wúih·m̀h·wúih sùng·jó ga?
    (make larger by pulling) màng·fut. /I thought I could stretch it. Ngóh yíh·wàih hó· yíh màng·fut kéuih.

(make larger by putting something inside) jaahng·daaih. /Let's see whether I can stretch it. Si·háh tái·háh jaahng·m̀h·jaahng·dāk·daaih kéuih.

(length or distance) gyuht, dyuhn. /The next stretch of road won't be so bad. Hah·yāt·gyuht louh jauh móuh gam yáih la.

(become larger when pulled) màng·hòi. /This elastic won't stretch. Nī·tìuh jeuhng·gàn m̀h·màng·dāk·hòi.

(become tight) làai·gán. /Stretch the clothesline. Làai·gán tìuh lohng·sāam·síng kéuih.

strict   yìhm, yìhm·gaak

strike   (hit) dá. /The man tried to strike him but he dodged. Gó·go yàhn séung dá kéuih daahn·haih kéuih sim·hòi·jó.

(collide) johng·màaih. /The ship struck a rock. Jek syùhn johng·màaih gauh sehk·syu.

(stop work) bah·gùng. /What are they striking for? Kéuih·deih waih·māt·sih bah·gùng a? /How long have they been on strike? Kéuih·deih bah·jó géi·nói gùng la?

strike a match waahk fó·cháai. /Be careful when you strike matches. Néih waahk fó·cháai ge sih·hauh hóu·sēng boh!

string   (thread or fine string) sin (M: tìuh); (cord, rope) síng (M: tìuh); (of a musical instrument) sin (M: tìuh); (series of things on a string) chyun: **a string of pearls.** Yāt·chyun jān·jyù.

to string chyùn·héi, chyùn·màaih. /Find a thread to string these beads. Wán tìuh síng lèih chyùn·héi dī jyū·jái kéuih.

strip   (as of cloth) tìuh; (undress) mōk, tyut

strive   (fight) jàang: **strive after fame** jàang·mìhng; **strive after wealth** jàang·leih; **strive to be first** jàang·sìn

stroke   (rub gently) hehng·hēng sou (háh). /The cat likes people to stroke her. Dī māau hóu jùng·yi yàhn hehng·hēng sou kéuih ge.

(as, of a Chinese character) waahk, bāt·waahk. /How many strokes does this character have? Nī·go jih yáuh géi·dò·waahk a?

stroll   saan·bouh. /They have gone for a stroll. Kéuih·deih chēut·jó·heui saan·bouh.

strong   (powerful) gau·lihk; yáuh·lihk. /Are you strong enough to swim that far? Néih gau·m̀h·gau·lihk yàuh gam yúhn a? /He has strong hands. Kéuih ge sáu hóu yáuh·lihk. /I'm not very strong yet (after an illness). Ngóh juhng·haih m̀h·haih géi gau·lihk.

(firm, solid) gau·lihk. /Is this ladder strong? Nī·lehng tài gau·m̀h·gau·lihk a? /Do you have a good strong rope? Néih yáuh móuh yāt·tìuh hóu gau·lihk ge síng a?

(concentrated) máahng; nùhng (for coffee and tea). /This drink is too strong. Nī·tíng jáu taai máahng. /He likes to drink strong tea. Kéuih jùng·yi yám nùhng chàh.

(large and able) kèuhng·daaih. /The United States has a strong army. Méih·gwok yáuh yāt·go hóu kèuhng·daaih ge hói·gwān.

strong and healthy kèuhng·jong; **strongly opposed** máahng·liht fáan·deui; **strong points** chèuhng·chyúh, hóu·chyúh

structure   (construction) kau·jouh; (a building) gin·jūk·maht

struggle   (against difficulty) fáhn·dau. /There is no success which has not been achieved without some struggles. Sìhng·gùng móuh wah m̀h·gìng·gwo fáhn·dau ge.

stubborn   ngaahng·géng, ngàahn·gu

student   hohk·sāang; **college student** daaih·hohk·sāang; **high school student** jùng·hohk·sāang; **elementary school student** siu·hohk·sāang; **student studying abroad** làuh·hohk·sāang. /She is a very serious student. is expressed as Kéuih duhk·syù hóu yihng·jàn.

studio   (of an artist) wá·sāt; (of a photographer) yíng·séung·póu (M: gàan); (of a film
    company) jai·pín·chóng (M: gàan); (of a broadcasting station) bo·yām·sāt

studious   (given to study) kàhn·lihk

study   (do research) yìhn·gau; (learn) hohk; (read) duhk·sỳu; (look at, read) tái. /He's
    studying medicine at the university. Kéuih hái daaih·hohk duhk·gán yī·fō. /I've studied
    the situation very carefully. Ngóh yíh·gìng hóu jí·sai yìhn·gau·gwo nī·go chìhng·yìhng la.
    /He's studying. Kéuih jing·joih duhk (or tái) gán syu. /Have you studied the map?
    Néih tái·gwo go deih·tòuh meih a? /He is studying law. Kéuih hohk faat·leuht.
    study, studies. /He is doing well in his studies. Kéuih duhk·sỳu duhk dāk hóu hóu.
    (reading room) syù·fóng. /He is in the study, please go in (and have a seat). Kéuih
    yìh·gā hái syù·fóng·syu, chéng yahp·heui chóh lā.
    make a study of yìhn·gau. /I think we'll have to make a study of this problem.
    Ngóh gok·dāk ngóh·deih yiu yìhn·gau·háh nī·go mahn·tàih.
    studying abroad làuh·hohk. /He wants to study abroad after graduation. Kéuih
    séung bāt·yihp jī·hauh heui làuh·hohk.

stuff   (thing) yéh. /Put some of that stuff on, it will keep the mosquitos away. Chàh dī
    gó·dī yéh, dī mān jauh m̀h·wúih ngáauh néih ge la. (Put some of that stuff on, the mos-
    quitos will not bite you.) /What's the stuff he is eating? Kéuih sihk·gán dī māt·yéh a?
    to stuff sāk. /Stuff your ears with cotton. Yuhng dī mìhn·fā sāk·jyuh néih ge yíh·
    jái. /I don't think you can stuff all these clothes into your suitcase. Ngóh gú néih go
    pèih·gīp m̀h·sāk·dāk·lohk gam dō sāam.
    (eating a lot). /I can't eat any more; I'm stuffed. Ngóh hóu báau la, m̀h·sihk·dāk·
    lohk la.

stuffing   háam. /What do you use for stuffing (for cooking)? Néih yuhng māt·yéh jouh
    háam a?

stuffy   guhk. guhk·hei. /Open the window! This room is so stuffy. Nī·gàan fóng gam
    guhk, faai dī hòi·jó go chēung kéuih.

stumble   /He stumbled on a rock and fell. Kéuih béi gauh sehk kwang·chàn diht·dóu.

stump   (of a tree) syuh·tàuh

stupid   chéun, bahn, sòh

sturdy   (healthy) hòn·gihn

stutter   lau·háu, lau·háu lau·siht. /He stutters. Kéuih sìh·sìh lau·háu ge.

style   (fashion) fún, yéung. /It's the latest style. Nī·go haih jeui·sàn ge fún. /I don't
    like the style of that dress. Ngóh m̀h·jùng·yi gó·gihn sāam ge fún (or yéung).
    (of speaking) taai·douh; (of writing) sé·faat, bāt·faat, johk·fùng; (of painting) waahk·
    faat, johk·fùng. /His style of speaking is very interesting. Kéuih góng·wá ge taai·
    douh hóu dāk·yi ge. /His work is in the style of the modern French painters. Kéuih
    ge waahk·faat haih fóng yihn·doih Faat·gwok ge wá·gā ge.
    in new style sàn·fún ge, sān·sīk ge; stylish sìh·fún (ge), hìng. /The clothes worn
    last year are not stylish now. Gauh·nín jeuk ge sāam gàm·nín yìh·gìng m̀h·hìng la.

subcommittee   síu·jóu wái·yùhn·wúi

subdivide   joi·fàn·wàih. /We'll subdivide them into eight groups. Ngóh·deih yiu jèung
    kéuih·deih joi·fàn·wàih baat·jóu.

subdue   (as an enemy) jai·fuhk; subdue pain jí·tung

subject   (topic) tàih·muhk. /What was the subject of his lecture? Kéuih yín·góng ge
    tàih·muhk haih māt·yéh a?
    (field) fō·muhk. /Mathematics is my favorite subject. Ngóh jeui jùng·yi ge fō·muhk
    haih sou·hohk.

(national) jihk·màhn, -yàhn. /He's a British subject. Kéuih haih Yìng·gwok·jihk màhn. <u>or</u> Kéuih haih Yìng·gwok·yàhn.

be subject to. /All passengers are subject to a search. Daap·haak go·go dōu yiu sauh gím·chàh.

(in grammar) jyú·chìh. /There is a subject for every sentence. Múih·geui·wá dōu yáuh yāt·go jyú·chìh.

subjective   jyú·gùn ge: **subjective view** jyú·gùn ge tái·faat

sublet   (rent to joint tenants) fān·jòu; (underlet) jyún·jòu

submarine   chìhm·séui·téhng (M: jek)

submerge   (sink into water) chàhm·yahp séui·dái; (put under a liquid) jam

submissive   (obedient) tèng·wah, fuhk·chùhng

submit   (hand in) gàau (as, a report); chìhng(·daih) (a petition). /Have you submitted your report? Néih gàau·jó néih ge bou·gou meih a? /This is the report we are going to submit to the President. Nī·go jauh haih ngóh·deih jauh·lèih yiu chìhng·daih béi júng·túng ge bou·gou·syù la.

subordinate   (under a certain command) bouh·hah, hah·suhk; (of another person) sáu·hah **subordinate to** daih·suhk·yù. /This department is subordinate to the school of liberal arts. Nī·yāt·haih haih daih·suhk·yù màhn·hohk·yún ge.

subpoena   chyùhn·piu (N); chyùhn (V)

subscribe   dehng. /I want to subscribe to a Chinese newspaper; which one do you suggest? Ngóh séung dehng yāt·fan Jùng·màhn·bou·jí, néih wah bīn·fahn hóu a? **to subscribe** (for donation) yihng·gyùn. /He subscribed fifty dollars per month to the Salvation Army. Kéuih múih·yuht yihng·gyùn ńgh·sahp·mān béi Gau·sai·gwān.

subscriber   dehng·wuh

subscription   (money donated) gyùn·fún; **appeal for subscription** jeun·hàhng mouh·gyùn. /We will start to appeal for subscriptions next month. Ngóh·deih hah·go·yuht yiu hòi·chí jeun·hàhng mouh·gyùn.

subsequently   hauh·lòih

subsidize   jèun·tip

subsidy   jèun·tip

substantial   (real) jàn·saht ge, saht·joih ge

substitute   (article) doih·yuhng·ban; (person) tai·gūng (for laborers); **to substitute** tai, tai·doih. /Can you find yourself a substitute? Néih hó·yíh wán·dóu yàhn tai néih ma? /He can't find himself a substitute and just doesn't know what to do. Kéuih wán·ṁh·dóu yàhn tai kéuih (<u>or</u> tai·gūng); ṁh·jì·dím·syun.

subtract   gáam: **subtract three from ten** sahp gáam sàam

subtraction   gáam·faat

suburbs   gāau·kēui

succeed   (come after) jip·jyuh; jip·yahm. /If he resigned, who would succeed him as manager? Yùh·gwó kéuih chìh·jīk, bīn·go jip·jyuh jouh gìng·léih a? /Do you know who will succeed him in office? Néih jì·dou bīn·go jip·yahm ma?

(reach a desired goal) sìhng·gùng. /If you work hard unceasingly, you will succeed indeed. Yùh·gwó néih bāt·dyuhn gám nóuh·lihk, yāt·dihng sìhng·gùng.

(finish a thing satisfactorily) dāk. /If at first you don't succeed, try again. Yùh·gwó héi·sáu ge sìh·hau ṁh·dāk, néih joi si·háh.

succeed in doing something is expressed with a verb of action followed by sèhng, dóu, yùhn, etc. /Did you succeed in getting that order (of business)? Néih yáuh móuh jouh·sèhng gó·dàan sàang·yi a? /Did you succeed in getting him on the phone? Néih dá·dihn·wá wán·dóu kéuih ma? /Did you succeed in writing the letter? Néih yáuh móuh sé·yùhn fùng seun a?

success   sìhng·gùng; (usually personal achievement) sìhng·jauh.

successful   hóu yáuh·sihng·jauh, hóu·sìhng·gùng. /His son is very successful. Kéuih go jai hóu yáuh sìhng·jauh. /Our plan was successful. Ngóh·deih ge gai·waahk hóu sìhng· gùng.
   (to follow another into office) sìhng·gai. /Can you tell me who succeeded Roosevelt as president? Néih hó m̀h hó·yih góng·béi ngóh dì bin·go sìhng·gai Lòh·sī·fūk jouh júng· túng a?

succession   **in rapid succession** maht·maht. /Today we had many visitors in rapid succession. Gàm·yaht mahn·maht gám yáuh yàhn lèih chóh.

such   gám. /There's no such person here. Nī·syu móuh gám ge yàhn. /I never heard of such a thing happening. Ngóh chùhng·lòih meih tìng·gin·gwo yáuh dī gám ge sih. /I've never tasted such food. Ngóh chùhng·lòih meih sihk·gwo dī gám ge yéh.
   such as (hóu·chíh) . . . jì·léui (ge yéh). /It's too warm for some fruit trees, such as apple and apricot. Yàn·waih nī·syu ge tìn·sìh taai yiht, pìhng·gwó a, hahng a, jì·léui ge gwó·syuh m̀h·jung·dāk.
   (so) gam. /I've seldom seen such beauty. Ngóh hóu síu gin·dóu gam leng ge.

suck   jyut: **suck out the poison** jyut dī duhk chēut·lèih; **baby sucks milk** bìh·bī sihk·náaih

sudden   fāt·yìhn(·gāan). /His friend died a sudden death. Kéuih ge pàhng·yáuh fāt·yìhn séi·jó. **all of a sudden** fāt·yìhn·gāan. /All of a sudden, the light went out. Fāt·yìhn· gāan dihn·dāng sīk·jó.

suddenly   fāt·yìhn (gāan)

sue   (take legal action) gou

suffer   (endure, undergo) sauh·fú. /The war accomplishes nothing but making people suffer. Dá·jeung jí·haih lihng yàhn·màhn sauh·fú, māt·yéh sìhng·jauh dōu móuh.
   (feel great pain) tung dāk hóu sàn·fú. /He suffered when he broke his arm. Kéuih dit·tyun jek sáu jì·hauh tung dāk kéuih hóu sàn·fú.
   (be harmed or hurt) sauh syún·sāt. /The crops have suffered because we have had no rain for the last two months. Yàn·waih móuh·yúh lohk, gàm·nin ge sàu·sìhng sauh hóu daaih ge syún·sāt.

sufficient   gau, jūk·gau. /Is it sufficient? Gau·m̀h·gau a? /We have sufficient coal and charcoal for the winter. Ngóh·deih yáuh jūk·gau ge mùih·taan ying·fuh gàm·nin ge láahng·tīn.

sugar   tòhng

sugar cane   je (M: pò, dau for a whole plant; sóng or gauh for a section)

suggest   wah (say); tàih·yih (propose). /Do you have any one to suggest for the job. Néih wah nī·gihn sih wán bīn·go lèih jouh hóu a? /What do you suggest we do tonight? Néih wah ngóh·deih gàm·máahn jouh māt·yéh hóu a? /I suggest that we ask him to come too. Ngóh wah ngóh·deih chéng·màaih kéuih yāt·chái lèih. /Are you suggesting that he's wrong? Néih haih·m̀h·haih wah kéuih m̀h·ngāam a? /I suggest that we go picnicking to-morrow. Ngóh taih·yih tìn·yaht heui yéh·chāan.
   (bring to mind) lihng . . . séung·héi (remind one of something one had forgotten); tái·héi·lèih hóu·chíh (look like); tèng·héi·léih hóu·chíh (sound like); sihk·héi·lèih hóu· chíh (taste like); màhn·héi·léih hóu·chíh (smell like); mò·héi·léih hóu·chíh (feel like).

/What does it suggest to you? Néih wah kéuih chíh māt·yéh a? /The shape of it suggests a large orange, the smell suggests a pumelo; oh, yes, it's a grapefruit. Mò·héi·lèih hóu· chíh yāt·go hóu daaih go ge cháang, màhn·héi·lèih hóu·chíh go sà·tìhn·yáu; O, haih la, yùhn·lòih haih yāt·go Méih·gwok lèih ge yùhn·syùn·yáu.

suicide   jih·saat; **commit suicide** jih·saat

suit   (clothes) sāam (M: tyut, tou). /This suit doesn't fit me very well. Nī tyut sāam ngóh jeuk·héi·lèih m̀h·haih géi ngāam. /How much is this suit? Nī·tyut géi·dò chín a?
    (legal) ngon, ngoh·gín. /Who is the lawyer handling the suit? Bīn·go leuht·sī dá·léih nī·go ngon(·gín) a?
    (be suitable) ngāam. /I'm afraid this color doesn't suit her. Ngóh pa nī·go ngàahn· sīk m̀h·ngāam kéuih. /I hope this color will suit your taste. Ngóh hèi·mohng nī·go ngàahn·sīk ngāam néih ge sàm·séui la.
    follow suit. /If you're going home early, I think I'll follow suit. Yùh·gwó néih jóu jáu, ngóh dōu gàn·jyuh néih jáu la.
    to suit lihng . . . múhn·yi (be satisfied); lihng . . . héi·fùn (be pleased). /I think this gift ought to suit him. Ngóh gú nī·gihn láih·maht yāt·dihng wúih lihng kéuih múhn·yi ge la.

suitable   ngāam, hahp·sīk

suitcase   pèih·gīp

sulphur   làuh·wòhng

sum   (amount, figure) sou·muhk; (total gained by adding numbers) júng·sou; **a sum of money** yāt·bāt·chín; **a large sum of money** yāt·daaih·bāt chín. /Is this sum correct? Nī·go sou·muhk ngāam ma? /The sum of all these numbers is 1,005. Nī·dī sou·muhk ge júng·sou haih yāt·chìn·lìhng·ńgh. /It's a small sum. Yāt·go hóu síu ge sou·muhk jē.
    to sum up júng·jì, júng yìh·yìhn·jì; (to conclude). /To sum up, the situation there is rather tense. Júng(·yìh·yìhn)·jì, gó·syu ge chìhng·yìhng sèung·dòng gán·jèung. /He summed up the situation in a few words. Kéuih yuhng géi·geui wá jauh jèung gó·go chìhng·yìhng góng·saai la.

summary   jaahk·yiu, daaih·yiu, daaih·gòng

summer   hah·tīn, yiht·tīn; hah·gwai (the season). /Does it rain much here during the summer? Nī·syu hah·tīn lohk·yúh lohk dāk dò ma?
    summer clothes hah·tīn·sāam, yiht·tīn·sāam; **summer resort** táu·syú·ge deih·fòng, beih·syú ge deih·fòng; **summer school** hah·lihng·gún, syú·kèih hohk·haauh; **summer camp** hah·lihng·yìhng; **summer vacation** syú·ga

summit   (the highest point, lit. & fig.) jeui·gòu·fūng; **the summit of a mountain** sàan· déng; **the summit talks** gihk·fūng wuih·yi

summon   (call or send for with authority, as by a court) chyùhn; **summons** chyùhn·piu

sun   yaht·táu (colloq.), taai yèuhng. /Stay out of the sun. M̀h·hóu kéih·hái yaht·táu hah· bihn. /The sun is very hot today. Gàm·yaht yaht·táu jàn·haih máahng la.
    sunbeam, sunlight, sunshine yaht·gwōng; **sunburned** saai·hāk·jó. /I got sunburned. Ngóh saai·hāk·jó. **sundial** yaht·kwài; **sunglass** hāk·ngáahn·géng; **sunrise** yaht·chēut; **sunset** yaht·lohk; **sunstroke** jung·syú, sauh·syú, gám·syú. /He had a sunstroke. Kéuih jung·jó syú.

Sunday   láih·baai(·yaht); sìng·kèih·yaht; **Sunday night** láih·baai·máahn; **Sunday school** jyú·yaht·hohk

sunflower   heung·yaht·kwàih

sundries   (articles) jaahp·fo; (odds and ends) sāp·seui·ge·yéh; (expenses) jaahp·fai

superficial   bíu·mihn·seuhng ge; chín·bohk ge (lit. shallow and thin) superfluous   dò·yùh ge

superior   (in quality) seuhng·dáng ge; (aesthetically) yàu·sau ge; (in office) seuhng·sî.
/He is my superior. Kéuih haih ngóh seuhng·sî. (in age, learning, merit, etc.) chîhn·
bui; (in age and generation) jéung·bui

supernatural   sàn·kèih ge; bāt·hó·sí·yih ge (inconceivable)

superstitious   màih·seun

supervise   gāam·dūk

supper   máahn·faahn. /What time do you have your supper? Néih géi·dím·jūng sihk
máahn·faahn ga?

supplement   bóu·chùng (V); (to a magazine, newspaper, etc.) jàng·hón (N); **supplementary
reader** bóu·chùng·duhk·bún; **supplementary tax** fuh·gà·seui; **supplementary volume**
juhk·pīn

supply   (supply a demand, or supply money) gùng·ying, gùng, gūng·kāp, chēut (give out).
/I don't know whether the drugstore has enough medicated cotton on hand to supply our
need. Ngóh m̀h·jî gó·gàan yeuhk·fòhng gau·m̀h·gau yeuhk·mìhn (·fà) gùng·ying ngóh·deih ge
sèui·yiu. /Who supplies the money for your schooling? Bīn·go gūng(·kāp) néih duhk·
syù a? /We'll supply anything you need. Néih yiu māt·yéh ngóh·deih dōu hó·yih gūng·
kāp néih. /They supply the money, and we'll do the work. Kéuih·deih chēut·chín ngóh·
deih chēut·lihk.
(available amount). /Our supply of medicine is running low. is expressed as Ngóh·
deih só·chyùhn·ge yeuhk yuht lèih yuht síu la.
a supply of. /We need another supply of rubbing alcohol. Ngóh·deih juhng sèui·yiu
dî fó·jáu.
a large supply daaih·pài (ge), hóu·dò. /We need a large supply of towels. Ngóh·deih
sèui·yiu daaih·pài mòuh·gān.
supplies (yaht·yuhng ge) yéh. /I'm going to town for groceries and other supplies.
Ngóh yìh·gā yahp·sèhng máaih dî sihk·maht tùhng kèih·tà (yaht·yuhng ge) yéh.

support   (provide maintenance for) yéuhng. /Who supports your parents? Bīn·go yéuhng
néih fuh·móuh a? /Are you supporting a family? Néih sái yéuhng·gà ma?
(approve) jaan·sìhng. /I support this idea. Ngóh jàan·sìhng nī·go baahn·faat.
(hold up) fùh·jyuh (keep something standing erect with hand); chàang·jyuh (support
something from beneath with poles); díng·jyuh (prop up or carry on one's head). /Do
you need someone's support to walk? Néih sái·m̀h·sái yàhn fùh·jyuh néih hàahng a?
/Go and get some wood to support it. Heui ló géi·tìuh muhk lèih chàang·jyuh kéuih.
/Get something to support it, otherwise it will fall. Ló dî yéh lèih díng·jyuh kéuih yeuhk·
m̀h·haih kéuih jauh dit·lohk·lèih la.
supporting role pui·gok; **a support** chyúh (pole); chèuhng (wall)

suppose   (think) gok·dāk, yíh·wàih. /He's all right, I suppose. Ngóh gok·dāk kéuih géi
hóu. /I suppose that this is true. Ngóh yíh·wàih haih jàn ge.
(assume true) gá·yùh. /Suppose he turns up, what then? Gá·yùh kéuih lèih jauh dím
a?
(assume wrongly) yihng·cho . . . haih . . . /They supposed me to be President Nixon.
Kéuih·deih yihng·cho·jó ngóh haih Nīk·sán júng·túng.
be supposed to yìng·fahn. /You're supposed to do it yourself. Néih yìng·fahn jih·
gēi jouh. /I was supposed to go with him. Ngóh yìng·fahn tùhng kéuih heui ge.

suppress   (put down by force) jan·ngaat: **suppress a riot** jan·ngaat bouh·duhng; (to prevent or prohibit publication) gam·jí: **suppress the publication of this book** gam·jí nī·bún
syù chēut·báan

sure   (be certain of something) kok·haih; gáam·wah (dare to say); **not sure** m̀h·gáam·
wah, m̀h·wah·dāk·saht. /I'm sure that I heard someone calling for help. Ngóh kok·haih

tèng·gin yáuh yàhn ngaai gau·mehng. /I'm sure this is the best way to solve the problem. Ngóh gáam·wah nī·go haih gáai·kyut nī·go mahn·tàih jeui hóu ge fòng·faat. /I'm
not sure whether or not this is true. Ngóh m̀h·gáam·wah nī·gihn sih haih·m̀h·haih jàn
ge. /I'm not sure whether I'm going or not. Ngóh m̀h·wah·dāk·saht heui·m̀h·heui.
(dependable) kaau·dāk·jyuh, wán·jahn. /This method is slow but sure. Nī·go fòng·
faat maahn dī daahn·haih kaau·dāk·jyuh.
(confident) yáuh·bá·ngāk. /They are sure of winning this ball game. Kéuih·deih
deui·yù yèhng nī·chèuhng·bō hóu yáuh·bá·ngāk.
be sure yāt·dihng. /Be sure to lock the door when you go out. Néih chēut·gāai ge·
sìh·hauh yāt·dihng·yiu só·mùhn.
feel sure that gok·dāk . . . yāt·dihng. /I feel sure that he'll be back on his feet soon.
Ngóh gok·dāk kéuih yāt·dihng hóu faai·cheui jauh hóu·fàan ge la.
(certainly) hóu; jàn·haih. /I'd sure like to see him, but I won't have time. Ngóh hóu
séung gin·háh kéuih, daahn·haih ngóh móuh·sìh·gaan. /You said it would rain, and sure
enough it did. Néih wah wúih lohk·yúh, jàn·haih lohk·héi·séuhng·lèih.

surface   mihn, mín: **the surface of the earth** deih·mín; **the surface of the sea** hói·mín

surgeon   ngoih·fō yī·sāng

surgery   (the treatment) ngoih·fō sáu·seuht; (the operating room) sáu·seuht·sāt

surgical   **surgical operation** sáu·seuht; **to perform a surgical operation** got

surname   sing; **surname and given name** sing·mìhng

surpass   (exceed) chìu·gwo; (excel) sing·gwo

surplus   jihng·yùh ge, yáuh·jihng ge (At); jihng·yùh maht·jī (N)

surprise   (something not expected) yi·séung·bāt·dou ge sìh (business,) or yéh (thing).
/I have a surprise for you. Ngóh yáuh yāt·gihn néih yi·séung·bāt·dou ge sih.
(amaze, take unaware) cha·yih; kèih·gwaai, chēut·kèih. /She was surprised to see
us. Kéuih gin·dou ngóh·deih fèi·sèuhng cha·yih. /Are you surprised that we came?
Ngóh·deih fāt·yìhn·gāan lèih·jó, néih gok·dāk kèih·gwaai (or chēut·kèih) ma?

surrender   (to the enemy) tàuh·hòhng; (as a criminal) jih·sáu; (as a rebel) tàuh·sìhng;
(a claim) fong·hei; (hand over) gàau·chēut

surround   (enclose on all sides) wàih·jyuh. (enclose a military unit, a fort, etc.)
bàau·wàih

surroundings (environment) wàahn·gíng

surtax   fuh·gà·seui

survey   (measure the size, shape, and position of an area) chāk·lèuhng

suspect   (to imagine to be) sì·yìh. /I suspect he doesn't like his job. Ngóh sì·yih kéuih
m̀h·jùng·yi nī·fahn gūng.
(think or believe guilty without being able to prove it) sì·yìh. /He suspects that man
stole his car. Kéuih sì·yìh gó·go yàhn tàu·jó kéuih ga chè.
(a person) yìhm·yìh·fáan

suspend   (cease for a time) tìhng·jí, tìhng—: **suspended from school** tìhng·hohk; **suspended
from office** tìhng·jīk; **suspend payment** tìhng·jí jì·fuh; **suspend publication** tìhng·báan,
tìhng·hón
(hang) gwa·hái, diu·hái. /The swing is suspended from a tree. Go chīn·chāu gwa·hái
pò syuh·syu.

suspension   **suspension bridge** diu·kìuh; **suspension of business** tìhng·yihp; **suspension
of hostilities** tìhng·fó, tìhng·jin; **suspension of publication** tìhng·hón

suspicion   yìh·sàm

suspenders   diu·dáai (M: tìuh)

suspicious   hó·yìh, yìhng·jīk hó·yìh. /The things he has done recently are rather suspicious. Kéuih jeui· gahn só·jouh· ge sih sèung·dòng hó·yìh. /The police said he was a suspicious character. Gíng·chaat wah kéuih yìhng·jīk·hó·yìh.

swagger   (walk in a bold, swinging way) daaih·yìuh daaih·báai gám hàahng

swallow   tàn, tàn·jó, tàn·dāk·lohk, tàn·m̀h·lohk. /Don't swallow it. M̀h·hóu tàn. /Swallow it. Tàn·jó kéuih. /Can you swallow it? Néih tàn·dāk·lohk ma? /I can't. Ngóh m̀h· tàn·dāk·lohk.
       (a bird) yin·jí, yín (M: jek)

swan   tìn·ngòh (M: jek)

swarm   jah (M): **a swarm of ants** yāt·jah ngáih

sway   (swing) yìuh·yìuh báai·báai

swear   saih·yuhn. /He swore that he wouldn't do such a thing again. Kéuih saih·gwo· yuhn joi dōu m̀h·jouh dī gám ge sih la.
       (to make a solemn pledge or promise; vow) faat·saih. /He says he swears not to drink anymore. Kéuih wah kéuih faat·saih m̀h·yám·jáu la.
       (to administer a legal oath to) syùn·saih

sweat   hohn (N); chēut·hohn (VO), làuh·hohn (VO). /Gee, it's hot, I'm sweating. Jàn· haih yiht la, yiht dou ngóh chēut·hohn. /Has he been sweating? Kéuih yáuh móuh chēut· hohn a? /Yes, he has been sweating a lot. Kéuih chēut·jó hóu·dò hohn.

sweep   sou: **sweep the floor** sou·deih (sweep the ground); **sweep away** sou·jó kéuih

sweet   (of taste) tìhm. /Is it sweet enough? Gau tìhm meih a? (of smell) hèung; (of sound) hóu·tèng
       (attractive) leng; (lovable) hó·ngoi. /She is so sweet. Kéuih jàn·haih leng la.
       sweets tóng, tòhng·gwó; **sweet potato** fàan·syú

swell   júng (enlarge because of infection); jeung (become bigger because of air, etc.). /How long have your feet been swollen? Néih sèung geuk júng·jó géi·nói la. /The balloon swells larger and larger. Go hei·kàuh yuht lèih yuht jeung.

swelling   (a swollen place) júng·héi·séuhng·lèih; **swelling has gone away** sìu·júng /When did the swelling start? Géi·sí júng·héi·séuhng·lèih ga? /The swelling on his foot has already gone away. Kéuih jek geuk yíh·gìng sìu·júng la.

swim   yàuh·séui (VO). /Do you know how to swim? Néih wúih yàuh·séui ma? /We have to swim this river and land over there. Ngóh·deih yiu yàuh·gwo nī·tìuh hòh hái gó·syu séuhng·ngohn. /I'm going out for a swim, are you coming? is expressed verbally Ngóh yiu heui yàuh·séui, néih heui ma?
       swim across yàuh·gwo; **swimming suit** yàuh·séui·yī (M: gihn); **swimming pool** yàuh· séui·chìh

swindle   ngāk·pin

swindler   lóuh·chīn, pin·jí

swing   (for recreation) chīn·chāu (N); (to sit on a swing and swing) dá·chīn·chāu
       (as a pendulum) fihng; **swing about freely** fihng·lèih fihng·heui

switch   (elec.) dihn·jai; **the main switch** júng·jai; **to switch off** sàan: /Switch (turn) it off! Sàan·jó go jai kéuih! **to switch on** hòi: /Switch it on! Hòi·jó go jai kéuih.

sword   dōu (M: bá); **officer's sword** jí·fài·dōu (M: bá); **double-edged sword** gim (M: bá)

syllabus   (course of study) fo·chìhng

symbol   (written or printed mark) fùh·houh, gei·houh; (something abstract) jeuhng·jìng: /The dove is a symbol of peace. Gaap·jí (or baahk·gáap) haih wòh·pìhng ge jeuhng· jìng.

sympathize   (to share or understand the feelings or ideas of another, be in sympathy) tùhng·chìhng

sympathy   tùhng·chìhng; (sameness of feeling; affinity between persons or of one person for another) tùhng·chìhng·sàm

symphony   gàau·héung·ngohk; **symphony orchestra** gàau·héung·ngohk·tyùhn

symptom   (sign, indication) jìng·hauh. /He doesn't have any symptoms of measles. Kéuih mouh chēut·chán ge jìng·hauh. This is expressed more colloquially as Kéuih m̀h·chíh chēut·chán.

synonym   tùhng·yih·jih

synthesis   júng·haahp

synthesize   júng·haahp

syphilis   mùih·duhk

syrup   tòhng·jēung

system   (of government) jai·douh: **educational system** gaau·yuhk jai·douh; **economic system** gìng·jai jai·douh; (method) fòng·faat. /You should have a system for doing this thing. Néih yìng·dòng yáuh go fòng·faat jouh nī·gihn sih.
    (a whole body) sàn·tái, sàn·jí. /The doctor said that his system was unusually strong. Yī·sāng wah kéuih ge sàn·tái fèi·sèuhng gihn·hòng.
    (biol., astron., etc.) haih·túng, haih: **nervous system** sàn·gìng haih·túng; **digestive system** sìu·fa·haih·túng; **solar system** taai·yèuhng·haih

systematically   yì·jiu·chi·jeuih gám, yāt·bouh yāt bouh gám. /We should do it systematically. Ngóh·deih yìhng gòi yì·jiu·chi·jeuih·gám jouh.

T

table   (furniture) tói (M: jèung); **tables and chairs** tòih·yí; **tablecloth** tói·bou (M: jèung); **table tennis** bīng·bōng·bō
    (array of data) bíu; **timetable** sìh·gaan·bíu; **table of contents** muhk·luhk. /Do you have a train timetable? Néih yáuh móuh fó·chè ge hàhng·chè·sìh·gaan·bíu a? /You can look it up in the table of contents. Néih hó·yíh chàh·háh muhk·luhk.
    set the table báai·tói. /Have you set the table yet? Néih báai·hóu tói meih a?

tablespoon   tōng·gāng, chìh·gāng; **a tablespoonful** yāt·chìh·gāng; **two tablespoonfuls** léuhng·chìh·gāng

tablet   (a pill) yeuhk·pín. /These tablets are very easy to swallow. Nī·dī yeuhk·pín hóu yùhng·yih tàn ge.
    ancestral tablet sàhn·jyú·páai. /Is this an ancestral tablet? Nī·go haih·m̀h·haih sàhn·jyú·páai a?

tackle   (deal with) deui·fuh, ying·fuh

tactics   (mil.) jin·seuht; (fig.) sáu·dyuhn (means)

tadpole   fō·dáu

tael   léung (a Chinese weight—1/16 catty—equivalent to 1 1/3 oz. or 37.80g.)

tail   méih (M: tìuh)

tailor   chòih·fúng, chòih·fùhng·lóu

take   (grasp, carry, bring, etc.) ja; nīk; nìng;;**take it away** nīk·hòi kéuih; **take (it) to**
nīk·heui; **take (it) out** nīk·cheut·lèih. /Take each other's hands to form a circle. Daaih·
gā jà·jyuh sáu wàih·sèhng yāt·go yùhn·hyūn. /Please take my suitcase. M̀h·gòi néih
tùhng ngóh nīk go pèih·gīp. /Take away these old newspapers. Nīk·hòi nī·dī gauh bou·jī
kéuih. /Take this letter to the post office and mail it. Nīk nī·fùng seun heui yàuh·jing·
gúk gei·jó kéuih. /You should take everything out before you clean (wash) the refrigerator. Sái bìng·gwaih jì·chìhn néih yiu nīk·saai só·yáuh·ge yéh chēut·lèih. /Why don't
you take it along? Dím·gáai néih m̀h·daai·màaih heui nē? /Why didn't you take them
along? Dím·gáai néih móuh tùhng kéuih·déih yāt·chái heui a?

      take someone **to** a place sung . . . heui. /Who's taking her to the station? Bīn·go
sung kéuih heui chè·jaam a? /Is anyone going to take him to the hospital? Yáuh móuh
yàhn sung kéuih heui yī·yún a? /When were you taken to the hospital? Keuih·deih géi·
sí sung néih yahp·lèih yī·yún ga?

      take something or someone **to** a place (of a vehicle or a route). /The plane will take
you there in an hour. is expressed as /Yùh·gwó néih chóh fēi·gèi, yāt·go jūng·dím jauh
dou la. (If you go by plane you can get there in an hour.) /Where will that road take
us? is expressed as Gó·tìuh louh tùhng·heui bīn·syu a? (That road goes where?)

      (want or accept) sauh; yiu or gáan (choose); máaih (buy). /I'll take the room with a
bath. Ngóh yiu yáuh chùng·lèuhng·fóng gó·gàan. /Which room will you take? Néih yiu
(or gáan) bīn·gàan a? /She'll take the blue one; isn't the blue one pretty? Kéuih máaih
gó·go làahm ge, gó·go làahm ge leng lā! /He refused to take the money. Kéuih m̀h·háng
sàu·chín.

      (appropriate without permission) nīk, ló, sái (drive). /Who took my umbrella? Bīn·
go nīk·jó ngóh bá jē a? /Who took the papers out of my drawer? Bīn·go hái ngóh gwaih·
túng ló·jó dī jí a? /Who took my car? Bīn·go sái·jó ngóh ga chè heui a?

      (use) yuhng. /Will you let me take your car? Ngóh hó·yíh yuhng néih ga chè ma?

      (require time) yiu. /How long does it take to go from here to there? Hái nī·syu heui
gó·syu yiu géi nói a? /It takes two hours. Yiu léuhng·go jūng·dím.

      (go by a means of transportation) sái if one operates the vehicle oneself, otherwise
chóh. /I am glad you took your car. Hóu·joih néih sái néih ga chè lèih. /We are taking the train tomorrow. Ngóh·deih tìng·yaht chóh fó·chè heui.

      (require personnel) yiu . . . ji dāk; (require additional personnel) juhng yiu dò . . .
ji dāk. /It will take two men to move this piano. Yiu léuhng·go yàhn ji būn·dāk nī·go
gong·kàhm. /It will take two more men to move this piano. Juhng yiu dò léuhng·go
yàhn ji būn·dāk nī·go gong kàhm.

      take a bath sái·sàn. /The children will take their bath at eight o'clock. Dī sai·mān·
jái baat·dím·jūng sái·sàn.

      take a break, take a rest yāu·sīk·háh, táu·háh. /Let's take a break. Daaih·gā yāu·
sīk·háh.

      take a chance si·háh. /Why don't we take a chance? Dím·gáai ngóh·deih m̀h si·háh
nē?

      take a nap fan (or táu) yāt·jahn·gāan; fan·ngaan·gaau (at noontime). /Why don't you
go and take a nap? Dím·gáai néih m̀h·heui fan yāt·jahn·gāan nē?

      take a seat chóh. /Is this seat taken? Nī·go wái yáuh yàhn chóh ma? /Take a seat,
please. Chéng·chóh.

      take a walk saan·bouh, hàahng·háh. /Would you like to take a walk? Néih séung
chēut·heui saan·háh·bouh (or hàahng·háh) ma?

      take advantage of chan·jyuh. /We should take advantage of the good weather and
go on a picnic. Ngóh·deih yìng·gòi chan·jyuh gam hóu tìng·sìh chēut·heui yéh·chāan.

      take advice tèng·wah. /I think you should take his advice. Ngóh yihng·wàih néih
yìng·gòi tèng kéuih wah.

      take care of a matter baahn. /Can you take care of this matter for me? Néih hó·
yíh tùhng ngóh baahn nī·gihn sih ma? /I've already taken care of that matter. Gó·gihn
sih ngóh yíh·gìng baahn·jó la.

      take care of a person dá·léih. /Who is going to take care of your children? Bīn·go
dá·léih néih ge sai·mān·jái a? /Who is taking care of your children? Bīn·go dá·léih·gán
néih ge sai·mān·jái a?

take charge of a house or family dá·léih, tái·mùhn·háu (as a servant does). /Who's taking charge of the house while you're away? [Néih heui·jó ji·hauh] bīn·go tuhng néih dá·léih ngūk·kéi a?

take care of matters dá·léih, gún. /Who is taking care of this section? Nī·bouh fahn bīn·go dá·léih a?

take it easy. Mh·sái gam gán·jèung. (Relax. Don't be so tense or anxious.) or Hóu·sēng. Maahn·máan. (in handling things)

take medicine sihk·yeuhk. /Have you taken your medicine this morning? Néih gàm·jìu·jóu sihk·jó yeuhk meih a? /You should take this medicine three times a day, one teaspoonful each time. Nī·jek yeuhk néih yāt·yaht sihk sàam·chi, múih·chi yāt·chàh·gāng.

take pictures yíng·séung. /Are we allowed to take pictures here? Nī·syu jéun yíng·séung ma? /I would like to take a picture of you, is that all right? Ngóh séung tùhng néih yíng fūk séung, hóu ma? /I would like to have my picture taken with you, how about it? Ngóh séung tùhng·màaih néih yāt·chái yíng fūk séung, hóu ma?

take place most events which in English are said to **take place** are expressed by verbs in Chinese, see **happen** or **occur**

take someone's **temperature** taam·yiht. /Have you taken his temperature? Néih yáuh móuh tùhng kéuih taam·yiht a?

take one's time. /Take your time. Maahn·máan, mh·sái pàhn·làhn.

take your choice chèuih néih gáan (select)

take notes or minutes (down) gei; sé·dài. /It's your turn to take the minutes today. Gàm·yaht lèuhn·dou néih gei géi·luhk. /Do you take notes in history class? Néih séuhng lihk·sí tòhng ge sìh·hauh néih gei bāt·gei ma? /Please take this (few words) down. Chéng néih sé·dài nī·géi·geui syut·wah.

take someone **for** someone yíh·wàih . . . haih . . . /Sorry, I took you for Mr. Chan. Deui·mh·jyuh, ngóh yíh·wàih néih haih Chàn·sīn·sàang.

take for granted. /Don't take everything for granted. Máih yíh·wàih yeuhng·yeuhng sih dōu haih gam yùhng·yih ge.

take off (of a plane) héi·fèi. /When does the plane take off? Fēi·gèi géi·sí héi·fèi a?

take off clothing, hats, and shoes, etc. chèuih. /We can take off our shoes and wade across to the other side. Ngóh·deih hó·yíh chèuih·jó deui hàaih gaang·séui hàahng·gwo deui·mihn.

take over jip: **take over** an office jip·yahm. /When will you take over that business? Néih géi·sí jip gó·pùhn sàang·yi a?

take part in chàam·gà. /I think everyone should take part in this work. Ngóh gok·dāk go·go yàhn dōu yìng·fahn chàam·gà nī·hohn gùng·jok.

take the place of tai, tai·doih. /Who's going to take his place? Bīn·go lèih tai kéuih a?

take it seriously. /Don't take it seriously. Mh·hóu gam yihng·jàn.

take turns lèuhn·láu. /How about taking turns to do it? Daaih·gā lèuhn·láu jouh hóu ma? /It's your turn. Lèuhn·dou néih la.

take precautions against tàih·fòhng. /Should take precaution against cholera. Yiu tàih·fòhng fok·lyuhn.

take up (begin working on) héi·sáu hohk, hòi·chí hohk. /I think I'll take up Mandarin this fall. Ngóh séung gàm·nín chāu·tīn héi·sáu hohk gwok·yúh.

take something **up with** someone wán; wán (or tùhng) . . . sèung·lèuhng (consult with). /You'll have to take up this matter with him. Nī·gihn sih néih yiu wán kéuih ji dāk. /Why don't you take this matter up with him? Dím·gáai néih mh·heui wán kéuih sèung·lèuhng·háh nē?

tale   (story) gú, gú·jái; to **tell a tale** góng·gú; **fairy tale** sàhn·sīn gu·sih

talent   chòih·gon, bún·sih; **talented** yáuh·chòih·gon, yáuh·bún·sih

talk   góng; góng·wá, góng syut·wah. /What were you just talking about? Néih·deih jing·wah góng·gán māt·yéh a? /Who is he talking to? Kéuih tùhng bīn·go góng·wá a? or Kéuih tùhng bīn·go góng·gán syut·wah a?

a talk yín·góng. /We would like to ask you to give a talk to our students some time next week; can you make it? Ngóh·deih séung chéng néih hah·go láih·baai lèih tùhng ngóh·deih ge hohk·sāang yin·góng; néih dāk·hàahn ma?

talk too much dò·háu, dò·jéui. /He talked too much. Kéuih taai dò·háu la.

talk something over hóu·hóu·déi kìng·háh (discuss); sèung·lèuhng·háh (consult). /I think you should go to see him and talk it over. Ngóh gú néih yìng·gòi heui wán kéuih tùhng kéuih hóu·hóu·déi kìng·háh. /Let us talk this over. Chóh·lohk hóu·hóu·déi kìng·háh.

talk someone **into** something góng·dou. /Can you talk him into selling this lot to us? Néih hó·yíh góng·dou kéuih maaih nī·faai deih béi ngóh·deih ma?

tall   gòu; **tall tale** daaih·paau; **to tell tall tales** chè·daaih·paau

tally   cháu, chàuh·máh (N); (make a count; keep score) gei·sou. /He's tallying the votes. Kéuih hái·syu gei·gán piu·sou. **tally with** tùhng . . . sèung·fùh. /Does his figure tally with yours? Kéuih ge sou·muhk tùhng néih ge sèung·fùh ma?

tame   sèuhn, sèuhn·fuhk

tank   (mil.) táan·hāk·chè (M: ga); **gasoline tank** yàuh·gòng

Taoism   Douh·gaau; **Taoist priest** douh·sí

tap   (faucet) séui·hàuh; **turn the tap off** sàan séui·hàuh; **turn the tap on** hòi séui·hàuh

tape   daai (N); **recording tape** luhk·yām·dáai (M: gyún 'reel'); **red tape** sáu·juhk. /It has to go through all the red tape. Yiu gìng·gwo só·yáuh·ge sáu·juhk ji dāk.

tar   (used for protecting and preserving surfaces) bá·màh·yàuh, yáu

target   (for shooting) bá; (things aimed at) muhk·bīu. **target practice** lihn·bá

tassel   séui (M: tìuh)

taste   (sense) meih·douh, mcih. /Do you like the taste? Néih jùng·yi nī·go meih·douh ma? /The five tastes are: sour, sweet, bitter, hot, and salty. Ngh·meih haih: syùn, tìhm, fú, laaht, hàahm.

(ability to choose). /She has good taste in clothes. Kéuih hóu wúih jeuk·sāam.

(preference). /Suit your own taste. Néih jùng·yi dím jauh dím lā.

to taste si; or expressed with the noun meih·douh. /Let me taste it. Dáng ngóh si·háh. /It tastes good. Meih·douh hóu hóu. /This wine tastes a little bit sour. Nī·jek jáu ge meih·douh yáuh dī syūn·syùn·déi.

tasteless móuh·meih(·douh). /It's tasteless. Móuh·meih·douh. or Yāt dī meih·douh dōu móuh.

tasty   hóu·sihk

tax   seui; **income tax** yahp·sīk·seui; **pay tax** naahp·seui; **levy tax** chàu·seui. /How much tax do you pay per year? Néih múih·nìhn naahp géi chín seui a?

taxi   dīk·sí (M: ga)

tea   chàh; (leaves) chàh·yihp; **to have tea** yám·chàh; **teacup** chàh·būi; **tea dance** chàh·móuh; **teahouse** chàh·gēui; **teapot** chàh·wú; **teaspoon** chàh·gāng; **a teaspoonful** yāt·chàh·gāng

teach   gaau; **teaching materials** gaau·chòih. /Can you teach me how to use chopsticks? Néih hó·yíh gaau ngóh jà faai·jí ma? /Who taught you how to drive a car? Bīn·go gaau néih sái·chè ga? /You have to teach them how to use this machine. Néih yiu gaau kéuih·deih dím·yéung yuhng nī·go gēi·hei.

teacher   (form of address) sīn·sàang, lóuh·sì: Chàhn sīn·sàang, Chàhn lóuh·sì; (general term) gaau·yùhn, gaau·sī.

teacher training class sī·jī·fan·lihn·bāan; **teachers training college** sī·faahn hohk·yún

teakwood   yáu·muhk

team   deuih; **a team** yāt·deuih; -déui: **football team** jūk·kàuh·déui; **basketball team** làahm·kàuh·déui

tear   (teardrop) ngáahn·leuih

tear   (something flat and flexible, like paper or cloth, and if it is done by one action) maak; (if into many small scraps) sī; either of these plus an appropriate postverb such as jó, hòi, laahn·jó, hòi·jó. /I tore my jacket. Ngóh maak·làahn·jó gihn sāam. /Someone has torn two pages out of the book. Nī·bún syù béi yàhn maak·jó léuhng·yihp. /As soon as he finished reading the letter he tore it up. Kéuih yāt tái·yùhn fùng seun jauh jīk·hāk sī·jó kéuih.
   tear down a building chaak; **tear open** chaak·hòi. /This old (storied) building soon will be torn down. Nī·gàan gauh láu jauh·lèih chaak la. /Who tore this package open? Bīn·go chaak·hòi·jó nī·go bàau·gwó a?

tease   lìuh (V). /She likes to tease her husband about getting fat. Kéuih hóu jùng·yi lìuh kéuih sīn·sàang, wah kéuih yuht lèih yuht feih. /He is a great tease. is expressed as Kéuih hóu·jung·yi lìuh yàhn ge. (He likes to tease people.)

technical   geih·seuht·seuhng ge. /This is a technical problem. Nī·go haih geih·seuht·seuhng ge mahn·tàih. **Technical school** gùng·yihp jyūn·fō hohk·haauh; **technical term** jyùn·mùhn·mìhng·chìh

technique   geih·seuht

tedious   lihng yàhn yim·muhn

teeth   ngàh (M: jek); **teeth** chēut·ngàh

telegram   dihn·bou (M: fùng); **send a telegram** dá·dihn·bou; **telegram of congratulations** hoh·dihn. /Here are two telegrams for you. Nī·syu yáuh néih léuhng·fùng dihn·bou. /I want to send a telegram to New York. Ngóh yiu dá fùng dihn·bou heui Náu·yeuk.

telegraph   (send a telegram) da·dihn·bou; (transmit a telegram) faat·dihn·bou. /Telegraph us when you get there. Dou·bouh ge sìh·hauh dá go dihn·bou fàan·lèih.
   by telegraph yuhng dihn·bou faat·chēut·heui. /Send this price list by telegraph. Nī jèung ga·chìhn·bíu yuhng dihn·bou faat·chēut·heui.
   telegraph office dihn·bou·gúk (M: gàan)

telephone   dihn·wá; **to telephone** dá·dihn·wá. /May I use your telephone? Ngóh hó·yíh je néih ge dihn·wá yuhng·háh ma? /Did anyone telephone me? Yáuh yàhn dá·dihn·wá béi ngóh ma? /Where can I telephone you this evening? Gàm·máahn ngóh dá·dihn·wá heui bīn·syu wán néih a?
   telephone directory dihn·wá·bóu; **telephone exchange** dihn·wá·gúk; **telephone number** dihn·wá·nām·bá, dihn·wá·houh·sou

telescope   chìn·léih·geng, mohng·yúhn·geng

television   dihn·sih; **watch television** tái·dihn·sih

tell   (say or speak about something) góng (béi) . . . jī or tèng; góng. **tell a story** góng gú·jái; **tell a joke** góng siu·wá. /Can you tell me how to get to the station? Néih hó·yíh góng ngóh jī dím·yéung heui fó·chè·jaahm ma? /Did he tell you our plan? Kéuih yáuh móuh góng néih tèng ngóh·deih ge gai·waahk a? /I told you so! is expressed as Ngóh dōu góng·gwo néih jī haih gám ge la! /What did he tell you? Kéuih góng·jó dī māt·yéh béi néih tèng a?
   (order, command) giu. /Tell the taxi to wait for us. Giu ga dīk·sí dáng ngóh·deih. /Tell them not to make so much noise. Giu kéuih·deih m̀h·hóu gam chòuh. /I was told

to wait here. Kéuih·deih giu ngóh hái nī·syu dáng. /Tell him to come right away. Giu kéuih jīk·hāk lèih. /Tell him to wait. Giu kéuih dáng·háh.
    (know) jī. /No one can tell what will happen tomorrow. Móuh·yàhn jī tìng·yaht dím ge chìhng·yìhng.
    tell the difference between fān·dāk·chēut (positive); fàn·m̀h·chēut (negative). /Can you tell the difference between these two materials (cloth)? Néih fàn·m̀h fān·dāk·chēut nī léuhng gihn yī·líu a?
    tell the truth jiu saht góng. /Tell me the truth. Jiu saht gong (m̀h·jeun góng daaih· wah). /Are you telling the truth? is usually expressed as Néih m̀h·haih gong daaih· wah lā ma? (You aren't lying, are you?)

temper (disposition, frame of mind) sing·chìhng, pèih·hei;(a tendency to become angry readily) pèih·hei. /She has a temper. Kéuih pèih·hei hóu yáih ge. /He lost his temper again. Kéuih yauh faat·pèih·hei la.

temperance jit·jai

temperate yáuh·jit·jai ge; wàn·wòh ge. /We live in a temperate climate. Ngóh·deih jyuh·hái hei·hauh wàn·woh ge deih·fòng.

temperature (of a person) yiht·douh; (of the weather and heat) douh, wàn·douh, yiht·douh.
    take one's temperature taam yiht, si wàn·douh. /Have you taken her temperature? Néih tùhng kéuih taam·jó yiht meih a? /Yes, I did; it's one hundred and two. Ngóh taam·jó la, yāt·baak·lìhng·yih douh.
    run a temperature faat·sīu (VO); **temperature recedes** teui·sīu (VO). /She ran a high temperature for three days. Kéuih faat·jó sàam·yaht gōu sīu. /Her temperature is gone. Kéuih yìh·gìng teui·jó sīu la. /Does he have a temperature? Kéuih yáuh móuh faat·sīu a? /What's his temperature? Kéuih yauh gei·do·douh yiht a? or Kéuih yiht·douh géi gòu a?

temple míu, jih·miuh (M: gàan); **temple keeper** miuh·jūk; **Buddhist temple** jih·mùhn, — jí; **Confucian temple** Húng·sing·míu; **Taoist temple** douh·gun, — gun; **Holy temple** sing·dihn

temporary (provisional) làhm·sìh ge; (not permanent) jaahm·sìh ge. /He wrote me a temporary receipt. Kéuih sé·jó jèung làhm·sìh ge sàu·geui béi ngóh. /This is only a temporary arrangement. Nī·go jí·haih yāt·go jaahm·sìh ge baahn·faat.

temporarily jaahm·sìh. /We may use this temporarily. Ngóh·deih jaahm·sìh hó·yíh yuhng nī·go. /We need some temporary help. Ngóh·deih jaahm·sìh sèui·yiu yāt·léuhng ·go yàhn bòng·sáu. (We need one or two persons to help us temporarily.)

tempt yáhn·yau; **tempting** yáhn·yàhn. /To tempt a person to steal is a sin. Yáhn·yau yàhn tàu·yéh haih yāt·júng jeuih·ngok.

temptation yáhn·yau

ten sahp; **the tenth** daih·sahp; **one tenth** sahp·fahn·jī·yāt; **ten cents** yāt·hòuh·jí; **ten commandments** sahp·gaai; **ten thousand** yāt·maahn; **ten million** yāt·chìn maahn; **ten times** sahp·púih; **ten times more** dò sahp·púih

tenant (of a house) jòu·haak; **subtenant** yih·fòhng·dūng

tend (look after) chau. /Who tends your baby when you're working? Néih jouh·gùng ge sìh·hauh bīn·go tùhng néih chau sai·mān·jái a? (take care of) dá·léih. /Who tends your lawn in the summer? Yiht·tīn ge sìh·houh bīn·go tùhng néih dá·léih chóu·déi a? (inclined or disposed to) sìh·sìh wúih. /Now that he's old he tends to forget things. Kéuih yìh·gā lóuh·jó la, sìh·sìh wúih m̀h·gei·dāk yéh.
    tend the sick jiu·liuh behng·yàhn, dá·léih behng·yàhn. /We need some help to tend the sick. Ngóh·deih séui·yiu yàhn bóng·sáu jiu·liuh behng·yàhn.

tendency kìng·heung

tender   (of meat) nàhm; (kind) hóu·sàm; (gentle) wàn·yàuh; (delicate; easily harmed) yau·
nyuhn

tendon   gàn (M: tìuh)

tennis   móhng·kàuh; **tennis court** móhng·kàuh·chèuhng; **tennis racket** kàuh·pák; **play
tennis** dá·móhng kàuh

tenor   (the highest male adult voice) nàahm·gōu·yām

tense   (showing mental or nervous strain) gán·jèung; (tightly stretched, as a rope) gán

tent   jeung·mohk

term   (in school) hohk·kèih. /When does the new term at school begin? Hah·hohk·kèih
géi·sí hòi·hohk a? /How many terms do you have in one school year? Néih·deih hohk·
haauh yāt·nìn yáuh géi·dò go hohk·kèih a?
    (in office) yahm·kèih, kèih·haahn, nìhn·haahn. /The term of the President is four
years. Júng·túng ge yahm·kèih haih sei·nìhn. /He was engaged for a term of five years.
Kéuih sauh·ping ge kèih·haahn haih ńgh·nìhn.
    (technical name) is generally expressed verbally as giu (jouh); mìhng·chìh: **geograph-
ical term** deih·léih mìhng·chìh. /Do you know the term for this part of the machine?
Néih jì·dou gèi·hei nī·bouh·fahn giu·jouh māt·yéh ma?
    terms (conditions) tìuh·gín. /What are their terms? Kéuih·deih yáuh māt·yéh tìuh·
gín a? /We can't accept their terms. Ngóh·deih bāt·nàhng jip·sauh kéuih·deih ge tìuh·
gín.
    be on good terms with tùhng . . . wóhng·lòih dāk hóu hóu. /They have been on good
terms with the people of that village. Kéuih·deih tùhng gó·tìuh chyūn ge yàhn wóhng·
lòih dāk hóu hóu.

terminate   (a contract) gáai·chyùh; (cease) tìhng·jí; (conclude) git·chūk; (end) yùhn, yùhn·
bāt

terminus   (as of a bus) méih·jaahm

termite   baahk·ngáih (M: jek)

terrible   gāau·gwàan, gán·yiu. added to intensify the unpleasant nature of something already made clear by other words. /Wasn't that a terrible storm last night. Kàhm·
máahn gó·chèuhng yúh jàn·haih daaih dāk gāau gwàan lo. /I've got a terrible cold. Ngóh
sèung·fùng dāk hóu gán·yiu.

terrify   haak; haak . . . yāt·tiu. /Don't tell the children ghost stories; that would terrify
them. Ṁh·hóu góng dī gwái·gú béi dī sai·màn·jái tèng wúih haak·chàn kéuih·deih. /You
terrify me! Néih haak ngóh yāt·tiu.

territorial   **territorial air** líhng·hùng; **territorial water** líhng·hói

territory   (of a state) líhng·tóu (M: faai); (land) tóu·deih (M: faai); (region) deih·fòng (M:
daat); **leased territory** jòu·je·deih; **New territory** (in Hong Kong) Sàn·gaai

terror   húng·bou; **terrorist** húng·bou·fahn·jí, bouh·tòuh

test   (examine a person) háau. /I test them once a month. Ngóh múih·go·yuht háau kéuih·
deih yāt·chi.
    (chemically) fa·yihm. /I think we'd better test this water before we drink it. Ngóh
tái jeui hóu fa·yihm·gwo nī·dī séui sìn·ji hóu yám.
    (medically) gím·yihm. /I think we have to test his blood. Ngóh tái ngóh·deih yiu
gím·yihm·háh kéuih ge hyut.
    (mechanically) gím·chà, si·yihm. /Take the machine back to the shop and have it
tested. Nīk nī·go gèi·hei fàan·heui chóng·syu gím·chà·háh. /We'll test it before we put
it on the market. Ngóh·deih yiu si·yihm·gwo sìn·ji nīk·chēut·heui maaih·dāk.

test (examination) háau·si; or expressed verbally with háau as above. /I have to take a test tomorrow. Ngóh tìng·yaht yiu háau·si. /What is the test about? Háau māt· yéh a? /It's a driving test. Háau sái·chè. /How long will the test take? Yiu háau géi nói a?

oral test háu·si; **written test** bāt·si; **test tube** si·gún

testament   (will) wàih·jūk; **New Testament** Sàn·yeuk (chyùhn·syù); **Old Testament** Gauh· yeuk (chyùhn·syù)

testify   (bear witness) jouh·jing; (certify) jing·mìhng

testimonial   jéung·johng

testimony   jing·chìh (such as given in a congressional committee); háu·gùng (such as given in court); jing·geui (proof)

text   bún·màhn, jing·màhn; **original text** yùhn·mahn; **the full text** chyùhn·mahn. /There is nothing about this in the text. Hái bún·màhn yahp·bihn bihng móuh gwāan·yù nī·gihn sih ge gei·joi. /Can you show me the original text? Néih hó·yíh béi yùhn·màhn ngóh tái· háh ma?

textbook   gaau·fō·syù

textile   fóng·jīk (At): **textile art** fóng·jīk gùng·ngaih; **textile fabrics** fóng·jīk bán; **textile machinery** fóng·jīk·gei; **textile materials** fóng·jīk yùhn·líu; **textile factory** fóng·jīk· chóng

than   béi: A béi B SV; -gwo: A SV-gwo B. /You're taller than he. Néih béi kéuih gòu. or Néih gòu·gwo kéuih.
    better than . . . bei . . . SV dī . . . ; . . . SV gwo·di. /Have you something better than this? Néih yáuh móuh béi nī·go hóu·dī ga? /This one is a little better than that one. Nī·go hóu·gwo gó·go dī.
    much better than . . . béi . . . SV hóu·dò; . . . SV-gwo . . . hóu·dò. /This one is much better than that one. Nī·go béi gó·go hóu hóu·dò. or Nī·go hóu·gwo gó·go hóu·dò.

thank   dò·jeh. /Did you thank him for us? Néih yáuh móuh tai ngóh·deih dò·jeh kéuih a? /Thank you. Dò·jeh. /Thank you very much. Dò·jeh·saai.
    polite expressions in which **thanks** or **thank you** are used. /Thank you. M̀h·gòi (for a favor); Dò·jeh. (for a present); M̀h·gòi néih. (for something not yet done such as a future favor). /Many thanks. M̀h·gòi·saai. (for a favor); Dò·jeh saai. or dò·jeh, dò·jeh. (for a present). /No, thanks. (for a thing offered) Dò·jeh, ngóh m̀h·yiu la. (Cordial); or M̀h·yiu la. (abrupt). (for more of something) Dò·jeh, ngoh m̀h·yiu la. or Gau la, gau la, ngóh·m̀h·yiu la. (for a service, as offered by the host) M̀h·gáam·dòng. (to a servant) M̀h·sái la. /Thanks for your coming. Dò·jeh néih séung·mín.

that   (someone or something indicated or understood by context) gó·go; gó plus some specific measure; gám. /I want that one. Ngóh yiu gó·go. /I left that (book) at home. Gó·bún ngóh lauh·jó hái ngūk·kéi. /That is the thing he wants. Kéuih yiu gó·gihn yéh. /What does that mean? Gám haih māt·yéh yi·si a? /That's what he wants. Kéuih jauh· haih yiu gám.
    (to such a degree) gam. /I didn't know the dress was that expensive. Ngóh m̀h·jī nī·gihn sāam yiu gam gwai ge. /It can't be that late (in the day)! M̀h·wúih gam ngaan gwa!
    as a relative pronoun, that is expressed with ge or without it. /Can we find anybody that knows this area? Ngóh·deih yáuh móuh faat·jí wán yāt·go suhk·sīk nī·yāt·daai deih· fòng ge yàhn a? /Who's the man that just came in? Ngāam·ngāam hàahng·yahp·lèih gó· go yàhn haih bīn·go a? /When was the last time that you came? Néih seuhng·chi haih géi·si lèih ga? /Show me the vase that was just placed in the showcase. Béi ngóh tái· háh ngaam·ngāam báai·yahp sīk·gwaih gó·go fā·jēun.
    as a conjunction, that is not expressed in Cantonese. /We always knew that the peace between these two countries wouldn't last long. Ngóh·deih yāt·heung jauh jī·dou nī·léuhng·gwok jī·gāan ge wòh·pìhng m̀h·wúih bóu·chìh·dāk géi nói ge la.

so that hóu. /Let's finish this right away so that we can do something else. Faai
dī jouh·yùhn nī·yeuhng hóu jouh daih·yih·yeuhng.
/That will do. Dāk la. /That won't do. Gám m̀h·dāk.

the   <u>Cases which in English take</u> the <u>require in Cantonese</u> nī <u>or</u> gó <u>plus a measure, or
no special expression.</u> /Do you know the person who just walked out? Néih sīk·m̀h·sīk
ngāam·ngāam hàahng·chēut·heui gó·go yàhn a? /I've been trying to find the store all
day. Ngóh wán gó·gàan pou·táu wán·jó ngóh sèhng·yaht la. /Have you ever seen the
President? Néih yáuh móuh tái·gin·gwo Júng·túng a?

the . . . the . . . , yuht . . . yuht . . . . /The sooner the better. Yuht faai yuht hóu.
/The faster the ship goes, the more severe the rocking gets. Jek syùhn hàang dāk yuht
faai yuht nóng dāk gán·yiu.

theater   hei·yún (M: gàan); **movie theater** dihn·yín·yún (M: gàan)

their   kéuih·deih ge, **theirs** kéuih·deih ge

them   kéuih·deih

theme   (a topic or subject) tàih·muhk

then   (at that time) dou gó·jahn·sí, gó·jahn·sí. /Return at four! I'll be ready by then.
Sei·dím·jūng fàan·lèih lā, dou gó·jahn·sí ngóh jauh yuh·beih hóu la. /Things will be different then. Dou gó·jahn·sí chìhng·yìhng jauh m̀h·tùhng la. /We ought to know then
whether he needs an operation or not. Dou gó·jahn·sí ngóh·deih jauh jī·dou kéuih sái·
m̀h·sái hōi·dōu la.
     (in that case) gám. /Then we had better not go. Gám ngóh·deih jauh m̀h·hóu heui la.
/Have your own way then. Gám, yàuh dāk néih dím la. /Then it is useless to go on.
Gám jauh mòuh·waih gai·juhk·lohk·heui la.
     (afterward) jī·hauh, hauh·lòih, hāu·mēi, sāu·mēi. /We arrived home, and then it
started to rain. Ngóh·deih dou·jó ngūk·kéi jī·hauh jauh lohk·héi·yúh·séuhng·lèih la.
/Then what happened? Hāu·mēi yauh dím a?
     now and then gáu·bāt·gáu, gáu·m̀h·gáu, noih·bāt·nói. /He drops in to see us now and
then. Kéuih gáu·bāt·gáu lèih taam·háh ngóh·deih. /We go to the movies now and then.
Ngóh·deih gáu·m̀h·gáu heui tái yāt·chi dihn·yíng.

theological **theological seminary** sàhn·hohk·yún

theology   sàhn·hohk

theoretically   joih leih·leuhn·seuhng. /Theoretically it's one of the best ways to attain
     world peace. Joih léih·leuhn·seuhng nī·go haih daat·dou sai·gaai wòh·pìhng jeui hóu ge
     fòng·faat jī·yāt.

theory   léih·leuhn; **the theory of evolution** jeun·fa·léun; **the theory of relativity** sèung·
     deui·léun; **the theory of music** yàm·ngohk·yùhn·léih

there   gó·syu, gó·douh. /You'll find him there. Néih hái gó·syu jauh wán·dóu kéuih ge la.
/Put it down there. Jài·hái gó·syu. /What do they sell there? Gó·douh maaih māt·yéh
a? /I've never been there. Ngóh móuh heui·gwo gó·douh. /How do you get there? Gó·
douh dím·yéung heui a?
     (exclamation). /There, there! Now it doesn't hurt anymore. Hóu la, hóu la, gám
jauh m̀h·tung la. /There, there! never mind, go to sleep. Hóu la, hóu la, m̀h·gán·yiu,
heui fan·gaau la. /There you are (meaning 'It works!' or 'It's finished!')! Dāk la!
     there is, there are, there was, there were. /Is there anyone home? Yáuh móuh
yàhn hái·kéi a? /There's no one home. Móuh yàhn hái·kéi. /There's not even a single
soul. Yāt·go yàhn dōu móuh. /There are plenty of them; have some more. Juhng yáuh
hóu·dò sihk dī tīm lā. /Are there vacancies? Yáuh móuh fóng (room) a? /Is there
room in your car? Néih ga chè juhng yáuh móuh wái a? /There are ten more days until
Christmas. Juhng yáuh sahp·yaht jauh haih sing·daan·jit la. /Is there any difference?
Yáuh móuh fàn·biht a? /There is some. Yáuh dò·síu fàn·biht.

therefore   só·yíh, yàn·chí. /I think that's the case, therefore I said so. Yàn·waih ngóh sèung·seun haih gám só·yíh ngóh gám góng. /The letter had been addressed to the wrong house therefore it never reached me. Gó·fung seun sé·cho·jó deih·jí yàn·chí ngóh yāt·jihk móuh sàu·dou.

thermometer   (for measuring one's temperature) taam·yiht·jām; (for meteorological use) hòhn·syú·bíu

thermos bottle   nyúhn·séui·wú

these   nī·dī. /What are these? Nī·dī haih māt·yéh a?

thesis   (dissertation) bāt·yihp·leuhn·màhn (M: pìn)

they   kéuih·deih

thick   (in dimension) háuh. /Don't cut the bread too thick. Dī mihn·bāau m̀h·hóu chit dāk taai háuh. /I need a board two inches thick. Ngóh yiu yāt faai léuhng·chyun háuh ge báan.
    (in consistency) giht. /The soup is too thick, isn't it? Dī tòng giht·dāk·jaih haih·m̀h·haih a?
    (in density) maht. /The weeds will get thicker if you don't get rid of them. Yùh·gwó néih m̀h·màng·jó gó·dī yéh·chóu jauh yuht lèih yuht maht la.
    (of fog) daaih. /Let's go back; the fog is getting thick. Fàan·heui lo, dī mouh yuht lèih yuht daaih lo.

thief   chahk

thigh   daaih·béi

thin   bohk (in dimension). /Give me a sheet of thin paper. Béi jèung bohk·jí ngóh.
    (of consistency) hèi. /It's too thin; put more rice in it. Hei·dak·jaih, jài dō·dī máih lohk·heui.
    (lean) sau. /Why is he so much thinner than before? Dím·gáai kéuih sau·gwo yíh·chìhn gam dò a?
    (of a sound or the voice) sai. /His voice was so thin we could hardly hear him. Kéuih ge sèng gam sai, ngóh·deih gèi·fùh tèng·m̀h·dóu kéuih góng māt·yéh.

thing   (indefinite material objects) yéh. /What are those things you're carrying? Néih nīk·jyuh dī mát·yéh a? /Take those things off the table. Jèung tói·mín dī yéh nìng·hòi.
    (indefinite nonmaterial entities) sih. /What is the thing on your mind? You can tell me about it. Néih sam·leuih·bihn yáuh māt·yéh sih a? Néih hó·yíh góng béi ngóh jî.
    not a thing māt·yéh·dōu . . . m̀h . . . ; māt·yéh·dōu móuh . . . . /I can't see a thing from here. Ngóh hái nī·syu māt·yéh·dōu tái·m̀h·dóu. /I haven't done a thing all week. Ngóh sèhng·go láih·baai māt·yéh·dōu móuh jouh.
    thing as it is used in some English sentences has no equivalent in Chinese. /He takes things too seriously. Kéuih taai gwo yihng·jàn·dāk·jaih. /It's a foolish thing to do. Gám·yéung jouh jàn·haih chéun lo. /You poor thing! Néih jàn·haih hó·lìhn la!

think   (conceive) séung. /Learning how to think is not enough; one has also to learn how to act. Yāt·go yàhn jihng·haih hohk dím·yéung séung m̀h·gau ge, juhng yiu hohk dím·yéung jouh sìn·ji dāk. /Think carefully before you begin. Séung·chìng·chó sìn·ji hóu yūk·sáu.
    (meditate; ponder) nám. /You may think it over. Néih nám·gwo sīn lā.
    (believe likely or possible) tái. /I think it will rain. Ngóh tái wúih lohk·yúh. /I think I'll go now. Ngóh tái ngóh yiu jáu la.
    (to hold as an opinion) yíh·wàih. /They thought that the earth was flat. Kéuih·deih yíh·wàih deih·kàuh haih pìhng ge.
    (to consider or regard something to be as specified) yihng·wàih. /He thought the lecture very interesting. Kéuih yihng·wàih gó·go yín·góng góng dāk hóu hóu.

(to anticipate or expect) séung·dou, seung·m̀h·dou (neg.). /I didn't think I would find you here. Ngóh séung·m̀h·dou hái nī·syu gin·dóu néih.

(to make a mental discovery; form or have a plan) séung·dóu, séung·chēut(·lèih). /He thought of it first. Nī·go faat·jí haih kéuih sìn séung·dóu ge. /Who thought this (method) up? Nī·go faat·jí haih bīn·go séung·chēut·lèih ga?

(to remember, recall) séung·dāk·héi; séung·m̀h·héi, m̀h·séung·dāk·héi (neg.). /Can you think of that man's name? Néih séung·dāk·héi gó·go yàhn ge méng ma? /No, I can't. Ngóh séung·m̀h·héi. /I can't think of his address. Ngóh séung·m̀h·héi kéuih ge deih·jí.

think of (have an opinion about) gok·dāk; deui(·yù) . . . dím·yéung tái·faat. /What do you think of that man? Néih gok·dāk gó·go yàhn dím a? /What do you think of the international situation? Néih deui·yù gwok·jai ge chìhng·yìhng dím·yéung tái·faat a?

think twice jí·sai séung·háh. /I'd think twice about this matter if I were you. Yùh·gwó ngóh haih néih, nī·gihn sih ngóh yāt·dihng jí·sai·séung·háh.

third   **the third** daih·sàm; **one third** sàm·fahn·jí·yāt

thirsty   géng·hot. /I'm very thirsty. Ngóh hóu·géng·hot.

thirteen   sahp·sàam; **thirteenth** daih·sahp·sàam

thirty   sàam·sahp, **thirty-one** sàam·sahp·yāt

this   (someone or something present, near, or just mentioned) nī·go or nī plus some specific measure. /What's this? Nī·go haih māt·yéh a? /Is this yours? Nī·go haih· m̀h·haih néih ga? /Do you like this book? Néih jùng·yi nī·bún syù ma? /Is this school big? Nī·gàan hohk·haauh daaih·m̀h·daaih a?

(to this degree) gam. /As long as we've done this much, we might as well finish it. Ngóh·deih gei·yìhn jouh·jó gam dò la, bāt·yùh jouh·màaih kéuih la.

this with certain periods of time requires special terms: **this morning** gàm·jīu·jóu; **this evening** gàm·máahn; **this year** gàm·nín, gàm·nìhn

after this chùhng·chí·jí·hauh. /After this I'll quit smoking. Chùhng·chí·jí·hauh ngóh jauh móuh sihk·yīn la.

thorn   chi (M: tìuh), lahk (M: tìuh)

thorny   (full of thorns) yáuh·chi ge, yáuh·lahk ge

thorough   (doing all that should be done) jàu·dou; yihng·jàn (with seriousness). /She is very thorough with her work. Kéuih jouh·sih hóu jàu·dou ge.

(fully executed) chit·dái. /The government will make a thorough investigation in this matter. Jing·fú yiu chit·dái diuh·chàh nī·gihn sih. /He is very thorough in everything he does. Kéuih jouh yeuhng·yeuhng sih dōu hóu chit·dái ge.

those   gó·dī; **those few** gó·géi·go; **those two** gó·léuhng·go

though   daahn·haih. /I'll come, though I may be late. Ngóh yāt·dihng lèih, daahn·haih ngóh wúih chìh·dī. /He may have spoken to me; I didn't hear him, though. Kéuih waahk· jé tùhng ngóh góng·gwo, daahn·haih ngóh móuh·tèng·gin.

(in spite of the fact that) sèui·yìhn. /I was on time, though I got up late. Ngóh sèui· yìhn héi·ngaan·sàn, daahn·haih móuh chìh·dou.

even though jīk·sí. /It's better to ask him even though he may refuse. Jīk·sí kéuih wúih kéuih·jyuht daahn·haih dōu haih màhn·háh kéuih sìn hóu.

as though hóu·chíh . . . (yiu) . . . gám. /It looks as though it may rain. Hóu·chíh yiu lohk·yúh gám. /He raised his hand as though to strike. Kéuih géui·héi jek sáu hóu· chíh yiu dá yàhn gám. /It seems as though I know him. Ngóh hóu·chíh sīk kéuih gám.

thought   (opinion) yi·gin. /I'll tell you my thoughts on the matter tomorrow. Ngóh tìng· yaht jèung ngóh gwàan·yù nī·gihn sih ge yi·gin góng·béi néih jì.

(thinking) sì·séung; nihm·tàuh. /His essay is full of striking thoughts. Kéuih pìn màhn·jèung léuih·bihn chùhng·múhn bāt·jí géi kèih·dahk ge sì·séung. /His one thought is how to win the scholarship. Kéuih wàih·yāt ge nihm·tàuh jauh·haih séung dāk·dóu gó·go jéung·hohk·gàm.

to think   séung·háh, háau·leuih·háh. /We'll have to give some thought to this matter. Nī·gihn sih ngóh·deih yiu hóu·hóu·déi séung·háh.

thousand   chìn; **ten thousand** yāt·maahn

thread   sin (M: tìuh); **thread a needle** chyūn·jàm (VO)

threaten   húng·haak

three   saam; **three-tenths** sahp·fahn·jì·sàam

thresh   (beat) dá: **to thresh grain** dá·wòh

threshold   mùhn·cháahn

thrice   sàam·chi

thrifty   hàan, hàan·gihm

thrill   (cause to feel excited) hìng·fáhn. /The children were thrilled when they heard
the band. Dī sai·mān·jái tèng·gin gú·ngohk·déui m̀h·jì·géi hìng·fáhn.

thrive   (be successful; get along well) (hìng·)wohng. /His new store is thriving. Kéuih
gàan sàn·pou·táu sàang·yi hóu wohng.

throat   hàuh·lùhng. /He has a sore throat, therefore he didn't go to school. Kéuih hàuh·
lùhng tung só·yíh móuh fàan·hohk.

throne   wòhng·waih

through   gwo is used as postverb with any suitable verb of motion **walk through** hàahng·
gwo; **pass through** gìng·gwo; **drive through** sái·gwo. /After you walk through the hallway, then turn to your lcft. Hàahng·gwo tìuh láahng·hón jì·hauh jyun jó. /Is the parade
going to pass through this street? Chèuhn·yàuh ge deuih·ngh gìng(·gwo) m̀h·gìng·gwo nī·
tìuh gāai a? /There are more than ten thousand cars driving through this tunnel every
day. Múih·yaht sái·gwo nī·go deih·douh ge hei·chè yáuh yāt·maahn·géi·ga.
    (from) yàuh, hái. /Which door did he come in through? Kéuih yàuh bīn·go mùhn·háu
yahp·lèih ga? /The burglar came in through the window. Go chahk haih hái chēung·mún·
syu yahp·lèih ge.
    (looking from one side to the other) hái; -chēut·heui. /You can see Victoria Peak
through this window. Néih hái nī·go chēung·mún hó·yíh mohng·dóu Taai·pìhng·sàan·déng.
/If you looked out this window then you could see Victoria Peak. Yùh·gwó néih hái nī·
go chēung·mún mohng·chēut·heui, néih jauh wúih mohng·dóu Taai·pìhng·sàan·déng la.
    (because of) yàn·waih. /He became sick through overeating. Kéuih yàn·waih sihk
dāk dò·dāk·jaih só·yíh sihk·behng·jó.
    (finished) -yùhn, fong·gùng (as an employee). /Are you through? Néih jouh·yùhn meih
a? /Can you get through with this book tonight? Néih gàm·máahn tái·dāk·yùhn nī·bún syu
ma? /I'll be through work at five o'clock. Ngóh ngh·dím·jūng jauh fòng·gùng la.
    through and through. /I read it through and through. Ngóh tai·gwo hóu·géi·chi la.
/He knows his business through and through. Keuih [deuì·yù kéuih nī·hòhng sàang·yi]
hóu joih·hòhng.
    through street. /Is this a through street? is expressed as Nī·tìuh gāai haih·m̀h·
haih gwaht·tàuh·hóng a?
    throughout the day sèhng·yaht; **throughout the night** sèhng·máahn. /Our neighbor's
baby was crying throughout the night; maybe she is sick or something. Ngóh·deih gaak·
lèih ge bìh·bī·jái haam·jó sèhng·máahn, waahk·jé yáuh behng dōu m̀h·díng.

throw   (cast, hurl) diuh. /I don't want it anymore; please throw it away. Ngóh m̀h·yiu
la, diuh·jó kéuih lā.
    throw a light in a direction jiu. /Throw that light this way. Jiu·gwo·lèih nī·bihn.
    throw out gón·chēut·heui, gón·chēut·lèih. /He told me yesterday his landlord said
to him, 'If you don't pay the rent tonight, I'll throw you out.' And just now he came and

told me that he was thrown out by his landlord this morning. Kàhm·yaht kéuih góng ngóh jī, kéuih ge ngūk·jyú deui kéuih wah: 'Néih gàm·máahn juhng m̀h·béi jòu, ngóh jauh gón néih chēut·heui ge la.' Jing·wah kéuih lèih góng ngóh jī, kéuih gàm·jīu·jóu yìh·gìng béi ngūk·jyú gón·jó chēut·lèih la.

    throw up (vomit) ngáu. /Did she throw up again after taking the medicine? Kéuih sihk·jó yeuhk jī·hauh yáuh móuh yauh ngáu·gwo a?

thumb   sáu·jí·gùng; **thumbtack** gahm·dēng

thunder   (the sound) hàahng lèuih, dá·lèuih. /Did you hear all that thunder last night? Néih kàhm·máahn yáuh móuh tèng·gin hàahng·lèuih a? /It is thundering. Hàahng·lèuih la.

thunderbolt   **struck by a thunderbolt** béi lèuih pek·chàn; **struck to death by a thunderbolt** béi lèuih pek·séi.

Thursday   láih·baai·sei, sìng·kèih·sei

thus   (in this way) gám·yéung; (so, this) gám; (therefore) só·yíh

ticket   fēi (M: tīuh); piu (M: jèung); **ticket for an opera** hei·fēi; **movie ticket** dihn·yíng fēi; **boat ticket** syùhn·fēi; **train ticket** fó·chē·fēi; **round trip ticket** lòih·wùih·fēi; **commuter's ticket** chèuhng·kèih·fēi; (ticket to be taken at a door or gate as one enters) yahp·chèuhng·hyun, fēi. /Have you got the tickets yet? Néih yáuh fēi meih a? /Please buy two tickets for me. Chéng néih tùhng ngóh máaih léuhng·tìuh fēi.

tickle   (to touch one's body lightly so as to cause laughter) jīt. /She likes to tickle children. Kéuih hóu jùng·yi jīt sai·mān·jái.
    (to have a tickling sensation) hàhn.

ticklish   (sensitive to being tickled) pa jīt. /She is ticklish. Kéuih hóu pa jīt ge; (delicate) mèih·miuh ge.

tide   chìuh·séui; chìuh·làuh (fig.); **high tide** séui daaih; **low tide** séui teui

tidy   kéih·léih, jíng·chàih (SV); **to tidy up** jāp(·sahp)·hóu. /Please tidy up the living room, we'll have company this afternoon. Chéng néih jāp·hóu go tēng kéuih, gàm·yaht hah·jau yáuh yàhn lèih chóh.

tie   (bind, fasten) bóng. /Tie these two bundles together. Jèung nī·léuhng·jaat bóng·màaih yāt·chái. /Tie the dog to the tree. Bóng jek gáu hái pò syuh·syu. /He knows how to tie his shoelace now. Kéuih jih·gēi wúih bóng hàaih·dáai la.
    (wrap string around) jaat. /Please tie this up for me. M̀h·gòi tùhng ngóh jaat·hóu kéuih.
    to tie (a knot, or tie, etc.) dá. /Tie a knot here. Hái nī·syu dá go lit. /Why is it so difficult to tie this tie? Nī·tìuh tāai dím·gáai gam nàahn dá a?
    a tie (neckwear) tāai (M: tìuh), léhng·dáai (M: tìuh); **bow tie** léhng·fā. /Do we have to wear a tie? Sái·m̀h·sái dá tāai a? /Why don't you wear the bow tie? Dím·gáai néih m̀h·dá go léhng·fā nē?
    be tied up. /Are you tied up this evening? is expressed as Néih gàm·máahn yáuh sih ma?
    (an equal score) bāt·fàn·sing·fuh, dá·go·wòh·gwó. /Yesterday's game ended in a tie. Kàhm·máahn gó·chèuhng·bō bāt·fàn·sing·fuh.

tiger   lóuh·fú (M: jek)

tight   (not loose) gán. /Hold it tight. Jà·gán kéuih. (not fit) jaak (narrow), sai (small). /She has grown so much that her dress is too small. Kéuih daaih·jó gam do, kéuih gihn sāam yìh·gìng taai sai la.

tighten   (as a screw) séuhng·gán; (as a rope) màng·gán; (as a top of a jar) náu·gán

tile   (for roof) ngáh (M: pin); (for floor) gāai·jyún (M: faai); **lay tiles for the roof** pòu ngáh·mín; **lay tiles for the floor** pòu gàai·jyùn

till   -dou; ji dou . . . (sìn) ji . . . /I waited till five o'clock. Ngóh dáng·dou ngh·dím·jūng.
/He did not come till today. Kéuih ji·dou gàm·yaht ji lèih. /He didn't tell me till this
morning. Kéuih ji·dou gàm·jìu·jóu ji góng ngóh jī.

(plow) làih. /The farmers have already started to till the land. Dī nùhng·yàhn yíh·
gìng hòi·sáu làih·tìhn la.

timber   muhk·líu (M: dī)

time   (most general term) sìh·gaan, sìh·hauh, yaht·jí. /Let's do it this way, it may save
us some time. Ngóh·deih gám yéung jouh, waahk·jé hó·yíh hàan dī sìh·gaan. /His children all are grown up; his hard time is over. Kéuih dī sai·mān·jái go·go dōu daaih lo,
kéuih dī gàan·nàahn ge yaht·jí dōu yíh·gìng gwo·saai lo. /I don't think we should sit and
wait for a miracle at a time such as this. Joih nī·go gám ge sìh·hauh, ngóh sèung·seun
ngóh·deih bāt·nàhng chóh·hái syu dáng sàhn·jīk ge chēut·yihn. /This has wasted a lot of
our time. Nī·gihn sih sàai·jó ngóh·deih hóu dò sìh·gaan. /Sorry, we have no time to
discuss this. Deui·m̀h·jyuh, ngóh·deih yìh·gā móuh sìh·gaan tóu·leuhn nī·gihn sih. /I'll
fix a time for seeing him. Ngóh yiu dihng·go sìh·gaan gin kéuih. /Do you think that
we'll have time to see him before we go? Ngóh·deih jáu jī·chìhn wúih·m̀h·wúih yáuh
sìh·gaan gin·dóu kéuih a? But /Time is up. is expressed as Gau jūng la. /It's time
to leave. Hóu jáu la.

(time consumed) géi·nói (how much time). /How much time do you need to fix it?
Néih yiu jíng géi·nói a?

(hour of day) dím·jūng. /What time is it? Géi dím·jūng la?

(day) yaht. /Let's talk about it some other time. Daih·yaht sìn·ji kìng la.

(era, age) sìh·doih. /The topic of his lecture is: 'The time of Confucius.' Kéuih yín·
góng ge tàih·muhk haih: 'Húng·jí ge sìh·doih.'

(occasion) chi, tong. **last time** seuhng(·yāt)·chi; **next time** daih(·yih)·chi, hah·chi.
/This is the first time that I have come to your school. Nī·chi haih ngóh daih·yāt·chi
lèih·dou gwai (your honorable) haauh. /I've been there three times. Ngóh yíh·gìng heui·
gwo sàam·chi la.

(rhythm) paak·jí. /Keep it in waltz time. Néih jiu·jyuh tiu Wàh·yíh·jī·móuh gám ge
paak·ji jauh dāk la.

(multiply) sìhng. /Two times two is four. Yih·sìhng·yih dáng·yù sei.

(-fold, doubling, tripling, etc.) púih. /The price has gone up four times since last
month. Ga·chìhn yíh·gìng gòu·gwo seuhng·go·yuht sei·púih la.

a long time hóu·noih. /It's been a long time since I've seen him. Ngóh hóu noih
móuh gin kéuih la.

at times yáuh·sìh. /At times he works twenty-four hours at a stretch in his lab.
Kéuih yáuh·sìh hái kéuih ge saht·yihm·sāt yāt jouh jauh jouh yah·sei go jūng·dím m̀h·
tìhng.

behind the times lohk·ngh. /These attitudes are behind the times. Nī·dī taai·douh
yíh·gìng lohk·ngh la.

for the time being jaahm·sìh. /Let's forget about it for the time being. Ngóh·deih
jaahm·sìh jèung nī·gihn sih dīu·hòi kéuih syun la.

from time to time noih·bāt·nói, gáu·bāt·gáu, yáuh·sìh. /She comes to see us from
time to time. Kéuih noih·bāt·nói lèih taam·háh ngóh·deih.

have . . . time. /Did you have a nice time? Néih·deih wáan dāk hóu ma? /He had a
hard time the last couple of years. Gwo·heui nī·léuhng·nìhn kéuih gwo dāk hóu gàan·
nàahn.

in no time máh·seuhng, (or jīk·hāk) jauh . . . /I can fix it in no time. Ngóh hó·yíh
máh·seuhng jauh jíng·fàan·hóu kéuih.

in time (soon enough) dou·sìh. /I'm sure we'll get it finished in time. Dou·sìh ngóh·
deih yāt·dihng jouh·yùhn (or jouh·héi) ge la.

on time (on schedule) yī·sìh. /Is the train on time? Fó·chè haih·m̀h·haih yī·sìh dou
a?

time after time géi·dò·chi. /Time after time I told him to stop gambling. Ngóh
góng·gwo géi·dò·chí giu kéuih m̀h·hóu dóu·chín la.

work against time pìng·mehng·gám. /His factory has been working against time to meet the order. Kéuih gàan gùng·chóng pìng·mehng·gám gón·fo.

to time. /Time it. Tái·jyuh go bíu, tái·háh yiu yùhng géi nói sìh·gaan.

timetable sìh·gaan·bíu

timid (harmless, gentle) sèuhn; (not bold, fearful) sai·dáam; (want of courage or self-confidence) noh·yeuhk

tin sek; tinned provisions gun·tàuh sihk·bán; tin opener gun·tàuh·dōu

tinkling tinkling sound līng·līng·sèng

tiny hóu sai; dī gam dāai M: a tiny doll yāt·go dī·gam·dāai·go ge gūng·jái; a tiny flower yāt·déu dī·gam·dāai·déu ge fā

tip (end) jīm: the tip of a pencil yùhn·bāt·jīm; the tip of the tongue leih·jīm; (money given for service) tīp·sí. /I gave him two dollars as a tip; is it enough? Ngóh béi·jó léuhng·go ngàhn·chín tīp·sí kéuih, néih wah gau meih a? (give money for service) dá·séung. /How much should I tip him? Yiu dá·séung kéuih géi·dò chín a?

tipsy bun jeui. /He is already tipsy. Kéuih yíh·gìng bun jeui la.

tire (become tired) guih. /Don't walk so fast or you soon will tire. Mh·hóu hàahng gam faai, yeuhk·mh·haih néih hóu faai·cheui jauh guih ge la.
(for vehicle) tāai, chē tāai

title (name of a thing) méng: title of a book syù méng; (topic) tàih·muhk. /What is the topic of your lecture? Néih góng māt·yéh tàih·muhk a? (official term for a person holding some position) gūn·jīk (in governmental service); hàahm·tàuh, mìhng·yih (as in school, etc.). /What title is he giving to you? Kéuih béi néih yāt·go māt·yéh mìhng·yih a?

to often a Chinese verb of motion contains within itself the to idea and no separate word is necessary, some verbs require a postverb such as hái, heui, etc. /Give it to me, it's mine. Haih ngóh ge, béi ngóh là. /I want to go. Ngóh yiu heui. /All children like to play. Sai·màn·jái go·go dōu jùng·yi wáan ge. /Rock the baby to sleep. Yìuh go bìh·bi fahn·gaau la. /Tie the dog to the railings. Bóng jek gáu hái tìuh làahn·gòn·syu. /I saw him walking to the woods. Ngóh tái·gin kéuih hàahng·yahp go syuh·làhm·syu. /You start to run when I count to three. Ngóh sóu·dou sàam ge sìh·hauh, néih·deih jauh hòi·sáu jáu la. /Send this letter to Mr. Lee. Sùng nī·fùng seun heui·béi Léih sīn·sàang. /We won the game 4 to 3. Gó·chèuhng bō ngóh·deih yèhng·jó, sei béi sàam.
(time before an hour). /It's ten minutes to four. is expressed as /Jàang léuhng·go jih sei·dím. (lack ten minutes (to) four o'clock.)
(with reference to, concerning, as regards) deui; deui·yù. /They're very kind to me. Kéuih·deih deui ngóh hóu hóu. /What do you say to this? Néih deui·yù nī·gihn sih yáuh māt wá góng a?

toad kàhm·kéui (M: jek)

toast hong (V); dō·sī, hong·mihn·bāau (N) (M: pin); toaster tōu·sí·lòuh

tobacco (leaves of any solanaceous plant prepared for smoking) yīn·chóu; (the prepared leaves used in cigarettes, cigars, and pipes) yīn·yíp; yīn·sī (fine cut)

today gàm·yaht

toe geuk·jí (M: jek); toenail geuk·(jí·)gaap

together yāt·chái. /Let's work together. Daaih·gā yāt·chái jouh là. /They play well together. Kéuih·deih daaih·gā yāt·chái wáan dāk hóu hóu. /Please add these figures together. Chéng néih jèung nī·géi·go sou·muhk gà·màaih yāt·chái kéuih.
together with (including also) lìhn·màaih. /The price of this table together with tax is forty dollars and fifty cents. Nī·jèung tói lìhn·màaih seui yāt·guhng sei·sahp·go·lìhng·ńgh.

get together (for fun, talk, etc.).hàahng·màaih. /Let's get together some evening next week; how about it? Daih·yih·go láih·baai wán yāt·máahn daaih·gā hàahng·màaih kìng·háh hóu ma?

toilet   (water closet) chi·só; sái·sáu·gāan (as in a hotel or restaurant); (bathroom) sái·sàn·fóng; **toilet paper** chi·só·jí, chóu·jí

token   (souvenir) géi·nihm·bán; (sign) gei·houh

tolerate   (bear; endure) dái; yáhn; **can tolerate the cold** dái·dāk·láahng; **can tolerate the pain** yáhn·dāk·tung

toll   (ring) johng: **toll the bell** johng·jūng

tomato   fàan·ké; **tomato catsup** ké·jāp, ké·jeung (M: jèun 'bottle'); **tomato juice** ké·jāp

tomb   fàhn·mouh, fàhn, mouh; **tombstone** mouh·bèi

tomorrow   tìng·yaht; **tomorrow morning** tìng·jìu·jóu; **tomorrow night** tìng·máahn

ton   dēun; **tonnage** dēun·sou

tone   (sound) sèng·yàm. /I prefer the tone of the organ to that of a piano. Ngóh jùng·yi fùng·kàhm ge sèng·yàm dò·gwo gong·kàhm.
     (voice) sèng, sèng·hei. /He told him in a very angry tone. Kéuih hóu ngók gám sèng góng·béi kéuih tèng.

tongs   kím

tongue   leih (M: tìuh); (language) wá. /What is his native tongue? Kéuih (bún·lòih) góng bīn·syu ge wá ga? **slip of the tongue** góng·cho·jó. /Sorry, it was a slip of the tongue. Deui·mh·jyuh, ngóh góng·cho·jó.

tonic   (invigorating; refreshing) yáuh·bóu·ge, bóu·hyut·ge, tàih·sàhn·ge; (medicine) bóu·yeuhk

tonight   gàm·máahn

tonsil   diu·jūng

too   (also) dōu, yihk, yihk·dōu (ref. each of these words in the C–E section). /I should like to go, too. Ngóh dōu séung heui. /I would like to have two pounds of these too. Ngóh yihk yiu léuhng·bohng nī·dī. or Nī·dī ngóh yihk yiu léuhng·bohng. /Are you going too? Néih yihk·dōu heui àh?
     (excessively) dāk·jaih, or gwo·tàuh is used after a SV (stative verb), if it is used after a verb, the word dāk is required: V dāk SV dāk·jaih or gwo·tàuh; taai is always used before a SV. /This is too expensive. Ni·go gwai·dak·jaih. /He's too tall. Kéuih gòu·gwo·tàuh. /This box is too big; it can't be sent by airmail. Nī·go háp daaih·gwo·tàuh, mh·gei·dāk fēi·gèi. /This box is too big. Nī·go hap taai daaih. /He ate too much. Kéuih sihk dāk dò·dāk·jaih. /He drank too fast so he choked. Kéuih yám dāk faai·gwo·tàuh só·yíh juhk·chàn.

tool   ga·sàang; gùng·geui (literary); (person used by powerful interests) faai·léuih

tooth   ngàh (M: jek). /Which tooth hurts? Bīn·jek ngàh tung a? /This tooth needs to be pulled. Nī·jek ngàh yiu baht.
     toothache ngàh·tung; **toothbrush** ngàh·cháat; **toothpaste** ngàh·gōu (M: tùhng); **toothpick** ngàh·chīm (M: jì); **false teeth** gá·ngàh; **to have a tooth filled** bóu·ngàh

top   -déng, mín. -tàuh. **top of one's head** tàuh·(·hok)·déng; **top of a car** chè·déng; **top of a mountain** sàan·déng; **top of a roof** ngūk·déng; **top of a tree** syuh·déng; **top of a table** tói·mín; **top of a wall** chèuhng·tàuh; **top of one's voice** daaih·sèng. /You don't have to shout at the top of your voice! Néih mh·sái gam daaih·sèng ngaai!

topic   tàih·muhk

torch   fó·bá; (flashlight) dihn·túng

torn   maak·laahn·jó

torpedo   yùh·lèuih; **torpedo boat** yùh·lèuih·téhng (M: jek); **to discharge a torpedo** fong·
yùh·lèuih

torture   (cause a person or animal to suffer greatly) yeuhk·doih

toss   (throw lightly with an upward movement) deng, diuh; **toss a ball** deng·bō

total   (entire amount) júng·sou, haahm·baahng·laahng. /What is the total? Júng·sou haih
géi·dò a? or Haahm baahng laahng géi dò a?
(whole, complete). /What is the total amount? Yāt·gung haih géi·dò a? /The car is
a total loss. Ga chè sèhng·ga laahn·saai. (The car is completely ruined.)
(add up to) yāt·guhng haih, yāt·guhng yáuh. /His income totals two thousand dollars
a year. Kéuih ge sàu·yahp yāt·nìhn haih yih·chīn·mān.
(add) gà·màaih yāt·chái. /Total 5 and 4 and 6, and you get 15. Jèung ńgh tùhng sei
tùhng luhk gà·màaih yāt·chái haih sahp·ńgh.

touch   (feel with the fingers) mò. /The blind man touched the elephant's ear and said,
'I know what an elephant looks like.' Go màahng·yàhn mò·háh go jeuhng ge yíh·jái wah,
'Ngóh jì·dou go jeuhng ge yéung haih dím·yéung ge.'
(be or come together so that they contact each other) ngàai·jyuh. /Put the books on
the table so that they touch each other. Jèung dī syù báai·hái tói·syu yāt·bún ngàaih·
jyuh yāt·bún.
(reach) dam·dou. /The curtain is too long; it almost touches the floor. Douh chēung·
lím taai chèuhng, chā·m̀h·dō dam·dou deih·háh la.
(strike lightly) dim·háh. /He just touched the balloon, and it flew away. Kéuih dim·
háh go hei·kàuh jē, go hei·kàuh jauh fēi·jó·heui la.
(land hands on) dau. /Don't touch it! M̀h·hóu dau! /Don't touch the dog. M̀h·hóu dau
jek gáu.
(evocative of emotion) gáam·duhng; **be touching** duhng·yàhn. /We were greatly
touched by the story of her troubles. Ngóh·deih tèng kéuih góng·yùhn kéuih ge gàan·
nàahn jì·hauh, ngóh·deih hóu gáam·duhng. /That movie is very touching. Gó·chēut dihn·
yíng hóu duhng·yàhn.
(one of the senses) chūk·gok. /Touch also makes us able to learn about things. Chūk·
gok yihk·dōu hó·yíh sí ngóh·deih hohk·dóu yéh.
(a slight or mild trace) yāt·dī, dī·dēu. /All this soup needs is a touch of salt. Dī
tòng jauh chà dī·dēu yìhm jē.
(a stroke of a brush or pencil) -bāt. /The painter gave the picture a few touches and
it was done. Go wá·gā hehng·hēng mìuh·jó géi·bāt jē, fūk·wá jauh waahk·hóu la.
in touch. /Keep in touch with me. Gáu·m̀h·gáu lèih chóh·háh ā. or Sìh·sìh tùhng
ngóh lyùhn·lohk·háh ā.
touch up. /The picture needs touching up. Nī·fūk séung yiu sàu·háh.

tough   (meat) ngahn; (overly aggressive, brutal in manner; rough) ngàuh·jìng

tour   (travel about for pleasure) yàuh·lihk, léuih·hàhng. /We plan to tour Europe before
we go back to the United States. Ngóh·deih dá·syun fàan Méih·gwok jì·chìhn heui Ngàu·
jàu yàuh·lihk.
(a journey for pleasure) is always expressed verbally. /We cannot take a tour this
year. Gàm·nín ngóh·deih m̀h·heui·dāk yàuh·lihk.

tourist   yàuh·haak; **tourist agency** léuih·hàhng·séh

tow   (drag) tò; **tow boat** tò·syùhn (M: jek)

toward   (direction) heung. /He's coming toward us now. Kéuih yìh·gā heung ngóh·
deih hàahng·gán·lèih la.

(near, close to) jauh·lèih·dou. /It's getting toward the time to quit work. Jauh·lèih dou fong·gùng sìh·hauh la.

(to) deui. /His behavior toward his classmates was not what it should be. Kéuih deui kéuih tùhng·bāan ge syù·yáu ge taai·douh m̀h·yìng·gòi haih gám. /They all feel very sympathetic toward him. Kéuih·deih go·go deui kéuih dōu hóu tùhng·chìhng.

towel   mòuh·gān (M: tìuh); **face towel** sáu·gān; sái·mihn sáu·gān; **bath towel** daaih·mòuh·gān, mòuh·gān

tower   **the church bell tower** gaau·tòhng ge jūng·làuh; **the tower of the British Parliament** Yìng·gwok gwok·wúi ge jūng·làuh; **bell tower** jūng·làuh; **water tower** séui·taap

town   (as an administrative unit) jahn, síh·jahn; (refers to a small community) sèhng, síh·táu. /How far is the next town. Daih·yih·go sèhng yáuh géi yúhn a?

toy   gūng·jái

trace   (mark left) hàhn·jīk, yìhng·jīk; **to trace** jèui·gau (follow the course of); mìuh, yan (through thin paper). /Get a sheet of paper and trace it out. Ló jèung jí mìuh·jó kéuih chēut·lèih.

trachoma   sà·ngáahn

track   (of a railroad) tit·gwái, louh·gwái; (trail left by walking) geuk·yan (horse racing track) páau·máh·déi, páau·máh·chèuhng; (running sports) gihng·choi; **track and field** tìhn·gihng·choi

    be off the track lèih·tàih. /In his lecture, he was off the track many times. Kéuih ge yín·góng m̀h·jí lèih·jó tàih géi·dò·chi.

    be on the right track jouh dāk ngāam. /You're on the right track. Néih jouh dāk ngāam la.

    keep track of. /Please keep track of the expenses of our trip. Chéng néih gei·jyuh ngóh·deih nī·chi léuih·hàhng yùhng·jó géi·dò chín.

    lose track of. /I have lost track of him recently. Jeui·gahn ngóh móuh·jó kéuih ge sīu·sīk.

tractor   tō·lāai·gēi (M: ga)

trade   sàang·yi, mauh·yihk, gàau·yihk. /They don't trade with the Communist countries. Kéuih·deih m̀h·tùhng guhng·cháan·jyú yih ge gwok·gà jouh·sàang·yi. /How is their trade this year? Kéuih·deih gàm·nín ge sàang·yi yùh·hòh a? /They don't have much foreign trade. Kéuih·deih ge gwok·ngoih mauh·yihk hóu síu. /They trade at the stock exchange. Kéuih·deih hái gú·piu gàau·yihk·só gàau·yihk.

    to learn a trade hohk·sáu·ngaih. /I think he should learn a trade. Ngóh gok·dāk kéuih yìng·fahn hohk yāt·mùhn sáu·ngaih.

    trade school jīk·yihp hohk·haauh; **trade union** jīk·yihp·gùng·wúi; **trading company** mauh·yihk·gūng·sī

trademark   māk·tàuh, sēung·bíu

tradition   chyùhn·túng

traffic   /The traffic is very heavy at noontime. Ngaan·jau ge sìh·hauh chè·leuhng hóu jài·yúng. **traffic lights** hùhng·luhk·dāng, gāau·tūng·dāng; **traffic police** gàau·tùng·gíng·chaat

tragedy   (event) bèi·cháam ge sih, cháam·sih (M: gihn); (drama) bèi·kehk (M: chēut)

tragic   bèi·cháam ge, chài·lèuhng ge

train   (of railway) fó·chè; **train fare** chè·geuk; **train ticket** chè·fēi; **get off the train** lohk·chè; **get on the train** séuhng·chè; **ride on a train** chóh·fó·chè; **express train** faai·chè; **local train** maahn·chè. /When does the train leave? Fó·chè géi·dím·jūng hòi a? /When does the express arrive? Faai·chè géi·sí dou a?

to train (by practice) fan·lihn, lihn. /We are training twenty nurses. Ngóh·deih jing· joih fan·lihn·gán yih·sahp·go hòn·wuh. /He's training for the tennis match next week. Kéuih jing·joih lihn·gán móhng·kàuh, jéun·beih chàam·gà daih·yih go láih·baai ge béi· choi.

be trained in (have studied and learned) hohk·gwo. /Have you been trained in nurs-ing? Néih yáuh móuh hohk·gwo hòn·wuh a?

a train of yāt·chyun. /I saw a train of trucks on the highway. Ngóh hái gùng·louh· syu tái·dóu sèhng·chyun gam dò fó·chè.

traitor   (one who betrays his country) maaih·gwok·chahk

tram   dihn·chè; **to go by tram** chóh·dihn·chè

trample   yáai, daahp

transact   baahn; **transact business** baahn·sih; **transact official business** baàhn·gùng (sih)

transcribe   (to make a copy by hand) chàau. chàau·sé

transfer   (to another post) diuh. /He has been transferred to Japan. Kéuih diuh·jó heui Yaht·bún la. /I'm asking for a transfer. Ngóh jing·joih chíng·kàuh diu ngóh heui daih· yih·go deih·fòng.

    (to another school) jyún hohk. /If you don't like to study here, you may transfer to another school. Yùh·gwó néih m̀h·jùng·yi hái nī·gàan hohk·haah duhk néih hó·yíh jyún hohk.

    (hand over) yìh·gàau, gàau. /He asked me to transfer these things to you. Kéuih giu ngóh jèung nī·dī yéh yìh·gàau béi néih.

transform   (the shape) bin(·fa)·sèhng, bin·wàih; (the character or personality) gói·bin. /Twenty years in China have transformed him. Hái Jùng·gwok jyuh·jó yih·sahp·nîhn jèung kéuih gói·bin·jó.

transfusion   **transfusion of blood** syù·hyut

transgress   (of a law, agreement, etc.) wàih·fáan: **transgress the immigration law** wàih·fáan yìh·màhn·faat; **transgress the law** faahn·faat

transient   (not permanent) jaahm·sìh ge

transitional   **transitional period** gwo·douh·sìh·kèih

translate   yihk, fàan·yihk. /How do you translate this sentence? Nī·geui wá néih dim· yéung yihk a?

    translate into yihk·sèhng, fàan·yihk·sèhng. /Please translate these English sen-tences into Chinese. Chéng néih jèung nī·géi·geui Yìng·màhn yihk·sèhng Jùng·màhn.

translator   fàan·yihk

transliterate   yihk·yām

transmit   chyùhn: **to transmit electricity** chyùhn·dihn; **air transmits heat** hùng·hei chyùhn yiht; tau: **glass transmits light** bō·lēi tau gwòng

transparent   (capable of being seen through) tau·mìhng ge

transplant   jung·gwo. /I want to transplant these roses. Ngóh séung jung·gwo nī·dī mùih·gwai kéuih.

transport   (from one place to another) wahn, wahn·syù. /The problem is how we will transport these bananas to the market to sell. Yìh·gā ge mahn·tàih haih dím·yéung jèung nī·dī hēung·jìu wahn·heui sìh·chèuhng maaih.

    (a ship that carries soldiers) wahn·syù·laahm, wahn·syù·syùhn (M: jek); (an airplane) wahn·syū·gēi (M: ga)

transportation   (a way of getting from one place to another) gàau·tùng. /The only transportation out to that place is the ship. Yàuh nī·syu heui gó·syu wàih·yāt ge gàau·tùng jí·
haih syùhn.
    (the carrying of goods from one place to another) wahn·syù. /Transportation is im-
portant to business. Wahn·syù deui sèung·yihp hóu juhng·yiu.

trap   (a device) haahm·jehng (for tiger, etc.); lùhng (for fox, etc.); gáap (for rat, etc.):
mouse trap lóuh·syú·gáap
    (to catch in a trap) jòng. /He is trying to trap the bird in a cage. Kéuih séung yuhng
go lùhng lèih jòng gó·jek jéuk.

travel   léuih·hàhng; yàuh·lihk. **traveling expenses** léuih·fai, louh·fai. /Where are we
going to travel next year? Ngóh·deih chēut·nìn heui bīn·syu léuih·hàhng a? /Do you
want to travel around the world? Néih séung yàuh·lihk sai·gaai ma?
    (go some place by car, train, etc.) chóh; (if one is operating the vehicle oneself) sái;
(if one sits astride, as on horseback or a bicycle) kèh. /Which is the best way to travel?
Chóh māt·yéh jeui hóu a? /By airplane. Chóh fēi·gèi jeui hóu la.
    travel (movement of traffic). /Travel on this road is always difficult. is expressed
as Nī·tìuh lóuh géi·sìh dōu m̀h·haih·géi hóu·hàhng.

traveler   léuih·haak

tray   tok·pún; **tea tray** chàh·pún

tread   (to walk) hàahng; (to step on) yáai. /Don't tread on the flowers. M̀h·hóu yáai·
chàn dī fā.

treasure   bóu·bui, bóu·maht

treasurer   (of a business firm) sì·fu; (as of a club) léih·chòih

treasury   **treasury of a country** gwok·fu

treat   (act toward) deui, doih. /He treats his students well. Kéuih deui kéuih dī hohk·
sāang hóu hóu. /How does your mother-in-law treat you? Néih ge gà·pó doih néih hóu
ma?
    (give medical attention to) yì, tái. /Who was the doctor that treated you before?
Bīn·go yī·sāng yíh·chìhn yì·gwo (or tái·gwo) néih a? or Néih yíh·chìhn tái·gwo bīn·go
yī·sāng a?
    (pay for someone else) chéng. /I'm treating this time. Nī·chi ngóh chéng.
    treat something **as** dong, dong·jouh, dong·wàih. /We shouldn't treat this as a small
matter. Ngóh·deih bāt·nàhng jèung nī·gihn sih dòng (jouh) yāt·gihn síu·sih.
    a treat. /It's a real treat! Jàn·haih gwo·yáhn la.

treatment   is usually expressed verbally except in few occasions. /He is under medical
treatment. Kéuih yìh·gā jing·joih yì·gán. /He said he couldn't tolerate such treatment
any longer. Kéuih wah kéuih joi bāt·nàhng yáhn·sauh nī·júng doih·yuh la.

treaty   tìuh·yeuk; **peace treaty** wòh·yeuk; **to sign a treaty** chìm·yeuk

treble   sàam·púih. /The price has trebled. Ga·chìhn héi·jó sàam·púih.

tree   syuh (M: pò, 'plant of'); **one tree** yāt·pò syuh

tremble   jan, dá·jan; **tremble with cold** dá·láahng·jan

tremendous   (very great) hóu·daaih ge. /The fire caused a tremendous loss for the
owners of the building. Nī·chèuhng fó·jūk deui yihp·jyú hóu daaih ge syún·sāt.

trench   (a ditch) hòuh (M: tìuh); (mil.) jin·hòuh (M: tìuh)

trend   (tendency) chèui·heung, chèui·sai; (incline in a specific direction) kìng·heung (yù)

trial   (a test) is expressed with si try. /Why don't you give it a trial? Dím·gáai néih
m̀h·si·háh nē?

(in court) <u>is expressed with</u> hòi·sám. /When will the case come up for trial? Gó·gihn ngon géi·sìh hòi·sám a?

triangle (geom.) sàam·gok; (used in drafting) sàam·gok·chek (M: bá); (a love affair involving a group of three) sàam·gok·lyún·oi

triangular sàam·gok(·yìhng) ge

tribe juhk. /There are five tribes of people living in this area. Nī·yāt·kēui yáuh ńgh·juhk yàhn jyuh·hái nī·syu.

tribute **pay tribute** (from one ruler to another) jeun·gung

trick (a clever act which amuses people) bá·hei. /He said he had learned some tricks from a magician. Kéuih wah kéuih hái go luhng·faat· ge gó·syu hohk·jó géi·tou bá·hei.
(cheat; deceive) ngāk, pin. /Don't let anyone trick you. M̀h·hóu béi yàhn ngāk néih.
play a trick on <u>is expressed verbally with</u> nán(·fa). /They played a trick on him by filling the whiskey bottle with vinegar. Kéuih·deih nán(·fa) kéuih jèung go hùng ge wài·sih·géi jáu·jēun yahp·jó dī chou yahp·heui.

tricky (complicated) hóu·líu·kíu ge

tricycle sàam·lèuhn·chē

trifle (a little unimportant thing) síu·sih.

trigonometry sàam·gok

trim (by cutting) jín; **trim the tree** jín·jī

trip (a journey) chēut·heui léuih·hàhng, chēut·heui wáan·háh. /We're going on a trip next week. Ngóh·deih daih·yih·go láih·baai chēut·heui léuih·hàhng.
(catch one's foot; stumble) kwang·chàn. <u>is expressed passively</u>. /I tripped on the broom and almost fell. Ngóh béi bá sou·bá kwang·chàn gēi·fùh daat·dài.
(cause to stumble) sin. /Did you or didn't you put out your foot to trip him? Néih haih·m̀h·haih sàn jek geuk chēut·heui séung sin kéuih a?

tripod (a three legged support for a camera, etc.) sàam·geuk·gá; (sacrificial vessel) dín

troop (soldiers) gwàn·déui

trophy (captured arms) jin·leih·bán; (a prize) jéung·bán; (a silver cup as prize) ngàhn·būi; (memorial or memento) géi·nihm·bán

tropical yiht·daai ge

tropics **the tropics** yiht·daai

trouble (to worry) lihng . . . m̀h·ngòn·lohk. /Her baby's sickness troubles her. Kéuih bìh·bī jái behng lìhng kéuih hóu m̀h ngòn·lohk.
(nuisance; additional work) fai·sih. /We will not stay for lunch if it is too much trouble for him. Yùh·gwó taai fai·sih, ngóh·deih jauh m̀h·hóu hái kéuih syu sihk·faahn la.
(something that causes worry, unhappiness, and so on) fàahn·nóuh ge sih. /His family has had many troubles. Kéuih ngūk·kéi jeui gahn yáuh hóu dò fàahn·nóuh ge sih.
(state of being troubled). /What's the trouble? Jouh·māt·sih a?
(put to inconvenience) màh·fàahn; lòuh·fàahn. /Sorry to trouble you. Màh·fàahn·saai néih. /May I trouble you for some catsup? Lòuh·fàahn néih béi jèun ké·jāp ngóh.
be in trouble. /I'm in trouble. Baih·gà·fó la.
look (or ask) **for trouble.** /Are you asking for trouble? Néih séung jáu fu·hei a?
/He is a trouble maker. <u>is expressed as</u> Kéuih nī·go yàhn jyùn·mùhn gáau·sih gáau·fèi ge.

to trouble (afflict physically) lihng . . . gok·dāk m̀h·jih·yĭhn. /Which part of your chest troubles you? Néih ge hùng·háu bīn·syu lihng néih gok·dāk m̀h·jih·yĭhn a?

troublesome   (characterized by inconvenience or additional work) fai·sih. /It's very troublesome indeed! Jàn·haih fai·sih lo. (causing trouble) dò·sih. /That man is very troublesome. Gó·go yàhn hóu dò·sih ge.

trough   chòuh; **watering trough** séui·chòuh

trousers   fu (M: tìuh); **one pair of trousers** yāt·tìuh fu

truce   tìhng·jin

truck   fo·chè (M: ga)

true   (factual) jàn; (genuine) jàn·jǐng ge. /Is it true? Haih·m̀h·haih jàn ga? /You are a true friend. Néih jàn·haih gau·pàhng·yáuh la. or Néih kok·haih yāt·go jàn·jing ge pàhng·yáuh.
 is it true that haih·m̀h·haih. /Is it true that he is out of a job? Kéuih haih·m̀h·haih móuh sih jouh a?

trumpet   la·bā: **to blow a trumpet** chèui·la·bā

trunk   (of a tree) syuh·sàn; (of an elephant) jeuhng·baht; (a suitcase) lùhng, pèih·lùhng

trust   sèung·seun. /Don't you trust me? Néih m̀h·sèung·seun ngóh àh? /We're looking for a servant that we can trust. Ngóh·deih séung wán yāt·go sèung·seun·dāk·gwo ge gùng·yàhn. /I guess we've got to trust what he has said. Ngóh tái ngóh·deih jí·yáuh sèung·seun kéuih góng ge syut·wah. /Fortunately his landlord trusts him so he can wait till payday to pay his rent. Hóu·joih ngūk·jyú sèung·seun kéuih dou chēut·lèuhng gó·yaht sìn·ji gāau·jòu.
 (faith) **is expressed verbally with** sèung·seun. /The children have complete trust in what their teacher tells them. Dī sai·mān·jái sahp·jūk sèung·seun kéuih·deih sīn·sàang góng ge syut·wah.
 trust something **to** someone jèung . . . gàau·béi . . . sàu·màaih kéuih. /They trusted the money to his care. Kéuih·deih jèung gó·bāt chín gàau·béi kéuih sàu·màaih kéuih.

trustee   (member of a group of persons appointed to manage the affairs of a college, hospital, etc.) dúng·si; **board of trustees** dúng·sih·wúi; (a person to whom another's property is entrusted) sauh·wái·tok·yàhn

truth   (exactly what happened) dòng·sìh ge sih·saht, sih·saht. /I want you to tell me the truth. Ngóh yiu néih jèung dòng·sìh ge sih·saht góng·béi ngóh tèng. /Are you telling the truth? Néih góng ge haih·m̀h·haih sih·saht a?
 (as in the Bible) jàn·léih

try   (attempt; make an effort) si. /I tried again and it works. Ngóh joi si·háh jauh dāk la. /Why don't you try? Dím·gáai néih m̀h·si·háh nē?
 (give a trial to) si. /Here, try my pen, see whether it's easier to write with. Sí·háh ngóh·jí·bāt, tái·háh haih·m̀h·haih hóu·sé dí. /I think I'll try the sweet and sour sparcribs. Ngóh séung si·háh tìhm·syùn·paai·gwāt. /Try one of these candies. Si·háh nī·dī tóng lā.
 (a test or trial) **is also expressed verbally with** si. /Let's give it another try. Joi si yāt·chi tìm.
 (give a court hearing to, before a judge) sám. /Who's going to try the case? Nī·go ngon yàuh bīn·go sám a? /The man was tried for stealing. Gó·go yàhn yàn·waih tàu·yéh só·yíh sauh sám.

tub   pùhn; (a low, wooden, barrel-like vessel) túng

tube   (in general) gún; (a radio part) jàn·hùng·gún; (when used as a measure) tùhng: **a tube of toothpaste** yāt·tùhng ngàh·gōu; (inner tube of a tire) noih·tāai tuberculosis   fai·behng, fai·lòuh·behng, fai·lòuh

tuck   **tuck in** sip·hóu: **tuck the shirt in** sip·hóu gihn sēut·sāam; **to tuck up the sleeves**
ngaap·héi go sàam·jauh; **tuck up the trousers** ngaap·héi go fu·geuk

Tuesday   láih·baai·yih, sìng·kèih·yih

tug   tò, làai; **tug boat** tò·syùhn (M: jek)

tuition   (the charge for instruction) hohk·fai

tumbler   (a drinking glass) séui·būi, bō·lēi·būi

tumor   láu; **malignant tumor** duhk·láu

tune   (melody) kūk (M: jek). /I know this tune. Ngóh jì nī·jek kūk. **to tune** gaau·yām.
/We should have someone tune our piano. Ngóh·deih yiu wán yàhn lèih gaau·háh go
gong·kàhm ge yām la.

tung oil   tùhng·yàuh

tungsten   wù

tunnel   (through a mountain) sāan·lūng; (passage underground) seuih·douh

turban   tàuh·gān

turkey   fó·gāi (M: jek)

turn   (change position of the body) nihng·jyun·mihn. /He turned and beckoned to us to
follow him. Kéuih nihng·jyun·mihn giu ngóh·deih gàn·jyuh kéuih. /He turned his head
and talked to his friend. Kéuih nihng·jyun·tàuh tùhng kéuih ge pàhng·yáuh góng.
    (change direction) jyun; **turn a corner** jyun wāan; **turn in** jyun yahp·heui; **turn out**
jyun chēut·heui; **turn left** jyun jó; **turn right** jyun yauh. /Don't make a turn at this
corner; turn in at the next one. M̀h·hóu hái nī·go gāai·háu jyun (wāan), hái daih·yih·go
gāai·háu jyun·yahp·heui. /Turn left at the next corner. Hái daih·yih·go gāai·háu jyun
jó.
    (a chance, opportunity, time) lèuhn·láu; lèuhn·dou; yāt·go·go gám lèuhn·jyuh. /We
took turns driving when we were coming back. Ngóh·deih fàan·lèih ge sìh·hauh daaih·
ga lèuhn·láu sái ge. /How about doing it by taking turns? Hóu·m̀h·hóu lèuhn·láu jouh
a? /Whose turn is it now? Lèuhn·dou bīn·go la. /You'll have to wait your turn. Meih·
lèuhn·dou néih. /Tell the children to form a line and wait their turn to get the food.
Giu dī sai·mān·jái pàaih·hóu·déui, yāt·go·go·gám lèuhn·jyuh lèih ló dī sihk·maht.
    (change, become, transform) bin·sèhng. /Ice turns to water when it gets warm. Dī
bīng yuh·dóu yiht jauh bin·sèhng séui ge la. /The storm turned the street into a river.
Nī·yāt·chèuhng daaih·yúh jèung tìuh gāai bin·jó·sèhng yāt·tìuh hòh. /My little friend
asked me if I could turn her dolly into a princess. Ngóh·ge síu·pàhng·yáuh mahn ngóh
hó·m̀h·hó·yíh jèung kéuih ge gūng·jái bin·sèhng yāt·go gùng·jyú.
    (to switch) hòi (turn on); sàan; sīk (turn off). /Turn on the lights. Hòi·jeuhk dī dāng
kéuih. /Turn on the switch. Hòi·jó go jai kéuih. /Turn off the light. Sàan·jó (or sīk·
jó) jáan dāng kéuih. /Turn off the switch. Sàan·jó go jai kéuih. /Turn off the water.
Sàan·jó go séui·hàuh kéuih.
    turn back fàan jyun tàuh. /Let's turn back. Fàan jyun tàuh lo.
    turn <u>something</u> **in** wàahn·fàan. /You should turn in all your books borrowed from
the library before leaving school for vacation. Fòng·ga jì·chîhn néih yiu wàahn·fàan·saai
tòuh·syù·gún ge syù sìn·ji hó·yíh lèih·hòi hohk·haauh.
    turn out (assemble) dou·chèuhng ge, chēut·jihk ge. /How many turned out? Douh·
cheuhng·ge yàhn yáuh géi dò a?
    turn out <u>in a certain way</u>. /How did the meeting turn out? /Gó·go wúi hòi·sèhng dim
a?
    turn <u>something</u> **out** (produce) chēut. /How many radios can your factory turn out in
a month? Néih·deih ge gùng·chóng yāt·go yuht hó·yíh chēut géi·dò·go sāu·yām·gēi a?

turn something **over** diuh·jyun, fáan·jyun. /Turn the table over. Diuh·jyun jèung tói kéuih. /Turn the box over (Turn the box upside down.) Jèung go háp fáan·jyun kéuih.

turn something **over to** someone gàau·béi. /He turned over all of his business to his sons. Kéuih jèung kéuih dī sàang·yi gàau·saai·béi dī jái la.

turn to a page kín·dou. /You'll find his address if you turn to page five. Néih kín· dou daih·n̄gh·yihp jauh wán·dóu kéuih ge deih·jí la.

turn to someone for help kàuh, wán. /You can always turn to him for help. Néih géi·sìh dōu hó·yíh heui kàuh kéuih bòng·mòhng néih ge.

turn something **up** (increase) hòi . . . dī. /Turn the radio up, will you? M̀h·gòi néih jèung go sāu·yām·gēi hòi (or náu) daaih·sēng dī.

a turn (a change in condition). /He was very ill last week, but he had taken a turn for the better. Kéuih seuhng·go láih·baai behng dāk hóu gāau·gwàan, daahn·haih kéuih fāt·yìhn·gàan hóu·fàan hóu dò la.

turn a somersault dá·gàn·dáu; **turn against** fáan·kong; **turning point** jyún·gèi; **turn red** bin·hùhng; **turn sour** bin·syùn

turnip lòh·baahk

turpentine (used in medicine) chùhng·jit·yàuh

turtle gwāi (M: jek)

tusk ngàh; **elephant tusks** jeuhng·ngàh

tutor sīn·sàang

tweezers gíp·jái

twentieth daih·yih·sahp; **twentieth century** yih·sahp·sai·géi

twenty yih·sahp; **twenty-one** yih·sahp·yāt

twice léuhng·chi. /I've been here twice already. Ngóh yih·gìng lèih·gwo léuhng·chi la.
twice as much dò·gwo yāt·púih. /He charged me twice as much as he asked for. Kéuih gai ngóh ge ga·chìhn dò·gwo kéuih yiu ge ga·chìhn yāt·púih.

twelve sahp·yih

twig syuh·jī

twill (cloth) chèh·màhn·bou, ché·bou

twin mà·ge; **twin brothers** mà·jái (M: deui); **twin sisters** mà·néui (M: deui)

twinkle jáam·jáam·háh; **in a twinkle** jáam·ngáahn jī·gāan

twist **twist together** náu·màaih·yāt·chái; **twist thread** chò·sin; **twist and turn** nihng· lèih nihng·heui, náu·lèih náu·heui

two yih; léuhng (couple of). /One, two, three, ... Yāt, yih, sàam, ... /Twenty-two. Yih·sahp·yih. /Two dollars. Léuhng·go ngàahn·chín. /Two hundred. Yih·(or léuhng)baak. /Two thousand. Yih·(or léuhng) chīn. **two or three days** leuhng·sàam yaht; **two hands** léuhng·jek sáu

type (kind; sort) tíng. /I don't like this type of person. Ngóh m̀h·jùng·yi nī·tíng yàhn. (used in printing) jih·tái; **to type** dá·jih. /Do you type? Néih wúih dá·jih ma?

typewriter dá·jih·gèi

typhoid chèuhng·yiht·jing

typhoon daaih·fùng; **have typhoon** dá·daaih·fùng

typist dá·jih·yùhn

U

U-boat   chìhm·séui·téhng (M: jek)

ugly   cháu·yéung, nàahn·tái

ulcer   **peptic ulcer** waih·kúi·yèuhng

ultimate   jeui·hauh ge: **the ultimate aim** jeui·hauh·ge muhk·dīk

ultimatum   jeui·hauh·tùng·dip

umbrella   jē (M: bá)

umpire   gùng·jing·yàhn, pìhng·pun·yùhn

un-   m̀h: **unhappy** m̀h·faai·lohk; **unfaithful** m̀h·jùng·saht; **unsteady** m̀h·wán·jahn; móuh-:
   unchanged móuh·bin·dou; **unprepared** móuh·yuh·beih, etc.

unable   m̀h . . . dāk; meih . . . dāk. /He is sick; he is unable to work. Kéuih yáuh
   behng, kéuih m̀h·jouh·dāk gùng. /He has been sick and is unable to go back to school
   yet. Kéuih behng·jó juhng meih fàan·dāk hohk.

unaccustomed   m̀h·(jaahp)·gwaan. /She is unaccustomed to this kind of life. Kéuih m̀h·
   jaahp·gwaan dī gám ge sàng·wuht.

unalterable   m̀h·gói·dāk

unanimously   (showing the agreement of everyone) chyùhn·tái yāt·ji. /The resolution
   was passed unanimously. Gó·go yi·ngon chyùhn·tái yāt·ji tùng·gwo.

unattainable   dāk·m̀h·dóu ge

unavoidable   bāt·nàhng beih·míhn ge

unaware   m̀h·jì. /We were unaware of his sickness. Ngóh·deih m̀h·jì kéuih behng·jó.

unbearable   hóu·nàahn·dái ge. /In the summer the heat is unbearable. Tìn·sìh·yiht ge
   sìh·hauh yiht dāk hóu·nàahn·dái ge.

unbelievable   hóu nàahn·sèung·seun. /It's unbelievable that he would have done this.
   Hóu nàahn·sèung·seun kéuih wúih jouh dī gám ge sih.

unbiased   hòuh·mòuh·pìn·gin ge

unbind   gáai·hòi, gáai·lāt

unbutton   gáai·hòi·nāp·náu; gáai·hòi·dī·náu (more than one button)

unceasingly   bāt·hit·gám, bāt·hit ge. /It rained unceasingly yesterday. Kàhm·yaht bāt·
   hit·gám lohk·yúh.

uncertain   wah·m̀h dihng, m̀h·dihng·dāk·saht. /I am uncertain about whether I'll go to
   the meeting or not. Ngóh wah·m̀h·dihng heui·m̀h·heui hòi·wúi.

uncivilized   yéh·màahn: **uncivilized methods** yéh·màahn sáu·dyuhn

uncle   (father's elder brother) baak·fuh; (father's younger brother) a·sūk; (mother's
   brother) káuh·fú

unclean   m̀h·gòn·jehng

uncomfortable   m̀h·syù·fuhk. /This chair is uncomfortable; don't sit on it, sit on that
   one. Nī·jèung yí m̀h·syù·fuhk, m̀h·hóu·chóh, chóh gó·jèung lā.

uncommon   (rare) síu·yáuh ge, hèi·hón ge. /This bird is very uncommon. Nī·tíng jeuk
   haih hóu·síu·yáuh ge. (special) dahk·biht ge. /This is an uncommon opportunity. Nī·
   go haih yāt·go hóu dahk·biht ge gèi·wuih.

unconditional mòuh·tìuh·gín (ge): **unconditional surrender** mòuh·tìuh·gín tàuh·hòhng

unconfirmed meih·jing·saht (ge). /This information is unconfirmed. Nī·go sīu·sīk juhng meih jing·saht. or Nī·go haih meih jing·saht ge sīu·sīk. (This is unconfirmed news.)

unconnected m̀h·sèung·lìhn ge, m̀h·sèung·gwàan ge

unconscious bāt·síng·yàhn·sih. /He has been unconscious for more than an hour. Kéuih yíh·gìng yáuh dím·géi·jūng bāt·síng·yàhn·sih la.

uncontrollable móuh·faat·ji hung·jai. /The situation is getting uncontrollable. Go chìhng·yìhng yíh·gìng juhk·jím móuh·faat·jí·hung·jai la.

uncooked juhng meih jyú·dāk·suhk (not done yet); sàang·ge (raw)

uncover kín·hòi, po·wohk. /Uncover the cooking pot. Kín·hòi go bō·goi kéuih. /The government agents uncovered a spy ring. Jìng·fú jìng·taam po·wohk·jó yāt·go gaan·dihp·móhng.

under hái . . . hah·bihn, hái . . . (hah·)dái. /Let's take a break under the tree. Hái gó·pò syuh hah·bihn táu yāt·jahn·gāan sìn. /Put your shoes under the bed. Jèung deui hàaih jài·hái chòhng·(hah·)dái.
(below) yíh·hah. /Is his monthly income under $150.00? Kéuih múih·go·yuht ge sàu·yahp haih·m̀h·haih hái yāt·baak·ńgh·sahp·mān yíh·hah a? /It cannot be bought under twenty dollars. Yih·sahp·mān yíh·hah máaih·m̀h·dóu. /Children under twelve years old are half price, under five years old are free. Sahp·yih·seui yíh·hah ge sai·mān·jái bun·piu; ńgh·seui yíh·hah ge míhn·fai.
(in the process of) jing·joih . . . gán. /The building is under repair. Joh láu jing·joih sàu·léih·gán. /She is under treatment. Kéuih jing·joih yì·gán. /This problem is under discussion. Nī·go mahn·tàih jing·joih tóu·léuhn·gán. /Your suggestion is under consideration. Néih ge gin·yi jing·joih háau·leuih·gán.
(by the provisions of) yi·jiu, gàn·geui. /Under the new law overtime parking can be punished by a heavy fine. Yì·jiu sàn·dihng ge tìuh·laih tìhng·chè chìu·gwo kwài·dihng ge sìh·gaan hó·nàhng fat dāk hóu chúhng ga.
under one's charge yàuh gún·léih. /This will be under your charge. Nī·gihn sih yàuh néih gún·léih.
under one's management joih . . . gún léih jì·hah, yàuh . . . gún·léih: **under one's rule** joih . . . túng·jih jì·hah. /The factory is getting more prosperous under his management. Gàan gùng·chóng joih kéuih gún·léih jì·hah yuht lèih yuht faat·daaht.
undersea, underside of, underwater -dái. /We have to build an undersea tunnel. Ngóh·deih yiu hái hói·dái jūk yāt·tiuh seuih·douh. /The underside of the boat needs painting. Go syùhn·dái yiu yàuh yáuh la. /Can you see anything underwater? Néih hái séui·dái hó·yíh tái·dāk·dóu yéh ma?
under the circumstances joih gám ge chìhng·yìhng jì·hah, . . . jí yáuh . . . ; gei·yìhn haih gám, . . . jí yáuh . . . . /Under the circumstances I have to accept his terms. Joih gám ge chìhng·yìhng jì·hah, ngóh jí yáuh jip·sauh kéuih ge tìuh·gin.
be under control. /Is everything under control? Yeuhng yeuhng yéh dōu tóh·dong lā máh?

underestimate gú·gai gwo·dài

undergraduate daaih·hohk·sāang

underground deih hah-: **the underground** (a group organized in strict secrecy) deih·hah·jóu·jīk; **the underground movement** deih·hah·gùng·jok; **member of the underground** deih·hah·gùng·jok yàhn·yùhn; **the underground subway** deih·dái·chè

undermine pò·waaih

underneath hái . . . hah·bihn. /They found a bomb underneath the car. Kéuih·deih hái ga chè hah·bihn wán·dóu yāt·go ja·dáan.

(the under side) hah·bihn, hah·dài, dái·hah. /Is there a crack underneath? Hah·bihn haih·m̀h·haih lit·jó a? /The box is paper on top and wooden underneath. Nī·go háp seuhng· bihn haih jî ge, hah·bihn haih muhk ge. /These pipes will have to be fixed from under- neath. Nī·dī gún yiu hái hah·bihn sìn·ji sàu·léih·dāk.

underpants   dái·fu (M: tîuh)

undershirt   dái·sāam, hohn·sāam (M: gihn)

understand   (get the meaning of) mìhng, mìhng·baahk. /I don't understand what you mean. Ngóh m̀h·mìhng(·baahk) néih ge yi·si. /Do you understand now? Néih mihng·baahk meih a?

(be thoroughly acquainted with) sām·jî. /It takes a long time to understand him. Yiu gìng·gwo hóu noih sìh·gaan sìn·ji hó·yíh sām·jî kéuih ge.

(have heard that) tèng·gin·wah. /I understand he's going away; is that true? Ngóh tèng·gin·wah kéuih jauh·lèih jáu la, haih·m̀h·haih a?

undertake   dàam·yahm. /He says he has so much work to do he will not undertake any more. Kéuih wah kéuih yáuh gam dò gùng·jok yiu jouh, kéuih m̀h·joi dàam·yahm kèih· tà ge gùng·jok la.

undertaker   (one who prepares the dead for burial) ngh·jok·lóu

underwear   dái·sāam·fu

underweight   m̀h·gau·chúhng

underworld   (Hades) deih·yuhk; (the place of departed souls) yām·gàan; (the debased, or criminal portion of humanity) hah·làuh·séh·wúi

undo   (untie) gáai

undoubtedly   mòuh·yih, hòuh·mòuh·yih·mahn. /He has undoubtedly taken a bribe. Kéuih mòuh·yih haih sauh·jó hāk·chín la.

undress   (to take the dressing from the wound) gáai·bāng·dáai; (to divest the formal gar- ments; to disrobe) chèuih·mín·sāam; (to divest of clothes; to strip) chèuih·saai·sāam

undue   (excessive) gwo·douh ge, gwo·fahn ge

uneasy   (uncomfortable) m̀h·syù·fuhk; (anxious) m̀h·ngon·lohk

unemployed   sāt·yihp. /He's been unemployed for two months. Kéuih sāt·yihp·jó léuhng· go·yuht la. /Many people have become unemployed recently. Nī·páai hóu dò yàhn sāt· yihp.

unequal   (not fair) m̀h·pìhng·dáng; (not uniform) m̀h·sèung·dáng

uneven   (not level) m̀h·pìhng. /The table rocks because the floor is uneven. Jèung tói yūk haih yàn·waih go deih·báan m̀h·pìhng.

(not the same size) m̀h·dahng·chan. /The four legs of the table are uneven. Jèung tói ge sei·jek geuk m̀h·dahng·chan.

(odd 'of numbers') dàan: **the uneven numbers** dàan·sou. /The houses on the north side of the street are even numbers; the ones on the south are uneven numbers. Tíuh gāai ge ngūk hái bāk·bín ge haih sèung·sou, hái nàahm·bin ge haih dàan·sou.

unexpected   séung·m̀h·dou, chēut·fùh·yi·liuh jî·ngoih. /It's completely unexpected. Jàn· haih séung·m̀h·dou la. or Jàn·haih chēut·fùh·yi·liuh jî·ngoih la.

unexpected calamity wàahng·woh (M: chèuhng); **unexpected income** wàahng·chòih (M: bāt)

unfair   m̀h·gùng·douh

unfamiliar   m̀h·suhk·sīk; **unfamiliar face** sàang·mín·yàhn, sàang·bóu·yàhn unfinished   meih·yùhn(·sìhng) ge

unfit   m̀h·ngāam

unfold   (as newspaper) dá·hòi: **unfold the newspaper** dá·hòi jèung bou·jí

unfortunate   m̀h·hóu·chói

unfortunately   hóu·sèui·m̀h·sèui; pīn·pīn. /Unfortunately there was a big storm on that day. Hóu·sèui·m̀h·sèui gó·yaht yauh daaih·fùng yauh daaih·yúh. /Unfortunately it happened that I didn't have enough money with me. Pīn·pīn ngóh gó·yaht m̀h daai·dāk gau chín.

unfounded   hòuh·mòuh·gàn·geui ge

ungrateful   mòhng·yàn·fuh·yih ge

unhappy   m̀h·faai·lohk; m̀h·fùng·héi (not glad)

unhealthy   (not conducive to health) m̀h·waih·sāng (ge)

unicorn   kèih·lèuhn (M: jek)

unify   túng yāt

uniform   (same) yāt·leuht sèung tùhng ge. /These boards are uniform in size. Nī·dī báan ge chek·chyun haih yāt·leuht sèung·tùhng ge.
    (clothes) jai·fuhk (M: tyut, suit)

union   **a labor union** gùng·wúi; **a trade union** gùng·wúi; **the Union** (the U.S. government) Méih·gwok lyùhn·bòng·jing·fú

unit   dāan·wái; **mechanized unit** (in army) gèi·haaih·fa bouh·déui

unite   (form a union) lyùhn·hahp·héi·lòih, hahp·màaih·yāt·chái. /The unions want to be united. Dī gùng·wúi yiu lyùhn·hahp·héi·lòih.
    (cause to form a union) túng·yāt. /Finally he united China. Jēut·jí kéuih túng·yāt·jó Jùng·gwok.

United States   Méih·gwok

unity   /We should fight for this in unity. Ngóh·deih daaih·gā yiu tyùhn·git yāt·ji waih nī·gihn sih lèih fáhn·dau.

universal   chyùhn·sai·gaai (the whole world); yàhn·yàhn (everybody). /We believe that there is a universal desire for peace. Ngóh·deih sèung·seun chyùhn·sai·gaai dōu hèi·mohng wòh·pìhng.

universe   (the creation; the cosmos) yúh·jauh; (the world) sai·gaai: **Miss Universe** sai·gaai·síu·jé

university   daaih·hohk; **university student** daaih·hohk·sāang

unjust   m̀h·gùng·pìhng, m̀h·gùng·douh

unlawful   m̀h·hahp·faat ge, faahn·faat ge

unless   chèuih·fèi. /I shall go unless it rains. Chèuih·fèi lohk·yúh ngóh yāt·dihng heui.
    (if) yùh·gwó. /Unless you try, you'll never succeed. Yùh·gwó néih m̀h·si·háh néih wíhng·yúhn m̀h·wúih sìhng·gùng ge.

unlike   m̀h·tùhng

unlimited   mòuh·haahn ge

unload   **unload cargo** héi·fo

unlock   /Unlock it! Hòi·jó bá só kéuih!

unloose   gáai·hòi

unlucky   m̀h·hóu·chói

unmarried   (juhng) meih (·git)·fàn

unnecessary   m̀h·sèui·yiu

unpack   dá·hòi. /The customs officer wants you to unpack your suitcase for examination. Seui·gwāan giu néih dá·hòi néih ge pèih·gīp béi kéuih gím·chàh.

unnoticeable   tái·m̀h·chēut ge

unoccupied   /This house is unoccupied. Nī·gāan ngūk móuh yàhn jyuh.

unofficial   (not authoritative) fēi·gūn·fōng ge; (not formal) fēi·jìng·sīk ge

unpaid   /This bill is unpaid. Nī·tìuh dāan juhng meih béi·chín.

unpleasant   m̀h·sóng. /Yesterday's weather was very unpleasant. Kàhm·yaht ge tìn·hei jàn·haih m̀h·sóng la.

unprepared   móuh·yuh·beih

unprecedented   hùng·chìhn ge

unprepared   Móuh·yuh·beih

unqualified   m̀h·hahp·gaak (ge), m̀h·gau·jì·gaak (ge). /He's unqualified. Kéuih m̀h·hahp·gaak. /What are you going to do with those who are unqualified? Gó dī m̀h·hahp·gaak· ge dím syun a?

unreasonable   /It's unreasonable! Móuh·póu ge!

unreliable   m̀h·hó·kaau, kaau·m̀h·jyuh. /This report (of news) is unreliable. Nī·go sīu· sīk m̀h·hó·kaau.

unripe   meih suhk

unroll   gyún·hòi

unsafe   m̀h·wán·jahn

unsatisfactory   m̀h·lihng·yàhn·múhn·yi. /The recent products of that factory are un- satisfactory. Gó·gàan gùng·chóng jeui·gahn ge chēut·bán m̀h·lihng·yàhn múhn·yi.

unsanitary   yáuh·ngoih·waih·sāng (ge)

unsealed   móuh fùng·háu ge; **unsealed letter** hòi·háu·seun

unseen   tái·m̀h·gin ge

unskilled   /I knew he wanted the job but he was unskilled in that kind of work. Ngóh jì· dou kéuih séung yiu jouh gó·fahn gūng, daahn·haih kéuih móuh gó·mùhn sáu·ngaih.

unsuccessful   m̀h·sìhng·gùng

unsuitable   m̀h·ngāam, m̀h·sīk·hahp

untidy   (of things) láau·gaauh; (of persons) lé·he

untie   (unfasten) gáai, gáai·hòi. /Do you know how to untie it? Néih sīk·m̀h·sīk gáai a? /Untie this knot. Gáai·hòi nī·go lit.

until   (up to a certain time) yāt·jihk . . . dou. /He told me to wait until four o'clock. Kéuih giu ngóh yāt·jihk dáng·dou sei·dím·jūng. /He didn't show up until four o'clock. Kéuih yāt·jihk ji·dou séi·dím·jūng ji lèih.
     (up to a certain point) yāt·jihk . . . dou. /Last night we didn't stop work until mid- night. Ngóh·deih kàhm·máahn yāt·jihk jouh·dou bun·yé. /We ate until we could eat no

more. Ngóh·deih yāt·jihk sihk·dou m̀h·sihk·dāk·lohk waih jí. /May I wait until he comes back? Ngóh hó·yíh yāt·jihk dáng·dou kéuih fàan·lèih ma?
(from . . . till . . . ; to) yàuh . . . ji (·dou) . . . . /We had to wait from noon until 4 o'clock for the plane to come. Ngóh·deih yàuh ngaan·jau ji sei·dím dōu hái syu dáng ga fēi·gèi lèih.
not until is either expressed with . . . jî·chìhn . . . m̀h . . . ; or . . . sìn·ji . . . . /This letter won't get there until next week. Nī·fùng seun hah·láih·baai jî·chìhn m̀h·wúih dou ge. or Nī·fùng seun hah·láih·baai sìn·ji dou.

untrained   meih·gîng·gwo·fan·lihn ge

untrue   m̀h·haih·jàn·ge, gá·ge

untrustworthy   m̀h·kaau·dāk·jyuh, kaau·m̀h·jyuh

unusual   fèi·sèuhng ge

unwilling   m̀h·háng, m̀h·yuhn·yi. /The workmen were unwilling to work after 6 o'clock in the evening. Dī gùng·yàhn m̀h·háng luhk·dím·jùng yíh·hauh jouh·gùng.

unworthy   (not deserving) m̀h·jihk·dāk. /His case is unworthy of your kindness. Kéuih ge chìhng·yìhng m̀h·jihk·dāk néih gam hóu·sàm.

up   **be up** (of a person, meaning out of bed in the morning) héi·sàn. /I wasn't up yet when they called on me. Kéuih·deih lèih wán ngóh ge sìh·hauh ngóh juhng meih héi·sàn.
be up (above the ground) chēut (lèih). /It's only five o'clock and the sun is already up. Ngh·dím·jūng jē, yaht·táu yíh·gîng chēut·jó·lèih la. /The grass will be up at the end of March. Sàam·yuht·méih dī chóu jauh chēut la.
be up to someone yàuh. /This is up to you to decide. Nī·gihn sih yàuh néih kyut·dihng.
be up to something. /What's he up to now? Kéuih séung jouh māt yéh a? (What trouble is he making now?)
up with a verb is to be found generally under the appropriate verb entry, some common ones are given as follows:
add up. /Please add up these figures. M̀h·gòi néih jèung nī·dī sou·muhk gà·màaih kéuih.
blow up. /They will use dynamite to blow up the rocks. Kéuih·deih yiu yuhng ja·yeuhk jà·hòi gó·dī sehk.
bring up a problem tàih·chēut. /I'll bring up this problem tomorrow. Ngóh tìng·yaht yiu tàih·chēut nī·go mahn·tàih.
close up (tightly). /Close up all the windows. Sàan·màaih·saai dī chēung·mún kéuih.
fill up yahp·múhn. /Fill it up. Yahp·múhn kéuih.
go up (price). /The price of eggs has gone up a lot recently. Nī·páai dī gài·dáan héi dāk hóu gán·yiu.
live up on. /We live up on a hill. Ngóh·deih jyuh·hái sàan·seuhng.
lock up. /Be sure to lock up the house before you leave. Néih jáu jî·chìhn gei·jyuh só·hóu douh mùhn.
put an umbrella **up.** /Put the umbrella up, it is raining. Lohk·yuh la, hòi hòi (or hòi·jó) bá jē kéuih.
time up. /Time is up. Gau jūng la. or Sìh·gaan dou la.
walk up. /There's no lift in this building; we have to walk up there. Nī·joh láu móuh dihn·tài, ngóh·deih yiu hàahng·séuhng·heui.
use up. /He just told me he has already used up his money. Kéuih jing·wah góng ngóh jî kéuih yíh·gîng yuhng·saai kéuih dī chín la.
up plus a verb that is usually covered by a single Chinese verb, such as: /We'll take that plan up at the next meeting. Ngóh·deih hah·chi wúi tóu·leuhn gó·go gai·waahk. /Hurry up. Faai dī. /Don't forget to call me up tonight. Gei·jyuh gàm·máahn dá·dihn·wá béi ngóh. /We invited our friends up for dinner tomorrow night. Ngóh·deih tìng·máahn chéng pàhng·yáuh lèih sihk·faahn.

uphold   (back up with agreement) jì·chìh, yúng·wuh. /In the last meeting the majority upheld his statement. Seuhng·chi·wúi daaih·dò·sou yàhn dōu jì·chìh kéuih ge yi·gin.

upkeep   /How much is the upkeep of this building per year? [Dá·léih] nī·joh·láu yāt·nìhn yiu géi·dò chìn sái·fai a?

upon   hái . . . seuhng·bihn. /Put the cup upon the table. Jài go būi hái tói·seuhng·bihn.

upper   seuhng·bihn. /Put the canned food on the upper shelves. Jèung dī gun·táu jài·hái seuhng·bihn gó·géi·gaak.
    upper classes seuhng·làuh·séh·wúi; **upper floors** làuh·seuhng; **upper lip** seuhng·sèuhn; **uppermost** ji·gòu ge; **upper part of a shoe** (above the sole) hàaih·mín; **upper part of the body** seuhng·sàn

upright   (straight up and down) jík·jihk. /Their baby can sit upright in her crib now. Kéuih·deih go bìh·bī·jái yìh·gìng hó·yíh hái jèung chòhng·jái·syu chóh dāk jík·jihk la.
    (honest) jing·jihk. /He is an upright man. Kéuih haih yāt·go hóu jing·jihk ge yàhn. or Kéuih go yàhn hóu jing·jihk ge.

upset   (turn over) fūk·jyun. /I saw the cat trying to upset the fish bowl this morning. Gàm·jìu·jóu ngóh tái·gin jek máau séung fūk·jyun go gàm·yùh·gòng.
    (disturbed; worried) m̀h·ngòn·lohk. /We were very upset when we were told that you quit school. Ngóh·deih tèng·gin·wah néih m̀h·duhk·syù la, ngóh·deih hóu m̀h·ngòn·lohk.

upside down   dou·jyun·tàuh. /Put the clean glasses upside down on the shelves. Jèung dī gòng·jehng būi dou·jyun·tàuh jài·hái gá seuhng·bihn.
    turn . . . upside down gáau·dou·lyuhn·saai. /The kids turned the room upside down. Dī sai·màn·jái jèung gàan fóng gáau·dou·lyuhn·saai.

upstairs   làuh·seuhng; **to go upstairs** séuhng·láu

up-to-date   (modern) jeui mō·dāng ge; (stylish) jeui sìh·hīng ge. **up-to-date information** jeui·gahn ge sìu·sīk; **up-to-date method** jeui sàn ge faat·jí. /This furniture is up-to-date. Nī·tíng gā·sī haih jeui mō·dāng ge la. /Her dress is up-to-date. Kéuih gihn sāam ge yéung haih jeui sìh·hīng ge la.

upward   heung·seuhng. /The helicopter flew upward for two minutes, then turned north. Ga jihk·sìng·gèi heung seuhng fèi·jó léuhng·fān·jūng jauh heung bāk fèi·jó·heui la.
    (toward a higher number) **fifty upward** ńgh·sahp·yíh·seuhng; **ten years upward** sahp·nìhn·yíh·seuhng

urge   (ask earnestly) ngài (beg); hyun (persuade). /The children are urging me to take them swimming. Dī sai·màn·jái ngài ngóh daai kéuih·deih heui yàuh·séui. /You must urge him to take a vacation. Néih·deih yāt·dihng yiu hyun kéuih yāu·sīk·háh m̀h·hóu jouh·yéh sìn la.
    an urge fèi·yiu . . . bāt·hó. /He felt a great urge to go back home. Kéuih gok·dāk fèi yiu fàan·ngūk·kéi bāt·hó. (He felt that he absolutely had to go back home.)

urgent   gán·gāp (ge). /Sorry, I have some urgent business which must be attended to immediately. Deui·m̀h·jyuh, ngóh yáuh gihn hóu gán·gāp ge sih máh·seuhng yiu baahn.
    in urgent need of gāp·sèui. /I'm in urgent need of money. Ngóh gāp·sèui chìn yuhng.

urinate   ngò·niuh, síu·bihn, ò·niuh

urine   niuh, síu·bihn

urn   ngung, ngung·gòng

us   ngóh·deih

use   yuhng. /How do you use it? Nī·go dím·yéung yuhng a? /What is it used for? [Nī·go] yuhng·lèih jouh māt·yéh ga? /May I use it for a while? Ngóh yuhng yāt·jahn·gāan

dāk·m̀h·dāk a? /Can you teach me how to use chopsticks? Néih gaau ngóh yuhng faai·
jí dāk ma? /You'll have to wait a minute; the telephone is in use now. Néih yiu dáng·
yāt·jahn·gāan; go dihn·wá yáuh yàhn yuhng·gán. /You may use my car. Néih hó·yíh
yuhng ngóh ga chè. /May I use your phone? Ngóh hó·yíh yuhng néih ge dihn·wá ma?
<u>or</u> Ngóh hó·yíh je néih ge dihn·wá dá·háh ma? (May I borrow your telephone?)
   (a way in which a thing is used) yuhng, yuhng·chyúh. /What are the uses of rubber?
Can you name some? Syuh·gāau yáuh māt·yéh yuhng a, néih hó·yíh góng géi·júng ngóh
tēng ma? /The most essential use of rubber is to make tires. Syuh·gāau jeui daaih ge
yuhng·chyúh haih jouh chē·tāai. /There's no use hurrying; we've already missed the
train. Gāp dōu móuh yuhng ge la, ngóh·deih yíh·gìng gón·m̀h·dóu nī·lèuhn fó·chē la.
   (a point; a value) yuhng. /What's the use of arguing? Ngaau·géng yáuh māt yuhng
nē?
   (need) yuhng·dāk·jeuhk. /He has no use for such a big house. Kéuih m̀h·yuhng·dāk·
jeuk yáuh gàan gam daaih ge ngūk. /There's no use for him to work so hard? Kéuih m̀h·
yuhng·dāk·jeuhk jouh dāk gam sàn·fú ā? /There's no use getting so angry. M̀h·yuhng·
dāk·jeuhk gam nāu ā?
   be used to gwaan·jó; **not used to** m̀h·gwaan. /I'm used to having a midnight snack;
I can't go to bed without it. Ngóh sihk·gwaan·jó sīu·yé, m̀h·sihk m̀h·fan·dāk. /I'm not
used to this kind of hot weather. Nī·dī gam·yiht ge tìn·sìh ngóh hóu·m̀h·gwaan.
   used to (past customary action) expressed <u>with a verb plus a time phrase, such as</u>
yíh·chìhn, chùhng·chìhn (formerly). /I used to eat there every day. Ngóh yíh·chìhn
yaht·yaht dōu hái gó·syu sihk·fàahn ge.
   use <u>something</u> **up**. yuhng·saai, sái·saai (especially money). /We've almost used up
our sugar. Ngóh·deih jauh·lèih yuhng·saai dī tòhng la. /He always uses up his money
before the end of the month. Kéuih sìh·sìh meih dou yuht·dái jauh sái·saai kéuih dī chín
ge la.

useful   yáuh·yuhng (ge). /How about giving him (as a gift) something more useful? Hóu·
m̀h·hóu sung gihn yáuh·yuhng·dī ge yéh béi kéuih nē?
   (helpful; of service) bōng·dāk·sáu. /She makes herself quite useful around the house.
Kéuih hái ngūk·kéi hóu bōng·dāk·sáu ge.

useless   móuh·yuhng. /This old machine has been useless ever since some of the parts
were broken. Nī·go gauh gèi·hei jih·chùhng yáuh géi·go gèi·gín waaih·jó yíh·gìng móuh·
yuhng la.

usher   (a person) jīu·doih·yùhn; **to usher** daai . . . yahp (·heui) . . . . /Would you please
usher the guests into the reception room? M̀h·gòi néih daai·dī yàhn·haak yahp jīu·doih·
sāt chóh.

usual   pìhng·sìh. /Does everyone go to work at the usual time in the summer? Tìn·sìh.
yiht ge sìh·hauh haih·m̀h·haih (go·go·dōu) yì·jiu pìhng·sìh gám ge sìh·gaan fàan·gùng a?
   (ordinary) pìhng·sèuhng·ge, chàhm·sèuhng ge. /He'll only ask you some very ordinary
questions. Kéuih jí·haih yiu mahn néih géi·go hóu pìhng·seuhng ge mahn·tàih jē.

usually   pìhng·sèuhng, pìhng·sìh. /How do you handle these matters usually? Néih·deih
pìhng·sìh dím·yéung ying·fuh dī gám ge mahn·tàih a? /We usually have our breakfast
at seven o'clock; Saturday and Sunday, a little later. Ngóh·deih pìhng·sìh chāt·dím·jūng
sihk jóu·chāan; láih·baai·luhk, láih·baai·yaht chìh·dī.
   as usual jiu·sèuhng. /There'll be school as usual tomorrow. Tìng·yaht jiu·sèuhng
séuhng·fo.

usurp   **usurp other's property** ba·jim·yàhn·deih ge cháan·yihp; **usurp someone's power**
chàm·dyuht yàhn·deih ge kyùhn·lihk; **usurp a throne** chyun·waih

utensil   **kitchen utensils** sā·bōu·ngāang·chāang (M: dī); **household utensils** sou·bá deih·
tō jí·léui ge yéh

uterus   jí·gùng

utilize   leih·yuhng. /I think we can utilize this stream for power. Ngóh tái ngóh·deih
hó·yíh leih·yuhng nī·tîuh hòh lèih faat·dihn. /Why don't you utilize this opportunity?
Dím·gáai néih m̀h·leih·yuhng nī·go gèi·wuih nē?

utmost   gihk·jì: **utmost importance** gihk·jì gán·yiu

utter   /No one uttered a word. Móuh·yàhn chēut·dou·sèng. (complete) /After that fire,
the business district was in utter ruin. Gìng·gwo gó·chèuhng daaih·fó jì·hauh sèhng·go
sèung·yihp·kēui yùhn·chyùhn wái·waaih·saai.

utterly   yùhn·chyùhn; jyuht·deui. /It's utterly different. Yùhn·chyùhn m̀h·tùhng. /It's
utterly impossible. Jyuht·deui bāt·hó·nàhng.

V

vacancy   kyut, hùng·ngák (an open job); hùng·ngák, hùng·wái (a position waiting to be
filled). /There are two vacancies in our teaching staff for next year. Ngóh·deih chēut·
nín ge gaau·yùhn yáuh léuhng·go·kyut. /There are two vacancies in our sophomore
class. Yih·nîhn·kāp yáuh léuhng·go hùng·ngák.
    (an empty space) móuh·deih·fòng (in general). /There is no vacancy. Gó·syu <u>móuh·</u>
<u>ngūk</u> (no house, <u>or</u> móuh fóng, no room) chēut·jòu (for rent).

vacant   **vacant house** hùng·ngūk, gāt·ngūk; **vacant lot** hūng·deih, gāt·deih; **vacant room**
hùng·fóng, gāt·fóng; **vacant spot** dò·yùh ge deih·fòng (<u>the word hùng 'empty' is a homo-</u>
<u>nym of</u> 'ominous,' <u>because of superstition, the word gāt 'auspicious' is preferably used.</u>)
/One house is vacant. <u>is expressed as</u> Yáuh yāt·gāan ngūk móuh yàhn jyuh.

vacation   (a period away from school, or work, including public holidays) fong·ga (VO);
summer vacation syú·ga; **to have a summer vacation** fong syú·ga; **winter vacation**
hòhn·ga, nîhn·ga; **to have a winter vacation** fong hòhn·ga; **spring vacation** chèun·ga.
/Do you have a summer vacation? Néih·deih yáuh móuh syú·ga ga? or Néih·deih fong·
m̀h·fong syú·ga ga? /When does the summer vacation start? Géi·sí hòi·sáu fong syú·
ga a?
    (a period of time chosen by oneself away from one's usual occupation to have fun or
rest) yàu·ga. /When's your vacation? Néih géi·sí yàu·ga a?

vaccinate   **vaccinate to prevent smallpox** jung·dáu. /Has he been vaccinated? Kéuih
jung·jó dáu meih a? /Has he ever been vaccinated? Kéuih yáuh móuh jung·gwo dáu a?

vaccine   (vaccine lymph) dauh·mìuh

vacuum   jàn·hùng; **vacuum tube** jàn·hùng·gún

vagabond   làuh·mòhng, mòuh·láai

vague   hàhm·wùh (speech); mòuh·wùh (impression)

vain   **vain desire** mohng·séung; **vain hope** mohng·séung
    in vain móuh·yuhng; baahk·baahk. /All our work is in vain. Ngóh·deih só·jouh gam·
dò·yéh yùhn·chyùhn móuh·yuhng. or Ngóh·deih baahk·baahk jouh·jó gam dò yéh.

valiant   yúhng·gáam

valid   /This ticket is valid for a month. Nī·jēung fēi yāt·go·yuht·noih yáuh·haauh. /This
contract is still valid. Nī·jèung hahp·yeuhk yîhng·yìhn yáuh·haauh.

valley   sàan·ngaau, sāan·gūk; **river valley** làuh·wihk

valuable   gwai·juhng ge: **valuables** gwai·juhng ge maht·gín

value   (worth; monetary) ga·chîhn <u>or as</u> jihk (be worth it). /The value of this house is
$10,000, but, because the owner must sell it quickly, he will sell it for $8,000. Nī·gāan   .

ngūk ge ga·chìhn haih yāt·maahn mān, daahn·haih yàn·waih go ngūk·jyú gāp·jyuh yiu
maaih·jó kéuih, só·yíh jí·haih maaih baat·chīn·mān jē. /What's the value of this house?
Nī·gāan ngūk jihk géi·dò chín a?

    (worth; non-monetary) ga·jihk. /The value of this book is that it contains some ever-
lasting truth. Nī·bún syù ge ga·jihk haih kèih·jùng bàau·hàhm yeuhk·gōn wíhng·gáu·bāt·
miht·ge jàn·léih.

    (given in another monetary system) is expressed with wuhn exchange for géi·dò·
chín so much money. /What's the value of the American dollar here? Nī·syu yāt·go
ngàhn·chín Méih·gām wuhn géi·dò chín a?

    to value an opinion juhng·sih. /People value his opinion very highly. Yāt·bùn yàhn
dōu hóu juhng·sih kéuih ge yi·gin.

    value something **at** such- and- such an amount gú·gai. /What do you value his
property at? Néih gú·gai kéuih ge cháan·yihp jihk géi·dò chín nē?

vapor   séui·hei

various   gok·júng bāt·tùhng ge; gok·júng ge; gok—ge; hóu dò. /Men's preferences are
various. Yàhn yáuh gok·júng bāt·tùhng ge si·hou. /There are various styles of dresses
in the window. Go sīk·gwaih·syu yáuh gok·yeuhng fún·sīk ge sāam. /This association
is composed of men of various occupations. Nī·go wúi haih yàuh gok·júng jīk·yihp ge
yàhn jóu·jīk ge. /People from various countries took part in this relief program. Gok·
gwok ge yàhn dōu chàam·gà nī·hohng gau·jai gùng·jok. /He suggested various places
we could go for a picnic. Kéuih wah·jó hóu·dò·daat deih·fòng ngóh·deih hó·yíh heui yéh·
chāan.

vary   bin·wuhn; bāt·tùhng. /He should vary his diet. Kéuih yìng·gòi bin·wuhn·háh kéuih
só·sihk ge yéh. /The laws of different countries vary. Gok·gwok ge faat·leuht bāt·
tùhng.

vase   fā·jēun

vaseline   fà·sih·líng

Vatican   (the papal authority or government) gaau·tìhng; **the Vatican hill** Wàh·tàih·gōng

veal   ngàuh·jái·yuhk

vegetable   choi, sò·choi

vehicle   chè (M: ga)

veil   mihn·sā

vein   jihng·mahk, jihng·mahk·gún

velvet   sì·yúng

venerate   jyùn·ging

venereal   **venereal disease** fà·láuh, mùih·duhk

venetian blind   baak·yihp·chēung

venison   luhk·yuhk

venomous   **venomous snake** duhk·sèh (M: tìuh)

ventilate   làuh·tùng·háh dī hùng·hei; lihng dī hùng·hei làuh·tùng·háh. /You must open the
windows to ventilate the house. Néih yāt·dihng yiu dá·hòi chēung·mún làuh·tùng·háh dī
hùng·hei. /We must think of a way to ventilate this building. Ngóh·deih yāt·dihng yiu
séung go faat·jí lihng nī·gàan·láu ge hùng·hei làuh·tùng·háh.

venture   (dare) gáam. /He did not venture a second request for money to spend on
candy after his father said no. Jih·chùhng kéuih bàh·bā wah·gwo m̀h·béi jì·hauh kéuih
jauh m̀h·gáam joi mahn kéuih bàh·bā ló·chín máaih tóng sihk la.

(risk) taam·hím. /He ventured into the African jungle twice. Kéuih heui Fei·jàu taam·gwo léuhng·chi hím.

nothing ventured, nothing gained bāt·yahp·fú·yuht, yīn·dāk·fú·jí

Venus	(planet) gām·sīng

veranda	(a roofed portion attached to the exterior of the building) kèh·láu

verb	duhng·chìh

verdict	pun·kyut

verify	(confirm) jing·saht. /Can you verify his statement? Néih hó·yíh jing·saht kéuih só·góng·ge haih jàn·ge ma?

vermilion	(color) jyù·hùhng·sīk, (the pigment) ngàhn·jyū

vernacular	**vernacular tongue** fòng·yìhn, tóu·tàahm, hèung·háh·wá (colloq.)

verse	(poetry) sī; (bib.) jit: /Book of John, chapter 6, verse 63. Yeuk·hon daih·luhk· jèung, daih·luhk·sahp·sàam·jit; (a stanza; a group of lines that go together in a poem) jit

   versed in jīng·tùng. /He's well versed in English literature. Kéuih jīng·tùng Yìng· gwok màhn·hohk.

version	(translation) (yihk)·bún. /Does this book have an English version? Nī·bún syù yáuh móuh Yìng·màhn (·yihk)·bún a? /I was told there's a Chinese version of this novel; have you read it? Ngóh tèng·màhn·wah nī·bún síu·syut yáuh jùng·màhn (·yihk)· bún, Néih yáuh móuh tái·gwo a?

versus	deui: **Yale versus Harvard** Yèh·lóuh deui Hà·faht

vertebra	jek·gwāt, jek·jēui·gwāt

vertical	sèuih·jihk ge

very	hóu. /He's a very easy person to get along with. Kéuih go yàhn hóu yùhng·yih sèung·chyúh ge. /I was very pleased to get your letter. Ngóh sàu·dou néih fùng seun hóu fùn·héi. /He spoke very fast, therefore I didn't understand what he said. Kéuih góng dāk taai faai, só·yíh ngóh m̀h·mìhng·baahk kéuih góng·māt·yéh.

   (exact, precise) ngāam·ngāam; jing·haih. /The very day I left Peking, the Sino Japanese war started. Ngóh ngāam·ngāam lèih·hòi Bāk·gìng gó·yaht, Jùng·yaht jin·sih jauh faat·sàng la. /He's the very man you want. Kéuih jing·haih néih só·sèui·yiu·ge yàhn.

   (mere) yāt·séung·héi (or séung·dou) . . . jauh . . . . /The very idea of Winter makes me shiver. Ngóh yāt·séung·héi láahng·tīn jauh dá·láahng·jan la.

   not very m̀h·haih·géi. /It's not very cold here in the winter. Nī·syu tìng·sìh láahng ge sìh·hauh m̀h·haih géi láahng jē. /The bank isn't very far from here. Gó·gàan ngàhn· hòhng lèih nī·syu m̀h·haih géi yúhn jē.

   It's very kind of you to say so. Hóu·wah, hóu·wah.

vessel	(a ship or boat) syùhn (M: jek); (blood vessel) hyut·gún; (a pot) bōu; (a bowl) wún; (a cup) būi; (a barrel) túng; (a bottle) jēun

vest	(a garment worn under a suit coat) bui·sām (M: gihn)

veteran	(a person who has been in the armed service) teui·ńgh·gwàn·yàhn; (experienced) yáuh·gìng·yihn·ge

veterinary	sau·yì

veto	fáu·kyut·kyùhn (N); fáu·kyut (V)

vex	(irritate, annoy, anger) gīk·nàu. /The boys' ridicule vexed the old man. Dī sai·lóu· gō gīk·nàu·jó go baak·yē·gūng.

via   gìng·yàuh. /These cargoes will be shipped to New York via Hong Kong. Nī·dī fo gìng·yàuh Hèung góng wahn·heui Náu·Yeuk

vibrate   jan·duhng

vibration   jan·duhng

vice   (bad or evil conduct) m̀h·hóu ge hàhng·wàih; jeuih·ngok ge hàhng·waih. /Laziness and cheating are vices. Láahn·doh tùhng góng·daaih·wah dōu haih m̀h·hóu ge hàhng· wàih.

        (deputy) fu: **vice-chairman** fu·jyú·jihk; **vice-consul** fu·lìhng·sì; **vice-president** (of a Republic) fu·júng·túng; **vice-principle** fu·haauh·jéung; **vice-minister** (of a ministry in the government) chi·jéung: **vice-minister of Foreign Affairs** ngoih·gàau·chi·jéung

vice versa   yihk dōu. /They didn't trust him, and vice versa. Kéuih·deih m̀h·sèung seun kéuih, kéuih yihk·dōu m̀h·sèung·seun kéuih·deih.

viceroy   júng·dūk

vicinity   fuh·gahn. /Is there a drugstore in the vicinity? Nī·syu fuh·gahn yáuh móuh sài·yeuhk·fòhng a?

vicious   ngok. /Be careful of that vicious dog. He is apt to bite people. Tàih·fòhng gó· jek ngok gáu, gó jek gáu hóu·jùng·yi ngáauh yàhn ga.

victim   (a person killed) yuh·naahn ge yàhn (in general); or is specified by the accident, such as: sìu·séi·ge yàhn (someone burned to death); jaahm·séi·ge yahn (someone drowned to death); dá·séi·ge yahn (being killed), etc.
        (a person harmed) sauh·sèung·ge yàhn. /The victims of the fire were removed to a hospital. Nī·chi fó·jūk sauh sèung·ge yàhn yíh·gìng sung·saai·heui yì·yúhn la.

victory   sing·leih; sing·jó; dá·yèhng·jó. /Their victory in this game made them the champion. Yàn·waih nī·chèuhng·bō ge sing·leih, só·yíh kéuih·deih dāk·dóu gun·gwān.
or Yàn·waih kéuih·deih sing·jó (or dá·yèhng·jó) nī·chèuhng·bō só·yíh kéuih·deih dāk· dóu gun·gwān.

view   (a scene) fùng·gíng. /The view from the mountaintop was beautiful. Hái sàan·déng· syu mohng·lohk·lèih ge fùng·gíng hóu leng.
        (a thought; an idea; an opinion) yi·gin. /Everyone may air his views on this problem. Gwàan·yù nī·go mahn·tàih múih·go·yàhn dōu hó·yíh góng kéuih jih·géi ge yi·gin. /What are your views on the subject? Néih deui·yù nī·gihn sih yáuh māt yi·gin a?
        (think about; consider) yihng·wàih. /The doctor viewed his illness with alarm. Yī· sāng yihng·wàih kéuih ge behng sèung·dòng ngàih·hím.
        (sight) tái·dóu. /The airplane soon came into view after we arrived at the airport. Ngóh·deih dou·jó fēi·gèi·chèuhng jì·hauh móuh·géi·nói jauh tái·dóu ga fēi·gèi la.
        in view of jiu . . . lèih tái. /In view of recent developments we do not think this step advisable. Jiu muhk·chìhn ge chìhng·yìhng lèih tái, ngóh·deih yihng·wàih nī·go baahn·faat m̀h·tóh·dong.
        viewpoint taai·faat

vigorous   hóu jìng·sàhn, hóu jong·gihn, jìng·lihk chùng·pui

villa   biht·séuih (M: gàan)

village   chyūn (M: tìuh)

villager   chyūn·màhn

villain   (a wicked person) waaih·yàhn, kwàaih·yahn

vine   (grape vine) pòuh·tàih·jí·syuh (M: pò); **mellon vine** gwà·tàhng; **vineyard** pòuh·tàih· jí·yùhn, pòuh·tòuh·yùhn; (climbing plants) làan·tàhng

vinegar   chou, syùn·chou; **dark vinegar** hāk·chou; **white vinegar** baahk chou viola   jùng·tàih·kàhm

violate   (break rules or laws) faahn: **violate school rules** faahn·haauh·kwài; **violate laws** faahn·faat

violence   kèuhng·bouh ge hàhng·wàih; **use violence toward a person** hèung·yàhn hàhng·hùng

violent   máahng·liht ge: **a violent blow** máahng·liht ge dá·gīk; **violent pain** tung dāk hóu gāau·gwàan. /Did you say you had a violent pain? Where was it? Néih wah néih tùng dāk hóu gāau·gwàan àh, bīn·syu tung a? **a violent speech** gīk·liht ge yín·góng; **a violent controversy** gīk·liht ge jàang·leuhn; **a violent storm** kwòhng·fùng·bouh·yúh. /Yesterday, the whole afternoon we had a violent storm. Kàhm·yaht sèhng go hah·jau kwòhng·fùng·bouh·yúh.

violin   wāai·ōu·līn, síu·tàih·kàhm; **to play the violin** ngàahn (or wáan) wāai·ōu·līn

violinist   síu·tàih·kàhm·gā

virgin   (an unmarried girl) chéuih·néuih

virtue   dāk·hahng. /Honesty is a virtue. Sìhng·saht haih yāt·júng dāk·hahng.

visa   chìm·jing. /Have you had a visa? Néih chìm·jó jing meih a? /I'm waiting for a visa. Ngóh jing·joih dáng·gán chìm·jing.

visible   tái·dāk·dóu. /It's visible even on a cloudy day. Tìn·sīk m̀h·hóu ge sìh·hauh dōu hó·yíh tái·dāk·dóu. /Is it visible? Tái·m̀h·tái·dāk·dóu a? /It's not visible. Tái·m̀h·dóu.

vision   (the ability to see; eyesight) ngáahn. /His vision is poor. Kéuih sèung ngáahn m̀h·hóu.
    (imagination) waahn·jeuhng; (something supernaturally revealed) yih·jeuhng

visit   taam; (if very formal) baai·fóng; **return a visit** wùih·baai; **visiting card** mìhng·pín; **visiting hours** wuih·haak·sìh·gaan. /We plan to visit them next Saturday. Ngóh·deih dá·syun hah·láih·baai·luhk heui taam kéuih·deih. /Come to visit us while you are on vacation. Fong·ga ge sìh·hauh lèih taam ngóh·deih lā.
    a visit is expressed verbally as above. /While we're there, we would like to pay a visit to some friends. Ngóh·deih heui·dou jì·hauh dá·syun heui taam·háh géi·go pàhng·yáuh. but /We had a pleasant visit. is expressed as Ngóh·deih daaih·gā gin·dóu·mihn hóu fùn·héi.
    (to or by a doctor) chi. /How many visits did you make to the hospital last month? Néih seuhng·go·yuht heui·gwo yì·yún géi·dò chi a? /How much does the doctor charge for a visit? Yī·sāng lèih yāt·chi yiu géi·dò chín a?

visitor   (guest) yàhn·haak, haak, lòih·bàn (formal); **visitors' book** lòih·bàn chìm·méng·bóu

vital   hóu gán·yiu ge. /Food is vital to life. Sihk·maht deui·yù sàng·mihng haih hóu gán·yiu ge.

vitamin   wàih·tà·mihng·yún

vivid   (bright; clear) sìn·mìhng. /Her dress is a vivid blue. Kéuih gihn sāam ge sīk·séui haih hóu sìn·mìhng ge làahm·sīk.
    (clear; plain) /I have a vivid picture in my mind of what happened to our city after the enemy's bombing. Dihk·gèi gwàng·ja ngúh·deih ge sèhng jì·hauh ge·chìhng·gíng joih ngóh ge sàm·muhk·jùng juhng yihk·yihk·yùh·sàng.

viz   jīk·haih

vocabulary   chìh·leuih, jih·leuih

vocal   **vocal cord** sìng·daai; **vocal music** sìng·ngohk

vocation   (a call; a career) sih·yihp; (trades, profession, or occupation) jīk·yihp

voice   (in speaking) sīng·yàm (M: go); sèng (M: bá). **lose one's voice** sèng·hàuh ngá·
jó. /You have such a nice voice; you could learn to sing. Néih ge sīng·yàm gam hóu
néih hó·yíh hohk cheung·gō. /I can _recognize your voice on the telephone. Ngóh hó·
yíh hái dihn·wá·syu yihng·chēut néih bá sèng. /She had a bad cold and lost her voice.
Kéuih yàn·waih sèung·fùng só·yíh sèng·hàuh ngá·jó.
      (right to express oneself) faat·yìhn·kyùhn. /Everyone has a voice in this meeting.
Nī·go wúi go·go dōu yáuh faat·yìhn·kyùhn.
      to voice faat·bíu: **to voice one's opinion** faat·bíu go·yàhn ge yi·gin; **to voice one's
desire** góng·chēut go·yàhn ge yuhn·mohng; **to voice the hope of people** bíu·daaht yàhn·
mahn ge hèi·mohng

void   (invalid; null) mòuh·haauh. /This is void. Nī·go yíh·gìng mòuh·haauh la.

volcano   fó·sàan

volleyball   pàaih·kàuh: **to play volleyball** dá·pàaih·kàuh

volt   wōu, wōu·dá

volume   (a book) bún. /This bookcase is small; it can't hold many volumes. Nī·go syù·
gá hóu·sai, m̀h·jài·dāk géi·dò bún syù.
      (one book in a set of books) bún, gyún. /This book has ten volumes. Nī·tóuh syu
yáuh sahp·bún.
      (loudness of sound). /Turn up the volume on the radio. Jèung go sāu·yām·gēi náu
daaih·sēng dī.

voluntary   jih·yuhn ge, jih·duhng ge; **a voluntary army** yih·yúhng·gwān, ji·yuhn·gwān

volunteer   (offer one's service without being asked or told to do so) jih·duhng ge, jih·
yuhn·ge, jih·gou·fáhn·yúhng. /He volunteered to join the army. Kéuih jih·duhng yahp·
ngh dòng·bìng. /He volunteered to carry the food pack up to the mountain top. Kéuih
jih·yuhn (or jih·gou·fáhn·yúhng) nīk dī sihk·maht séuhng·heui sàan·déng.
      (a person) is always expressed verbally. /He's a volunteer. Kéuih haih jih·duhng
chàam·gà ge. /How many volunteers do we have so far. Jihk·dou muhk·chìhn wàih·jí,
ngóh·deih yáuh géi·dò jih·yuhn chàam·gà ge yàhn a? /We need some volunteers.
Yáuh·móuh yàhn jih·yuhn chàam·gà jouh nī·gihn sih a?

vomit   ngáu. /Did she vomit? Kéuih yáuh móuh ngáu a? /She vomited twice this morning. Gàm·jìu·jóu kéuih ngáu·jó léuhng·chi.

vote   (for someone for an office) syún. /Whom are you going to vote for? Néih syún
bīn·go a? (authorize by vote) tùng·gwo; tàu·piu (by balloting) tùng·gwo; géui·sáu (by
raising hands) tùng·gwo. /The board voted one thousand dollars for relief yesterday.
Dúng·sih·wúi kàhm·yaht tùng·gwo buht yāt·chīn·màn jouh gau·jai·fai. /The proposal was
voted down. Gó·go tàih·yíh móuh tùng·gwo.
      a vote piu, syún·piu. /If you have fifty votes you'll be elected. Yùh·gwó néih yáuh
ngh·sahp piu néih jauh beih·syún la.
      (act of voting) bíu·kyut; tàu·piu (by balloting) bíu·kyut; géui·sáu (by raising hands)
bíu·kyut; **to cast a vote** tàu·piu. /Let's vote for it by show of hands. Ngóh·deih géui·
sáu bíu·kyut la.
      put to a vote fuh bíu·kyut; **the right to vote** syún·géui·kyùhn; **voter** syún·géui·yàhn;
syún·màhn (the voting public)

voucher   sàu·geui

vow   (make a promise; take an oath) saih·yuhn (VO). /Didn't he vow that he wouldn't
gamble again? Kéuih m̀h·haih saih·gwo yuhn m̀h·dóu·chín la mē?

vowel   móuh·yām

vulgar   (unrefined) chòu·lóuh (ge); (low) hah·làuh (ge). /His language is always so vulgar.
Kéuih góng wá géi·sìh·dōu haih gam chòu·lóuh ge.

W

wade   (walk along or through a body of water) gaang·séui. /Almost every child likes to
wade. Chā·m̀h·dō go go sai·mān·jái dōu jùng·yi gaang·séui ge. /We may wade across.
Ngóh·deih hó·yíh gaang·séui gwo·heui.

wag   báai; to wag the tail báai·méih

wage   yàhn·gùng. /I understand he works for a small wage. Ngóh jì·dou kéuih ge yàhn·
gùng·hóu síu. /Your wages will be four hundred dollars a month. Néih ge yàhn·gùng
haih sai·baak mān yāt·go yuht.

wagon   (used to carry loads) fo·chè (M: ga)

wail   (cry loudly from pain or grief) haam. /Please ask her why she is wailing. M̀h·gòi
néih mahn·háh kéuih haam māt·yéh?

waist   (the middle part of the body) yìu; (the part of a garment that goes around the
waist) yìu·wàih; waistband yìu·dáai (M: tìuh); waistline yìu·wàih

wait   dáng. /I'm sorry to keep you waiting for so long. Deui·m̀h·jyuh, lihng néih dáng·
jó ngóh gam noih. /You can see him if you will wait until he comes back. Néih hó·yíh
gin kéuih yùh·gwó néih hó·yíh hái·syu yāt·jihk dáng·dou kéuih fàan·lèih. /I'll wait for
you here until 5 o'clock. Ngóh hó·yíh hái·syu dáng néih dáng·dou ńgh·dím. /Please
wait a moment. M̀h·gòi néih dáng yāt·ján. /Let's wait a little longer. Dáng yāt·jahn·
gāan tìm. /They've waited for a long time. Kéuih·deih dáng·jó hóu·noih la. /Wait till
the bus stops. Dáng ga bā·sí tìhng·jó sìn. /Whom are you waiting for? Néih dáng·gán
bīn·go a? /I'm waiting for a friend. Ngóh dáng·gán yāt·go pàhng·yáuh.
      (the time spent waiting) is expressed verbally with dáng. /The plane was late, so
we had a long wait. Fēi·gēi lèih chìh·jó, só·yíh ngóh·deih dáng·jó hóu·noih. /There
will be an hour wait before the plane gets in. Yiu dáng yāt·go·jūng·tàuh fēi·gēi sìn·ji
dou.
      (put off; delay) dáng. /Do not wait dinner for me. M̀h·hóu (or m̀h·sái) dáng ngóh
sihk·faahn.
      wait on jiu·fù, jiu·doih. /Who waited on this table? Bīn·go jiu·fù nī·jèung tói ga?
      wait till, wait until dáng·dou. /We can let that job wait till tomorrow. Gó·gihn sih
ngóh·deih hó·yíh dáng·dou tìng·yaht sìn·ji jouh. /Wait until tomorrow and then we'll see
what happens. Dáng·dou tìng·yaht sìn·ji syun la.

waiter   fó·géi (generally used in Hong Kong); kéih tóng (in Southeast Asia) kéih tói (in
North America)

waitress   néuih·jiu·doih

wake   séng. /I woke up early this morning. Gàm·jìu·jóu ngóh hóu·jóu jauh séng la.
/Wake up! is mostly expressed as Héi·sàn lo. (Get up!) /When did he wake up?
Kéuih géi·sí séng ga?
      wake someone up -séng: giu·séng (by calling); ngúng·séng (by pushing); chòuh·séng
(by disturbing); etc. /Please wake me up at seven o'clock. Chéng néih chāt·dím·jūng
giu·séng ngóh.

walk   hàahng. /How long will it take us to walk there? Yiu hàahng géi·nói ji dou·dāk
(gó·syu) a? /Do you think we can walk it in an hour? Yāt·dím·jūng hàahng·dāk·dou ma?
      a walk louh (path). /There are flowers on both sides of the walk. Tìuh louh léuhng·
bihn dōu haih fā.
      (act of walking). /It's a long walk from here to the station. Hái nī·syu heui chè·jahn
yiu hàahng hóu·noih háh.

take a walk, go for a walk hàahng·háh, saan·háh·bouh. /Let's go for a walk. Chēut·
heui hàahng·háh hóu ma? /I take a walk after supper every day. Ngóh múih·yaht sihk·
yùhn máahn·faahn dōu chēut·heui saan·háh·bouh.

in all walks of life gok·fòng·mihn ge yàhn, gok·gaai yàhn·sih (formal expression);
gok·hòhn·gok·yihp ge yàhn.

wall   chèuhng (M: buhng); (if it makes an enclosure) wàih·chèuhng (M: douh). /Who is
the man in the portrait hanging on the wall. Gwa·hái chèuhng·seuhng·bihn gó·fūk séung
haih bīn·go a?

wallet   hòh·bāau, ngàhn·bāau

walnut   hahp·tòuh

want   (desire) yiu. /I want a watch. Ngóh yiu yāt·go bīu. /I want to buy a watch. Ngóh
yiu máaih yāt·go bīu. /I want some more sugar. Ngóh juhng yiu dī tòhng tìm.
        (plan) séung. /I want to buy something for her birthday. Ngóh séung máaih dī yéh
sung béi kéuih jouh sàang·yaht.
        (asking a person for a favor) séung·chéng. /I want you to do me a favor. Ngóh
yáuh yāt·gihn sih séung·chéng néih bòng·mòhng·háh.
        a want kyut·faht. /After the war, there was terrible want in the world. Dá·yùhn
jeung jī·hauh māt·yéh dōu hóu kyut·faht.
        in want kùhng (poor). /That family has always been in want. Gó·gà yàhn sìh·sìh
dōu·haih gam kùhng ge la.

war   jin·jàng (M: chèuhng); **World War** sai·gaai daaih·jin. /After a long war the country
finally gained its independence. Gìng·gwo yāt·chèuhng chèuhng·gáu ge jin·jàng jī·hauh
gó·go gwok·gà jēut·jī bihn·sèhng yāt·go duhk·lahp ge gwok·gà.
        be at war dá·jeung. /Our country has been at war for five years. Ngóh·deih ge
gwok·gà yíh·gìng dá·jó ngh·nìhn jeung la.
        war news jin·sih sīu·sīk; **warplane** gwàn·yuhng·gēi (M: ga); **warship** jin·laahm (M:
ga); **wartime** jin·sìh; **war zone** jin·kèui

ward   (in hospital) behng·fóng, daaih·fóng. /I think we have to place him in a ward until
there's a private room. /Ngóh tái ngóh·deih jī·yáuh fong kéuih hái daaih·fóng sìn, dáng·
dou yáuh <u>dàan yàhn fóng</u> (or sī·gà·fóng) sìn·ji yáu kéuih bùn yahp·heui.
        (prevent, push off) dóng·jyuh. /He tried to ward off the blow with his arm, but he
was too slow. Kéuih si·háh yuhng sáu dóng·jyuh kéuih ge kyùhn·tàuh, daahn·haih yíh·
gìng taai chìh, lèih·m̀h·chit la. /They are trying to ward off the disaster. Kéuih·deih
jing·joih séung faat·jī dóng·gwo nī·chèuhng jòi·naahn.

wardrobe   sāam·gwaih, yì·gwaih

warden   (of a prison) dín·yuhk·jéung; (of a school) séh·gāam

ware   fo·maht. /The wares in that store are very dear. Gó·gàan pou·táu ge fo·maht
hóu·gwai.
        (utensils) -hei; **silverware** ngàhn·hei; **copperware** tùhng·hei; **chinaware** chìh·hei;
tinware sek·hei

warehouse   jaahn·fòhng; fo·chōng (godown)

warfare   -jin: **chemical warfare** fa·hohk·jin

warlike   hou·jin ge

warlord   gwàn·faht

warm   nyúhn. /It's not warm enough in this room. Nī·gàan fóng m̀h·gau nyúhn.
        (hot) yiht. /We were uncomfortably warm at the theater. Ngóh·deih hái gàan hei·
yún yahp·bihn yiht dāk hóu sàn·fú.
        warm up yiht. /The soup is cold, take it into the kitchen and warm it up. Dī tòng
dung·jó la, nīk yahp·heui chyùh·fóng yiht·háh kéuih là.

warn   gíng·gou. /We should put up a sign warning people that this bridge is dangerous. Ngóh·deih yiu gwa yāt·go pàaih gíng·gou dī hàahng·yàhn, nī·tìuh kìuh ngàih·hím.

warning   gíng·gou. /This is the second warning. Nī·go haih daih·yih chi gíng·gou la.

warrant   (for arrest) kèui·piu; (to attend court) chyùhn·piu.
   (guarantee) /This is warranted for a year. Nī·go bàau yuhng yāt·nìhn.
   (a fair cause) léih·yàuh. /You have no warrant to say such a thing. Néih móuh léih·yàuh góng dī gám ge syut·wah.

wash   sái. /Don't wash these clothes; they have to be dry-cleaned. M̀h·hóu sái nī·dī sāam, nī·dī sāam yiu gòn·sái ji·dāk.
   (carry, sweep) chùng. /The hard rain washed away the huts on the side of the hill. Daaih yúh jèung sāan·bīn géi·gàan muhk·ngūk·jái chùng·jó heui.
   washable sái·dāk ge; **washbasin** mihn·pún; **washboard** sái·sāam·báan; **wash clothes** sái·sāam; **washing machine** sái·sāam·gèi, sái·yī·gèi; **wash the face** sái·mihn; **wash the hands** sái·sáu

wasp   wòhng·fūng (M: jek)

waste   sàai. /Do not waste your paper. M̀h·hóu sàai dī·jí. /It's a waste of time to argue further. Joi ngaai·lohk·heui dōu móuh·yuhng ge la, jáan sàai sìh·gaan ge jē.
   (useless things) móuh·yuhng ge yéh. /We need someone to move away the waste. Ngóh·deih sèui·yiu yāt·go·yàhn lèih bùn·saai nī·dī móuh·yuhng ge yéh heui.
   wastepaper jih·jí; **wastepaper basket** jih·jí·lāp

watch   (keep looking at) tái·jyuh. /I like to watch a plane taking off. Ngóh hóu·jùng·yi tái·jyuh ga fèi·gèi héi·fèi.
   (mind, care for) hòn(·jyuh). /Watch my car, will you? Tùhng ngóh hòn·jyuh ga chè. /We need someone to watch our baby in the afternoon. Ngóh·deih hah·jau sèui·yiu yāt·go yàhn tùhng ngóh·deih hòn bìh·bī·jái.
   (look out for) hàu·jyuh. /The cat watched the door all day for a chance to steal into the house. Jek māau seng·yaht hàu·jyuh douh mùhn séung jáu·yahp gāan ngūk.
   (a turn to stand guard) gàang. /Everyone has to stand a watch; each watch is four hours. Múih·go yàhn dōu yiu hòn·gàang; múih sei·go jūng·tàuh yāt·gàang.
   (a timepiece) bīu, sáu·bīu. /Does your watch keep correct time? Néih go bīu jéun·m̀h·jéun a?
   watch out (be careful) gu·jyuh. /Watch out when you move that box of dynamite. Néih bùn gó·sèung ja·yeuhk ge sìh·hauh néih yiu gu·jyuh boh.
   watch out for (guard against) tàih·fòhng, gu·sàang. /You have to watch out for him; he is quite an operator. Néih yiu tàih·fòhng kéuih ji·dāk, kéuih hóu·dò fà·yéung ge.
   be on the watch for fòhng·beih. /The police were ordered to be on the watch for trouble tonight. Gíng·chaat yíh·gīng jip·dóu mihng·lihng fòhng·beih gàm·máahn yáuh·māt sih·gon faat·sàng ge la.

watchmaker   (one who repairs watches) jūng·bīu lóu

watchman   hòn·gàang ge

water   séui. /Please give me a glass of water. M̀h·gòi néih béi bùi·séui ngóh.
   (put water on) làhm. /Don't forget to water the flowers. M̀h·hóu m̀h·gei·dāk làhm·fā.
   by water (of travel) chóh·syùhn; yàuh séui·louh. /At this time of the year the only way you can get there is by water. Múih·nìhn nī·go sìh·hauh yùh·gwó néih séung heui gó·syu jí·yáuh <u>chóh·syùhn</u> (or yàuh séui louh) heui.

water buffalo   séui·ngàuh (M: jek)

water chestnut   máh·tái

water closet   séui·chi

watercolor   (a painting) séui·chói·wá. /Do you know how to paint in watercolor? Néih wúih waahk séui·chói·wá ma? /How much does this watercolor cost? Nǐ fūk séui·chói· wá géi·dò chín a?

waterfall   buhk·bou

waterfront   (land at the edge of a harbor or the part of a city on such land) hói·pèih

water level   (a leveling instrument) séui·pìhng; (water table) séui·pìhng·sin; (height of the surface of still water) séui·wái

watermelon   sài·gwà; **watermelon seeds** gwà·jí (M: nāp 'grain')

water polo   séui·kàuh

waterpower   séun·lihk

waterproof   m̀h·yahp·séui ge, fòhng·séui ge. /This hat is waterproof. Nǐ·déng·móu m̀h· yahp·séui ge.

wave   (in water) lohng, bò·lohng; **waves in a storm** fùng·lohng. /The waves were very rough this morning. Gàm·jìu·jóu lohng hóu daaih.

    to wave báai·sáu (with the hand); jìu·jín, pìu·yèuhng (as of a flag). /I waved twice but the taxi wouldn't stop. Ngóh báai·jó léuhng·chi sáu, daahn·haih ga dīk·sí m̀h·tìhng /The flags are waving in the breeze. Dǐ kèih chèuih fùng jiù·jín.

    wave (in the hair) bō; **wavelength** bō·chèuhng; **electrical waves** dihn·bó; **heat waves** yiht·lohng; **light waves** gwōng·bō; **long waves** chèuhng·bō; **short waves** dyún·bō; **sound waves** yām·bō, sìng·lohng

wax   laahp (N); dá·laahp (V); **wax paper** laahp·jí (M: jèung)

way   (route, path) louh. /Is this the right way to the airport? Nǐ·tìuh louh haih·m̀h·haih heui fèi·gèi·chèuhng ge louh a? /Which way do you think we should take? Néih wah ngóh·deih yìng·gòi hàahng bīn·tìuh louh ji·ngāam a?

    (distance) <u>is expressed with</u> yúhn (be far). /The village is still quite a way off. Gó· tìuh chyūn juhng yáuh hóu yúhn.

    (manner) yéung. /I don't like the way he acts (or looks). Ngóh m̀h·jùng·yi kéuih gám yéung.

    (means, method) faat·jí, fòng·faat. /We still haven't found a way of solving this problem. Ngóh·deih juhng méih séung·dóu go faat·jí lèih gáai·kyut nǐ·go mahn·tàih. /Can you find a way to get him here? Néih yáuh móuh faat·jí wán kéuih lèih a?

    across the way deui·mihn. /That store is just across the way from our school. Gó· gàan pou·táu jauh hái ngóh·deih gàan hohk·haauh deui·mihn jē.

    be in the way jó·jyuh. /Don't get in their way. M̀h·hóu jó·jyuh kéuih·deih.

    by the way waih. /By the way, are you going tonight? Waih, néih gàm·máahn heui· m̀h·heui a?

    by way of yàuh. /They came back by way of Europe. Kéuih·deih yàuh Ngàu·jàu fàan·lèih ge.

    by way of joking góng·síu jē. /He said it only by way of joking. Kéuih góng·síu jē.

    go out of one's way to jeuhn·lihk, gihk·lihk. /They indicated that they would go out of their way to help him get elected. Kéuih·deih bíu·sih kéuih·deih yiu jeuhn·lihk bòng· joh kéuih syún·géui.

    have a way with deui . . . hóu·yáuh·baahn·faat ge, hóu·wúih tam . . . ge. /She has a way with children. Kéuih deui sai·màn·jái hóu·yáuh·baahn·faat ge. <u>or</u> Kéuih hóu·wúih tam sai·màn·jái ge.

    in some ways, in a way. /His plan in some ways is better than the other one. Kéuih ge gai·waahk joih máuh·géi·fòng·mihn lèih·góng hóu gwo lihng·ngói gó·go. /In a way they are lucky to be here. Joih máuh·yāt·fòng·mihn lèih·góng kéuih·deih hóu·joih haih hái nǐ·syu.

    pay one's way jih·gēi béi·chín. /Let's each of us pay his own way; how about it? Gok·yàhn jih·gēi béi·chín, hóu ma?

this way gám·yéung; **that way** jing·wah gám·yéung, gó·yéung. /You should do it this way, not that way. Néih yiu gám·yéung jouh, m̀h·haih jing·wah gám·yéung jouh.

work one's way through. /He's working his way through college. Kéuih yìh·gā jih·gēi gùng kéuih jih·gēi duhk daaih·hohk.

we   ngóh·deih. /We must hurry or we shall be late. Ngóh·deih yāt·dihng yiu faai·dī, yeuhk·m̀h·haih jauh chìh la.

weak   (lacking strength) yeuhk, yúhn·yeuhk. /He was weak after his sickness. Kéuih behng·hauh sàn·jí hóu yeuhk.

   (not solid, frail) m̀h·gau·lihk. /This bridge is too weak to hold so many people. Nī tiuh kìuh m̀h·gau·lihk, m̀h·kéih·dāk gam dò yàhn.

   (not very good) m̀h·haih géi·hóu, chā·dī. /He is a little weak in history. Kéuih ge lihk·sí m̀h·haih géi·hóu.

   (diluted) táahm. /The soup is rather weak; don't add any water to it. Dī tòng yíh·gìng hóu·táahm la, m̀h·hóu gà séui la.

weakness   (a weak point) yeuhk·dím, dyún·chyúh

wealth   (riches) sàn·gà, chìhn·chòih. /He's a man of great wealth. Kéuih yáuh daaih·ba sàn·gà.

   (much, or a large amount) daaih·bá, hóu·dò. /He has a wealth of antiques. Kéuih yáuh daaih·bá gú·dúng.

wealthy   yáuh·chín; **a wealthy man** chòih·jyú·lóu; **wealthy and honored** yauh·fu·yauh·gwai; **wealthy and powerful** fu·kèuhng. /The United States is a wealthy and powerful country. Méih·gwok haih yāt go fu·kèuhng ge gwok·gà.

   become wealthy faat·choih. /Since he became wealthy, he moved away. Jih·chùhng kéuih faat·jó·chòih jì·hauh, kéuih jauh bùn·jó·heui daih·syu la.

wean   (to cause a child to stop suckling) gaai·náaih (VO). /How long since she was weaned? Kéuih gaai·jó·náaih géi·nói la?

weapon   móuh·hei: **atomic weapons** yùhn·jí·móuh·hei; (arms) gwàn·haaih; (used in criminal action) hùng·hei

wear   (for clothes, trousers, socks, boots) jeuk; (hat, cap, spectacles, pins, earrings, rings, wristwatch, gloves, bracelets) daai; (necklace, scarf, suspenders) laahm; (something tied, as neckties, belts) jaat. /What are you going to wear to dinner tonight? Néih gàm·máahn jeuk māt·yéh sāam heui sihk·faahn a? /This dress was meant for evening wear. is expressed as Nī·gihn·sāam haih máahn·táu jeuk ge.

   wear off gwo. /The effect of the drug will wear off in a couple of hours. Dī yeuhk·lihk léuhng·sàam·go jūng·tàuh jauh gwo ge la.

   wear out. /He wears his shoes out very fast. is expressed as Kéuih ge hàaih hóu·faai jauh laahn ge la. (His shoes are worn out very fast.)

   be worn out (fatigued) guih·séi, guih·dou·yiu·séi. /I'm completely worn out. Ngóh jàn·haih guih·séi la.

   (rub or be rubbed away) mòh. /The record is almost worn smooth. Go cheung·díp jauh·lèih mòh·dou pìhng la.

   (service) /This suit will give you good wear. Nī·tyut sāam néih hó·yíh jeuk hóu·noih.

   men's wear nàahm·yán sāam. /Does that store sell men's wear? Gó·gàan pou·táu maaih nàahm·yán sāam ma?

weather   tìn·hei; tìn·sih; **good weather** hóu·tìn. /What kind of weather will we have tomorrow? Tìng·yaht ge tìn·hei dím a? /If tomorrow's weather is not good, we had better not go. Yùh·gwó tìng·yaht tìn·hei (or tìn·sih) m̀h·hóu, ngóh·deih jeui·hóu m̀h·heui la. /In hot weather the grass grows especially fast. Tìn·sih yiht ge sìh·hauh dī chóu chèuhng·dāk dahk·biht faai. /They very seldom go out in cold weather. Tìn·sih láahng kéuih·deih hóu·siu chēut·gāai. /What do you do at home in rainy weather. Lohk·yúh tìn·sìh néih hái kéi jouh māt·yéh a? /We had good weather yesterday. Kàhm·yaht hóu tìn.

weave   jīk: **weave cloth** jīk·bou; **weave baskets** jīk·láam; **weave mats** jīk·jehk

web   (any woven fabric) móhng; (of a spider) kàhm·lòuh sī·mōng

wed   (to become married) git·fàn; **wedding** fàn·láih; (to take a wife) chéui; (to take a husband) ga. (see marry)

wedge   /Put a wedge under the door to keep it open. Dá·hòi douh·mùhn béi gauh muhk sip·jyuh kéuih.

Wednesday   láih·baai·sàam, sìng·kèih·sàam

weed   yéh·chóu (M: dī); **weed out the useless plants** màng·saai dī yéh·chóu kéuih; **weed out** (some useless elements) chìng·chèuih . . . ; **pull out the weeds** màng·chóu

week   láih·baai, sìng·kèih; **this week** nī·go láih·baai; **last week** seuhng·go láih·baai; **next week** hah·go láih·baai, daih·yih·go laih·baai; **weekend** jàu·muht; láih·baai·méih (used in Chinese community in North America); **weekly** múih·go láih·baai yāt·chi (once a week). /We pay it weekly. Ngóh·deih múih·go láih·baai béi yāt·chi (chín); jàu·hón (a magazine or paper). /We take two weeklies. Ngóh·deih dehng·jó léuhng·fahn jàu·hón. **weekly meeting** jàu·wúi

weep   haam. /Why is she weeping? Kéuih haam māt·yéh a?

weigh   bohng·háh; bohng·gwo. /Please weigh this package for me. M̀h·gòi néih tùhng ngóh bòhng·háh nī·go bàau·gwó géi chúhng. /Have you weighed yourself lately? Néih jeui·gahn yáuh·móuh bohng·gwo néih géi chúhng a? /Please weigh this piece of meat for me? M̀h·gòi néih bohng·háh nī·gauh yuhk géi chúhng?
      weigh a certain amount (yáuh) NU M. /This piece of meat weights three pounds. Nī·gauh yuhk sàam·bohng.
      weigh anchor (begin a voyage) hòi·sàn, hòi·syùhn
      weigh one's words háau·leuih. /He weighed his words carefully before answering. Kéuih háau·leuih·jó yāt·jahn·gāan sìn·ji daap·fūk.

weight   juhng·leuhng. /What is the weight of the new space ship? Nī·go sàn·ge taai·hùng·syùhn ge juhng·leuhng haih géi·dò a?
      (piece of metal used on a balance) faat·máh; (anything heavy) chúhng·ge·yéh. /Put a weight on it. Béi dī chúhng·ge·yéh jaahk·jyuh kéuih.
      gain weight chúhng, fèih; **lose weight** hèng, sau. /She said she wanted to lose some weight, but I'm thinking of gaining some. Kéuih wah kéuih séung hēng·dī (or sau·dī), daahn·haih ngóh séung ngóh chúhng·dī (or fèih·dī).

welcome   (act of welcoming) fùn·yìhng. /The students gave them a warm welcome when they came back. is expressed as Kéuih·deih fàan·dou·lèih ge sìh·hauh dī hohk·sāang yiht·liht fùn·yìhng. (When they returned the students welcomed them warmly.)
      (receive gladly) fùn·yìhng. /Welcome, welcome! Fùn·yìhng, fùn·yìhng! /Welcome (you, our honorable guest) to our school! Fùn·yìhng (néih) ga·làhm ngóh·deih hohk·haauh. /Welcome home again! Fàan·lèih la, fùn·yìhng, fùn·yìhng! /They welcomed us to the club. Kéuih·deih fùn·yìhng ngóh·deih gà·yahp gó·go wúi.
      (permitted) m̀h·sái haak·hei. /You are welcome to use my car. Néih géi·sí yiu yuhng [ngóh ge] chè, m̀h·sái haak·hei. (Whenever you want to use my car, please feel free.)
      (in answer to thanks offered) m̀h·sái haak·hei. /You are welcome. M̀h·sái haak·hei.
      welcome news hóu·sīu·sīk; **a party to welcome someone** fùn·yìhng·wúi

weld   hohn. /Weld the ends of the wires together. Jèung léuhng·tìuh sin·háu hohn·màaih kéuih.

welfare   fūk·leih: **social welfare** séh·wúi·fūk·leih

well   (in a good or desired way) hóu; tóh·dong; seuhn·dihm. /They do their work very
well. Kéuih·deih jouh·dāk hóu hóu. /He's doing very well in his business. Kéuih ge
sàang·yi jouh·dāk hóu hóu. Nī·gihn sih jouh·dak hou tóh·dong.
/Everything went well. Yeuhng·yeuhng dōu hóu seuhn·dihm.
    (thoroughly) /Stir it well before you fry it. Gáau·wàhn kéuih sìn·ji hóu jìn. /Chew
it well before you swallow it. Jiuh·laahn kéuih sìn·ji hóu tàn.
    (in good health) hóu. /Is your mother feeling well these days? Néih màh·mā nī·páai
(sàn·jí) géi hóu ma?
    (an introductory expression of a sentence) gám·àh. /Well, then I'll let you take care
of it by yourself. Gám·àh, néih jih·gēi gáau·dihm kéuih la.
    as well, as well as (in addition, in addition to) yihk . . . yihk, yauh. /She sings, and
she plays the piano as well. Kéuih yihk wúih cheung·gō yihk wúih tàahn·kàhm. /She
bought a hat as well as a new dress. Kéuih máaih·jó déng móu yauh máaih·jó gihn sāam.
    might as well bāt·yùh. /We might as well go back. Ngóh·deih bāt·yùh fàan·heui lo.
    a well jéng (for water); yàuh·jéng (an oil well)
    well dressed jeuk dāk hóu chàih·jíng, dá·baahn (for woman) dāk hóu chàih·jíng; **well
to do** hóu yáuh·chín, hóu fut·lóu; **well versed in** jìng·tùng. /He's well versed in the
Chinese classics. Kéuih jìng·tùng (Jùng·gwok·ge) gīng·sí. **well worth** dái. /It's well
worth it, indeed! Jàn·haih dái lo!

well known   chēut·méng (ge). /He's well known in the business world. Kéuih hái sèung·
yihp·gaai hóu chēut·méng ge.

west   sài: **southwest** sài·nàahm; **northwest** sāi·bāk. /You go west for two miles then
you'll see the bridge. Néih heung sài hàahng yih·léih jauh tái·gin tìuh kìuh la.
    (indicating a part or area) sài·bouh. /In the west the mountains are higher than they
are here. Sài·bouh ge sàan béi nī·syu ge gòu. /They live in the west part of the country.
Kéuih·deih jyuh·hái bún·gwok ge sài·bouh.
    (indicating an area beyond the border) sài·bihn, sài·bín; **to the west of** hái . . . ge
sài·bín. /To the west of this river is Chinese territory. Tìuh·hòh ge sài·bihn jauh·haih
Jùng·gwok ge deih·fòng la. /The little island is three miles west of the big one. Go
síu·dóu hái go daaih·dóu sài·bihn sàam·léih.

western   sài·bihn, sài·fòng ge; **westerner** sài·fòng·yàhn. /We lived in the western part
of the city. Ngóh·deih jyuh·hái sèhng ge sài·bihn. /The western countries seem still
not to understand oriental civilization very well. Sài·fòng ge gwok·gà juhng hóu·chíh
haih meih·haih géi líuh·gáai dùng·fòng ge màhn·fa.

westward   heung sài. /We should go westward. Ngóh·deih yiu heung sài hàahng.

wet   sāp. /The child wet his pants. Gó·go sài·mān·jái laaih·jó·niuh. /He wet the bed.
Kéuih laaih·sāp jèung chòhng.
    to wet jíng·sāp, put·sāp, etc., the main verb indicating the method used. /Wet it
with hot water. Yuhng yiht·séui jíng·sāp kéuih.

whale   kìhng·yùh (M: tìuh)

wharf   máh·tàuh

what   (used interrogatively) māt·yéh, mè·yéh. /What's the matter? Jouh māt·yeh a? or
Jouh māt sih·gon a? /What does he want? Kéuih yiu māt·yéh a? /What is your surname?
Néih sing māt·yéh a? or (polite) Gwai sing a? or Gòu sing a? /What is he doing? Kéuih
jouh gán māt·yéh a? /What is he doing here? Kéuih hái syu jouh māt·yéh a? /What did
he say? Keuih wah māt·yéh a? /What do you mean? Māt·yéh wá? /What does that mean?
Gám haih māt·yéh yi·si a? or Gám haih dím·gáai a? /What is that? Gó·go haih māt·yéh
a? /What is this called? Nī·go giu·jouh māt·yéh a? /What is your name? Néih giu mè·
yéh méng a? /What do you want for supper? Néih gàm·máahn séung sihk māt·yéh a?
/What's the quarrel about? Kéuih·deih jàang māt·yéh a?

     mãt. /What can I do for you? Yáuh mãt gwai·gon a? /What's the difference? Yáuh mãt fàn·biht a? /What's the good of it? Yáuh mãt hóu·chyúh a? /What for? Waih mãt sih·gon yiu gám a?

     dím. /What is the meaning of it? Dím·gáai a? /What is your opinion? Néih gok·dāk nī·gihn sih (yìng·fahn) dím nē? /What shall we do? Dím·syun a? /What then? Gám yauh dím a?

     géi. /What size does he wear? Kéuih jeuk géi dáai (or géi dò houh) ga? /What time is it now? Géi dím·jūng la? /What percentage? Géi·dò sìhng a?

     só (that which). /What he said is right. Kéuih só·góng·ge hóu·ngāam. /Give him all of what is left. Jihng jó gó·dī béi saai kéuih là. /What he has done is different from what we did. Kéuih só·jouh·ge·sih tùhng ngóh·deih só·jouh·ge m̀h·tùhng.

     (exclamation) mãt·yéh·wá. /What! Isn't he here yet? Mãt·yéh·wá! Kéuih juhng meih lèih? /What a pity! Jàn·haih hó·sīk la. /What? Mãt·yéh·wá? /What a beautiful day! Gàm·yaht tìn·sìh jàn·haih hóu la.

     what about dím a. /What about your children? Néih·dī sai·mān·jái dím a? /What about the other tooth? Néih gó·jek·ngàh dím a?

     what if yùh·gwó (or yeuhk·haih) . . . gám yauh dím a? /What if the train gets in late? Yùh·gwó ga fó·chè lèih·chìh·jó gám yauh dím a?

     what kind of dím·yéung ge. /What kind of a house are you looking for? Néih yiu wán gàan dím·yéung ge ngūk a?

     I'll tell you what gám là. /I'll tell you what; let's go to a movie tonight. Gám·là, gàm·máahn heui tái dihn·yíng hóu ma.

whatever   (anything that). /Eat whatever you want to eat. Néih jùng·yi sihk mãt jauh sihk mãt. /Do whatever you like. Néih jùng·yi dím maih dím lō.

     (no matter what) mòuh·leuhn dím·dōu. /Come, whatever happens. Mòuh·leuhn dím·dōu yiu lèih.

wheat   mahk

wheel   chē·lūk

when   (at what time) géi·sí, géi·sìh. /When will you come? Néih géi·sí lèih a? /When did you come? Néih géi·sí lèih ga? /When does he begin? Kéuih géi·sí héi·sáu (jouh) a? /When will it be finished? Géi·sí hó·yíh jouh·yùhn a?

     (at the time that) gó·jahn (sí), ge sìh·hauh. /I wasn't home when he called. Kéuih lèih taam ngóh gó·jahn·sí ngóh ngāam·ngāam m̀h·hái·kéi. /When the work is done, you can go. Néih jouh·yùhn (ge sìh·hauh) jauh hó·yíh jáu la.

     (although) kèih·saht. /He bought two cars when he needed but one. Kéuih màaih·jó léuhng·ga chè kèih·saht kéuih jí·haih sèui·yiu yāt·ga jē.

whenever   (when) géi·sìh, géi·sí. /Come to see us whenever you have time. Néih géi· sìh dāk·hàahn jauh lèih taam ngóh·deih lā.

     (any time that) mòuh·leuhn géi·sí; chèuih·sìh. /Whenever you ask him, he says no. Mòuh·leuhn géi·sí néih mahn kéuih kéuih dōu wah m̀h·dāk ge. /He may go home whenever his work is done. Mòuh·leuhn géi·sí kéuih jouh·yùhn jauh hó·yíh fàan ngūk·kéi la. /You may go there whenever you like. Néih hó·yíh chèuih·sìh heui.

where   (at or in what place) bīn·syu, bīn·douh. /Where do you live? Néih jyuh·hái bin· syu a? /Where's the airport? Fèi·gèi·chèuhng hái bīn·syu a?

     (to what place) heui bīn·syu, heui bīn·douh. /Where are you going? Néih heui bīn· syu a? /Where has he gone? Kéuih heui·jó bīn·syu a?

     (from what place) hái bīn·syu (or bīn·douh) lèih. /Where did you get those flowers? Néih gó·dī fā hái bīn·syu ló·lèih ga? /Where do you come from? Néih hái bīn·syu lèih ga?

     (at or in or to which) is expressed with ge. /The house where I used to live is on this street. Ngóh yíh·chìhn jyuh·gwo gó·gāan ngūk hái nī·tìuh gāai·syu. /The restaurant where we used to go was closed. Ngóh·deih yíh·chìhn sìh·sìh heui sihk·faahn gó·gàan jáu·gún yíh·gìng jāp·jó·lāp la.

wherever   bĭn·syu . . . bĭn·syu, bĭn·douh . . . bĭn·douh. /I'll go wherever you go. Néih
heui bĭn·syu, ngóh heui bĭn·syu.

whether   (not matter if) mòuh·leuhn . . . m̀h . . . /Whether you like it or not, I shall do
it. Mòuh·leuhn néih jùng·yi m̀h·jùng·yi ngóh dōu yiu gám jouh ge la.
    (if) haih·m̀h·haih. /I don't know whether he has gone out or not. Ngóh m̀h·jĭ kéuih
haih·m̀h·haih heui·jó gāai.

which   bĭn <u>plus a measure, or</u> dĭ. /Which one do you want? Néih yiu bĭn·go a? /Which
book do you want? Néih yiu bĭn·bún syù a? /Which house does he live in? Kéuih jyuh
bĭn·gāan ngūk a? /Which road should we take? Ngóh·deih yiu hàahng bĭn·tìuh louh a?
/Which kind do you like? Neih jùng·yi bĭn·tíng a? /Which style do you like? Néih jùng·
yi bĭn·go yéung ga? /Which books are yours? Bĭn·dĭ syù haih néih ga? /Which month?
Bĭn·go yuht a? /Which day? Bĭn·yaht a?
    daih·géi . . . /Which number is it? Daih·géi·houh a? /Which one in order? Daih·gei·
go a?
    <u>as a relative noun is expressed with</u> ge. /I think this is the book which you wanted
to read. Ngóh tái nī·bún jauh·haih néih yiu tái ge syù la. /Why don't you choose the one
you like best? Dím·gáai néih m̀h·gáan néih jeui jùng·yi gó·go nē?

while   (a time) yāt·jahn·gāan; (a little while); hóu noih (a long while). /He will be back
in a little while. Kéuih yāt·jahn·gāan jauh fàan·lèih la. /I have not seen him for a long
while. Ngóh hóu·noih móuh·gin kéuih la.
    (during the time that) . . . gó·jahn·sí, . . . ge sìh·hauh. /While we were eating he
came. Ngóh·deih sihk·gán·faahn gó·jahn·sí kéuih lèih ge. /While the students were
studying the teacher fell asleep. Dĭ hohk·sāang duhk·gán·syù ge sìh·hauh go sīn·sàang
fan·jeuhk·jó. /It happened a long while ago. Nī·gihn sih faat·sàng·jó hóu·noih lo.
    (temporarily) jaahm·sìh. /That is enough for a while. Jaahm·sìh gau yuhng la.
    (and yet, but, though) sèui·yîhn . . . , daahn·haih . . . . /While I admit his good points,
I can see his bad. Sèui·yîhn ngóh sìhng·yihng kéuih ge chèuhng·chyúh, daahn·haih ngóh
yihk tái·dóu kéuih ge dyún·chyúh. /While she spoke loudly, I didn't hear her. There was
too much noise in the theater. Yàn·waih hei·yún yahp·bihn hóu·chòuh, sèui·yihn kéuih
góng dāk hóu daaih·sèng [daahn·haih] ngóh móuh·faat·jí tèng·dóu kéuih góng māt·yéh.
    be worth one's while jihk·dāk. /Do you think it is worth your while to do it? Néih
gok·dāk nī·gihn sih jihk·dāk jouh ma? /It is quite worth while to see the new museum.
Nī·go sàn ge bok·maht·yún hóu jihk·dāk tái.
    once in a while gaan·jūng, gaan·waahk. /I go there once in a while. Ngóh gaan·jūng
heui·háh.
    to while away the time sìu·mòh·sìh·gaan. /How did you while away your time in the
summer? Néih [gàm·nín] hah·tìn ge sìh·hauh dím·yéung sìu·mòh néih ge sìh·gaan ga?

whip   (beat; strike) bîn; (a switch) bĭn (M: tìuh); (beat with a beater or a fork, etc.) faak

whirl   /The children whirled about the room. Dĭ sai·màn·jái hái gàan fóng·syu tàhm·
tám·jyun. /The boy whirled the rope about his head. Gó·go sai·màn·jái jèung tìuh síng
hái go tàuh·hok·déng seuhng·bihn tàhm·tám·jyun gám fihng.

whirlpool   syùhn·wò, séui·jyuhn

whirlwind   syùhn·fùng

whisk   hehng·hēng sou. /She whisked away the scraps of paper from her desk. Kéuih
hehng·hēng sou·jó·heui syù·tói seuhng·bihn gó·dĭ seui·jí.

whisker   sòu, wùh·sòu

whiskey   wài·sih·géi

whisper   sai·sái·sèng gám góng. /What are they whispering about? Kéuih·deih hái syu
sai·sái·sèng gám góng māt·yéh a?

whistle   (used by the policeman or used for calling for help) ngàhn·gāi; **blow a whistle**
chèui·ngàhn·gāi
       (make a sound like a whistle) chèui·háu

white   baahk; (white color) baahk·sīk. /Do you like the white one? Néih jùng·yi gó·go
baahk ge ma? /Would it be all right to wear white shoes? Jeuk baahk·hàaih dāk ma?
/I want all the walls painted white. Ngóh yiu gam·dò buhng chèuhng dōu yàuh·saai
baahk·sīk ge.
       the white (part of an egg) gài·daahn·chēng, gài·daahn·báak. /What do you need the
white of the eggs for? Néih yiu dī gài·daahn·chēng jouh māt·yéh a?
       white hair baahk·tàuh·faat; **White House** baahk·gùng; **whitewash** fùi·séui; **to white-
wash** yàuh·fùi·séui

who   bīn·go. /Who are you? Néih haih bīn·go a? /Who's that person? Gó·go yàhn haih
bīn·go a? /Who said that? Bīn·go gám wah a? /Who told you? Bīn·go góng néih jì ga?
       as relative pronoun is usually expressed with ge. /We want to hire a man who knows
how to run this machine. Ngóh·deih yiu chéng yāt·go wúih sái nī·go gèi·hei ge yàhn.
/Who is the man who just walked in? Jing·wah hàahng·yahp·lèih gó·go yàhn haih bīn·go
a?
       who would have thought séuih·jì, dím·jì, bīn·go wúih séung·dou. /Who would have
thought it would rain so hard! Sèuih·jì lohk·héi daaih·yúh séuhng·lèih. /Who would have
thought that he would resign! Bīn·go wúih séung·dou kéuih jàn·haih chìh·jīk gá!
       Who's Who mìhng·yàhn·lūk. /Do you have the latest edition of Who's Who? Néih
yáuh·móuh jeui·gahn chēut·báan ge mìhng·yàhn·lúk a?

whole   sèhng: **whole body** sèhng·sàn (or jàu·sàn, múhn·sàn); **whole book** sèhng·bún syù;
whole day sèhng·yaht; **whole face** sèhng·mihn; **whole family** sèhng·gà; **whole hour**
sèhng·dim·jūng; **whole morning** sèhng·jìu; **whole night** sèhng·máahn, sèhng·yeh; **whole
piece** sèhng·go; **whole room** sèhng·gàan·fóng; **whole street** sèhng·tìuh gāai, **whole year**
sèhng·nìhn
       chyùhn: **whole body of students** chyùhn·tái hohk·sāang; **the whole body of faculty and
staff** chyùhn·tái gaau·jīk·yùhn; **the whole body of the members** chyùhn·tái wúi·yùhn;
the whole city chyùhn·sèhng; **the whole city** (municipality) chyùhn·síh; **whole country**
chyùhn·gwok; **whole school** chyùhn·haauh; **whole world** chyùhn·sai·gaai
       a whole lot of hóu dò. /He ate a whole lot of candy this morning. Kéuih gàm·jìu·
jóu sihk·jó hóu dò tóng.
       on the whole daaih·ji·seuhng. /On the whole I agree with you. Daaih·jì·seuhng ngóh
tùhng·yi néih ge yi·gin.

wholesale   pài·faat. /He's in the wholesale business. Kéuih jouh pài·faat sàang·yi.

wholly   yùhn·chyùhn, jyuht·deui. /The decision is wholly up to you. Nī·gihn sih yùhn·
chyùhn yàuh néih kyut·dihng. /This is wholly out of the question. Nī·gihn sih jyuht·deui
baahn·m̀h·dou (or m̀h·baahn·dāk·dou).

whom   bīn·go. /Whom are you looking for? Néih wán bīn·go a? /Whom should I speak
to? Ngóh yiu tùhng bīn·go góng a?

whooping-cough   gāi·kāt, baak·yaht·kāt

whore   (prostitute) lóuh·géui

whose   bīn·go ge. /Whose pen is this? Nī·jī bāt bīn·go ga? /Whose is this? Nī·go haih
bīn·go ga? /Whose house is that? Gó·gāan ngūk haih bīn·go ga?

why   jouh·māt·yéh, waih·māt·sih, dím·gáai. /Why didn't he come? Jouh·māt·yéh keuih
móuh·lèih a? /Why were you late? Waih·māt·sih néih lèih·chìh·jó a? /I don't see why
you don't come with us. Ngóh m̀h·jì·dou dím·gáai néih m̀h·tùhng ngóh·deih yāt·chái heui.

wick   (of lamp) dāng·sàm; (of candle) laahp·jūk·sàm

wicked   (malevolent) hāk·sàm (ge). /He's a wicked man. Kéuih nī·go yàhn hóu hāk·sàm
ge.

wide   fut. /Is it wide enough? Gau fut meih a? **wide apart** gak·dāk hóu yúhn. /The two
poles are wide apart; you need a longer rope. Gó·léuhng·tìuh chyúh gak·dāk hóu·yúhn,
néih yiu tìuh chèuhng dī ge sing sìn·ji dāk.

widen   jíng·fut

widow   gwá·fúh, gwá·móuh·pó; **remain a widow** sáu·gwá (VO). /She has been a widow
for ten years now. Kéuih yíh·gìng sáu·jó sahp·nìhn·gwá la.

widower   sāt·fàn. /He has been a widower for ten years. Kéuih yíh·gìng sāt·fàn sahp·
nìhn la.

wife   lóuh·pòh; taai·táai, fù·yán (polite)

wig   gá·(tàuh·)faat

wild   **wild animal** yéh·sau; **wild country** fòng·yéh, fòng·sàan·yéh·léhng; **wild flowers**
yéh·fā

wilderness   kwong·yéh, fòng·yéh

will   (indicating future time) jauh·lèih; yāt·dihng. /He will be here soon. Kéuih jauh·
lèih lèih·dou la. /I will let you know. Ngóh yāt·dihng tùng·jì néih. Sometimes it is not
translated, such as: /I will not go to New York tomorrow. Ngóh tìng·yaht m̀h·heui
Náu·yeuk. /Will you do it? Néih jouh·m̀h·jouh a? /It will not do. Gám m̀h·dāk. /It
will do. Dāk·la. /Will you please . . . M̀h·gòi néih . . . /Will you please send my best
regards to him? M̀h·gòi néih tùhng ngóh mahn·hauh kéuih.
    (denoting capacity or ability) hó·yíh; nàhng·gau. /This theater will hold a thousand
people. Nī·gàan hei·yún hó·yíh chóh yāt·chìn yàhn. /The cat will go for days without
drinking water. Jek māau nànhg·gau géi·yaht m̀h·yám·séui.
    will something **to** hái wàih·jūk seuhng sé·jyuh jèung . . . gàau béi . . . /He willed
all his property to the hospital. Kéuih hái wàih·jūk seuhng sé·jyuh jèung kéuih ge
cháan·yihp yùhn·chyùhn gàau·saai·béi yì·yún.
    as . . . **will.** /You may do as you will. Néih jùng·yi dím jauh dím. but /We'll have
to do as he wills. Kéuih dím wah ngóh·deih jauh yiu dím jouh.
    a will wàih·jūk. /Does he have a will? Kéuih yáuh·móuh wàih·jūk a?

willfully   (intentionally) dahk·dāng, jyūn·dāng

willing   háng. /Is he willing to do so? Kéuih háng gám jouh ma?

willingly   sàm·gàm·chìhng·yuhn. /He finished the job willingly. Kéuih sàm·gàm chìhng·
yuhn jouh·sèhng jó nī·gihn sih.

willow   láuh·syuh, yèuhng·láuh (M: pò)

wily   gwái·máh (ge)

win   yèhng. /Which team do you think will win? Néih wah bīn·yāt·deui wúih yèhng a?
/The two of them like betting each other and he always wins. Kéuih·deih léuhng·go hóu
jùng·yi syù·dóu, daahn·haih géi·sí dōu haih kéuih yèhng ge.
    (attain) dāk·dóu. /They hope they will win the first prize in the contest. Kéuih·deih
hèi·mohng nī·chi béi·choi hó·yíh dāk·dóu tàuh·jéung.
    win a battle or victory dá·yèhng (jeung), dá·sing (jeung). /The war will be over if
they win this battle. Yùh·gwó kéuih·deih dá·yèhng nī·chèuhng jeung, jin·sih jauh wúih
git·chūk ge la.
    win a prize in lottery jung. /He won the first prize (in the lottery). Kéuih jung·jó
tàuh·jéung.
    win money in gambling yèhng·chín. /He won two hundred dollars last night playing
mahjong. Kéuih kàhm·máahn dá·màh·jéuk yèhng·jó léuhng·baak·màn.

wind   fùng; **against the wind** ngahk·fùng; **with the wind** seuhn·fùng. /The wind is stiff;
it makes it difficult for the boat to reach the shore. Yîh·gā fùng hóu máahng jek syùhn
hóu nàahn kaau·ngohn.
   get wind of tèng·dóu dò·síu . . . ge sīu·sīk. /He said yesterday he'd already got wind
of the sharp decline of the stock market. Kéuih wah kàhm·yaht kéuih jauh yíh·gîng tèng·
dóu dò·síu gú·piu yiu dit·ga ge sīu·sīk la.
   get winded hei·chyún. /He's not a good swimmer because he gets winded easily.
Kéuih yàuh·(séui·yàuh) dāk m̀h·haih géi·hóu jē, yàn·waih kéuih taai yùhng·yih hei·chyún.

wind   (of a spring) séuhng·lín. /I forgot to wind my watch. Ngóh go bīu m̀h·gei·dāk
séuhng·lín.
   (wrap or twine around) jaat; jihn. /Don't wind the bandage too tight. Tîuh bàng·dáai
m̀h·hóu jaat dāk taai gán. /Wind up the rope. Jihn·hóu tîuh síng kéuih.
   wind up a business git·chūk; liuh·léih. /He plans to wind up his business at the end
of this year. Kéuih dá·syun gàm·nín nìhn·dái git·chūk kéuih nī·pùhn sàang·yi. /He has
two weeks to wind up his affairs before entering the army. Kéuih yahp·ngh jî·chîhn
yáuh léuhng·go láih·baai ge sìh·gaan liuh·léih kéuih go·yàhn ge sî·sih.
   wind up a speech jauh yiu góng·yùhn la; git·chūk. /I thought he was winding up his
speech half an hour ago. Ngóh yíh·wàih kéuih bun·dím·jūng yíh·chîhn jauh yiu góng·yùhn
la. /He should have wound up his speech half an hour ago. Kéuih bun·dím·jūng yíh·
chîhn jauh yìng·gòi git·chūk kéuih nī·pìn yín·chîh ge la.
   winding lyūn·kūk ge, lyūn·lyūn kūk·kūk ge. /That is a very winding road. Gó·tîuh
lóuh hóu lyūn·kūk ge.

windmill   fūng·chē

window   chēung·mún

windpipe   hei·gún (M: tîuh)

wine   jáu

wing   (of a bird or plane) yihk (M: jek)

wink   jáam·ngáahn. /He winked at me, seeming to tell me to follow him. Kéuih tùhng
ngóh jáam·háh·ngáahn hóu·chíh giu ngóh gàn·jyuh kéuih hàahng.

winnow   bo·gēi (N); sàai (V)

winter   láang·tīn, dūng·tīn; **winter season** dùng·gwai; **winter solstice** dùng·ji; **winter
vacation** hòhn·ga

wipe   maat. /Have you wiped the table? Néih maat·jó tói meih a?
   (make a thing dry) maat·gòn. /Wipe these dishes. Maat·gòn nī·dī díp kéuih.
   (rub away or off) maat·lāt. /Can you wipe it off? Maat·m̀h·maat·dāk lāt a?
   wipe it clean maat·gòn·jehng. /Use some soap to wipe it clean. Yuhng dī fàan·gáan
maat·gòn·jehng kéuih.

wire   (electric) dihn·sin (M: tîuh); (iron or zinc) tit·sín (M: tîuh); (copper) tùhng·sín (M:
tîuh); (steel) gong·sín (M: tîuh)
   (put electric wires in) ngòn dihn·sin. /Have you wired the garage yet? Chè·fòhng
ngòn jó dihn·sin meih a?
   (a telegraph message) dihn·bou. /I've already sent in the order by wire. Ngóh yíh·
gîng dá·jó dihn·bou heui dehng·fo la.
   (send a message by telegraph) dá·dihn·bou. /I've already wired our general office
in New York. Ngóh yíh·gîng dá·jó dihn·bou béi Náu·yeuk júng·gūng·sī la.

wireless   mòuh·sin·dihn: **wireless station** mòuh·sin·dihn·tòih; **wireless telegraph**
mòuh·sin·dihn·bou

wisdom   ji·waih

wise   chùng·mìhng

wish   (want, want to) hèi·mohng, héi·mohng yiu, séung·yiu. /I wish I could stay here longer. Ngóh hèi·mohng ngóh nàhng·gau hái syu jyuh noih·dī daahn·haih m̀h·dāk. /What do you wish for most? Néih <u>jeui hèi·mohng</u> (or jeui·séung) yiu māt·yéh a? /I wish we had a dog. Ngóh hèi·mohng ngóh·deih yáuh jek gáu jauh hóu la. /I wish to buy a piano. Ngóh séung yiu máaih yāt·go gong·kàhm.

(in giving an order) chéng. /I wish you would come on time tomorrow morning. Ngóh chéng néih tìng·jìu·jóu yì·jiu sìh·gaan lèih.

(expressing hope to a person for something pleasant). /I wish you a happy birthday. Tùhng néih hoh·sauh. /We wish you luck. Jūk néih sih·sih·yùh·yi.

(an expressed desire) yuhn·mohng; <u>or often verbally.</u> /Her wish of studying abroad came true. Kéuih yiu chēut·yèuhng làuh·hohk ge yuhn·mohng saht·yihn la. <u>or</u> Kéuih hèi·mohng chēut·yèuhng làuh·hohk yìh·gā gwó·yìhn saht·yihn la.

wit   gèi·gíng. /He has all his wits about him. Kéuih go yàhn hóu gèi·gíng ge.

witchcraft   chèh·seuht

with   (accompanying; going together) tùhng, tùhng·màaih. /I disagree with you. Ngóh tùhng néih ge yi·gin m̀h·tùhng. /Who is going to go with us? Bīn·go tùhng·màaih ngóh·deih yāt·chái heui a? /Are you going with me? Néih haih·m̀h·haih tùhng·màaih ngóh yāt·chái heui a? /Can you have lunch with me today? Néih (gàm·yaht) ngaan·jau hó·yìh tùhng ngóh yāt·chái sihk·faahn ma? /Whom did he quarrel with? Kéuih tùhng bīn·go ngaai·gāau a?

(having) yáuh, daai. /I want a room with bath. Ngóh yiu yāt·gàan yáuh sái·sàn·fóng ge (fóng). /I have no money with me. Ngóh móuh daai·chín.

(using as an instrument) yuhng. /I haven't learned to eat with chopsticks. Ngóh juhng meih·wúih yuhng faai·jí sihk. /You can cut it with a knife. Néih hó·yíh yuhng dōu·jái chit·hòi kéuih.

(including) lìhn. /The price of gasoline is thirty cents a gallon with tax. Dihn·yàuh ge ga·chìhn haih sàam·hòuh·jí yāt·gà·léun lìhn seui.

(because of) yàn·waih. /I went home with a cold. Ngóh yàn·waih yáuh·dī sèung·fùng só·yíh fàan·jó ngūk·kéi. /The price of television went up with the increasing demand. Yàn·waih máaih ge yàhn dò·jó, só·yíh dī dihn·sih ge ga·chìhn yauh héi·jó.

(despite) sèui·yìhn. /With all the work he's done on it, the lawn is still full of fallen leaves. Sèui·yìhn kéuih jouh·jó hóu·dò gùng·fù la, daahn·haih chóu·déi seuhng·bihn juhng·haih bāt·jì géi·dò lohk·yihp.

with each other béi·chí jī·gāan. /The two countries were at war with each other for many years. Nī léuhng gwok béi·chí jì·gāan dá·jó hóu·dò·nìhn jeung la.

be pleased with fùn·héi. /Are you pleased with the view from your windows? Néih fùn·héi néih chēung·mún ngoih·bihn ge fùng·gíng ma?

leave . . . with gàau·béi; jài·hái. /You can leave your child with her. Néih hó·yíh jèung néih go sai·mān·jái gàau·béi kéuih tùhng néih chau. /You can leave your key with the hotel clerk. Néih hó·yíh jèung tìuh só·sìh jài·hái léuih·gún ge gwaih·mín·syu.

with one's own . . . chàn—: . . . <u>eyes</u> chàn·ngáahn; . . . <u>hands</u> chàn·sáu; . . . <u>mouth</u> chàn·háu. /He said he saw it with his own eyes. Kéuih wah kéuih chàn·ngáahn tái·gin ge.

with all of one's strength jeuhn·lihk, cheut·jeuhn·lihk. /He pushed the door with all of his strength. Kéuih jeuhn·lihk ngúng douh·mùhn.

with the exception of cheuih·jó . . . jī·ngoih. /They all know how to swim with the exception of him. Chèuih·jó kéuih jī·ngoih, kéuih·deih go·go dōu wúih yàuh·séui.

with high speed. /The ambulance drove to where the accident had taken place with high speed. Ga gau·sèung·chē jeuhn·faai hòi·heui chēut·sih ge deih·dím.

with the whole heart jeuhn·sàm. /He has always supported our church with his whole heart. Kéuih yāt·heung dōu sahp·fàn jeuhn·sàm wàih·chìh ngóh·deih ge gaau·wúi.

withdraw (take back) sàu·wùih, sàu·fàan. /The publisher withdrew that book from circulation. /Go chēut·báan·gā yíh·gìng jèung gó·bún syù sàu·wùih.

withdraw from business tìhng·yihp; **withdraw from a race** tèui·chēut béi·choi; **withdraw (troops) from a position** chit·teui, yàuh . . . chit·teui; **withdraw a motion** chit·wùih duhng·yi, jèung tàih·yi chit·wùih; **withdraw the hand** sūk·faan·màaih jek sáu

wither (of flower) jeh, chàahn; (of plant) kù

within (inside) yahp·bihn, leuih·bihn. /The dog is hiding within the house. Jek gáu nī·màaih·hái gāan ngūk yahp·bihn.
(not beyond) jī·noih, yìh·noih. /I'll be back within an hour. Ngóh yāt·go jùng·tàuh jī·noih jauh fàan·lèih. /This house will be torn down within a year. Nī·gāan ngūk yāt·nìhn yìh·noih jauh yiu chaak la.

without (not having) móuh. /You can't get there without a boat. Yùh·gwó néih móuh syùhn m̀h·heui·dāk gó·syu. /She passed without seeing us. Kéuih hàahng·gwo móuh tái·gin ngóh·deih.
without a break yāt·hei. /He worked for six hours without a break. Kéuih yāt·hei jouh jó luhk·go jūng·tàuh móuh·tìhng·gwo.
without ceasing m̀h·tìhng, bāt·hit. /He talked for two hours without ceasing. Kéuih m̀h·tìhng gám góng·jó léuhng·go jūng·tàuh.
without delay gón·gán; máh·seuhng. /I want this suit made without delay. Nī·gihn sāam ngóh yiu gón·gán jouh·héi kéuih. /Send this letter out without delay. Nī·fùng seun yiu máh·seuhng sung·chēut·heui.

withstand (stand against) dóng·jyuh; (resist) dái·kong; (oppose) fáan·kong

witness (see) chàn·ngáahn tái·gin. /I witnessed the fight between them. Ngóh chàn·ngáahn tái·gin kéuih·deih léuhng·go dá·héi·sèuhng·lèih.
(testify to having seen) jouh·gin·jing·yàhn. /They want me to witness the signing of the contract. Kéuih·deih yiu ngóh jouh nī·go hahp·yeuk (or hahp·tùhng) ge gin·jing·yàhn.
(a person) jing·yàhn, gin·jing·yàhn. /Can you find a witness to testify for you? Néih hó·m̀h·hó·yíh wán·dóu go jing·yàhn lèih tùhng néih jouh·jing a?

wolf chàaih·lòhng, lóng (M: jek)

woman néuih·yán; in compound néuih—. /Who is that woman? Gó·go néuih·yán haih bīn·go a? /We need a woman doctor. Ngóh·deih sèui·yiu yāt·go néuih·yī·sāng.

womb jí·gùng

wonder (strange, wonderful things) kèih·jīt. /Have you seen all the seven wonders of the world? Sai·gaai·seuhng chāt daaih kèih·jīt néih tái·gwo·saai meih a?
wonder why m̀h·jī·dím·gáai; m̀h·mìhng·baahk. /I wonder why he doesn't call me up. Ngóh m̀h·jī·dím·gáai kéuih m̀h·dá·dihn·wá béi ngóh. /I wonder why he spent that much money buying this hat. Ngóh m̀h·mìhng·baahk kéuih waih māt·sih sái gam·dò·chín maaih nī·déng móu.
no wonder m̀h·gwaai·dāk. /No wonder it's cold in here, the window is open. M̀h·gwaai·dāk gàan fóng gam láahng là, yùhn·lòih go chēung·mún dá·hòi·jó.

won't m̀h. /I won't blame you. Ngóh m̀h·gwaai néih.

wood muhk (M: gauh); **firewood** chàaih (M: dī); **woods** syuh·làhm (M: go)

woodcut muhk·hāk

wooden (made of wood) muhk·ge, muhk·tàuh jouh ge

woodpecker deuk·muhk·níuh (M: jek)

wool yèuhng·mòuh

woolen (made of wool) yèuhng·mòuh ge; **woolen blanket** yèuhng·mòuh·jīn (M: jèung); (of or relating to woolen cloth) yúng·ge; **woolen cloth** yúng

word   jih. /How do you write this word? Nī·go jih dím sé a? /How do you spell that
word? Gó·go jih dím·yéung chyun a?

(meaning message or speech) syut·wah, wá. /Did he leave any word? Kéuih yáuh·
móuh làuh·dài māt·yéh syut·wah a? /May I have a word with you? Ngóh yáuh geui syut·
wah tùhng néih góng háh. or Ngóh séung tùhng néih góng geui syut·wah. /She didn't
say a word. Kéuih yāt geui syut·wah (or wá) dōu móuh góng.

(message other than oral: letter) seun. /Have you had any word from your son
lately? Nī·páai néih ge jái yáuh móuh seun fàan·lèih a?

beyond words góng·m̀h·chēut. /The palace is beautiful beyond words. Gó·go wòhng·
gùng góng·m̀h·chēut gam·leng.

give one's word wah·gwo. /He gave his word that he would finish the job. Kéuih
wah·gwo yāt·dihng jèung nī·jihn sih jouh·yùhn.

put in a good word góng geui hóu wá. /He wants me to put in a good word for him
with his boss; I think it's quite difficult. Kéuih séung ngóh hái kéuih lóuh·báan mihn·
chìhn góng geui hóu·wá, Ngóh tái hóu·nàahn.

to word chou·chìh. /How do you want to word the telegram? Nī·fùng dihn·bou dím·
yéung chou·chìh a?

work   (general or of brain work) jouh·sih, jouh; (public or government work) baahn·gùng;
(of physical labor) jouh·gùng, jouh. /Where is he working? Kéuih hái bīn·syu jouh·sih
a? /We work forty hours a week. Ngóh·deih yāt·go láih·baai jouh sei·sahp go jūng·tàuh.
/How many days do you work in your office, five days or six? Néih·deih yāt·go láih·
baai baahn géi·dò yaht gùng a? ńgh·yaht yīk·waahk luhk·yaht a? /Is he working? Kéuih
yáuh·móuh jouh·gùng a? (compare /Does he have a job? Kéuih yáuh·móuh gùng jouh
a?) /They work seven days a week. Kéuih·deih yāt·go láih·baai jouh·jūk chāt·yaht. /Is
your wife still working? Néih lóuh·pòh (only be used to workers, etc.) juhng jouh·sih
ma? /She has not been working recently. Kéuih nī·páai móuh jouh·sih.

work oneself. /Don't work yourself too hard. Néih m̀h·hóu jouh dāk taai sàn·fú.

work hard at something yuhng·sàm. /He really worked hard at his studies. Kéuih
hóu yuhng·sàm duhk·syù.

work loose sung. /A screw worked loose. Yáuh go lòh·sī sùng·jó.

work on a book jouh, sé. /He is working on a book. Kéuih yìh·gā jouh·gán yāt·bún·
syù.

work on something (repair) sàu·jíng, sàu·léih. /They're working on your car now.
Kéuih·deih yìh·gā sàu·jíng·gán néih ga chè la.

work out a plan. /They are working out a plan to solve this problem. Kéuih·deih
jing·joih jouh·gán yāt·go gai·waahk lèih gáai·kyut nī go mahn·tàih.

work out a solution séung·chēut go baahn·faat lèih gáai·kyut. /We hope you can
work out a solution for this problem. Ngóh hèi·mohng néih·deih nàhng·gau séung·chēut
go baahn·faat lèih gáai·kyut nī·go mahn·tàih.

work something **over** joi . . . /I hope you work your speech over a couple of times.
Ngóh hèi·mohng néih jèung néih ge yín·góng·chìh joi jàm·jeuk yāt·léuhng·chi.

work one's way through college. /He plans to work his way through college. Kéuih
dá·syun gùng kéuih jih·gēi duhk daaih·hohk.

work something **with one's hands** yuhng sáu . . . : jēut (to rub); chàai (to knead
dough, clay, etc.); chò (to roll or shape)

work (general, but especially brain work) sih; gùng·jok;(physical labor) gūng. /What
kind of work do you do? Néih yìh·gā jouh·gán māt·yéh sih a? /Where does he work?
Kéuih hái bīn·syu jouh·gūng a? /He's doing government work. Kéuih yìh·gā jouh (or
dá) jing·fú·gūng.

work of art. /That's a work of art. (a general statement) Gó·go haih yāt·gihn ngaih·
seuht·bán. (The following expressions refer specifically to different areas of creative
work.) Gó·gihn yéh jouh·dāk (or, of composing or writing, jok·dāk, sé·dāk; or, of calligraphy, sé·dāk; or, of painting, waahk·dāk; of carving, hāk·dāk; etc.) hóu hóu.

a nice piece of work. /That bridge is a nice piece of work. Gó·tìuh kìuh héi·dāk
hóu·hóu.

be out of work móuh·sih·jouh; móuh·gūng·jouh. /He has been out of work for two months now. Kéuih yíh·gìng móuh·sih·jouh léuhng·go·yuht la.

do light work. /After he has completely recovered, he may do some light work to start with. Kéuih yùhn·chyùhn hóu·fàan jì·hauh, kéuih hó·yíh hòi·sáu jouh dī hèng·chèhng ge sih.

take a lot of work. /It took a lot of work to get it done. Yuhng·jó hóu daaih sàm·gèi sìn·ji jouh·sèhng nī·gihn sih.

worker   (a person who works for wages, especially in a factory) gùng·yàhn

workmanship   sáu·gùng

world   (the earth) sai·gaai; (the globe) deih·kàuh   **the whole world** chyùhn sai·gaai, (all mankind) sai·gaai·seuhng só·yáuh ge yàhn, yàhn·leuih; **world power** kèuhng·gwok, sai·gaai·seuhng ge kèuhng·gwok; **World War I** daih·yāt·chi sai·gaai daaih·jin; **World War II** daih·yih·chi sai·gaai·daaih·jin. /Do you want to travel around the world? Néih séung wàahn·yàuh sai·gaai ma? /Next year we'll study world history. Hah·hohk·kèih ngóh·deih duhk sai·gaai·lihk·sí. /He is the world heavy weight boxing champion. Kéuih haih sai·gaai juhng·kāp kyùhn·wòhng.

business world sèung·gaai; **industrial world** gùng·yihp·gaai; **the scholastic world** hohk·seuht·gaai; **the occidental world** sài·fòng gwok·gà, sài·fòng gok·gwok; **the oriental world** dùng·fòng gwok·gà, dùng·fòng gok·gwok; **world famous** sai·gaai màhn·mìhng ge; sai·gaai chìh·mìhng ge

worm   chùhng (M: tìuh)

worry   dàam·sàm; (sàm·)fàahn; gwa·jyuh; sàm·gāp. /You worry too much! Néih taai· gwo dàam·sàm la! /What are you worrying about? Néih fàahn dī māt·yéh a? or Néih jouh·māt gam sàm·faahn a? (inquisitive); or Néih sái·māt gam sàm·fàahn a! (admonishing). /She worries a lot about her children. Kéuih sìh·sìh gwa·jyuh kéuih dī sai·màn·jái. /We were worried when you didn't get there on time. Néih móuh yì·sìh heui·dou gó·syu, ngóh·deih m̀h·jì géi sàm·gāp. /We were worried (about your safety) when you didn't get there on time. Néih móuh yì·sìh heui·dou gó·syu, ngóh·deih m̀h·jì géi dàam·sàm.

worry (anxiety) yàuh·leuih; gu·leuih; or expressed verbally as above. /The more money he has the more worries he gathers. Kéuih dī chín yuht dò kéuih ge yàuh·leuih (or gu·leuih) yuht dò. /Quit worrying! Neih m̀h·sái gam yàuh·leuih ge!

worse   juhng SV gwo . . . /This typhoon is worse than the one we had last month. Nī chèuhng daaih·fùng juhng gán·yiu·gwo seuhng·go·yuht gó·chi. /The quality of this oil is worse than what we bought last time. Nī·jek yàuh ge jāt·déi juhng yáih·gwo ngóh· deih seuhng·chi máaih gó·jek.

get worse or **worse and worse** yuht·lèih·yuht SV. /His condition got worse and worse. Kéuih ge chìhng·yìhng yuht·lèih·yuht yáih. /The patient felt worse this morning than he did last night. Go behng·yàhn gok·dāk gàm·jiu·jóu juhng sàn·fú·gwo kàhm·máahn.

worship   baai: **to worship ancestors** baai·jou·sin; **to worship an ancestor at the tomb** baai·sàan; **to worship Buddha** baai·pòh·saat, baai·faht; **to worship Heaven and Earth** baai·tìn·deih; **to worship the Spirit** baai·sàhn

worst   jeui·yáih (in quality); jeui·baih (in degree). This is the worst kind of orange produced here. Nī·dī haih bún·deih chēut·cháan ge jeui·yáih ge cháang. /The worst of it is that their car is not insured. Jeui·baih ge haih kéuih·deih ga chè móuh máaih·dou yin·sō.

worth   (of a commodity) jihk. /How much is that horse worth? Gó·pāt máh jihk géi·dò chín a? /It isn't worth a penny. Yāt·go·sīn dōu m̀h·jihk.

(value) ga·jihk. /The real worth of this painting is not its beauty. Nī·fūk wá ge jàn· jing ge ga·jihk m̀h·haih kéuih waahk·dāk dím·yéung hóu.

so much money's **worth** of something NU M ge. /Give me forty cents' worth of pea-nuts. Béi sei·hòuh·jí ge fā·sāng ngóh.

get one's money's worth V fàan·gau·bún. /We certainly got our money's worth out of our car. Ngóh·deih ga chē jàn·haih yuhng·fàan gau·bún la. /I certainly got my money's worth out of my pen. Ngóh nī·jī bāt jàn·haih sái·fàan gau·bún la.

worth seeing jihk·dāk tái. /Is that picture worth seeing? Gó·chēut dihn·yíng jihk·dāk tái ma?

worthless   móuh ga·jihk ge

worthwhile   jihk·dak. /It's worthwhile. Hóu jihk·dāk.

worthy   yáuh·yi·yih ge. /He leads a worthy life. Kéuih sàng·wuht dāk hóu yáuh·yi·yih. /This money is solicited for a worthy cause. Nī·bāt·chín haih gyùn·lèih jouh yāt·gihn hóu yáuh·yi·yih ge gùng·jok ge.

would   nàhng (·gau); or not expressed. /I wish he would come tomorrow. Ngóh hèi·mohng kéuih tìng·yaht nàhng·gau lèih. /I would go swimming every day if I had time. Yùh·gwó ngóh yáuh sìh·gaan ngóh yaht·yaht heui yàuh·séui.
    (to express a condition). /I would tell you if I knew. Yùh·gwó ngóh jī ngóh yāt·dihng góng béi néih tèng.
    (to express willingness) yuhn·yi. /He wouldn't take the job for any amount of money. Kéuih géi·dò chín dōu m̀h·yuhn·yi jouh nī·gihn sih.
    (to show something that went on regularly for some time) sìh·sìh. /He would study for hours without stopping. Kéuih sìh·sìh duhk·syù yāt·duhk·jauh·duhk géi·go jūng·tàuh m̀h·tìhng ge.
    (to make a request) m̀h·gòi. /Would you close the door for me? M̀h·gòi néih tùhng ngóh sàan·màaih douh mùhn. /Would you please give me a cup of tea? M̀h·gòi néih béi bùi chàh ngóh.
    (wish) séung. /I would that I lived in the country. Ngóh séung jyuh·hái hèung·háh.
    would like to séung yiu, séung. /What would you like to drink? Néih séung yiu yám dī māt·yéh a?
    would you kindly tell me . . . Chéng·mahn . . . /Would you kindly tell me how far the airport is from here? Chéng·mahn fèi·gèi·chèuhng lèih nī·syu yáuh géi·yúhn a?

wouldn't   /I wouldn't go if I were you. Yùh·gwó ngóh haih néih ngóh jauh m̀h·heui la.

wound   sèung; sauh sèung; V sèung. /How many were wounded? Sèung·jó géi·dò·go yahn a? Yáuh géi·dò·go yàhn sauh·jó sèung a? /He was beaten. Kéuih béi yàhn dá·sèung·jó (wounded by beating). /He was wounded by falling on the ground. Kéuih dit lohk deih·háh dit·sèung·jó.
    a wound sèung·háu. /It'll be a couple of months before the wound in his leg will heal. Kéuih geuk·syu gó·go sèung·háu yiu léuhng·go·yuht sìn·ji hóu·dāk.

wrangle   jàang. /Tell the children not to wrangle over the toys. Góng béi dī sai·màn·jái jī giu kéuih·deih m̀h·hóu jāang dī gūng·jái wáan.

wrap   bàau; **wrap up properly** bàau·hóu. /Do you want me to wrap it up for you? Néih yiu ngóh tùhng néih bàau·hóu kéuih ma?

wreath   (which is placed on a statue or coffin) fā·hyūn

wreck   **shipwreck** laahn·syùhn; **automobile wreck** laahn·chè

wrench   (a tool) sih·bāan·ná

wrestle   gwaan·gāau; **wrestling** gwaan·gāau. /Do you know how to wrestle? Néih wúih gwaan·gāau ma?

wring   (twist) náu, náu·gòn. /I've already wrung it several times. Ngóh yíh·gìng náu·jó géi·chi la. /Please wring out the dishcloth. M̀h·gòi néih náu·gòn tìuh maat·wún·bou kéuih.

wrinkle   (make folds or ridges in) jíng·chàauh; jau·héi. /Don't wrinkle your dress. Ṁh
hóu jíng·chàau gihn sāam. /She always wrinkles her forehead when she does arithmetic.
Kéuih yāt·jouh sou·hohk jauh jau·héi go mèih·tàuh ge la.

wrist   sáu·ngaau; **wrist watch** sáu bīu. /He sprained his wrist. Kéuih náu·chàn go sáu·
ngaau.

write   sé; sé·jih. /Don't forget to write your name. Ṁh·hóu ṁh·gei·dāk sé·méng. /Has
he learned how to write yet? Kéuih wúih sé·jih meih a?
     write a book, an essay, a song, etc. sé, jok. /Who wrote the book you are reading?
Néih tái·gán nī·bún·syù haih bīn·go sé ga? /He is writing an essay. Kéuih sé·gán yāt·
pīn màhn·jèung.
     write a check hòi jèung jí·piu, sé jèung chēk. /I'll write you a check. Ngóh hòi (or
sé) jèung jí·piu béi néih.
     write a letter sé seun. /Have you written your family a letter yet? Néih sé·jó seun
béi néih dī gà·yàhn meih a?
     write a receipt sé jèung sàu·geui, sé go sàu·tìuh. /Can you write me a receipt?
Néih hó·yíh sé jèung sàu·geui béi ngóh ma?
     write something **down** sé·dài, sé·lohk. /Write down that telephone number before
you forget it. Sé·dài go dihn·wá nām·bá, yeuhk·ṁh·haih jauh ṁh·gei·dāk ge la.
     write something **off** jyu·siu. /We've already written off that account. Ngóh·deih
yíh·gìng jyu·siu·jó gó·go wuh·háu lo.

writer   jok·gā

written   **written examination** bāt·si; **written language** màhn·jih

wrong   cho; ṁh·ngāam. /We're sorry that we have come late. We took the wrong road.
Jàn·haih ṁh·hóu yi·si la, ngóh·deih lèih chìh·jó. Ngóh·deih hàahng·cho·jó louh. /These
figures are wrong. Nī·dī sou·muhk ṁh·ngāam. /Did I say the wrong thing? Ngóh haih·
ṁh·haih góng·cho a?
     be (or go) **wrong with** (mechanically) waaih·jó. /Something is wrong with the tele-
phone. Dihn·wá waaih·jó. /Something went wrong with the plane, so the pilot decided
to land. Yàn·waih yáuh·dī gèi·gìn waaih·jó, só·yíh go gēi·sī kyut·dihng gong·lohk.
     be in the wrong cho. /He admitted he was in the wrong. Kéuih sìhng·yihng kéuih
cho·jó.
     to wrong yùn·wóng. /They wronged him. Kéuih·deih yùn·wóng·jó kéuih.
     be wronged sauh·jó·yūn·wāt. /They feel that they have been wronged for many
years. Kéuih·deih gok·dāk kéuih·deih sauh·jó hóu·dò·nìhn yūn·wāt la.

X

x-ray   ēk·sìh·gwōng

Y

yacht   yàuh·téhng (M: jek)

yam   fàan·syú

Yangtze River   Yèuhng·jí·gòng, Chèuhng·gòng (M: tìuh)

yard   (measure of length) máh. /How much is this material a yard? Nī·jek bou(·líu)
géi·chìn máh a?
     (a courtyard, such as in North China) yuhn·jí; (a small enclosure in the house or a
storied building in Kwangtung and neighboring provinces) tìn·jéng; (lawn) chóu·déi;
(empty land) hùng·deih
     lumber yard muhk·chóng; **railroad yard** fó·chè tìhng·chè·chèuhng, sāu·chè·chóng
(especially for repair)

yardstick   máh·chek (M: bá)

yarn   sā; **cotton yarn** mìhn·sā

yawn   dá·hahm·louh

year   nìhn, nín: **this year** gàm·nìhn, gàm·nín; **last year** gauh·nín; **next year** chēut·nín, mìhng·nìhn; **the year after next** hauh·nín; **the year before last** chìhn·nín; **leap year** yeuhn·nìhn; **school year** hohk·nìhn. /What was the year of your birth? Néih bīn·nìhn chēut·sai ga? /I hope to come again next year. Ngóh hèi·mohng chēut·nín joi lèih. /I haven't ridden a horse for years. Ngóh hóu·dò·nìhn móuh kèh·máh la. /It will take a whole year to finish this work. Nī·gihn sih yiu sèhng·nìhn gam·chèuhng sìn·ji jouh·dāk· yùhn.

yeast   (for making bread) mihn·júng; (for fermentation) bàau·móuh

yell   (shout) ngaai, daaih·sèng·gám·ngaai. /What is he yelling about? Kéuih hái syu ngaai māt·yéh a?

yellow   wòhng, wòhng·sīk (ge). /The yellow color is too strong; I don't like it. Wòhng· dāk·jaih, ngóh m̀h·jùng·yi. /Do you like the yellow one? Néih jùng·yi wòhng·sīk gó·go ma?

Yellow River   Wòhng·hòh (M: tìuh)

yes   The affirmative answer to a question is given by repeating the verb of the question in the affirmative (simple) form. This may be reinforced with It is so. Haih, haih la. /Yes, I'll ge glad to go. Haih, ngóh hóu fùn·héi heui. /Were you born there? Yes. Néih haih·m̀h·haih hái gó·syu chēut·sai ga? Haih.

yesterday   kàhm·yaht, chàhm·yaht, johk·yaht; **yesterday morning** kàhm·yaht·jíu; kàhm· yaht·jìu·tàuh·jóu; **the day before yesterday** chìhn·yaht

yet   (up to now; before this time) dou yihn·joih wàih·jí . . . juhng . . . /This is the tallest building yet. Dou yihn·joih waih·ji nī·joh lau juhng·haih jeuih gou ge lau.
(nevertheless) sèui·yìhn . . . daahn·haih . . . /He is old yet active. Kéuih sèui· yihn lóuh, daahn·haih juhng hóu hóu jîng·sàhn.
not yet juhng meih (·chahng). /The train has not come yet. Fó·chè juhng meih·lèih.

yield   (give way) yeuhng, teui·yeuhng. /If only they would yield to each other, there would be no problem. Jí·yiu kéuih·deih sèung·yeuhng·háh jauh móuh·mahn·tàih la.
(produce). /How many oranges does each tree yield on the average? Pìhng·gwàn yāt·pò syuh git géi·dò cháang a? /His business yields him great profit. Kéuih pùn sàang·yi tùhng kéuih wán hóu·dò chín.

Y. M. C. A.   Chìng·nìhn·wúi, Gēi·dūk·gaau·chìng·nìhn·wúi

yoke   (a wooden frame) ngaahk; (especially for oxen) ngàuh·ngaahk

yolk   daahn·wóng, dáan·wóng

you   (one person) néih; (several persons) néih·deih; **your** néih ge or néih·deih ge; **yours** néih ge, or néih·deih ge. /What do you want? Néih yiu māt·yéh a? /Is this your car? Nī·ga haih·m̀h·haih néih ge chè a? or Nī·ga chè haih·m̀h·haih néih ga? /Where is your school? Néih·deih ge hohk·haauh hái bīn·syu a? /This is for you. Nī·go haih béi néih (or néih·deih) ge.
(meaning some indefinite person) is usually not expressed. /You take the bus and then the ferry. Néih sìn chóh·bā·sī yìhn·hauh chóh douh·syùhn gwo·hói. /It makes you sick to hear about it. Tèng·gin jauh fàahn la.

yourself   néih jih·gēi

young   hauh·sāang, nìhn·hèng; **young man** hauh·sāang·jái; **young people** nìhn·hèng yàhn; **younger brother** sai·lóu; **younger sister** múi; **youngster** haauh·sāang·jái. /She is very young for her age. Kéuih sāang·dāk jàn·haih hauh·sāang la. /He isn't young anymore. Kéuih yíh·gìng m̀h·nìhn·hèng la.

youth   (a young person) chìng·nìhn(·yàhn), nìhn·hèng·yàhn. /We should do something for the youth of this area. Ngóh·deih yìng·gòi waih nī·syu ge chìng·nìhn jouh dī sih. /This letter was sent by a youth in search of a job. Nī·fùng haih yāt·go chìng·nìhn kàuh·jīk ge seun.

    (time of being young) siu·nìhn·sìh·doih; chìng·chèun. /He doesn't talk much about his youth. Kéuih m̀h·haih géi góng kéuih siu·nìhn·sìh·doih ge sih ge. /Once upon a time, there was an emperor who wanted to search for the secret of keeping one's youth . . . Gú·sìh yáuh go wòhng·dai séung wah chàhm·kàuh bóu·chìh chìng·chèun ge bei·kyut . . .

youthful   nìhn·hèng, hauh·sāang. /Her green dress makes her look very youthful. Kéuih jeuk gihn luhk sāam yíng·dāk kéuih hóu nìhn·hèng.

Y. W. C. A.   Néuih·chìng·nìhn·wúi, Gēi·dūhk·gaau·néuih·chìng·nìhn·wúi

<h1 style="text-align:center">Z</h1>

zealous   yiht·sàm

zebra   bàan·máh

zero   lìhng; (point of a scale) lìhng·douh; **above zero** lìhng·douh·(yíh·)seuhng; **below zero** lìhng·douh·(yíh·)hah

zigzag   (characterized by a zigzag) lyūn·lyūn kūk·kūk ge

zinc   sàn

zone   (geog.) — daai: **frigid zone** hòhn·daai; **temperate zone** wàn·daai; **tropic zone** yiht·daai; (location) deih·daai: **zone of military operations** jok·jin·deih·daai; **danger zone** ngàih·hím·deih·daai

zoo   duhng·maht·yún

zoology   duhng·maht·hohk

A

a 呀 (P) sentence particle for choice type questions

a·fēi 亞飛 (N) young hoodlum

a·gù 亞姑 (N) aunt (paternal)

a·gùng 亞公 (N) mother's father

àh 吖 (P) sentence particle changing a previous statement into a question

ai·yàh 哎吔* (Ex) exclamation (lament; regret; surprise)

āk·sáu 握手 (VO) shake hands (when greeting someone)

a·màh 亞嫲* (N) grandmother (father's mother)

ān·jín 引擎 (N) engine (transliterated)

a·pòh 亞婆 (N) grandmother (mother's mother)

A·sī·pāt·lìhng 亞斯匹靈 (N) Aspirin (M: pin, tablet)

a·sūk 亞叔 (N) uncle

a·yèh 亞爺 (N) grandfather (father's father)

a·yī 亞姨 (N) aunt (maternal)

B

bá 把 (M) measure for voice and knife

bà·bai 吧閉 (SV) clamorous

bà·git 巴結 (V) toady, flatter

ba·jim 霸佔 (V) usurp; take by force (a property, etc.)

bá·la 罷嘑 (P) sentence finals meaning 'how about' or 'you'd better'

Bà·làih 巴黎 (PW) Paris

bá·ngāak 把握 (N/V) have confidence in doing something /grasp, seize

bā·sí 巴士 (N) bus (M: ga)

baahk 白 (SV) white

baahk·baahk 白白 (A) in vain

baahk·ché 白斜 (N) white twill (cloth)

baahk·gáap 白鴿 (N) pigeon (M: jek)

baahk·gām 白金 (N) platinum

baahk·jih 白字 (N) character misused for another one of the same pronunciation. /sé baahk·jih, write wrong characters (comparable to misspelling a word in English)

baahk·johng·yúh 白撞雨 (N) rain with sun shining

baahk·júng·yàhn 白種人 (N) a member of the white race

baahk·lāan·déi 白蘭地 (N) Brandy (transliterated)

baahk·mihn 白面 (N) heroin

baahk·sáu·hīng gà 白手興家 (Ph) self-made (Lit. with empty hand to prosper one's family)

baahk·sihk 白食 (V) get a free meal

baahk·tòhng 白糖 (N) sugar

baahk·wá 白話 (At/N) colloquial, vernacular/vernacular writing

baahk·wá·kehk 白話劇 (N) a play in colloquial language

baahk·wá·màhn 白話文 (N) vernacular writing

baahk·wá·síu·syut 白話小說 (N) novels written in vernacular style

baahk·yàu 白油 (N) soy sauce

baahn 辦 (V) run, manage; set up (an establishment) and keep it going. /baahn hohk·haauh, to run a school; baahn·bou·gún, to run a newspaper

baahn·faat 辦法 (N) way or idea of doing, managing or arranging

baahn·fo 辦貨 (VO) order (merchandise), purchase goods

baahn·gùng 辦公 (VO) conduct or do official business

baahn·gùng·chóng 辦工廠 (VO) run a factory

baahn·gūng·sāt 辦公室 (N) office room (usually used for public office, but Cantonese people in Hong Kong and overseas are more accustomed to say sé·jih·làuh)

baahn·hóu 辦好 (RV) arrange satisfactorily

baahn·sáu·juhk 辦手續 (VO) go through the necessary procedure

baahn·sòh 辦傻 (V) to pretend stupidity

báai 擺 (V) arrange; display

baai 拜 (V) the act of clasping the hands together before the chest, usually involving some motion of hands and bowing in reverence

báai·dong 擺檔 (VO) to display for sale (e.g. hawkers setting up a stall for business)

baai·fóng 拜訪 (V) pay a visit

baai·jóu·sīn 拜祖先 (VO) worship ancestors

baai·nìhn 拜年 (V) give New Year's greetings

_____
*Indicates a coined character.

baai·nìhn·pín 拜年片 (N) New Year's greeting card

baai·sàan 拜山 (VO) worship at the graves

baai·sàhn 拜神 (VO) worship a god

baai·sauh 拜壽 (VO) wish someone a happy birthday (usually a senior or a superior)

baai·tok 拜托 (V) to ask a favor, entrust /Ngóh séung baai·tok néih yāt·gihn sih. I would like to ask you to do me a favor.

báai·wái 擺位 (VO) arrange table and chairs

baaih 敗 (SV) be defeated in a battle or a war /Bīn·gwok baaih·jó a? Which country was defeated?

baak 百 (NU/M) hundred

baak 伯 (N) father's elder brother, uncles

baak·fahn·jî·géi 百份之幾 (Pat) what per cent of /Baak·fahn·jî·géi? What per cent? /baak·fahn·jî·ńgh 5%

baak·gà·sing 百家姓 (N) "The one hundred Common Chinese surnames"

baak·maahn 百萬 (Nu) a million

baak·maahn·fu·yūng 百萬富翁 (N) millionaire

baak·sih·hó·lohk 百事可樂 (N) Pepsi-Cola (transliterated)

baak·sing 百姓 (N) all the people

baak·yē·gūng 伯爺公 (N) old man

baak·yē·pó 伯爺婆 (N) old woman

baak·yihp·chēung 百葉窗 (N) venetian blinds

baak·yim 百厭 (SV) naughty; mischievous

bàan 班 (M) batch, group, gang

bāan 班 (M) class

báan 板 (N) board (wooden), plank (M: faai)

báan 版 (N) a page, a column (newspaper)

báan·héi go mín 板起個面 (Ph) wear a long face

baat 八 (NU) eight

baat·yām 八音 (N) The eight musical instruments (Chinese)

Baat·yuht·jit 八月節 (N) Mid-autumn Festival (15th day of 8th lunar month)

bàau 包 (V/M) wrap /package

bàau 包 (V) guarantee

báau 飽 (SV) full (from eating)

bāau 飽 (N) stuffed steamed bread

baau 爆 (V) explode

bàau·bei 包庇 (V) harbor; screen

bàau·fuhk 包袱 (N) a package, bundle, parcel

bāau·gùng-bàau·líu 包工包料 (Ph) labor and materials included /Bāau·gùng-bàau·líu géi chín a? How much will it cost including both labor and materials?

bàau·gwó 包裹 (N) a parcel (P.O)

bàau·hàhm 包含 (V) contain

baau·ja 爆炸 (V) explode

bàau·kwut 包括 (V) include

bàau·láahm 包攬 (V) monopolize

bàau néih 包你 (Ph) assure you... that

baau·sehk 爆石 (Ph) blast rocks

bàau·wàih 包圍 (V) surround (as by soldiers)

bàau wuhn 包換 (Ph) guarantee to exchange

bāau yì 包醫 (Ph) guarantee to cure

bàh·bā 爸爸 (N) daddy

bah·fo 罷課 (VO) student strikes

bah·gùng 罷工 (VO) strike

bah·síh 罷市 (VO) to refuse to do business; to shut up shops, in protest against the authorities, etc.

bahn 笨 (SV) be stupid

baht 拔 (V) pull up; uproot

baht·chèuih 拔除 (N) uproot; eradicate

bài 跛 (V) hitch, walk lamely

bai·ngai 閉翳 (SV/V) worried /worry

baih 弊 (SV) be bad

baih·dauh 弊竇 (N) corrupt practices

baih·gà·fó·la 弊傢伙嘑* (IE) gee, gosh!

baih·gūng·sī 敝公司 (N) our company (polite form)

baih·gwok 敝國 (N) my country (polite form)

baih·haauh 敝校 (N) my school, our school (polite form)

baih·la 弊嘑* (IE) too bad! what a mess!

baih·sing 敝姓 (N) my surname (polite form)

bāk 北 (BF) north

bāk·gihk 北極 (N) North Pole

Bāk·gihk·lóuh·yàhn 北極老人 (N) Santa Claus

bām 泵 (N) pump

bān·bò 奔波 (SV) toilful, toilsome

bàn·haak 賓客 (N) visitor, guest

bán·hahng 品行 (N) character; conduct

bán·sing 品性 (N) temperament, disposition

bāt 筆 (N) pen, pencil

bāt 筆 (M) amount, sum (of money)

bāt·bīt 不必 (A) not need to

bāt·chēut 不出 (A) not beyond; within

bāt·dāk·líuh 不得了 (A) extremely, terrifically

bāt·dāk·yíh 不得已 (Ph) compelled to /Kéuih bāt·dāk·yíh sìn·ji gám jouh ge jē. He is compelled to do so.

bāt·dyuhn 不斷 (A) unceasingly, continuously

bāt·fòhng 不妨 (A) why not . . . ; it will do no harm to . . . /Go·go dōu wah gó·chēut dihn·yíng gam hóu·tái, bāt·fòhng heui tái·háh ā? Everyone says that movie is so good, why don't we go and see it?

bāt·gáu 不久 (MA) before long

bāt·gu yāt·chai 不顧一切 (IE): give no consideration to any risk in doing something

bāt·gwái 不軌 (At) irregular, improper

bāt·gwo 不過 (MA) but, however

bāt·hahng 不幸 (SV) unfortunate

bāt·hàm·chit·séung 不堪設想 (IE) a calamity beyond imagination

bāt·hit 不歇 (A) incessantly

bāt·jeuhn 不盡 (At) endless; numerous

bāt·jī·bāt·gok 不知不覺 (A) unconsciously; unnoticeably

bāt·jí·géi 不知幾 (A) extremely, beyond description

bāt·jīk 筆跡 (N) handwriting

bāt·lāu 不嘹 (A) has always been so

bāt·míhn 不免 (V) cannot avoid

bāt·nàhng 不能 (AV) cannot (variant of m̀h·nàhng·gau)

bāt·nàhng·bāt 不能不 (Ph) have to, cannot but; be compelled to

bāt·nghng·gau 不能夠 (AV) cannot (variant of m̀h·nàhng·gau)

bāt·ngoih (·fùh) 不外 (乎) (A) nothing but . . . ; only . . .

bāt·sám jē 不甚啫 (Ph) not very . . . , nothing particular

bāt·sau 不銹 (At) stainless

bāt·sìhng-mahn·tàih ge 不成問題嘅 (IE) It won't be any trouble.

bāt·sìhng-tái·túng 不成體統 (Ph) improper; unseemly

bāt·síng·yàhn·sih 不省人事 (Ph) passed out, faint

bāt·tùhng 不同 (SV) different

bāt·tùng 不通 (SV) illogical, ungrammatical

bāt·waahk 筆劃 (N) "strokes" of a character

bāt-yih-ga 不二價 (Ph) one price only

bāt·yihp 畢業 (VO) be graduated

bāt·yùh 不如 (V) be inferior to

bāt·yùh . . . gam SV 不如 … 咁 (V) not be as . . . as

bāt·yùh . . . la /lā 不如 … 喇 (IE) it is better to; rather; had better

behng 病 (N) sick

behng·chìhng 病情 (N) condition of a patient; symptom

behng·dài 病低 (V) be sick in bed

behng·fóng 病房 (N) room or ward in a hospital

behng·séi 病死 (RV) die of sickness

béi 畀 (V) to give

béi 比 (CV) than; compared with

béi·chí 彼此 (A) each other

béi·chí·gāan 彼此間 (A) each other

béi·choi 比賽 (V/N) contest, compete /contest, competition

béi dōu Neg. V 畀都唔… (Pat) no one will . . . 'even if it's free' /Nī·jèung yí gam gauh béi dōu móuh yàhn yiu a. This chair is so old, no one wants it even if it's given away free. /Gó·dī gam ge deih·fòng béi dōu m̀h·hou heui a. No one should go to such a place 'even if it's free.'

béi·gaau 比較 (V) compare

bēi·gùn 悲觀 (SV) pessimistic

béi gwán·séui luhk·chàn 被滾水淥親 (Ph) injured by boiling water

bèi·jihn 卑賤 (SV) mean; plebian

béi·kyut 秘訣 (N) secret (in doing things)

béi·laih 比例 (N) proportion

bei·maht 秘密 (A/SV/N) secretly /secret /secret

bēi·ngòi 悲哀 (SV) grief stricken; sad

bei·syū 秘書 (N) secretary

beih 被 (CV) by (a more formal and less common form of the passive CV béi)

beih (·hòi) 避 (開) (V) avoid

beih 避 (V) to flee from

beih·hòi 避開 (RV) keep away from, dodge

beih·duhng 被動 (A) involuntarily

beih·fùng·tòhng 避風塘 (N) inner harbor

beih·gō 鼻哥 (N) nose

beih·gou 被告 (N) defendant

beih·lèuih·jām 避雷針 (N) lightning rod

beih·míhn 避免 (V) avoid

beih·tai 鼻涕 (N) drivel from the nose

beih·yúh 避雨 (Ph) keep out of the rain

béng 餅 (N) cake (M: go; gauh, a piece)

béng·gōn 餅乾 (N) cookie; cracker (M: faai)

beng·màaih 뷰埋 (V) hide (things)

bihk·bihk·bahp·bahp 壁壁僕僕 (On) sounds made by the heart when it pounds bihn, bín 邊 (M) side; part

bihn·bok 辯駁 (V/N) argue; dispute /argument, dispute

bihn·faahn 便飯 (N) simple or ordinary meal

bihn·jūng 便中 (MA) at your convenience /Bihn·jūng néih tùhng ngóh mahn·háh lā. Please inquire about it for me at your convenience.

bihn·leuhn 辯論 (V/N) debate /debate

bihng 並(幷) (BF) (used before a negative expression to give emphasis)

bihng·ché 並且 (MA) furthermore, moreover

bihng·fèi 並非 (A) not . . . at all, by no means

bihng·mh·haih 並唔係 (A) not . . . at all, by no means

biht·séuih 別墅 (N) resort

bīk 逼 (SV/V) be congested; be over-crowded /crowd; squeeze (in a crowd)

bīk 逼 (V) force

bín 扁 (SV) flat (having broad surface and little thickness)

bin 變 (V) transform; undergo a change

bīn 辮 (N) queue, braid (M: tìuh)

bīn 邊 (SP) which, who, whom /Néih yiu bīn·go a? Which one do you want? /Kéuih haih bīn·go a? Who is he?

bìn 邊 (BF) side /Nī·bìn, this side

bīn·dī 邊的 (N) which? (plural)

bin·fa 變化 (N/V) transformation, change /transform, undergo a change

bin·gàng 變更 (V) change, alter

bìn·gaai 邊界 (N) border, border region

bin·tùng 變通 (V/SV) accommodate /adaptable; accommodating

bin·sīk 變色 (SV) faded in color

bin·sèhng 變成 (V) become, change into, transform into

bīn·syu (wúih) . . . 邊處(會) (Ph) how could . . . /Bīn·syu wúih yáuh·dī gám ge sih ga! How could such a thing have happened!

bìng 冰 (N) ice (M: gauh, piece)

bìng 兵 (N) soldier

bìng·gwaih 冰櫃 (N) refrigerator

bīng·sāt 冰室 (N) cafeteria (generally with a fountain) (M: gāan)

bìng·tòhng 冰糖 (N) hard candy

bīt·dihng 必定 (A) certainly (in an as-sertion or decision)

bīt·sèui 必需 (SV) indispensable

bīt·yiu 必要 (N) necessity

biu 裱 (V) to mount (scrolls, wallpaper, etc.)

bíu 表 (N) form (for information; ref. tíhn); chart

bīu 錶 (N) watch

bíu·chēut·heui 飈出去 (V) dash out

bíu·jéun 標準 (N) standard

bíu·mìhng 表明 (V) indicate clearly

bíu·mihn·seuhng 表面上 (MA) super-ficially, outwardly, on the surface

bíu·sih 表示 (V/N) express; show; sig-nify (indication of opinion) /expression

bíu·wùh 裱糊 (V) paste; mount

bíu·yín 表演 (V) perform; act (in a play)

bíu·yihn 表現 (N/V) expression, mani-festation /exhibit, reveal, show forth

bō 波 (N) ball (transliterated)

bō 波 (N) gear

bō·chèuhng 波場 (N) ball field

bō·chèuhng 波長 (N) wave length

bō·choi 菠菜 (N) spinach

bō·lēi 玻璃 (N) glass (M: faai)

bō·lohng 波浪 (N) waves

bō·lēi·jēun 玻璃樽 (N) glass bottle

bohk 薄 (SV) thin

bohk·doih 薄待 (V) treat coldly

bohk·hòh 薄荷 (N) peppermint; menthol

bohk·yúng 薄絨 (N) fine woolen materi-al

bohng 磅 (V) to weigh

bohng 磅 (M) a pound

bok 駁 (V) refute; talk back

bok 駁 (V) connect (a telephone, etc.)

bok 博 (V) to take a chance

bok·jéui 駁嘴 (V) to contradict; argue

bok·màaih 駁埋 (V) to join together

bok·maht·yún 博物院 (N) museum (M: gàan)

bok·sih 博士 (N) doctorate degree, Ph.D.

bok·tàuh 膊頭 (N) shoulder

bok·tùng 駁通 (RV) connected (a tele-phone)

bòng 幫 (V/CV) help

bóng 榜 (N) placard; pass list (for a matriculation examination, etc.)

bòng·báan 幫辦 (N) police officer (in Hong Kong)

bòng·bóu 幫補 (V) assist (with money)

bòng·chan 幫襯 (V) patronize

bòng·gàau 邦交 (N) diplomatic relations

bòng·joh 幫助 (V) help, assist

bóng·saht 綁實 (RV) tie firmly (with a string, etc.)

bòng·sáu 幫手 (N/VO) assistant, helper /help (lit. help with hand) bòu 煲 (V) boil; cook (in water)

bóu 簿 (N) notebook; book of record or account

bóu 補 (V) mend; patch; fill up (a vacancy)

bou 布 (N) cloth, material

bōu 煲 (N) kettle, pot (used in kitchen)

bòu·chàh 煲茶 (VO) prepare tea (lit. boil water to make tea)

bóu·chìh 保持 (V) keep, maintain /bóu·chìh lyùhn·lohk, keep contact; bóu·chìh wèn·douh, maintain the temperature

bóu·chyùhn 保存 (V) preserve, keep intact; store safely

bou·daap 報答 (V) to pay back the kindness or generosity of others; repay (a favor), recompense

bou·dìn 布甸 (N) pudding (transliterated)

bòu·faahn 煲飯 (VO) cook rice

bóu fó him 保火險 (VO) take out fire insurance

bou·fuhk 報復 (V) retaliate

bou·gaai 報界 (N) the press

bou·gou 報告 (N/V) report /make a report

bou·gou·báan 佈告板 (N) bulletin board

bóu·gún 保管 (V) safeguard

bou·gún 報館 (N) newspaper (office)

bóu·gwai 寶貴 (SV) precious

bóu·gyun 寶眷 (N) your wife; your family (polite form)

bóu·hyut 補血 (SV) tonic

bóu·jaahp 補習 (V) make up (in studying)

bòu·jéung 襃獎 (V) to laud, praise

bou·jí 報紙 (N) newspaper (M: fahn, a copy)

bou·ji 佈置 (V) arrange (furniture, stage-scenery, etc.)

bóu·joh 寶座 (N) a throne; shrine

bóu·juhng jih·géi 保重自己 (Ph) take good care of oneself

bóu·juhng sàn·tái 保重身體 (Ph) take good care of one's health

bóu·lám 寶藍 (At) bright blue

bóu·maht 寶物 (N) valuables

bou·méng 報名 (V) register (as in a school, etc.)

bou·on 報案 (VO) report a case

Bóu·sáu·dóng 保守黨 (N) Conservative Party

bou·sàuh 報仇 (VO) to take revenge

bóu·sauh·hím 保壽險 (VO) take out life insurance

bóu·sehk 寶石 (N) precious stones

bóu·taap 寶塔 (N) pagoda

bóu·wuh 保護 (V/N) protect /protection

bóu·yauh 保祐 (V) bless; care for (used only with a deity or ancestor as subject)

bóu·yeuhk 補藥 (N) tonics

bou·yùn 報冤 (VO) avenge

bouh 步 (M) pace, step

bouh 部 (M) part, section

bouh·hah 部下 (N) those under a command

bouh·bìng 步兵 (N) foot soldier

bouh·déui 部隊 (N) troops

bouh·duhng 暴動 (V/N) riot /riot

bouh·fahn 部份 (M) department; part; portion; section

bouh·louh 暴露 (V) expose; uncover

bouh·sáu 部首 (N) radical of a character

buhk·bou 瀑布 (N) waterfall; cascade

buhk·hái 撲*喺* (V) put one's head and arms on

buhk·yàhn 僕人 (N) a servant

buhn·lòhng 伴郎 (N) best man

buhn·nèuhng 伴娘 (N) bridesmaid

buht 撥 (V) dial (as a telephone); move with extended finger; set (as a clock); adjust; allocate (as of money)

bùi 杯 (M) cup /yāt·bùi séui, a glass of water

bui 輩 (M) generation

būi 杯 (N) glass, a drinking container (M: jek or go)

bui·gíng 背景 (N) background

bui·hauh 背後 (A) behind (one's) back

bui·jek 背脊 (N) the back (of the body)

bui·sām 背心 (N) a vest; waistcoat (M: gihn)

buih 焙 (V) to warm or dry by fire

būk·gwa 卜卦 (VO) to divine by using the hexagrams

bùn 搬 (V) move

būn (·ngūk) 搬屋 (VO) to move from one dwelling to other

bún 本 (M) for books

bún 本 (BF) main; principal (principal part of a large organization); this, our (when referring to the same organization to which the speaker belongs) /bún·haauh, our school

bun 半 (Nu/M) half/ half: /bun·go, 1/2; /(yāt·) go bun, 1 1/2; sàam·go bun·go, 3 halves

bún·chìhn 本錢 (N) capital (money invested in fixed assets)

bún·deih, bún·déi　本地　(At) local, indigenous, native

bún·deih·yàhn　本地人　(N) natives (of a place)

bun·dóu　半島　(N) peninsula

bún·fahn　本份　(N) duty

bun·ga　半價　(N) half price

bún·haauh　本校　(N) mother school (versus branch school); this (or our) school (when referring to the same school to which the speaker belongs)

bún·hòhng　本行　(N) one's own line

bún·líhng　本領　(N) one's ability

bún·lòih　本來　(MA) originally

bun·lóu, bun·louh　半路　(PW/A) halfway /enroute

bún·sàm　本心　(N) conscience

bún·sàn　本身　(N) itself; oneself

bún·sih　本事　(SV/N) be able, capable/ ability, capability

bun·tàn·bun·tou　半吞半吐　(Ph) to slur (facts)

bun·tòuh·yìh·fai　半途而廢　(Ph) to give up halfway

bùn·wahn　搬運　(V) transport; move

bun·yé　半夜　(TW) midnight (generally refers to midnight and the few hours following)

C

chā　叉　(N) fork

chā·sīu　叉燒　(N) grilled pork (ref. sīu·yuhk)

chā·sīu·bāau　叉燒飽　(N) steamed bread stuffed with grilled pork

chaahk　賊　(N) thief

chàahm·chúng　蠶蟲　(N) silkworm

chàahm·kwái　慚愧　(SV/IE) feel mortified /You put me to shame (by your praise)

chàahn·dáu　蠶豆　(N) horse bean, kidney beans

chàahn·fai·behng·yún　殘癈病院　(N) convalescent home for disabled persons

chaahn·huhk　殘酷　(SV) pitiless, merciless, cruel

chaahn·saat　殘殺　(V/N) massacre /massacre

chaahn·yáhn　殘忍　(SV) remorseless; cruel

chàai·gún　差館　(N) police office or headquarters (in Hong Kong)

chàai·hín　差遣　(V) send as envoy

chàai·múi　猜枚　(V) play finger-guessing game (for drinks at dinner)

chàai·yàhn　差人　(N) police; policeman (in Hong Kong)

chàaih　柴　(N) firewood (M: gàn, catty; daam, picul)

chàaih·lòhng　豺狼　(N) wolf (M: jek)

chaak　拆　(V) tear down (a building, house, etc.), rip

chaak·hòi　拆開　(V/RV) open (parcel, letter, etc.), /disassemble, rip off, tear off

cháam　慘　(SV) miserable, sorrowful, tragic

chaam　杉　(N) a species of pine used for lumber

chaam·báan　杉板　(N) pine boards

chāam·gà　參加　(V) participate in; attend (a meeting)

chāam·gùn　參觀　(V) to pay a visit to (e.g. school, museum, etc.)

chàam·háau　參攷　(V) refer, collate

chàam·háau·syù　參攷書　(N) reference book

chāan　餐(舘)(M) measure for 'faahn' – meal

chāan　餐　(N) meal

cháan·deih·pèih　剷地皮　(VO) squeeze by government officials

chāan·díp　餐碟　(N) dinner plate

cháan·fō　產科　(N) obstetrics or maternity department

chāan·gān　餐巾　(N) napkin (M: tìuh or faai)

chāan·tēng　餐廳　(N) dining room

chāan·tói　餐枱　(N) dining table

chāan·wúi　餐會　(N) dinner party

cháan·yihp　產業　(N) real estate, property

chàang　撐　(V) pole

cháang　橙　(N) orange

chàang·héi　撐起　(V) prop up

cháang·jāp　橙汁　(N) orange juice

chàang·jyuh　撐住　(V) prop up

chàang·syùhn　撐船　(VO) pole a boat

chaap　插　(V) to put in

cháat　刷　(N) brush (generally for things with handles)

chaat　刷　(V) brush

chaat·jí·gàau　刷紙膠　(N) eraser (rubber)

chaat·ngàh　刷牙　(VO) brush one's teeth

chàau　抄　(V) copy; transcribe

cháau　炒　(V) fry (with constant stirring); sauté

chāau·dài　抄低　(V) copy down

cháau·faahn　炒飯　(N/VO) fried rice/fry rice

chaau·háh 　嘸嚇　 (V) look for something (in a drawer, box, etc.)

cháau·mihn 　炒麵　 (N/VO) fried noodles /fry noodles

chā·bāt·dō 　差不多　 (A) almost, nearly

chā·dāk·yúhn 　差得遠　 (Ph) very different

chā·gwōng·geng 　乂光鏡　 (N) X-ray

chà·m̀h·dō 　差唔多　 (A) almost, nearly

chàh 　茶　 (N) tea

chàh 　擦　 (V) apply, put on

chàh 　查　 (V) detect; investigate

chàh·bōu 　茶煲　 (N) teakettle

chàh·chēut 　查出　 (RV) find out (by investigation)

chàh·fán 　擦粉　 (V) apply powder

chàh·fēi 　查飛　 (VO) check tickets; punch tickets

chàh·gēi 　茶几　 (N) tea-table

chàh·gēu 　茶居　 (N) teahouse (M: gàan)

chàh·jih 　查字　 (VO) look up words

chàh·jih·dín 　查字典　 (VO) consult a dictionary

chàh·làuh 　茶樓　 (N) teahouse

chàh·wú 　茶壺　 (N) teapot

chàh·wúi 　茶會　 (N) tea party

chàh yeuhk·gōu 　擦藥膏　 (Ph) rub on salve

chàh·yihp 　茶葉　 (N) tea leaf

chàh-yīn-fuhng-haak 　茶煙奉客　 (Ph) to offer tobacco and tea to visitors

chahk·táu 　賊頭　 (N) a bandit chief

chàhm 　沉　 (V) sink

chàhn 　塵　 (N) dust; dirt

chàhng 　層　 (M) point (as in 'on this point')

chàhng·gìng 　曾經　 (A) have already V

Chàhn sīn·sàang néih·deih 　陳先生你哋　 (Ph) Mr. Chen you and yours (friends, family, etc. understood)

chai 　砌　 (V) to lay (bricks, tiles, wood, etc.); assemble, put things together (as in a puzzle)

chài·cháam 　悽慘　 (SV) sorrowful, melancholy

chài·lèuhng 　凄涼　 (SV) sad and lonely

chāi·sàn 　樓身　 (VO) to live on a meager salary

chàih 　齊　 (SV) complete

chàih·beih 　齊備　 (SV) complete

chàih·chyùhn 　齊全　 (SV) complete

chàm·faahn 　侵犯　 (V) invade

chàm·leuhk 　侵略　 (V) invade

chàn 　親　 (SV) closely related

chàn 　嚫　 (BF) suffix to monosyllabic verbs means something like 'get', 'on' or 'at'. It is used mostly in connection with the

human body and usually in an undesirable or unpleasant sense. /Kéuih johk·máahn láahng·chàn àh? Did he catch cold last night? /Ngóh ga chè béi yàhn·deih ge chè pung·chàn. My car was hit by somebody else's.

chan 　趁　 (V) take opportunity to (used somewhat like the English conjunction 'while') /Nī·dī yéh yiu chan yiht sihk. You've to eat it while it's hot.

chān·bāt 　親筆　 (A) with one's own hand (in writing)

chān·chīk 　親戚　 (N) relative

chan·gà 　親家　 (N) relatives by marriage

chán·gām 　診金　 (N) clinic fee, the charge for professional service by a doctor

chàn·hìng·daih 　親兄弟　 (N) bloodbrothers

chàn·jih 　親自　 (A) personally, in person; by oneself

chán·jing 　診症　 (VO) examine a patient

chán·jing·sāt 　診症室　 (N) examining room

chan·jóu 　趁早　 (A) do something early

chán·lìuh·só 　診療所　 (N) clinic

chàn·maht 　親密　 (SV) very near; very dear; intimate

chan·nīgo·gèi·wuih 　趁呢個機會　 (Ph) take this opportunity; avail oneself of this opportunity

chàn·sàn 　親身　 (A) personally, in person; by oneself

chàn·sáu 　親手　 (A) with one's own hands (in doing a thing)

chàn·suhk 　親屬　 (N) kinfolk and relatives

chàn·yàhn 　親人　 (N) members of one's family or people who are very close relatives

chāt 　七　 (Nu) seven

Chāt·héi 　七喜　 (N) Seven-Up

Chāt·jīk 　七夕　 (N) the Milky Way Romance festival

Chāt·sahp·yih·hòhng 　七十二行　 (N) all business circles, all lines of business (lit. seventy-two trades)

chau 　嚊　 (V) to nurse or take care of (a baby or a child)

chau 　臭　 (SV) stench, smell

chāu·chīm 　抽籤　 (VO) to draw lots

chāu·gàn 　抽筋　 (VO) have a muscle spasm

chau·háau 　凑巧　 (MA) by lucky chance

chau·hāng·hàng 　臭哼哼　 (SV) nasty (smell)

chāu·lāu 　秋樓　 (N) spring coat, light overcoat

chau sai·mān·jái 嘈細蚊仔 (Ph) to take care of children

chau·séui 臭水 (N) carbolic acid, disinfectant

chāu·tīn 秋天 (N) autumn

cháu·yéung 醜樣 (SV) ugly

chau·yún 臭丸 (N) mothballs

chàuh·beih 籌備 (V) prepare, plan

chàuh·chèuih 躊躇 (V) hesitate

chàuh·fún 籌款 (VO) to solicit funds

chè, chē 車 (N) car; automobile (M: ga)

chè 車 (V) circulate, move around

ché 扯 (V) go away

che 斜 (V) be sloping; be slanting

chē 車 (V) sew by machine, make (clothes) by machine

ché·beih·hòhn 扯鼻鼾 (V) snore

chē·daaih·paau 車大砲 (V) lie; brag

chē·jái 車仔 (N) rickshaw (M: ga)

ché·kèih·sàan 扯旗山 (PW) Mount Victoria (on the Island of Hong Kong)

ché·kèih·sàan·déng 扯旗山頂 (PW) Victory Park (in Hong Kong)

che·lóu 斜路 (Ph) sloping road

chè·méih 車尾 (N) rear of a vehicle, the rear seats in a vehicle

chè·pàaih 車牌 (N) license plate (for car)

chē·sāam 車衫 (VO) make (clothes) by machine

chè·tàuh 車頭 (N) front of a vehicle, the front seats in a vehicle

chèh·màhn 斜紋 (At) twilled

chek 尺 (N/M) a ruler /a chinese foot

chēk 踱 (V) check (transliterated)

chēk 展 (N) check (M: jēung)

chek·douh 赤道 (N) equator

chéng 請 (V) please; ask (invitational sense), invite, request; hire (a person)

chèng·choi 青菜 (N) green vegetables

chèng·dáu 青豆 (N) green peas

chéng fó·gei 請伙記 (Ph) hire a man (for a business firm)

chéng·ga 請假 (VO) request leave of absence

chéng·gaau 請教 (V) ask for advice (polite form)

chéng gùng·yàhn 請工人 (Ph) hire a worker (for a home or factory)

chéng·haak 請客 (VO) to give a party (lit. to invite guests)

chéng mahn . . . 請問 (IE) may I ask . . . , would you please tell me . . .

chéng néih joi góng yāt·chi 請你再講一次 (IE) Please say it again.

chéng·pòh·mā 請婆媽 (Ph) hire a maid

chèng·tòih 青苔 (N) moss

chéng·wùih 請回 (IE) please return, don't escort me further

chéng·yám 請飲 (VO) give a dinner party (lit. invite to drink)

chéng·yī·sāng 請醫生 (VO) to call a doctor

Chèuhn·chí·wòhng 秦始皇 (PN) Chin Shih Huang, the first emperor of the Ch'in Dynasty (221-206 B.C.)

chèuhn·gíng 巡警 (N) a policeman

chèuhn·yèuhng·laahm 巡洋艦 (N) cruiser (navy) (M: jek)

chèuhn·kwài·douh·géui 循規蹈距 (Ph) to observe proper decorum

chèuhng 長 (SV) long

chèuhng 墻 (N) wall (M: buhng)

chèuhng 場 (M) showing of a motion picture, play, concert, etc.

chèuhng·bō 長波 (At) long wave

chèuhng·chyu 長處 (N) strong point (of people); advantages

chèuhng·dang 長凳 (N) bench; the wooden stands that support boards to make a bed (M: jèung)

chèuhng·gok·lōk·táu 墻角落頭 (N) corner of a wall

chèuhng·jauh·sin·sāam 長袖線衫 (N) long-sleeved undershirt

chèuhng·kèih 長期 (At) long-term

chèuhng·kèih·fēi 長期囉 (N) pass; long-term ticket

chèuhng·mehng 長命 (SV) long-lived

chèuhng·sāam 長衫 (N) gown (men's or women's) (M: gihn)

chèuhng·sai 詳細 (A) in detail

chèuhng·sìhng 長城 (PW) the Great Wall

chèuhng·tòuh 長途 (BF) long-distance

chèuhng·tòuh·dihn·wá 長途電話 (N) long-distance call

chèuhng·yiht·jing 腸熱症 (N) typhoid fever

chèui 吹 (V) blow

chèui 催 (V) urge (someone to speed up in doing something), rush

chéui 鎚 (N) hammer

chéui 娶 (V) take a wife /Kéuih juhng meih chéui lóuh·pòh àh? He hasn't gotten married yet?

cheui 脆 (SV) delicate; brittle; crisp

chèui·heung 趨向 (V/N) tend to /tendency

cheui·meih 趣味 (N) interest (a feeling)

chèui·sai 趨勢 (N) trend, tendency, current

chéui·sîu 取消 (V) cancel, rescind, eliminate

chèuih 除 (V) take off (clothes, shoes, hat, gloves, etc.)

chèuih bín lā 隨便啦 (IE) it doesn't matter (nothing to be particular about)

chèuih·chùhng 隨從 (N) attendants

chèuih·dài 除低 (V) take off (something and lay it down)

chèuih·deih 隨地 (A) at all places

chèuih·fèi 除非 (MA) unless; except

chèuih-gèi-ying-bin 隨機應便 (Ph) expedient

chèuih·hàaih 除鞋 (Ph) take off shoes

chèuih·háu 隨口 (A) say very casually (without much thinking)

chèuih·jái 鎚仔 (N) hammer

chèuih néih 隨你 (IE) It's up to you.

chèuih·jó . . . jî·ngoih 除咗 … 之外 (Pat) besides

chèuih . . . jùng·yi lā, chèuih . . . bín lā 隨 … 鍾意啦 (Ph) as one pleases, whatever one likes

chèuih·móu 除帽 (VO) take off hat

chèuih·sìh 隨時 (A) at all times, at any moment

chèuih·syu 隨處 (PW) everywhere (used only in subject) / hèuih·syu dōu yauh pou·táu. There are stores everywhere.

chéun·chòih 蠢材 (N) a fool

chēun·tīn 春天 (N) spring (season)

cheung 唱 (V) sing

chēung 鎗 (N) light firearm piece (as a rifle, revolver or pistol) (M: jì or hám)

chéung·gau 搶救 (V) rush to the rescue

chéung·gip 搶劫 (V/N) rob/robbery

chēung·lím 窗簾 (N) window curtain (M: tìuh)

chēung·mún 窗門 (N) window

chēung·paau 鎗砲 (N) arm (lit. small arms and guns)

chēut 出 (V) make; produce; put out, issue

chēut 齣 (M) measure for show or play

chēut·báan 出版 (V) publish

chēut·bán 出品 (N) product (M: gihn)

chēut·cháan 出產 (V/N) produce/product

chēut·chín 出錢 (VO) offer or contribute money; invest money

chēut·dáu 出痘 (VO) to have smallpox

chēut·faat 出發 (V) set out, set forth

chēut . . . fahn 出 … 份 (VO) pay one's share

chēut·fùng·tàuh 出風頭 (VO) show off, crave popularity

chēut·ga 出嫁 (V) to marry a husband; to give a daughter in marriage

chēut·gāai 出街 (VO) go out (onto the street)

chēut·gíng 出境 (VO) to leave a country

chēut·gíng·jing 出境証 (N) permit for leaving a country

chēut·háu 出口 (At/V) export/leave port

chēut·háu·fo 出口貨 (N) export commodity

chēut·heui 出去 (V) go out (there)

chēut·hòhn 出汗 (VO) perspire

chēut·jeuhn-baat·bóu 出盡八寶 (IE) exhaust all that a person can do (lit. using all the tricks)

chēut·jihk 出席 (V) attend a meeting

chēut·jòu 出租 (V) be for rent, to let (ref. jòu)

chēut·kèih 出奇 (SV) strange (unnatural; inexplicable, puzzling)

chēut·làih, chēut·lèih 出來 (V) come out (here)

chēut·lèuhng 出粮 (VO) pay wages. /Géi·sí chēut lòuhng a? When will pay day be?

chēut·lihk 出力 (A/VO/V) energetically, wholeheartedly/put more effort into/serve /Néi yiu chēut·lihk ji dāk gá. You have to put out more strength in doing it. /waih gwok·gà chēut·lihk, to serve one's country

chēut·lòuh 出爐 (VO) just come out of the oven

chēut·méng 出名 (SV) famous

chēut·sai 出世 (N) born (lit. come out and be into the world)

chēut·sèng 出聲 (VO) utter, say something

chēut·sòng 出喪 (VO) funeral procession

chēut·tàih·muhk 出題目 (VO) to assign subject for composition

chēut·yahm 出賃 (V) for rent; rent out

chēut·yahp 出入 (V) go from one place to another (lit. go out and come back)

chēut·yaht·táu 出日頭 (VO) sun comes out; has sunshine

chēut·yèuhng 出洋 (VO) go abroad

chēut·yún 出院 (VO) leave hospital

chì 嗜 (V) adhere

chi (or tong) 次 (M) a time or occasion

chi 賜 (V) grant, endow

chí·chóng 始創 (V) found

chi·daih 次第 (N) order; sequence

chi·dōu 刺刀 (N) bayonet (M: bá)

chi·gīk 刺激 (V/N) to stimulate; a shock

chi·jeuih 次序 (N) sequence, in order

chi·ngoih 此外 (Ph) beside this

chí·sí 吱士 (N) cheese (transliterated)

chi·só 廁所 (N) washroom, toilet

chi·só·jí 廁所紙 (N) toilet tissue

chìh 遲 (SV) late; later

chìh 詞 (N) word (linguistic term)

chíh 似 (V) looks like, resemble

chíh 恃 (V) rely on (look to the protection or support of . . .)

chìh·bēi 慈悲 (SV) merciful; compassionate

chíh·béng 柿餅 (N) dried persimmon

chìh·dáai 臍帶 (N) umbilical cord

chìh·dou 遲到 (V) be late

chíh·fùh 似乎 (A) as if; seem, seem or look as if (a variant of hóu·chíh as adverb)

chíh·gāng 匙羹 (N/M) spoon /spoonful

chíh·gok 似覺 (V) seem, feel, under the impression that

chìh·gū 慈姑 (N) caladium; arrowhead

chìh·hàhng 辭行 (VO) say goodbye to someone staying behind, to bid farewell

chìh·hei 磁器 (N) porcelain, chinaware

chìh·jóu 遲早 (A) sooner or later; eventually

chíh·sai 恃勢 (V) to take unfair advantage of power or influence

chìh·sàm 慈心 (SV) tenderhearted; affectionate

chìh·sehk 磁石 (N) loadstone

chìh·sihn 慈善 (At) charitable

chìh·tóng 祠堂 (N) ancestral hall (M: gàan)

chìhm·fuhk 潛伏 (V) conceal

chìhm·séui·téhng 潛水艇 (N) submarine

chìhn NU M 前 (Ph) ago. /Chìhn·léuhng·yaht, two days ago

chìhn·bihn 前邊 (PW) front

chìhn·gán 纏緊 (RV) bind tightly

chìhn·hauh·yāt·guhng 前後一共 (Ph) all told, altogether (from beginning to end)

chìhn·jeun 前進 (V/SV) to make progress /advanced

chìhn·mún 前門 (N) front door

chìhn·sin 前線 (N) front line

chìhn·tòuh 前途 (N) future

chìhng 晴 (V) (sky) be cleared

chìhng·bou 情報 (N) intelligence (information)

chìhng·douh 程度 (N) level, qualifications, standards /hohk·sāang ge chìhng·douh, the student's level; sīn·sàang·ge chìhng·douh, the teacher's qualifications

chìhng·yìhng 情形 (N) circumstance, condition, situation

chìhng·yún 情願 (A/V) rather; prefer

chìm 籤 (N) divining slip, lot

chìm·jí 簽字 (N/VO) signature/sign one's name

chìm·jing 簽証 (VO) visa

chìm·méng 簽名 (VO) sign one's name

chìm·sàu 簽收 (V) sign the receipt

chìm·túng 籤筒 (N) tube for holding lots

chìn 千 (M) thousand

chín 錢 (N) money

chín 淺 (SV) be shallow, light

chìn·bin·maahn·fa 千變萬化 (Ph) A thousand changes and ten thousand variations, frequent changes, extremely variable

chìn·chāu·gá 鞦韆架 (N) swing

chìn·fahn·jī·yāt 千份之一 (Ph) one thousandth

chìn·fòng·baak·gai 千方百計 (Ph) by every means to make it possible

chìn·gām 千金 (N) daughter (a formal way of addressing other people's daughter)

chìn·kèih 千祈 (A) by all means, without fail, be sure (used in imperative mood only)

chín·làahm·sīk 淺藍色 (N) light blue

chín·lauh 淺陋 (SV) mean, vulgar

chìn·léih·geng 千里鏡 (N) a telescope

chìn·maahn 千萬 (MA) by all means

chín·sīk 淺色 (N) light color

ching 秤 (N) steelyard (M: bá)

chìng·chèun 青春 (N) youth (literary)

chìng·chìng·chó·chó 清清楚楚 (Ph) very clear

Chìng·chìuh 清朝 (At) Ch'ing Dynasty (A.D. 1644-1912)

chìng·chó 清楚 (SV) distinct, clear (from ambiguity)

chìng·fù 稱呼 (V) address (with proper title as in a letter or in speaking)

chìng·ga 請假 (VO) to ask for leave

chìng·gáam 清減 (V) look thin (undesirably, e.g. after a sickness)

chìng·hàahn 清閒 (SV) have plenty of time

chìng-jihng-mòu-wàih 清靜無為 (IE) be inactive and tranquil

chǐng·kàuh 請求 (V) request

chìng·lèuhng 清涼 (SV) cool, breezy

chìng·mìhng·jit 清明節 (N) tomb-sweeping festival (usually occurs about April 5th)

chìng·nìhn 青年 (N) youth, young people

chìng·sau 清秀 (SV) handsome, genteel, well-bred

chìng·sóng 清爽 (SV) be clear and pleasant (of the air)

chìng·syun 清算 (V/N) purge, liquidate /purge

chìng·tìhm 清甜 (SV) fresh and sweet

ching·tòh 秤鉈 (N) steelyard weight

chǐng·yuhn 請願 (N) a petition

chip·sih 妾侍 (N) concubine

chit 切 (V) cut

chit·beih 設備 (N) furnishings; facilities

chit·bīng 撤兵 (VO) withdraw troops

chit·dái 徹底 (SV/A) thorough/thoroughly

chit·faat 設法 (V) devise ways and means, plan

chit·faat·jí 設法子 (VO) devise ways and means

chit·hòi 切開 (V) cut (into slices or strips)

chit·ji·gèi 切紙機 (N) paper cutting machine

chit·lahp 設立 (V) to establish

chìuh 朝 (M) dynasty

chìuh·douh 朝代 (N) dynasty

chìuh·sāp 潮濕 (SV) humid, damp, moist

chìuh·séui 潮水 (N) tide

chò 初 (BF) used before NU from one to ten, indicates first ten days of a lunar month: chō·yāt, the first day of the lunar month, etc.

cho 錯 (SV/V/N) be wrong/make mistake/error, fault

chò·chi 初次 (TW) the first time

Chó-chòih-Jeun-yuhng 楚才晉用 (IE) A talented person employed by a nation other than his own.

cho·gok 錯覺 (N) wrong impression; illusion

chō·jūng 初中 (N) junior high

chō·jūng·bouh 初中部 (N) the junior high section

chò·màaih-yāt·tyùhn 搓埋一團 (Ph) roll it into a ball

cho·ngh 錯誤 (N) mistake, error

chò·sìh 初時 (MA) at the beginning

chóh 坐 (V) sit, go by (bus, train)

chóh·dài 坐低 (V) sit down

chóh·dāk·lohk 坐得落 (RV) be able to seat (so many people)

chóh·gāam 坐監 (V) to be a prisoner in jail

chóh·héi·sàn 坐起身 (V) sit up

chóh·lohk 坐落 (RV) sit down (see chóh·dāk·lohk, chóh·m̀h·lohk)

choh·m̀h·lohk 坐唔落 (RV) be unable to seat (so many people)

chóh·múhn 坐滿 (RV) fill by sitting in (many people)

chòhng 床 (牀) (N) bed (M: jèung)

chòhng·màaih 藏埋 (V) to lay by, to hide away

chòhng·pòu 床鋪 (N) bedding

chòhng·tàuh 床頭 (N) head of bed

chòhng·tàuh·dāng 床頭燈 (N) nightlamp (at bedside) (M: jáan)

chói 睬 (V) pay attention to, to give heed; to respond to another's address /Dím·gáai néih m̀h·chói kéuih a? Why do you ignore him?

choi 菜 (N) vegetable; dish of food as those served in restaurants

choi·dōu 菜刀 (N) a cook's chopper (M: bá)

choi·gáu 賽狗 (VO/N) dog race

chói·hùhng 彩虹 (N) rainbow

choi·máh 賽馬 (VO) to race horses /Géi·sí choi·máh a? When will the race be?

choi·páai 菜牌 (N) menu

choi·páau 賽跑 (N) a foot race

chói·sīk(ge) 彩色 (At) variegated; many colored

chói·yuhng 採用 (V) adopt, use (lit. to select for use)

chòih·jyú·lóu 財主佬 (N) a rich man

chòih·cháan 財產 (N) property, estate

chòih·fúng 裁縫 (N) tailor

chòih·gon 才幹 (N) ability; talent

chòih·jing 財政 (N) finance

chòih·líu 材料 (N) material

chòih·pun·kyùhn 裁判權 (N) jurisdiction

chòih-sò-hohk-chín 才疏學淺 (IE) of slight ability and little education

chok 嘬 (V) jolt

chóng 廠 (N) factory (M: gàan)

chong·jouh 創造 (V) create

chòu 粗 (SV) be rough; coarse

chou 醋 (N) vinegar

chou·bouh 燥暴 (SV) rash; blustering

chòu·chúhng 粗重 (SV) bulky; heavy

chóu·déi　草地　(N) lawn; meadow

chóu·góu　草稿　(N) a rough draft

chóu·hàaih　草鞋　(N) straw sandals

chóu·jí　草紙　(N) coarse paper

chòu·juhk　粗俗　(SV) vulgar; uncouth

chòu·lihn　操練　(V) drill (mil.)

chòu·lòuh　操勞　(SV) working hard (used either for an old person or one who is doing manual labor)

chòu·lóuh　粗魯　(SV) rude; awkward

chóu·móu　草帽　(N) straw hat (M: déng)

chóu·yéung　草羊　(N) sheep (M: jek)

chòuh　嘈嘈(SV/V) be noisy /to make a noise, causing disturbance; argue

chóuh　貯　(V) save (money)

chòuh·séng　嘈醒　(V) wakened by noise

chùhng　蟲(虫)(N) worm, insect

chúhng　重　(SV) heavy

chùhng·chí·jí·hauh　從此之後　(Ph) since then

chùhng·chìhn　從前　(MA) formerly

chùhng·gàm·yíh·hauh　從今以後　(Ph) from now on

chùhng·gwàn　從軍　(VO) to join the service, to be a soldier

chùhng·lòih　從來　(MA) from the beginning; heretofore

chùhng·syú　松鼠　(N) squirrel (M: jek)

chùhng·syuh　松樹　(N) pine tree

Chùhng·yèuhng　重陽　(N) the Height-ascending festival

chūk·douh　速度　(N) velocity; speed

chūk·gei　速記　(N) shorthand

chūk·sàng　畜牲　(N) animals

chūk·sìhng·fō　速成科　(N) short course of study

chùng　沖　(V) make (tea or coffee) /chùng·chàh, make tea

chūng　葱　(N) scallions

chùng·chàh　沖茶　(VO) make tea

chùng·daht　衝突　(V/N) conflict, clash/ conflict

chùng·fahn　充份　(SV) ample

chùng·fut·lóu　充濶佬　(VO) pretend to have lots of money

chùng·ga·fē　沖咖啡　(VO) make coffee

chùng·johng　衝撞　(V) offend

chùng·jūk　充足　(SV) sufficient

chùng·lèuhng　沖涼　(VO) take a shower bath

chùng·lèuhng·fóng　沖涼房　(N) bathroom; shower

chùng·mìhng　聰明　(SV) be clever

chùng·mòhng　匆忙　(SV) be in a hurry

chyú·ji　處置　(V) settle (a matter)

chyúh·chòhng sāt　貯藏室　(N) storeroom

chyúh·chūk·ngàhn·hòhng　儲蓄銀行　(N) savings bank

chyùh·fèi　除非　(MA) unless

chyùh·fóng　廚房　(N) kitchen

chyùh·fóng·lóu　廚房佬　(N) cook

chyúh·sai　處世　(VO) engage in the business of life; deal with people

chyùhn　傳　(V) to hand down, to pass on

chyùhn　全　(BF) entire; whole

chyùhn　存　(V) deposit

chyùhn·bouh·sàn·gà　全部身家　(N) whole property (all that one owns)

chyùhn·dāan　傳單　(N) circulars; hand-bills

chyùhn·daih　傳遞　(V) pass from one to another

chyùhn·douh　傳道　(VO) preach the gospel

chyùhn·douh·yàhn　傳道人　(N) mission-ary, evangelist

chyùhn·fo　存貨　(N/VO) goods in stock/ stock goods

chyùhn·fún　存欵　(N) deposited money

chyùhn·gān　存根　(N) counterfoil or stub

chyùhn·haauh　全校　(N) the school as a whole

chyùhn·háp　全盒　(N) partitioned tray (for sweets)

chyùhn·joih　存在　(V) exist

chyùhn·sai·gaai　全世界　(N) the whole world

chyùhn·séui　泉水　(N) spring water

chyùhn·syut　傳說　(N) legend

chyùhn·tái　全體　(N) the whole body of (an organization)

chyùhn·túng　傳統　(At/N) traditional/ tradition

chyùhn·yíhm　傳染　(V) infect; spread (a disease)

chyùhn·yíhm·behng　傳染病　(N) con-tagious disease

chyùn　穿　(RVE/V) pierce through/leak out　/Yiu jíng·chyùn nī·buhng chèuhng sìn·ji dāk. We have to pierce through this wall. /Ngóh go dói yauh chyùn·jó la. There is a hole in my pocket again.

-chyun　寸　(M) inch

chyūn·bōu　穿煲　(VO) the secret is out

chyun-bouh-nàahn-hàahng　寸步難行　(IE) unable to move even an inch, hence com-pletely obstructed

chyūn·gwo　穿過　(RV) go through, pass through

chyún·hei 喘氣 (VO) gasp
chyūn·jàm 穿針 (VO) thread a needle
chyūn·lūng 穿窿 (At/VO) there's a
hole in . . . /Ngóh m̀h·yiu nī·go
chyūn·lūng ge. I don't want this one,
it has a hole in it. /Buhng chèuhng
chyùn·jó yāt·go lūng. There's a hole
in the wall.
chyun·màaih 串埋 (V) gang up with;
string together

D

dá 打 (V) hit
dā 打 (M) a dozen
dá·bá 打靶 (VO) to execute by shooting
dá·baaih·jó 打敗咗 (V) defeat; be defeated /Yùhgwo A dabaaih·jó B, if A
defeats B; B dabaaihjó. B was defeated.
dá·baahn 打扮 (V) dress up; make up
dá·bō 打波 (VO) play ball
dá·chek·laak 打赤 (Vi) be naked
dá·chìn·chāu 打韆鞦 (VO) to swing (on
a swing)
dá·chūng·fùng 打衝鋒 (VO) charge
(mil.)
dá·dāan 打單 (VO) blackmail
dá·dái 打底 (VO) lay a foundation (fig.)
dá·dihn 打掂 (A) vertically; straight
dá·dihn·bou 打電報 (VO) send a telegram
dá·dihn·wá 打電話 (VO) to make a
phone call
dá·dóu 打倒 -(V/Ph) knock down /Down
with . . . !
dá·dou·tan 打倒褪 (V) walk backward;
do something falteringly
dá·fó·gèi 打火機 (N) lighter
dá·fùng 打風 (VO) have a typhoon
dá·fú·tàuh 打斧頭 (VO) to cheat,
squeeze
dá·gàang·lóu 打更佬 (N) watchman
dá·gāau 打交 (VO) fight (as in a brawl)
dá·gip 打劫 (V) rob, plunder /dá·gip
ngàhnhòhng, rob a bank
dá·gú 打鼓 (VO) beat a drum
dá·gú 打估 (VO) ask a riddle
dá·gūng 打工 (VO) work (conf. jouh·sih)
dá·gùn·sì 打官司 (VO) go to court, have
a lawsuit
dá·gwàn·dáu 打筋斗 (VO) perform a
somersault
dá·haahm·louh 打喊路 (VO) yawn
dá·hāt·chi 打乞痕 (VO) sneeze
dá·hòi 打開 (RV) open

dá·jàai 打齋 (VO) religious services for
the dead (by Buddhist monks or Taoist
priests)
dá·jáap 打雜 (N/VO) household help
(servant) /doing household work
dá·jām 打針 (VO) have an injection or
inoculation
dá·jeung 打仗 (VO) make war, fight
dá·jih 打字 (VO) to type
dá·jiu·fù 打招呼 (VO) hail, greet
dá·jung 打中 (RV) hit the bull's eye
dá·léih 打理 (V) take care of; manage
dá·lèuih 打雷 (VO) thundering
dá·lòh 打鑼 (VO) beat a gong
dá·màh·jéuk 打麻雀 (VO) play Mah-Jongg
dá·m̀h·tùng 打唔通 (Ph) cannot put
through a phone call
dá·páai 打牌 (VO) play cards
dá·pē·páai 打啤牌 (VO) play poker
dá·pūk·ká 打撲卡 (VO) playing poker
dá·séi 打死 (RV) killed (by beating); shot
to death
dá·séng·jìng·sàhn 打醒精神 (Ph) to be
fully alert
dá·séung 打賞 (V) to reward, tip
dá·sí·īk 打使噎 (VO) hiccup
dá·sím 打閃 (VO) lightning flashes
dá·sing·jeung 打勝仗 (VO) win a battle
dá·syun 打算 (V/N) plan to, plan
dá·syun·pùhn 打算盤 (VO) use an abacus to figure
dá·ting 打聽 (V) inquire
dá·tòi 打胎 (VO) secure abortion
dá·wàahng 打橫 (A) crosswise
dá·yíuh 打擾 (V) trouble
dá·yuh·fòhng·jām 打預防針 (VO) have a
preventive inoculation
daahm 啖 (M) mouthful; puff (of smoke,
breath, etc.)
daahm, táahm 淡 (SV) insipid
daahm·dihng 淡定 (SV) calm (as used for
describing a person)
daahn·gā 蛋家 (N) 'Boat people,' floating
population
daahn·gōu 蛋糕 (N) sponge cake
daahn·gūng 彈弓 (N) spring
daahn·gūng·chòhng 彈弓床 (N) bed with
springs
daahn·haih 但係 (MA) but, however
daahn·yuhn 但願 (Ph) wish, hope (for
formal use)
daahp 沓 (M) pile
daahp·héi 沓起 (V) to pile up
daahp·jeng 搭正 (V) be exactly at (a
given time)

daaht·dou 達到 (RV) reach, attain

daaht·dou·muhk·dīk 達到目的 (Ph) to attain one's goal

dáai 帶 (N) belt, strip of cloth

daai 帶 (V) take or bring along

daai 戴 (V) wear; put on (a hat, etc.)

daai 帶 (M) region, area, zone

daaih 大 (SV) be large, big

daaih·bá 大把 (At) a great deal of, plenty of

daaih·bá·sai·gaai 大把世界 (IE) having a very promising future; very rich

daaih-bāt-sèung-tùhng 大不相同 (IE) there is a big difference

daaih·béi 大脾 (N) thigh

daaih·bīu·tàih 大標題 (N) headlines

daaih·dáam 大胆 (SV) daring, foolhardy, brave

daaih·dò·sou 大多數 (N/At) majority

daaih·fòng 大方 (SV) be dignified; generous; open-minded

daaih·fūk·gú 大腹賈 (N) rich merchant

daaih·gā 大家 (N) we all; all of us

daaih-gāt-leih-sih 大吉利是 (IE) Very lucky! (an expression which also may be used to counteract an ominous or foreboding event)

daaih·guhk 大局 (N) general situation (of a nation or of the world)

daaih·gwōng·dāng 大光燈 (N) pressure lamp

daaih·hah 大廈 (N) mansion (M: gàan)

daaih·hohk 大學 (N) university (M: gàan)

daaih·ji·ge chìhng·yìhng 大致嘅情形 (Ph) general condition of ...

daaih·ji·ge yi·si 大致嘅意思 (Ph) general idea

daaih·ji·seuhng 大致上 (A) in general; generally speaking; roughly

daaih·jung 大眾 (N) the people, the masses

daaih·kói 大概 (A) probably, approximately

daaih·kwài·mòuh 大規模 (A/SV) on a large scale

daaih·lāu 大縷 (N) overcoat (M: gihn)

daaih·leuhng 大量 (SV) generous, liberal, openhanded

daaih·lihk 大力 (SV) be strong

daaih·léuk 大略 (N) outline

Daaih·luhk 大陸 (N) mainland (usually China's Mainland)

daaih·paau 大砲 (N) field piece, cannon

daaih·pài 大批 (At) a large group, a large amount

daaih·sàhn 大臣 (N) minister (in a monarchy)

daaih-sai-só-chèui 大勢所趨 (Ph) the tendency of the world. /Yìga daaih·sai· swó chèui, go·go hauh·sāang·jái dōu haih gám ge la. This is the tendency of the world, every youngster acts like this.

daaih·sèng 大聲 (A/SV) loudly (lit. big voice) /be loud

daaih·sèng gám ngaai 大聲嗌喂 (Ph) yell loudly

daaih·sèung·fùng 大傷風 (N) a bad cold; influenza

daaih·tàuh·jām 大頭針 (N) pin (M: jì)

daaih-tùhng-síu-yih 大同小異 (IE) not very different, for the most part alike

daaih·wah 大話 (N) bragging; lies

daaih·wái 大位 (N) seat of honor

daaih·yàhn 大人 (N) adult

daaih·yi 大意 (SV) careless

daaih·yi 大意 (N) general idea

dàam 擔 (V) carry on the shoulder with a pole (by one person)

dàam·bóu 担保 (V/N) guarantee/guarantor

dàam·bóu·yàhn 担保人 (N) guarantor

dàam·gok 躭擱 (V) to hinder, delay

dáam·hip 胆怯 (SV) timid, cowardly

dàam·sàm 担心 (V) worry about

dàam·séui 担水 (VO) carry water

dàam·yahm 担任 (V) undertake

dàan, dāan 單 (At) single; odd in number

dàan 單 (M) measure for a business transaction /yāt·dāan sàang·yi, a business transaction

daan 誕 (N) birthday (for deities) /Yèh·sōu·daan, Christmas; Tìn·hauh· daan, birthday of the Queen of Heaven

dāan 單 (N) list; bill (M: jēung, tìuh)

dāan·chē 單車 (N) bicycle (M: ga)

dàan·sou 單數 (N) odd number

dāan·wái 單位 (N) unit

dàan·yàhn·fóng 單人房 (N) single room

daap 搭 (V/CV) to board train, boat or airplane /daap·syuhn, to board a boat; /daap·chè, to board a vehicle ... train, or bus; daap·gèi, to board a plane

daap 答 (V) answer, reply (general)

daap·fūk 答覆 (V) answer, reply (in a serious or thoughtful manner)

daap·haak 搭客 (N) passengers

daap·kìuh 搭橋 (VO) to build a small bridge

daap·pàahng 搭棚 (VO) to erect a scaffolding or mat-shed

daap·sihk 搭食 (VO) to board with

daap·sou 答數 (N) the answer (in mathematics)

daap·tói 搭枱 (VO) to share a table with others (in a bar or teahouse, etc.)

daap·ying 答應 (V) promise

daat 笪 (M) measure for place

daat 撻 (V) fall down flat, flounder

daat·dài 撻低 (V) fall flat

dahk·biht 特別 (A/SV) distinctively, unusually, especially; strange

dahk·dāng 特登 (A) specially, particularly

dahk·dím 特點 (N) special features, special characteristics

dahk·sīk 特色 (N) distinctive

dahk·sing 特性 (N) peculiarity

dahk·yi 特意 (A) intentionally, purposely, specially

dahk·yìhn·gāan 突然閒 (A) suddenly

dahm·geuk 霎腳 (VO) stamp the foot

dahn 燉 (V) steam with low heat

dahp 溚 (V) get wet by rain, in the rain; drip

dahp 揢 (V) hammer /Béi gó chéui dahp·háh kéuih. Hammer it a little.

dahp 揢 (V) pound /dahp·seui, pound to bits; dahp·laahn, to break, to pound to a pulp

dahp·sāp 溚濕 (RV) get wet by rain. /Kéuih jauh gam kéih·hái gó·syu béi yúh dahp woh, néih wah kéuih sòh mh·sòh a? Isn't he crazy, just standing in the rain and getting wet? /Dahp·sāp go sàn yáuh māt·yéh hóu nē? Was there any point in getting yourself wet in the rain?

daht·chēut·làih 凸出来 (At) project, jut out, bulge

daht·yìhn·gāan 突然閒 (A) suddenly, without warning

dài 低 (BF) down

dái 抵 (SV) be worth; worthwhile

dái 底 (BF) bottom; end

dái·dāk·jyuh 抵得住 (V) able to stand

dái·dāk·ngoh 抵得餓 (V) be able to endure hunger

dái·fu 底褲 (N) underpants (M: tìuh)

dai·gwok·jyú·yih 帝國主義 (N) imperialism

dái·hah 底下 (PW) underneath, beneath (interchangeable with hah bihn)

dái·jai 抵制 (V) boycott

dái·kong 抵抗 (V/N) resist /resistance

dái·ngaat 抵押 (V/N) pledge; mortgage; /pledges, securities

dái·sāam 底衫 (N) undershirt (M: gihn)

dái·wái 詆譭 (V) villify, slander

daih 遞 (V) hand to; deliver by hand

daih 第 (BF) when prefixed to cardinal numbers makes them ordinals /daih·yāt, the first; daih·yih, the second, etc.

daih·hìng 弟兄 (N) brethen

daih·jí 弟子 (N) pupils, disciple

daih·yih (plus M) (N) another; other /daih·yih go, another one; daih·yih dī, other; daih·yih·dī yàhn, other people

dāk 得 (V) get, receive, gain; infected with (disease)

dāk 得 (P) can, may /Néih heui·dāk ma? Can you go? /Ngóh heui dāk ma? May I go?

dāk·dóu 得到 (RV) got, attained, obtained

dāk·faat 得法 (SV) cleverly devised; well done

dāk·gwo-ché-gwo 得過且過 (IE) to manage on what little one has; indolent

dāk·hàahn 得閒 (SV) having leisure time

dāk·hahng 德行 (N) virtue

dāk·jaih 得滯 (A) more (or less) than enough; (suffix to SV indicating a regrettable degree) /dò·dāk·jaih, too much; siu·dāk·jaih, too little

dāk·jeuih 得罪 (V) offend; displease

dāk·jéung 得獎 (VO) win a prize

dāk·lihk 得力 (SV) capable /sèui·yiu yāt·go dāk·lihk·ge bòng·sáu, need a capable helper

dāk·yàhn·gèng 得人驚 (SV) terrifying

dāk·yàhn·sàm 得人心 (SV) popular

dāk·yi 得意 (SV) be interesting; strange; cute; pleased; satisfied

dám 揼 (V) throw away, discard

dam 喋 (V) suspend (by, from)

dám·gwāt 揼骨 (VO) Chinese massage

dám·jó 揼咗 (V) throw away

dám·laahn 揼爛 (RV) pound to pieces

dám·yan 揼印 (VO) to stamp a mark

dán 壆 (M) measure for storied building

dán 壆 (V) store away; store up; hoard

dán·fo 壆貨 (VO) to store up goods; to buy up goods

dán·syùhn 壆船 (N) a storage hulk

dàng 登 (V) publish (in a newspaper, magazine, etc.); insert (an advertisement, notice, etc.)

dáng 等 (V) wait

dáng 等 (N) class

dáng 等 (V) let, allow (let one have time to do something)

dang 凳 (N) bench (for sitting) (M: jèung)

dāng 燈 (N) lamp, light (M: jáan)

dāng·dáam 燈胆 (N) light bulb

dáng·dáng 等等 (Ph) and so on, and so forth, etc.

dàng·deui 登對 (SV) well matched

dàng-fó-fài-wòhng 燈火輝煌 (IE) all lit up and busy

dàng·gei 登記 (V) register

dáng·hauh 等候 (V) wait for

dāng·gwòng 燈光 (N) light /Nī·gàan fóng ge dāng·gwòng m̀h·gau boh. The light in this room is not adequate.

dāng·jaau 燈罩 (N) lampshade

dāng·jai 燈掣 (N) light switch

dāng·jit 燈節 (N) Lantern Festival (15th day of the 1st lunar month)

dáng·kāp 等級 (N) rating, grade, rank

dāng·lùhng 燈籠 (N) lantern

dáng·ngóh·tái·háh 等我睇吓 (IE) Let me see

dāng·sam 燈芯 (N) lampwick

dāng·taap 燈塔 (N) lighthouse

dāng·túng 燈筒 (N) lamp chimney

dáng·yù 等於 (EV) amounts to, equals

dàp·dài (go) tàuh 嗒低頭 (Ph) look downward (lit. bend down one's head)

dàu 篼 (M) for trees

dáu 豆 (N) bean

dáu 斗 (M) peck

dau 鬥 (V) compete, race /dau·jáu, to run a race; dau·syùhn, a boat race; dau·faai, to race

dau 嗲* (V) touch

dau 竇 (M) den (of animals), nest (of birds)

dau·géng 鬥頸 (V) to act contrarily

dàu·hei 鬥氣 (V) tilt up; take up things as water, rice sand, etc. in the hands

dau·jàng 鬥爭 (V/N) struggle

dau·lùhng·jàu 鬥龍舟 (VO) race dragon-boats

dau·lùhng·syùhn 鬥龍船 (VO) race dragon-boats

dau·muhk 鬥木 (N) carpentry

dàu·sàang·yi 兜生意 (VO) solicit business

dauh·fuh 豆腐 (N) bean curd

dauh·làuh 逗留 (Vi) tarry, loiter /Néih dauh·lauh·hái nī·syu jouh mātyéh a? What are you tarrying here for?

dauh·sā 豆沙 (N) skinless beans cooked and sweetened

dé 嗲 (SV) childish

dé·diu 嗲吊 (SV) procrastinate

dehk·máih 糴米 (VO) buy rice

dehng 定 (V/N) make reservation; order something, /deposit

dehng 定(訂)(V) subscribe to (a periodical, etc.)

dehng 定(訂)(V) reserve /dehng gàan fóng, reserve a room; dehng go wái, reserve a seat

dehng·fo 定貨 (VO) order goods

dehng·jouh 定做 (Ph) made to order

déi 哋 (P) used as a suffix for the reduplicated form of a monosyllabic SV, meaning 'rather,' e.g. fèih·féi·déi, rather fat; ai·ái·déi, rather short; etc.

deih 地 (N) land

deih·báan 地板 (N) floor

deih·bouh 地步 (N) place, footing, position, state, condition; address

deih·dím 地點 (N) site, location

deih·fòng 地方 (N) place

deih·há 地下 (N) ground floor

deih·jí 地址 (N) address

deih·jīn 地氈 (N) rug (M: faai)

deih·jyú 地主 (N) landlord (lit. landowner)

deih·kàuh 地球 (N) the earth

deih·kēui 地區 (N) area, section

deih·léih 地理 (N) geography

deih·lòuh 地牢 (N) basement, cellar

deih·pìhng·sin 地平線 (N) horizon

deih·tòuh 地圖 (N) map (M: fūk)

deih·waih 地位 (N) position, status

deih·yìhng 地形 (N) terrain

dék 笛 (N) flute; fife

dèng 釘 (V) nail

dèng 訂 (V) bind

deng 揿* (V) throw, smash

dēng 釘 (V/N) nail/nail (M: háu)

dèng·náu 釘鈕 (VO) sew button on

dèng·syù 訂書 (VO) bind books

deuhn 鈍 (SV) blunt; stupid

dèui 堆 (M) pile, heap

déui 隊 (BF) corps; unit /sìu·fòhng·déui, fire brigade

deui 對 (CV/V) to, toward (facing)

deui 對 (V) check, compare

deui·fòng 對方 (N) opponent

deui·fuh 對付 (V) cope with, handle (a tough problem or person)

deui·lyún (M: fu) 對聯 (N) couplet, parallel sentences (such as written on a scroll found in a Chinese parlor or the gate of a temple, etc.) (M: fu)

deui·mihn 對面 (PW) opposite

deui·mihn·hói 對面海 (PW) the other side of the harbor

deui·m̀h·jyuh 對唔住 (IE) I'm sorry

deui . . . móuh·hing·cheui 對…冇興趣 (Ph) be not interested in

deui·ngohn 對岸 (N) on the opposite shore

deui . . . yáuh·hing·cheui 對…有興趣 (Ph) be interested in

deui·yù 對於 (CV) with respect to, in regard to, toward

déui·yùhn 隊員 (N) member of a corps

deuih 隊 (M) corps; unit (a group of persons organized for a particular purpose)

deuih·jéung 隊長 (N) head of such corps

deuk 斲 (V) mince, chop

deuk·muhk·níuh 啄木鳥 (N) woodpecker (M: jek)

dōun 噸 (M) a ton

dèun·háuh 敦厚 (SV) sincere; honest

dèung 啄 (V) peck

dī 啲 (M) (indicates the plural form of the noun following) /nī·dī·yéh, these things; gó·dī·syù, those books

(yat) dī 啲 (M) a little /M̀h·gòi néih béi (yāt·)dī ngóh. Please give me a little.

dī·dá 啲打 (N) a trumpet

dī·gam·dēu 啲咁哚 (N) a tiny bit

dihk 滴 (M) a drop

dihk 敵 (BF) enemy, rival /dihk·yàhn, enemy; dihk·gwok, enemy country; dihk·dóng, rival party

dihk·yàhn 敵人 (N) enemy

dihn 電 (N) electricity

dihn·báan 電版 (N) plate (for printing)

dihn·bìng·gwaih 電冰櫃 (N) refrigerator

dihn·bīu 電錶 (N) electric meter

dihn·bò 電波 (N) radio wave

dihn·bou 電報 (N) telegram (M: fùng)

dihn·bou·gúk 電報局 (N) telegraph office

dihn·chè 電車 (N) tramcar

dihn·chìh 電池 (N) electric battery

dihn·dāng 電燈 (N) electric light

dihn·fai 電費 (N) electricity bill

dihn·fùng·sin 電風扇 (N) electric fan

dihn·hei 電器 (At) electrical

dihn·jūng 電鐘 (N) electric bell

dihn·làuh 電流 (N) electric current

dihn·lòuh 電路 (N) electric stove

dihn·máh 電碼 (N) telegraph code

dihn·màhn 電文 (N) telegram message

dihn·sām 電芯 (N) battery (for flashlight)

dihn·sih 電視 (N) television set

dihn·sin 電線 (N) electric wire (M: tìuh)

dihn·syùhn·jái 電船仔 (N) motorboat (M: jek)

dihn·tòih 電台 (N) broadcasting station

dihn·tong·dáu 電燙斗 (N) electric iron

dihn·túng 電筒 (N) flashlight (M: jì)

dihn·wá 電話 (N) telephone

dihn·yàuh 電油 (N) gasoline

dihn·yíng 電影 (N) movie (M: chēut)

dihn·yíng·pín 電影片 (N) movies; movie film

dihng (·haih) 定係 (MA) or /Haih nī·go dihng gó·go a? Is it this one or that one?

dihng 定(初)(V) set up (a project, rules or laws), make (plans)

dihng 定(訂)(V) subscribe to (a periodical, etc.)

dihng 定 (SV) calm, undisturbed; steady

dihng·fān 訂婚 (VO) become engaged

dihng·ga 定價 (N) list price

dihng·gai·waahk 訂計劃 (VO) make plans

dihng·jeuih 定罪 (VO) sentence, condemn

dihng·kèi·chyùhn·fún 定期存欵 (N) savings account

dihng·ngáak 定額 (N) a fixed quantity or number

dihng·saht 定實 (V) already decided

V dihng . . . sìn V定先 (Pat) do something beforehand, to have something prepared in advance. /Néih yiu wah·dihng kéuih tèng ngóh·deih yiu géi·dō sìn·ji dāk boh. You should tell him first how much we want. /Nà, ngóh yìh·gā tùhng néih góng·dihng sìn la. Now let me make this point clear to you first. /Néih béi·dihng dò·síu chín go gùng·yàhn sìn, tìng·jiu·jóu yāt tīng·gwòng jauh hó·yíh heui máai sung la. You give some money to the amah tonight, so she can go to the market and buy some food at daybreak. /Ngóh·deih yìh·gā gai·dihng tìuh sou sìn, gám ngóh·deih jauh ji·dou juhng yiu chàuh géi dò chín la. Let's figure out exactly how much money it costs, then we'll know how much more money we should raise.

dihng·yeuk 訂約 (VO) make an agreement

dihng·yih 定義 (N) definition

dihp 碟 (M) measure for dish of food

dihp·héi 疊起 (V) pile up

dihp·hóu 疊好 (RV) pile up carefully

diht·jeuih 秩序 (N) order, orderliness

dīk·dong 的當 (SV/A) proper /properly, satisfactorily

dīk·kok 的確 (A) really

dīk·sí 的士 (N) taxi (M: ga)

dím 點 (M) point

dím 點 (N) a dot, speck, comma

dím(·jūng) 點(鐘) (M) hour

dím 點 (V) count

dím 點 (V) ignite, light up

dim 喵' (V) touch

dím(·yéuhg) 點' (MA) how?

dím·choi 點菜 (VO) to order (dishes for a Chinese meal)

dím·gáai 點解 (MA) why? how is it that . . . ?

dím·jeuhk 點着 (V) light up (a fire, a lamp or a stove)

dím·méng 點名 (VO) call the roll

dím·sām 點心 (N) confections; pastry; refreshment (M: gihn)

dìn·dóu 顛倒 (V) upset, turn upside down; topsy-turvy

dìn·gáu 癲狗 (N) a mad dog

dìn·jáu 碘酒 (N) iodine

dìn·jó 癲咗 (V) went crazy

dìn·kwòhng 癲狂 (SV) insane

dín·láih 典禮 (N) ceremony, ritual

ding 梃' (N) stem of fruit

díng·dihng 定定 (A) firmly, unmovingly

díng·dò 頂多 (A) at the most

ding hahp·tùhng 訂合同 (Ph) sign a contract

díng·hēung 丁香 (SV) tiny, delicate

díng·hēung·fā 丁香花 (N) lilac

díng·m̀h·jyuh 頂唔住 (Ph) can't hold out any longer

dīng·yàu 丁憂 (N) in mourning for parents. /Kéuih jing·joih·dīng·yàu. He is in mourning for his parents.

dit 跌 (V) fall, drop

dit 跌 (V) fall (of price)

dit·chān 跌親' (RV) fell down and got hurt

dit·dài 跌低 (RV) fell down

dit·dóu 跌倒 (V) fall down

dit·ga 跌價 (VO) a fall in price

dit·lohk 跌落 (V) fall down

dìt·lohk·heui 跌落去 (RV) drop down, fall down (away from the speaker)

dit·lohk·lèih 跌落來 (RV) drop down, fall down (toward the speaker)

dìu·gá 丟架 (VO) lose face, blast reputation

diu·géng 吊頸 (VO) to hang oneself

dīu·hāk 彫刻 (V) carve, engrave, inscribe, cut

diu·héi 弔起 (V) hang up, suspend

diu·jūng 吊鐘 (N) uvula

diu·jūng·fā 吊鐘花 (N) bellflower

dìu·màahn 刁蠻 (SV) perverse; unreasonable

diu·sòng 吊喪 (VO) tribute to the dead at a funeral

diu·yú 釣魚 (VO/N) fish/fishing

diuh 丟 (V) throw, throw away

diuh·chàh 調查 (V/N) investigate/investigation

diuh·diu·fihng 掉掉捀' (SV) swaying; dangling

diuh·hoi 丟開 (V) throw away

diuh·jyun·tàuh 掉轉頭 (V/A) turn around (a thing) /as soon as (one turns one's head). /diuh·jyun·tàuh ji dāk. It won't work, unless you turn it around. /Kéuih diuh·jyun·tàuh jauh m̀h·gei·dāk ge la. As soon as he turns his head he will forget.

diuh·wuhn 掉換 (V) exchange

dò 多 (SV) be many, be much

dò 多 (BF) excessively, used as a verb suffix

dō·dāk 多得 (Ph) thank you for /Dō·dāk néih bòng ngóh. Thank you for your help. Dō·dāk·saai. Many thanks.

dō·dāk·néih 多得你 (Ph) thanks to you. /Dō dāk néih bòng·mòhng. Thanks to your help

dò·fàahn·néih 多煩你 (IE) May I trouble you to . . . Would you please . . . ?

dò·jeh (·néih) 多謝你 (IE) Thank you.

dò·jéui 多嘴 (SV) talkative

dò·jó 多咗' (SV) be more, excessive; too much, too many

dó·láahn 躲懶 (VO) to shirk work

dō·sí 多士 (N) toast (M: faai)

dò·síu 多少 (A) a little, some; somewhat

dò·sou 多數 (A/At) majority

dò·yùh 多餘 (SV) superflous, overdone

doh·lohk 墮落 (V) fall into decay, deteriorate

dohk 度 (V) measure (length or distance)

dohk·sàn 度身 (VO) take the measurements of a person

dohng 蕩 (V) wander

dohng·sāt·jó (·louh) 蕩失咀 (Ph) lose one's way

dói 袋 (N) pocket

doih 代 (M) a generation

doih 待 (V) treat

doih·bíu 代表 (V/N) represent/representative

doih·bíu·yàhn 代表人 (N) representative

doih·léih 代理 (V/N) to be a commercial agent /commercial agent

doih·maahn (·saai) 怠慢(嗮) (Ph) I
have treated you shabbily

doih·sou 代數 (N) Algebra

doih·yuh 待遇 (N) treatment; salary

dóng 黨 (N) political party

dong 檔 (BF/M) a sidewalk stall /mea-
sure for sidewalk stalls

dong 當 (V) consider as, treat as,
regard as

dong·jok 當作 (V) to regard as

dōng·bìng 當兵 (VO) to join the service,
to be a soldier

dōng·chò 當初 (MA) at the beginning

dòng·deih 當地 (At) local

dòng·gà 當家 (VO) to manage a household

dòng-guhk-jé-màih 當局者迷
(IE) confused, bewildered (when it is
one's turn to move, as in chess, one is
easily confused)

dong·háu 檔口 (N) stall

dong·haih 當係 (V) consider as, regard
as

dong·jouh 當作 (V) consider as, regard
as

dōng·jùng 當中 (PW) in the midst,
middle, center

dóng·jyuh 擋住 (V) to block up (a passage, road, etc.); prevent (a passage)

dòng·mihn 當面 (A) face to face

dóng·paai 黨派 (N) parties, factions

dòng·mín 當面 (A) face to face

dong·póu 當鋪 (N) pawnshop

dōng·sàm 當心 (V) beware of

dòng·sìh 當時 (A) at that time; at that
moment

dòng·tòhng 當堂 (A) on the spur of the
moment

dòng·yìhn 當然 (MA) naturally, of
course

dòng·yín 當然 (MA) naturally, of
course

dóu 島 (N) island

dóu 到 (RVE) ending of a RV /wán·dóu,
has found

dóu 倒 (V) pour; pour out (dispose of)

dóu 度 (P) approximately /Ńgh·sahp·
màn dóu. Approximately fifty dollars.

dóu (·jou) 倒灶 (VO) go out of business,
bankrupt

dou 到 (V) arrive at, reach

dou 到 (RVE) ending of a RV /duhk·dou
daih·luhk·fo, read up to lesson six

dou 到 (P) a verbal suffix used for euphony

dōu 都 (A) also; too, likewise; in all cases;
in either case

dōu 刀 (N) knife (M: jēung)

dóu·bok 賭博 (V/N) gamble /gamble

dou·bouh 到埗 (V) arrive

dou·chàih 到齊 (RV) all arrive

dóu·chín 賭錢 (VO) gamble /gambling

dou·chyu, dou·syu 到處 (PW) everywhere (only used in subjective case)

dou·daaht 到達 (V) arrive

dou·dái 到底 (A) after all; finally (lit. to
the bottom)

dou·geih 妒忌 (V/SV) to be jealous
/jealous

dou·gihk 到極 (A) suffix to SV, indicating superlative or exaggerated degree
/Hóu·dou·gihk. Great!

dōu haih . . . la 都係⋯嘑' (Ph) still
(it) is (better)

dōu haih m̀h hóu la 都係唔好嘑'
(Ph) still it is not good to do it

dōu·háu 刀口 (N) edge of knife, blade

dōu·jái 刀仔 (N) pocket knife (M: bá)

dōu·juhng·haih . . . hóu la 都重係⋯好嘑'
(Ph) still it is much better

dou·kèih 到期 (V) reach a fixed date

dóu·laahp·saap 倒擸𢶍 (Ph) take out
or throw out the garbage

dóu·máh 賭馬 (VO) to bet on a horse

dóu seui 倒水 (Ph) pour water

dou·sìh 到時 (A) when the time comes;
by that time /Dou·sìh sìn·ji syun la.
When the time comes we'll see.

douh 度 (M) measure for door, gate,
window

douh 度 (M) trip (made by boat or car)

douh 道 (BF) road, street /Castle Peak
Road, Chīng·sàan douh

douh 度 (M) degree

douh·dāk 道德 (N) virtue, morality

Douh·dāk·gìng 道德經 (N) the Scripture of Taoism

Douh·gaau 道教 (N) Taoism

douh·gām·ge 鍍金嘅 (At) gilded

douh·geih 妒忌 (V) to be jealous

douh·gwo 渡過 (V) cross (river, ocean,
etc.) /pass through /douh·gwo nàahn·gwàan,
passing through the bottleneck

douh·gyūn·fā 杜鵑花 (N) red azalea

douh·léih 道理 (N) logical reason; the
truth

douh·louh 道路 (N) path, road, way

douh·sí 道士 (N) Taoist priest

douh·yaht 度日 (VO) to spend or pass the day

duhk 讀 (V) study; read

duhk 毒 (N) poison, venom /yáuh·duhk, poisonous; móuh·dahk, nonpoisonous

duhk·bún 讀本 (N) a reader (a textbook)

duhk·lahp 獨立 (V/N) independent (as a country) /independence

duhng 洞 (N) cave, hole

duhng·gèi 動機 (N) motive

duhng·jok 動作 (N) action, motion

duhng·kéih 棟企 (At) perpendicular /dá duhng·kéih, be set perpendicularly

duhng·maht 動物 (N) animal

duhng·maht·yún 動物園 (N) zoo

duhng·sàn 動身 (VO) start (on a trip)

duhng·sáu·seuht 動手術 (VO) have a surgical operation

duhng·yàhn 動人 (SV) touching (emotional)

dūk·gùng 督工 (V) superintend; to act as overseer of work

dūk·jyuh 督住 (V) compel; supervise

dūk·seun 篤信 (V) firmly believe

dùng 東 (PW/BF) east

dung 凍 (SV) cool, cold

dúng 懂 (V/RVE) understand/indicates what's heard is understood

Dūng·fòng 東方 (PW) the East; the Orient

dūng·gù 冬菇 (N) a kind of mushroom (Chinese mushroom)

dung·gwán·séui 凍滾水 (N) cold boiled water

dung·séui 凍水 (N) cold water

dūng·tīn 冬天 (N) winter

dúng·yàhn·chìhng 懂人情 (SV) considerate, to understand human nature

dyuhn 段 (M) item; paragraph; section

dyuhn·jyuht 斷絕 (V) cease; cut off /dyuhn·jyuht gāau·tùng, cut off the communication (traffic)

dyún 短 (SV) short

dyún·bō 短波 (At) short wave

dyún·chūk 短促 (SV) short (in time)

dyún·chyu 短處 (N) shortcomings

dyun·dihng 斷定 (V) decide, to give judgment

dyún·jauh·sin·sāam 短袖線衫 (N) short-sleeved undershirt

dyún·kèih 短期 (At) short-term

dyún·mehng 短命 (SV) die young

Dyùn·ngh·jit 端午節 (N) Dragon Boat Festival (5th of 5th lunar month)

dyún·pín 短片 (N) featurette (short motion picture)

F

fā 花 (N) flower (M: déu) /yāt·déu fā, a flower; a bundle of flowers, yāt·jaat fā

fā·báan·báan 花斑斑 (SV) streaked; spotted

fā·bīn 花邊 (N) lace

fā·dáan 花旦 (N) the heroine in an opera (could either be played by a woman or impersonated by a man)

fā·fā·fīt(·fīt) 花花爺 (SV) capricious

fā·gāai·jyùn 花階磚 (N) tile (M: gauh or faai)

fà·gíu 花轎 (N) bride's sedan chair (M: déng)

fa·hohk 化學 (N/SV) chemistry/flimsy, feeble

fà·hùhng 花紅 (N) reward

fā·jēun 花樽 (N) vase

fà·kàuh 花球 (N) a bouquet of flowers

Fà·kèih, Fà·kéi 花旗 (At) U.S.A. (lit. 'flowery flag,' meaning 'Stars and Stripes' used colloquially for Méih·gwok). /Fà·kèih ngahn·hòhng, Bank of American (in Hong Kong)

fà·méng 花名 (N) nickname

fà·pùhn 花盆 (N) flowerpot

fā·sāng 花生 (N) peanut (M: nāp, a piece)

fà·síh 花市 (N) flower market

fa·yihm·sāt 化驗室 (N) laboratory

fa·yihm·sī 化驗師 (N) laboratory technician

fà·yún 花園 (N) flower garden

faahn 飯 (N) food; cooked rice; meal

fàahn 煩 (SV) be troubled, be annoyed

faahn 犯 (V) offend; do wrong

faahn·bōu 飯煲 (N) pot for cooking rice

fàahn·haih . . . dōu or yātkoi . . . 凡係 … 都 (一概) (Pat) all . . . /Fàahn·haih yàhn dōu yáuh léuhng·jek sáu, léuhng·jek geuk. All men have two hands and two legs. /Fàahn·haih ngh seui yíh·seuhng ge sai·mān·jái, yāt·koi yiu duhk·syù. All children who are over five must go to school.

faahn·jeuih 犯罪 (VO) commit a crime; sin against

fàahn·jìu 飯焦 (N) crusts of boiled rice

fàahn·muhn 煩悶 (SV) chagrined

fàahn·syùhn 帆船 (SV) sailboat (M: jek)

faahn·tēng 飯廳 (N) dining room

faahn·wàih 範圍 (N) scope, sphere; limits; jurisdiction

fàahn·wìhng 繁榮 (SV) prosperous

faai(·cheui) 快(趣) (SV) fast

faai·chè 快車 (N) express

faai·faai·cheui·cheui 快快趣趣 (A) quickly

faai·jí 筷子 (N) chopstick (M: sèung or deui) /yāt·sèung faai·jí, a pair of chopsticks

faai·jiht 快捷 (SV) fast (of motion)

faai·lohk 快樂 (N/SV) pleasure; happiness/be joyful or happy

faai·wuht 快活 (SV) cheerful, happy

fàan 返 (V/RVE) return to/indicating something has returned to original position or condition

fàan- 番 (BF) foreign /fàan·gáan, (foreign) soap

fàan 番 (M) measure for spoken words

fáan 反 (BF) contrary to, oppose

fáan·bok 反駁 (V) rebut

fáan·dáu 反哚 (SV) mischievous, naughty

fáan·deui 反對 (V) oppose

fáan·duhng 反動 (At) reactionary

fáan·fūk 反覆 (SV) unsteadfast, wavering

fàan·gáan 番梘 (N) soap (M: gauh)

fáan·guhng 反共 (At) anti-communist

fāan·gùng 返工 (VO) go to work

fáan·gúng 反攻 (V) counterattack, counteroffensive

fàan·gwái·lóu 番鬼佬 (N) foreigner (lit. foreign devil)

fáan·gwāt 反骨 (SV) unsteady, disloyal, changing allegiance facilely

fáan·gwòng 反光 (N) reflection

fáan·gwo·làih·góng 反過來講 (Ph) looking at it from another angle; on the contrary

fàan·heui 返去 (V) go back (to)

fàan·hohk 返學 (VO) go to school

fáan·jyun·minh 反轉面 (V/SV) turn over/inside out

fàan·jyun·tàuh 返轉頭 (A) one's return /Dáng yāt·jahn·gāan ngóh fàan·jyun·tàuh lèih máaih. A little later, I'll be back to buy it.

fáan·jyun·tàuh 反轉頭 (A) contrary to expectations /Kéuih mh·jí mh·dò·jeh ngóh, fáan·jyun·tàuh naauh·jó ngóh yāt·chàan. He did not even thank me, but rather gave me quite a lecture.

fàan·ké 番茄 (N) tomato

fáan·kong 反抗 (V) to rebel; turn against

fàan·lèih 返來 (V) come back (to), return (to)

fàan·lèih 返來 (RVE) return /hàahng·faan·lèih, return by walking

fàan·màhn 番文 (N) foreign language (written)

fáan·mín 反面 (N/VO) opposite side /break off friendship or relationship with another person

fàan·syú 番薯 (N) sweet potato, yam

fāan·tāan 番攤 (N) fantan, a kind of gambling game

fāan·wá 番話 (N) foreign language (spoken)

fáan·yìh 反而 (A) on the contrary, things turn up just the opposite; but rather /Kéuih mh·jí mh·dò·jeh ngóh fáan·yìh naauh·jó ngóh yāt·chàan. He did not even thank me, but rather gave me quite a lecture.

fàan·yihk 繙譯 (N/V) translation; translate

fàan(·yihk)·sèhng 繙(譯)成 (V) translate into (another language)

fáan·ying 反應 (N) response

faat 法 (BF) way of /sé·faat, the way of writing

faat 發 (M) round (of ammunition)

faat 發 (V) issue, send forth

faat·bíu 發表 (V) publish (an article etc.), to make known

faat·bíu·tàahm·wah 發表談話 (Ph) to make a statement

faat·bíu·yi·gin 發表意見 (Ph) to express an opinion

faat·bou·gèi 發報機 (N) transmitting set

faat·chòih 發財 (VO) earn a large amount of money; work (coll.)

faat·daaht 發達 (SV) be rich and famous; be prosperous

faat·dihn·gèi 發電機 (N) generator

faat·dìn 發癲 (VO) to go mad; to have a mental disease

faat·duhng 發動 (V) start (a motor)

faat·fà·dìn 發花癲 (VO) to have nymphomania

faat·fāi 發揮 (V) show forth (one's opinion)

faat·fō 法科 (M) school of law

faat·fùng 發瘋 (VO) get leprosy

faat·hòhng 發行 (V) sell wholesale

faat·héi 發起 (V) initiate, launch (a campaign); sponsor (a cause)

faat·jí 法子 (N) method, way, device

faat·jín 發展 (V) develop; expand

faat·láahng 發冷 (N/V) malaria/have a chill (due to fever)

faat·leuht 法律 (N) law

faat·leuht·seuhng·ge mahn·tàih 法律上嘅問題 (Ph) problem of law, legal problem

faat·mìhng 發明 (V/N) invent/invention

faat·mòu 發毛 (V) become moldy

faat·muhng 發夢 (VO) have a dream

faat·ngahm·wah 發哈話 (VO) talk wildly; lie; talk in one's sleep

faat·ngohng 發戇 (V) act stupidly or idiotically

faat·sàng 發生 (V) happen; occur /faat·sàng gáam·chìhng, friendship grows; fall in love (with each other) faat·sàng kwan·nàahn, difficulty occurs

faat·séng·muhng 發醒夢 (Ph) wake up from a dream

faat·sìu 發燒 (VO) have a fever

faat·yām 發音 (VO/N) pronounce/ pronounciation

faat·yèuhng·diu 發羊吊 (VO) have epilepsy

faat·yihn 發現 (V/N) discover/discovery

faat·yiht 發熱 (VO) have a fever

faat·yùhn 發源 (V) originate (as of a river or a culture). /Jùng·gwok màhn· fa haih hái bīn·syu faat·yùhn ga? Where did Chinese culture originate?

fahn 份 (M) share; divided part

fahn 份 (M) copy of

fàhn 墳 (N) a grave, mound

fahn·jì 分之 (Pat) fraction of a unit/ one third, sàam·fahn·jì·yāt; one-tenth, sahp·fahn·jì·yāt; four-fifths, ńgh·fahn· ji·sei

fàhn·chèuhng 墳場 (N) a graveyard

fàhn·mouh 墳墓 (N) grave, tomb

fahn·ngoih 份外 (A) beyond measure

fahn·noih 份內 (At) one's duty or obligation

faht 罰 (V) punish; fine

faht·chín 罰錢 (VO) fine (impose a fine on)

faht·dihn 佛殿 (N) the hall of Buddha in temples

faht·fún 罰欵 (N) fine

Faht·gaau 佛教 (At/N) Buddhist/ Buddhism

Faht·gaau·tòuh 佛教徒 (N) Buddhist

fai 費 (BF) fee /dihn·fai, fee for elec- tricity (electricity bill); séui·fai, water bill

fai·behng 肺病 (N) tuberculosis

fai·nóuh·gàn 費腦筋 (SV) annoying, vexing

fai·sàm 費心 (IE) I have put you to too much trouble

fai·sih 費事 (SV) laborious, trouble- some

fai·yuhng 費用 (N) expenses, expendi- ture

faih 吠 (V) bark

fàn 分 (BF) a prefix to a noun, meaning 'branch' /fàn·houh or fàn·dim, branch store; fàn·hóng, branch office of a bank or a firm

fàn 分 (V) discriminate, see the dif- ference in or between

fán 份 (M) share; divided part

fán 粉 (N) rice noodle

fān (jūng) 分 (M) minute

fān(·sou) 分(數) (N) grade, mark (given on examination)

fàn·biht 分別 (N/V) difference/be sepa- rated from each other

fan·dài 瞓低 (V) lie down

fàn·dāk·chēut 分得出 (RV) can distinguish, make out (something)

fàn·déui 分隊 (N) detached unit

fan·fóng 瞓房 (N) bedroom

fàn·fu 吩咐 (V/N) instruct/instruction

fan·gaau 瞓覺 (VO) sleep

fàn·gúk 分局 (N) branch office (when the head office is called 'gúk,' bureau)

fàn·haauh 分校 (N) branch of a school (Chinese system)

fàn·hòi 分開 (RV) separate

fàn·hóng 分行 (N) branch of a bank or a firm

fàn·kèih-fuh·fún 分期付欵 (Ph) pay in in- stallments

fàn·láih 婚禮 (N) wedding ceremony

fan·lihn 訓練 (V/N) train/training

fán·mihn 粉麵 (N) noodles (rice or wheat)

fàn·sáu 分手 (V) separate (away from each other)

fàn·sèhng 分成 (RV) divide into

fan·séng 瞓醒 (RV) awake

fàn·sīk 分析 (V/N) analyze/analysis

fāt 揬 (V) remove (dirt, rice, etc.)

fāt·laaht·saap 揬擸搚 (VO) take up garbage

fāt·yìhn 忽然 (A) suddenly

fāt·yìhn·gāan 忽然間 (A) suddenly

fauh 埠 (N) port; city

fàuh 浮 (V) float

fàuh·chou 浮燥 (SV) rash, frivolous

fàuh·kìuh 浮橋 (N) pontoon bridge

fáu·yihng 否認 (V) deny

fēi 飛 (N) ticket (M: jèung)

fèi·dáan 飛彈 (N) guided missile

fèi·faat 飛髮 (VO) have a haircut

fèi·fèi·há 飛飛吓 (Ph) while flying

fèi·gèi 飛機 (N) airplane (M: ga)

fèi·gèi·chèuhng 飛機場 (N) airfield, air- port

fèi·gèi·seun 飛機信 (N) airmail letter

fèi·gèi·seun·fūng 飛機信封 (N) airmail
envelope

fèi·hàhng 飛行 (V/N) take a plane
trip /flight, trip (by plane)

fèi·hàhng·yùhn 飛行員 (N) flier,
aviator

fèi·jìng·sīk·ge 非正式嘅 (A) in-
formally

fēi·lám 菲林 (N) film (M: tùhng)

fèi·sèuhng 非常 (A) extraordinarily

fèih 肥 (SV) fat

fèih·daaih 肥大 (SV) portly, bulky

fèih·jong 肥壯 (SV) robust

fèih·neih 肥膩 (SV) greasy; fatty foods

fèih·tìhn·líu 肥田料 (N) fertilizers

fihng 揈 (V) swing

fihng·lāt 揈甩 (RV) shake it off

fo 課 (M) lesson

fo 貨 (N) goods, commodity; freight

fō, fò 科 (M/BF) course (of study)
/school (of a university); department
or section of hospital, government,
etc.)

fo·bún 課本 (N) textbook

fó·chàai 火柴 (N) match (M: jì, a
stick; hahp, a box)

fó·chè 火車 (N) train

fo·chè 貨車 (N) truck (M: ga)

fó·chè·jaahm 火車站 (PW) railroad
station

fó·chè·tàuh, chè·tàuh 火車頭 (N) locomotive

fo·dāan 貨單 (N) invoice

fo·chìhng 課程 (N) course of studies

fó·gāi 火雞 (N) turkey (M: jek)

fó·gei 伙記 (N) waiter; helper; partner;
employee

fó·gíng 火警 (N) fire alarm

fó·gwán 火滾 (SV) infuriated (lit.
something boiling on the fire)

fō·hohk, fò·hohk 科學 (N) science

fō·hohk·jéng 科學井 (N) a well dug
the modern way

fo·hohng 貨項 (N) goods

fó·jáu 火酒 (N) alcohol

fó·jin 火箭 (N) rocket

fó·jūk 火燭 (V) have a fire

fó·jūk·chè 火燭車 (N) fire engine

fó·kìhm 火鉗 (N) fire tongs

fó·lihk 火力 (N) firepower, fire

fó·lòuh 火爐 (N) stove; furnace

fo·maht 貨物 (N) goods, commodity;
freight

fō·muhk 科目 (N) subjects

fo·sāt 課室 (N) classroom

fòhng·beih 防備 (V/N) guard against, take
precautionary action; ready for/precau-
tion

fòhng·hoih 妨害 (V) impede

fòhng·hùng 防空 (N) air defense

fòhng·hùng·yín·jaahp 防空演習 (N) air
defense drill

fòhng·ngoih 妨礙 (V/N) impede; hinder /
impediment; hindrance

fòhng·yihk 防疫 (At) take precautions
against epidemic

fòhng·yuh 防禦 (V) guard against

fok·lyuhn 霍亂 (N) cholera

fóng 房 (PW) room (M: gàan)

fòng 慌 (V) be nervous; fearful; alarmed

fōng- 方 (BF) square

fòng 方 (BF) direction; locality /dūng·
fòng, the east; nàahm·fòng, the south

fong 放 (V) put; let loose

fòng·bihn 方便 (SV) convenient

fóng·chàh 訪查 (V) investigate

fong·ché 況且 (MA) moreover

fòng·chek 方呎 (M) square foot

fong·daaih 放大 (RV) enlarge (e.g. a picture)

fong·daaih·hei 放大器 (N) enlarger; amplifier

fong·dài 放低 (V) put down

fong·deih 荒地 (N) uncultivated land

fong·dohng 放蕩 (SV) dissolute, dissipated
and immoral

fòng·faat 方法 (N) method, way

fong·fai 荒廢 (V) devastate, waste

fong·fó 放火 (VO) to set a fire

fong·ga 放假 (VO) to grant a holiday; have
a holiday

fong·gùng 放工 (VO) off from work

fōng·gùng·léih 方公哩 (M) square kilometer

fóng·haauh 仿效 (V) imitate

fong·hái 放喺 (V) put at or on

fong·hei 放棄 (V) abandon, pass up

fòng·heung 方向 (N) direction

fong·hohk 放學 (VO) off from school

fōng·jām 方針 (N) direction (of policy)

fōng·jèung 慌張 (SV) be in a hurry

fóng·jīk 紡織 (V) spinning and weaving

fong·jung 放縱 (V) indulge; leave un-
checked

fòng·jyuh 慌住 (Ph) be afraid of, to be
afraid that

fóng·mahn 訪問 (V) interview (news)

fòng·mauh 荒謬 (SV) ridiculous; irrational;
fictitious

fòng·mihn 方面 (N) circle; side; phase

fóng·mùhn 房門 (N) door of room

fong·ngaan·jau 放晏畫 (VO) leave work at lunch time

fong·pei 放屁 (VO) to break wind; talk nonsense

fóng·sā 紡紗 (VO) to spin

fong·sām·lā 放心啦 (IE) Don't worry.

fong·si 放肆 (V) to give rein to one's lusts; licentious, dissolute

fong·sùng 放鬆 (V) loosen, ease off

fòng·tòhng 荒唐 (SV) exaggerative

fōng·tòhng 方糖 (N) sugar in cubes (M: gauh)

fòng·yìhn 方言 (N) dialect

fong·yíng 放映 (V) project (on a screen)

fong·yíng·dihn·yíng 放映電影 (Ph) show a movie

fong·yíng·gèi 放映機 (N) projector

fóng·yùhn 訪員 (N) newspaper reporter

fó·séui 火水 (N) kerosene (M: gā·léun, gallon)

fó·séui·lòuh 火水爐 (N) kerosene stove

fó·sí 火屎 (N) sparks

fó·sihk 伙食 (N) provisions, food (provided in the mess hall)

fo·syùhn 貨船 (N) freighter

fó·syùhn·jái 火船仔 (N) ferryboat; tug (M: jek)

fó·táu 伙頭 (N) cook (for a store, or office, etc.)

fo·tòhng 課堂 (N) classroom

fó·yeuhk 火藥 (N) gunpowder

fú 苦 (SV) be bitter

fù 敷 (V) to apply (medicine on)

fu 褲 (N) trousers (a pair of trousers is 'yāt·tìuh·fu') (M: tìuh)

fu 副 (BF) vice-, deputy /fu·líhng·sí, vice-consul

fu 副 (M) measure for set of fork and knife, etc.

fú·chó 苦楚 (SV/N) distressing/ distress

fu·fòhng 庫房 (N) storehouse, warehouse

fù·fúh 夫婦 (N) a couple (husband and wife) (M: deui)

fú·gwā 苦瓜 (N) bitter gourd

fu·gwai 富貴 (SV) rich and prominent

fu·jyú·jihk 副主席 (N) vice-chairman

fū·kāp 呼吸 (V/N) breathe/breath

fu·kèuhng 富強 (SV) prosperous (only used to describe a country)

fù·lòuh·tàuh 骷髏頭 (N) a skull

fú·naahn 苦難 (N) tribulation

fú·seuhng 府上 (N) your home, residence (polite form)

fú·tàuh 斧頭 (N) hatchet

fu·tàuh·dáai 褲頭帶 (N) a belt (for trousers) (M: tìuh)

fú·tàuh·jái 斧頭仔 (N) hammer

fù·yán 夫人 (N) wife (polite form) (M: wái)

fù·yeuhk 敷藥 (VO) apply medicine

fu·yūng 富翁 (N) millionaire

fùh 扶 (V) support (with hand or hands)

fuh·baaih 腐敗 (SV) demoralized; deteriorated

fuh·chàn 父親 (N) father

fuh·daai 附帶 (Ph) in addition to, besides /Ngóh fuh·daai góng yāt·sèng . . . In addition to what I've said, I would say . . .

fuh·dàam 負担 (V) to bear, to take responsibility for

fúh·fō 婦科 (N) gynecology department

fuh·gà 附加 (V) add in extra

fùh·hahp 符合 (V) to tally; agree

fùh·houh 符號 (N) a mark; countersign

fuh·jaak 負責 (SV/V) be responsible/take on responsibility; be in charge

fùh·joh 扶助 (V) assist

fuhk·chùhng 服從 (V) obey, follow orders

fuhk·mouh 服務 (V) serve

fuhk·séui·tóu 服水土 (V) acclimate

fuhk·sih 服侍 (V) to serve (to render service to the parents, the sick, etc.)

fuhk·sīk 服式 (N) style of clothing; fashion

fuhk·wuht 復活 (N) the Resurrection

Fuhk·wuht·jit 復活節 (N) Easter

fuhk·yùhn 復原 (V) recover (from sickness)

fuh·laahn 腐爛 (V) become putrid

fuh·lóuh 父老 (N) village elders

fuh·luhk 附錄 (N) an appendix

fuh·màhn 訃聞 (N) letter or card announcing death

fuh·móuh 父母 (N) parents

fúh·néuih 婦女 (N/At) women in general

fuh·woh 附和 (V) accept, agree to /Ngóh fuh·woh kéuih ge yi·gin. I agree to his proposal.

fuhng·mihng 奉命 (VO) under order to

fuhng·sung 奉送 (V) present (a gift)

fuhng·wòhng 鳳凰 (N) phoenix (M: jek)

fūi·sīk·ge 灰色嘅 (At) gray

fùi·fuhk 恢復 (V) recover, get back; resume

fui·gói 悔改 (V) to repent and reform

fùi·hàaih 詼諧 (SV) funny; comical

fui·hahn 悔恨 (V) regret; feel remorse

fui·jeuih 悔罪 (VO) to repent of one's sin

fùi·sà 灰沙 (N) lime and sand

fùi·sàm 灰心 (SV) despondent

fùi·séui 灰水 (N) whitewash

fūk 幅 (M) measure for cloth, picture, etc.

fūk·fahn 福份 (N) fortune, bliss, luck, happiness (share of happiness allotted by fate)

fūk·hei 福氣 (SV/N) be lucky; be happy/ happiness; welfare

fūk·jaahp 複雜 (SV) be complicated

fūk·jyún 覆轉 (V) capsize

fūk·leih 福利 (N) welfare

fūk·sé·jí 複寫紙 (N) carbon paper (M: jèung)

fūk·seun 覆信 (VO/N) reply to a letter/ reply

fūk·syú 蝠鼠 (N) a bat (M: jek)

fūk·yām 福音 (N) the Gospel

fún(·sīk) 欵(式) (N) style, pattern, design /Néih jùng·yi bīn· go fún(·sīk) ga? Which style do you like?

fùn·doih 欵待 (V) treat liberally, treat with clemency

fùn·héi 歡喜 (SV/AV) be happy/to like, to be fond of

fún·hohng 欵項 (N) sum of money, ready money

fùn·sung·wúi 歡送會 (N) formal gathering for saying goodbye to someone

fùn·syu 寬恕 (V) to pardon; forgive; to show leniency

fùn·yìhng·wúi 歡迎會 (N) formal gathering to welcome someone

fùn·yùhng 寬容 (V) be lenient

fùng 風 (N) wind (M: jahm)

fùng·chi 諷刺 (V/N) satirize/sarcasm

fùng·chìuh 風潮 (N) disturbance; a social commotion or agitation

fùng·fu 豐富 (SV) be rich; be abundant

fùng·gíng 風景 (N) landscape; scenery

fùng·hei 風氣 (N) mannner; spirit (of a school, society)

fùng·hím 風險 (N) risk (lit. the threat of a storm)

fùng·juhk 風俗 (N) custom (M: júng)

fūng·jūk 豐足 (SV) plentiful

fùng·kàhm 風琴 (N) organ (musical instrument)

fùng·léut 風栗 (N) chestnut

fùng·lohng 風浪 (N) storm at sea, on a river or lake (lit. wind and waves)

fùng·lòu 風爐 (N) wind furnace or stove

fùng·màhn 風聞 (V) hear (it is rumored that . . .)

fūng·maht 蜂蜜 (N) honey

fùng·ngáh 風雅 (SV) refined

fūng·sāp 風濕 (N) rheumatism

fùng·séui 風水 (N) geomancy

fūng·sēung 風箱 (N) bellows

fùng·táan 風癱 (N) paralysis

fut 濶 (SV) be wide

fut·daaih 濶大 (SV) spacious

fut·lohk 濶落 (SV) ample, spacious

fut·lóu 濶佬 (N/SV) a rich man/spendthrift

G

gà 加 (V) add, increase

gà 家 (M) family

gá 假 (SV) be false, untrue, imitation, counterfeit

ga 架 (M) measure for car, airplane, etc.

ga 嫁 (V) get married (said of a woman) /Kéuih·ge daaih néui ga·jó meih a? Has her eldest daughter gotten married yet? /Kéuih·ge daaih néui ga·jó bīn·go a? Whom is her eldest daughter marrying?

gā 家 (BF) specialist, scholar /séh·wúi· hohk·gā, sociologist

gá·baahn 假扮 (N) to make believe (to be a certain person), to disguise oneself as

gà·cháan 家產 (N) property, holdings

ga·chìhn 價錢 (N) price

gà·dái 家底 (N) family possessions

gá·dihng 假定 (MA) supposing

gá·fā 假花 (Ph) artificial flower

ga·fē 咖啡 (N) coffee

ga·fē wùh 咖啡壺 (N) coffeepot

gà·fó 傢伙 (N) guy

gà·fuh 家父 (IE) my father (polite form)

gà·gíng 家境 (N) family financial situation

gā·gūng 家公 (IE) father-in-law

gà·gyun 家眷 (N) family (wife and children)

gà·hèung 家鄉 (N) hometown, native village

gā·hìng 家兄 (N) my elder brother (polite form)

gà·jahn 家陣 (TW) now, at present

gā·jē 家姊 (N) elder sister

gà·jéung 家長 (N) head of the family; student's parents

gà·jéung 嘉長 (V) encourage and praise

ga·jihk 價值 (N) value

ga·jòng 嫁妝 (N) trousseau, dowry

gà·juhk 家族 (N) clan, family

ga·kèih 假期 (N) vacation; holiday

gà·kwài 家規 (N) family discipline

ga·lēi 咖哩 (N) curry

gā·léun 加侖 (M) gallon

gà·móuh 家母 (IE) my mother (polite form)

gà·mouh 家務 (N) household affairs

gá·mouh 假冒 (V) counterfeit; impersonate

ga·muhk·bíu 價目表 (N) price list

ga·néui 嫁女 (VO) marry (of a daughter)

gà·pó 家婆 (N) mother-in-law

gà·púih 加倍 (VO) double the number

ga·sái 駕駛 (V) pilot, fly a plane

ga·sai 架勢 (SV) fantastic, gaudy; swanky

ga·sái·yùhn 駕駛員 (N) pilot, flier

gà·sèuhng·bihn·faahn 家常便飯 (N) potluck, ordinary family food

gā·sì 傢私 (N) furniture (M: gihn, for piece; tou, for set)

gá·sí·gāan 假使間 (MA) supposing, if

gà·suhk 家屬 (N) relatives

gà·tìhng 家庭 (N) family, household

gà·yàhn 家人 (N) the family

gà·yahp 加入 (V) join

gà·yíh 加以 (A) furthermore, moreover

gà·yuhng 家用 (At) for home use

gáai 解 (V) untie

gáai 解 (V) explain; interpret

gaai 界 (BF) circles, line or profession /sèung(·yihp)·gaai, business circle

gaai 鋸 (V) saw; cut

gāai 街 (PW) street (M: tiuh)

gáai·chèuih 解除 (V) remove; expel

gáai·fōng 街坊 (N) neighbor

gáai·fong 解放 (V/N) liberate/liberation (the term used for the Chinese Communist takeover of Mainland China)

gāai·háu 街口 (PW) end of street; intersection of streets

gaai·háu 戒口 (VO) to diet, abstain from certain foods

gaai·hòi 鋸開 (V) saw (it into two parts)

gáai·hot 解渴 (V) quench thirst

gāai·jīu 街招 (N) street poster

gàai·jyùn 階磚 (N) tiles

gāai·kāp 階級 (N) rank, class

gáai·kyut 解決 (V) solve (a problem); settle (a question)

gaai·laaht 芥辣 (N) mustard paste

gāai·méih 街尾 (PW) end of a street (lit. the tail of a street)

gáai·mìhng 解明 (V) explain clearly

gáai·nàu 解鈕 (VO) unbutton

gáai·páu 解剖 (V) dissect

gáai·saan 解散 (V) break (formation), dissolve (an organization)

gāai·síh 街市 (N) market

gáai·sīk 解釋 (V) explain, interpret

gaai·siuh 介紹 (V) introduce

gaai·siuh·seun 介紹信 (N) letter of introduction

gāai·tàuh 街頭 (PW) end of a street (lit. head of a street)

gàai·yàn 皆因 (Ph) all because, merely because

gaak 隔 (CV) skipping certain specified members of a series

gaak·chèuih 革除 (V) to get rid of; to expel (e.g. student)

gaak-hèu-sòu-yéuhng 隔靴搔癢 (IE) labor in vain; no relief; poor compensation (to scratch an itch through a boot)

gaak·hòi 隔開 (RV) separate by partition

gaak·jīk 革職 (VO) to remove from office or position

gaak·jó gei·yaht 隔咗幾日 (Ph) a few days later

gaak·lèih 隔籬 (PW) next (in position); neighbouring; next door

gaak·mihng 革命 (N/VO) revolution/revolt

gaak·ngoih 格外 (A) extra; extraordinary

gaak·sīk 格式 (N) form, pattern; model

gaak·yaht 隔日 (A) every other day

gaak·yeh 隔夜 (At) (food) left over from the day before /gaak·yeh sung, left-overs

gaak·yìhn 格言 (N) maxim, adage

gàam(·jyuh) 監(住) (CV) force; supervise

gáam 敢 (AV/V) dare

gáam 減 (V) subtract; lessen; reduce

gáam·bāt·jih 減筆字 (N) abbreviated form of characters

gáam·dài 減低 (V) to lower (the price, etc.)

gāam·dán 監躉 (N) a jailbird

gáam·duhng 感動 (V) move, arouse feeling or sympathy

gāam·dūk 監督 (V) supervise; oversee

gáam·ga 減價 (VO) reduce the price; at reduced price

gáam·gīk, gám·gīk 感激 (V) be grateful to, be thankful (for)

gáam·hèng 減輕 (V) lighten (a load); mitigate; relieve (from pain, anxiety, etc.)

gāam·gùng 監工 (VO) to oversee work

gáam·fáan 監犯 (N) a convict

gáam·síu 減少 (V) lessen; reduce

gàam·yuhk 監獄 (N) prison

gàan 間 (M) measure for building, house, room, etc.

gáan 揀 (V) select

gaan·chék 間尺 (N) a ruler (for measuring)

gáan·dàan 簡單 (SV) be simple

gaan·dihp 間諜 (N) a spy
gaan·fóng 間房 (VO) partition (a room into so many parts)
gaan·gaak 間隔 (N) partition
gáan·gáan·dàan·dàan 簡簡單單 (A) in a simple way
gàan·hím 奸險 (SV) wicked
gàan·hím 艱險 (SV) difficult and dangerous
gáan·jaahk 揀擇 (V) select
gáan·jihk 簡直 (A) simply /Gáan·jihk móuh·baahn·faat. There is simply no solution.
gaan·jip 間接 (A) indirectly
gaan·jūng 間中 (TW) sometimes
gàan.nàahn 艱難 (N/SV) difficulty, hardship/be difficult
gàan·sai 奸細 (N) spy
gáan·séui 鹼水 (N) liquid lye
gàan·sèung 奸商 (N) dishonest merchant
gáan·sihng 揀賸 (At) what remains after choosing
gáan·tái·jih 簡體字 (N) simplified character
gàan·waaht 奸滑 (SV) crafty
gàan·yàhm 姦淫 (N) adultery
gaang·séui 梗水 (VO) wade
gàang·tìhn 耕田 (VO) to farm, to till the soil
gàang·tìhn·lóu 耕田佬 (N) farmer
gaap 夾 (V) put together
gaap·chín 夾錢 (V) pool the money together
gaap·daai 夾帶 (V) carry secretly; to smuggle
gaap·fán 夾份 (V/A) cooperate, be a partner/cooperatively /Ngóh·deih léuhng·go gaap·fán hóu ma? How about being my partner? /gaap·fán máaih máh·bīu, pool money together to buy a sweepstake ticket
gaap·màaih 夾埋 (RV) put together
gaap·maanh 夾萬 (N) safe, vault
gaap·ngáang 夾硬 (A) compulsorily, by force
gaap·sáu-gaap·geuk 夾手夾脚 (A) cooperatively
gaap, yuht, bíng, dìng 甲,乙,丙,丁 (SP) The first four of the Ten Stems, used as ordinal numbers, or to indicate a series, etc., — as the Westerners use a, b, c, etc.
gàau 膠 (N) glue
gáau 攪 (V) stir up; meddle
gaau 教 (V) to teach
gaau 教 (N) religion
gaau 較 (V) set (a watch, etc.)
gaau 鉸 (N) hinge
gàau·béi 交畀 (V) hand over to, turn over to
gáau·chèuhng·sà 絞腸痧 (N) cholera (ref. fok·leuhn)
gàau·chìhng 交情 (N) friendship
gàau·daai 交帶 (V) tell, instruct (in the sense of order)
gáau·dāk·dihm 攪得掂 (RV) can arrange or manage; manageable
gaau·deui 校對 (V/N) proofread/proofreader
gáau·dihm 攪掂 (RV) fix, arrange
gáau·dihm(·jó) 攪掂咀* (RV) be well fixed up; well arranged
gàau dihn·fai 交電費 (Ph) pay electricity bill
gàau·doih 交代 (V) hand over to successor
gáau·dou . . . 攪到… (V) to a point that . . .; . . . to such an extent: /Kéuih gáau·dóu yāt·go sīn dōu móuh·saai. /He became penniless. /Kéuih gáau·dou yāt·dī baahn·faat dōu móuh. He has come to the end of his rope.
gaau·douh 教導 (V) teach and guide
gaau·fan 教訓 (V/N) upbraid/lesson, lecture (lengthy scolding)
gaau·fō·syù 教科書 (N) textbook
gāau·gā 交加 (N) a cross /dá (or waahk) go gāau·gā, to make a cross or X mark.
gàau·gaai 交界 (N/At) boundary, border region/adjoining
gàau·gwàan 交關 (SV/A) serious/seriously; terribly
gàau·hàaih 膠鞋 (N) sneakers, tennis shoes (M: deui, pair)
gàau·jai 交際 (V) participate in social activities
gàau·jai·fā 交際花 (N) society belles
gaau·jín 鉸剪 (N) scissors (M: bá: yāt·bá, one pair of)
gàau·jòu 交租 (VO) pay rent (ref. jòu)
gáau·lyuhn 攪亂 (V) to throw into disorder
gáau·m̀h·dihm 攪唔*掂 (RV) can't arrange or manage; unmanageable
gaau·m̀h·tèng 教唔*聽 (RV) can't make one obey what has been taught (these RV can only be used in the potential form, i.e. 'gaau·dāk·tèng', 'gaau·m̀h·tèng' or 'm̀h·gaau·dāk·tèng'. There is no such saying as 'gaau·tèng la' or 'móu gaau·tèng').

gaau·ngāam 較啱 (RV) set accurately, to set (watch to the correct time), to tune in (precisely on a particular radio station)

gàau·ngoih 郊外 (PW) outskirts of a city, suburbs

gàau·pàhng·yáuh 交朋友 (VO) make friends

gaau·sāt 教室 (N) classroom

gáau·séi 絞死 (RV) strangle to death

gàau·séui 膠水 (N) glue

gàau·séui·fai 交水費 (Ph) pay water bill

gàau·sip 交涉 (V/N) negotiate/negotiation

gàau·syù 教書 (VO) teach

gàau·tàuh·jip·yíh 交頭接耳 (Ph) to whisper in someone's ear

gaau·tòhng 教堂 (N) chapel, church (the building) (M: gàan)

gàau·tok 交托 (V) to entrust with

gàau·tòuh 教徒 (N) church member

gàau·tùng 交通 (N) communications; transportation system

gàau·tùng·kwài·laih 交通規例 (N) traffic law

gáau·waaht 狡猾 (SV) cunning; crafty; sly

gáau·wàhn 攪勻 (RV) to mix evenly

gàau·wuhn 交換 (V) exchange; interchange

gaau·wúi, gaau·wuih 教會 (N) church (lit. religious society)

gaau·wúi·hohk·haauh 教會學校 (N) church or mission school

gaau·wúi·yī·yún 教會醫院 (N) church or mission hospital

gaau·yáuh 教友 (N) church member

gàau·yihk 交易 (V/N) trade, transact/transaction

gaau·yuhk 教育 (V/N) educate/education

gaau·yuhk·gúk 教育局 (N) Bureau of Education

gaau·yùhn 教員 (N) teacher

gahm 撳 (V) press on

gahm-deih-yàuh-séui, 撳地游水 (wán·jahn gwo·dái) (IE) swimming with one's hands on the ground, not taking any risks

gahn(jyuh) 近住 (V) near

gahn·doih 近代 (At) modern age

gahn·lói 近來 (MA) recently

gahn·sih·ngáahn 近視眼 (N) near-sightedness

gāi 雞 (N) chicken (M: jek)

gai 計 (V) calculate, figure out

gái 髻 (N) tuft of hair

gai·chaak 計策 (N) a plan, a strategem

gai·chēut 計出 (RV) figure out

gài·dáan 雞蛋 (N) chicken egg

gài·daahn·chēng 雞蛋青 (N) white of an egg

gài·daahn·wóng 雞蛋黃 (N) egg yolk

gai·fuh 繼父 (N) stepfather

gài·hòng 雞糠 (N) chicken feed

gài·hóng 雞項 (N) a pullet

gai·juhk 繼續 (A/V) continuously/continue

gai·màaih 計埋 (V) count in

gai·màuh 計謀 (N) plan, strategem

gài·méih·jáu 雞尾酒 (N) cocktail

gài·méih·jáu·wúi 雞尾酒會 (N) cocktail party

gai·móuh 繼母 (N) stepmother

gài·mòuh·sóu 雞毛掃 (N) (chicken) feather duster

gài·ngáahn 雞眼 (N) corns (on toes)

gài·pèih·jí 雞皮紙 (N) brown paper

gai·sou 計數 (VO) to reckon accounts

gai·syun 計算 (V) calculate

gài·tàih 雞啼 (Ph) cock crow

gai·waahk 計劃 (N/V) plan/plan to

gàm 甘 (SV) sweet; pleasant

gám 噉 (A) in this way; or in that way, in that case, well, . . .; then

gam 咁 (A) so

gām 柑 (N) loose-skinned orange (Citrus nobilis)

V gám NU M ···噉··· (Pat) 'gám' is used as a suffix for verbs indicating the action has been completed /Gó·sáu gō kéuih cheung·gám léuhng·chi jé, kéuih jauh sīk la. He learned that song after singing it only twice. /Kéuih yám·gám léuhng·daahm jē jauh m̀h·yám·dāk·lohk la. He couldn't drink any more after taking only two gulps.

gàm·chóu 甘草 (N) licorice

. . . gám dōu . . . ···噉都··· (Pat) even though . . . still /Néih gám dōu m̀h·háng? Even though . . . , you still won't say yes? /Go tìn gám dōu m̀h·lohk·yúh. Weather like this for so long and it still won't rain!

(lìhn) gám . . . dōu 噉···都 (Pat) . . . . even though /Lìhn gám néih dōu hóu seun kéuih gé. It's so simple and obvious and yet you believe him. /Lìhn gám kéuih dōu m̀h·seun néih? He still won't believe you?

gàm·gai·naahp 金雞納 (N) quinine

gám gīk 感激 (SV/V) deeply affected; very grateful to

gám·gok 感覺 (V/N) feel/feeling

gam·jaih 咁滯 (A) to that extent (indicates an undesirable degree) /Kéuih wàhn·jó gam·jaih. He almost fainted.

gám·jeh 感謝 (V) to give thanks to

gam·jí 禁止 (V) prohibit; forbid

gàm·jih·taap 金字塔 (N) a pyramid

gàm·jìu·jóu 今朝早 (TW) this morning

"Gàm·jìu yáu jáu gàm·jìu jeui, mìhng·yaht sàuh lòih mìhng·yaht dòng." 今朝有酒今朝醉, 明日愁來明日當.

(IE) happy-go-lucky (lit. have wine today while there is some, let tomorrow's worries take care of themselves)

gám juhng m̀h·jí 噉重唔止 (Ph) moreover

gām·lín 金鍊 (N) gold necklace (M: tìuh)

gàm máahn 今晚 (TW) tonight

gām·ngáak 金鈪 (N) golden bracelet

Gām·sāan 金山 (PW) U.S.A. (lit. Golden Mountain, a loose term used by Cantonese to mean 'the United States.' Equivalent to 'Fà·kéi')

gàm·sàng 今生 (Ph) this life

gàm·sàng-lòih·sai 今生來世 (Ph) this life and the next

gam·seuhng·há 咁上下 (Ph) almost; about /Sahp·dím·jūng gam·seuhng·há, about ten o'clock

gám-seuhng-tìm-fà 錦上添花 (IE) to gild refined gold; to gild the lily

gām·sīk 金色 (N) gold color

gām·sīk·ge 金色嘅 (At) golden

gàm·suhk 金屬 (N) minerals

gàm·taap 金塔 (N) burial urn

gàm·yaht 今日 (TW) today

gám·yàn·jit 感恩節 (N) Thanksgiving Day

gám yauh m̀haih 噉又唔係 (IE) no, it isn't so, not really

gám·yéung 噉樣 (A) then; in such a way; so that (a variant of gám)

gàn 筋 (N) sinews

gàn(·jyuh) 跟住 (V) follow

gán 緊 (P) indicating continuance of action

gán 緊 (SV) be tight

gàn 斤 (M) a catty, pound (Chinese) (1 1/3 English pounds)

gàn·bún 根本 (A) at all; entirely /Gàn·bún m̀h·haih gám·yéung ge mahn·tàih. It is entirely a different problem. /Kéuih gàn·bún fáan·deui nī·gih sih.

He doesn't approve of this at all. /Ngóh kàhm·yaht gàn·bún móuh heui. I didn't go yesterday at all.

gàn·bún·seuhng 根本上 (A) basically

gàn·chèuih 跟隨 (V) follow

gàn·dáih 根底 (N) background (information which will help to explain something)

gàn·dāk·séuhng 跟得上 (RV) catch up

gán·gán·gau 僅僅夠 (Ph) barely enough

gán·gāp 緊急 (SV) be urgent, critical, crucial

gàn·geui 根據 (V/N) base on, according to/base/gàn·geui kéuih gám góng, based on what he said

gàn·geui·deih 根據地 (N) base of operations

gán·jèung 緊張 (SV) be excited, exciting; tense

gàn·jùng 跟踪 (V) to trace a person

gàn·jyuh 跟住 (V/A) follow

gàn·jyuh·méih 跟住尾 (Ph) to follow closely; right after that

gàn·m̀h·séuhng 跟唔上 (RV) cannot keep up

gán·sahn 謹慎 (V/SV) to be careful/prudent

gán·yiu 緊要 (SV) important; serious (in nature, grave)

. . . gán·yiu·gwo māt 緊要過乜 (Ph) . . . more important than anything else.

gàn·yuhk 筋肉 (N) muscles

gáng 梗 (SV) unyielding, stubborn; stiff (in neck, arm, etc.)

gáng 梗 (A) certainly

gang 更 (A) more, further

gang·gà 更加 (A) all the more

gàng·gói 更改 (V) change, reform

gáng·haih 梗係 (A) certainly, must be

gáng·jihk 梗直 (SV) upright; honorable

gàng·jing 更正 (V) to correct; rectify

gàng·wuhn 更換 (V) to replace; substitute

gāp·chit 急切 (SV) urgent; pressing

gāp·dihn 急電 (N) urgent telegram

gāp·jing 急症 (N) acute disease, medical emergency

gāt 桔 (N) mandarin orange

gāt 刮 (V) puncture; stab

gāt·hùng 吉凶 (N) good fortune and misfortune

gáu 九 (NU) nine

gau 救 (V) save, help from danger /Gau·mehng a! Help!

gau 夠 (V/RVE) have enough /Gau meih a? Have you had enough? /Gau la. Yes. /Meih gau. No.

gau·dáam 狗胆 (SV) brave, stout-
hearted

gáu·dau 狗竇 (N) dog house

gáu faih 狗吠 (Ph) the dog barks

gau·fó 救火 (VO) fight a fire

gau·fó·chè 救火車 (N) fire engine

gau·gíng 究竟 (MA) after all /Kéuih
gau·gíng làih m̀h·làih a? After all, is
he coming or not?

gau gòu 夠高 (Ph) tall enough

gau gwòng 夠光 (Ph) bright enough

gau·jai 救濟 (V/N) relieve/relief

gau·jì·gaak 夠資格 (At) be qualified

gau·ji·hei 夠志氣 (V) ambitious

gau·lihk 夠力 (SV) be strong

gau·mehng 救命 (VO) save a life

gau·mehng·a! 救命呀 (Ph) Help! Help!
(used only when in danger of losing
life)

gáu·m̀h·gáu 久唔久 (A) from time to
time; once in a while

gau·sàang·téhng 救生艇 (N) lifeboat
(M: jek)

gau·sāang·yī 救生衣 (N) life jacket (M:
gihn)

gau·sāang·hyūn 救生圈 (N) life belt

Gau·sai·jyú 救世主 (N) the Savior

gau·sēung·chē 救傷車 (N) ambulance
(lit. car to rescue the wounded) (M: ga)

gau·sèung·déui 救傷隊 (N) ambulance
corps or unit

gau·wuh 救護 (V) rescue

gauh 舊 (SV) be old (opposite of new)

gauh 嚿 (M) piece, lump /yāt·gauh
fàan·gáan, a piece of soap

gauh·jahn·sí 舊陣時 (TW) in the past

gauh·lihk 舊曆 (N) Chinese calendar
(old calendar)

gauh·sìh 舊時 (MA) formerly, in the
past

gauh·sīk 舊式 (SV) old style

Gauh·yeuk 舊約 (N) Old Testament

ge 嘅 (P) particle indicating modifica-
tion; sentence final

. . . ge yéh . . . 嘅嘢 (Ph) things
such as . . .

géi 幾 (A) fairly, rather (pos.) not
very (neg.)

géi (dò) 幾 (NU) how many, how
much

géi 幾 (NU) few, several; odd, more
than

gei 寄 (V) send, mail

gèi·bún 基本 (N/At) basis/fundamental

gèi·chó 基礎 (N) basis; foundation

géi·dáai 幾大 (Ph) no matter how 'great'
it is . . . /(Ngóh) géi·dáai dōu m̀h·pa.
I don't give a darn.

gei·dāk 記得 (V) remember

gèi·deih 基地 (N) base (e.g. air base)

Gēi·dūk 基督 (N) Christ

Gēi·dūk·gaau 基督教 (At/N) Protestant/
Protestantism

gēi·dūk·tòuh 基督徒 (N) a Christian

gèi(·hei)·fòhng 機器房 (N) printing room;
machine room

gèi·fòng 飢荒 (N) famine

gèi·fùh 幾乎 (A) almost

gèi·fúng 譏諷 (V) satirize, mock

géi(·gam) 幾(咁) (A) how (precedes stative verbs to indicate an extreme, extent
or amount) /Géi(·gam) gòu a! Gee, it's
tall! How tall it is!

gēi·gām 基金 (N) fund (money set aside
for some particular purpose)

géi·gau·ji·hei 幾夠志氣 (Ph) quite ambitious

gèi·gín 機件 (N) the parts of a machine

gèi·gíng 機警 (SV) alert

gèi·gwàan 機關 (N) government offices
and bureaus

gēi·gwāan·chēung 機關槍 (N) machine
gun

gèi·hei 機器 (N) a machine

géi·hòh 幾何 (N) geometry

gei·houh 記號 (N) distinguishing mark

gei·jé 記者 (N) reporter; correspondent

gei·jeung 記賬 (VO) put on account;
charge

gei·joi 記載 (V/N) put on record/record

gei·luhk 記錄 (V/N) make a written record of, take minutes/record, minutes

géi·luhk 記錄 (N) record, minutes

gèi·maht 機密 (N/SV) official secrets/
confidential

gèi·ngoh 饑餓 (N) hunger

gei·nihm, géi·nihm 紀念 (V/N) com-
memorate/memorial

géi·nihm·bán 紀念品 (N) souvenir; re-
membrance

géi·nihm·yaht 紀念日 (N) anniversary

géi·sí 幾時 (TW) when (?), at what time?

gei·sing 記性 (N) memory

gei·siu 譏笑 (V/N) ridicule; mock/scoff

gei·sūk 寄宿 (V) live in a school dormitory

gei·sūk·sāng 寄宿生 (N) boarding student

gei·wóhng·bāt·gau 既往不咎 (IE) let bygones be bygones

gèi·wuih 機會 (N) opportunity; chance

gei-yàhn-lèih-hah 寄人籬下　(IE) lodging under another's shelter, one who depends on another to earn a living

gei·yìhn 既然　(A) since

géi·yùhn 紀元　(N) the first year of a new era

géi·yùhn·chìhn 紀元前　(At) B.C. (Before Christ)

géi·yùhn·hauh 紀元後　(At) A.D. (Anno Domini, in the year of the Lord)

geih 忌　(V) to be jealous; envy; be allergic to

geih·nàhng 技能　(N) ability, skill

geih·seuht 技術　(N) technique, sleight of hand, skill

gèng 驚　(SV) be afraid; surprised

géng 頸　(N) neck (M: tìuh)

géng·gàn 頸巾　(N) scarf (M: tìuh)

geng 鏡　(N) mirror (M: mihn)

geng·gá 鏡架　(N) frame (of a mirror)

géng·hot 頸渴　(SV) thirsty

géng·lín 頸鍊　(N) necklace (M: tìuh)

geng·tàuh 鏡頭　(N) lens

géui 舉　(V) cite

geui 句　(M) measure for 'syut·wah' or 'wá' —spoken language

geui, geu 鋸　(V/N) saw

géui·hàhng 舉行　(V) hold (a meeting); perform (a ceremony); give, put on (an exhibit)

géui·héi 舉起　(V) lift up

géui·jin 舉薦　(V) recommend

géui·kèih-bāt-dihng 舉棋不定　(IE) indecisive; changing one's mind often (to hesitate in making a move at chess)

géui·laih 舉例　(VO) give an example

gēui·làuh·jing 居留証　(N) residence permit

geui·muhk·gèi 鋸木機　(N) buzz saw

géui·muhk·mòuh·chàn 舉目無親　(IE) not a single relative is around

géui·sáu 舉手　(VO) raise one's hand

gèui·yìhn 居然　(A) contrary to expectations; simply

geuk 腳　(N) foot (M: jek)

géuk 腳　(N) one of the four players in a Mahjong game

geuk·bouh·sèng 腳步聲　(Ph) sound of footsteps

geuk·jàang 腳踭　(N) the heel

geuk·jai 腳掣　(N) foot brake

geuk·ji·gaap 腳指甲　(N) toenail

geuk·jīk 腳跡　(N) footprints

geuk·sīk 腳色(角色)　(N) role in a play; cast of a play

gèung, gēung 薑　(N) ginger

gihk·dím 極點　(N) extreme limit; crowning point

gihk·dyùn 極端　(A/N) extremely; extremity

gihk·lihk 極力　(A) with all one's strength

gihn 件　(M) article, piece, item (measure for 'sih(·gon)'—affair, or 'yéh'—thing, etc.)

gihp 挾　(V) carry something under one's arm; hold; clip

gihp 挾*　(V) to crowd; to pinch

gīk 激　(V) provoke; rouse; excite

gīk·hei 激氣　(SV) exasperating, irritating

gìm 兼,兼　(V) to hold another job or position concurrently

gim 劍　(N) two-edged sword (M: bá)

gím·chàh 檢查　(V/N) to inspect, check, examine/check, inspection; examination /gím·chàh sàn·tái, have a physical examination

gin 見　(V/RVE) meet; visit (rather formally)/ending of RV

gin(·dāk) 見(得)　(AV) feel /Néih gin·dāk dím a? How do you feel? (as in asking a patient or one who is not feeling well) /Ngóh gin tàuh-wàhn. I feel dizzy.

gìn·bok 肩膊　(N) shoulder

gìn-bouh-haahng-bouh 見步行步　(IE) make an expedient move

gìn·chìh 堅持　(V) insist

gin·chit 建設　(V/N) build up, institute/reconstruction

gin·gáai 見解　(N) opinion

gìn·gu 堅固　(SV) firm, stable, strong, lasting, firm

gin·haauh 見效　(SV) effective (lit. to show effect) /Gó·jek yeuhk gin m̀h·gin·haauh a? Is that medicine effective?

gin·jaahp 見習　(V) undergo field training

gin·jouh 建造　(V) construct, build

gin·jūk 建築　(V/N) build, erect, construct /architecture, buildings

gin·jūk·maht 建築物　(N) buildings, structures

gìn·kyut 堅決 (SV) firm; determined

gin·lahp 建立　(V) establish, set up; found; erect

gin·leuhng 見諒　(V) excuse, forgive

gin·mihn 見面　(VO) meet, see personally

gin·sīk 見識　(N) knowledge, wisdom

gin·yih 建議　(N/V) suggestions/suggest

gíng·bou 警報　(N) air raid alarm

gíng·chaat 警察　(N) police; policeman

gíng·chè 警車　(N) police car

gìng·dín 經典　(N) the classics

gìng·dòu 京都　(N) capital; metropolis

gìng·fai 經費 (N) fund

gìng·fòng 驚慌 (V) be frightened, nervous, fearful; alarmed

gìng·géi 經紀 (N) agent, broker

gìng·gou 警告 (V/N) warn/warning

gìng·gwo 經過 (V) pass through

gìng·hōng 京腔 (N) Peking accent

gìng·jai 經濟 (N/SV) economy; economics/be economical

ging·jàng, gìhng·jàng 競爭 (N/V) contest, competition/compete, contend

ging·jáu 敬酒 (VO) propose and drink a toast to; raise cup and drink to express respects or thanks

gìng·ji 景緻 (N) scenery, picturesque view

ging·juhng 敬重 (V) respect

gìng·kèih 驚奇 (SV) unbelievable

gìng·léih 經理 (N) manager

gìng·sáu 經手 (V) handled (by an agent)

gìng·sáu·yàhn 經手人 (N) an intermediary

gìng·sī 警司 (N) police commissioner, police officer

gìng·sin 經線 (N) meridian of longitude

gìng·wáih·sin 經緯線 (N) map coordinates

gìng·yihm 經驗 (N) experience

gìng·yihn 竟然 (A) actually

gìng·yīn 敬煙 (VO) offer a cigarette

gìng·yuh 境遇 (N) circumstances, conditions

gip 夾 (N) clip, pin

gip 劫 (V) to rob by force

gīp·jāp 喼汁 (N) Worcestershire sauce

git·baai·hìng·daih 結拜兄弟 (N) sworn brothers

git·bìng 結冰 (VO) freeze up, ice up

git·chūk 結束 (V) to wind up; close

git·fàn 結婚 (VO) marry; get married

git·gwó 結果 (N/A) result/as a result

git·guhk 結局 (N) end; conclusion

git·hahp 結合 (V) unite

git·náu 結組 (VO) button up

git·saht 結實 (SV) strong, durable

git·sīk 結識 (V) be acquainted with

git·sou 結數 (VO) calculate the total financial take of a business, close the account; pay the bill

giu 繳 (V) to pay (tax, membership dues, etc.)

giu 轎 (N) sedan chair (M: déng)

giu 叫 (V/CV) call; call loudly, yell; order (dishes)/tell, order

giu(·jouh) 叫(做) (RV) named, is called, considered as

gìu·gwai 嬌貴 (SV) highborn

gìu·ngouh 驕傲 (SV) proud; arrogant

gìu·nyuhn 嬌嫩 (SV) delicate, soft

giu·séng 叫醒 (RV) to wake up

giuh 撬 (V) to pry up

giuh·chèuhng·geuk 撬墙脚 (VO) to supplant (through scheming)

giuh·hòi 撬開 (V) pry open with a knife or a crowbar

gō 歌 (N) song (M: sáu)

gō 哥 (BF) elder brother

gó 嗰 (SP) that (there)

go 個 (M) for persons or things

gó·dī 嗰啲 (N) those

gò-gùng-juhng-dāk 歌功頌德 (Ph) eulogize

gó·jahn·sí 嗰陣時 (TW) when . . ., at the time of . . .; at that time . . ., meanwhile

gó·páai 嗰派 (MA) those days

go·sàm·séung·wah 個心想話 (Ph) wish to say . . .

go·sing 個性 (N) character (pattern of behavior or personality)

go·yàhn 個人 (At) individual; personal

gòh·gō 哥哥 (N) elder brother

gói 改 (V) change, alter, correct

gói·bin 改變 (N) change

gói deih·ji 改地址 (Ph) change address

gói·gaak 改革 (V/N) reform

gói·gwo 改過 (VO) to mend one's ways

gói gyún 改卷 (Ph) correct exercises or tests

gói·jeng 改正 (V/N) correct/amendment

gói·jeun 改進 (V/N) improve/improvement

gói·jōng 改裝 (V) remodel

gói·jóu 改組 (V) reorganize

gói·jouh 改造 (V) reconstruct

gói·kèih 改期 (VO) change a date

gói·lèuhng 改良 (V) reform; improve

gói·méng 改名 (VO) give a name; change a name

gói·sāam 改衫 (VO) alter a dress

gói·sihn 改善 (V) reform, to better, improve

gói·wàih 改為 (V) change into

goi·yan 蓋印 (V) to seal; stamp

gok 各 (SP) each, every

gok 覺 (V) notice

gok·chín 擱淺 (V) run aground

gok·dāk 覺得 (AV) feel

gok·douh 角度 (N) angle

gok·fòng·mihn 各方面 (Ph) all circles; all aspects

gok·hah 閣下 (N) you sir (polite address)

gok·lōk·táu 角落頭 (N) corner

gok·ngh 覺悟 (V) become enlightened; roused to a comprehension (of one's failing)

gok·sīk 角色 (N) role in a play; cast of a play

gok·sīk·gok·yeuhng 各式各樣 (Ph) various

gok·wàahn·gok 各還各 (Ph) each for himself

gòn 乾(爛)(SV) dry

gón 趕 (V) to drive out

gòn·chou 乾燥 (SV) parched; feverish

gón·dāk·chit 趕得切 (RV) there is time; can make it

gón·faai 趕快 (A) in a hurry

gón·gán 趕緊 (A) speedily, at once, promptly

gòn·gòn·jehng·jehng 乾乾淨淨 (SV) very clean

gòn·jehng 乾淨 (SV) clean

gòn·jehng kéih·léih 乾淨企理 (Ph) clean and neat

gón·jyuh 趕住 (A) speedily, in a hurry

gòn·lèuhng 乾糧 (N) dry provisions

gón·mh·chit 趕唔切 (RV) there isn't enough time; can't make it

gòn·sip 干涉 (V) interfere with

gòn·són 乾爽 (SV) dry, airy

góng 講 (V) say; talk, speak

góng . . . jì (or tèng) 講···知 (Ph) to tell /Chéng néih Góng kéuih jì. Please tell him.

gong 鋼 (N) steel

góng·baih 港幣 (N) Hong Kong dollar (H.K. currency)

gong·chēung 鋼窗 (N) steel window

góng·daaih·wah 講大話 (VO) to lie (lit. to talk big)

góng·dou 講到 (V) mention

góng·douh 講道 (V) preach (to an audience)

góng·dūk 港督 (N) the Governor of Hong Kong

góng·faat 講法 (N) way of speaking

góng·gahp 講及 (V) mention

gong·gàn 鋼筋 (N) steel bar

góng·gau 講究 (SV) particular about, meticulous

góng·gú 講古 (VO) to tell stories

góng·héi·séuhng·lèih 講起上來 (Ph) by the way; incidentally

góng hòi yàuh góng la! 講開又講喇 (IE) while we are on this subject, . . .

góng·jàn 講真 (Ph) speak clearly

góng·ji 港紙 (N) Hong Kong dollar (H.K. note)

gong·kàhm 鋼琴 (N) piano

góng·léih 講理 (VO) talk reasonably; listen to reason

gong·lohk 降落 (V) land

gong·lohk·saan 降落傘 (N) parachute

góng·màaih 講埋 (V) finish talking about

góng·mh·chēut 講唔出 (A/RV) indescribable (lit. can't say or tell) /can't put it into words

gòng·muhk 綱目 (N) general outline

góng·ngán 港銀 (N) Hong Kong dollar (H.K. silver)

gòng·sàan·yih·gói bún·sing·nàahn·yìh 江山易改本性難移 (IE) A fox may grow gray, but never good (rivers and mountains may be easily changed but it is hard to alter a man's nature)

góng·síu 講笑 (VO) to crack a joke

góng·tàahn 講壇 (N) altar

gong·tit 鋼鐵 (N) iron of superior quality

góng·tòih 講台 (N) speaker's platform

góng·yàhn·chìhng 講人情 (VO) to ask someone to do a favor by 'bending the rule' a little bit

gòu 高(髙) (SV) be tall, high

góu 稿 (N) manuscript; rough draft

gou 告 (V) sue

gou·baahk 告白 (N) advertisement (M: dyuhn)

gōu·bāt·sèhng, dāi·bāt·jauh 高不成,低不就 (IE) to be particular in selecting a job (unqualified for a high position, and refusing to take a low position)

góu·dái 稿底 (N) original copy

gòu·douh 高度 (N) height

gou·ga 告假 (VO) request leave of absence

gòu·gin 高見 (N) counsel, wise advice (polite expression)

gòu·gwai 高貴 (SV) high-class; dignified; stately

gòu·hing 高興 (SV) be delighted; joyful

gōu·jàang 高踭 (N) high heel (of shoes)

gōu·jūng 高中 (N) senior high

gōu·jūng·bouh 高中部 (N) senior high school

gōu·kāp 高級 (N) high class, high rank

gòu·ngouh 高傲 (SV) arrogant; haughty

gòu·seh·paau 高射炮 (N) antiaircraft gun

gòu·sing a? 高姓呀 (IE) What is your last name?

gòu·seuhng 高尚 (SV) high-principled; noble; magnanimous

gòu·yeuhk 膏藥 (N) sticking plaster (M: tip)

gú 估 (V/N) guess, presume, think (that); riddle

gú 古 (BF) ancient /gú·sìh, ancient times; gú·yàhn, ancient people

gú 股 (M) share (of stock)

gú 鼓 (N) drum

gu·dāk·dihm 顧得掂 (RV) can take care of, look after

gu·dihng 固定 (SV) fixed, stationary

gú·doih 古代 (TW) ancient times

gú·dóu·la 估到嘑 (RV) guessed it

gù·duhk 孤獨 (SV) friendless; alone

gú·dúng 古董 (N) antique, curio

gú·dūng 股東 (N) shareholder

gú·fahn, gú·fán 股份 (N) share of stock

gú·fán-sàang·yi 股份生意 (Ph) corporate business

gú·gai 估計 (V) estimate

gú·gwaai 古怪 (SV) strange, odd, peculiar

gù·hòhn 孤寒 (SV) stingy, closefisted, niggardly; selfish

gú·jái 古仔 (N) story

gu·jāp 固執 (SV) obstinate

gú·jōng 古裝 (At) ancient style of dress

gu·jyuh 顧住 (V) be alert to, be careful of, take care of, keep an eye on /Gu.jyuh dī chè boh! Be careful of car! /Chéng néih tùhng ngóh gu·jyuh dī sai·mān·jái. Please take care my children. /Gu.jyuh (m̀h hóu) pung·chàn yàhn boh! Be careful, not to bump into someone!

gù·lahp 孤立 (SV) without assistance; isolated

gú·laih 鼓勵 (V/N) encourage /encouragement

gū·lēi 咕喱 (N) coolie

gú·lóuh 古魯 (古老)(SV) be antique; be old style

gū·mā 姑媽 (N) paternal aunt

gu·mahn 顧問 (N) adviser

gú·m̀h·dou 估唔到 (V/A) do not expect/unexpectedly

gu·m̀h·dihm 顧唔掂 (RV) cannot take care of, or look after /Ngóh gu·m̀h·dihm gam do la! I can't take care of them anymore!

gù·mòuh·leuhn 姑無論 (A) no matter what

gù·nèuhng 姑娘 (N) young lady; miss

gú·piu 股票 (N) stock (for exchange), stock certificate (M: jèung)

gú·sìh 古時 (TW) ancient times

gu·tái·mihn 顧體面 (VO) careful of one's reputation

gú·waahk 蠱惑 (SV) not straightforward; devious

gú·wún 古玩 (N) antique curio

gú·yàhn 古人 (N) ancient people

gu·yi 故意 (A) intentionally, purposely

gu·yì 故衣 (N) secondhand clothing

gù·yìh 孤兒 (N) orphan

gù·yìh·yún 孤兒院 (N) orphanage

gu·yìhn 固然 (A) of course, unquestionably

gùh·gúh·sèng 咕咕聲 (Pat) the sound or noise of . . . /guh·gú·sèng or gùh·gùh·sèng, the sound of snoring; Wàhng wáng sèng, the zooming sound of an airplane; fùh·fú sèng, the sound of wind; sàh·sá·sèng, the sound of rain.

guhk 焗 (V) roast (in oven); bake

guhk·bouh 局部 (N) local, partial

guhk·chūk 侷促 (SV) hampered; cramped

guhk·jéung 局長 (N) one in charge of a bureau (office)

guhk·lòuh 焗爐 (N) oven

guhk·mihn 局面 (N) condition, situation

Guhng·cháan·dóng 共產黨 (N) Communist party

guhng·cháan·jyú·yih 共產主義 (N) communism

guhng·tùhng 共同 (A) collectively

Guhng·wòh·dóng 共和黨 (N) Republican party

guih 癐 (SV) be tired

gūk·fà 菊花 (N) chrysanthemum species

gūk·gú 咖咕 (N) cocoa

gūk·gùng 鞠躬 (VO) to bow

gun 灌 (V) irrigate; to pour in; to fill in (a container)

gun 罐 (M) measure for canned foods

gùn·chaat 觀察 (V) observe; study

gùn·chòih 棺材 (N) coffin

gún·chūk 管束 (V) curb, restrain; control

gun·gwān 冠軍 (N) the champion (in athletics, games, etc.)

gún·haht 管轄 (V) supervise (people, as a foreman or a department head does)

gún·léih 管理 (N/V) management, administration /manage, administer; govern

gùn·mohng 觀望 (V) hesitate, to be undecided; to dally

gùn·muhk 棺木 (N) coffin (M: fu)

gùn·nihm 觀念 (N) concept

gun·táu 罐頭 (N) canned food (M: gun)

gùn·wá 官話 (N) Mandarin (lit. officials' language; 'gwok·yúh' is preferably used nowadays)

gūng 公 (At) male (for animals)

gūng (·kāp), gùng 供 (V) supply /gùng séui, supply water

gùng·bou 公佈 (V) to make public

gùng·chek 公尺 (M) meter

gùng·chèuhng 工場 (N) workshop

gùng·chìhng 工程 (N) construction work (M: gihn)

gùng·chìhng·sī 工程師 (N) engineer

gùng·chóng 工廠 (N) factory (M: gàan)

gùng·chyun 公寸 (M) centimeter

gùng·dihn 宮殿 (N) palace

Gùng·dóng 工黨 (PN) Labor party

gùng·douh 公道 (SV) fair; fair priced; equitable

gūng·fān 公分 (M) decimeter

gùng·fo 功課 (N) schoolwork; course of study (M: mùhn)

gūng·fō 工科 (N) school of engineering

gùng·fo·bíu 功課表 (N) schedule of daily classes (M: jèung)

gūng·fù 工夫 (N) work /Gam dò gùng·fu, géi·sìh jouh dāk saai a! There is so much work, when can it be finished!

gūng·gà 公家 (At) public (a group of people having common interests or characteristics)

gūng·gīk 攻擊 (V/N) attack (by word or deed)

gùng·ging 恭敬 (V) to respect, venerate

gùng·guhng 公共 (At) public

gùng·gún 公館 (N) residence (polite formal term)

gùng·haauh 功效 (N) effect; efficacy

gùng·héi 恭喜 (V) congratulate

gùng-héi-faat-chòih 恭喜發財 (IE) best wishes for your prosperity

gùng·héi, gùng·héi 恭喜, 恭喜 (IE) congratulations!

gung·hin 貢獻 (N/V) tribute (something given or contributed voluntarily as due or deserved: a gift or service showing respect, gratitude, or affection) /contribute

gùng-hòh-sān-hèi 恭賀新禧 (IE) best wishes for a happy New Year

gūng·hòi 公開 (SV) made public

gūng·jái 公仔 (N) doll, toy

gūng·jái·syù 公仔書 (N) comics; book or magazine containing many pictures (M: bún)

gùng·jin 弓箭 (N) bow and arrow

gùng·jok 工作 (N) job, work (M: gihn)

gūng·kāp 供給 (V) furnish; supply with

gùng·lahp 公立 (At) established by government or community (school, hospital, etc.)

gùng·léih 公理 (N) commonly accepted principle

gùng·léih 公里 (M) 0.6214 mile

gùng·louh 公路 (N) highway, public road

gùng·lòuh 功勞 (N) merit

gùng·màhn 公民 (N) citizen

gùng·màhn 公文 (N) public documents

gùng·pìhng 公平 (SV) just; fair

gūng·sèung·gún·léih 工商管理 (N) business administration

gūng·sí, gùng·si 公使 (N) minister (diplomatic)

gūng·sī 公司 (N) company (business); corporation

gùng·sih 公事 (N) official business, public business

gùng·sih 工事 (N) defense works, fortifications

gùng·sih·dói 公事袋 (N) briefcase

gùng·yàhn 工人 (N) servant; worker (in a factory or the like)

gūng·yīk 公益 (N) the common good

gùng·yuh 公寓 (N) inn

gùng·yún 公園 (N) public park

gwā 掛 (V) hang

gwā 瓜 (N) melon; gourd (edible vegetable)

gwā·fàn 瓜分 (V) partition among several, to divide in shares

gwá·fúh 寡婦 (N) widow

gwa·héi 掛起 (V) hang up

gwa·houh 掛號 (VO) register (of mail)

gwa·houh·seun 掛號信 (N) registered letter

gwa·kèih 掛旗 (VO) fly a flag

gwà·jí 瓜子 (N) melon seed

gwa·jyuh 掛住 (V) to be concerned with; to worry; to be anxious about

gwa·sàm 掛心 (V) to be concerned with; to worry; to be anxious about

gwàai 乖 (SV) be good (as in 'be a good boy')

gwaai 怪 (V) blame

gwaai·cho 怪錯 (V) misjudge, wrong

gwáai·daai 拐帶 (V) kidnap

gwáai·jéung 拐杖 (N) a walking stick

gwáai·jí·lóu 拐子佬 (N) a kidnapper

gwáai·pin 拐騙 (V) kidnap

gwaan 慣 (RVE) denoting being accustomed to doing something

(jaahp·) gwaan 習慣 (V) be accustomed to

gwàan·haih 關係 (N) relation; relationship
gwàan·jiu 關照 (V) to pay special
attention
gwāan·sàm 關心 (V) concern
gwāan·yù 關於 (CV) about; concerning;
with regard to; as to
gwaat 刮 (V) scrape
gwaht 掘 (V) dig; excavate
gwaht 榾 (SV) blunt
gwái 鬼 (N) ghost, devil, spirit
gwai 貴 (SV) be expensive
gwai 貴 (BF) your honorable—as to
country, school, store, factory, etc.
/gwai·haauh, your school
gwai 季 (M) measure for seasons
gwái·douh 軌道 (N) track; railway; orbits
of heavenly bodies
gwái·gam 鬼咁 (A) very, exceedingly
(lit. as . . . as a devil)
gwài·gàn 歸根 (A) finally
gwài·gàn-dou-dái   (Ph)
finally, eventually
gwai·gàng 貴庚 (IE) your age (polite)
gwai·gon 貴幹 (N) your business (lit.
your noble business) /yáuh māt gwai
gon a? What can I do for you?
gwai·gūng·sī 貴公司 (N) your
company (polite form)
gwai·gwok 貴國 (N) your country
(polite form)
gwai·haauh 貴校 (N) your school
(polite form)
gwai·houh 貴號 (N) your store (polite
form)
gwai·jit 季節 (N) season
gwái·máh 鬼馬 (SV) crafty; cunning
gwái . . . . máh (mē) 鬼 . . . 馬 (Pat)
how could . . . /Giu ngóh fan gwéi fan
máh mē. How could I sleep in such a
condition? Ngoih·bihn gam chòuh, duhk
gwéi duhk máh mē. It's so noisy outside
how could I study?
gwai·sáang 貴省 (N) your province
(polite form)
gwai sing a? 貴姓呀? (IE) What is
your surname?
gwái·syú 鬼 (SV) with a suspicious
look
gwaih 櫃 (N) closet; wardrobe; cabinet
gwaih 跪 (V) kneel
gwaih·mín 櫃面 (N) counter (of a store);
information desk (of a hotel)
gwaih·túng 櫃桶 (N) drawer (as of a
desk)

gwaih·túng·jái 櫃桶仔 (N) small
drawer
gwān 軍 (M) army (a military unit)
gwán 滾 (SV/V) be boiled /boil
gwan 棍 (N) a stick; club; rod (M: tìuh)
gwàn·déui 軍隊 (N) armed forces;
military unit
gwàn·fó 軍火 (N) ammunition
gwàn·fuhk 軍服 (N) military uniform
gwán·gáau·saai 滾攪晒 (IE) Sorry I
have troubled you.
gwàn·góng 軍港 (N) navy base, naval
dock
gwān·gùn 軍官 (N) military officer
gwàn·haaih 軍械 (N) weapons
gwán·séui 滾水 (N) boiled water
gwàn·sih 軍事 (At) military
gwàn·yàhn 軍人 (N) soldier; servicemen
gwán·yiht·laaht 滾熱辣 (Ph) boiling hot
gwàn·yuhng 軍用 (At) military (of, or for,
the armed forces) /gwān·yuhng gēi, military airplane
gwàng·ja 轟炸 (N/V) bombing attack
/bomb
gwàng·ja·gèi 轟炸機 (N) bomber (M:
ga)
gwāt·jí 骨子 (SV) be exquisite;
meticulous
gwāt·jit 骨節 (N) joints
gwāt·sō 骨梳 (N) comb made of bone
gwāt·yuhk 骨肉 (N) a group of persons
connected by birth (lit. bone and flesh)
gwo 過 (V) pass, exceed, cross
gwo 過 (P) verb suffix, indicating experience; indicating 'across to'; used in
a sense more or less like the word 'háh'
gwo 過 (P) used in comparison, similar
to the English '-er than' in the pattern
'X is taller than Y' /Ngóh gòu·gwo kéuih.
I am taller than he.
gwo 過 (V) go to
gwo·chúhng 過重 (SV) be overweight
gwo·dāk·heui 過得去 (SV) passable;
tolerable
gwo·douh·sìh·kèih 過渡時期 (N)
transitional period
gwo·fahn 過份 (V/SV) overdo/excessive
gwo·heui 過去 (V/At) pass /passed; in
the past
gwo·hói 過海 (VO) cross over by ferry
gwo·kèih 過期 (VO) overdue, expired
gwó·jāp 果汁 (N) fruit juice
gwó·jeung 果醬 (N) jam, fruit sauce,
preserves
gwo·jéung 過獎 (IE) You flatter me.

gwo·jit 過節 (VO) observe a festival
gwo·jūng 過鐘 (V) pass a set time
gwo·nìhn 過年 (VO) celebrate the New Year
gwo·sàn 過身 (V) passed away, died
gwo·sāt 過失 (N) fault; error
gwó·tāan 菓攤 (N) fruit stalls
gwo·tàuh 過頭 (A) more than enough; (suffix to SV indicating to a regrettable degree)
gwo·wàhn·yúh 過雲雨 (N) passing shower
gwo·yáhn 過癮 (SV) craving satisfied
gwo·yaht·jí 過日子 (VO) spend one's life
gwo·yeh 過夜 (V) to stay overnight
gwó·yìhn 果然 (A) it has turned out as expected
gwo·yù 過於 (A) excessively, overly
gwok 國 (N) country
gwok·dòu 國都 (N) capital (national)
gwok·fu 國庫 (N) national treasury
gwok·gà 國家 (N) state; country; nation
gwok·hing 國慶 (N) national celebrations
gwok·hing (·yaht) 國慶(日) (N) anniversary of the Republic of China, October 10th
gwok·jai 國際 (At) international
gwok·jihk 國籍 (N) nationality
gwok·kèih 國旗 (N) national flag
gwok·mán 國文 (N) Chinese (as a subject in school)
gwok·màhn 國民 (N) citizens
Gwok·màhn·dóng 國民黨 (N) the Chinese Nationalist party
gwok·mouh·yún 國務院 (N) U.S. Department of State
gwok·wòhng 國王 (N) king
gwok·wúi 國會 (N) congress
gwok·yúh 國語 (N) Mandarin Chinese (language)
gwòng 光 (SV) be bright
gwóng·bo 廣播 (N) broadcast
gwòng·gíng 光景 (N) prospects, state of affairs
gwòng·gwan 光棍 (N) rascal
gwòng·làhm 光臨 (N/V) your gracious visit / honor (someone) with a visit
gwòng·máahng 光猛 (SV) be bright
gwòng·mìhng 光明 (SV) bright (literary)
gwòng·sìn 光鮮 (SV) bright and fresh
gwòng·sin 光線 (N) lighting
gwòng·waaht 光滑 (SV) smooth; polished

gwòng·wìhng 光榮 (N/SV) glory, honor /glorious
gwōng·yàm·chíh·jin 光陰似箭 (IE) Time is like an arrow. It goes so fast.
gyuht 橛 (M) part, section
gyùn 嚉 (V) squeeze through
gyùn 捐 (V) donate, contribute
gyùn·béi 捐畀 (V) donate to
gyùn·chín 捐錢 (VO) donate money; solicit donation; raise money by donation
gyún·héi 捲起 (V) to roll up

H

hà 嘎 (P) a particle meaning 'look!' /Hà! kéuih wah kéuih m̀h·yiu woh! Look! He said that he doesn't want it!
hà 嗄 (V) bully
hā 蝦 (N) shrimp (M: jek)
hà·gáau 蝦餃 (N) shrimp dumpling
hà·máih 蝦米 (N) dried shrimps
hàahm 鹹 (SV) be salty
hàahm·bāau 鹹包 (N) steamed bread stuffed with meat
hàahm·choi 鹹菜 (N) salted vegetables
hàahm·dáan 鹹蛋 (N) salted eggs
hàahm·fú 鹹苦 (N) full of toil and suffering
haahm·hoih 陷害 (V) ensnare; involve
haahm·jehng 陷阱 (N) a pitfall
hàahm·sāp 鹹濕 (SV) lecherous
hàahm·sauh·hohk·haauh 函授學校 (N) correspondence school
hàahm·yú 鹹魚 (N) salted fish (M: tìuh)
haahn 限 (V) limit /Yāt·yàhn haahn máaih yāt·go. Limited one to a customer.
haahn·dihng 限定 (V) fix, assign, allot, set a limit on /Haahn·dihng yāt yàhn yāt go. Assign one for each person.
haahn·jai 限制 (V/N) restrict, set a limit for someone /limit, restriction
haahn·kèih 限期 (V) give a time limit (as in a command)
hàahn·sih 閒事 (N) trifling matters
hàahn·wá 閒話 (N) gossip
hàahng 行 (V) walk; go (of watch, cars, etc.
hàahng·duhng 行動 (N) action, activity
hàahng·gāai 行街 (VO) stroll about; window shopping
hàahng·gwo 行過 (V) by or through
hàahng·háh 行吓 (V) take a walk; take a short trip
hàahng·màaih 行埋 (A) get together
hàahng·wàhn chyùhn·sai·gaai 行勻全世界 (Ph) travel all over the world

hàahng·yàhn·louh 行人路 (N) sidewalk

hàaih 鞋 (N) shoe (M: deui)

hàaih 唯* (SV) rough, not smooth

hàaih 唉 (P) an exclamatory particle
indicating sighing, i.e. oh, gee, gosh

hàaih·chāu 鞋抽 (N) shoehorn

hàaih·dáai 鞋帶 (N) shoelace

hàaih·gōu 鞋膏 (N) shoe polish

hàaih·gwāt 骸骨 (N) bones, skeleton

hàaih·jàang 鞋踭 (N) heel of shoe

hāak, hāk 黑 (SV) black, dark

hāak, hāk 刻 (V) engrave

hāak·báan, hāk·báan 黑板 (N) blackboard

hāak·bohk, hāk·bohk 刻薄 (V/SV) to
browbeat /haughty and stern (in look
or speech)

haak·chàn 嚇親 (V) be frightened (by
someone or something)

hāak·fuhk, hāk·fuhk 克服 (V) overcome

haak·gā·yàhn 客家人 (N) Hakka

haak·gēi 客機 (N) passenger plane

haak·hei 客氣 (SV) polite, stand on
ceremony

haak·jáan 客棧 (N) inn

hāak·jai, hāk·jai 克制 (V) overcome;
restrain

hāak (·júng)·yàhn, hāk (·júng)·yàhn 黑
種人 (N) negro

haak·séi 嚇死 (RV) scared to death

haak·tēng 客廳 (N) living room, parlor

hāak·yíng, hāk·yíng 黑影 (N) dark
shadow

haam 喊 (V) cry

hàan 慳 (V/SV) save / be thrifty

hàan·chín 慳錢 (SV/VO) economical,
thrifty /save money

hàan·gihm 慳儉 (SV) thrifty

hāang 坑 (N) pit; ditch; gully

hàang·kèuih 坑渠 (N) gutter, sewer

haap 呷 (V) sip; suck

haap·jaak 狹窄 (SV) narrow; small
capacity

haap yāt·dahm 呷一啖 (Ph) take a
mouthful

háau 考 (V) examine; take an examination; give an examination (test of knowledge or skill)

hàau 敲 (V) knock

hàau·chyún 嗜喘 (N) asthma

haau·douh 孝道 (N) filial piety

haau·ging 孝敬 (V) reverence

hāau·jūk·gong 敲竹槓 (VO) to blackmail

háau·leuih 考慮 (V) consider, think over

háau·miuh 巧妙 (SV) ingenious; skillful;
clever

hàau·mùhn 敲門 (VO) knock on door

haau·seuhn 孝順 (SV/V) filial, respectful
to one's parents /to serve the parents
with filial obedience

háau·si 考試 (VO/N) take an examination;
give an examination /examination

haauh·gwó 效果 (N) results

haauh·jéung 校長 (N) principal, president
(of a college)

haauh·ji 校址 (N) school grounds

haauh·kwài 校規 (N) school rules

haauh·yì 校醫 (N) school physician

háh 吓 (M) for one occurrence of an
action

háh 吓 (P) 'a little' /Mh·gòi béi ngóh
tái·háh. Please let me take a look.

hah·bihn 下邊 (PW) bottom, below, underneath

hah·bou 夏布 (N) grass cloth

hah·chèuhn 下旬 (TW) last 10 days of
month

hah·chi 下次 (TW) next time

hah·dáng 下等 (At) low class; poor
quality; inferior

hah·jau 下畫 (TW) afternoon

hah·ji 夏至 (N) summer solstice

hah·jihn 下賤 (SV) low class (people)

hah·lohk 下落 (N) whereabout

hah·máh·wài 下馬威 (N) bluff (to
frighten by a pretense of strength)

hah·pàh 下爬 (N) chin

hah·tīn 夏天 (N) summer

hah·yāt·bui 下一輩 (N) the next
generation

hah·yéh 下野 (VO) to retire to private
life (only used to refer to important
political figures)

hah·yih·yún 下議院 (N) House of
Representatives

hahm·baahng·laahng 喊嘿唥* (A) altogether, all told

hahm·jūng 唅*盅 (N) jar; chinese porcelain
tea bowl with lid for holding back tea
leaves

hàhn 痕 (SV) be itchy

hahn 恨 (V) hate

hahn 恨 (AV) desire

hàhn hán déi 痕痕地* (Ph) itch a little

hàhn·jīk 痕跡 (N) marks; pricks

hahng 杏 (N) apricot

hàhng·chi 行刺 (V) assassinate

hàhng·duhng 行動 (N) activities, behavior;
conduct

hahng·fūk 幸福 (N/SV) happiness, blessings /be blessed

hàhng·jing 行政 (N) administration

hàhng kéuih 恆佢 (Pat) a verb suffix indicating the continuation of an action /Yíh·gìng sahp·yāt·dim géi, jauh·lèih sihk ngaan·jau la, kéuih juhng hái syu fan hàhng kéuih. It is already past eleven, soon it will be lunch time, and he is still sleeping.

hahng·kwài 幸虧 (MA) fortunately, luckily

hàhng·láih 行禮 (VO) perform a ceremony

hàhng·léih 行李 (N) baggage (M: gihn)

hàhng·sàm 恆心 (N) perseverance; constancy

hàhng·wàih 行為 (N) conduct; behavior

hahng·yàhn 杏仁 (N) almonds, apricot pits

hàhng·yì 行醫 (VO) practice medicine

hahp 合 (V) close

hahp 合 (V) in accord with

hahp 盒 (M) box of

hahp·faat 合法 (SV) legal, legitimate

hahp·dái 盒底 (PW) bottom of a box

hahp·fán 合份 (A) jointly

hahp·fó 合夥 (A) in partnership

hahp-fú-túng-chíng 闔府統請 (IE) Your whole family is invited

hahp·fùh 合乎 (V) meet (the standard of qualification)

hahp·gaak 合格 (At) eligible

hahp·jok 合作 (V/N) cooperate (with) /cooperation

hahp·léih 合理 (SV) be reasonable

hahp·màaih·yāt·chái 合埋一齊 (Ph) put together; altogether

hahp·ngáahn 合眼 (SV) pleasing, pleased with

hahp·sàm·séui 合心水 (SV) to be exactly what one wants

hahp·sìh 合時 (SV) at the proper moment; timely

hahp·sīk 合適 (SV) be suitable

hahp·tòuh 合桃 (N) walnuts

hahp·tùhng 合同 (N) contract

hahp·waih·sāng 合衛生 (SV) be sanitary

hahp·yi 合意 (SV) satisfactory, pleasing

hahp·yuhng 合用 (SV) useful

haht·jéun 核准 (V) to authorize after examination

hái 喺* (V) at, in, on

hái 喺* (CV) from

hái 喺* (P) suffix to a verb, means at, in, or on

haih 係 (EV) to be; equal; it is

haih 係 (V) have (a disease)

haih·gam·là 係嗽啦 (IE) O.K.; all right

haih . . . lèih, m̀h haih . . . lèih 係…來, 唔係…來 (Pat) is . . . , is not . . . /Nī·go haih sing lèih m̀h·haih méng lèih. This is a surname, not a given name.

haih yiu 係要 (Ph) insist

hāk, hāak 刻 (V) carve

hāk·bohk 刻薄 (V/SV) treat harshly /merciless, grim

hāk·chín 黑錢 (N) bribes; squeeze

hāk·mā·mā 黑孖孖 (SV) pitch dark

hāk·mohk 黑幕 (N) hidden corruption

hāk·sàm 黑心 (SV) malevolent

hán·chit 懇切 (SV) sincere

hán·kàuh 懇求 (V) supplicate

háng 肯 (AV/V) willing /to consent to

háng·dihng 肯定 (SV) positive

háp 盒 (N) box

hāp·ngáahn·fan 恰眼瞓* (VO) doze

hāt·sihk 乞食 (V) to beg (as a beggar)

hāt·yī, hāt·yìh 乞兒 (N) beggar

háu 口 (N/M) mouth /mouthful; puff

háu·chí 口齒 (N) elocution; articulation

háu·chòih 口才 (N) eloquence

háu·ging 口徑 (N) caliber (of guns, etc.)

háu·hei 口氣 (N) in a boastful tone /gam daaih ge háu·hei, in such a boastful tone

háu·hēng·hèng 口輕輕 (A) speak hastily (without consideration of the consequence) /Kéuih háu hēng hèng jauh góng·jó béi kéuih ge pàhng·yáuh jì la. He told his friend without much consideration.

háu·houh 口號 (N) a shout in a political mass meeting, slogan; a password

hàu·jyuh 喉住 (V) watch, keep one's eye on

hāu·mēi 後尾 (A) later, later on

háu·sèuhn·gōu 口唇膏 (N) lipstick

háu·séui 口水 (N) saliva

háu·tàuh·bou·gou 口頭報告 (N) oral report

háu·yām 口音 (N) accent, pronunciation

háuh 厚 (SV) be thick

hauh·bihn 後邊 (PW) rear, back

hauh·chán·sāt 候診室 (N) waiting room (in a doctor's office)

hauh·doih 後代 (N) descendant, posterity

hauh·fòng 後方 (N) the rear (as opposed to the front lines)

hauh·fui 後悔 (V) regret, repent

hàuh·gāp 喉急 (SV) hasty; impatient

hauh·gēi·sāt 候機室 (N) waiting room at an airport

hauh·lòih 後來 (MA) afterwards, later on

hàuh·lùhng 喉嚨 (N) throat

hauh·móuh 後母 (N) stepmother

hauh·mún 後門 (N) back door

hauh·sāang 後生 (N) office boy

hauh·sāang 後生 (SV) young, in the prime of life

hauh·sāang·jái 後生仔 (N) young fellows

hauh·sai 後世 (N) the future generations

hauh·yàhn 後人 (N) descendants; posterity

hauh·yeuih 後裔 (N) descendants; posterity

hehng·hēng (·déi) 輕輕 (吔) (A) lightly (usually used in relation with motion, weight and pressure), tenderly, softly

hèi 稀 (SV) watery

héi 起 (V) build

héi 起 (V) rise (of price)

héi 起 (RVE) ending of RV

hei 戲 (N) play (dramatic), show

hei 器 (BF) implement or device (utensil, gadget, furniture, etc.)

hei·bām 汽泵 (N) an air pump

hei·chè 汽車 (N) automobile (M: ga)

hei·chìhng 起程 (V) to start a journey

hei·dék 汽笛 (N) steam whistle

héi·dím 起點 (N) starting point

héi·fèi 起飛 (V) take off (aero)

héi·fo 起貨 (VO) unload cargo

hèi·fuh 欺負 (V) bully

héi·góu 起稿 (VO) make a draft

hei·gùn 器官 (N) an organ of the body

hei·haaih 器械 (N) instruments; equipment, tools

héi·haak 喜客 (SV) hospitable

héi·hàhng 起行 (V) to begin a journey

hei·hauh 氣候 (N) climate, temperature

hèi·hèi·déi 稀稀吔 (At) watery

hèi·hón 希罕 (SV/V) rare /cherish, treasure, prize

hèi·ja 欺詐 (V) extort, deceive

hei·jí 戲子 (N) opera actor

héi·jòng 起贓 (N) to recover stolen property

hei·kehk 戲劇 (N) drama; theatrical performance

hèi·kèih 稀奇 (SV) curious, marvelous

hei·kūk 戲曲 (N) theatrical songs

hei·làuh 氣流 (N) air current

hei·lihk 氣力 (N) strength (physical)

hei·luhng 戲弄 (V) make sport of

héi·méng 起名 (VO) give a name to

hèi·mohng 希望 (V/N) hope /hope

hei·ngaat 氣壓 (N) atmospheric pressure

hei·ngaat·bíu 氣壓表 (N) barometer

hèi·pin 欺騙 (V) cheat; deceive

héi·póuh 起泡 (VO) to bubble, hiss, and foam

hèi·sàn 起身 (VO) get up

hèi·sàng 犧牲 (V/N) sacrifice /sacrifice

héi·sáu 起首 (AV/V/At) begin to /start /the first . . . , at the beginning /héi·sáu gó·léuhng yaht, the first two days; héi·sáu gó·jahn·si, at the beginning; héi·sáu gó·páai, at the beginning

héi·séuhng·lèih 起上來 (P) ending of monosyllabic verb to indicate something happening as a surprise or tending to happen followed by a result that is not usually expected /haam·héi·séuhng·lèih, start to cry

hei·séui 汽水 (N) carbonated water, soft drink /sà·sí (·hei)·séui, root beer; cháang·séui, orange drink

héi·síh 起市 (SV) sell at a high price

héi·sih 喜事 (N) an occasion for joy (e.g. wedding, birthday party, etc.)

héi·sīk 起色 (N) improvement /Yáuh héi·sīk, showing improvement (in referring to a business, a patient's condition) /Kéuih ge sàang·yi nī·páai yáuh dī héi·sīk. His business has picked up a little bit recently. /Keuih ge behng yáuh móuh héi·sīk a? Is there any improvement in his condition?

hei·sīk 氣色 (N) complexion; appearance

hei·tòih 戲台 (N) stage

héi·yáuh·chí·léih 豈有此理 (IE) Darn it! (lit. there is no such rule! There is no such principle!)

héi·yùhn 起源 (N) beginning, origin

hei·yún 戲院 (N) theatre (M: gàan)

hek·kwài 吃虧 (VO) 'get stung'; suffer a loss

hèng 輕 (SV) light (opp. heavy)

hèng 輕 (SV) young (always used with nìhn·géi) /Kéuih nìhn·géi juhng hèng. He's still young.

hèng·yih·mh 輕易唔 (A) very seldom

hèu 靴 (N) boots (M: jek); deui, pair)

heui 去 (V) go

hēui (·síh) 墟(市) (N) a market place in
the rural area

heui·duhk 去毒 (VO) to clear out poi-
sons

hèui gam chòuh bà gam bai 墟咁嘈
巴咁*閞 (Ph) noisy as a market

héui·hó 許可 (V/N) permit /permission

heui·sai 去世 (V) pass away

hēui·sàm 虛心 (SV) unprejudiced

hèui·yeuhk 虛弱 (SV) weak

hèung 香 (SV) fragrant

heung 向 (CV) toward (in the direction
of)

héung 響 (V/SV) sound, ring /loud (in
sound) /Dihn·wá héung la. The telephone is ringing. Dihn·wá m̀h·héung
àh? The telephone doesn't work?
/Dím·gáai gam héung ga? Why is it
so loud?

hēung 香 (N) incense stick (M: jì)

hēung·bān·jáu 香檳酒 (N) champagne

héung·fūk 享福 (VO) enjoy happiness

hèung·há 鄉下 (N) the country (rural);
one's native place (which is not a city)

hèung·há·lóu 鄉下佬 (N) country
folk

hēung·jīu 香蕉 (N) banana (M: jek)

hèung·léih 鄉里 (N) people from the
same rural area

héung·leuhng 響亮 (SV) clear sounding,
be loud and clear (in voice)

heung·lòih 向來 (A) hitherto, before
this

hèung·màhn 鄉民 (N) villagers

hèung·meih 香味 (N) aroma; fragrance

héung·sauh 享受 (V/N) enjoy /enjoy-
ment

hèung·séui 香水 (N) perfume

hèung·seun 香信 (N) kind of mushroom

héung·ying 響應 (V) quick reply echo,
response

him (·lohk) 欠 (V) owe

hīm (·hèui) 謙 (SV) humble, modest

him·chín 欠錢 (VO) owe money

him·dāan 欠單 (N) promissory note

him·hohng 欠項 (N) debts, liabilities

him·jaai 欠債 (VO) be in debt (owe
money)

him·kyut 欠缺 (V) lack of

hìm·ngok 險惡 (SV) dangerous and
injurious

hìm·yeuhng 謙讓 (SV) yielding, give
way to others

hím·yiu 險要 (SV) strategically important
(such as mountain pass)

hìn 牽 (V) lead (a person or an animal
with one's hand)

hin·bìng 憲兵 gendarmes; military police

hin·chēut, yíng·chēut 顯出 (V) show,
manifest

hin·faat 憲法 (N) constitution (supreme
law)

hìn·gwa 牽掛 (V) be anxious; worry

hīn·hā 牽蝦 (V) having asthma

hín·hok 蜆殼 (N) clamshells

hín·jaak 譴責 (V) censure, reprimand

hin·jai 牽制 (V/N) hamper, obstruct;
harass (mil.) /hindrance, obstruction

hin·leuih 牽累 (V) incriminate; implicate

hìn·lìhn 牽連 (V) implicate

hín·mèih·geng 顯微鏡 (N) microscope

hín·mìhng 顯明 (SV) obvious, evident

hìn·sip 牽涉 (V) involve

hín·yìhn 顯然 (A) evidently, obviously

hìng 興 (AV) like, fond of, go for /Néih·
deih hìng m̀h hìng dá·paai ga? Do you
like to play mahjong?

hìng 興 (V) be in style /Nī·paai hìng
bīn·go fún a? Which is in style?

hìng 兄 (BF) elder brother. /lìhng·hìng,
your elder brother; gā·hìng, my elder
brother

hìng·cheui 興趣 (N) interest

hìng·daih 兄弟 (N) brothers /Chàn·hìng·
daih, full brothers; tùhng·bàau hìng·dàih,
full brothers; (sò·) tòhng hìng·daih,
cousins of same surname

hìng·fáhn·jāi 興奮劑 (N) a stimulant

hìng·fàuh 輕浮 (SV) superficial; frivolous, light

hing·hoh 慶賀 (V) congratulate

hìng·jūk 慶祝 (V) celebrate

hìng·sih 輕視 (V) look down on

hìng·wohng 興旺 (SV) prosperous

hìng·yih 輕易 (SV) easy (usually used
negatively) /Gam hìng·yih mē! You
think it would be that easy!

hip 怯 (SV) timid; fearful, nervous

hip·lihk 協力 (A) to work, in coopera-
tion with

hip·wúi 協會 (N) association /Jùng·méih·
màhn·fa·hip·wúi, Sino-American Culture
Association

hip·yeuk 協約 (N) treaty of alliance

hit yāt ján 歇一陣 (Ph) rest awhile,
have a pause /Hit yāt ján sìn·ji jouh lā.
Let's take a break!

híu 曉 (V) understand, know

hó·faú 可否 (Ph) will it . . ., or not?
/Néih hó·fáu bòhng·háh kéuih a? Can
you give him a hand?

hó·gin 可見 (Ph) it is evident

hō·hāak 苛刻 (SV) needless severity

Hó·háu·hó·lohk 可口可樂 (N) Coca-
cola

hò·jing 苛政 (N) cruel government

hó·kaau 可靠 (SV) dependable

hò·kàuh 苛求 (V/N) to importune
/importunity

hó·lìhn 可憐 (SV/V) be pitiful /have
pity on

(hó·háu)·hó·lohk (可口)可樂 (N) Coca-
Cola

hó·nàhng 可能 (SV/A/N) be possible
/possibly/possibility

hó·oi 可愛 (SV) be lovable

hó·pa 可怕 (SV) be fearful

hó·séung-yìh-jì 可想而知 (Ph)
conceivable

hó·sīk 可惜 (SV/MA) be regretful
/it is a pity that . . .

hó·wu 可惡 (SV) detestable; abominable

hó·yìh 可疑 (SV) suspicious

hó·yíh 可以 (AV) can, be permitted

hòh 河 (N) river (M: tìuh)

hoh 賀 (V) to congratulate

hòh·fà 荷花 (N) lotus flower

hoh·láih 賀禮 (N) congratulatory
presents

hòh·bāau 荷包 (N) purse, pouch, a
belt purse

hòh·bīt 何必 (MA) why should it be
that . . . ? /Hòh·bīt nē? Why should
it be so?

hòh·fong 何況 (A) furthermore, moreover; how much more that

hòh·fú 何苦 (Ph) why take so much
trouble

hòh·lāan·séui 荷蘭豆 (N) aerated
water

hòh·lāan·syú 荷蘭薯 (N) potato

hoh·sauh 賀壽 (VO) extend birthday
congratulations

hoh·típ 賀帖 (N) congratulatory cards

hohk 學 (V/AV) learn; study /learn to,
study how to

hohk 學 (BF) -logy; science of /séh·
wúi·hohk, sociology

hohk·haauh 學校 (N) school (M: gàan)

hohk·jaahp 學習 (V) learn by practice

hohk·jé 學者 (N) scholar

hohk·jūk 學足 (Ph) studied for exactly
a certain period of time /Ngóh hohk·

jūk sàam·nìhn. I studied for exactly three
years.

hohk·jūk·saai gam do 學足晒咁多
(Ph) learn completely what has been
taught

hohk·kèih 學期 (N) semester; school
term

hohk·mahn 學問 (N) learning

hohk·sāang 學生 (N) student

hohk·sì 學師 (VO) to be an apprentice

hohk·si·jái 學師仔 (N) apprentice

hohk·syut 學說 (N) doctrine, theory

hohk·wái 學位 (N) academic degree

hóhn 旱 (SV) dry, drought

hohn 銲 (V) solder

hòhn·ga 寒假 (N) winter recess (from
school)

hóhn·jòi 旱災 (N) drought

hòhn·láahng 寒冷 (SV) cold (weather,
literary expression)

hòhn·sāam 汗衫 (N) undershirt (M: gihn)

hóhn·tìhn 旱田 (N) fields which cannot be
flooded

hòhng 行 (M) row; line (of writing)

hòhng 行 (M) trade, line of business

hohng 項 (M) sort, item

hòhng·chìhng 行情 (N) condition, market
price

hòhng·chìhng 航程 (N) flying range; sailing range

hòhng·hói 航海 (VO) navigate

hòhng·hùng 航空 (At) aviation, flight

hòhng·hùng·deih·tòuh 航空地圖 (N)
air map

hòhng·hūng·gūng·sī 航空公司 (N) air
line company or its office

hòhng·hùng·móuh·laahm 航空母艦
(N) aircraft carrier

hòhng·kwèi 行規 (N) guild rules

hòi 開 (V) open; start away (train, bus,
ship)

hòi 開 (P/RVE) a verb suffix indicating
'away from,' or indicating something
has been going on /ending of RV

hói 海 (N) sea

hòi·baahn 開辦 (V) to establish and put
in operation

hói·bīn 海邊 (PW) beach; seashore

hōi·chāan 開餐 (VO) serve a meal

hòi·chēung 開槍 (V/VO) open fire
/fire a shot

hòi·chí 開始 (V) begin, commence

hòi·dāan 開單 (VO) make out a list,
make out a bill

hói·dái 海底 (PW) the bottom of the sea

hòi·dong 開檔 (VO) open the stall
(ready for customers)

hói·dóu 海島 (N) island

hòi·dōu 開刀 (VO) have a surgical
operation

hòi·douh 開導 (V) enlighten, show a
person the right way to avoid making
mistakes

hòi·faahn 開飯 (VO) serve a meal

hòi·fòng 開荒 (VO) reclaim, bring
under cultivation

hòi·ga 開價 (VO) state a price, quote
a price

hói·góng 海港 (N) seaport

hòi·gùng 開工 (V) to begin work

hói·gwāan 海關 (N) the customhouse

hói·gwān 海軍 (N) navy

hói·gwān·luhk·jin·déui 海軍陸戰
隊 (N) marine corps

hòi·hán 開墾 (V) to bring under cultivation, reclaim

hói·háu 海口 (N) estuary; seaport

hòi·hohk 開學 (Ph) start school

hòi·jèung 開張 (V) to open a shop

hói·léih 海哩 (N) nautical mile

hói·méi 海味 (N) seafood delicacies

hòi·mohk 開幕 (VO) open for business
for the first day, have a grand opening

hói·ngohn 海岸 (N) seacoast, seashore

hói·pèih 海皮 (N) shore area (a term
used primarily in Hong Kong)

hōi·pīk 開闢 (V) to open up; develop,
reclaim

hòi·sàm 開心 (SV) amused, happy,
contented

hòi·sàn 開身 (V) start sailing away
(said of boat); leave from station (said
of train)

hói·sáu 開首 (A/V) at the beginning
/start, begin

hói·sīn 海鮮 (N) seafood

hói·sīn·jeung 海鮮醬 (N) sauce for
seasoning seafood

hòi·tàuh 開投 (V) auction off

hòi·tòih 開台 (V) to begin a performance (of an opera)

hòi·tùng 開通 (SV) liberal, open-
minded

hòi·wàahn·siu 開玩笑 (VO) crack a
joke, make fun of

hói·wāan 海灣 (N) bay

hòi·wuh·háu 開戶口 (VO) open an
account in a bank

hòi·wúi 開會 (VO) have a meeting; attend a meeting (lit. open a meeting)

hói·yèuhng 海洋 (N) the ocean

hòi·yín 開演 (V) begin performing

hoih 害 (V) harm

hoih·chyúh 害處 (N) harm, disadvantage

hók 鶴 (N) crane (M: jek)

hok 殼 (N) shell /hìn·hok, clamshell;
gài·dáan·hok, eggshell

hok 壳 (N) ladle /séui·hok, ladle

hòn (·jyuh) 看住 (V) keep an eye on,
watch; take care

Hon·chìuh 漢朝 (At) Han Dynasty (206 B.C.
-220 A.D.)

hòn·doih 看待 (V) treat

hòn·gàan·lóu 看更佬 (N) night watchman

hòn·sáu 看守 (V) guard; watch

Hon·yàhn 漢人 (N) Han people

hòn·wuh 看護 (N) nurse

hòng 糠 (N) husks, chaff

hóng 行 (BF) a store (such as a jewelry
store, electrical appliance store, etc.)

hóng 巷 (N) small street, lane, alley
(M: tìuh)

hong (·gòn) 烘(乾) (RV) to dry (by fire)

hòng·gihn 康健 (SV) hale; hearty; strong

Hōng·hèi 康熙 (PN) K'anghsi, the second
emperor of the Ch'ing dynasty (A.D.
1662-1723)

hong·mihn·bāau 烘麵包 (VO/N) to
toast /a piece of toast (M: faai)

hot 喝 (V) shout at

hot·chói 喝彩 (VO) to clap, shout for an
encore, to applaud

hot·jyuh 喝住 (V) to stop by shouting

hot·mohng 渴望 (V) aspire

hot·síh 渴市 (SV) short in supply

hóu 好 (SV) be good, well; O.K.

hóu 好 (A) very, quite; may

hóu 好 (RVE) ending of RV

hou 好 (AV) like to, be fond of

hóu a 好呀 (IE) 'Fine.' The 'a' is merely
a sentence final, it is not the 'a' particle
used in the choice-type question.

hóu·chíh 好似 (V/A) resemble; look like
/seemingly; it seems that

hóu·chíh . . . jì·léui 好似 … 之類
(Ph) such as . . . and the like

hóu·chói 好彩 (SV) be fortunate, lucky

hóu·deih·deih 好地地 (A) in good
condition; in good health

hou·duhng 好動 (SV) active; fond of
change

hóu faai·cheui 好快趣 (Ph) very soon

hóu·géi·go 好幾個 (NU) quite a few,
a good many

hóu·gei·sing 好記性 (SV) have good memory

hóu·géng 好頸 (SV) good tempered (colloq.)

hóu·gihk 好極 (IE) very good; excellent

hou góng·síu 好講笑 (Ph) fond of joking

hóu·gwo 好過 (V) excel (in quality, value, etc.)

hóu·hàahn·jē 好閒啫* (IE) It doesn't matter.

hou·hohk 好學 (SV) fond of study

hóu·hóu·déi 好好哋* (A) nicely; in a decent manner

hóu·jìng·sàhn 好精神 (SV) be cheerful

hóu·joih 好在 (MA) fortunately

hóu·joih . . . ja 好在 … 嗻 (A) fortunately . . .

hou·kèih 好奇 (SV) curious

hou·kèih·sàm 好奇心 (N) curiosity

hóu·meih·douh 好味道 (SV) be tasty, flavorous, delicious

hóu·m̀h·hóu 好唔好 (Ph) how about

hóu·sàm 好心 (SV/A) be kind, good-hearted /kindly, with good intentions

hóu·sàm·gèi 好心機 (SV) devoted; enthusiastic; attentive

hóu·sēng 好醒* (A) be careful /Hóu sēng boh! Be careful!

hóu·sèung·yúh 好相與 (SV) affable, kind

hóu·siu 好笑 (SV) funny, ridiculous

hóu·siu·yùhng 好笑容 (SV) cheerful /Kéuih go yàhn sìh·sìh dōu haih gam hóu·siu·yùhng ge. He is a man who always wears a smile.

hóu·tìn 好天 (SV) fine day, fine weather

hóu·wáan 好玩 (SV) amusing, interesting

hóu·wah 好話 (IE) you are welcome; you flatter me; good of you to say so

hóu wah m̀h·hóu·tèng 好話唔好聽 (IE) to tell the truth; the ugly truth is . . .

hóu·yàhn·sí 好人事 (SV) affable, considerate

hóu·yáuh·yi·yih 好有意義 (Ph) very meaningful

hóu·yéung 好樣 (SV) good looking

houh 號 (M) day (of month); number (of house, room, etc.)

houh·fai 耗費 (V) squander; waste

hòuh·giht 豪傑 (N) hero

hòuh·jí 毫子 (N) dime

houh·máh 號碼 (N) number

houh·ngoih 號外 (N) extra (newspaper)

hòuh·sí 蠔豉 (N) dried oysters

hùhng 紅 (SV) red

hùhng·fūk 洪福 (N) great happiness

hùhng·jong 雄壯 (SV) strong, masculine, resounding

hùhng·mòuh·nàih 紅毛泥 (N) cement

Hùhng·sahp·jih·wúi 紅十字會 (N) Red Cross

hùhng·sīk 紅色 (N) red color

hùhng·sīk·ge 紅色嘅* (At) red

hùhng·yán 熊人 (N) a bear

hūk 哭 (V) weep, wail, cry

hūk·hūk·tàih·tàih 哭哭啼啼 (Ph) weep and wail

hùng 凶 (At) unfortunate; malignant

hùng·deih 空地 (N) unused land

hūng·gāan 空間 (N) space

Húng·gaau 孔教 (PN) Confucianism (as a religion)

hung·gou 控告 (V) sue

hūng·gwān 空軍 (N) air force

hūng·gwāt 胸骨 (N) breastbone

hùng·hàahn 空閒 (SV) unoccupied; at leisure

húng·haak 恐嚇 (V) frighten

hùng·háu 空口 (A) just words without proof /Hùng·háu góng yáuh māt yuhng ā! What's the use of just talking!

hùng·háu 胸口 (N) chest

hùng·hei 空氣 (N) air

hūng·hèui 空虛 (SV) empty; unoccupied

hùng·hím 凶險 (N) disaster

hùng·jaahp 空襲 (N) air raid

húng·jéuk 孔雀 (N) peacock (M: jek)

hūng·jùng 空中 (PW) space, in the sky

hūng·jùng·síu·jé 空中小姐 (N) air hostess

hūng·kàm fut 胸襟濶 (Ph) magnanimous, generous in overlooking injury or insult

hùng·kwong 空曠 (SV) vacant and spacious (refers to outdoor space)

hùng·máahng 兇猛 (SV) fierce

hùng·ngok 兇惡 (SV) wicked; malignant

húng·pa 恐怕 (MA) afraid that /Ngóh húng·pa keuih m̀h·dāk·hàahn bo. I'm afraid that he will be busy.

hùng·sáu 兇手 (N) a murderer

hùng·sáu 空手 (A) empty-handed

hùng·séung 空想 (N) daydreams

hyūn 圈 (N/M) circle, ring /a round of mahjong

hyun 勸 (V) persuade; advise; console

hyun·chēut·lèih 楦出來 (V) scoop out

hyun·douh 勸導 (V) educate (lit. persuade and guide)

hyun·gou 勸告 (V) admonish

hyūn·tou 圈套 (N) a snare

hyut 血 (N) blood

hyut·gún 血管 (N) blood vessels (M: tìuh)

hyut·hohn·chín 血汗錢 (N) money gained by hard labor

hyut·túng 血統 (N) blood relation

J

jà 渣 (N) sediment; dregs

jà 揸 (V) hold in one's hand; grasp

ja 炸 (V) to explode

ja, jaau 炸 (V) fry (in deep oil)

ja 嗱 (P) sentence final

jā·chè 揸車 (VO) drive (a car)

ja·dáan 炸彈 (N) a bomb

ja·dai 詐諦 (V) falsify; pretend to be; fake

ja·dé 詐嗲 (V) to act peevishly

ja·gā·yi 詐假意 (A) falsify, feign

ja·m̀h·ji 詐唔知 (Ph) pretend ignorance

ja·yeuhk 炸藥 (N) dynamite

jaahk 摘 (V) pick (fruit or flower from tree)

jaahk 碦 (V) put a paperweight or other object on something to hold it down

jaahk·yát 摘日 (VO) pick a luck day

jaahk·yaht·jí 摘日子 (VO) pick a lucky day

jaahm 站 (N) stop (as a bus stop) or station (of a railroad)

jaahm·sìh 暫時 (A/At) temporarily /temporary

jaahn 賺 (V) make profit, gain (in business); earn

jaahn 濺 (V) spatter, splash /jaahn sāp sàn, got wet from spattering; jaahn wū·jòu, spattered

jaahn·chín 賺錢 (SV/VO) be profitable /make profit

jaahn·fóng 棧房 (N) warehouse

jaahp 閘 (N) gate

jaahp·fai 雜費 (N) sundry expenses

jaahp·fo 雜貨 (N) miscellaneous goods

jaahp·fo·póu 雜貨鋪 (N) general store, variety store (M: gàan)

jaahp·gwaan 習慣 (N) habit; customary practice

jaahp·hahp 集合 (V) gather, rendezvous

jaahp·ji 雜誌 (N) magazine (periodical) (M: bún, copy; issue, kèih)

jaahp·jih·típ 習字帖 (N) copy book

jaahp·juhk 習俗 (N) habit and custom

jaahp·jùng 集中 (V) concentrate

jaahp·lèuhng 雜糧 (N) foodstuff (other than rice)

jaahp·sīk·ge 雜色嘅 (At) of various or spotted colors; of various kinds

jàai 齋 (N) fast

jaai 債 (N) debt

jaai·jyú 債主 (N) creditor

jaai·kyùhn 債權 (N) right of creditor

jaai·mouh 債務 (N) obligation of debtor

jáak 宅 (BF) family dwelling /Leih jaak, Lee's residence

jaak 窄 (SV) be narrow

jaak·beih 責備 (V) reprove, rebuke

jaak·faht 責罰 (V/N) punish/punishment

jaak·yahm 責任 (N) responsibility, duty, obligation

jáam 嘶 (V) wink, blink

jáam 斬 (V) chop, hack; cut down or off; behead

jáam·hòi 斬開 (RV) cut apart

jáam·ngáahn 嘶眼 (VO/A) blink (one's eye) /in a wink

jáam·seui 斬碎 (RV) to chop fine

jáam·tyúhn 斬斷 (RV) cut in two

jáan 棧 (N) a warehouse

jáan 盞 (M) measure for lamp, light

jáan 嘈 (A) in vain /Jáan jíng ge jē. It is no use fixing it. Jáan mahn ge jē. It is no use asking it.

jaan 讚 (V) praise

jaan·joh 贊助 (V/N) sponsor, aid /sponsorship

jaan·méih 讚美 (V) praise

jaan·méih·sī 讚美詩 (N) hymn; doxology (M: sáu)

jaan·séung 讚賞 (V) commend (and reward)

jaan·sìhng 贊成 (V) concur, agree

jàang 踭 (N) heel or elbow

jàang 嘈 (V) lack, be short; differ by; owe

jàang 爭 (V) wrangle, contend; strive

jāang·dī 爭的 (A) almost

jāang·jāp 爭執 (V/N) wrangle /disagreement

jàang·jyuh 爭住 (CV) fighting to be the first to do something

jaat·jyuh 紮住 (V) tie up

jaat·saht 紮實 (RV) tie firmly (with a string or the like)

jáau 爪 (N) claws; talons

jaau 罩 (N) a cover

jaau, ja 炸 (V) fry (in deep oil)

jáau·fàan 找迴 (V) return the change (the balance) after paying

jáau·juhk 找續 (V) exchange (of money)

jáau·wuhn 找換 (V) change money

jahm 唪＊ (M) for odors, breeze, etc.

jahng·sung 贈送 (V) give away, present; confer on

jahng·yì·sì·yeuhk 贈醫施藥 (Ph) give medical care free

jaht, ját 侄 (N) nephew

jaht·néui 姪女 (N) niece (brother's daughter)

jái 仔 (N) son

jái 仔 (P) diminutive suffix to nouns /tói·jái, small table

jài(·hái) 擠＊ (V) put (at)

jai 掣 (N) brake; switch

jai 唔濟＊ (V) do (colloq.) /Néih jai m̀h·jai a? Will you do it? /M̀h·jai. No.

jài·dài 擠低祇 (V) put down

jai·douh 制度 (N) system

jai·fuhk 制服 (N) uniform (M: tou, suit)

jai(·jih) 祭(祀) (V) sacrifice

jai·jouh 製造 (V) manufacture, make (with a machine)

jai·m̀h·jyuh 制唔住 (RV) ungovernable, uncontrollable

(NU) jái·ná 仔姆＊ (Ph) mother and total number of children /sàam·jái·ná, mother and two children

jai·náu·gèi 製鈕機 (N) button-making machine

jai·séui 制水 (VO) water control

jai·tàahn 祭壇 (N) altar for sacrifice

jài·yúng 擠擁 (SV) crowded

jaih 滯 (SV/RVE) sluggish; obstinate /having indigestion /Kéuih sihk·jaih·jó jē, m̀h·gán·yiu ge. It's nothing serious, he just ate too much. (He just has indigestion, that's all.)

jāk 側 (V/SV) lean to one side /be tilted, askew

jāk·mihn 側面 (N) profile

jàm 斟 (V) pour

jàm 斟 (V) discuss, negotiate; make a deal (colloq.)

jàm 針 (N) needle (M: háu)

jam 浸 (V) immerse; soak, dip

jām 針 (N) hands (of watches, etc.) /chèuhng jām, the long hand (of a watch); /dyún jām, the short hand (of a watch)

jàm·báan 椹板 (N) chopping board

jam·tau 浸透 (RV) soak thoroughly

jám·tàuh 枕頭 (N) pillow

jám·tàuh·dói 枕頭袋 (N) pillowcase

jàn 真 (SV) be true

jan 震 (SV) jerky, shaky

jān·bóu 珍寶 (N) precious gem

jan·dihng 鎮定 (SV) calm, undisturbed

jan·duhng 震動 (V) vibrate

jàn·gà·fó 真傢伙 (A) really, truly

jàn·haih 真係 (A) certainly, really

jàn·haih fa·hohk la! 真係化學嘢＊ (Ph) a phrase always used to suggest something flimsy

jàn·haih m̀h·wah·dāk la 真係唔＊話得嘢＊ (IE) There should be no complaint!

jan·haih ngāam la! 真係啱＊嘢＊ (IE) What a coincidence! What an opportunity!

jan·hìng·gwok·fo 振興國貨 (Ph) encourage and promote native goods

jān·hùng 真空 (At/N) vacuum /a vacuum

jān·hùng·gún 真空管 (N) tube (of radio, television, etc.)

jan·jihng 鎮靜 (SV) imperturbable, calm

jàn·jing 真正 (SV) genuine, real, true

jān·jyù 珍珠 (N) pearl (M: nāp)

jāng·gà 增加 (V) add to, increase

jāng·syūn 曾孫 (N) great grandson

jāp 執 (V) pick up

jāp 汁 (N) juice; sauce /cháang·jaap, orange juice; nihng·mūng·jāp, lemon juice

jāp·fóng 執房 (VO) tidy up a bedroom

jāp·hàhng 執行 (V) put into operation; carry out (an order); enforce (a law)

jāp·hàhng·léih 執行李 (VO) pack luggage

jāp·lāp 執笠 (V) close out (a business)

jāp·màaih 執埋 (V) gather up (things)

jāp·sahp 執拾 (V) tidy up (things)

jāp·yeuhk 執藥 (VO) get medicine with a prescription (from a pharmacy)

ját 侄 (N) nephew

jāt 質 (BF) substance, nature, constitution /tit·jāt, iron (in medicine)

jāt 枳 (N) a plug; cork /jēun·jāt, a bottle cork

jāt·déi 質地 (N) quality, natural disposition

jàu 州 (M) state (of the United States); continent /Nga·jàu, Asia; Méih·jàu, America

jáu·jáu 走 (V) run; leave

jáu 酒 (N) wine

jáu·bā 酒吧 (N) bar

jāu·bō 週波 (N) frequency (radio)

Jàu·chìuh 周朝 (At) Chou Dynasty (B.C. 1122-255)

jáu·dim 酒店 (N) hotel (M: gàan)

jàu·dou 週到 (SV) circumspect, prudent, considerate, thoughtful

jáu·gā 酒家 (N) restaurant (M: gàan)

jáu·gún 酒館 (N) restaurant

jau·héi 縐起 (V) crinkle, wrinkle

jáu·jēun 酒樽 (N) wine bottle

jàu·jyún 週轉 (V) meet a financial need

jáu·leuhng 酒量 (N) capacity for liquor

jāu·leuht 週率 (N) frequency (radio)

jáu·lóu 走佬 (V) run away; walk out (from marriage)

jau·màaih 縐埋 (V) be wrinkled; crumpled

jau·màhn 縐紋 (N) wrinkles, folds, ripple

jáu·naahn 走難 (VO) flee from disaster (war or famine)

jau·ngohk 奏樂 (VO) to perform music (by orchestra or band)

jāu·sàn 週身 (A) whole body (of a living thing)

jáu·sāt·jó 走失咗* (V) lose contact with a group in traveling

jáu·sì 走私 (V) smuggle

jàu·sìh 週時 (A) all the time

jáu·wùh 酒壺 (N) winepot

jauh 就 (A) then (introduces subsequent action); at once; only, just

jauh 就 (A) contradicts a previous statement, usually stressing the contradiction by giving an example

jauh 袖 (N) sleeve

jauh·hái 就喺 (Ph) it is right at (some place)

jauh·haih 就係 (EV) is (more emphatic)

jauh·haih yàn·waih ... só·yíh (or sìn·ji) ... 就 係 因 為 … 所 以 (先至) (Pat) It is precisely because ... (therefore) ... /Jauh·haih yàn·waih kéuih m̀h·dāk·hàahn sìn·ji pàai ngóh làih ge jē. It is precisely because he is tied up that he sent me here. /Jauh·haih yàn·waih yàhn·háu taai dò la, só·yíh nī·dī mahn·tàih gam nàahn gáai·kyut. It's precisely because the population is so big that it is so difficult to have these problems solved.

jauh·jān·bún 袖珍本 (N) pocket edition

jè (·jyuh) 遮(住) (V) shade (from light); block or conceal (from sight); protect against (the sun or rain, etc.)

je 借 (V) borrow

je 蔗 (N) sugarcane (M: tiuh, stick; gauh, piece)

jē 遮 (N) umbrella (M: bá)

jē 啫* (P) and that's all, only

jē (k) 啫* (P) a final particle generally used in a negative sentence /Mh·haih jē(k). No, it isn't so.

je·béi 借畀 (V) lend to

jé·fù 姐夫 (N) elder sister's husband

je·fún 借款 (N) loan (money)

je·ging 借敬 (V) drink a toast (said by a guest in toasting the group, or another guest) (lit. propose a drink by borrowing it from the host)

jè·jyuh 遮住 (V) shade (from light); block or conceal (from sight); protect against (the sun or rain, etc.)

je nī·go gèi·wuih 借呢個機會 (Ph) avail oneself of an opportunity

je·syù·jing 借書証 (N) library card

Jeh·sàhn·jit 謝神節 (N) Thanksgiving Day

jeh-tìn-jeh-deih 謝天謝地 (Ph) thank heaven (and earth)

jehk 蓆 (N) mat for a bed or chair (M: jèung)

jek 隻 (M) measure for ship, boat; hand, foot; domestic animals, etc.

jek 隻 (M) kind, brand (for gasoline, cigarette, etc.)

jèng 精 (SV) be clever; shrewd; witty

jéng 井 (N) well

jeng 正 (SV) accurate, correct (like pronunciation, etc.); be rightly placed

jeuhk 着 (RVE) ending of verbs like; 'fan,' sleep; 'hòi,' turn on

jeuhk 着 (V) entitled to have

jeuhk·gán 着緊 (SV) diligent; attentive

jeuhk·gāp 着急 (SV) impatient

jeuhk·sou 着數 (SV) being in the gaining position as in getting a bargain, etc. /Néih déng móu máaih dāk jàn·haih jeuhk·sou la. Your hat is sure a good buy. /Kéuih béi yàhn wán·jó jeuhk·sou. He has been a victim of some swindler.

jeuhn 盡 (RVE) to do the utmost, to the full extent /Chēut·jeuhn sām·gèi dōu haih móuh·yuhng ge la. No matter what you have done, it's useless.

jeuhn·jaak·yahm 盡責任 (VO) fulfill one's duty

jeuhn·joih 盡在 (A) just because /Jeuhn·

joih yàn·waih ngóh m̀h·gau chín, só·yíh séung heui dōu m̀h·heui·dāk. Just because I don't have enough money I can't go.

jeuhn·leuhng, jeuhn·léung 盡量 (A) as much (many) as possible; at the full capacity or extent; resort to every means

jeuhn·lihk 盡力 (VO) put the utmost effort into, do one's best

jeuhn·sàm 盡心 (A) put all of one's heart (thought) into

jeuhn·sàm-jeuhn·lihk 盡心盡力 (IE) wholeheartedly

jeuhn yàhn· sih 盡人事 (Ph) to do what one can do (in a desperate situation)

jeuhng 丈 (M) ten Chinese feet (141 in English inches)

jeuhng 像 (N) image, picture

jèuhng-cho-jauh-cho 將錯就錯 (IE) to make the best of a mistake

jeuhng·fù 丈夫 (N) husband

jeuhng·kéi 象棋 (N) Chinese chess (M: pòu, game)

jeuhng·ngàh 象牙 (N) ivory

jeuhng·ngàh·sō 象牙梳 (N) ivory comb

jèui 追 (V) chase, pursue

jéui 嘴 (N) mouth

jeui 醉 (SV/RVE) intoxicated /M̀h·hóu yám·jeui bo! Don't get drunk!

jeui 最 (A) the most

jeui·cho 最初 (At) at the very beginning

jeui·gahn 最近 (A) recently (lit. more recently)

jèui·gau 追究 (V) investigate; follow up

jeui·mahn 追問 (V) intensely inquire

jeuih·chāan 聚餐 (VO) a group of people such as alumni who get together for dinner

jeuih·jaahp 聚集 (V) observe or attend church services

jeuih·jyuh 縋住 (V) to weight down something which hangs

jeuih·yàhn 罪人 (N) sinner; criminal

jéuk 雀 (N) bird (M: jek)

jeuk 着 (V) wear

jeuk·fuhk 着服 (VO) to go into mourning (lit. wearing mournful dress)

jeuk·níuh 雀鳥 (N) bird (a collective term)

jeuk·sih 爵士 (N) knight

jeuk·sih·haahm·tàuh 爵士銜頭 (N) an honorable title, as 'Knight'

jèun 樽 (M) bottle of

jéun 准 (V) permit; allow

jéun 準 (SV/RVE) accurate (as a watch); hit the bull's eye /sure, accurate

jēun 樽 (N) bottle

jéun·beih 準備 (V/N) prepare, make ready to /preparation

jeun·bouh 進步 (V/N) progress /progress, improvement /Kéuih nī·páai jeun·bouh dāk hóu faai. He has been making great progress recently.

jèun·chèuhn 遵循 (SV) compliant; obedient

jeun·hàhng 進行 (V) engage (in doing); progress /Kéuih jing·joih jeun·hàhng nī·gihn·sih. He is engaged in doing this. /Nī·gihn gùng·chìhng jeun·hàhng dāk taai maahn. The construction is progressing too slowly.

jeun·hēung 進香 (V) be a pilgrim

jēun·jāt 樽枳 (N) bottle corks

jéun·kok 準確 (SV) accurate

jèun·tip 津貼 (V/N) aid, subsidize /subsidy, allowance

jèung 將 (CV) used to bring an object to the front of a main verb /Jèung nī·jèung tói bùn·heui gó·syu. Move this table to there.

jèung 章 (M) chapter (of book)

jèung 張 (M) for table, chair, paper, etc.

jéung 長 (BF) head (of an organization, etc.) /haauh·jéung, headmaster, president (of college); syùhn·jéung, captain (of ship)

jeung 醬 (N) thick sauce or paste

jeung 漲 (V) rise

jeung 脹 (SV) filled with air, water, gas, etc.

jéung·bán 獎品 (N) prize (an article)

jéung·bui 長輩 (N) seniors

jèung·chìhng 章程 (N) rules; bylaws

jèung·daaih 長大 (V) grow up

jèung·gahn, jèung·gán 將近 (A) about to

jéung·gwái 掌櫃 (N) manager (jéung·gwái is used for an old-fashioned or small store; gìng·léih is used for a modern and large business firm, etc.)

jéung·hohk·gām 獎學金 (N) scholarship (gift of money)

jéung·laih 獎勵 (V/N) encourage by means of reward /reward

jèung·lòih 將來 (MA) in future

Jéung·lóuh·wúi 長老會 (N) Presbyterian church

jeung·muhk 賬目 (N) accounts, books

jeung·ngoih 障礙 (N) obstacle
jèung·wùh 漿糊 (N) paste
jēut·jì 卒之 (MA) finally
jì 枝 (M) for writing instruments
jì (·dou) 知 (道) (V) know; know about
jì 枝(曲)(BF) branch /jì·dim, branch store
jí 指 (V) point at
jí 紙 (N) paper (M: jèung)
jí 祇(只)(A) only /jí yáuh, only have; jí nàhng, only can
jí, jih 寺 (N) Buddhist temple
jí 止 (V) relieve, stop (as pain, etc.) /jí·tung, relieve pain; jí·hyut, stop bleeding
ji 置 (V) buy (furniture or property)
ji 至 (BF) superlative degree /ji·hóu, the best; ji·faai, the fastest
ji 至 (A) 'not . . . until,' 'must . . . before,' 'then and only then'; only /Gàm·yaht hàh·jau ji dak. It won't be ready until this afternoon.
V-jì-bāt jeuhn 之不盡 (Ph) endless /Yìhn-jì-bāt-jeuhn. It's a long story. /Yùh·gwó néih yáu kéuih góng, kéuih jauh góng-jì-bāt·jeuhn ge la. If you let him talk as he wants to, there will be no end to it.
ji·boh 至㗭'(P) sentence final meaning 'only'; or 'that is all'
jì·bún 資本 (N) capital (money invested in fixed assets)
jì·bún·gā 資本家 (N) capitalist
jì·bún·jyú·yih 資本主義 (N) capitalism
ji·chìh 支持 (V/N) support /support
ji·chìh 至遲 (A) at the latest
jì·chìhn 之前 (MA) before . . . . . . ago /sihk·faahn jì·chìhn, before eating; léuhng·go yuht jì·chìhn, two months ago
jí·dáan 子彈 (N) bullets, ammunition
jí·dihng 指定 (V) assign, designate
jí·dím 指點 (V) to show, direct
ji·dò 至多 (A) at the most
jí·dói 紙袋 (N) paper bag
jí·douh 指導 (V/N) direct, guide /direction, guidance
jí·fāi 指揮 (V) command; direct
jì·gaak 資格 (N) qualification
jī·gāan, jī·gàan 之間 (Ph) between . . .; among . . . /nī·léuhng·go jī·gāan, between these two; gó·sàam go jī·gàan, among those three
jí·gaau 指教 (V/N) instruct /instruction (only used in polite saying)

jī·gám 之嘅 (IE) yet, nevertheless
ji·gàm 至今 (MA) up to the present day
ji·gán 至緊 (A) be sure to (lit. very important)
jì·géi 知己 (N) intimate friends
jì·gihk 之極 (A) an adverbial suffix meaning extremely /hó·wu jì·gihk, most disgusting
jí·gún 只管 (A) try to, will give it a try
jí·gùng 子宮 (N) the womb; uterus
jí haih 只係 (Ph) is only
jí·háp 紙盒 (N) cardboard box
jì·hauh 之後 (MA) after . . . /sihk·yùhn máahn·faahn jì·hauh, after eating supper
jì·hei 志氣 (N) ambition; strength of will
jì·heung 志向 (N) ambition, aspiration
jí·hot 止渴 (VO) to quench thirst
jí·hùhng·sīk·ge 紫紅色嘅' (At) purple
jí·hyut 止血 (VO) stop bleeding
ji·joih 志佐 (V) set one's mind on, aim at (fig.)
ji·jóu 至早 (A) at the earliest
jī·jūk 知足 (SV) content
jì·jūng 之中 (Ph) among . . .; between . . .; of . . .
jī·jyū 蜘蛛 (N) spider
jī·jyū·móhng 蜘蛛網 (N) spider's web
jí·kāt 止咳 (VO) stop coughing
jì·màh·yàuh 芝蔴油 (N) sesame oil
jì·meih 滋味 (N) taste; flavor
ji·mihng, ji·mehng 致命 (A) fatal
jí·múi 姐妹 (N) sisters
jí·nàahm·jām 指南針 (N) compass
jí nàhng 只能 (Ph) can only
jì·ngoih 之外 (Ph) beyond a certain number or limit
jì·noih 之內 (Ph) within a certain number or limit
jì·piu 支票 (N) (bank) check (M: jèung)
jì·piu·bóu 支票簿 (N) checkbook
jì·sai 仔細 (A) carefully, in detail
jī·sí 之士 (N) cheese (transliterated)
jì·sìh 之時 (TW) at the moment of
jí·sih 指示 (V/N) instruct /instructions
jī·sīk 知識 (N) knowledge
ji·síu 至少 (A) at least
. . . jì só·yíh . . . ···之所以 (Pat) the reason that . . . /Kéuih jì só· yíh m̀h·lèih nē, gáng·haih kéuih béi yàhn màng·jó heui dá·páai la. The reason that he didn't come must be that he was forced by somebody to go play Mahjong.
jí·sou 指數 (N) index number
jí·syùn 子孫 (N) son and grandsons, posterity

jì·tung 止痛 (VO) stop or relieve pain

ji·wai, ji·waih 智慧 (N) wisdom; sagacity

jì·yàhn·gung 支人工 (VO) pay an employee; get paid

jì·yāt 之一 (Ph) one of ... /Kèih·jūng jì·yāt haih ngóh·ge hohk·sāang. One of them is my student.

jì yáuh 只有 (Ph) only have

jì yáuh ... hái lā 只有···喺嘴 (IE) all I (or we) can do is ... (I guess) /Jí jáuh maaih·jó kéuih hái lā. All we can do is to sell it. /Jì yáuh m̀h chēut·sèng hái lā. All I can do is to keep my mouth shut.

jì·yi 指意 (AV/V) in hope of /hope

ji·yihp 置業 (VO) acquire property

jí·yíu 紙鷂 (N) paper kite (M: jek)

jí·yiu 只要 (MA) all one needs to do is; it is only required (that) ... /Jí·yiu hòi·jo go jai jauh dāk la. All one needs to do is to turn on the switch.

ji·yù 至於 (A) regarding ... as to ...

ji·yuhn 志願 (N) aspiration

jih 字 (N) word; character, ideograph

jih 寺 (N) Buddhist temple

jih·bèi 自卑 (V) to abase (oneself)

jih bin 自便 (Ph) do as one wishes (lit. do at one's own convenience)

jih·chuhng 自從 (MA) ever since; since

jih·dín 字典 (N) dictionary

jih·duhng 自動 (A/At) voluntarily /automatic

jih-gàm-yìh-hauh 自今以後 (Ph) from now on

jih·géi, jih·gēi 自己 (N) self, oneself

jih·geui 字據 (N) contract; written evidence

jih-gú-gàai-yìhn 自古皆然 (IE) It has been this way since the dawn of the world

jih·hei 自棄 (V) give oneself up to wickedness

jih·houh 字號 (N) label, name (of a store or firm)

jih·jih 自治 (V/N) self-govern /self-government, autonomy

jih·joih 自在 (SV) comfortable

jih·jok·yihp 自作孽 (Ph) self-wrought evils

jih·jyùn·jih·daaih 自尊自大 (SV) self-important; conceited

jih·lahp 自立 (V) support oneself financially

jih·lòih·séui 自來水 (N) tap water

jih-mìhng-dāk-yi 自鳴得意 (IE) singing one's own praises

jih·miuh 寺廟 (N) temple

jih·móuh 字母 (N) alphabet

jih·mùhn 寺門 (N) temple

jih·nāp 字粒 (N) movable type

jih·ngáahn 字眼 (N) diction, expression

jih·òn 治安 (N) public order (absence of lawlessness)

jih·saat 自殺 (V) commit suicide

jih sai 自細 (Ph) since childhood or youth

jih·sàu 自修 (V) self-study; private study

jih-sèung-màauh-téuhn 自相矛盾 (IE) self-contradictory

jih·sì 自私 (SV) selfish

jih-sì-jih-leih 自私自利 (SV) selfish

jih·tái 字體 (N) shape of a character; style of type

jih·wá 字畫 (N) decorative painting or scrolls (M: fūk)

jih·yām 字音 (N) syllable, sound of a written character

jih·yàuh 自由 (N/SV) freedom /be free

Jíh·yàuh·sàhn·jeuhng 自由神像 (N) Statue of Liberty

jih·yìhn 自然 (SV/A) natural /of course, naturally

jih·yìhn·fò·hohk 自然科學 (N) natural science

jih·yuhn 自願 (AV) of one's own free will. /Ngóh jih·yuhn gám jouh. I want to do it of my own free will.

jihk 席 (M) table (in a banquet)

jihk 值 (V) have value of, is valued at, worth

jihk·baahk 直白 (SV/A) frank /frankly

jihk chèuhng jihk tóuh 直腸直肚 (Ph) outspoken

jihk·chìhng 直情 (A) simply

jihk·chín 值錢 (SV/VO) be valuable

jihk·dāk 值得 (AV) worthwhile

jihk·gun 籍貫 (N) one's native place

jihk·háu 藉口 (V/N) make a pretext of /pretext

jihk·jip 直接 (A) directly

jihk·màhn 籍民 (N) citizen

jihk·maht 植物 (N) plant

jihk·maht·hohk 植物學 (N) botany

jihk·mohk 寂寞 (SV) lonely, lonesome

jihk·sin 直線 (N) direct line

jihk·sīng·gèi 直升機 (N) helicopter (M: ga)

jihk·yát 值日 (VO) on day duty

jihk·yé 值夜 (VO) on night duty

jihm·jím 漸漸 (MA) gradually

jihn 纏 (V) bind up

jihn 賤 (SV) cheap, held in little esteem

jihng 靜 (SV) be quiet

jihng, sihng 賸 (V) remain, be left over

jihng (·fàan), sihng·fàan 賸返 (V) have left, have remaining, leave behind (to let remain unmoved or undone)

jihng·haih 靜係 (A) only

jihng·jíng 靜靜 (A) quietly

jiht·jí 截止 (V) end, be over (e.g. a deadline) /Géi·sìh jiht·jí bou·méng a? When does registration end?

jiht·jyuh 截住 (V) intercept; interrupt

jiht·tyúhn 截斷 (V) cut off

jīk 織 (V) weave

jīk 積 (V) save (money, etc.)

jīk 則 (N) blueprint, design

jīk (·jí) 累(紙)(N) check (M: jèung)

jīk·chūk 積蓄 (V/N) save /savings

jīk·gihk 積極 (SV) positive; energetic

jīk·hāak, jīk·hāk 即刻 (A) at once, immediately

jīk·haih 即係 (EV) is, are (emphatic)

jīk·jouh·chóng 織造廠 (N) textile factory

jīk·lāang·sāam 織冷衫 (VO) knit a sweater

jīk·sí . . . , . . . dōu 即使 ···都 (A) even if . . . /Yùh·gwó haih gám, jīk·sí néih m̀h·lèih dōu m̀h·gán·yiu la. If this is the case, it'll be all right even if you can't come.

jīk·sìh 即時 (A) immediately, right now

jīk·yaht 即日 (A) the same day

jīk·yihp 職業 (N) occupation; profession; job

jīk·yùh 即如 (V) the same as

jīk·yùhn 職員 (N) staff member; officer; clerk

jim 佔 (V) constitute; occupy

jìm 尖 (SV) pointed; sharp-pointed

jim(·geui) 佔據 (V) occupy by force

jim·líhng 佔領 (V) occupy (territory)

jìm·máih 粘米 (N) rice

jìn 煎 (V) fry (in a skillet without stirring, as a fried egg)

jín 剪 (V) cut with scissors

jin 墊 (N) cushion, mattress /Yí·jín, a cushion for chair

jin(·jyuh) 墊住 (V) cushion

jin 薦 (V) recommend

jin 箭 (N) arrow (M: jì)

jín 氈 (N) blanket (M: jēung)

jìn·cháau 煎炒 (At) frying in general

jin·dau 戰鬥 (N/V) combat

jin·jàng 戰爭 (N) war

jín·kèih 展期 (VO) postpone; defer

jín·láahm 展覽 (V) exhibit, display

jin·laahm 戰艦 (N) warship (M: jek)

jín·láahm·wúi 展覽會 (N) exhibition (public display, as of works of art, manufacture, etc.)

jin·leuhk 戰略 (N) military strategy

jin·seuht 戰術 (N) tactics

jin·sih 戰事 (N) warfare, battle

jín·tyúhn 剪斷 (RV) cut with scissors

jìng 蒸 (V) cook (by steam)

jíng 整 (V) repair; fix; prepare (dishes)

jing 証 (N) identification or certification paper

jing 正 (At) main; principal (versus branch or subordinate)

jing 症 (N) disease (M: tìng)

jìng·bìng 徵兵 (N/VO) conscription of soldiers /conscript soldiers

jing·chaak 政策 (N) policy; administrative policy

jìng·chàh 偵查 (V) investigate, secret inquiry

jíng·chàih 整齊 (SV) neat, in good order

jìng·chói 精彩 (SV) great, beautiful, terrific, fantastic (exclamatory expression of a masterwork or a performance of exceptional quality)

jíng·dihng 整定 (A) by destiny; determined by fate

jing·dong 正當 (SV) right, proper; what should be, legitimate; fair, honest

jing·fàn 證婚 (VO) officiate at a marriage

jing·fàn·yàhn 證婚人 (N) officiator at a marriage

jing·fú 政府 (N) a government

jing·gaai 政界 (N) government circles

jing·geui 證據 (N) proof, evidence

jing·gín 證件 (N) certificate

jing·gìng 正經 (SV) serious-minded; honest, open

jing·guhk 政局 (N) political conditions

jing·haak 政客 (N) politician

jíng·háh jíng·háh, jíng·jíng·há 整吓整吓, 整整吓 (A) gradually (usually implies a deteriorating condition)

jìng·hei 蒸氣 (N) steam

jìng·ji 精緻 (SV) be exquisite; fine and delicate

jing·jih 政治 (At/N) political /politics

jing·jih·gā 政治家 (N) statesman; politician

jing·jihk 正直 (SV) honest, upright

jíng-jíng-chaih-chaih 整整齊齊 (Ph) neat, in good order

jing·joih V-gán . . . 正在 V 緊 (Ph) in the midst of (a progressive action)

jing·joih V-gan gó·jahn·sí, . . . 正在 V 緊 咽*陣 時 (Ph) during, just at the moment of

jing·joih yiu . . . 正在要 (Ph) just about to

jing·káai 正楷 (N) the proper printed form of a Chinese character

jìng·kàuh 徵求 (V) solicit

jing·kok 正確 (SV) correct

jing·mìhng 證明 (V/N) prove /proof

jing·mìhng·syù 證明書 (N) certificate

jing·pín 正片 (N) main feature (of a movie)

jìng·sàhn 精神 (N/SV) spirit /be cheerful; be in good health

jing·saht 證實 (V) confirm

jìng·sàu 徵收 (V) collect (tax)

jing·sèuhng 正常 (SV) normal

jing·sīk 正式 (At/A) formal, official /formally, officially; properly

jing·só·waih 正所謂 (IE) the saying that . . . (used to begin a quotation of a common saying or a literary phrase)

jing·syù 證書 (N) credentials, diploma

jìng·taam 偵探 (V/N) scout; spy; detect /detective

jing·yàhn 證人 (N) witness, attestor

jìng·yuht 正月 (TW) the first month of the lunar year

jing·wah 正話 (MA) just (a moment ago)

jip 接 (V) meet (to be present at the arrival of); receive (a letter, a thing, a telephone call, etc.)

jip·gahn 接近 (V/SV) approach, adjoin /near to, adjoining

jip·hāp 接洽 (V) make contact and negotiate

jip·jūk 接觸 (V/N) contact /contact

jip·jyuh 接着 (A) without stopping, without a break, continuously /Kéuih duhk·yùhn daih·yāt·dyuhn jì·hauh, chéng néih jip·jyuh duhk daih·yih·dyuhn. After he has finished reading the first paragraph, please go on reading the second paragraph without a break.

jip·sàang·yi 接生意 (VO) take an order (in business) /Kéuih jeui·gahn jip·jó léuhng·dàan hóu daaih ge sàang·yi. Recently he took two big orders.

jip·sāng 接生 (VO) deliver a baby

jip·sàu 接收 (V) take possession of

jip·sin·sāng 接線生 (N) telephone operator

jit 節 (M) paragraph, passage; section (of writing)

jit 節 (N) festival

jit 折 (BF) certain percentage off /baat·jit, 20% off; chāt·jit, 30% off

jit·chou 浙醋 (N) vinegar

jit·gihm 節儉 (SV) thrifty; frugal

jit·ging 捷徑 (N) short cut; easy method

jit·hohk 哲學 (N) philosophy

jit·hohk·gā 哲學家 (N) philosopher

jit·jai 節制 (V) temperate; moderate

jit·kau 折扣 (N) discount

jit·lihng 節令 (N) the 24 solar terms of a Chinese year; February 5, Spring begins; February 19, The rains; May 5, Summer begins; June 21, Summer Solstice; etc.

jit·muhk 節目 (N) program (of entertainment or a ceremony)

jìu 朝 (M) morning

jiu 照 (V) shine upon

jiu (·jyuh) 照 (CV) according to . . . accordingly /jiu(·jyuh) gám jouh, do it accordingly

jīu, hēung·jīu 蕉, 香蕉 (N) banana (M: jek)

jìu·dím 焦點 (N) focus

jìu·doih 招待 (V) receive and attend (a guest), entertain

jìu·fù 招呼 (V) usher; greet; take care of (a person); receive a friend and serve him beverage, food, etc.

jiu·gai 照計 (Ph) in my opinion (lit. as it is figured)

jiu·gauh 照舊 (A) as before, as formerly

jiu·geng 照鏡 (VO) look in a mirror

jiu·gu 照顧 (V) to patronize; to care for

jiu·jeng 照正 (MA) normally

jiu·liuh 照料 (V) look after, take care of

jiu·ngóh·só·ji 照我所知 (Ph) according to what I know; as far as I know

jìu·pàaih 招牌 (N) signboard with the name of a business establishment, private, or public office

jiu·pín 照片 (N) slides

jiu·sèuhng 照常 (A) as usual

jìu·tàuh·jóu 朝頭早 (TW) morning

jiu·X-gwōng 照X光 (VO) take X-ray

jiu·ying 照應 (V) look after, take care of

jìu·yìuh 招摇 (V) loiter

jiuh 嚼 (V) chew; masticate

jiuh·jaahp 召集 (V) convene, call together

jó 左 (SV) left

jó (·jyuh) 阻(住) (V) obstruct; hold up

jó 咗 (P) verb suffix, indicating completed action

jó·gaak 阻隔 (V) hinder; obstruct

jó·gán 左近 (PW) vicinity, near-by

jó·jí 阻止 (V) hinder, prevent, stop,
impede

jó·léun 左輪 (N) revolver (M: jì)

jó·yáu, jó·yauh 左右 (A) approximately
/léuhng·go ngàhn·chín jó·yáu, approximately two dollars

jó·yauh·wàih·nàahn 左右為難
(IE) in a dilemma

joh 座 (M) measure for storied building — 'láu'

johk 鑿 (V) gouge, chisel

johk·chyùn 鑿穿 (V) puncture

johng 撞 (V) bump into, run into

johng·báan 撞板 (VO) run up against a
stone wall (lit. run into a board)

johng·sī 狀師 (N) solicitor, lawyer

joi 再 (A) once more, or more; again

joi 載 (V) to carry (as by vehicle or
vessel)

joi·geuk 儀脚 (N) freight rate

joi·gin 再見 (IE) good-bye

joi·haak 載客 (VO) carry passengers

jòi·pùih 栽培 (V) cultivate; render
assistance to the younger generation
or the inferior

jói·seung 宰相 (N) prime minister;
premier

joih·chèuhng 在場 (V) to be present

joih·fùh 在乎 (V) care about, be concerned with

joih gai·waahk·seuhng 在計劃上
(Ph) on paper, on the drawing board
(i.e. in theory)

joih gwàn·sih·seuhng 在軍事上
(Ph) militarily speaking

joih·hòhng 在行 (SV) be expert, experienced, well-versed in

joih·noih 在内 (V) included /Nī·go joih
m̀h·joih·noih a? Is this included? /Nī·
go m̀h·joih·noih. This is not included.

joih sèung·yihp·seuhng 在商業上
(Ph) commercially speaking

joih yáuh·yìh·seuhng góng 在友誼上
講 (Ph) speaking of friendship

joih·yi 在意 (V) be attentive to

joih yùhn·jāk·seuhng 在原則上
(Ph) in principle

jok·gā 作家 (N) authors, writers

jok·gwaai 作怪 (VO) make trouble /Kéuih
yauh jok·gwaai la. He is making trouble
again.

jok·jé 作者 (N) author, writer

jok·yāp 作揖 (VO) to make a bow (slight
bow with hands clasped and raised as a
gesture of greeting or congratulation)

jok·yuhng 作用 (N) function, purpose

jòng 裝 (V) pack

jòng 覘 (V) peep

jong 葬 (V) bury (the dead)

jòng·baahn·sèhng 裝扮成 (V) disguise
as; dress as, make up to look like

jōng·háu 莊口 (N) wholesale firm

jòng·hóu 裝好 (RV) be installed

jong·láih 葬禮 (N) funeral rites

jòng·maht 贓物 (N) stolen goods; loot

jòng·múhn 裝滿 (RV) fill

jōng·sàu 裝修 (V) decorate (refurnish)

jòu 租 (V/N) rent /rent

jóu 早 (SV) early

jóu 棗 (N) dates, jujube

jóu TW ... 早 ... (Pat) ... ago
/jóu·léuhng·yaht, couple of days ago

jou 竈,灶 (N) stove; furnace

jóu·chāan 早餐 (N) breakfast

jóu·chỳuhn 祖傳 (At) hereditary; handed
down from ancestors

jóu·fuh 祖父 (N) grandfather

jòu·gaai 租界 (N) the foreign concessions

jòu·gip 遭劫 (VO) to meet with disaster

jou·gwàn 灶君 (N) the kitchen god

jóu·gwok 祖國 (N) fatherland, mother
country

jóu·jīk 組織 (V/N) organize /organization

jóu·jùng 祖宗 (N) ancestors

jóu·máahn 早晚 (MA) sooner or later

jóu·móuh 祖母 (N) grandmother

jóu·páai 早啡 (A) not very long ago

jóu·sàhn 早晨 (IE) good morning

jóu·sìh 早市 (N) market in early morning

jóu·táu 早 (IE) good night

jóu·yāt·máahn 早一晚 (TW) the
previous night

jouh 做 (V) do; make; be (a doctor, teacher,
etc.); act as (a character in a play, etc.);
be used as (with ngoi·lèih)

jouh·chéui 做廚 (VO) to be a cook

jouh·dāk 做得 (IE) It's O.K. All right.
Can be done

jouh·dāk·lèih 做得嚟 (RV) something
would (or could) be done

jouh·gùn 做官 (VO) be an official

jouh·gùn·ge 做官嘅* (N) government officials

jouh·jing 做證 (V) act as witness

jouh·gùng 做工 (VO) do a job; work

jouh·gùng·fo 做功課 (VO) do homework

jouh·gūng·fù 做工夫 (VO) work on (to put in some work on); to 'fix'

jouh·hei 做戲 (VO) play drama or opera; act in drama or opera (as an actor)

jouh·jok 做作 (SV) forced or artificial

jouh·láih·baai 做禮拜 (VO) observe or attend church services

jouh·lihn·jaahp 做練習 (VO) do an exercise

jouh·māt (·yéh) sih·gon a? 做乜*(嘢) 事幹呀? (IE) What happened?

jouh·māt·yéh 做乜*野* (MA) why

jouh·māt·yéh a? 做乜*嘢*呀? (IE) What is the matter?

jouh·pún 做伴 (VO) be in the company of, keep company with (a person)

jouh·sauh 做壽 (VO) to give a birthday party for an elderly person

jouh·sèhng, jouh·sìhng 做成 (V) create; make into

jouh·yìuh 做謠 (VO) make up a rumor

juhk 逐 (SP) every single one /juhk·bún syù, every single book

juhk 續 (V) give change (after payment)

juhk 俗 (SV) common, unrefined, vulgar

juhk 族 (N) tribe; clan

juhk·chín 續錢 (VO) make change (money)

juhk·fàan 續返 (V) return the change (the balance) after paying

juhk·go 逐個 (A) one by one; every single one

juhk·go láih·baai 逐個禮拜 (Ph) every single week

juhk·hei 俗氣 (SV) unrefined, vulgar

juhk·jím 逐漸 (A) gradually

juhk·wá 俗話 (N) common saying

juhk·yúh 俗語 (N) proverb, common saying

juhk·yúh wah 俗語話 (Ph) there is a saying

juhng 重 (A) still, yet

juhng·daaih 重大 (SV) heavy, important

juhng·haih 重係 (A) as before, as usual

juhng·hóu . . . ? 重好 (A) why should . . . ? should still . . . ? (expresses surprise or admonishment)

juhng·yáuh 重有 (A) furthermore

juhng·yiu 重要 (SV) be important

juhng·yiu·sing 重要性 (N) importance

jūk 捉 (V) catch; net

jūk 粥 (N) rice gruel, congee

jūk 祝 (V) wish

jūk 足 (RVE) sufficient, enough /Yùh·gwó néih nàhng·gau hohk·jūk sàam·nìhn, néih ge Gwóng·jàu·wá jauh hóu hóu la. If you can study Cantonese for three full years, your Cantonese will be excellent. /Néih sái nī·gihn sāam yiu lohk·jūk fàan·gáan·fán ji dāk boh. You should put in enough soap powder when you wash this coat.

jūk 竹 (N) bamboo

jūk·chìuh 觸礁 (VO) to run on a rock

jūk·daat 竹笪 (N) split bamboo mats

jūk·fu 囑咐 (V) to order; command

jūk·gòu 竹篙 (N) bamboo pole

jūk·hei 竹器 (At/N) bamboo /bamboo furniture, utensil, etc.

jūk·jūk 足足 (A) exactly, whole /Ngóh kàhm·yaht jàn·haih guih la, ngóh kàhm·máahn jūk·jūk fan·jó sahp·go jūng·tàuh. I was really tired yesterday, last night I slept ten whole hours.

jūk·jyuh 提住 (V) grasp, hold

jūk·kàuh 足球 (N) soccer ball; soccer

jūk·kéi 捉棋 (VO) play chess or checkers (M: pòu or pùhn)

jūk kìuh 築橋 (Ph) to build a bridge

jūk louh 築路 (Ph) to build a road

jūk máh·louh 築馬路 (Ph) build roads

jūk·nī·nī 捉呢呢 (VO) play hide and go seek

jūk·séun 竹筍 (N) bamboo shoot

jùng 舂 (V) pound, ram down

júng 種 (M) kind of, sort of; race (of people)

júng 腫 (V) swell

júng 粽(糭)(N) dumplings (made by wrapping glutinous rice or millet in broad bamboo leaves and boiling it)

jung 種 (V) plant; cultivate; grow

jung 中(甶)(RVE/V) hit the center /win (a prize /dá·jung, hit a bull's eye; seh·jung, hit a bull's eye by shooting (with gun or arrow) /jung·jó máh·bīu, won a lottery.

jūng 鐘 (N) clock, bell

júng 總 (BF) general; total /júng·gìng·léih, general manager; júng·pìhng·gwàn·fān·sou, total average grade

jùng·chàu·jit 中秋節 (N) mid-autumn festival (15th day of 8th lunar month)

jùng·chèuhn 中旬 (TW) middle ten days of month

jùng·dáng　中等　(At) mediocre

jūng·dím　鐘點　(N) hour

jung·duhk　中毒　(V) take poison by accident

júng·dūk　總督　(N) governor (of Hong Kong)

jūng·gāan　中間　(PW) the center

jùng·gaau　宗教　(N) religion

jùng·gaau　中校　(N) lieutenant colonel

jung·gai　中計　(VO) fall into a trap

júng·gìng·léih　總經理　(N) general manager

jùng·gou　忠告　(V/N) admonish /admonition

Jùng·guhng　中共　(At/N) Chinese Communist Party (abbreviation of Jùng·gwok Guhng·cháan·dóng) /Communist China

júng·guhng　總共　(A) totally

Jùng·gwok　中國　(N) China

Jùng·gwok·gwok·màhn·dóng　中國國民黨　(N) Chinese Nationalist Party

júng·haih　總係　(A) always, all the way along /Ngóh júng·haih jìu·tàuh jóu ngh·dím·jūng jó·yáu jauh séng la. I always wake up around 5:00 a.m., lately.

jùng·háuh　忠厚　(SV) honest, trustworthy

jung·hohk　中學　(N) high school; middle school (term used in China); secondary school

júng·jaahm　總站　(N) the terminus (of a bus line)

jùng·jeung　中將　(N) lieutenant general, vice admiral

júng·jì　總之　(A) to sum up in short /Júng·jì kéuih m̀h·lèih ge la. In short, he will not come.

jùng·jí　中指　(N) middle finger

jùng·jí　宗旨　(N) the leading idea; purpose

jùng·jihk　忠直　(SV) upright, honest, and sincere

júng·juhk　種族　(N) tribe, race

jùng·lahp·gwok　中立國　(N) neutral country

júng·léih　總理　(N) premier

júng·leuih　種類　(N) type, kind

júng·lìhng·sí　總領事　(N) consul general

júng·lìhng·sí·gún　總領事館　(N) consulate general

jung·máh·bīu　中馬票　(VO) to win a prize (or the first prize) of a lottery or a horse race

Jùng·màhn　中文　(N) Chinese (written language)

jùng·ńgh　中午　(TW) noon

jūng·sām　中心　(PW/N) in the middle /center

jūng·sàm　忠心　(SV) loyal

jūng·sīk　棕色　(N) brown color

jūng·sīk·ge　棕色嘅*　(At) brown

júng·sou　總數　(N) total number

júng·túng　總統　(N) president (of a Republic)

Jùng·wàh·màhn·gwok　中華民國　(N) Republic of China

Jùng·wàh·yàhn·màhn·guhng·wòh·gwok　中華人民共和國　(N) Chinese Peoples Republic

jùng·wai　中尉　(N) first lieutenant

júng·wúi　總會　(N) general office, headquarters

júng·wúih　總會　(A) eventually it will be

jùng·yi　鐘意　(V/AV) to like, be fond of /like to

jūng·yì　中醫　(N) physician trained in Chinese medicine

jùng·yìhn·yihk·yíh　忠言逆耳　(IE) Honest advice is unpleasant to the ear.

jyū　豬　(N) pig (M: jek)

jyú　煮　(V) to cook

jyu·chaak　註冊　(V) register, enroll

jyú·chìh　主持　(V) be in charge of

jyu·gáai　註解　(N) explanatory notes

jyú·gok　主角　(N) hero (of a play)

jyū·gū·līk　朱咕叻*　(N) chocolate

jyú·jèung　主張　(V/N) advocate, propose, favor (a proposal, motion, plan) /advocacy, suggestion

jyú·jihk　主席　(N) chairman

jyu·jok　著作　(V/N) compose /work (writings)

jyu·juhng　注重　(V) emphasize

jyu·mìhng　著名　(SV) famous, well-known

jyú·yahm　主任　(N) head of a section, director

Jyú·yaht·hohk　主日學　(N) Sunday school

jyu·yām·jih·móuh　注音字母　(N) phonetic writing

jyú·yán　主人　(N) host; hostess

jyu·yi　注意　(V) pay attention to, take notice of

jyú·yi　主意　(N) determination

jyú·yih　主義　(N) doctrine; -ism

jyú·yiu　主要　(At) chief, main, essential

jyù·yuhk 豬肉 (N) pork

jyuh 住 (V) stay, live

jyuh 住 (P) suffix to verbs indicating firmness

jyuh·gā 住家 (N) a residence

jyuh·gā·kēui 住家區 (N) residential area

jyuh·haak 住客 (N) tenant (of a house); guest (in a hotel, etc.)

jyuh·jaat 駐紮 (V) stationed at (military)

jyuh·jí 住址 (N) address, dwelling-place

jyuh·lohk 住落 (V) settle down

jyuh·yún 住院 (VO) hospitalize (lit. stay in hospital)

jyuh·yún·ge·yī·sāng 住院嘅病人 (N) resident doctor; intern

jyuhn·gei 傳記 (N) biography

jyuht·deui 絕對 (A) absolutely, definitely

jyùn 專 (A) solely, specially

jyún 轉 (V) forward (a letter) (when written means 'in care of')

jyùn 磚 (N) brick (M: gauh or faai)

jyun, jyún 轉 (V) turn to

jyùn·chùhng 遵從 (V) to act in accordance with

jyún·daaht 轉達 (V) convey, transmit

jyūn·dāng 專登 (A) specially, particularly; intentionally

jyún·gā 專家 (N) expert, specialist

jyún·gàau 轉交 (V) forward (a letter) (when written means 'in care of')

jyùn·ging 尊敬 (V) respect, esteem

jyún·gou 轉告 (V) relay (a message)

jyùn·jai 專制 (SV) despotic, tyrannical

jyùn·juhng 尊重 (V) respect; to feel or show honor or esteem for; to show courteous regard for /Kéuih·deih hóu jyùn·juhng kéuih ge yi·gin. They respect his opinion.

jyùn·mùhn 專門 (At/A) specialized (in a field of study or a skill) /exclusively

jyūn·sàm 專心 (A/SV) with undivided attention

jyùn·sáu 遵守 (V) to observe; obey

jyun·sehk 鑽石 (N) diamond (M: nāp, 'grain')

jyun·wāan 轉灣 (VO/V) make a turn /circle, turn around in a circle

jyùn·yahm 專任 (At) employed full time

jyun yauh·sáu·bihn 轉右手邊 (Ph) make a right turn

K

kā 卡 (N) railroad car

kaau 靠 (V) depend upon

kaau·dāk·jyuh 靠得住 (SV) be reliable, dependable

kaau·hoih 靠害 (V) have intention of harming; implicate

kaau·m̀h·jyuh 靠唔住 (SV) undependable

kàhm 琴 (N) stringed or wind instrument

kàhm 擒 (V) climb

kàhm·máahn 噚晚 (TW) last night

káhm·móuh 妗母 (N) wife of mother's brother

kàhm·sau 禽獸 (N) animals

kàhm·yaht 噚日 (TW) yesterday

kàhm·yaht·jīu 噚日朝 (TW) yesterday morning

káhn 近 (SV) near

kàhn·gihm 勤儉 (SV) industrious and frugal

kàhn·lihk 勤力 (SV) industrious, diligent

kai 契 (N) deed to property (M: jèung)

kài·chá 稽查 (N) inspector

kài·gaan 溪澗 (N) brook

kai·mā 契媽 (N) godmother

kai·yèh 契爺 (N) godfather

kàm 噙 (A/SV) take a long time to . . . /durable

kám 擒 (V) cover; cap

kàm·dáng 噙等 (Ph) take a long time to materialize

kàm·hìng·daih 襟兄弟 (N) men who marry sisters

kàm·jeuk 噙着 (SV) wear well (for clothing, etc.)

kàm·sái 噙洗 (SV) durable

kàm yuhng 噙用 (Ph) take a long time to use up

káng 骾 (VO) be choked with

kāp 吸 (V) inhale

kāp 級 (M) step (of stairs)

kāp 給 (V) to put on (as a seal); affix

kāp·chàhn·gèi 吸塵機 (N) vacuum cleaner

kāp·lihk 吸力 (N) attracting force, gravity

kāp·sàu 吸收 (V) to take up or in by sucking

kāp·tòuh·jēung 給圖章 (VO) stamp with a seal

kāp·yáhn 吸引 (V) draw, attract

kāp·yan 給印 (VO) put on a seal

kāt 咳 (V) cough /Kéuih kāt·jó géi nói la? How long has he been coughing?

kāt·pín 咭片 (N) calling card (M: jèung)

kāt·sau 咳嗽 (V) cough

kàu 搞 (V) to mix up

kau(·chèuih) 扣(除) (V) deduct

kàu·hèi 搞稀 (RV) dilute

kau·jouh 構造 (N) structure, construction

kàu·kèuih 溝渠 (N) a drain; sewer; gutter

kau·làuh 扣留 (V) detain; arrest

kàu·lyuhn 搞亂 (V) mess up, put things in disarray or disorder

kàu·màaih 搞埋 (V) mix up with

kau·máaih 購買 (V) buy

kau·náu 扣鈕 (VO) button up

kàu·wàhn 搞勻 (RV) to mix evenly

kau·yàhn·gùng 扣人工 (VO) deduct from wages

kàuh 求 (V) beg; implore; seek after

kàuh·chèuhng, bō·chèuhng (N) ball field

kàuh·chìm 求籤 (VO) to divine by lots

kàuh·fàn 求婚 (VO) propose (marriage)

káuh·fú 舅父 (N) mother's brother

kàuh·kèih 求其 (MA) any (whatever); at one's convenience

kàuh·yàhn 求人 (VO) ask for help or a favor

ké·jāp 茄汁 (N) catsup; tomato sauce

kèh 騎 (V) ride on (a horse or other animal, etc.) /kèh máh, ride horseback

kèh·bok·máh 騎膊馬 (VO) to carry a child on shoulders

kèh·láu 騎樓 (N) veranda; balcony

kehk 屐 (N) wooden slippers (M: deui, pair)

kehk·chìhng 劇情 (N) synopsis of a play

kéi 棋 (N) chess

kèih 旗 (N) flag, banner (M: jì)

kèih 期 (BF) period of time

kéih 企 (V) stand

kèih·fo 期貨 (N) dated order

kèih·gōn 旗杆 (N) flagstaff (M: jì)

kèih·gwaai 奇怪 (SV) strange, queer

kèih·haahn 期限 (N) time limit

kéih·héi·sàn 企起身 (V) stand up

kèih·jí 棋子 (N) chessman

kèih·jùng 其中 (A) inside, therein, among them

kéih·léih 企理 (SV) be neat

kéih múhn yàhn 企滿人 (Ph) (a room) filled with standing people

kèih·póu 旗袍 (N) lady's dress (Chinese style)

kèih·pún 棋盤 (N) chessboard

kèih·saht 其實 (MA) actually; in fact

kèih·tà(·ge) 其他嘅 (SP) other

kèih·tà·ge 其他嘅 (N) the other, the rest

kèih·tóu 祈禱 (V/N) pray (to God) /prayer

kèih·tóu·màhn 祈禱文 (N) Lord's prayer; written prayer

kèih·yùh·ge 其餘嘅 (N) the other, the rest

kèih·yùh gó·dī 其餘嗰啲 (N) the rest, the other

kèuhng 強 (SV) strong and powerful (as of a country)

kéuhng·bīk 強逼 (V) force

kèuhng·gàan 強姦 (V) rape

kèuhng·jim 強佔 (V) take by violence

kèuhng·jong 強壯 (SV) be strong (of body)

kèuhng·ngaahng 強硬 (SV) resolute; obstinate

kēui 區 (M) area, section (of land)

kēui·chūk 拘束 (SV/V) be restrained /restrain

kēui·juhk.laahm 驅逐艦 (N) destroyer (Navy) (M: jek)

kéuih 渠佢 (N) he, she, him, her

kéuih·deih 佢哋 (N) they, them

kéuih·deih léuhng·fù·fúh 佢哋兩夫婦 (Ph) he and his wife

kéuih·jyuht 拒絕 (V) refuse, reject

kéuih·lèih 距離 (N) distance

kìhm 鉗 (V) use pliers

kìhn·sìhng 虔誠 (SV) religiously devout

kím 鉗 (N) pliers; pincers; tongs

kín 揵 (V) thumb through (a book)

kín·hòi 揵開 (V) open (a book)

kìng·gái 傾偈 (VO) chat, converse

kíu 嬌 (SV) coincident, opportune /Jàn·haih kíu la! What a coincidence!

kìuh 橋 (N) bridge (M: douh or tìuh)

kíuh 繞 (V) to wind (to turn or coil around)

kòhng·fùng, kwòhng·fùng 狂風 (N) gust

kok·dihng 確定 (V) make certain

kok·haih 確係 (A) actually; really (interchangeable with jàn·haih)

kok·saht 確實 (SV) be true; reliable

kok·saht·haih 確實係 (Ph) actually be

kong·chóng 匡牀 (N) couch for two to sit on

kong·jin 抗戰 (N) war of resistance

kùhng 窮 (SV) be poor

kùhng·fú 窮苦 (SV) be poor

kūk 曲 (N) tune (M: jī)

kūk 曲 (SV) crooked; bent; perverse

kūk-gòu-woh-gwá 曲高和寡 (IE)
to be too high-brow to be popular;
high-brow (When the song is 'high-
brow,' you will find very few people
who will sing it with you.)

kūk·sin 曲綫 (N) curve

kut·wùh 括弧 (N) parentheses; brackets

kwà·háu 誇口 (V/SV) boast, brag
/boastful

kwà·jèung 誇獎 (V) praise; extol

kwàaih 嘥 (SV) bad (in character),
mischievous, mean

kwàaih·yàhn 嘥人 (N) villain, hoodlum

kwàhn 裙 (N) skirt (M: tìuh)

kwàhn 羣 (V/M) to mix with a group of
people /group, flock (of birds), pack
(of dogs), school (of fish), herd (of
sheep), etc.

kwàhn·dóu 羣島 (N) archipelago, group
of islands

kwài·dihng 規定 (V) make a regulation
to

kwài·géui 規矩 (N) regulation, rule

kwāi·hùng 虧空 (V) have a deficit

kwāi·jāk 規則 (N) regulations, rules

kwàih·laih 規例 (N) regulation, rule; law

kwài·mòuh 規模 (N) scale (scope)

kwán 綑 (M) a bale; ream

kwán·héi 綑起 (V) bind, tie, bale

kwan·nàahn 困難 (N) difficulty

kwong 礦,鑛 (N) a mine

kwong·chùng 擴充 (V) expand (e.g.
business, school, etc.)

kwong·jèung 擴張 (V) spread (influence);
enlarge (area)

kyùhn 權 (N) authority; power

kyùhn·beng 權柄 (N) authority; right-
ful power

kyùhn·leih 權利 (N) right, legal right

kyùhn·lihk 權力 (N) power, authority

kyùhn·tàuh 拳頭 (N) fist

kyut·dihng 決定 (V) decide

kyut·dím 缺點 (N) defect; weakness

kyut·faht 缺乏 (V) lack, be short of,
be in short supply

kyut·liht, kyut·lit 決裂 (V) to break
off relations

kyut·sàm 決心 (A/N) determinedly
/determination

kyut·síu 缺少 (V) lacking; lack of

L

la 嚹 (P) sentence final

la, lo 喇,囉 (P) indicating changed status

la 罅 (N) crevice; rift; crack (M: tìuh)

lā 啦 (P) sentence final, used with commands or requests, or final agreement

làahm (·sīk)·ge 藍(色)嘅 (At) blue

laahm·chè 纜車 (N) cable car

làahm·dihn 藍靛 (N) indigo dye

làahm·kàuh 藍球 (N) basketball (game or
ball)

laahm·sīk 藍色 (N) blue color

láahn 懶 (SV) lazy

laahn 爛 (SV) broken; rotten; overripe

láahn·doh 懶惰 (SV) lazy

làahn·fà 蘭花 (N) orchid

làahn·gōn 欄杆 (N) railing; balustrade

laahn·háu 爛口 (N) obscene language

láahng 冷 (SV) be cold

láahng·chàn 冷親 (V) catch cold

láahng·daahm 冷淡 (SV) indifferent; slow
(business)

láahng·hei·gēi 冷氣機 (N) air condi-
tioner

láahng·hóng 冷巷 (N) hallway, corridor

láahng·tīn 冷天 (N) winter

láahng·yiht·séui·hàuh 冷熱水喉
(N) faucet (hot and cold)

laahp 臘,腊(BF) dried and salted meats
/laahp·yuhk, cured pork; laahp·chéung,
dried sausages; laahp·ngaap, cured duck

laahp·chéung 臘腸 (N) dried sausage

laahp·jaahp 攞雜 (SV) mixed

laahp·jūk 蠟燭 (N) candle (M: jì)

laahp·méi 臘味 (N) cured meats

laaht 辣 (SV) be hot or peppery

laaht 捋 (M) a row

laaht·taat 辣撻 (SV) dirty

làai 拉 (V) drag, pull

làai 拉 (V) apprehend, arrest

làai·hòi 拉開 (V) pull open

lāai·mēi 孻尾 (At/A) the last (of series)
/later

lāai·sán 孻臣 (N) license (transliterated)

làai·sáu 拉手 (VO) shake hands

láam·jyuh 攬住 (V) embrace, hug

làan 躝 (V) crawl, creep

lán 蘭 (N) orchid

làan 欄 (N) a wholesale market /choi·
làan, wholesale vegetable market; jyū·
làan, wholesale pig market

láau·gam·gaauh 嘮咁噭 (Ph) in a
mess

làauh 撈 (V) fish for, dip up with a net or slotted spoon, etc.

làh 喇 (P) fusion of 'la' and 'àh'

làh·lá·sèng 喇攊聲 (A) hurriedly

lahk 勒 (V) restrain a bridle; strangle

lahk·dahk 勒特 (SV) queer (person)

lahk·sok 勒索 (V) extort

làhm 臨 (A) just before, at the point of, on the verge of, when about to

làhm 淋 (V) water

lahm(·héi) 淋(起) (V) pile up

làhm·gāp 臨急 (A) at the very last minute

làhm·sìh 臨時 (A) on the spur of the moment, provisional

làhm-sìh-póuh-faht-geuk 臨時抱佛脚 (IE) to do a thing when it is urgently needed (one holds the buddha's foot imploringly when one is in trouble)

lahp·hāak, laahp·hāak 立刻 (A) immediately

lahp·jing 立正 (Ph) stand at attention

lahp·ngon 立案 (VO) register with government (for organization)

lahp·sàm 立心 (A) determinedly; have in mind; plot to

láih 禮 (N) decorum, rites

laih 例 (N) example (actual case)

láih·baai 禮拜 (N) week

láih·baai·tòhng 禮拜堂 (N) chapel, church (the building) (M: gàan)

láih·béng 禮餅 (N) wedding cake

láih·fuhk 禮服 (N) formal dress (M: tou, suit)

làih gwaan làih suhk 嚟(咪)慣嚟熟 (Ph) come very often

... làih ... heui ⋯嚟⋯去 (Pat) V back and forth /haahng·làih haahng·heui, walk back and forth

laih·jī 荔枝 (N) lichee, litchi (fruit)

láih·jit 禮節 (N) ceremony, formality

láih·maauh 禮貌 (N) manners, courtesy

láih·maht 禮物 (N) gift, present (M: gihn)

laih·ngoih 例外 (N) exception

(daaih·)láih·tòhng (大)禮堂 (N) auditorium

lam 淋 (V) cave in (as 'a building')

lām 冧 (N) bud (of flower)

lāp 笠 (N) a tall basket

lāt 甩 (RVE) off

lāt·jó 甩咗 (V) drop off, fall off

lāt·sòu 甩鬚 (SV) disgraceful, lose face

láu, làuh 樓 (N) storied building (M: joh)

láu 樓 (M) story, floor /yāt·láu, first floor; main floor (in Hong Kong)

lau 餾 (V) induce, urge

làuh 留 (V) save, reserve

lauh 漏 (V) leak; overlook; leave something behind unintentionally /Gāan ngūk lauh yúh. The roof leaks. /Ngóh lauh·jó yāt·go jih. I overlooked one word. /Neih lauh·jo māt·jéh a? What have you left behind?

làuh 流 (V) flow

làuh·bouh 留步 (IE) Please don't escort me any further (by a visitor when leaving)

làuh·cháan 留產 (V) stay in the maternity ward before giving birth to a baby

làuh·chyùhn 留傳 (V) pass on, hand down

lauh-dāk-chīng-sàan-joih, bāt-pa-móuh-chàaih-sìu 留得青山在,不怕冇柴燒 (IE) As long as the green hills remain, you don't have to be afraid there will be a shortage of firewood.

làuh·hah 樓下 (PW) downstairs; the main floor

làuh·hàhng·jing 流行症 (N) epidemic disease

làuh·hàhng·sing·gáam·mouh 流行性感冒 (N) a bad cold, influenza

làuh·hái·PW 留喺 (V) stay (or leave something) at a certain place

làuh·hohk 流落 (V) study abroad

làuh·hohk·sāang 留學生 (N) student in a foreign country; student returned from a foreign country

làuh·hyut 流血 (VO) bleed

làuh·ji 留字 (VO) to leave a note

làuh·jih 留字 (VO) to leave a note

lauh·jó 漏咗 (V) leave behind, left behind

làuh·nàahn 留難 (V) hold up, detain a person unnecessarily

làuh·sàm 留心 (V) give attention to; take notice of

làuh·seuhng 樓上 (PW) upstairs; second floor

làuh·sìng·fèi 留聲機 (N) record player (M: ga)

làuh·sòu 留鬚 (VO) to grow a beard

làuh·tài 樓梯 (N) stair, staircase (M: douh)

láuh·tíu 柳條 (N) stripes

lauh·yeh 漏夜 (A) during the night

làuh·yì 留醫 (V) be in the hospital (as a patient)

lìhng, leng 零 (NU) plus, odd, more than, over /sahp·lèhng·go, ten plus; yih·sahp lèhng·seui, a little over twenty years old

léhng 領 (V) apply for; receives (by application)

léhng 領 (N) collar (M: tìuh)

léi 梨 (N) pear (in general)

lèih 離 (CV) distant from

lèih, làih 嚟,嘜 (V) come (làih more formal)

lèih 釐 (N) percent (interest)

leih 脷* (N) tongue (M: tìuh)

léih 里 (M) a Chinese mile (1/3 of an English mile)

léih 理 (V) pay attention to; take care of, mind /M̀h·hóu léih keuih. Don't pay any attention to him. Néih yiu léih·háh kéuih ji dāk ga? You should take care of him, shouldn't you?

leih·bihn 利便 (V/SV) facilitate; be convenient

lèih·chàih 嚟齊 (RV) all arrive

leih·chìhn 利錢 (N) interest (on money)

lèih·dāk·chit 嚟得切 (RV) there is time; can make it

lèih·dáng 釐戥 (N) steelyard to weigh gold, drugs, etc.

lèih·fàn 離婚 (VO) divorce; be divorced /Kéuih·deih jeui·gahn lèih·jó fan. They were divorced recently.

léih·fō 理科 (N) school of natural science (university)

lèih·gaan 離間 (V) cause a rift between two friends; to sow dissension or discord among people

leih·hòi 離開 (RV) leave (a place)

leih·hoih 厲害 (SV) severe

lèih·kèih 離奇 (SV) strange, inexplicable

léih·leuhn 理論 (N) theory

lèih·m̀h·chit 嚟唔切 (RV) there isn't enough time; can't make it

lèih·póu 離譜 (VO/SV) act rather strangely /erratic

léih·séung 理想 (N/SV) ideal /ideal

leih·sih 利是 (N) a token of good luck (a sum of money contained in a small red envelope)

leih·sīk 利息 (N) interest (on capital)

léih·yàuh 理由 (N) reason

leih·yīk 利益 (N) gain, advantage, profit

lèih·yúhn 離遠 (A) from afar (abbr. of 'lèih dāk hóu yúhn')

leih·yuhng 利用 (V) utilize

lēk 叻* (SV) be smart

leng 靚 (SV) be pretty, handsome

lèu·háu·séui 擸口水 (VO) spit

lèuhn 輪 (V) standing in line

lèuhn·dou 輪到 (V) to be (someone's) turn /Lèuhn·dou néih la. It's your turn.

lèuhn·haahm 淪陷 (V) fall of a city or country to the enemy

lèuhn·haahm·kēui 淪陷區 (N) occupied area

lèuhn·jāt 燐質 (N) sulphur (as a natural element)

leuhn·jeuhn 論盡 (SV) be clumsy

lèuhn·láu 輪流 (AV) to take turns doing something

lèuhn·màhn, lèuhn·mán 論文 (N) thesis

lèuhn·séh 鄰舍 (N) neighbor

lèuhng 量 (V) survey, measure

léuhng 涼 (SV) cool

léuhng 兩 (NU) two or couple

léuhng·fū·chài 兩夫妻 (N) couple, husband and wife

léuhng·fù·fúh 兩夫婦 (N) a couple, husband and wife

léuhng·gā 兩家 (NU+M) . . . two /Gàm·yaht ngóh m̀h·heui la, néih·deih léuhng·gā heui lā? I won't go today, you two may go. /Kéuih·deih léuhng·gā dou wah m̀h·dāk·hàahn. Both of them say that they are not free tonight.

léuhng·gùng·pó 兩公婆 (N) couple, husband and wife (a common term, but not as refined as léuhng·fū·fúh)

léuhng·háh 兩吓 (NU+M) twice

lèuhng·pàahng 涼棚 (N) mat awning to keep off the sun

lèuhng·sàm 良心 (N) conscience

lèuhng·sihk 糧食 (N) foodstuff, provisions

lèuhng·sóng 涼爽 (SV) cool

lèuhng·tíng 涼亭 (N) pavilion

leuht·sī 律師 (N) lawyer, solicitor

leuht·sī·làuh 律師樓 (N) solicitor's office

lèuih 雷 (N) thunder

leuih 累 (V) implicate, involve /leuih dāk ngóh jàm·haih cháam la. It got me quite involved.

léuih·bihn 裏邊 (PW) inside

léuih·daaht 雷達 (N) radar

léuih·fai 旅費 (N) traveling expenses

léuih·gún 旅館 (N) hotel (M: gàan)

léuih·hàhng 旅行 (N/V) journey/travel

léuih·hàhng·séh 旅行社 (N) travel agency

leuih·jeuih 累贅 (SV) cumbersome

lèuih·kàuh 壘球 (N) baseball (game or ball)

léuih·sung·yīn 呂宋煙 (N) cigars (M: háu)

léung 兩 (M) an ounce (1/16 of a catty)

lihk 力 (N) strength; energy; effort

lihk·leuhng 力量 (N) strength

lihk·sí 歷史 (N) history

lìhn 連 (A) even

lìhn 煉 (V) refine; smelt

lihn·bá 練靶 (VO) practice shooting

lìhn·daai 連帶 (V) be connected with

lìhn·hei 連氣 (A) successively, continuously

lihn·jaahp 練習 (N/V) exercise (as in a lesson) /practice (in order to learn)

lihn·jaahp·bóu 練習簿 (N) exercise book

lìhn·jip 連接 (V) connect, join together

lìhn·juhk 連續 (A) one after the other; unbroken series of

lihn·kàhm 練琴 (VO) practice a stringed or wind instrument

lìhn·wàahn 連環 (N) connecting link

lìhng 零 (NU) zero (where one or more zeros stand between numbers, 'lìhng' is used)

líhng, léhng 領 (V) apply for and get; receive /Líhng sàn·fahn·jing, apply for and get an identification card

lihng·(dou) 令到 (V) to cause

lìhng·dái 令弟 (N) your younger brother (polite form)

lìhng·déui 領隊 (N) leader (of a group)

lìhng·dìng 伶仃 (SV) lonely, alone

líhng·dóu 領到 (RV) receive /líhng· dóu la, has received (what was applied for, or given by the government or an institution); meih lìhng·dóu, hasn't received yet.

lìhng·douh 零度 (N) zero degrees

lìhng·douh 領導 (V) take the lead, lead, guide

lìhng·gín 零件 (N) spare parts

lìhng·hìng 令兄 (N) your elder brother (polite form)

lìhng·jauh 領袖 (N) leader

lìhng·jyūn(·yūng) 令尊 (N) your father (polite form)

lìhng·leih 伶俐 (SV) clever; smart

lìhng·lohk 零落 (SV) deserted; withered

lìhng·lóng 令郎 (N) your son (polite form)

lìhng·ngoi 令嬡 (N) your daughter (polite form)

lìhng ngoih juhng . . . 另外重 . . . (Ph) in addition; besides

lìhng·sái 領洗 (V) receive baptism

lìhng·seui 零碎 (SV) fragmentary

lìhng·sí 領事 (N) consul

lìhng·sí·gún 領事館 (N) consulate

lìhng·sìng 零星 (SV) miscellaneous

lìhng·táu 零頭 (N) a surplus

lìhng(·sauh)·tóng 令(壽)堂 (N) your mother (polite form)

lìhng·tùng 靈通 (SV) well-informed /sīu·sīk·lìhng·tùng, well-informed

lìhng·wàhn 靈魂 (N) the soul

lìhng yàhn gáam·duhng 令人感動 (Ph) be touching, moving

lìhng·yàhn tóu·yim 令人討厭 (Ph) cause men to be disgusted

lihp·yàhn 獵人 (N) hunter

lik 繿 (N) knot

lín 鍊 (N) chain (M: tìuh)

lit·hòi 裂開 (V) crack; split

líuh·bāt·dāk 了不得 (SV/A) terrific /extremely

líuh·gáai 了解 (V) understand

líuh·git 了結 (V) to settle /Gó·gihn sih líuh·git·jó meih a? Has that case been settled yet?

líuh·jih 療治 (V) treat (disease)

líuh·jung 料中 (V) to guess rightly

líuh·sih 了事 (Ph) be finished. /Yíh· gìng líuh·sih la. It's over. (The affair is finished.)

ló 攞 (V) fetch

ló 攞 (V) get married (of a woman) (See example sentences given under 'chéui')

lò·sò 囉嗦 (SV) fastidious, annoying

lòh 鑼 (N) gong

lòh 籮 (N) bamboo basket

lòh·pùhn 羅盤 (N) compass

lòh·sī(·dēng) 螺絲(釘) (N) screw (M: nāp)

lòh·sī·pāi 螺絲批 (N) screwdriver

lohk 落 (PV/RVE) indicates downward /down

lohk·bohk 落雹 (VO) hail (hail is falling)

lohk·chè 落車 (VO) get off (a train, bus, etc.); get out of (a car)

lohk che 落斜 (Ph) going downhill

lohk·dehng 落定 (VO) to pay a deposit, put down a deposit

lohk·déi 落地 (VO) get down on the floor

lohk-gihk-sāang-bèi 樂極生悲
(IE) Too much joy brings sorrow.

lohk·gùn 樂觀 (SV) optimistic

lohk·hauh 落後 (V/At) fall behind (in work, studies, etc.) /underdeveloped /lohk·hauh·gwok·gà, underdeveloped countries

lohk·heui 落去 (V/RVE) go down /ending of certain verbs, indication 'downward'; 'without stopping', 'continuously'

lohk·lèih 落嚟* (V) come down

lohk·lihk 落力 (SV) be enthusiastic (in doing something); work hard

lohk·mouh 落霧 (VO) foggy, misty

lohk·on 落案 (V) put into police record

lohk·syut 落雪 (VO) snow

lohk·tòhng 落堂 (VO) class dismissed

lohk·yi 樂意 (AV) be glad to; be a pleasure to, willingly

lohk·yihp-gwāi-gàn 落葉歸根 (Ph) to return to the origin

lohk·yúh 落雨 (VO) raining

lohk·yúh·mēi 落雨微 (VO) drizzling (rain) /Yìh·ga ngoih·bihn lohk·gán yúh·mēi. It's drizzling out now.

lohng 浪 (N) wave

lohng 晾 (V) spread out to dry

lòhng·bui 狼狽 (SV) awkward, hard to manage

lohng·fai 浪費 (V/SV) waste /wasteful

lohng·gòn 晾乾 (V) to dry in the air

lohng·héi 晾起 (V) to hang up to dry or air (clothes, etc.)

lohng·sāam 晾衫 (VO) to dry or air clothes

lòih·bàn 來賓 (N) guest (can be used to address the guests in an audience)

lòih·hàahm 來函 (N) the letter received

lòih·lihk 來歷 (N) antecedents

lòih·wóhng 來往 (V/N) associate (with people) /association (with people), contact

lòih·wùih 來回 (N) round trip

lòih·wùih·fēi 來回飛* (N) round-trip ticket

lòih·yùhn 來源 (N) origin, source

long·héi 挪起 (V) shore up, to raise up by putting something beneath

lòu 撈 (V) to make a living; gain, procure; to mix and stir (in preparing a dish)

lóu 佬 (P) suffix means 'fellow' /gòu·lóu, a long fellow

lòu·dāk·dihm 撈得掂 (RV) make a fairly good living

lou·dāk·dihm·dihm 撈得掂掂 (Ph) make a very good living

lòu·m̀h·dihm 撈唔掂 (RV) can't make a living

lòu·sai·gaai 撈世界 (VO) to make a living (colloq.)

lóuh 老 (SV) old

louh 路 (N) road (M: tìuh)

louh 路 (M) route (M: tìuh)

lóuh·báan 老板 (N) boss, manager

lóuh·baak·sing 老百姓 (N) common people

lóuh·chóu 潦草 (SV) careless (e.g. in writing)

lòuh·fàahn 勞煩 (V) trouble (as in 'may I trouble you . . .')

louh·fai 路費 (N) travel expenses

lóuh·fú 老虎 (N) tiger (M: jek)

lóuh·gùng 老公 (N) husband (a colloquial expression, not as refined as jeuhng·fù, or sīn·sàang)

louh·háu 路口 (N) end of the street

lòuh·lihk 勞力 (N) labor

lóuh·pòh 老婆 (N) wife (a colloquial expression; the polite term used to refer to another's wife is 'fū·yán' or 'taai·táai'; for one's own wife one says 'noih·yán' or 'noih jí'.)

lóuh·sì 老師 (N) teacher (usually used as a polite form in greeting)

louh·sūk 露宿 (V) to sleep in the open

lóuh·syú 老鼠 (N) rat, mouse (M: jek)

lóuh·yàhn·gà 老人家 (N) you sir (literally means person of age; can be preceded by néih (you) or kéuih (he, she) for polite use)

lóuh·yàhn·yún 老人院 (N) home for aged people

lóuh·yèh 老爺 (N) old gentleman — term of respect (obsolete)

luhk 六 (NU) six

luhk 漉 (V) soaked or hit by boiling liquid

luhk·chāt·sìhng 六七成 (A) 60 or 70 percent

luhk·deih 陸地 (N) land (as distinguished from sea)

luhk(·sik)·ge 綠(色)嘅* (SV) green

luhk·gwān 陸軍 (N) army (land force)

luhk·sīk 綠色 (N) green color

luhk·yām 錄音 (V/N) record /recording

luhk·yām·dáai 錄音帶 (N) tape

luhk·yām·gèi 錄音機 (N) tape recorder

lùhng 聾 (SV) be deaf

lùhng 龍 (N) dragon (M: tìuh)

lùhng 籠 (N) cage

luhng·dou 弄到 (V) cause

lúhng·dyuhn 龍斷 (V) monopolize
lùhng·hā 龍蝦 (N) lobster (M: jek)
lūk 碌 (V) roll
lūk 轆 (N) wheel
lūk·làih·lūk·heui 擁嚟擁去 (Ph) tossing around
lūk·yau 樣柚 (N) chinese grapefruit; pomelo
lyuhn 亂 (SV) be in disorder; be confused
Lyùhn·hahp·gwok 聯合國 (N) United Nations
lyuhn·lok 聯絡 (V/N) liaison
lyùn 嚹 (SV) crooked, bended

M

ma 嗎 (P) sentence particle to simple type questions
mā·fù 嗎唬 (SV) not serious minded
mā·mā·fū·fù 嗎嗎唬唬 (SV) not serious minded
maahn 慢 (SV) slow
maahn 萬 (M/NU) ten thousand /yāt·maahn·mān, ten thousand dollars; yāt·maahn·go hohk·sāang, ten thousand students
máahn·chāan 晚餐 (N) super
máahn·hāak 晚黑 (TW) night, evening, nighttime
maahn·hahng 萬幸 (SV) very fortunate
maahn·jih·gíp 万字夾 (N) paper clip
maahn·léih·chèuhng·sìhng 萬里長城 (PN) Great wall of China
maahn·māan, maahn·máan 慢慢 (A) slowly
maahn·mò 慢模 (SV) slow (in action)
máahn·táu 晚頭 (TW) night, evening, nighttime
máahn·tauh·hāak 晚頭黑 (TW) night, evening, nighttime
maahn·wá 漫畫 (N) comics, cartoon (M: fūk)
maahn·yāt 萬一 (MA) in case
máahng 猛 (SV/A) violent, fierce /with gusto /máahng cheung yāt·lèuhn, sing with gusto; máahng sihk yāt·lèuhn, eat with gusto; máahng yám yāt·lèuhn, drink with gusto
màahng·chéung 盲腸 (N) appendix
màahng·chùhng 盲從 (V) to follow blindly
máahng·gūng 盲公 (N) a blind man
máahng·liht 猛烈 (SV) fierce; violent
máahng·sau 猛獸 (N) wild animal, beast (M: jek)

màahng·yàhn·gaau·yuhk 盲人教育 (N) education for the blind
māai 咪 (M) mile (transliterated)
màaih 埋 (P) a verb suffix indicating 'with', 'along with', 'also with'; 'close to'
màaih 埋 (V) bury
máaih 買 (V) buy
maaih 賣 (V) sell
máaih·báan 買辦 (N) comprador
máaih·chàih 買齊 (RV) buy everything one intends to buy, get everything on one's shopping list
màaih·dāan 埋單 (Ph) figure up a bill (usually used in restaurant)
máaih·dāk·héi 買得起 (RV) can afford to buy (there is no such form as 'máaih-hei' in this particular RV)
maaih·fàan·lèih ge chín 賣返嚟嘅錢 (Ph) sale, money made by a financial return from a sale
máaih·fā·daai . . . 買花帶… (IE) money earned as 'pocket money' not as a means of supporting the family (lit. buying flowers to wear)
màaih·fuhk 埋伏 (V/N) to set up an ambush /ambush
maaih·gou·baahk 賣告白 (VO) put an advertisement in the paper, a magazine, etc.
màaih·jihk 埋席 (VO) proceed to dinner table
màaih·jong 埋葬 (V) bury
máaih·jung 買中 (RV) bought something which meets one's desire
máaih·mh·héi 買唔起 (RV) can't afford to buy
màaih·tàuh 埋頭 (V) dock
máaih·yin·sō 買燕梳 (Ph) have insurance for (lit. buy insurance for) /Máaih·jó yin·sō mcih a? Has it been insured?
màaih·yun 埋怨 (V) blame, hold someone responsible
maak·hòi 擘開 (V) open, break apart with hands /maak·hòi sèung ngáahn, open one's eyes; maak daaih go háu, open one's mouth wide
maat 抹 (V) wipe
maat·gòn·jehng 抹乾淨 (RV) wipe clean
māau 貓 (N) cat (M: jek)
màauh·téuhn 矛盾 (N) contradiction
máh 馬 (N) horse (M: pāt)
máh 碼 (M) yard
màh 麻 (N) hemp
máh·chè 馬車 (N) horse-cart
máh·chòuh 馬槽 (N) horse's manger

màh·fàahn 麻煩 (N/V/SV) troubles /bother, trouble /bothersome

màh·fūng 麻瘋 (N) leprosy

màh·fūng·behng·yún 麻瘋病院 (N) hospital for lepers

máh·jí 碼子 (N) bullets, cartridge (M: nāp)

máh·kwá 馬褂 (N) outer jacket (for formal use)

máh·lihk 馬力 (N) horsepower (M: pāt)

máh·lāu 馬騮 (N) monkey (M: jek)

máh·louh 馬路 (N) road, boulevard (M: tìuh)

màh·mā 媽媽 (N) mother

màh má déi 麻麻哋* (IE) it is passable

máh·seuhng 馬上 (MA) immediately, at once

máh·tái 馬蹄* (N) water chestnut

máh·tàih 馬蹄 (N) horsehoof

máh·tàuh 碼頭 (N) wharf, pier

máh·wúi 馬會 (N) Jockey Club

mahk 墨 (N) ink

mahk·fán 麥粉 (N) oatmeal

mahk·jāp 墨汁 (N) Chinese liquid ink

mahk·ngàh·tóng 麥芽糖 (N) malt candy

mahk·pin 麥片 (N) oatmeal

mahk·séui 墨水 (N) liquid ink

mahk·séui·bāt 墨水筆 (N) fountain pen

mahk·syù 默書 (VO) to write from memory or dictation

mahk·tóu 默禱 (V/N) say a silent prayer /silent prayer

mahk·yín 墨硯 (N) ink-stone

màhn 聞 (V) smell

mahn 問 (V) ask

màhn·fa 文化 (N) civilization; culture

màhn·fa·seuhng·ge gàau·làuh 文化上嘅交流 (Ph) cultural interchange

màhn·faat 文法 (N) grammar

màhn·fō 文科 (N) school of liberal arts

mahn·gahp 問及 (V) inquire about

màhn·geuih 文具 (N) stationery

màhn·gwok 民國 (N) the Republic of China (the contraction of Jùng·wàh·màhn·gwok)

mahn·hauh 問候 (V) to ask the health of another; to send kind regards to . . .

mahn·héi 問起 (V) raise a question about

màhn·hohk 文學 (N) literature

màhn·jèung 文章 (N) composition; essay

màhn·jih 文字 (N) written language

máhn·jit 敏捷 (SV) nimble; active

màhn·juhk 民族 (N) the nation (in the sense of the people), race

màhn·jyú 民主 (N/SV) democracy /be democratic

màhn·jyú·dóng 民主黨 (N) Democratic Party

màhn·jyú·jing·jih 民主政治 (N) democracy

mahn·louh 問路 (VO) ask for directions

màhn·mìhng 文明 (SV) civilized

màhn·mìhng·yíh·gáu 聞名已久 (Ph) meaning 'have heard of (you) for a long time'

màhn·ngáh 文雅 (SV) refined; polished; cultured

màhn·pàhng 文憑 (N) diploma; certificate

mahn·sih·chyu 問事處 (N) information desk

mahn·tàih 問題 (N) problem; question

màhn·yìhn 文言 (At/N) in literary style /literary-style writing

màhn·yìhn·mán 文言文 (N) literary writing

màhn·yìhn·síu·syut 文言小說 (N) novels written in literary style

màhn·yuhng 民用 (At) for civil use

maht 密 (SV) be close (to one another); be dense

maht 襪 (N) stocking; sock (M: deui, pair)

maht·chit 密切 (SV) be close (in relationship)

maht·fūng 蜜蜂 (N) bee (M: jek)

maht-gihk-bīt-fáan 物極必返 (IE) "The pendulum will swing back"

maht·léih 物理 (N) physics

maht·léih·hohk 物理學 (N) physics

maht·máh 密碼 (N) secret code

maht·tòhng 蜜糖 (N) honey

māi·dīng 咪丁 (VO) get stung, be made a sucker; to swindle

máih 米 (N) rice (uncooked) (M: gàn, catty)

máih 咪 (V) do not (colloq.) /Máih lā! Stop it! /Máih gám lā! Please don't!

maih 咪 (V) fusion of m̀h haih /Gám maih hóu baih! That would be very bad, wouldn't it?

máih·faahn 米飯 (N) food, provisions

máih·hòng 米糠 (N) rice husk

máih·lèih 咪喱 (M) millimeter

mān 蚊* (M) dollar

mān 蚊 (N) mosquitoes (M: jek)

mān·jeung 蚊帳 (N) mosquito net

mān·jí 吆紙 (BF) bank note /n̂gh·mān·jí, five-dollar bill

màng 掹 (V) pull

māt (·yéh) 乜(嘢) (N) what?

màu 踎 (V) squat on the heels

màu·dài 踎低 (V) stoop, squat down

máuh 畝 (M) Chinese acre (6.6 máuh in an English acre)

màuh·hoih 謀害 (V) to plot harm to someone

màuh·sàng 謀生 (V) earn a living

màuh·sih 謀事 (VO) seek a job

màuh-sih-joih-yàhn, sìhng-sih-joih-tìn 謀事在人成事在天 (IE) Man proposes, God disposes (It is man's to scheme; it is Heaven's to accomplish.)

mauh·yihk 貿易 (N) trade, commerce

mè 孭 (V) to carry on the back

mé 歪 (V) be awry, be askew, be not straight

mē 咩 (P) indicating surprise, doubt, etc.

mehng 命 (N) life (M: tìuh)

mēi·jí 尾指 (N) the small finger

méih 尾 (N) tail (M: tìuh)

meih 未 (P) negative indicating incompletion of action

meih 味 (N) (measure for dish of food)

meih·bīt 未必 (A) may not; not necessarily

méih·chāau 美鈔 (N) U.S. currency

meih·chàhng 未曾 (AV) not yet

meih·douh 味道 (N) flavor; taste

méih·fóng 尾房 (N) the last room on a floor (farthest from the street)

méih·gām 美金 (N) U.S. dollar

méih·gùn 美觀 (SV) beautiful (of things)

Méih·gwok 美國 (N) America (U.S.A.)

méih·jàu 美洲 (N) the Americas (north and south)

mèih·jihn 微賤 (SV) low, mean

mèih·sai 微細 (SV) very small; minute; trifling

mèih·sàng·maht 微生物 (N) germs, bacteria

méih·seuht 美術 (N) fine art

meih·séui 沬水 (V) submerge

méng 名 (N) name

m̀h 唔 (P) negative prefix to verbs

m̀h·cho 唔錯 (Ph) it's not bad

m̀h·dāk·dihm 唔得掂 (V) will be in trouble

m̀h·dāk·hàahn 唔得閒 (SV) busy

m̀h·dāk·líuh 唔得了 (SV) in for it (in deep trouble)

m̀h·dáng·sái 唔等使 (SV) not useful for the time being

. . . m̀h·dihng . . . m̀h·dihng . . . 唔定 … 唔定 … (Pat) maybe (this), maybe (that)

m̀h·fong·sām dāk lohk 唔放心得落 (Ph) be worried, concerned

m̀h·gáam·dòng 唔敢當 (IE) you are flattering me! (lit. I am not entitled to . . .)

m̀h·gai·daai 唔芥蒂 (V/SV) not to notice/not care about (e.g. not concerned about money, not bearing grudges, etc.)

m̀h·gán·yiu 唔緊要 (IE) never mind, it doesn't matter

m̀h·gau·dáam 唔夠胆 (SV) weak-kneed

m̀h·gau·yìhng·yéuhng 唔夠營養 (Ph) undernourished

m̀h·gei·dāk 唔記得 (V) unable to remember, forget

m̀h·gin·dāk 唔見得 (Ph) not necessarily

m̀h·gin·jó 唔見咗 (V) to lose or lost

m̀h·gòi 唔該 (V/IE) please /thank you; sorry

m̀h·gok·yi 唔覺意 (AV) unintentionally, by mistake

m̀h·gwaai·dāk 唔怪得 (MA) no wonder that . . .

m̀h·gwaai·dāk 唔怪得 (V) cannot blame

m̀h·gwàan néih sih 唔關你事 (IE) none of your business

m̀h·gwàan ngóh sih 唔關我事 (IE) I have nothing to do with it

m̀h·hàahng·dāk·hòi 唔行得開 (RV) can't pull oneself away

m̀h·haih 唔係 (A) negative used instead of 'm̀h' before compound, phrase or a clause

m̀h·haih·gám·góng 唔係噉講 (IE) that's not so

m̀h·haih géi jìng·sahn 唔係幾精神 (Ph) be not feeling well

m̀h·hóu 唔好 (AV) better not; don't (imperative)

m̀h·hóu gai·daai 唔好芥蒂 (Ph) don't be bothered by trifles

m̀h·hóu gai·daai la! 唔好芥蒂罐 (IE) Don't hold grudges!

m̀h·hóu gin·gwaai 唔好見怪 (IE) don't take offense

m̀h·hou haak·hei 唔好客氣 (IE) make yourself at home; help yourself; please (accept what is offered)

m̀h·hou (tùhng ngóh) haak·hei boh! 唔好(同我)客氣嗻 (IE) Please! (don't refuse . . .)

m̀h·hóu·yi·si 唔好意思 (SV) embarassed; ashamed to

m̀h·jàang·hei 唔爭氣 (SV) dispirited, lack of fighting spirit

m̀h·jí 唔止 (MA) not merely . . .; not only . . .; not as little as you say

m̀h·jì·géi 唔知幾 (A) extremely, beyond description

m̀h·ji·joih 唔志在 (V/AV) not give a damn/not care a bit

m̀h·jí·jūk 唔知足 (SV) discontented

m̀h·jih·yìhn 唔自然 (SV) not feeling well; ill

m̀h·jìng·sàhn 唔精神 (SV) be not well; be sick

m̀h·joih·fùh 唔在乎 (Ph) not be concerned with, not care a bit

m̀h·jùng·yuhng 唔中用 (SV) no use, not helpful

m̀h·kèui 唔拘 (IE) doesn't matter

m̀h·máaih·dāk·hei 唔買得起 (RV) can't afford to buy

m̀h·ngāam 唔啱 (IE) no; it is not correct

m̀h·ngāam . . . 唔啱… (A) might as well

m̀h·ngāam·neih . . . ā 唔啱你… (Pat) why don't you . . . /Mh·ngāam néih heui ā? Why don't you go? Mh·ngāam néih maaih·jo kéuih ā? Why don't you buy it?

m̀h·sàam·m̀h·sei (IE) improper

m̀h·sái·fòng 唔駛慌 (Ph) I bet . . . will not /Mh·sái·fòng tìng·yaht wúih lohk·yúh a. I bet it'll not rain tomorrow.

m̀h·sái·haak·hei 唔駛客氣 (IE) don't mention it

m̀h·sái·jí·yíh 唔使指意 (Ph) it's hopeless

m̀h·sái kèui 唔駛拘 (IE) make yourself at home; don't stand on ceremony /Chèuih·bín choh, m̀h·sái kèui. Make yourself at home, sit anywhere you want to.

m̀h sàm·gáp dāk lèih ge 唔心急得嘅嘅 (IE) worry won't help at all

m̀h·sé·dāk 唔捨得 (AV/V) to begrudge, to be loth to part with

m̀h·sé·dāk·lohk 唔寫得落 (RV) not be able to write down (not have enough room)

m̀h·sèng·m̀h·hei 唔聲唔氣 (A) quietly, sneakily

m̀h·sèung·tùhng 唔相同 (At) different

m̀h·siu·fa 唔消化 (SV) have indigestion

m̀h·syun 唔算 (Ph) it doesn't seem to be . . . /Mh·syun yáih lā. It doesn't seem to be bad.

m̀h·tūng 唔通 (MA) could it be possible that; do you mean to say

m̀h·wah·dāk·saht 唔話得實 (RV) can't say definitely

m̀h·yáhn·dāk·jyuh 唔忍得住 (RV) can't endure, can't tolerate

m̀h·yáhn·sàm 唔忍心 (At) softhearted; compassionate

m̀h· . . . yauh . . . 唔 … 又 … (Pat) if not . . . . then /Néih m̀h·jouh yauh jouh māt·yéh a? If you don't do this what else would you do?

mihn 面 (N) face

mihn·bāau 麵包 (N) bread (M: go, roll; faai, piece; tìuh, loaf)

mihn·chìhn 面前 (PW) front

míhn·dāk 免得 (A) lest, for fear that; avert (something from happening)

mihn·deui·mihn 面對面 (Ph) face to face

mìhn·fà 棉花 (N) cotton

mihn·fán 麵粉 (N) wheat flour

míhn·ji 免致 (A) lest; avoid (damage, etc.) /Nī·gihn yéh yiu sàu·maai kéuih míhn·ji béi dī sai·mān·jai jíng·laahn·jó. Put this thing away lest the children break it.

mihn·jí 面子 (N) face, dignity

mihn·jīk 面積 (N) area

míhn·kéuhng 勉強 (V/SV) impose on/be unwilling, reluctant

míhn·laih 勉勵 (V/N) encourage/encouragement

mihn·pùhn, mihn·pún 面盆 (N) washbasin

mihn·sihk 麵食 (N) pastry, dumpling, noodles, etc.

mìhn·tòi 棉胎 (N) cotton quilt (generally refers to the inner cotton pad of a cotton quilt); cf. mìhn·peih, cotton quilt

mìhn·baahk 明白 (V/SV) understand (clearly) /clear, easy to understand

mìhng·chìh 名詞 (N) term (of speech), noun

mìhng·chìng 名稱 (N) term, name

mìhng·chìuh 明朝 (At) the Ming Dynasty (A.D. 1368-1644)

mìhng·chóng 名廠 (At) name brand, well-known brand

mìhng·hā 明蝦 (N) prawn (M: jek)

mihng·lihng 命令 (N/V) order, command /order

mìhng·mìhng 明明 (A) obviously

mìhng·nìhn 明年 (TW) next year

mìhng·pín 名片 (N) calling card (M: jèung)

mìhng·seun·pín 明信片 (N) postcard (M: jèung)

mìhng·wahn 命運 (N) fate, destiny

mìhng·yuh 名譽 (N) reputation

mìhng·yuh·wúi·yùhn 名譽會員 (N) honorary member of a society

mín·sāam 面衫 (N) coat (M: gihn)

mīt·hòi 搣開 (RV) peel off; tear into sections

míu 廟 (N) temple (M: gàan or joh)

míuh 秒 (M) second (of time)

miuh·jóun 瞄準 (V) aim

mìuh·sé 描寫 (V) sketch; describe vividly

mò 摸 (V) feel with hand

mō·dá 摩打 (N) motor (transliterated)

mò·gwái 魔鬼 (N) devil; satan

mòh 磨 (V) grind; refine

moh 磨 (N) a grinder (stone grinder)

mohk-mìhng-kèih-miuh 莫名其妙 (IE) very mysterious and abstruse, very strange, peculiar

mohng 望 (V) look at from a distance

móhng 網 (N) net; network; system web

mohng·dou ngáahn dōu chyùn·jó 望到眼都穿咀 (IE) expect something anxiously

mòhng·gei 忘記 (V) forget

mohng·gin 望見 (RV) see from a distance

mòhng·gwok 亡國 (VO) the nation perishes

mohng·jyuh 望着 (V) stare at

móhng·kàuh 網球 (N) tennis ball; tennis

mohng·yúhn·geng 望遠鏡 (N) telescope

mōk 剝 (V) flay; peel; lay bare

móu 帽 (N) hat (M: déng)

móu 模 (N) mold

móu·sī 舞獅 (VO/N) to perform the lion dance /the lion dance

móuh 冇 (V) have not

mouh 霧 (N) fog, mist

móuh·bá·ngāak 冇把握 (SV) have no confidence

móuh·baahn·faat 冇辦法 (VO/SV) don't know how to do it; there is no way to do it /be incapable

móuh·PN baahn·faat 冇...辦法 (IE) has no way to deal with him (you or me)

mòuh·bāt 毛筆 (N) Chinese pen (actually a brush used for writing) (M: jī)

móuh·behng 毛病 (N) flaw; ailment; defect; failing; fault

móuh·chàn 母親 (N) mother

móuh·cheui 冇趣 (SV) flat; uninteresting

móuh·chēut·sīk 冇出息 (SV) can't make out in life

móuh cho 冇錯 (IE) it is right

móuh cho la! 冇錯嘞! (IE) That's right.

mouh·chùng 冒充 (V) to be an imposter, to pretend to be

móuh·dāk·sihk 冇得食 (Ph) in want of food

móuh·douh·dāk 冇道德 (SV) immoral

móuh·douh·léih 冇道理 (SV) be wrong; be ridiculous; be unreasonable

mòuh·dyùn·baahk·sih 無端白事 (MA) without reason or cause

mòuh·dyùn·dyùn 無端端 (MA) without reason or cause

mòuh·faahn 模範 (N) model; mould, pattern

móuh·faat·jí 冇法子 (A) no way to

móuh·faat·jí mh V... 冇法子唔... (Ph) have to, cannot but

móuh·fán 冇份 (V) have nothing to do with it; have no part of it; have no share in it /Kéuih wah kéuih móuh·fán. He said he had nothing to do with it.

mòuh·fēi 無非 (A) simply; solely /Kéuih mòuh·fēi séung ló dō·dī chin jē. He simply wants to get more money.

mòuh·fóng 模仿 (V) imitate, copy

mòuh-gà-hó-gwài 無家可歸 (Ph) homeless

mòuh·gān 毛巾 (N) bathtowel (M: tìuh)

móuh·gán·yiu 冇緊要 (IE) never mind; it doesn't matter

móuh·géi·nói 冇幾耐 (Ph) after a while (lit. not very long)

mòuh·gù 無辜 (SV) innocent; guiltless

mòuh·gún 毛管 (N) pores of skin

móuh·gwàan·haih 冇關係 (Ph) unrelated; irrelevant; it doesn't matter

mòuh·haahn 無限 (At) limitless, unlimited

móuh·haauh 母校 (N) alma mater (M: gàan)

mòuh·haauh 無效 (At) invalid, ineffectual

móuh·háu·chí 冇口齒 (SV) not keeping one's word

móuh·hei 武器 (N) weapon

mouh·hím 冒險 (VO/SV) risk danger; adventure /risky

mòuh-hó-noih-hòh 無可奈何 (Ph) there is no other way out /Mòuh-hó-noih-hòh jí yáuh gám jouh la. Since there is no other way out, we have to do it this way.

móuh·jí 母子 (N) mother and son

móuh·jyú·yi 冇主意 (SV) have no determination

mòuh·kùhng 無窮 (At) endless

mòuh·kùhng·jeuhn 無窮盡 (At) inexhaustible; infinite

mòuh·laaih 誣賴 (N) implicate other by false charges

mòuh·leuhn 無論 (MA) no matter . . .; whether . . . or not

móuh·líu 冇料 (SV) be empty-headed

mòuh·lìuh 無聊 (SV) tedious

móuh·màhn·tàih 冇問題 (Ph) there is no problem

móuh·māt . . . 冇乜 (Pat) nothing . . . /Mou·māt shih. Nothing important. Mou·māt gán·yiu. Nothing serious.

móuh·māt·m̀h 冇乜唔 (Pat) a variation of the pattern 'móuh wah . . . m̀h . . .'

móuh·māt·só·waih 冇乜所謂 (IE) it doesn't matter

móuh·māt·yéh 冇乜嘢 (IE) It is nothing.

mòuh·mìhng·jí 無名指 (N) ring finger

móuh·póu 冇譜 (SV) unmethodical; unsystematic, erratic, strange

móuh·sām·gèi 冇心機 (SV) downhearted, depressed, listless

móuh·sáu·méih 冇手尾 (SV) one who never finishes what he has started

móuh·sèng·hei 冇聲氣 (Ph) not hopeful

mouh·séui 霧水 (N) dew

móuh·séung·dou 冇想到 (RV) didn't expect

mòuh·sin·dihn·sāu·yām·gèi 無線電收音機 (N) radio set

mòuh·sin·dihn·tòih 無線電台 (N) radio station

móuh·só·waih 冇所謂 (IE) it doesn't matter

móuh só·waih . . . 冇所謂 . . . (Ph) there is no such thing as . . .

mòuh·sou 無數 (At) endless; numerous

mòuh tà ge 無他嘅 (IE) it's nothing in particular

móuh·tēng 舞廳 (N) dance hall

móuh wah . . . m̀h 冇話 . . . 唔 (IE) there's no such thing as . . .

mòuh·waih 無謂 (A/SV) it is no use to /meaning less, unnecessary

mòuh waih la! 無謂囉 (IE) Don't bother!

móuh·wúi 舞會 (N) dancing party

mòuh·wùh 模糊 (SV) blurred

mòuh·yàhn·yìn 冇人煙 (At) unpopulated

mòuh·yi·jūng 無意中 (A) unintentionally; accidentally

móuh·yi·si 冇意思 (Ph) dull, flat, uninteresting; no meaning

mòuh·yìh 無疑 (A) doubtlessly

mouh·yihng 冒認 (V) claim falsely

móuh·yim·jūk 冇厭足 (SV) insatiable greedy

mòuh-yíng-mòuh-jùng 無影無蹤 (Ph) not a trace of

móuh·yīu·gwāt 冇腰骨 (SV) unreliable (lit. no backbone)

mòuh·yùhn·mòuh·gu 無緣無故 (MA) without reason

móuh·yuhng 冇用 (SV) useless

muhk·bīu 目標 (N) target; goal; objective

muhk·chìhn 目前 (TW) at present; the present

muhk·dīk 目的 (N) goal, aim, object

muhk·dīk·deih 目的地 (N) destination (place)

muhk·gūng 木工 (N) carpentry

muhk·hei 木器 (N) wooden furniture, utensil

muhk·jéung 木匠 (N) carpenter

muhk·luhk 目錄 (N) index

muhk·ngūk 木屋 (N) hut; wooden house

muhk·sī 牧師 (N) minister (clerical); priest

muhk·yíh 木耳 (N) fungus

mùhn 門 (N) door (M: douh)

mùhn 門 (M) for trades, skills, (school) courses

múhn 滿 (SV/RVE) full

muhn 悶 (SV) dull, bored, distressed

mùhn·háu 門口 (N) door (the entrance)

mùhn·pàaih 門牌 (N) number of house

mùhn·sēut 門恤 (N) door bolt

mùhn·sìh 門匙 (N) door key

mùhn·tòuh 門徒 (N) disciple; follower

múhn·yi 滿意 (V) be satisfied with /Ngóh deui nī·gihn·sih hóu muhn·yi. I'm very satisfied about this.

múhn·yuht 滿月 (V) first month after birth

muhng 夢 (N) dream

muhng·gin 夢見 (V) dream of (lit. see in dream)

mùhng·lùhng 矇矓 (SV) obscure, misty, blurred

muht·sàu 沒收 (V) confiscate

múi 妹 (N) younger sister

múi 梅 (N) plum

mùih 煤 (N) coal (M: gàn, catty)

múih 每 (SP) each, every

múih·fùhng 每逢 (A) whenever, every occasion of

mùih·gwai 玫瑰 (N) rose (M: déu)

múih·síu·sìh 每小時 (TW) per hour

mùih·yán 媒人 (N) matchmaker

múng·dúng 懵懂 (SV) muddleheaded

N

ná 乸 (At) female (for animals)

nàahm 南 (BF) south

nàahm·chìng·nìhn·wúi 男青年會 (N) Y.M.C.A.

nàahm·fòng 南方 (PW) the south

nàahm·gà 男家 (N) bridegroom's family

nàahm·gaai 男界 (N) men (exclusively)

nàahm·gūng 男工 (N) male worker

nàahm·gùng·yàhn 男工人 (N) man-servant

nàahm·jái 男仔 (N) boy

nàahm·jyú·gok 男主角 (N) hero (as in a play, movie, etc.)

nàahm-pà-yahp-cho-hòhng, néuih-pa-ga-cho-lòhng 男怕入錯行,女怕嫁錯郎 (IE) It is a predicament for a man to get into the wrong trade, and a girl to marry the wrong chap.

nàahm·yán 男人 (N) man

nàahn 難 (SV) be difficult

nàahn·fùhng 難逢 (Ph) hard to meet with, unlikely

nàahn·gwo 難過 (SV) feel bad

nàahn·hàm 難堪 (SV) hard to bear, intolerable; unendurable

naahn·màhn 難民 (N) refugee

nàahn wái néih lo, nàahn wàih néih lo 難為你咯 (IE) I am sorry that you have had such a hard time.

nàahn·yíh 難以 (A) difficult to /nàahn·yíh gáai·sīk, difficult to explain

naahp·fūk 納福 (V) to enjoy happiness

nāai·lōng sì·maht 尼龍絲襪 (N) nylon stockings

naauh 鬧 (V) scold

naauh·jūng 鬧鐘 (N) alarm clock

naauh·siu·wá 鬧笑話 (VO) make a fool of oneself

nàh·sáu 拿手 (SV) dexterous; expert

nàhm 腍 (SV) tender; soft; well cooked

nàhng(·gau) 能(夠) (AV) be able to, can

nàhng·gon 能幹 (SV) able, competent

nàhng-wāt-nàhng-sàn 能屈能伸 (IE) adaptable to circumstances (one who can both stoop and stand erect)

nahp 溼 (SV) sticky; slow

nàih 泥 (N) mud

nàih·jāt 泥質 (N) substance containing mud

nàih·séui 泥水 (N) bricklayer's work

nám 諗 (V) think, contemplate

nām·bá 冧巴 (N) number (transliterated)

nám·lohk 諗落 (V) i.e. nám·lohk·heui, to think it over continuously

nán·fa 撚化 (V) play a prank on

nang·jyuh 嚟住 (V) cleave to

nāp 粒 (M) measure of seeds, grains, etc.

nāp·yahp·heui 凹入去 (V) be dented

nàu 嬲 (SV/V) angry /getting angry

náu 鈕 (N) button (M: nāp)

náu 扭 (V) turn (with fingers or a tool); twist

náu·jeuhk 扭着 (RV) turn on (as a switch)

nē 呢 (P) a question particle

néih 你 (N) you (singular)

néih·deih 你地 (N) you (plural)

néih·fū·yán 你夫人 (N) your wife (polite form)

néih·haak·hei·jē 你客氣啫 (IE) You are just too humble.

nèih·saat 彌撒 (N) Mass

néih wah dím maih dím lō 你話點咪點囉 (IE) Whatever you say.

néih yāt . . . ngóh yāt . . . 你一···我一··· (Pat) one after another, in turn /Néih yāt sèng, ngóh yāt sèng, yuht góng yuht chòuh. They speak very loudly one after another, and it becomes noisier and noisier. /Néih yāt geui, ngóh yāt geui, yùh·sih léuhng·go·yàhn ngaai·héi·gāau séuhng·lèih. After exchanging angry remarks in turn, they finally start arguing.

néui 女 (N) daughter

néuih 女 (BF) female /Néuih·sīn·sàang, female teacher

néuih·gà 女家 (N) bride's family
néuih·chìng·nìhn·wúi 女青年會 (N) Y.W.C.A.
néuih·gaai 女界 (N) women (exclusively)
néuih·gūng 女工 (N) female worker
néuih·gùng·yàhn 女工人 (N) maid-servant
néuih·jái 女仔 (N) girl
néuih·jí 女子 (At) girls' /girls' school, néuih·jí hohk·haauh
néuih·jí·jùng·hohk 女子中學 (N) girls' high school
néuih·jyú·gok 女主角 (N) heroine (as in a play, movie, etc.)
néuih·jyú·yán 女主人 (N) hostess
néuih·sai 女婿 (N) son-in-law
néuih·syūn 女孫 (N) granddaughter (paternal)
néuih·wòhng 女皇 (N) ruling queen
néuih·yán 女人 (N) women
ngá 啞 (SV) be mute
ngá·jái 啞仔 (N) deaf mute
ngaahk·fùng 逆風 (N) head wind, adverse wind
ngaahk·tàuh 額頭 (N) forehead
ngáahn 眼 (N) eye (M: jek; sèung, pair)
ngáahn·baahk·baahk 眼白白 (A) no recourse
ngáahn·chìhn 眼前 (TW/PW) the present, at present (a variant of muhk·chìhn) /in front of the eyes
ngáahn·daht·daht 眼凸凸 (A) with bulging eyes
ngáahn·fà 眼花 (SV) be dazzled
ngáahn·fan 眼瞓* (SV) sleepy
ngáahn·fō 眼科 (N) ophthalmology department
ngáahn·gaai 眼界 (N) taste or judgment in selecting /hóu ngáahn·gaai, good taste, good judgment
ngáahn·géng 眼鏡 (N) eyeglasses (M: fu)
ngáahn·géng·kwāang 眼鏡框 (N) eyeglass frames
ngáahn·gwōng 眼光 (N) foresight /hóu yáuh ngáahn·gwōng, having good judgment
ngáahn·jihk·jihk 眼直直 (A) with eyes fixed on, look attentively
ngáahn·jūng·dēng 眼中釘 (IE) 'needle in the eye,' pain in the neck
ngáahn·leuih 眼淚 (N) tear (from crying)
ngáahn·mèih 眼眉 (N) eyebrows
ngàahn·sīk 顏色 (N) color
ngaahng 硬 (SV) hard (in texture)
ngaahng·géng 硬頸 (SV) stubborn
ngàai 挨 (V) lean on
ngaai 哎 (V) yell, scream
ngaai·gāau 哎交 (VO) wrangle; argue
ngāai·māan 挨晚 (TW) evening
ngàaih 捱 (V) bear, endure
ngàaih·dāk·dihm 捱得掂 (RV) can manage to survive (by meager substance); can endure
ngàaih·faahn·chàan 捱飯餐 (IE) suffer hunger
ngàaih·m̀h·dihm 捱唔掂 (RV) cannot manage to survive (by meager substance); cannot endure
ngàaih·sai·gaai 捱世界 (VO) to manage to survive (by meager substance)
ngáak 鈪 (N) bracelet (M: jek)
ngáak 額 (N) a fixed number; settled portion
ngāak, ngāk 詎 (V) deceive; cheat; fool
ngāak·sáu, ngāk·sáu 握手 (VO) shake hands
ngāam 啱* (SV) right, correct /Ngāam ma? Is this correct? /Ngāam la. Yes, that is right.
ngāam·kīu 啱*譑* (SV) on good terms
ngāam·ngāam 啱*啱* (A) just (a moment ago)
ngāam saai la! 啱*晒嚹* (IE) What luck!
ngaan 晏 (SV) late (in the day)
ngaan·gaau 晏覺 (N) a nap
ngaan·jau 晏晝 (TW/N) noontime /lunch
ngāang 罌 (N) jar
ngáang·haih 硬係 (A) persistently
ngáap, ngaap 鴨 (N) duck (M: jek)
ngaap·dáan 鴨蛋 (N) duck egg
ngaat 壓 (V) press
ngaat·jai 壓制 (N/V) suppress, subdue
ngaat·gwái 押櫃 (N) deposit (a pledge or part payment)
ngaat·jyuh 壓住 (V) keep down, hold in
ngaat·lihk 壓力 (N) pressure
ngáau 拗 (V) break, snap
ngaau·géng 拗頸 (VO) argue
ngáau·hòi 拗開 (RV) break asunder
ngáau-saht-ngàh-gàn 咬實牙根 (IE) determinedly (ready to take any consequence)
ngáauh 咬 (V) bite; gnaw
ngáh 瓦 (N) roof tile (M: faai or pin)
ngàh·cháat 牙刷 (N) toothbrush
ngàh·chaat·chaat 牙刷刷 (SV) chattering
ngàh·chīm 牙籤 (N) toothpick

ngàh·fō 牙科 (N) dentistry department
ngàh·fùi 牙灰 (N) ashes
ngàh·gōu 牙膏 (N) tooth paste (M: ji)
ngáh·mín 瓦面 (N) top of roof (of tiles)
ngàh·yìn 牙煙 (SV) dangerous, precarious
ngàhm 掅 (V) feel in pocket or bag;
draw from pocket or bag
ngàhn·bāau 銀包 (N) wallet; purse
ngàhn·chín 銀錢 (N) dollar
ngàhn·hòh 銀河 (N) milky way
ngàhn·gāi 銀雞 (N) whistle
ngàhn·hòhng 銀行 (N) bank (M: gàan)
ngàhn·jí 銀紙 (N) currency (paper
money)
ngàhn·sīk·ge 銀色嘅 (At) silver
color
ngahp·táu 揢頭 (VO) nod one's head;
agree
ngái 矮 (SV) low; short (opp. gòu)
ngàih·hím 危險 (SV/N) dangerous
/danger
ngàih-joih-daan-jihk 危在旦夕
(IE) a person's life (or the existence of
an institution) is only a question of
hours
ngaih·seuht 藝術 (N) art
ngám 揞 (V) cover with the hand
ngam 暗 (SV) dark (destitute of light),
dim; gloomy
ngam·houh 暗號 (N) code, password,
secret sign
ngam·jùng 暗中 (A) secretly; privately
ngám·jyuh sèung·ngáahn
(Ph) cover the eyes
ngàm·taam 暗探 (N) private detectives
ngán 銀 (N) money
ngán·ge 銀嘅 (At) silver
ngāng·gō 鸚哥 (N) parrot (M: jek)
ngāp 噏 (V) babble
ngāt 扤 (V) press (with hands or fingers)
ngāt·saht 扤實 (RV) press solid
ngáu, aú 嘔 (V) vomit, throw up
ngáu·hyut 嘔血 (VO) to spit blood (from
lungs)
ngàuh 牛 (N) cattle (cow and ox) (M:
jek)
ngáuh·jeuhng 偶像 (N) idols, image
ngàuh-m̀h-yám-séui, m̀h-gahm-dāk-ngàuh-
tàuh-dài 牛唔飲水唔撳
得牛頭低 (IE) no one can be
forced to do what he doesn't want to do;
you can lead a horse (lit. cow) to water
but you can't make him drink
ngàuh·náaih 牛奶 (N) cow's milk

ngàuh·pá 牛扒 (N) steak
ngàuh·yàuh 牛油 (N) butter
ngáuh·yìhn 偶然 (A) accidentally; occasionally; by chance
ngàuh·yuhk 牛肉 (N) beef
ńgh 五 (NU) five
ńgh·gūk 五穀 (N) grain in general
ńgh·gùn 五官 (N) the five senses
ńgh·lèuhn 五倫 (N) the five relationships
(sovereign and subject, father and son,
brothers, husband and wife, friends)
ńgh·meih·gá 五味架 (N) cruet set (lit.
five-flavor stand, a set of four or five
bottles of seasonings or condiments in a
rack at table)
ńgh-ngàahn-luhk-sīk 五顏六色
(Ph) colorful; gaudy (lit. five or six
colors)
ngh·wuih 誤會 (V/N) misapprehend; mis-
understand /misapprehension; misunder-
standing
ńgh·yuht·jit 五月節 (N) Dragon-Boat
Festival (5th day of the 5th lunar month)
ngò·jòu, wū·jòu 齷齪 (SV) dirty
ngóh 我 (N) I, me
ngoh, tóuh·ngoh 餓, 肚餓 (SV/V) hungry
ngóh·deih 我哋 (N) we, us
ngóh·deih-léuhng·fù·fúh 我哋兩夫婦
(Ph) my wife and I
ngóh·deih m̀h gin·jó gam dò nìhn 我哋唔
見咀咁多年 (IE) we haven't seen each
other for many years
ngóh m̀h tùhng néih haak·hei la 我唔同
你客氣嘞 (IE) Then I won't
refuse your hospitality.
ngóh·tái 我睇 (Ph) I guess; I think
ngohk·héi 愕起 (V) raise (the head)
ngohn 岸 (PW) shore (seldom used by itself) /Ngohn·seuhng yāt·go yàhn dōu
móuh. There is no one on the shore.
ngohn·bīn 岸邊 (PW) at the shore
ngoi 愛 (V) to love
ngoi·chìhng 愛情 (N) feelings of affection (spiritual)
ngoi·gwok 愛國 (SV) patriotic
ngoi·lèih 愛嚟 (CV) used (or needed) for
ngói·ngòih·gám 㗎㗎噉 (A) expres-
sionless
ngoi·sīk 愛惜 (V) love and care
ngoih 外 (BF) foreign; other; outside
ngoih·bihn 外邊 (PW) outside
ngoih·fō 外科 (N) surgical department
ngoih·fō yī·sāng 外科醫生 (N) surgeon
ngoih·fú 外父 (N) wife's father
ngoih·gā 外家 (N) wife's family

ngoih·gàau 外交 (N) diplomatic rela-
　tions
ngoih·gàau·bouh 外交部 (N) ministry
　of foreign affairs
ngoih·gàau·gā 外交家 (N) diplomat
ngoih·gwok 外國 (At/PW) foreign
　/foreign country
ngoih·hóng 外行 (N/SV) a raw hand;
　an outsider, one who is outside of a
　trade, layman /ignorant
ngoih·móu 外母 (N) wife's mother
ngoih·pòh 外婆 (N) maternal grand-
　mother
ngòih·saai 呆嘥* (SV) dumbfounded
ngoih·sáang 外省 (At/PW) another
　province (a term used by natives of
　one province talking about another)
ngoih·sāang 外甥 (N) sister's child
ngoih·syūn 外孫 (N) a daughter's son
ngoih·yèuhng 外洋 (PW) abroad,
　foreign places
ngok 惡 (SV/A) hot-tempered; wicked;
　vicious/used as an adverbial prefix
　means 'hard', 'difficult' /Nī·gihn sih
　hóu ngok·jouh ge. This thing is hard to
　manage.
ngok·dái 惡抵 (SV) unbearable; un-
　comfortable
ngok·jaahp 惡習 (N) bad habits
ngok·jok·kehk 惡作劇 (N) practical
　joke; trick at another's expense
ngok·yàhn 惡人 (N) bad or wicked man
ngòn 按 (V) install /ngòn dihn·wá, to
　install a telephone
ngon·gín 案件 (N) case, crime
ngòn·ji 安置 (V) place (a person in a
　job, or position, etc.)
ngòn·lohk 安樂 (SV) contented, com-
　fortable
ngòn·pàaih 安排 (V) arrange
ngòn·sàm 安心 (A) put the mind at
　rest
ngòn·wai 安慰 (V/N) comfort, console
　/consolation
ngòuh 㩒* (N) shake violently
ngūk 屋 (PW) building, house
ngūk·déng 屋頂 (N) rooftop
ngūk·haak 屋客 (N) tenant (of a house)
ngūk·jòu 屋租 (N) house rent
ngūk·jyú 屋主 (N) landlord (of house)
ngūk·kéi 屋企 (PW) home
ngúng 擤* (V) push
ngúng·lohk·heui 擤落去 (RV) push
　down
ngúng·séuhng·heui 擤上去 (RV) push
　up

nī 呢 (SP) this (here)
nì 匿 (V) hide, conceal (oneself) /Kéuih
　nì(·màaih)·hái bīn·syu a? Where is he
　hiding himself?
nī·dī 呢啲* (N) these
nì·màaih 匿埋 (V) hide
nī·páai 呢牌* (MA) recently (used inter-
　changeably with gahn·lói)
nī tàuh . . . gó tàuh . . . 呢頭 … 嗰頭
　(Pat) as soon as one thing is done (or
　about to be done), another thing follows
　immediately /Ngóh nī·tàuh juhng meih
　góng·yùhn kéuih gó·tàuh yíh·gìng giu yàhn
　ló·jó léuhng·bùi jáu lèih la. Before I had
　finished what I was saying he had already
　ordered two glasses of wine. /Kéuih nī·
　tàuh wah 'm̀h·yám la, m̀h·yám la.' gó·
　tàuh yauh jà·héi go jáu jēun yám gán la.
　He had just about finished saying 'No more,
　no more,' when he picked up the bottle and
　drank again.
nìhm 黏 (V) glue on, stick on, stick together
nihm 唸 (V) recite, memorize
nìhn, nín 年 (M) year
nìhn·chō·yāt 年初一 (TW) the first day
　of the Chinese New Year
nìhn·dái 年底 (TW) end of the year
nìhn·ga 年假 (N) New Year's vacation
nìhn·géi 年紀 (N) age (of a person)
nìhn·gwàan 年關 (N) the end of a year
　(or lit. the pass of a year)
nìhn·hèng 年輕 (SV) young
nìhn·kāp 年級 (BF) grade in school /sàam·
　nìhn·kāp, third grade
nìhn·leih 年利 (N) annual interest
nìhn·lìhng 年齡 (N) age (formal term as
　it is used in a form, etc.)
. . . nìhn·(yìh)·lòih · · · 年(以)來 (Ph)
　during the past . . . years
nìhn·lóuh 年老 (SV) aged
nìhn·méih 年尾 (TW) end of the year
nìhn·sà·ah·máahn 年卅晚 (TW) Chinese
　New Year's Eve
nìhn·sīk 年息 (N) annual interest
nihng·jyun 擰轉 (V) turn
nihng·mūng·jāp 檸檬汁 (N) lemon juice
nīk, nìng 搦,擰 (V) take hold of, take, carry
　(small article)
nīk·jyuh 搦住 (V) hold in one's hand
nìng 擰 (V) take hold of, take, carry (small
　article)
nìng·jyuh 擰住 (V) hold in one's hand
noh·máih 糯米 (N) glutinous rice
noih, nói 耐 (SV) a long time
noih·bāt·nói 耐不耐 (A) from time to
　time; once in a while

noih·bouh 内部 (N) internal section
noih·deih 内地 (PW) inland
noih·fō 内科 (N) internal medicine department
noih·fō yī·sāng 内科醫生 (N) doctor of internal medicine (as distinguished from a surgeon)
noih·hóng 内行 (SV/N) expert /an expert
noih·jí 内子 (N) my wife (polite form; usually preceded by ngóh)
noih·jūng 内中 (A) among them; sometimes
noih·lyuhn 内亂 (N) internal disorder (of a country)
noih·mohk 内幕 (N) the inside story
noih·yùhng 内容 (N) contents
nóuh (·gàn) 腦(筋) (N) brain
nóuh·lihk 努力 (V/A) work hard /arduously
nùhng 濃 (SV) strong (as in tea); strong flavor (as in cooking)
nùhng·chèuhng 農場 (N) farm
nùhng·fō 農科 (N) school of agriculture
nùhng·fù 農夫 (N) farmer
nùhng·yàhn 農人 (N) farmer
nùhng·yihp 農業 (N) agriculture
nùng 燶 (SV) be scorched
nyúhn 暖 (SV) be warm
nyúhn·séui·wú 暖水壺 (N) thermos bottle

O

ò 痾 (V) to go to stool /ò·sí, to ease nature; ò·niuh, to urinate; ò·hyut, to pass blood; ò·pei, to break wind
ò·fèih·sí 阿肥史 (N) office
ò·leih 痾痢 (VO) having dysentery
ò·niuh 痾尿 (VO) urinate
o·sí 痾屎 (VO) to ease nature
oi·sàm 愛心 (N) love (lit. heart's love)
òn·mìhn·yeuhk 安眠藥 (N) hypnotic (any drug inducing sleep)
ōn·sí 安士 (M) ounce (transliterated)
on·tàuh·yaht·lihk 案頭日曆 (N) desk calendar
on yuht gai 按月計 (Ph) charge by month
ou·miuh 奥妙 (SV) mysterious; marvelous
oùh 撽* (V) shake

P

pa 怕 (V) to be afraid of . . . ; fear
pa·cháu 怕羞 (SV) timid, bashful
pàahng 棚 (N) shed; mat-shed
pàahng·jeung, pàhng·jeung 膨脹 (V) expand, swell
páai 牌 (N) playing cards (various kinds)
páai 咈* (BF) suffix indicating time /Nī·páai, recently
paai 派 (V) send (a person with a mission or duty)
paai 派 (V) issue, hand out, distribute (food or clothing as relief)
paai 派 (M) factions, schools (of thought, etc.)
paai·biht 派別 (N) faction
paai·dihng 派定 (V) assign, appoint
pàaih 牌 (N) plate; brand; placard; sign
pàaih(·jí) 牌(子) (N) brand-name
pàaih·chèuhng·lùhng 排長龍 (VO) stand in line (lit. in line like a long dragon)
pàaih·déui 排隊 (VO) stand in line, line up
pàaih·fōng 牌坊 (N) memorial arch
pàaih·gwāt 排骨 (N) pork ribs (M: gauh)
pàaih·kàuh 排球 (N) volley ball
paak 拍 (V) pat; to clap
paak 泊 (V) dock
paak 拍 (V) compare
paak·dāk·jyuh 拍得住 (RV) can match (can be a peer with)
paak·jéung 拍掌 (VO) clap the hands
paak·maaih 拍賣 (V) to sell at auction
paak·máh·tàuh 泊碼頭 (VO) dock a ship
paak·mùhn 拍門 (VO) knock on the door
paak·syuh 柏樹 (N) cypress tree
paan·mohng 盼望 (V) expect eagerly; hope for
pāat·ná 巴那 (N) partner (transliterated)
paau 砲 (N) cannon
paau 泡 (V) soak
paau·dáan 砲彈 (N) artillery shells
pàau·lohng·tàuh 拋浪頭 (VO) to frighten one (with words)
paau·má 砲碼 (N) cannonball, shell
pàh·chín 扒錢 (VO) extort money
pàh·sàan 爬山 (VO) climb up a mountain
pàh·téhng 扒艇 (VO) to row a boat
pàhn·jihn 貧賤 (SV) poor and mean
pàhn·làhn 頻䜩* (SV) be hurried
pàhng·geui 憑據 (N) proof; evidence
pàhng·hūng 憑空 (A) without proof
pàhng·yáuh 朋友 (N) friend
pài 批 (M) batch, group
pài 批 (V) to wittle, to skin (a potatoe, etc.)
pài·faat 批發 (At) selling goods wholesale /Kéuih jouh pài·faat sàang·yi. He runs wholesale business.

pài·yeuk 批約 (N) lease
pài·dohng 批蕩 (V/N) plaster/plaster
pài·jéun 批准 (V) grant; ratify
pài·pìhng 批評 (V/N) criticize /criticism
pan 噴 (V) to breathe out; spout out
pan·séui·chìh 噴水池 (N) fountain
pāt 匹 (M) a bolt (of cloth); (M) for horse /yāt·pāt·máh, a horse
paau·jéung 炮仗 (N) firecracker (M: chyun, string)
pèhng 平 (SV) inexpensive, cheap
péi 皮 (N) fur (coat, etc.) (M: gihn)
péi·yàhn 鄙人 (N) my humble self (polite form)
pei·yùh (wah) 譬如 (MA) for instance; if, in case
pèih·dáai 皮帶 (N) leather belt (M: tìuh)
pèih·dáan 皮蛋 (N) preserved eggs
péih·dāan 椀單 (N) sheet (for a bed) (M: jèung)
pèih·fai 皮費 (N) business expenses
pèih·fù 皮膚 (N) skin (human)
pèih·hei 皮氣 (N) temperament
pèih·gīp 皮篋 (N) suitcase
pèih·hàaih 皮鞋 (N) leather shoe
pèih·hèu 皮靴 (N) boots
pìhng 平 (SV) level; even; smooth
pìhng·dáng 平等 (SV/N) be equal /equality
pìhng·deih 平地 (N) level ground
pìhng·fūng 屏風 (N) a movable screen
pìhng·gwàn 平均 (SV) be average
pìhng·gwàn·fān (·sou) 平均分 (N) average grade
pìhng·gwó 蘋果 (N) apple
pìhng·gwo·jāp 蘋果汁 (N) apple juice
pìhng·hàhng 平行 (SV/N) balanced /balance
pìhng·jihng 平靜 (SV) peaceful, tranquil
pìhng·màhn 平民 (N) the common people
pìhng·ngòn 平安 (SV) peaceful; safe; in good health (all are used in regard to people)
pìhng·pìhng·ngòn·ngòn(·ge) 平平安安嘅 (A) safely
pìhng·pun 評判 (V) judge
pìhng·sèuhng 平常 (SV/MA) ordinary /ordinarily
pìhng·sìh 平時 (MA) usually, ordinarily
pìhng·táan 平坦 (SV) level, smooth
pìhng·wán 平穩 (SV) safe, steady

pìhng·yaht 平日 (MA) generally; daily
pìhng·yùhn 平原 (N) plain
pīk 僻 (SV) secluded; one-sided
pīk·jihng 僻靜 (SV) secluded; quiet
pìn 偏 (V/SV) inclined to one side /bias
pìn 篇 (M) leaf of a book; (M) for an article /yāt·pin màhn·jèung, an article, an essay
pín 片 (N) movie, film (abbrev. of dihn·yíng·pín)
pin 騙 (V) deceive, cheat, swindle
pīn·chāp 編輯 (V/N) to edit; compile /editor
pin·guhk 騙局 (N) plan to cheat people; plan for swindling
pīn·pīk 偏僻 (SV) out of the way, not populated
pīn·sàm 偏心 (SV) partial; prejudiced
pìng·yām 拼音 (N/VO) spelling /spell phonetically
pìng·yām·jih 拼音字 (N) romanization
piu·leuhng 漂亮 (SV) attractive, smart looking
pò 篹 (M) measure for a plant
po·cháan 破產 (VO) bankrupt
po·chòih 破財 (VO) to suffer loss
po·fai 破費 (V) lavish; waste
po·fú·chàhm·jàu 破釜沉舟 (IE) victory or death; "to burn the bridges" (to sink the boats and break up the pots and pans)
po·gaak 破格 (A) make an exception; in defiance of rule or custom
po·geng·chùhng·yùhn 破鏡重圓 (IE) old lovers reunited (two broken pieces of mirror coming together again)
po·lohk·wuh 破落戶 (N) a decayed family
po·waaih 破壞 (V) destroy; smash
pòh·mā 婆媽 (N) maidservant
pòhng·bīn 旁邊 (PW) the side of, flank, beside
pòhng·gùn·ge·yàhn 旁觀嘅人 (N) bystander
pòhng·gùn·jé·chìng 旁觀者清 (IE) the onlooker (of a chess game) seems always to have the clearest mind
pòhng·tèng 旁聽 (V) to audit (a college class
pòhng·yàhn 旁人 (N) bystander
pok 撲 (V) dash into
pōk(·jái) 泡(仔) (N) blisters
pok·saht 樸實 (SV) simple-hearted, artless or unsophisticated in nature

pok·sou 樸素 (SV) unpretentious, simple

pòu 鋪 (V) spread on

póu·pin 普遍 (SV) general, common

pou·táu 鋪頭 (N) store, shop (M: gàan)

póu·tùng 普通 (SV) common, general

póu·tùng·wá 普通話 (N) southern Mandarin

póuh(·jyuh) 抱(住) (V) hold (in one's arm or arms); embrace /pouh(·jyuh) go bìh·bī jai, holding a baby; pouh(·jyuh) nī·júng sàm·léih, having such a state of mind; pouh(·jyuh) nī·júng taai·douh, holding such an attitude

póuh 泡 (N) a bubble

póuh·hahm 抱憾 (Ph) with regrets, sorry

póuh·bāt·pìhng 抱不平 (V) to be indignant (when others are wronged)

póuh·hip 抱歉 (V) regret; sorry /Ngóh fèi·sèuhng póuh·hip, I'm very sorry.

pòuh·saat 菩薩 (N) statue or image of Bodhisatva

pòuh·tàih·jí 菩提子 (N) grape (M: nāp, for a grape; chàu, a bunch)

pùhn 盆 (N) basin, pot

pùhng 蓬 (N) mat-awning; sail

pui 配 (V) pair; mate; match; fit /Ngóh yiu pui yāt·tìuh só·sìh. I want to make a key to fit that lock.

pui·fuhk 佩服 (V) admire; respect

pui·hahp 配合 (V) to match; pair; to fit

pùih 陪 (V) accompany, go along with; keep someone company

púih 倍 (M) time, fold /léuhng·púih, two-fold

pùih·haak 陪客 (V/N) to entertain a visitor /a guest (who is not the honorary guest)

pùih·sám·yùhn 陪審員 (N) jury

pùih·sèuhng 賠償 (V/N) compensate /compensation

pūk·dóu 仆倒 (V) fall down

pún 伴 (N) company (as of a person)

pun 判 (V) to judge; to sentence

pun·dyun, pun·dyuhn 判斷 (V) judge

pun·dyuhn·lihk 判斷力 (N) sense of judgment

pun·láan 拌爛 (V) act recklessly (headlong and irresponsible)

pun·séi 拌死 (A) act desperately

pung 碰 (V) hit; crash into

pung·dóu 碰到 (RV) bump into, meet (by accident)

put 潑 (V) to throw out (water)

put·sin 撥扇 (VO) to wave a fan

S

sà, sā 紗 (N) gauze; yarn (used in manufacturing cloth)

sá 灑 (V) to sprinkle (liquids); scatter

sà·ah 卅 (NU) thirty (abbrev. form)

sà·chàhn 沙塵 (SV) proud, haughty

sā·dīn·yú 沙甸魚 (N) sardine (partly transliterated from English)

sà·jí 沙紙 (N) sandpaper

sà·mohk 沙漠 (N) a desert

sà·ngáahn 砂眼 (N) trachoma

sā·tāan 砂灘 (N) sand bank, beach

sà·tòhng 砂糖 (N) granulated sugar

sàai 徙* (V) waste /Jàn·haih sàai·saai la! What a waste!

saai 晒 (V) sun

saai 嘥* (P) verb suffix, used as 'all' or 'whole'

sáai·ji·daaih·hah 徙置大廈 (N) resettlement building (in Hong Kong)

saai·páang 晒棚 (N) drying platform (usually on the rooftop)

saai·yaht·táu 晒日頭 (VO) sun oneself

sāak, sāk 塞 (V) stuff, fill by crowding

sàam 三 (NU) three

sāam 衫 (N) clothes, dress, gown (M: gihn; tyut, suit)

sàam·dáng 三等 (N) third class

sàam·báan 舢板 (N) sampan (M: jek)

sāam·dói 衫袋 (N) pocket on a coat

sāam·fu 衫褲 (N) shirt (or coat) and trousers (M: tyut, suit)

sàam·géi·yaht 三幾日 (Ph) a couple of days

sàam·jéung 三獎 (N) third prize

sàam·lèuhn·chè 三輪車 (N) pedicab

sàam·léuhng·yaht 三兩日 (Ph) a couple of days

sàam·màhn·jih 三民治 (N) sandwich (a transliteration from English)

sàam·màhn·jyú·yih 三民主義 (N) Three people's principles

sàan 閂 (V) close (door, gate)

sàan 刪 (V) expunge, delete

sàan 山 (N) mountain; hill

sáan 散 (SV) loose, scattered

sāan·bīn 山邊 (PW) hillside

sāan·bō 山坡 (N) slope of a hill

saan·bouh 散步 (V/N) take a walk /a stroll

saan·chèuhng 散場 (V) the show has ended

sàan·déng 山頂 (N) summit

sàan·déng·laahm·chè 山頂纜車 (N) cable car (to the peak; in Hong Kong)

sàan·duhng 山洞 (N) a cave; cavern

sàan·geuk 山脚 (N) foot of a mountain

sāan·gūk 山谷 (N) valley

saan·jihk 散席 (VO) leave table (lit. disperse from table)

sāan·lūng 山窿 (N) mountain cave

sáan·ngán 散銀 (N) small coins; small change

sàan·séui·wá 山水畫 (N) A Chinese picture depicting a landscape (M: fūk)

saan·wúi 散會 (VO) adjourn or close a meeting

sáang 省 (M) province

sáang 擤 (V) scour

sàang·bóu 生保 (SV) be strange (to a community, or a place)

sàang·bóu·yàhn 生保人 (N) stranger

sàang·choi 生菜 (N) lettuce

sàang·chōng 生瘡 (VO) have boils

sàang·chùhng 生蟲 (VO) contain worms or insects

sàang·dāk hóu sī·màhn 生得好斯文 (Ph) be well bred

sàang·duhng 生動 (SV) lifelike; vivid

sàang·gāi 生雞 (N) a cock (M: jek)

sàang·gwó 生果 (N) fresh fruit

sàang·gwó·dong 生果檔 (N) a fruit stall

sàang·hòuh 生蠔 (N) oyster

sàang·jì 生蝨 (VO) to have mange

sàang·máahng 生猛 (SV) lively; active

sàang·mín·yàhn 生面人 (N) stranger

sàang·sau 生銹 (VO) rust

sáang·sèhng 省城 (N) capital city of a province; Canton

sàang·sò 生疏 (SV) become estranged; out of practice

sàang·tit 生鐵 (N) cast iron

sàang·wuht·séui·jéun 生活水準 (N) living standard

sàang·yaht 生日 (N) birthday

sàang·yi 生意 (N) business (buying and selling)

saap·hei 噪氣 (V) wrangle

saat 撒 (V) to sow (seed); scatter

saat 殺 (V) kill; slay

sahm 甚 (A) very

sahm·ji 甚至 (A) even, even to the extent of /Ngóh sahm·ji lìhn kéuih ge sing dōu m̀h·gei·dāk·jó. I have even forgotten what his surname is.

sàhn 神 (N) god, gods

sàhn·bei 神秘 (SV) mysterious

sàhn·fuh 神父 (N) Catholic priest

sàhn·gìng 神經 (SV) crazy, insane

sàhn·gìng·behng 神經病 (N) mental disorder

sàhn·gìng behng·yún 神經病人 (N) a hospital for the mentally ill

sàhn·gìng·sèui·yeuhk 神經衰弱 (SV) nervous breakdown

sàhn·hei 神氣 (N/SV) expression/to put on airs

sàhn·sīn 神仙 (N) god, gods; fairies; immortals

sahp 十 (NU) ten

sahp·chyùhn·sahp·méih 十全十美 (IE) be (a hundred percent) perfect

sahp·fahn·jì . . . 十分之… (Pat) . . . tenths /sahp·fahn·jì·sàam, three-tenths

sahp·fan 十分 (A) completely; 100%

sahp·gaai 十誡 (N) the Ten Commandments

sahp·jih·gá 十字架 (N) the Cross

sahp·jih·louh·háu 十字路口 (PW) street or road intersection

sahp·jūk 十足 (SV) ideal; complete

sahp·jūk·sahp gám 十足十噉 (A) one hundred per cent (emphatic)

sahp·mān·jí 十蚊紙 (N) ten-dollar bank note

saht 實 (RVE) ending of resultative verb indicating firmness

saht·ga 實價 (N) set price

saht·hàhng 實行 (V) put into practice; carry out; practice

saht·jai 實際 (SV) practical

saht·jai seuhng 實際上 (A) actually, in actuality

saht·maht 實物 (N) substance, a solid matter

saht·yihn 實現 (V) realize (as hopes, etc.)

saht·joih 實在 (SV/A) honest /really

saht·yuhng 實用 (SV) practical

saht·wá 實話 (N) truth (not lie)

saht·yihp 實業 (N) real estate

sài 西 (BF) west

sái 使 (V) to use; to spend

sái 使 (CV) to send; to tell; to need to

sái 洗 (V) wash

sái 駛 (V) drive (a car), operate (a plane)

sai 細 (SV) be small, little, fine

sai 細 (SV) young

sai·bāau 細胞 (N) cells

sài·béng 西餅 (N) pastry (M: gihn)

sāi·chāan 西餐　(N) Western food

sài·chèh 西斜　(At) afternoon sun

sái·chìh·mohk·gahp 噬臍莫及
(IE) repentance is too late (How can one
reach to bite one's navel?)

sāi·fòng 西方　(At/PW) the West /sài·
fòng gwok·gà, the Western countries

sai·gà 世家　(N) nobility; aristocracy

sai·gaai 世界　(N) world

sai·gaai·daaih·jin 世界大戰　(N)
world war

sai·gaai·seuhng 世界上　(Ph) in the
world

sai·géi 世紀　(N) century

sai·guhk 世局　(N) world situation

sāi·gwà 西瓜　(N) watermelon

sāi·jōng 西裝　(N) Western dress (M:
gihn; tyut or tou, suit)

sāi·jōng·póu 西裝舖　(N) Western
tailor shop

sài·lihk 西曆　(N) Western calendar

sai·lihk 勢力　(N) influence, strength,
power, prowess

sai·lóu 細佬　(N) younger brother; I
(polite form)

sai·lóu·gō 細佬哥　(N) small boy

sai·māan·jai 細蚊仔　(N) child, children

sái·māt 使乜　(IE) why should . . .

sái·māt·gam 使乜咁　(IE) why
should . . . so . . .

sai·sái·sèng 細細聲　(A) in a soft
voice

sai·sàm 細心　(SV) meticulous

sái·sàn 洗身　(VO) take a bath

sái·sàn·fóng 洗身房　(N) bathroom

sai·sèng 細聲　(A/SV) in a low voice
(lit. small voice) /be soft-spoken

sai-seuhng-mòuh-nàahn-sih, jí·pa·yáuh-
sàm·yàhn 世上無難事,只怕
有心人　(IE) There is nothing hard
in this world which a determined man
cannot do.

sai·sih ge yéh 世事嘅野　(Ph) the
ways of the world

sāi·sīk 西式　(At) Western style

sài·yàhn 西人　(N) Westerner

sài·yèuhng 西洋　(At) Occidental

sāi·yì 西醫　(N) physician trained in
Western medicine

sái·yī·gèi 洗衣機　(N) washing
machine

saih·yuhn 誓願　(VO) swear, take an
oath

sāk, sāak 塞　(V) to block up; stop up;
obstruct

sàm 深　(SV) be deep; be dark (of colors)

sàm 心　(N) mind; heart

sám 嬸　(N) wife of father's younger brother

sám 審　(V) try, judge (as in a trial)

sám 潘　(V) sprinkle

sàm·behng 心病　(N) heart disease; 'love-
sickness'

sàm-daaih-sàm-sai 心大心細
(IE) indecisive

sàm·fàahn 心煩　(SV) irritated, distressed

sàm·fū·kāp 深呼吸　(N) deep breath

sàm·fūk 心腹　(N) confidant

sàm·gáau·ge 深交嘅　(SV) have intimate
friendship /Ngóh·deih hóu sàm·gàau·ge.
We are very close friends.

sàm·gāp 心急　(SV) be impatient

sàm·gèi 心機　(N) attentiveness; interest;
effort

sàm·hāk 深刻　(SV) deep (deeply inscribed),
profound

sàm·hèui 心虛　(SV) afraid of being discovered, apprehensive

sàm·hip 心怯　(SV) timorous; fearful;
nervous

sàm·hòhn 心寒　(SV) disheartened

sàm·johng·behng 心臟病　(N) heart
disease

sàm·làhm 森林　(N) forest

sàm·léih 心理　(N) state of mind

sàm·léih·jok·yuhng 心理作用　(N)
imagination, fascination

sàm·léih·seuhng·ge 心理上嘅
(Ph) psychological influence

sàm·luhk·sīk 深綠色　(At) dark green

sám·mahn 審問　(V) try in court; interrogate

sám·móuh 嬸母　(N) wives of brothers
(younger and elder respectively)

sàm·múhn·yi·jūk 心滿意足
(Ph) perfectly satisfied

sàm·ou 深奧　(SV) profound (marked by
intellectual depth)

sàm·sih 心事　(N) personal concerns

sàm·sīk 深色　(N) dark color

sàm·táahm 心淡　(SV) to lose interest in

sàm·tiu 心跳　(Ph) heart beating

sàn 新　(SV) be new

sàn 伸　(V) stretch out; stick out

sàn 身　(N/M) body /the measure for a
suit of clothes (lit. body)

san·beih·tai 擤鼻涕　(VO) to blow
the nose

sàn·bīn 身邊　(A) along with (in carrying)

sàn·chíng 申請　(V) to apply

sàn·chíng·bíu 申請表　(N) application form

sàn·chíng·syù 申請書 (N) application form

sàn·chòih 身材 (N) figure, height

sàn·fán 身份 (N) status, rank (of a person)

sàn·fán·jing 身份證 (N) identification card

sàn·fú 辛苦 (SV) torturing, labor with pain and fatigue

sàn·fún·ge 新款嘅 (A) new style

sān·gà 身家 (N) property a man owns

sàn·jí 身子 (N) health /Kéuih nī·páai sàn·jí m̀h·haih géi hóu. He has not been in good health recently.

sàn·kèih 新奇 (SV) new, novel

sàn·lihk 新曆 (N) New Calendar (adopted from the West and therefore called 'new,' interchangeable with sài·lihk, yèuhng·lihk)

sàn·lóng 新郎 (N) bridegroom

sàn·lòhng·gō 新郎哥 (N) bridegroom

sàn·mán 新聞 (N) news

sàn·màhn·gwóng·bo 新聞廣播 (N) news broadcast

sàn·màhn·pín 新聞片 (N) newsreel

sàn·néung 新娘 (N) bride

sàn·póuh (N) daughter-in-law

sàn·sàn·fú·fú 辛辛苦苦 (A) by hard working; laboriously

sàn·sáu 新手 (N) an inexperienced person

sàn·séui 薪水 (N) salary

sàn·sí 紳士 (N) gentry; village elders

sān·sīk 新式 (SV) new style

sān·sìn 新鮮 (SV) be fresh

sān·sīn hùng·hei 新鮮空氣 (Ph) fresh air

sàn·tái 身體 (N) body; health

Sàn·yeuk 新約 (N) New Testament (of the Bible)

sān·yùn 申寃 (V) to obtain redress

sāng·cháan 生產 (V) give birth; produce

sāng·chyùhn·gihng·jàng 生存競爭 (Ph) the struggle for existence

sāng·háu 牲口 (N) cattle

sāng·jéung 生長 (V) grow, develop

sāng·mihng 生命 (N) life

sāng·pìhng 生平 (A) during a lifetime

sāng·wuht 生活 (N) (daily) life; livelihood

sāp 濕湮 (SV/V) wet/wet

sāp·douh 濕度 (N) humidity

sāp·hei 濕氣 (N) dampness, humidity

sāp·sāp·seui·seui 濕濕碎碎 (SV) be miscellaneous

sāp·seui 濕碎 (SV) be miscellaneous

sāp·sīng 濕星 (SV) be miscellaneous

sāt 失 (V) lose

sāt·baaih 失敗 (V/N) fail; be defeated /defeat; failure /Kéuih yíh·gìng sāt·baaih jó léuhng·chi, kéuih m̀h·háng jouh la. He has failed twice, he won't do it again.

sāt·gok 失覺 (V) inattentive; unconscious of

sāt·jùng 失踪 (V) to be missing (as of a person)

sāt·láih 失禮 (SV) impolite

sāt·mìhn 失眠 (V/N) have insomnia /insomnia

sāt·mohng 失望 (V) be disappointed, be in despair

sāt·sih 失事 (V) have an accident

sāt·tàuh·gō 膝頭哥 (N) knee

sāt·yéh 失野 (VO) lose something

sāt·yìhng 失迎 (IE) fail to receive a guest at the door

sàu 收 (V) take in; receive; collect (money, letter, etc.)

sáu 手 (N) hand (M: jek)

sáu 首 (M) measure for song

sáu 搜 (V) search out

sau 瘦 (SV) thin

sau 銹 (N) rust

sáu·bei 手臂 (N) arm

sàu·bou·gèi 收報機 (N) teletype

sáu·chàh 搜查 (V) search

sáu·chēung 手鎗 (N) pistol; revolver (M: jī)

sàu·chòhng 收藏 (V) collect /sàu·chòhng gú·wún, curio collecting

sáu·dói 手袋 (N) handbag

sàu·dou 收到 (RV) received; have received

sáu·dòu 首都 (N) capital (place)

sáu·dyuhn 手段 (N) inproper means

sau·fā·ge 繡花嘅 (At) embroidered

sáu·gān 手巾 (N) towel (M: tìuh)

sáu·gān·jái 手巾仔 (N) handkerchief (M: tìuh)

sàu·geui 收據 (N) a receipt

sàu·gói 修改 (V) revise, amend

sáu·gùng 手工 (N) handicraft; manual skill; 'handicrafts' (as a subject taught in school)

sáu·gùng·yihp 手工業 (N) handicraft industry

sáu·hah 手下 (N) persons who work under one's command

sáu·hàhng·léih 搜行李 (VO) to examine luggage

sàu·hohk·fai 收學費 (VO) charge for tuition

sáu·jàai 守齋 (VO) to fast

sáu·jàang 手睜 (N) the elbow

sáu·jai 手掣 (N) hand brake

sàu·jeung 收賬 (VO) collect debts

sáu·jí 手指 (N) finger (M: jek)

sáu·jí·gaap 手指甲 (N) fingernail

sáu·jí·gùng 手指公 (N) thumb

sáu·jí·mēi 手指尾 (N) the little finger

sàu·jíng 修整 (V) repair

sáu·juhk 手續 (N) procedure; process; formality

sáu·jùng·lahp 守中立 (Ph) maintain neutrality

sáu·láih·baai 守禮拜 (VO) observe or attend church services

sáu·làuh 收留 (V) accommodate

sáu·làuh·dáan 手榴彈 (N) hand grenade

sàu·léih 修理 (V) fix, repair

sáu·líhng 首領 (N) leader

sàu·màaih 收埋 (V) put away, put aside

sáu·mát 手袜 (N) glove

sāu·mēi 收尾 (MA/At) afterward, later on /last /sāu·mēi gó·go, the last one

sáu·méih 手尾 (N) unfinished business (M: dī)

sáu·mùhn·háu·ge·yàhn 守門口嘅人 (N) doorman

sáu·ngaih 手藝 (N) skill, trade

sàu·ngán 收銀 (V) take in money (as done by a cashier)

sàu·pún 收盤 (VO) to wind up business

sàu·sahp 收拾 (V) put in order, tidy up

sáu·sai 手勢 (N) hand gestures

sáu·sàn 搜身 (VO) to search the person

sáu·seuhng 手上 (PW) in one's hand

sáu·seung 首相 (N) prime minister

sáu·seuht 手術 (N) skill; surgical operation

sáu·seuht·sāt 手術室 (N) operating room

sàu·síh 收市 (VO) close up for the day (as a store)

sàu·sìhng 收成 (N) harvest

sáu·sīk 首飾 (N) jewel; jewelry

sāu·sīk 收息 (VO) receive interest

sáu·sìn 首先 (A) first; at first

sáu·sing·chāan 守聖餐 (VO) receive Holy Communion

sáu·tàih 手提 (At) portable /sáu·tàih dá·jih·gēi, portable typewriter

sàu·tìuh 收條 (N) a receipt

sàu·tói 收枱 (VO) clear the table

sáu·tou 手套 (N) gloves (M: fu, deui)

sàu·wùih 收回 (V) take back

sàu·yahp 收入 (N) income

sāu·yām·gēi 收音機 (N) radio set (M: ga)

sau·yì 獸醫 (N) a veterinarian

sau·yuhk 瘦肉 (N) lean meat

sàu·yùhng 收容 (V) accommodate (students in school, patients in hospital, workers in factory, etc.)

sàuh 愁 (V/SV) worry /worrisome

sàuh 仇 (N) enmity

sauh·chi·gīk 受刺激 (VO) have a shock

sauh·dá·gīk 受打擊 (VO) to suffer reverses

sauh·fan·lihn 受訓練 (VO) receive training

sauh·fú 受苦 (VO) suffer hardship

sauh·fùn·yìhng 受歡迎 (SV) be welcomed (i.e. a person whom everyone is glad to see)

sauh·gáam·duhng 受感動 (V) be moved by

sauh·gaau·yuhk 受教育 (VO) receive education

sauh·hei 受氣 (VO) be scolded; to endure wrong /sauh lóuh·báan hei, to bear boss' scolding

sauh·sái 受洗 (V) receive baptism

sauh·sèung 受傷 (VO) suffer injury; be wounded ('sauh' can be omitted without affecting the meaning)

sauh·syún·sāt 受損失 (VO) suffer loss, damage

sauh yíng·héung 受影响 (Ph) influenced by, affected by . . .

sàuh-yùhng-múhn-mihn 愁容滿面 (IE) having a sad look /Dím·gáai kéuih gàm·yaht sàuh-yùhng-múhn-mihn gám a? Why is he wearing such a sad look today?

sè(·jyuh) 賒(佢)(V) to buy or sell on credit

sé 寫 (V) write

se 瀉 (V) have diarrhea

sé·dāk 捨得 (AV/SV) to be willing to part with /to be generous

sé·dāk·lohk 寫得落 (RV) be able to write down (have enough room)

sé·héi·kéuih 寫起渠 (Ph) take it down (in writing)

sé·jih·làuh 寫字樓　(N) office (M: gàan)

sé·jih·tói 寫字枱　(N) writing table, desk (M: jèung)

sé·lohk 寫落　(V) write down

sè·síu 些少　(UN) small amount, little bit, a few

sè·sou 賒數　(V) to buy or sell on credit

se·yìhm 瀉鹽　(N) Epsom salts

sèh 蛇　(N) snake, serpent (M: tìuh)

seh 射　(V) to shoot out; discharge

séh·dái 舍弟　(N) my younger brother (polite form)

séh·gàau 社交　(N) social intercourse

seh·gīk 射擊　(V) fire (a gun), shoot

séh·hah 舍下　(N) (my) house or home (lit. humble house)

seh·jin 射箭　(VO) to shoot an arrow

seh·jung 射中　(RV) to hit a target by shooting

séh·léun, séh·leuhn 社論　(N) editorial

séh·wúi 社會　(N) society in general; community

séh·wúi·hohk 社會學　(N) sociology

séh·wúi·hohk·gā 社會學家　(N) sociologist

séh·wúi·jyú·yih 社會主義 (N) socialism

sehk 石　(N) stone (M: gauh)

sehk·dang 石凳　(N) stone bench

sehk·fùi 石灰　(N) limestone, lime

sehk·sí 石屎　(N/At) broken stone for concrete /concrete

sehk·sí·láu 石屎樓　(N) cement building (M: joh)

sehk·tàuh 石頭　(N) stone; boulder

sehk·tói 石枱　(N) stone table

sèhng 城　(PW) walled city; city, town /sèhng ngoih·bihn, outside the city

sèhng 成　(BF) whole, entire /sèhng go, a whole one, the whole /sèhng·gàan hohk·haauh, the whole school

sèhng 成　(RVE) into /bin·sèhng, change into; yihk sèhng, translate into

sèhng 成　(V) become, be considered /Nī·bún·syù juhng meih sèhng yāt·bun syù. This 'book' cannot be considered a book yet (i.e. not finished yet).

sèhng·bún syù 成本書　(Ph) whole book

sèhng·gàan hohk·haauh 成間學校 (Ph) whole school

sèhng·yaht 成日　(Ph) whole day

séi 死　(V) die; (N) death; (RV) /Kéuih béi yàhn dá·séi·jó. He was beaten to

death. (A) stubbornly /Kéuih séi m̀h·háng yihng. He stubbornly refused to admit it.

sei 四　(NU) four

sei·fōng 四方　(SV) be square (shape), be four-sided

sei·fōng·tói 四方枱　(N) square table (M: jèung)

sei·gwai 四季　(N) four seasons

sei·gwai·pìhng·ngòn 四季平安 (Ph) be in good health throughout the year

séi·gwo·fàan·sàang 死過返生 (IE) a near escape from death

séi·lo! 死囉！(IE) exclamation (desperation; sorrow); damn!

sei·sei·fōng·fōng·ge 四四方方嘅* (At) square

séi·sèung 死傷　(N) casualties

séi·sì 死屍　(N) corpse

Sei·syù 四書　(N) the four books (of the Confucian Cannon), i.e. The Analects of Confucius, Mencius, The Great Learning, The Golden Mean

sei·wàih 四圍　(A) around; on all sides; in every direction

sek 錫　(N) pewter

sèng 聲　(N) sound; voice

séng 醒　(SV) awake

sèng·hei 聲氣　(N) news, sign (of hope)

sèng·jan·jan·gám 聲震震嘅* (A) in a trembling voice

sēng·yàm, sīng·yàm 聲音　(N) sound; voice; noise

sèuhn 純　(SV) pure; unmixed

seuhn(·jyuh) 順(住)　(V/CV) follow (naturally) /follow, along

sèuhn·bán 純品　(SV) honest and obedient

seuhn·bín 順便　(A) at your convenience, when convenient; while . . .

seuhn·chùhng 順從　(V) follow obediently, obey, to comply with

seuhn·fùng 順風　(N) favorable wind, tail wind

seuhn·gíng 順境　(N) favorable circumstances

sèuhn·háuh 純厚　(SV) sincere; honest

seuhn·jyuh 順住　(CV) follow; along

seuhn·leih 順利　(SV) smooth (free from interruptions, difficulties, etc.)

seuhn·louh 順路　(A) on the way

sèuhn·mòhng·chí·hòhn 唇亡齒寒 (IE) People rely on each other (when the lips are gone the teeth will feel cold).

seuhn séui 順水　(Ph) with the stream; a fair tide

sèuhn·seuih 純粹 (SV) pure; unadulter-
ated

seuhn·seuih 順遂 (SV) compliant;
agreeable to

sèuhn·suhk 純熟 (SV) at home in, skillful

seuhng 上 (P) suffix to terms pertaining to subjects of learning, government,
ideology, and some other terms of abstract nature, with similar meaning of
'ge', 'of' or 'in' /jing·jih·seuhng, political, politically; sì·séung·seuhng,
ideological, ideologically

séuhng 上 (BF) ascend

séuhng·bā·si 上巴士 (VO) get on or
board a bus

séuhng·bāan 上班 (VO) go to work; go
to class

seuhng·bihn 上邊 (PW) top, above

séuhng·chè 上車 (VO) get in a car; get
on a train or bus

seuhng·chèuhn 上旬 (TW) first 10 days
of month

seuhng·chi 上次 (TW) last time (i.e.
previous to this time, not the final time)

séuhng·choi 上菜 (V) serve food at the
table

Seuhng·dai 上帝 (N) God

seuhng·dáng 上等 (At) first class, best
quality

séuhng·dong 上當 (VO/SV) tricked,
fooled, swindled

séuhng·fēi·gèi 上飛機 (VO) get on
or board a plane

séuhng·fo 上課 (VO) go to class

séuhng·fó·chè 上火車 (VO) get on
or board a train

seuhng·goi 上蓋 (N) the top part of a
building

séuhng·hcui 上去 (V) go up

seuhng·jau 上晝 (TW) forenoon

seuhng·jùng·hah 上中下 (At) first,
second and third (in grading)

seuhng·kèih (·jòu) 上期(租) (N) pre-
paid rent (to be paid at the beginning
of period)

séuhng·lín 上鍊 (V) wind (e.g. watch,
etc.)

séuhng·láu 上樓 (VO) go upstairs

séuhng·lèih 上嚟* (V) come up

séuhng·ngohn 上岸 (VO) go ashore,
disembark

séuhng·sàan 上山 (VO) go up a hill

séuhng·sàm 上心 (V) take something
very hard, be very upset

seuhng·sìng 上升 (V) soar, ascend

séuhng·syùhn 上船 (VO) get on or board
a boat

séuhng·tái·chòu 上體操 (VO) take
physical training, attend athletic drill

séuhng·tòhng 上堂 (VO) go to class

séuhng·yahm 上任 (VO) take over duties
of a post

séuhng·yáhn 上癮 (VO) become an addict;
be addicted to; develop a craving for

seuhng·yāt·bui 上一輩 (N) the last
generation

seuhng·yi·yún 上議院 (N) senate

séui 水 (N) water

seui 歲 (M) year(s) old /sahp·ńgh seui,
fifteen years old

seui 碎 (SV) broken, be in fragments

seui 稅 (N) tax

séui·dāan 稅單 (N) custom clearance
certificate

séui·bàm 水泵 (N) a water pump

séui·chí 水柿 (N) yellow persimmon

séui·chi 水廁 (N) water closet

séui·chìh 水池 (N) pond

séui·chòuh 水槽 (N) groove

séui daaih 水大 (Ph) flow (opposite of ebb)
/Séui daaih lo! The tide is rising!

séui·dáu 水痘 (N) chicken pox

séui·fai 水費 (N) water bill

séui·gáau 水餃 (N) boiled dumplings

séui·geuk 水腳 (N) fare, passage (for
ship)

séui·gún 水管 (N) tube, pipe

seui·gwāan 稅關 (N) the customhouse

séui·hàuh 水喉 (N) faucet, hose

séui·jaahp 水閘 (N) sluice gate

séui·jéun 水準 (N) standard, level

séui jeung 水漲 (Ph) flow, the water is
rising

sèui jì 須知 (Ph) (You) should know
that . . .

séui·kèuih 水渠 (N) sewer, channel, drain

séui·sáu 水手 (N) sailor, seamen

séui·táhm 水氹* (N) puddle

séui teui 水退 (Ph) the water recedes, ebb

sèui·tèuih 衰頹 (SV) tottering; feeble

séui·tìhn 水田 (N) fields which can be
flooded

séui·tòhng 水塘 (N) pond; reservoir

séui·túng 水桶 (N) water barrel, bucket

sèui·yìhn 雖然 (MA) although

sèui·yiu 需要 (N/V) need /in need of;
necessary /Nī·gihn sih sèui·yiu gám jouh.
It is necessary to do so.

sèuih·bāt·ji 誰不知 (A) a variation of
'sèuih ji' (who would have thought that . . .)

seuih·douh 水道 (N) tunnels (M: tiuh)

seuih·jì 誰知 (MA) who would have thought that . . .

seuih·yī 睡衣 (N) pajamas (M: tyut, suit)

seun 信 (V) believe; believe in

seun 信 (N) letter (M: fùng)

seun-bāt (or m̀h)-seun-yàuh-néih 信 不 (or 唔) 信 由 你 (IE) believe it or not

seun·dāk·gwo 信得過 (V/SV) trust /trustworthy

seun·fūng 信封 (N) envelope

seun·gaau 信教 (VO) believe in a religion

seun·houh 信號 (N) signal

seun·jí 信紙 (N) letter paper (M: jèung, sheet)

seun·jīn 信箋 (N) letter paper (M: jèung, sheet)

sèun·mahn·chyu 詢問處 (N) information desk

seun·sàm 信心 (N) faith

seun·sēung 信箱 (N) mailbox (for receiving mail only)

seun·yahm 信任 (V/N) trust

seun·yéuhng 信仰 (N/V) religious belief /believe in

seun·yuhng 信用 (N) trustworthiness; credit

sèung 鑲 (V) inlay; inlay with

sèung 雙 (At) double; even

séung 想 (AV) consider, plan to, want to

séung 相像 (N) photograph (M: fūk)

sèung·bīu 商標 (N) trademark

sèung·chèuhng 商場 (N) market (business world)

Sèung·chìuh 商朝 (At) Shang Dynasty (1766–1122 B.C.)

sèung·chyu 相處 (V) be a friend (of) or be working together (with); be acquainted with, be associated with

seung·dái 相底 (N) negative (film)

sèung·dáng·yù 相等於 (EV) equal to

sèung·dòng 相當 (A) somewhat; to a considerable degree; fairly, quite; rather

sèung·fáan 相反 (At) quite the opposite /Kéuih·ge yi·gin tùhng ngóh·ge ngāam·ngāam sèung·fáan. His opinion is just the opposite of mine.

séung·fàan·jyun·tàuh 想返轉頭 (IE) look back on what one has been through

séung·faat 想法 (N) way of thinking

sèung·fauh 商埠 (N) commercial port

sèung·fùng 傷風 (V/N) having a cold /a cold

sèung·gaai 商界 (N) business circles, commercial world

sèung·góng 商港 (N) seaport

sèung·hàhn 傷痕 (N) scar from a wound

sèung·hòhn 傷寒 (N) typhoid fever

sèung·hóu 相好 (V) friendly, on good terms

séung·jeuhn-baahn·faat 想盡辦法 (Ph) exhaust all the ways

sèung·lèuhng 商量 (V) discuss; talk about, consult with

sèung·lìhn 相連 (At) adjoining

sèung·líu·ge 雙料嘅 (At) double strength, heavy-duty

sèung·màh·yáu 雙麻柚 (N) Chinese grapefruit, pomelo

séung·m̀h·dou 想唔到 (MA) unexpectedly

séung·mín 賞面 (IE) favor with one's presence (at a party, etc.) /Néih jàn·haih séung·mín la! Thank you for coming!

sèung·nóuh·gàn 傷腦筋 (SV) annoying, vexing

sèung·sàm 傷心 (SV) grieved; broken-hearted

sèung·sáu 雙手 (A) with both hands

sèung·seun 相信 (V) believe

sèung·sīk 相識 (V) know or be acquainted with each other (to be used in the pattern N tùhng N V, never in the pattern N V N)

sèung·sou 雙數 (N) even number

sèung·tùhng 相同 (At) similar

séung·wah 想話 (AV) thinking of /Ngóh séung·wah m̀h·heui ge la, daahn·haih yauh m̀h·heui m̀h·dāk. I was thinking of not going but I just have to go.

sèung·yàhn 商人 (N) merchant

sèung·yàhn·fóng 雙人房 (N) double room (M: gàan)

sèung·yìh 相宜 (SV) reasonable (in price)

sèung·yihp 商業 (N) business, commerce

sèung·yihp chyúh·chūk ngàhn·hòhng 商業 儲蓄銀行 (N) commercial savings bank

sèung·yihp·je·fún 商業借款 (N) commercial loan

sèung·yihp·kēui 商業區 (N/PW) business area

séung·yút 賞月 (VO) enjoy the moonlight

sēut·jihk 率直 (SV) frank, outspoken

sēut·lìhng 率領 (V) lead out

sēut·sāam 恤衫 (N) shirt ('sēut' being a transliteration of 'shirt') (M: gihn)

sì 絲 (N) silk

sí 使 (CV) cause, make (cf. lihng)

sí 氏 (BF) a word used to indicate a woman's maiden name, e.g. Chàhn sí, maiden name Chàhn

sí 屎 (N) excrement; dung

si 試 (V) try, taste

sì 詩 (N) poem; poetry (M: sáu)

sì 師 (M) division (military)

sì·dohk 司鐸 (N) a catholic priest (lit. he who attends the bell)

sì·chàuh 絲綢 (N) silk fabric

sì·faat 絲髮 (N) silk material

sì·faahn·hohk·haauh 師範學校 (N) teachers' college

sì·fú 師傅 (N) master (opp. of apprentice)

sí·gā 私家 (A) privately (owned by oneself)

sì·gēi 司機 (N) driver

sì·gìng 詩經 (N) The Book of Odes

sì·gō 詩歌 (N) hymn; poetry (lit. poem and song) (M: sáu)

sì·gū 師姑 (N) nun (Buddhist)

si·gyún 試卷 (N) examination paper (M: fahn)

sì·hòi 撕開 (RV) tear open

si·hou 嗜好 (V/N) be addicted to /things one is crazy about

sì·jí 獅子 (N) lion (M: jek)

sì·jih 私自 (A) without authorization

sì·lahp 私立 (At) privately established (school, hospital, etc.)

sì·léih 司理 (N) manager of a company

sì·lihng 司令 (N) commander

sì·lihng·bouh 司令部 (N) headquarters (military)

sì·lìng 士令 (N) shilling (transliterated)

sì·màhn 斯文 (SV) be cultured, gentlemanlike, refined

sì·mìhn 絲棉 (N) silk wadding

sì·nāai 師奶 (N) Mrs.

sì·sáu 屍首 (N) corpse

sì·sé 施捨 (V/N) helping others by giving (money, food, etc.)

sì·séung 思想 (N) thought; thinking; ideology

sí·túng 屎桶 (N) commode, potty chair (for adults in houses that don't have plumbing)

sì·yàhn 私人 (At) private (owned by oneself)

sì·yàhn 詩人 (N) poet

sì·yèh 師爺 (N) one who works in an attorney's office or some government office in Hong Kong

sì·yìh 思疑 (V/N) suspect; presume, guess /suspicion

si·yihm 試驗 (V/N) experiment

si·yuhng 試用 on probation (in employment)

síh 市 (N) city, municipality

sih(·gon) 事(幹) (N) affair, undertaking

sì·hàaih 屍骸 (N) corpse

sí·hāang 屎坑 (N) latrine; privy

sìh·bāt·sìh 時不時 (MA) occasionally

sih·bìt 事必 (A) must be, certainly

sih·chìhn 事前 (A) beforehand

sih·chìhng 事情 (N) affair

sih·daahn 事但 (IE) do whatever one wishes

sih·dāam 士担 (N) stamp

sìh·doih 時代 (N) period, era, epoch, age

sih·fèi 是非 (N) scandal

sih·fuhng 侍奉 (V) to serve, wait on (parents, elders, superiors, etc.)

sìh·fún 時款 (SV) in style, stylish

sìh·ga 市價 (N) market price, current price

sìh·gaan 時間 (N) time

sìh·gaan·bíu 時間表 (N) timetable

sih·gín 事件 (N) incident

sìh·guhk 時局 (N) political situation at a certain time

sìh·gwàan 事關 (MA) because

sìh·hauh 時候 (N) time, a period

sìh·hīng 時興 (SV) stylish, fashionable

sìh·jái 侍仔 (N) waiter in a westernized hotel or restaurant; in a Chinese restaurant etc. the word 'fó·gei' is used instead

síh·jing·fú 市政府 (N) municipal government

sìh·kèih 時期 (N) period (of time)

sìh·máhn·tóu 士敏土 (N) cement

síh·mihn 市面 (N) market (economic term)

sih, nùhng, gùng sèung 士農工商 (N) scholars, farmers, artisans, merchants (general classification according to their occupation)

sih·saht 事實 (N) fact

sih·saht·seuhng 事實上 (A) in fact

sìh·sìh 時時 (A) often, always, frequently

sìh·sìh·hāk·hāk 時時刻刻 (A) constantly, always

sih·sìn 事先 (A) beforehand, in advance

síh·táu 市頭 (N) market

sih·táu 事頭 (N) boss; proprietor of a
business; head of office

sih·yáu, sih·yàuh 豉油 (N) soy sauce

sih·yihp 事業 (N) enterprise, career,
work

sihk 食 (V) eat

sihk·baahk·mihn 食白麵 (Ph) take
heroin or marijuana

sihk·báau 食飽 (RV) eat until full

sihk·jàai 食齋 (VO) to eat only vegetables; to abstain from meat as a
religious observance

sihk·gau 食夠 (RV) eat enough

sihk·jaih 食滯 (V) have indigestion

sihk-m̀h-báau-yauh-ngoh-m̀h-séi
食唔飽又餓唔死
(IE) to live on merely for the sake of
existence

sihk·maht 食物 (N) foodstuff

sihk·yīn 食煙 (VO) smoke

sihk·yīn·dáu 食烟斗 (VO) smoke a pipe

sìhm, sím 蟬 (N) cicada, broad locust
(M: jek)

sihn 善 (At) good, virtuous

sihn·mouh 羨慕 (V) envy

sihn·ngok 善惡 (N) good and evil

sihn-ngok-bāt-fàn 善惡不分
(IE) can't make the distinction between good and evil

sihn·sih 善事 (N) benevolence, an act
of kindness, charitable gift

sihn·tóng 善堂 (N) a benevolent organization

sihn-yáuh-sihn-bou-ngok-yáuh-ngok-bou
善有善報惡有惡報
(IE) goodness has a good recompense,
wickedness has a bad recompense

sìhng, sèhng 成 (RVE) into /bin·
sìhng, change into

sìhng 成 (P) ten percent (only used in
telling a percentage, i.e. 'baat·sìhng
sàn' eighty percent new, etc.)

sìhng 乘 (V) multiply

sihng 賸 (V) remain over (as a remainder)

sìhng·chèuhng 城墻 (N) city wall

sìhng·gai·jái 承繼仔 (N) adopted
son

sìhng·gèi 乘機 (A) take advantage of
an opportunity

sìhng·gin 承建 (V) to be the contractor
of a building project

sìhng·gin 成見 (N) prejudice

sìhng·gùng 成功 (N/SV) success /be
successful

sìhng·jái 繩仔 (N) cord

sìhng·jauh 成就 (N) achievement

sìhng·jīk 成績 (N) achievement, results
or grades gained, average marks

sìhng·jip 承接 (V) to contract for a job

sìhng·lahp 成立 (V) establish

sìhng·lèuhng 乘涼 (VO) to enjoy the cool
air

sìhng·saht 誠實 (SV) honest, sincere

sìhng·síh 城市 (N) city

sìhng·suhk 成熟 (SV) ripe; mature

sìhng·wàih 成為 (V) become

sìhng·waih 承惠 (IE) Thank you.

sìhng·yàhn 成人 (N/VO) adult /become a
man

sìhng·yihng 承認 (V) recognize; confess;
acknowledge

sìhng·yúh 成語 (N) proverb, idiom,
idiomatic expression

siht 蝕 (V) lose money in business or
speculation

siht·bún 蝕本 (VO) lose in business (lit.
lose from capital money)

siht·dái 蝕底 (SV/V) suffer loss, be
cheated

sīk 識 (V/AV) know, recognize /know how
to

sīk 式 (BF) style, type

sīk 熄 (V/SV) turn off (the light) /be off
(the light is . . .)

sīk·dong 適當 (SV) suitable, fit

sīk·jái 骰仔 (N) dice

sīk·jó 熄咗 (V) turn off (the light); (the
light) is out

sīk·jùng 適中 (SV) well located

sīk·séui 色水 (N) color

sím 閃 (V) gleam, flash (as lightning)

sím 蟬 (N) cicada, broad locust (M: jek)

sím·beih 閃避 (V) avoid; dodge

sím·dihn 閃電 (VO) lightning

sìn 先 (A) first (in Cantonese 'sin' as an
adverb can be used after the verb. This
is different from the Mandarin usage.)

sin 線 (N) thread (M: tìuh)

sin 扇 (N) fan (M: bá)

sīn 仙 (N) cent; penny

sìn·bāt·sìn 先不先 (A) first

sìn·fuh 先父 (N) my late father

sìn·fūng 先鋒 (N) vanguard

sìn·hauh 先後 (N) sequence, order (lit.
first and after)

sìn·ji 先致 (A) then and only then

sin·sāam 線衫 (N) undershirt (M: gihn)

sìn·sàang 先生 (N) Mr., sir, gentleman;
teacher; husband (polite)

sīn·sí 仙士 (N) a cent

sīn-tīn-bāt-jūk 先天不足 (Ph) a feeble constitution

sìng 升 (M) measure (for grain, or rice, etc.)

sìng 升 (V) rise, raise

sìng 繩 (N) rope (M: tìuh)

sing 姓 (EV) be surnamed

sing 勝 (V) win; excel (literary)

sing 性 (P) (suffix) the nature of . . . , -ity /ngàih·hím·sing hóu daaih, contain the potentiality of great danger

sīng 星 (N) star

sīng·bāan 升班 (VO) promotion to a higher class

sing·biht 性別 (N) sex (as appears in application forms, etc.)

Sing·chāan 聖餐 (N) Last Supper, Lord's Supper

sing·chìhng 性情 (N) temper; disposition

sing·daan·gō 聖誕歌 (N) Christmas carol

sing·daan·jit 聖誕節 (N) Christmas

sing·daan lóuh·yàhn 聖誕老人 (N) Santa Claus

sìng·díu, sìng·diuh 聲調 (N) tone

sing·gaak 性格 (N) character, personality

sing·gāp 性急 (SV) impatient; quick tempered

Sing·gìng 聖經 (N) Bible (M: bún, bouh)

sìng·gong·gèi 升降機 (N) elevator; lift (British term for elevator)

sìng·gùn 升官 (VO) be promoted (primarily used for officials)

sing·gwo 勝過 (V) excel, surpass (in quality, value, etc.)

sīng·kàuh 星球 (N) planet

sìng·kèih 星期 (TW) week

sìng·kèih 升旗 (VO) to raise the flag

sìng·kèih·yāt 星期一 (TW) Monday

sing·leih 勝利 (N) victory

Sìng·lìhng 聖靈 (N) Holy Ghost

sìng·mìhng 聲明 (N/V) declaration, statement /declare, state

sing·mihng 性命 (N) life

sing·mihng 姓名 (N) full name

sìng·sàhn 星辰 (N) stars

sing·sī 聖詩 (N) sacred song, hymn

sīng·tìn 升天 (VO) ascend to heaven

sing·yàhn 聖人 (N) sage, saint

sīng·yàm 聲音 (N) sound, noise

sip 㡓 (V) cushion, make something steady (by filling or wedging something in)

sit·lauh 洩漏 (V) to leak out, divulge

sìu 銷 (V) sell

sìu 燒 (V) burn; put fire to; roast

síu 少 (SV) be few; less

siu 笑 (V) to laugh, smile

sìu·chēng 燒青 (At) enameled

síu·daih 小弟 (IE) I (a polite saying, of a man only)

siu·dou tóuh dōu tung·jó 笑到肚都痛咀 (Ph) laugh heartily

sìu·fa 消化 (V) digest

sìu·gihk 消極 (At) negative, listless

sìu-go-chīng-gwòng 燒個清光 (IE) burn to the ground

síu·hei 小氣 (SV) petty; ungenerous; narrow minded

sìu·hín 消遣 (V/N) amuse /amusement, pastime, hobby

síu·hohk 小學 (N) primary school

síu·hohk·haauh 小學校 (N) primary school

siu·tàuh 兆頭 (N) an omen, a sign

síu·jé 小姐 (N) miss; daughter (polite)

sìu·jeuhk 燒着 (RV) burn, set fire to

siu·mēi·mēi 笑微微 (Ph) smile slightly

sìu·miht 消滅 (V) exterminate; extinguish; annihilate

siu·nāai 少奶 (N) Mrs. (young woman)

síu·néui 小女 (N) my daughter (polite form)

síu·sàm 小心 (V/SV) look out for /be careful

síu·sìh 小時 (N) hour (lit.)

sìu·sīk 消息 (N) news, information

sìu·sīk lìhng·tùng 消息靈通 (Ph) well informed /Ha, néih jan·haih sīu·sīk lìhng·tung la. My! you are really well informed!

síu·sing 小姓 (N) my humble name (polite form)

síu·sou 少數 (N/At) minority

síu·syut 小說 (N) a novel (M: bún)

síu·tàih·kàhm 小提琴 (N) violin

siu·wá 笑話 (N) joke

sìu·yé 消夜 (N) midnight snack (M: chàan)

síu·yìh 小兒 (N) my son (polite form)

síu·yìh·fō 小兒科 (N) pediatrics department

síu yi·si jē! 小意思嗻! (IE) It's merely a token!

sìu·yuhk 燒肉 (N) roast pork

sō 梳 (V) comb /sō tàuh, comb the hair

só 鎖鎖 (V) lock (M: bá)

sō 梳 (N) comb

sō·fa 梳化 (N) sofa (M: 'jèung' for piece; 'tou' for set)

so·gái 梳髻 (VO) dress the hair; arrange the hair in a bun or chignon

só·lín 鎖鍊 (N) fetters; chains

só·sìh 鎖匙 (N) key

sò·tàuh 梳頭 (VO) comb hair

sò·tòhng 疏堂 (At) the relationship with uncles, aunts, or cousins on the father's side

só·waih 所謂 (At) so-called

só yáuh ge 所有嘅 (Ph) all, all there is, whatever there is, all one has

só·yíh 所以 (MA) therefore

sòh 傻 (SV) be stupid; be foolish

sok·hei 索氣 (VO) panting (lit. keep inhaling); inhale

sok·sing 索性 (A) simply (used to modify verbs only) /sok·sing maaih·jó kéuih, simply sell it

sóng·jihk 爽直 (SV) be straightforward; be openhearted

sòng·sih 喪事 (N) funeral affairs

sóu 掃 (N) brush

sóu 嫂 (N) elder brother's wife

sou 掃 (V) sweep

sou·bá 掃把 (N) broom (M: bá)

sou·bóu 數簿 (N) book of account

sòu·cheui 蘇脆 (SV) crisp

sou·deih 掃地 (VO) sweep floor

sou·gàau 塑膠 (At) plastic

sou·hohk 數學 (N) mathematics

sòu·hòhng·póu 蘇杭鋪 (N) dealer in imported goods

Sòu·lyùhn 蘇聯 (N) U.S.S.R. Soviet Russia

sou·mouh 掃墓 (VO) to care for a grave

sou·muhk 數目 (N) sum, amount, figure (number)

Sòu·ngòh 蘇俄 (N) U.S.S.R., Soviet Russia

sóu·yāt·sóu·yih 數一數二 (Ph) be one of the best

sòu·yíuh 騷擾 (V) disturb; trouble, bother

suhk 熟 (SV/V) be familiar with each other /be familiar with (a thing); know well (used with 'deui' or 'deui·yù')

suhk·hòhng 熟行 (SV) know the trade well, well-versed in

suhk·jeuih 贖罪 (VO) to atone for a crime or sin

suhk·sáu 熟手 (SV) experienced hand

suhk·sīk 熟悉 (V) know something

well (used with or without 'deui' or 'deui·yù')

suhk·tit 熟鐵 (N) wrought iron

suhk·yù 屬於 (V) belong to

sūk 叔 (N) father's younger brother, uncle

sūk 縮 (V) draw back; contract; shrink

sūk·chìng 肅清 (V) exterminate, eradicate

sūk·jihng 肅靜 (SV) be in deep silence

sūk·máih 粟米 (N) corn; maize

sūk·se 宿舍 (N) dormitory (M: gàan)

sūk·séui 縮水 (V) shrink; shorten

sùng 鬆 (V/SV) loosen /loose

sung 餸 (N) dish of Chinese food (M: dihp, meih)

sung 送 (V) send, deliver (things); escort; send off; present (a gift)

sung·ban 送殯 (VO) to attend a funeral

sung·chè 送車 (VO) see someone off by train

sung·chìuh 宋朝 (At) Sung Dynasty (A.D. 960–1280)

. . . sūng·dí ⋯鬆啲 (Pat) a little over /Léuhng·go láih·baai sūng·dí. A little over two weeks. /Yāt·chek sūng·dí. A little over a foot.

sung·(fēi·)gèi 送(飛)機 (VO) see someone off by plane

sung·hàhng 送行 (V) to see someone off

sung·jong 送葬 (VO) to attend a funeral

sung·láih 送禮 (VO) give or send a gift

sung·syùhn 送船 (VO) to see someone off by ship

sung·syún 送船 (VO) to see someone off by ship

sùng·yàhn 鬆人 (VO) sneak away

syù 書 (N) book (M: bún)

syù 輸 (V) lose (as a game, etc.)

syu 處 (P) a place /nī·syu, here; gó·syu, there

syù·chín 輸錢 (VO) lose money by gambling

syù·dóu 輸賭 (V) bet; wager

syù·fóng 書房 (N) study room (M: gàan)

syù·fuhk 舒服 (SV) comfortable

syú·ga 暑假 (N) summer vacation

syù·gá 書架 (N) bookshelf

syù·gei 書記 (N) a secretary

syù·gún 書館 (N) school

syù·gwaih 書櫃 (N) bookcase

syù·hyut 輸血 (VO) give a blood transfusion

syu·mouh 庶務 (N) an office manager, one who takes care of the general affairs in an organization syù·pèih 書皮 (N) book cover

syù·seun·gún 書信館 (N) post office (term used in Hong Kong)

syū·sīk 舒適 (SV) comfortable

syù·tói 書枱 (N) desk (M: jèung)

syuh 樹 (N) tree (M: pò)

syuh·gàau 樹膠 (N) rubber

syùh·jái 薯仔 (N) potato

syuh·jī 樹枝 (N) branches of a tree, bough

syuh·làhm 樹林 (N) woods

syuh·muhk 樹木 (N) trees (collectively)

syuh·pèih 樹皮 (N) bark (of a tree)

syuh·yihp 樹葉 (N) leaf of a tree

syuh·yíng 樹影 (N) shadow of a tree; or a tree's reflection on water

syùhn 船 (N) ship, boat, steamship

syúhn 舐* (V) suck, lick

syùhn·chōng 船艙 (N) cabin (in a ship)

syùhn·fùng 旋風 (N) cyclone

syùhn·jéung 船長 (N) captain (of a ship)

syùhn·jyún 旋轉 (V) to whirl; revolve

syùhn·méih 船尾 (N) stern

syùhn·sàn 船身 (N) hull (of a ship)

syùhn·tàuh 船頭 (N) bow (of a ship)

syùn 酸 (SV) be sour

syún 選 (V) select; elect

syun 算 (V) be regarded as

syūn 孫 (N) grandson

syùn·bou 宣佈 (V) announce

syún·chēut·lèih 選出離* (V) select; elect (lit. select out)

syùn·chyùhn 宣傳 (N/V) propaganda /propagate

syún·géui 選舉 (N/V) election /elect

syun·haih 算係 (Ph) consider as

syun·haih gám la 算係嘅*啦 (IE) It is all right, I think you can't be too fussy about it.

syún·hoih 損害 (V/N) damage; injure /injury; damage

syún·hou 損耗 (N) damage, loss

syún·jaahk 選擇 (V) select; choose

syūn·jī 酸枝 (N) Chinese ebony

syun·mehng 算命 (VO) tell fortunes

syun·pùhn 算盤 (N) abacus

syún·sāt 損失 (V/N) lose /loss

syún·sèung 損傷 (V/N) injure; damage /injury; damage

syun·tàuh 蒜頭 (N) garlic

syún-yàhn-leih-géi 損人利己 (IE) to injure others and benefit one-self

syut 雪 (N) snow

syut·chòhng 雪藏 (V) keep something cold; on ice

syut·gōu 雪糕 (N) ice cream

syut·gwaih 雪櫃 (N) icebox, refrigerator

syut·jùng-sung-taan 雪中送炭 (IE) to give timely aid (lit. to send charcoal to a friend when it snows)

syut·lèih 雪梨 (N) russet pear

syut·wah 說話 (N) speech (spoken words)

T

táahm 淡 (SV) insipid

tàahm·pun 談判 (V/N) negotiate /negotiation

tàahm·wá 談話 (V/N) converse /conversation

tàahn·hēung·muhk 檀香木 (N) sandalwood

tàahn·kàhm 彈琴 (VO) play a stringed or wind instrument

tàahn·ngaat 彈壓 (V) suppress (a mob)

taai 太 (A) too

tāai 呔* (N) necktie (M: tìuh)

tāai 呔* (N) tire (transliterated) (M: tìuh)

taai·douh 態度 (N) attitude

taai·gwo 太過 (Ph) to go too far; out of proportion; overdo

taai·hauh 太后 (N) mother of the emperor

taai·hùng 太空 (N) outer space

taai·jí 太子 (N) the crown prince

taai-pìhng-mòuh-sih 太平無事 (IE) peaceful

taai·táai 太太 (N) Mrs., madam; wife (polite)

taai·yèuhng 太陽 (N) the sun

táaih 胦* (N) steering wheel; rudder

tàam 貪 (SV/V) covetous; greedy /because of /Ngóh jyuh·hái nī·syu tàam kéuih lèih hohk·haauh káhn. I live here because it's close to the school.

taam 探 (V) visit

taam·behng 探病 (VO) visit a patient

taam·jiu·dāng 探照燈 (N) search-light

tàam·sàm 貪心 (SV) covetous, greedy

tàam·tòuh 貪圖 (V) desire greedily /tàam·tòuh mìhng·leih, desire greedily fame and gain

taam·yiht 探熱 (VO) take temperature

taam·yiht·jām 探熱針 (N) thermometer (for taking a person's temperature) (an atmospheric thermometer is called 'hòhn·syú·bíu')

taan 嘆* (V) enjoy (oneself) /Néih jàn·haih wúih taan la! You really know how to enjoy yourself!

taan 嘆 (V) sigh; moan

taan 炭 (N) charcoal (M: gauh)

táan·baahk 坦白 (SV/V) frank /tell the truth

tàan·dung 攤凍 (V) cool; to wait till something gets cold

taan·hei 嘆氣 (VO) sigh

taan·hei 崇氣 (N) carbon dioxide

táan·hāk·chè 坦克車 (N) tank (military)

tàan·hòi 攤開 (RV) to spread out (books, papers), spread thin

táan·wuh 袒護 (V) to side with, to protect a person (with prejudice)

taap 塔 (N) pagoda (M: joh)

taat·sà·yú 撻沙魚 (N) sole (fish)

taat·sou 撻數 (VO) to get away without paying one's debts

táhm 氹 (N) a hole in the ground (with water or mud in it), a pit

tàhng 籐 (N) rattan

tàhng·gip 籐篋 (N) rattan case

tàhng·jehk 籐蓆 (N) rattan mat

tàhng·láam 籐籃 (N) rattan basket

tài 梯 (N) ladder (M: bá)

tái 睇 (V) look; read; watch; check

tái 睇 (V) depend on, determined by, contingent upon

tai 替 (CV/V) in place of /substitute for

tai 剃 (V) shave /tai·sòu, shave (beard)

tái·baahk 睇白 (MA) obviously

tāi·bōu 鋁煲 (N) aluminum pot

tái·chòu 體操 (N) physical training, athletic drill

tái·chúhng 體重 (N) body weight

tái·chyùn 睇穿 (RV) be beyond all earthly cares

tái·dài 睇低 (RV) despise; undervalue

tái·dāk·chēut 睇得出 (RV) able to find out by seeing

tai·doih 替代 (V) in place of

tái·faat 睇法 (N) way of looking at things

tái·fùng·tàuh 睇風頭 (VO) waiting to see how the wind blows

tái·gàang 睇更 (VO) to watch (a night watch)

tái·gin 睇見 (V) see

tai·gūng 替工 (VO) to take another's place in work

tái·gwo 睇過 (V) seeing how things are before a decision is made; see how . . .; see whether . . .

tái·hèng 睇輕 (V) to hold lightly

tái·jàn 睇真 (Ph) look more carefully

tái·jing 睇症 (VO) diagnose, examine disease

tái·jung 睇中 (RV) find something which meets one's desire

tái·jyuh 睇住 (V) stare at; keep one's eyes on

tái lèih chau la 睇嚟湊 (IE) It all depends.

tái·lihk 體力 (N) physical strength

tái·mahk 睇脈 (VO) to diagnose

tái . . . mihn·seuhng 睇 . . . 面上 (Pat) for (someone's) sake /Tái ngóh mihn·seuhng yùhn·leuhng kéuih nī·yāt·chi lā. Please forgive him this time for my sake.

tái·mùhn·háu 睇門口 (VO) to take care of a house

tai·sān 替身 (N) a substitute

tái·síu 睇小 (V) despise; to hold lightly

tai·sòu 剃鬚 (VO) shave (beard)

tái·tau 睇透 (RV) see through

tái·tip 體貼 (V) be considerate of; sympathize with

tai·wuhn 替換 (V/N) replace, substitute /replacement

tái·yuhk·gún 體育館 (N) gymnasium (M: gàan)

tàih 堤 (N) dike

tàih·baht 提拔 (V) promote; elevate

tàih·chèung 提倡 (V) promote; advocate

tàih·chìhn 提前 (A) give precedence to (an item of business); advance the schedule

tàih·fòhng 提防 (V) beware of

tàih·gahp 提及 (V) mention

tàih·gòu 提高 (V) raise (price, morale, etc.); elevate

tàih·muhk 題目 (N) theme; subject; heading

tàih·sàhn 提神 (SV) stimulant (such as tea, coffee)

tàih·séng, tàih·síng 提醒 (V) caution; warn, remind

tàih-siu-gàai-fèi 啼笑皆非 (IE) a situation in which one can neither laugh it off nor lose one's control

tàih·yi 提議 (V) to propose for discussion

tam 氹 (V) coax (a child); fool, deceive

tam·sai·mān·jai 氹細蚊仔 (V) to amuse children

tàn 吞 (V) devour, swallow

tan (·hauh) 褪(後) (V) back up

tan·lāt 褪 (V) slip off

tàu 偷 (V) steal

táu 抖 (V) rest

tau·chit 透切 (SV) to the point, thorough

tau·fó　透火　(VO) light a fire

táu·hei　唞*氣　(VO) breathe; exhale

tàu·jáu　偷走　(V) steal away, sneak away

tau·jeuhk　透着　(RV) kindle a fire

táu·lèuhng　唞*涼　(V) to cool oneself outdoors or in a shady area

tau·sàm·lèuhng　透心涼　(Ph) refreshingly cool

tāu·tāu·déi　偷偷哋　(A) stealthily

tàu·yéh　偷野*　(VO) steal, steal things

tàuh　頭　(N/V) head /end (of a street etc.)

tàuh　頭　(SP) first (ordinalizing prefix—denotes the first one of a series)

tàuh·bīu　投標　(VO) bid for contract

tàuh·bō　頭波　(N) first gear

tàuh·chèuhng　頭場　(Ph) first show

tàuh·dáng　頭等　(N) first class

tàuh·faat　頭髮　(N) hair (on the head)

tàuh·gēi　投機　(V) speculate

tàuh·gēi·sāang·yi　投機生意　(N) speculation

tàuh·hòhng　投降　(V) surrender

tàuh·hói　投海　(V) to drown oneself (in the sea)

tàuh·hok　頭壳　(N) head

tàuh·hok·déng　頭壳頂　(N) top of the head

tàuh·jéung　頭獎　(N) first prize

tàuh·jì　投資　(V) invest money in

tàuh·piu　投票　(VO) vote by ballot

tàuh·séui　投水　(VO) to drown oneself

tàuh·sīn　頭先　(MA) just a while ago

tàuh·séuih　頭緒　(N) clue; way; means connection (lit. thread of a thing)

tàuh-syú-geih-hei　投鼠忌器　(IE) one hesitates to throw something at the rat when the rat is next to something valuable

tàuh·tung　頭痛　(V/N) have a headache /headache

tàuh·wàhn　頭暈　(V/N) to feel dizzy /dizziness

téhng　艇　(N) small boat or sampan (M: jek)

téhng·gā　艇家　(N) "Boat People" floating population

tek　踢　(V) kick /tek bō, play football; tek yīn, kick 'shuttlecock' (a Chinese game)

tèng　聽　(V) listen

tēng　廳　(N) living room

tèng jān　聽真　(Ph) listen more intently

tèng·màhn　聽聞　(V) hear

tèng màhn góng　聽聞講　(Ph) it is said

tèng màhn wah　聽聞話　(Ph) it is said

tèng·túng　聽筒　(N) stethoscope

tèng·wah　聽話　(SV) obedient

teui(·yeuhng)　退讓　(V) to give precedence

tēui·chāk　推測　(V) conjecture; infer

teui·chēut　退出　(V) evacuate; withdraw from

tèui·chìh　推辭　(V) decline, refuse (generally used intransitively)

tèui·séung　推想　(N) inference; deduction

teui·sìu　退燒　(VO) return to normal temperature

teui·yiht　退熱　(VO) return to normal temperature

tìhm　甜　(SV) be sweet

tìhm·bāau　甜包　(N) steamed bread with sweet stuffing

tìhm·maht　甜蜜　(SV) sweet

tìhm-yìhn-maht-yúh　甜言蜜語　(Ph) flattery (sweet and honeyed words)

tìhn　填　(V) fill up; fill in

tìhn　田　(N) rice field; farmland (M: faai; máuh, acre)

tìhn·bīn　田邊　(PW) side of rice field

tìhn·bíu　填表　(VO) fill in a form

tìhn·fòhng　填房　(N) wife of a remarried widower

tìhn·gāi　田雞　(N) frog (M: jek)

tìhn·gēi　田基　(N) field dikes

tìhn·mehng　填命　(VO) to be held responsible for a life lost

tìhn·pìhng　填平　(RV) fill up (a hole in the ground, etc.)

tìhng　停　(V) stop, cease, discontinue; park /tìhng gùng, cease work; tìhng chè, stop a vehicle; tìhng jin, stop fighting; tìhng ga chè hái gó·syu, park the car there

tìhng·chè·chèuhng　停車場　(N) parking area

tìhng·deuhn　停頓　(V) be suspended; come to a halt

tìhng·dihng　停定　(V) stop, come to a standstill

tìhng·jí　停止　(V) cease, discontinue

tìm　嚐*　(P) a sentence final meaning 'more' or 'also' /Sihk dī tīm fā. Eat some more. Tim dī lā? How about adding a little more to your offer? — i.e. salesman trying to persuade customer to go a little higher in his bargaining. /Yiu dī tim. (I) need more. /Hóu pèhng tìm. Moreover, it is quite cheap.

tīm dìng　添丁　(VO) bear a son

tīm-dìng-faat-chòih　添丁發財　(IE) wish you to have a baby and make a fortune (New Year's greeting) tìm·ji 添置 (V) buy and add to what one already has

tìn 天 (N) sky; heaven

tìn·bīn 天邊 (PW) great distance (lit. skyline)

tìn chìhng 天晴 (Ph) the weather has cleared

tìn·fā 天花 (N) smallpox

tìn·fà·báan 天花板 (N) ceiling

tìn·gwòng 天光 (Ph) day breaks, day dawns

tìn·hāak, tìn·hāk 天黑 (Ph) the day gets dark

tìn·hùng 天空 (PW) sky, space

tìn·hei 天氣 (N) weather

tìn·hei·bou·gou 天氣報告 (N) meteorological reports

tìn·hóhn 天旱 (At) dry weather

tìn·jéng 天井 (N) a small courtyard (usually with glass roof)

tìn·jí 天子 (N) the emperor (lit. Son of Heaven)

tìn·jòi 天災 (N) natural disasters

Tìn·jyú 天主 (N) God (Roman Catholic term)

Tìn·jyú·gaau 天主教 (At/N) Catholic /Catholicism

tìn·jyú·tòhng 天主堂 (N) a Catholic church

tìn·léih·chèuhn·wàahn 天理循環 (IE) heaven's law works around in time

tìn·màhn 天文 (At) astronomy

tìn·màhn·hohk·gā 天文學家 (N) astronomer

tìn·màhn·tòih 天文台 (N) astronomical observatory

tìn·mòuh·jyuht·yàhn·jì·louh 天無絕人之路 (IE) while there is hope, there is a way (lit. the heavens never lead one to a dead end road)

tìn·mūng·gwòng 天矇光 (At) at dawn

tìn·páang 天棚 (N) rooftop terrace

tìn·sàang 天生 (At) innate, born with

tìn·sàang·tìn·yéuhng 天生天養 (IE) heaven produces, heaven will nourish

tìn·si 天使 (N) angel

tìn·sìh 天時 (N) weather

tìn·sin 天線 (N) antenna

tìn·sing 天性 (N) natural disposition; instinct

tìn·tói 天台 (N) a terrace, rooftop

tìn yàm 天陰 (Ph) cloudy weather

tìn-yáuh-bāt-chāk-jì-fùng-wàhn, yàhn-yáuh-daan-jihk-jì-woh-fūk 天有不測風雲,人有旦夕禍福 (IE) There are always unpredicted storms in the sky and unpredicted bliss or misfortune in this world.

tìn·yìhn, tìn·yìn 天然 (At) innate; natural

tíng 梃 (M) kind, sort of

ting 聽 (V) allow, let /Ting kéuih la. Let him do as he will.

ting·hauh 聽候 (V) wait for /ting·hauh sīu·sīk, wait for news

tìng·jìu·jóu 聽朝早 (TW) tomorrow morning

tìng·máahn 聽晚 (TW) tomorrow evening

tìng·yaht 聽日 (TW) tomorrow

tip 貼 (V) paste up, glue on, stick on; affix /tip gou·sih, to post up a proclamation; tip gòu·yeuhk, to put on a medicated plaster

tīp·sí 貼士 (N) tips (transliterated)

tit·chéui 鐵鎚 (N) hammer

tit·dēng 鐵釘 (N) iron nail (M: háu)

tit·gaap 鐵甲 (N) armor plates

tit·gaap·chè 鐵甲車 (N) armored car; armored train

tit·gwái 鐵軌 (N) rail (railroad)

tit·jaahp 鐵閘 (N) iron gate

tit·jāt 鐵質 (N) iron (as a natural element)

tit·kìuh 鐵橋 (N) steel bridge (M: tìuh)

tit·louh 鐵路 (N) railroad (M: tìuh)

tit·pín 鐵片 (N) iron plate

tit·sín 鐵線 (N) iron wire (M: tìuh)

tiu·gòu 跳高 (VO) to make a high jump

tiu·láu 跳樓 (VO) to jump down from a building (suicide)

tiu·móuh 跳舞 (VO) dance

tiu·pèih 佻皮 (SV) mischievous

tiu·saan 跳傘 (VO) bail out, jump with a parachute

tiu·séui 跳水 (VO) to jump into the water (suicide); diving

tiu·síng 跳繩 (VO) jumping rope; rope jumping

tiu·syún 挑選 (V) select, choose

tīu·tīk 挑剔 (SV) fastidious

tiu·yúhn 跳遠 (VO) to make a broad jump; broad jump

tìuh 條 (M) measure for 'gāai' street, 'só·sìh' key, etc.

tìuh·gín 條件 (N) condition, terms of contract, articles; item (of documents, etc.)

tìuh·jíng 調整 (V) adjust, regulate

tìuh·laih 條例 (N) rules, regulations, bylaws

tìuh·meih 調味 (VO) to season

tìuh·wàhn 調勻 (RV) to blend

tìuh·yéuhng 調養 (V) recuperate

tìuh·yeuk 條約 (N) treaty

tò 拖 (V) pull, tow, drag

tò 拖 (V) stall

tò·chèuhng 拖長 (V) prolong

tò·háai 拖鞋 (N) slippers (M: deui, pair)

tò lāai sáu 拖拉手 (Ph) hand in hand

tò·jyuh 拖住 (V) to lead by hand

tòh 舵 (N) helm, rudder

tóh 妥 (RVE) properly, suitably; agreeably /Gó·gihn sih yíh·gìng jouh·tóh la. That matter has already been taken care of properly.

tòh·bui 駝背 (N) humpbacked

tóh·dong 妥當 (SV) well-fixed, well-settled, well-managed

tòh·leuih 拖累 (V) involve, implicate

tòhng 糖 (N) sugar

tòhng·chāan 唐餐 (N) Chinese food

Tòhng·chìuh 唐朝 (At) the T'ang Dynasty (A.D. 618–907)

tòhng·gwó 糖菓 (N) candies and preserves

tòhng·hìng·daih 堂兄弟 (N) male cousins on the father's side

tohng·mēi 塘蝨* (N) dragonfly (M: jek)

tòhng·jí·múi 堂姊妹 (N) female cousins on father's side

tòhng·jōng 唐裝 (N) Chinese dress (M: gihn; tyut, suit)

Tòhng·yàhn·fauh 唐人埠 (PW) Chinatown

tòi 胎 (N) the pregnant womb

tói 枱 (N) table, desk (M: jèung)

tói·bō 枱波 (N) billiard

tói·dái 枱底 (PW) underneath a table

tói·mín 枱面 (PW) tabletop

tòih 抬 (V) carry between two or more persons

tòih·gíu 抬轎 (VO) carry a sedan chair

tok 托 (V) hold in the palm

tok 託,托 (V) entrust; request

tok 托 (V) to carry on the shoulder

tok·daaih·geuk 托大脚 (VO) to act or speak in an obsequious or servile manner; to flatter

tok·laaih 托賴 (IE) Thank you (in answering the greeting 'How are you?' Lit. 'I am fine, due to your blessing')

tok pún 托盤 (N) tray

tok·yàhn·chìhng 托人情 (VO) to

rely on someone's good will to do something

tòng 劏 (V) kill, butcher

tòng 湯 (N) soup

tóng 糖 (N) candy (M: nāp, piece)

tong 趟 (N) a time, occurence, trip

tong 攤* (V) open (sliding window or door)

tong·dáu 熨斗 (N) a flatiron

tóng·waahk 倘或 (MA) if, supposing

tóng·yeuhk 倘若 (MA) if, supposing

tóu·cháan 土產 (N) local produce

tóu·féi 土匪 (N) bandits

tóu·gou 禱告 (V/N) pray (to God) /prayer

tou·háu·séui 吐口水 (VO) spit

tou·jái 兔仔 (N) hare; rabbit (M: jek)

tóu·leuhn 討論 (V/N) discuss (in order to solve a problem) /discussion

tòuh 圖 (N) chart; drawing (M: fūt)

tòuh 淘 (V) wash out /tòuh máih, wash the rice; tòuh jéng, clean a well

tóuh 肚 (N) belly

tòuh·dái 徒弟 (N) apprentice

tòuh·jáu 逃走 (V) run away from, flee

tòuh·jēung 圖章 (N) personal seal

tòuh·jùng 途中 (TW) on the road

tòuh-lòuh-mòuh-gùng 圖勞無功 (Ph) to labor in vain

tóuh·ngoh 肚餓 (SV) hungry

tóuh·ngò, tóuh·ò 肚痾 (V/N) have diarrhea /diarrhea

tóuh·se 肚瀉 (V/N) have diarrhea /diarrhea

tòuh·syù·gún 圖書館 (N) library

tóuh·tung 肚痛 (V/N) stomach-aches /stomach-ache /Ngóh tóuh·tung. My stomach aches. /Ngóh yáuh dī tóuh·tung. I have a little stomach-ache.

tòuh·wá 圖畫 (N) picture (not photograph) (M: fūk)

tùhng 同 (CV) be similar; be alike (should be used in the following patterns) A tùhng B sèung·tùhng, A and B are similar; A tùhng B m̀h·sèung·tùhng, A and B are not similar

tùhng(·màaih) 同(埋) (CV) with, and, for /Ngóh·tùhng(·màaih) néih heui. I will go with you.

tùhng·bàau 同胞 (At/N) children of same parents /brethren /Kéuih·deih haih tùhng·bàau hìng·daih. They are full brothers.

tùhng·behng-sèung-lìhn 同病相憐 (IE) in the same boat

tùhng·chè 同車 (A/VO) on the same car or train /go on the same car or train

tùhng·chìhng 同情 (V) sympathize

tùhng·chìhng·sàm 同情心 (N) sympathy

tùhng-chòhng-yih-mùhng 同牀異夢 (IE) partners having contrary objectives; party members holding opposite views (lit. to be in the same bed dreaming different dreams)

tùhng . . . dá yuh·fòhng·jām 同 . . . 打預防針 (Ph) give an inoculation to

tùhng·gèi 同機 (A/VO) on the same plane /go on the same plane

tùhng·hēung 同鄉 (N) fellow townsmen (persons from the same town or village)

tùhng·hohk 同學 (VO/N) go to the same school together /schoolmate

tùhng·hohk·wúi 同學會 (N) alumni association

tùhng . . . hōi dōu 同 . . . 開刀 (Ph) perform an operation on

tùhng-jàu-guhng-jai 同舟共濟 (IE) (people) helping each other while in the same boat (i.e. in difficulty)

tùhng·jeuhng 銅像 (N) statue

tùhng·ji 同志 (N) comrade

tùhng·jùng 同宗 (At) having a common ancestor

tùhng·júng 同種 (At) of same species

tùhng·ngūk (·jyú) 同屋(主) (VO/N) live in the same house

tùhng·pín 銅片 (N) plate of copper or bronze (M: faai, sheet)

tùhng·sìh 同時 (MA) at the same time, meanwhile

tùhng·sih 同事 (VO/N) work in the same place /co-worker, colleague

tùhng·syùhn 同船 (A/VO) on the same ship /go on the same ship

tùhng . . . tùhng . . . 同 . . . 同 (Pat) to work (or study or travel) together with /Ngóh tùhng kéuih tùhng·sih. He and I work together (at the same office, etc.).

tùhng·yàuh 桐油 (N) wood oil

tùhng·yàuh·fùi 桐油灰 (N) wood oil putty

tùhng·yi 同意 (V/N) agree /agreement, permission

túng 桶 (M/N) bucket /barrel, pail

tung 痛 (SV) hurt, ache; be sore

tung·faai 痛快 (SV) delighted; content

tung·fú 痛苦 (SV/N) bitter /suffering

túng·gai 統計 (N/V) statistics /to conduct a statistical study

tùng·gou 通告 (N) notice, a bulletin

tùng·gwo 通過 (V) pass through /pass (a bill, a proposition, etc.)

tùng·hàhng·jing 通行証 (N) identification card, pass

tùng·hei 通氣 (SV) be ventilated; accommodating

tùng·heui 通去 (V) pass through to

tùng·jì 通知 (V) inform, notify

tùng·jì . . . yāt·sèng 通知 . . . 一聲 (Ph) notify (the word 'yāt·sèng' meaning 'one sound' is superfluous, but it's quite commonly used in speaking)

tùng·sèuhng 通常 (MA) usually

tùng·seun 通信 (VO) correspond

tùng·sèung 通商 (V) commerce (with foreign nation)

tūng·sèung·háu·ngohn 通商口岸 (N) a port

tùng·seun·séh 通訊社 (N) news agency

tùng·sing 通勝 (N) almanac

tūng·sīu 通宵 (N) whole night through

tūng·tūng 通通 (A) all in all

túng·yāt 統一 (V) unify

tùng·yùhng 通融 (V) facilitate, ask for a favor

tyúhn 斷 (SV) be broken (into two parts)

tyùhn·git 團結 (V/SV) unite /closely united

tyùhn·tái 團體 (N) a group, an organization

tyùhn·yùhn 團圓 (V) have a family reunion

tyut 脫 (V) to undress; to take off

tyut 脫 (M) suit for clothes

tyut·hím 脫險 (Ph) out of danger

tyut·fuhk 脫服 (VO) to put aside mourning clothes

tyut·lèih 脫離 (V) disengage from; disentangle; clear

U

ung·gòng 甕缸 (N) water jar

W

wá 話 (N) spoken language

wá 畫 (N) painting (M: fūk)

wá 擇 (V) scratch

wá·bou 畫報 (N) pictorial periodical (weekly, monthly, etc.) (M: bún)

wá·gā 畫家 (N) painter

wá·pín 畫片 (N) slides

waahk·fàn 劃分 (V) to divide; distinguish between

waahk·jé 或者 (MA) may, maybe; perhaps; or

waahk·jīk·sī 畫則師 (N) architect; designer

waahk·tòuh 畫圖 (VO) draw a chart or map

waahk·wá 畫畫 (VO) paint a picture

wàahn 還 (A) still; yet (lit.)

wàahn 還 (V) return (something)

waahn-dāk-waahn-sāt 惠得惠失
(IE) while they have not attained their
anxiety is how to attain them; when they
have attained them, their anxiety is
that they might lose them.

waahn·dāng 幻燈 (N) slide show

wàahng·dihm 橫掂 (MA) anyway; any-
how

wàahn·ga 還價 (VO) offer a price

wáahn·gau 挽救 (V) save (a situation)

wàahn·gíng 環境 (N) environment

wàahn·gu 頑固 (SV) obstinate, stubborn

wáahn·làuh 挽留 (V) detain

wáahn·lyún 輓聯 (N) funeral scrolls

waahn·naahn 患難 (N) adversity

wàahn·pèih 頑皮 (SV) naughty; disobedient

waahn·seuht 幻術 (N) magic, magical
arts

wàahn·sàhn 還神 (VO) offer a sacrifice
to thank a god

wàahn·sèui 還需 (Ph) still need (lit.)

wàahn·yàuh-sai-gaai 環遊世界
(Ph) tour around the world

waaht 滑 (SV) be slippery; smooth

waaht·kài 滑稽 (SV) be comical, funny,
humorous

waaht·lauh 滑漏 (SV) smooth, slippery

wāai·ōu·lín 歪嘔哽* (N) violin
(transliterated)

waaih 壞 (SV) bad (in character); things
out of order

waaih·chyu 壞處 (N) bad (aspect), disadvantage

wàaih·yahn 壞人 (VO) pregnant

wàaih·yìh 懷疑 (V) suspect, to harbor
suspicion

wáan 玩 (V) play, enjoy or amuse oneself, play (musical instruments)

wāan 灣 (V) bend

wāan·kūk 彎曲 (SV) winding, crooked
bent

wàan·màaih 彎埋 (V) to anchor, tie up

waat 挖 (V) dig, scoop out

wah 話 (V) say

wah 話 (V) advise, admonish (as for
discipline)

wah·jauh·gám·wah·là 話就嗽話啦
(IE) Yes, you may say so but . . . ;
It is easy to say so.

wah·jauh·wah . . . daahn·haih . . .
話就話 · · · 但係
(IE) it is said . . . but . . . ; so to
speak, but . . .

wah·jauh·wah . . . kèih·saht . . .
話就話 · · · 其實 · · ·
(IE) it is said . . . ; but . . . ; so to speak,
but . . .

wàh·kìuh 華僑 (N) overseas Chinese

wàh·léih 華里 (M) Chinese li (measure
of distance)

wah·méng 話名 (A) make a pretense
that . . .

wah·m̀h·tèng 話唔聽 (RV) can't make
one obey what has been said (these RV
can only be used in the potential form, i.e.
'wah·dāk·tèng' 'wah·m̀h·tèng' or 'm̀h·wah·
dāk·tèng'. There is no such saying as
'wah tèng la' or 'móuh wah tèng').

wah·saht 話實 (RV) say definitely

wah·sih 話事 (V) be in charge

wàhn 雲 (N) cloud (M: pin)

wàhn 暈 (SV/V) be dizzy /faint

wàhn 匀 (RVE) all over

wàhn 匀 (P) variant of the verb suffix
'gwo' indicating experience

wahn 運 (V) transport

wàhn·chèuhn 匀純 (SV) evenly

wahn·chēut·háu 運出口 (V) export

wahn·duhng 運動 (V/N) exercise
(physically) /movement, campaign

wahn·duhng·chèuhng 運動場
athletic field; stadium

wahn·hahp 混合 (V) mix

wahn·hei 運氣 (N) luck

wahn·hòh 運河 (N) canal

wàhn·lohng 暈浪 (SV) be seasick; be
dizzy

wàhn·paak 魂魄 (N) spirit, apparition

wàhn·sehk 雲石 (N) granite

wàhn·wán·déi 暈暈哋 (SV) be a little
dizzy

wahn·yahp·háu 運入口 (V) import

wái 位 (M) for person (polite)

wái 位 (N) seat

wai 喂 (V) feed; suckle

wái·bóng 譭謗 (V) to slander; backbite

wài·hip 威脅 (V/N) threaten /menace

wái·kūk 委曲 (SV) grievous; unjust

wai·mahn 慰問 (V) make a visit to the
sick or poor

wái·miht 毀滅 (V) exterminate

wái·saht 委實 (A) really; certainly

wài·sih·géi 威士忌 (N) whisky

waih 喂 (P) hello, 'hey'

waih 為 (CV) for, for the sake or purpose
of

waih·bìng 衛兵 (N) bodyguard

wàih·bui 違背 (V) disobey; violate

wàih·cháan 遺産 (N) legacy

wàih·chèuhng 圍墻 (N) wall (surrounding something) (M: douh)

wàih·chìh 維持 (V) maintain, support

waih . . . chit·séung 為 ⋯ 設想 (Ph) to be concerned about /Ngóh·deih yìng·gòi·waih kéuih chit·séung·háh ji dāk boh. We should put ourselves in his place.

wáih·daaih 偉大 (SV) great

waih·dāk 為得 (V) be altruistic

wáih·douh 緯度 (N) degrees of latitude

wàih·duhk 唯獨 (A) with the exception of, only

wàih·faahn 違反 (V) violate

waih . . . fuhk·mouh 為 ⋯ 服務 (Ph) render service to . . .

waih gwok·gà chēut·lihk 為國家 出力 (Ph) to serve the country

waih·háu 胃口 (N) appetite

waih . . . héi·gin 為 ⋯ 起見 (Pat) for the sake of /waih·òn·chyùhn·héi·gin, for the sake of safety

waih·ji 位置 (N) position, location

wàih·jūk 遺嘱 (N) will

wàih·jyuh 圍住 (V) surround

wàih·kwán 圍裙 (N) apron

wàih·maht·léun 唯物論 (N) materialism

wàih·néih·sih·mahn 唯你是問 (IE) I will hold you responsible. /Nǐ·gihn·sih wàih·néih·sih·mahn. I'll hold you responsible for this matter.

waih·sāng 衛生 (At) sanitary

wàih·sihn-jeui-lohk 為善最樂 (IE) There is nothing better in this world than to be benevolent.

wáih·sin 緯綫 (N) parallel of latitude

waih·sīng 彗星 (N) a comet

waih·yahn 為人 (SV) be altruistic

wàih·yāt 唯一 (At) only one; unique

wán 搵 (V) look for

wán·bahn 搵笨 (VO) to make someone a sucker

wán·chín 搵錢 (VO) make money (usually refers to a person; i.e. a person who has the knack of making money)

wán·dihng 穩定 (SV) steady

wàn·douh 溫度 (N) temperature

wán·gūng 搵工 (VO) looking for a job

wàn·jaahp 溫習 (V) review

wán·jahn 穩陣 (SV) be safe; careful; firm

wán·jeuhk·sou 搵著數 (VO) make a sucker out of somebody

wán·sihk 搵食 (V) make a living

wán·wahn 搵勻 (V) look all over

wát·hó 核 (N) fruit stone; pits

wāt·kūk 屈曲 (RV) to bend

wìhng·hahng 榮幸 (SV) privileged (as used in 'It is my privilege . . .')

wìhng·yuh 榮譽 (N) honor, good reputation

wìhng·yúhn 永遠 (A) eternally, forever

woh-bāt-dàan-hàhing 禍不單行 (IE) misfortunes never come singly

wòh 禾 (N) rice (the plant); rice seedling

wòh·gón 禾稈 (N) stalk of rice

wòh-hei-sàng-chòih 和氣生財 (IE) affability brings wealth

wòh·pìhng 和平 (SV/N) be peaceful /peace

wòh·séung 和尚 (N) monk

wohk·cháan 鑊鏟 (N) spatula

wohng 旺 (SV) be prosperous, flourish

wòhng·chyùhn 黃泉 (N) hades

wòhng·dai 皇帝 (N) emperor

wòhng·dáu 黃豆 (N) soybean

wòhng·fūng 黃蜂 (N) wasp

wòhng·gā 皇家 (N) royal family; government (as colloquially used in Hong Kong)

wòhng·gùng 皇宮 (N) the imperial palace

wòhng·gwā 黃瓜 (N) cucumber

wòhng·hauh 皇后 (N) queen

wòhng·júng·yàhn 黃種人 (N) a member of the yellow race

wóhng·sí 往時 (MA) formerly, in the past

wòhng·sīk 黃色 (N) yellow color

wòhng·sīk·ge 黃色嘅 (SV) yellow

wòhng·dáam·behng 黃疸病 (N) jaundice

wòhng·tòhng 黃糖 (N) brown sugar

wóng-fai-sàm-gèi 枉費心機 (IE) waste of effort

wú, wùh 壺 (N) pot

wùh·jìu·fán 胡椒粉 (N) ground pepper

wù·jòu 齷齪 (SV) dirty

wùh 湖 (N) lake

wùh·bīn 湖邊 (PW) lake-side

wùh·díp 蝴蝶 (N) butterfly (M: jek)

wuh·háu 戶口 (N) account in a bank; family (term used in census)

wuh·jiu 護照 (N) passport

wuh·sèung 互相 (A) mutually, each other /Wuh·sèung bòng·joh. Help each other.

wuh·sih 護士 (N) nurse

wùh·tòuh 糊塗 (SV) stupid; muddled, doltish

wuhn 換 (V) change

wuhn·sìhng 換成 (V) change into (other currency), exchange for

wuhn·yìhn·jì 換言之 (Ph) in other words

wuht·duhng 活動 (SV/N) active /activi-
ty
wuht·kèih·chyùhn·fún 活期存欵
(N) commercial bank account
wuht·put 活潑 (SV) be active; be lively
wùi 煨 (V) roast in ashes
wúi 會 (N) meeting, conference; society;
association; union
wúi·yùhn 會員 (N) member (of a society, association, union)
wùih 回,囘(V) reply
wúih 會 (AV) can, know how to, be able
to; may, likely to, might
wùih·baai 回拜 (V) repay a visit
wúih·dá·syun·pùhn 會打算盤
(SV) shrewd
wùih·daap 回答 (V/N) answer
wuih·deui 滙兑 (V) remit
wuih·fai 滙費 (VO) the charge of
remittance
wuih·fún 滙欵 (N) remittance (M: bāt)
Wùih·gaau 回教 (N) Moslem; Islam
wuih·gai 會計 (N) cashier, treasurer;
accountant
wuih·gai·sī 會計師 (N) certified
public accountant
wùih·ging 回敬 (V) return a toast (to
the host or to someone who has toasted
you)
wùih·gwok 回國 (VO) return to one's
country
wuih·haak·sāt 會客室 (N) reception room
wùih·nàahm 回南 (At) (the wind) changing to southward
wuih·piu 滙票 (VO) cashier's check
(M: jèung)
wùih·seun 回信 (VO/N) reply to a letter /reply
wùih·séung 迴想 (V) to recall, recollect
wùih·sìng 迴聲 (N) echo
wùih·típ 回帖 (N) card of acknowledg-
ment (of an invitation, etc.)
wuih·yih, wuih·yi 會議 (N) meeting
for discussion; conference
wún 碗 (N/M) bowl

X

X·gwōng(·geng) 乂光鏡 (N) X ray

Y

yaahp 揰* (V) wave one's fingers in
signaling someone to come over
yáai·dāan·chē 嘥單車 (VO) ride a
bicycle

yah 廿 (NU) twenty
yàhm 淫 (SV) lewd; obscene; dissolute
yahm·hòh 任何 (At) any (has to be followed by a noun when it is used)
yahm gáan 任揀 (Ph) free to choose
yahm·kèih 任期 (N) term of office
yahm·mihng 任命 (V) appoint
yahm·mouh 任務 (N) mission, duty, as-
signment
yahm·sing 任性 (SV) headstrong
yahm(·yàuh) 任(由) (CV) as one pleases;
at one's pleasure, let
yahm·yuhng 任用 (V) employ; appoint
yàhn 人 (N) man, person
yáhn 忍 (V) bear, endure
yáhn 癮 (N) craving; habit
yàhn·chìhng 人情 (N) favor; indulgence
yàhn·chòih 人才 (N) talented person
yáhn·dāk 忍得 (V) bear
yáhn·dāk·jyuh 忍得住 (RV) can endure,
can tolerate
yàhn·deih 人哋 (N) other people
yàhn·deih wah māt maih māt lō 人哋
話乜*咪乜*咯 (IE) whatever people
say, it doesn't matter
yáhn·douh 引導 (N) direct, guide
yàhn·gà 人家 (N) family
yàhn·gaak 人格 (N) personality
yàhn·gùng 人工 (N) wage /yàhn·gùng
hóu góu, the wage is high; yàhn·gùng hóu
dài, the wage is low
yàhn·gùng·jouh·ge 人工做嘅* (At) artificial
yàhn·haak 人客 (N) guest
yàhn·háu 人口 (N) population
yàhn·háu·pìhng·ngòn 人口平安 (IE)
everyone in the family is safe and sound
yàhn·héi 引起 (V) arouse
yáhn·jouh·ge 人造嘅* (At) artificial
yáhn·jyuh·daahm·hei 忍住唥氣
(Ph) hold back one's temper or breath
yàhn·leuih 人類 (N) human race
yàhn·màhn 人民 (N) people (of a country)
yàhn·màhn·baih 人民幣 (N) 'peoples'
currency' (the paper money used in Communist China)
yàhn·màhn·gùng·séh 人民公社
(N) people's commune
yáhn·m̀h·jyuh 忍唔住 (A) can't keep
oneself from . . . /Kéuih yáhn·m̀h·jyuh
siu·hei·séuhng·lèih. He can't keep himself from laughing. /Kéuih yáhm·m̀h·
jyuh nàu·hei·seuhng·leih. He can't keep
himself from being angry.
yàhn·sàan·yàhn·hói 人山人海 (IE)
crowded, masses of people

yáhn·sàm 忍心 (SV) hardhearted; be without emotion

yàhn-sām-bāt-jūk, sèh-tàn-jeuhng 人心不足蛇吞象 (IE) The eyes are always larger than the stomach. (People are always discontented, just like a snake wishing it could swallow an elephant.)

yàhn·sāng·gūn 人生观 (N) philosophy of life

yàhn·sauh·yin·sō 人壽無梳 (N) life insurance

yàhn·só·guhng·jì 人所共知 (IE) it's known by everyone

yáhn·yáuh 引誘 (V) entice; induce

yahp 入 (V) put in; enter; get in; admit (to a club, etc.)

yahp·bihn 入邊 (PW) inside

yahp·gaau 入教 (VO) be a follower of a religion (mostly used to mean 'to be a Christian')

yahp·gíng 入境 (VO) enter a country

yahp·gíng·jing 入境證 (N) permit for entering a country

yahp·háu 入口 (N/VO) import /enter port; import

yahp·háu·fo 入口貨 (N) import commodity

yahp·heui 入去 (V) go in

yahp·jihk 入席 (VO) proceed to dinner table (in a formal party)

yahp·jihk 入籍 (VO) naturalize

yahp·lèih 入嚟 (V) come in

yahp·mùhn·jing 入門証 (N) entrance permit

yahp·sáu 入手 (V) begin (to do something) /Nī·gihn·sih dím·yéung yahp·sáu a? How does one begin this thing?

yahp·sīk 入息 (N) income

yaht 日 (M) day

yaht·gei 日記 (N) diary

yaht·gei·bóu 日記簿 (N) diary (the book)

yaht·hauh 日後 (A) at a later date

yaht·jouh·yeh·jouh 日做夜做 (IE) working day and night

yaht·kèih 日期 (N) an appointed time, date

yaht·lihk 日曆 (N) calendar

yaht·sèuhng 日常 (A) daily

yaht·sihk 日蝕 (N) eclipse of sun

yaht·táu 日頭 (TW/N) daytime/sunshine; sun

yáih 吟 (SV) be bad or poor (in quality)

yám 飲 (V) drink

yám (jáu) 飲(酒) (V) attend a dinner party /Gàm·yaht yáuh·yàhn chéng·(ngóh) yám (·jáu). I'm invited to a dinner party today.

yám·chàh 飲茶 (VO) drink tea; have tea in a teahouse

yám·jeui (·jáu) 飲醉(酒) (V) be drunk

yàm·lihk 陰曆 (N) lunar calendar

yām·diuh 音調 (N) pitch (in music and speech)

yàm·màuh 陰謀 (N) secret plots

yàm·ngohk·gā 音樂家 (N) musician

yàm·ngohk·wúi 音樂會 (N) concert (musical performance)

yám-séui-sì-yùhn 飲水思源 (IE) not to forget the source of good gifts (While one drinks the water, one should think of the origin of the water.)

yám·sihk 飲食 (N) food and drink; diet

yan 印 (V/N) print /seal (used as attestation or evidence of authenticity)

yan·chaat 印刷 (V/N) print /printing

yàn·chí 因此 (A) therefore; for this reason

yán·chòhng 隱藏 (V) conceal

yàn·dín 恩典 (N) favor (given by authority)

yan·jeuhng 印像 (N) impression; image (fig.)

yan·jih·gún 印字館 (N) printing office

yán·mùhn 隱瞞 (V) conceal (a fact)

yàn·saht 殷實 (SV) reliable; well-to-do

yan·séui·jí 印水紙 (N) blotter

yan·sīk 印色 (N) red stamping ink

yàn·sou 因素 (N) element

yan·syù 印書 (VO) printing of books

yàn·waih 因為 (MA) because

yàn·waih ... gwàan·haih 因為...關係 (Ph) due to, because of

yāt 一 (NU) one

yāt·bouh·yāt·bouh 一步一步 (Ph) step by step

yāt·bùn 一般 (At) in general /yāt·bùn yahn, people in general

yāt·bùn·lèih·góng 一般來講 (IE) generally speaking

yāt·chái, yāt·chàih 一齊 (A) together

yāt·chai 一切 (At) all

yāt·chàuh·mohk·jín 一籌莫展 (IE) be at the end of one's wits; have no way out

yāt·chèuhng·hèui·gèng 一場虛驚 (IE) it's a false alarm

yāt·dihng 一定 (A) definitely, certainly, sure

yāt·jài 一劑 (NU+M) one dose (of Chinese herb)

yāt·gaau fan·dou tīn·gwòng 一覺瞓到天光 (IE) sleep the whole night through

yāt-gà-daaih-sai 一家大細 (Ph) the whole family

yāt-gà-sou-háu 一家數口 (Ph) a family of a few people

yāt·go·gwāt 一個骨 (NU+M) one quarter

yāt·guhng 一共 (A) altogether, all told, totally

yāt·hah 一吓 (NU+M) once

yāt·hạh 一吓 (MA) accidentally; suddenly

yāt·háu·yīn 一口煙 (Ph) one cigarette

yāt·hei 一氣 (A) in one action without pause (lit. in one breath) /Nī·gihn sih yùh·gwó yāt·hei·gam jouh·lohk·heui m̀h·sái sàam·go·jūng·tàuh (or jūng·dím) jauh hó·yíh jouh·yùhn la. If we can keep on doing this, it won't take three hours to have it finished.

yāt·heung 一向 (MA) heretofore, from the beginning, until now

yāt·jahn·gāan 一陣間 (TW) (in) a moment, (after) a short while

yāt·jàu·nìhn 一週年 (N) first anniversary

yāt·ji 一致 (V/A) uniform, to be unanimous /uniformly, unanimously

yāt·jihk 一直 (A) directly; straight ahead; has always been (since the beginning)

yāt V V jo 一……咗 (Pat) used for emphasis /kéuih yāt·behng behng·jó léuhng·go·yuht. He was sick for two months. Kéuih yāt·heui heui·jó sàam·nìhn. He had been away for three years.

yāt·jóu 一早 (A) very early

yāt·koi 一概 (A) all, the whole of

yāt·laaht 一剌 (NU+M) a row of

yāt·leih . . . yih·leih . . . 一來…二來… (Pat) in the first place . . . in the second place . . .

yāt·leuht 一律 (A) uniformly, without distinction

yāt·lihn 一連 (A) successively

yāt·louh 一路 (A) along the road; during the whole trip, enroute

yāt-louh-pìhng-ngòn 一路平安 (Ph) A pleasant journey! (A safe trip!)

yāt-louh-seuhn-fùng 一路順風 (Ph) Have a nice trip! (May you have favorable wind all the way!)

yāt.mān·jí 一文*紙 (N) one-dollar banknote

yāt·méi 一味 (A) insistently, persistently

yāt·ngáahn·tái·dóu 一眼睇到 (Ph) see at a glance

yāt-ńgh-yāt-sahp 一五一十 (Ph) (tell something) item by item; (count something) by fives /Kéuih yāt-ńgh-yāt-sahp gám góng·saai béi·ngóh·tèng. He told me everything, item by item. /Yāt-ńgh-yāt-sahp gám sóu·gwo·saai kéuih. He has counted them by fives.

yāt-nìhn-bun-jói 一年半載 (Ph) a year or so

yāt·nìhn·kāp 一年級 (N) first grade

yāt-pàhn-yùh-sái 一貧如洗 (IE) flat broke

yāt·saht 一實 (A) undoubtedly, definitely

yāt·sai 一世 (NU+M) whole lifetime

yāt·sàm 一心 (A) devotedly

yāt·sàng 一生 (N) (in) one's whole life; lifetime

yāt-sāt-jūk-sìhng-chìn-gú-hahn, joi-wùih-tàuh-yíh-baak-nìhn-sàn 一失足成千古恨，再回頭已百年身 (IE) an irremediable mistake (One fall becomes a thousand years of regret; a return is impossible except in a rebirth.)

yāt·sìh 一時 (A) at a certain moment, all of a sudden

yāt·sìh·m̀h·gok·yi 一時唔覺意 (A) slip out

yāt·tyùhn·wòh·hei·gám 一團和氣噉* (A) genially

yāt·waahk 一劃 (NU+M) a stroke (in writing Chinese characters)

yāt·yaht . . . gwo yāt·yaht 一日…過一日 (Pat) day by day /Dī yéh yāt yaht gwei·gwo yāt·yaht. Things are getting more expensive day by day.

yāt·yaht·yāt·yaht·gám 一日一日噉* (A) day by day /Yàhn·háu yāt·yaht yāt·yaht·gám jāng·gà. The population is increasing day by day.

yāt·yeuhng 一樣 (At) the same (kind)

yāt-yìhn-nàahn-jeuhn 一言難盡 (Ph) it is a long story (a literary phrase, literally meaning 'difficult to tell all in a few words')

yāt-yìhn-wàih-dihng 一言為定 (Ph) a promise is a promise

yāt·yù 一於 (A) definitely; insistently, surely will, determinedly

yáu 由 (V) let; leave it (him) as it (he) is

yàu·dím 優點 (N) merits

yàu·doih 優待 (V/N) give a special offer (by a commercial firm) /special offer

yàu·ga 休假 (N) furlough

yàu·jihng 幽靜 (SV) secluded, quiet

yàu·leuih 憂慮 (V/N) worry

yau·sai 幼細 (SV) be fine (in skill or quality)

yàu-sing-lyuht-baaih 優勝劣敗 (IE) survival of the fittest

yàu·yàuh 優遊 (SV) living easily and leisurely

yàuh 遊 (V) tour

yàuh 油 (N) oil

yàuh 由 (CV) through . . . ; by (indication agent) /Yàuh nī·go mùhn·háu chēut·heui. Go out through this door. /Nī·gihn·sih yàuh kéuih dá·léih. This thing will be managed by him.

yáuh 有 (V) have

yauh 又 (A) again

yauh 右 (SV) right

yáuh·bá·ngāak 有把握 (SV/VO) certain /sense of security; have confidence

yáuh·baahn·faat 有辦法 (VO/SV) know how to do it, there is a way to do it /be capable

yáuh·behng 有病 (SV) be sick (cannot be preceded by an adverb, such as hóu, m̀h·haih géi; used as opposite of healthy)

yáuh-beih-mòuh-waahn 有備無患 (IE) forethought prevents distress

yàuh·chàai 郵差 (N) mailman

yáuh·cheui 有趣 (SV) amusing

yáuh·chēut·sīk 有出息 (SV) can make good in life

yàuh-chín-yahp-sàm 由淺入深 (IE) from easy to difficult

yáuh·dī 有啲* (A) somewhat, rather; a little /Yàuh·dī m̀h·haih géi fōng·bihn. It's rather inconvenient. /Gihn sāam yáuh·dī sai. The clothes are a little small.

yáuh·dī 有啲* (N) some, some of, certain (used only in subject) /Yáuh·dī yàhn wah, some people said; yáuh·dī taai sai, some are too small

yáuh·douh·dāk 有道德 (SV) virtuous

yáuh·douh·léih 有道理 (SV) be right; be truthful; be logical, reasonable

yàuh·fai 郵費 (N) postage

yáuh·fán 有份 (V) has something to do with it; has some part in it; has some share in it /Nī·pùhn sàang·yi kéuih dōu yáuh fán ge boh. As far as I can see, he is one of the owners of this business also.

yáuh fàn·sou ge la 有分數嘅*嘛* (Ph) knows how to manage it

yáuh·gāai 遊街 (V/N) parade /a parade

yáuh gam ngāam dāk gam kíu 有咁*啱* 得咁*翹* (Ph) it's such a coincidence

yáuh géi hó nē 有幾何呢 (Ph) have a rare chance /Dím·gáai gam po·fai a? Why should you spend so much money (on me)? /Yáuh géi hó nē. We so seldom have the opportunity to have you as our guest.

yáuh gihn sih faat·sàng 有件事發生 (Ph) a certain thing happens

yáuh góng yáuh siu 有講有笑 (Ph) chatting and laughing

yàuh (·jing)·gúk 郵(政)局 (N) post office

yáuh·haahn 有限 (SV) be limited

yàuh·haak 遊客 (N) tourist

yàuh . . . héi·sáu 由 … 起首 (Pat) start from . . .

yáuh·hing·cheui 有興趣 (SV) be interesting (said of book, story, news, etc.)

yàuh·ja 油炸 (V) cooked in oil

yáuh·jeun·bouh 有進步 (SV) improved (having made progress)

yàuh . . . ji or dou or ji·dou . . . 由 … 至；由 … 到；由 … 至到 (Pat) from a certain time or place to another

yáuh·jyú·yi 有主意 (SV) determined

yáuh·kèih·sih 尤其是 (A) especially

yáuh kéuih góng móuh néih góng 有渠 講冇你 (IE) never give anybody a chance to talk

yàuh·láahm 遊覽 (V) tour

yàuh·láahm·jí·nàahm 遊覽指南 (N) tourist's guidebook

yàuh·láih(·maauh) 有禮(貌) (SV) polite

yàuh·lihk 遊歷 (V) tour

yáuh·lihk 有力 (SV) be strong enough; powerful

yáuh·líu 有料 (SV) learned, intelligent

yáuh māt gwai·gon a? 有乜貴幹呀？ (IE) What can I do for you? (lit. what is your business with me?)

yáuh māt jí·gaau a? 有乜指教呀？ (IE) What can I do for you? (lit. what instruction do you have for me?)

yauh ngò (or ò) yauh ngáu (or áu) 又疴 又嘔 (Ph) has diarrhea and nausea

yáuh·ngoi 友愛 (SV) affectionate to each other (as brothers and sisters)

yàuh·piu 郵票 (N) stamp (M: go)

yáuh·sàm 有心 (IE/SV) It is kind of you to inquire /be thoughtful, considerate

yáuh·sàm·gèi 有心機 (SV) devoted, enthusiastic

yáuh·sàn·géi 有身妮* (At) pregnant

yáuh·sèng·hei 有聲氣 (Ph) hopeful

yàuh·séui 游水 (VO) swim

yàuh·séui·yī 游水衣 (N) swimming suit

yáuh·sìh 有時 (MA) sometimes

yàuh·wihng·chìh 游泳池 (N) swimming pool

yàuh·wihng·yī 游泳衣 (N) bathing suit

yáuh·yahn 有孕 (VO) pregnant /Kéuih yáuh·jó yahn gei nói la? How long has she been pregnant?

yáuh·yi 有意 (A) intentionally

yáuh·yīk 有益 (SV) be beneficial; conducive

yáuh·yīk chyúh 有益處 (3V) be beneficial; conducive

yáuh·yùh 有餘 (V) have more than sufficient

yáuh·yuhng 有用 (SV) useful, helpful

yéh 嘢* (N) thing (M: gihn, or go)

yeh 夜 (M/SV) night /be late at night

yéh·chāan 野餐 (N) picnic (M: chi)

yèh·jí·tóng 椰子糖 (N) coconut candy

yéh·màahn 野蠻 (SV) uncivilized; truculent

yéh·sau 野獸 (N) wild animals

yeh·síh 夜市 (N) night market

Yèh·sōu 耶穌 (N) Jesus

Yèh·sōu·gaau 耶穌教 (At/N) protestant /Protestantism

yèhng 贏 (V) win (as a game, battle, etc.)

yèhng·chín 贏錢 (VO) win money by gambling

yeuhk 藥 (N) medicine

yeuhk·chòih 藥材 (N) herbs used for medicinal purpose

yeuhk·chóng 藥廠 (N) pharmaceutical supply factory

yeuhk·doih 虐待 (V) maltreat; ill-treat; oppress

yeuhk·fai 藥費 (N) medicine charge

yeuhk·fán 藥粉 (N) medicine powder

yehk·fòhng 藥房 (N) drugstore

yeuhk·fōng 藥方 (N) medical prescription

yeuhk·haih 若係 (MA) if; in case

yeuhk·jāi·sī 藥劑師 (N) pharmacist

yeuhk·mh·haih 若唔係 (MA) otherwise

yéuhng 養 (V) raise or keep (animal)

yeuhng 樣 (M) kind; sort

yeuhng·bouh 讓步 (V) give in

yèuhng·chūng 洋蔥 (N) onion

yèuhng·fo 洋貨 (N) foreign goods

yéuhng-fú-wàih-waahn 養虎為患 (IE) to invite misfortune (lit. raising a tiger to cause trouble)

yéuhng gāi 養雞 (Ph) raise or keep chickens

yéuhng gàm·yú 養金魚 (Ph) raise or keep goldfish

yéuhng gáu 養狗 (Ph) keep a dog

yéuhng·hei 氧氣 (N) oxygen

yèuhng·hóng 洋行 (N) foreign firm

yéuhng jéuk 養雀 (Ph) keep a bird

yèuhng·jūk 洋燭 (N) candle (lit. imported candle, the term for candle locally made is laahp·jūk)

yéuhng·jyū 養珠 (N) cultured pearl

yèuhng·lihk 陽曆 (N) solar calendar

yeuhng·louh 讓路 (V) give the right of way

yéuhng māu 養貓 (Ph) keep a cat

yèuhng·tóu 楊桃 (N) carambola (a kind of fruit in Canton area)

yèuhng·yuhk 羊肉 (N) mutton

yēui 錐 (N) an owl

yēui·lūng 錐窿 (VO) to bare a hole

yeuk 約 (V/N) invite, make a date or appointment with /date; appointment

yeuk·mók 約摸 (A) approximately

yeuk·wuih 約會 (N) engagement, appointment

yeuk-yiu-yàhn-bāt-jì, chèuih-fèi-géi-mohk-wàih 若要人不知，除非己莫為 (IE) If you don't want a thing to be known, you must not do it.

yéung 樣 (N) appearance (look), style

yéung·háh 揚吓 (V) shake (a cloth or piece of clothing) /Yéung·háh jèung jīn. Shake the blanket a bit.

yì 醫 (V) give medical care to, cure, treat

yì 衣 (BF) clothing; coat

yì 椅 (N) chair (M: jèung)

yī 姨 (N) maternal aunt

yī·chē 衣車 (N) sewing machine

yì·chi·jeuih 依次序 (Ph) follow an order (succession or sequence)

yì·douh 醫道 (N) medical skill, technique, and experience

yì·fuhk 衣服 (N) clothing

yì·gá 衣架 (N) clothes rack

yì·gauh 依舊 (A) same thing over again, as before, as usual

yi·gin 意見 (N) opinion

yì·gwaih 衣櫃 (N) wardrobe, cabinet for clothes

yi·hohk 醫學 (N) medical science

yì·jiu 依照 (CV) according to

yì·jyuh 依住 (V) according to /Néih maih yì·jyuh kéuih·ge yi·si jouh lō. Just do it according to his will.

yì·kaau 倚靠 (V/N) rely upon, depend upon /reliance

yì·kèih 依期 (A) according to a fixed time

yì·laaih 倚賴 (V/N) depend /dependence

yì·lìuh·só 醫療所 (N) clinic

yì·ngóh·ge·chín·gin 依我嘅淺見 (IE) in my humble opinion, as far as I can see

yi·ngoih 意外 (At/N) unforeseen /un-expected events /Yùh·gwó faat·sàng māt·yéh yi·noih, gam jauh dím·syun a? If something unexpected has happened then what are we going to do?

yì·sāng 醫生 (N) physician

yì·sèuhng 衣裳 (N) clothes

yì·seuht 醫術 (N) medical skill, technique

yi·si 意思 (N) meaning, idea, intention

yi·yih 意義 (N) significance

yì·yún 醫院 (N) hospital (M: gàan)

yih 二 (NU) two

yih 易 (SV) easy

yíh 以 (CV) with

yíh-beih-hàuh-fō 耳鼻喉科 (N) ear-nose-throat department

yìh·bíu 姨表 (N) maternal first cousins

yíh-bīn-fùng 耳邊風 (Ph) to give no heed to; to pay no attention to

yíh·buih 耳瘺* (Ph) hard of hearing

yìh·ché 而且 (MA) besides, moreover, furthermore

yìh·chèuhng 二場 (Ph) second show

yíh·chìhn 以前 (MA) formerly, before, previously; before . . . ; . . . ago (see 'before' and 'ago' in E–C section)

yih·dāk 宜得 (AV/V) would like to be /in need of

yíh-dāk-bou-yun 以德報怨 (IE) to return good for evil

yíh·déu 耳朵 (N) ear (M: jek)

yíh·dáng 二等 (N) second class

yìh·gā 而家 (TW) now, at present

yíh·gìng 已經 (A) already

yíh·hah 以下 (Ph) below a certain number or grade

yíh·hauh 以後 (MA) thereafter, after-wards; from now on; after . . . (see 'after' in E–C section)

yìh·hèi 兒戲 (SV) not serious; superficial; uncertain; precarious (lit. child's play)

yìh·hei 儀器 (N) instruments

yìh-hohk-nàahn-jìng 易學難精 (IE) easy to pick up but hard to learn well

yìh·jái 耳仔 (N) ear (M: jek)

yìh·jéung 姨丈 (N) husband of maternal aunt

yih·jéung 二獎 (N) second prize

yih·jí 二指 (N) forefinger

yih·láu 二樓 (N) second floor; first floor (British system in Hong Kong)

yíh . . . lèih . . . 以 . . . 來 (Pat) to use or employ . . . to . . . /Ngóh·deih yìng·gòi yíh ngóh·deih ge nàhng·lihk waih séh·wúi fuhk·mouh. We should employ our ability to serve society.

yih·leuhn 議論 (V/N) criticize; discuss /criticism

yìh lùhng 耳聾 (Ph) deaf

yìh·mā 姨媽 (N) elder maternal aunt

yìh·míhn 以免 (AV) in order to avoid /Yìh·míhn faat·sàng sih·gu, in order to avoid any accident

yih·móuh 姨母 (N) maternal aunt

yih·mouh 義務 (N) obligation

yìhm·yìh 嫌疑 (N) suspicion

yíh ngóh lèih góng 以我來講 (Ph) take me for instance

yíh ngoih 以外 (Ph) beyond a certain number or limit

yíh noih 以內 (Ph) within a certain number or limit

yìh·sahp·sai·géi 二十世紀 (N) twentieth century

yìh·sàm 疑心 (V) suspect

yíh·seuhng 以上 (Ph) above a certain number or grade

yìh·tēng 二廳 (N) family sitting room

yìh·túng 耳筒 (N) earphone, headset

yíh·wàih 以為 (A) to think that, suppose

yíh . . . wàih . . . 以 . . . 為 . . . (Pat) consider . . . as the . . .

yíh-yāt-tìm-jok-ńgh 二一添作五 (IE) share equally

yíh·yún 議院 (N) parliament

yíh·yùhn 議員 (N) member of parliament

yihk 譯 (V) translate

yihk 亦 (A) also; too, likewise

yihk 翼 (N) wing (bird), (M: jek)

yihk·dōu 亦都 (A) also; too, likewise

yihk bāt·gwo 亦不過 (Ph) nothing but

yihk·chēut 譯出 (RV) translate

yihk·gíng, ngahk·gíng 逆境 (N) adverse circumstances

yihk hóu 亦好 (Ph) all right (lit. also good)

yihk·sìhng 譯成 (V) translate into (other language)

yìhm 嫌 (V) object to, consider with dislike

yìhm 鹽 (N) salt

yìhm 嚴 (SV) be strict

yìhm 染 (V) infect; dye

yìhm·gam 嚴禁 (V) strictly order

yìhm·hei 嫌棄 (V) dislike

yìhm·hyut 驗血 (VO) have or do a blood test

yìhm·juhng 嚴重 (SV) be serious, severe, grave

yìhn·chìh 延遲 (V) delay

yìhn·chín 現錢 (N) cash

yìhn·chèuhng 延長 (V) prolong; extend /yìhn·chèuhng sìh·gaan, increase the time; /yìhn·chèuhng làuh·gîng ge kèih·haahn, extend a visa

yìhn·doih 現代 (At) modern, present time, this generation

yìhn·doih·fa 現代化 (V) modernize

yihn·fo 現貨 (N) regular stock; goods in stock

yìhn·fún 現款 (N) cash

yìhn·gām 現金 (N) cash

yìhn·gau 研究 (V) make special investigation of, make a study of

yìhn·hauh 然後 (A) afterwards; then

yìhn·jeuhng 現象 (N) phenomenon

yìhn·jì·hauh 然之後 (Ph) (a variation of yìhn·hauh)

yìhn·kèih 延期 (V) postpone

yihn·sîng·ge 現成嘅 (At) ready-made

yihng·cho 認錯 (VO) to acknowledge oneself to be in the wrong

yihng·dāk 認得 (V) recognize

yihng·dāk·chēut 認得出 (RV) recognize

yihng·dóu 認到 (RV) recognize

yihng·jàn 認真 (A) seriously

yìhng·jìk hó·yìh 形跡可疑 (Ph) suspicious looking

yìhng·jip 迎接 (V) receive (a guest, visitor, etc.)

yìhng·johng 形狀 (N) shape, form

yìhng·sai 形勢 (N) configuration; features

yìhng·sīk 認識 (V) know (a person); become acquainted with

yìhng·sīk·seuhng·ge fàn·biht 形式上嘅分別 (Ph) difference in form

yìhng·sìhng 形成 (V) form

yìhng·wàih 認為 (AV) consider

yìhng-yàhn-yìh-gáai 迎刃而解 (IE) to solve a problem with ease (lit. it is split as soon as it meets the knife)

yìhng·yéuhng 營養 (N) nutrition

yìhng·yìhn 仍然 (A) still

yìhng·yùhng 形容 (V) describe

yihp·mouh 業務 (N) commercial transactions

yiht 熱 (SV) hot

yiht·douh 熱度 (N) temperature

yiht·douh·jām 熱度針 (N) thermometer

yiht·laaht 熱辣 (SV) piping hot

yiht·naauh 熱鬧 (SV) hustling and bustling

yiht·sàm 熱心 (SV) enthusiastic

yiht·séui·hàuh 熱水喉 (N) hot water faucet

yiht·tīn 熱天 (N) summer

yīk 億 (NU) one hundred million

yīk·chyu, yīk·chyúh 益處 (N) benefit

yīk·waahk 抑或 (MA) or

yim 厭 (RVE) get bored with or get tired of

yim·faahn 厭煩 (SV) troublesome, wearied

yim·gyuhn 厭倦 (V) get tired of

yim·hei 厭棄 (V) disdain

yím·màaih 掩埋 (V) shut (a door, etc.)

yìn 煙,烟 (N/SV) smoke /smoky

yín 燕 (N) swallow (bird)

yín 演 (V) perform (a play, etc.)

yīn 煙,烟 (N) cigarette (M: háu) /yāt·háu·yīn, a cigarette

yīn·dáu 煙斗 (N) pipe (for tobacco)

yìn·fó 煙火 (N) fireworks

yīn·fùi 煙灰 (N) ashes; cigarette ashes

yín·góng 演講 (V/N) to give a speech /a speech

yín·jaahp 演習 (V/N) maneuver /maneuver, drill

yīn·jái 烟仔 (N) cigarette (M: háu)

yīn·jái·dong 烟仔檔 (N) a cigarette stand

yin·jí 燕子 (N) swallow (M: jek)

yin·sō 燕梳 (N) insurance

yīn·táu 烟頭 (N) cigarette butt

yīn·tùng 烟道 (N) chimney

yin·wō 燕窩 (N) edible birds-nest

yin·wuih 宴會 (N) feast, lunch or dinner party

yīn·yēung 鴛鴦 (N) the mandarin duck

yīn·yíp 烟葉 (N) tobacco

yín·yùhn 演員 (N) performer, actor

yíng 影 (N) shadow; reflection

ying 應 (V) answer (the door); respond (to a remark)

yīng 鷹 (N) eagle (M: jek)

yìng.bohng 英鎊 (N) pound sterling

ying·chàuh 應酬 (N/V) social engagement /have a social engagement

ying·chàuh·wá 應酬話 (N) conventional polite greetings

yìng·fahn 應份 (MA) ought to, should

yìng·gòi 應該 (MA) ought to, should

ying·fuh 應付 (V) cope with

yíng·héung 影響 (N/V) influence, affect /influence, effect

yìng·hùhng 英雄 (N) hero

yìng·màhn 英文 (N) English

yíng·pín 影片 (N) movie, film

yíng·séung 影相 (VO) photograph

yíng·séung·gèi 影相機 (N) camera

yìng·sìhng 應承 (V) promise

yìng·tòuh 櫻桃 (N) cherry

yip 醃 (V) preserve; pickle; salt

yiu 要 (AV) want to; have to

yiu 要 (V) want

yìu·gwaai 妖怪 (N) elf

yiu·gwāt 腰骨 (N) backbone

yiu·kàuh 要求 (V/N) demand

yiu·lèih 要嚟 (CV) used (or needed) for

yìuh 搖 (V) shake

yíuh·lyuhn 擾亂 (V/N) disturb /disturbance

yíuh·lyuhn·jih·òn 擾亂治安 (Ph) disturb the peace

yíuh·yìhn 謠言 (N) rumor

yú 魚 (N) fish (M: tìuh)

yú 瘀 (V) bruise

yù·sih 於是 (MA) then, thereupon

yuh·beih 預備 (V) prepare

yùh·chi 魚翅 (N) shark's fins

yuh·dihng 預定 (V) decide beforehand

yuh·dóu 遇到 (V) to meet with; to encounter

yùh·gòn·yàuh 魚肝油 (N) codliver oil

yùh·gwó 如果 (MA) if, in case

yúh·jauh 宇宙 (N) the universe

yuh·jūk 預祝 (V) wish, or congratulate in advance

yúh·làu 雨樓 (N) raincoat (M: gihn)

yùh·leuhn 輿論 (N) public opinion

yùh·lèuih 魚雷 (N) torpedo

yuh·ngāam 遇啱 (MA) coincidentally, happened to be (at that time)

yuh·sìn 預先 (A) beforehand

yuh·syun 預算 (V/N) prefigure, expect /budget

yúh·yī 雨衣 (N) raincoat (M: gihn)

yúh·yìhn·hohk 語言學 (N) linguistics

yuhk 肉 (N) meat

yuhk·hei 玉器 (N) jade (jewel)

yuhk·gaai·jí 玉戒指 (N) jade ring (M: jek)

yuhk·syùn 肉酸 (SV) ticklish; unpleasant; nasty

yuhk·wòhng·daaih·dai 玉皇大帝 (N) king of gods in the Chinese pantheon

yuhk·yíh·wáan 玉耳環 (N) jade earrings (M: fu)

yuhk·yīng·tóng 育嬰堂 (N) a foundling home

yuhk·yīng·yún 育嬰院 (N) a foundling home

yùhn 圓 (SV) be round, spherical

yùhn 完 (P) verb suffix indicates finishing of an action

yúhn 遠 (SV) far

yúhn 軟 (SV) be soft, yielding

yuhn 縣 (N) county

yùhn·bāt 鉛筆 (N) pencil (M: jì)

yùhn·bāt·páau 鉛筆鉋 (N) pencil sharpener

yùhn·bún 原本 (A) originally

yúhn·chyu 遠處 (PW) a place in the distance

yùhn·chyùhn 完全 (A/SV) completely, entirely /complete, perfect

yùhn·daan 元旦 (N) New Year's day (in solar calendar)

yùhn·góu 原稿 (N) original copy

yùhn·gou 原告 (N) plaintiff

yuhn·gu 原故 (N) cause, reason

yuhn·hyūn 圓圈 (N) a circle

yuhn·jāak, yùhn·jāk 原則 (N) principle

yùhn·jí 原子 (N) atom

yùhn·jí·dáan 原子彈 (N) atom bomb

yùhn·jí·nàhng 原子能 (N) atomic power (energy)

yùhn·jihk 原籍 (N) one's native place

yúhn·joih·tīn·bīn, gahn·joih·ngáahn·chìhn 遠在天邊近在眼前 (IE) Phrase means "It is right in front of your eyes (lit. it seems it is as far as toward the skyline, actually it is right in front of your eyes").

yùhn·kwāi 圓規 (N) compass
yùhn·léih 原理 (N) principle
yùhn·leuhng 原諒 (V) to excuse
yùhn·lòih 原來 (MA) 'now I have found out . . .' (lit. originally)
yùhn·màhn 原文 (N) original text
yùhn·sìhng 完成 (V) complete, accomplish
yùhn·tòuh 沿途 (Ph) along the whole way
yùhn·yàn 原因 (N) reason; cause
yùhng 融容 (V) melt
yùhng·syuh 榕樹 (N) bastard banyan
yuhng 用 (V/N) use /use
yuhng·chyu 用處 (N) use, usage
yúhng·gám 勇敢 (SV) brave
yuhng·geuih 用具 (N) tool, instrument, appliance
yuhng·gùng 用功 (VO/SV) put time and effort into /work or study hard
yúhng·hei 勇氣 (N) courage
yuhng-jeuhn-sàm-gèi 用盡心機 (IE) be at the end of one's wits
yuhng·lèih 用嚟 (CV) used for
yùhng·maauh 容貌 (N) appearance, look
yuhng·naahp 容納 (V) contain; embrace
yuhng·sàm 用心 (A) put one's heart into (doing something)
yuhng·tòuh 用途 (N) usage
yùhng·yáhn 容忍 (V) be patient; forbear
yuhng·yi 用意 (N) intention, intent

yùhng·yih 容易 (SV) easy
yuht 月 (N) month
yuht·béng 月餅 (N) mooncake
yuht·dái 月底 (TW) end of the month
yuht·fahn·pàaih 月份牌 (N) calendar
yuht·gwōng 月光 (N) moon; moonlight
yuht·láahm·sāt 閱覽室 (N) reading room
yuht·leih 月利 (N) monthly interest
yuht lèih yuht 越嚟越 (Pat) getting more and more /yuht lèih yuht gwai, getting more expensive; yuht lèih yuht nàahm, getting more difficult
yuht·lihk 閱歷 (V/N) undergo; experience /experience
yuht·méih 月尾 (N) end of the month
yuht·sihk 月蝕 (N) lunar eclipse
yuht·sīk 月息 (N) monthly interest
yuht·tòih 月台 (N) station, platform
yúk 玉 (N) jade (M: faai or gauh)
yūk 郁 (V) touch; move
yūk·háh 郁吓 (A) might easily
yún·jyún 婉轉 (A) subtly (in presenting a point)
yùn·sàuh 寃仇 (N) vindictive grudges
yūn·wāt 寃屈 (N) a wrong, injustice
yùn·wóng 寃枉 (V/SV) wrong /be wronged
yùn·yùhn 淵源 (N) source (lit.)
yúng 絨 (N) woolen material (M: fūk)
yúng 佣 (N) commission; brokerage

CHARACTER INDEX

CHARACTER INDEX

I. The characters in this index are arranged according to (1) the number of the strokes of the character, (2) the sequence of the radical system generally used in the Chinese dictionary, (3) the number of strokes of the character under the radical system.

II. The characters listed are those used in both the Mandarin and the Cantonese dialects of Chinese. The coined characters of Cantonese are not included.

III. To find the Cantonese pronunciation and the meaning of a Chinese character or of the first character used in an expression, first count the number of strokes of the character. Next, in the section listing characters with the given number of strokes, look for the radical of the character. Then, after finding the character given under the radical, use the romanization to look up the character or expression in the Cantonese-English section of the dictionary.

中文求英文之用法

（一）

欲查中文字之英文字義及用法

（甲）數出中文字之筆劃多少，

（乙）照部首尋求該字，

（丙）尋得該字後即用該字之英文拼音出該字在粵語英文拼音部份查出該字領頭之詞，凡用該字領頭之詞句、或成語，均詳載粵英即粵語英文拼音部份。

（二）

欲查語英文拼音部份。

可直接查英文字如何解法及用法，英文部份

詳附英粵對照之例句，乃練習

日常所用英文對照最好之資料。

一劃
1 stroke

[一部] 一　yāt

二劃
2 strokes

[一部] 七　chāt
丁　dīng
[乙"] 九　gáu
[｜"] 了　líuh
[二"] 二　yih
[人"] 人　yàhn
[八"] 八　baat
[刀"] 刀　dōu
刁　dīu
[入"] 入　yahp
[力"] 力　lihk
[十"] 十　sahp
[卜"] 卜　būk
[又"] 又　yauh

三劃
3 strokes

[一部] 三　sàam
上　seuhng
下　hah
丈　jeuhng
[乙"] 乞　hāk
[几"] 凡　fàahn
[十"] 千　chìn
[又"] 叉　chà
[口"] 口　háu

[土"] 土　tóu
[大"] 大　daaih
[女"] 女　néuih
[寸"] 寸　chyun
[小"] 小　síu
[山"] 山　sàan
[工"] 工　gùng
[己"] 己　yíh

四劃
4 strokes

[一部] 不　bāt
丑　cháu
(clown)
卅　sà·ah
[｜"] 中　jùng
中　jung
[二"] 五　ńgh
井　jéng
互　wuh
[人"] 仇　sàuh
仁　yàhn
今　gàm
仍　yìhng
介　gaai
仆　pūk
[儿"] 元　yùhn
[入"] 内　noih
[八"] 公　gùng
六　luhk
[凵"] 凶　hùn
[刀"] 分　fān
切　chit
[勹"] 勻　wàhn
[匕"] 化　fa

[十"] 升　sìng
卄　yah
[又"] 反　fáan
友　yáuh
[大"] 天　tìn
夫　fù
太　taai
[子"] 孔　húng
[小"] 少　síu
[尢"] 尤　yàuh
[尸"] 尺　chek
[己"] 巴　bà
[幺"] 幻　waanh
[弓"] 引　yáhn
弔　diu
[心"] 心　sàm
[户"] 户　wuh
[手"] 手　sáu
[支"] 支　jì
[文"] 文　màhn
[斗"] 斗　dáu
[方"] 方　fòng
[斤"] 斤　gàn
[日"] 日　yaht
[月"] 月　yuht
[木"] 木　muhk
[欠"] 欠　him
[止"] 止　jí
[比"] 比　béi
[毛"] 毛　mòuh
[氏"] 氏　shih

[水"] 水　séui
[火"] 火　fó
[爪"] 爪　jáu
[父"] 父　fuh
[片"] 片　pin
[牙"] 牙　ngàh
[牛"] 牛　ngàuh
[王"] 王　yúk, yuhk
(ref.王)

五劃
5 strokes

[一部] 世　sai
[丶"] 主　jyú
[人"] 令　lihng
代　doih
他　ta (he)
以　yíh
付　fuh
仔　jí
仙　sīn
[儿"] 兄　hìng
[冂"] 冊　chaah
(volume)
[冬"] 冬　dùng
[凵"] 出　chēut
凸　daht
凹　nāp
[力"] 加　gà
功　gùng
[勹"] 包　bàau
[匕"] 北　bāk
[十"] 半　bun
[厶"] 去　heui

[口 "]	可	hó
	古	gú
	召	jiuh
	司	sì
	叫	giu
	只	jí
	叩	kau
	右	yauh
	史	sí
	句	geui
	另	lihng
["]	四	sei
[夕 "]	外	ngoih
[大 "]	失	sāt
[女 "]	奶	náaih
[子 "]	孕	yahn (pregnant)
[工 "]	巧	háau
	左	jó
[巾 "]	布	bou
	市	síh
[干 "]	平	pìhng
[幺 "]	幼	yau
[心 "]	必	bit
[手 "]	打	dá
	扒	pàh
[木 "]	本	bún
	末	meih
[止 "]	正	jing
	正	jeng
[氏 "]	民	màhn
[水 "]	汁	jāp
	永	wíhng
[犬 "]	犯	faahn
[玉 "]	玉	yúk
	玉	yuhk
[瓜 "]	瓜	gwà

[瓦 "]	瓦	ngáh
[甘 "]	甘	gàm
[生 "]	生	sàang
	生	sàng
[用 "]	用	yuhng
[田 "]	田	tìhn
	甲	gaap
	由	yàuh
[疋 "]	疋	pāt
[白 "]	白	baahk
[皮 "]	皮	pèih
	皮	péi
[目 "]	目	muhk
[矛 "]	矛	màauh
[石 "]	石	sehk
[禾 "]	禾	wòh
[立 "]	立	lahp
[母 "]	母	móuh

六劃

6 strokes

[一部]	百	baak
	再	joi
	丢	dìu
[亠 "]	交	gàau
	亦	yihk
[人 "]	休	yàu
	任	yahm
	伙	fó
	件	gihn
	份	fahn
[儿 "]	先	sìn
	充	chùng
	光	gwòng
	兄	hùn
[入 "]	全	chyùhn

[八 "]	共	guhng
[冫 "]	冰(氷)	bìng
	決(决)	kut
[卩 "]	危	ngàih
	卯	yan
[口 "]	同	tùhng
	向	heung
	名	mìhng
	名	méng
	合	hahp
	各	gok
	吃	hek
[囗 "]	回	wùih
	因	yàn
[土 "]	在	joih
	地	deih
[夕 "]	多	dò
[女 "]	好	hóu
	奸	gàan
	如	yùh
[子 "]	字	jih
	存	chyùhn
[宀 "]	安	on
	安	ngon
	宇	yúh
	守	sáu
[寸 "]	寺	jih
[小 "]	尖	jìm
[巾 "]	帆	fàahn
[干 "]	年	nìhn
[手 "]	扣	kau
	托	tok
[攴 "]	收	sàu
[日 "]	早	jóu
[曰 "]	曲	kūk
[月 "]	有	yáuh
[木 "]	朱	jyù

[欠 "]	次	chi
[止 "]	此	chí
[歹 "]	死	séi
[水 "]	江	gòng
	汗	hohn
[火 "]	灰	fùi
[竹 "]	竹	jūk
[米 "]	米	máih
[羊 "]	羊	yèuhng
[老 "]	老	lóuh
	考	háau
[而 "]	而	yìh
[耳 "]	耳	yíh
[肉 "] (月 ")	肉	yuhk
[自 "]	自	jih
[至 "]	至	ji
[血 "]	血	hyut
[行 "]	行	hàahng
	行	hàhng
	行	hòhng
	行	hóng
[衣 "]	衣	yì (clothing)
[西 "]	西	sài
[邑 "] (阝 ")	邦	bòng
[虫 "]	虫	chùhng

七劃

7 strokes

[丨部]	串	chyun
[二 "]	些	syē
[人 "]	伶	lìhng

住 jyuh
伴 pún
似 chíh
佔 gú
佑 gu
位 wái
位 waih
佈 bou
作 jok
伯 baak
伸 sàn
佔 jim
何 hòh
你 néih
但 daahn
佛 faht
低 dài
  (low)
佣 yúng

[儿 "] 兒 míhn
   兜 hăk

[兵 "] 兵 bìng

[冫 "] 冷 láahng
   况 fong

[刀 "] 利 leih
   別 biht
   初 chò
   判 pun
   删 sàan

[力 "] 劫 gip
   努 nóuh

[口 "] 吸 kāp
   吠 faih
   吩 fàn
   吹 chèui
   告 gou
   呀 a
   吞 tàn
   否 fáu
   呂 léuih

[囗 "] 困 kwan

[土 "] 坐 chóh
   坐 joh
   坑 hāang

[女 "] 妒 douh
   妨 fohng
   妖 yìu

妥 tóh

[子 "] 孝 haau

[宀 "] 完 yùhn
   宋 sung

[尸 "] 局 guhk
   尾 méih

[巾 "] 希 hèi

[广 "] 床(牀) chòhng

[廴 "] 延 yìhn

[廾 "] 弄 nuhng

[弓 "] 弟 daih

[彡 "] 形 yìhng

[心 "] 快 faai
   志 ji
   忍 yáhn
   忘 mòhng
   忌 geih

[戈 "] 我 ngóh
   戒 gaai
   成 sìhng
   成 sèhng

[手 "] 技 geih
   扶 fùh
   批 pài
   投 tàuh
   抄 chàau
   折 jit
   抗 kong
   抑 yīk
   找 jáau
   扭 náu
   扮 baahn
   把 bá

[攴 "] 改 gói
   攻 gùng

[日 "] 旱 hón
   (draught)

[曰 "] 更 gèng
   更 geng
   更 gàang

[木 "] 杏 hahng
   材 chòih
   村 chyūn
   杜 douh
   杲 ngòih
   李 léih
   (as a
    surname)
   李 léi

[止 "] 步 bouh

[水 "] 求 kàuh
   沒 muht
   汽 hei
   沙 sà
   沉 chàhm
   冲 chùng
   決 kyut

[火 "] 災 joi
   (calamity)
   灶 jou

[犬 "] 狂 kwòhng

[田 "] 男 nàahm

[禾 "] 私 sì

[穴 "] 究 gau

[母 "] 每 múih

[肉 "] 肚 tóuh
   肝 gòn
   (liver)
   肛 gòng

[艸 "] 芝 jî

[艮 "] 良 lèuhng

[見 "] 見 gin

[角 "] 角 gok

[豆 "] 豆 dáu

[赤 "] 赤 chek

[走 "] 走 jáu

[足 "] 足 jūk

[身 "] 身 sàn

[車 "] 車 chè

[辛 "] 辛 sàn

[辵 "] 巡 chèuhn

[里 "] 里 léih

[阜 "] 防 fòhng
   附 fuh

八劃
8 strokes

[一部] 並 bihng

[丿 "] 乖 gwàai

[亅 "] 事 sih

[二 "] 亞 nga

[亠 "] 京 gìng
   享 héung

[人 "] 來 lòih
   來 lèih
   使 sí
   供 gùng
   例 laih
   佩 pui
   侍 sih
   依 yì
   佻 tiu

[儿 "] 兔 tou
   兒 yìh

[入 "] 兩 léuhng

[八 "] 其 kèih
   典 dín

[冖 "] 函 hàhm

[刀 "] 刺 chi
   到 dou
   刷 chaat
   刷 cháat
   制 jai
   刮 gwaat
   刻 hāk

[十"] 卑 bèi	[彳"] 往 wóhng	松 chùhng	花 fā
協 hip	彼 béi	[止"] 武 móuh	[虍"] 虎 fú
[又"] 取 chéui	[心"] 忠 jùng	[水"] 沿 yùhn	(tiger)
受 sauh	忽 fāt	注 jyu	[辵"] 近 gahn
叔 sūk	性 sing	法 faat	迎 yìhng
[口"] 周 jàu	怪 gwaai	泥 nàih	返 fáan
和 wòh	恆 hàhng	油 yàuh	返 fàan
呼 fù	怕 pa	泡 paau	[金"] 金 gàm
命 mehng	[戈"] 或 waahk	泡 póuh	(gold)
命 mihng	[戶"] 所 só	治 jih	[長"] 長 chèuhg
咖 ga	房 fóng	波 pò	長 jéung
味 meih	[手"] 抽 chàu	河 hòh	[門"] 門 mùhn
呢 nē	承 sîhng	[火"] 炒 cháau	[阜"] 附 fuh
呷 haap	拍 paak	[父"] 爸 bàh	(卩") 阻 jó
[囗"] 固 gu	拒 geuih	[爪"] 爭 jàang	[雨"] 雨 yúh
[土"] 坦 táan	拉 làai	爬 pàh	[青"] 青(靑) chìng
[夕"] 夜 yeh	抱 póuh	[爿"] 牀 chòhng	青(靑) chèng
[大"] 奇 kèih	拐 gwáai	[片"] 版 báan	[非"] 非 fèi
奔 bàn	拖 tò	[牛"] 物 maht	
奉 fuhng	抹 maat	牧 muhk	**九劃**
[女"] 委 wái	抵 dái	[犬"] 狗 gáu	**9 strokes**
姑 gù	招 jiu	(犭")	[人部] 侮 móuh
姊 jé	拆 chaak	[玉"] 玩 wáan	侵 chàm
姐 jé	拔 baht	玫 mùih	便 bihn
妹 múi	拘 kèui	[白"] 的 dīk	俗 juhk
妾 chip	担 dàam	[目"] 盲 màahng	保 bóu
姓 sing	拾 tòih	直 jihk	信 seun
始 chí	拼 pìng	[矢"] 知 jì	偈 guhk
[子"] 季 gwai	[攴"] 放 fong	[示"] 社 séh	[冂"] 冒 mouh
孤 gù	[斤"] 斧 fú	[穴"] 空 hùng	冠 gun
[宀"] 定 dihng	[方"] 於 yù	[耳"] 耶 yèh	[刀"] 前 chîhn
定 dehng	[日"] 明 mîhng	[肉"] 肥 fèih	剃 tai
官 gùn	易 yih	股 gú	[力"] 勇 yúhng
宗 jùng	旺 wohng	肩 gìn	勉 mihn
[尸"] 居 gèui	[月"] 服 fuhk	肯 háng	[十"] 南 nàahm
屈 wāt	朋 pàhng	育 yuhk	[卩"] 即 jĭk
[山"] 岸 ngohn	[木"] 枝 jì	[舌"] 舍 séh	[厂"] 厚 háuh
[巾"] 帖 típ	杯 bùi	[艸"] 花 fà	
[干"] 幸 hahng	杯 būi		
[广"] 底 dái	枉 wóng		
府 fú	東 dùng		
	果 gwó		
	枕 jám		
	板 báan		
	林 lahm (as a surname)		

[口"] 咳 ngáauh
咳 kāk

[土"] 城 sèhng
城 sìhng

[大"] 契 kai
奔 bàn
奏 jau

[女"] 威 wài
姦 gàan
姨 yìh
姪 jāt

[宀"] 客 haak
宣 syùn

[寸"] 封 fung
(to seal)

[厂"] 屋 ngūk
屍 sì
屎 sí

[己"] 巷 hòn

[巾"] 帝 dai

[幺"] 幽 yàu

[广"] 度 douh

[廴"] 建 gihn
廻 wùih

[彳"] 後 hauh
律 leuht
待 doih
很 hán

[心"] 怨 yun
恃 chíh
思 sì
忽 fāt
急 gāp
恆 hàhng
怠 doih
恢 fùi
恨 hahn

[戶"] 扁 bín

[手"] 括 kut
拼 pīng
指 jí

挑 tìu
拜 baai
按 ngon
挖 waat

[攴"] 政 jing
故 gu

[方"] 施 sì

[日"] 昨 johk
春 chèun
是 sih
星 sìng
星 sīng

[木"] 柿 chí
架 ga
柳 láuh
查 chàh
染 yíhm
柏 paak
柺 gwái
柴 chàaih
柑 gām

[止"] 歪 méh

[殳"] 段 dyuhn

[水"] 洗 sái
活 wuht
洪 hùhng
洋 yèuhng
洞 duhng
津 jèun
派 paai
泉 chyùhn
洒 sá

[火"] 炭 taan
炮(砲) paau
炸 ja
炸 jaau

[牛"] 牲 sàang

[犬"] 狡 gáau

[玉"] 珍 jàn
玻 pō

[甘"] 甚 sahm

[田"] 界 gaai

[白"] 皆 gàai
皇 wòhng

[皿"] 盆 pùhn

[目"] 省 sáang
相 sèung
眉 mèih (eye-brow)
看 hon
看 hòn
盼 paan

[石"] 砂 sà

[示"] 祈 kèih
祠 chìh

[禾"] 秋 chàu
科 fò
科 fō
秒 míuh

[穴"] 突 daht
穿 chyùn

[母"] 毒 duhk

[糸"] 紅 hùhng
紀 géi
約 yeuk

[缶"] 缸 gòng

[羊"] 美 méih

[襾"] 耐 noih

[肉"] 肺 fai
背 bui
胡 wùh
胃 waih
胎 tòi

[艸"] 苦 fú
苛 hò
英 yìng
若 yeuhk
茄 ké

[舟"] 舢 sàam

[虍"] 虐 yeuhk

[衣"] 表 bíu
衫 sāam

[西"] 要 yiu

[言"] 計 gai
訂 dèng
訂 dehng
訂 dihng
訃 fuh

[貝"] 負 fuh

[車"] 軍 gwàn
軌 gwái

[邑"] 郊 gàau
(阝)

[里"] 重 chúhng
重 chùhng
重 juhng

[門"] 問 sàan

[阜"] 恨 haahn
(阝)

[ ] 降 gong

[面"] 面 mihn

[革"] 革 gaak

[音"] 音 yàm

[頁"] 頁 yihp

[風"] 風 fùng

[飛"] 飛 fèi

[食"] 食 sihk

[首"] 首 sáu

[香"] 香 hèung

十劃
10 strokes

[丿部] 乘 sìhng

[人"] 倍 púih
個 go
借 je
倒 dóu
值 jihk
倘 tóng

修 sàu	[弓 "] 弱 yeuhk	消 sìu	紗 sà
俻 fóng	[彡 "] 彩 chói	浪 lohng	紗 sā
侍 sìh	[彳 "] 徒 tòuh	[火 "] 烟 yìn	納 naahp
倚 yí	[心 "] 恐 húng	烤 haau (to roast)	紙 jí
候 hauh	困 yàn	烝 jìng (to steam)	純 sèuhn
[八 "] 兼 gìm	悔 fui		素 sok
[冫 "] 准 jéun	慕 gùng	[牛 "] 特 dahk	級 kāp
凍 dung	[戶 "] 扇 sin	[犬 "] 狼 lóng (wolf)	[缶 "] 缺 kyut
凄(凄) chài	[手 "] 捉 jūk	狼 lòhng	[耒 "] 耗 hou
涼(涼) lèuhng	拳 kyùhn	狹 haahp	耕 gàang
[刀 "] 剝 mōk	拿 nàh	[玉 "] 珠 jyū	[肉 "] 能 nàhng
[厂 "] 原 yùhn	捐 gyùn	班 bàan	脊 jek
[口 "] 哲 jit	振 jan	[田 "] 畜 chūk	脈 mahk (pulse)
嗥哭 hàau hūk	撲 ngàai	畝 máuh	脆 cheui (brittle)
哥 gō	摧 ngàaih	留 làuh	胸 hùng
唇 sèuhn	挾 gihp	[广 "] 痛 behng	[自 "] 臭 chau
[土 "] 埋 màaih	挽 wáan	症 jing	[至 "] 致 ji
[夊 "] 夏 hah	[攴 "] 效 haauh	痂 gà	[舟 "] 航 hòhng
[女 "] 娛 yùh	[方 "] 旅 léuih	[皿 "] 益 yīk	[艸 "] 茶 chàh
[子 "] 孫 syùn	旁 pòhng	[目 "] 真(眞) jàn	草 chóu
[宀 "] 宮 gùng	[日 "] 曼 ngaan	[石 "] 破 po	荔 laih
富 hoih	時 sìh	砲(炮) paau	荒 fòng
家 gà	[曰 "] 書 syù	砧 jàm	[虍 "] 虔 kìhn
宴 yin	[木 "] 案 ngon	砌 chai	[虫 "] 蚊 mān
容 yùhng	格 gaak	[示 "] 祕 bei	[言 "] 討 tóu
宰 jói	核 haht	神 sàhn	訓 fan
[寸 "] 射 seh	核 wát	祝 jūk	記 gei
[尸 "] 展 jín	桑 sòng (mulberry)	祖 jóu	託 tok
屐 keh	桃 tóu (peach)	祠 chìh	[豆 "] 豈 héi
[山 "] 島 dóu	校 haauh	[禾 "] 租 jòu	[豸 "] 豹 paau
[工 "] 差 chā	校 gaau	秩 diht	豺 chàai
差 chàai	桐 tùhng	秤 ching	[衣 "] 衰 sèui
[巾 "] 席 jihk	根 gàn	稟 chèuhn	[貝 "] 財 chòih
席 jehk	栽 jòi	[穴 "] 窄 jaak	貢 gung
師 sì	[殳 "] 殷 yàn	[立 "] 站 jaahm	[走 "] 起 héi
[广 "] 座 joh	[气 "] 氣 hèi	[竹 "] 笑 siu	[辵 "] 逆 ngaahk
庫 fu	[水 "] 酒 jáu	[米 "] 粉 fán	逃 tòuh
唐 tòhng	漫 jam	[糸 "] 紡 fóng	追 jèui
	浮 fàuh		
	海 hói		

送	sung	[口"] 問	mahn	[心"] 情	chìhng	淫 yàhm
迷	màih	商	sèung	悽	chài	淡 daahm
退	teui	啄	deuk	患	waahn	淡 táahm
[酉"] 配	pui	啤	bē (beer)	惜	sek	淺 chín
[金"] 針	jàm	啞	ngá	[手"] 接	jip	淋 lahm
釘	dēng	唱	cheung	推	tèui	淘 tòuh
釘	dèng	唯	wàih	採	chói	添 tìm
[門"] 閃	sím	[囗"] 國	gwok	掛	gwa	淒 chài
[阜"] 除	chèuih	圈	hyūn	捨	sé	涼 lèuhng
[佳"] 隻	jek	[土"] 堆	dèui	捲	gyún	液 yiht
[馬"] 馬	máh	培	puih	探	taam	淵 yùn
[骨"] 骨	gwat (bone)	基	gèi	排	pàaih	湊(凑) chau
[高"] 高	gòu	堂	tòhng	掘	gaht	淚 leuih
[鬥"] 鬥	dau	埠	fauh	掃	sou	(tear)
[鬼"] 鬼	gwái	執	jāp	撤	kín	[爻"] 爽 sóng
		堅	gìn	掩	yím	[犬"] 猛 máahng
十一劃		[夕"] 夠(够)	gau	[攴"] 敏	máhn	猪 jyù
11 strokes		[女"] 娶	chéui	教(敎)	gaau	猪 jyū
[乙部] 乾	gòn	婚	fàn	救	gau	[玄"] 牽 hìn
[人"] 假	gá	婦	fúh	敗	baaih	率 sēut
做	jouh	婉	yún	[斗"] 斜	che	[玉"] 理 léih
偶	ngáuh	[宀"] 密	maht	[斤"] 斬	jáam	球 kàuh
停	tìhng	寄	gei	[方"] 旋	syùhn	現 yihn
健	gihn	宿	sūk	族	juhk	[廿"] 甜 tìhm
偷	tàu	寂	jihk	[无"] 既	gei	[生"] 產 cháan
偏	pìn	寬	yùn	[日"] 晚	máahn	[田"] 畢 bāt
側	jāk	[寸"] 專	jyùn	[月"] 望	mohng	[广"] 痕 hàhn
偉	wáih	將	jèung	[木"] 條	tìuh	痔 jih
俱	jìng	[尸"] 屏	pìhng	桶	túng	[皿"] 盒 háp
[刀"] 副	fu	[巾"] 帶	daai	梳	sō	盒 hahp
剪	jín	常	sèuhng	梳	sò	[目"] 眼 ngáahn
[力"] 動	duhng	[广"] 庶	syu	梨	léi	[石"] 研 yìhn
勒	lahk	康	hòn	梅	múi	[示"] 祭 jai
[匕"] 匙	chìh	[弓"] 強(强)	kèuhng	梅	mùih	票 pun
[匚"] 區	kèui	張	jèung	梯	tài	(ticket)
[厶"] 參	chàam	[彐"] 彗	waih	梘	gáan	[立"] 章 jèung
		[彳"] 從	chùhng	[欠"] 欲	yuhk	竟 gíng
		得	dāk	[毛"] 毫	hòuh	[竹"] 笛 dék
		徙	sái	[殳"] 殺	saat	笨 bahn
		[彡"] 彩	chói	[水"] 深	sàm	符 fùh
		彫	dìu	清	chìng	第 daih
				混	wahn	

[米"] 粒 nāp
粗 chòu

[糸"] 細 sai
累 leuih
紮 jaat
組 jóu
紳 sàn
紫 jí

[羽"] 習 jaahp

[肉"] (月部) 脫 tyut
腳 geuk

[舟"] 船 syùhn
舵 tòh

[臼"] 舂 jùng

[艸"] 荷 hòh
莫 mohk

[虍"] 處 syu
處 chyúh

[虫"] 蛋 dáan
蛇 sèh

[衣"] 袋 doih
袋 dói
袒 táan
袖 jauh
被 péih
被 beih

[見"] 規 kwài

[言"] 許 héui
設 chit
訪 fóng
訛 ngāk

[貝"] 貪 tàam
貧 pàhn
責 jāk
責 jaak
貨 fo

[赤"] 赦 se

[車"] 軟 yúhn

[辵"] 通 tùng
透 tau
速 chūk
逗 dauh
逐 juhk
連 lìhn
造 jouh
逛 gwaahng
途 tòuh

[邑"] (阝部) 郵 yàuh
部 bouh

[里"] 野 yéh

[金"] 釣 diu
釬(銲) hohn (to solder)

[阜"] (阝部) 陸 luhk
陰 yàm
陳 chàhn (as a surname)
陪 pùih
陷 haahm

[隹"] 雀 jéuk

[雨"] 雪 syut

[頁"] 頂 díng

[魚"] 魚 yú

[麥"] 麥 mahk

[麻"] 麻 màh

十二劃

12 strokes

[人部] 傢 gà
傘 saan (umbrella)

[儿"] 兜 dàu

[刀"] 割 got
創 chong
剩 sihng

[力"] 勞 lòuh
勝 sing

[十"] 博 bok

[厂"] 厨 chyùh

[口"] 喜 héi
喘 chyún
善 sihn
喇 la
喉 hauh
喪 song
喪 sòng
喝 hot
單 dàan
喊 haam
啼 tàih
喂 wai

[囗"] 圍 wàih

[土"] 場 chèuhng
報 bou
堤 tàih

[士"] 壺 wùh

[大"] 奢 chè

[女"] 媒 mùih

[宀"] 富 fu
寒 hòhn

[寸"] 尊 jyùn

[尢"] 就 jauh

[山"] 嵌 hahm (inlay)

[广"] 廁(厠) chi

[巾"] 帽 móu
幅 fūk

[幺"] 幾 géi

[彳"] 循 chèuhn
復 fuhk

[心"] 悲 bèi
惡 ngok
悶 muhn

[手"] 提 tàih
描 mìuh
握 ngāak
捷 jit
插 chaap
掌 jéung
掣 jai
揀 gáan
換 wuhn

[攴"] 散 saan
散 sáan
敢 gáam
敦 dèun
敝 baih

[斤"] 斯 sì

[日"] 普 póu
智 ji
景 gíng
晾 lohng
晴 chìhng

[曰"] 最 jeui
曾 chàhng
曾 jàng (as a surname)
替 tai

[月"] 朝 chìuh
期 kèih

[木"] 極 gihk
植 jihk
棉 mihn
棚 pàahng
椅 yí
棋 kèih
棋 kéi
棺 gùn
棗 jóu
棲 chài
棕 jùng
森 sàm
棧 jaahn
棍 gwan

[欠"] 款 fún
欺 hèi

[歹"] 殖 jihk
殘 chàahn

[殳"] 殼 hok

[水"] 減 gáam
渴 hot (thirsty)

渣 jà	結 git	[辵"] 進 jeun	[囗"] 圓 yùhn
渡 douh	絲 sì	週 jàu	園 yún
湯 tòng	統 túng		(garden)
港 góng	絕 jyuht	[邑"](阝") 都 dōu	
湖 wùh	絞 gáau		[土"] 塘 tòhng
測 chāk		[酉"] 酥 sòu	(pond)
溫 wàn	[肉"](月") 脹 jeung		填 tìhn
游 yàuh	脾 pèih	[里"] 量 lèuhng	塔 taap
		量 leuhng	塊 faai
[火"] 無 mòuh	[舌"] 舒 syù		塞 sāk
焦 jiu		[金"] 鈍 deuhn	
然 yìhn	[艸"] 萍 pìhng	鈕 náu	[大"] 奧 ou
焙 buih	華 wàh		
	菊 gūk	[門"] 開 hòi	[女"] 嫌 yìhm
[瓜"] 爲(瀉)wàih	菜 choi	間 gàan	嫁 ga
	等 pùh	閒 hàahn	嫂 sóu
[片"] 牌 pàaih	菌 kwán	閏 yeuhn	媽 mā
	渡 bò		
[犬"] 猪 jyū		[阜"](阝") 階 gāai	[干"] 幹 gon
	[虍"] 虛 hèui	隊 deuih	
[玉"] 琴 kàhm		陽 yèuhng	[彳"] 微 mèih
	[行"] 街 gāai		
[田"] 番 fàan		[隹"] 集 jaahp	[心"] 意 yi
畫 wá	[衣"] 裙 kwàhn	雄 hùhng	愛 oi
	裂 lit		愛 ngoi
[疒"] 痛 tung	裁 chòih	[雨"] 雲 wàhn	感 gáam
痧 sà	補 bóu		想 séung
		[頁"] 順 seuhn	慈 sàuh
[癶"] 發 faat	[言"] 評 pìhng	項 hohng	慌 fòng
登 dàng	註 jyu		
	診 chán	[黃"] 黃 wòhng	[手"] 損 séun
[目"] 着 jeuhk	証 jing		搭 chàh
	詞 chìh	[黑"] 黑 hāk	搶 chéung
[矢"] 短 dyún	詆 dái	黑 hāak	搖 yìuh
			搜 sáu
[石"] 硬 ngaahng	[豕"] 象 jeuhng		搬 bùn
		十三劃	搭 daap
[禾"] 稀 hèi	[貝"] 貯 chyúh	**13 strokes**	
稅 seui	貴 gwai		[戈"] 敬 ging
程 chìhng	買 máaih	[乙部] 亂 lyuhn	
	貼 tip		[斗"] 斟 jàm
[穴"] 窗 chēung	貿 mauh	[人"] 傳 chyùhn	
	費 fai	傳 jyuhn	[斤"] 新 sàn
[立"] 童 tùhng	賀 hoh	傾 kìng	
		傷 sèung	[日"] 暗 ngam
[疋"] 疏 sò	[走"] 趁 chan	債 jaai	暖 nyúhn
	越 yuht	僅 gán	暈 wàhn
[竹"] 答 daap		催 chèui	暑 syú
等 dáng	[足"] 跌 dit	傻 sòh	
筋 gàn	跛 bài		[曰"] 會 wúi
筆 bāt	距 géuih	[力"] 勤 kàhn	會 wúih
筒 séun	跑 páau	勢 sai	會 wuih
[米"] 粥 jūk	[身"] 躭 dàam	[口"] 嗜 si	[木"] 楊 yèuhng
			葉 yihp
[糸"] 絨 yúng			椰 yèh

	楚 chó	[羊"]	義 yih	[辵"]	達 daaht	[囗"]	團 tyùhn
[欠"]	歇 hit		群(羣) kwàhn		運 wahn		圖 tòuh
[止"]	歲 seui		羨 sihn		逼 bīk	[土"]	境 gíng
[殳"]	毀 wái	[耳"]	聖 sing		違 wàih		塾 jin
[水"]	準 jéun	[聿"]	肅 sūk		過 gwo		塵 chàhn
	溝 gàu	[肉"]	腰 yìu		遊 yàuh	[夕"]	夥 fó
	滑 waaht		腦 nóuh		道 douh		夢 muhng
	滋 jì		腸 chéung		遏 yuh	[大"]	奬 jéung
	滙 wuih		腸 chèuhng	[邑"]	鄉 hèung	[女"]	嫩 nyuhn
	溪 kài		腫 júng	[金"]	鉛 yùhn	[宀"]	實 saht
[火"]	煩 fàahn	[臼"]	舅 káuh		鉗 kìm		寡 gwá
	照 jiu	[舟"]	艇 téhng	[門"]	閘 jaahp	[寸"]	對 deui
	煤 mùih	[艸"]	萬 maahn	[阜"]	隔 gaak	[巾"]	幕 mohk
	煎 jìn		葉 yihp	[雨"]	電 dihn	[心"]	慚 chàahm
	煮 jyú		落 lohk		零 lìhng		態 taai
	煉 lihn		葬 jong		零 lèhng		慘 cháam
	煨 wùi		葡 pòuh		雷 lèuih		慢 maahn
[犬"]	獅 sì		葱 chūng	[革"]	靴 hèu		慈 chìh
[田"]	當 dong		著 jyu	[頁"]	預 yuh		慣 gwaan
	噹 dòng	[虍"]	號 houh		頑 wàahn	[戈"]	截 jiht
[疒"]	瘩 tàahm	[虫"]	蜆 hín	[食"]	飲 yám	[手"]	摘 jaahk
	瘀 yú	[衣"]	裝 jòng		飯 faahn		摸 mò
[皿"]	盞 jáan		裏(裡) léuih	[馬"]	馴 seuhn		摺 jip
[目"]	督 dūk	[角"]	解 gáai	[鼓"]	鼓 gú	[攴"]	敲 hàau
	睡 seuih	[言"]	誇 kwà	[鼠"]	鼠 syú	[方"]	旗 kèih
[矢"]	矮 ngái		試 si		(rat)	[木"]	構 kau
[石"]	碗 wún		詳 chèuhng				槍 chēung
	碎 seui		詼 fùi	**十四劃**			榮 wìhng
	碰 pung		詢 sèun	**14 strokes**		[欠"]	歌 gō
[示"]	禁 gam		話 wá			[水"]	演 yín
[禸"]	禽 kàhm		詩 sì	[人部]	像 jeuhng		漏 lauh
[竹"]	筷 faai	[貝"]	資 jì		僕 buhk		漲 jeung
[糸"]	經 gìng		賊 chak	[八"]	凳 dang		滯 jaih
	綁 bóng		賊 chaak	[刀"]	劃 waahk		滿 múhn
	綑 kwán	[足"]	跳 tiu	[厂"]	厭 yim		漢 hon
[网"]	罪 jeuih		跪 gwaih	[口"]	嘆(歎) taan		漂 piu
	罩 jaau		路 louh		嘔 ngáu		滴 dihk
	置 ji		跟 gàn		嘉 gà		漸 jihm
		[車"]	載 joi				漠 maahn
		[辰"]	農 nùhng			[火"]	熄 sīk

[足"] 疑 yìh

[皿"] 畫 jeuhn
鑒 gàam

[石"] 碟 díp
碩 sehk

[示"] 福 fūk
禍 woh

[禾"] 稱 chìng
種 jung
種 júng

[立"] 端 dyūn

[竹"] 算 syun
管 gún
劄 daahp

[米"] 精 jīng
粽 júng

[糸"] 網 móhng
綱 gòng
維 wàih
綠 luhk
緊 gán
綢 cháuh

[四"] 罰 faht

[耳"] 聚 jeuih
聞 màhn

[肉"] 膏 gòu
腐 fuh
腦 nóuh

[舛"] 舞 móuh

[艸"] 蓋 goi
蒸 jing
蓆 jehk

[虫"] 蜜 maht
蜘 jī
蜚 daahn

[衣"] 製 jai
裱 bíu

[言"] 誓 saih
語 yúh
說 syut

認 yihng
誤 ngh
誠 sìhng
誣 mòuh
誕 daan

[豕"] 豪 hòuh

[貝"] 賒 sè
賓 bàn

[車"] 輕 hèng
輓 wáahn

[辛"] 辣 laaht

[辵"] 遠 yúhn
遞 daih

[酉"] 酸 syùn

[金"] 銅 tùhng
銀 ngán
銀 ngàhn

[門"] 閣 gok

[阜"] 障 jeung

[雨"] 需 sèui

[頁"] 領 léhng
領 lihng

[食"] 飽 báau

[馬"] 駁 bok

[骨"] 骰 sīk

[鬼"] 魂 wàhn

[鳥"] 鳳 fuhng

[鼻"] 鼻 beih

[齊"] 齊 chàih

十五劃
15 strokes

[人部] 價 ga
僻 pīk
儀 yìh

億 yīk

[刀"] 劈 pek
劍 gim
劇 kehk

[厂"] 厲 leih

[口"] 噴 pan
嘴 jéui
嘵 jiuh

[土"] 增 jàng
墮 doh
墳 fàhn
墨 mahk

[女"] 嬌 gìu

[宀"] 審 sám
寫 sé
寬 fùn

[尸"] 層 chàhng

[广"] 廢 fai
慶 hing
廟 miuh
廚 chyùh
廠 chóng
廣 gwóng

[弓"] 彈 tàahn
彈 dáan

[廾"] 弊 baih

[彡"] 影 yíng

[彳"] 德 dāk
徵 jìng

[心"] 憂 yàu
慰 wai

[手"] 撥 buht
撕 sì
摩 mò
撲 pok
播 bo
撈 làauh
撑 chàang
撒 saat
撞 johng
撤 chit
撬 giuh

[攴"] 敷 fù
敵 dihk
數 sóu
數 sou
整 jíng

[日"] 暫 jaahm
暴 bouh

[木"] 標 bīu
模 mòuh
樂 lohk
樣 yéung
樣 yeuhng
樓 láu
樓 làuh

[水"] 漆 lóuh
漿 jèung
潛 chìhm
潮 chìuh
潑 put
澈 chit

[火"] 熟 yiht
熟 suhk

[疒"] 瘦 sau
瘡 chōng

[石"] 碼 máh
磅 bohng
磁 chìh
確 kok

[禾"] 稿 góu

[宀"] 窮 kùhng

[竹"] 箭 jin
箱 sēung
箱 sèung
節 jit
篇 pīn

[米"] 糊 wùh

[糸"] 編 pīn
練 lihn
緯 wáih
線 sin
緣 yùhn

[四"] 罷 bah

[肉"] 膠 gàau

膝 sāt

[舌"] 鋪 pou

[艸"] 蕉 je

[虫"] 蝦 hā
蝴 wùh

[行"] 衛 waih

[衣"] 複 fūk
褻 bòu

[見"] 靚 leng

[言"] 請 chéng
請 chíng
調 diuh
調 tìuh
課 fo
論 leuhn
談 tàahm
誰 sèuih

[貝"] 賠 pùih
質 jāt
賣 maaih
賦 fuh
賬 jeung
賞 séung
賜 chi
賤 jihn

[走"] 趣 cheui
趟 tong

[足"] 踢 tek

[車"] 輪 lèuhn
輩 bui
輝 fāi

[辵"] 適 sīk
遭 jòu
遮 jè
遲 chìh

[邑"] 鄰(鄰) lèuhn

[酉"] 醉 jeui
醃 yìm
醋 chou

[金"] 鋪 sìu
鋤 sau

[門"] 閱 yuht

[雨"] 霉 mùih
震 jan

[非"] 靠 kaau

[革"] 鞋 hàaih
鞠 gūk

[食"] 養 yéuhng
餅 béng

[馬"] 駝 tòh
駐 jyu
駕 ga
駛 sái

[骨"] 骸 hàaih

[鬥"] 鬧 naauh

[麥"] 麵 mihn

十六劃
16 strokes

[刀部] 劑 jài

[厂"] 歷 lihk

[口"] 器 hei
噸 dēun

[子"] 學 hohk

[心"] 憲 hin
懂 dúng
憑 pàhng

[戈"] 戰 jin

[手"] 擔 dàam
操 chòu
撻 taat
擋 dóng
擇 jaahk

[攴"] 整 jíng

[木"] 機 gèi
橋 kìuh
樹 syuh
橘 gāt

橫 pok
橫 wàahng
樽 jèun
橙 cháang
檸 nìhng

[水"] 激 gīk
濃 nùhng

[火"] 燒 sìu
燈 dāng
燃 yìhn
燐 lèuhn
燕 yin
燕 yín
燉 dahn

[犬"] 獨 duhk

[石"] 磚 jyùn
磨 mòh
磨 moh

[禾"] 積 jīk

[竹"] 築 jūk
範 faahn
篤 dūk

[米"] 糖 tòhng
糖 tóng

[糸"] 縐 jau
縣 yuhn

[肉"] 膨 pàahng
臟 neih

[臼"] 興 hìng

[艸"] 薑 gēung

[虫"] 融 yùhng

[行"] 衡 waih

[衣"] 褲 fu

[見"] 親 chàn

[言"] 諷 fúng
謀 màuh

[豸"] 貓 māau

[貝"] 賭 dóu

[車"] 輸 syù

[辛"] 辦 baahn

[辵"] 選 syún
遺 wàih
遵 jyùn

[酉"] 醒 séng

[金"] 錢 chín
銅 gong
錯 cho
鋸 geu
錫 geui
錐 sek
錄 yēui
錄 luhk
錦 gám
錶 bīu

[阜"] 隨 chèuih
隧 seuih
險 hím

[佳"] 雕(鵰) dīu

[雨"] 霍 fok

[青"] 靜 jihng

[頁"] 頭 tàuh
頸 géng

[食"] 餓 ngoh
餐 chāan
餐 chàan

[髟"] 髻 gái
鬆 yàuh

[鳥"] 鴨 ngáap
鴛 yūn

[黑"] 默 mahk

[龍"] 龍 lùhng

[龜"] 龜 gwāi

十七劃
17 strokes

[人部] 優 yàu

[口"] 嚇 haak	[艮"] 艱 gàan	[手"] 擾 yíuh
[土"] 壓 ngaat	[艸"] 薄 bohk	擺 báai
[巾"] 幫 bòng	薑 gēung	擴 kwong
[弓"] 彌 mèih	薪 sàn	[斤"] 斷 tyúhn
彌 nèih	薦 gin	[月"] 朦 mùhng
[心"] 懇 hán	[虍"] 虧 kwāi	[木"] 檸 nìhng
應 yìng	[言"] 謝 jeh	櫃 gwaih
懞 múng	謙 hìm	[止"] 歸 gwāi
[戈"] 戲 hei	講 góng	[水"] 瀉 se
[手"] 擡(抬)tòih	謠 yìuh	瀑 buhk
擱 gok	[貝"] 賽 choi	濺 jaahn
擦 chaat	購 gau	[爪"] 爵 jeuk
摩 maak	賺 jaahn	[犬"] 獵 lihp
擤 jài	賸 jihng	[田"] 疊 léuih
[木"] 檢 gím	賸 sihng	[示"] 禮 láih
檀 tàahn	[走"] 趨 chèui	[竹"] 簡 gáan
[毛"] 氈 jīn	[車"] 輿 yùh	[米"] 糧 lèuhng
[水"] 濕(湿)sāp	[足"] 避 beih	[糸"] 織 jīk
[火"] 謍 yìhng	還 wàahn	繡 sau
[片"] 牆 chèuhng	[酉"] 醜 cháu	[羽"] 翻 fàan
[玉"] 環 wàahn	[金"] 鍍 douh	翼 yihk
[广"] 療 lîuh	鍊 lín	[耳"] 職 jīk
[竹"] 篷 pùhng	鐘 jūng	[肉"] 臍 chìh
[米"] 糠 hòn	[門"] 闊 fut	[臼"] 舊 gauh
糢 mòuh	[阜"] 隱 yáhn	[艸"] 藉 jihk
[糸"] 縮 sūk	[隹"] 雖 sèui	藍 làahm
總 júng	[黍"] 黏 nìhm	藏 chòhng
縫 fùhng	[黑"] 點 dím	[虫"] 蟬 sím
繁 fàahn	[齊"] 齋 jàai	蟲 chùhng
[耳"] 聲 sìng		[西"] 覆 fūk
聰 chùng	**十八劃**	[言"] 謹 gán
聯 lyùhn	**18 strokes**	[豆"] 豐 fùng
[肉"] 膽 dáam	[人部] 儲 chyúh	[車"] 轉 jyun
膿 nùhng	[女"] 嬸 sám	轉 jyún
[匚"] 臨 làhm	[戈"] 戴 daai	
[臼"] 舉 géui		

[酉"] 醫 yì
醬 jeung
[里"] 釐 lèih
[金"] 鎮 jan
鎮 jahn
鎗(槍)chēung
鎖(鎖)só
鎔 yùhng
[隹"] 雙 sèung
雙 sòng
雜 jaahp
雞(鷄)gāi
[革"] 鞭 bìn
[頁"] 額 ngáak
顎 ngaahk
顏 ngaahn
題 tàih
[馬"] 騎 kèh
[彡"] 鬆 sùng

十九劃
19 strokes

[土部] 壞 waaih
壟 lúhng
[宀"] 寶 bóu
[心"] 懷 wàaih
懶 láahn
[火"] 爆 baau
[犬"] 獸 sau
[示"] 禱 tòuh
禱 tóu
[禾"] 穩 wán
[竹"] 簽 chìm
簿 bòu
[糸"] 繳 gíu
繩 sìng
繩 sìhng

[四"] 羅 lòh
[肉"] 臘 laahp
[艸"] 藥 yeuhk
　　 藝 ngaih
[衣"] 襟 kàm
[言"] 譏 gèi
　　 證(証) jing
　　 識 sīk
[貝"] 贊 jaan
　　 贈 jahng
[車"] 轎 gíu
[辛"] 辭 chìh
[辵"] 邊 bīn
　　 邊 bín
　　 邊 bihn
[金"] 鏈 lín
　　 鏡 geng
[門"] 關 gwàan
[隹"] 離 lèih
　　 難 nàahn
[雨"] 霧 mouh
[頁"] 顛 dìn
　　 類 leuih
[馬"] 騙 pin

二十劃
20 strokes

[力部] 勸 hyun
[口"] 嚴 yìhm
[心"] 懺 chaam
[牛"] 犧 hèi
[石"] 礦 kwong
[立"] 競 ging

[竹"] 籌 chàuh
　　 籃 làahm
　　 籃 láam
　　 籍 jihk
[米"] 糯 noh
[糸"] 辮 bīn
　　 繼 gai
[缶"] 罌 ngāang
[舟"] 艦 laahm (war-ship)
[艸"] 蘇 sòu
　　 蘋 pìhng
[虫"] 蠔 hòuh
[衣"] 襪(袜) maht
[見"] 覺 gok
[言"] 議 yih
　　 議 yi
　　 譬 pei
　　 譯 yihk
　　 譟 wái
[貝"] 贏 yèhng
[足"] 躁 chou
　　 躉 dán
[金"] 鐘 jūng
[馬"] 騷 sòu
[齒"] 鹹 hàahm
[黑"] 黨 dóng
[齒"] 齣 chēut

二十一劃
21 strokes

[口部] 嚼(嚐) jiuh
[尸"] 屬 suhk
[木"] 欄 làahn

櫻 yìng
[水"] 灌 gun
[火"] 爛 laahn
[宀"] 竈(灶) jou
[竹"] 籐 tàhng
[糸"] 纏 jihn
　　 纏 chìhn
[艸"] 蘭 láan
　　 蘭 làahn
[虫"] 蠟(蝋) laahp
　　 蠢 chéun
[言"] 護 wuh
　　 譴 híng
[足"] 躊 chàuh
[車"] 轟 hùng
　　 轟 gwàang
[辛"] 辯 bihn
[金"] 鐵 tit
[雨"] 露 louh
　　 霸 ba
[頁"] 顧 gu
[食"] 饑 gèi
[馬"] 驅 kèui
[鬼"] 魔 mò
[鳥"] 鶴 hók
　　 鶴 hohk
　　 鶯 ngāng
[齒"] 齦(咬) ngáauh

二十二劃
22 strokes

[口部] 囉 lò
[弓"] 彎 wàan

[手"] 攤 tàan
[木"] 權 kyùhn
[欠"] 歡 fùn
[水"] 灑(洒) sá
[疒"] 癮 yáhn
[竹"] 籠 lùhng
[米"] 糴 dehk
[耳"] 聾 lùhng
　　 聽 tèng
[言"] 讀 duhk
[貝"] 贖 suhk
[音"] 響 héung
[馬"] 驕 gìu
[髟"] 鬚 sòu

二十三劃
23 strokes

[手部] 攬 gáau
[日"] 曬(晒) saai
[竹"] 籤 chìm
[言"] 變 bin
[頁"] 顯 hín
[馬"] 驚 gèng
　　 驗 yihm
[骨"] 體 tái
[鳥"] 鷹 yīng

二十四劃
24 strokes

[口部] 嚼 jūk

[广"] 廟 dìn

[皿"] 鹽 yìhm

[缶"] 罐 gun

[虫"] 蠶 chàahn
蠶 chàahm

[言"] 讓 yeuhng

[雨"] 靈 lìhng

[鬥"] 鬮(鬥) dau

[鹵"] 鹼(視) gáan

[齒"] 齷 wū

二十五劃
25 strokes

[广部] 廳 tēng

[水"] 灣 wàahn
(bay)

[竹"] 籮 lòh

[見"] 觀 gùn

[貝"] 贜 jòng

[金"] 鑲 sèung

二十六劃
26 strokes

[言部] 讚 jaan

二十七劃
27 strokes

[糸部] 纜 laahm

[金"] 鑽 jyun
鑼 lòh

二十八劃
28 strokes

[金部] 鑿 johk

LIST OF GEOGRAPHICAL NAMES AND COMMON CHINESE SURNAMES

Afghanistan 阿富汗 Ò·fu·hon

Albania 阿爾巴尼亞 À·yíh·bàan nàih·nga

Algeria 阿爾及利亞 À·gèi·leih·a

Anhwei 安徽 Ōn·fài (a province of China)

Argentina 阿根廷 A·gàn·tìhng

Athens 雅典 Nga·dín

Atlantic Ocean 大西洋 Daaih·sài·yèuhng

Australia 澳大利亞 Ou·jàu or Ou·daaih·leih 澳大利

Austria 奧地利 O·deih·leih

Baltic Sea 波羅的海 Bò·lòh·dìk·hói

Bangkok 曼谷 Maahn·gūk

Belgium 比利時 Béi·leih·sìh

Berlin 柏林 Paak·làhm

Bombay 孟買 Maahng·máaih

Boston 波士頓 Bò·sih·deuhn

Brazil 巴西 Bā·sāi

Bulgaria 保加利亞 Bóu·gà·leih·a

Burma 緬甸 Míhn·dihn

Cambodia 柬埔寨 Gáan·póu·choi (same as 高棉 Gòu·mìhn)

Canada 加拿大 Gà·nàh·daaih

Cairo 開羅 Hòi·lòih

Canton 廣州 Gwóng·jàu

Central America 中美洲 Jùng·méih·jàu

Central China 華中 Wàh·jùng

Ceylon 錫蘭 Sek·làahn

Chahar 察哈爾 Chaat·hà·yíh (a province of China)

Chang 張 Jèung

Chao 趙 Jiuh

Chekiang 浙江 Jit·gòng (a province of China)

Chen 陳 Chàhn

Cheng 鄭 Jehng

Ch'eng 程 Chìhng

Chia 賈 Gá

Chiang 蔣 Jéung

Chiang Chung—Cheng 蔣中正 Jéung Jùng—Jing (same as Chiang Kai-shek, Jéung gaai·sehk)

Ch'ien 錢 Chìhn

Chicago 芝加哥 Jī·gā·gō

Chile 智利 Ji·leih

Chin 金 Gàm

Ch'in 秦 Chèuhn

China, People's Republic of 中華人民共和國 Jùng·wàh·yàhn·màhn guhng·wòh·gwok

China, Republic of 中華民國 Jùng·wàh·màhn·gwok

Chou 周 Jàu

Chou En-lai 周恩來 Jàu Yàn·lòih

Chu 朱 Jù

Chu Te 朱德 Jyū·dāk

Chung 鍾 Jùng

Congo Republic 剛果 Gòng·gwó

Cuba 古巴 Gú·bā

Czechoslovakia 捷克斯拉夫 Jit·hāk·sī·lāai·fū

Dahomey 達荷美 Daaht·hòh·méih

Denmark 丹麥 Dàan·mahk

East China 華東 Wàh·dùng

Egypt 埃及 Òi·gahp

Fan 范 Faahn

479

Fang 方 Fòng

Feng 馮 Fùhng

Finland 芬蘭 Fàn·làahn

France 法國 or 法蘭西
    Faat·gwok or Faat·lāahn·sāi

Fukien 福建 Fūk·gin
    (a province of China)

Geneva 日內瓦 Yaht·noih·ngáh

Germany, East 東德 Dūng·dāk

Germany, West 西德 Sāi·dāk

Ghana 甘那 Gām·nàh

Greece 希臘 Hèi·lihp

Hague, The 海牙 Hói·ngàh

Hainan 海南 Hói·nàahm
    (a province of China)

Haiphong 海防 Hói·fòhng

Han 韓 Hòhn

Hankow 漢口 Hon·háu

Hanoi 河內 Hòh·noih

Heilungkiang 黑龍江 Hāk·lùhng·gòng
    (a province of China)

Ho 何 Hòh

Hollywood 荷里活 Hòh·léih·wuht

Honan 河南 Hòh·nàahm
    (a province of China)

Hong Kong 香港 Hèung·góng

Hopeh 河北 Hòh·bāk
    (a province of China)

Hsia 夏 Hah

Hsiao 蕭 Sìu

Hsieh 謝 Jeh

Hsu 許 Héui

Hsu 徐 Chèuih

Hsueh 薛 Sit

Hu 胡 Wùh

Huang 黃 Wòhng

Hung 洪 Hùhng

Hunan 湖南 Wùh·nàahm
    (a province of China)

Hungary 匈牙利 Hùng·ngàh·leih

Hupeh 湖北 Wùh·bāk
    (a province of China)

Iceland 冰島 Bìng·dóu

India 印度 Yan·douh

Indonesia 印度尼西亞
    Yàn·douh·nàih·sài·nga or Yàn·nàih

Iran 伊朗 Yì·lóhng

Iraq 伊拉克 Yì·lāai·hāk

Ireland 愛爾蘭 Oi·yíh·làahn

Israel 以色列 Yíh·sīk·liht

Italy 意大利 Yi·daaih·leih

Japan 日本 Yaht·bún

Jordan 約但 Yeuk·daan

Kao 高 Gòu

Kiangsi 江西 Gōng·sài
    (a province of China)

Kiangsu 江蘇 Gōng·sòu
    (a province of China)

Kirin 吉林 Gāt·làhm
    (a province of China)

Korea 高麗 Gòu·laih
    (same as 朝鮮 Chosen)

Korea, North 北韓 Bāk·hòhn

South Korea 南韓 Nàahm·hòhn

Kowloon (H.K.) 九龍 Gáu·lùhng

Ku 顧 Gu

Kualu Lumpur 吉隆坡 Gāt·lùhng·bō

Kuan 關 Gwàan

K'ung 孔 Húng

Kuo 郭 Gwok

Kwangsi 廣西 Gwóng·sài
    (a province of China)

Kwangtung 廣東 Gwóng·dùng
    (a province of China)

Kweichow 貴州 Gwei·jàu
    (a province of China)

Laos 寮國 Louh·gwok
    (same as 老撾)

Lebanon 黎巴嫩 Làih·bà·nyuhn

Lei 雷 Lèuih

Leningrad 列寧格勒 Liht·nìhng·gaak·lahk

Li 黎 Làih

Li 李 Léih

Liang 梁 Lèuhng

Liaoning 遼寧 Lìuh·nìhng
(a province in China)

Libya 利比亞 Leih·béi·nga

Lin 林 Làhm

Lin Piao 林彪 Làhm·bìu

Liu 劉 Làuh

Liu 柳 Láuh

Lo 羅 Lòh

London 倫敦 Lèuhn·dēun

Los Angeles 羅省 Lòh·sáang

Lu 呂 Léuih

Lu 盧 Lòuh

Lu 陸 Luhk

Ma 馬 Máh

Macao 澳門 Ou·mùhn or Ou·mún

Madrid 馬德里 Máh·dāk·léih

Malasia 馬來西亞 Mah loih sai nga

Manila 馬尼拉 Màh·nàih·lā

Mao 毛 Mòuh

Mao tze-tung 毛澤東 Mòuh·jaahk·dūng

Mediterranean Sea 地中海 Deih·jùng·hói

Mei 梅 Mùih

Meng 孟 Maahng

Mexico 墨西哥 Mahk·sāi·gō

Middle East 中東 Jūng·dùng

Mongolia 蒙古 Mùhng·gú

Montreal 滿地可 Múhn·deih·hó

Morocco 摩洛哥 Mò·lohk·gō

Moscow 莫斯科 Mohk·sī·fō

Nanking 南京 Nàahm·gìng

New Delhi 新德里 Sān·dāk·léih

New York (city) 紐約 Náu·yeuk

New Zealand 紐西蘭 Sān·sài·làahn

Ningsia 寧夏 Nìhng·hah
(a province of China)

North America 北美洲 Bāk·méih·jàu

North China 華北 Wàh·bāk

Northeast China (Manchuria) 東北 Dūng·bāk

Norway 挪威 Nòh·wāi

Ouyang 歐陽 Ngàu·yèuhng

Pacific Ocean 太平洋 Taai·pìhng·yèuhng

Pai 白 Baahk

Pakistan 巴基斯坦 Bā·gēi·sī·táan

P'an 潘 Pùn

Panama 巴拿馬 Bà·nàh·máh

Pao 鮑包 Bàau

Paris 巴黎 Bà·làih

Pearl Harbor 珍珠港 Jān·jyù·góng

Pearl River 珠江 Jyū·gōng, Jyū·gòng

Peking 北京 Bāk gìng or
Bāk·pìhng 北平

P'eng 彭 Pàahng

Persia 波斯 Bō·sī

Peru 秘魯 Bei·lóuh

Philippines, The 菲律賓 Fèi·leuht·bān

Poland 波蘭 Bò·làahn

Portugal 葡萄牙 Pòuh·tòuh·ngàh

Rangoon 仰光 Yéuhng·gwōng or
Yéuhng·gwòng

Red Sea 紅海 Hùhng·hói

Rome 羅馬 Lòh·máh

Rumania 羅馬尼亞 Lòh·máh·nàih·nga

Saigon 西貢 Sài·gung

San Francisco 三藩市 Sàam·fàahn·síh
(same as 舊金山 Gauh·gām·sāan)

Shanghai 上海 Seuhng hoi

Shangtung 山東 Sāan·dùng
(a province of China)

Shansi 山西 Sāan·sài
(a province of China)

Shen 沈 Sám

Shensi 陝西 Sím·sài
(a province of China)

Shih 石 Sehk

Siberia 西伯利亞 Sài·baak·leih·nga

Sidney 雪梨 Syut·lèih

Singapore 星架坡 Sìng·ga·bō

Sinkiang 新疆 Sān·gèung
(a province of China)

South America 南美洲 Nàahm·méih·jàu

South China 華南 Wàh·nàahm

South China Sea 南海 Nàahm·hói

Southwest China 西南 sài·nàahm

Soviet Union 蘇聯 Sòu·lyùhn

Spain 西班牙 Sāi·bàan·ngàh

Ssutu 司徒 Si·tòuh

Stalin 史太林 Sí·taai·làhm

Stanley (H.K.) 赤柱 Chek·chyúh

Star Ferry (H.K.) 尖沙咀 Gìm·sà·jéui

Su 蘇 Sòu

Suez Canal 蘇彝士運河 Sòu·yìh·sih·wahn·hòh

Suiyuan 綏遠 Sèui·yúhn
(a province of China)

Sun 孫 Syùn

Sung 宋 Sung

Swatow 汕頭 Saan·tàuh

Sweden 瑞典 Seuih·dín

Switzerland 瑞士 Seuih·sih

Syria 叙利亞 Jeuih·leih·nga

Tai 戴 Daai

Taiwan 台灣 Tòih·wāan

Taan 譚 Tàahm

Teng 鄧 Dahng

T'ang 唐 Tòhng

Thailand 泰國 Taai·gwok

Netherlands 荷蘭 Hòh·lāan

Tibet 西藏 Sài·johng

T'ien 田 Tìhn

Ting 丁 Dìng

Tokyo 東京 Dūng·gìng

Trinidad 千里達 Chìn·léih·daaht

Ts'ai 蔡 Choi

Ts'ao 曹 Chòuh

Tseng 曾 Jàng

Tso 左 Jó

Tu 杜 Douh

Tung 董 Dúng

Tunisia 突尼西亞 Daht·nàih·sài·nga

Turkey 土耳其 Tóu·yíh·kèih

Union of Soviet Socialist Republics 蘇維埃聯邦, 蘇聯 or 蘇俄 or 俄國 Sòu·lyuhn or Sòu·ngòh or Ngòh·gwok

United Kingdom (Great Britain and Northern Ireland) 英國 Yìng·gwok

Versailles 凡爾賽 Fàahn·yíh·choi

Vienna 維也納 Wàih·yáh·naahp

Vietnam, North 北越 Bāk·yuht

Vietnam, South 南越 Nàahm·yuht

Vladivostok 海參威 Hòi·sām·wāi

Wan 萬 Maahn

Wang 王 Wòhng

Wang 汪 Wòng

Washington, D.C. 華盛頓 or 美京 Wàh·sihng·deuhn or Méih·gìng

Wei 魏 Ngaih

Wei 衛 Waih

Western Hemisphere 西半球 Sài·bun·kàuh

Wu 吳 Ngh

Wu 伍 Ngh

Yokohama 橫濱 Wàahng·bàn

Yang 楊 Yèung

Yangtze River 揚子江 Yèuhng·jí·gòng
(same as 長江 Chèuhng·gòng)

Yeh 葉 Yihp

Yellow River 黃河 Wòhng·hòh

Yellow Sea 黃海 Wòhng·hói

Yen 顏 Ngaahn

Yen 嚴 Yìhm

Yu 于 Yù

Yu 余 Yùh

Yuan 袁 Yùhn

Yugoslavia 南斯拉夫 Nàahm·sī·lāai·fū

Yunnan 雲南 Wàhn·nàahm
(a province of China)

CONVERSION TABLE OF ROMANIZATION

COMPARATIVE TABLE—Initials

Yale	Meyer-Wempe*	IPA†
p	p'	p'
b	p	p
t	t'	t'
d	t	t
k	k'	k'
g	k	k
ch	ch', ts'	tɕ'
j	ch, ts	tɕ
kw	k'w	k'w
gw	kw	kw
m	m	m
n	n	n
ng	ng	ŋ
f	f	f
l	l	l
h	h	h
s	s, sh	ɕ
y	i, y	y
w	oo, w	w

COMPARATIVE TABLE—Finals

Yale	Meyer-Wempe	IPA
a	a	a:
aai	aai	a:i
aau	aau	a:u
aam	aam	a:m
aap	aap	a:p
aan	aan	a:n
aat	aat	a:t
aang	aang	a:ŋ
aak	aak	a:k
ai	ai	ai
au	au	au
am	am, om	əm (or am)‡
ap	ap, op	əp (or ap)
an	an	ən (or an)
at	at	ət (or at)
ang	ang	əŋ (or aŋ)
ak	ak	ək (or ak)

---

*Bernard F. Meyer and Theodore F. Wempe, Student's Cantonese-English Dictionary (Maryknoll, New York, 1947).

†International Phonetic Alphabet (but with ü for y and y for j)

‡Some writers use short a to represent these sounds, while others use ə.

COMPARATIVE TABLE—Finals (cont.)

Yale	Meyer-Wempe	IPA
e	e	ɛː
eng	eng	ɛːŋ
ek	ek	ɛːk
ei	ei	ei
eu	oeh	œː
eung	eung	œːŋ
euk	euk	œːk
eui	ui	ɵü
eun	un	ɵn
eut	ut	ɵt
i	i	iː
iu	iu	iːu
im	im	iːm
ip	ip	iːp
in	in	iːn
it	it	iːt
ing	ing	eŋ
ik	ik	ek <u>or</u> Ik
o	oh	ɔ
oi	oi	ɔi
on	on	ɔn
ot	ot	ɔt
ong	ong	ɔŋ
ok	ok	ɔːk
ou	o	ou
u	oo	u
ui	ooi	uːi
un	oon	uːn
ut	oot	uːt
ung	ung	oŋ
uk	uk	ok
yu	ue	üː
yun	uen	üːn
yut	uet	üːt

COMPARATIVE TABLE—Tones

Yale			Meyer-Wempe
high falling	à	a	upper even
high rising	á	á	upper rising
middle level	a, at	à	upper going
		àt	middle entering
high level	ā, āt	a	upper even
		at	upper entering

COMPARATIVE TABLE—Tones (cont.)

<u>Yale</u>			<u>Meyer-Wempe</u>
low falling	àh	ā	lower even
low rising	áh	ǎ	lower rising
low level	ah, aht	â	lower going
		ât	lower entering

LIST OF BOOKS CONSULTED

Chao, Yuen Ren, Cantonese Primer, Cambridge, Mass. , Harvard University Press, 1947.

Chiang Ker Chiu, A Practical English-Cantonese Dictionary, Singapore, Chin Fen Book Store, 1941.

Huang, Parker Po-fei, Cantonese Sounds and Tones, New Haven, Far Eastern Publications, 1963.

Huang, Parker Po-fei, IFEL Vocabulary, New Haven, Far Eastern Publications, Yale University, 1955.

Kok, Gerald P., coauthor Parker Po-fei Huang, Speak Cantonese, Book I, New Haven, Institute of Far Eastern Languages, Yale University, 1956.

Huang, Parker Po-fei, Speak Cantonese, Book II, New Haven, Far Eastern Publications, Yale University, 1963.

Huang, Parker Po-fei, Speak Cantonese, Book III, New Haven, Far Eastern Publications, Yale University, 1967.

Institute of Far Eastern Languages, Dictionary of Spoken Chinese, New Haven, Yale University Press, 1966.

Meyer, Bernard F., and Wempe, Theodore F., The Student's Cantonese-English Dictionary, New York, Field Afar Press, 1947